Rd

MW01282341

REF

HEINRICH HEPPE

REFORMED DOGMATICS

SET OUT AND ILLUSTRATED
FROM THE SOURCES

FOREWORD BY KARL BARTH

REVISED AND EDITED BY
ERNST BIZER

———————

ENGLISH TRANSLATION BY
G. T. THOMSON

BAKER BOOK HOUSE
Grand Rapids, Michigan

FIRST PUBLISHED IN GREAT BRITAIN
IN 1950

Translated from the original German
Reformierte Dogmatik

Reprinted 1978 by Baker Book House
with permission of George Allen & Unwin Ltd.

ISBN: 0-8010-4207-0

PHOTOLITHOPRINTED BY CUSHING - MALLOY, INC.
ANN ARBOR, MICHIGAN, UNITED STATES OF AMERICA
1978

FOREWORD

I shall never forget the spring vacation of 1924. I sat in my study at Göttingen, faced with the task of giving lectures on dogmatics for the first time. No one can ever have been more plagued than I then was with the problem, could I do it? and how? My Biblical and historical studies to date had more and more expelled me from the goodly society of contemporary, and, as I began to realise ever more clearly, of almost the whole of the more recent theology; and I saw myself, as it were, alone in the open without a teacher. That H. Scripture must be the controlling element in an evangelical dogmatics I also realised to the full. I was equally quite clear that the right thing was, in particular, to link up again with the Reformed, as more than one designed to do at that time. But how to do it, without a guide? I was more terrified of the footprints of modern Biblicism than attracted by them. Was it not too akin to what it would attack, to attack it effectively? What soul in the last two centuries of Protestant theological history had not meant to hitch everything on to the Reformers? What was the effect of that on Protestant dogmatics? What could I see happening right and left of me, over and over again?

Then it was that, along with the parallel Lutheran work of H. Schmid, Heppe's volume just recently published fell into my hands; out of date, dusty, unattractive, almost like a table of logarithms, dreary to read, stiff and eccentric on almost every page I opened; in form and content pretty adequately corresponding to what I, like so many others, had described to myself decades ago, as the " old orthodoxy."

Well, I had the grace not to be so slack. I read, I studied, I reflected; and found that I was rewarded with the discovery, that here at last I was in the atmosphere in which the road by way of the Reformers to H. Scripture was a more sensible and natural one to tread, than the atmosphere, now only too familiar to me, of the theological literature determined by Schleiermacher and Ritschl. I found a dogmatics which had both form and substance, oriented upon the central indications of the Biblical evidences for revelation, which it also managed to follow out in detail with astonishing richness—a dogmatics which by adopting and sticking to main lines of the Reformation attempted alike a worthy continuation of the doctrinal constructions of the older Church, and yet was also out to cherish and preserve continuity with the ecclesiastical science of the Middle Ages. I found myself visibly in the circle of the Church, and, moreover, in accordance with such prototypes, in the region of Church science, respectable of its kind. I had come to be amazed at the long, peaceful breathing, the sterling quality, the relevant strictness, the superior style, the methods confident at least themselves, with which this "orthodoxy" had wrought. I had cause for astonishment at its wealth of problems and the sheer beauty of its trains of thought. In these old fellows I saw that it can be worth while to reflect upon the tiniest point with the greatest force of Christian presupposition, and, for the sake of much appealed-to "life," to be quite serious about the question of truth all along the line. In other words I saw that Protestant dogmatics was once a careful, orderly business, and I conceived the hope that it might perhaps become so again, if it could reacquire its obviously wandered nerves and return to a strict, Churchly and scientific outlook.

At the same time I was also aware that a return to this orthodoxy (in order to remain at its side and to compete with it!) could not be contemplated, because Israel's disgrace, with which hitherto I had been closely acquainted only in its neo-Protestant form, had already been prepared and set in motion in that earlier period. The dogmatics of these centuries had already been too closely bound up with a form not taken from the thing itself but from contemporary philosophies, for the substance itself not to have suffered thereby as a whole as well as in detail. All too confidently the heroes of orthodoxy, in their justifiable attempt to adopt the Early and Mediaeval Church tradition, overloaded it with presuppositions which were bound sooner or later to jeopardise Reformed knowledge of God and of salvation. And they were too lively and hilarious in imagining that they would really master revelation today with the schematisms of their supposedly enlightened understanding; they were too extreme—this is particularly in their doctrine of Scripture— in turning revelation in all its mystery into something like a handy intellectual principle, to be able to express and defend it effectively to their followers in the eighteenth century, to set up the still and recurrently most unillumined understanding even of the Christian as a pattern alongside of and ultimately over the mystery of revelation. With great respect I preferred not to follow them in these respects. Undoubtedly, Protestant dogmatics will have to acquire the decisive items of knowledge by Biblical exegesis in the actual Reformers' school and not in the utterances of those theologians of the older or more recent orthodoxy. Orthodoxy may be but one stop on the way to this goal. Nevertheless and notwithstanding, I did and still do maintain that it is a good thing at least not to push on over hastily to a Biblical-Reformed theology, but to linger at least on real fundamentals at the stop "orthodoxy". The "push through" far too frequently means, just merely pushing through once more to a new mixture of Enlightenment and Pietism. Success can come only if we have previously learned to read the Reformers as the *Church's* teachers and, with them, Scripture as the document for the Church's existence and nature, and therefrom to ask what Church science might be. That precisely may be learned, nay must be, from the early Orthodox men.

Now as regards Heppe in particular; he has done me the service, which he can and will do for others, of bringing me to understand the special direction in which dogmatic science has proceeded in the early Reformed Church. He might be described as in this respect a more reliable guide than the better-known work of Alexander Schweizer (*Die Glaubenslehre der ev.-ref. Kirche*, 1884 ff). Of course Heppe has his notable weaknesses. According to modern claims and viewpoints it is anything but a source book. On Heppe's historical outlook we should note that according to him, wonderful to relate, not Calvin but the later Melanchthon must have been the Father of Reformed theology. And he has paid his tribute to the spirit of the nineteenth century, in that for him the incursion of the covenant-theology of Cocceius and his pupils, proclaimed alongside of Cartesianism, into the line of the older expositors of Reformed dogma seems not to involve any deeper problem; so that we ask in vain how it came about, that, in this particular, Reformed orthodoxy in the eighteenth century can be so marvellously and painlessly "intellectual," i.e., pietistically rationalist. In spite of such weaknesses and amid them all we acquire from Heppe incomparably far better information about early Reformed dogmatics than from Schweizer, because—from the systematic viewpoint incomparably less gifted, interested and equipped than the latter—he is at least free from his tendency to suspect and to insist on predestination and to make all roads end at Schleiermacher. The results were that most of the more modern German dogmaticians of Lutheran provenance have all derived their acquaintance with Reformed theology manifestly from Schweizer and not from the more modest but ultimately sterling and more logical Heppe. Obviously, to acquire a knowledge of orthodoxy we need not stop at either Schmid or Heppe, but must seek out and traverse the more arduous road to the sources, in which once more everything often enough acquires an appearance quite different from that which the excerpts offered by Heppe might lead us to suppose.* But for a start and an introduction we should handle him with nothing but confidence. So long as we have nothing better, we have every cause to be thankful that we have him and have him now again after long seasons of gross oblivion.

Bonn, February, 1935   KARL BARTH

---

* One of the classical sources, Johannes Wolleb's *Compendium Christanae Theologiae*, Basel 1926, appears simultaneously with this book in the same new edition.—*Publisher's note.*

CONTENTS

PREFACE

The first edition of this book appeared as volume 2 of Heppe's writings on Reformed Theology in the year 1861. The author in his foreword states that his aim has been to expound the orthodox system of doctrine in the Reformed Church faithfully and without addition. "All the written sources I could lay hands on, I have carefully researched and compared, in order to transmit the thought material brought to light and disseminated by the acknowledged representatives of Reformed orthodoxy. Where differences were found, I have given an account of them and have at the same time attempted to set forth, which view is to be regarded as that truly corresponding to the spirit of Reformed Church doctrine. The extracts from the sources which I have imparted for the illustration of Reformed Church doctrine are (particularly in the fundamental *Loci*) given so copiously and so fully that the reader can himself test the reproduction of the Reformed system which I have given him."

Because of this fidelity with which Heppe has handled his material we once more present the book today. Its content is the doctrine of the Reformed Church as it was wrought out by the important teachers of the same. Whereas all around it events of world history took place bound up with Confessional rivalries, these men saw their life-task in jealously guarding and working up in ever fresh attacks the gift which the Reformation had made them. They believed that thus they were fulfilling their task and were convinced that they were thereby executing as important a task as the diplomats and mercenaries in these wars—if not a more important one!

Now we stand at least in historical connection with the Church, and, however it is to be done, have also to manage their inheritance. Whether we do so on the Fathers' side or against them—we cannot, we must not do so, without living, coming and going with them. Even if their way should have been just a wrong way, it was still a wrong way which was pursued with passionate fidelity and which must at some point be actually founded upon the business of our Church herself, which, therefore, even menaces us and must accordingly be at least acknowledged and known.

It is of course our conviction that this way was not a wrong way. From start to finish orthodox theology has steadfastly maintained that for good or ill theology has a "doctrine", and that this is not its smallest merit. The Church works through the Word, and so must for good or ill be able to state *what* word she intends to work by. There is no Christian Church which is not in duty bound to strive for purity in her doctrine and to give an account of it. That is why she has her confession; nay, that is why she should always be in process of working it up and developing it afresh. A Church which refuses to be "orthodox" is quite ignorant as to where her task lies. People, therefore, ought to stop reproaching orthodoxy with "rationalism" and the like; it is no reproach against a *doctrine* that it is rational. It must still be so, even when speaking of the "irrational." Its passion is to be found only in the thing itself.

So our way out of Church chaos can fundamentally be none other than that of a new orthodoxy. But it is another question whether the Fathers themselves continually clung to their matter, or whether they did not themselves there and then diverge from their track. Here it is not possible to carry through the discussion with orthodox doctrine. But by walking in its tracks, we shall have pretty thoroughly to ask ourselves whether the old doctrine has always been stated and with sufficient clarity, so that substantially it could be nothing else than a challenge to *faith,* and whether it has validated this fact at all points with the necessary modesty and decisiveness. However surely in substance we are bound to no other presuppositions and however surely for long stretches we cannot take any other way, I as little imagine that the latter is the case. The very first chapter of this book betrays a definite uncertainty in the treatment of natural Knowledge of God, so that Schleiermacher may be directly quoted as the Consummator of orthodoxy. This lack of clarity, then as now, was not confined to the one *locus.* The consequence of this in my view is the philosophical attitude to the doctrine of God, because it ceases to be sufficiently clear that in dogmatics we are dealing only with the *revealed* God. A further consequence is the here and there tentative attitude on the question of certainty of salvation. On this orthodoxy has itself prepared the way for its adversaries. In the struggle for *libertas philosophandi* it knuckles under to the German high schools and could not hold its ground against the attack of philosophy, because it encountered the latter on its own ground. On the other hand it was at a loss, for all its learning, to confine pietism and fanaticism within their limits. Finally, the doctrine of inspiration could not stand against the sense of truth in historical investigation, and thus at the same time unmasked itself as the product of a false striving after false certainties. Of course it must still be observed, that even "orthodoxy" is not a self-enclosed unity. It was a broad road which led from Calvin to Keckermann and finally to Endemann and Wyttenbach, and it is an of course unavoidable error of the book before us that the stages on this journey cannot be expressed with perfect clarity.

The idea of it is not that orthodoxy, in its historical forms, might be our schoolmistress in each and all. But that does not alter the fact that its presupposition, its method and its purpose are binding for us too, and that consequently reflection upon its results cannot be spared us. The ancient contrast between Lutherans and Reformers cannot have much significance. This contrast has made its own contribution to the downfall of orthodoxy; for the truth can only be *one*. It must be overcome, but the path to its conquest can honestly be found only in scientific consideration of the twofold situation and of the matter itself, i.e., of the common presupposition. In this work Reformed and Lutherans must join hands.

To conclude, there is little to say about this new edition. The Latin quotations have everywhere been checked. Here I have to thank the University libraries of Marburg, Tübingen, Münster, Berlin, Münich, Breslau, Bonn and Herborn, as well as the Information Office of the German Libraries for many meetings and much patience. In the course of this test only few quotations remained completely unaltered. The correct spelling—an adequate reproduction being out of the question anyhow on technical printing grounds—was assimilated to our modern spelling, and in the punctuation, which was handled very variously in the sources, I assumed the liberty which seemed to me necessary to make the book as readable as possible, without painfully adhering to the usual rules. Absolute adequacy of reproduction no understanding reader will demand, since the written sources from time to time were at my disposal only for a limited period; but I hope I have achieved the possible. Mistakes in the sources were only corrected where an obvious printing error was in question; in doubtful cases they were gladly left. I therefore ask the reader not to assume an oversight in every case where something seems unusual. The quotations from Alting and the Leiden Synopsis, as well as from Trelcatius, Crocius and Beza were tested by Miss Hannelore Reiffen and Pastor Schneider of the Educational Union in Neuekirchen. For very valuable help in revision I thank, in addition to those named, my wife as well as Miss Maria Eppinger of Schwenningen on the Neckar.

Tailfingen (Wttbg),

14 September, 1934

ERNST BIZER

Footnote on Bizer's strictures in his preface, on the worth of Heppe's work.

Every Christian with access to Heppe will be grateful to Ernst Bizer for his accurate work upon Heppe's text and citations. I know how valuable they can be, even in Latin and German, to English-speaking subscribers to the Westminster Confession. But we are by no means as critical as Bizer is of Heppe's "orthodoxy". The very concept of revealed truth, discoverable under God in Scripture, *implies* an orthodoxy which, while never *possibly* immaculate, may yet, like our Credal statements, largely approximate to the ideal *systematic* truth. I know from the experience and study of years, that Heppe can work wonders in theological students. He is not only instructive. To an age fed on the husks of human enlightenment and today craving for the true light of direct revelation Heppe is manna, and that in plenty. And so, while deprecating the editor's strictures upon Heppe, we tender personal thanks to him for giving us—Heppe. To so many of us in this country, his source-book is, under God, anything but outworn. It can and does bring men back to right paths. May it continue to do so many fold in completely English dress!— G.T.T.

CHAPTER I

NATURAL AND REVEALED THEOLOGY

1.—To man there belongs naturally and essentially a consciousness that there is a God, and that Him he is bound to honour.—CALVIN (I, iii, 1): "God has Himself implanted in all some kind of grasp of His *'numen.'* "— P. MARTYR: (*praef.*) "Knowledge of God—is naturally innate in the minds of all."—BURMANN (I, ii, 16): "Religion flows from the very nature of God and man; hence religion is the necessary and natural sequel to reason, and so natural religion *datur* (is something given)."

Later Reformed theology defended these propositions against the *Socinians* in particular, who taught that man's soul is originally a *tabula rasa*. At the same time there are warnings against a false conception of an innate idea of God.—Says RIISSEN (I, 5): "Certain more recent writers explain the natural sense of deity (*numen*) *by the idea of God impressed on our minds;* upon which it must be observed, that the idea of God is said less properly to be impressed upon us, if by it some species and image of God is intended, intelligible to and in our minds, which clearly and distinctly represents to us the nature and essence of God. This is not only rejected by the infinite majesty of God ; our finite and frail intelligence is incapable of grasping it—how could the image of an infinite entity be given in a finite mind whether adequately or clearly and distinctly? Nor, even if it can be held for certain that God is because of this common notion and the instinct of conscience, does it follow forthwith that we might at once infer, by a clear and distinct concept such as the idea we are speaking of is supposed to be, who He is and what His nature. In any case it is certain that if a clear and distinct idea of God is given us, it is held, in the last resort, in consequence not of a nature thoroughly blinded by sin, but of a supernatural revelation of the Word, in which God openly reveals Himself to us, although this actual knowing in respect of glory is but a speculation and an enigma, i.e., imperfect as yet and mighty obscure."

2.—This innate knowledge of God, *notitia Dei insita,* is formed in man by his reason and his conscience into a *notitia acquisita.* Hence there is a *religio naturalis.*—RIISSEN (I, 4): " Is there given a natural theology or ingrained (*insita*) knowledge of God drawn from the book of conscience by κοιναὶ ἔννοιαι partly acquired, being sought in this book of created things discursively? Yes, against the *Socinians*—6 : This *cognitio Dei* is called *naturalis,* "(1) because it is from nature, (2) accompanies nature, (3) teaches none but natural things." The most essential content of natural religion is given by RIISSEN thus (I, 7): "(1) that God is, (2) and that He must be worshipped, (3) that we must live good lives, (4) that the soul is immortal, (5) that a reward is due to virtue, punishment to wickedness".

3.—Reason allows man to know the idea of God immanent in him and teaches him to conclude from the visible world as God's work to its invisible originator and ruler. At the same time conscience teaches man to know God as Him who loves and rewards goodness, abhors and punishes evil and to whom he is absolutely responsible. Hence at its most perfect man's natural knowledge of God is formed (apart from what it becomes by revelation) by the fact that he considers himself to be the image of God.

CALVIN (I, v, 1): "He not only endued the minds of men with that which he calls the need of religion. He so revealed it in the whole creation of the world and so openly offers Himself every day, that they cannot open their eyes without being compelled to behold Him."

HEIDEGGER, (I, 7,): "After sin entered the world, the sinner did not therefore so far completely unlearn God. Corrupt nature still preserved for him a natural theology and religion, although very imperfect. (i) Man the sinner retained reason, to which nature and an ingrained idea and notion of Deity suggested that which was known of God (Rom. 1. 19): God making the revelation through nature; and (ii) God's ποιήματα brought to their notice and view the invisible things of Him from the creation, namely His everlasting divinity and power ; and (iii) conscience, which, bearing in its bosom the work of the law written in man's heart and so the good and bad taught by that law, as it were powerfully defends man in things rightly done before God the Judge, accusing him in those badly done (Rom. 2. 15.). I say nothing of the countless and pregnant proofs by which reason incontrovertibly (ἀναντιρρήτως) maintains that God the rewarder of good and the punisher of evil exists without the help of any revelation or tradition.

How far this *cognitio innata* is acquired, is taught by RIISSEN (I, 1): "Natural knowledge of God is usually acquired in a threefold way: (1) by the way of causality, when we understand a cause from its effects, (2) by the way of *eminentia*, when we attribute to God eminently and κατ' ἐξοχὴν anything perfect there is among created things, (3) by the way of negation, when we remove from God things which mark imperfection in creatures. Preferably man's divine-image character is emphasised, and thereby the description of it as a microcosmos is quite familiar. E.g., CALVIN (I, v, 3,): "Man is a microcosmos, because he is a rare specimen of the divine power, wisdom and goodness.—Within, individuals feel the heavenly grace by which they grow;—to apprehend God we need not go outside ourselves".—PETER MARTYR (2): " Our own nature chiefly shows us God, we being made in His image."—HYPERIUS

(77): "From the pre-eminence of man who is a μικρόκοσμος and the most absolute image of the whole world, in fact of God Himself—and because of course God's existence and to a great extent God's nature may most clearly be noted from the nature of man".

4.—Of course natural knowledge of God is inadequate to achieve eternal blessedness. Man convicted by his consciousness of sinfulness learns thereby that God punishes us, but of himself he knows nothing of what God's will is for the sinner according to His grace. *Religio naturalis* is thus not *salutaris*, and can only make man inexcusable, for not accepting revelation. Besides this man by himself cannot so know what he does know about God through reason and conscience, as he ought to know about Him.

HEIDEGGER (I, 9): "The kind of knowledge of God and of divine things that may be drawn from nature and its principles *cannot be so connected with salvation as to be saving*. Man the sinner—can in no wise know the will and good pleasure of God outside of His revelation. In addition what man can naturally know about God under the leading of reason and wit, man the yet unsatisfied animal does not know as it can and ought to be known".—DANAEUS (*Isag.* 1, p. 102 ff.) enumerates the distinguishing marks of natural knowledge of God, as distinguished from revealed: "First of all, this knowledge, derived only from God's visible works or from this world, is true enough; but it is insufficient for salvation, because a peculiar knowledge of redemption is required for salvation. Secondly, this general knowledge does teach that God exists and that He is to be worshipped; for it knows that He is mighty and righteous and wise. But it does not recognise either who this God is or how He is to be worshipped. Thirdly, this general knowledge of God is chiefly sustained by the witness of conscience, which is given by God to every man that cometh into the world (Jn. I. 17). And so, as for a host of reasons this power and voice of our conscience is either suffocated or disappears or is destroyed or corrupted, the same befalls this general knowledge of God in us. Still, it cannot be abandoned, just as the force of conscience cannot be abandoned either. In short, as appears from the above, this general knowledge of God only renders us inexcusable in God's sight, but does not contain or transmit the doctrine of salvation. By it we know the one God to be an august majesty and an incomprehensible power. But we do not understand that He is merciful to us in His Son".

5.—Yet what natural religion teaches about God, although imperfect is not therefore untrue. At the same time "this knowledge", says COCCEIUS (*Summ. Theol., I, 4*), "*is true although it is not adequate. The things known of*

God, partly negatively by the setting apart of those that belong to weakness and imperfection, partly by the image, partly by the attribution of inaccessible eminence (for we recognise that He dwells in light inaccessible), are devoid of falsehood: even though there is more in the actual fact than can be perceived by us."

6.—Natural religion is also useful. On the one hand man is deprived of every excuse, as against God, for not believing in God and not fulfilling His lawful will. On the other hand the natural man who seeks peace with God through *religio naturalis* will the more joyfully and thankfully accept the revelation of God's grace, if it is imparted to him. And the regenerate man who has received the revelation of grace and believes in it will be all the better able to understand and see through God's revelation in nature.

HEIDEGGER (I, 12): "In short, natural knowledge of God is not useless because not saving. As regards God it has this use, that it renders the man who blames fate, the μεμψίμοιρος, without excuse, ἀναπολόγητος, Rom. 7. 20, as regards man it profits to this extent, that both the not yet regenerate seeking God and His salvation in nature, if haply they may grope after and find Him Ac. 17. 27, in grace or by the Word of God, the Spirit of God taking the lead, take it up and greet it when found: and the regenerate already taught from God's word about the true God and the way of His salvation, a return as it were to nature having been instituted, look up more also from God's admirable works to His power, wisdom and goodness, worship His majesty and put all their trust in the one and only God of Israel, who alone doeth such things."

7.—Man is aware in his conscience that he is a transgressor against God's commandment and thereby guilty in God's sight; and yet by his natural knowledge of God he knows God only as the righteous judge of good and evil. *Religio naturalis,* then, cannot ensure any man peace with God or be in any sense a *religio* satisfying to Himself or to man. It actually points beyond itself, since it arouses in man the need and longing for a revelation, by which man must first rightly conceive what it means for a God to exist, and by which he must recognise, that God may also be the sinner's God, that God will also be sought of the sinner and how He will also be found of him.—COCCEIUS (*S.T.*, I, 17): "There was every need for revelation, not only that man might be roused to a νόησις and attention to God's creatures, so as to behold in them the invisible things of God and so feel after God and find Him; but much more that he might learn what it means that God exists, and in this perfection might be aware of the second one which drives him nearer to God, *that God may*

be the sinner's God; then that he might perceive that grandest glory of God,"
which is *to will to be sought and found of the sinner ; lastly, how He must be
sought in order that He may be found.* Without this knowledge and faith it
is impossible to please God, i.e., to approach Him, to walk with Him,
to do things pleasing to Him and to worship Him, Heb. 11. 6."
Similarly HEIDEGGER (I, 13).

8.—Only, then, as faith in revelation does religion become what it ought
to be according to its idea: not an awareness of God or even an observance
of the divine commands *per se*, but a determination of the immediate
self-consciousness, a feeling (Schleiermacher!) which rests upon experience
of God as absolute love.

The concept of theology is treated by the dogmaticians in a far more
thoroughgoing style than the concept of religion. Regularly they discuss
the distinction between *theologia archetypa* (i.e., "The knowledge which
God has of Himself and in Himself") and *th. ectypa* (i.e., man's knowledge
of God). The latter they divide into *theologia beatorum* and *theologia
viatorum*, the second being theology proper. On the other hand none of
the older men arrives at a proper, adequate, definitive concept of religion.
—CALVIN (I, ii, 2) says: "What is pure and genuine religion but *faith
conjoined with serious fear of God*, so that fear may contain in itself voluntary
reverence and involve a legitimate worship, such as is prescribed in the
law."—DANAEUS (*Isag.* p. 107) says: "He who knows either the law or
God in word alone is not on that account pleasing to God. But he who
worships God, as Himself prescribes in His word, is indeed favoured in
His sight, Rom. 2. 13 (not the hearers of the law are just before God, but
the doers of the law shall be justified), Mt. 24. 46 (Blessed is that slave,
whom his Lord when he cometh shall find so doing), Lk. 12. 47 (and that
slave, which knew his Lord's will, and made not ready, nor did according
to His will, shall be beat with many stripes). Otherwise our poor knowledge is both thoroughly useless and even thoroughly dangerous, Rom.
1. 21 (knowing God, they glorified him not as God, neither gave thanks),
Lk. 12. 47. By the Latins indeed the worship of God is called now godliness, now religion as *Lactantius* says, now even the veneration of the
numen. p. 110: *True* worship of God may be defined generally thus:
Worship of God is the true honour shown to God from a sense of His
kindness and power towards us, as resulting from His word. But this
honour—is not civil, but divine and religious and is seated mainly in the
heart and mind. Thus worship arises from the sense of God's power
and kindness.—Hence this definition explains the nature of the worship
called filial, which is due to God by the Christian man, as to an excellent
parent and his God."

Later dogmaticians like WYTTENBACH (*Tent. theol. prol.* 11) define religion as "the right way of knowing God and worshipping Him," and he further adds that "strictly therefore religion does not differ from theology." SCHLEIERMACHER was the first able to give conceptual determination to the thoughts on religion which were expressed by the earlier dogmaticians descriptively and in a scattered way. Generally three elements in the concept of religion were set forth by the dogmaticians, (1) that religion is not a knowing but a living, and a determination of man's inward existence, (2) that it can only revive in man through experience of God as absolute pardoning love and (3) that it rests upon the recognition of the absolute dependence of man upon God.—CALVIN (I, v, 9): "It is to be noted that we are to be invited to the knowledge of God; not a knowledge which, satisfied by empty speculation, merely flutters in the brain, but knowledge which strikes root in the heart. God is revealed by his virtues, because we feel within us the power of which we also enjoy the benefits; and so we must be much more vividly affected by this knowledge, than if we were to imagine a God, no sense of whom could reach us. Wherefore also it behoves us to be insistent in our search after God, which holds the mind in such suspense of wonderment that it at the same time touches the very root of effective sense".—Here also let us quote what COCCEIUS says *(S.T.* I, 28*)*: "He is at last able to subject himself to Scripture, who has begun to love God. But this no one can do, unless he has seen that in it is contained a doctrine, which is both worthy of God and sets *a lovable God before the sinner."* According to OLEVIAN religion in the first instance consists essentially in man acknowledging his absolute dependence upon God and affirming it by unconditional obedience to the absolute will. He says (*De subst. foed.* p. 170) "Since God's majesty is supreme, as it says in the beginning of His law, 'I am the Lord thy God', from Whom we all have being itself; and since He alone is wise, to Whom no one was counsellor, and to Whom no one first gave him something in order that He might pay it back, and who therefore testified that nothing pleased Him except obedience, by which *we look up wholly to His majesty and depend upon it,* or that He would not be honoured otherwise than according to His will revealed by Him in a sure word, Who alone is fit to testify to Himself, so that His majesty may stand out in all things: surely we ought to judge only that right which He prescribes and in the way in which He prescribes it."

9.—Man then may with complete certainty recognise what real revelation of God is. If he compares what is proclaimed to him as revelation with his natural consciousness of God, he finds that the latter is satisfied by the former, that revelation enables him to know God in His absolute majesty, his own heart in its sinful misery and at the same time a sure comfort regarding it. If a man is in addition convinced that the fact of revelation is vouched for by perfectly credible witnesses and that the prophecies which the revelation contains have attained fulfilment, he may be certain that what is proclaimed to him as revelation is also the real revelation of God.—HEIDEGGER (I, 26): "The best way of discerning revelation that can be applied is, that first conscience, which *is conscience towards God,* 1 Pet. 2, 19, as being so to speak the lamp which God Himself has placed in man, should accurately compare with the revelation made, the things which it discovers in its own bosom and in the works of divine providence, and find out whether the revelation illumines the glory of God manifested in them and explains the duty and status of man, whether by reason of the wretchedness in which he feels himself involved or by reason of the bliss for which he pants. The next thing to this is to examine how and *by what evidences of truth revelation has taken place.*—In short, if revelation has created faith in itself, *predictions being proved by the upshot,* it cannot be doubted that it was emitted on God's authority, who alone foreknows things to come."

10.—But this knowledge is not imparted to man by flesh and blood, but solely by the Spirit of grace, who opens a man's eyes and directs his heart, that he may achieve a certain knowledge of revealed fact. —HEIDEGGER (I, 27): "This watchfulness man possesses not by nature but by grace and the Spirit of God, who renders him spiritual and bends his heart thereto and opens his eyes, 1 Jn. 5. 7 (it is the Spirit that beareth witness, because the Spirit is truth)".—The doctrine of the *Arminians* is rejected (RIJSSEN, I, 9): "who lay it down that the light of grace is acquired by the right use of natural light and that by grace we reach glory".

11.—Although in and for itself reason is capable of absorbing super-natural truths, it is impossible for fallen man's reason to conceive them for itself.—VOETIUS (I, p. 3): "We presuppose that the supernatural truths of divine faith surpass the reason of man as such. He does not perceive them unless he is raised up and informed by a higher light. But they are not repugnant to him *per se* or as such, only through the accident of corruption and the wicked disposition which inheres in our mind."

12.—Generally then *religio naturalis* and *religio revelata* are so related to one another, that the latter is the confirmation of the former (since it absorbs it into itself); and the latter mediates revelation's point of contact in man. Yet it must by no means be concluded from this that reason, i.e., "the faculty of the rational soul in man by which he apprehends and adjudicates upon things intelligible" (VOETIUS I, 1), may *in any way* be the principle of knowledge by faith. Not for a moment can this be said of the reason illumined by revelation. On the contrary the sole principle of religious knowledge must be the light from which even the Christian's reason has its illumination, namely, revelation; or (since as a matter of order God only reveals Himself by the Word) the word of H. Scriptures.—VOETIUS (I, 3-4): "With these provisos we say that no human reason is the principle *by which or through which or in consequence of which or by reason of which* we believe, or the foundation or law or norm of what is to be believed, by the prescription of which we judge".— HEIDEGGER (I, 33) says that "we must not judge by reason even healed by grace, but according to the principle admitted by illuminated reason, namely, according to Scripture."—RIISSEN (I, 11, 1) quotes the following arguments: "Although reason is the instrument or the means by which we may be led to faith, it is not the principle on which dogmas of faith are proved or the foundation on which they rest: (1) (because) the reason of unregenerate man is blind as regards law, Eph. 4. 17. 18 (. . . ye no longer walk . . . in the vanity of the mind, being darkened in understanding, alienated from the life of God because of the ignorance that is in (you), because of (the) hardening of (your) heart), Rom. 8. 7 (the mind of the flesh is enmity against God), Eph. 5. 8 (ye were once darkness . . .), 1 Cor. 2. 24 (the natural man receiveth not the things of the Spirit of God; (for) they are foolishness unto him); (2) the mysteries of faith are above the sphere of reason, and to them animal man cannot rise; (3) faith is ultimately resolvable not into reason, so that I ought to believe because I thus understand and grasp, but into the Word, because God thus speaks in Scripture; (4) reason cannot be the norm of religion, either as corrupt (because it is not only beneath faith but against it), or as sound (because such reason is not found in corrupt man)."—Thus "the solid and sure architectonic principle of theology" is "divine revelation" (COCCEIUS *Aphor. prolixiores*, 11, 7) and revelation mediated by the Word. "Ordinarily God reveals nothing apart from the Word" (COCCEIUS *ibid.* II, 8).

13.—Of course, Christianity is called by the apostle a "reasonable service", Rom. 12. 1. This, however, must only imply that it consists not in Levitical ordinances, usages and works, but in the worship of God in spirit and truth. In consequence of this, on the other hand, it must also be insisted that Christianity is not directed against reason, that it would not kill it or set it aside, but that it would rather work upon man directly through reason, i.e., not magically but morally.—HEIDEGGER (I, 39): "The Christian religion is indeed a reasonable service *(cultus)*

Rom. 12. 11 not because it is built up from reason or to its norm and scale—but because it is not σωματική, σαρκική, as Israel's was in part, but inward, spiritual.—Thus faith conquers reasoning and leads every reason captive to obedience in Christ, yet so that it does not remove sobriety and light of mind or truth naturally known, but actually conquers by it, by the leading of God's Spirit and His Word. In revealing God does not push men about like ζῶα ἄλογα or automata, but He speaks to φρόνιμοι, 1 Cor. 10. 15 (who can judge what an apostle says). Faith does not destroy reason but stimulates it, does not get it involved but directs it, does not blind the mind but illuminates it."

14.—Hence the use of reason in theology is perfectly justified. By it (1) the true God must be proved to be the author of revelation; (2) the logical harmony or (and of course it holds only on the supposition of faith!) the rationality of revealed truths must be set forth; (3) the connection of conclusions resulting from each of them is to be developed; and (4) the entire natural, historical, linguistic, etc., knowledge of theology to be made use of. But only faith makes it possible for man to use reason in this correct way and, in dealing with truths which belong only to revelation, to limit it to such an *usus organicus,* in which illumined and led by the H. Spirit it adopts revelation, distinguishes the true from the false by the plumb-line of the Word of God, scientifically illumines the mysteries of faith and demonstrates the connection of the separate truths of faith.—HEIDEGGER (I, 39): "Illumined reason is of no contemptible use to theology. And its chief use consists in the fact that forthwith it brings forth from its own treasury arguments on behalf of faith. This happens in four ways. Firstly, reason urged and directed by the Spirit of God through sure and undoubted criteria and signs of divinity discovers that he who reveals the way of salvation, God, is not an imposter, demon or man suspected of falsehood.—Secondly, illumined reason puts forth arguments for the principles of Christian faith, by which it shows to the unbelieving of those who embrace it its worthiness of credit, which is not a thing impossible, irrational or contrary to man's uncorrupted nature; and it dissolves subtleties adduced to the contrary by a perverse reason. —Thirdly, reason occasionally proceeds in accordance with its own principles by collecting suitable arguments on behalf of faith, in those matters which are known both by faith and by reason; or arguments at least known by faith, which stimulates reason in many, are confirmed by reason.—Fourthly, in a word reason, accompanying the use of words and of the things signified by these words, whether natural ideas and reasons which we have of and for the things and which revelation presupposes, has power of judgment on equal terms, i.e., those considered apart from construction or conjunction. Use is the judge in familiar words which are not proper and peculiar to revelation. Faith alone judges upon the supernatural construction and conjunction of simple words or terms which belong to revelation alone. The *H. Spirit alone secures our right use of reason and the propriety of our faith.*" The result of this is that "the use of reason in things which depend on sheer, pure revelation is merely instrumental *(organicus)*", i.e., "(1) a man humbly receives and tests revelation in the bosom of reason by the previous Spirit and His Word; (2) in the doctrine of religion reason is an instrument for judging true and false, certain and uncertain, etc., but only if preceded by the light of the divine Word and the inward illumination of the H. Spirit; (3) by the aid of languages and the arts reason throws light upon mysteries solidly proved from the Word of God; (4) reason compares one word of God with another word of God, the OT with the NT, etc., one dogma of faith with another."—RIISSEN (I, 11): "The use of human reason in theology is (1) to perceive things revealed, Mt. 13. 51 (Have ye understood these things? . . . Yea!); (2) to compare them with other things, Ac. 17. 11 (received the word with all readiness, examining the scriptures daily whether these things were so); (3) to explain, Neh. 8. 8 (they read in the book . . . and they gave the sense so that they understood the reading); (4) to distinguish the false; for it is necessary to search out things that differ, Phil. 1. 10 (prove or approve the things that differ); (5) to clear it of objections, Rom. 9 (the 'God forbids!')."

15.—Thus by believing surrender to revelation and by a use of reason which puts reason at the service of faith in revelation there grows up a *theologia revelata,* which, as the first rightly to prove that "natural theology" is preliminary knowledge of God in its true significance, is "the doctrine of God reconciling man the sinner to Himself in Christ and duly to be known of him and worshipped in godly-wise, a doctrine taught of God who reveals it by His Word, and purely instituted as in His presence for man the sinner's salvation and for the glory of God's name" (HEIDEGGER I, 14). On this view theology is a science which rests essentially on the facts of revelation and is meant to be not a pure awareness but a life. Hence it does not, like the purely human science, belong only to a spiritual power of man's. It pertains to his whole personality, so that in cultivating it the whole man with all the powers of his spiritual and moral life must play his part with reason and understanding, with heart and soul, with knowledge and conscience.—TURRETIN (I, vi, 4): "None of the intellectual functions as treated in ethics and contradistinguished from each other can constitute the true and proper genus of theology. (1) All these habits are habits of knowing. But theology is a habit not of knowing but of believing. (2) Natural habits were discovered and developed by the ingenuity of man. Theology is supernatural and θεόδοτος; its principle is not human reason but divine revelation. (3) They are all theoretical or practical simply. Theology is of a mixed category, partly theoretical, partly practical.—But although theology cannot properly and strictly be called any one of these habits, it is nevertheless well said that it includes them all in itself in an eminent degree."

16.—Since theology has also to acknowledge and to expound what belongs to natural religion, we may distinguish between "simple (pure) articles", which rest purely upon revelation, and "mixed articles", in the exposition of which reason too has its substantial share. Only it must be maintained that the basic doctrines of theology (Trinity, Fall of human race, Redeemer, True Blessedness and the Single Way to it) may be known purely from revelation, and that withal H. Scripture in every part of its doctrinal system is the sheer authority.—ALSTED (*Theol. Didact.*, p. 7): "Since theological questions are of two kinds, simple and mixed, of which the former consist of purely theological terms, the latter of a theological term and a philosophical, no one of sound mind could fail to see that philosophy can be applied to proof only in the latter category, in the former merely to assertion and explanation."

CHAPTER II

HOLY SCRIPTURE

1.—The one source and norm of all Christian knowledge is H. Scripture, i.e., the (inner) content of all the books which God has allowed to be recorded by Prophets, Evangelists and Apostles. "H. Scripture is the Word of God described on the authority of the H. Scripture through Moses and the prophets in the OT, through the evangelists and apostles in the NT, and made up into canonical books, in order to teach the Church fully and plainly about God and things divine and to be the single norm of faith and life unto salvation" (HEIDEGGER, II, 6).—Other definitions of Holy Scripture: PETER MARTYR (p. 29): "(Holy Scripture is) a sort of expression of the wisdom of God inspired by the Holy Spirit in godly men, then consigned to memorials and letters (i.e., literary records)" —BEN. ARETIUS (p. 15): "Divine Scripture is the evidence of the divine will towards the race of mortals, originally unfolded by the Spirit of God, but afterwards consigned to letters through men at God's instigation for the salvation of believers."—WENDELIN (Collat. p. 41): "H. Scripture which we call canonical is the infallible rule of faith and morals transmitted by God through the prophets and apostles to the Church and comprised in fixed books."—RIISSEN (II, 1): "Scripture is the collection of books written through the Spirit by men of God concerning the things which men must know, believe and do for the glory of God and their own salvation."—MASTRICHT (I, ii, 6): "By H. Scripture we understand nothing else than the doctrine of living for God, so far as it is contained and described in writing (literis)." In explanation of this definition MASTRICHT remarks: "Since the art of living to God is not a natural power but an acquired faculty, it really demands a rule by which it may be directed, one prescribed by God, which, apart from the life of Christ and our own conscience, we have earlier placed in the Word of God or Scripture."

2.—To H. Scripture therefore belong only the books written by prophets and apostles, i.e., by those persons whom God illumined in a special way with His Spirit, in order to avail Himself of them as the instruments of revelation.—WENDELIN (Collat. p. 47): "Besides the prophets and apostles there are no canonical and authentic doctors in the Church of Christ."

3.—Since these books have from early times been recognised and accounted as prophetic and apostolic by a canon of the Church, they are called canonical.—COCCEIUS (S. Th., IV, ii): "The Church possessed a fixed canon of both OT and NT, i.e., a κατάλογος or list of divine books, which they have therefore called canonical (κανονικοί), i.e., put on the list, as ὄντας ἐν τῷ κανόνι. Others, they declared, were outside the canon and they have called them ἀκανόνικοι. Against the *Socinians* and *Anabaptists* it is insisted that the OT also has canonical authority for the Christian, e.g., RIISSEN (II, x): "The *Socinians* and *Anabaptists* deprive the OT Scriptures of canonical effect as beneath the NT, supposing a difference in substance between OT and NT. Although we do not deny that the O.T. has been done away as regards the Mosaic dispensation, we lay it down that it still continues doctrinally." The books were called הכתדב, τὸ γεγραμμένον; הספרים, τὰ βιβλία; ספד יהוה; מכתב אלהים (sic !); γραφαὶ ἅγιαι; ἱερὰ γράμματα.

[These books are given usually in the Authorised Version order without any classification, save that they speak of the five books of Moses which are then named].

The following books belong to the canon of the Old and New Testaments (*Confess. Gall.* III): "The five books of Moses, namely Genesis, Exodus, Leviticus, Numbers, Deuteronomy. That of Joshua. Judges. Ruth. Samuel two books. Kings two Books. Chronicles or Paralipomena two books. Ezra one Book. Nehemiah. Esther. Job, Psalms, Proverbs of Solomon, Ecclesiastes, Song of Songs, Isaiah, Jeremiah, with the Lamentations, Ezekiel, Daniel, Minor Prophets XII, namely, Hosea, Joel, Amos, Obadiah, Jonah, Micah, Nahum, Habakkuk, Zephaniah, Haggai, Zechariah, Malachi [all in LXX forms].

"The Holy Gospel of Jesus Christ according to Matthew, according to Mark, according to Luke, according to John. Acts of the Apostles. The Epistles of Paul, namely to the Romans one, to the Corinthians two, to the Galatians one, to the Ephesians one, to the Philippians one, to the Colossians one, to the Thessalonians two, to Timothy two, to Titus one, to Philemon one. The Epistle to the Hebrews. The Epistle of James. Peter's Epistles two. John's Epistles three. Jude's Epistle one. John's Apocalypse."

4.—The writings preserved and transmitted along with them, which are not of prophetic or apostolic origin, are on the other hand called apocryphal books. "These books are and are called apocryphal, which have neither prophets nor apostles for their authors" (WENDELIN, *Coll.* 44). Such apocryphal books are to be found only in the OT as an appendix to it. Those books of the NT which were regarded as apocryphal (i.e., as not emanating from the apostles) by the Reformers and in part by their pupils (namely the epistles 2 Peter, 2 and 3 John, Jude, Hebrews, and the Revelation of John) have long been known and acknowledged by the Church to be canonical.

To begin with the Reformed distinction between the Word of God and Holy Scripture and the conception of Holy Scripture peculiar to original Protestantism, which was not dogmatic but historical (as in German Protestant and even in the later Lutheran theology right into the seventeenth century), seemed to lead to the restoration of the Eusebian canon in the NT Hence, e.g., MUSCULUS (*Loci*, p. 175) on the epistles 2 Peter, 2 and 3 John, Jude, Hebrews and Revelation comments: "The effect of these judgments of the early men is that I am less bound to them than to the rest of the Scriptures." At the same time HYPERIUS (p. 48) had already remarked that these writings could undoubtedly be used for the exegetical basis of dogmas. From that time it held (e.g., as early as ZANCHIUS, p. 3) in Reformed dogmatics as a *res comperta,* that the books cited had for long enough been wrongly regarded as uncanonical (Cf. HEPPE, *Altprot. Dogm.* I, p. 254), and ever after the identification of the concepts "Word of God" and "H. Scripture" had become prevalent, Reformed Dogmaticians began to declaim against the Old Protestant distinction between canonical and apocryphal writings in the NT, as against a delusion of the devil. Cf. COCCEIUS (*S.T.* IV, 36): "Among them" (the writings of the NT) "although the de-authorisation, or stamping as forgery, of certain books or parts of them has been attempted, the more notably has their authority shined forth by the zeal and proof of the godly in the early Church. Thus neither the Epistle of James nor the two of John nor the second of Peter nor the Revelation are reasonably counted by some apocryphal. And these books are sufficiently commended as θεόπνευστοι both by the godliness and sanctity of the doctrine in agreement with Moses, the prophets and every gospel, as well as by the truth of prophecy and their conformity with προάγουσα προφητεία and by the antiquity of the witness that is theirs."

As regards the OT apocrypha we are informed by BUCAN (IV, 8), why they have no canonical authority: "(1) because they were not written either by prophets or by apostles, and they are not αὐτόπιστοι; (2) in them ἐνεργεία, force and majesty do not shine forth as in the canonical books; (3) and in them are things which are at variance with the canonical books, either ἀσύστατα or quite openly false (Tob. c. 8 and 12 against the Word of God, 1 Macc. 6 and 2.14 and 2.12.   In Baruch 6 it is said that the Jews would be in captivity seven generations instead of seventy years, contrary to the custom of Scripture; (4) they were not transmitted to the Jews (to whom yet were entrusted the oracles of God), because they are not even extant in the Hebrew tongue; and (5) their credit in the Church was always doubtful and t' re was hesitation as to their authors."

5.—These canonical books of the Old and New Testaments not only contain God's Word but are God's written word itself.—The older Reformed theology distinguished between the "Word of God" and "Holy Scripture" most definitely. By the first term they meant all that God had spoken to the fathers in diverse ways and in latter times by His Son. It was therefore taught by CALVIN and his immediate successors in Church teaching (and in Germany still by HYPERIUS), that the "Word of God," i.e., the manifold revelations or words in which God had spoken to men, were transmitted orally at the start and that it was only later that they were recorded; cf. HEPPE *A.-P. Dk.* I, p. 251-2. According to this account, then, the "Word of God" was the word spoken by God to individual men. The later dogmaticians on the contrary, separating the idea of inspiration from that of revelation unanimously teach that the "Word of God" rests, not upon God's personal acts of revelation, but upon the manner of their recording, upon inspiration. On this view the "Word of God" is "the word brought to record by inspiration," whereby the concepts "Word of God" and "Holy Scripture" were identified. This as early as *Conf. Helv.* II: "The canonical scriptures are the actual true word of God." And WOLLEB (3) concludes by saying: "The query, whether the scriptures or sacred books are the Word of God, is unworthy of a Christian. As in a school we do not dispute with one who denies first principles, so we ought to adjudge a man unworthy to be listened to, if he denies the first principle of the Christian religion." Of course, even Reformed scholasticism was in the habit of continuing still the old definition of "Word of God" and "H. Scripture". How this was done is clear from the answer given by VOETIUS (V, 1) to the question, "whether it is an article of faith or *de fide* or a necessary *credendum*, that Scripture is the Word of God." VOETIUS replies: "Distinguish between the thing itself (or the material and content of this Scripture) and the external forms and special modes of writing, such as, e.g., that this part is written in such and such a language, such and such a phrasing, etc.; again, between the canon taken collectively and its integral parts indefinitely, and the same canon taken distributively (or its separate parts, greater, less and least, considered *definite* and *sigillatim*); in addition between faith (or the inference from the principle of faith) and the conclusion from a principle of faith upon some other theological truth."

In a manner quite different from that in which a distinction was drawn between the *verbum* ἄγραφον (i.e., the word spoken by God to the individual exponents and instruments of the dispensation of salvation, or the word of revelation proper) and the *verbum* ἔγγραφον (or the recording of the revealed word), a distinction was now drawn between the *verbum internum* and *externum*. The former was reckoned the content, the latter the expression of inspiration (which is conceptually different from revelation). "The inward word is the private inspiration of prophets and apostles; the outward is the preaching of it by their mouths, done in the public canon" (HEIDEGGER I). The distinction between the unwritten and the written word was only discussed in opposition to the Catholic doctrine of tradition; e.g., RIJSSEN II, 3: "The distinction of the word into unwritten and written is not a division into genus and species, as the Papists would have it, but of the subject into its accidents. It happens to the same word that once it was not written but now it is."

6.—The record of the canonical books came into existence by the special and direct activity of the Holy Spirit, which urged the authors to write, gave them the thoughts and words they were to record, and preserved them from any error in their writing. In other words, the canonical writings were in content and in form inspired in their authors by the H. Spirit.

At the root of the original Reformed doctrine of inspiration lay the distinction *between*, at the root of the later Church doctrine the identification *of* the concepts "Word of God" and "H. Spirit". Hence for CALVIN the authority of H. Scripture rested purely on the fact that it reports upon real acts of God in revelation. In other words, it is the original document of revelations, which were followed before their recording and were for a time transmitted orally. CALVIN (I, vi, 1-2) insists that from the beginning God imparted Himself to individuals, as Adam, Noah, Abraham, etc.: "this they were then to transmit by hand to their successors. . . . *In the end*, in order that by a continuous advancement the truth of doctrine might survive in the world in all ages, it was His will that the same oracles which He had deposited with the patriarchs should be consigned, so to speak, to public records. It was with this in view that the law was promulgated and to it the prophets were later added to interpret it." There is no word of a peculiar inspiration of the record. The authority of Scripture then rests not upon the form of its recording, but upon its content, i.e. upon the reality of the revealed facts attested in the writing. Hence God is described not so much as the "author" of scripture, as rather the author of the doctrine attested in it, which He Himself has announced to men. (I, vii, 4)—"It must be held that faith in doctrine is not established, until we are convinced that God is its author. Therefore the highest proof of Scripture is uniformly derived from the person of God who speaks it (*a Dei loquentis persona*). For HYPERIUS' exactly similar teaching see HEPPE, *Altprot. Dogm.* I, p. 251. URSIN also is still on the whole unacquainted with the mechanical theory of inspiration. He says (*Loci*, p. 446): "In order that the reason may be understood for distinguishing between H. Scripture and other writings, we must take account of the degrees of those who teach in the Church. The authority of the prophets and apostles is far superior to that of other ministers of the Church; God called them directly to proclaim His will to the rest of men, and He equipped them with the testimonies of miracles and other things, by which He testified that He illumined and controlled their minds in this way by His Spirit, so that He might prevent them from erring in any part of doctrine." Accordingly the trustworthiness of the canonical books rests not upon the special way and manner in which God has effected their recording, but upon the state of grace which their authors permanently enjoyed, upon their life in the Holy Spirit. The ground upon which the infallibility of their narratives rests is not the operation of the Holy Spirit at the time of writing out the canonical scriptures, but the abiding fellowship of the Spirit in which God kept the prophets and apostles, the knowledge of the truth which the Biblical authors enjoyed generally through the illumination of the H. Spirit.

But as early as the end of the sixteenth century the conception of inspiration had changed; it was now completely severed from the idea of revelation. Scripture was therefore now regarded as inspired, purely because it was dictated to the Biblical authors by God.

Already COCCEIUS completely represents this conception of inspiration, at least with the reservation that there may still be noted in him at least a few effects of the earlier way of viewing it. In his *S.T.* IV. 39 his teaching is: "The author and giver of these books is God (not the Father only but also the Son), who ordered them to be written, and by His Spirit inspired, urged and guided His ministers to write them. (40): The men of God, called prophets in general parlance, were God's *assistants and amanuenses, who wrote exactly as they spoke, not by their own will but driven by the H. Spirit.* COCCEIUS adds (41): *"By their sheer function of amanuenses* these men described things partly seen and heard from God in ecstasy or in apparition to the eye or in dreams, the Spirit also revealing many things in them by a supernatural light. Other things also they referred to by historical narration and by teaching "according to the wisdom given" them, 2 P. 3. 15. Some things they dictated for writing. *In these it was given them to be faithful,* not without the witness of the H. Spirit:—whence it follows that they never deviated from the thing to be written about by infirmity of memory or of λογισμός nor by lack of skill or care in the use of words. So that every word, as being contained in letters which were sacred as signs, should be accepted and held as the word of the H. Spirit, useful and most wisely compounded to meet every exigency of edification *without the slightest danger.* Upon this wisdom moreover is stamped *the impress of speech (often a repentant mind and a special gift of ministry,* when the Spirit of God *has tempered His gifts pleasantly,* being the θεὸς εἰρήνης) and a *disposition worthy of its author."*

Thus H. Scripture carries its *certitudo* (authority) in itself, since it is essentially a beam of divine light and divine wisdom. And since Scripture gives this account of itself, it cannot base its reliability upon any alien authority or allow it to be so based. H. Scripture desires only such an acknowledgement of its certainty as is conceded to it purely because of its inspiration. Hence Cocceius attacks the *Papists* who assert (III, 3) "that they do not deny the divine authority of Scripture in itself, but only ask how it obtains authority *quoad nos,* i.e. with us, or how we agree that Scripture is divine." For "they reduce Scripture to the level of things which men say, so that it may be doubted whether God has spoken to them or not. This is a signal insult inflicted upon Scripture, as though there were no radiance of divinity in Scripture." See note on Paragraph 7, (which combats the idea that there is any need for the Church's authority. But we must of course never forget that Scripture has neither authority nor validity apart from the direct opening of our minds by the H. Spirit. The same Spirit which inspired the authors must inspire us, if Scripture is to be Scripture for us as for them).

Henceforward the "divineness" of Scripture was derived purely—not from the participation of its authors in the facts of revelation and in God's saving activity, but from the manner of its recording.—Heidegger (*Corp. Theol.* II, 32): "The compulsion to write was enjoined upon them, not by a *direct calling* to the prophetic and apostolic—not on *chance occasions* only—not by the *will of man*—but alike by *God's mandate* both *general* (by which they were commanded to teach all nations), and *special*—and by inspiration or *the divine inward mandate."* Hence of course it was assumed that the inspiring H. Spirit did not efface the individuality of the authors, but used them as tools to set forth revealed truth in manifold form. Heidegger *S.T.* II, 36: "Nor does the variety in style of the writers obstruct the divine inspiration of things and words. The H. Spirit, as the θεὸς εἰρήνης in His inspiration, so directed and sanctified, that they might expound one and the same doctrine, though in varying words."—Leiden Synopsis (III, 7): "The writers did not always regard themselves purely παθητικῶς or passively, but also ἐνεργητικῶς or effectually, as those who applied both skill and mental activity and discourse and memory, arrangement and order and their own style (whence the difference in manner of writing among them) Amos 7. 14-15 (I was no prophet, neither was I a prophet's son; but I was an herdman and a dresser of sycamore trees; and the Lord took me from following the flock, and the LORD said unto me, Go, prophesy unto my people Israel) 2 Cor. 10. 10 (His letters . . . are weighty and strong ; but his bodily presence is weak and his speech of no account) 11. 6 (though I be rude in speech, yet am I not in knowledge; nay in everything we have made it manifest among all men to you-ward); but under the presidency of the H. Spirit who so drives and guides them, that they are preserved on all sides from any error of mind, memory, language and pen 2 Sam. 23. 1-2 (David . . . The Spirit of the Lord spake by me, and His word was upon my tongue) 1 Cor. 7. 25. 40 (. . . I give my judgment, as one that hath obtained mercy of the Lord to be faithful: ...after my judgment: and I think that I also have the Spirit of God)."

The theologians of the ACADEMY OF SAUMUR, of course, made an attempt later to restore the Reformed conception of H. Scripture to its rights once more. But they encountered the opposition of the entire Reformed orthodoxy, which in the *Form. Cons. Helv.* declared with regard to the Hebrew text of the OT, that it is θεόπνευστος regarding both the vowels (whether the very points or at least the power of the points) and regarding things as well as words."

On the basis of this thought the *Scholastics* proceeded in their disquisitions on H. Scripture and its inspiration.

The question "whether the writers of the New Testament thought in a different language (i.e. Syriac) from the one they wrote in", is denied by VOETIUS (I, p. 14): "No one produces anything correctly and reasonably, whether orally or in writing, unless he has previously thought it correctly. If therefore they wrote in Greek or in Hellenistic, they also thought in Greek, and that by the inspiration and dictation of the H. Spirit."

The question "whether the sacred writers, i.e. the prophets and the apostles, understood everything they wrote" is affirmed by VOETIUS I, pp. 45, 47.

The question "whether the sacred writers wrote unwillingly and because compelled to write" VOETIUS answers in the negative, I, p. 46.

The question "whether, when they wrote afresh, the H. Spirit stirred up their thought and memory of what they had taught previously or acquired by revelation" VOETIUS affirms, "with the distinction that He stirs up afresh not only things habitually known by infusion of the charism of infallibility and of the direct impress of supernatural light (which we conceive after the manner of a habit), but also things actually known afresh, as regards the formal concept of course and the actual recollection, but not the impress of the intelligible things: once impressed these persist and do not flare up and die down like fireworks," I, p. 46.

VOETIUS I, p. 46: "Only the apostles and apart from them Luke also and Mark were θεόπνευστοι. On the other hand this cannot be said of the evangelists *Barnabas, Titus, Timothy, Silvanus* and *Epaphroditus*."

Similarly the amanuenses of the prophets and apostles were as little inspired as the *librarii et typographi* who prepare copies of the Bible.

The question, "whether the inscriptions or titles of the books of Scripture are authentic", VOETIUS answers, (V, p. 2): "So far I do not see that the case has been made out for the canonicity and inspiration of all the titles prefixed." Authenticity is even not to be assumed, "where in the actual sacred text either the whole title or the author's name is learnedly written down". The only result is that in such cases the titles are "credible indirectly and *per consequentiam*".

To answer the question "whether the accents of the original Hebrew and Greek text are authentic" VOETIUS V, p. 4 distinguishes between the musical and the tonic accents. "As regards the euphonic or musical accents of the Hebrews according to which they chant when reading, I do not see why they should be affirmed. As for the tonics I fail to see why they should be rejected. We prefer to concede that the former, which make for the integrity of etymology and syntax, may be on an equal footing with the vowel points, rather than to attack the opposite standpoint. In the matter of Greek accents in the NT, I prefer the simple assertion that they unmistakably belong not only to the elegance of the language and script but also to its integrity at that time."

Quite individually MASTRICHT defines the concept of the inspiration of H. Scripture by linking up the concept of divine canonisation with the revelation of the Biblical books. He says (I, ii, 13): "God made Scripture (a) partly by revelation, which was carried out; (1) by writing, as is clear in the decalogue ; (2) by a behest that it should be written ; Dt. 31. 19 (. . . write ye this song for you, and teach thou it the children of Israel; put it in their mouths, that this song may be a witness for me against the children of Israel) ; Rev. i. 19 (write the things which thou sawest, and the things which are, and that thing which shall come to pass hereafter); (3) by inspiring it, 2 Tim. iii, 16 (every scripture inspired of God is also profitable for teaching, for reproof, for correction, for instruction (in discipline) which is for righteousness), i.e. by suggesting the things to be written and by infallibly directing the writing, so that in everything, whether they were occupied in law or in deed, He not only inspired the actual things but also dictated the separate words: (b) partly by canonisation, by which inspiration the writings were transmitted to the Church.— For it does not suffice, to constitute a part of Scripture, if some book is written through some extraordinary servant of God and by the sure direction of the Spirit, unless it is also given by the divine authority of the Church and sanctified for the purpose of her (the Church's) sanctified rule."

7.—Upon this incomparable peculiarity in the origin of H. Scripture, i.e. upon its divineness rests its peculiar attributes, "those by which its divineness is sufficiently declared" (L. CROCIUS *Synt.*, p. 117). These are "authority and certitude, sufficiency and perfection, necessity and perspicuity".—The assertion usual in Roman theology of the seventeenth century, that "Scripture being absolutely and in itself authentic is divine, but that relatively and *quoad nos* that authority depends on the Church, so that the only way it becomes known to us is by the kindness of the Church", is nicely countered by RIISSEN (ii, 9): "Since authority belongs to the genus of the things related, it must not be viewed absolutely but relatively. And so Scripture cannot be authentic in itself without it also having regard to us. The proofs which acquire it authority in its own right ought also to move us to assent to them. [But this proof is the H. Spirit! And the nerve of the Roman position is that the Church as such is guided by the H. Spirit].

8.—The divineness or the inspired character of H. Scripture is revealed to the believer first of all as the attribute of authority itself. "The authority of H. Scripture is the dignity and excellence pertaining to H. Scripture alone, above all other writings, by which it is and is held to be *authentic*, i.e., infallibly *certain*, so that by absolute necessity it must be believed and obeyed by all because of God its Author" (POLAN, i, 16). In virtue of this H. Scripture is the principle of the whole of theology, the exclusive norm of Christian doctrine and the infallible judge in all doctrinal disputes; and in such wise that all that the vocabulary of Scripture or its indubitable inferences contain is dogma; whereas the opposite of it is error; and anything else, even if it does not contradict H. Scripture, is indifferent for the soul's salvation.—LEIDEN SYNOPSIS (iii, 18-19): "This Scripture alone is the *principle* from which and the *substance* from which all saving truth is to be deduced, the *canon* and *norm* by which every true and so every false doctrine of things divine must be measured—in a word the αὐτόπιστος and irrefragable *witness* and judge, i.e. its own evidence, by which every controversy raised about divine things should be judged.—The criterion or norm of judgment is contained in the following axioms; (1) whatever is contained in it or agrees with it either expressly or by a valid inference is true dogma; (2) that which disagrees must necessarily be false; (3) while whatever is not contained in it, although it does not directly disagree with it, is not a dogma necessary to salvation."

9.—The attributes or affections of H. Scripture are very variously listed. CROCIUS (*Synt.*, p. 117) mentions "authority, perfection, clarity of feeling and of interpretation, effectiveness". MASTRICHT (I, ii, 14-21) recounts the following: "(1) its supreme and independent *authority*, whereby neither in itself nor as regards others does it depend on any source other than God." In virtue of this it possesses "(a) the *power to decide* all theological controversies, (b) to *direct* life and morals, (c) to *judge* ourselves"; nevertheless the distinction must be preserved between the "αὐθεντία of history" and the "αὐθεντία of the norm": (2) "*truth and certainty*": (3) the *integrity* by which through God's singular providence it exists immune from all corruption: (4) *holiness* and *purity*, and that by reason of (a) God the principal cause, (b) the amanuenses who are called God's holy men, (c) the holy matter, i.e. the will of God, (d) the *end*, which is our sanctification: (5) *perspicuity*: (6) *perfection* from which nothing at all is lacking which makes for living unto God: (7) *necessity*, not indeed absolutely, but presupposing the divine will: (8) *efficacy*. By many dogmaticians only 'authority', 'perfection', and 'perspicuity' are brought forward.

10.—The authority, i.e. the divineness and authenticity in no wise rests, even *quoad nos*, upon the Church's acknowledgement, but simply and solely upon Scripture itself, which as God's word is αὐτόπιστος and ἀνυπεύθυνος. The sole evidence which with absolute certainty assures the Christian of the divineness and authority of H. Scripture is therefore the evidence which Scripture bears to itself or which God bears to it in the conscience of the believer, the evidence of the H. Spirit. This is given to the believer in the fact that the longing for salvation which fills him reaches full satisfaction through the H. Spirit, that the Spirit of God which animates him is recognised again in H. Scripture and that his own life of faith is furthered by it more and more, in an ever more benedictory fashion. But as a result the divineness and authority of Scripture can also be recognised only by the Christian who can experience the evidence of the H. Spirit. Other proofs which are used to ground the divine authenticity of Scripture have therefore value for the Christian only so far as they can be used to uphold the authority of Scripture from without. To these belong the evidence of the Church, which transmits H. Scripture to the individual Christian as the word of God acknowledged by it at all times (which tradition has no more value than the evidence of heretics, Jews and heathen, which likewise certifies that H. Scripture was acknowledged in the Church as God's Word from the beginning); as well as the fulfilled predictions of H. Scripture (especially the destruction of Jerusalem and the earlier divine guidance of the Jewish nation, as well as its later dispersion); and the miracles by the performance of which the authors of H. Scripture are certified by

God Himself to be men of God. The question of the authority is identical with the question of the knowability of its divineness or inspiration. In answering this question all Reformed dogmaticians are in essential agreement, since all adduce the *testimonium Spiritus sancti* as the real proof, besides which (with various deviations from each other) they adduce various other arguments as auxiliary proofs of lesser value.

CALVIN argues thus (I, vii, 4): If we are asked for a proof of the divineness of the content of H. Scripture, we must reply that "the testimony of the H. Spirit is more outstanding than all reason. As God alone can properly bear witness to His own words, so these words will not obtain credit in the hearts of men, until they are sealed by the inward testimony of the Spirit. Thus the same Spirit who spake by the mouth of the prophets must penetrate to our hearts, to persuade us that they have faithfully delivered what they were entrusted with by God, Is. 59. 21 (as for me, this is my covenant with them, saith the Lord: my spirit that is upon thee, and my words which I have put in thy mouth, shall not depart out of thy mouth, nor out of the mouth of thy seed, nor out of the mouth of thy seed's seed, saith the Lord, from henceforth and for ever)". Only for him who has this witness of the H. Spirit can other arguments have significance as supports of faith, to convince him of the divineness of Scripture; namely, (1) the "dispensation of divine wisdom", which shines forth from Scripture, (2) "the doctrine savouring of nothing earthly, (3) the fair mutual agreement of all its parts, (4) the humbleness of mean words which yet displays the profoundest and most sublime mysteries of the heavenly kingdom, (5) the antiquity of the writings of Moses, who yet does not tell of a new God, but sets forth one well known to all Israelites, (6) the prophecies of Isaiah, Jeremiah and Daniel's soothsayings, before even an appearance of future events was patent, in fact when rather it was the opposite of the things they were preaching," (7) the simplicity and majesty of the evangelists and apostles, (8) the general " consent" of the Church, the witness of the martyrs, etc. (I, viii).—Scripture is thus αὐτόπιστος, its repute rests purely on itself and is therefore in no wise dependent on the authority of the Church. The expression of *Augustine* adduced by the *Papists* to contradict this statement: "I should not believe the Gospel, were I not moved thereto by the authority of the Catholic Church" is rightly connected by CALVIN with *Augustine's* situation, in which "he was involved with the *Manichees*"; so that his view was: "since he was a stranger to the faith, he could not otherwise be brought to embrace the gospel as the sure truth of God, unless he was overcome by the authority of the Church".—All later dogmaticians explain this expression in exactly the same way. WOLFGANG MUSCULUS rightly remarks, p. 181, that here '*crederem*' is equivalent to '*credidissem* .

Those who assert that "all authority of Scripture depends on the Church" act foolishly (as VIRELLIUS says in *Relig. Christ. compend.*, p. 3), "as though one should say that the light of the sun depends upon the testimony of man. As the sun will not cease to shine although all men should be blind, so the divine word will never take harm, whether it be approved of men or not". URSIN (*Loci*, p. 436) teaches exactly the same. The most essential "evidence" of the "certainty of Scripture" is the testimony of the H. Spirit. "This testimony is unique, proper only to those reborn by the Spirit of Christ and known only to them. And it has such power that it not only attests and seals abundantly in our souls the truth of the prophetic and apostolic doctrine, but also effectually bends and moves our hearts to embrace and follow it." URSIN expounds this thus: Faith in the word of Scripture is nothing else than "the firm assent by which we assent to every word of God transmitted to us and the trust by which severally we recognise and declare that God is gracious to us according to the voice of Scripture. This trust is followed by gladness which rests in God and invokes Him, with the certain hope of obtaining good things which we ask for in accordance with the prescription of the Word. But godly individuals with the quick and sure feelings of their hearts have experience, that both these things, the assent or certainty regarding doctrine and the lively consolation which springs from it, depend not on any man's or creature's testimony, but are kindled and confirmed by the power of the divine Spirit Himself through no other teaching than that of the prophets and apostles read, heard and pondered". Only for him who has experienced this testimony of the H. Spirit in his heart can the other arguments (antiquity of doctrine, prophecies, miracles, etc.) adduced for the inspiration of the canonical books in Scripture, have the real force of proof.

For the individual of course, the authority of the Church may be the means by which he attains to belief in Scripture, since it stimulates and educates him, etc. But it does not follow that the repute of Scripture is dependent upon the authority of the Church. It is rather the same here with the Church as it is with the woman at Sychar, Jn. iv. 42. "Many of the Samaritans are said to have believed in Christ because of the woman's words in testimony, that he had told her all things that she had done. But after they had had Christ with them for two days, many more believed because of his words.—Therefore as the men of Sychar were first moved by the woman's tale to believe in Christ, after they had seen and heard Christ himself they were so confirmed, that they now said that they would believe, even if the woman were silent. So it may be the case that those not yet converted or still weak, may, by the testimony of the Church as more impressing them visually, be most moved to have faith in Scripture;

yet after they have been irradiated by the richer light of faith, they experience confirmation that Scripture is the word of God by a far higher and surer testimony—though all angels and men should be persuading them of something different" (Ursin ?).

Thus the solely real witness to the divineness of Scripture is the witness which Scripture gives of itself, "because God Himself bears this witness". Hence the constant description of H. Scripture as αὐτόπιστος and ἀνυπεύθυνος.—Bullinger (I, 2) is most precise in describing the Reformed Church conception of the *certitudo* of H. Scripture : "Briefly, since Scripture is the Word of God, it must be believed without doubt."

Summing up the most essential statements in this doctrinal development Piscator (p. 16) teaches that H. Scripture proves itself to be θεόπνευστος and αὐτόπιστος, purely by the witness of the H. Spirit; in addition to which he emphasises the following "proofs for establishing faith in Scripture": "(1) its heavenly majesty, (2) the mutual consent of all its parts, (3) the admiration which it draws us into, (4) the number and greatness of its miracles, (5) the wonderful fulfilment of prophecies, (6) the consent of the Church, (7) the blood of the martyrs."

Even later this conception of H, Scripture was retained unchanged alike in the Federal theology and in Scholasticism, and the nature of the *test. Sp. s.* was defined with special care, e.g. by Heidegger (*Corp. Theol.* II, 14): "This witness of the H. Spirit is not a bare persuasion of mind which may be liable to error, or an irrational movement of the heart such as enthusiasts hawk as divine. But it is its glow and shining in our dark hearts, affording us the light of the knowledge of the glory of God in the face of Jesus Christ, 2 Cor. 4. 6, so that, natural obstacles having been thus removed, we may be able to look within at all the excellency and wealth of the divine word."—The relation of the witness of the Church about Scripture to that of the H. Spirit is described by Heidegger (*Medull. Theol.* II, viii): "The witness of the Church" is "not authentic and fundamental but εἰσαγωγικὸν and ὑπηρετικόν".—In the same sense Wolleb p.3: "This witness is twofold, fundamental and ministerial. The witness of the H. Spirit is fundamental (*principale*)— while the witness of the Church is ministerial."

Similarly Voetius V, 14: "As there is no objective certainty about the authority of Scripture, save as infused and imbued by God the Author of Scripture, so we have no subjective certainty of it, no formal concept of the authority of Scripture, except from God illuminating and convincing inwardly through the H. Spirit. As Scripture itself, as if radiating an outward principle by its own light (no outsider intervening as principle or means of proof or conviction), is something ἀξιόπιστόν or credible *per se* and *in se*—so the H. Spirit is the inward, supreme, first, independent principle, actually opening and illuminating the eyes of our mind, effectually convincing us of the credible authority of Scripture, from it, along with it and through it, so that being drawn we run, and being passively convicted within we acquiesce."

ALSTED 31 gives the strongest expression : "The authority and certitude of Scripture depends on the witness of the H. Spirit and this proof is the greatest of proofs. For the authority of any saying or writing depends upon its actual author. Much depends upon this rule, which is the basis of the whole of theology."

[One should note how confused VOETIUS is for instance, and the confusion is that of the entire "verbal inspiration" school. At one moment he declares that Scripture shines by its own light: the next he (rightly) declares that the intervention of the Holy Spirit is indispensable. In fact the H. Spirit is the light by which H. Scripture shines. But then, to change the metaphor, the Spirit bloweth where it listeth, and is not at the disposal of any man or book or other creative thing. But the fact that Reformed theology has such a strong hold upon the H. Spirit as the so-called subjective principle helps us to appreciate the other fact that verbal inspiration is nearly right and an excellent rule of thumb. It is abolished as a theological dogma by the fact that God alone controls the essential light of His Spirit. It is so difficult to realise that God alone is, and that by Him alone can we ever know Him, even through Scripture. If we do so know Him, it is because He so brought it to pass by His direct intervention.—Be very careful to note how, even in the next section, the "subjective principle of the H. Spirit" is automatically put aside in favour of a false autonomy of H. Scripture].

11.—Since the authority of H. Scripture coincides with the authority of God (!), it is essentially an absolute authority. At the same time there is founded on the contents of Scripture a distinction in its authority. So far as everything that Scripture recounts is absolutely certain historical truth, it possesses "historical authority or authenticity". But so far as it contains the absolutely divine norms of faith and life, it possesses "normative authority or authenticity". From this it is clear that the "historical" stretches further than the "normative" authority. The former applies to the entire content of Scripture, the latter on the contrary only to a part of it, since what Scripture relates of the works, words and thoughts of the devil and the godless has historical authority but not normative.

This distinction is discussed most adequately by VOETIUS I, p. 30-31: The authority of H. Scripture is distinguishable as an *authentia historica* and *normalis,* the latter of which is also called *authentia praecepti.* The former, *auth. hist.*, is that attribute of H. Scripture, "by which H. Scripture is understood to be infallibly true with a *veritas θεόπνευστος*, so far as the historical writers, in setting forth historically all the dogmas, decrees, words, deeds, good or bad, which are contained in the Bible, are believed to have received them from the mouth and by the direct revelation of God, and to have shewn them to us without any error". *Authentia normalis* is the attribute of H. Scripture, "by which the actual matter of the things contained in the Scriptures (e.g. decrees, sayings, doings) apart from the knowledge of them, oblige and constrain our consciences to faith in, observance and imitation of the things which are there said to be necessary to believe, observe and imitate". VOETIUS continues: "On this premise we say that the whole of Scripture is authentic with the authenticity of history, i.e. that infallible and *θεόπνευστος* truth is diffused through its parts one and all, so that the writers have put forth their views one and all both in matter and in phrasing, not of their own private impulse or whim but at the dictation of the H. Spirit." The stylistic peculiarities of the Biblical writings should not be adduced to contest this idea of inspiration; even these are inspired by the H. Spirit (p. 33). Even the *puncta vocalia* in the OT are inspired (p. 33). On the other hand the " marginal readings " (*τὸ κέρι*) are not to be regarded as authentic.

As regards the *authentia normae s. praecepti* no one would wish to say that "it is just as broadly evident as the *authentia historiae*" (p. 38f.). In determining it we may err by excess as well as by defect. Hence we must distinguish between "sayings and writings and decrees and acts" and between "persons and persons". We must distinguish "(1) persons whose words, deeds, plans are in every way authentic without distinction" (the persons of the Trinity, angels), and from these "God's extraordinary and special injunctions", like His behest to Abraham to slay his son, are to be excepted; (2) "persons whose words, plans, deeds are in no way authentic" (devils, the godless); (3) the persons of believers and godly men, whose words, etc., are authentic, so far as they are supported "by prophetic or apostolic presence and direction"; (4) the "deeds, plans or private administrations", private utterances and regulations of the prophets and apostles are not authentic, unless they have a dogmatic significance ("dogmatise and instruct the Church of God"), in which case of course they acquire authentic standing.

TURRETIN (II, iv, 2) says more briefly: "One *authentia* is of history or of narrative: there is another over and above of truth and of norm. According to the former whatever is narrated in Scripture is most true, just as it is narrated, whether good or bad, true or false. But the latter those things are said to possess, which are true in themselves, so that they may be transmitted as the norm of faith and morals. Not everything in Scripture has *authentia normae*, as those recorded to have been said by the godless or a devil. Yet everything has *authentia historiae*." Likewise pretty well all the dogmaticians.

12.—Further, upon the divineness of H. Scripture rests its perfection. "The perfection of Scripture is the perfection of its parts, by which it contains all the heads of faith and morals, and of its degrees, by which it embraces all degrees of revelation" (BURMANN, 45). In relation to the purpose of Scripture its perfection is exhibited as sufficiency: Scripture contains everything man needs, in order to become acquainted with the nature and will of God as well as of himself, in such wise that thereby his consciousness of sin is awakened and the salvation he requires is transmitted to him. But this does not mean that Scripture expounds all truths completely in express words, but that "implicitly" or "explicitly" it unveils the truth in a perfection, which leads the believer into all truth, since it instructs man in everything he needs to know in order to obtain eternal life.

TURRETIN (II, xvi, 9): "The question comes back to this, whether H. Scripture contains perfectly, not all things absolutely, but those necessary for salvation: not expressly and in so many words, but equivalently and by legitimate deduction; so that there is no need to take refuge in some *verbum ἄγραφον* ;—we accept this." If science proves that all sorts of foreign ingredients have worked their way into Scripture, nothing follows from this against its perfection, since RIISSEN (II, xvi, 3) rightly remarks: "The question is not whether the springs are so pure, that no flaw has crept into many MSS.—but whether they are so corrupt, that they can no longer be regarded as the judge in controversies and the norm".

13.—We must distinguish "essential perfection", according to which H. Scripture sufficiently contains the truths of revelation necessary for obtaining the eternal salvation of grace; and "integral perfection", according to which the sacred writings are by God's grace so preserved from destruction and adulteration that altogether no canonical book and no essential part of such a book has gone astray.

HEIDEGGER (*Medull. theol.* II, 24): "The Scripture of both testaments has its own perfection, which is either the essential perfection of the saving articles of faith, though in different ways, constant in the fulness of the things explained, according to the age and measure of the divine revelation; or integral, and that both simply so, being reflected in plenary fashion in the canon of the conjoined books of OT and NT; and relatively conspicuous in the whole canon whether of the OT or the NT and, as regards parts of the whole Scripture, in each book of it."

Earlier of course they thought differently about *perfectio integralis* in the Reformed Church (in accordance with CALVIN's idea of inspiration). PETER MARTYR e.g. acknowledges that writings which originally belonged to the canon were lost (p. 40): "Of those books which dropped out are noted the book of Enoch (Gen. 5. 22), the book of Jasher (2 Sam. 1.18), the book of the Wars of the Lord (Num. 21. 14), the exploits of David, also of Solomon and of Jehoshaphat, the annals of the kings of Israel (1 K. 2. 41). Besides them, the book of the chronicles of the Kings of Israel (1 K. 14. 19, 16. 27, 22. 39), also the forecasts of the Sons of the Prophets (2 K. 2. 3). In short 3,000 parables of Solomon and 1,005 of his songs, as well as his discussions on plants, 1 K. 4. 32 (in which passage it is explained why God wished to excise so many volumes from these words) [! ?]. Further many famous memorials have been lost. But by the providence of God many have also been preserved, especially those which have been of the greatest use and are most conducive to the instruction of man. Nor must it be thought to have happened by accident that so many great labours have perished: not even a sparrow falls to the ground by chance."

Other Reformed teachers also represented this view, which was also still thoroughly familiar even in later times. RIISSEN, e.g. (II, xvi, 4) to the question "whether complete books, especially of the Old Testament, have perished", gives the answer: "Certain also of ours, like *Musculus*, *Whitaker*, following *Chrysostom*, make the same assertion, etc." But this acknowledgment was later rejected and the present view dogmatically justified, it being taught that not only the recording but also the collection of the Biblical books was effected directly and indirectly by God Himself. [You could assert that of anything at all! !]. The LEIDEN SYNOPSIS teaches (III, 12-13): "The συλλογή or collection or digest of them was actually also made divinely, and that partly directly, partly indirectly. Directly, of those books which, as first written for the whole Church, were committed and commended to it by the divine writers, Rom. 32 (. . . they were intrusted with the oracles of God), as in the OT the books of Moses (which, brought into the *sacrarium* by himself, were placed by divine injunction next to the ark, Dt. 31. 26 (take this book of the law, and put it by the side of the ark of the Covenant of the Lord your God, that it may be there for a witness against thee), and in the NT the Gospels, which, as they were common in subject, display no special inscription, except Luke. And in these is the foundation of saving truth. Indirectly, of those which, written by the authors themselves primarily to particular races, churches, and those the tiniest and

the metropolitan, or their adversaries, had a first, particular use; and by
them they were preserved, not rashly or by accident, but by God's
singular providence (which looks after the Churches in things necessary)
—and by a divine instinct were accepted by practically all of them as
divine; and that not by a free act of the Church, but by a necessary
adoption." Cf. especially MARCK (II, 16): "Nor did any canonical books
completely perish, as *Socinians* and *Papists* would commonly have it, the
latter indeed to prove the imperfection of Scripture, some counting more
than twenty out of the OT alone.   There subscribed, we admit, very
well-known theologians of our own, who yet rightly reject the Papacy,
since canonical doctrine comprised in several books does by the abundant
goodness of God most surely survive in books today.   But this irrelevance
in proof noted, we are of opinion still, that this assumption as to books
completely lost must not be admitted in company with certain *Papists*,
most learned men, because of (1) God's immutability in his decrees, (2)
His provident care actually proved under OT and NT and (3) repeated
promises, Mt. 5. 18 (. . . Till heaven and earth pass away, one jot or one
tittle shall in no wise pass away from the law, till all things be accomplished), Lk. 21. 33 (Heaven and earth shall pass away, but my words
shall not pass away), 1 Pet. 1. 23 (begotten again, not of corruptible
seed, but of incorruptible, through the Word of God, which liveth and
abideth), and also (4) the almost excessive and superstitious watchfulness
of the Church in later times, both Christian and Jewish".—ALTING
(p. 78): "Scripture has lost nothing canonical. The books that are lacking
were not of this kind: God had preserved it otherwise (*alias?*)." RIISSEN
(ib.) says: "It is safer to follow the common view, that no canonical book has
perished". [At least until you have realised that, the canon being as it is today, you more and more feel how complete the dogmatic system is: nothing
is lacking for our human confidence in the divine mystery of redemption].

14.—This being so, there is no need of a tradition to complete the doctrinal content of H. Scripture. Tradition can only be concerned with the
government, discipline and worship of the Church.—RIISSEN (II, xi, 2):
"The question is not as to all traditions. Historical and ritual traditions
are given. Also divine and apostolic ones, i.e., dogmas handed down by
Christ and the apostles. The question is as to dogmatic and ethical
traditions, whether such are given over and above Scripture; which we
deny."—WYTTENBACH (*Tent. theol.* I, 212-312): "Be it noted moreover
that *Protestants* do not reject outright all tradition (e.g., the famous
COCCEIUS, *Admonit. de princip. fidei*, p. 19): they admit historical tradition, if it is certain. This consists in the consent of every age of the
Christian Church or in its testimony as to what it has believed, what books

it has received as divine, how this or that passage of Scripture was understood, etc. They yield a place to such fixed tradition as to canonical and apocryphal books. But they reject the dogmatic tradition, which prescribes *credenda* and *agenda* not contained in Scripture."

15.—Just as essentially as the attribute of 'perfection' and 'sufficiency' the attribute of 'necessity' also belongs to H. Scripture. Owing to the weakness of man's heart and the power of error dominant in the world H. Scripture is necessary, in order that pure knowledge of revealed truth may be maintained on earth. Scripture is necessary, not alone for the well-being of the Church, but for her being at all; she would lose herself, did she not possess an absolutely sure record of revealed truth. Meanwhile be it noted that the necessity for H. Scripture is not absolute, but is a *necessitas ex hypothesi dispositionis*. Had it been God's good pleasure, He could have maintained the pure knowledge and attestation of His truth even without the medium of a H. Scripture.—CALVIN says (I, vi, 3): "If we consider how slippery is the lapse of man's mind into forgetfulness of God, how great his proclivity for every kind of error, how great his passion for fashioning simultaneously new and fictitious religions, it will easily be realised, how necessary such a sealing of heavenly doctrine has been, to prevent its extinction in oblivion, its disappearance in error or its corruption by man's presumption."

MUSCULUS infers the necessity for H. Scripture from the need for an authority to which man must be subject *a priori*, in order to reach experience and knowledge of the truth (p. 176): "It is impossible for unskilled man, persuaded instantaneously at the outset by understanding the actual things, to be guided by the nature of the truth. Necessity itself requires that, moved first by some authority, they should submit to *doctrina*, the spirit and mind of which they can scarcely grasp at once, until having acquired trained senses they understand the things themselves, in which they are commencing their training. Thus authority is rightly regarded as a gate, through which in general all disciples must enter in order to gain knowledge of the things to be learned."

TURRETIN (II, ii, 6): "Three things confirm the need for Scripture, (1) the preservation, (2) the vindication, (3) the propagation of the Word. It was necessary for the written word to be transmitted to the Church, in order that there might be a fixed immovable canon of true religion for faith, which might more easily be preserved pure and intact from the infirmity of memory, the perversity of men and the brevity of life; that it might be more surely defended from the deceits and corruptions of Satan; that it might more conveniently be spread and transmitted, not only to the absent but also to posterity."

COCCEIUS (*S. T.* II, 1-20) means by *necessitas* the attribute of Scripture by which it "will enjoin" on us the "necessity of retaining it and attending to it", and proves it in five different connections. The written word of God is necessary (1) because without it the theologian neither has nor knows of the thing to say, namely, God's word; (2) because without Scripture no one can so consider God's works, as to be able in them to know, praise and exalt God Himself; (3) because without it man cannot truly love God; (4) because without it justification and its cause is not known; (5) and in addition, because God's word had of necessity to be recorded "(*a*) because of the forgetfulness of nations, (*b*) because of confirmed idolatry and the Jews' ἀπιστία and heresies and the defection that will exist in the last times, (*c*) because of faith in Christ" (so far as Christ is announced in prophecy and accredited by it); and (*d*) "because of the clarity of the Gospel and of the NT."

In opposition to R.C. dogma POLAN starts with the statement (I, 35): "Ever since H. Scripture was given by God to the Church it has been and is and will be necessary not only to the Church's *bene esse* but also to the Church's *esse*". Which is to be taken thus: "When only the books of Moses existed, they were necessary to the Church: there was no Scripture of the NT in Moses' time". To the Church's *esse* (ordained but not absolute) Scripture was necessary, "because true doctrine could not have been and could not be preserved amid so many heresies and scandals, had Scripture not been ordained for its preservation by God and commended to the Church". Therefore the Church needed Scripture, exactly as "the daily bread is necessary, which this life cannot do without". But here be it noted that Scripture is necessary, "not by an absolute or single necessity—God might have taught and maintained the Church, had He so willed, even without Scripture—but by the so-called *necessitas ex hypothesi dispositionis*".—HEIDEGGER speaks in the same sense (*Corp. theol.* II, 4): "God might also have preserved the Church without Scripture: with God all things are possible." However "once God had emitted proof of His grace and did not wish any other norm of His revelation to exist in the world, Scripture was so necessary to the Church, that she can no more do without it, than the world without the sun, or indeed without God Himself".

16.—If then H. Scripture is necessary for obtaining life eternal and for preserving the Church upon earth, its essential content must also be of such clarity, that it may be understood even of the unlearned, who reads H. Scripture with a believing heart or one desirous of salvation. Therefore H. Scripture has the attribute of perspicuity—[attributing to the book what is the gift of God?]—"by which the things necessary to be known for salvation are so plainly and clearly unfolded in Scripture, that they may be understood even by unlearned believers who read with devotion and attention" (WENDELIN, *Proleg., c.* 3). This does not imply that every separate word and sentence should be unambiguously clear. Rather the perspicuity of Scripture is to be connected only with the basic doctrines of revelation, which condition blessedness.

With the greater or less measure of spiritual illumination enjoyed by the salvation-hungry reader we are not concerned (LEIDEN SYNOPSIS, V, 9): "The chief dispute between us and the *Papists* is about man being illumined by the Spirit of Christ in differing measure and for different ends. Against them we assert with *Augustine,* that God has so tempered style and phraseology in the Scripture, that those things which contain faith and the morals of living, hope of course and love, may be found placed openly in the Scriptures and may be discerned by all according to their calling and measure of faith and be applied to themselves savingly."

POLAN (I, 44) rightly insists that Scripture is clear "in itself" and "by its own nature", that meanwhile this perspicuity refers not to "single passages" of it, but to "the single heads of Christian doctrine necessary to faith and the worship of God".

17.—In this connection it must further be noticed that true knowledge of it is only possible to the reader desiring salvation [this may not be possible!]: whereas the unconverted can at best appropriate only a theoretical and purely external knowledge of the truths of faith. As an animal can quite see the body of a man but not his spirit because it hasn't one itself, even the unspiritual man may see and understand the letter but not the Spirit of Scripture [capitals mine].

POLAN I, 44, BUCAN IV, 20. Even VOETIUS (V, p. 9) answers the question "whether understanding of Scripture happens also to the unconverted or unregenerated", by decisively denying this, so far as it has to do with "sanctifying and saving understanding". On the other hand VOETIUS allows the unconverted the capacity for a knowledge of Scripture, by which they may be convinced theoretically of the "truth of the Gospel and of other dogmas of faith", but also considers it possible "only by a general assistance or a kind of general grace of the illumining and convincing Spirit."

18.—The perspicuity of Scripture does not exclude its need of exposition. "The interpretation of H. Scripture is the explanation of its true sense and use, an explanation set forth in clear words for the glory of God and the edification of the Church" (POLAN I, 45).

18*b*.—So it follows from the divineness of Holy Scripture, that the exposition of Scripture passages which offer difficulties must be made to depend, not on another judge like the authority of the Church, but only on the Spirit of God, whose work alone Scripture is, or on Scripture itself. All doctrines, then, the knowledge of which is necessary for eternal life, are presented with undoubted clarity in H. Scripture for him who reads it with a believing mind, i.e., according to the *regula fidei et caritatis*. It follows from this that the obscure passages of Scripture are to be explained by the unambiguously clear ones or by the *analogia fidei* based on them.

"Not the Church but Scripture itself (i.e., the H. Spirit) and the *analogia fidei* teaches and shows how all individual passages in Scripture must be expounded"—it is from this thought that the doctrine of Scripture exposition is developed by all dogmaticians. It is required therefore that the believer submit to the guidance of the "rule of faith and love" when investigating Scripture (*Conf. Helv.* I, 2: "The interpretation of H. Scripture is to be sought from it alone, that it may be the interpreter of itself, the rule of faith and love being in the chair (*moderante)*"). If the believer reads Scripture in this spirit, i.e., in the H. Spirit, he has a guarantee that he also understands Scripture, which is prompted by the same Spirit. Above all the statement was fixed that "Scripture is its own interpreter". Which was also expressed thus: "The H. Spirit is the only interpreter of Scripture." If further the Church is also mentioned as a third term, it is done as in the following exposition of PETER MARTYR (p. 31): "I have always reckoned that there are two signs by which we grasp the truth of the divine literature. I mean the H. Spirit and the actual Word of God. And anent the Spirit, Jn. 8 has it that Christ spoke thus: 'If ye have God for your Father (v. 42) . . . why do ye not understand my speech?' (v. 43)." The Word itself comes in here as the norm, "since for one part of Scripture that is more obscure, it is meet to judge it by a second which we see to be clearer". As a third element the "constant consent and authority of the Church" may still be added, not as though the Church had a judicial power to control faith and doctrine, but so far as she possesses "three offices regarding the Word of God", that she (1) "as a witness preserves the sacred books," that she (2) "as their herald ... publishes and preaches the words committed to her by God," and that she (3) as "imbued with the divine spirit, distinguishes pure and germane books of divine literature from the adulterated and apocryphal". It is the same with the last point as with the following case: "When a royal epistle is brought, the prefects of cities and administrators of provinces are able sufficiently to recognise from use and civil skill, whether it is genuine or forged that is given them in the

King's name. But when they have realised that it has not been vitiated or tampered with, they may not invent or twist it at their own will. In the same way we must think of the Church" [and Scripture].

BUCAN sums up the main positions on the doctrine of Scripture exegesis in the following three theses (IV, 21-24): (1) "Interpretation of Scripture is the unfolding of the true and genuine sense of Scripture and the application of it to the manifest use of the Church"; (2) Scripture exegesis is to be gained, "not from a man's private feelings and already formed opinions, but from the actual context, from attention to and comparison of what precedes and follows with other passages of Scripture": wherein the rule of the *analogia fidei* is to be insisted upon, "namely, the constant and unchanging sense of Scripture expounded in open passages of Scripture and agreeing with the Apostle's Creed, the Decalogue and the Lord's Prayer, etc."; (3) The "use of Scripture" is portrayed by the Apostle, 2 Tim. 3. 16 (Every scripture inspired of God *is* also profitable for teaching, for reproof, for correction, for instruction [discipline?] which is in righteousness: that the man of God may be complete, furnished completely unto every good work).

The most penetrating discussion of the question, "who is the lawful interpreter of H. Scripture?" is to be found in the LEIDEN SYNOPSIS (*Disp.* V). It says first of all: "In order that this question may be correctly explained according to the norm of God's Word, we say that Scripture is its own interpreter, or rather God, speaking in the Scriptures and through the Scriptures. In the clearer and essential passages He openly indicates His will to believers, as was previously shown. In obscure passages He more and more confirms the same will of His for them by comparison of them with clearer passages."—(27): Since then God avails Himself of the ministry of men, it must be acknowledged, "that in Christ's true Church there is also another class of interpreters, the ministerial, constituted under both God and His Word, to which also in H. Scripture the power of judging is assigned, 2 Chron. 19. 8 (the King set of the Levites and the priests, and of the heads of the fathers' houses of Israel, for the judgment of the Lord and for controversies), Ezek. 44. 24 (in a controversy they shall stand to judge: according to my judgments shall they judge it: and they shall keep my laws and statutes in all my appointed feasts; and they shall hallow my sabbaths), Zech. 3. 7 (. . . if thou wilt walk in my ways, and if thou wilt keep my charge (Joshua), then thou shalt also judge my house, and shalt also keep my courts, and I will give thee a place of access among these that stand by), 1 Cor. 2. 15 (he that is spiritual judgeth all things, and he himself is judged by no man), 10 . 15 (I speak as to wise men; judge ye what I say), 14 . 29 (and let the prophets speak by two or three, and let the others discern), etc."

(28): This *potestas interpretandi* or *iudicandi* is a twofold one, a *potestas publica* and a *potestas privata,* both of which rest upon special calling and attainments. (29): "The power of private judgment on the true and false sense of H. Scripture in things necessary for salvation is competent for all true believers, for strengthening their own faith and edifying that of others, according to the law of love, the measure of the gift received, and the nature of the differing calling. (This is eloquently exhorted in Jn. 10. 3f.: "The sheep hear the true shepherd's voice . . . and they follow him; for they know his voice. And a stranger they will not follow, but will flee from him; for they know not the voice of strangers"; and Mt. 7. 15: "Beware of false prophets"; Paul speaks thus, 1 Cor. 10. 15: "I speak as unto wise men: judge ye what I say." 1 Jn. 4. 2: "Beloved, believe not every spirit, but prove the spirits, whether they be of God."). (30): This *potestas* is based upon the *donum* διακρίσεως which is the subject of 1 Cor. 2.15. Of course this gift is not imparted to all believers in the same measure. But it is thoroughly necessary (31) "that we recognise it at least in some measure in all Christ's sheep and true believers. Otherwise their faith would be resting, not on the Word of God but solely on human witness, contrary to what the apostle says, Rom. 10. 17 (belief cometh of hearing, and hearing by the word of Christ), and all the sheep have some knowledge of their own shepherd's voice, as Christ (John 10) bears witness. The (32) "power of publicly interpreting Scripture and of publicly judging of the interpretation does not belong to all but to certain persons only, who have been instructed to this end both by gifts and by calling." At the same time by such endowment is not meant a spiritual equipment independent of the Word of God (36): "Both of these gifts and the faculty of interpreting are subject to the Word of God and to the H. Spirit speaking in Scripture: for those who are adorned with the public gift of interpretation and preaching form their own judgment from H. Scripture."

19.—"The analogy of faith is the argument from general dogmas which contain the norm of all that is to be taught in the Church" (CHAMIER I, 17). At the same time it must be insisted that not only what plainly confronts us in the vocabulary of H. Scripture, but also what is derived as a necessary conclusion from it, must be regarded as the content of Scripture and as the truth of revelation.

Since the beginning of the seventeenth century the question is habitually discussed in Reformed dogmatics (TURRETIN I, xii, 6): "whether the dogmas of faith and morals are to be proved only by the express word of God, or may also be lawfully proved by inferences drawn from Scripture," and the latter is asserted against the Catholics. (Cf. VOETIUS I,

5-7, HEIDEGGER I, 40). Here is TURRETIN's account of the meaning and origin of this discussion (I, xii, 1): "The question arose from the new method of discussion among the *Agyrtae* and *Circulati* among the *Papists*. [*Agyrtae=Circulati*: a de Aguire (Spanish) was secretary of the Inquisition]. The more easily to disencumber themselves of our arguments, by which we invincibly build up our views from Scripture and transfix their errors, they have imagined they will have no more convenient way of giving us the slip than by forcing us to prove that all our dogmas are contained word for word in Scripture, all use of inference having been rejected. The first among the *Papists* to have thought out this trick is apparently *Perronius Cardin* in his reply to the King of Great Britain. He was followed by several others of the same kidney, *Gunter, Cotton, Arnold* and especially *Veronus,* who also invented the singular method of disputation hence called Veronian; these were joined by the *Wallemburgian* Brethren in Germany (I, xii, 1)." Be it noted however that H. Scripture contains the truths expressed in it either κατὰ λέξιν or κατὰ διάνοιαν ; whence we say that "everything is comprised in Scripture not in the first but in the second way" (I, xii, 3). For "the sufficiency and perfection of Scripture does not rest on the fact, that in it all errors and heresies are condemned by name, but only that all positive dogmas are clearly transmitted" (I, xii, 7).

20.—As is already included in the concept, Scripture exposition includes two things, namely, (1) an "account of the true sense of Scripture" and (2) "making it suitable for use" (POLAN I, 45).—All dogmaticians most specifically declare against a Scripture exegesis in principle manifold. POLAN clears up (I, 45) the meaning of the fourfold interpretation usual at an earlier date. (1) "They call it the *literal* sense, which the words directly bear; (2) they term it the *allegorical* sense, when words of Scripture signify over and above the literal sense something in the NT which pertains to Christ or the Church, especially in the mystery of salvation and of eternal life ; (3) they call it the *tropological* sense, when acts or words refer to some signification referring to morals; (4) they call it the *anagogical* sense, when words or facts are referred to signifying eternal life." Then he proceeds: "In truth there is only one true and genuine sense for each passage of H. Scripture, and that is the literal."— At the same time this "one literal sense" is either "simple" or "composite": and the former is once more either the "strict" literal sense or the "figurative". The "strict literal sense" is generally to be insisted upon in Scripture, "unless it be false". The "compound sense is that of which part is in type, part in the truth of the type, as it is in all those passages of H. Scripture in which something is described under a type".

—Similarly TURRETIN (II, xix, 2): The proof that every Scripture passage can have only one meaning TURRETIN derives from (1) "the unity of truth—truth is one and single; (2) the unity of form—of one thing only a single essential form is given, but sense is the form of Scripture; (3) the perspicuity of Scripture, which cannot admit various foreign and diverse senses."—The *sensus literalis* is only to be abandoned when it goes contrary to the *fidei articuli* or the *praecepta caritatis*, or when "the language is manifestly understood to be metaphorical from the same or other parallel passages".

For that matter it is insisted that alongside the 'sense' of Scripture passages we have still to recognise its 'application', and that in this case allegorical exegesis of Scripture is justified. Hence TURRETIN says (II, xix, 6): "Distinguish the sense of Scripture from its application. The sense is one—but the application may be different;—thus allegory, anagogy and tropology are not so much different senses, as applications of the one literal sense."—Similarly HEIDEGGER (*Corp. theol.* II, 80-81): "Whence arises the distinction of the applied allegorical sense, when the literal sense is transferred to describe faith or something spiritual in the NT."

Only DANAEUS (*Isagoge Christ.* IV, iii, 6) adduces the fourfold exposition of Scripture of *Augustine* in an apparently deviating sense and remarks: "Every Scripture says something either plainly and openly, or figuratively. Many things H. Scripture says in grace to us who are carnal, earthy and animal, which are yet to be taken in a different way from that which they sound in words, as when it ascribes to God a nose and eyes. When it propounds to us eternal life and the Church's felicity under the name and figure of a crown, a garden or earthly riches, these things are certainly metaphorical and to be received otherwise than as they are said, but not literally. The same thing is to be observed in every manner of speech when the subject is the sacraments, since the manner of speaking in the case of the sacraments is typical, figurative or sacramental."

20*b*.—Thus the true meaning of Scripture expressions which exposition has to fix, can never be anything but a single, and generally speaking the proper, literal meaning, the *sensus literalis*, which is either the *sensus literalis simplex* or the *sensus literalis compositus*. As a rule the former must be adhered to. On the other hand the latter must be recognised, where in Scripture something is expounded as a type; and only where the literal sense would be at variance with the "articles of faith" or the "precepts of love", where, that is, Scripture itself demands another exposition of its words, is the "figurative meaning" of it to be transmitted. Otherwise, in the application of Scripture passages to the very manifold circumstances of life, allegorical interpretation has its rights in the *accommodatio ad usum.*

21.—Of course for correct interpretation of H. Scripture every kind of human precondition, item of knowledge and dexterity is desirable, as general spiritual education, knowledge of language and history, etc.— Hence the SECOND HELV. CONF. (II, 2) sets up the following signs and guarantees of a correct Scripture exegesis: "We recognise that interpretation to be orthodox and genuine, which, culled from the Scriptures themselves (according of course to the spirit of the language in which they are written, weighed likewise to suit circumstances, and expounded in the light of passages either like or unlike, which are also more numerous and clearer), agrees with the rule of faith and love and makes outstandingly for the glory of God and the salvation of men."—WOLLEB (p. 7) adduces the following "means of investigating the true sense of Scripture"— "frequent prayers; knowledge of tongues; inspection of sources; con- sideration of theme and scope; distinction between strict and figurative expressions; the noting and logical analysis of causes, circumstances, antecedents and consequents; the comparison of the more obscure with the more manifest, of like with like, or unlike with unlike; in a word, the analogy of faith."

22.—But the most essential requisite is faith and life in the fellowship of the H. Spirit, who even in the apparent contradictions of Scripture (the ἐναντιοφανῆ) teaches us to realise the perfect harmony of the contents of Scripture.—Reformed dogmaticians concede that in Scripture an ἐναντιοφανές but not an ἐναντίον arises, and occupy themselves anxi- ously in solving the individual ἐναντιοφανές. Cf. WENDELIN (*Exercit. theol.* p. 1): "I have conceded the ἐναντιοφανές, not an ἐναντίον; (p. 3): so I deny a true contradiction in God's will, concede an apparent one and reconcile the ἐναντιοφανές in the two examples adduced from the Penta- teuch, Gen. 22. 2 (offer up Isaac sequel), Exodus 9. 1-12 (bid him let my people go: God hardens Pharaohs' heart) cf. 10, 20-27)".—HEIDEGGER (*Medull. theol.* II, 12): "Nor are a few ἐναντιοφανῆ and ἄλυτα any obstacle. These may be composed both by Scripture as the foundation and by right reason as the instrument of reconciliation."

23.—For the H. Spirit leads into all truth all who are of a believing heart and call upon Him for enlightenment by Himself alone. The believer has thus the consolation that God really gives Him the true understanding of Scripture and that true knowledge of the Word will be maintained for ever on earth by God's gracious care.—URSIN (*Loci.* p. 453-454): In the disputes that arise "we acknowledge as judge not the Church but the H. Spirit Himself speaking to us and declaring His words in Scripture". The Church has only to mediate and proclaim ("she inquires, shows and announces") the infallible verdict of the H. Spirit. Of course the believer is aware that "the contentious are constantly in search of sophisms by which to dodge the testimonies of Scripture". But he is aware that they do so "in the face of conscience" (*reclamante conscientia!*), and therefore, if they will not accord with the verdict of the H. Spirit, he must not look for another judge but just leave them to the "judgment of God". On the other hand the believer may console himself, that if (1) with believing mind he searches in Scripture, and takes account of the *analogia fidei* and of the context, (2) in addition (but *longo intervallo*) he also compares the *consensus ecclesiae catholicae* contained in the purer writings of the Fathers, and (3) unceasingly asks God for enlightenment—the right understanding of Scripture will certainly be vouchsafed to him. "In disputes on religion this is enough to fortify the consciences of individual godly men."

The certainty that regenerated Christians at all times attain to a right understanding of Scripture is thus a comfort which only exists for faith. Hence declares the LEIDEN SYNOPSIS V, 39: "Our sole advice here by way of conclusion is this, that God by His Spirit and His Word is so continually present to His true church that neither she nor her living members err to their destruction, at least in the necessary fundamentals of faith and morals. Otherwise she would cease to be the true Church of Christ, contrary to Christs' promise, Mt. 16. 18 (Thou art Peter, and upon this rock I will build my Church; and the gates of hell shall not prevail against it), Jn. 10. 5 (a stranger will they not follow, but will flee from him; they know not the voice of strangers)."—COCCEIUS (*S. T.* VI, 64, 65): "Not only does H. Scripture possess in itself such perspicuity that by it a man may be saved even though destitute of other instrument and aid. But also by His grace God brings it to pass, that interpretation of Scripture and manifestation of the truth arises from it. So there is no longer need to discover from the Scriptures truth unusual as it were, and unheard of (as we are forced to look for the meanings of the Jews from the Talmud and its exegetes, for those of the Turks from the Qur'an, the stone-dead opinions of other races from the tomes of the ancients). By propagating the Church once gathered by the prophets, Christ and the apostles to the end of the World, and by preserving the truth in it so that it does not depart from her mouth, Is. 59. 21 (as for me, this is my covenant with them, saith the LORD: my spirit that is upon thee, and my words which I have put in thy mouth, shall not depart out of thy mouth, nor out of the mouth of thy seed, nor out of the mouth of thy seed's seed,

saith the LORD, from henceforth and for ever) God brings it about that
the gospel is preached in the world till the end of the world, and that it is
put in everyone's way together with the sacred literature itself, and that
it is a short cut to learn and approve the truth from it."—But above all
it holds (RIISSEN I, 10): "We teach that without the H. Spirit's aid a man
cannot either rightly perceive H. Scripture or be subject to it." Similarly
the GENERAL GERMAN-REFORMED CONFESSION, II (Cf. HEPPE, *Bekenntnisschriften,* p. 265): "For another thing we believe that no one can rightly
understand God's Word, except God illumine him by His Spirit."

CHAPTER III

THE FOUNDATION OF HOLY SCRIPTURE

1.—The attributes of "sufficiency" and "perpetuity" belong to H. Scripture, because the whole doctrine of it rests upon a foundation, from which all revealed truths are derived and in which all doctrines of salvation are already contained in essence. This basic truth of Scripture is the comfortable doctrine, that Christ is the way, the truth and the life and the believer's inalienable possession. In the Son become man not only does the truth of the law appear afresh : in Him it is also the eternal, forgiving grace of the Father; that is, law and gospel offered to the world, and not just offered but given to believers, so that they can never lose it again. This then is the sum of all doctrines of Scripture, that Christ is not just the salvation of the world in general but is also "my" salvation, and that because "I" have become "the Lord's property", I shall likewise remain so for ever. The basic foundation of all revealed truths in Scripture is thus the covenant of God with believers in Christ.

The distinction between a *fundamentum Scripturae* and the individual doctrines in it, and the conviction that the latter are essentially present in the former, is so essential not merely to the Federal theology but to the Reformed system in general, that the latter cannot be understood at all without recognition of the former. At the same time this proposition is the basis of the really scientific nature, the method in principle of Reformed dogmatics. German-Reformed theology described this fundamental concept of Revelation (HEPPE, *Altprot. Dogm.* p. 144ff.) from the very beginning by the expression *foedus Dei* (also *regnum Christi*, κοινωνία *cum Christo*). Thereby it was asserted that Christ is salvation, not merely because He acquired salvation, but because He can never be conceived otherwise than in a definite relation to the individual believer, as Redeemer, Mediator and Bringer of bliss, and so the Redeemer of really redeemed men who are implanted in Him. Hence the concept of the name of Christ exactly coincides at this point with the concept of the covenant of God. Cf. URSIN, *Loci* p. 427: "If the covenant which exists between God and believers is described in these (prophetic and apostolic) books, it is necessary that it should be explained in them, what God promises us and provides us with, viz., His grace, remission of sins, the H. Spirit, righteousness and eternal life, and the preservation of the Church in this life through and on account of His Son our Mediator; and what He requires of us in return, namely faith by which to receive these benefits and a life ordered by His precepts, whereby we declare our thankfulness. Now these are the things taught in law and gospel."

Thus the concept of the *foedus Dei* is the essence of all revealed truths. Meanwhile URSIN continues: "Nor does the H. Spirit mean anything else when it says in one word that Christ is taught in the whole of Scripture, and that he alone is to be sought in it.—(428): True and complete acknowledgment of Christ comprises the whole doctrine of H. Scripture and the Church".

COCCEIUS (who in *Summa theol.*, I, vii, 2 deals "*de fundamento*") likewise says: "The foundation is expressed in more than one way in Scripture. First, it denotes him to whom they are added and with whom they are united, that they may be in him and live in him and lean on him in hope." But then he closes with the remark: "Hence the Catechism (Heidelberg) also rightly sets forth in the first question the sum of consolation which supports the mind in life and in death, that we belong to Jesus Christ our most faithful Lord" (VII, 57).

2.—Hence it follows (1), that the distinction between fundamental and derivative articles of doctrine is well worth observation. The doctrinal propositions in which the real foundation of doctrine is expressed and expounded have a higher and more essential meaning than those which do not impinge upon it directly.—All Reformed dogmaticians discuss this distinction with peculiar interest. E.g. VOETIUS II p. 513: "The first hypothesis is, that everything that occurs in Scripture is not equally necessary to saving faith or to Church union and communion, or needs to be taught the faithful and inculcated upon them with a like necessity. This we gather from 1 Cor. 3. 10, 12, 15 (according to the grace of God which was given me, as a wise master-builder I laid a foundation— Jesus Christ—if any man's work be burned he shall suffer loss: but he himself shall be saved: yet as through fire) Phil. 3. 15-16 (let us therefore, as many as be perfect, be thus minded: and if in anything ye are otherwise minded, even this shall God reveal unto you: only, whereunto we have already attained, by that same rule let us walk) 2 Tim. 1. 13 (hold the pattern of sound words which thou hast heard from me, in faith and love which is in Christ Jesus) Tit. 1 (an apostle, according to the faith of God's elect and the knowledge of the truth which is according to godliness) 1 Tim. 6. 3 (if any man—consenteth not to sound words, even the words of our Lord Jesus Christ, and to the doctrine which is according to godliness). There is the additional reason that as in all disciplines so in the Scriptures the essentials and οἰκεῖα of religion, or the axioms or precepts are to be distinguished from the commentaries upon them.— p. 531: These (fundamental) articles are the principal theses in the separate dogmatic heads of the Christian catechism; or they are the common ἔννοιαι and aphorisms of Christian doctrine, necessary for promoting and preserving the practice and profession of faith and holiness in the unity and society of the Church".—Similarly FRANZ TURRETIN I, xiv, 5: "Although all truths which are revealed in Scripture are necessary to be believed as divine and infallible, they are not all equally necessary. Here we must accurately distinguish between the scope (*amplitudo*) and extension of the faith, and its *necessity*. Not everything within the scope of faith is at once of its necessity".

The opposition of the Reformed to the rationalistic and Lutheran conception of this point of doctrine is described by RIISSEN, I, 12: "As regards the doctrine of the fundamental articles of faith the *Socinians* err in defect, excluding from the fundamentals the dogma of the Holy Spirit, the Trinity, the Person and Satisfaction of Christ, etc. So do the *Arminians*, who embrace the fundamentals in these three points, faith in the divine promises, obedience to the divine precepts and the reverence due to the Scriptures. Sin in excess lies at the door of both *Papists* who obtrude as fundamentals the traditions of the Roman Church; and the *Lutherans*, the more rigid of them who, to render coalescence with us more difficult, extend the fundamentals too widely. We take the middle way and regard those dogmas as fundamental, (1) which contain the necessary causes and conditions of salvation; (2) knowledge of which is transmitted by Scripture as being necessary to salvation and ignorance of which as leading to destruction".—The answer to the question, which dogmas then belong to the fundamental doctrinal statements, is of course not fixed in the Church's system of doctrine. HOTTINGER says (*Curs. theol.* p. 7): "Theological *loci* on the Trinity, the eternal deity of the Son, and the hypostasis of the H. Spirit, original sin and the perfection of the law, the person of Christ and his satisfaction etc., are necessary and fundamental to Christian doctrine." In proof of this the Scripture passages mainly adduced are Jn. 17. 3 (this is life eternal, that they should know thee, the only true God, and him whom thou didst send, even Jesus Christ) Mt. 28. 19 (—baptizing them in the name of the Father and of the Son and of the Holy Ghost) Jn. 5. 20 (the Father loveth the Son and sheweth all things that himself doeth; and greater works than these will he shew him, that ye may marvel) Jn. 3. 5-6 (Except a man be born of water and the Spirit, he cannot enter into the kingdom of God. That which is born of the flesh is flesh; and that which is born of the Spirit is spirit) Rom. 5. 12 (as through one man sin entered into the world, etc.) Mt. 22. 37-38 (Which is the great commandment, etc.) Rom. 1. 1-2 (—the gospel of God which he promised afore by his prophets in the Holy Scriptures) Mt. 20. 28 (—the Son of man came not to be ministered unto but to minister, and to give his life a ransom for many). Others make similar declarations, e.g. FRANCIS TURRETIN I. xiv. 25: "The question as to the number of the fundamental articles, promptly hurled at us by our adversaries beyond what is rash, since Scripture makes no precise definition on this point, is useless as well, and unnecessary, for the controversies which intervene between us and them".

3.—But the distinction of fundamental and non-fundamental doctrines of H. Scripture still does not suffice for understanding the connection which permeates all the separate truths of Scripture and links them up. Since the institution of a covenant relationship with man is the purpose of all God's revelations, the Christian must (2) regard the separate revealed truths in the light of the covenant idea, in such a way as recognises them as a whole only in relation to that idea and grasps them with believing trust precisely in their special validity and significance for his individual person.

This thought OLEVIAN above all develops in his *Fester Grund* pp. 13-14. To the question, "Give me a lead as to how I should act, so as to draw a sure confidence and certain trust from the articles of faith", he gives the answer: "Firstly, in each and all of the articles of faith I remember the promise of God, that to thee is promised and given by God what stands in the article, if thou hast trust in thy heart and confessest it with thy mouth. As an example: in confessing, "He suffered under the judge Pontius Pilate", thou must not just remember the story as it took place in the Passion; the wicked Enemy is also aware of that. But believe that God truly promiseth thee in the article, that he suffered for thee and that it is thine own, as though thou hadst *had* the suffering of it thyself. Likewise when thou confessest "crucified" (i.e. for me), when God promises thee that He has let His Son be crucified for thee; as Paul saith, "who loved me and gave Himself for me" (Gal. 2. 20), and that therefore He belongeth none the less to thee, than if thou thyself hadst been nailed to the Cross, when Christ was nailed thereon to pay for thy sins. In fine; in every single article aye be mindful, that what stands therein was promised and given thee for blessedness. Therefore sayest thou also, "*I* believe", namely that all that happened to me for my good and to me as well as to the most holy was promised and given by God. Yea of this thou shouldst be certain, that if thou hadst been the only poor sinner on earth, like a single lamb, Christ would have left the ninety and nine sheep that were already in heaven, and would have come down for thee from the heavenly glory, to look for thee, to bear thee on His shoulder, and to redeem thee, as Himself teacheth in the gospel."

"For another thing, if a man will rightly apply and appropriate to himself the promise of Jesus Christ, he clings to this plumb-line, that his body and soul were formed for the Son of God, in order that all that had contributed to them might happen in the name and for the sake of believers one and all. This is the unchangeable will and eternal counsel of God, on which we may confidently build."—The rule and plumbline are taken from the following testimonies in Scripture: Heb. 10. 5. 27 (sacrifice and offering thou wouldest not, but a body didst thou prepare for me) ; v. 27 (a certain fearful expectation of judgment) ; Psalm 40. 6 (Burnt offering and sin offering thou hast not required) ; v. 9 (I have published righteousness in the great congregation); 1 Cor. 1. 30 (of him are ye in Christ Jesus) Rom. 10. 6-7 (the righteousness of faith saith thus, Say not in thy heart—but what saith it? the word is nigh thee, etc.) Luke 1. 10 (the multitude praying without at the hour of incense) Hebrews 2. 14-15 (Christ took flesh that through death he might destroy him that had the power of death (the devil) and might deliver all who through the fear of death were all their lifetime subject to bondage) Rom. 5. 12-18 (Therefore, as through one man sin entered into the world, and death through sin; and so death passed unto all men, for that all sinned:—for until the law sin was in the world: but sin is not imputed when there is no law. Nevertheless death reigned from Adam until Moses, even over them that had not sinned after the likeness of Adam's transgression, who is a figure of him that was to come. But not as the trespass, so also is the free gift. For if by the trespass of the one the many died, much more did the grace of God and the gift by the grace of the one man, Jesus Christ, abound unto the many. And not as through one that sinned, so is the gift: for the judgment came of one unto condemnation, but the free gift came of many trespasses unto justification. For if, by the trespass of the one, death reigned through the one; much more shall they that receive the abundance of grace and of the gift of righteousness reign in life through the one, even Jesus Christ. So then as through one trespass the judgment came unto all men to condemnation; even so through one act of righteousness the free gift came unto all men to justification of life).

1 Cor. 15. 20. 21. 23 ("But now hath Christ been raised from the dead, the first fruits of them that are asleep. For since by man came death, by man came also the resurrection of the dead—each in his own order: Christ the first fruits; then they that are Christ's at his coming).

1 Thess. 4. 14 (if we believe that Jesus died and rose again, even so them also that are fallen asleep in Jesus will God bring with him).

1 Thess. 5. 3 (When they are saying, Peace and safety, then sudden destruction cometh upon them, as travail upon a woman with child; and they shall in no wise escape).

CHAPTER IV

THE EXISTENCE AND NOTION OF GOD

1.—To establish the doctrine of God's covenant with man is primarily to fix the doctrine of God.—COCCEIUS (*S.T.* VIII, 1): "In order that the doctrine of the covenant and testament of God may be transmitted, it is necessary that the mind of the hearer be strengthened in the thought that God exists. Unless a man surely fixes this, he cannot seek God and approach Him and attend to His witness."

2.—In it we distinguish the doctrine of God Himself and of His activities and works.—HOTTINGER (p. 36): "There are two parts of theology: one is the doctrine of God, the other the doctrine of His acts and works".

3.—In the former we have again to distinguish the way in which God has revealed Himself through the creation of the world and man, and how He has done so through the redemption of the world. First of all we must treat of God in the first relation.—CALVIN (I, ii, 1): "Because the Lord appears first as the Creator simply, alike in the making of the world and in the general doctrine of Scripture, then as the Redeemer in the face of Christ, a twofold knowledge of Him arises in consequence, the former of which must be treated now, and then the other will follow in its order".

4.—The existence of a personal creator and ruler of the world, dependent on nothing, rather holding everything in dependence upon Himself, of course requires no proof for one who does not seal himself against the revelation of God in the world. Hence arguments for the existence of God in general are to be used at all only for the regulation of those who deny God.—VOETIUS (I, p. 167) raises the question "whether the existence of God may be proved by disputation", and gives the answer: "(1) Where there is danger from the frenzies of atheists, this must be done sparingly, cautiously, compendiously and clearly. Where there is none it may be avoided, especially before the ruder and weaker and in catechetical institutions. There it will as a rule be sufficient to assume and adopt the principle. (2) The treatment must be taught κατασκευαστικῶς rather than ἀνασκευαστικῶς i.e., proofs must rather be brought forward for the truth than adversaries' objections refuted...lest such things be taught by the very mention of them, and the devil take occasion of corrupt flesh to confuse men's minds with horrible thoughts of the kind. (3) But the way with books that are published differs from

47

that of instructions given by word of mouth. In the former, especially if dogmatic or argumentative, this proof can scarcely be passed over. In the latter it may, according to the matter under discussion. (4) One method is that of academic instructions and disputations, another that of the ecclesiastical. In the former theologians should be armed against antagonists of every kind. But this should be done with such care and circumspection, that it does not appear to be an airing of a dialectical problem. These distinctions being applied, we agree that (since the importunity of the ungodly does not create the necessity for us) there should be no dispute among Christians as to "whether there be a God".

5.—That there is an absolute spiritual and moral power on which the world is utterly dependent for its origin and for its continuation, man realises from the physical, moral and civil order, which he apprehends in the world and in the human race, and from the spirituality and moral bondage which characterises himself.—That a natural knowledge of God is possible was shown by the earlier German-Reformed dogmaticians entirely after the precedent of MELANCHTHON. URSIN (*Loci*, p. 459) adduces the following eleven *argumenta naturae*: (1) The order apprehensible in nature; "it is impossible that order, i.e. the disposition of parts and the succession of movements and actions, constant in fixed and lasting laws and changes, should either exist or be preserved by chance or fortune, the results of which we see to be neither perpetual nor of one kind; or because of their matter, which being a brute business, the institution of order cannot be assigned to it". (2) The rationality of man's spirit; "for since it cannot be that a cause is worse than its effect in the same category, i.e. that anything should be contributed to a second thing, by that which the supposed giver does not itself possess, it is sufficiently clear that rational nature, being the product of something different, could not have arisen from a brute, but only from an intelligent nature. Since therefore the human mind is neither without beginning— man's nature begins to exist—nor exists of itself—none of the things which begin to exist can be the cause of itself—and therefore has some effectual cause: it is necessary that there should be some creating, intelligent and wise nature, to which we give the name of God". 460: (3) The moral and rational ideas innate in man: "both the nature and consent and perpetuity of these can have their rise neither in matter nor in accident." (4) The indubitable truth that the items of knowledge given in natural self-consciousness are right; "since therefore even without doctrine all men feel by a natural judgment that God exists, this principle is the less to be called in doubt, the more its steadiness and certainty compared with that of any other are necessary to the life of men and to the preservation of their whole nature". (5) The voice of conscience punishing the sinner, "tortures and tremblings could not strike hearts and minds after the admission of sins, save in a nature that understood and sanctioned the difference between things good and bad, that hated and avenged crimes, and exercised judgment upon minds". 461: (6) The general experience that as a rule evil is already punished here on earth; "There is therefore a Mind that discerns things good and bad, a Judge of the human race who punishes the wicked and protects the good". 462: (7) The presence of a civic order in human society; "which political society could not be proved from any other source than a mind which perceives and approves this order for men". (8) The extraordinary spiritual endowment, the *motus heroici*, which individual men enjoy; since man cannot appropriate them himself and since neither can they be explained by the activity of any "second cause", it follows that they are bound to proceed "from a cause superior to all second causes, i.e. from God". 463: (9) The historically existing prophecies of quite incalculable future events, e.g. the Flood, Abraham's posterity, which allow the conclusion "that they were revealed to men by a Mind with foreknowledge of these matters". (10) The teleological order of the world, "the evidence of which caused even philosophers to say that the world and everything whatsoever it contains was made for the sake of God and men". 464: (11) The "series of causes and effects, which must be a finite one, and so posits a First Cause which produces and moves them". No *progressus in infinitum* can be assumed for causes which mutually condition each other; otherwise it would follow, "that either within the area of finite time there occurred infinite movements and changes, or that at no time did those infinite causes ever reach their goal, i.e. their appointed effect". Therefore the start of the movements must depend upon a Cause unchangeable, eternal and almighty."

The other dogmaticians express themselves similarly. E.g. POLAN (II, 4): "The proofs of the existence of God have nothing to do with "innate knowledge of God", but with "acquired knowledge of God". They are as follows: "(1) Consideration of the world, of which the mass, workmanship, form, continued maintenance, wise government, countless variety, order of bodies, various movements, wonderful power teach, that there exists an Intelligent Nature from which all these things proceed.—(2) The principles innate in us, which are the sources of doctrines which must necessarily have been impressed on man's mind by an Intelligent Nature.—(3) The special knowledge, naturally innate in us, that God exists.—(4) The peculiar evidence of our conscience in its terror of the thunderings and other unusual storms and earthquakes, in its fear of God the Judge because of crimes committed, in fact shuddering with a certain trembling.—(5) Punishments of crimes inflicted on the wicked even in this life. (6) The institution and preservation of political order.—(7) Virtues and unusual emotions in heroic souls.—(8) Intimations of things to come (CICERO, *De divinatione: "Si est divinatio, sunt Dii"*).—(9) The goal (*finis*) of all things natural. Since it is very certain in all of them, but very few of them look ahead to that to which they constantly tend and proceed or perceive it, it is altogether necessary that there be some mind that perceives everything, controls them in detail and directs them to their ends.—(10) The series of causes, which does not proceed to infinity, as though leading us by the hand to a Prime Mover, on Whom all movements, acts and effects depend.—(11) Worship itself, whether religious or superstitious, introduced by fear of the Numen.—(12) The common confession and consent of all races, even the most savage.—(13) The sense of God's goodness, i.e. of God's immense benefits, spiritual and bodily.—(14) The excellence of our mind;—(15) The immortality of our soul.—(16) The wonderful, outstanding and unlooked-for events, which cannot be done save by a most potent Nature, with which the theatre of human life is filled."—THOMAS OF AQUINO therefore and other *Scholastics* are wrong in denying "that God is known *per se.*" "

From the time the influence of WOLF's philosophy began to appear in Reformed dogmatics and when it in its turn began to die, the "proofs for the existence of God" were set up by rule (*scientifice*)—exactly as in *Lutheran* dogmatics. *Cf., e.g.,* ENDEMANN *Compend.* of 1782, pp. 19-24.

6.—Since for all this an intelligent and absolute causality must be present, the existence of a God is therefore an absolute necessity.—VOETIUS (V. p. 64): "Problem—whether God alone is a necessary being? Ans: Absolutely, *in se, per se, per existentiam.* Necessity however is not assigned to creatures except *secundum quid.* The creature exists with a mixture of contingency and independence upon the prime necessity, i.e. on God."

7.—And therewith to man is at the same time guaranteed the unity or singleness of God, which utterly excludes the existence of another divine being. The divine perfection, resting as it does upon God's absoluteness which conditions only itself, and displayed in the unity of the divine government of the world, cannot be divided up into several beings.

DANAEUS (*Isag.* I, p. 5) and URSIN already rightly insist that the concept of the absolute perfection of God can only be thought on the hypothesis that there is but one God. URSIN says (*Loci*, p. 464): "There cannot exist but one of that, the perfection of which is supreme.—

Therefore divine essence is single. Scattered among several gods, divinity would not be universal in any of them, and so none of them would be perfect and accordingly none would be the true God: Dt. 4. 35. 39 (. . . the Lord he is God: there is none else beside him—the Lord he is God in heaven above and upon the earth beneath: there is none else); 6. 4 (. . . The Lord our God is one LORD): 32. 39 (See now, that I, even I, am he, and there is no God with me: I kill, and I make alive; I have wounded, and I heal: and there is none that can deliver out of my hand): Is. 44. 6 (. . . I am the first, and I am the last; and beside me there is no God); 45. 18. 22 (. . . I am the Lord and there is none else. Look unto me and be ye saved, all the ends of the earth: for I am God and there is none else): 1 Cor. 8. 4. 6 (concerning the eating of things sacrificed to idols, we know that no idol is anything in the world, and that there is no God but one. For though there be that are called gods, whether in heaven or on earth; as there are gods many, and lords many; yet to us there is one God, the Father, of whom are all things and we unto him; and one Lord, Jesus Christ, through whom are all things, and we through him); Eph. 4. 5. 6 (One Lord, one faith, one baptism, one God and Father of all, who is over all, and through all, and in all)."—Similarly POLAN (II, 5): "When it is asked whether there is one essence of God or several, we answer that there is but one, or rather a sole and single One, and accordingly not by aggregation or consent, not in genus or species—but in number or rather prior to number, just as essence is never predicated of God in the plural number—whence also God is more suitably called *unicus* than *unus*". The most essential proofs of the *unitas Dei* are the following three: (1) "There cannot be more than one *ens a se*. (2) God is supremely perfect. What is supremely perfect cannot exist save as one. He who alone has the whole is finally perfect; and there are imperfects, who have something distributed among them. So the divine essence is single. (3) The government of the world does not admit of several gods".—RIISSEN III, 10: "God is called one, not only because He is undivided in Himself and divided from anything else, as the human individual is one numerically, but exclusively of all others. He is one, i.e., single, as the sun is called one because it is single".—BUCAN I, 11 : "God is called one neither generically nor specifically, but essentially and numerically, or by reason of nature, because there is only one, an individual essence of God."—HEIDAN 73: "God is one, not only with that unity by which He is undivided in Himself and divided from everyone else, but also by that unity by which He is *Deus solus et unicus*, i.e., has an essence void of multiplication and division, and with which no other essence is equal or on a par, which is called numerical unity. Since God is conceived as an *ens perfectissimum*, He cannot be conceived save as one."

8.—Of course, man cannot discern the nature of this single God. The finite spirit cannot perfectly grasp the infinite 1 Tim. 6. 16 (who only hath immortality, dwelling in light unapproachable; whom no man hath seen or can see: to whom be honour and power eternal. Amen). 1 Jn. 3. 2 (now are we children of God, and it is not yet made manifest what we shall be. We know that if he shall be manifested, we shall be like him; for we shall see him as he is) Rom. 11. 34 (who hath known the mind of the Lord? or who hath been his counsellor?). Whence also no real definition of God is possible.

All Reformed dogmaticians present the statement which, e.g., Musculus (p. 430) expresses, that "what is finite cannot express the infinite", and hence dispute the idea that God's nature can really be defined. For (says Hyperius p. 84) "if you labour to weave an essential definition by dialectical reason, where will you find a genus more lofty or more extensive than God Himself? Where will you look for a genuine or proper differentia?"—Similarly Cocceius (*Aphorism. prolix.* IV, 5): "We do not form an adequate positive concept of God".—Chamier III, 5: "We know that God cannot be defined, not only because He is infinite, i.e., is no wise defined, but also because every definition consists of genus and differentia. But these things are not appropriate to God; for things that consist of genus and species must needs be composite. Therefore God can only be described."—Polan II, 3: Every definition of God is a "kind of description of God, so far as He has been revealed to us." For "God cannot be defined". Even if God is described as Spirit, this can only be done *formae notione,* but not with a view to describing a *genus praedicabile,* which God might share with angels and men. The concept of genus cannot be applied to God: "(1) there is nothing superior to God even in thought, which He might be brought under as a part, since God shares no one's essence; (2) for God is not one by genus or species in the philosophical acceptation, but by number or individuality; (3) no cause of God can be given which is denoted by a genus; (4) God is not composite; for things that have a genus are composite according to genus and specific differentia."

9.—In the first instance therefore it can only be said (Riissen III, 1) that: "God is (1) an independent being, (2) upon whom all things depend, (3) who takes care of everything else".—Alsted 56: "God is an independent essence.—There is no perfect definition of God, though there are various descriptions of Him. God is incomprehensible—and yet it is true, as Bernard concludes, that it is God alone who can never be sought in vain, even when He cannot be found".—Polan defines thus (II, 3): "God is a Spirit; increate; existing by Himself; one in essence; trine in the persons, Father, Son and H. Spirit". Meanwhile this is just a "sort of description of God as He is revealed to us;" for "God is indefinable" (Cf. Para. 8 *Supra*.)—Other dogmaticians frame definitions of God by insisting on the parallelism of the attributes and the tri-personality, e.g., HOTTINGER p. 37: "God is a most single Spirit, un-changeable, immense, eternal, supremely living, wise, good, righteous, free, mighty and blessed, and He is the Father, the Son and the H. Spirit".—WOLLEB p. 7: "God is a Spirit existing of Himself from eternity, one in essence trine in persons, Father, Son and H. Spirit".—HEIDAN p. 68: "God is a Spirit existing by Himself" or "a thinking independent substance" or "the *ens perfectissimum*".

10.—Next it has to be acknowledged that in the absolute essence essen. tiality is completely identical with personality, existence and substance- In creaturely substances these differ from each other, because in their case the one is carried by the other. God in His essence is life *par excellence* and absolutely unifold life and absolutely unifold actuosity (*actus puris-simus et simplicissimus*).

POLAN (II, 5): " God's essence is Deity itself, by which God is and exists absolutely *a se* and *per se*". At the same time the concept of "God's essence" is not made properly clear, until the difference between it and the concept of creaturely truth is visualised. Three points require consideration here. " (1) Essence and ὁ ὤν, he who is, differ in creatures : God alone is that which He is and is who He is, i.e., an οὐσία which does not depend on another. (2) Though essence and existence differ in creatures, they do not do so in God. (3) Essence and substance differ in the same way in creatures, because essence is contained in substance, and besides the essence itself, all the things that naturally inhere in the essence. But in things divine they mean the same thing."—The statement that God is *actus purissimus* or *simplicissimus,* or that " God is essentially actuosity," is stereotyped in Reformed dogmatics, as will be shown in the following *Locus*.

11.—In this way of course God's nature is not really defined yet. But although to man God remains uncaused for conceptual knowledge, He is yet not hidden for religious and moral knowledge of Himself, and can therefore be found of everyone that seeks Him.—DANAEUS (*Christ. Isag.* I, 2): "No definition of God can be adduced, which completely covers His nature. And yet it is true as BERNARD says (Bk. V, *De considerat.*) that God alone is and can never be sought in vain, even when He cannot be found." [See ALSTED para. 9 *Supra*.].

12.—Even after his fall some remnants of his original knowledge of God survived for man. He may therefore by consideration of himself and of nature still know God's nature to some extent, indeed so that he may enter into living fellowship with God as with his God and Lord. Only, if man would attain to a certain knowledge of God that satisfies him, he must not limit himself to this *cognitio Dei naturalis*. Rather he must give heed to God's acts of revelation to which Holy Scripture gives testimony. Man only possesses right knowledge of God, when he is aware—and this is the whole point—what God is, not in and for Himself but for man. But even outward knowledge of God's outward acts of revelation still does not ensure any *living* knowledge of the divine nature. This is imparted to man only by God attesting Himself to him by the Holy Spirit, by His letting him experience within himself the truth of the facts of revelation.—CALVIN I, ii, 1: "Neither shall we say that, strictly speaking, God is known where there is no religion or godliness. 2: They are therefore merely toying with cold speculations, whose purpose in this question is to insist upon what God is. Our interest is much more to know what He is like and what belongs to His nature. What is the point of confessing with EPICURUS to a God who has thrown aside care for the world and merely delights in leisure? What good is it to know a God with whom we have nothing to do? Nay, rather knowledge of Him ought to be sufficient to put us in fear and reverence, then by its leading and instruction to teach us to look for all good at His hand and to account it to Him."

Under these leading thoughts all Reformed dogmaticians develop the doctrine of the knowledge of God in the following way:—MUSCULUS (p. 5) aptly says of evangelical knowledge of God: "He who has not this knowledge of God plainly knows not what God is, even although he hold to a knowledge of His essence, which is quite past finding out; nor can he use the knowledge of God for those things which are necessary and are only displayed by God. It is very true, as *Augustine* quotes from *Varro* in his *De civ. Dei* iv, 22, how valueless it is for anyone to know a doctor's name and appearance and to be ignorant what a doctor is. So it is no advantage that you know that God exists and are not ignorant of His name and essence, if you don't know that He is the creator, preserver and ruler of all things, and so do not know why you ought to supplicate Him."

Who God is may, so far as his spiritual sight extends, be known by a man correctly, yet only imperfectly. URSIN (*Loc.* p. 456): "God's infinite majesty cannot be comprehended by the understanding of any finite nature." In general man knows God (COCCEIUS S.T. IX) not "by His essence" but "by His effects, and by His name by which He Himself willed to manifest His excellences to us". To man generally knowledge of God is only possible, because God has revealed Himself to him and would be known by him. Hence URSIN (*ibid.*) says: "With mind and faith we know as much as He Himself reveals of Himself to us of His infinite mercy." This self-revelation of God is threefold: (1) by God's works, of course, which exist and take place in the whole nature of things, (2) by the Word transmitted to the Church and (3) by the Holy Spirit, by whom the elect are enlightened unto eternal life." The knowledge of the divine nature gained from God's revelation in the works of nature is but inadequate and uncertain, after the Fall has utterly defaced the divine image in man. It leads only to the definition of *Plato* and *Aristotle,* quite useless for the heart and sinful consciousness of man. (URSIN, p. 467): "God is eternal mind, sufficient unto itself for blessedness, most excellent and the cause of good in nature." So if man would attain to a true knowledge of God, he must not "exist on items of natural knowledge and testimony", but must "hear the Word divinely transmitted". Hence it must above all be insisted (URSIN, p. 466) "that He alone is true God, who right from the beginning of the human race has revealed Himself not only in the footprints of His divinity that shine in the nature of things, but especially in the Church by His transmitted word and by other shining testimonies of miracles, deliverances and consolations, by which He eloquently teaches us, as who and as of what sort He would be recognised and preached by us". But also the merely human and external knowledge of God's revealed facts is not yet sufficient to afford man a true and lively knowledge of the divine nature. In addition it is still necessary (URSIN, p. 457), "that at the same time God should reveal Himself to us in our hearts by His Spirit"; which God does by means of the Word in the hearts of the elect. Only then man learns really to grasp and inwardly to understand that God is an "essence spiritual, intelligent, eternal, different from all creatures, incomprehensible, most perfect in itself, unchangeable, of immense power, wisdom and goodness, righteous, truthful, pure, merciful, beneficent, most free, wrathful at sins. This essence is the Father everlasting, who has begotten the Son, His own image, from eternity; and the Son, the co-eternal image of the Father; and the H. Spirit proceeding from Father and Son, as the divinity has been disclosed in the sure Word transmitted through prophets and apostles and in divine testimonies; that the eternal Father with the Son and the H. Spirit created heaven and earth and all the creatures in them and is present to all the creatures to preserve and rule them by His providence and to work all good things in them all; and that in the human race created in His image He elected and gathers for Himself an everlasting Church for the Son's sake and through him, that from her this one and true Divinity might be recognised according to the Word divinely transmitted and worshipped and celebrated in eternal life and be the judge of the righteous and the unrighteous" (URSIN, p. 468).

13.—Thereby also God let man know His name, i.e., that which God has revealed of His essence to man.—Cocceius (*S.T.*, IX, 2): "The name of God in Scripture signifies all that can be known of God and that God wished to be known of Himself by us to His highest praise." Cocceius here collects the designations of God to be found in the Old Testament: אלהים, אלוה, שׁדי, אדני, יהדה.

14.—As only the spirit of man knows what man is, so only the truly godly man knows what God is; viz., through the Spirit dwelling in him.— Bullinger II, 2: "As none knows what is in man save the spirit of man which is in him, so, too, none can explain what God is, save God in His Word. But whosoever feign other opinions and attempt to obtain knowledge of God in a different way, deceive themselves and worship the idols of their own heart."

15.—Roused by the light of nature and furthered by the light of grace this knowledge of God attains its consummation in eternal life by the light of glory.—The distinction of the threefold *lumen naturae, gratiae,* and *gloriae* is very frequent with the dogmaticians in treating the doctrine of the knowledge of God. So, e.g., Eilshemius in the *Ostfriessl. Kleinod,* p. 389, says: "God gives men a threefold light, by which they know that there is truly a God. The one is a light of nature (within the heart, and without 'at the construction of the world'), the second a light of grace, the third a light of glory. By this threefold light the mind of man is led and guided as by three different staircases to knowledge of the eternal Godhead in this and in the future life."

CHAPTER V

THE ATTRIBUTES OF GOD

1.—Since the nature of God is manifested to the limited comprehension of man, man is aware in the unity of the divine nature of a manifold of attributes of God. "The essential properties of God are the divine attributes, by which the truth of the divine essence is both known in itself and distinguished from all other essences" (POLAN II, 7). The divine attributes are not something different from the nature and existence of God, so that the latter may be thought of as distinct from the former: nor are they parts of the divine nature, so that their total makes up the unity of the divine nature; nor are they something accidental, so that God's nature would be thinkable without the attributes; in God's nature there is nothing which is not God Himself. Rather the attributes of God are the divine nature itself in its relation to the world. And since God is essentially nothing else but absolutely single actuosity, every separate attribute of God is the identity of the whole divine being, as the latter is displayed in relation to a definite object.

The doctrine of the divine attributes is touched upon with but quite scanty remarks by CALVIN and his immediate pupils, as well as even by VIRELLIUS and the German-Reformed dogmaticians emanating from the School of MELANCHTHON and is carefully illustrated for the first time not until HYPERIUS and DANAEUS. It rests upon the proposition of the Reformed dogmaticians that "God is *actus purissimus et simplicissimus*" (purest and most single activity). Hence all insisted on the saying, e.g., of ZANCHIUS (*De nat. Dei. I*): "It is quite clear that there is no quality or accident in God, by which He may be said to be such or such; He is whatever He is by His own most single essence. Otherwise I should be saying that there is something in God which is not God." From this ZANCHIUS concludes that "God is more truly called life than living, wisdom than wise, light than shining and so with the rest. Why? Because He lives by Himself and is wise by His own essence, not by a wisdom which is added to the divine essence".—God's nature is (BUCAN I, 14) "most single essence, which admits of no composition or division". In God there is (16) no "accident; for everything is essential in God".—The separate propositions which result from this for the conception of God's attributes are most fully set forth by POLAN (II, 7): "(1) God's essential attributes are *really His very essence;* and they do not actually differ from God's essence or from each other. Not from the essence; they are in the essence in such wise as to be the essence. Not from each other; whatever there is in God is one. Moreover there ought to be absent from the prime unity all difference and all number whatsoever. In God there is nothing which is not either essence or person.—(2) No elements in God are distinguished essentially. All the things in God are one indivisible and most single essence.—(3) As God's essential attributes are not distinguished *realiter*, so too they are not distinguished by the nature of the thing but rather by the *ratio* or rather mode; i.e., by our conception and comprehension, or by our mode of understanding them.—(4) God's attributes are not parts of the divine essence. Any essential attribute you like is the actual essence of God whole and entire. So that God's essence and God's essential attribute are not one thing and another, but one and the same thing.—(5) God's essential attributes are inseparable *realiter*.—(6) Whatever God is or does in Himself, He is it or does it in Himself by one and the same act, which is His essence. Thus by one and the same act He is single (unifold!) infinite, unchangeable; by one and the same act He lives, knows, wills, animates, etc.—(7) God's essential attributes are in God from eternity to eternity, even though He does not declare them in outward works, whether not always or not upon certain persons or not in the same way.—(8) God's essential attributes are not subsequent to His essence, because they are actually the same thing.— (9) God's essential attributes are not accidental forms or accidents in God, but are essential ideas and forms. There is nothing in God which is not subsistent *per se*. Nor are there quantities in Him by which He might be said to be so much or so much; by His essence He is immense [the meaning is dealt with later] and great. Nor are there qualities in Him by which He might be said to be such and such. Whatever kind God is, He is so by His essence. His essence is whatever He is. His essence is wise, His essence is good, His essence is powerful, His essence is merciful, etc. In God *being* is the same as *being* wise, or good, or powerful, or merciful. Conclusion: God is immense and great without quantity; good, true and righteous without quality; action without movement, merciful without passion; present everywhere without position; first and most recent without time and beyond time; the Lord of all things without habit or addition.—(10) God's essential attributes are *actus*, exactly as God is purest and most single *actus* [activity].—(11) Without essential divine attributes God cannot exist, lest He exist without Himself; for He Himself is *ipsissima sapientia, bonitas, potentia;*" [i.e., identical with wisdom, goodness, power].

2.—Any distinction, therefore, of the divine attributes from each other and from the nature of God is not objective in God, either by a "real" or by a "modal distinction". It is based solely on the limitation of man's powers of comprehension. However, this subjective decision is not devoid of all objective foundation. In itself the divine nature is the most perfect and the purest unity of living being. But in its indications of manifold objects it reveals itself as a manifold, in which man does recognise the unchangeable unity and identity of the divine nature, yet also the distinguishable reflections of it.

BRAUN (*Doctr. foed.* I, ii, 2, 17): "Thus the attributes are not distinguished from the essence of God nor in turn from each other either *realiter* or by a real distinction. Such a distinction has place only between things and things, and necessarily posits composition.—Nor are the attributes distinguished from the essence by a modal distinction. Attributes are distinguished from an essence modally, because there is a modal distinction between a thing and its mode, as between a hand clenched or opened. But such a distinction posits composition between thing and mode, as well as variation; for every mode is changeable. God however is most single, without composition.—(18) Thus God's attributes are distinguished from His essence and from each other *distinctione rationis,* since it is by thought alone that we abstract attribute from essence and one attribute from another."—All dogmaticians pronounce accordingly, e.g., HOTTINGER, p. 44: "The attributes are distinguished neither from the essence nor from each other but only by our conceiving".—Hence, since every attribute is a manifestation of the same absolutely simple essentiality of God, it may justifiably be said (BRAUN I, ii, 2, 19) that "God's righteousness is His goodness, is His knowledge, is His will; or His mercy is His righteousness, etc. But it would be wrong for me to say that the concept I have of the righteousness is the same concept which I have of the deity, mercy or eternity".

At the same time it should be noted that man's distinction between the divine attributes is not a purely subjective one. Hence Reformed dogmaticians in this connection make use of the Scholastic distinction between *ratio ratiocinans* and *ratio ratiocinata*. They teach that the distinction of attributes is objectively based on the manifestation of God over against the various elements in the actual life of the world. In this sense we have VOETIUS saying, I, p. 233: "Although the divine essence and perfection is one and unifold, it does not operate in its own adequate way. So we say that God punishes the wicked in the way of righteousness, saves His own in the way of mercy.—Actually the attributes of righteousness and mercy—are not multiplied or distinguished in God himself. Virtually they are distinguished solely in their actual effects or in their finish up in such and such a work or effect."—BRAUN I, ii, 2, 18: "The distinction of *ratio ratiocinata* is founded on fact in respect of God's various acts and of the diverse objects in which God exercises His powers."— This point is most adequately developed by MASTRICHT (II, v, 5): The divine attributes, "if you mean the fact, are nothing but the one, infinite, perfection of God, according as it is apprehended by us in various inadequate concepts. To our so-called formal concepts, really differentiated from each other, there answer on God's side various objective concepts, the note of which in God is but the one infinite perfection, apprehensible by our understanding, owing to its native finitude and weakness, only in various acts, in parts as it were." Hence it must especially be maintained (II, v, 6), that "everything generally in God is nothing but one most single and pure *actus*, His very essence, His infinite perfection". And that on the following grounds: "(1) neither can one thing and another fall under the absolutely prime being by composition; (2) nor even under infinite being; for if this or that thing so fell, they would be either infinite or finite: not infinite, because several infinites involve an infinite contradiction; not finite, for out of several finites one infinite cannot take shape; (3) nor further under unchangeable and incorruptible being; for where thing is compounded with thing, thing is also torn from thing and so they can be altered and corrupted." From this then it follows that God's attributes are distinguished from each other not so much "on God's side" but rather "from the side of our conceiving", and so not *realiter* but "by our reason or thought". In any case this distinction rests not merely upon *ratio ratiocinans*, which is destitute of ways of distinguishing, but also upon *ratio ratiocinata*, which receives its ways of distinguishing from God Himself."

3.—A division of God's attributes is possible in manifold ways, namely, into attributes strict and metaphorical, positive and negative, absolute and relative, inward and outward, into attributes of God in and for Himself, and those of divine, active life or living. Most usually the division of God's attributes is into "incommunicable" and "communicable". This is not to be understood as though individual perfections of God might be imparted by God to certain creatures. This distinction is rather to be related to "analogical communication, by which nominally a common concept of the attributes of God and of creatures may be formed" (MARCK IV, 9), i.e., single attributes which God possesses in absolute perfection are also to be found in man in creaturely limitation, but others not.

BRAUN (I, II, 2, 20) gives the following divisions of God's attributes, (1) Into "proper, like goodness, righteousness, wisdom, etc., (2) figurative (*metaphorica*), as when God is called the Rock, the Lion, Fire, etc., (3) positive, like goodness, wisdom, righteousness, (4) negative, like immensity, infinity, immutability, etc., (5) absolute ones are reason and will, (6) relative, e.g., when He is called the LORD, Creator, Governor, etc. (21): The most notable distinction of God's attributes is that by which they are distinguished into communicable and incommunicable. Strictly speaking none are communicable, since they are *proprietates* (God's very own). Still analogically and equivocally certain ones may be called communicable, because certain traces of them are found among creatures, such as knowledge, will, goodness, justice."—TURRETIN (III, 6): "Among the various distinctions of the divine attributes none occurs more frequently than that by which they are divided into communicable and incommunicable."

Already among the older dogmaticians we find this division of the divine attributes which later became predominating. E.g., SOHNIUS, who in his *Method. theol.* (*Op. Th.* I, p. 103) says: "Attributes of the first kind are those which have nothing ἀνάλογον or like in anything else that we can see, whence this class is called by some ἀκοινώνητον.— Attributes of the second kind are those which have something ἀνάλογον and like in something else that we can see. Whence this class is called by some κοινωνητόν : not because these attributes are communicated or inhere in other things of themselves, but because in a way like effects are seen in them." In the former class SOHNIUS counts "singleness", "infinity", "eternity", and "immensity"; in the latter "life", "wisdom", "will" and "might".—COCCEIUS (*S.T.* IX, 34) understands by "incommunicable attributes" those which "separate God from the creatures not only οὐσία but also in name", and at once adds that "we reach their *res* by negation, although in God it (*res*) exists ὄντως (essentially)". Among these attributes COCCEIUS counts "singleness, eternity, immensity, immutability". The "communicable attributes" are partly the "life", partly the "virtue", partly the "power of God". The "life of God" includes, God being "most single Spirit", "intelligence" and "will". [int.≡knowledge].—The LEIDEN SYNOPSIS (VI, 23, 30) reckons as incommunicable attributes *simplicitas* [unifoldness!] ("on which depend unity and immutability") and "infinity", i.e., "eternity and immensity", and among the "communicable attributes" "life", "wisdom", "will" and "power".

To explain the difference in which the communicable attributes are present in God and man, POLANUS (II, 14) emphasises as follows, that "(1) By these attributes in God is understood the divine essence. But in the creatures they are only certain qualities actually different from their essence. Thus God lives by Himself by His essence, and also understands or knows, is wise and good, etc. Thus in God they exist essentially, in creatures accidentally.—(2) They are in God by nature, but in the creatures only by participation.—(3) In God they are infinite, because of course, they are eternal, because they are immense and incomprehensible. In the creatures they are finite.—(4) In God they exist in a more excellent fashion; they are absolutely perfect. Therefore God is not only living, immortal, wise, but also life itself, wisdom, immortality, blessedness itself; whereas in the creatures they are imperfect.—(5) In God they are actually one thing, the one and single essence; for by the same essence by which He is living, He is blessed, wise; among the creatures they are many and diverse. By one form man understands, by another he is righteous. The same must be felt about other attributes of the second class.—(6) In God they are ἀρχέτυποι, in creatures ἔκτυποι.—(7) They are assigned to God πρώτως i.e., firstly (primarily), *per se* and so strictly (*proprie*). But they are predicated of the creatures δευτέρως, secondarily, *per aliud* and ἀναλογικῶς, that is, by a sort of similitude, on the analogy of both act and use in creatures. (8) In God they exist immutably, in creatures mutably."

Upon the interest with which the distinction between communicable and incommunicable attributes was contested by the LUTHERANS and the CARTESIANS and upheld by the Reformed, MASTRICHT (II, iv, 12) remarks: "In order to secure the ubiquity of Christ's flesh and his presence in a peculiar way in the H. Supper the LUTHERANS insist that by the hypostatic union of the two natures of Christ the attributes of the divine nature have been communicated to the human nature; and so they sufficiently abolish the distinction into communicable and incommunicable.—The *Cartesian* theologians, in order to be able more conveniently to substitute the division, more suited to their philosophy, into understanding (knowledge) and will, think that it should be removed from its place. The Reformed are of opinion that, although no attribute of God is strictly and univocally communicable or common, because all are infinitely remote, there are yet some, traces of which of a kind are observed κατ' ἀναλογίαν in the creatures, and so the division is quite tolerable, since others are given in which no such trace is discernible, e.g., independence, aseity, immutability. For (1) along with Scripture experience itself teaches us that life, reason, will, goodness, love, grace, righteousness, holiness are shared by God with the creatures in the way we have specified; (2) the distribution in question is useful and necessary alike, regarding the proof of the homoousian deity of Son and Holy Spirit as one which we can and are used to prove not by the communicable but solely by the incommunicable attributes; and (3) Scripture teaches that God made man in His image (Gen. 1. 25)."

4.—The incommunicable attributes or "God's essential properties of the first order are those which are predicated of God as it were *a priori*, as He is; i.e., they declare the essence of God as it is in Himself absolutely; and in Him alone they inhere and to Him are attributed according to essence *actus* and force", and for that reason they are incommunicable *simpliciter*. The communicable attributes or "God's properties of the second order are those which are predicated of God *a posteriori*, as He is the *principium agendi*." They are "incommunicable as they exist in God". On the other hand they are called communicable κατ' ἀναλογίαν, because a kind of likeness of them is discovered in the creatures". For "there is no perfection in created things, of which the idea or manner is not most perfect in God" (POLAN II, 7, 14).—The incommunicable attributes of God (HEIDEGGER, III, 30) are His "independence, simplicity, infinity (eternity and immensity) and immutability".

"It is independence by which in being and operating God depends on no one else but possesses for Himself an essence sufficient to make Him *a se* in essence and also in operation, so that everything outside Him depends upon Him in existing and in operating" (HEIDEGGER, *Corp. Theol.*, III, 30).

"It is God's simplicity or singleness, by which He is devoid of all composition, coalescence, concretion, admixture, confusion and diversity, in such wise that whatever is even thought in God is God Himself and that so there is the most absolute identity of the divine essence and attributes and even of the attributes among themselves" (HEIDEGGER, III, 32).—God's "simplicity" embraces His "spirituality, invisibility and incomprehensibility" (III, 35).

"Independence" and "simplicity" are reckoned by the dogmaticians among the attributes of God, since it is recognised that they are just determinations of the divine in and for itself, and that in particular the mention of "singleness" is only repeated here in order to guard against a false conception of the relation of the attributes to one another. Cf. KECKERMANN, 98: "I see that among the attributes are usually counted those things which must be mentioned before all attributes; like singleness, which is not to be conceived as an attribute, since in the first instance it is predicated of the essence. It is a recognition that there are no such distinctions in God".—BRAUN I, ii, 6, 19: "Although so many attributes are assigned to God,—none the less God is most single. He recognises no composition; neither logical by genus and differentia; nor physical by matter and form, whether partially or by subject and accident; nor metaphysical, by action and power, by essence and existence, or by nature and *suppositum*. Therefore God is most single."—HEIDAN, p. 95: "God's singleness is—the individual unity of all God's perfections". Aptly HEIDAN remarks further that *simplicitas* is but an expression of God's absoluteness in and for Himself. For "all composition involves some dependence. In every compound one of the components is either subordinated to the other, or is the principle of the other, or is more perfect than the other, or at least the whole composite depends upon both." The singleness of God is upheld against *Socin* and *Vorstius,* who (RIISSEN III, ii, 1) deny that singleness can be attributed to God, purposely the more easily to collapse the mystery of the Trinity by insisting that God's essence is composite." At the same time the question is answered in the negative (RIISSEN *ibid.* 27): "whether God enters into composition with any created things, in order to have reason for some part, whether matter or form" (as, e.g., the Platonists say that "God is the world's soul").

The doctrine of the "singleness" and "spirituality" of God gained a practical significance in the system, because from the standpoint of it the Catholic and Lutheran use of pictures was rejected. This was of course given more expression by confessional writers than by dogmaticians. DANAEUS (*Isag.* II, p. 113ff.) is of opinion that the use of pictures even as ornaments is very doubtful.

MASTRICHT raises the question (II, iv, 12): "whether it is right in divine worship when praying to objectify God to oneself as an old man", and answers the question thus: "Because the *Lutherans* have long since lost the use of images in public worship, which cannot but generate such stupid conceptions in onlookers, they cannot with any sort of ἐπιείκεια find fault. They declare that such conceptions of God in the guise of an elderly man do not import any sin, provided they do not insist that God's essence has such a figure. See *Francis Balduin, Cas. conscient. cap. 2 casus 1, Pruknerus* in *Mille casibus consc.,* and others. In order to get at them with both nails the *Reformed* say that it is lawful to have a concept of God, in fact it is highly necessary, unless we would be atheist: yet they hold that a concept of God under the guise of a man or anything else corporeal is quite out of order". The reasons are as follows: (1) "The Saviour Jn., 4. 24 bids us hold such a conception of God, as agrees with God's nature, describes God as Spirit and of course He wishes to be worshipped and adored in spirit, i.e., spiritually, without any sort of figures; and in truth, or with true thoughts agreeable to the concept. (2) Such conceptions of God are false, according as they do not agree with the God conceived; in fact they are illicit. (3) Such concepts are vain Rom., 1:21. (4) They obscure the glory of the incorruptible God and as it were change it ἐν ὁμοιώματι εἰκόνος φθαρτοῦ ἀνθρώπου. (5) By these concepts the heart is clouded and the mind rendered foolish".

5.—"It is God's infinity by which His Deity embraces all perfections in the highest degree, without any limit, mode or end" (HEIDEGGER III, 39)— BRAUN (I, ii, 6, 1): "Infinity signifies God's supreme perfections, so far as God recognises no limits in any of His perfections. Hence God's essence and all His attributes ought to be called infinite. His immensity is often taken in the same sense. At the same time by immensity writers are often in the habit of signifying some relative attribute, so far as nothing is given by which God's perfection can be limited or measured." As a rule "God's infinity" means two things: (1) the absolute perfection of the moral attributes and (2) the timeless and non-spatial character of God. WOLLEB e.g. says (p.9): "It is infinity by which God is known as a being infinitely true and good and devoid of all measure or limit". Meanwhile other dogmaticians in agreement with HEIDEGGER, like the LEIDEN SYNOPSIS VI, 65, say: "Infinity, i.e. eternity and immensity".

6.—Infinity appears as "eternity", so far as it excludes from God's existence any temporal limit, and as "immensity", or "omnipresence", so far as it excludes from it any spatial limit. " 'Eternity' is that infinite and interminable duration, which is at once whole without any innovation or succession" (POLAN, II, 11).—The dogmaticians endeavour to define the concept of eternity in various ways. Says ALSTED 75: "It is God's eternity by which He is devoid of time as regards limit and succession"; VAN TIL, Comp. I, 26: "Eternity is actual interminable and simultaneous possession of essence".—WENDELIN (Systema, p. 14): "Eternity is God's attribute by which He excludes all limitations of duration, being devoid of beginning and end of existence."—RIJSSEN III, 12: "It is God's eternity, by which God is everything that exists without beginning and end."—In a closer exposition of the concept of eternity MASTRICHT distinguishes three measures of duration, time, aeon and eternity, as follows (II, xi, 8:) "The first (measure of duration) is that of things by their nature changeable and liable to age; it rejoices in a beginning and an end and is called time. The nature of this consists in the continual succession of moments, so that only one strictly speaking exists at a time, since those preceding have ceased to exist and those subsequent do not exist yet. The second measure (of duration) is of things essentially incorruptible or non-material. It has a beginning but no end and is called an aeon. The third, which is simply unchangeable and so lacks beginning and succession—this at last is the eternity which the Scholastics define as endless, indivisible and independent duration. Endless, because it lacks each extremity; indivisible also as lacking succession; finally independent, being devoid of all imperfection and change. So that in eternity these three combine, absence of beginning, of end (which all admit) and of succession, which Vorstius denies with the Socinians".—Similarly MARCK IV, 31.

7.—"God's immensitas is the essential attribute of God, through which the divine essence is signified as not being limited, circumscribed or bounded by any place, but as penetrating and filling places one and all everywhere and being present to all things" (POLAN II, 12).—Many dogmaticians speak like HEIDEGGER III, 41: "God's infinity removes from His existence beginning, end and succession by eternity, and from His essence local (spatial) circumscription by immensity; so that there is no difference between 'immensity' and 'omnipresence'." On the other hand RIISSEN III, 16: "It is God's immensity by which, devoid of measure and limit, God is everything that is. This immensity is distinguished from omnipresence; the former states an eternal and absolute attribute in God, while the latter denotes a dwelling locally which exists in time".

The concept likewise of "omnipresence" the dogmaticians seek to define in various ways. Says ALSTED (73): "Strictly God is not in any place but contains all places. He is *totus* in all *res*, *totus* in single things, *totus* in Himself". VAN TIL (*Compend. theol.*, p. 33): "Omnipresence is the very actuality of existing related to corporeal creatures, which depend for their being and continuance on God".—When it is desired to explain that God's omnipresence is not merely of an operative but of an essential kind, the verse is often adduced and explained:

Enter, praesenter Deus hic et ubique potenter.

In explanation of the definition "God is not circumscribed by any place" POLAN remarks (II, 12) upon the concept of *locus*: "By the term place we understand not only bodily and physical space but also spiritual and supernatural, wherever that is: not only in activity whether in heaven at its highest or on earth right at its centre, but also δυνάμει and so even beyond the highest heaven. Place is no less above the highest heaven than in heaven and beneath heaven. It is a human error that there is no place above heaven; also that heaven is not a place. But place is either circumscriptive or definitive. Now God is not in a circumscriptive place, like corporeal things contained by their corporeal place which is divisible into its own sizeable parts also divisible; nor in a definitive place, as are intelligent forms, i.e. angels and human souls, because although the place of intelligent forms is not corporeal or circumscribed as regards us, it is yet defined in itself, so that one intelligent form cannot define (limit) two places at the same time, i.e. operate in two places at the same time".—To do away with the error contained in the statement that God is also *extra mundum* RIISSEN (III, 19) remarks: " By His immensity God is also outside the world. Not indeed positively, as though we had to conceive of spaces outside the world which God fills with His presence; but negatively, so far as all the spaces in the world do not exhaust the immensity of God, that He should be contained in them. He is therefore at present outside the world in Himself, as once upon a time, before the creation of the world."

8.—Yet the immeasurable being of God must not be thought of as infinite extension. It rather consists in the divinity "being whole and one in itself, whole and one in individual places and things, and so as to be entire within all things and entire (*tota*) outside everything" (POLAN II, 12). Hence the immeasurability of God as an " absolute attribute" is also more correctly described as "immensity" than as "omnipresence", since it belonged to God even before the creation of the world and hence must not be confined to God's relation to the world (MARCK IV, 27). It also follows from this, that God's omnipresence is to be thought of not as an operative but as an essential allpresentness in the world.—MASTRICHT (II, x, 9): "Although the Reformed do not deny that God is omnipresent virtually and functionally (*virtute et* ἐνεργείᾳ); yet, because both virtue and function are one and the same thing in God, if you except work produced, they do deny that the divine essence is omnipresent". Similarly all other Reformed dogmaticians represent in the development of the doctrine of God's omnipotence the strictly theistic conception of God; e.g., HEIDEGGER (*Corp. theol.*, III, 47): "Detestable is the godlessness of *Socinus, Vorstius* and certain *Anabaptists*, who obtrude upon Christianity a God who in essence is in heaven, but works everywhere by mediating causes physical or hyperphysical, as a king living in a palace works through his ministers. This sort of presence of God in the world beyond heaven is not even presence in the true sense, not to mention immensity or omnipresence, but is rather absence". In particular it is stressed by ZANCHIUS (II, 6) that "God is anything but said to be or is more in heaven than on earth, or more in saints than in the ungodly because of His essence; He is so because of His operation and grace".

9.—"Immutability" is that attribute of God, "by which He alone is *per se* and *a se*, in actuality and in potency, devoid of all succession, change or variation, remaining the same eternally without even the faintest shadow of transmutation" (HEIDEGGER III, 49). This unchangeability of God is: (1) "an immutability of essence"; for it is not "liable to any conversion into another essence, to any alteration, to any change of place: (2) an "immutability of nature or essential attributes"; for the latter "are and remain unchangeable to all eternity"; and (3) an "immutability of God's decrees and promises": for "whatever God has decreed from eternity or whatever He has promised is immutable, Is. 46, Rom. 11, Heb. 6, 17-18."—HEIDAN 95: "From God's singleness we rightly infer His immutability, by which God is necessarily that which He is or such as He is".—RIISSEN (III, 21) regarding the question, "whether God is immutable as regards both essence and will" makes the following point against the *Socinians*: "Opponents also carp at this immutability of God, especially that concerned with acts of will, as though God could now unwill what He previously willed, and will now what formerly He refused to will. We are of opinion with the orthodox that complete immutability must be attributed to Him as well regarding His nature as regarding His will".

10.—The communicable attributes of God are *vita, intellectus* and *voluntas,* as well as the "virtues" of the latter, especially *bonitas, iustitia* and *libertas,* and finally *potentia* and *beatitudo* (HEIDEGGER III, 52).

"It is God's life by which God both lives Himself, by nature perpetually *actuosus* in Himself, and is the fountain of life to others, imparting it beyond Himself in various ways" (HEIDEGGER III, 53). To give a closer explanation of this determination of the concept the following is to be stressed (POLAN II, 15): "(1) *Vita* and *vivere* do not differ in God, but are the same thing; (2) God's life is God Himself, is God's own *esse,* so far as He is God; (3) it has no cause of itself, so as not to be a divine thing as well; (4) it is eternal; (5) it is so sure, that with the utmost propriety GOD ALONE MAY BE SAID TO LIVE".

HOTTINGER, p. 50: "It is God's life by which He both lives Himself by nature perpetually *actuosus* in Himself and is the source of life for others, communicating it in a variety of ways outside Himself".—MASTRICHT describes the difference between absolute, divine and creaturely human life thus (II, xii, 8): "Although life is common to God and to rational creatures not just in name only; for in that case we could not possibly be led through the life of the creatures into that of the Creator; yet really the fact is still not such that it is not remote from ours *toto coelo,* as finite is from infinite, as detailed pretty much under these heads: "(1) while creatures are only living, God is life itself, 1 Jn. 5. 20 (we know that the Son of God is come, and hath given us an understanding, that we know Him that is true, and we are in Him that is true, even in His Son Jesus Christ. This is the true God and eternal life). Or, what is the same thing, whereas creatures have a life different from their essence, a life which is a sort of faculty of the essence, God rejoices in a life which plainly coincides with His essence. (2) Creatures precariously carry the life imparted to them by God who is the spring of life, Ps. 36. 9 (with thee is the fountain of life: in thy light shall we see light) Acts 17.28 (in him we live and move and have our being...For we are also his offspring); God has life in Himself. Accordingly (3) whereas creatures possess a life not their own, God has His own; (4) The life of creatures is finite, either both ways, from head and from heel, or at least from the head; and so at one time they did not possess life; and some day they will not possess it. God rejoices in life infinite, immortal and eternal, which He is accordingly said to possess in the present; (5) The life of creatures slips by in movement, succession and continual flux : to God belongs the endless possession of life at once whole and perfect " ;—(the latter is a definition of BOETHIUS much used by dogmaticians: *interminabilis vitae tota simul et perfecta possessio*). Chief stress is laid on what BRAUN (I, ii, 2, 12) says: "God's life is His *ipsissima essentia,* while ours is conceived as an *actus secundus*".

11.—In its essence God's life is knowledge and will. In the former according to Scripture, Rom. 11. 33 (O the depths both of the wisdom and the knowledge of God! How unsearchable are his judgments and his way past finding out!) we must distinguish between God's *cognitio* and God's *sapientia*. God's *cognitio, intelligentia* or *scientia* is that perfection of the divine *intellectus*, by which in a most perfect and plainly divine manner, by essence and in a unique and perfectly single act He understands and knows all things outside Himself, present, past, future and possible" (HEIDEGGER III, 56). God's knowing is thus an absolute one, since God knows (1) Himself and (2) the things outside Himself (as posited and conditioned solely by Him) purely by Himself, by His own being.

As regards the divine *scientia,* the dogmaticians above all insist upon the difference between it and human knowledge, since all stress the statement, that man has the capacity for knowledge, but God is essentially knowledge. Cf. WENDELIN (*System*. 145): "Knowledge is the actual intelligent essence of God".—VAN TIL 32: God's life is the actual actuosity of the divine essence. This actuosity is His intellectual, intelligent and active life."— BRAUN: I, ii, 3, 2: "Knowledge and will are in God, not in the way of a faculty or habit, since not even in man is knowledge distinguished *realiter* from will, but should be conceived merely as a different mode of thinking. Thus it is in God in the way of most single *actus*, because in God there is but the sole and most single idea, whereby He perfectly contemplates and knows once and for all by a single intuition His own perfections and all things present and future, necessary, contingent and possible".— In complete agreement with this COCCEIUS says (*S.T.*, X, 6, 8, 9, 14) that God's life comprises knowledge and will, since God is "most single Spirit". Knowledge is present in God neither as a *potentia* nor as a *facultas* but as an *actus,* and He is therefore more correctly described as knowing than as possessing knowledge. For it is the direct living utterance of the knowing Absolute. Hence since God's knowledge is an eternal one, nothing new can occur in it. "If we admit something new in God, He cannot be eternal. Therefore neither can a new object come to God's knowledge; for new knowledge would exist in God." This is to be explained as that God simply knows Himself and that, the nature of which it is, "to attest the perfection of God".

12.—Hence the divine awareness must never be conceived as though God took up things from without into His knowledge, i.e., changed, expanded or modified Himself. Of course reasoning creatures can only know things *ratiocinando*, discursively. Whereas God knows the same things intuitively, "without the discursiveness of reasoning, by the absolute spirituality of His own nature in its relation to His own being and to all realities and possibilities outside Himself" (POLAN II, 18).

From the remarks made about the difference between divine and human knowledge there result still wider variations of both. Above all (KECKERMANN 97): "God's knowing is a most single *actus*; (man's) knowledge has distinct *actûs*". From this it follows that God's knowledge is not discursive and successive but intuitive and simultaneous, and that God has knowledge of things not through a survey of them which extends and changes His consciousness, but in such a way that He conditions them Himself and therefore knows them because He knows Himself; for God's knowing is the being of God and the actuosity of the divine being itself. Cf. BRAUN I, ii, 3, 2: "From this it is clear that God's knowledge is noetic only, not dianoetic or discursive; and that therefore God knows everything through His essence, since His knowledge is nothing else than His most single essence, with some connotation of things knowable. Thus He does not know like a man, who by much laborious reasoning deduces from the better known that which is less known. But in one intuition and act He knows all things that ever were, that are and that are destined to be for ever".—HEIDAN, p. 113: "There is a great difference between our knowledge and God's. All our knowledge is through ideas, some of which are innate, others adventitious, others manufactured by ourselves, like chimeras....Of these the ones most specially to be considered are those called adventitious, knowledge of which man acquires by analysis, which is gathered from the things themselves. And so things exist first of all in themselves, before they can reach man's senses and through them his reason, there to form an idea of themselves. So that the things themselves are in us an instance and a prototype, but the knowledge of them is an image. In God it is otherwise. Because He knows everything by genesis and not by analysis, all things exist in His mind before they exist in themselves; nor does He borrow His knowledge or beg it from things. Whence also knowledge in God is the prototype and actual things are the image or express likeness of it. This is true only of the things which God knows outside Himself; for He knows Himself. He is therefore strictly all-knowing".

HEIDEGGER (*Corp. theol.* III, 56) develops this point most completely: "In God there is no new and old, prior and subsequent, potency and activity, ignorance and knowledge, things which in no wise become God eternal, infinite and perfect, in whom therefore is not διάνοια but νοῦς, not dianoetic knowledge which belongs to the ignorant, but noetic which belongs *simpliciter* to the intelligent. Nor does He receive kinds of knowledge, because He Himself is first of all Is. 44. 6 (I am the first, and I am the last; and beside me there is no God) Rev. 1. 8 (Alpha and Omega), eternal, Rom. 1. 20 (everlasting power and divinity), and depends upon no one else. Rather, all things live, move and have their being in Him. Nor is it by knowing that He receives form or idea from a thing perceived; all things are γυμνὰ before Him, Heb. 4, 13. He rather gives to the thing perceived. Where would He receive species or ideas from? From things? But none were present to God, who knows from eternity. Or from one who knows? In this way there would exist something superior to God, and we should have progress *in infinitum*, and that would be anything but glorious for God. In God there is nothing different or distinct from His most single *esse*, nothing potentially otherwards; nothing prior and posterior, nothing changeable. But also by perceiving steadily creatures are worn out and become bored, whether because they do not achieve perfect knowledge, or because they hurry to another act of perceiving something else, or because they are busy perceiving alien things. God is not so. He understands by one infinite act; nor does He understand anything but Himself and what is of Himself in Himself. Hence His knowledge is pure, most single, one, perpetual, never weary, continuing from eternity to eternity. It is activity without beginning or end, and so essence itself, by which as being infinite and the cause of all things He comprehends at once all things and sundry".

13.—The divine awareness is thus the direct actuosity of the being of God itself and isᵉ therefore one, absolutely simple, unconditioned, infinite, simultaneous, eternal, unchangeable and absolutely perfect and certain intuition.—VOETIUS sets forth the attributes of the divine awareness thus (I, p. 249): "The attributes of divine knowledge are: (1) That it is one, undivided in itself and most single, although we distinguish it in terms of objects. And so God Himself is knowing (*intelligens*). God and His understanding and knowledge or το *intelligere* are one and the same thing, and He Himself understands in one act. (2) That it is prime and independent in essence and not by participation, not caused by things upon which all knowledge of created things depends; ἀρχέτυπος not ἔκτυπος, lacking no revealing principle, no intelligible species, no revelation, revealing light, experience or observation, because He knows all things of Himself, in Himself, through Himself. Is. 40. 13-14 (who hath directed the Spirit of the Lord or being his counsellor hath taught him ? With whom took he counsel and who instructed him, and taught him in the path of judgment and taught him knowledge, and shewed him the way of understanding?) Rom. 11. 34 (who hath known the mind of the Lord ? or who hath been his counsellor ?). (3) That it is eternal. (4) That it is unchangeable and consequently simultaneous, so that there is no succession in it, no before and after, accession or withdrawal, although we may conceive of elements or instances of reason in it in its ordering towards objects. (5) That it is perfect not only in apprehension but also in comprehension, in single intuition, not by discursion from known to unknown, seeing into things directly and intimately; not by composition or division, not by inadequate or analogical concepts, or universal or confused or non-evident ones: because it fully and most distinctly knows things as they are, Ps. 7. 10 (the righteous God trieth the hearts and reins), 139, 2-5, Jer. 17. 10 (I the Lord search the heart, I try the reins:..), Heb. 4. 13 (there is no creature that is not manifest in his sight; but all things are naked and laid open before the eyes of him with whom we have to do). (6) Necessary, determined and sure, even when it is dealing with things free, contingent and lightly indeterminate in their nature; so that it cannot be liable to any ignorance, error or doubt, even at the remotest remove. (7) Actual, not like potency or habit; so that it could not be actuated by any idea or intelligible species either co-eternal with itself or accepted by things, or by any means: for He Himself as purest activity is His own idea, species, copy, perception, understanding. (8) Infinite both intensively and extensively, i.e., both in itself and by reason of the object; and so nowhere abstract; precise, so that it knows or conceives of one thing not by having known another, e.g., subject without accident, whole without part or apart from its part, the universal in abstraction from instances or apart from instances".

14.—In the divine awareness are distinguished "(1) *scientia necessaria naturalis,* which precedes every act of will in the order of nature, and by which God knows at the first direct and highly necessary act (*a*) Himself in Himself and through Himself; then (*b*) all things possible, not in themselves but in His essence as their necessary cause, and (*c*) *scientia libera,* by which after the decree of His will He knows determinately all matters existing, in whatsoever difference of time they are, whether present, past or future" (VOETIUS I, p. 247).—HEIDAN (p. 117): "Although one in God this knowledge is yet a varying mode of knowing, according as the *actus* itself varies in its various objects. Moreover, the *actus* of knowing is nothing else than the actual conjunction of the knowable object with the knowing faculty, or the real occupation of the knowing faculty with the knowable object. Hence the distinctions of knowledge into necessary and free, etc.—Necessary is that which precedes every act of will in the order of nature, because its object is simply eternal and can never not be; as when God knows Himself and all things possible.—Free, which follows a free act of will, i.e., whose object so depends on the divine will, that by nature it may not be; and so an object to which the divine *intellectus* inclines not by the direct necessity of nature but by the mediation of will. Now such an object is whatever God has decreed to make or to allow outside Himself".—VAN TIL (I, 41): "God's knowledge is distinguished into necessary, by which He cannot not know Himself, and free, by which He knows all His works produced by Himself or to be produced; free, because it depends upon His will".—ALSTED 97: "It is God's natural knowledge by which God knows Himself and all things possible; by reason of the previous *actus* it is called necessary knowledge; it is free knowledge by which He knows all other existents. 98: God's necessary knowledge precedes every free act of the divine will, free knowledge follows the act of will. All God's knowledge is necessary; given any sort of necessary object, the divine *intellectus* knows it."

VOETIUS (I, 248) thus sets forth the elements to be distinguished in God's knowledge:

"God knows Himself firstly, necessarily and intuitively; Things other than Himself, namely:

(1) Possible things undefined by natural knowledge or by the necessary knowledge of single intelligence. These He knows (i) precisely in Himself and in abstraction from any act of will, the name for which is speculative knowledge; or (ii) conjointly with the act of the divine will, which is practical knowledge.

(2) Existing things: (i) Generally, things future, past and present; this is free knowledge, knowledge of sight, definite knowledge; (ii) Specially, things that exist, only in the difference of future time; this is called foreknowledge."

"Necessary or natural knowledge" is thus the direct awareness which in virtue of His being God has of Himself and of all possibilities, in so far as He is the conditioning cause of them. "Free knowledge" is an awareness comprising all realities, which rests upon the absolute decree of the divine will and is determined by it.

15.—(2) *Scientia visionis* (or intuitive knowledge). It "is that by which God knows the things which are and those which are altogether future, and sees them as present; and (*a*) He knows them in Himself not only as powerful, i.e., as being able to do them, but also as willing them to be done eventually: (*b*) He knows them also in their second or proximate causes": and (*c*) "God knows them in their very selves". And there is "knowledge of simple intelligence, by which in His omnipotent essence only God knows the things which might eventuate and exist, but which never eventuate, will never exist; but not in willing them, because He does not will them to eventuate either in their second causes (they haven't any!) or in themselves, because they will never exist" (POLAN, II, 18).— POLAN (*ib.*) adds: "This is called knowledge of simple intelligence, because things which do not actually exist are only known, *intelliguntur;* and this pertains to Deity alone, so that it is not even competent for the soul of Christ, although there is a created similitude of knowledge of vision in Christ's soul". By "single intelligence" then (which is not a *scientia* proper) God surveys not "what is independent of or discharged from His will and results from the will of finite beings" (which in the Reformed view do not exist at all), but the area of His own absolute freedom and of the possibilities resident in it, which He does not allow to come into being.—HEIDAN (p. 117): "Knowledge of single intelligence is the same as natural knowledge with a secondary object, namely things possible, but not as regards the primary object, God. It is also called intuitive. It is knowledge of vision, by which God views things which actually exist now or did so once or are certain to do so in the future. These continually pass before God and are present to Him".

Thus "knowledge of vision" and "knowledge of simple intelligence" are so distinguished from each other that the former is a proper awareness by which God's vision pierces everything which is not Himself, since He can and wills to effect all that exists and takes place outside Himself. Whereas the latter is not knowledge (*scientia*) proper, but an *intelligentia* by which God reviews the realm of His absolute freedom; in which lie countless possibilities, which however He will not allow to be realised.

We can only speak of a divine foreknowledge from the viewpoint of man's conception of the divine nature. God knows the future in virtue of the spirituality and absoluteness of His being. The only thing that is future and happens at all is (1) what is possible, i.e., what may be a means of glorifying God and (2) what God will allow to be realised. ("God foreknows the things which he wishes to happen in the future" BUCAN, XXXVI, 2). Hence by His will determining things He sees and knows the future as the present, and as regards His foreknowledge it necessarily possesses the character of infallibility, as regards His determining counsel the character of immutability.

16.—"God's foreknowledge is that knowledge by which God is signified as foreseeing and foreknowing from eternity everything that is said to be future, as far as we are concerned" (POLAN II, 18).—CALVIN III, xxi, 5: "When we attribute foreknowledge to God, we mean that everything has always been and will always remain under His eye; so that there is nothing future or past in His knowledge but everything is present; and present in such a way that He does not picture them merely by ideas (as things pass before us, of which our minds retain a recollection) but truly views and discerns them as though set down in front of Him". Since as the actuosity of the divine Being foreknowledge is the proof of God's nature over against the world, it is determinative and is therefore to be distinguished from *notitia*.—BUCAN XXXVI, 2: "Generically it is prescience or πρόγνωσις, by which with single understanding God foreknows and precognosces all created things. By some it is called *notitia* but God's *notitia* is of wider extent than His prescience. Knowledge extends not only to things present, past and future, but also to things which will never be, whether they be possible or impossible. Now, prescience is of things which are to be. And so prescience demands will, which comes first in order. Nothing will come to be, unless God wills it to be; otherwise He would hinder it. Therefore God foreknows what He wills to come into being, but so that to His knowledge nothing is future or past; all things are present, Heb. 4. 13 (there is no creature that is not manifest in his sight; but all things are naked and laid open before the eyes of him with whom we have to do). This universal knowledge does not imply necessity of effects. Prescience itself is the cause of things *simpliciter*, as though they were future because He foreknows them. He foreknows them because He has decreed that they shall come to be."

In adequate accord with the basic thought of the Reformed system HOTTINGER bases prescience upon the decrees of God (p. 76): "As God's decrees are unchangeable, prescience is infallible. And hence arises a twofold necessity for things future; both hypothetical; the one that of immutability since it is a decree, the other that of infallibility as regards prescience, which indeed is also the tradition of Scripture, Lk. 24. 26-27, 44-46 (Behoved it not the Christ to suffer these things, and to enter into His glory? And beginning from Moses and all the prophets, he interpreted to them in all the Scriptures the things concerning Himself. . . . These are my words which I spake unto you, while I was yet with you, how that all things must needs be fulfilled, which are written in the law of Moses, and the prophets, and the psalms, concerning. . . . Thus it is written, that the Christ should suffer, and rise again from the dead the third day) 1 Cor. 2. 9 (Things which eye saw not, and ear heard not, and which entered not into the heart of man, whatsoever things God prepared for them that loved him). God's prescience is partly theoretical, partly practical. The former is bare knowledge of things future, posited in nothing more than the contemplation of them. Concerning it the words of Heb. 4. 13 (there is no creature that is not manifest in His sight, but all things are naked and laid open before the eyes of him with whom we have to do), Ac. 15. 18 (the LORD . . . maketh these things known from the beginning of the world) are to be taken strictly. The latter is knowledge of things future, together with the conjoined will by which God resolved to produce them; a metaphorical expression for Him who effects.   In this sense by a characteristically Hebrew usage πρόγνωσις is used Ac. 2. 23 (. . . by the determinate counsel and foreknowledge of God) Rom. 8. 28-29 (we know that to them that love God all things work together for good, even to them that are called according to his purpose. For whom he foreknew, he also foreordained to be conformed to the image of his Son, that he might be the first-born of many brethren) compared with each other".—Yet the explanation of prescience causes difficulty for the dogmaticians.—HEIDEGGER (III, 59) discusses the question "what the reason, cause, foundation is of prescience or the knowledge of those things which are outwith God, on account of which all things are known by God, even the contingent and the particularly free", and denies that this question can be answered with complete satisfaction speculatively ("here if anywhere we are certainly as blind as bats"). Really, therefore, the task of dogmatics can only be to reject every wrong answer to the question, in course of which it must preeminently be insisted that "actual future events or any object cannot be the object of God's knowledge, according as in our mode of understanding the object moves the faculty and is in a sense the cause of the act arising from it". But we must also insist, "that there is in God a manner and way of prescience agreeable to His nature, whether men are aware of it or not". And at the same time it must be acknowledged that "the cause of the knowledge of all things in God is the knowledge belonging to His infinite essence, which is the cause of all things" (60). How far this is so cannot of course be proved. But it can be made moderately explicable, if we insist that in virtue of absolute knowledge of Himself God has also an absolute knowledge of all the existences which are possible, i.e., which are so made that, conditioned solely by Him, they can serve "to His glory", and "He can be their end"; for "not otherwise can anything be said to be possible for God". Since then God only really wills what (in this sense) is possible, and since only what He wills becomes real, God in virtue of His absolute knowledge of Himself is also in possession of an absolute knowledge of all that humanly speaking is future.—RIISSEN raised the question (III, 23): "whether God foreknows contingent things of the future and the actions of free creatures", and (in opposition to *Socin*) answers it in the affirmative, in the following manner which carefully preserves the Reformed doctrinal principle: "The question is not about any future things which have a necessary cause; about these there is no doubt. It is about contingent things which have a cause free and ἀδιάφορος. Not in respect of the First Cause, in which sense contingent things are also extremely necessary ; for they may be and not be. But in respect of the second contingent causes : Whether God knows them, not indeterminately only and probably, but determinately and most surely; which the *Socinians* deny, in order more easily to introduce the indifference of *liberum arbitrium*, an indifference immune even from that necessity which arises from God's prescience."

17.—Prescience is to be distinguished from permission; for "prescience is an act of knowing, permission is an act of the will—the former has its object in itself, the latter has it outside itself" (POLAN II, 18).—On the other hand the distinction invented by the *Jesuits* and adopted by the *Arminians* is utterly untenable and objectionable, of a "middle knowledge of God, a conditioned knowledge of future contingencies, by which from eternity, not absolutely but conditionally, God knows what men and angels would be doing for their freedom, if they are put with these or those circumstances in such and such an order of events" (VOETIUS I, p. 254). Possibilities presumed to be independent of God and a divine awareness of things which did not rest upon the absolute decree of God do not exist.

On the origin and history of the distinction of God's middle knowledge GISBERT VOETIUS I, pp. 254-7, gives the following account here transmitted in summary : " After the rise of the new sect of *Jesuits* great contentions existed between it and the other clergy both secular and regular. The Jesuits were generally out to diminish the authority of others, mainly of the *Dominicans*, pretty much like Carthage, the rival of the Roman Empire. Hence pretexts were sought, all plausible occasions were snatched at. Among others they thought that the most favourable to their purpose would be the famous controversies on the conception of Mary and on the concurrence of grace and free-will, where they hoped that the applause of the majority, both clerical and lay, would not fail them. The disputations on grace and free will (we must speak elsewhere on the conception of Mary) were first condemned for Pelagianism or semi-Pelagianism by the Louvain theologians at Louvain in the person of *Leonardo Lessius,* then also by the *Duaceni* and the Belgian bishops : the *Jesuits* complain of him in the

Imago futuri saeculi, Bk., 6, p. 847 which see. Later, such heat arose between *Jesuits* and *Dominicans* in Spain, when the former charged the *Dominicans,* along with the *Lutherans* and *Calvinists,* with abolishing free will and with *syncretism;* the *Dominicans* in turn charging the *Jesuits* with *Pelagianism;* that a four years' silence was imposed on them by the Pope and the supreme Inquisitor of heresy, which might scarcely be lifted but on condition that they should have power to dispute and write on the controversy without insults or censures to or upon the other side, according to VASQUEZ, *Praefat. dedicat. ad commentar. in Thomam.* Of that tragedy there is some account in *Petrus Matthaeus,* the French historian, Bk. 7, 493. Not to appear openly to declare war upon *Augustine* and *Thomas* with their followers or to συγκρητίζειν with the *Pelagians,* the *Jesuits* thought out *scientia media,* which to this day is the refuge of all Pelagianisers. Some make *Fonseca* the first author of this καινοφωνία, others *Molina.* At all events each of them boasts of it. The state of affairs is this. In 1566 in his public lectures and dictations *Fonseca* had proposed this way of reconciling free will and grace and had communicated his ideas also verbally to his hearers (as he bears witness, *Met.,* VI, *c.* 2, *qu.* 4, *sect.* 8). But because of the kind of innovation he had published nothing in type before 1596, since he was publishing vol. 3 of his *Comm. on Metaphysics.* First to perfect and gradually to tame the bearlike offspring of *Fonseca* by licking it (as *Fonseca* says) and to bring it to light was *Louis Molina* in his treatise on the agreement of free will and grace, first published 1588, then repeated in an enlarged edition 1595, published at Antwerp by Trognaesius in quarto and in a commentary on I *qu.* I, 3, where he even explicitly claims that, to date, this way of conciliation had not been transmitted by anyone he knew. He wishes to appear αὐτοδίδακτος and does not mention *Fonseca.* So let us grant that, driven by the same spirit, both had made up this lie, although nothing had become known to the one about the other's ideas. They were followed by *Fr. Suarez* on p. 3 *qu.* 1, but chiefly in a queer tract, which was first published in quarto among the theological *opuscula,* and separately, and then in folio along with all his works. By twisting everything that was here contorted by the subtlety of his mind, he had no small share in boosting this novelty. And no less also after him VASQUEZ *Comment. ad.* 1, *qu.* 4 and MENDOZA somewhere or other. In their steps were several others of the same kidney, like *Becanus* in scholastic theology, *Lorinus* and *A Lapide* at random in commentaries, together with professors at Cologne, Moguntum (?), Ingoldstadt, etc. This *Jesuit* innovation, scarcely known when new, not even examined in Holland, has seemed to our *Remonstrants* most suitable for fortifying the baseless and unbridled hair-splittings of *Castellio, Cornhert, Cuolhasius, Wiggert,* etc., against the grace of God and predestination."

Of course, some *Reformed* teachers, e.g., *Gomarus, Walaeus, Ludwig Crocius*, assumed a "conditioned or middle knowledge" on God's part, which was related to a "conditional proposition as to its object" (as HEIDEGGER *Corp. Theol.* III, 22 remarks) "in respect of bad actions, in which divine providence concurs not effectively but permissively and on the supposition of a conditional or permissive decree". ALSTED too (97) says that "there is a middle knowledge, by which He knows that if this exists that will exist." For the rest the distinction of a *scientia media* was decisively rejected by all dogmaticians. VOETIUS (I, p. 257) generally makes good against them the two following statements: "(1) Conditions which are opposed, as it said in the science of conditionals, are either about to be or not. If the former they are already the object of knowledge of vision; if the latter, they are already the object of knowledge of single intelligence. Therefore there is no middle knowledge. (2) Everything is absolutely foreordained by God and depends on His will, therefore God decreed them independently of knowledge of conditionals. For He also ordained the actual, free, conditional causes as the effect of His providence".—VOETIUS contradicts it more adequately in the following agreements (I, 309-318): "1. The division of divine knowledge into knowledge of single intelligence and that of vision exhausts the entire nature of the knowable object. Therefore there is no middle kind. 2. Whatever object is not knowable, there is no knowledge of it with God. But a conditioned future, one prior to any *actus* of the divine will is not knowable. Therefore there is no knowledge of it with God. 3. If there is any middle knowledge in God, there ought to be some cause by dint of which His will on this or that occasion is infallibly determined on the one side and not on the other. But there is no such cause. Therefore neither is there a middle knowledge. 4. If there be such a middle knowledge in God, there will be a calling to suit, by which God so attunes place, time, preacher, words and all the circumstances to suit the nature and capacity of the person called, that the man in such circumstances most surely assents to the divine call to faith, an assent which he could not give in other circumstances and occasions. But there is not any such calling to suit, so neither is there a middle knowledge. 5. The object of middle knowledge is simply not-being and nothing. Therefore the knowledge itself is not knowledge."—VOETIUS in addition brings up a series of logical and dogmatical absurdities which arise from this distinction. He shows (I, 318) that the assumption of a *scientia media* "impinges upon theological truth handed down by nature herself; which is, that if a declared connexion is true, it is necessary, and if it is not necessary it is not true, because what is before us is the truth, not of parts but of inference, which may be conceded, if both parts are untrue."

In particular the contradiction of this distinction is proved by essential truths connected with God's *voluntas* or *intellectus* or *potentia*. In the first respect VOETIUS (I, 320) presents the following four propositions: "(1)— This view posits the absurdity of absurdities, that in created things there is given a fixed futurition prior to every divine decree and that it suffices to produce futurition that a decree be posited on the condition laid down or a decree accompanying the object of this knowledge, not actual but possible *ad modum*.—(2) In a like class it lays down something else not less seriously absurd, that there still remains after the divine determination some futurition of what is in every way a non-futurition of things.—(3) From this knowledge we on our part will be able to assign the reason and cause of divine predestination.—(4) Thus, predestination as regards this knowledge will have to be called postdestination rather than predestination, as regards the temporary object."

As regards God's *intellectus* it has to be considered "(1) that middle knowledge makes knowledge of single intelligence void in God. (2) This knowledge makes God's understanding depend upon an external object, makes His idea come to Him from another source and so makes the eternal reasons of events in the priority of nature to be in the creature before they are in God and creatures here not to depend on God, but God to depend on the creatures as His pattern. (3) This knowledge lays down a counsel strictly pronounced in God, concerning which *Jul. Caesar Scaliger* rightly says that 'a voice in the divine counsels is as godless as plurality in the Deity'" (*Exerc.* 365, *sect.* 8).—Similarly VOETIUS discusses the absurdities which are the joint result of *potentia* and the three faculties named and closes with the apposite comment (I, p. 336): "From the points which have been so far upheld against middle knowledge it is clear that the whole difficulty in the present controversy reduces to this one point: Could free conditioned things, from eternity indifferent by nature to futurition or non-futurition, have passed over into the state of a future event otherwise than by the divine decree? This is the fundamental of fundamentals, on which the whole weight of the case rests. This is that postulate, which both we cannot concede to our adversaries and they cannot prove to us. This is the centre from which are drawn the shapeless and absurd hypotheses with which these hypothetical D.D.s wretchedly spatter both philosophy and also sacred theology, viz., that God's will were a blind potency in making decrees, but for the previous shining light of middle knowledge. Middle knowledge is effective and congruous for any end by its nature. Upon it God is forced to wait in the wise framing of His decrees, which are bound to have a fixed result. The truth or falsity of future conditioned free ones is not known from their causes or from the divine decree, but from the actual occurrence of the thing. Before every act of His will God can see certainty in things quite uncertain by their nature. In short, there is an *ens* independent of the supreme *ens*." The main thing is, then, that for God there can be no possibility or object of knowing, which precedes His decrees and is independent of them. Whence RIISSEN says (III, 24) that "no conditioned thing in the future can be knowable before the decree"; and BRAUN (I, ii, 3, 7) finds fault, when by *scientia simplicis intelligentiae* it is meant "that before His decree God conceives everything in His nature and in His ideas, whether they are possible or impossible, true or false, contingent or necessary"—because "whatever is not future is not future, because God decreed that it should not be future, therefore it is impossible".

18.—God's will.—To explain the concept of *voluntas* MASTRICHT (II, xv, 4) remarks that "the word *voluntas* denotes three things: (1) That power of our mind which is the *principium* θελητικόν or faculty of willing; (2) the *actus* of that faculty or θέλησις, volition itself; (3) lastly, its willed object (θελητόν), the thing willed. The first two have most to do with this *locus*. And so will is the faculty of acting ἐκ προαιρέσεως or by rational consent, the *actus* of which is called *appetitus rationalis* (reasonable desire).—(II, xv, 5): Further the activities of this rational *appetitus* as such are of two kinds: the elicited *actus* or volition, and another, the enjoined one, concerned with the *actus* of each faculty, mind, senses, limbs. The elicited one is either harmonious by being willed or discordant by not being willed. And this *actus* usually presupposes an end, which it could not acquire by means; therefrom arises hope and longing. But if on the other hand it thinks of the end as unobtainable, it produces *velleitas* and *votum* (which is not *velleitas* save as that imperfect activity of will which is destitute of the power to obtain").—There can then be no *velleitas* in the divine nature: WENDELIN (*Exercit.* 13, 13): "Strictly, *velleitas* does not apply to God, since it denotes imperfection". "Strictly, *velleitas* applies to him who has an obstacle to his will, which he does not want to or cannot remove. And in addition progress from *velleitas* to perfect *voluntas* savours of movement and change unworthy of the unchangeable, almighty and most wise God."

19.—God's will is that attribute of God (POLAN II, 19) "by which He wills good as an end and everything for good, from all eternity, of His own self and independently and by one constant act", or (MASTRICHT, II, xv, 8): "God's will is His most wise propension towards Himself as the supreme end and towards the creatures as means for His own sake". The divine will is thus the being of God Himself, so far as it is active actuosity in relation to Himself and to everything outside Himself.

SOHNIUS (*Op.* I, p. 105f.): "It is will by which the divine essence is described as freely decreeing what it wisely knows; or, by which the divine essence is described as being free to approve or disapprove of what it knows: and in a most single sense, so that this will is the actual living essence of God. And as God's wisdom is the actual essence of God or the wise God Himself; and further as in one and the same *actus* God wills whatever He wills by His essence: so in one and the same act He knows and sees by His essence; and so that the whole of Him wills, just as the whole of Him (*totus*) knows and sees and does not wish at the same time". —COCCEIUS (*S.T.* III, x, 48): "What God wills, i.e., orders to be, He orders and calls not at different times or in distinct acts, but in one most single act. And so in God we must not discern different decrees". Hence COCCEIUS says that the stereotyped proposition in *Reformed* dogmatics, that "what is last in execution is first in intention", is true *apud Deum* only in the formulation that "what is last in execution is primary in intention".

20.—Like all attributes of the absolute nature, His will also is essentially a single actuosity eternally identical with itself, which appears like a manifold of various indications and effects only in relation to the manifold of objects.—BRAUN (I, ii, 3, 13): "As God knows everything by one intuition and a single act of thinking, so also He wills and has willed by one act of will, i.e., by a single volition, Himself and all things present, past, future, necessary, contingent, absolute and conditioned, good and bad from eternity, by a most free and immutable will: so that nothing can be conceived, in whatsoever state it be, which does not therefore depend upon the will of God. Therefore by one and the same act of will He wills to create and to destroy, to set up and to pull down, to love and to hate, to punish and to condone: so that no difference ought to be made among these volitions save in respect of our conceiving and of the various concepts which we form regarding various effects and objects. So that even God's single act of will is His very counsel and decree, is creation and preservation, stability and change in things, even annihilation itself, if there be such a thing".—Since then the divine will is the actuosity of the divine being eternally identical with itself, which only to man appears an infinite manifold of expressions of will, it may be said that in the same act of will God may will otherwise but not that He may otherwise will".—HEIDEGGER (III, 69): "Although God wills all things in one most single *actus*, e.g., to create and to destroy the world, to save some and condemn others, etc., yet we conceive various acts of the divine will by our reason and distinguish them by our conception. He cannot, it is true, will a thing otherwise, i.e., by a different act. Yet by one and the same act of willing He may will differently; e.g., that events should be one way and another and so that different sets of things should exist. Thus God wills one thing to exist for the sake of another. But that one thing is not strictly speaking the cause by which God's will is inwardly moved to decree the second."

21.—In and for itself the divine will is absolutely single, absolutely independent, eternal, infinite, immutable and absolutely active. The "affections" of the divine *voluntas* were pretty unanimously set out by the dogmaticians. According to MASTRICHT (II, xv, 9-16) God's *voluntas* "is (1) independent; its essence is the first cause of things, Rev. 4. 11 (thou didst create all things and because of thy will they were, and were created); (2) most single; it is God Himself willing; (3) unchangeable, Mal. 3. 6 (I the Lord change not) 1 Sam. 15. 29 (the Strength of Israel will not lie nor repent; for he is not a man, that he should repent) Ps. 33.11 (the counsel of the Lord standeth fast for ever, the thoughts of his heart to all generations); so that He not only wills now this, now that, but wills everything He wills always at one and the same time; (4) eternal, Eph. 1. 4 (he chose us in him before the foundation of the world); it is God Himself willing, so He does not begin to will what He did not will previously; nor does He cease to will what He willed previously; nor does He will one thing before another; although from the order which we observe in our own *voluntas* we conceive that God wills the end before the means in order of intention, and the means before the end in order of sequence; (5) infinite; God himself is infinite, not indeed because He wills all things willable to exist, as He understands all things intelligible, but because He wills Himself infinite and on His own account wills all things partly to exist and partly not; (6) free and most free; freedom is of the essence of will. This freedom is either antecedent to the thing willed as its principle, in which sense God freely wills only things different from Himself, Rev. 4. 11 (above) ; or as its concomitant, in which sense God wills Himself and all that is His; (7) effective; whatever He wills and as He wills it, He gives it effect in His own time and in His own way; nor is there anything which does not happen, if He wills it, or does not happen as He wills it".

22.—"Since God's will is not a blind urge but an *appetitus intelligens,* it must indeed be distinguished from *scientia.* Yet it coincides with it in such a way, that it may be conceived as just the obverse of it, i.e., God wills precisely because He wills it: the divine willing is the divine nature itself."—HEIDEGGER (*Corp. theol.* III, 68): "God's *voluntas*, or His *appetitus intelligens* does not differ from His *intellectus*. In God there is nothing save

what is single. Nothing is different. The creature may understand what
it does not will, and will what it does not understand. But God wills
whatever He understands. By His understanding (far otherwise than the
creature!) He forms the essences of things and so cannot not will them.
And whatever He wills, by the very fact that He wills it, He at once
understands it. By the very fact that understanding and will in God are
completely identical, His understanding and willing must be one and
the same perpetual *actus* continuing from eternity to eternity, so that in
it nothing before and after, antecedent and consequent may be posited.
If God's understanding and will is the actual high singleness of God, one
intellection or volition cannot succeed another as in men. One that arose
afterward in Him would not have existed previously in Him, and so there
would be room in God for being and not-being".—HEIDAN is different
(p. 211): "The nature of will is not the same as that of knowledge and
power in God. His knowledge knows everything knowable and His
power can do everything possible. But by will He does not will all that
He can will. The things He decreed needed willing and are future in
act. Hence, although He is called omniscient and omnipotent, He is
not therefore omnivolent". Similarly AMESIUS (*Medulla,* p. 31). [This
is not really different from HEIDEGGER].

23.—We have to distinguish the way in which God wills Himself, and
that in which He wills things outside Himself. Himself God wills necessarily; since He is the highest good and goal of all things, He cannot not
will Himself. Things on the other hand God wills freely, because as
creatures they are not necessary but for God contingent; so that He wills
all things in such a way that He might also not will them.—RIJSSEN,
III, 28: "God wills some things necessarily, some freely. Himself He wills
necessarily; He is the final end and the highest goal, which He cannot not
will and love, because He cannot not will His own glory or deny Himself.
All other things He wills freely; nothing created is necessary as regards
God, but contingent, since because He could have done without them,
He wills them all in the sense that He might not have willed them".

24.—So in no way can it be said that any element in creaturely life can
be a determining reason for the divine will. In the temporal course of
things God does not will the subsequent for the sake of what precedes it;
He wills freely (and He might even alter it), that what precedes should
condition what follows, by arranging along with the ends the means
as well for its attainment.—VOETIUS (V, 87): "Query: whether God wills
one thing on account of another? Ans.: If the 'on account of' (*propter*)
is put above the *velit* or *velle,* or united with the *velle,* no. But if it is put

above the *hoc* or joined to it, admitted, in the sense that one thing willed is the cause or condition or antecedent of a second willed thing: but t is anything but the cause or condition or antecedent of the actual divine will, i.e., of God Himself.—And this is what *Thomas* has shrewdly expressed in this axiom: *Deus vult hoc propter hoc, sed non propter hoc vult hoc* (God wills A to cause B, but He does not will A at the instance of B)".—
COCCEIUS (*S.T.* III, x, 51): "It is rightly said that 'God wills one thing on account of another'; i.e., God co-ordinated these means with that end: but not that 'God wills this because of that', as though God's will were moved from without."

25.—The will of God directed to the world is by many distinguished as *voluntas beneplaciti* and *voluntas signi*, in the sense that it is *voluntas beneplaciti* by which He wills us to be saved and we understand what He has established with Himself concerning our salvation from eternity.—It is (*voluntas*) *signi* by which He requires the things which we ought to supply (SEEGEDIN, p. 23).

Many dogmaticians approve the distinction between *voluntas signi* and *voluntas beneplaciti*; POLANUS (II, 19): "It is called *voluntas signi*, because it signifies what is pleasing to God, what belongs to our duty, what He wishes to be done or omitted by us, etc." These "*signa voluntatis*, from which it is known what God wills", are "precept, prohibition, permission, counsel, and the fulfilment of predictions."—They were wont to describe the content of *voluntas signi* by the hexameter used by DURANDUS :
Praecipit et prohibet, permittit, consulit, implet.

Similarly WALAEUS, p. 171: "A famous distinction of great importance and use, employed by the Scholastics and also accepted by ours, is the division into *voluntas signi et beneplaciti*"; and HOTTINGER, who (p. 80) explains that "the distinction of will into that which is of sign and that which is of good pleasure is convenient. It is confirmed by famous sayings of H. Scripture, Dt. 29. 29 (the secret things belong unto the Lord our God; but the things that are revealed belong unto us and to our children for ever, that we may do all the words of this law); Tobit 12, 14, 18 (not of any favour of mine (the angel Raphael) but by the will of our God I came: wherefore bless Him for ever)". HOTTINGER identifies this distinction with the difference between *voluntas revelata* and *voluntas arcana*. For he continues "*Voluntas signi* is sometimes called *revelata*, *voluntas beneplaciti arcana*". Then he says that by this distinction is expressed merely the difference between *voluntas praecipiens* and *voluntas decernens*. In this latter sense the distinction is also used by BRAUN (I, II, 3, 18): "It is also divided into *voluntas beneplaciti et voluntas signi*. By others rather into *voluntas praecepti*; which division seems more convenient.

Voluntas signi (or *praecepti*) is that will by which God signifies to men what He wishes to be done by them; *voluntas beneplaciti* or *decreti*, by which God has decreed what He wishes to do in man, e.g., God wills, *voluntate signi vel praecepti*, that parents should provide all things for their children which are necessary for long life, although He has perhaps decreed *voluntate beneplaciti et decreti*, that the children should die suddenly. So God willed *voluntate signi et praecepti* that Abraham should gird himself to sacrifice his son Isaac, although *voluntate decreti et beneplaciti* He willed to preserve him in life. But if we wish to speak accurately, *voluntas beneplaciti et signi* are not two different wills—it has just been proved that in God there is only a single will—but only a single one which deals with men in different ways and manifests itself variously. By one and the same will God manifests Himself differently to Abraham. First He commands him to sacrifice Isaac, although by the same will He has decreed to preserve Isaac in life. Next He revealed to Abraham, what He had not revealed to him in the first instance, that He would preserve Isaac. By the first act of His will towards Abraham He declares His lordship over the life of men and at the same time exacts obedience from Abraham. For this act the will of God is conceived by us as *voluntas signi sive praecepti*. But in the second act He revealed His decree and this act we call *voluntas decreti vel beneplaciti*. Thus God's commands are to be viewed not absolutely but in comparison with His ends". Then BRAUN continues (19): "Yet if we would speak correctly, it is certain that no will can be called *voluntas signi*. Rather by a universal order we must say that it is the sign of an approving will. All injunctions, promises and threats are but signs of God's will, i.e., of what God wishes to be done by us, but not of what He has decreed. Nor are there different wills. Every will is strictly speaking *voluntas beneplaciti*. When God enjoins, approves, promises and threatens, this is always done in terms of His *beneplacitum*. And although at first sight His entire *consilium* is not clear, it becomes so in its own time, when it has pleased God"—Similarly, others explain themselves, e.g., HEIDAN, who describes *voluntas signi* as *voluntas revelata signi approbans*, and *voluntas beneplaciti* as *voluntas arcana*; yet in this connection he remarks (p. 135): "There is this difference between *voluntas beneplaciti* and *arcana*, that although all *voluntas arcana* is *beneplaciti*, not all that is hidden is *beneplacitum*. Even God's *beneplacitum* is sometimes revealed: as when God revealed His judgments to the Prophets, Am. 3. 7 (Surely the Lord God will do nothing, but He revealeth his secret unto his servants the prophets); as when He suggests (Is. 38. 5) the fifteen years of life added to Hezekiah. Moreover the *voluntas* revealed this in the actual issue and we know from Scripture that such is the will of God."—ALTING (p. 78): "Some *voluntas* is called *signi*, also revealed and *praecepti*:

other is called *beneplaciti*, also *arcana* and *decreti*. The difference is subjective ; the latter is in God, the former outside God in the Word : and objective; the latter refers to the fact of God, the former to the duty of men. To the latter obedience is not demanded, nor is disobedience punished, since no law was given. But obedience to the former is demanded and disobedience punished, because a law was given''.

To meet the *Arminian* reproach that by such a distinction two *voluntates sibi contrariae* are assumed HEIDAN, (pp.136-7) insists: ''(1) Strictly speaking there is but a single will of God called *beneplaciti*, whereby God determines by Himself what He wills to do in and concerning the creature. The second is but the sign and indication by which He shows what He wishes creatures to do. But He does not wish them to make His *beneplacitum* universal, but only the things which He reveals to them, Dt. 29. 29 (p. 85).

(2) God often wills the same thing by *voluntas beneplaciti* and *signi;* the same thing as happens He enjoins in His holy law, e.g., the conversion of the Gentiles. Although God wills some things *voluntate signi*, like the repentance of the reprobate, the faith of Judas, the non-slaying of Christ, which he nevertheless anything but decreed by *voluntas beneplaciti* as things that would never happen; and He wills some things *voluntate beneplaciti*, which He can anything but will *voluntate signi*, like the selling of Joseph or the slaying of Christ.

(3) But these wills are not contrary, because they are not concerned with the same things, nor is their connection and reference the same. The object of the *beneplacitum* is an existent eventuating in the nature of things, which is to have or not to have an actual existence, be it a good or a bad existent, consonant or not with the *voluntas signi*. But the object of the *voluntas signi* is approval of the morally good and honourable or disapproval of the unjust and wicked.

(4) Whence as a result of *voluntas beneplaciti* fixed inference may be drawn as to the issue of the matter, though this cannot be done as a result of *voluntas signi*. That is merely moral regulation of human actions, whether they eventuate or not. In His law God did not formally decree our moral acts to exist or not to exist; He only enjoins their ordination, forbids their non-ordination. The existence and non-existence of things is determined by God's *voluntas beneplaciti*, not *signi*.

(5) Hence it often happens that man's unrighteous will is discovered to be conform with God's *voluntas beneplaciti*, which is yet not in accord with His *voluntas signi*, as if a bad son should wish his father to die, whom God also wills to die; and man's will may not agree with God's will, as though a godly son should wish his father not to die, whom God does not will to live longer.''

The most representative verdict in Reformed theology on this distinction is expressed by HEIDEGGER (III, 71): ''God's will in relation to the things outside Him is variously named. In one way when He insists, forbids, allows, threatens; in another when He calls or orders how things should be. The former will is called by the *Scholastics*, on the authority, it is thought, of Hugh of St. Victor, *voluntas signi,* whether because it is signified by some sign, like a word, precept, interdict, etc.; or because it signifies God's will as the effect and adjunct of it; by others *voluntas εὐαρεστίας,* of good pleasure or delight; θέλημα εὐάρεστον, the gracious, acceptable will, Rom. 12. 2; the latter is called by the same scholastics *voluntas beneplaciti* or by the Scripture term εὐδοκία Mt. 11. 26 (well-pleasing) Eph. 1. 5, 9 (good pleasure) Phil. 2. 13, because He willed His good pleasure (*beneplacitum*) that this or that should exist. But it is pretty clear that both distinctions *signi* and *beneplaciti,* εὐαρεστίας καὶ εὐδοκίας, as constants, when the terms are not opposed formally, labour under an ambiguity and are not altogether significant. Both what, God enjoins, promises, etc., by the sign of a word is of His good pleasure: and not seldom He reveals by the sign of revelation His good pleasure also concerning the things which ought to exist; in fact even will, revealed in a word, is strictly not a sign (as being rather the effect of will than that will itself) but will signified through a word".—Hence we must say that generally Reformed theology has disapproved of the distinction between *voluntas signi et beneplaciti.*

26.—Be that as it may, much more in correspondence with H. Scripture than this distinction invented by the *Scholastics* of the Middle Ages is the distinction of the divine will into *voluntas praecipiens sive moralis* and *voluntas decernens sive efficax* on the one hand, and into *voluntas revelata* and *valuntas arcana* on the other. "*Voluntas Dei praecipiens sive moralis* is the rule of every created will, from which alone as a rule comes the difference between equity and iniquity, good and evil." "*Voluntas Dei decernens et efficax* is not the rule of created will, but the deepest cause of events and of the existence of all things" (HEIDEGGER, III, 73-74). The *voluntas decernens* is sheerly effective, while *voluntas praecipiens* is not, not because God's power is in any way limited in it, but because God will help only the elect with His *voluntas decernens* and only in them does He let His *voluntas praecipiens* achieve execution.

HEIDEGGER III, 77: "Between God's preceptive and discerning will there is this difference, that the former does not always find effect. The latter, which is effective, is never deprived or can be deprived of effect. Not that *voluntas praecipiens* is ineffective as regards God Himself or is robbed of all success. It effects all that God wills and intends in laying down the precept; i.e., it declares the duty and obligation of the creature who wishes to be saved and explains the perpetual connection between duty and benefit, and in short renders ἀναπολογήτους those who disobey the precept. But it is ineffective in respect of certain people who do not obey the precipient will. As regards them the former cannot achieve. Precipient will is not the cause of events, but only the law of created will, which God often leaves to itself. But this will isn't never-unfulfilled. This is the case when effective will concurs with this will by grace. Whence it is clear, that it is not by defect of power in God that His preceptive will does not take effect with all men, but by the judgment of God or by His actual effective or decerning will, by which He has decreed not to impart grace to all, but to abandon some to themselves. God does not act necessarily but voluntarily. Whence it is not necessary that His attitude to everything should be the same, and He was equally powerful in fulfilling His law through Paul and Judas, although in the fulfilment of it He was not equally present to Judas and to Paul". In the same way MASTRICHT (II, xiv, 8) divides the will of God into legislative, by which He wills and determines what we ought to do or not to do *de iure* only, but not *de eventu*; and *decretive*, by which He wills and determines what He Himself wills to do or what is or is not to be *de facto* only, but not what should or should not be done *de iure*. In this way God wills many things by legislative will, which actually do not come to pass, e.g., He willed that Pharaoh should let Israel go *de iure*, i.e., He willed this to be Pharaoh's duty, but He did not will it *de facto*. On the other hand He wills many things to be done *de facto*, e.g., all the sins that are committed, which He does not will *de iure* or as our duty. Consequently we answer the objections thus: that He wills not the death of the sinner by legislative will, so far as He seriously wills that there be an individual connection between the conversion of the sinner and his salvation. Whence He seriously invites certain men to conversion and to those who do seriously convert He promises life; although at the same time He does not will it by His decerning will, or although He has not decreed from eternity to confer faith and repentance by grace upon all sinners and so actually to save them".—RIISSEN similarly distinguishes between *voluntas moralis* and *voluntas decernens sive permittens* (III, 32): "Moral will does not extend beyond the moral goodness or badness of a thing which God wills to propose to the creature; wherefore it is often not fulfilled. But the decerning or permissive will is always fulfilled".—TRELCATIUS 53, "by means of objects and effects good and bad," divides the will of God into *beneplacitum* and *placitum*.

27.—There is the division of *voluntas decernens* into *voluntas efficiens* and *voluntas permittens*. By the former God executes what in conformity with His absolute holiness He has positively and directly resolved to do. By the latter (*voluntas efficaciter permittens*) God lets the evil happen, which He wills to let happen for the revelation of His glory. The divine *permissio* is thus not to be thought of as indifference but as likewise a positive action of the divine will.—HEIDEGGER (III, 78): "The decerning or effective will of God is twin; efficient, whereby it effects what it wills and operates it itself, and permissive, whereby it wills to allow what it neither effects nor operates or can operate, as sin; and sin as such God can simply neither will nor decree at all. What God wills, He approves, esteems, delights in, He orders, causes and ordains to exist, either as an end or as a means, things which in no way fit sin. Nor whether He is willing or refusing is God's permission like man's permission, which admits of an eclipse which he neither wills nor refuses, as the LOMBARD and with him the Scholastics assert. It is effective, mighty, and not separate from God's will at all. Otiose permission of sin separated from God's will is repugnant both to the nature of the First Cause and to the divine and almighty foresight, to His nature and to Scripture".

28.—Besides there is the distinction of "God's revealed" and His "secret will" to be considered. The former is that which God reveals as His will, partly by the word of Law and Gospel, partly by experiences which He sends to man. The latter is God's decree, in so far as it is still hidden and is only to be revealed in the future at a definite date (HEIDEGGER III, 79). On the other hand the distinction set forth by many dogmaticians, of an "absolute" and a "conditioned" will, a will "antecedent" and "consequent", etc., must be rejected, they are so very open to misinterpretation.

The earlier dogmaticians mostly adhere to the distinction of a "will of God absolute" and "conditioned", "antecedent" and "consequent"; e.g., HYPERIUS, who (p. 138ff.) assumed the "conditional will" for the Biblical statement that "God would have all men to be saved." Many of the older dogmaticians also describe "absolute will" as *voluntas beneplaciti*. So, e.g., POLAN who (II, 19) makes this distinction: "It is the absolute will of God by which He wills separate things singly and absolutely beyond all conditions which may or are likely to exist among creatures. This is what is meant in Rom. 9. 18-19 (so then He hath mercy on whom He will, and whom He will He hardeneth. Thou wilt then say to me, Why doth He still find fault? For who withstandeth His will?). It is also called the *voluntas beneplaciti divini* or the *beneplacitum* of the divine will". On the other hand the later dogmaticians almost without exception dropped this distinction. Says VOETIUS (V, 88): "Query: whether the will is rightly distinguished into antecedent and consequent. Answer: If by antecedent is meant the declaration of the divine will and of the order laid down by it as between condition and thing conditioned, Yes; e.g., if a man believes and if he perseveres, he will be saved: this is equivalent to the categorical pronouncement that 'everyone that believes and perseveres will be saved'. But if by ante-cedent will is meant the will strictly speaking, or the *beneplacitum*, No. For in God, whether in the act of God willing or apart from the act of willing there is neither before and subsequent, nor antecedent and consequent, nor condition and conditioned, but the pure, single and indivisible *actus* of the will, by which He wills everything He wills; just as by one most single *actus* He knows the things that are knowable." HEIDEGGER directly warns us against using this distinction when he says (*Corp. Theol.* III, 76): "If by *voluntas antecedens* are meant God's precepts sanctioned by promises and threats and prior to the action of created will; and by consequent (will) the effects of the divine will following the obedience or disobedience of the created will, according as God either followed it up by His grace or left it to itself; and if likewise by God's conditioned will is meant the will by which God prescribes the conditions for those to be saved (as when He wills and bids the man who would live do something; or him who would be saved He wills and bids to believe something), and by absolute will, that by which He wills to save the believer by His grace and to damn the non-believer, not after either a foreseen or actual existing faith or unbelief but by decreeing prior to it that He wills to bestow faith by His grace on this man and that, and so to save that believer but to damn others left to themselves and unbelieving; these distinctions, as having an orthodox and prior meaning, having been first used by CHRYSOSTOM also, by the DAMASCENE also, and by more recent orthodox, we do not altogether reject. In this way as regards meaning antecedent and conditioned will will actually be preceptive: consequent and absolute will be decerning. But owing to the danger of abuse and to ἀκυρολογία it is best to avoid both." Still more definitely MASTRICHT declares against the assumption of a conditioned divine will (II, xv, 27): "Query, Whether there is in God such a will as depends upon a condition to be fulfilled by creatures? The stupid *Pelagians* of old, to whom today are to be added the *Socinians*, through love of an independent free judgment, by which it may do whatever it wills apart from any predetermination by the divine will, used to posit such a will in God as wills if the creature but wills, as is sad and pained because the creature refuses what He Himself wills. The LUTHERANS, from hatred of the absolute divine will, particularly in the matter of reprobation and from love of universal salvation for men all and singly, admit a will such that by it He wills their salvation, the condition being just that they themselves will it. All (these heretics) agree upon the fact that in many God's volition is suspended by a condition to be supplied first by the *liberum arbitrium* of creatures, and if this condition is not fulfilled, God is very often frustrated in His intent. Thus, according to them He wills, e.g., that all His injunctions are kept as exactly as possible, if of course men wish it; He also wills that one and all should be saved, just if they themselves wish to believe in Christ, to repent of their sins and to attend to good works. And so in place of God's volition they admit no more than a kind of suspended wishfulness (*velleitas*). The *Reformed*, although acknowledging a will in God which hangs this or that event upon this or that condition, e.g., Peter's salvation on his faith, which in this sense may also be called conditioned, yet acknowledge no will of His which depends upon any condition.—Similarly RIISSEN III, 31, MARESIUS 21, WENDELIN 62, and others.

29.—To the will of God pertain its "affections and virtues", i.e., "the acts of will (or the will itself), according as it has different relations with objects which severally have a different basis" (HEIDEGGER III, 86). The "chief virtue of God embracing all the rest in its bosom is His holiness, righteousness or goodness, by which in all His words and deeds He is of Himself, by unchangeable necessity of essence, good, righteous and holy; nor does He say or do anything to deny or hide Himself and the truth of His divinity" (HEIDEGGER III, 88).

Many dogmaticians conceive of holiness (preferably lawgiving) and righteousness (preferably judicial) as identical concepts (e.g., RIISSEN III, 38: "It is righteousness and holiness by which without any *iniquitas* God is all that He is)", or describe the latter (holiness) outright as righteousness.—COCCEIUS regards holiness as veracity and defines it (*S. T.* III, 10, 52): "Holiness consists in God necessarily loving truth and saying and doing nothing by which to deny or obscure truth".—BULLINGER defines thus, presupposing the concept of *malum* as *non ens* or *privatio entis*: "By holiness we understand that which possesses realities alone, not mixed with their opposites" (DILUCID§ 453).—MASTRICHT (II, 19, 1): God's holiness is the "moral goodness by which God is at most imitable".— LEIDEN SYNOPSIS VI, 40: "It is holiness by which being most pure in Himself God approves all cleanness and abhors the contrary".—STAPFER sees in holiness absolute perfection or God's good pleasure in it (I, 139): "God embraces all that can be conceived of perfection and indeed perfections alone with nothing diverse or contrary, all imperfection being excluded, and in this sense He is called holy—(140): Theologians commonly define holiness as God's love for Himself because He loves His perfections". Similarly the later dogmaticians as a body, e.g., WYTTEN-BACH I, p. 285: "(God) possesses perfections with no imperfections to oppose them, and alone does so, since He is set apart and segregated from all imperfection, which means being holy; therefore God is holy". ENDEMANN distinguishes a twofold *sanctitas* of God, namely (*Instit.* 28), "(1) essential holiness—according as God's essence, nature and attributes are so perfect as to render any imperfection in God impossible," and (2) "moral holiness, which separates moral imperfection from actions and purifies them, so that they are right and just."

30.—Since holiness like all other attributes of God is the divine nature itself and so present in God in absolute perfection, it cannot be conceived as God's agreement with the law of the good. God Himself is rather the essential idea and principle of holiness.—MASTRICHT (II, 198): "Holiness belongs to God (1) not as an accessory but as His actual essence; nor (2) as something received from another source but as the fountain of all holiness in all things, Lev. 20. 8; 21. 15 (I am the Lord which sanctify you (him) Ezek. 20. 12 (I am the Lord that sanctify) 1 Thess. 5. 23 (the God of peace himself sanctify you wholly); nor (3) by fixed measure; but without measure in an infinite degree, which accordingly cannot be increased or diminished, because this is its very essence, although it can and ought to be declared more and more, Mt. 6. 9 (hallowed be thy name); nor (4) fashioned after the holiness of the law or anything (else), but as the idea and pattern and norm of all holiness, 1 Pet. 1. 15 (like as he which called you is holy), Eph. 4. 24 (the new man which after God hath been created in . . . holiness . . .): and not so much (5) as a particular attribute of it; but as a universal affection, affecting all and any of its attributes; not, in a word (6) some common *affection* of it, but by far the chief."

31.—But as little can it be said that God's act of willing is simply the nature of the divine holiness.   For man, of course, God's will is the utterly holy law. But as regards God Himself the divine will is holy, because God only wills what corresponds with the holiness immanent in him, i.e., with His own will. As the absolute nature God is no way dependent on a law situated outside Him. As the morally perfect Spirit God cannot be other than true to Himself and thereby in His entire action display His own moral perfection as law immanent in Him.

Reformed dogmaticians as a whole are occupied with the question, whether goodness is good because God wills it, or whether God wills the good because it is good. Recognition of the absoluteness of God seemed to many reconcilable with the former. Hence, e.g., POLAN (II, 26) says: "(1) God does, what by His own law He prohibits us; He passed the law for us, not for Himself. E.g., He does not bring it about that we admit no sin while living here, though He might most easily have done so.—(2) The supreme rule of divine righteousness is His most perfect and infallible will. God is a law to Himself. Whatever He wishes done, it is right by the very fact that He wills it. Whatever God does He knows and wills."—Yet the later dogmaticians let this idea drop. VOETIUS (I, 364ff.) discusses the question, whether there is in the divine nature an immanent, necessary and independent law, which, if God would not deny Himself, God must maintain, and he answers Yes. In reply to the objection that, if there is something good and right antecedently to God's will, then God must dutifully will and do it, which contradicts the absolute nature of God, VOETIUS rightly (!) insists (373) that "God is under no moral duty *ab extra*; He is due no one and there is no cause outside God which could bind or determine Him. But *ab intra* He may be bound (if I may so say) but not be subject (*subesse*); He is indebted to Himself and cannot deny Himself. So the Father in divine things is bound to love the Son, for He cannot not love. The Son is bound by the necessity of the divine nature to work from the Father, for he cannot not operate from the Father, as often as operation has to be instituted outside of God. So, too, in actions outwardly, it being given that creation has been produced, God is obliged to preserve it by His continual hold and continual influx (as long as He wills it) and in addition as the prime Mover, to move and govern it to His own glory, Prov. 16. 4 (the Lord hath made everything for its own end: yea even the wicked for the day of evil) Rom. 11. 36 (of Him and to Him and through Him are all things). This is immutably good and righteous, the opposite of which He cannot will". Similarly VOETIUS answers the objection, that God is "simply without law for everything outside Himself", in the same sense (I, 375): "(1) He is *exlex* from the law which He fashioned for man, by formally adopting law as it is the law. But He is not free and absolute from all matter and content of law, so that He may enjoin or Himself make its opposite; e.g., as to believe that He is not God and to enjoin others to believe so, in opposition, of course, to the first precept of the decalogue. (2) By hypothesis, as and when He wills to give precepts, He necessarily gives them good and righteous, nor in general can He do or will the opposite. (3) Specifically He also gives some righteous things antecedently to His free will, those in which He necessarily ends, being of course derived from His instrinsic nature and goodness". Similarly I, p. 379: "There is in God an idea, which has the nature of the art and exemplar and principle of God's operations *ad extra*. If then some rule, norm, law or principle of the divine will and of the laws it makes for the creatures, with the help of outward methods concerning the creature, be posited in God as acceptable and fitting for God, it of course anything but overturns God's essence and will, prime, independent, ἄναρχον".

This thought is most fully and precisely expounded by HEIDEGGER (*Corp. Theol.* III, 89-90): "Whatever the nature of the creature's holiness, righteousness and goodness, its first rule and norm with respect to God is not His free will and commands but His actual, essential righteousness. Things are not good, holy and righteous in themselves, because God willed and ordered them. He willed and ordered them because they ought to agree with the holiness of His most pure nature and essential righteousness. With respect to us indeed the source of all righteousness is to be sought nowhere else than in His will, which as most perfect is thus the rule of all righteousness and holiness. But with respect to God, although in those things which have free and positive goodness, as in ceremonies so instituted as also to admit of abolition, God's will is the first rule of righteousness; in those, however, which have innate goodness, the actual will of God derives a rule from no other source than from His essential holiness, righteousness and goodness or from His most Holy nature. Just as we are forthwith held to follow the free will and order of God of whatever kind, so we are bidden imitate God's holiness and righteousness, Lev. 19. 2 (ye shall be holy, for I the Lord your God am holy) Eph. 5. 2 (walk in love, even as Christ also loved you) 1 Cor. 11. 1 (hold fast the traditions) 2 Pet. 1. 4 (that through the promises ye might become partakers of the divine nature) Eph. 4. 24 (the new man which after God hath been created in righteousness and holiness of truth). God is not subject to moral duty *ad extra*. He can be bound by no one. Nor does He depend either on another outside Himself or is liable to any law. But because He cannot deny Himself or conceal His excellences, He cannot fight against Himself and His holiness and truthfulness. He is a law unto Himself. Nor is He so absolved from all matter of law, that He can always do, enjoin and sanction the opposite. And God is also free *ad extra*, but not indifferent."

32.—God's holiness is manifested generally as perfect kindness and love and as perfect righteousness. Both rest upon a "certain benevolent and beneficent propension towards the creatures", which is present in God (MASTRICHT II, xvii, 3). "The love of God is the essential property or essence of God, whereby delighting Himself in it He wishes it the good which He approves." To be distinguished are the "general love of God", the object of which is creation generally, so that "no one either of men or even of demons may say that he is not loved by God"; God hates the sin in the godless, but loves the nature created by Him—and the "special love of God, by which He peculiarly pursues the separate elect" (POLAN, II, 122). Herein is manifested the "goodness of God", according to which God is in and for Himself "supremely good" and towards creation "beneficent" (Riissen III, 41). Since then God's love for the creature is essentially a "love not due", it appears as grace. "God's grace is His virtue and perfection, by which He bestows and communicates Himself becomingly on and to the creature beyond all merit belonging to it" (HEIDEGGER III, 94). Over against the misery of the creature God's love is manifested (1) as mercy. Etymologically *misericordia* is wretchedness of heart due to a sense of another's wretchedness together with alacrity in succouring the wretched. Actually in God it is nothing but grace towards the wretched" (MASTRICHT II, xvii, 22); (2) as patience and long suffering. "*Patientia Dei* is His most benign will, by which He so controls His anger, that He either bears sinning creatures long and puts off punishment, awaiting their repentance, or He does not pour forth all His anger in one moment upon them, lest they should be reduced to naught"; and (3) as gentleness: "God's clemency is His most benign will, by which mindful of His mercy in wrath He is propitious to us and spares us, although we have deserved otherwise, preferring our repentance and conversion to our death" (POLAN II, 24 and 25).

The other side of the divine holiness, righteousness in the broader sense of the word, comprises the attributes of righteousness in the narrower sense of the word, and truthfulness. Since righteousness in general is "agreement with His law and rule" (MASTRICHT II, xvii, 4), so the "righteousness of God" is the order or "nature of the divine mind and will, by which God immutably and ineffably wills and approves, Himself does and effects in others, such things as He has laid down in His law; and all the things at variance with this order He neither wills nor approves nor works nor effects nor helps, but hates and detests" (POLAN II, 26). God manifests this righteousness of His partly as world-ruler (*iustitia dominica et gubernans sive regiminis*—dominical and governing righteousness or righteousness of rule) partly as lawgiver and judge of all, good and bad (*iustitia iudicialis et retribuens sive iurisdictionis*—judicial and retributive righteousness or righteousness of jurisdiction).—On the necessity of God's judicial activity COCCEIUS remarks (*S.T.* III, 10, 61): "He cannot not punish [*sc.* man], because he is an intelligent copy and creation, made in His image"; and HEIDEGGER (III, 98): "By the very fact that God has an intelligent creature accountable to Himself alone, He must of necessity become his judge, because He cannot leave him to himself, or not reward him if righteous, or not punish him if unrighteous".—The dogmaticians reject the assumption of a commutative righteousness, e.g., BRAUN (I, ii, 4, 17): "Commutative righteousness is not to be ascribed to God in the same sense as to men, in whom through *iustitia* there arises a sort of reciprocal obligation of the parts as the result of natural communion or of fixed contracts, by which No. 1 is bound to No. 2 to stand by his promises. For this there can be no room save among men who are equal and of the same condition. But since we were created by God and depend on Him and have no rights of our own but are bound to God, no law holds for us against God, by which He would be bound to us". Similarly RIISSEN (III, 39) and others. [And see Chapter VII, The Decree].

33.—Yet God manifests His righteousness in such a way, that He thereby allows not merely His righteousness to prevail but withal His love too, and so in His righteousness reveals His whole nature.—HYPERIUS, p. 160f.: "When God punishes, He not only enacts righteousness but also mercy attested by all. Whenever He mulcts, He never does so as severely as men have actually deserved." Hence we must maintain "that although mercy and righteousness produce different effects, they are in no wise contrary, nor as contraries have they a place in God, nor can they be distinguished in the mind in turn; but as things most conjoined and inseparable, one of which exists for the sake of the other, they always exceedingly befit the one and unchangeable God" (Cf. Chapter VII).— HEIDEGGER (III, 97): "God so uses this righteousness that He never lets it crash—on the rest of His attributes, holiness, goodness, wisdom.— That absolute law and worship of His He so modified by a gracious covenant, that we look up to and revere Him not only as Lord, but also as a kindly Father."

34.—The question whether the nature of righteousness depends wholly upon the will of God or whether God is tied to a law immanent in Him, is like answering the question whether goodness is good because God wills it or whether God wills goodness because it is good (independently of His will). Righteousness is God's actual nature which in virtue of His moral perfection God cannot deny. Hence everything that corresponds with the nature of God and with His image in the creature is a law immanent in God Himself, in the sense that God cannot destroy or infringe it.—MASTRICHT (II, xviii, 11): "Regarding legislative righteousness the question is whether all righteousness depends on the sole will of God, or whether a thing is righteousness because God wills it to be righteous, or on the other hand God wills it because it is right. From which there also results another question, whether God by righteousness could have enjoined things plainly contrary to the things He did enjoin." To this MASTRICHT replies: "(1) Of course God is $\pi\rho\omega\tau o$-, in fact $\alpha\dot{\upsilon}\tau o$-$\delta\dot{\iota}\kappa\alpha\iota o\nu$. Yet from this God's will as such is not forthwith the cause of all righteousness. Certain things we conceive to be righteous antecedently to God's will, although they are not so antecedently to His nature. At once (2) some things are righteous just because God wills them, i.e., those which are *iuris positivi*. Some things God wills because they are righteous, those which are *iuris naturalis*, so far as they agree with the holiness of His nature, or with the nature of man, so far as he bears the image of God. (3) God could not therefore enjoin things contrary to those which He enjoins, except so far as they are *iuris positivi et arbitrarii*".—In this sense VOETIUS discusses single questions, as (I, 392) "whether God can afflict an innocent man with hellish tortures; whether God has the right to bind man to something impossible".

35.—Therefore God can only forgive the guilt of sin, because He lets the sin be punished and the guilt be atoned for.—COCCEIUS (*S.T.* III, 10, 61): "The *Socinians* detract from the divine nature and dignity, when they put remission and punishment of sins among the things which may be both done and omitted without danger to the dignity of the intelligent nature (divine of course)".—To the question whether God's essence is so just, that He cannot let sin go unpunished, RIISSEN replies (III, 40): "The more easily to destroy Christ's satisfaction the *Socinians* deny that there is any attribute in God which exacts satisfaction for necessary sin; if He punishes sin, that is the most free effect of His will. Among orthodox also there is some diversity of opinions about the exercise of this righteousness. Some lay it down as necessary, others as free and indifferent, from which God may abstain, if He wills. Hence their diversity of opinion on the necessity for satisfaction. Some regard it as merely hypothetical, i.e., on the hypothesis of the divine will and decree, as God could not remit sins without satisfaction, not because His righteousness absolutely and necessarily exacted it, but because He so decreed. This view is followed by the most learned *Twiss* after certain of our doctors, who spoke more securely before the rise of *Socinus*. Others posit absolute satisfaction, which does not depend on the decree alone, but also arises from divine righteousness. But although both sides are agreed on the hinge of the question against the *Socinian* denial of the necessity of satisfaction, it is yet certain that the latter view, which we follow, is far more effective in strangling the *Socinian* heresy and more suited to the nature of God and to the words of Scripture".

36.—"God's truth is His essential attribute by which He is understood to be true in Himself, veracious in His words and deeds and the author of all truth in the creatures, most foreign to everything false and lying and to all dissimulation and forgetfulness" (POLAN II, 27). God's truthfulness is displayed as faithfulness in what He plainly promises. "Truth in words is named God's faith, because the things spoken by Him exist.

and eventuate with an immutable certainty".—The question "whether God could deceive, if He wished", which was affirmed by the *Cartesians*, was not so much denied by the dogmaticians as rather rejected as being absurd in and for itself. MASTRICHT (II, xiv, 10) says: "The Reformed are of opinion that He neither can nor wills to deceive, and that the nexus 'could if He would' is false and impious"; and mainly on these grounds: "(1) it is against the Scriptures, for which it is ἀδύνατον ψεύσασθαι θεόν; (2) against the nature not only of prime truth but of truth's very self that He even could deceive, since without doubt it is a greater perfection in a witness that he cannot deceive, than that he can; (3) contrary to God's nature, in whom on this principle there would be ναί καί οὔ, in spite of the Apostle 2 Cor. 1. 18; also (4) against the goodness of a most merciful Creator, that He could deceive His wretched creatures."

37.—The activity of the divine will is manifested as God's omnipotence. "God's power (is that attribute) by which He adequately carries out whatsoever He wills suitably to His nature" (HEIDEGGER III, 104).— VOETIUS (I, 405) collects a series of definitions of God's omnipotence: "It is the essential property of God by which He can and does effect all things in one and all." Elsewhere thus: "It is that one by which He acts outside Himself with free will and can do all possible things." Not a bad thing also to extract the definition from the works of SUAREZ *sect. cit.* 5, 45: "It is nothing but the actual divine nature which, so far as it is actual being in essence, is of itself capable of any participated or participable being, if there be added will to apply and knowledge to direct." Others describe it thus: "God's power is the infinite and single strength to do all the things which are in harmony with His essence and attributes." —BRAUN (I, ii, 4, 3) defines thus: "The power of God is His most effective will, so far as He exerts it towards the creatures".

38.—Omnipotence is the omnipotent nature of God Himself and is therefore eternal, bound to no means and infinite, since it is never exhausted in what it produces.—MASTRICHT (II, 20, 14): "The power of God is (1) His very essence or powerful Deity; in God there is not thing and thing: (2) infinite, not only in itself, so far as He is actually God Almighty, Genesis 17. 1 (. . . to Abram . . . I am God Almighty (El Shaddai); walk before me, and be thou perfect); nor merely by perfection of operation, so far as He operates by a nod whatever He does operate, Ps. 33. 9 (He spake, and it was done; and he commanded and it stood fast) Is. 40. 28 (fainteth not, neither is weary) Eph. 1. 12 (according to the working of the strength of his might) Phil. 3. 21 (the working whereby

He is able to subject even all things unto Himself); but also *ex objecto,*
Lk. 1. 37 (no word of God shall be void of power), so far as it extends
to all things possible (just like the understanding, because of its infinite
power, extending to all things understandable); nor does it ever effect
anything by power, but that it might effect more, Eph. 3. 20 (able to do
exceeding abundantly beyond all that we can ask or think). For although
things which He can make cannot exist at the same time, because so the
infinite would be given inactivity beyond Himself, and His power would
as it were have been exhausted, and so He would not be almighty, yet
power is not lacking in God by which He can produce, if existence is not
repugnant to the things; (3) independent, so that it can act by means,
without means, against means, 1 Sam. 14. 6 (there is no restraint to the
Lord to work by many or by few); in short (4) eternal (Rom. 1. 20);
for although from eternity He had not operated outside Himself, He yet
had power from eternity, and the same power by which He willed, when
He made the world. And by it also He would have produced the world
from eternity, if only the world could have existed from eternity".

39.—The object of divine omnipotence is all that is possible at all, i.e.,
all that may be a means of glorifying God and that God will also really
let be realised for this purpose. What is not of this kind is impossible,
i.e., ideally it is not real at all; rather absolutely non-existent; and
therefore cannot be the object of divine omnipotence.—The concept of
possible and impossible is variously defined by many dogmaticians.
POLAN distinguishes (II, 29) "the impossibles of nature, which surpass
the usual course and order of nature", and "things impossible by nature",
which are against the definition of the thing." VOETIUS compares the
concepts of possible and accidental as follows (I, p. 408): "The possible
is generally described as that which may be though it is not. It is distinguished from the contingent, which, though it is, may yet not be.
Impossible, that which cannot be or of which there is no objective or
passive power. Moreover, as logical and physical power is twofold, so
possible and impossible are twofold; naturally, I mean, or *secundum quid,*
and absolutely or logically, when there is no opposition in the terms."
    But most dogmaticians develop the concepts of possible and impossible
in conformity with Reformed principle by saying: "That is possible,
which God in conformity with His nature is able and willing really to
let come into being for His own glory, as, e.g., HEIDEGGER (III, 106):
"The object of divine power is δυνατὸν, the possible; not in itself,
as though there were anything outside God, which had the cause of its
possibility in itself, outside the power and will of God; but in the power
and will of God, which alone is the foundation and root of all possibility.

All things outside of God derive their essence and reality from the fact that, as God understands how to make them for His own glory, so He wills that they be and produces them.—(107): Thus then that is possible, which God can will, order, call, do for His glory; impossible, which God cannot order, call, do for His glory. We do not recognise in God absolute power of the kind which separates from the essence of possible things their relation to the end, the glory of God, of whom, to whom and from whom exists whatever does exist".

HEIDAN is different (p. 88): "Things which are the object of divine power, so far as concerns themselves, derive neither from understanding nor from will nor from omnipotence itself the fact that they are possible and objects of that power. They are the objects of omnipotence, according as of themselves they do not involve a contradiction. Only then is God related to them as omnipotent". From which it follows that "The absolutely possible (as distinguished from that which is called possible comparatively and in relation to this or that power) is that which does not involve a contradiction. Implying a contradiction is nothing else than repugnance of terms in the connection of predicate with subject and of subject with predicate. But what is repugnant to happening thus cannot possibly happen. All implication or impossibility consists in our conceiving alone, vilely conjoining ideas which are mutually opposed to each other".

40.—In the impossible however is displayed not a limitation but the moral perfection of God's power. It is precisely in virtue of perfection, freedom and power that God cannot will and so cannot do what contradicts the moral and spiritual order, which is a copy of His own divine glory.

What holds of God's will holds also of God's omnipotence. HEIDEGGER (III, 107): "From this we may readily gather that God cannot do certain things, not because of defect, as *Pliny* once raved, but because of abundance and perfection of power. This consists in the fact that He can do θεοπρεπῆ, things worthy of God the supreme, infinite and most perfect Being; not those which degenerate from His nature and entity and point to nothingness.—Therefore He cannot do, nay, He most powerfully cannot do things which are repugnant to His nature, as to destroy Himself, suffer, die, because in *Augustine's* words He is omnipotent in doing what He wills, not by suffering what He does not will. He cannot not love, not bear witness to His Son eternally. He cannot do those things which argue impotence, weakness, defection from Himself and His perfections, like lying, Tit. 1. 2 (God cannot lie), denying Himself, 2 Tim. 2. 13, beholding evil and looking upon perverseness, Hab. 1. 13, forgetting the laborious work of charity, Heb. 6. 10, things which even among creatures we do not contemplate without cursing. He cannot do things which involve contradiction, i.e., which are so enunciated that subject recoils from predicate, as that things done are undone, that in a triangle there are four angles, that twice two is five and the like. *Esse* or *non esse* may be predicated of an individual, but not both at the same time. God also cannot bring it about or predicate it, that the same thing should at once be and not be: it would make Him a liar. He cannot make a thing infinite; to make a thing is to give a beginning to a thing which was not. But beginning is as opposed to the infinite, as affirmation to negation".

The rest of the dogmaticians also express themselves in the same way, conceiving the idea of omnipotence purely in terms of the idea of the divine will, e.g., OLEVIAN (*Fester Grund*, p. 23): The nature of divine omnipotence is not just that God can do all that He wills and put it into action, but that He also hinders, smashes, destroys and brings to naught what He entirely refuses to will and has decided otherwise. Similarly VOETIUS (I, p. 409), who adds that "on this principle God is being denied not some power but impotence and imperfection".—ALSTED, p. 93 : " It is God's power by which out of the freedom of His will God can work outwardly whatever things He can freely will and does work whatever He freely wills.—WOLLEB, p. 11: " The object of omnipotence is whatever is not adverse to its nature and does not imply a contradiction, and so is rather not of ἀδυναμία than of δύναμις. So lying, making the done undone, making man's body infinite, and the like, cannot be attributed to God."

To meet the objection founded on this, that Reformed theology does not recognise the true omnipotence of God, the opposite is therefore insisted on with special emphasis, e.g., by BRAUN (I, ii, 4, 5): "Thus it does not follow that God is not omnipotent (1) because He cannot perform contradictories—contradictories are nothing and overturn His supreme perfection. (2) Nor is His omnipotence therefore to be denied, because He cannot produce an infinitely perfect creature—infinite perfection involves necessary existence, which does not fall to a creature; what exists necessarily cannot be created".—DANAEUS (*Isagog.* I, 17): "Certain things God is said to be unable to do, like lying, Tit. 1. 2, denying Himself, 2 Tim. 2. 13, lying, Num. 23. 19 ; which things, as is taught by ATHANASIUS, BASIL, AUGUSTINE, the DAMASCENE, do not assign ἀδυναμία to God, but rather prove and assert His truth and power. These may belong to weakness, but not to power. But neither can God perform contradictories. This is not constancy but extreme inconstancy. Nor can God do what the fool thinks; God's omnipotence is united to His wisdom".
—In particular it is emphasised, that God's omnipotence is not exhausted

in what really happens; HEIDAN 84: "Whatever it wills, it really effects. Indeed it can make more than it wills and it suffers no resistance from any created thing".

41.—A distinction is to be drawn between "God's absolute power (by which) He is said to be capable of everything that can throw light on His glory" and "God's ordered or actual power (by which) He has willed what He decreed to do from eternity" HEIDEGGER (III, 108).— LEIDEN SYNOPSIS VI, 35: "God's power is the attribute by which the living, intelligent and will-ing God is by strength and ability strong enough to act outwardly. Considered singly and apart from will it is absolute and covers everything possible, not just what is simply impossible, Mt. 3. 9 (from these stones . . . children unto Abraham) 19. 26 (with God all things are possible) Lk. 1. 37 (no word from God shall be void of power); conjoined with will it is actual, Ps. 115. 3 (hath done whatsoever he hath pleased) Eph. 1. 11 (worketh all things after the counsel of His will), and is exercised directly or indirectly (whence He is called the Lord of hosts or armies).—MASTRICHT II, xx, 13: "While power is one and most single in God, because it is His essence, it is yet usually divided by us into absolute, according as we conceive it as preceding His will, Eph. 3. 20 (able to do . . . above all, etc.) Mk. 5. 4. 7 (what have I to do with thee? (daemon speaking)) ; and ordered, according as we conceive it to follow the will; by which He is now not merely able to do it if He wills it, but He also effects what He wills, Ps. 135. 6 (whatsoever the Lord pleased he hath done).—RIJSSEN III, 36, further adds: "From actual power to effect is a valid inference. It is otherwise in the case of absolute power. This absolute power CALVIN has rejected, not absolutely but relatively, abusing the method of the *Scholastics*, who constructed from it many portentous dogmas : as that God can lie, sin, etc."—VOETIUS distinguishes also between " God's omnipotence actual and ordained ", since (I, 407) he answers the question " whether the actual, or effective and operating omnipotence of God falls in with ordered or ordinary omnipotence" thus: "This is what POLAN wants (*lib.* 2 *synt. c.* 24), but the statement is short of accurate; for the ordered extends more widely than the actual. By ordered power God can, e.g., extract this boy who is falling into the fireplace, help this one who is hungry, staunch blood for this wounded man, extinguish this blaze, etc., by ordinary, i.e., men's labour, and according to the laws of nature; and yet He does it."

42.—Thus ordered power is the "actual effectiveness of God's will". But besides this we have to distinguish God's *potentia* and His *potestas*. God's *potestas* is the concept of the absolute right by which God makes use of His omnipotence over against the creature.—HEIDEGGER further distinguishes (III, 110) *potestas* absolute and ordered. The former is τὸ αὐτεξούσιον in God's will, or the power of free will dependent on no one outside Himself." The latter is that "by which He has the right to act according to what He has ordered, in virtue of His absolute right and power."

43.—The content of these attributes is the perfection and complete adequacy, the glory and majesty, and the blessedness (of God).—LEIDEN SYNOPSIS VI, 43: "In all these divine attributes consists the perfection of God, as one in whom is no defect; His excellency and surpassingness over all things, so that nothing is His match or like; His glory or majesty, both inward in His attributes whereby He is glorious in Himself, Is. 48. 11 (my glory will I not give to another), and outward in light inaccessible Ex. 33. 18-22 (Moses' sight of God at Sinai) 1 Tim. 6. 16 (dwelling in light unapproachable); and blessedness by which He enjoys Himself and rests in Himself, in need of nothing and the complement of everything good, 1 Tim. 6. 15 (the blessed and only potentate) Ac.17. 25 (not . . . as though he needed anything), and so singly to be upheld, blessed, honoured, worshipped, the only object of service, adorable, praiseworthy, to be called upon and in words and deeds to be glorified, Rom. 1. 21 (as the unrighteous do not) Tit. 1. 16 (those who profess to but do not know Him). And He is the end and use of divine knowledge".

MASTRICHT (II, xxi, 1): "From the primitive attributes so far recounted three derivatives emerge: omnisufficiency and perfection by which He is most perfectly sufficient unto Himself and to all, majesty and glory by which He is such as to be most worthy to be praised and made famous, and blessedness by which He is most happy (*felicissimus*) in every detail. The perfection and sufficiency which we claim for God is regarded as not limited to a fixed genus or to any fixed use which suits any creatures and excludes privative imperfection alone, but as universal, including every good, sufficient in every category and in every man for everything up to infinite beatitude, which thereby rules out all negative imperfection".—(II, xxii, 5-8): "For glory these four elements concur: (1) an infinite eminence; (2) the brilliance of this perfection and eminence; (3) recognition of this eminence, from which it is called God's face; (4) the making famous or manifest of the eminence recognised by its brilliance, more appropriately termed glorification than glory.—(II, xxiii, 1): There remains of the derived attributes the third and last of all God's attributes, by which He rejoices in and enjoys Himself and all His perfections and imparts Himself to His own for the enjoyment of His joy, which is called blessedness as described by Ps. 16. 2 (I have no good beyond thee)".

CHAPTER VI

THE HOLY TRINITY

1.—A basic doctrine of Christianity, the foundation of the entire doctrine of the covenant of grace and of Christian faith in God *simpliciter*, is the doctrine of the Three-in-oneness of God.—The dogmaticians are at pains to prove (against *Socinians* and *Arminians*) that the dogma of the Trinity is a basic doctrine and must necessarily be believed for the soul's salvation's sake, because the concept of the Trinitarian God coincides completely with the concept of the revealed God (the "Christians' God).' Cf., e.g., Voetius I, p. 467ff. Hence Bullinger says II, 2: "Since the unity in trinity of the Deity is simply and plainly taught in H. Scripture, it is fair that we also should agree with Scripture and not investigate inquisitively or seek a fuller knowledge in this life, than that which God has revealed. Therefore, the Christian emperors a thousand years from today were right to appoint capital punishment for those who should spread new teaching on this dogma and teach different things with insult to God".—But also for that very reason Calvin recommends a treatment of the dogma as simple as possible and related purely to the vocabulary of Scripture, I, xiii, 21: "Here if ever among the hidden mysteries of Scripture I recommend sober philosophising of extreme restraint, with the further condition of great caution, lest either thought or tongue go beyond the point to which the territories of God's word extend".— It is likewise insisted by the dogmaticians, that the use of the description οὐσία, *persona, Trinitas,* etc., should be adhered to, although they are not found in Scripture. Calvin I, xiii, 5: "The terms were not discovered anyhow and care must be taken, not to be convicted of haughty rashness in spurning them. Yet I am not of such a precise austerity as to persist in swordplay over empty expressions."—Wolleb, p. 12: "The words *persona,* triad and ὁμοούσιος, although not found in so many syllables in the Scriptures, are yet in agreement with the Scriptures and are usefully employed in the Church." Bucan justifies the use of the word *Trinitas* with the remark, that at least the sense of it is to be found in the passage 1 John 5. 7 (ὅτι τρεῖς εἰσιν οἱ μαρτυροῦντες τὸ Πνεῦμα καὶ τὸ ὕδωρ καὶ τὸ αἷμα ; καὶ οἱ τρεῖς εἰς τὸ ἕν εἰσιν—*tres, trinitas* (I. 5, 7) [although this is not in the best MSS.!]). Others like Keckermann and Martyr venture to regard the passage as not precisely genuine.

2.—For human reason this doctrine remains an eternally inexplicable mystery.—Generally the inconceivability of the doctrine of the Trinity is recognised by all dogmaticians. Therefore the use of analogous phenomena from the world of nature or from ideas of a similar appearance belonging to the realm of a heathen outlook is disapproved of. CALVIN (I, xiii, 18) is already saying that: "To express the force of the distinction I am not sure that it is expedient to borrow analogies from human affairs. Sometimes the ancients are in the habit of doing so. At the same time they admit that it makes a tremendous difference what they adduce by way of simile". (Similarly HYPERIUS, p. 109). Among the German Reformed dogmaticians PEZEL and SOHNIUS of course objected to *Melanchthon's* attempt at a speculative construction of the doctrine of the Trinity. But URSIN was already completely departing from this in his *Corp. doctr. Christ.* (Cf. HEPPE *Altprot. Dogmatik*, Vol. 1, p. 300). Of the later dogmaticians only KECKERMANN (72) linked up with *Melanchthon* or *Augustine.* P. 20ff. he seeks to expound as follows the necessity of God's trinitarian existence in God's actual essence: "It is our duty meticulously to explore their basis and so to make it plain to the Anti-trinitarians, that the trinity of persons emanates from God's actual essence and that God cannot be God, unless He have three distinct modes of existing or persons.—God has most excellent knowledge, is in fact knowledge itself in the highest degree.—But knowledge is the actual *actus* of God's essence, in fact the essence itself in activity.—Therefore this *actus* of knowing is infinite and eternal like the essence itself.—But eternal knowledge has an eternal object—which it cognises.—But since the divine knowledge is most perfect, its object ought to be most perfect. But there is nothing more perfect than God. Therefore the object of divine knowledge will be none other than God Himself.—Thus God's knowledge returns and bends back from eternity upon itself, i.e., upon God. Just as the soul thinks of itself . . . and this thought or intellection is called reflex.—But now, since no knowledge knows without an image of the object which it knows, it is necessary, whereas God has known Himself most perfectly from eternity, that He has conceived and begotten in His very self the most perfect image of Himself. (All intellection is the conceiving of some image. Either, therefore, we must attribute such an image to God or make Him irrational and ἀνόητος). This most perfect production of an image in the divine essence is rightly called conception and generation. Because of course the bending back of the divine knowledge upon itself is the conception or production of a thing most like God, in fact, God Himself. Moreover, the conception and production of the most perfectly like is nothing else but generation.—Generation which takes place in the actual genderer is called conception. The more perfect the nature of the Genderer, the closer generation is to essence and the more akin is the thing gendered.—Since then God is most perfect life, and since His entire life is knowledge, He needs must have a conception most akin to knowledge and most inward.—And this conception, which is the most perfect of the divine knowledge, will be a generation, positing a mode of existence in God or a second person, which is rightly called both the image of God and the Son.—Since then in God being known and existing are the same thing and since moreover the being known is actually the *esse* of the Son, it is necessary for the essence and existence of God and of the Son to be constituted the same.—Since also God's knowing is active from eternity, He Himself is eternal *actus*. But since the knowing is not without an image, it follows that this image or the Son which He has conceived is just as eternal,—and will not be less than the Genderer.— In God's essence two modes of existence or persons are inferred, Father and Son. So I now think it plain—that these two modes are founded on the actual nature and essence of God, so that God is not God, if He have not the co-eternal Son.—The aphorisms now to follow will prove that a third existence is also rooted in God's actual essence.—Since knowing is comprised in the divine essence, so also will be volition.—The more knowing there is in things, the more will there will be.—So there must needs be the most perfect will in God.—God wills nothing except so far as He knows it. And as He knows Himself as the most perfect *ens*, so by His will He desires and wills Himself as the supreme and most perfect good. Thus in its activity God's will returns upon itself, and rests in God Himself as the infinite good.—Since God's infinite will embraces and always achieves its object entire, there must therefore be produced from it supreme pleasure and love.—So whereas the Father conceives and with most perfect will desires the image of Himself, His Son: it follows that the most perfect love and the fullest pleasure proceed from Father to Son and from Son to Father, as from image to archetype; and that so by the conjunction of the knowledge and will of both a third mode of existence or person is posited in the divine essence, called the H. Spirit. It is called the Spirit—because the *dilectio* is a sort of impulse and beat of the will, by which it is borne to the good of the beloved Object as though breathed from the will.—Since then by most perfect will and love the Father so to speak aspires to the Son and the Son for his part to the Father, the Spirit is therefore rightly said to proceed from the mutual longing of both.—Thus then we have from the very essence of God, by unchangeable principles, demonstrated three modes of subsistence or persons, Father, Son and Holy Spirit; and that in such wise, that they cannot be more or fewer, unless it be denied that God is God. We shall wind up the whole proof by a single syllogism. In an essence in which there is perfect knowledge bending back upon itself, an Image is begotten and a Spirit proceeds on the impulse of the will. And yet these things inhere in the one, most single essence of God. Therefore there will be in the same essence the Begetter, the begotten Image and the proceeding Spirit".

ALSTED also sought to give explanations of the dogma. Yet he declared that (104): "The mystery of the Trinity can neither be discovered by the light of nature nor be understood by the light of nature or by the light of glory, by any creature". Hence the stereotyped description, *mysterium Trinitatis.*—Similarly take the LEIDEN SYNOPSIS VII, 14: "Hence the mode of this mystery, inexplicable as it is by human reason, is rather to be adored in humble faith than defined by risky phrases (*periculosis locutionibus*)".—On the attitude of later Reformed Orthodoxy to this whole question MASTRICHT (II, xxiv, 21) expresses himself most completely: "Starting from the nature of God as knowing some *Scholastics* have tried to accomplish it in pretty much this fashion: reason teaches that God knows (*intelligere*); of this knowledge is born the idea or image; and since the thing known is something good, love arises: but since the image and also the love are not accidents in God but substance, it cannot but be that there is one substance in Knower, Known and Loved. Hence they called the Father God knowing, the Son God known and the H. Spirit God loved. Others among them like *Scotus* (*Sent.* Bk. 1, *dist.* 2, 9 and 10) attempt to arrive at Trinity from production thus: To produce is a perfection which does not involve any imperfection: hence it befits the most perfect being, and that eternally before the production of a universe. And since eternal production demands an eternal product, which in turn, since it involves no imperfection in its conception, must also be received as an eternal product; and since producing and being produced involves perfection without imperfection, it too must be admitted to complete perfection. Whence it results that the Father is God producing, the Son God producing and produced, and the Holy Spirit God produced only. *Gabriel Biel* (*Sent. disc.* 100. 1) and *Raimundus de Sabunde* in his *Theol. natur. cc.* 46-55 follow the same proof. Some of the *Cartesians* (others objecting) like *John Clauberg,* have adopted the same proof in their disputations and with laborious prolixity he follows it up with some disputations. Later men add other proofs, e.g., that the possession of no good is pleasant without a partner; and since in God there has always been most pleasant possession of the highest good, he says it may easily be concluded that God has never been without a partner [!]. *Thomas Aquinas* in his *Summa, part* I, *qu.* 32, *art.* 1 rages at the Scholastics, that in making this attempt they derogate from faith in more than one way. Others of the Scholastics declare that in all things created there is some *vestigium* of the Trinity, but in the human soul an image of it, since mind remembers itself, knows itself, loves itself: if we see this we see the Trinity; we do not yet see God but the image of God—quoting this from

Augustine, De Trin., XIV, *c.* 8. Nor are there lacking some of ours who endeavour, if not to prove at least to declare the Trinity from the three primary attributes of God, power, wisdom and goodness: so, the Father is as it were God mighty, the Son wise, the H. Spirit good. The common view of the Reformed is that the Trinity can neither be investigated nor solidly proved by natural reason. Meanwhile it is declared that as to possibility it may be proved by similes and reasons *a posteriori*, because (1) it is a mystery to all acknowledgers who acknowledge its truth; (2) as *Aquinas* warns us, in more ways than one it derogates from the dignity of this dogma, whereby it deals with things rationally unsearchable even by faith, so far as anti-Trinitarians believe that by such miserable arguments we merely raise an edifice of trouble. Add that to seek in faith a reason for this mystery is to stretch a shadow over a weak eye, that it may not be transfixed by brighter light, as *Richardus* tells us in *De Trin., lib.* 1, cap. 1 ; (3) no philosopher, nor all the philosophers together, have reached ἐπίγνωσις for all the acuteness of their reason put together; (4) the dogma of the Trinity is the basis of the whole Christian faith: hence, if it is resolved into reason, it thereby degenerates from faith into philosophy; (5) no natural reason can be set up which impregnably concludes that God is therefore one in essence, trine in persons."

The manner in which dogmaticians sought to explain the doctrine of the Trinity *a posteriori* may be realised from the following passage of POLAN's *Syntagma*, III, 4: "There is a certain similitude and adumbration of the divine generation in physical generation; God the Father begets *per se* a like offspring, as do all bodies which beget naturally; *persona* begets *persona*, as men do. There is also a similitude and adumbration of the divine generation in mental or metaphysical generation. As mind begets by nature, not by power, so also does God. As mind begets a spiritual begetting (*genitura*), so too God. As mind begets a co-essential and συναΐδιος *genitura,* so too God. As a unifold and perfect mind begets a unifold and perfect *genitura*, so too God. As a mind begets immutably, so too God. As a mind begets of itself in itself, so too God. As a mind does not beget of matter outwith itself, so neither does God. As mind always begets and cannot not beget, so too God the Father. As metaphysical generation persists, so too does the divine. This is just what the ancients have said, that God begets the Son by a mode of knowing (*intellectus*), teaching that in some way there is a likeness to divine generation in the generation of *intellectus*.—Once more, there is a great dissimilitude between divine and metaphysical generation. The mind begets merely an inexistent faculty or attribute, but God the Father begets a *persona* existent *per se*. Mind begins to beget in time; but God does not begin to beget, but always begets *ab aeterno in aeternum* beyond any limitation of time."

3.—In a word, this doctrine [thus shrouded in mystery] rests simply on revelation.   H. Scripture teaches (in OT as well as in NT), that the one God, who has made Himself known alike in the creation and government of the world and in the planting and preservation of the Church, is three-in-one from eternity as Father, Son and H. Spirit.—GISB. VOETIUS I, p. 467: The doctrine of the Trinity rests "upon these capital theses: (1) that there are three truly distinct Father, Son and H. Spirit; not distinct as names or attributes, or as effects, offices or functions of one and the same person; but distinct, so that they are and may be called *alius et alius;* i.e., they are distinct hypostases; (2) that these three and each of them singly is the one true God, the Creator, Preserver, Redeemer whom we worship *una religione;* (3) there is an order, as of substance, so also of operation among these hypostases; i.e., that the Father is *a nemine,* the Son from the Father alone by generation, the H. Spirit by procession from Father and Son ".—The most important NT passages of Scripture, upon which the doctrine is based, are: Mt. 3. 16-17 (Jesus, when he was baptised, went up straightway from the water; and lo, the heavens were opened, and he saw the Spirit of God descending and coming upon him; and lo, a voice out of the heavens, saying, This is my Son, the Beloved, in whom I am well-pleased); 28. 19 (Go ye therefore and make disciples of all the nations, baptizing them into the name of the Father and of the Son and of the H. Ghost); 2 Cor. 13. 13 (Benediction) ; 1 Jn. 5. 7f. [read to v. 12 in AV] ; Revelation 1. 4, 5 (Grace to you and peace, from him which is and which was and which is to come, and from the seven spirits which are before the throne and from Jesus Christ the faithful witness, etc.).

4.—The Godhead is thus manifested over against the world as a single nature; in its inward being it exists as a threeness of persons.—KECKERMANN (18) warns us against a confusion between triplicity and trinity. "Strictly, that which is composed of three things is triple(x), which it is blasphemous even to think concerning God;—that which in a single (*unica*) nature has three modes of existence is trine; the modes plainly do not imply composition".

5.—"Trinity is that relation in God, whereby in His divine and single essence three persons subsist, truly and actually distinguishable from each other by their own attributes or by a distinct mode of existence, namely Father, Son and H. Spirit, which single persons are the same one true God" (BEZA, *Tract. theol.,* I. 1). The relation of the three persons to the unity of the divine nature results from the relation of the concepts of person and nature to each other. URSIN, *Loci.,* p. 489: "Essence or οὐσία is a thing existing *per se*, although communicated to several. Person is an *individuum* existing, alive, intelligent, incommunicable, not based upon any other, nor part of a second."—The words "nor part of a second" are the Reformed addition to *Melanchthon's* definition, which WENDELIN explains thus, *Collat.*, p. 54: "By this limitation *persona* is distinguished from a rational soul, which is single, living, knowing, subsistent, but not a *persona*, because it is part of a man, who is a person consisting of two parts, body and soul".—Other definitions are LEIDEN SYNOPSIS, VII, 3: "The word *persona* in Latin is equivalent to πρόσωπον in Greek. Sometimes it denotes the mask and quality of a man or an outward condition, as Ac. 10. 34 (God is no respecter of persons); sometimes a subsistence endowed with reason as 2 Cor. 1. 11 (for the gift . . . thanks may be given by many persons). Suiting the word by analogy to the *personae* of the Trinity, we use it in the latter sense."—RIISSEN IV, 1: "To be called a *persona*·it is required (1) that it be a substance, (2) knowing, (3) not part of a second, (4) not supported by anything else. Person therefore denotes the complete status of a knowing substance." *Lutheran* dogmatics retains *Melanchthon's* definition without adding "nor part of a second".

6.—Hence *persona Deitatis* (POLAN III, 2) "is a subsistence in the divine essence, having in itself by nature the whole of that divine essence, but distinguished by its incommunicable attribute from the other *personae* to which it is related".—RIISSEN IV, 2: "A divine *persona* signifies neither essence only nor a mode of subsistence only, but the essence to be found in such a mode". More definitely WOLLEB says, p. 12: "A divine *persona* is neither a species of God or of Deity, nor part of it, nor a thing other than Deity, nor a bare relation, nor merely a τρόπος τῆς ὑπάρξεως but the essence of God *cum certo* τῆς ὑπάρξεως τρόπῳ. Nor is a *persona* a composite of being and being; nor are the essence of God and the τρόπος τῆς ὑπάρξεως thing and thing: it is a thing or *ens* and a *modus entis.*"

7.—Accordingly the three *personae* are equal to each other (1) so far as each of them has the same nature of God as each of the other two—they are ὁμοούσιοι to each other; (2) so far as each of them possesses the same divine majesty as each of the other two, so that the Father holds no advantage over the other two persons; and (3) so far as each of the three persons exists (ἐνυποστατικῶς) in the nature of each of the other two. On the other hand the three persons are distinct in name ; in the order of their being, in the mode of their action, in their external effects; which indeed proceed from the entire Trinity, in which nevertheless the separate persons are active in a different way; and finally in the special attributes which belong to each person.

MARCKIUS (V, 5-6): "The explanation may be made in four positions: (1) that there is in God a single most thoroughly unifold and singular essence.—(2) that there are besides three true *personae*, which abstractly are incommunicable modes of subsistence of the divine essence, relatively and terminatively related as it were to the more absolute and broader essence.—(3) that these *personae* meet mutually (α) in one essence: which was wisely expressed by Nicaea in the term ὁμοούσιος.—(β) in ἰσότης or equal participation in the dignity and honour flowing from the one supreme nature, so that there also should not be fixed here any ὑπεροχὴ of the Father as such.—(γ) in ἐμπεριχώρησις, *mutua inexistentia.* —(4) that these *personae* are at the same time distinguished among themselves (α) by name, (β) by order, (γ) by mode of operation, (δ) by *opera ad extra*, which of course as regards the operative principle belong undividedly to the Trinity, but according to the order of the persons and the special dispensation are terminatively appropriated to the separate *personae* 1 Cor. 8. 6 (yet to us there is one God, the Father, of whom are all things, and we unto Him; and one Lord, Jesus Christ, through whom are all things and we through him) Ac. 20. 28 (Take heed unto yourselves, and to all the flock, in which the H. Ghost hath made you bishops, to feed the Church of God, which he purchased with his own blood) 1 Cor. 6. 11 (. . . but ye were washed, but ye were sanctified, but ye were justified in the name of the Lord Jesus Christ and in the Spirit of our God), (ε) by personal attributes, notions or operations, which they call characteristic, diacritical, gnoristic, which belong, not to the essence or to the persons *in abstracto*, but to the latter *in concreto;* nor are the perfections absolute but relative, so that they place as much real perfection in one as in a second *persona*, even if they are set forth in passive terms."

8.—First of all then each of the three persons is according to its nature the ONE living and perfect God. But just as real and essential as the oneness in nature of the three persons is the distinction of persons in the divine nature.—POLANUS III, viii, 5-6: "The persons of the deity according to essence are one thing. Compared with each other they are *pares seu aequales,* holding in common an essential perfection, which is entire (*tota*) in all and each of the *personae.* Entire Deity is equal in the perfection of itself.—The *persons* of the Deity are distinguished among themselves not essentially (according to the *esse* common to them all) but nevertheless really; because one *persona* is produced by another. And at once they differ in their incommunicable attribute, i.e., according to the subsistence peculiar to each *persona.* Hence in the Trinity there is *alius et alius*, but not *aliud et aliud*. The Father is one, the Son another, the H. Spirit another (*alius*); because the *persona* of the Father is one, that of the Son another; that of the H. Spirit another (*alia*). But the Father is not one thing, the Son another thing, the H. Spirit another thing (*aliud*). Because there is not one essence of the Father, another of the Son and another of the H. Spirit. But there is the numerically one essence. The Father's *esse* is the *esse* of the Son and of the H. Spirit: therefore the essence of the Father is the Son and the H. Spirit. But to be the Father is not to be the Son or the H. Spirit. As there is a supreme and single (*individua*) unity of the divine essence in the three *personae*, so there is a real and discrete distinction of the persons in the unity of the essence. The divine nature is God; therefore it is common to all three *personae* of the divine nature as the appellation God. The divine nature of the Father is the Father, the divine nature of the Son is the Son, and the divine nature of the H. Spirit is the H. Spirit. The nature is viewed as being determined and subsistent in the *persona;* each is unifold, both nature and person, yet they are both distinct *ratione* [in function?]; while the *personae* are distinct *realiter*. Therefore Father, Son and Spirit differ personally, not essentially."

9.—The oneness, or the *communio personarum divinarum* is to be considered as ὁμοουσία, as ἰσότης, and as περιχώρησις ἐνάλληλος.—"The ὁμοουσία or *consubstantialitas* or *coessentialitas* of the divine persons is that whereby the three persons are of one and the same substance or essence, but singular and sole (*unicae*) numerically; or whereby they are one thing according to essence, the essence of all of them is one, and by no means one for the Father, another for the Son and another for the H. Spirit, 1 John 5. 7 (the Spirit is the truth) John 10. 30 (I and the Father are one).—ἰσότης of the divine persons is that by which the three persons are equal to each other by the essential attributes of Deity, by the act of subsisting, and in works and dignity and honour.— Περιχώρησις or ἐμπεριχώρησις ἐνάλληλος in the divine persons is the completely close union, whereby one person is in another, not like an accident in a subject, but in the way in which one person permeates and embraces in every direction the whole of another always and inseparably because of the numerically one and same essence, the whole of which the separate persons possess, Jn. 1. 1 (in the beginning was the Word, and the Word was with God, and the Word was God) 10. 38 . . . know and understand that the Father is in me and I in the Father) 14. 10f. (believest thou not that I am in the Father, and the Father in me? the words that I say unto you I speak not of myself: but the Father biding in me doeth the works)" (POLAN III, 8).

The distinction of the persons is a twofold one; the persons are to be distinguished from the essence of the Deity and from each other. From the essence of Deity they are distinguished not *realiter* nor yet *rationaliter*, but *modaliter*, that is, in the manner of their subsisting.—KECKERMANN 59: "(Persons) are distinguished from essence, not *sola ratione* nor by a real distinction, nor even formally, as the *Thomists* in fact would have it— but modally or by a modal distinction, which is between the *ens* and the order or mode of the *ens*."—RIJSSEN IV. 6: "The divine *personae* differ from the essence not really, i.e., essentially, like thing and thing; but modally, like mode from thing. The personal attributes, by which the *personae* are distinguished from the essence, are definite modes by which the essence is characterised, not formally and strictly as in creatures which are affected by modes, but eminently (as limiting or extreme instances) and analogically, all imperfections being removed."

10.—From each other the three persons of the Trinity are distinguished, not *essentialiter* nor *rationaliter*, but *realiter* (though incomprehensibly).— BUCAN I, 8 : "This *discrimen* [discrimination] is not essential as in creatures, where each one has its own definite, measurable *esse*: there is not one essence of the Father, another of the Son, another of the H. Spirit, but one and the same one, which the Father communicates entire to the Son, and Father and Son communicate to the H. Spirit. It is not rational, because it is not ἐπινοίᾳ or verbally that one speaks of Father, Son and H. Spirit. Nor do we say this *respective*, in the relative sense in which a man may be and is called a father and a son. It is a real and yet incomprehensible *discrimen*. Each *persona* has its own peculiar definition or subsistent and incommunicable attribute, and differs from another not οὐσίᾳ, but τρόπῳ ὑπάρξεως. Erroneous conceptions are (RIJSSEN IV, 7): "1. *Sabellianism*, from *Sabellius* of Pentapolis, who came from the Egyptian city of Ptolemais, introduced about A.D. 260, later followed by *Praxeas Asiaticus* and *Hermogenes Afer* and some centuries later by *Michael Servetus*, who put only the distinction of *ratio* between the persons, so that there is but a single *persona*, which because of the various results is now called the Father, now the Son, now the H. Spirit. 2. The tritheism of *Philoponus* and *Valentinus Gentilis*, which out of the three *personae* fashions three eternal and unequal spirits, mutually distinct in essence."—A DIEST 18: "Distinction of the *personae* is partly from the essence, partly among themselves. The former is one of *ratio* as between mode and thing, the latter real, as between mode and mode."

11.—[The persons then differ not οὐσίᾳ but τρόπῳ ὑπάρξεως.]— "Distinction of persons is that by which one person is distinguished from the other persons by a fixed notion (*certa notione*)." This distinction depends upon the relation in which the three persons stand to each other. "The relation of the divine persons is the τρόπος ὑπάρξεως, the mode of existence, proper to each person and incommunicable, which does not compose the person, but composition apart constitutes it and distinguishes it from other persons." Hence the *relatio* or *notio personalis* of the Father is *paternitas*, that of the Son *filiatio* or *nativitas*, that of the H. Spirit *processio*.—BUCAN III, 12: "(The attributes by which they are persons and really distinct from each other): (1) Ἀγεννησία or *paternitas* is the incommunicable attribute of the first *persona* of the Trinity, by which it comes about that the Father is a *nullo* but *a seipso*, not made, not begotten, but begetting the Son *ab aeterno*. (2) Γέννησις *generatio* or *filiatio*, in the passive sense of course, by which the Son receives and has in himself his whole and complete essence from the Father. (3) Ἐκπόρευσις, emanation or *processio*, also in the passive sense, by which the H. Spirit from eternity receives the same complete essence from Father and Son, not when he is sent or outpoured upon the house of David, but in respect of the essence which he receives from eternity, imparted to Him by Father and Son."

12.—This intrapersonal relationship results in the distinction of the divine persons according to origin, order and operation. The origin of the divine *personae* is the procession of one person from another. In this respect the Father is described as the *fons totius divinitatis*, as God καθ' ὑπεροχήν. Order of persons means that one person is, not *a prius*— in eternity a *prius* and a *posterius* are not to be looked for, CALVIN (I, xiii, 18)—but *prior* by nature or by cause: in this sense a first, second and third person is spoken of. The distinction of persons resting upon this according to operation is a twofold one, namely according to order and the mode of action in essential operations and according to personal operation.—Order of operations in the divine *personae* is the same in action as it is in existing. As therefore the Son has His existence from the Father, and the H. Spirit His from the Father and from the Son, so too in divine action the Father's will takes precedence, so that the Son's will follows; and similarly the H. Spirit follows the will of the Father and of the Son, yet not in time but in order.—The *modus agendi* in *opera essentialia* is as follows. The Father acts through the Son in the H. Spirit. Also the Father acts *a nullo*. The Son acts *a Patre* Gen. 19. 24 [? 49. 24 From thence is the shepherd, the stone of Israel?] Jn. 5. 19 (the Son can do nothing of himself, but what he seeth the Father doing: for what things soever he doeth, these the Son also doeth in like manner) 30 (I can of myself do nothing: as I hear, I judge: and my judgment is righteous; because

I seek not mine own will, but the will of him that sent me) 8. 28 (when ye have lifted up the Son of man, then shall ye know that I am, and I do nothing of myself; but as the Father taught me, I speak these things). The H. Spirit acts *ab utroque* John 16. 13 (when He, the Spirit of truth is come, he shall guide you into all truth: for he shall not speak from himself; but what things soever he shall hear, these shall he speak; and he shall declare unto you the things that are to come).—KECKERMANN 71: "As is the order of existing, so also is the order of acting in the *personae* of the sacrosanct Trinity. The Father acts *a sese*, the Son *a Patre* and the H. Spirit *ab utroque*. As regards the essence, which is the first principle of action, all the persons act *a sese*. But as regards the order and determination of action they do not all act *a sese*, because they do not all possess their mode of existence *a sese* Jn. 5. 14."

13.—Hence creation is ascribed to the Father, redemption to the Son, sanctification to the H. Spirit: yet in such a way that these works are none the less common to the three persons. The personal operation which displays the *character hypostaticus* or *personalis* or the *notae personales* of each separate person is twofold, an internal and an external. The former, or the *opus Dei ad intra* (so called because in it there is no sort of relation to the world) consists in these, that "the Father begets the Son and in so doing gives him and bestows upon him essence, power and all other essential things. The Son is born of the Father and receives divine essence and all essentials of deity by being born. The H. Spirit proceeds from Father and Son, receiving from Father and Son divine essence and all essentials of Deity by being breathed" (POLAN III, 8). These are the *opera Dei ad intra*, also called *opera divisa* (i.e., works shared among the separate persons) or *incommunicabilia*.

BUCAN III, 13: "These attributes are called *opera trinitatis ad intra*, because they take place within the actual essence, without any regard to things created, in an incomprehensible way. They are also called *opera divisa*, or distinct and incommunicable. *Paternitas* belongs to the Father alone, *filiatio* to the Son alone ἐκπόρευσις to the H. Spirit alone."

14.—"The external operations of the persons" or the *opera ad extra* (also called *opera indivisa*), are those "which are performed in respect of the creatures by the whole divinity or which the three persons together operate in the works of creation and redemption" (BUCAN III, 14).— Cf. *ibid*: "The *opera divinitatis ad extra* are called *indivisa*, because they are common to the three persons. Hence the rule: *opera trinitatis ad extra sunt indivisa*. Gen. 1. 26 (Let us make man in our image) and Jn. 5. 17-19 (what the Father does, the Son also does likewise), but all the while

preserving the *proprietas* of the persons, the order and distinction of action
1 Cor. 15. 57 (thanks be to *God* which giveth us the victory through
our Lord Jesus Christ). So the incarnation taken actively is an *opus*
of the whole Trinity, *ratione ἀποτελέσματος* Rom. 11. 36 (of him
and through him and to him), if you look to the effect, although the Son
alone was incarnate."—LEIDEN SYNOPSIS VII, 21—26: "The marks by
which these divine *personae* are distinguished from each other are either
inward or outward. The former [inward] are recognised by three
different characteristic attributes, implying that their *opera* are *ad intra*.—
22: The first of these attributes is, that the unbegotten Father has begotten
the Son from eternity by communication of the same essence. This
attribute of the Father the Greeks call *ἀγεννησία*; we less fitly
call it innascibility.—23: The second is that the Son begotten of the
Father has partaken of the same essence as the Father. This attribute
of the Second Person the Greeks express by the noun *γένεσις*, we by
nativitas.—24: The third is that the Holy Spirit emanates from the Father
and the Son, which attribute of the H. Spirit the Greeks call *ἐκπόρευσις*,
we *processio*.—25: By these three characteristic attributes connoting inward
personal actions the three persons of the Trinity are not only distinguished
from each other by a mutual difference, but are also opposed in turn
by a mutual relation, the Father begetting the Son begotten, and both
breathing to the one breathed and *vice versa*.—26: The outward marks,
in consequence of which the distinction of the same persons is noticed,
are the *operationes ad extra*, which are partly essential, so far as they
proceed from the principle of the whole essence equally common to the
three persons; partly personal, or so far as the order of the persons acting
in them is considered, as creation, which as regards order is peculiarly
attributed to the Father as the first person *κατ᾽ ἐξοχήν*; or so far as
the singular *οἰκονομία* or dispensation of the divine wisdom is
viewed in them, in respect of which the sending of the Son to redeem
is ascribed to the Father, redemption to the incarnate Son, and sanctification to the H. Spirit."

15.—In considering the separate persons of the H. Trinity there are
accordingly four points to be distinguished: (1) the divine essence common
to all three, (2) the personal peculiarity, (3) the *ordo in operando*, (4) the
special way in which each of them along with the rest achieves the works
of the dispensation of salvation.—HEIDEGGER (IV, 37): "As to the separate
personae of the Deity the treatment is under four heads. It considers
in each of them (1) what they have in common with the others, namely,
Deity; (2) the *ἰδιότης* or attribute by which each is distinguished
from any other; then (3) the order in operation; (4) the singular way

in which the individual persons co-operate mutually in the business of salvation which the mystery of the Trinity serves: theologians are in the habit of calling this οἰκονομία, as the works usually assigned to the separate persons, because of the individual mode of co-operation, are called economic."—LEYDECKER 52 gives an exacter explanation of the concept of *oeconomia*: "The word *oeconomia* in Greek stands for any dispensation, disposition or government. In Scripture it is transferred to God's special providence which is saving. The foundation is, that God one and trine is our saviour and He solely (*unicus*)."

16.—Touching the last point (4) the works of dispensing salvation as such are common to all the three persons of the Trinity in an undivided way (*operationes communes*). Yet in the manner of being executed the activity of each separate person is a special one (an *operatio personalis*).— HEIDEGGER (IV, 45): "The persons of the Trinity have among them a certain economy, according to which the works common and undivided as to operation are claimed as proper to certain persons in respect of mode of operation. The principle of operation is the same, common Deity, will, power. It is a common operation of all the persons. As to inception and operation the work is common. As regards mode of operating it is peculiar and distinct, according to the resemblance to that which is truly proper to any person, and according to the dispensation of the mystery of godliness and of human salvation. According then to the order of subsistence and action, just as the Father is *a se*, exists and operates through Son and H. Spirit, the Son exists and operates *a Patre* through the H. Spirit, the H. Spirit exists and operates *a Patre et Filio*. So, suitably to this order of subsistence and action *ad intra*, there is also assigned to the Father *ad extra* the inauguration of things, or creation; to the Son their continuation, or redemption; to the H. Spirit their consummation, or sanctification and regeneration. Likewise, because of the goal of the action and of the habitude peculiar to the work of the fixed person whose operation shines out most in any *opus*, the incarnation, although the work of the entire Trinity, is referred singly to the Son."— ALSTED 125: "The *opera deitatis ad extra* are common to the three persons —because they proceed from the essence. (But) as the essence is marked in the Father by a peculiar mode, and likewise in the Son and in the Spirit, so also the essential operations are distinct in the order and determination of the action."

17.—As to the three separate persons of God the following is to be said: "The Father is the first person of the Deity, owing existence to none, who from eternity has begotten the Son the essential image of Himself"

(HEIDEGGER IV, 46).—ALSTED 130: "The Father derives the origin neither of essence nor of person from any; not of essence, because He is God ; nor of person, because he exists *a se ipso*. Whence He is called simply ἄναρχος, ἀγέννητος."—LEIDEN SYNOPSIS (VIII, 6) : "The characteristic and inward property of the Father by which He is distinguished ὑποστατικῶς from Son and Spirit, is active generation. Although active breathing also belongs to the Father, that is nevertheless not His characteristic attribute, because He shares it with the Son."

18.—Of course, the name of Father serves to describe the Deity in general, when it is being considered in relation to the creature, so that in that case all three persons of God are intended by this name. But in quite a special way the first person of the Trinity is so named because of His relation to the Son, whom He has also begotten from Himself.

POLAN (III, 4): "God the Father is called in Scripture the Father, when God is spoken of, in two ways, οὐσιαδῶς and ὑποστατικῶς; —οὐσιαδῶς, i.e., *essentialiter*. He is so called with respect to the creatures which He either has created or regenerates, so far as God is one in essence, trine in persons, Father, Son and H. Spirit; and accordingly in this sense the Son also and the H. Spirit are contained in the appellation Father, as in Mt. 6. 26 (your heavenly Father feedeth them —the birds of heaven), Eph. 4. 6 (one God and Father of all, who is over all and through all and in all;—ὑποστατικῶς, i.e., personally, the Father means one definite person of Deity according to His relation to the eternal person of the Son begotten by Him in the unity of the essence, Jn. 1. 18 (No man hath seen God at any time: God only-begotten, who is in the bosom of the Father, he hath declared Him."—LEIDEN SYNOPSIS (VIII, 2): "When we call the first person in the H. Trinity Father, we do not relate this to the creatures who have been produced out of nothing by God; nor to believers who are the adopted of the Son of God, regarding whom in Scripture God is sometimes also called their Father. We relate it to the Son who is begotten of Him from eternity; and we use the name ὑποστατικῶς or personally."—ALSTED 130: "The name Father when assigned in Scripture to God is taken in three ways, as regards creation, adoption and eternal generation. In the first two ways it is taken essentially, in the last personally; and in the last meaning it is taken in this argument.—As regards the creation of things, according to which the very Gentiles know God the Father, Ac. 17. 28 (in him we live and move and have our being).—As regards the adoption, by which He adopted believers as sons to Himself, Gal. 4. 5 (God sent forth the Spirit of His Son into our hearts, crying Abba, Father). In both these ways it is taken essentially; i.e., it is used commonly of the three persons

of the Trinity, Mt. 6. 26 (above), Ephesians 4. 6 (*ib.*). But in this passage Father signifies God according to the relation which He has to the Son."
—That the Father in particular is described as the first person, is justified by the LEIDEN SYNOPSIS (VIII, 5) on the following three grounds: "We say that the Father is described as the first person: in respect of His subsistence which is from no other person, and from which the remaining ones have their origin; in respect of the divine *operationes ad extra,* derived from Him as the first source through the Son and the H. Spirit: finally, in respect of the order which H. Scripture here and there uses, especially in the formula of our baptism Mt. 28. 19."

19.—The *opera Patris ad intra* are to beget the Son and to breathe the Holy Spirit, the former exclusively, the latter in common with the Son.— This *generatio Filii* is proved (SYNOPSIS VIII, 9) by the following passages of Scripture: Ps. 2. 7 (The Lord said unto me, Thou art my son; this day have I begotten thee), Prov. 8. 23-24 (I (Wisdom) was set up from everlasting, from the beginning, or ever the earth was. When there were no depths, I was brought forth, when there were no fountains abounding in water) Mic. 5. 2 (But thou, Beth-lehem Ephratah, which art little to be among the thousands of Judah, out of thee shall one come forth unto me that is to be ruler in Israel; whose goings forth are from of old, from everlasting) Jn. 1. 14 (the Word became flesh and dwelt among us) Rom. 8. 32 (He was led as a sheep to the slaughter; and as a lamb before his shearer is dumb, so he openeth not his mouth) Col. 1. 15 (the image of the invisible God, the first-born of all creation) Jn. 5. 18 (. . . he not only brake the Sabbath but also called God his own Father, making himself equal to God) Prov. 8; Jn. 5; Col. 1; Heb. 1.

20.—The begetting of the Son is the "inward and personal action of God the Father, by which in a spiritual and ineffable manner He has begotten His Son as His image from eternity out of Himself in the same essence, and by the same essence has communicated to him the same infinite essence entire" (LEIDEN SYNOPSIS VIII, 7). But the Father's begetting is not to be compared with His creative activity. It proceeds indeed from the Father's will but not from a decree of His, and is therefore not a work of the will of the Father, but an attribute of the person of the Father who begets the Son eternally in virtue of His essence and is eternally the Father.

 POLAN (III, 4): The Father begat the Son "not βουλήσει, i.e., by will or decree; nor by compulsion; because neither does any violent necessity befall God nor does will forestall wisdom.—Generation is not a work of His will, but a property of His nature. Of course, the Father begets willingly or by a perfectly free will, i.e., not by compulsion; but yet not by will or through will, i.e., as though resolve were supervening upon fresh deliberation, as He created things by will.—He does not beget as essence but as the Father, and accordingly He begets hypostatically.— He begets by personal attribute, not by essential power.—He begets an intellection of Himself, the same as and equal to Himself in the same way, because he does not know *per speciem* (by species) but *per sui ipsius praesentiam* (by His own presence). Further, divine generation is not a physical movement but an *actus purus*, not from *non esse* to *esse*, but from that which is both ways at the same time *ἀϊδίως gignens et genitum, principium* and *principatum* (so to speak!) or rather *principium de principio*.—Then the Father does not beget by a power according to which He may beget or may not beget; He begets *naturâ*, according to which He is as He is and cannot be otherwise."—HEIDEGGER (IV, 51): "In this way God the Father begat His Son from eternity of His own substance, giving him to have life in Himself, as He also had life in Himself Jn. 5. 26 (as the Father hath life in himself, even so gave He to the Son to have life in Himself), and so begetting not another God, but only another person in the same common Deity, and that by a natural and necessary *actus;* but yet by a will not disjoined, not of course precedent, but concomitant, because will itself is for God His own nature and necessity; although naturally the mode of that obviously divine generation cannot be defined by us, because it is hidden in the deep secrecy (*penetralia*) of the divine wisdom.—Let us then say with the godly of old, that this generation took place both ἀκαταλήπτως (incomprehensibly) ἀχρόνως, (timelessly), ἀχωρίστως (inseparably) and ἀπάθως (dispassionately)."

21.—Nor must it be said that the divine essence produced the Son, nor that the essence of the Son was produced by the Father, nor that the Father produced the Son of His own essence, nor that the Son has had his essence imparted by the Father. When earlier Church teachers used these expressions, they are only to be understood in the sense that the opinion is rejected of the Son being produced from any sort of material. But it is more correct to say that the personality of the Father produced the personality of the Son, since the divine essence is common to the Father and to the Son, and the only thing conditioned by the eternal generation is the presence of the personal relation of the Father and Son in the essence of God.

POLAN (III, 4): "The Fathers sometimes say that the divine essence generates the Son; because the essence of the Son is generated by the Father. But such expressions are figurative, not strict, the noun divine essence not being taken absolutely or abstractly, that is, the person wholly apart and as it is common to the three persons and entire in each; but relatively, as it is in the person of the Father or in the person of the Son, and so ὑποστατικῶς, exactly as the name God is not always taken οὐσιαδῶς, but often ὑποστατικῶς as well.   For subjects as such are allowed by the predicates. Accordingly, metaphorical expressions of this kind are rejected and not admitted without suitable exegesis for two reasons. The first is, because, acts strictly belonging to the hypostaseis, or *supposita*, the essence itself strictly does not beget the Son, but the Father does so (*Thomas Aquinas*, Pt. I, *qu.* 31, *art.* 5).   "The second reason is because by this kind of talk, 'the divine essence begat the Son', one may easily be led into the mistake of thinking, that the Son's essence is unlike and numerically other than the Father's essence in divine things, as in human affairs the essence of fathers and sons is different at least in number; or into the mistake of believing that Father and Son consist of some common essence such as matter, from which both Father and Son were conflated and composed."

The main thought, on the basis of which these and similar expressions may be rejected, is the statement that the Father is not the *essentiator* of the Son. Cf. CALVIN (I, xiii, 2): "Certain rascals, to escape the invidiousness of *Servetus'* godlessness, have confessed that there are of course three persons, but with the additional argument that the Father who is truly and strictly the one God, in forming the Son and the Spirit, transfused His deity into them; the Father to be distinguished by this mark from the Son and Spirit, that He alone is the essentiator." Only moderately valid in opposition to *Arian* tendencies.

Cf. POLAN (III, 4): "The Father begets the Son not of His essence strictly, meaning as of matter: for God is void of matter. Therefore what the Fathers say, that the Father begat the Son of His essence, is to be taken metaphorically, because He did not do so outside of His essence ἐκ τῶν μὴ ὄντων (of things that were not), as the *Arians* once used to say.   So the Fathers used the phrase 'of His essence', not to posit any matter (for God is void of matter, as was already said), but to deny all matter whatsoever."

To exclude pertinent misinterpretations of these manners of speech found in the Fathers, modifications of them are proposed. URSIN (*Loci*, p. 542) would have *a se existens* added to *essentia Filii*: "The Son is begotten of the Father of the Father's essence, but the Son's essence is not begotten, but existent *a se* is communicated to the Son at birth by the Father.— And what is said of the Son's generation is also to be said of the H. Spirit's procession."—KECKERMANN (62) adds to essence "considered along with the mode" (namely, the *persona*): "I do not deny", he says, "that there are many who say that the Son has his essence communicated by the Father, because the Father's knowledge reflected upon Himself begets the Son. But this phrasing should be received very cautiously; indeed it should be considered altogether false, if it is used of the essence considered absolutely. The Son possesses it *a se ipso* as much as the Father does; and not the Son only but the Holy Spirit also. So it follows that, if the phrase in question is to be preserved, it must be understood of the essence considered along with the mode, so that to say that 'the Son's essence was communicated' is the same as if I should say that 'the second mode of existing in the Trinity, which is called the Son, is communicated by the Father."

Generatio is thus (1) *aeterna et perpetua,* (2) *hyperphysica, non physica,* "in order that there may be removed thence all imperfection, dependence, succession, change, division, multiplication", and (3) *propria, non metaphorica,* " so far as the actual *filiatio* flowing from it is true, as the Son Himself is truly the image of the invisible God".

22.—As then the Father begets the Son, He also (with the Son) sends forth the H. Spirit, which mission of the Spirit is likewise to be conceived as an eternal so-called attribute of the person of the Father (and of the Son).—Leydecker, 28: "*Spiratio* also is neither *creatio* nor *essentiatio,* but the ineffable communication of essence. No one will explain how it differs from generation."

Upon this personal relation of the Father to the Son whom He begets eternally, and to the H. Spirit whom He, with the Son, eternally sends forth, rests the nature of the Father's activity, namely that the Father acts through the Son in the H. Spirit (*opera ad extra*). From this *ordo subsistendi et operandi* it follows as regards the Father's *officium oeconomicum* that the Father is (1) the Lord (*dominus*), (2) *creator mundi,* (3) *legislator,* (4) upholder of the law passed, sanctioned and violated (*vindex legis latae, sancitae et violatae*), (5) *misericors Pater,* who according to His eternal counsel of peace, chose, sent, anointed and gave a Mediator for sinners, when given visited him with every sort of punishments so that he might redeem them; in addition He sends the H. Spirit to apply by faith the redemption acquired, to regenerate, convert, sanctify; at last He calls them through the ministry of the Word to participate in redemption, those called He adopts, sanctifies and glorifies" (Mastricht II, xxv, 7).

23.—"The Son of God is the second person of the Deity, always generated by the Father, not according to essential but according to personal being, and with the Father, breathing the H. Spirit" (Polan III, 5).—Wolleb p. 13 gives the proofs for the Deity of the Son as follows: "The Son's deity is proved by

I.—The divine names". In OT the Angel of the Lord Mal. 3. 1 (Behold, I send my messenger, and he shall prepare the way before me:

and the Lord (*sic*), whom ye seek, shall come suddenly to his temple; and the messenger of the covenant, whom ye delight in, behold, he cometh, saith the Lord of hosts). Next, Jehovah and God Gen. 16. 13 (Thou art *El roi*) 18. 1 (the Lord appeared unto (Abraham) by the oaks of Mamre, the appearance of the "three men" addressed as "my Lord") 32. 9 (And Jacob said, O God of my father Abraham and God of my father Isaac, O LORD) Ex. 3. 15 (the Lord, the God of your fathers . . . hath sent me) Josh. 6. 2 (The Lord said unto Joshua, See, I have given into thy hand Jericho), Zech. 2. 12 (and the Lord shall inherit Judah) 3. 1-2 (. . . the high-priest standing before the angel of the LORD, . . . and the Lord said unto Satan, The Lord rebuke thee, O Satan . . .). In the NT Jn. 1. 1 (In the beginning was the Word, and the Word was with God and the Word was God) 17. 3 (this is life eternal, that they should know thee the only true God, and him whom thou didst send, even Jesus Christ) 20. 31 (these are written that ye may believe, that Jesus is the Christ the Son of God; and that believing ye may have life in his name) Ac. 20. 28 (. . . the Church of God which he hath purchased with his own blood) Rom. 9. 5 (Christ . . . who is over all, God blessed for ever) Tit. 2. 13 (. . . our great God and Saviour, Jesus Christ).

II.—The divine attributes.—(1) Eternity Jn. 8. 58 (. . . Before Abraham was, I am) Rev. 1. 8 (I am the Alpha and the Omega, saith the Lord God, which is and which was and which is to come, the Almighty). (2) Omniscience Jn. 2. 24–25 (Jesus did not trust himself unto them, for that he knew all men, and because he needed not that anyone should bear witness concerning man; for he himself knew what was in man). (3) Omnipresence Mt. 28. 20 (. . . lo, I am with you alway, even unto the end of the world). (4) Omnipotence Jn. 5. 19 (Verily, verily, I say unto you, the Son can do nothing of Himself, but what things he seeth the Father doing; for what things soever he doeth, these the Son also doeth in like manner) Heb. 1. 3 (. . . being the effulgence of his glory, and the very image of his substance, and upholding all things by the word of his power, when he had made purification of sins, sat down on the right hand of the majesty on high . . .).

III.—The divine works.—Jn. 14. 11 (Believe me that I am in the Father and the Father in me; or else believe me for the very works' sake).

IV.—The divine honour.—Jn. 3. 16 (God so loved the world, that He gave His only-begotten Son, that whosoever believeth in him should not perish, but have everlasting life) Mt. 28. 19 (. . . baptizing them into the name of the Father and of the Son and of the H. Spirit) Phil. 2. 10 (that in the name of Jesus every knee should bow, of things in heaven and things on earth and things under the earth).

24.—As such the Son is not created or made by God or adopted by grace or because of merit. He is God the Son according to his nature and is therefore true αὐτοθεὸς like the Father and the H. Spirit.—POLAN III, 5: "He who is called the Son of God is either the Son *per naturam;* or by creation in the image of God, like Adam Lk. 3 last verse [38] (the Son of Adam, the Son of God); or by the grace either of personal union with the Λόγος, like Christ according to his human nature; or of adoption, like all the elect in Christ, both the good angels who are called the sons of God, and men predestined to eternal life. Here is meant the Son of God not created nor made, not by grace, and so made the Son not by merits but by nature; in other words, the natural and proper Son of God. He is called the Son in the strictest sense and in a single sense (*univoce*); among men they are not called sons in principle, but secondarily."—MUSCULUS, 158: "The origin of a son is to be made from another. The Word was not made but was."—MASTRICHT (II, xxvi, 16) discusses the question "whether Christ is the Son of God by eternal generation alone". This discussion was caused by the assertion of the *Socinians*, "that he himself is the Son of God, but by no means from eternal generation, but by his nativity of the B.V., since he was conceived in a clearly unusual way by the H. Spirit, who here played the part of the male and mingled some extraordinary substance with the female seed; also because there was imparted to him by grace a certain resemblance to God, since (*a*) he was sanctified by the Father and sent into the world Jn. 10. 34–36 (is it not written in your law, I said: Ye are gods? If he called them gods, unto whom the word of God came (and the Scripture cannot be broken), say ye of him, whom the Father sanctified and sent into the world, Thou blasphemest? because I said, I am the Son of God?); (*β*) by his rising from the dead as he was born Ac. 13. 32–33 (we bring you good tidings of the promise made unto the fathers, how that God hath fulfilled the same unto our children, in that He raised up Jesus: as also it is written in the second psalm, Thou art my son: this day have I begotten thee); (*γ*) by exaltation he was raised to God's right hand Heb. 1. 4–5 (having become by so much better than the angels, as he hath inherited a more excellent name than they. For to which of the angels hath he said at any time, Thou art my Son, this day have I begotten thee? and again, I will be to him a Father and he shall be to me a Son?)." As an orthodox reply to the question MASTRICHT frames this statement: "The Reformed insist that he is the Son of God solely by eternal generation, although this eternal *filiatio* was manifested in his sanctification and his being sent into the world, as well as in his resurrection and exaltation."

25.—The Son is also called the Word (1) as regards his person, because he is the perfect image of the Father that proceeded from the Spirit of God; and (2) on account of his office, because the Father does everything through him, and because he is the revelation of the Father.—POLAN (III, 5): "Λόγος is predicted both of the person and of the office: of the person, because it proceeded from the mind and is the image of the *Genitor*, expressing and displaying the *Genitor* entire in itself; just as our speech is the effigy or image of our entire thought and mind: of the office, however, Λόγος is predicated, both because by him all things were made, since it was he (Λόγος) who spoke and they were made, whatsoever things were made; and because he is the Father's interpreter to angels and men, disclosing God's will to both."—COCCEIUS (*Aphor. Ob.* VI, VII, 13): "The word Λόγος is the word of οἰκονομία but presupposing φύσις. Of course (1) it is the object of all God's language pertaining to life; (2) of it is the eternal promise by which all things are produced and sustained as the ῥῆμα δυνάμεως (the utterance of power); (3) of it it is λαλεῖν τὰ ῥήματα τοῦ θεοῦ Jn. 3. 34 (he whom God hath sent speaketh the words of God; for he giveth not the Spirit by measure); (4) he ἐξηγεῖται τὸν πατέρα Jn. 1. 18 (no man hath seen God at any time; the only begotten Son which is in the bosom of the Father, he hath declared Him) ὡς εἰκών."—KECKERMANN 65: "The Son is called the Λόγος of the Father, as being alike inward and outward. Inward, because the divine *intellectus* bent back upon itself from eternity begat His Son or Λόγος. Outward, because the Λόγος expounds and explains to the human race, and first of all to the elect sons of God, the decrees or counsels of his eternal Father. In order, of course, that we may know the Father, through His image.—He is called the Wisdom of the Father, both inward and outward; inward, because it is God's highest wisdom that He knows Himself, and by knowing Himself He begets the Son in the image of Himself;—outward wisdom he is called, because he instructs the sons of God in that inward wisdom of his Father and concerning the wisdom which for us leads to eternal salvation."

26.—The dispensation of the Son (*opera ad extra*) is redemption; wherefore all utterances of H. Scripture, in which God is expounded as revealing Himself for the salvation of the world, are to be connected with the Son.—HEIDEGGER IV, 69: "There remains the *oeconomia Filii* in regard to which, as creation is assigned to the Father as His peculiar work, so is redemption to the Son as his. As Christ is the second and middle *persona* of the H. Trinity, and is *a Patre*, and lives because of the Father who liveth, and hath received it of the Father to have life in himself; so he could and willed to become the μεσίτης, mediator, sponsor, priest, Ἰησοῦς our Saviour and Redeemer, to be sent into the world, to enter the flesh and as our גֹּאֵל to assume the seed of Abraham Heb. 2. 16 (not of angels doth he take hold, but he taketh hold of the seed of Abraham), to offer himself by the eternal Spirit to God the Father, to enter the holy place once for all by his own blood, to find an αἰωνία λύτρωσις Heb. 9. 12–14 (not through the blood of goats and calves, but through his own blood he entered in once for all into the holy place, having obtained an eternal redemption . . . the blood of Christ, who through the eternal spirit offered himself without blemish unto God, shall cleanse your conscience from dead works to serve the living God), to demand an outstanding inheritance for himself by right of his merit Ps. 2. 8 (ask me and I will give thee the nations for thine inheritance and the uttermost parts of the earth for thy possession), to become the king of his Church and judge of the world; one God, one mediator also between God and men, the man Jesus Christ 1 Tim. 2. 5. Therefore all the things said here and there in the Scriptures about Jehovah the God and Holy One of Israel, about Jehovah going to be or having become their God, of the goël, avenger and upholder of the people, of the ·Saviour and the sinner's righteousness, of the Rock or Ark of salvation, of the angel of Jehovah, of His countenance, of the covenant and testament, of the Redeemer, mediator, sponsor, priest, intercessor with the Father by virtue of merit, of the Reconciler, etc., should be ἰδιοποιεῖσθαι [appropriated] to the Son for οἰκονομία [dispensation] (passim as in OT Gen. 17. 8 (I will give unto thee, and to thy seed after thee, the land of thy sojournings, all the land of Canaan, for an everlasting possession and I will be their God) 48.16 (the angel which hath redeemed me from all evil, bless the lads; and let my name be named upon them, and all the name of my fathers Abraham and Isaac; and let them grow into a multitude on the face of the earth) Ex. 3. 2–4 (the angel of the Lord appeared unto him in a flame of fire—and Moses said, I will turn aside now—and when the Lord saw that he turned aside to see, God called unto him out of the midst of a bush . . .) Deut. 32. 35 (vengeance is mine and recompence . . . the day of their calamity is at hand . .) Ps. 82. 1 (God standeth in the congregation of God: he judgeth among the gods) Ps. 95. 1 (. . . let us make a joyful sound to the rock of our salvation) Is. 40. 5, 9 (. . . the glory of the Lord shall be revealed, and all flesh shall see it together. . . O thou that tellest good tidings to Zion (bis)), 41. 14 (. . . thy redeemer is the Holy One of Israel), 45. 21, 24, 25 (. . . who hath declared it of old? have not I, the Lord? and there is no God else beside me; a just God and a Saviour; there is none beside me. . . . Only in the Lord is righteousness and strength . . . all they that were incensed against him shall be ashamed. In the

Lord shall all the seed of Israel be justified . . .) 50. 1–6 ((the bill of your mother's divorcement) is my hand shortened that it cannot save? . . .) 63. 9 (. . . the angel of his presence saved them . . .) 64. 1 (O that thou wouldst rend the heavens and come down . . .) Jer. 23. 6 (In his days Judah shall be saved, and Israel shall dwell safely: and this is his name whereby he shall be called, The Lord is our righteousness) 33.16 (in those days shall Judah be saved . . . and this is the name whereby she shall be called, The Lord is our righteousness) Mal. 2. 2 (to give glory unto my name), etc., and in the NT)).

27.—"The H. Spirit is the third person of the Deity, proceeding from Father and Son by an eternal and single breathing" (POLAN III, 6).— ALSTED 142: "The voice of the Spirit—principally signifies God, and that either essentially concerning the essence of Father, Son and H. Spirit; or personally, concerning the third person. It is assigned to Him by a kind of reason of its own. In this third person is manifested the virtue, power and community of Father and Son, from which comes the capacity of all created things, as the power of sanctification is poured in. Therefore He is called *Spiritus* κατ᾽ ἐξοχήν, and *sanctus*, not by reason of an essential attribute (for in this way Father and Son are also holy) but because of His special operation."

28.—The H. Spirit is thus a personality. The arguments for the personality of the H. Spirit are given by RIISSEN (IV, xii, 1): "(1) Actual personal acts are ascribed to him Jn. 14. 16 (another Comforter, that he may be with you for ever, (17) even the Spirit of truth) 15. 26 (. . . the Comforter, whom I will send) 1 Cor. 2 [the *locus classicus* on the H. Spirit], Gen. 22 (Abraham's offering: v. 8 "God will provide himself the lamb for a burnt offering, my son"), 1 Cor. 12. 11 (all these gifts worketh the one and the same Spirit, dividing to each one severally even as he will) Rom. 7. 11. 8. 9 (the law, the commandment) Gen. 4. 10 (the voice of thy brother's blood crieth from the ground).—(2) He is other than Father and Son, being sent by both Jn. 14. 16 (I will pray the Father, and he will send you another Comforter, that he may be with you for ever) 15. 26 (when the Comforter is come, whom I will send you from the Father) 16. 27 (the Father himself loveth you, because ye have loved me, and have believed that I came forth from the Father [who sends the Comforter]). He is emphatically called the Paraclete, because that suggests a personal office. Emphatically, too, πνεῦμα is conjoined with the masculine pronoun Jn. 16. 13 (ὅταν ἔλθῃ ἐκεῖνος τὸ πνεῦμα τῆς ἀληθείας).—(3) He vies in equal power with Father and Son Mt. 28. 19, 2 Cor. 13. 13, 1 Jn. 5. 7.—(4) He appears under a visible species,

as at Christ's baptism and on the day of Pentecost.   But the assumption
of visible species belongs to persons, not to attributes or accidents.—(5)
There is sin against the H. Spirit.   Now he against whom we sin cannot
fail to be a divine person.—(6) He is distinguished from his gifts
I Cor. 12. 4 (diversities of gifts but the same Spirit), etc."

29.—The Spirit is also Deity.—The proofs of the divinity of the H. Spirit
are derived by RIISSEN (IV, 12, 2) from: "(1) the name of God attributed
to Him Ac. 5. 3 (to lie to the Holy Ghost); (2) from the attributes such
as (a) eternity: in the beginning of creation the Spirit was brooding on
the face of the waters Gen. 1. 2; (b) omnipresence: Ps. 139. 7 (whither
shall I go from thy spirit? or whither shall I flee from thy presence);
(c) omniscience: 1 Cor. 2. 10 (the Spirit searcheth all things, even the
deep things of God; (d) omnipotence, which is manifest from His works;
(3) The divine works as: (a) the creation of all things Ps. 33. 6 (by the
word of the Lord were the heavens made; and all the host of heaven by
the breath of His mouth) Job 26. 13 (by his Spirit the heavens are beauty);
(b) the preservation of all things Gen. 1. 2 (the Spirit of God moved upon
the face of the waters); (c) the mission and unction of Christ Is. 61. 1
(The Spirit of the Lord God is upon me; because the Lord hath anointed
me to preach good tidings unto the meek, etc.); (d) gifts of tongues and
miracles 1 Cor. 12. 4 (diversities of gifts); (4) divine honours: He must
be believed according to the Creed; baptism must be into Him Mt. 28. 19;
to Him prayers are to be directed Rev. 1. 4 (the benediction at the
opening)."

WOLLEB, p. 15: "These prove the deity of the H. Spirit:
I. The name, God. Acts 5. 3, 4 (. . . how is it that thou hast conceived this thing in thy heart? Thou hast not lied unto men but unto God).
II. The Attributes.—(1) Eternity Gen. 1. 2 (the Spirit of God moved
upon the face of the waters).—(2) Omnipresence Ps. 139. 7 (whither
shall I go from thy Spirit?).—(3) Omniscience 1 Cor. 2. 10 (the Spirit
searcheth all things, even the deep things of God).—(4) Omnipotence:
this is clear from His works.
III. The divine works.—(1) The Creation of all things Gen. 1. 2,
Ps. 33. 6 (By the word of the Lord were the heavens made and the host
of them by the breath of his mouth) Job. 26. 13 (By his Spirit the heavens
are beauty) 34. 14 (can gather up the spirit of man again).—(2) Preservation of all things Gen. 1. 2 (brooding).—(3) Mission and unction of Christ
Is. 61. 1 (The Spirit of the Lord God is upon me, etc.).—(4) Gifts of
tongues and miracles, 1 Cor. 12. 4 (diversity of gifts, but the same Spirit).
IV.—Divine honours.—(1) He is to be believed in according to the
Creed.—(2) Baptism is to be into His name Mt. 28. 19. To him prayers

are to be directed 1 Cor. 12. 13, Rev. 1. 4, where the seven spirits are mentioned in respect not of numbers but of gifts. Whence the early Church sings '*Tu septiformis munere*'."

30.—The Spirit is all these in the same way as the Father and the Son, but is distinguished from them (1) by being the third person; (2) as regards His *modus subsistendi*, by so proceeding from both that He thereby possesses the full essence of Father and Son as His own essence. The procession or *emanatio* of the H. Spirit is the mode of imparting the divine essence, by which the third person of the Deity as the Spirit receives from Him whose Spirit He is the same unimpaired essence as Father and Son have and hold.—SOHNIUS (*Op.* I, p. 89): "As to how the Son's nativity differs from the procession of the H. Spirit, i.e., what the property is and, as it were, the formal distinction between generation and procession, on account of which the second person only is and is called the Son and the third only the Spirit, the doctors of the Early Church *Augustine* and the *Damascene* and others admit their ignorance, since it has not been expressly defined in God's Word."—ALTING 18: " '*Ἐκπόρευσις* is distinguished from generation. But how, we don't know."

HEIDEGGER IV, 41: "Venturing to turn aside from the restraint of the ancients and the path of Scripture the *Scholastics* so defined the difference between generation and procession, that they assigned the former to *intellectus*, the latter to will and love. This is plainly ἄλογον. Since Father, Son and Holy Spirit have *intellectus* and will equally, it would follow that the Son is generated by His *intellectus*, the Spirit breathed by His *voluntas*."—It is discussed by RIISSEN in more detail (IV,14): "What the difference is between generation of the Son and the procession of the H. Spirit cannot be explained and it is safer not to know than to enquire into it. The *Scholastics* would look for the difference in the operation of *intellectus* and *voluntas*, so that the generation of the Son is brought about by means of *intellectus*, whence he is called the wisdom of God; but procession by means of *voluntas*, whence it is called love and charity. But as this is said without Scripture, it involves rather than explains matters. Those talk more sanely, who babbling in such a difficult matter find the distinction in three things. (1) In principle: because the Son emanates from the Father alone, but the H. Spirit from Father and Son at once. (2) In mode: because the Son emanates *per vim generationis*, which culminates not only in personality but also in likeness, on account of which the Son is called the image of the Father and according to which the Son receives the property of communicating the same essence to another person. But the Spirit does so by *spiratio*, which ends only in personality, and through which the person who proceeds does not receive the property of communicating that essence to another. (3) In order: because, as the Son is the second person, but the H. Spirit the third, generation by our way of thinking, precedes *spiratio*, although really they are co-eternal."

31.—The H. Spirit thus proceeds from the Father and the Son "by one and the same breathing" and "in equal measure from both".—RIISSEN IV, 13: "Query, whether the Holy Spirit proceeds from Father and Son? Answer, This was formerly a famous controversy between the GREEKS and the LATINS. The GREEKS laid it down, that He proceeded from the Father alone: the LATINS from the Father and the Son. At last in the *Council* of *Florence* 1439 a modification (*temperamentum*) was sought, that it be laid down that the H. Spirit proceeds from the Father through the Son. But although the Greeks should not be indicted for heresy on account of their view, nor should it have been the occasion of a schism, yet the Latins' view is better retained, both because the H. Spirit is sent by the Son Jn. 16. 7 (. . . if I go I will send the Comforter to you), and because He is also called the Spirit of the Son Gal. 4. 6 (God sent forth the Spirit of the Son into our hearts, crying, Father), and because, whatever He has, He has it from the Son Jn. 16. 13–14 (he shall take of mine and shall declare it unto you), and because Christ breathed the H. Spirit upon the disciples Jn. 20. 22."

From this it is clear that Reformed dogmatics does not precisely reject the Greeks' doctrine of the outpouring of the H. Spirit as heterodoxy. The other dogmaticians express themselves in a way similar to RIISSEN'S, e.g., the LEIDEN SYNOPSIS, IX, 19: "To moderate and compose the controversy, some said not unsuitably, according to the expression of the ancients, that the Father breathes the H. Spirit through (*per*) the Son, and the H. Spirit proceeds from the Father through the Son. By this way of speaking it is signified that He derives from both. And the manner of subsistence is further signified, namely, that in a mediate and subordinate way He proceeds from the Father through the Son; whereby also the breathing and procession of the H. Spirit is not removed from the one principle of the Greeks, which is also the personal one of the Father, because of the antecession of origin and order in the Father. And the relation and subordination of the Spirit to the Son is stabilised Jn. 15. 26 (when the Comforter is come, whom I will send unto you from the Father. . . .) 16. 14 (He shall glorify me: for he shall take of mine and shall declare it unto you. All things whatsoever the Father hath are mine: therefore said I, that he taketh of mine, and shall declare it unto you)."

32.—The Holy Spirit proceeds not "by will" but by nature or the necessity of nature, not "through or by the act of the Father's and Son's will", but "according to an act of will" or "through the mode of will"; not "of essence as of material" but "from the person of Father and of Son in unity of essence", not "by accident" but "substantially". The *processio* is just an internal one, in the essence of God.—LEIDEN SYNOPSIS IX, 10: "The word procession is not to be taken as an emanation of virtue and efficacy from God, as God's works proceed from the Worker; nor as an inward and immanent action in God's essence, which yet tends to an object outside God (as the decrees are God's and proceed from God): but according to God's *actio ad intra* (as the schools say), i.e., whereby God acts in His essence, as that bent back upon Himself He sets up a real relation in the fellowship of the divine essence."

33.—The *processio* is relatable to the same thing, and is an eternal one, and not to be confused with the *missio* of the H. Spirit, by which the Father and the Son are active in the world (POLAN III, 2).—CALVIN (I, xiii, 14): "What the Scriptures attribute to the H. Spirit is far removed from the creatures, and we ourselves learn it in the experience of piety [godliness]. It is He who everywhere diffused upholds, stimulates and quickens them in heaven and on earth. He is already ruled out of the number of creatures by the very fact that He is not to be confined by any limits. But by the transfusion of His own vigour into everything to breathe life and nature into them is clearly divine.—Scripture teaches in many passages that by His own energy He is the author of regeneration."—BEZA (1, 6): "The infinite power and efficacy of the H. Spirit was unfolded in the creation and preservation of all creatures right from the beginning of the world. In this particular treatment it will be primarily assessed by us from the things He has effected in the sons of God, whose gifts He of course brings with Him, in order to make them participators in them; and, to be brief, to bring them by degrees to the end for which they were destined before the foundations of the world were laid."

CHAPTER VII

THE DECREES OF GOD

1.—Since God is purely life (*actus purissimus*) He cannot be thought of apart from an activity immanent in and essential to Him, which is the pure cause of His activity in creation.—At this point the dogmaticians link up with what has already been said regarding the *opera Dei*. POLAN first of all divides God's works into *opera personalia* and *essentialia*. The former are "those which belong to the separate persons of the Deity, each person acting by its own personality, or according to the nature of its person as its formal principle". The latter are once more "either *opera Dei simpliciter personalia,* which one person of the Deity in the divine essence effects upon a second according to the relation existing between themselves, without the intervention of any foreign go-between". Consequently they are also called "*opera relationis* (the Father begets the Son, the Son is begotten and with the Father breathes the H. Spirit, etc.), or *opera certo modo personalia,* which are brought to a common end, it is true, and in which the principle of action is the divine strength common to all the persons, but yet are done principally by one person of the Deity according to the special dispensation competent for it alone." These latter are the economic works of the individual persons of the Trinity (POLAN IV, 2).—The *opera Dei essentialia* are those "which proceed from the divine essence common to Father, Son and H. Spirit, and cease in the creature" (POLAN IV, 3).

The other dogmaticians similarly, e.g., WOLLEB, pp. 16–17: "The works of God are essential or personal. Essential works are those common to the whole sacrosanct Trinity. Personal works are those peculiar to the individual *personae*. Both essential and personal works are *ad intra* or else *ad extra*. An *opus Dei ad intra* is one which is not referred to a goal outwith God; such as the *intellectio* with which God *intelligit* Himself, the begetting of the Son, the production of the H. Spirit. An *opus Dei ad extra* is one which is referred to a goal outwith the most H. Trinity; such are predestination, creation and the like, which have to do with creatures, a goal as it were outwith God."—Hereupon these statements follow: I. "One and the same *opus ad extra* is in a different respect personal and essential. In this way Christ's incarnation is in its inception an essential work common to the whole sacrosanct Trinity; but in its goal it is a personal work of the Son alone. Although the Father also, and the H. Spirit, is each the cause of Christ's incarnation, yet the Son alone is incarnate. In this way although creation, redemption and sanctification are essential works of the entire sacrosanct Trinity, yet in another sense they are called personal. For the Father is called the Creator, because He is the Source or *fons* alike of that operation and of the sacrosanct Trinity; and the Son and the H. Spirit act *a Patre*. The Son is called the Redeemer, because by the assumption of human nature he carried out the work of redemption. The H. Spirit is called the Sanctifier, because He is sent by Christ to comfort and to sanctify. II. *Opera ad extra sunt indivisa seu omnibus personis communia*: this axiom follows the preceding one; since essence is common to all the *personae*, so too are the *opera essentialia*. III. Nevertheless each remains a single work, in its essential origin, in the act of being effected and in the actual effect. The *opera ad extra* are ἐμμένοντα, immanent or inward, or else μεταβαίνοντα, transeunt and external. The first class are works performed within the essence of God; and to this class belong the decrees of God."

Next the works of God are divided into inward and outward. The former are those "which in their very essence are due to God's inward and external *actus*". And these inward works are either "personal" or "essential." "*The inward personal works of God* are divine acts which do not belong to the deliberative will but to the nature of deity according to the attributes of each person" (e.g., the Father's work is the begetting of the Son). "By *inward* essential *works of God* are meant those of the deliberative will, the inward *actus* of the divine wisdom and most free will, i.e., *God's eternal counsel and decree*" (POLAN IV, 4–6).

Biblically the concept of the *consilium Dei* is based on Eph. 1. 11 (who does all things according to the counsel of his will). Relating the dispute between *J. L. Vives* and *J. C. Scaliger* over the question, "whether it is godly to ascribe *consilium* to God," POLAN (IV, 6) decides thus: "*John Ludovic Vives*, a man of great parts and judgment, says that God's providence is His will governing all things by His counsel. *Julius Caesar Scaliger* on the other hand says (*De subtilitate ad Cardanum, exercitatione* 365, *sectione* 8) "God has no need of counsel as a means or idea or instrument for governing. A voice in the divine counsels is as godless as plurality in the Deity. God does not dispute or reason or propound or infer; He does not confer with another or receive from anyone." But, as I shall say with all deference to *Scaliger*, *Vives* does not attribute counsel to God in the sense in which we usually attribute it to men, but in that in which Scripture itself attributes it to God, Ps. 33. 11 (The counsel of the Lord standeth fast for ever) Is. 46. 10–11 (declaring the end from the beginning, and from ancient times things that are not yet done, saying: My counsel shall stand, and I will do all my pleasure . . . I have spoken, I will also bring it to pass; I have purposed, I will also do it), Ac. 2. 23 (him, being delivered up by the determinate counsel and foreknowledge of God, etc.) 4. 28 (to do whatsoever thy hand and thy counsel foreordained to come to pass) 13. 36 (after David had in his own generation served the counsel of God) Eph. 1. 11 (who executeth all things according to the counsel of his will) Heb. 6. 17 (God being minded to show more abundantly unto the heirs of the promise the immutability of his counsel . . .). In these and other passages *consilium* is attributed to God, but apart from all reasoning or consultation."

2.—This immanent, essential activity of God is the eternal, unalterable counsel [=decision] of His will. "The eternal counsel of God is the essential inward work of God, the judgment so to speak of the divine mind and wisdom upon all matters, the doing of which He willed for a good end" (POLAN IV, 6).—COCCEIUS, in the *S.T.*, *Loc.* V. xiv, 3, 4, *De consilio Dei in genere,* starts from the concept of the possible: "That is possible [sc. for God], which can be for the glory of God.—Moreover that is to God's glory, which attests God's perfection and obscures no perfection or virtue of God." God's absolute omnipotence can therefore only be displayed in such wise that its effects are determined by the holy character of the divine nature. Hence we must not say with the *Scholastics*, that "by His absolute power God can do everything that can be thought of by men, as though the ordinance of power, as they say, came from the decree alone and did not depend on sense of fitness and wisdom". 8: Meantime, in order that "transition may be made from possibility to existing thing", it is necessary that "God's will also intervene". 10: "So Scripture attributes to God Eph. 1. 11 a "counsel of His will". That is, God's will is referred back to a "counsel", "because in the things which God's hand has ordained, reason, beauty and wisdom are recognised". 14: This *consilium* is "one; prior and subsequent thoughts do not 'fall into' God". 15: On the contrary, we must insist that God "from eternity knows in Himself, what He could and what it becomes Him to do and to emit and also to let be done under His dispensation." 17: So too the rules of human cleverness should not be applied without more ado to God's decree. In the sphere of human action the rule of course holds, that "what is last in execution is first in intention". With men volition of one thing is the cause of the volition of a second thing." On the other hand, "in things which God wills, the order of ends and means, causes and effects, antecedent occasions and consequent κατορθίοματα is seen. At the same time neither is anything the cause of the divine volition, nor one volition the cause of a second volition." 19: Of course God's works possess "such beauty, that single things in themselves befit God and show God's strength, above all in their time and in their order, according as either cause has preceded effect or means the appointed end or occasion a κατόρθωμα; in a word, in a whole series that which

is last most shows forth God's glory as compared with all that went before
it." 20–21: "If therefore we also allow the rule of human foresight to
be ἀνθρωποφαδῶς adjusted *in this sense,* namely, that the last in
being done is the first in intention", we must not therefore conclude
"that every consequence is so related to what precedes, that obviously
the latter are caused by the former, and that the former are therefore more
desirable then the latter".

Since then all that happens happens necessarily, but likewise only in
virtue of the divine counsel, and since all God's works are designed to
proclaim God's glory, God had for this purpose to make intelligent beings.
Unconscious creatures cannot see or praise God's glory, and on the other
hand God had no need to see works of His omnipotence and to delight
in them. "Wherefore we conclude that it befitted God's wisdom, if He
wished to create or produce anything outside Himself, not to produce
only bodies in which there can be no recognition, but also (1) to make
mind (26),—and not just mind, to contemplate the rest of His works
but also (2) in some way to use them, or to perceive some usefulness in
them from the things created" (27). Since then God exercises "all government glorious to Himself" over the conscious as over the unconscious
creation, God has of course made and arranged everything in full freedom; yet in it all, in order to reveal precisely His glory; God has observed
a *necessitas ex hypothesi,* since God is aware "what it becomes Him to do
at any time or on any occasion" (29–30).

3.—From the concept of the divine counsel (εὐδοκία, *decretum, beneplacitum, voluntas, etc.,* Is. 46. 10, Eph. 1. 11, Ac. 2. 23, 4. 28 (see p. 134)
Jer. 30. 14, [≡forsakenness] 29, 11 [≡acceptability] Ps. 2. 7, 8 (I will
tell of the decree)) are naturally to be excluded the creaturely imperfections of *inscitia, dubitatio* and *sapientia aliunde accepta* [wisdom derived
from another source], in short, everything associated with the eventuation
of a human counsel (MARCK VI, 2).—BRAUN (I, ii, 9, 3): "In every
decree of men these three things are required: (1) an idea or concept
of the thing in the mind; (2) a will approving or disapproving; (3) the
end and aim proposed. These things necessarily posit some dependence
and imperfection in us; we cannot have the idea of a thing, unless the
thing first exists outside our mind, wherefore our mind is affected by the
thing which presents itself extrinsically; so also with our will. Strictly
speaking, therefore, these three things cannot be attributed to God. Still
according to our way of conceiving, the idea or concept of God may be
called His supreme wisdom; the will approving or disapproving, and
its goal the most actual will of God."—HEIDAN, p. 209: "God does
nothing in time, which He has not decreed to do from eternity.

Otherwise—He would have been borrowing counsel and manifold under-standing from things themselves, or at least taking occasion from what was offered to think of many things."

4.—The expression therefore of God's counsel, the decree of it, is to be distinguished only conceptually from the counsel, as from the nature of God Himself; it is not different essentially.—PICTET (III, i, 7): "It is to be observed that when we are considering the actual act of the divine will in the decree, we are not distinguishing the decree from the actual essence of God. The will of God and God Himself are the same thing, and there is nothing in God which is not God Himself."—WOLLEB (p. 18): "The decree is truly the veriest will of God. But for the sake of teaching the will is held to be the efficient cause and the decree to be its effect."—BRAUN (I, ii, 9, 4): "Since the will of God is His actual essence, it follows that His counsels and decrees must not be distinguished from His essence except to suit our methods of conception".—These statements are upheld against the *Socinians*, who asserted "that God's decrees differ from God *realiter*" and "that not all (decrees) are eternal, but certain ones are temporal". *Cf.* RIISSEN (V. 8).—COCCEIUS rejects the question raised as an unprofitable one, noting (*S.T.* XIV, 56) that: "it is superfluous to ask in what respect God's decrees differ from His essence. We are content with what John says (1 Jn. 4. 8) that God is love. We know nothing about God previously or more distinctly than that holy and good will, by which He wills to be glorified in the intelligent creation." At the same time COCCEIUS naturally asserts the essential eternity of the decrees (*Loc.* V. *De consilio Dei in genere*, Ch. XIV, 40): "If any fresh will exists in God, it exists in time. Therefore God's will will be subject to time; therefore God Himself will be temporal, not eternal."

5.—"The decree of God is the act of God, by which from eternity, according to His utterly free will, He has by an unchangeable counsel and purpose specified and resolved on the things that were to come into being outwith Himself in time, together with their causes, operations and circumstances and the manner in which they are bound to be made and to exist, for proof of His glory" (HEIDEGGER V, 4). Or more briefly: "The decree of God is the inward act of the divine will, by which from eternity He has most freely and most surely decreed concerning the things which had to be made in time " (WOLLEB 17).—Other definitions: v. TIL (4, *De decret. Dei*, p. 61): "God's decree is our name for God's eternal and immutable purpose to manifest His glory in things possible; concerning which, according to His infinite wisdom and most free εὐδοκία, He has determined both what He wished to be done or not to be done

in time, both in setting up natures and also in appointing their futurition".
—PICTET (III, i, 2): "By the decree we understand the firm and unchangeable purpose in God's mind concerning what He was to make
in time or to allow".—HOTTINGER, p. 73: "The decree is God's inward
action or His eternal counsel anent things to come into being outwith
Himself, which things He foreknows with an infallibility equal to the
immutability with which He has predetermined them."

6.—Since then the divine decree is the being and will of God Himself,
it is unconditioned by anything else and is absolute, eternal and unchangeable. For that very reason it is also absolutely determinative of all
that achieves reality, including its conditions, and is thereby the first
cause of things.—BRAUN (I, ii, 9, 6): "Since God's decree is His will and
His decreeing His most actual willing, it follows that His decrees can
have no cause and that God cannot be so moved by anything as to will
this or that".—RIISSEN (V, 8): "God's decrees are called absolute (1) so
far as they are definite and fixed *sententiae*, not the longings of a mind in
suspense, nor ones not yet clearly defined; (2) so far as they do not depend
on any previous condition; (3) so far as God does not will to hinder them
or cut them out". From this it follows that: "all the decrees are absolutely
and simply eternal" and that they (V, 4) are attributed to God, not
by way of Him finding out, but of surely fixing, the eventuation of things,
according to which He does nothing rashly but acts deliberately, i.e.,
knowingly and willingly." The divine decrees are thus essentially "(1)
free, (2) eternal, (3) absolute, (4) immutable, (5) the first cause of things."
—We should note the remark of BRAUN: (I, ii, 9, 11): "Although God
may decree certain things on some fixed condition, e.g., Peter's salvation on condition of his belief, yet only the thing decreed is conditioned,
not the decree itself; He decreed absolutely to give Peter salvation
and its condition, faith and perseverance in faith".—RIISSEN clears up
the question in more detail (V, 8): "In this *locus* it is not a question
of the decree being absolute, or conditioned *a posteriori* and *logically,*
or *in respect of the things decreed* and *the objects willed* outside God. The
question is not whether there are such decrees as either possess or involve
no condition or means in their execution (for in this sense we do not
deny that various decrees may be termed conditioned, although the
expression is less proper); we are dealing with the decree conditioned
a priori and *antecedently, on the side of the decree itself,* and the question
is whether there are any such decrees, as are suspended by some potential
condition outwith God and of uncertain issue; or whether they are
absolute, depending upon His good pleasure alone. This is proved"
[Anti-Arminian].—HOTTINGER, 79: "The decree may be described as

absolute and conditioned, if conditioned be taken to mean that which is absolved of all means, which has no means subordinate to itself"; on the other hand the distinction is false, "if conditioned means that it depends on some condition of things to come, which is outside God".

7.—The decree is not an accident of the divine nature.—BRAUN (I, ii, 9, 4): "Hence also it follows that the decrees do not inhere in God in the manner of an accident and inherently, changing hourly, as the *Socinians*, *Vorstius* and the *Arminians* madly suggest, but more perfectly, by attribution and denomination, like God's attributes, which do not differ in reality from His essence. Things decreed, then, posit nothing in God save outward denomination, which imports no change in His actual nature."—RIISSEN V, 5: "*Socinus* and *Vorstius* will have it that the decrees exist in God inherently and accidentally, in order to overturn God's *simplicitas* (singleness) and to prove that there is real composition present in Him. We prove that there cannot be accidents given in God in such a way that, etc."—HOTTINGER, p. 74: "Decrees are in God not as accidents in a subject, but as acts of will with a tendency to externalisation (*cum schesi ad extra*)"

8.—Nor yet is the decree a world of ideas present in God in Plato's sense, nor yet the will of God in and for itself, but an activity or tendency of the divine will corresponding to the nature of God, to do in the course of time what can and ought to serve the revelation of God's glory.— MARCK VI, 5: "As to the general nature of the decrees we must hold (1) that they are not, as the *Socinians* would have it according to *Vorstius*, accidents really distinct from the essence, because of its utter singleness and unchangeable perfection;—(2) that they are not ideas of things, things existing from eternity outwith the divine essence, as in the Platonic ideas;—(3) that they are not the actual divine will in itself, considered formally, absolutely and abstractly, since from this no *res* could follow;— (4) but that they are the acts of the divine will, as it tends towards the future existence in time of things known from their ideas, and towards their just limits, or towards the actual will tending in this direction".

9.—It follows that in the decree of God three distinctions are to be observed: (1) the *actus decernens*, which is the divine nature of God Himself; (2) the "tendency and relation to the object to be secured in time", in which the difference is brought out between the *decretum* and the *essentia* of God; and (3) the *res decreta* which is distinguished from God *realiter*. As regards the first point the decree is *unicum*, *simplicissimum*, *necessarium* and *aeternum*, so that there is neither *prius* nor *posterius*.—

BRAUN (I, ii, 9, 5): "Although God's decrees do not differ *realiter* from His own will and so from His essence, nevertheless, since we can scarcely conceive them otherwise than in a human fashion, we usually contemplate in God (1) the act of the will, through the mode of vital action, namely, knowledge and volition, but while they are God's actual essence (God knows and wills everything through His essence), we note the knowledge and will as being still indifferent towards the creatures; (2) the tendency and relation out towards the creatures, which in respect of God is nothing but a new extrinsic denomination, positing nothing *in re* and so asserting no new perfection or change in God; (3) the thing actually decreed, as it were the object of God's decree. In the former way the decree of God was considered necessary, since knowledge and will are essential and so of course are the actual essence. In the second way it is free, since God might by the same will and the same decree not have decreed the thing or have decreed it otherwise."

WOLLEB, p. 19: "In itself God's decree is *unicum et simplicissimum,* nor is any *prius* or *posterius* to be found in it. But as regards the things decreed the distinction is that God is said to have decreed their eventuation in the order in which they do eventuate."

As regards its tendency it is free and manifold comparable to a circle which has one centre, to which all its countless radii point (MASTRICHT III, i, 15).

10.—This *res decreta* cannot be described as the object of the divine decree in the strict sense of the term. Since it is first determined by the divine decree what abstract possibilities are to become real in time, by it also the objects of the divine activity are first called into existence. At the same time, in the improper sense of the word, everything is described as the object of the divine decree, which God has resolved to do in conformity with His holiness; i.e., (1) anything possible at all which may really hold a purpose of good or of glorifying God in time, and (2) anything of the possible, which God really means to let happen, to do or to permit. In all this the divine decree is not just a purely efficient cause but also a prototype; not in the sense that the idea of the world and of what happens in the world is present independently of the divine will in God, but in such a way that from eternity it exists potentially in the knowledge and will of God.

HEIDEGGER (V, 12): "There is no object of the divine decree existing outwith God. It is however improper to give the name of object to what He has decreed to do, i.e., has wisely known that He could do for the glory of His name and accordingly resolved from eternity to do and produce in time. And that means all that He has hitherto done or permitted to be done and in due course all that He is about to do or allow to be done. As regards all these, so far as they contain any measure of entity, the decree of God imports the notion of a twofold cause, efficient and exemplary. Efficient, because everything done or about to be done is done or about to be done, because God so decreed. No other higher, prior or superior cause of His works can be given (Gen. 45. 8 so it was not you that sent me (Joseph) hither, but God . . .; 50. 20 Ye meant evil against me; but God meant it for good, to bring to pass, as it is this day, to save much people alive; Ps. 115. 3 our God . . . hath done whatsoever he pleased; Is. 14. 24 The Lord of hosts hath sworn, saying, Surely as I have thought, so shall it come to pass; and as I have purposed so shall it stand; Mt. 11. 25–26 . . . thou didst hide these things from the wise and understanding and didst reveal them unto babes . . . so it was well-pleasing in thy sight; Ac. 2. 23 . . . delivered up by the determinate counsel and foreknowledge of God; Rom. 9. 18 (he hath mercy on whom he will, and whom he will he hardeneth). Exemplary, because the decree of God not only supposes in God's mind the idea of all the perfections He can produce: which idea is God's actual essence not as known (as the *Scholastics* insist, feigning in God's Trinity a mirror or images of all things which they behold, as often as they behold God in heaven) but as knowing and willing; but also God's actual decree is the παράδειγμα or idea of all works outwith Himself, in accordance with which as ἀρχέτυπος they are actually expressed in time as ἔκτυπα."

POLAN (IV, 6): "Whence all things which become in time are said to have been in God from eternity; not by their own real essence, not by formal substance, but by knowledge and decree; not through a formal *esse* but through the virtual *esse*".—HOTTINGER, p. 76: "Because as regards the object, which is not τὰ δυνατά, things possible *simpliciter*, but τὰ μέλλοντα, the things about to be, the decree is of the nature both of an efficient and of an exemplary cause: of the former, because things past or future are past or future, because God has decreed it; of the latter, because God's decree is the sort of idea of all works outside Himself, in accordance with which as archetype the remainder are expressed as ectypes".

RIISSEN (V. 7): "God's decree is as it were the idea of all things outside Himself, in accordance with which as archetype the actual ἔκτυπα, as it were, are expressed in time."—At this point as a rule the dogmaticians discuss the question (RIISSEN V, 10, 1), "whether by His decree God has appointed for each man a certain, fixed term to life". This was denied by the *Remonstrants* and *Socinians*. To this question VOETIUS devoted an express writing, *Dissertatio epistolica de termino vitae,* in which

he emphasises the following pair of parallel statements: (1) (p. 92):
"If the absolute decree meant a decree excluding or cutting out means,
because precisely and absolutely, without any foreordination of means and
circumstances, it decreed the bare end and finished up in that alone, the
(*Arminian*) conclusion would be true. But such an absolute never occurs
to us or to any Christian ever, even in a dream. We neither imagine that
God only decrees that the Son die, but that he die here and now and thus.
Since means and end are equally fixed and sure in God's predetermination, how is it left uncertain and how can it be present or absent in the
execution?" And (2) (p. 129): "God's decree, by which the term of
human life is predestined, is not the cause of all the evils that intervene,
if a man by excess break off his own life αὐτοχειρία".—The dogmaticians unanimously answer the question, so that as regards a second
cause the answer is no, as regards the first cause it is yes. E.g., RIJSSEN
[no reference]: "The question is not as to the end of life in respect of
second causes; we admit that it may be contracted or lengthened by
good or bad ordering: it has regard to the first cause, and to the divine
decree and divine ordination.   Likewise the question is not whether each
man's life and death are decreed absolutely without any respect to
necessary means, so that whatever men have done or not done, what
God has decreed will assuredly be the upshot. This none of us asserts.
We recognise that the term is so fixed that we may not exclude the necessity of means. But the question is whether by God's decree the term
of each man's life is so constituted in fixity and immobility along with its
circumstances, that he cannot die at another moment of time or by
another kind of death than that by which he happens to die. Which
we affirm."

11.—Hence what we have to regard as the object of the divine decree
is not the abstract order of the physical, moral and saving dispensation
in the abstract which is present in the world and in God's kingdom of
grace, but the concrete existence and life of the world and of individual
men with their complex of causes and effects.

HEIDEGGER (V, 13): "This being so there can in no wise be attributed
to God an indefinite and general decree, not concerned with the persons
included in the genus but with the qualities of the persons, and these
not as existing or seen in persons but as possible: as though God had
decreed to save believers but has decreed nothing about the faith and
salvation of Peter, Paul, etc. In this way the chief part would be withdrawn from God's decree and God would exist in a manner in His own
right and unto Himself."—BEZA (*Op.* I, p. 171): "The ways of God
omnipotent are past searching out. Without His eternal and changeless

decree nothing is done anywhere by anyone either universally or specially, not even excepting those things which are evil and accordingly detestable; although not as decreed by an ever good and righteous God but as happening through Satan and other evil instruments."

12.—"The decree of God is the effectual *principium* of all things without exception and of their order" (POLAN IV, 6). God's decree is sheerly the efficient cause of everything good, the effectually permissive cause of evil. For it is God who effects that which in a sinful act bears the stamp of a real *res*, namely the substance of the act, in order even thereby to reveal His glory. The really bad in it, which has not true being at all, He merely permits.—POLAN makes an adequate distinction (IV, 6): "So far as (*malum culpae*) is sin, i.e., an aberration from divine law, God decreed it by a permissive but not by an efficient decree. So far as it achieves a substance or action in which sin inheres (i.e., attains to the government and ordering of sin) then both as to principle and as to upshot and consummation that (substance or action) was decreed by an efficient decree.—When we say that all things are effects of God's eternal decree, we mean both substances, and created accidents, and their results good and bad; but we exclude sin because it is not a *res*."—WOLLEB (p. 18–19): "III. Even the things that are counter to God's will do not take place apart from His will.—Many things may take place counter to the *voluntas signi*, which are yet conform to the *voluntas beneplaciti*. By will of sign God did not will man's fall, indeed He most severely forbade it: yet He willed and decreed it by the will of His good pleasure, according as it was a means of revealing His glory".—IV. Thus by God's decree and will things good and bad take place; the former by efficient, the latter by permissive decree.—V. Yet God's decree or will is not the cause of any evil or sin, although whatever God has decreed necessarily happens.— For since evil things were decreed by a will efficient but not permissive, God's decree is not the cause of evil. So God's will is not the cause of evil, because God's decrees are ἀμεταμέλητα and inevitable; they do not occur by necessity of compulsion but only by the necessity of immutability."

RIISSEN V, 10: "By no means did (God) also decree to effect all He decreed to enjoin; in that case countless decrees would be void every day. And since He enjoins upon all men holiness and the fulfilment of the law, He would have decreed to save all by the law. But He only decrees to effect the things which are done, whether they are moral or natural goods."—BEZA (*De praedestin. Op.* III, p. 407): "Although what God ordains to be is always good, He is said to will the good, not to will the evil. Consequently, if with some we infer that no will of God intervenes in things which are done evilly but His bare foreknowledge, not only will everything fall to the ground which we said about Adam's fall and the eternal decree of both damnation and the reasons for which damnation ensues. But we should also have the most absurd and false conclusion, that demons and all men according to their badness are exempted to a great extent from God's sway; i.e., so far as He does not hinder their actions but only puts certain limits to them. Hence the distinction between the decreeing will and permission, which it is not difficult to prove to be ill understood of some. Of course, if rightly explained, we do anything but reject it; indeed we assert that it must be retained."— Expressions of reproach at the distinction between *voluntas decernens and permittens* are to be found now and again in Reformed dogmaticians, but are usually connected merely with the conception of this distinction usual in *Lutheran* theology, *e.g.,* in DANÄUS (*Christ. isag.,* pp. 54–55; see p. 145).

13.—Since therefore all evil takes place *contra voluntatem mandantem* (counter to the enjoining will), but absolutely nothing *praeter voluntatem efficientem* and *efficaciter permittentem* (outwith the efficient and effectually permissive will) of God, everything that takes place is necessitated by God, not *necessitate coactionis* but *necessitate hypothetica* and *consequentiae.* Everything ensues as ordered on the *hypothesis decreti divini,* so that the divine decree abolishes neither the freedom of personal creatures (who always do self-determinedly what God determined should be done), nor, as regards *causa secunda,* the contingency of things (which latter ceases to be contingency solely in relation to the divine counsel).

WOLLEB 19: "The necessity of God's decrees does not do away with freedom in rational creatures";—reason : "because it is not a necessity of compulsion but one of immutability. As regards the divine decree Adam's fall took place of necessity. Yet meanwhile Adam sinned freely, being neither ordered nor forced nor impelled by God, having in fact been most severely admonished not to sin. Nor does it (the necessity of the decrees) do away with contingency in second causes. Many things are contingent as regards second causes, which occur necessarily as regards God's counsel."—BEZA (*Op.* I. p. 1-2): "Nothing happens anyhow or without God's most righteous decree, although God is not the author of or sharer in any sin at all. Both His power and His goodness are so great and so incomprehensible, that at a time when He applies the devil or wicked men in achieving some work, whom He afterwards justly punishes, He Himself none the less effects His holy work well and justly.— These things do not hinder but rather establish second and intermediate causes, by which all things happen. When from eternity God decreed whatever was to happen at definite moments, He at the same time also decreed the manner and way which He wished it thus to take place; to such extent, that even if some flaw is discovered in a second cause, it yet implies no flaw or fault in God's eternal counsel."—BEZA (*Op.* III, p. 408): "We must therefore know that as God, as the first and supreme Mover, determined one and all what things were to happen with that most wise and excellent will of His, He also created of more than one kind the mediate causes, by means of which He determined the occurrence of the things which He resolved upon. Thus it is necessary to place the beginning and true efficient cause of human actions, so far as they are human, in the actual will of men, so far of course as men act spontaneously and of their own motion. But so far as they execute their work by their own inner strength, so that God does through them what He has determined, this work is to be regarded as not human but divine, the beginning of which is the general will of God in question; so that it is a twofold work that looked like a single one, and each of them is to be measured by the diverse nature of the *principium*."

DANAEUS (*Christ. Isag.* 54): "The second condition and quality of God's providence is, that it imposes inevitable necessity upon things, but not, however, force or compulsion. For things which occur by God's providence are ordained by His will and decree, and accordingly happen by necessity. For God's will is unchangeable, nor can it be hindered in any way. But this necessity differs from force and compulsion, as we already warned you. (55): Although whatever happens to us happens necessarily, since it happens by God's providence, the things we do are not done by us against our will and consent. So although whatever we do we do it necessarily according as God's providence has decreed it to be done, yet we do not therefore do them under compulsion and against our will and consent, so far as regards the principles of the action in us. They are also *our* actions. We eat and drink of necessity but not unwillingly, because by the inward movement of our minds we choose it so to happen to us. But though this necessity is inevitable, so far as it is held to depend on and to have been constituted by God's providence; yet so far as this same necessity is in our wills, as viewed in that *principium* of action which we have within us, it is a spontaneous act. Consequently, away with the sophistic distinction usually foisted by them between God's permission and His decree or will. Since whatever is done by God's permission is also done by His will, it is likewise done by His decree also."

14.—A distinction is to be made between "God's general decree (the decree of creation and providence, i.e. the eternal *praefinitio* of the things to be created, preserved and governed in time)" and "God's special decree (the decree of predestination)" i.e. "God's counsel concerning the salvation or damnation of intelligent creatures" (HEIDEGGER V, 19, 20). This distinction is based not on the decree in and for itself, which essentially is but one, but solely upon man's conception of it. Nevertheless it merits as careful consideration as the *ordo decretorum Dei*.—HEIDEGGER V 14: "But although God's decree is *unicum* by reason of its *principium*, yet for our mode of conceiving even it has different parts as it were, one of which God deemed it not suitable to Himself to decree without the second: and it has its τάξις καὶ σύνταξις of the *res decreta* depending on the same decree, just as one act of vision perceives at once many objects mutually distinct in order".—WOLLEB, 20: "God's decree about creatures is general or special. It is the general decree by which He has resolved to declare the glory of His power, wisdom and goodness in the creation and preservation of all things. The special decree has been called predestination. In it He resolved to manifest the glory of His grace, mercy and righteousness in electing or reprobating rational creatures."

15.—The order of the decrees ought not in any sense to be a speculative construction, but must be derived purely from Scripture. According to it the following is the fixed *ordo rerum creatarum*: "(1) God decreed to manifest His glory abroad in all its multifariousness and not for His own but for creation's good, so that all things might respond to His wise counsel as to their end, the praise of His Name; (2) He decreed to create the world, and in it both minds to know, love and celebrate His glory and exceeding excellency and to perceive some advantage in the rest of His works; and bodies acknowledged by minds to proclaim His glory profoundly by their order, usefulness and beauty; (3) God resolved to preserve and govern the world created and the things in it and to expose the changeable men created to temptation and fall, whereby along with their entire posterity they would rush headlong into sin and destruction; (4) God decreed of the fallen already involved in their destruction to select some in Christ, in time to call, justify and glorify them with the glory of His gracious mercy; others to abandon to their sins and to damn eternally to the praise of His righteousness" (HEIDEGGER V, 16).

In this sense the *ordo salutis* is expounded by the prevailing Church doctrine in the infralapsarian sense. The contrast between the supralapsarian and the sublapsarian basis is clearly and skilfully set forth by RIISSEN VI, 20, 23: "Although in the decrees regarded formally and *a parte Dei* no order can properly be expected, because they are an *actus unicus et simplicissimus*, there is nothing to prevent the institution of some order in them, considered objectively and from our side according to our mode of conceiving.—As to what order they are to be arranged in for the purposes of comparison, there is no one unanimous finding. Those who ascend *supra lapsum* (above the Fall) or above creation to constitute the decree of predestination are of opinion that the decrees must be so arranged, that they place the decree of predestination before the decree of creation and of permission to lapse, and God is conceived as having first thought of manifesting His glory in the exercise of mercy and righteousness in the salvation or damnation of men, before He thought of creating man or permitting his fall; so that creation and permission to fall are of the nature of a means for revealing His mercy and righteousness. Thus the first decree about men concerns the manifestation of God's glory in the exercise of mercy and righteousness by the salvation and damnation of men; the second concerns creation; the third, permission to lapse; the fourth, the sending of Christ for the salvation of those whom He had decreed to save. But although this order contains nothing absolutely repugnant to the foundation of salvation and the analogy of faith, and was the approved view of great men who deserved well of the Church, there are nevertheless various obstacles to its acceptance.—23: For the orthodox (1) the first decree is the creation of man, (2) permission for his fall, (3) the election of certain of the human race from lapse to salvation and the abandonment of others to the corruption in which they were born, (4) for sending Christ into the world as Mediator of the elect to obtain them salvation, (5) the effectual calling of the latter and their presentation with faith, their justification, sanctification and final glorification. And because these decrees occurred in this order and this order answers to the nature of the thing itself, to this order we justifiably adhere, having rejected the rest."

In the supralapsarian sense BEZA is fullest in his *ordo rerum decretarum* in his *Summa totius Christ. (Op.* I p. 170), as follows:—

"The Sum of all Christianity, or the description and distribution of the causes of the salvation of the elect and of the destruction of the reprobate, collected from the sacred writings.

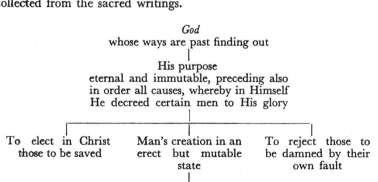

God
whose ways are past finding out

His purpose
eternal and immutable, preceding also
in order all causes, whereby in Himself
He decreed certain men to His glory

| To elect in Christ those to be saved | Man's creation in an erect but mutable state | To reject those to be damned by their own fault |

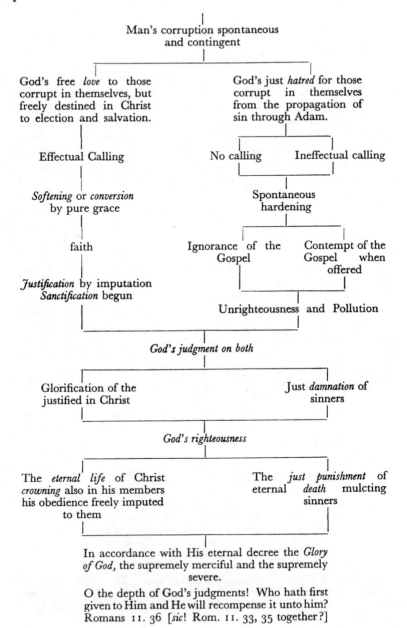

Man's corruption spontaneous
and contingent

God's free *love* to those corrupt in themselves, but freely destined in Christ to election and salvation.

God's just *hatred* for those corrupt in themselves from the propagation of sin through Adam.

Effectual Calling

No calling　　Ineffectual calling

Softening or *conversion*
by pure grace

Spontaneous
hardening

faith

Ignorance of the
Gospel

Contempt of the
Gospel when
offered

Justification by imputation
Sanctification begun

Unrighteousness and Pollution

God's judgment on both

Glorification of the
justified in Christ

Just *damnation* of
sinners

God's righteousness

The *eternal life* of Christ
crowning also in his members
his obedience freely imputed
to them

The *just punishment* of
eternal *death* mulcting
sinners

In accordance with His eternal decree the *Glory of God,* the supremely merciful and the supremely severe.

O the depth of God's judgments! Who hath first given to Him and He will recompense it unto him? Romans 11. 36 [*sic*! Rom. 11. 33, 35 together?]

16.—Thus (on the infralapsarian view), the decrees of the revelation of God's glory, of creation, of providence, and with the latter the decrees of the permission of the fall and of predestination, stand in a relation of successive subordination, in the consummation of which "the decree of the manifestation of the divine glory" reaches its goal.—HEIDEGGER (V, 16): "Thus in the order which Scripture transmits the actual event, sealed especially in Gen. 1, 2, 3 etc., proves that the decrees of the manifestation of the divine glory, of creation, of providence and thereunder of permission of sin, of predestination, or election to life and reprobation to death, are most harmoniously (παναρμονικῶς) subordinate to one another".

CHAPTER VIII

PREDESTINATION

1.—The doctrine of the *decretum Dei speciale* or of predestination belongs to those parts of doctrine, which because of their significance and their difficulty must be set forth with quite unusual circumspection and care; the result being that, since the doctrine is revealed in H. Scripture, it must on the one hand quite definitely be taught, but on the other hand must be handled only within the limits which God has fixed in the revelation of this mystery.—*Canones Synod. Dordr.* 14: "As this doctrine of divine election has by the most wise counsel of God been preached through the prophets, Christ himself and the apostles, alike under the OT and under the NT, and thereafter entrusted to the memoirs of sacred literature ; so also today it is to be propounded in the Church of God, for which it was peculiarly designed, religiously and holily with the spirit of discretion, in its own place and time, all inquisitive spying of the ways of the Most High being ruled out, and this to the glory of the most sacred divine name and the lively consolation of His people".—LEIDEN SYNOPSIS (XXIV 1-2): "Although the doctrine of God's eternal predestination is stiff and full of difficulty, we must not therefore maintain silence about it in the Church of Christ, as certain preposterously canny folk think. We neither can nor should we wish to be more cautious than the H. Spirit, who frequently propounds that same doctrine as well in the prophets as in the addresses and letters written to whole churches. And it comprises matter full of consolation and of other fruits contributory to the edification of the Church, as will afterwards be shown by us. But we recognise that it must be handled with all moderation and spiritual foresight, and above all meticulous care must be exercised not to disclose a wisdom here which goes beyond what is written. Let us follow the leading of the divine Word alone, to whose obedience Christ's true disciples gladly surrender themselves."—HYPERIUS 182: "Knowledge of predestination lights up God's glory, consoles consciences; but its treatment is parlous".—CALVIN (III, xxi, 1): "Before I enter upon the actual subject, I have a twofold preface to address to two classes of men. The discussion of predestination, in itself attended with considerable difficulty, is rendered exceedingly perplexing and so dangerous by man's inquisitiveness, which no barriers can restrain from wandering into forbidden snares and propelling itself into heaven, refusing if possible to leave God anything secret without him (man) scanning and embroidering it.—2: Let it then be our first and obvious consideration, that to seek any other knowledge of predestination than that unfolded in the Word of God is no less mad than to wish to walk where there is no road or to peer in darkness. Nor let us be ashamed of a little ignorance, where it is an instructed ignorance. Nay let us rather renounce investigation of a knowledge, to claim which is foolish and dangerous and so destructive.—3: There are others who in their desire to cure this disease would all but order every mention of predestination to be buried: indeed they advise us to flee any question of it as we would a rock. But although their restraint is rightly to be praised, since they think mysteries should be sipped with such sobriety: yet because they fall so short of the mean, they cut no ice with the mind of man, which does not lightly submit to restraint. So to keep the lawful course even in this matter, we must go back to the Lord's word, in which we possess a sure rule of understanding. Scripture is the school of the H. Spirit, in which as nothing necessary or useful in the way of knowledge has been left out, so nothing is taught but what conduces to knowledge. Whatever then is transmitted in Scripture about predestination, we must be careful not to shut believers off from it; lest we seem evilly to cheat them of their God's benefit, or to convict and insult the Spirit, who has published things which it is forsooth politic to suppress anyhow. Let us, say I, allow the Christian to open the mind and ears of all directed to him to the words of God, only observing this restraint, that once the Lord has closed His holy mouth, he too should block his own path to inquisitiveness. The best goal of soberness will be, not only in teaching to follow the lead of God invariably, but when He has made an end of teaching, to cease from wishing to be wise."

2.—*Praedestinatio* is generally "the appointing of a thing to an end before it exists or is made" (ALTING, *Meth. theol.* 4).—That there really is "a specific predestination pertaining to rational creatures", POLAN (IV, 7) proves by the passages Eph. 1. 4, 11 (he chose us in him before the foundation of the world, that we should be holy and without blemish before Him in love—foreordained according to the purpose of him who worketh all things after the counsel of his will); Rom. 8. 29 (whom he foreknew, he also foreordained to be conformed to the image of his son); Jude 4 (. . . they who were of old set forth unto condemnation); and on the following grounds: "(1) He who is all-wise predestines all his *res*, before they come into being, not to an uncertain issue but to a fixed end. God is all-wise, therefore God has predestined all His *res* before they were made, not to an uncertain issue, but to a fixed end, and accordingly His rational creatures also;—(2) He who has the freest power and is ἀνυπεύθυνος, does what he pleases with his own; but God has the freest power, etc.—(3) In him in whom there is a counsel and decree anent things future, there is predestination, because predestination is such a counsel and decree: but in God there is a counsel and decree anent future things, therefore, etc.—(4) There is providence in God, predestination is a part of providence, therefore, etc.;—(5) In him in whom there is foreknowledge, love and purpose of will, there is predestination, because the latter cannot be separated from the former items; now there is foreknowledge, etc., in God, therefore, etc.;—(6) all perfection exists in God; predestination is perfection, therefore it (predestination) is in God."—COCCEIUS insists (*S. th.* XXXVII, 1-4) that Scripture attests, that God has resolved not only in His mercy to be gracious and to re-adopt us as his children, but also in rich proof of His longsuffering to reveal to a section of them His power and His wrath, the result being that "there is really a testament with God and that He has elected heirs of life to whom He should give life by the testament; others likewise He has rejected and held in hatred Mal. 1. 2, 3 (I have loved you, saith the Lord, Yet ye say, wherein hast thou loved us? Was not Esau Jacob's brother? saith the Lord: yet I loved Jacob; but Esau I hated and made his mountains a desolation, and gave his heritage to the jackals of the wilderness), quoted Rom. 9. 13; and thus some He has predestinated unto the adoption of sons, others He has set unto wrath; which counsel we commonly designate by the name predestination. And not badly, since in both parts of this counsel there is a ὁρισμός, *definitio,* and a προορισμός, *praedefinitio,* concerned also with the actions of them that perish Lk. 22, 22 (the Son of man indeed goeth as it hath been determined, but woe unto that man through whom he is betrayed) Ac. 4, 28 (gathered together, to do whatsoever they hand and thy counsel foreordained to come to pass)." For the rest be it noted that in these words Scripture prefers describing the *ordinatio et definitio certorum hominum ad bonum,* Rom. 8. 29-30 (whom he foreknew, he also foreordained to be conformed to the image of His Son, that he might be the first-born among many brethren: and whom he foreordained, them he also called: and whom he called, them he also justified: and whom he justified, them he also glorified)."

3.—As the *decretum Dei de specialis gloriae suae manifestatione in creaturarum rationalium statu aeterno* (MASTRICHT III, ii, 7) predestination applies to all the rational creatures of God, i.e., to angels and to men. As to angels predestination is that counsel of God, by which "God has decreed of His grace to preserve some from lapse and to confirm them in their primeval integrity unto salvation, to condemn the rest beyond hope, who had been allowed to lapse and been left in it" (HEIDEGGER V, 21).—As to the difference in predestination as regards angels and men HEIDEGGER (*ibid.*) remarks: "There is this difference between the two predestinations: (1)

that of the angels precedes, that of men follows, as is clear from the order of creation and fall; (2) the former was made as regards elect in a state of integrity, God considering the unimpaired angel; the latter in a state of sin, God considering him as having lapsed; (3) the former was made neither in Christ as redeemer and mediator (for in him was the perpetual well-spring of all grace) Jn. 1. 14-16 (The Word became flesh and dwelt among us (and we beheld His glory, glory as the only begotten from the Father, full of grace and truth) . . . of his fulness we all received, and grace for grace) *and the medium conjoining the creature, infinitely distant from the Creator, with Himself* [i.e., the Creator] Eph. 1, 10 (to sum up all things in Christ) *they might have been elected*) nor (4) through calling, justification, sanctification, as subordinate means to their predestination: the latter succeeded both in Christ as redeemer and through the means invoked, made subordinate to their election; the former finally (5) decreed by a greater grace as regards election, to save the elect angels without misery at all; as regards reprobation it abounded in a greater ἀποτομία, since He resolved to condemn sinning angels beyond all hope of pardon 2 Pet. 2, 4 (God spared not angels when they sinned but cast them down to Tartarus (hell), and committed them to pits of darkness, to be reserved unto judgment); the latter involves for elect men greater grace, since it saves them though sinners and worthy of Gehenna; as to the reprobate it is accompanied by a greater severity, since they suffer not only for their own actual sins, but also for original sin."

That there is really a *predestinatio* of angels is proved by 1 Tim. 5, 21 (the elect angels) 2 Pet. 2, 4 (above) Jude 6 (angels which kept not their own principality, but left their proper habitation, he hath kept in everlasting bonds under darkness unto the judgment of the great day) Mt. 25. 41 . . . to them on the left hand, Depart from me, ye cursed, into the eternal fire which is prepared for the devil and his angels).—In this connection RIISSEN and others discuss two questions. First of all it is asked: "what sort of angels encounter God in His predestination?"—This was involved in the great controversy between *supra-* and *sublapsarianism*. RIISSEN replies (VI, 14): "Some would have them to have been equal, not unequal, that is, still unimpaired and standing, but liable to lapse, some of whom He decreed to save from lapse, others of whom He decreed to allow to lapse; which may be said, if *reprobatio* is taken in a wider sense, so as to include the decree to permit lapse; but if it is taken more strictly and appropriately, according as it denotes the decree of desertion in lapse and of damnation because of lapse, angels as lapsed should be kept in view here, (1) because liability to fall does not render the creature worthy of reprobation, but actual fall; (2) Scripture seems to bring us to this point 2 Pet. 2, 4 (above) Jude 6 (*ibid.*). Therefore they are rather

conceived as having sinned and deserted their origin than conceived
as reprobate."—Next the question is raised: "Whether angels are elected
in Christ?" RIISSEN replies (15): "All theologians agree that they were
not elected in Christ the Redeemer: they disagree as to whether any
reason exists for him being called their Mediator, not indeed of redemption, but of preservation, and confirmation. But although there is in
their view nothing repugnant to the analogy of faith, the view of those
is truer, who deny that the election of angels took place in Christ the
Mediator. We agree of course that this confirmation of grace befell them
per λόγον, so that from him from whom they had received their being
they also borrowed the preservation of it; but we do not think that this
can be said in like terms of Christ the θεάνθρωπος and Mediator."
—This view became the prevailing one. Hence for example HOTTINGER
(p. 85) also teaches: "The election of angels was made in Christ, not as
mediator and redeemer, but as the perennial spring of all grace and the
means by which the creature, infinitely remote from the Creator, is yet
united to Him".

4.—As to men the idea of predestination is to be defined thus: "Predestination is God's decree by which He has appointed rational creatures
from eternity to fixed limits beyond this temporal and natural life, they
to be led thereto by fixed means likewise foreordained from eternity"
(POLAN IV, 7). Or more briefly: "It is the predestination of men by
which from the entire human race to be created and destined to fall God
foreordains some to life eternal, others to death eternal" (RIISSEN,
VI, 19).—CALVIN (III, xxi, 5): "Predestination is our name for God's
eternal decree, whereby He has fixed with Himself, what He wishes to
happen to each individual. We are not all created under the same conditions; for some eternal life, for others eternal damnation is foreordained.
So according as each has been created for one or the other end, so we
say that he has been predestined to life or death."—BRAUN (I, ii, 9, 12):
"Predestination is God's eternal and immutable decree to manifest His
glory by the exercise of His righteousness and mercy" (in the supralapsarian sense, without the addition "in hominibus lapsis")!—HOTTINGER
86: "It is predestination of men by which out of the whole human race
to be created and about to fall God foreordained some to life eternal,
others to death eternal".—ALSTED 190: "In this locus the word predestination is used by synecdoche. Most broadly it signifies the appointment of a thing to a fixed end. In this locus it is restricted to rational
creatures considered apart from this temporal and animal life. Hence
God's predestination is defined as God's counsel concerning the rational
creature's ultimate end or state outwith this animal life."—WOLLEB 20:

"It is the predestination of men by which out of the human race created in His image but destined to lapse spontaneously into sin God has resolved to save some for ever through Christ, to damn others eternally by leaving them in their wretchedness, in order to manifest the glory of His mercy and His righteousness".

5.—Thus the *causa efficiens primaria* is God Himself, the *causa προηγουμένη* is God's free will, i.e., the *decretum Dei absolutum* (POLAN IV, 7). Its *finis summus* is the *gloria Dei*, its *finis subordinatus* is the *salus electorum*. Its *effectus* are the creation of intelligent beings and the permission of sin. It embraces the *"praefinitio*, by which from eternity God has appointed fixed ends for individual men", and the *"ordinatio*, by which He has appointed certain means", by which the individual is to attain to his eternal determination (ALSTED 149). In first intention predestination is a *decretum absolutum;* in a more ultimate intention it is a *decretum* not *conditionatum* but *ordinatum s. respectivum.*—KECKERMANN 168; WOLLEB 20: "Although in God's mind predestination is a single and most unifold *actus*, to suit the weakness of our powers of knowledge it is distinguished into predestination *ad finem* and predestination *ad media*. One predestined *ad finem* is also predestined *ad media.*—21: Predestination is an absolute decree and it is not. It is absolute as regards the efficient cause; it is not absolute as regards its matter or object, and its means. Destination or predestination is the constituting of the end and the ordering of the means to the end.—ALSTED 168: "The decrees contemplate a fixed end and means and so in this way they are not absolute but *respectiva*".—WENDELIN (*Theol. syst. maius,* 298): "(The decree) is in a different respect absolute and not absolute: absolute in respect of the impelling cause existent in man or different from the divine good pleasure; not absolute in respect of the means for obtaining salvation through the actual decree of election of those destined; among these last means the merit of Christ and faith hold the first place".

6.—Predestination is eternal, i.e., it is fixed from within eternity and for eternity, it is unsearchable and unchangeable.—BUCAN (XXXVI, 12): "This decree is profound and admirable, inscrutable, eternal (in respect of its origin and by the nature of its end) and accordingly unshakable, immutable and infallible.—BUCAN (*ib.* 7) distinguished accordingly three degrees of predestination, namely (1) "the decree itself in God's mind to save and reject men; (2) the execution of progress of that actual eternal decree through mediate causes and (3) the grandly outstanding architectonic end, the glory, of course, of God Himself, who thus reveals both His power and His mercy".

7.—So it is on the one hand eternal election, on the other hand eternal rejection of individuals.—MASTRICHT proves on the following grounds, that *reprobatio* is to be reckoned to *praedestinatio* and that the latter is therefore twofold (III, ii, 24): "(1) Because the paronym of predestination used in the matter of reprobation, is read in Ac. 4, 28 (those who acted violently towards Christ "were gathered together", "to do whatsoever thy hand and thy counsel foreordained to come to pass"); (2) Because in more than one way the matter of predestination is referred in Scripture to reprobation Prov. 16, 4 (The Lord hath made everything for its own end, yea, even the wicked for the day of evil) Mt. 25, 41 (Then shall he say also unto them on the left hand, Depart from me, ye cursed, into the eternal fire which is prepared for the devil and his angels) Rom. 9. 22 (What if God, willing to show His wrath, and to make his power known, endured with much longsuffering vessels of wrath fitted unto destruction?) 1 Thess. 5. 9 (God appointed us not unto wrath, but unto the obtaining of salvation through our Lord Jesus Christ) Jude 4 (. . . they who were of old set forth unto condemnation); (3) Because Scripture refers reprobate Pharaoh and his blinding and hardening, as means of reprobation, to the predestining will of God Rom. 9. 17-18 (the Scripture saith unto Pharaoh, For this very purpose did I raise thee up, that I might shew in thee my power, and that my name might be published abroad in all the earth. So then he hath mercy on whom he will, and whom he will he hardeneth) 1 Pet. 2. 8 (. . . they stumble at the word, being disobedient; whereunto also they were appointed) Mt. 11. 25-26 (. . . I thank thee, O Father, Lord of heaven and earth, that thou didst hide these things from the wise and understanding and didst reveal them unto babes: yea, Father, for so it was well-pleasing in thy sight): (4) Because in reprobation the appointment of means to an end is exactly as it is in election: vessels of wrath or the reprobate in their just condemnation (on account of their sins) are appointed as a means by God for the manifestation of His wrath or vindictive righteousness, exactly as vessels of mercy and their free beatification are appointed to manifest His glorious grace Rom. 9. 22-23 (22 above ; 23, that he might make known the riches of his glory upon vessels of mercy, which he afore prepared unto glory).—Definitions which conceived predestination merely as election were stigmatized as deficient by the later orthodoxy, e.g., that of HYPERIUS, p. 183: "It is predestination by which God elects us in Himself, before the foundations of the world were laid—in order that He might adopt us as sons through Jesus Christ unto Himself, according to the good pleasure of His will".

8.—The object of God's predestinating decree is not so much man in and for himself or to be created by God or created in a state of innocence, as fallen man whom God has resolved either to redeem in Christ or to reject.—COCCEIUS (*Summ. theol.* XXXIX, 6-7): "Thus the object of election or of the will to separate (men) through salvation from the perishing and of predestination or of the will to save, i.e., to redeem, sanctify, justify, glorify, is that which it is necessary for us to think of as extant, before we can think worthily and fittingly of God, that He is executing the act which we say He has decreed, or that which must necessarily be known as future by God when decreeing the salvation of man. Therefore the object of election and of predestination will thus be taken to be a wretched man among many wretches, one for whom it is impossible to attain to life apart from grace."—HEIDEGGER (V, 33) explains this thought, first of all remarking with regard to election that "Men are the object of the decree of the election of men, men marked out from eternity to be given to Christ for redemption and salvation by him and so regarded by God as wretches and sinners lying in the common mass of wretchedness and corruption and in blood. Neither does either the counsel of election or of universal predestination ascend higher or include in itself the creation of the first man and the guidance of transgression, but it rather supposes the decree already. Whence neither does Scripture anywhere give us a lead in fixing this counsel above that part of the decree which views the creation and lapse of man. Indeed, in asserting that we have been elected and predestinated unto holiness and sonship Eph. 14. 5 (. . . chose us in him before the foundation of the world that we should be holy. . . . Having foreordained us unto adoption as sons . . . according to the good pleasure of his will), it implies that we were elect as aliens from Christ, impure and children of wrath, because only aliens from Christ were elected in Christ, i.e., to be redeemed by him Rom. 8. 29 (p. 151) Jn. 15. 19 (I chose you out of the world).—Nor could election by any other way be described as an act of mercy preparing vessels of mercy to the glory of God Rom. 9. 23 (p. 156), since all mercy has to do with the wretched man. For if election, yea and all predestination preceded creation and the prevision of a fall, there would also take place in the execution of the same a transition from predestination or election to creation and the fall. But the transition is always to redemption, calling, justification Eph. 1 : 4, 5, 7, 8 (Even as he chose us in him before the foundation of the world, that we should be holy and without blemish before him in love: having foreordained us unto adoption as sons through Jesus Christ unto himself, according to the good pleasure of his will . . . in whom we have our redemption through his blood, the forgiveness of our trespasses, according to the riches of his grace, which he made to abound toward us in all wisdom and prudence) Rom. 8. 29-30 (whom he foreknew, he also foreordained to be conformed to the image of His Son, that he might be the first-born among many brethren: and whom he foreordained, them he also called: and whom he called, them he also justified: and whom he justified, them he also glorified) 9. 22-23 (that he might make known the riches of his glory upon vessels of mercy, which he afore prepared unto glory) 2 Tim. 1. 9 (God saved us and called us with a holy calling, not according to our works, but according to his own purpose and grace, which was given us in Christ Jesus before times eternal); but to creation and the fall never. Whence it is plain that its place is below creation and the fall."—HEIDEGGER now tries to meet the supralapsarians' objection, especially *Gomarus'* statement, that if man was only predestined to life or death after the fall, God created him *incerto fine*. HEIDEGGER remarks in contradiction (V. 34): "He created man with a fixed end, just as He predestined him with a fixed end. For the distinct decrees of creation and predestination have also distinct ends in respect of God; each has in view the glory of God, but not illustrated in the same way. Thus God created man for His own glory. 'Of Him, through Him and to Him are all things. To Him be the glory for ever' Rom. 11. 36. Now God's glory is illustrated through man in two ways, either according to law or according to Gospel. In the former way in creation and in the fall; in the latter after the fall in the state of grace and of glory, to which the state of the reprobate is opposed."

In the same sense the LEIDEN SYNOPSIS (XXIV, 23) says: "We agree that neither was man created with an ambiguous end, nor did the lapse of man occur without God's special providence. If not a sparrow falls to the ground without our Father, much less the whole human race. But God willed first to show what *liberum arbitrium* amounted to in man, and then what the benefit of His own grace. So with the infinite light of His own knowledge foreseeing that it would turn out, that man created in His image would with his entire posterity abuse his *liberum arbitrium* God, in order that the more manifest way of an admirable righteousness and mercy might be opened up, considered it more in accord with His most almighty goodness to make well of ill, than not to let evil live, as *Augustine* rightly reminds us."—WENDEDLIN (*Collatio*, p. 249): "In God's view the object of predestination was fallen man, dead in sin".—WOLLEB 21: "The *materia* or object of election and reprobation is not man considered absolutely, but man destined to fall of his own free will into sin".—HOTTINGER, p. 94: "The object (of predestination) is the human race to be created and about to fall in Adam or, considered in the mind of God predestinating, as created, fallen and corrupted by original sin".—Similarly SEEGEDIN, p. 110, and others.

HEIDEGGER next compares the *finis creationis* and the *finis praedestinationis* (V, 34): "Now the glory of creation consists in the fact that God's invisible power, wisdom and goodness was laid bare not only in all His works, particularly in the invisible image conferred upon man through creation: it also shone out thus, that the *liberum arbitrium* left him made no advance as regards righteousness and life. God the Creator secured this end exactly as He intended. Now in the mystery of predestination God testified to the power of the benefit of His grace and of the judgment of His righteousness. Proceeding therefore from that He resolved to display the glory of His grace, mercy and righteousness. As then the end of every divine decree concerning man is the illumination of the divine glory, so it is (the end) both of the power, goodness and wisdom in the decree of creation, and of the grace, mercy and righteousness in the decree of predestination." At this point HEIDEGGER also tries to resist the conclusions drawn up by the *Supralapsarians* from the statement that "what is first in intention is last in execution". The *Supralapsarians* asserted this: "Because the illumination of God's glory by mercy in the salvation of the elect and by righteousness in the damnation of the reprobate is last in execution, it ought to be conceived in the divine intention as the first of them all and so as actually older than and prior to the intention to create man".—HEIDEGGER rightly remarks against this position: "There is a double confusion in the argument, which clearly betrays itself, (1) that of the absolutely and the relatively ultimate end, as well as (2) that of the decree of creation and that of predestination. Since the axiom about the absolutely ultimate end must be understood, it is sufficiently clear from what we have said, that the illumination of the glory of mercy and righteousness is not *simpliciter* and absolutely the ultimate end as regards the government of man generally, but derivatively and relatively, as regards the government of fallen man, and so not (the ultimate end) of the decree of creation and of permission to lapse, but of the decree of predestination: yet in the latter itself, since it is last in execution, the illumination of the divine glory by the salvation or damnation of the sinner is likewise first in intention and must begin with men fallen and sinning. For in the same order either of nature or of grace, but not in things disparate, that which is last in execution is most truly laid down as first in intention."— RIISSEN (VI, 19, 1) makes the same point with the following arguments: "(1) *Non ens* cannot be the object of predestination, for predestination does not make its object, like creation, but supposes it. But *homo creabilis vel labilis* is *non ens*, because by creation he was brought from non-being into being.—(2) He who is exposed to divine predestination should be either "eligible" by mercy or "reprobable" (!) by righteousness:

but this cannot be said of *homo creabilis* or *labilis*, but only of him created and fallen.—(3) If predestination looks to man *creabilis* or *labilis*, creation and fall will be the means of predestination. But this cannot be said rightly (i) Because Scripture never speaks of them as of the means of predestination, but as of an antecedent condition. (ii) Otherwise sin would be on account of damnation, whereas on the contrary damnation is on account of sin. (iii) A necessary means has a connection with the end, so that given the necessary means the end should be posited in due course. And neither creation nor the fall have any such connection either with election or with reprobation; for men could be created and fall, yet not be elected. (iv) If they were means, God would have inaugurated a counsel to save or destroy man before He had decreed anything as to his futurition and fall, which is absurd. Therefore creation and the fall are presupposed as a pre-requisite condition in the object, like existence and ductility in clay.—(4) The view in question is ἐνδιάβλητος (open to criticism), as though God had reprobated men before they were reprobable through sin, nor therefore did He wish to damn them because they were sinners, but He allowed them to become sinners, so that they might be punished and He resolved to create in order to destroy.—(5) God "chose us out of the world" Jn. 15, 19. Therefore not as creatable and liable to fall, but as having fallen. Objection: "It is not a question of eternal predestination but of calling in time." Answer: "These things are not contrasted but combined; God has elected man from the same mass from which He calls man in time."—(6) The election of men takes place in Christ, therefore contemplates man as lapsed, because men cannot be elected in Christ, except as being in need of redemption through him, therefore as sinners and wretches.—(7) The mass of which Paul speaks Romans 9. 21 is the object of predestination (the potter's 'lump' of clay), but it is none other than a corrupt mass: (1) Because that lump (*massa*) is meant, from which are made vessels of mercy and vessels of wrath vv. 21, 22, 23; but wrath and mercy presuppose sin and misery: (2) that lump is meant, lying in which men may be held in hatred by God, as Esau. But such ought to be a corrupt lump, because God could not have hated a perfect (*integra*) creature: (3) that lump is meant from which Pharaoh was roused; but no one can have said that Pharaoh was raised from a perfect lump."

To those dogmaticians who uphold supralapsarianism belongs e.g. BRAUN, who speaks of the controversy before us as follows (I, ii, 9, 24): "Some institute parts or acts of predestination from creation itself or from the fall of man; they are called sublapsarians because they so arranged things as if creation and the fall preceded every act of predestination. Others start its actions at the actual end which God has set before Himself in the creation of man, namely at the manifestation of His glory through the exercise of His justice and mercy. For creation itself and the lapse of man were predestinated by God; therefore predestination precedes creation and the fall.—25. Therefore the parts or acts of predestination should be ordered in this way. (1) God decreed to manifest His glory by manifesting His mercy and righteousness. (2) He decreed to create a creature endowed with reason and after His own image, to whom He could manifest His glory. (3) He decreed to create that creature liable to lapse. (4) He decreed to permit his lapse. Who does not see so far that the object of predestination is man creatable and liable to lapse? There follow the remaining acts of predestination, which look to the means and execution or actual exercise of justice and mercy; therefore (5) He decreed to free certain men already lapsed from lapse and misery, to leave others in that state. In this sense the object of predestination is *homo lapsus,* not *labilis* ; for he who is freed from wretchedness or left in it must of course have already lapsed into wretchedness. Those who say that lapsed man is the object of predestination, in arranging the act of predestination begin with this fifth and last act, that God wishes to free some from wretchedness, to leave others in wretchedness; but this is bad, since the end precedes the execution in every intention. Since then the end is the manifestation of God's glory, by the manifestation of His righteousness and mercy, at that point we must undoubtedly begin, since it is the first act in God's intention and so the first act in predestination.— 26. Thus strictly speaking the object of predestination as regards the end *homo creabilis et labilis.*"

To render supralapsarianism tenable TRELCATIUS 61 has recourse to the distinction between *praeordinatio finis* and *praeordinatio mediorum.* Since consequently according to him the *massa* or *objectum praedestinationis* is generally man in and for himself, namely man to be carried out of the common nature of his kind above nature, TRELCATIUS explains it in this way : " If you are looking at the foreordination of the end, the matter of predestination is man commonly or absolutely, but if of the means to the end, it is man of himself and in himself ready to perish and guilty (*reus*) in Adam".—On ZWINGLI's Supralapsarianism cf. ZELLER, *Das theol. System Zwinglis,* p. 54ff. The main assertion upon which ZWINGLI bases his supralapsarianism is to be found in the statement of it (*De provid.* 108) : " Since righteousness was to be known by both angels and men and would be obscure and ignoble without the opposite unrighteousness, He prescribed what is right and holy for both.—Both therefore transgress it, because both ought to have known what righteousness and innocence were—God wrought both of these but through an impeller or instrument, in the angel through an ambitious mind, in man through the impeller demon or flesh."

Since the sublapsarian conception of the object of predestination became the dominant one in the Reformed Church, the opposite supralapsarian theory is to be regarded merely as a private theory of individuals. By far the predominant number of dogmaticians (e.g. LEIDEN SYNOPSIS (XXIV, 21): "The matter from which God graciously elects some, is the human race fallen from its primaeval integrity into sin by its own fault and accordingly also liable to condemnation before Him") and the confessional writings of the Church together (*Conf. Gall.* 12; *Belg.* 16; *Helv.* II, 10 etc., as well as the German Reformed confessional writings generally) are expressed in the sense here expounded. At the same time mediations were also sought for. MASTRICHT e.g. attempts to mediate the opposition between the supra- and infra- lapsarian ways of looking at it by distinguishing a fourfold *actus praedestinationis* (III, ii, 12): "Four acts of God are here to be observed: (1) the purpose to manifest the glory of mercy and of punishing righteousness; (2) the statute to create all men and permit them to lapse in a common beginning; (3) of those created and fallen to choose one in whom He would acquire the glory of mercy, and to reprobate another in whom He would obtain the glory of avenging righteousness; (4) an intention to prepare and direct the means corresponding to election and to reprobation. By reason of the first act of predestination the object could only have been *homo creabilis et labilis,* since no decree so far is presupposed to have been made concerning creation and the fall: by reason of the second act it is strictly *homo creandus et lapsurus*; by reason of the third *homo creatus et lapsus*; by reason of the fourth *homo electus et reprobus*. Since therefore, so far as it is distinguished from election and reprobation, predestination consists of two prime acts, you would be most accurate in saying that the object of predestination is *homo creabilis et labilis, creandus et lapsurus*; while at the same time the object of election and reprobation is *homo creatus et lapsus*. Thus most conveniently you will have reconciled specifically dissident views and most safely removed difficulties with which each side wants to saddle the side opposed to it."—BRAUN even remarks in conclusion : " From all these considerations, if one weighs the matter with an attentive mind, a peaceful soul and no party zeal, it is manifestly plain that there is no discrepancy between supra- and sub- lapsarians, as they are usually called and so their views may easily be reconciled."

9.—At the same time it follows that predestination does not first appear temporally after the Fall. On the contrary it belongs to God's eternity, to His essential being.—BUCAN (XXXVI, 11): "This decree does not begin precisely after men have been created or have begun to sin; but before the foundations of the world were laid, from eternity, that very thing was purposed by God".

A.—ELECTION.

10.—Since a portion of fallen humanity is saved from eternal damnation, its redemption and entry into bliss rests upon the eternal counsel of the triune God, in virtue of which the Son vowed to make satisfaction for a portion of humanity. This vow the Father accepted by resolving to give a definite part of the human race to the Son and to awaken it by the H. Spirit to living participation in the righteousness and in the holy life of Christ. "The election of men, who are to be saved for ever is a predestination, whereby from eternity God has given Christ the men on whom He wished to have mercy, that he might give them eternal life; i.e. whereby he decreed personally from eternity, which men He wished some day to adopt out of the rest and, exempted from their common destruction, to adopt as sons in Christ, to call effectually into communion with Christ, to justify in Christ and to glorify, so that they might behold the glory of Christ eternally and in him be partakers of the heavenly heritage and life eternal" (POLAN IV, 9). Or more briefly: "Election is the predestination of certain fixed men, in whose eternal salvation is manifested the glory of the divine mercy" (MASTRICHT III, iii, 5).— *Can. Syn. Dordr.* 7: "Election is the immutable purpose of God, whereby before the foundations of the world were laid He elected from the whole human race, that had fallen from its primeval integrity into sin and destruction by its own fault, according to the most free good pleasure of His will, out of pure grace, a fixed number of men neither better nor worthier than others, but prostrate with the others in a common wretchedness, to salvation in Christ, whom He appointed mediator right from eternity and the head of all the elect and the foundation of salvation; and resolved to give him them to save and to call and bring them effectually into his own communion through His own word and Spirit; or He decreed to present them with true faith in Himself, to justify and sanctify them, and at last, being powerfully protected in the communion of His Son, to glorify them, for a proof of His mercy and for the praise of His glorious grace."

LEIDEN SYNOPSIS (XXIV, 14): "We define the election in question as God's eternal and immutable decree, by which from the entire human race that had fallen by its own fault from primaeval integrity into sin and destruction He elected a fixed multitude of individual men, neither better nor worthier than the rest, of His sole good pleasure, to salvation in Christ Jesus, and resolved to give them to His Son to redeem, and by a peculiar and effectual mode of operating to bring them to living faith in Himself and to a sure perseverance in the same living faith, and that for a proof of His gracious mercy and for the praise of His glorious grace."— Almost word for word the same WALAEUS 369, and others.—Now and again the distinction between πρόθεσις, πρόγνωσις and προορισμὸς is mentioned, e.g. by WOLLEB 22: "These three words, although sometimes taken to be the same, should for the sake of teaching be so distinguished, that πρόθεσις indicates the actual purpose to save, πρόγνωσις the free benevolence with which He recognises us as His, while προορισμὸς indicates predestination to Christ and the other means to salvation". At the same time most dogmaticians, as e.g. HOTTINGER, p. 105, teach that these expressions are to be used *sensu apostolico*, "in which πρόγνωσις is πρόθεσις and προγνῶναι the same as προτιθέναι as the connection and comparison of passages shows Ac. 2. 23 τῇ ὡρισμένῃ βουλῇ, the determinate counsel and πρόγνώσει, foreknowledge of God) 4. 28 (to do whatsoever...thy counsel (βουλή) foreordained (προώρισε) to come to pass)".

11.—In H. Scripture this truth is guaranteed by the passage Eph. 1. 3-8: "Blessed be the God and Father of our Lord Jesus Christ, who hath blessed us with every spiritual blessing in the heavenly places in Christ: even as he chose us in him before the foundation of the world, that we should be holy and without blemish before him in love: having fore-ordained us unto adoption as sons through Jesus Christ unto himself, according to the good pleasure of his will, to the praise of the glory of his grace, which he freely bestowed on us in the Beloved: in whom we have our redemption through his blood, the forgiveness of our trespasses, according to the riches of his grace, which he made to abound toward us in all wisdom and prudence . . ." The *causa electionis princeps* is the triune God, in such a way that to the Father particularly belongs the *electio* in and by itself, to the Son the *sponsio*, to the H. Spirit the *obsignatio* of the election.—HEIDEGGER (V, 28): "The cause of election is God alone, and He is Father, Son and H. Spirit. For this counsel has been disponed from eternity by way of a testament or a decreeing and immutable will, by which God appointed with Himself in Christ heirs of His righteousness and kingdom; but administratively in this counsel God the Father's election is simply called election; and for the promise on behalf of the elect it is assigned to the Son, for their sealing to the H. Spirit."—BUCAN (XXXVI, 16): "The principal cause of election is— God (Jn, 6. 37, all that which the Father giveth me; 44, no man can come to me except the Father . . . draw him; 17.9 . . . I pray . . . for those whom thou hast given me, for they are thine; Eph. 1. 4. . . . he chose us in him before the foundation of the world)—and Christ, because he is not another than the Father Jn. 15. 16 (I chose you . . . that whatsoever ye shall ask of the Father in my name He may give it you),—and the H. Spirit Ac. 13. 2 (. . . the H. Spirit said, Separate me Barnabas and

Saul for the work whereunto I have called them)."—MARTINI (*Method. theol.* p. 25) distinguished in the eternal counsel of grace the *decretum proprium* of the individual persons of the Trinity as follows: "It is the decree of the Father, by which He gave His Son of His own will fixed persons out of the number of men to be created and about to lapse into sin, that he might redeem them in a human nature.—It is the decree of the Son, by which of his own will he received of the Father those to be redeemed and resolved to assume a human nature etc.—It is the decree of the H. Spirit, by which He has received from the Father and the Son for sanctification unto life eternal those whom the Father had given the Son, and that on account of the satisfaction provided by him" [i.e. the Son].

12.—The *causa impulsiva* of election is the love with which Father, Son H. Spirit would love one another and glorify one another.—HEIDEGGER (V.29): "To elect some God generally was impelled by the love of His glory, the riches of which He wished to prove openly by this stupendous work and as a result of it to prepare praise of the glory of His grace, Rom. 9. 23 (that he might make known the riches of his glory upon vessels of mercy, which he afore prepared unto glory), 11. 33 (O the depth of the riches both of the wisdom and the knowledge of God! how unsearchable are his judgments and his ways past finding out!) Eph. 1. 6 (to the praise of the glory of his grace, which he freely bestowed on us in the Beloved).—Specifically the love of the persons of the H. Trinity, by which they are borne to each other reciprocally with great ardour for their mutual glorification, is the cause of election within God. The Father loves the Son, shows him what works He is doing Himself, opening to him His counsel for undertaking them Jn. 5. 20 (the Father loveth the Son, and sheweth him all things that himself doeth . . .) 8. 50 (I seek not mine own glory: there is one that seeketh and judgeth) Eph. 1. 6 (to the praise of the glory of his grace which he freely bestowed on us in the Beloved). The Son in turn glorifies the Father in the work of salvation Jn. 17. 4 (I glorified thee on the earth, having finished the work, which thou gavest me to do), and the H. Spirit glorifies the Father and in the same way also the Son."—BUCAN (XXXVI, 17): "What is its efficient impulsive cause?—The intrinsic one is only in God, *videlicet*, His sheer love of Himself and the sole εὐδοκία τοῦ θελήματος τοῦ θεοῦ, —the sole grace and mercy and love of God,—God's mere pleasure, contemplating Himself alone, excluding moreover every other outward cause, which exists or might exist in men."—Particular election is thus and so far not absolute, as though it were arbitrary: it rather has its moral ground (inconceivable of course to man) in God's essentiality.

Cf. WALAUS 385: "Although no cause outside God can be given on man's side, as we warned you earlier, why this man rather than that is elect or reprobate, as Isaac rather than Ishmael, Jacob than Esau, since in themselves they were both equals and equally unworthy of election: still we must not think that on His side God had no reasons or causes for so doing : since the divine will always conspires with His wisdom and does nothing without reason or rashly ; although these reasons and causes have not been revealed to us, and accordingly they neither ought to nor can be probed by us apart from His will.—And it is this also which the chief doctors of the Reformed Church are often repelling from themselves, when they are reproached with setting up here some absolute will of God. Firstly they say it is not absolute, because it includes means by which the appointed end is achieved ; next because God also does not lack just reasons for having acted thus or thus, although these are hidden from us. Thus CALVINUS says (*De occulta Dei provid.* p.1013 *statim in initio*) : " Although for me God's will is the supreme cause, yet I everywhere teach, that where in His counsels and works no cause is apparent, it is yet hidden with Him, so that He has decreed nothing save justly and wisely. Therefore the triflings of the *Scholastics* on absolute power I not only repudiate but also detest, because they separate His righteousness from His rule." So too speaks BEZA in *Colloq. Mompelg.* p.162 : " This will or this decree of His we never sever from righteousness and true right reason, and as always most orderly, although we believe it to be inscrutable even for the very angels ; and accordingly we admire and adore it and refuse to recognise any other absolute will in God".

13.—Thus in no way may the ground of election be sought in anything that is outside God : not in the will of man, not in the use of the means of grace, not in the foreseen faith of the twice-born, not in his persistence in faith, not in his diligence in sanctification, nor yet in the merit of Christ, but solely in the good pleasure of God.—POLAN (IV 9) : " The efficient impulsive cause on account of which our eternal election was made is nothing outside God, and accordingly not the will of man; not a good use of the grace we may have received from God; not our foreseen faith; not men's foreknown merits; not our own prayers or those of others; not our perseverance in good, i.e. in faith and zeal for good works; not dignity of race or privilege in any other thing; not Christ's merit, nor yet a prevision of any of these things, which was and is in God; nor finally the actual final end of election; but the sole good pleasure of God founded on His gratuitous love towards us Lk. 12. 32 (. . . it is the Father's good pleasure to give you the kingdom) Rom. 9, 11. 16. 18 (the children being not yet born, neither having done anything good or bad, that the purpose of God according to election might stand, not of works, but of him that calleth; 16, it is not of him that willeth nor of him that runneth, but of God that hath mercy; 18 so then he hath mercy on whom he will, and whom he will he hardeneth) Eph. 1. 5. 11 (Having foreordained us unto an adoption as sons through Jesus Christ unto himself, according to the good pleasure of his will . . . 11: in whom also we were made a heritage, having been foreordained according to the purpose of him who worketh all things after the counsel of his will) Dt. 7. 7-8 (The Lord did not set his love upon you, nor choose you, because ye were more in number than any people: for ye were the fewest of all peoples. 8: But because the Lord loveth you and because he would keep the oath which he sware unto your fathers, hath the Lord brought you out with a mighty hand, and redeemed you out of the house of bondage, from the hand of Pharaoh king of Egypt) 10.15 (only the Lord had a delight in thy fathers to love them, and he chose their seed after them, even you above all peoples, as at this day), Rom. 8. 29 (whom he foreknew he also foreordained . . .) 1 Pet. 1.2 (according to the foreknowledge of God the Father, in sanctification of the Spirit unto obedience and sprinkling of the blood of Christ . . .) Jer. 1. 5 (before I formed thee in the belly I knew thee, and before thou camest out of the womb I sanctified thee; *I* have appointed thee a prophet unto the nations). Add to these testimonies the reason sought from the nature of God: Because the highest good could not behold an object other than Himself, even in doing good or conferring it upon someone: therefore it is necessary that the cause of our election and of all the benefits linked up with it should exist from eternity in God alone."—WOLLEB 21: "Of course faith or foreseen holiness is not the cause of election: a man is not elected because he is going to believe; he believes because he is elect Ac. 13. 48 (as many as were ordained to eternal life believed).—RIISSEN (VI, 19,3): "With one consent the orthodox insist that alike for glory and for grace election is sheerly gratuitous, so that there was no cause or condition or reason in man, by intuition of which God has chosen one rather than another, but that this depended solely upon His εὐδοκία".

WENDELIN (*Collatio* p. 225f.): "We deny that the decree of election has flowed from Christ's merit as its meritorious cause and from faith persevering to the end by a cause whether impulsive or instrumental. Even if these are causes of life decreed from eternity and to be conferred in time, they are not causes of the actual decree or election, but are rather its effects. God did not elect us to life, because we were to believe in Christ and persevere to the end in faith; we believe and persevere in faith because we are elect unto life eternal."—RIISSEN (VI, 19, 2): "We admit that Christ is the meritorious cause and foundation of the salvation decreed, from the standpoint of guilty man (*reus*), but not of the decree of salvation from the standpoint of God."

14.—Of course the person of Christ is the foundation of election. To a certain extent he is the sole object of it, in so far as all are elected whom the Father hath given to the Son and by the H. Spirit hath implanted in Him from eternity; so that from eternity they are the mystical body of Christ, the guarantor of their election.—HEIDEGGER (V. 30): "In the eternal testament then Jesus Christ the Son of God has been written the principal heir, προεγνωσμένος before the laying of the foundation of the world (1 Pet. 1.20 . . . foreknown indeed before the foundation of the world, but manifested at the end of the times for your sake), partly as heir of all things, partly as claimant and assertor of the inheritance given him (Heb. 1. 1-2 God . . . hath at the end of the days spoken to us in his Son, whom he appointed heir of all things, through whom also he made the worlds) (Psalm 2. 7 thou art my son etc.)—Whence it is clear that the Son's inheritance is certain men given him, so that saved by him as the author of their salvation Heb. 2. 10 and snatched out of Satan's power they might exist an inheritance worthy of himself, nay might even become the consorts and joint-heirs of his glory Jn. 17. 24 (that they also may be with me; that they may behold my glory . . .) Rom. 8. 17 (. . . joint-heirs with Christ . . . glorified with him).—Accordingly there is neither Son without us, nor an heir without an inheritance and coheirs; nor a brother firstborn without the other brethren, but all together were foreknown and elected in the one and indivisible decree (Eph .1. 4 . . . chose us in him before the foundation of the world).—MASTRICHT (III, iii, 8): "It is an advantage to note that the object of election is the whole mystical Christ, i.e. Christ with all his own".—LEIDEN SYNOPSIS (XXIV, 24): "In this decree of election we assign first place to Christ as the head and redeemer of the Church.—27: And by this pact there is between Christ as head and the elect, as his ordained and presented members which he received for quickening and reduction to one body, a fixed respect and mutual relation, even before they are fully united to him by faith, but are in themselves as yet his enemies".—WALAEUS (p. 380 ff.) discusses the controversy which attached to this point of doctrine. It is the question, "how we can be deemed 'in Christ' even before we believe". Some think that by 'in Christ' is here meant: "That Christ is the substratum of election, as it were the basis (*fundamentum*) for conferring the salvation to which we were elected, so that Christ is held elected only after our election". WALAEUS says: "This view is defended by many orthodox, and I agree that it is true, although I don't think it goes far enough". For "(1) that we were elected before our Head was elected does not seem appropriate to the nature of a head, which as first thing in dignity is likewise first thing in order; (2) Paul says that we were predestinated to be conformed to the image of His Son, that he might himself be the firstborn among many brethren (Rom. 8. 29). But to be predestinated to be conform to an image already presupposes that image; and how is a firstborn who is among brothers, appointed last-born because of the brethren? (3) And those who fell thus will find the difficulty, so hard to solve, which opponents here contrive, that to save His righteousness God has appointed salvation for us before He has appointed the satisfaction for the sins of those to be elected; a point they keenly press. So WALAEUS explains that with ZANCHIUS and POLAN he follows *Augustine's* view, and accordingly teaches, "that Christ as our head was first elected and then his members in Christ", i.e. "with respect to Christ and his future merit", not as though we had been elected "because of Christ's merit", but because we are not elected "save with respect to Christ's merit, by which we were to be redeemed from our misery". Some distinguish here "two respects of Christ", as "Head" and as "Redeemer", so that "the election of us" in the first respect precedes, and the second follows. In any case it may be said that "before any decree both end and means were present, but He elected the two at the same time, both end and means, by the one decree of election".

15.—Hence, so far as the Father elected a portion of humanity to eternal life in view of the future merits of Christ (that is, relatively), Christ is rightly called the *causa electionis,* just as he is literally the *medium* of it: by electing individuals the Father at the same time ordained the redemptive work of Christ, as the means of executing the counsel of grace. At the same time it must not be concluded from this that Christ's redemptive work and merits are the *causa meritoria* simply of God's counsel of grace and of election.—HEIDEGGER (V. 31): "Therefore in a different respect Christ is the cause and the means of eternal election. The cause, because election took place on account of him having been written the heir in the testament, and could not have taken place otherwise. We have proved that this whole counsel was undertaken from love of the Son. Now he on whose account or by whose grace a thing takes place, is the cause of the thing. Therefore Christ is at once foreknowing and by reason of this end foreknown. And the means, so far as God in His counsel foreknew and had respect to Christ not only as the heir, but also as the mediator of the testament, the redeemer of his inheritance and the blameless lamb without blemish 1 Pet. 1. 19-20 (. . . foreknown indeed before the foundation of the world, but manifested at the end of the times for your sake).

HEIDEGGER (V, 32): "Meanwhile we may not allow to certain *Remonstrant* and *Lutheran* (*Augustani*) theologians, that Christ may be called, as our mediator and saviour, by reason of his merit and redemption, the meritorious cause or foundation of eternal election, not merely to be executed, but also to be decreed, because it is not a phrase of Scripture, which makes Christ the cause and foundation of election Ac. 4. 12 (in none other is there salvation) 1 Cor. 3. 11 (other foundation can no man lay than that which is laid, which is Jesus Christ) Heb. 2. 10 (. . . the author of our salvation), as well as of the Church Eph. 2. 20 (being built upon the foundation of prophets and apostles, Christ Jesus himself being the chief corner stone); but nowhere of election; nor has the election of us any meritorious cause at all outside God; moreover in Him it has no other cause or foundation than His love of the Son and, in the Son, of us and so the sheer good pleasure of Him that elects".—LEIDEN SYNOPSIS (XXIV, 29): "Although then Christ's merit is not the cause of our election, because even Christ's very merit is in consequence of election; yet our election was not accomplished without respect to the Christ's future merit, because Christ's future merit and his whole mediation are among the objects of this election and at the same time the foundation of all those benefits appointed for us through election".— HOTTINGER (p.104-105): "Nor do we deny outright that election enters in in respect of faith. This phraseology of Scripture is appropriate 2 Th. 2. 13 (. . . God chose you from the beginning unto salvation in sanctification of the Spirit and belief of the truth, whereunto he called you through our gospel, to the obtaining of the glory of our Lord Jesus Christ) Ac. 13. 48 (. . . as many as were ordained to eternal life believed), if respect is understood to the consequent effect or subordinate means. Alleged testimonies of Scripture attest this. But if there is respect of antecedent faith as the efficient and impulsive cause, as the patrons of foreseen faith accept it, our answer is No. Faith is subsequent to election as the means of execution, and consequently as a thing strictly effected it depends upon its proper cause Rom. 8, 29-30 of (whom he foreknew he also foreordained . . .) Ac. 13. 48 (above).

Nor do we deny either that election took place by intuition of Christ's merit or that Christ the Mediator is the foundation of election. Only ambiguity must be removed. Intuition of Christ's merit in election is either of the impulsive cause preceding election, on account of which it actually took place:—or it is either of the subordinate means or of the consequent effect: which God subordinated to the execution of election to prove His righteousness. In this sense election is rightly said to have taken place by intuition of the merit of Christ, as is the case Eph. 1. 4 (. . . chose us in him before the foundation of the world); 1 Th. 5. 6.

(God appointed us . . . unto the obtaining of salvation through our Lord Jesus Christ); Rom. 8. 29 (whom he foreknew he also foreordained . . .). But in the former sense the assertion is not correct.

16.—17.—Christ's redemptive work° and merits are not the absolute *causa electionis,* which is to be sought only in the absolute counsel of love of the Trinity. They are the sheer *causa salutis* and therefore, with faith in Christ and persistence in faith, the means by which the salvation promised them by the Father is imparted and applied to the elect in the manner corresponding to the holiness and righteousness of God, which must receive satisfaction for sin, in order to be able to forgive it. In consequence the elect are elected not only to salvation but also to the means thereto; for the H. Spirit instils faith in Christ, sanctification and persistence in faith.—LEIDEN SYNOPSIS (XXIV, 25-26): "Although we recognise that God the Father had the will or affection to pity certain men, since He has appointed Christ redeemer in the same eternity— nevertheless this will or affection alone is not yet called election in Scripture, because that pity was prevented by the righteousness from ordaining salvation for sinners in a complete act without the intervention of a satisfaction, and because this election embraces not only the end but also the means necessary to salvation. It is only then called and is election, when Christ has been appointed the head and mediator of those to be elected and they have been ordained his members. And in this respect we are called elect in Christ Jesus, Eph. 1. 4 (. . . chose us in him before the foundation of the world), Rom. 8. 29 (whom he foreknew he also foreordained . . .).—HEIDEGGER (V, 48): "God elected those few not to salvation only but also to the means of salvation, which are Christ's merit apprehended by faith and so actual faith towards Christ and sanctification conjoined with perseverance, which some unavailingly summon from another than the decree of election".—WOLLEB 22: "The decree for saving us is predestination to an end, whereas the decree for giving us Christ as our Head is predestination to means".—LEIDEN SYNOPSIS (XXIV, 18): "Although we willingly concede that election to salvation and to the means of salvation may be considered separately,— we still deny that on that account these acts in God's decree are truly different.—19: When it is objected to us that ordination of means is superfluous, when the elect have already been absolutely ordained to salvation by some antecedent act, this arises from sheer ignorance of the orthodox view, because God never elected anyone absolutely to salvation, if 'absolutely' excludes the means which God has ordained for securing salvation. That ordination to salvation involved in God's purpose the consideration of the means necessary to salvation, always involved them from eternity in that very same act."

The means of election are most subtly distinguished by BUCAN (XXXVI 30): "The strict and peculiar means ordained by God for the elect are six. In relation to the election or predestination of the elect they are strictly its effects. As compared with each other and with the end of election they may be called both causes and effects. In fact three of them are equal to causes, three equal to effects. The first means is Christ—as the mediator in whom God elects.—The second means is effectual calling by inspiration of the H. Spirit to true repentance and acknowledgement of Christ.—The third means is faith in Christ or the application of Christ through faith.—From these follow three effects: justification in God's sight,—sanctification—and glorification".

18.—Election is as much an act of God's will determining all things in the world, as of His knowledge—BRAUN (I, ii, 9, 17): "Like election reprobation also should be referred to God's will, not only to His knowledge".— WENDELIN (*Collatio* p. 266): "Is there no fixed and defined number of the elect except as regards the divine prescience and omniscience? Hardly anything more absurd could be thought of or more unworthy of God. These fellows (namely the *Lutherans*) fashion God as seated in a watchtower and encountering with His eyes this bottom-most world and seeing what men are doing or likely to be doing, not ordering or disposing things future or present."

19.—Therefore the number of the elect has been fixed by God from eternity. His universal love and grace God of course shows to all His creatures. But His redeeming grace is not universal but particular. It has only chosen those whom according to His unsearchable counsel God wished to elect, in order to make known to them the glory of His sin-forgiving love, which rescues them from eternal death.—HEIDEGGER (V, 43): "The uniform subject of gratuitous election is the definite number of persons separated from the common sin-corrupted mass and liable to accusation, before the separation no better than others worthy of reprobation; this number God alone knows and has established in complete freedom by His secret will, to be revealed to no mortal". Dt. 32. 3-4 (I will proclaim the name of the Lord: Ascribe ye greatness unto our God. The Rock, His work is perfect; For all his ways are judgment: a God of faithfulness and without iniquity, just and right is He) 29. 29 (the secret things belong unto the Lord our God; but the things that are revealed belong unto us and to our children for ever, that we may do all the works of this law) 2 Tim. 1. 9 (saved us and called us with a holy calling . . . according to his own purpose and grace, which was given us in Christ Jesus before times eternal); Mt. 25. 34 (Then shall the king say unto them on his right hand, Come, ye blessed of my Father, inherit the kingdom prepared for you from the foundation of the world) Rom. 8. 29-30 (whom he foreknew, etc.).

Riissen (VI, 18, 2): "The question is not of God's general love and φιλανθρωπία, which He exercises towards all creatures, but of His special saving love, by which He has willed to pity them unto salvation".— Wendelin (*Collatio*, p. 253): "As to why God has not elected all but only some, and why these rather than those, there is no other reason but God's εὐδοκία, since for God predestinating all men are objects equally dead in sins and of themselves unfit for any good and liable to eternal death".—Bucan XXXVI, 21: "Why did God not elect all? Let us not enquire more carefully, says *Augustine*, if we do not wish to go astray. Let us not doubt that the reasons for this counsel are most just but past searching out".

The arguments for the particularity of grace and election are given by Mastricht (III, iii, 16): "The Reformed do not admit universal election at all, because (1) Scripture has no trace (γρύ) of universal election; (2) on the contrary it only teaches particular election (Mt. 20. 16 the last shall be first and the first last; 22.14 many are called but few are chosen; Jn. 15. 19 I chose you out of the world, therefore the world hateth you; 17.6 the men whom thou gavest me out of the world; Rom. 8. 29, 9. 13, Jacob I loved, but Esau I hated; 15, I will have mercy on whom I will have mercy; 18, he hath mercy upon whom he will, and whom he will he hardeneth; 22, What if God willing to show his wrath and to make his power known endured with much longsuffering vessels of wrath fitted unto destruction? 1 Th. 5. 9 God appointed us not unto wrath, but unto the obtaining of salvation through our Lord Jesus Christ); nor is there an unlike example; because (3) to elect is to take from several, to prefer one to another, or having accepted one to reject another Dt. 7. 7 (the Lord did not set his love upon you, nor choose you because ye were more in number than any people; for ye were the fewest of all peoples) Jn. 15. 19 (above). Accordingly universal election is σιδηρόξυλον or contradictory; because (4) in such a case there would be no reprobation, upon which Scripture insists Rom. 9. 18. 22 *sup*: Jude 4 (of old set forth unto condemnation) Prov. 16. 4 (the Lord hath made everything for its own end: yea, even the wicked for the day of evil) Mt. 25. 41 (. . . the eternal fire which is prepared for the devil and his angels); because (5) the elect are said to be entered in the book of life Lk. 10. 20 (rejoice that your names are written in heaven) Phil. 4. 3 (. . . whose names are in the book of life), which is eloquently denied of those about to perish Rev. 13. 8.

(every one whose name hath not been written in the book of life of the
Lamb that hath been slain from the foundation of the world) 17. 8 (they
whose name hath not been written in the book of life from the foundation
of the world); because (6) the elect are called προορισθέντες εἰς
υἱοθεσίαν Eph. 1.5 (foreordained us unto adoption as sons), which
is nowhere said of all nor can be said; because (7) the elect are
called foreknown, i.e. loved already (Rom. 8. 29, 11. 2 (God's people which
he foreknew), 2 Tim. 1. 9 (saved us and called us with a holy calling . . .
according to his own purpose and grace, which was given us in Christ
Jesus before times eternal) 1 Pet. 1. 2 (according to the foreknowledge of
God the Father, in sanctification of the Spirit, unto obedience and
sprinkling of the blood of Jesus Christ) Ps. 1. 6 (the Lord knoweth the way
of the righteous: but the way of the wicked shall perish), which is denied
of the reprobate Mt. 7. 23 (I will profess unto them, I never knew you:
depart from me, ye that work iniquity); because (8) the elect are called
μέλλοντες πιστεύειν 1 Tim. 1. 16 (for this cause I obtained
mercy, that in me as chief might Jesus Christ shew forth all his long-
suffering, for an ensample of them which should hereafter believe on Him
unto eternal life), which is not true of the reprobate; because (9) in that
way many elect would perish, contrary to Paul Rom. 8. 29; because (10)
the universal election would either be *rata* or *irrita*. If the former, men
one and all would be saved, which is counter to what precedes, namely
against Mt. 25 (parables of the virgins, the talents, the last judgment);
if in the latter case, it should be in vain even on God's part; but He
changeth not Mal. 3. 6 (I the Lord change not, therefore ye, O sons of
Jacob, are not consumed) nor does He change His counsels Is. 46. 10
(My counsel shall stand and I will do all my pleasure) Heb. 6. 17 (God,
being minded to shew more abundantly to the heirs of the promise the
immutability of his counsel, interposed with an oath), even at the instance
of another, because he that changeth the counsels of another is prior and
superior to and more powerful than Him also."

Against the universalism of the Berne theologian *Samuel Huber* (1624,
cf. *Alex. Schweizer's Central-dogmen,* Vol. I, p. 501ff.) who called the doctrine
of the Reformed about gracious election a "botched election", and
asserted the universality of grace, and thereby of course also rejected the
doctrine of election *propter praevisam fidem* as Pelagianism, HEIDEGGER
(V, 45) remarks: "Nor accordingly were all men elect, which once was
the lunacy of *Puccius* and that giddy *Samuel Huber*. The latter concocted
a distinction, by which Scripture calls some elect nominally, others
participially: establishing a few elect nominally, but all eligible
participially. This distinction Scripture refutes, saying: Except the Lord
had shortened the days no flesh would have been saved. But διὰ

τοὺς ἐκλεκτούς οὓς ἐξελέξατο he shortened the days (Mk. 13. 20).
Whence also he calls the participially elect τεταγμένους ad vitam
aeternam (Ac. 13. 48). For the same universal election to some
extent some *Augustan* (i.e. *Lutheran*) theologians also put up a fight,
asserting that by His antecedent will God had decreed from eternity to
save all men universally who were destroyed by sin, through Christ the
Saviour who was to be apprehended by faith; but consequently He
resolved to save believers and to damn unbelievers; in this will, they
declare, the cause of particularity arises from the fact that some obey
and believe God's kindly and universal good pleasure: others do not.
But the fiction of an antecedent and a consequent will derived from the
Damascene and some scholastics we sufficiently pinned down earlier on.
There is one definitely fixed, effectual and immutable will of God,
which always achieves its end Is. 14. 27 (the Lord of hosts hath proposed,
and who shall disannul it? and his hand is stretched out, and who shall
turn it back?) 46. 10 (My counsel shall stand and I will do all my pleasure)
Rom. 9. 19 (why doth He find fault? for who withstandeth His will?)
11.7 (that which Israel seeketh for, that he obtained not; but the election
obtained, and the rest were hardened), Heb. 6. 17 (God, being minded
to shew more abundantly to the heirs of the promise the immutability
of his counsel, interposed with an oath). Nor has anyone yet been able
so to explain this twin will, without one seeming to quarrel with the
other, or man's salvation seeming rightly to be situated in his *arbitrium*."

20.—Therefore in spite of their scattering by the way and their power to
wander far from God the state of the elect is unchangeably and unshakably
fixed.—SEEGEDIN p. 111: "Can the elect perish? Not at all and that
on account of unchangeable causes."—RIISSEN (VI, 19, 4): "Although
the orthodox admit that the elect may fall away on their own part,
because they found it to be too true, if they are left to themselves, yet
they insist that they cannot fall away on the side of the decree, by which
they are elect unto salvation".—BUCAN XXXVI, 48: "Can the elect
perish? They cannot even be seduced finally Mt. 25. 34 (come, ye blessed
of my Father, inherit the kingdom prepared for you from the foundation
of the world).—The distinction between complete and incomplete
election is therefore rejected, LEIDEN SYNOPSIS (XXIV, 17): "Thus
altogether removed from the truth is the division of some, by which they
distinguish between complete and incomplete, revocable and irrevocable
election".

21.—Of course the number of the elect is known to God alone, and therefore no man can know about the other man with full certainty, whether

he is elect or not. But of his own election, yes!—not of course *a priori*, i.e. not by useless poring over the mystery of the divine counsel of grace, but only *a posteriori*, i.e. the moment he is converted and born again— the individual elect may have the most undoubted certainty, resting not upon a conviction gained or derived from reflection, but upon faith in Christ, given with Christ himself. For since election has its God-ordained means (the Word and Sacraments, and the offer of them to individuals), it has also its definite signs, namely living faith in Christ, zeal in sanctification and the witness of the H. Spirit: which, if the believer experiences them in himself, assure him of his election. Since therefore, the believer in a personal and living way, has in himself the power of the Word of God, the communion of the life of Christ, and lives the life of a redeemed and sanctified child of God, he knows thereby on the basis of his faith in God's Word, that he too is called by it to Christ and to the Kingdom of God, and is aware by the peace of God which fills his soul, and which is higher than all reason, that already he is really implanted in Christ by the Father's free grace, and is also preserved eternally in the communion of Jesus Christ by the same grace, which calls no one to a temporary, transitory faith.

KECKERMANN describes the rule by which the individual's state of grace may be recognised (306): "We must judge of election not *a priori* but *a posteriori*.—Because it includes means, we must draw our conclusions about it from the means; it is not our business to judge and conclude concerning God's secret decrees except from revelation. Now God reveals His decrees precisely when He displays and bestows their means." Upon the presence of these *media electionis* rest the "sure marks of election". The former are mainly the Word and the Sacraments, the latter faith in Christ, the witness of the H. Spirit and zeal in sanctification (in good works). Hence says BUCAN (XXXVI, 33): "The marks of election are many: their source is true faith to Christ effectual through love; from them spiritual life is certainly diagnosed; and accordingly our election, like the life of the body, is perceived by its movement". All Reformed dogmaticians therefore insist, that the individual may become sure of his election not *a priori*, not through foolish brooding over God's counsel but *a posteriori* by a practical or analytical syllogism. E.g. WOLLEB 23: "In exploring our election we must advance by the analytic method from the means of execution to the decree, beginning with our sanctification, with a syllogism like this: Whoever feels in himself the gift of sanctification, by which we die to sin and live unto righteousness, is justified, called or presented with true faith and elect. But I feel this by the grace of God. Therefore I am justified, called and elect."

The comfortable consciousness of one's own election which is imparted to the individual, is not acquired by him from intellectual reasons as a derivative conviction, but rests upon personal experience of the H. Spirit, who fills the heart with this certainty of salvation. COCCEIUS, *Aphorism, brev.* (*Op.* VI, x, 5): "The sign of election is true faith in God through Christ, which being explored and proved by trials affords the faithful sure hope, consolation and glorying in the hope of glory.—This certainty is a divine testimony to the heart, according to the testimony extant in sacred letters; it is not a fallible conjecture". In this sense HEIDEGGER for example says (V, 49): "Besides, the certainty of divine election to salvation and to the means of salvation is in respect of God who elects supreme; in respect of man elected to salvation and its means it is so great as to suffice for salvation and its consolation in this life. In respect of God supreme, because by His eternal and immutable counsel He has defined a fixed number of the elect, which can in no wise admit of increases or decreases and of which none can be lost or fail to obtain eternal salvation.—(V, 51): Already too in respect of man elected, the certainty of election is so great, as to suffice him for salvation and necessary consolation. For although it is anything but fixed for a man as to the election of others, save by a judgment of love, by which he does not rashly assign anyone to the reprobate, yet as to his own he may admit it to himself, with a certainty not moral or conjectural, which might deceive him, but by faith which cannot deceive."

POLAN (IV, 9) distinguishes four 'divine benefits' and four 'divine testimonies', by which "eternal election may be rendered certain to the elect, and that after their regeneration". To these POLAN reckons "(1) effectual calling to the communion of Christ Rom. 8. 30 (whom he foreordained he also called) 9. 23-24 (and that he might make known the riches of his glory upon vessels of mercy, which he afore prepared unto glory, even us, whom he also called, not from the Jews only, but also from the Gentiles); (2) the gift of saving faith Ac. 13. 48 (. . . as many as were ordained to eternal life believed) 2 Th. 2. 13 (God chose you from the beginning unto salvation in sanctification of the Spirit and belief of the truth, whereunto he called you through our gospel, to the obtaining of the glory of our Lord Jesus Christ) Tit. 1. 1 (. . . according to the faith of God's elect . . .); (3) gratuitous justification in the sight of God, Rom. 8. 30 (whom he foreordained he also called); (4) glorification, i.e. regeneration or sanctification or fresh creation, by which we have been created in Christ Jesus unto good works, which God hath prepared that we should walk in them". The "divine testimonies" are partly "outward", partly "inward". The former are (1) the "witness of the gospel, which reveals and attests to all and sundry who truly believe in Christ, that they are elect unto life eternal", and (2) the "witness of the sacraments, instituted by God to confirm our faith". The two "inward witnesses" are (1) the "witness of our own spirit, when our conscience has been made calm as the result of justification through faith in the sight of God Rom. 5. 1 (being justified by faith let us have peace with God through our Lord Jesus Christ)", and (2) the witness of the H. Spirit, i.e. "that inward revelation in the heart of each elect human, that God the Father has predestined him whom He was adopting as a son, which revelation takes place through the infusion of inward grace, by which the H. Spirit effectually persuades the elect human, to believe surely that he is the son of God, and that by the sole goodness of God the Father and by the grace of Christ; and to be filled with trust and love to God, such that he calls upon Him from the heart, from love of Him hates his sins and is gripped by a sincere desire to do His will".—LEIDEN SYNOPSIS XXIV, 41-42: "The uses of this doctrine are many and outstanding in the Church of Christ.—But these uses reach their full effectiveness, only when the elect are made surer of their election. This happens not by any enthusiasm or rash review of divine judgments, but by its fixed results and marks, which the profane are ignorant of and despise, but which the godly in serious self-examination joyfully detect in themselves".—The inmost core of the doctrine of the *certitudo electionis* is described by SEEGEDIN p.117: "This (certainty of our salvation) consists in Christ Jesus. Although our salvation has always been hidden with God, Christ is yet the channel by which it flows down to us, and is received by us in faith, that it may be firm and fixed in our hearts. Upon him therefore we must cast the eyes of faith, in order that we may surely hold that we are of the order of the sons of God. God's predestination is hidden in Himself; moreover in Christ alone He makes it plain to us. Nor does He will to save anyone, unless he believes in Christ."—MARTINIUS (*Dispp. decas* I, p.173): "First we must believe in the Gospel, then we must believe that we are elect."— *Confession of the Reformed Church of Germany* (HEPPE, p. 275): "Whoso will know whether he is elect, let him believe in Christ, then he knows it. For all who believe are elect.—Whoso will grow the longer the surer of his gracious choice, let him become the longer the more godly.—And though faith be in us somewhat very small, we should not therefor despair".

B.—REPROBATION.

22.—The other side of God's predestinating decree is the rejection of those, on whom God will not have mercy. "Reprobation is the decree of God, by which out of the mere good pleasure of His will He has resolved to leave fixed men, whom He does not elect, in the mass of corruption and piling up sins on sins and, when they have been hardened by His just judgment, to visit them with eternal punishments, in order to display the glory of His righteousness" (HEIDEGGER V, 54). Or: "(Reprobation is) that by which God has resolved to leave certain men whom He has not elected in the mass of corruption and to condemn them eternally because of sin" (RIISSEN, VI, 16). That there really is such an eternal and unalterable *reprobatio* of individual men is clear from H. Scripture, which teaches that God chose a part of men from eternity, whence the remainder are not chosen, but purposely passed over; which H. Scripture likewise expressly attests. If there were no *reprobatio*, absurdities would have to be inferred, which would contradict essential truths of faith. A part of men would in that case have a life quite undetermined and aimless. In that case God's punishing righteousness could not be revealed, and Christ would not have been justified in expressly not interceding for a part of humanity, those namely who are of this world.—HEIDEGGER (V, 55): "It cannot be doubted that from eternity God has reprobated some. Election itself also teaches this. He who elects some passes over those whom He does not elect, leaves and appoints them to merited judgment, as sinners not elected for giving to Christ for redemption, left to themselves and to the increases of their corruption. Apart from such appointment the majority of men would run down to their end without any counsel of God and would be allowed an unfixed outcome, and God could not have resolved anything from eternity anent the exercise of righteousness and judgment. Without impiety this cannot be thought of God, the supreme Lord of all things and of good and bad men, alike a merciful and a just distributor. In addition, God θέλων, willing to show His wrath against vessels of wrath Rom. 9. 22, held it necessary to set up an example of some, when He spared others. The righteous is delivered out of trouble, and the wicked cometh in his stead (Prov. 11. 8). And this very fact also does not a little to illumine oppositely the glory of God's mercy."—WALAEUS 357: "The election of some necessarily supposes the preterition and rejection of others".

By the following arguments POLAN proves that there is a decree of God, in accordance with which God "from eternity has reprobated and passed over certain rational creatures", and that accordingly a number of men are rejected (IV, 10): (1) from the Scripture passages Jer. 6. 30 (refuse silver shall men call them, because the Lord hath rejected them) Mt. 7. 23 (and then will I profess unto them, I never knew you; depart from me, ye that work iniquity) Jn. 17. 9 (I pray for them: I pray not for the world, but for those whom thou hast given me; for they are thine) Rom. 9. 22 (what if God, willing to shew his wrath, and to make his power known, endured with much long-suffering vessels of wrath fitted unto destruction?) 1 Pet. 2, 7-8 (for you which believe is the preciousness, but for such as disbelieve, The stone which the builders rejected . . . was made . . . a stone of stumbling and a rock of offence) Jude 4 (of old set forth unto condemnation) Rev. 13. 8, (every one whose name hath not been written in the book of life of the Lamb that hath been slain from the foundation of the world) 17. 8 (they whose name hath not been written in the book of life from the foundation of the world) 20. 15 (if any was not found written in the book of life, he was cast into the lake of fire); also (2) from the following arguments: "(a) If not all are elected to eternal life, then the rest are reprobate; but the former stands, therefore so also the latter.— (b) Whomsoever Christ drives from himself in the last judgment, these are forthwith reprobated from eternity by God. This proposition is fixed, because Christ will not drive from himself those who are elect Jn. 6. 37 (all that which the Father giveth me shall come unto me; and him that cometh to me I will in no wise cast out). But Christ will reject many in the last judgment Mt. 7. 23 (and then will I profess unto them, I never knew you: depart from me, ye that work iniquity) 8. 12 (the sons of the Kingdom shall be cast forth into the outer darkness) 25. 41 (depart from me, ye cursed, . . .).—(c) If not all are sheep, but many are goats or disgraceful, who shall depart into eternal punishment, then there are those reprobated by God. But the former is the case as Mt. 25 (the judgment) teaches. So Christ says to the Jews, (Jn. 10. 26) "Ye believe not, because ye are not of my sheep".—(d) If there are some for whom Christ did not pray, for whom he did not die effectually, who are of the world; then they are reprobated by God. But the first is true, as Christ testifies Jn. 17; therefore so is the last.—(e) If some are reprobate, then there is reprobation. *Illud est, ergo et hoc.* The assumption is proved by the examples of Cain, Ham, Ishmael, Esau, Judas Iscariot."

23.—Essentially *reprobatio* includes two elements, *praeteritio* or the denial of grace not due, and *praedamnatio* or the appointment of punishment due. For God resolved (1) as absolute Lord of His creation to pass over in His redeeming grace a part of fallen mankind which really merited damnation because of its guilt of sin, and (2) as the righteous judge of all His rational creatures to deal with them according to law and righteousness.— WOLLEB 23: "In order to the teaching of reprobation two acts are laid down: the denial of grace not due, called *praeteritio* and the appointment of due punishment, called *praedamnatio*".—KECKERMANN 308: "Reprobation is God's decree for leaving certain men in sin and for damning them eternally on account of sin. Reprobation comprises a double act. The first act is God's purpose to abandon certain men and leave them to themselves; this act is absolute, depending on the sole and absolute *arbitrium* of God.—Act No. 2—is the purpose to damn on account of sins;

this act is not absolute, but involves respect to the state of sin.—310: It is rightly said that we are saved because of election; but it cannot with equal fitness be said that certain are damned because of reprobation. Election is the positive *principium* of salvation, but reprobation strictly speaking is not a principle but the removal of a principle. Nor can it be said strictly that men were ordained from eternity to damnation, unless with this addition: on account of sin".—LEIDEN SYNOPSIS XXIV, 46: "A twofold way of enunciating this eternal reprobation occurs in the Word of God. The first is negative, the second affirmative. Both evince the fact of reprobation and both by synecdoche are sometimes used for the whole of reprobation.—49: From this twin mode of speaking arises a distinction, employed by great theologians in this matter, into negative and affirmative reprobation, which others call *praeterition* and *predamnation*. By explaining these the nature of this dogma will be made the plainer.—50: Negative reprobation means the eternal act of the divine power and judgment, by which according to the counsel of His will He did not resolve to pity the rest whom He did not elect to the extent of presenting them with the peculiar grace of election not due to them. The affirmative kind is the act by which He resolved to impose upon the same men, justly left in the lump of perdition or of their own free will variously abusing the light of nature and the gospel, the punishment they had earned.—52: But neither must we take this as though the two acts were really different: God has determined all things from eternity by Himself in a single *actus*. But we have given this explanation because of the different things contained in the same decree and because of their different relations, namely of *terminus a quo* and *ad quem*."

24.—God is not bound to give His redeeming grace to any man: all have fallen away from Him and are liable to eternal death. Hence when God refuses His grace to some men, He does what He might do to all according to His righteousness; He bestows no mercy on them, He denies them communion with the Redeemer and effectual calling to him and punishes them with increasing hardness and blindness. Thus the reason of their damnation is neither the sinfulness of their condemnation foreseen by God nor their eternal rejection. Otherwise, since they are all alike sinful, God would have had to damn them all; and whilst of course for the elect election is the positive ground of their salvation, for the damned rejection is only the withholding of the ground of salvation, but not the ground of damnation itself. That consists purely and solely in the sinfulness of the rejected, while rejection itself has its sole ground in the absolute will of God, who fulfils His decree of reprobation by means of a completely just *damnatio*.

HEIDEGGER (V, 56): "The nature of universal reprobation resolves into these parts, that God as αὐτοκράτωρ, absolute Lord, disposing, that is, by His sheer freewill of those who are called reprobate from this disposition, then as a just judge, decreeing damnation to none but the sinner, has, in order to illuminate the glory of His righteousness, partly passed over certain men lying in the common lump of sinners and so no worse than the rest, partly appointed them to destruction, partly by the same decree subordinated means suitable to this end. Moreover He has passed them over in the preparation both of glory and of grace. In the preparation of glory, so far as He has prepared a kingdom of heaven for those alone who are blessed of the Father. Come, ye blessed of my Father, approach the inheritance of the kingdom prepared for you from the foundation of the world: depart from me, etc. Mt. 25. 34, 41. In the preparation of grace, so far as He has not given the others to the Son to be redeemed the same as the elect Jn. 17. 9 (I pray not for the world but for those whom thou hast given me) Mt. 13. 11 (unto you it is given to know the mysteries of the kingdom of heaven, but to them it is not given) 11. 26 (Yea, Father, for so it was well-pleasing in thy sight)."—WOLLEB 23: "As Christ is the cause not of election but of salvation, so unbelief is the cause not of reprobation but of damnation. Reprobation differs from damnation, as the means of executing differs from the decree".—BUCAN (XXXVI, 36): "Are not foreseen sins like unbelief etc. the causes of the decree why a man is reprobated?—No! If sins were the cause of reprobation, there would be no elect, since God has foreseen that all men are sinners. But only God's purpose (is the cause), the will which in any work of His is both righteous and the single rule of all righteousness."—RIISSEN VI, 17: "Reprobation no less than election is considered either absolutely in respect of one, or comparatively and relatedly in respect of several. In the former sense it may be asked, why God has reprobated this or that man. The answer is, because on the score of sin he was worthy to be reprobated; not because sin is strictly the cause of reprobation, otherwise all had been reprobate, who were equally sinners; but, because it is the condition and quality in the object previously from which "reprobability" arises in man. In the latter sense it may be asked, why He has reprobated this man rather than that, since both are equally sinners and so "reprobable". Here sin cannot be alleged because it is common to both, and no reason can be given save the sole good-pleasure of God, because it so pleased Him."—These points of doctrine are most completely and comprehensively lit up by HEIDEGGER (V. 59): "Above all the decree of reprobation and that of damnation are not the same thing. The former embraces (1) not only the purpose of damning, but also several acts in some ways higher in their scope, such as are the purpose (a) of not pitying unto salvation Rom. 9. 16-17-18 (So then it is not of him that willeth, nor of him that runneth, but of God that hath mercy. For the Scripture saith unto Pharaoh, For this very purpose did I raise thee up, that I might show my power, and that my name might be published in all the earth. So then he hath mercy on whom he will, and whom he will he hardeneth); (b) of not ordaining Christ as Redeemer Jn. 17. 9 (. . . I pray not for the world, but for those whom thou hast given me; for they are thine); (c) of not calling, but of leaving them in the ways of ignorance Ac. 14. 16 (suffered all the nations to walk in their own ways), or at least of not calling them effectually Mt. 11. 25-26 (I thank thee, O Father, Lord of heaven and earth, that thou didst hide these things from the wise and understanding and didst reveal them unto babes: Yea, Father, for so it was well-pleasing in thy sight); (d) of blinding and hardening Rom. 11. 7-8-9 (the election obtained it, and the rest were hardened . . . God gave them a spirit of stupor, eyes that they should not see, ears that they should not hear, unto this very day; then Ps. 69. 22f. ((Let their table before them become a snare ; and when they are at peace let it become a trap). (2) There are also different causes of reprobation and of damnation. Of the latter there is sin alone, of the former there are other causes, as we shall presently see. Nor does the objection hold here that Christ as judge will be unjust, if he admits one cause of decerning punishment, another of executing it. It is enough that he condemns no one save for sin, nor will he have decreed to damn any save a sinner, although not on account of sin, because otherwise he would have been obliged to the damnation of all. Besides that God in reprobation is not merely a just judge who reprobates none but the sinner. He is also αὐτοκράτωρ and the Lord of absolute power, in light of which just as He ordains some sinners to grace and glory, so He passes others over, excluding them from this grace and glory and ordaining them to the deserved punishment of the sin. (3) The formal act of reprobation is now negative, now positive. The former act is emitted negatively and denies the reprobate saving grace and the glory not due, both of them ; the latter affirms of the same people something positive, judgment and penalty. The former is called praeterition, the latter predamnation. Scripture plainly distinguishes these acts. It not only speaks of reprobation either negatively Mt. 7. 23 (I never knew you!) Jn. 10. 26 (ye believe not, because ye are not of my sheep) etc., or affirmatively Prov. 16. 4 (the Lord hath made . . . the wicked for the day of evil) Mt. 25. 41 (Depart from me, ye cursed) Rom. 9. 11, 18, 22; 11 (for the children being not yet born, neither having done anything good or bad, that the purpose of God according to election might stand, not of works but of him that calleth), . . . 18 (supra); 22 (What if God, willing to shew his wrath, and to make his power known, endured with much long suffering vessels of wrath fitted unto destruction) Jude 4 (of old set forth unto condemnation), but also by predamnation terms some vessels of wrath unto dishonour Rom. 9. 22, sons of perdition Jn. 17. 12, but as to praeterition it opposes election and reprobation or the dereliction of those who are not elected and approves it by the actual result Is. 41. 9 (thou art my servant I have chosen thee, and not cast thee away) Mt. 24. 40-41 (two men in the field . . . two women at the mill, one shall be taken, one left).   But the actual fact also demands this distinction, because reprobation fails to elect some set in the common lump, but leaves them in the lump and in addition appoints them to eternal damnation.   And in fact in the negative act is presupposed sin or guilt, which, since Adam's guilt, rests on the whole human race ; while in the positive act there is also in addition natural corruption and some other sins, of whatever kind, because they do not seek God, who at least in nature has not left himself without a witness; and whom they cannot ignore they do not glorify, they do not wait upon His works in order duly to acknowledge Him; and if the Gospel is revealed to any of them, they either do not receive it in good faith or when received they do not behave in a way worthy of it and they deem Christ's blood common by which he was sanctified, and harden themselves in evil; in word every sin is acquired, whether against the law of nature or against the voice of the gospel.   Further the distinction into negative and positive act is not either of genus into species or of whole into parts or of object into accidents, but of one formal act in respect of objects and terms which consist of ἄρσις and θέσις.   The objects of praeterition are grace not given, glory not prepared; the judgment of predamnation is the penalty due to sin.   The terms of it also are different; a quo=dereliction in common guilt and corruption ; ad quem=damnation either common because of original sin, or particular according to greater or lesser degrees of the actual sins committed against law and gospel.   (4) Fourthly, in a word, reprobation is taken either absolutely of the decree of praeterition and damnation (or of predamnation) ; or relatedly or comparatively of the will by which God has passed over the one lot for the other in the preparation of grace and glory; likewise the one He has predestined over the other for punishment to be inflicted by a just judgment for sins.   After these observations we assert that no one is damned except for sin; that no one is reprobated or passed over by eternal decree or appointed to destruction, except the sinner, not because sin is the cause of the decree itself or of the decerning will (otherwise all men as undistinguishable in the same lump would have had to be reprobated), but because it is the condition in the object passed over, and the cause of its destruction and damnation, so that the condition of the object of the reprobation and the cause of the actual destruction should be altogether assigned to sin."

25.—But while by *praeteritio* God refuses His redeeming grace to the rejected He does not deprive them of His common grace, which latter would have sufficed man in his original state to attain to eternal blessedness, and of which man continues to receive so much that he has no ground for excuse left at the judgment seat of God.—LEIDEN SYNOPSIS (XXIV, 54-55): "For this to be understood correctly, careful note must be taken that this praeterition does not remove or deny all grace in those passed over, but that only which is peculiar to the elect. But that which through the dispensation of common providence, whether under the law of nature or under gospel grace, is dispensed to men in varying amount, is not by this act of praeterition removed but is rather presupposed; the non-elect are left under the common government of divine providence and the exercise of their own *arbitrium*.—55: Moreover this dispensation of common providence always involves the communication of outward and inward benefits; which indeed sufficed for salvation in the unimpaired nature, as is clear in the rejected angels and the whole human race considered in the first parent before the fall. But in the corrupt nature so much has survived or been superadded to nature under the gospel, that they have been stripped and deprived of every pretext of excuse before the divine judgment, as the apostle testifies Ac. 14. 27 (they rehearsed all that God had done with them, and how they had opened a door of faith unto the Gentiles), Rom. 1. 20 (the invisible things of him since the creation of the world are clearly seen, being perceived through the things that are made, even his everlasting power and divinity, that they may be without excuse) 2. 1 (Wherefore thou art without excuse, whosoever thou art that judgest: wherein thou judgest another, thou condemnest thyself: for thou that judgest practisest the same things); also Jn. 15. 22 (If I had not come and spoken to them, they had not had sin, but now they have no excuse for their sin) 1 Cor. 4. 3 (with me it is a very small thing that I should be judged of you, or of man's judgment: yea I judge not mine own self) and elsewhere."—WALAEUS 490-491: "But reprobation does not deny in the reprobate all grace or every gift saving in itself: for we see that even to the reprobate many even supernatural things are communicated above the gifts of nature, as the propounding of the gospel, many other charisms, and illumination of the mind, and some improvement of the affections or joy, and a taste of future benefits (Heb. 6; Mt. 13); by these gifts they are set in order for salvation, did they not suppress them themselves and render God's counsel towards themselves of no effect, as saith Scripture in Lk. 7, and Rom. 1, also Ac. 7, resist the H. Spirit. For it must assuredly be held that they first

desert God before they are deserted by God, as *Augustine* often says.
For God endures with much longsuffering vessels of wrath, etc. Rom. 9. 22.
In fact we say more with the same *Augustine*, that it does not conflict with
reprobation that even grace sufficient for salvation is given them, as is
clear from the example of the reprobate angels, as well as of all men
created in Adam in the image of God.   Only they are *denied grace infallibly
effectual for salvation.*   In Adam all had strength to keep the law, even also
to believe in Christ, had it been revealed to them (as even theologians
themselves confess who ascend above the fall in this article), and they lost
it in him (sc. Adam).   Therefore grace sufficient for salvation is consistent with the decree of reprobation."

26.—We must not conclude from the fact that the godless man is predestined to eternal rejection, that he is also predestined to persist in
godlessness or in sin generally.   Of course a distinction must be made in
sinful action between the action itself and the sinful inclination revealed
in it.   To the action in which a man is proved to show a sinful tendency
of the heart the sinner is as much predestined by God as the punishment
consequent upon it is predestined.   On the other hand the sinful nature
is altogether man's concern.—HEIDEGGER (V, 66): "Is it therefore easy
to judge whether reprobate are as much predestinated to the actual sins
of unbelief and impenitence as to paying the penalty for their sins?—
The wholly important thing is to distinguish the sin; because when it is
concretive, containing many different subheads, the question may be
affirmed or denied.   In sin there are the action or inclination, which is
considered in the genus of being; the *vitium* or ἀνομία of inclination
and action, its form so to speak; and God's judgment consistent with
both, the accident as it were.   First and third come under predestination
as its effect, because God has decreed both to operate the action or inclination reckoned in the genus of being and to exercise His judgment for sin
in accordance with the action.—God is the author both of the action
itself and of the judgment or ἀντιμισθία and of the penalty, whether
He executes them through bad or through good instruments.   Nevertheless it is only improperly that He is said to have thus predestinated to sin:
strictly action and judgment are not sins.   The former (action) is
subordinated to sin first, the latter (judgment) follows sin.   And much
less has God predestinated anyone to sin, so far as sin is ἀνομία and
opposed to the divine law."

27.—And that is why we cannot reproach God with respect of persons
in the election and rejection of individuals (God has not rejected the
reprobated because of their foreseen sinfulness, neither is He the cause
of their sinfulness) or with arbitrary action in rejection (He only judges

and damns the rejected according to His holy law).—Cocceius (XXXVIII, 17): "There is nothing in the objection some make to this doctrine, that God is not an acceptor of persons. God truly is not an acceptor of persons, because (1) He does not judge save according to His law, which is the mirror of God's truth, righteousness and judgment. (2) He does not recognise anyone worthy of His justifying and sanctifying grace: and He values nothing so highly in man the sinner, as that it should constitute a reason for Him donating grace."—Braun (I, ii, 9, 21): "But it does not therefore follow (1) that God is to be accused of cruelty. There is no cruelty, when God intends the manifestation of His righteousness. (2) Nor is He an acceptor of persons, because He has elected one, passed over another. (1) He is an acceptor of persons, who regards something in man as worthy as it were of a reward, which is, nevertheless, nothing; (2) God would be an acceptor of persons, had He elected on account of faith and good works, which latter nevertheless deserve nothing; (3) Nor is God to be called the author of sin: not reprobation, but the actual will of man, must be called the cause of sin."—Leiden Synopsis (XXIV, 58): "Nor is this will absolute as though lacking reason, or tyrannical (perish any blasphemy in the word), as some understand the word absolutely, when they attempt in that respect to create ill-feeling in us. It is most wise, most ordered and most holy. Firstly it cannot be accused of tyranny, if it exacts its right from one delinquent and criminal, although it does not exact it from other criminals in like wise; secondly, if it does so for good and holy ends. For if both lots were liberated, the due reward for sin through righteousness would remain obscure, while if no one was liberated, we should not know what grace would bestow, as *Augustine* remarks in agreement with the *Apostle* (Rom. 9. 22-23 God willing to show His wrath . . . that He might make known the riches of his glory upon vessels of mercy).—59. In fact it is not even absolute, as though no reason is fixed for the divine wisdom, why it should have rejected this man rather than that, although that reason is not to be sought in diversity of merits."

28.—The purpose of reprobation is twofold: "The supreme end is the glory of God reprobating;—the subordinate end is the righteous condemnation of the reprobated to death for their sins" (Heidegger V, 64).—Alting, p.80: "The end (of reprobation) (1) in respect of God, which is the supreme end, is God's glory, (2) in respect of man, which is the subordinate end, is the righteous condemnation of the reprobate".

29.—The means by which God consummates rejection are: "desertion of the reprobate, their separation from Christ and from the grace of redemption or reconciliation, the omission to call them or at all events ineffectual calling, the retention of their sins, their blinding or induration and their final impenitence" (HEIDEGGER (V, 65).—BUCAN (XXXVI, 39): "What are the peculiar means of executing God's decree for the reprobation of men?—Six in number. (1) The infinite proliferation of actual sins.— (2) 'Απιστία, infidelity, or alienation and separation from Christ.— (3) Desertion, or no calling, or an ineffectual one through the preaching of the Word, or no inward response to calling; for neither was the gospel preached to individuals separately and to the whole age, nor is it now preached in the entire globe, nor was it given to individuals to believe Matthew 11. 25 (thou didst hide these things from the wise and understanding and didst reveal them unto babes) also 28 (come unto me, all ye that labour and are heavy laden, and I will give you rest). All are called upon, who labour and are laden; i.e. they faint under their burden of sins, which only fits those who recognise themselves as sinners and take refuge with Christ.—(4) Pertinacity or hardening and complete blinding in sins.—(5) Hence comes constant aversion from God, contempt and progress from sin to sin.—(6) Finally their most just condemnation follows therefrom."

30.—Therefore it can only be said of those who persist in deadly sins to the end, that they are rejected.—POLAN (IV, 10): "The signs of reprobation are these: (1) every kind of denial of God's benefits which necessarily follow election, namely those of effectual calling, saving faith, justification and sanctification. These God has reprobated, to whom He has utterly refused such benefits; (2) blinding and induration in evil or sin. The reprobate are blinded and hardened by the just judgment of God, to persevere and to perish in sins."—COCCEIUS (Aphor. prolix. Op. VI, 11, 21, 27): "The sign of reprobation in this life is sin against the H. Spirit and final impenitence."

31.—Otherwise each must think of other in this respect according to the law of love and hope the best for him. Instead of giving entrance to thoughts of despair, each must seek for himself by a believing grasp of the Gospel and by steady zeal in sanctification to establish confidence in his own election more and more.—HEIDEGGER (V. 67): "From the means of reprobation rehearsed, no one except those who sin unto death ought to or can determine anything certain before the end of life, concerning the eternal reprobation of himself or of others. Of others indeed we must have good hopes by the judgment of love 1 Cor. 1. 37 (beareth, believeth, hopeth, endureth all things), nor should anyone discard hope of his own salvation, but rather strive vigorously to effect by zeal for faith and good works to make his own calling and election sure."

32.—In this sense the doctrine of the eternal rejection of the godless must be taught in the Church according to Scripture, to comfort the faithful and to rouse sinners, and must not be hushed up from false avoidance and disinclination.—HEIDEGGER (V, 70): "We do not approve the affected ταπεινοφροσύνη of some, who overcome either by the stupor of ignorance or by errors either advise or command concerning the dogma of predestination ἐχεμυθία or a sacred silence in the Church. Indeed their temerity is detestable, who with the Icarian wings of their own blind reason, outwith the barriers of God's Word, extolling themselves to the heights, endeavour to penetrate the secrecies of the divine will, and exactly as if they had been God's counsellors, thundering as it were from heaven, they are not ashamed inadvisedly to drag into the light things which God has covered up in the mist of a deep night, and to attach to God Himself the concatenations of the divine decrees which they have designed in their own brains.—Be that as it may, let us avoid these and other rocks; let us regard this dogma soberly and publicly in an order analytic rather than synthetic, not by peering into its causes in heaven, but by explaining signs on earth and in our own hearts, for instance, and in the Christian conversation of men (as one about to examine a tree beholds and tastes its flowers and fruits, does not try to dig or furrow up its roots), and so expound it that everywhere, with Luther as godly consultant even in this matter, we may behold and strictly follow a God not hidden but manifested or speaking in His Word; if in addition, above all in the doctrine of reprobation, a prudent συγκατάβασις is applied for the capture and complicity of those in whose presence there is discussion of that matter, it is not only a useful one to know and to transmit and above all saving, but it is also necessary."—LEIDEN SYNOPSIS (XXIV, 61): "So we see the spontaneous collapse of all the calumnies with which this doctrine is weighed down by some. And accordingly in Christ's Church, although with all sobriety, it must sometimes, we declare, be dealt with out of H. Scripture. By this comparison God's goodness the more shines out towards us, as Paul reminds us Rom. 11. 22 (the goodness of God etc.), and hence we so much the more humble ourselves beneath God's judgments, that we venerate and adore His righteousness and wisdom although at times hidden from our eyes, as the same Apostle also anticipates us in doing Rom. 9. 20 (O man, who art thou, that repliest against God ? . . .) 11. 33 (O the depth of the riches both of the wisdom and the knowledge of God! how unsearchable are his judgments and his ways past finding out)."

CHAPTER IX

CREATION

1.—The outward realisation of God's *operationes internae* or the execution of His eternal decree is the *operationes externae*, i.e. the *opus naturae* and the *opus gratiae*.—MASTRICHT III, v, i: "So much for the inward operations of God. Follow the outward, which look to the inward as their ideas and in addition put into execution the counsel of manifesting the glory of His mercy and righteousness. They are two in number, creation by which the creature is produced, and providence by which He beholds what He has produced."—MARCK (VIII, 1): "God begins to execute the eternal decrees in creation, which is the first outward transeunt and temporal work and along with providence is called the *opus naturae*, as opposed to the *opera gratiae ac redemtionis*: although all the works of nature also proceed from God's commoner grace and tend towards the grace to be conferred on the elect".

2.—In respect of these *operationes Dei externae* we must maintain (1) that they occur outwith the divine nature, since its strength is unfolded outwardly; (2) that they are executed in definite temporal form; and of course (3) in conformity with the eternal decree.—POLAN (V, 1): "In the definition of the outward works of God three things are distinctly propounded about them, to distinguish them from the inward works; (1) They take place outside God's essence, He exerting His power *ad extra*; (2) God does them at a fixed time; (3) God does them in accordance with the eternal decree or counsel of His will".

3.—The *opus naturae* includes the creation of the world and providence.—WOLLEB 24. "So much for the inward works of God. The outward ones are those which are done outside God's essence; and they are both the creation and the government of the creatures, or the actual providence of God."

4.—"Creation" (generally: "the production of things out of nothing"; RIISSEN, VI, 3) "is strictly the name of God's first outward work, by which directly and of Himself at the beginning of time He produces things which previously were not, purely by His almighty command, from simple non-being into being, without change, by His own free will, and that out of nothing or out of material previously made out of nothing but by nature incapable of assuming such form as the Creator imposed upon it, when the material was made out of nothing" (POLAN V, 2): or more briefly: "Creation it is, by which God produced the world and the things in it partly out of nothing, partly out of naturally inert matter, to manifest the glory of His power, wisdom and goodness." (WOLLEB 24).

The subject of creation as a divine act utterly incommunicable to the creature is the triune God.—WOLLEB 24: "The work and honour of creation must not be assigned to any creature, not even to the angels, but to God alone".—LEIDEN SYNOPSIS (X, 14): "We emphatically reply that the creation of the world is quite incommunicable to creatures".

5.—The triune God is the Creator, but in such a way that the Father as the "source of the Trinity" is also the proper source of the works of creation, which He has executed through the Son and the H. Spirit.— Usually along with the statement that "creation is the work of the entire Trinity" it is further insisted that "as God the Father is the *fons sanctae Trinitatis* or *divinitatis,* so too He is the *fons* of all the things which are from God and outside God, i.e. of the creatures" (WENDELIN, *Collat.* p.104): e.g. in the LEIDEN SYNOPSIS (X, 9): "The Father of Himself created the world through the Son and the H. Spirit; the Son of the Father through the H. Spirit; and the latter of the Father and the Son."

6.—In fact God completed creation without being in any way determined by any outward co-operating cause, or by objective ideas by which He took His bearing, solely by the efficacy of His free will and good pleasure. —HEIDEGGER (VI, 14): "Like the eternal decrees of God the temporal creation had itself no cause outside God whether principal or instrumental; could not have had one. In the beginning nothing existed outside God, and no ideas even or exemplars of work outside God had been set up, such as *Plato* imagined that God had in view when creating; this on the evidence of *Aristotle,* though others contradict this".

7.—By His free will and good pleasure God called everything outside Himself out of nothing into existence for a definite purpose and made them the object of his good pleasure.—MASTRICHT (III, v, 8): "The command of creation included three things: (1) the production of the thing by that most effective *Esto* or *Fiat* (Gen. 1. 3,6,7), by which creation received existence: (2) the ordering of it: let it be for this or that end, e.g. to give light upon the earth Gen. 1. 16; by which its use was assigned to each thing and the office as it were which it was to fulfil universally; (3) approval of it; God saw that it was good Gen. 1.4, whereby of His goodness He approved the excellence and perfection of the creation and blessed it to the use assigned to it."

8.—Of course the world is the reflection of ideas present in God. These, however, are not something objectively confronting God's consciousness but are God's very nature, which is described as the essence of the ideas, so far as the nature of God is for man an imitable copy.—POLAN (V, 6): "Let it stand fixed and sure that in the divine mind there had been and were ideas of everything that was created, according to which they were made, knowledge of which is not only necessary to the study of wisdom, but is also highly useful to the discipline of morals, as is admitted since *Augustine*.—The divine ideas of the things created are forms existing in the divine mind from eternity, not really distinct from the divine essence, but which are actually the same as the divine essence. These ideas created things imitate by God's intention as their Creator, who determines the end for Himself.—These ideas are in the divine mind or in God, as in the source of all being. In God in fact they have one *ratio*, but outside Him they issue into numerous ones. They are in God like numbers in unity.—The words "existent from eternity" distinguish divine ideas from human conceits in the knowledge of artificers. The words following "not distinct really from the divine essence etc." exclude the ideas from the number of forms created, whether substantial or accidental, actually distinct from the essence of their subject. God is not a subject endowed with many forms, substantial or accidental. He is most single essence, self-existing and singly existent and existent in that way. And like the essential attributes of Deity the ideas also in the divine *intellectus* do not differ *realiter* from the divine essence itself.—So the divine ideas are not creatures actually known by God, but they are objective reasons, i.e. the actual divine essence conceived by God, according as it is imitable by things created, just as the divine exemplar is infinitely more perfect than the things created, since it is the actual divine essence known as imitable."

9.—Above all it is fixed, that the creation of the world is a thoroughly free act of God, in fact an act of God free *libertate contradictionis* (MARCK, VIII, 12), so that God could also refrain from creating. Only in relation to God's eternal decree did creation follow *ex necessitate consequentiae*.— URSIN (*Loci*, p. 548): "God created the world not by an absolute necessity but by the one which is termed *consequentiae*, or *ex hypothesi, sc. suae voluntatis*, although by His eternal and immutable, yet utterly free decree. Neither was God tied down to creating things, nor if He had never created the world, or were reducing it to nothing when created, would He be on that account less good or less blessed."—VOETIUS (I, 566): "*Creatio* is an *actio ad extra*, and therefore free, and so accords with the decree. In addition it is outward and emanative, and so is distinguished from the decree."

10.—So the creation of the world substance resulted in a moment without trouble on God's part and without any sort of omnipotence in its origination.—MASTRICHT (III, v, 14): "Since therefore the δημιουργός of creation is infinite, who in addition created by the sole nod of His will, it is clear that individual things emerged—(1) not by a laborious effort but by a word, Ps. 33. 9 (he spake and it was done; he commanded and it stood fast);—(2) nor by a successive movement circuitously and by twists, but in a moment of time (*ibid.*), because creation excludes all matter prepared by deprivation of its original form, in order that a new one might be substituted for it, in which successive elements are required; finally (3) without any difficulty or fatigue, Is. 40. 28 (. . . the everlasting God, the LORD, the Creator of the ends of the earth, fainteth not neither is weary; there is no searching of his understanding").—BUCAN (V, 10): "The creation of the world took place (1) by the production of the matter or seed-bed of the whole world; (2) by informing that, and this by the sole command of God in a moment of time."

11.—Hence *creatio activa* is nothing but the effectiveness of the divine will in relation to its definite purpose; whereas *creatio passiva* is the coming of the world into existence, (not, however, its construction out of already existing material).—HEIDEGGER (VI, 16): "Since it is agreed that it was by His sheer will and command that God created the world, in accordance with the Scriptures quoted above, it appears according to the same Scriptures, that creation in the active sense is nothing else than the efficacy of the divine will, or the divine volition as put into execution through the power of God; and that passive creation is the becoming, arising, beginning to be, because of God's will, and so the rise of the thing which is created, together with the relation which it has to Him who creates, as of effect to cause. This they call passive creation improperly and καταχρηστικῶς, since where there is no subject, it cannot strictly be said to experience (*pati*) anything. Yet we say it experiences this, because since the becoming is a *passio* in the subject changed, so too becoming in the creature is a kind of *passio*, because as a rule it has the same relation to the Creator, as any change has to its end. Therefore creation is active in God the Creator, passive in the creature. The former is not distinguishable from God's will and effectual decree. For though to will and to do may seem to be distinguished according to the word of Ps. 115. 3 (our God . . . hath done whatsoever he pleased) and the eternal decree is called temporal creation, yet what is thus expressed ἀνθρωποπαθῶς should be understood soberly, as that God's doing is God's willing plus effectuality".

12.—Since then the counsel to create the world existed in God from eternity and since the execution of this counsel is nothing else than the absolute energy of the divine will, the result is that the making of the world produced absolutely no change or completion in the being or blessedness of God. "Creation is a transition not of the Creator but of the creature from potency to actuality" (WOLLEB 24), since it was neither a transition from rest to activity nor a continuation from mere possibility to action. Hence it cannot be said that before creation God was idle and first became active through it. The eternal decree with all that pertains to it is an eternal act of God.—WOLLEB 25: "No perfection was added to God by the creation of the world".—MARCK (III, 11): "Hence it may be clear, how creation differs from the decree and at the same time imports no change into God, as though He had passed from leisure to labour and from potency to action. Here there is and has been and always will be the same will in God, by which He wills the existence of things in the beginning of time appointed by Himself, which, when by action it produces a work, is called creation, the creature but not God then receiving new perfection, according as a fresh outward relation is added. Hence the problems of God's occupation in eternity raised by the inquisitive fall to the ground."—URSIN (*Loci* p. 547) replies to the objection, "that it seems absurd that from all eternity to the creation of the world God has been idle, and that therefore the world has always existed", by saying that "from all eternity God contemplated His wisdom, and elected us to life eternal in the Son before the foundations of the world were laid."—CALVIN (I, xiv, 1): "Nor should we be moved by the profane jest, that it is strange why it did not occur sooner to God to create heaven and earth, but He idly let an immense interval elapse.— It is neither right nor expedient for us to ask why God put off for so long." —BUCAN (V, 36): "What was God doing, before He created this world ? The question is inquisitive and so *Augustine* (*Confessions*, II, 12) writes, that a certain senior made a knowing answer to such an inquirer: "He was fashioning a hell for Nosey Parkers". Our answer is, that God had been sufficient and blessed in Himself and had needed for nothing and had delighted Himself in His eternity with His Wisdom, i.e. the Son and the Spirit, of one substance with Himself, Jn. 1. 1, 16.13 (the Son: the Spirit of truth)."—LEIDEN SYNOPSIS (X, 27): "Could He ever have been idle, who apart from Himself contemplated from eternity all that He was to create, and is said to have known and elected us in Christ His beloved Son before the foundations of the world were laid, Rom. 8.28 (. . . the called according to his purpose) Ephesians 1.4 (chose us in him before the foundation of the world . . .) ?"

13.—Since there is nothing higher than the divine will, the cause of creation can only be found in that itself and in its goodness. God created the world, not as though He needed the creature for His majesty and blessedness, but purely because in His goodness and wisdom He wanted to create it.—VOETIUS (I, 558): "There are no outward impelling causes (if one may indeed use this expression of God). The divine goodness is inward; the good diffuses and communicates itself."—POLAN (V. 3): "No προηγούμεναι causes of creation are to be sought outwith God, but only in God. These are God's will, goodness, wisdom and power".—BUCAN (V, 5): "The impelling cause of the creation of things was God's immense goodness joined to His supreme wisdom, which He willed to communicate and by communicating to manifest, because the good is communicative of itself."—HEIDEGGER (VI, 17): "As to the cause that impelled God to create, *St. Augustine, lib.* 83, p. 28 thus piously speaks: "He who asks why God ever wished to create the world, is asking for the reason of God's will. Every efficient cause is greater than that which is effected. But nothing is greater than God's will." But he also (*Enchirid.*, c. 19) alleges His goodness as the cause of His will.— Necessity or need did not move Him to create the world, because He needs nothing, Ac. 17.25 (neither is he served by men's hands, as though He needed anything, seeing he himself giveth to all life, and breath, and all things),—but His most free will, by which He willed to set up a kingdom in the world, and in it to communicate Himself to the creatures as the supreme good and to offer Himself for their enjoyment, and so in them ἐνδοξασθῆναι καί θαυμασθῆναι, "to be glorified and to be marvelled at", 2 Th. 1.10.

14.—This likewise makes clear the *finis creationis*, the purpose of the making of the world. God would let the glory, power, wisdom and goodness of His nature be revealed. Therefore He created the world, in order to render Himself to it, and especially to the intelligent creatures, as the absolute *Bonitas* for their possession and enjoyment.—All dogmaticians stress the *gloria* or *celebratio Dei* as the real ground and final aim of creation, by coalescing its *finis* and its *causa προηγουμένη*, as does COCCEIUS (S.T. XV, 39, 40, 42): "The end of creation is the glory of God, i.e. the manifestation of the eminence, power and virtues of God in the creature and to the creature. God's goodness is the *causa προηγουμένη* of creation". From this it follows that the goodness of the creature consists in it being a witness and evidence of the divine glory. "Thus in all things created there had to be at least some trace of God's perfection and goodness."—LEIDEN SYNOPSIS (X, 29): "The end (of the world) is the manifestation of God's wisdom and power and the perpetual celebration of these virtues among all creatures, especially among rational creatures." URSIN (p. 550 f.) describes the *fines creationis mundi* in the same sense (Cf. HEPPE, *Altprot. Dogmatik*, I p. 317).—Hence we must say that "the supreme end of creation" is "the glory of God or the celebration of God to all eternity." The "subaltern end of creation" is "our use of it" (POLAN, V., 5).

15.—That of which God made the world was not a material existing with God from eternity.—COCCEIUS (S.T. XV, 10-11): "If the eternal changes, it changes from eternity and so changes at the same time in its potency to change and in the act of it, which is a contradiction. Secondly, what is liable to any kind of motion or change must itself have begun to be and must have a certain mode of its duration; in fact, what has countable elements cannot be without a beginning, just as every number starts with unity".—MASTRICHT gives (III, v, 22) the following arguments against assuming the eternity of the world: "Had the world existed from eternity, (1) it would have been infinite in duration; and since duration in reality is not far removed from essence, it would have been *eadem opera* infinite in essence, and in consequence either God Himself, or—(there are) two infinite essences, and therefore neither of them simply infinite; (2) this year would have been preceded by an infinite number of years, to which years would be continually being added, and, by an open contradiction, the infinite would be being increased; in fact (3) since this infinite number of years would achieve a much greater number of months, days, hours and minutes, infinite would be greater than infinite, by an open contradiction once more; and since (4) throughout eternity an infinite number of days would have had to precede the existence of this day, how pray could this one have succeeded? For the infinite number of those preceding would never have been achieved; and since (5) in the world's duration succession could not be absent, importing order of before and after, some beginning is necessarily required, from which such before and after should be derived; which beginning excludes eternity".

16.—The material of the world, then, is nothing.—BUCAN (V, 7): "All things were created and produced *ex nihilo*, the word being taken negatively, i.e. out of no other pre-existent or prejacent material. The preposition *ex* here signifies not a material cause from which something is made, but order, as though to say: Since there was nothing at first, whatever there is afterwards, was made. Or it signifies the possession of a material cause; which is simply denied."—HOTTINGER, p. 110: "The preposition *ex* here denotes neither efficient cause nor matter but limit (*terminus*) and order.—In this way the world is said to be *ex nihilo,* i.e. *post nihilum,* since there could have been nothing before".

17.—Out of nothing along with time God created heaven and earth, so that while the world was not a formless chaos, it was not yet the idea of individual existences, which God first created from its matter in the following days of creation. Hence are to be distinguished *creatio prima,* the result of which was *materia inhabilis,* and *creatio secunda.* This latter was also a real creation, since the first-created world mass, the *materia prima,* was incapable of producing from itself forms and single entities, which only God's almighty power could achieve.—RIISSEN (VII, 4): "One creation is first and direct; it is simply *ex nihilo.* Another is secondary and indirect; while made of some material, it is quite formless and unarranged and not disponible by any power in second causes for producing a *terminus*; in it the only power given is that of obedience or non-repugnance in order to the first cause, acting with infinite power." —VOETIUS (I, p. 554) "Creation may be distinguished into first and second. The former is the production of a thing *ex nihilo,* and those produced in this way are heaven, the elements, light; and even now human souls are daily produced, so far as they are a spiritual essence. The latter is the production of essential or accidental form in a pre-subjected but plainly undisposed material, and that by the direct operation of the divine power. And so were produced the works of the five days, as also were most of the miraculous works when the order of nature had already been constituted."—MARCK (VIII, 14): "Concerning the second creation, of bodies, made after the beginning I don't see how certain most learned men hesitate to find it of a matter not absolutely formless but yet confused and inelegant, which because of the inability is usually called *nihilum secundum quid* (nothing in the relative sense). For (α) Moses most clearly suggests that the common mass was made first, Gen. 1. 1; unless we are to say that he has made no mention of the earth created; (β) he teaches that it was vast and shapeless plainly through the confusion of bodies presently added; (γ) next there appeared, according to Him openly, the upper waters also, plants, animals and the human body; whence (δ) also ὕλη ἄμορφος is well-known not only among Jews and Christians but also the Gentiles under the name, whether of Phoenician or Greek origin, chaos; for they rather received it elsewhere than transmitted it themselves."—For the rest be it noted that in Reformed dogmatics regarding the doctrine of creation it came to be the rule expressly to reject the *Lutheran* doctrine of the original creation of a formless chaos. It was assumed that as early as the first day of creation the real world, earth and water, was created, but that of course (1) on this day

the substance of the two completed bodies were jumbled together, and
that (2) individual existences were not called into being therefrom until
the following days.   Cf. e.g. WENDELIN (*Coll.* p. 105): "We do not
recognise a rude and unassimilated mass commonly called chaos, i.e.
matter void of substantial form, which actually contained in it no kind
of completed body.—The matter which Moses (Gen. 1) calls *Tohu and
Bohu,* i.e. according to some interpretations a rude and unassimilated
mass, commonly called chaos, i.e. matter void of substantial form,
which actually contained in it no kind of completed body, was not the
Aristotelian πρωτὴ ὕλη devoid of substantial shape, as some would
have it, but the confusion of two complete bodies, substantially
perfect, namely earth and water."—Similarly the other dogmaticians, e.g. HOTTINGER 113: "Under the name of first matter we
understand neither nothing nor substance void of all form and created
together, but the rough mass of the earth created on the first day."—
Since God prepared the works of the last days of creation from the mass
called into being on the first days of creation, it is insisted by the Reformed
theologians (WENDELIN, *Collat.* p. 102): "Creation is not perfectly defined
by the action by which something is created out of nothing, because
something is also created strictly out of something."—COCCEIUS'
definition (S.T. XV, 4): "Creation is the production of a new thing by
command, whether it be new relatively to the whole that exists, or
generically or individually."   The main thing is that the sheer dependence
of the existence of a thing upon God is expressed in the concept of
creation. For (COCCEIUS XV, 2) "what is increate is eternal, is necessary,
does not depend on God, is not subject to God, is God."

18.—The result of this is the concept of the creature (POLAN V, 6). "The
creature is everything produced outside God by God with His sole potent
word and command, out of nothing or of matter previously made out of
nothing and in itself incapable of assuming the form with which the
Creator endued it".—In POLAN's definition the emphasis is on the
concept of *res,* whence POLAN (V, 6) remarks: "Be that as it may, in the
proposed definition we must first perpend the genus creature, which is
res, i.e. the *ens* which has a true *esse* created by God, which has a true
existence in itself, which is something in itself.   In this class sin and
death are excluded from the number of creatures.   Neither of these is an
ens with a true *esse* created by God and an existence in itself.   Neither
has the *ratio* of a *res.*   Although original sin comprises not only deprivation
of good but also aversion to God who is the *summum bonum,* propension to
evil, a natural impulse counter to God's Word and other similar things;
although moreover it dwells in us, as the Apostle says Rom. 7. 21 (I find

the law, that, to me who would do good, evil is present); although there is a law in our members warring against the law of the regenerate mind (Rom. 7. 23), yet, if we would speak strictly, it is not a definite *res*, since it has not a true *esse* produced by God; hence sin is not a creature. In this way death is not a particular *res*, i.e. it is not an *ens* having a true *esse* produced by God and a true existence in itself: it is therefore not a creature."—The real meaning of all creatures is the world, their essential attributes are those of relative perfection, unity, spatio-temporal limitation and mutability (HEIDEGGER VI, 20-23).

19.—The creation of the world resulted in the beginning of time ; i.e. with the world time was created, or: the world was created in the form of time.—RIISSEN (VII, 5): "God created all things in or with the beginning of time".—MARCK (VIII, 19): "All this production took place in the concreated beginning of time, before which nothing existed save God eternal".

20.—And God completed the creation of matter and of the creatures made from it in the course of six successive days; not as though God could not have called every item into existence in one moment, but in order to manifest the variety and wise ordering of His creatures.— HEIDEGGER (VI, 36): "We can scarcely doubt that those things which, directly produced from nothing, passed simply from non-being to being, came forth in a moment of time; not because they were made by the order or command of God,—but because the transition from *non esse* to *esse* cannot be made save in a moment. Thus it is right (*par est*) to believe that what is extended, or heaven and earth, light, spirits, were things created in a moment. The remainder, which He created by the same power of His almighty word out of matter produced from nothing on the first day by the preceding creation, by separating, arranging, moulding, shaping and adorning it, may appear to have been subjected to a certain delay and succession in work, not because of a defect of power in God but because of the state of the creature to be made. (VI, 34): So both the variety, distinction and excellence of its works, as well as God's wisdom, shone forth more plainly and fully from the superb work thus unfolded in the connection and order throughout its parts. And the order was displayed, by which God can always first prove His own power and goodness in the weakness and imperfection of the creature and then in its consummation 2 Cor. 4. 6 (It is God that said, Light shall shine out of darkness, who shined in our hearts, to give the light of the knowledge of the glory of God in the face of Jesus Christ), and the structure of the works themselves may more easily be learned by man".

21.—Therefore He made not only unconscious but also intelligent, personal beings, able to recognise, enjoy and praise the revelation of God's majesty and love.—COCCEIUS (S.T. XV, 41): "Therefore it is necessary that there should be a creature to understand through creation the excellence and virtues of God, to love and seek God, and to enjoy God as its good.—So if the whole creation testifies to the intelligent creature, it aims to tell it that its true and single good is God."

22.—The most attractive creatures of God are therefore the angels and men.—COCCEIUS (S.T. XVI, 1): "The most outstanding of God's creatures are the intelligent ones, angels and men".

23.—To their purpose the world as God had created it corresponded perfectly. As the creaturely expression of the *bonitas Dei* the world was essentially good.—AMESIUS (*Med.* I, viii, 17): "Everything was created very good, because not made anyhow or in vain, but for an end which it effectively pursued." Hence the ineradicable draw of the creature to God. (21.22): "By this goodness all things (*res*) created tend in their own natural manner to God, from whom they came forth". This is shown in a threefold connection: "(1) in that they shew forth God's glory; (2) in that they give us an occasion for both knowing and seeking God; (3) in that they sustain our life, in order that we may live well unto God".

CHAPTER X

ANGELS GOOD AND BAD

1.—In the heavenly sphere God created personal, purely spiritual beings in His own image, i.e. angels, whose appointment it is to be sent out by God on appointed functions, namely to fulfil the eternal decrees.— URSIN (*Loci* p. 551) : "On the testimony of H. Scripture angels both good and bad are spirits, by which term we here understand a spiritual person".—COCCEIUS (*S.Th.* XVI, 2) is more definite: "We have learned the term angel from Scripture. It denotes generally one who says or does something in the name of someone else. However in contradistinction to men God's angels are called πνεύματα λειτουργικά, ministering spirits, endowed with unusual mind and will and power of self-movement and of action." Hence in the dogmatic conception of angels the main thing is what CALVIN stresses (I, xiv, 5): "Angels", he says, "are heavenly spirits, whose ministry and obedience God uses to execute all that he has decreed, as it says in Scripture *passim*. The name is also applied to them, because God uses them as a kind of go-between messengers for revealing Himself to men".

2.—"Angels are spirits created by God in righteousness, void of all matter, self-existent, endowed with extraordinary intelligence, will and power, some of whom persevering in their righteousness and confirmed in the same by God serve Him by proclaiming His praises as well as in ordering the world, especially the Church. Others falling away therefrom were cast out of heaven and are now beginning to pay the penalty and as the executors of God's judgments they will undergo punishment by fire for ever after the end of the world" (HEIDEGGER, VIII, 3).— LEIDEN SYNOPSIS (XII, 2): "The name angels signifies spiritual creatures, subsistent in themselves, equipped with knowledge and free will, but surpassing all the other creatures in extraordinary power and strength so as to cope outwardly with the works suited to their nature.—RIISSEN (VII, 26): "Angels are spiritual substances, created, complete, endowed with knowledge, will and power".

3.—Angels are thus pre-eminently (not subjective emotions or ideas in man or accidents and qualities, but) real personal entities.—CALVIN (I, xiv, 9): "It was at one time the view of the *Sadducees* that by angels nothing was meant but either motions with which God imbues men, or things which He emits as instances of His power. But this delusion is rejected by so many evidences in Scripture, that it is extraordinary that

such crass ignorance could have been tolerated in that nation."—
WOLLEB 27: "Angels are not accidents or qualities but true ὑφιστάμενα".
—LEIDEN SYNOPSIS (XII, 8): "In consequence of this peculiar creation
of them we maintain against the *Sadducees* of old Acts 23. 8 (The Sadducees
say that there is no resurrection, neither angel, nor spirit; but the
Pharisees confess both) and the *Libertines* of our own day, that angels are
true hypostases or substances, subsisting separately and by themselves.
God is said to have created no accidents in separation".

4.—Angels are in fact bodiless and therefore immortal spirits.—WOLLEB
27: "Angels are intelligent spirits, free from a body".—HEIDEGGER
(VIII, 6): "The question has been put whether (angels) are ἀσώματοι
simply and whether they have at least a body in which they live in their
natural condition and as incomplete beings are ordained to animate and
develop a body.—To this view not only the ancient philosophers *Plato,
Proclus* and others incline—but also the early fathers not a few,
Tertullian, Origen, Lactantius, Macarius, Gennadius and others, so that *John*
Bishop of Thessalonica (*Conc. Nic.* II *act.* 5) has ventured to assert that
such is the sentiment of the Catholic Church.—Not to mention some
Scholastics, *Bonaventure, Richard, Aureolus* and even our *Zanchius,* who under
his tutors *Dionysius* and the *Damascene,* insist that they are material. But
they are more correctly said to lack all matter".—LEIDEN SYNOPSIS
(XII, 11): "From this spiritual nature of theirs follows also their immortality. By the same power by which they have been produced out of
nothing, they might also be reduced to nothing. Since however their
essence was not composed of diverse inward principles, they cannot of
and by themselves be resolved into other principles, nor will they ever
be so resolved by the will of God".—In his own fashion HYPERIUS (p. 273)
describes the angels as *ignitae naturae,* since "Scripture teaches that a
fiery character inheres in them."

5.—Angels are not eternal, do not emanate from God's nature, but are
created by God out of nothing (according to Biblical indications on the
first day of creation, after heaven and earth were called into existence).—
HEIDEGGER (VIII, 8): "It is admitted that angels did not emanate from
God, because they were not cut from the infinite essence. Besides they
were created at all not before nor after the visible world, both because
whatever is before the world is fixed as eternal Jn. 17. 5 (and now, O
Father, glorify thou me with thine own self with the glory which I had
with thee before the world was) Eph. 1. 4 (even as he chose us in him before
the foundation of the world, that we should be holy and without blemish
before him in love) 1 Pet. 1. 20 (who were foreknown indeed before the

foundation of the world, but was manifested at the end of the times for your sake, and because whatever was before the world is God)."— ALSTED 263: "Angels are not eternal because, as ministers, they depend on God."—URSIN (*Loci* p. 552) "Angels were created by God out of nothing in the very beginning of the world Ps. 148, 2, 5 (Praise ye him, all his angels, praise ye him, all his hosts. Let them praise the name of the Lord: For he commanded and they were created), Col. 1. 16 (in him were all things created, in the heavens and upon the earth, things visible and things invisible, whether thrones or dominions or principalities or powers).— COCCÆIUS (*S.T.* XVI, 12) finds it probable that the angels were created on the day "on which the expanse (*Firmament*) separated the upper from the lower waters". So the other Reformed dogmaticians, e.g. MASTRICHT (III, vii, 4): "That angels were created on the first day of creation along with their dwelling-place seems highly probable, from the fact that they are said to have applauded God when He was founding the earth Job 38. 4-7 (Where wast thou when I laid the foundations of the earth? Declare if thou hast understanding. Who determined the measures thereof, if thou knowest? Or who stretched the line upon it? Whereupon were the sockets thereof sunk? Or who laid the cornerstone thereof; when the morning stars sang together, and all the sons of God shouted for joy?). It is certain that they had not been created prior to the first day of creation, since before that there was only eternity, in which a beginning is not admitted: whence being before that beginning and being from eternity are in the Scriptures equivalent terms (ἰσοδυναμοῦντα) —it is also certain that they were not created after man, whom they seduced."—Similarly LEIDEN SYNOPSIS (XII, 6), WOLLEB (p. 25), RIISSEN (VII, 30), WENDELIN (*Coll.* p. 108).

6.—They are also essentially finite spirits, equipped with limited gifts, though far surpassing the natural powers of man.—URSIN (*Loci* p. 552): "(Angels) are finite, that is, of a limited essence, and endowed with a fixed measure of strength and wisdom."—HEIDEGGER (VIII, 12): "This knowledge though many miles (*parasangs!*) ahead of ours, is finite": "because (LEIDEN SYNOPSIS, XII, 21) a finite nature cannot contain the infinite (*finita natura infiniti capax non est*)."

7.—Hence their *cognitio*, their *voluntas* and their *immortalitas* call for special notice. What the angels know and are aware of, they know, not like God in virtue of their own essentiality (hence they have no natural knowledge of the hidden thoughts of man or of things of the future); they know not intuitively, but discursively, by the ideas implanted in them and by their natural consciousness of God, by the experience which they acquire in dealing with God, themselves and man, and by special revelation, since God reveals His eternal counsels to them. (It is thus a *cognitio naturalis s. concreata, experimentalis* and *revelata*).

HYPERIUS p. 274ff: The angels enjoy a threefold way of knowledge, (1) a created knowledge; (2) a knowledge *ex revelatione*; "for in progress of time angels learn additional things and by so doing advance, especially where God, when it has seemed good to Him, deigns to reveal to them some of His secret counsels; (3) [a knowledge] by experience. For from the things done here on earth by men they perceive a great deal forthwith and note what is the will and dispensation of God".—MASTRICHT (III, vii, 9): "Although it (angels' knowledge) is far more perfect than ours as not depending on sense images and impressions and so possessing more fixed and constant thoughts, it does not know by its own essence, because it is by no means the pattern and cause of all things; or even in God's essence as in a mirror, since God's operations are free: nor do they know all things, because this belongs to God alone; nor do they know future contingents severally, except by conjectures and long use and experience of things Is. 41. 22-23 (Let them bring them forth, and declare, unto us what shall happen: declare ye the former things, what they be, that we may consider them and know the latter end of them; or shew us things for to come. Declare the things that are to come hereafter, that we may know that ye are gods; yea, do good or do evil, that we may be dismayed, and behold it together), or hidden corners of the human heart Jer. 17. 10 (I the LORD search the heart, I try the reins, even to give to every man according to his ways, according to the fruit of his doings) 1 K. 8. 39 (then hear thou in heaven thy dwelling place, and forgive, and do, and render unto every man according to all his ways, whose heart thou knowest; (for thou, even thou only, knowest the hearts of all the children of men)); or the day of judgment Mk. 13. 22 (But of that day or that hour knoweth no one, not even the angels in heaven, neither the Son, but the Father); whatever they do know they realise through intelligible species, whether ingrained in them by creation or revealed by God or derived from things, perceptually or discursively, so that a triple knowledge appears in them (1) a natural or *increate* John 8. 44 (Ye are of your father the devil, and the lusts of your father it is your will to do. He was a murderer from the beginning, and stood not in the truth, because there is no truth in him. When one speaketh a lie, he speaketh of his own, for his father also is a liar), (2) a revealed Dan. cc. 8, 9 (Belshazzer, and the prophet's visions), Rev. 1. 1 (the revelation of Jesus Christ, which God gave him to shew unto his servants, even the things which must shortly come to pass; and he went and signified it by his angel unto his servant John), and (3) an experimental derived from seeing and hearing

Eph. 3. 10. (. . . that now unto the principalities and the powers in the heavenly places might be made known through the church the manifold wisdom of God), 1 Tim. 3. 16. (Every scripture inspired of God is also profitable for teaching, for reproof, for correction, for instruction (discipline ?) which is in righteousness) 1 Pet. 1. 12 (to whom (prophets) it was revealed, that not unto themselves, but unto you, did they minister unto you . . . ; which things the angels desire to look into.)"

· HEIDEGGER (VIII, 13): "The principle of angelic knowledge is threefold: nature, use and revelation, whence also their actual knowledge of them is either natural or experimental or revealed. Nature supplies them both with innate notions and ideas and with the concreated image of God and therewith with reason and νόησις, in fact with that διάνοια or reasoning by which things unknown are inferred from known and both are connected. Hence by the innate idea of God they know God's existence, from God's image His virtues, as well as the difference between honourable and base, good and bad; [they know] the principles, both those speculative of things naturally knowable and those practical ones of things moral and the inferences flowing from them, and other things of the kind, by a reasoning the subtlety, acumen and swiftness of which is theirs far beyond human reasoning; [they know] far more things than man knows about themselves, God and creation. Use too and experience combined with their perception suggests much to them that nature denies. For by conversing with God, their beginning and end, with one another and with men they daily see and experience much hitherto unseen or not experienced.—Finally revelation supplies angels with things which they acquire neither by nature nor by use. To this category belong the decrees and counsels of God, which He reveals to those sent to carry them out, etc."—RIISSEN (VII, 34-37): "Angels' knowledge is threefold: (1) natural, imbued in angels from the beginning of creation and common to good and bad alike; (2) revealed, by which they are aware of much in the revelation of God, of which previously they were ignorant as in Dan. 8 and 9 (p. 204) is revealed to the angel Gabriel the mystery of the 70 weeks, and (3) experimental, arising from things that happen in the world. These are dealt with in Eph. 3. 10 (above). Moreover (35) angels know: (1) God and things divine; not that they grasp the divine essence, but so far as they apprehend to a certain extent rays of His majesty, as the infirmity of the creature can bear it; (2) themselves and men; (3) other creatures, and that far more perfectly than men. But they do not know (36): (1) future contingencies, which are God's alone to know Is. 42. 9 'Behold the former things are come to pass, and new things I declare: before they spring forth I tell you of them;' (2) the hearts and thoughts of men." (37): Concerning the mode of angelic knowledge we must maintain: (1) that angels' knowledge is only intellective, not sensory, which pertains to bodies; (2) that angels do not know by their essence, because in that case angelic essence would contain everything and would be the image and cause of all things, which belongs to the infinite God alone; but by fixed species and ideas or similitudes of things, which are partly inborn and ingrained, partly acquired, either by God's revelation or by experiences through species drawn from the things themselves. Further although it is not clear to us how they can draw such species or images from things since they are devoid of outward senses, it must not therefore be denied that they actually do so, as may be gathered from the fact that in conversation with the saints they perceive their voices and reply to them; (3) their knowledge is not intuitive and noetic, but dianoetic and discursive, because an angel perceives everything not by simple intuition but by a manner of discourse" (i.e. discursiveness).

8.—Like their knowledge the angels' will is also finite and limited, so that they cannot like God work by their mere will, but need power which God supplies them with to carry out their will—RIISSEN (VIII, 39): "The angels' will is not independent and operative, as though they acted by will alone, because to operate by mere will and command most powerful belongs to God alone; but beyond their will, all creatures lack the power, which is the effective beginning of operations *ad extra* and which really has an influx into the effect. But it is the most free principle of willing, in consequence of which manifold and various actions are elicited spontaneously according to the nature of the objects at the dictates of practical reason".

9.—Like their knowledge the power lent to angels also far transcends any human capacity. At God's pleasure they have free disposal of the forces of nature: indeed, they can affect human powers of knowledge and will, at least indirectly.—HEIDEGGER (VIII, 17): "The angels were also created with outstanding power.—And first of all their great force and power over corporeal things is natural.—Thus by God's permission and ordinance they have in their power all natural causes and nature as a whole, so that they can retard, hinder, repress, promote, impel its impulses. And perhaps as a rule, as often as the course of nature is affected, it is by the agency of angels, at all events where the effect does not exceed the force of a second cause.—And albeit they do not directly influence man's knowledge and will,—nevertheless indirectly in their own way they can impinge upon both: upon knowledge, when as instruments and σύνεργοι of God, by arousing phantasms of the spoken word and stimulating the spirits of the brain they confront the mind with truth and goodness and urge assent to most potent attractions;—upon the will, when through the mind affected in the way mentioned they bend the will, and arouse reactions in the senses, by which the will itself is in a sense stampeded into choosing the object."

10.—These gifts are the special advantages with which the image of God in angels is adorned. God created the angels personal spiritual beings in His image in truth, i.e. in holiness and righteousness.—POLAN (V, 11): "The image of God in angels is the likeness of the divine nature impressed on angels by God at their first creation, that as sons of God they may call Him their Father. The parts of the image of God in angels are two: the first is the actual incorporeal substance of the angels, by which they suggest the incorporeal God; the second consists in the excellent attributes assigned to the angelic substance by God."—LEIDEN SYNOPSIS (XII, 7): "We assert, then, that in the beginning all the angels were created good—and in the image of God, against the *Manichees* and the *Priscillianists*".

11.—Those angels who freely, though not without God's gracious aid, persisted in the truth God so established in the same in virtue of His eternal counsel by His H. Spirit, that to all eternity they cannot fall away from Him or lose blessedness; whereby the freedom of their will is not impaired but really established (because they have achieved complete freedom from sin).—COCCEIUS: (*S. T.* XVI, 36-38): "The first state of the angels is that they have all been created in truth Jn. 8. 44 (unlike the devil's angels). This involves the realisation of the honour due to God and of the duty to be rendered through their ministry both *per se* and by the ordering of other things Godward, and the inclination of the will to love and prosecute this. Thus they were created good and upright, like man too.—In that grace the elect angels persisted 1 Tim. 5. 21 (I charge thee in the sight . . . of the elect angels), with readiest will of course, but also with the most sure and effectual aid of the Creator.—Nor will those who have persisted ever fall in the future, as bound to be preserved by the power of God.—URSIN (*Loci.* p. 553): The angels are created in perfect righteousness and holiness, "by which they are confirmed to God", and the angels who persist in obedience "are so confirmed in the holiness and bliss in which they were being created, that although they serve their Creator with the height of free will, they could yet never fall from Him or lapse from the state of righteousness and felicity in which they are". This perseverance however they possess "by God's sheer and gratuitous love to them through God's Son who preserves and rules over them".

HEIDEGGER (VIII, 28): "Their confirmation in original goodness and uprightness and so their actual glorification the good angels acquired neither by their own words in the strict sense, nor by desert, nor by the alien merits of Christ the Mediator".

BUCAN (VI, 12): "But since they cannot sin and turn wretched any more, have they ceased to have freewill? On the contrary! Whatever they will, they will freely. Nay, they are freer than before, when they were able to sin and not to sin. Now they are so free from sin, that they cannot even sin, and from wretchedness, that they could not be wretched any longer. They have become at once most holy and most blessed."

All this rests upon the eternal decree of God. BUCAN (VI, 10): "Why is it that some of the angels falling away from the truth others have persisted in grace and truth? The proximate and direct cause is the good will of the particular angels wherein they were created in the beginning by God."

"Midway or higher is God's free kindness by which their will was assisted, so that they might and did will to persist in the truth, others to whom this grace was not imparted refusing to persist and so coming short of the truth by their own fault Phil. 2. 13 (it is God which worketh in us both to will and to do).

"But supreme are the eternal, fixed and changeless decree and counsel of God proceeding from His own wisdom, by which He elected and predestined the former to communion and perseverance in His grace, while others in His righteous good pleasure He reprobated for His own glory 1 Tim. 5. 21 (I charge thee in the sight of God, and Christ Jesus, and the elect angels . . .) "I bear witness", saith the Apostle, "in the sight of God and the Lord Jesus Christ and the elect angels". If elect, therefore some, not all."

12.—These latter are the good angels.—HEIDEGGER (VIII, 26) gives us the Biblical descriptions of them: angels of Jehovah Ps. 103. 20 (ye angels of his; ye mighty in strength that fulfil his word, hearkening unto the voice of his word); Ps.104 .4 (who maketh his angels winds, his ministers a flaming fire), ἐκλεκτοί 1 Tim. 5. 21 (I charge thee in the sight of God, and Christ Jesus, and the elect angels) ἅγιοι, Dt. 33. 3., Job. 15. 15 (he putteth no trust in his holy ones: Yea, the heavens are not clean in his sight), Mt. 25. 31 (fellow-servants of the faithful) Rev. 19. 10 (. . . see thou do it not: I am a fellow-servant with thee and with thy brethren that hold the testimony of Jesus) cf. 22. 9, sons of God, hosts of heaven, Cherubim, Seraphim, etc.

13.—The number of these angels is fixed for all eternity, like those of the heavenly spirits generally.—HEIDEGGER (VIII, 19): "The number of them is assuredly great.—And that number is quite sure and fixed without possibility of increase or decrease, because they neither gender nor perish."

14.—Since they are not mere thoughts but substantial beings they exist spatially, but in such wise that space is not for them an obstructive barrier. In the same way angels exist temporally as beings created for a definite time, but in such wise that for them time never ends.—WOLLEB 27: "Angels are in a place not circumscriptively but definitively."— BUCAN (VI, 17): "Angels move in space, not however circumscriptively, but definitively, because they are in one place in such a way that they are not in another."—MASTRICHT (III, vii, 28): "It is the common view of the *Reformed* that, because angels are of a substance different from their thoughts regarded as actions, by reason of that substance they are truly and strictly in a place (localised), although definitively only; they are so in one place as not to be in another".—HEIDEGGER (VIII, 21): "Angels have limits both to their essence and to their operation, or, as it is termed, a sphere of activity. But it is difficult for us to understand the way in which angels are in a place, so that neither is it our business to know it. It is enough that both believers are sure of their presence and protection by God's will and command; and unbelievers know them as present executors of God's judgment. It is at least certain that they are not in a place strictly or locally so as to be extended or diffused in it; for they are not bodies, which alone are extended in space of their own and commensurate with it. The *Scot* is content with a presence transcending operation by way of being in a place. *Thomas* is more correct in denying that they are in a place without operating, because they are everywhere and operate by knowledge and will, even *ad extra*, by glorifying God, and serving Him among men and all other creatures. So that they may be said to be in a place not because they are bounded by a place but because they themselves rather bound the place by their operation, as *Thomas* rightly says.—22: Therefore angels whom no medium resists must move very swiftly; much more, assuredly, than a corporeal thunderbolt, which is borne from east to west in a most destructive movement. Nor does it follow from this that angels move in a moment or by deserting their localisation acquire a new one in a moment. Although the medium is not resistant, succession is and so is a fresh act succeeding a former one, as well as the distance between the termini, which involves some measure of delay. For it is impossible that in the same νῦνι and present it should have a *locus* and when it leaves it should acquire a new one. Nor may we accept outright without a grain of salt *Tertullian's* words: "As spirit hath wings, in a moment it is everywhere."

HEIDEGGER (VIII, 23) : " The duration of angels is neither eternity, which befits God alone as existing necessarily and through His nature; nor time or a continuance consisting of material things measurable by movement; or something separate (*discretum*), which suits things that succeed each other without continuity, not permanent things; nor a permanent instant which is defectible. Therefore what is usually attributed to them is αἰών, *aevum*, as it were ἀεὶ ὤν, always (at least *a posteriori*) existing, because of their prolonged duration, the origin of which man does not attain to by living, and of which there shall be no end at all."

15.—Although the endowment and appointment of all good angels is the same, it must still be assumed that there are among them certain gradations, about which Scripture meantime has not revealed anything adequate.

In general it is recognised that in the realm of heavenly spirits there must be an order, in so far as everything must be done by the angels *ordinate*; by which none the less the *Catholic* comparison of it with the Church hierarchy and similar subtileness is rejected. CALVIN says (I, xiv, 8): "As to the number and degrees (of angels), let those who dare define look to the sort of foundation they have". HYPERIUS agrees with CALVIN. He recognises that according to Scripture certain orders of angels are distinguishable, but disputes the necessity for regarding them as permanent gradations of rank (p. 287); "To distinguish perpetual rankings, according to which some angels are always pre-eminent, others always subordinate, in short to insist upon a fixed number of them and grades of dignity in particular cases is the mark of the inquisitive and rash fellows rather than of those who follow the authority of the Scriptures". Most of them like BUCAN (VI, 19) teach that "No one versed in the Scriptures can deny that there is some order among angels, because order and distinction in things is an outstanding and divine thing; for some of them are called Cherubim, others Seraphim, others angels, others archangels. But this order does not depend upon the dignity or excellence of the nature of the angels, as that some are by nature more worthy than others, but rather upon different kinds of functions.—But that hierarchies and degrees of hierarchies among angels exist, as the *Papists* think, cannot be proved by any evidence of Scripture".— MASTRICHT (III, vii, 30): "The Reformed recognise that there is indeed some order among angels, because not only is God their Maker a God of order, 1 Cor. 14. 33, 40 (not a God of confusion: things should be done decently and in order), but because the various names of the angels challenge us to that view, Col. 1.16 (thrones, dominions, principalities,

powers; all things have been created through him and unto him),
Eph. 3.10 (to the intent that now unto the principalities and the powers
in the heavenly places might be made known through the church the
manifold wisdom of God). Cf. Ezek. 9. 3 (the glory of the God of Israel
was gone up from the cherub, whereupon it was, to the threshold of the
house . . .) Is. 6. 2 (Above (the Lord) stood the seraphim) 1 Th. 4. 16
(the Lord himself shall descend from heaven with a shout, with the voice
of the archangel, and with the trump of God) Gen. 3. 24 (God placed
at the east of the garden of Eden the Cherubim and the flame of the
sword which turned every way, to keep the way of the tree of life), Jude 9
(Michael); especially since the disjunctive particles whether thrones or
dominions (Col. 1. 16) seem to confirm some order among angels, not to
add that there is some order among the evil spirits themselves, Matt. 12.24
(devils: Beelzebub their prince). But what the order is among angels,
they believe cannot be determined by men in their imperfection."

16.—Angels are appointed to glorify God, to serve God as messengers
to men, to watch over the elect, to support them in bodily and spiritual
need, and to bring their souls to eternal rest.—The most essential
qualification of angels is watching over the elect. CALVIN (I, xvi, 6):
"And so relates that they keep watch over our safety, undertake our
defence, direct our ways, etc."—COCCEIUS (S.T. xiv, 45): "They are sent
on service on behalf of those who are to inherit salvation, Heb. 1. 14
(Are they not all ministering spirits sent forth to do service for the sake
of them that shall inherit salvation?), whether to indicate God's will,
or to suggest good thoughts, or to resist the devil and his angels, or to
protect and aid, avert harms, mitigate evils, strengthen and confirm the
fearful, gather the dispersed, deliver from the company of evil men and
from scandals, lastly to convey their souls to Abraham's bosom".
POLAN distinguishes the angels' tasks thus (V, 12): "The duty of good
angels is twofold, either (1) towards God, or (2) towards men". The
first consists in them "(a) ministering to God and doing His will" and
"(b) in celebrating and adoring God with unceasing praises". To this
also pertains the "duty they show to Christ", so far as he is the God-man
and the head of the Church. As to men the "office" is laid on them
"(a) to dispense and administer God's benefits to those who have been
elected to eternal life" and "(b) to execute God's judgments on men".
The former they do as follows: "(α) they teach the elect and reveal
to them God's will, judgments and mysteries, announce His works and
benefits, instruct the doubtful and perturbed in the truth, etc. (β) they
protect the elect against all dangers of soul and body; (γ) both by
addressing them and by declaring their presence they console the

prostrate, afflicted and anxious; (δ) they carry the souls of the dying elect to heaven; (ε) on the last day and glorious advent of Christ they will gather elect people from the four winds, from the extreme of earth to the extreme of heaven".

17.—God allows all this, which He could do Himself, to be carried out by angels, in order on the one hand to help our weakness and sinfulness by manifold means and in the most various ways, and on the other hand to reveal His power in the angels also.—CALVIN (I, xiv, 11): "God, of course, does not do this of necessity, as though He could not do without them. As often as He likes He passes them over and accomplishes His own work by His mere nod: so far is He from needing their aid to remove a difficulty. He does this, then, to comfort our weakness, that we may lack nothing to quicken good hope in our souls or to confirm them in freedom from care. It should of course be enough and more than enough that the Lord declares Himself to be our protector".

URSIN (*Loci.* p. 554): "God moreover does many things through angels and sometimes through many of them, things which He could equally well accomplish either without them or through them one at a time (1) both in the interests of our weakness which, unless it sees itself girt about by many guards and instruments of the divine power and benificence, forthwith slips into doubts of the providence, protection and presence of God; (2) and in order to show also His power over the angels by which He uses their labour and service according to His own judgment."

The view that there are special guardian angels for individual persons, places or callings is contested almost by all dogmaticians (after CALVIN's precedent) as a *Popish* heresy. CALVIN says (I, xiv, 7): "Whether separate angels are posted to individual believers for their protection I should not dare to affirm as a certainty.—What is certain is that not merely is each of us in the care of one angel, but that the whole body of them with one accord watch over our salvation. It is said of all the angels together, that they rejoice more over one sinner turned to repentance, than over ninety and nine righteous persons who persist in their righteousness, Lk. 15. 7. It is also said of many angels, that they bore the soul of Lazarus to Abraham's bosom, Lk. 16. 22."—Accordingly RIISSEN (VII, 34) gives to the question: "Whether any man has his own particular guardian angel, or even one good, another bad" the answer that "it is denied against the *Papists*". Of course individual doctors represented the opposite view, e.g. BUCAN (VI, 28) who teaches: "That as a rule to each elect person a certain particular good angel is appointed by God to guard him, may be gathered from Christ's words, Mt. 18. 10, where it is said 'Their angels do continually behold the face of my Father.' Also from

Ac. 12. 15 where the believers who had assembled in Mark's house said of Peter knocking at the door, 'It is his angel.' These believers were speaking according to the opinion received among the people of God."—But it was only now and again that belief in guardian angels was represented in the Reformed Church. This is VOETIUS' account (I, 900): "There are some of ours who putting their co-religionists in the second place admit as a probable opinion that a good angel guards individual men, or is at least assigned to believers, among whom ZANCHIUS *De oper. creat. lib.* 3 c.13. And recently the view has been specifically defended by ALSTED in the supplement to Chamier's *De eccles. lib.* 5 c. 7. Most recently also VOSSIUS pretty plainly indicates his inclination towards this view, *lib. 1. De idolol. c. 7.* In his notes on Matt. 18. 10 (see that ye despise not one of these little ones; for I say unto you, that in heaven their angels do always behold the face of my Father which is in heaven) *Grotius* seems to stand for this opinion: ultimately however, he put it aside or left it undecided. Both of them seem to be moved to some extent by patristic authority. We, however, embrace the view of CALVIN (in *Instit. lib.* I *cap.* 14, 7 and *comm. in Ps.* 91 and *in Mt.* 18) and of other Reformed, who reject the view in question as vain and curious, and we think that something has stuck here to the early Fathers from the *Platonic* philosophy and the mythological theology of the Gentiles."—MASTRICHT (III, vii, 31) gives an account of the view later prevalent in the Church: "The Reformed believe that the angels as a whole minister to the salvation of the elect, because Scripture attests this, Heb. 1. 14 (Are they not all ministering spirits sent forth to do service for the sake of them that shall inherit salvation?), Ps. 34. 7 (The angel of the Lord encampeth round about them that fear him), Ps. 91. 11 (He shall give his angels charge over thee, to keep thee in all thy ways) compared with Mt. 4.6, Lk. 15. 10 (joy over one sinner that repenteth) 16. 22 (angels took Lazarus to Abraham's bosom). But they cannot believe with divine faith in single angels appointed to single tasks, spheres, men, because (1) Scripture nowhere says so, nor can it be made known to us from any other source; in fact (2) it rather says the opposite, when it at times assigns several angels to one as well as one angel to several, Gen. 28. 12 (Jacob's ladder) 32. 12 (angels who met Jacob at Mahanaim) Ps. 34. 7 (The angel of the Lord encampeth round about them that fear him, and delivereth them) 2 K. 6. 16-17 (the chariots and the horsemen of Elisha) Lk. 16. 22 (Lazarus); because (3) it paves the way for ἀγγελοθρησκεία; because (5) it means collusion with Gentiles, Moslems, Jews."

18.—In their functions angels at times assume bodily form but only in passing. It is not a corporeality proper to them or essentially belonging to them, but only a temporary form of manifestation which they can immediately drop or exchange for another.—WOLLEB 27: "The bodies in which the angels appeared were not mere φαντάσματα nor ones hypostatically united to them, but ones freely assumed for the sake of a particular ministry.—RIISSEN (VII, 50-51): "Those bodies in which the angels appeared were neither empty phantasms nor proper bodies hypostatically united to them, but administrative (*oeconomica*).— Still they were so united to these bodies, that they could not therefore be called men, because the union was not personal and inward, but outward and accidental".—URSIN (*Loci.* p. 552): "These visible species or bodies which can be seen and touched are different substances from the incorporeal essence of spirits, whether formed of nothing or of some matter and temporarily worn and moved by spirits for effecting certain actions. For they are both laid aside again by them and other and varying forms are assumed, as the serpent through which the devil conversed with Eve."—Later dogmaticians devote the most circumstantial investigations into the nature of the bodies in which angels appear, asking for example whether God produced these bodies *ex nihilo an ex elementis,* whether angels take possession even of living men (*cohibita tantisper eorum phantasia*), in order to appear in their form, whether human bodies temporarily assumed by angels were also occupied by a human soul, etc.

19.—Some men plunge into the intricacies of the nature of this assumed body and ask whether or not they have a human soul. Now that the revelation of God has been consummated, manifestations of angels are no longer to be expected, since their sole service was to revelation.—RIISSEN (VII, 53): "As in the time of the patriarchs, when the word of God had not yet been written and thick night still bound the Church, God frequently used apparitions of angels to console believers and to confirm faith: so now, when the radiance of the gospel had arisen, the Son of God had been manifested in the flesh, the H. Spirit most abundantly poured out upon the Church and the canon of Scripture closed, the Church no longer needs such aids. Hence it has come to pass that although at the start of the Gospel there were still some ἀγγελοφανείαι for exhibiting Christ's ministry and creating faith in the doctrine of it, later, when the gospel had been established, they ceased, so that although the invisible God uses the ministry of angels in the world, He no longer or very rarely brings them within the vision of men."—BUCAN (VI, 33): "What is the reason that, whereas angels once upon a time were wont to appear frequently to the fathers in human form and to converse and talk familiarly with them, they now no longer do so? Because now that Christ is incarnate and sits at the right hand of the Father in heaven and

His H. Spirit has been widely bestowed, he wishes that our conversation should be in heaven, and not with angels on earth (visibly). Secondly, because in the beginning the Church used to need such heavenly confirmations; now God's Word has been more than sufficiently confirmed, Hebrews 1. 1. (God having of old time spoken unto the fathers by the prophets by divers portions and in divers manners . . .)."

20.—In their holiness and blessedness the angels provide us with an example of the righteousness of works, so that Christ was their Lord but not their Mediator.—Cocceius (*S.T.*, XVI, 52-53): "In the good angels is an example of the righteousness of works; and so Christ is not called their Mediator that they may become heirs of his righteousness, but still head, prince, lord, as of a family, in whom we also are reconciled and made one with them, because he is the Son."

21.—To angels, of course, no sort of worship is due (*nec λατρεία nec δουλεία nec θρησκεία nec προσκύνησις*); but as the holy witnesses of God's glory they are to be held by us in honour and enjoyed with devotion. And therefore faith in the angels and their service in the kingdom of God should not entrench at all upon trust in God, but should establish it.

Cocceius (*S.T.* XVI, 51): "Neither service nor slavery nor worship nor adoration is due to them (the angels), but reverence as to holy witnesses, that they may be thrilled through us, walking as we do in all modesty and fear, and not be put to flight through unbridled desires, unrestrained talk, drunkenness, luxury, pride, talkativeness 1 Cor. 11. 10 (the woman ought to have a sign of authority upon her head, because of the angels) 1 Tim. 5. 21 (I bear witness, saith the Apostle, in the sight of God and the Lord Jesus Christ and the elect angels), Lk. 15. 7-10 (lost sheep, lost coin: the joy in heaven at finding it)"—Calvin (I, xiv, 12) aptly remarks: "Accordingly whatever is to be said about angels, let us direct it to the aim of expelling all diffidence and more strongly establishing our hope in God. These defences are devised for us by the Lord, to banish fear at the numbers of our enemies, as though they should prevail against His help, so that we should flee to the refuge of Elisha's statement, that those for us are more than those against us."

22.—Like the good spirits the bad ones are also real personal existences. —Calvin (I, xiv, 19): "As above we refuted the trifling philosophy anent the holy angels, which teaches that they are nothing but good inspirations or motions inspired by God in the minds of men; so here too those are to be rebutted, who lightly declare that devils are evil affections or upsets imported into us by our flesh."

23.—The bad spirits were originally created as angels in perfect righteousness and holiness, but have fallen away from God.—Cocceius (*S.T.* XVI, 54): "By a παρατροπὴ τῆς γνώσεως many spirits who had been created good by God did not maintain their beginning, did not persist in the truth and abandoned their domicile" Jn. 8. 44 (Ye are of your father the devil, and the lusts of your father it is your will to do. He was a murderer from the beginning, and stood not in the truth, because there is no truth in him. When he speaketh a lie, he speaketh of his own: for he is a liar and the father thereof) Jude 6 (angels which kept not their own principality, but left their proper habitation, he hath kept in everlasting bonds under darkness unto the judgment of the Great Day). That they are many is clear from Mk. 5. 9 (. . . my name is Legion; for we are many) Lk. 8. 30 (. . . Legion; for many devils were entered into him).—The angels fell (Heidegger VIII, 47), "the author and instigator being a certain individual, who consequently is distinguished κατ᾽ ἐξοχὴν as *Diabolus*, Satan, the great Dragon, Belial, the Evil One, Beelzebub, the prince of devils".—As to the time at which the fall of the angels took place Voetius (I, 919) remarks: "The time of the lapse Scripture does not determine. This at least is indefinitely admitted, that it preceded the fall of Adam; and therefore could not have been a longer stay of their integrity than from the first creation down to and excluding the fall of Adam."

24.—The cause of this rebellion apparently consisted in proud denial of creaturely dependence upon God and in wanton striving after equality with God, as well as in an unbounded hatred of the Son of God as the Redeemer of the world.—Heidegger (VIII, 46): "Scripture does not define the nature of the angels' first sin. So whether it could have been pride and affectation of divinity; or envy, by which the apocryphal book of Wisdom *cap.* 2.24 says death was introduced into the world; or lying, which some infer from Jn. 8. 44 (Ye are of your father the devil, and the lusts of your father it is your will to do. He was a murderer from the beginning, and stood not in the truth, because there is no truth in him. When one speaketh a lie, he speaketh of his own, for his father also is a liar); or singular contempt and violation of some divine law; or remissness or diminished attention in contemplating God, as it appeared to *Molinaeus*, is not clearly certain. One thing is admitted, that it was not the lust of which the sons of God made themselves guilty; they were of course not angels but the children of Seth, Gen. 6. 1-8, *q.v.*—the more probable thing is that it would have been pride and a claim to divinity."—Leiden Synopsis (XII, 28) "What the first sin of the angels was into which they fell by a free abuse of will, is not expressed so clearly in the Scriptures. Still it is highly probable that it had consisted in some affectation of divinity and in a peculiar contumacy towards God's Son. This is inferred from the temptation by which Satan seduced our first parents, and from the perpetual effort by which he is zealous to transfer God's glory to himself; but specifically out of the hatred with which he persecutes Christ and his Church".—VOETIUS (I, 920): "We shall maintain that here an instructed ignorance is the surest, that none of all the opinions is sure, though that anent pride seems more probable than the rest."

25.—Their fall then was to be sought in the angels' own free will.—URSIN (*Loci.* p. 554): "Although those who are now the evil spirits or angels have once actually been good—yet they turned from God by their own and their free will and accordingly by their own special fault."—POLAN (V, 13): "The bad angels are bad not by God's effecting, not by their nature according to which they were created good, but by their very own will".

26.—Hence God was right to punish them and with eternal damnation at that, since they are so utterly abandoned by Him, that they can never again repent or ever again have the will to repent, but must in consequence persist in their godlessness.—URSIN (*Loci.* p. 555): "Although moreover, they rush against God of their own and their free will, they are yet by God's just judgment in such wise deserted and cast away by Him, that they are unchangeably bad and liable to eternal punishments." —POLAN (V, 13): "Because they have been eternally rejected and incurably hardened in evil, they can do nothing but sin, i.e. mentally approve and voluntarily choose only what things are evil and displease God, and will manage to do so sucessively to eternity". To give some idea of the persistence of the evil spirits in their godlessness and damnation, VOETIUS (I, 921) distinguishes a threefold instance in their case, which is the effect of their falling away from God: "The consequences of the sin of the demons was a threefold fall among them ; from the state of grace which they possessed, from the state of glory which they were to have possessed, and from heaven their home. Hence their perpetual continuance and obstinacy in sinning and wretchedness." —To the question "whether some are right in inferring, from Col. 1. 20 where it is said that God through Christ reconciles all things to Himself, that devils and the damned will some day be saved," BUCAN (VII, 19) gives this answer : "Certainly not. By the word "all" we must understand the whole body of the Church, which is divided as it were into two parts, namely into those things which are in heaven (by which we understand simply the believers who died before Christ's coming), and those things which are on the earth".

27.—Of course we must insist that like every result in time the fall of the evil spirits from God rests upon an eternal counsel of God, according to which God resolved not to hinder it—which, in fact, in no way makes God the cause of the fall, since God had equipped the angels with adequate powers of righteousness, and hence was not bound to restrain them from falling."—WENDELIN (*Collat.* p. 117): "Although Satan was not led to apostasy by God's decree, it must yet be noted that he had not sinned without a decree at all. The reason is plain. Whatever God does in time, He has decreed to do from eternity. And yet God allowed Satan to rebel in time. Therefore from eternity He decreed to allow him.— 118: Yet (Satan) fell away by his own fault, not by that of God who permits or decrees to permit; God was not bound to prevent apostasy, after He granted him sufficient strength in his integrity, as also in the case of the first human beings."

28.—The *finis* for which God allowed the evil spirits to fall was, that He wished (1) to reveal in them and their punishment His wrath against sin, (2) by them to punish the godless while still here on earth, and also (3) by them to test the elect and to exercise them in humility and patience. —URSIN (*Loci*, p. 556): "Into this wickedness God allowed them to slip, (1) not only to indicate His wrath against sin in their eternal punishment, but also (2) through them to punish the ungodly in this life, and also (3) to chastise or search and exercise the elect with temptations".— BUCAN (VII, 18): "For what ends did God ordain evil spirits? (1) In order that by their temptations the godly may be exercised in humility and patience and the latter's salvation be in this way promoted; (2) in order that through them as torturers He may afflict the ungodly with spiritual as well as with corporal punishments; to sum up, in order that God might use their effrontery to magnify His own glory".

29.—Thus the power which the kingdom of evil spirits with their head, the Satan, exercises upon the elect in passing and according to God's purpose for their salvation, is a different one from that which God has eternally fixed for that kingdom to exercise against the rejected.— BUCAN (VII, 11): "Is the power of bad angels over elect and reprobate equal? No! God, it is true, lets His elect be exercised by them for a time; but never to be overcome, because the promise, that the woman's seed shall crush the serpent's head, Gen. 3. 15, applies to Christ and all his members. But against the reprobate they have more power: whence the Apostle (Eph. 2. 2) says that the devil accomplishes his work in the sons of disobedience".

30.—The Satan with his kingdom has received his judgment, through the judgment with which sin is judged by Christ.—Cocceius (*Summ. theol.* XVI, 64): "The devil was judged and condemned as an importunate accuser, when sin was condemned in Christ's flesh Jn. 16. 11 (of judgment, because the prince of this world is judged) Rom. 8. 3 (God sending his own Son condemned sin in the flesh)".

31.—Therefore he can only be effective, so far as God allows him to be.—Calvin (I, xiv, 17): "Let it remain fixed that except by God's will and assent he (Satan) can do nothing."

32.—Therefore even faith in the existence and activity of the devil and his kingdom should rouse the believer to all the firmer trust in God, to all the greater assiduity in sanctification, and to all the more insistent prayer for God's gracious aid against the assaults of the Evil One.—Bucan (VII, 20): "What is the use of the doctrine of demons ?—That we may so much the more beware of offending God, that we may so much the more be watchful and stand on guard, and so may fight against our hordes of enemies, as though for our altars and hearths, with spiritual weapons, especially with assiduous prayers to Christ, etc."

CHAPTER XI

MAN

1.—In order to have creatures upon earth, in whom the whole creation was microcosmically set forth as in a picture, and who at the same time manifested the picture of the divine nature in creaturely form, who consequently, although creations of God like all other creatures, were yet justified in lording it over all other creations and in whom consequently by all this the glory of God was reflected at its loftiest, God made man.—BUCAN (VIII, 2): "Why did God make man last of His works?—(1) In order that, since He was proposing to create him fixed in body and soul, He might before his creation have everything prepared pertaining to the happiness of both the parts, body and soul;—(2) that he might use the things created for the Creator's glory;—(3) in order that the sum of the whole world might be described in man as in a small map; and so he would be a μικρόκοσμος of God and a kind of compendium of the things previously created;—(4) because God wished to commune with him and to acquiesce in him".—LEIDEN SYNOPSIS (XIII, 2): "Man is the consummation and end of the lower nature, the congener of the higher, the compend and bond of the whole, by which things heavenly are united to things earthly".—To emphasise the significance which man has in the eyes of God Himself, the SYNOPSIS (XIII, 7) insists that "in addition, to swell and to magnify his dignity, He brings it about that in proposing to create him He did not after the manner of the other creatures produce him by a word alone, but consulted and decreed concerning his creation, or rather, girt Himself to the work, in order to contrive laboriously a singular and outstanding labour".—MASTRICHT also aptly states the purpose of man's creation (III, ix, 4): "Nor did He thus create him rashly or in vain, but for His own glory, Ps. 89. 48 (. . . for what vanity hast thou created the children of men?) Is. 43. 7 (every one . . . whom I have created for my glory) Prov. 16.4 (The Lord hath made every thing for his own end; yea, even the wicked for the day of evil); of course in order (1) to recapitulate all created things so speak in one man and to present the sum of this vast universe in a stupendous work of art in such tiny compass and as a sort of μικρόκοσμος: (2) to repeat Himself in man and survey Himself as in a mirror, exactly as man has that in him in which he can see God as his own πρωτότυπος Jn. 14. 9 (. . . he that hath seen me hath seen the Father): (3) that He might have one through whom everything that has flowed from Himself might so to speak flow back to Him, one who like a quaestor of His on earth might undertake the provenance of all creatures and recognise that they had proceeded from Himself and as it were restore them by a suitable rendering of thanks, Rom. 11.36 (of him and through him and to him are all things, to him be the glory for ever). For although both angel and man are blessed with reason, to acknowledge the creator and the creatures as emanating from the Creator; yet man alone is fitted to experience the goodness of all creatures in himself and to render thanks to God accordingly. Further (4) in order that the ἄλογοι creatures might have a lord by whose agency they should be ruled, Gen. 1. 26 (let them have dominion). Hence they are all brought to man as their Lord, to receive their names and functions, Gen. 2. 19. In short (5) that in the three and functions Gen. 2. 19. In short (5) that in the three persons who had co-operated in producing us we might acknowledge the Father's love, the Son's grace and the H. Spirit's communion, 2 Cor. 13. 13.

The remaining dogmaticians variously stress single elements in the *finis hominum*, e.g. URSIN (*Loci*. 567-569) says that man's real end is God Himself, namely "(1) the glory or eternal celebration of God, which is accomplished by both spirit and words and by complete obedience according to the divine law; (2) true acknowledgment of God and (3) the manifestation of God (*patefactio*) or the declaration of God's mercy in the elect unto life eternal—and of God's righteousness and wrath against sins—in the reprobate". As subordinate ends of man's existence there are still to be added "the society, conjunction or aggregation of the human race", and the "mutual beneficence and duties which men ought to show to men, each individual according to his calling".

POLAN (V, 33): "Man's supreme end is God or God's glory; his sub-ordinate ends are twin, some belonging to this, others to the future aeon." The former are "(1) dominion over the creatures of the lower orders, (2) honest labour pleasing to God, (3) society with other men in the fellow-ship of life, religion and mutual duties, according to each's calling to mutual aid and mutual preservation". The latter "is distinct according to the distinction between men made by God from eternity. Men elected to eternal life are created for eternal life, but the reprobate are created for eternal death".

2.—Man means creatures made out of a material body and a soul or personal spirit.—The trichotomic consideration of man (i.e. the distinction of soul and spirit in his meaning) is rejected by Reformed theology; VOETIUS (I, 765): "On the whole we feel bound to hold that there is only one soul in individual men".—CONF. HELV. (II, 7): "We say that man consists of two substances and these different."—ENDEMANN (*Instit.* I, p. 191): "It is without reason that fanatics ascribe three essential parts to man. The passages to which they appeal, 1 Th. 5. 23 (. . . may your spirit and soul and body be preserved entire, without blame at the coming of our Lord Jesus Christ) Heb. 4. 12 (the word of God is . . . piercing even to the dividing of soul and spirit), merely teach that the human mind may be regarded as a spirit, and as a soul." Similarly SOHNIUS (*Opp.* I, 64), BULLINGER (*Compend.* II, 5), WALAEUS (p. 221) and others.—Hence WOLLEB defines (p. 27): "Man is a creature consisting of a body originally formed of earth, thereafter propagated by the transmission of seed, but endowed with a rational soul of divine origin."

3.—The two constituents, soul and body, are so fashioned as to be a single personal being.—HEIDEGGER (VI, 91): "God did not so create man's body and spirit as to be diverse ὑφιστάμενα but so as by the intimate union of both to make one man.—And each of them compounded and by God's will most straitly united constituted one man, one ὑφιστάμενον, one living, knowing, speaking person. And this direct union (i.e. the co-existence, or the composition and essential nexus of soul with organic body, which is succeeded by the interchange of mutual movements and thoughts), rather than the soul, is the form of man. For man's soul or better the form of the organic body is neither informing nor assisting."

4.—Like the body the soul is not an accident of something else but a self-existing living substance (WALAEUS p. 223). The mutual relationship is such, that the connection between soul and body is not accidental but entirely essential, so that the body belongs essentially to the soul and to its Ego.—VOETIUS (I, p.757) : " The body is an essential part of man.— (p. 762): Problem : whether the true and substantial form of man is both thus united to the body and substantially actuates and informs it ? Answer in the affirmative, provided the union is not *per accidens* but *per se*, not accidental but substantial ". Hence the soul is called " the essential form of man " BUCAN (VIII, 137), "the body's informing form" (*forma informans*) VOETIUS (I, 781) ; whereas the body is called *formata*.

5.—God made man's body of earth.—BUCAN (VIII, 9) : " Man's body was taken from the slime or mud of the earth ".

6.—The soul was made of nothing, Hence man's soul " differs by its whole nature from the body and the body's affections " (BRAUN I, ii, 13, 10). Man's soul must therefore be regarded neither as refined corporeality nor as an efflorescence of the body, as a *modus, temperamentum* or κρᾶσις of corporeal life, nor as a part of the substance of God.—All dogmaticians insist that the soul is not in any sense a part of the physical body, nor an efflorescence of the bodily life, nor yet a part of God's substance either. Referring to the latter point VOETIUS e.g. (I, 783) answers the question, " whether man's soul is of the substance of God and not *ex nihilo* ", in the negative. One as early as URSIN is strong against the conception of man's soul as a physical life-power or efflorescence of human corporeality, most emphatically insisting that man's soul is personal, i.e. self-supporting life. (*Loci.* p. 559) : " Because there have been and are even today those who have taught, that man's soul exactly like that of the beasts is nothing else than life or vital force resulting from the admixture and projection of the body and accordingly perishes and is extinguished along with the body—and that as the body dies, it goes to sleep, i.e. is without motion or sensation till the resuscitation of the body, because really it is just a mortal mind, i.e. merely a quality or δύναμις of the body, but nothing after the body has been dissolved—the testimonies of the divine voice against such men must be adhered to anent the spiritual and immortal substance of the human soul." For Scripture teaches (Ps. 49. 8, the redemption of their soul is costly and must be let alone for ever, 2 Sam. 11.11, as thou livest and thy soul liveth, 2 Pet. 1. 13-14, And I think it right, as long as I am in this tabernacle, to stir you up by putting you in remembrance, knowing that the putting off of my tabernacle cometh swiftly, Heb. 12.9,21-23 shall we not be in subjection to the Father of spirits . . . ? . . . Moses said, I exceedingly fear and quake . . . but ye are come . . . unto the city of the living God . . . to the general assembly and Church of the first-born . . . , 2 Cor. 2.11, who among men knoweth the things of a man save the spirit of man, which is in him ? . . .) " that man's soul is not only the form and perfection or the admixture or force or potency or agitation resulting from the mingling with the body, but an incorporeal substance, living, knowing, dwelling in the body and supporting and moving it ".— BRAUN (I, ii, 14, 22) : "Impious is the dogma of those who teach, that mind is just a *crasis* or *temperamentum* of body, etc."—HEIDAN (p. 326): " We thus maintain that the soul is a substance, distinct from the body, which comes from without ; not an accident or quality, nor a mode or modification and κρᾶσις of the body."

A man's spirit is distinguished from an angel's spirit by its determination to bodily existence, by its predisposition and by the urge dwelling in it to unite with a body. VOETIUS (I, 738) : " Does man differ specifically from an angel, and does he know that which is rational through his form ? Answer, yes : for angels are not to be called rational animals. They are complete spirits and not appointed to an animal body."—LEIDEN SYNOPSIS (XIII, 17) : " (The human soul) differs from the angelic nature (who are also spirits), because angels are essences so separate from body, that they have no natural drawing (*affectio*) to a body : the soul on the contrary ".

7.—" Man's soul is a spiritual substance in a human body, created by
God out of nothing and united to the body for the effecting of one
ὑφιστάμενος or person" (BUCAN VIII, 25).   It is through and through
a living, spiritual being, so that a distinction is possible between its
substance and its individual thoughts, but not between its substance and
its power to live generally.   It is essentially a *substantia cogitativa,* a
substantia cogitans, i.e. an *actus substantialis cogitandi.*

Corresponding to the conception of God as *actus purissimus,* or absolute
" living ", is the description of man's soul as an *actus cogitandi.*—BRAUN
(I, ii, 13, 7) : "The human mind (or soul) is thus strictly and by its
nature a *substantia cogitans* or a *cogitatio substantialis,* or, if you prefer it, an
actus substantialis cogitandi ".   This *actus cogitandi* is " a substance whose
whole nature consists in *cogitare* " ; hence it is the principle and the cause
of all individual thoughts.   Therefore for the *actus cogitandi* which constitutes the nature of the soul no sort of " substrate matter in which thinking
inheres " must be assumed.—Others of course, e.g. MASTRICHT (III,
ix, 14), contest this conception of the soul. However, MASTRICHT still
recognises that the soul must be regarded as a " *substantia cogitativa* ".

8.—Since man's soul is a personal spirit, its essential powers (*facultates*)
must be distinguished. They are those of knowing and willing. " *Intellectus* is the faculty by which objects are discerned for approval or for
disapproval ", and in fact it is on the one hand " practical understanding
by which we distinguish good from evil ", on the other hand " theoretical
understanding, by which we distinguish true from false. Will is the
faculty of the soul by which we either choose or reject objects, according as
the understanding judges them to be good or bad" (BUCAN VIII, 30-31).
However, since the soul is essentially a *substantia cogitativa,* an *actus cogitans,*
the two faculties of the soul are distinguished from the soul only as
modi rei from the *res ipsa,* and the two faculties are distinguished only as
various *modi* of one and the same subject.—BRAUN (I, ii, 14, 2): "Knowledge and will are not distinguished from mind itself, except as mode from
thing modified, as figure, position, movement, rest are distinguished from
extension. Nor are knowledge and will distinguished mutually from each
other, save that as different modes in the same substance, as mode of
mind from mode of mind : so that one mode is knowing, another will ;
as a round figure is distinguished from a square-sided one, which both
exist in the same extension at different moments. Hence knowledge and
will are just different modes of thinking in our one mind ".

9.—Further, the soul is immaterial and absolutely simple, so that the
attributes of spirituality and unity belong to it essentially.—MASTRICHT

(III, ix, 8-9): "Among the affections of the soul the first is its unity ;—
the second its spirituality or immateriality, by which it is all altogether
and utterly immune from matter, not only the grosser but even the most
subtle, such as *Vorstius* and the *Socinians* along with certain ancients
actually assign to it ".

10.—Thus it is essentially non-spatial and only enters upon a spatial
relationship by its union with the body, in such a way that alike in its
separate parts as in its totality the body sets forth in space the activity
of the soul.—HEIDEGGER (VI, 92): "The reasonable soul, consisting of
pure knowledge and thought, is spiritual, indissoluble, immortal."
Besides this the majority, like WOLFGANG MUSCULUS, teach that "the
soul has its seat in the body", but in such wise that it "is not contained in
any part of the body and is yet in them all."—VOETIUS (I, 767): "The
soul is entire in the entire body and entire in any part." Chief reason:
otherwise "the soul would be one with the body *per accidens* and so a
compound, or not a whole essentially and *per se*".—BRAUN (I, ii, xiv,
7, 10, 12, 13, 14): "The union (of body with soul) is not to be conceived
of by a local presence, as though mind were co-extensive with body"
(otherwise it would not be a *unio* but a *mixtio*).—"Body and spirit are
united by relative attributes," since the *unio* of the two consists "in their
inherent ability to act, and in their action". From this it is clear "that
the soul is not joined to the body as a navigator is joined to a ship, an
angel to an assumed body or a friend to a friend;" and also that the
statement "the soul is entire in the entire body and entire in any part of
the whole" must not be taken as though a "local presence", a "co-
extension" or a "confusion" with the body were to be expressed about
the soul. Only "with regard to *operationes ad extra*" may an *esse in loco*
be attributed to souls as to angels.—The teaching is different on the other
hand in BUCAN (VIII, 27-28) (though he recognises the difficulties which
counter his view), in HEIDAN (p. 327) and in others.

11.—And for the same reason [§9] the soul is indissoluble, i.e. essentially
immortal, not *per gratiam* but *per naturam suam*. As a specific personal
substance existing for itself the soul is not essentially affected by what
happens to the body. So when the latter is destroyed it lives on as a
self-aware ego, but without corporeality.—WOLLEB 29: "The human
soul is immortal not ἁπλῶς and because it cannot be reduced to
nothing by God; but by God's ordinance and so far as it is indestructible
by second causes.—HEIDEGGER (VI, 87): "Sane reason confirms the
immortality of the soul. If it is spiritual, as earlier we said that it testified,
it must also be immortal. Neither has spirit in itself any principle of

division or dissolution; much less can it be destroyed by others who are not its creators. The members of the body are exposed to the violence of hands and weapons. The ἀΰλος spirit cannot be touched or injured, far less destroyed by sword, fire, water or force of hand or weapon. In that case a man's soul does not depend upon any created thing, not even upon its own body. Since it is a substance it is bound to have an existence; and since it is a non-material substance, its existence can neither be produced nor propped up by a material body. To be a substance is to be a subject of existence. To be an immaterial substance is to be a subject of existence apart from the aid of matter and quantity.— When therefore the body is torn or plucked asunder, the soul remains a substance, remains thinking, remains what is signified by the word "I", in no wise diminished save that it is divested of its integument".

MASTRICHT (III, ix, 17): "The Reformed are of opinion that the rational soul is immortal, and that not merely by grace but also by its own nature, and that this is fixed for us not only from Scripture, but also by its nature and by natural reasons, because: (1) being purely spiritual the rational essence of the soul is not liable to any dissolution and so has no principle of death; because (2) by divine righteousness it cannot be that the plan for the good should not be in one way and the statute for the evil not in another way; because moreover (3) it seems most foreign to the wisdom of God that men and brutes should have the same outgoing, when we have already taught that their origins are most unlike; without adding (4) that all religion labours and perishes where it is believed, that nothing survives man's death except his body, so soon to be reduced to ashes."

That the human soul is essentially immortal is proved principally by the following arguments, by BUCAN (VIII, 26): "(1) from its nature, because it is a unifold essence, having nothing of admixture, concretion, copulation or augmentation, whence it cannot be secreted, divided, dispersed and accordingly is not liable to dissolution (interitus). For death is as it were the departure, secretion and disruption of those parts which before death, were held together by some conjunction;—(2) from the witness of conscience, which conceives horrible terrors by its responsibility for sins. In fact, unless men's souls survived after death, the godless would have no need to have the slightest fear of future punishment." Exegetically the immortality of men's souls is proved from Ps. 49. 15 (God will redeem my soul from the power of Sheol . . .) Eccles. 12. 7 (. . . the spirit shall return to God who gave it) 1 Sam. 28. 9 (Endor) Mt. 10. 28 (able to destroy) Phil. 1. 22-23 (But if to live in the flesh—if this is the fruit of my work, then what I shall choose, I wot not. But I am in a strait betwixt the two, having the desire to depart and be with Christ; for it is very far better) 1 Pet. 3. 18 (Christ . . . that he might

bring us to God) Rev. 6. 9 (souls under the altar) 7. 9 (the great multitude . .
before the throne and before the Lamb). With more completeness
WALAEUS recounts the following arguments for the immortality of the
soul (p. 226): "The reason is sought (1) from the unifoldness of the soul
and its spiritual nature, which cannot be resolved into parts nor does it
possess anything contrary by which it might be resolved or destroyed;—
(2) from the outstandingness of the faculties of the soul: it knows all
things (*res*), even the immortal and eternal, which befalls no other faculty
natural or moral; things such as God, angels, the state of life to come
and the means leading thereto; and that combined with love and
inclination for these things—(3) from man's desire (*appetitus*), whereby
he desires the highest good, eternal felicity, immortality, etc., a desire
which exists in no other animate creatures and cannot be in man for
nothing and originates in God; so it will also have its fulfilment;—(4)
from the operations of the soul that are independent of the body, as
when within itself by reflex perception it contemplates itself or considers
first principles;—(5) from God's righteousness and goodness, which demands that it be well with the good, ill with the evil; this does not always
happen in this life, since life here is often more splendid and jolly for wicked worldly men than for the good, 2 Cor. 5. 10 (we must all appear before
the judgment seat);—(6) from the pangs of conscience in many scoundrels,
who have no one to fear in the world, since their crimes are hidden,
or when their power is so great, that they ought to fear no one here;—
(7) to this add the consent of all nations and the acknowledgement of all
ancient and outstanding philosophers, the *Epicureans* alone excepted,
whom *Cicero* in his *De Senectute* therefore calls finickin, and recent
philosophers".

12.—Concerning the origin of souls after the creation of the protoplasts
it can neither be said that they are continued by bodily generation nor
that God created them in the beginning of the world and brought them
successively from their pre-existent condition into union with bodies.
It must rather be admitted that God creates a soul for each newly
begotten body and unites it with it.

Whereas Lutheran dogmatics in the doctrine of the origin of man's
soul (almost completely) defends traducianism and rejects creatianism,
by the Reformed (apart from individual older Church teachers) traducianism as well as pre-existence is rejected. Says RIISSEN (VII, 52, 2): "Rather
common is the view of those who insist that the soul is *ex traduce*, i.e. that
the soul is transmitted (*traduci*) from soul, not by de-cision or partition
from the parent soul, but in a certain spiritual fashion, as light is kindled
at light " (a coarser and more spirit-like traducianism). We lay it down

that all souls are created by God directly and are infused by being created, and so are produced *ex nihilo* apart from any pre-existent matter ".

Against the assumption of an eternal existence of the soul VOETIUS adduces the following arguments (I, 796 f.) : " (1) Before union with a body souls have committed no sin, Rom. 5. 12-13 (therefore as through one man sin entered into the world . . . (and became universal), 13 : for until the law sin was in the world : but sin is not imputed where there is no law) compared with Rom. 9. 11 (the children being not yet born, neither having done anything good or bad, that the purpose of God according to election might stand, not of works, but of him that calleth, it was said unto (Rebecca) etc.) 2 Cor. 5. 10 (we must all be made manifest at the judgment seat of Christ, that each one may receive the things done in the body, according to what he hath done, whether it be good or bad). (2) If soul were united with body for a punishment, the union would not be natural nor would it be a boon and a perfecting of nature, but rather an evil, as all punishment is ; which would be most absurd. (3) In any thing, that which is natural to it is prior to what is beyond nature ; but the separation of the soul and separate existence is beyond nature while union is according to nature, therefore the latter was prior to the former and not the contrary. (4) If in the beginning God had created separated souls, in that case He would not have created all things in the perfection appropriate and due to the nature of each. This is a *ratio consequentiae* [a reason based on inference], because in the body the soul secures the perfection proper and natural to it, not outside the body. It has a native propension to its own body, as is commonly taught by writers on the separate soul and by the *Scholastics* on *Qu. 1, Art. 76, 1.* (5) If souls exist before the body, either they are on the way or at their finish (or, in their fatherland or in a neutral land). Not the first, as was already said in accordance with 2 Cor. 5. 10 (we must all be made manifest at the judgment seat of Christ, that each one may receive the things done in the body, according to what he hath done, whether it be good or bad), for there is no way or course of salvation save in this world and this life. Not the second, because the end and the reward are not secured save after the toil and struggle of this life, Heb. 12. 1-2 (looking unto Jesus the author and finisher of our faith) 1 Cor. 9. 25-27 (striving in the games: I . . . bring my body into bondage, so that I may not lose in the end) 2 Cor. 5. 1-3 (we look from the earthly tabernacle to the house not made with hands. In the former we groan for our habitation from heaven) 2 Tim. 2. 5, 12 (no contest no prize : . . . " if we endure we shall also reign with him ; if we shall deny him, he will also deny us) compared with 4. 5 (be thou sober in all things, suffer hardship, do the work of an evangelist, fulfil thy ministry). Nor the last, because there is no rational creature which is not ὑπόδικος and ὑπόνομος, subject to God in the category of morals, and whose actions in consequence are not allotted the nature of virtue and vice ".

That the souls of children are not begotten by the parents and are not transmitted by generation POLAN proves by the following arguments (V, 23): " (1) Because the soul is ἀμέριστος, i.e. *impartibilis,* therefore it neither generates nor is generated ; it is an incorporeal or spiritual substance ; just as angel is not generated by angel, because it is a *substantia* ἀμέριστος.—(2) Because it is inorganic, it does not require the instrument of a body to perform actions. According to a thing's attitude towards action is its attitude to existing, and according to its attitude to existing is its attitude to action. Since then the rational soul acts without a body (for even while it is in the body it has reflex activities [of its own] : it counts, it knows both singles and universals, it infers from adjacent causes, it knows and wills in separation from the body), it follows that it is also brought into being without the action of a body.—(3) Because it is intelligent and immortal ; nothing intelligent and immortal can be elicited from a faculty and potency in matter.—(4) Because Christ's soul was not propagated from the soul of a father. Had it been propagated from the soul of a father, it would undoubtedly have been propagated with the infection of sin.—(5) If God alone is the Father of spirits or souls, then they are not generated by parents. The antecedent is true, therefore so is the consequent. The antecedent is clear from Heb. 12. 9 (fathers of our flesh . . . the Father of spirits). The antithesis would not be consistent, had the Apostle not understood by the " fathers of our flesh " those who generated with the body and by " Father of spirits " Him who directly created spirits or souls. For God also creates human bodies, but indirectly, by the instrument of this nature.—(6) Because what ever is propagated by the parents along with the flesh dies with the flesh. But a rational soul does not die with the flesh ; hence the rational soul is not propagated by parents along with the flesh ".

Hence Reformed dogmaticians teach in the sense of creatianism, as MASTRICHT (III, ix, 20) relates: "The Reformed with *Jerome* and the common Church of that time (*Hieron., Apol. ad Rufin. lib.* II) teach : " that new souls are created daily by God out of nothing and that individuals are united to their individual bodies within a human being ". The reasons for this are given by VOETIUS (I, 798) as follows : " We advise making a choice of reasons, lest we snatch promiscuously at everything adduced. For us they are these. (1) From Genesis 2. 7, where the soul is not roused from its own transient matter, namely earth (which was at that time analogically the seed or seed-bed of the human body), but was formed by God and united to a body. Moreover this story of man's creation should be compared with the creation of the rest of the animals.—(2) From Eccles. 12. 7 (the dust returns to the dust as it was, the spirit to God its Maker) with Heb. 12. 9 (fathers of our flesh . . . Father of our spirits), with the possible addition of Zech. 12. 1 (God forms the spirit of man). In these passages something peculiar is assigned to God in the production of souls : as opposed to the production of other living things.—(3) From the conception of Christ, who since he became a participator in flesh and blood in like fashion as ourselves Heb. 2. 11-15, had a soul by creation and not *ex traduce*. Had he had it *ex traduce*, of course it would be from the Father (for by most He is made the sole author of transmission and the chief author by all). But He had no father. Even although he had not borne a soul of his mother's seed, he was yet his mother's son and David's, Abraham's, Isaac's.—(4) No bodily virtue can achieve the effecting of a spiritual substance, because no virtue acts outside its genus. Now the intellective soul exceeds the whole genus of bodily substance.—(5) If the generation of the body is the cause producing the soul, then the dissolution or corruption of the body will be the corrupting cause : but the latter is absurd. Therefore ! Moreover transmission of seed is the proper cause of generation of the body.—(6) Every natural agent which acts in dependence on matter produces nothing but what is dependent on matter ; but the soul is not dependent on matter, because it can exist outside the body.—(7) There is added the consent of all the Fathers (with one or two exceptions) and the ancient philosophers, for all of whose words see ZANCHIUS ; in addition that of the writers of the middle period and of the *Scholastics,* finally of more recent theologians, philosophers, medicals both *Papist* and those who walked out of Papacy except SOHNIUS (*tom.* 2 p. 563), PEUCER (*Tractat. de ortu animae*), COMBACHIUS, (*Anthropol. c.* 2), TIMOTHY BRIGHT (*In Physicam*) SCRIBONIUS (p. 18) and all who call themselves *Lutherans,* whom LUTHER'S authority has forced into a contrary opinion or at least into an ἐποχή. Of our own men MUSCULUS (*in loc. comm.*) and PISCATOR (*Disput. de peccato*) leave the matter *in medio*. MARTYR thinks that traduction cannot be refuted from Scripture ".

Similarly WOLLEB p. 28: "Today the following reasons prove that the soul, created by God out of nothing, is breathed into man: (1) Because our souls would be from a different source from Adam's, ours from pre-existent matter, Adam's from none. Nor can it be objected that there is one way of generation, another of creation; nothing is generated from matter save what was also created of matter from the beginning. (2) Because Christ's soul is not from the transmitter of seed: He was conceived not by the ministry of a husband but by the operation of the Holy Spirit from the blood of the Blessed Virgin. (3) Because Scripture speaks of the rise of our souls as of a work of creation, not of nature, Job 33. 4 (the spirit of the Lord hath made me and the breath of the Almighty hath given me life), Zech. 12. 1 (. . . the Lord . . . stretcheth forth the heavens and layeth the foundations of the earth and formeth the spirit of man within him) where manifestly he [the prophet] is inflamed by the works of creation. (4) Because the genesis of each is as its analysis [break-up or dissolution]. But the analysis of man is that the body return to the dust, but the spirit to God Eccles. 12. 7. Since then in the analysis of man the spirit returns directly to God, it was undoubtedly made by Him. (5) Because Scripture openly distinguishes between the fathers of bodies and of spirits, Heb. 12. 9 (we had the fathers of our flesh to chasten us, and we gave them reverence: shall we not much rather be in subjection to the Father of spirits and live?). (6) Because the soul is ἀμέριστος and so is not produced except out of nothing. (7) Because if it were generated by a transmitter, it would be generated either from a soul or from a body or from body and soul together. But it is not generated from a soul, because nothing is generated from an incorruptible. Nor from a body, because the soul is not corporeal. Not from body and soul together, because it would be partly corporeal, partly incorporeal. But if it is produced out of nothing it is produced by God alone, whose alone it is to produce something out of nothing".—Upon the controversy touched on here and its course cf. in particular VOETIUS I, 858ff.

To the question "when is the soul infused and when does it arrive in the body?" BUCAN (VIII, 26) answers: "When the body in the mother's womb is already radically organised and disposed to receive such a soul, as appears from the manner of the first soul, which is the type of all creatures".

POLAN here notes (V, 31) that the uniting of the newly-made souls with the newly-begotten bodies takes place "in males, according to common opinion, about the *40th*, in females about the *80th* day".

13.—Man's body on the other hand because of its specific materiality is *per se* essentially spatial and mortal.—HEIDEGGER (VI, 92): "(The life of the body) is material, dissoluble, mortal". But by this it is only acknowledged (as will be seen better, later on), that man's body could die, not that it had to die.

14.—Above all man's body is sexual, since after the creation of the first pair it was only reproduced by generation.—VOETIUS (I, 1093): "After the first creation of man from earth God had fixed this law of nature, that man should generate man".—ENDEMANN (*Institut.* I, p. 192): "Wherefore God gave them the faculty of propagating their kind and joined them in wedlock".

15.—In its original state the nature of man was the perfect image of God in creaturely form: God had made man in His own image. Generally speaking this divine likeness in man is (MASTRICHT III, ix, 29) "that conformity of man whereby in his own way (i.e. as a creature) he reproduces the highest perfection of God". This was set forth first of all in the substance of man, i.e. in his spirit-body personality; man's immortal spirit with the faculty of self-consciousness and of self-determination was an image of the divine nature and the body was an organ completely corresponding and completely serviceable to the life of the spirit. Thus the image of God in man was declared in the gifts with which this spirit-body personality was adorned.

For the understanding of the Reformed Church doctrine of the divine image in man it should be noted that it is thoroughly connected with man as such, indeed with the entire man, with his entire spirit-body being, and that accordingly any hesitation in view is shown only in the conception of the question, whether the divine image is to be understood only of the original *praestantia* of the human nature or also of this itself, the spirit-body personality of man. CALVIN distinguished in the concept of the *imago Dei* between the "substance of the soul" and the "qualities of the soul" but adhered to the former view. *Instit.* IX, v, 3: "The principle I have just laid down I adhere to, that the image of God extends to everything in which the nature of man surpasses that of all other species of animals. Accordingly by this term is denoted the integrity with which Adam was endued when he was full of right knowledge, when he kept his affections composed to reason, all his senses duly regulated, and when he truly ascribed all his excellencies to the admirable gifts of his Maker. And though the primary seat of the divine image was in the mind and the heart, or in the soul and its powers, there was yet no part, down even to the body, in which some sparks of glory did not gleam." This view was also represented later. COCCEIUS (*Summ. theol.* XVII) finds the divine image not in the "substance of the soul", nor yet in the "faculties of the soul", nor yet in the "*imperium* which man had over the living", but in the *rectitudo* which he explains (§ 22) as moral reciprocity with God in all a man's parts, in the soul of course as the ἡγεμονικὸν and in the body and limbs as the σκεῦος. Similarly HEIDEGGER (VI, 19), BRAUN (I, ii, 15), RIISSEN (VI, 60) etc.

Individual teachers attractively saw the divine image in the original, quite untrammelled dominion of man over the other creatures, since in this man appeared to a certain extent as God's representative; whereby, on a broad view, man's *dominium* was regarded not as the *imago divina* itself, but as the purpose of it. So e.g. MARTYR p.156: "So man was made in the image of God from the beginning, that he might be at the head of all things created, as a kind of representative (vicar) of God". ZANCHIUS combines both views (p. 20): "We believe that the image of God consisted chiefly in this, both that just as God is absolute Lord of all things, so to man all things were subjected, so much so as to make him king of the whole world; but chiefly that as God is most holy and righteous, so also man was created upright (*rectus*) etc.". Anyhow the conception of the *imago Dei* which came to be supreme in Reformed theology is a different one. The prevailing majority of dogmaticians distinguished (in agreement with *Melanchthon* and O.P. dogmatics) (See HEPPE, *Altprotest Dogmatik*, vol. I p. 356) the substance and the original endowments (*dotes*) or attributes of the divine image, finds the former in the personal nature of man, and assigns the original righteousness to the latter.

In the interests of this distinction the concepts of the *imago* and the *similitudo* of God (although on other grounds it was frequently disapproved of, e.g. by WALAEUS p. 235) were differentiated, e.g. by BUCAN (IX, 2): "*Similitudo* is a broader concept than *imago*. Where there is *imago* there is also *similitudo*, but not *vice versa*. An egg is said to be like an egg, but yet an egg is not the image of an egg. However in this dispute over the image of God in man the word *similitudo* was added to the word *imago* by way of exposition, as Phil. 2. 7 ("form of a servant" and "likeness of a man"). Similarly POLAN (V, 11): "If we would talk accurately, similitude and image differ, because *similitudo* has a broader range than *imago*, as AUGUSTINE (T. IV, *libro* LXXXIII, *quaest.*, 73) teaches, namely that where there is *imago* there is at once *similitudo* as well, but not *vice versa*."

The German Reformed dogmaticians belonging to *Melanchthon's* school represent this conception almost without exception: e.g. PEZEL (*Argum. et Object.* II, p. 83; see HEPPE I, p. 356) and URSIN (*Corp doctr.* p. 39, see HEPPE), where the latter insists that above all as a nature rational man is in the image of God, and that therefore the *imago divina* must in the first instance be recognised in the " incorporeal knowing and willing substance of the soul". In the *Loci* (p. 558) URSIN indeed begins his expositions of the divine image in man with the statement that " it will have to be estimated not by the state in which men began to be after the entry of sin, but by the reparation made through Christ, i.e. from the nature of man born again ", and hence explains that " further, the image of God is not to be sought in the sole substance of the soul, but particularly in the virtues and gifts with which it was adorned by God in the creation." In any case URSIN continues : " Nevertheless since soul is knowing Spirit, the more excellent part of man's substance, separable from the body, immortal, the beginning and the cause of life and movement in the living body, it must be confessed that, even if it be not reborn, its substance is a shadow of divinity. But since the substance as of spiritual natures generally so also of the human soul is unknown in the fog of this life, the *imago* must be considered in those faculties and operations in which we see that man excels other creatures, and are aware that he is conform with God in consequence of the divine word and works." Now there are two *facultates animae* in which the image of God in man is set forth, namely " (1) the faculty that cognises things unifold, singular and universal, and compounds or divides them, and reasons from what is compounded, having by nature ingrained *notitiae*, which are the principles of doctrines and the rules of living, and a reflex action that judges of appropriate actions " ; and " (2) the will, which is the faculty that freely chooses or rejects the object which knowledge indicates for choice or rejection. In these faculties and actions of the soul and in those effects and signs which necessarily accompany them the *imago Dei* is to be sought ". From this URSIN derives the definition (p. 559): " Thus the image of God in man is the mind rightly realising God's nature, will and works and the will freely obeying God and the conforming of all inclinations—with God's will and mind ; and in short the purity and integrity of the soul's spiritual and immortal nature, perfect blessedness and joy acquiescing in God and the dignity of man and the majesty by which he excels and dominates the other creatures ". In the dominion which has been given to man over creation URSIN already finds an element of God's image in him, because in Ps. 82. 6 it is said regarding government *vos dii estis*;—and adds (*Loci* p. 565): " Now as for the fact that many things now fight against and harm man, that happens because of sin, by which he has lost his rights but which does not do away with his dominion altogether ".—all that has been discussed URSIN in conclusion sums up in these words (p. 559): " Thus the chief parts of the image are wisdom, righteousness, and a human mind capable of these divine properties. Nor is the fact that the soul is an immortal spirit to be excluded from the likeness to God, since God too is spirit ". As regards the difference of condition in which man displays himself before and after the fall we must insist (p. 566) that " (the image of God) had been unimpaired before the fall, but by the fall had been obscured, so that barely do there survive slender traces of it ".

But the other dogmaticians too express themselves on the main topic in exactly the same way, e.g. POLAN (V, 11), who, to expound the doctrine of the divine image in man, first of all propounds the statement that : " The parts of the image of God, for which rational creatures were made are two. The first is the actual spiritual substance, incorporeal and immortal, Jn. 4. 24 (they that worship God must worship him in spirit and truth) 1 Tim. 6. 16 (men are to attend the appearing of the Potentate, " who only hath immortality ").—The second part is the " endowments or attributes assigned to the rational creature." Hence POLAN rightly distinguishes in the image of God in man the " soul's substance " and the gifts imparted to it (V, 34): " The substance of a soul reports the nature of God according to its condition for these reasons : (1) As God is Spirit unifold and non-material, so too man's soul is spirit unifold in respect of things material, and non-material in respect of bodies. (2) As God is one essence, although there is more than one person in Him, so the soul of man is one, although it consists of several faculties. (3) As God is incorporeal and invisible, so too the human soul is incorporeal and invisible, possessing no corporeal dimensions. (4) God knows and wills ; so the soul is endowed with the faculty of knowledge and will. Moreover these endowments and attributes, of which God is the archetype, the image and likeness moreover in the human soul, are natural life and immortality, bliss and glory." To " natural blessedness " belong " wisdom, righteousness, power " and " natural liberty in man's soul ". Note the examples following.

LEYDECKER (p. 126) distinguishes: (1) " The image in nature so far as man is presented with a spiritual soul, knowing and willing ", and (2) " in wisdom, righteousness and holiness ". Similarly MARESIUS (*Art.* 146) : " God's image in man has respect partly to his nature, partly to the endowments conferred on him. (*Syst. theol.* p. 93)—The image of God in man (1) looked to the essence and state of the soul, spiritual, immortal, knowing, willing ; (94) it shone out (2) in the soul's endowments and its accidental perfection, that is, in the light and rectitude of the mind, in the holiness and righteousness of the will, in the harmony of the senses and affections and in their promptness after good ".—On ALSTED and WENDELIN cf. HEPPE, *Altprotest. Dogm.* I. p. 357.

WOLLEB 26 : " The image of God consists partly in natural gifts, the unifold and invisible substance of angels of course and of the human soul, life, knowledge, will and immortality, partly in supernatural gifts, primaeval bliss naturally, rightness of knowledge and will and in majesty and dominion over the other creatures."

A DIEST, p. 37: "The image of God (which cannot be lost) was the spiritual, immortal, rational substance of the soul, with the powers of knowing and freely willing : the divine image, which can be lost, lay for knowledge in wisdom, for the will and its effects in true righteousness and holiness ".

BUCAN distinguishes (IX, 8-11) the divine image in man "by the nature of man's substance, by the nature of his gifts or qualities" and "by the nature of his attributes or dignity". In the first respect Adam was in the image of God, "(1) because the soul put in man by God is by nature spiritual, knowledgeable, incorporeal, immortal, invisible essence, which in its petty measure reproduces the nature of God ; (2) the single (*unica*) soul existing in man, endowed with several faculties, like memory, thought, will is a symbol (as *Augustine* will have it) displaying the unity of the divine essence and the plurality of the persons" ; in the second respect "(a) because God in the beginning had kindled in man's mind the aspect (*facies*) of heavenly wisdom, by which he rightly apprehended God and His will revealed to him, and so all God's works and the natures and attributes of all things ; (b) next because God had adorned man in his will with perfect righteousness and holiness, by which he represented and imitated God's righteousness and holiness as in a mirror ; He had also equipped him with powers suited to every good thing, in short, with a body most beautifully fitted to obey the soul, moving it with the utmost readiness and without trace of weariness ; in the third respect "because by the dominion which he held over all animals and all creatures of this earth, he represented on earth God Himself, the Lord of all things."

MARCK (XIV, 5): "More truly to embrace the unimpaired divine image the nature of the soul is called spiritual and immortal along with its faculties".

MASTRICHT (III, ix, 29-30): "The image of God in man is . . . both in man's actual essence and in the prime faculties of the soul, at all events in the virtues of these faculties.—Hence man's first conformity with God is in man's actual essence and all of that in body and soul".—Hence MASTRICHT remarks in conclusion (III, ix, 38): "The *imago Dei* as we call it has neither perished completely through sin, nor does it completely survive sin. It remains therefore (as regards Gen.9. 6; "whoso sheddeth man's blood, by man shall his blood be shed: for in the image of God made he man"; Ja. 3. 9 "with the tongue bless we the Lord and Father; and therewith curse we men, which are made after the likeness of God"; 1 Cor. 11. 7 "a man indeed ought not to have his head veiled, forasmuch as he is the image and glory of God; but the woman is the glory of man", where undoubtedly it speaks of a state not past but present), it remains, I say, so far as it consists (1) of the actual nature of man's body and soul; (2) of the natural faculties of the soul, knowledge and will; (3) of certain gifts of knowledge and will, so far as in the worst there is still detectable some use of reason and even a propension to a good even moral Rom. 1. 19 (that which may be known of God is manifest in them (the ungodly); for God manifested it unto them) 2. 15 (they shew the work of the law written in their hearts, their conscience bearing witness therewith and their thoughts one with another accusing or else excusing them) 1 Cor. 5. 1

(incest); further (4) of some remnants at least of the original *dominium* Gen. 7. 2 (Noah choosing the beasts for the Ark)."

HEIDAN p. 333: "(Man's divine image consists) in three things: (1) in the rational and immortal nature or essence so far as it is a thinking substance, i.e. knowing and willing; (2) in dominion over lower things and beasts; (3) in gifts".

MARTINIUS (*De creat. mundi* p. 97): "So in the soul and its powers and endowments—the divine image is specially placed; but in the body too in a secondary sort of way.—But of this image of God some rough, rotten and confused ruins remain after the fall, the soul's essence indeed being preserved but robbed of its heavenly adornments, being vicious and wretched; and unless He who made remakes it, it is absolutely all over with its entire salvation".

WALAEUS (*Loci*, p. 238): "So we say that the image of God consists in those gifts and priviliges in which man surpasses all other living beings, as David Ps. 8 for this reason outstandingly proclaims here God's goodness to man. These privileges are first to be considered in man's essential attributes, as in his soul spiritual and immortal, also in his mind, free will and the power answering thereto; wherefore even unregenerate men are called God's offspring Acts 17.—Secondly, these privileges are to be placed in original wisdom and righteousness, as Paul says Eph. 4. 24. (*we* are to "put them on")".

TRELCATIUS 309: "By the image of God we mean the likeness by which man conveniently reports the nature of the Creator to his own nature, both in the soul strictly, and in the body because of the soul, and finally in the entire and unimpaired person, because of the union of the two. In the soul, whether you regard its nature, or its faculty of substance, or its faculties or finally the qualities of the *habitus* by which these are produced. The substance of the soul reports the nature of God according to its condition and the measure of its condition, for three reasons: (1) the former like the latter is also one;—(2) the former like the latter is also unifold, spiritual, and non-material;—(3) as the latter so too the former is incorporeal and immortal." Cf. EILSHEMIUS, *Ostfriessl. Kleinod* p. 13.

CONFESSION OF THE REFORMED CONGREGATION AT FRANKFURT 1554: "God made man in His image and likeness. A soul was given him which is a spirit like God Himself and also immortal, although it has a beginning. The soul He adorned with every endowment of His goodness, power, wisdom, holiness, righteousness and all the virtues, just because in man you might as with the eye see God Himself".

Those dogmaticians who declared against this conception of the doctrine and took sides with COCCEIUS, unanimously made three distinctions in the *imago divina*, namely (1) the "antecedent of the image", (2)

its "consequent" and (3) the "actual formal nature of the image of God",
understanding by the first "the spiritual essence of the soul which alone
is fit for the *imago Dei* to be stamped on it", by the second the "uprightness of the soul", by the third Adam's *dominium* (HEIDEGGER, BRAUN,
WITSIUS, RIISSEN and others). For the rest it is insisted by almost all, that
even in man's original corporeality the *imago divina* in it was set forth,
so far as the body was an instrument perfectly corresponding with the
godlike spirit and ministering to it (by not hindering it etc.), and at the
same time, being the peak of material creation, sets forth a microcosmic
figure of the whole world, as of the figure of God. Cf. BUCAN (IX,13):
"How does the image of God shine in man's body?—Not as it is a body
simpliciter and endowed with such a figure, but according as the body
linked to a rational soul bears part of God's image and in a way contains
the whole world in itself. Whence also man is called a μικρόκοσμος,
in which the Creator and Archetype of the whole world shines forth".—
LEIDEN SYNOPSIS (XIII,)13): "Now the body thus shaped by God was
δεκτικόν of the human soul and so equipped as to be the fit instrument of such a soul and its actions and of no spiritual nature *per se* besides".
—TRELCATIUS 309: "The *imago Dei* is "both in the soul strictly, and in
the body because of the soul". That also the "terrestrial bliss in Paradise"
was accounted to the original gifts and ornaments of the godlike condition, pretty well accords with this".—MARTINIUS: (*Summula* p. 10) "Man's
bliss (besides the joy, glory, and peace in the contemplation of God)
also embraced health of body and a pleasant surfeit of all things for leading
life on earth etc.".

16.—These gifts were (1) "original wisdom", i.e. a perfect knowledge of
man himself as well as of God and nature, above all "right reason"
and a "good conscience"; (2) "original righteousness, i.e. complete
pleasing of God; (3) free will (*liberum arbitrium*), i.e. the capacity of being
able to will effectively what is good and well-pleasing to God; (4) being
made capable of bodily immortality; (5) unlimited dominion over all
the other creatures; and (6) perfect earthly blessedness of soul and body
in Paradise. — POLAN (V, 34): "The original wisdom in man's soul was
that excellence and perfection of knowledge, by which unimpaired man
rightly knew God and God's works and himself and wisely understood
all things unifold, singular and universal, and rightly compounded or
divided them and reasoned from the composites rightly and without
error,—*in sum*: knowledge, judgment, foresight not only sufficed to
govern the animal life, but also ascended with them to God. So *ratio*
in unimpaired man was *recta*. But also in man's state of innocence
conscience was good and could accuse him of nothing".

17.—These original attributes of man as a whole are not supernatural but, since they belong to man's divine image, natural gifts, i.e. gifts of human nature in its original state, and therefore transmissible by the "protoplasts" to their posterity.—COCCEIUS (*Summ. Theol.* XVII) : " The image of God was natural to man, not because it flows from the actual substance and faculties, but because it would have been unbecoming in God not to make man upright (*rectus*)".—RIISSEN (VII, 61): "This image may be called natural to man, not as though it were an essential part of his nature, but (1) because it was created along with the nature; (2) because it was not contrary to it; (3) it was necessary to the end of created man ; (4) it would have had to be propagated along with the nature, as the remnants of it now are".—HOT-TINGER (p.118-119): "Now this original righteousness and immortality of the first man were natural gifts, not supernatural, so far as that is *natural* which the first man received with his actual nature; while *supernatural* is what is above the intact nature and its condition". Only so far as these gifts are "above the nature corrupted by sin, and only as they are restored by supernatural grace", may they be called supernatural gifts.

18.—Among these gifts, that of "original righteousness" calls for special mention. "Original righteousness" was that uprightness of the will, by which man perfectly obeyed the divine will according to the whole law, both inwardly and outwardly; consequently he had all the motions of his heart composed to obey reason and rightly adjusted according to their order: he loved and worshipped God and was holy; his desires were good and ordered,—the inclinations and affections of a right reason observed moderation; this absolute adjustment to its harmony was followed in the body by a kind of equable proportion towards that order as its necessary effect, so that the body as the soul's instrument obeyed right reason" (POLAN, V.34).—BUCAN (X, 5): "Original righteousness was (1) the light in man's mind by which he knew God and His will; (2) the writing of God's law in his heart, by which he inclined to obey Him, and the uprightness of the whole man, by which the spirit was subject to God, the soul to the spirit, the body to the soul and was obedient; (3) the acceptance of the whole man, by which he was pleasing to and accepted by God, but which was separable from man himself, as the actual event proved."

19.—This original righteousness was of course—since only God Himself is righteousness—not the substance but an accident of Adam's nature, being precisely its *rectitudo* and its *integritas*.—BUCAN (X, 4): "Was this original righteousness in which Adam was created substance or accident?—It was not substance, but was the uprightness and integrity in his nature and so a quality which might be present or absent irrespectively of the corruption of the subject, i.e. of the soul. An upright nature and uprightness of nature are different, as a straight line and straightness of line are different, since line is the subject of straightness. Accordingly Adam's soul was the subject of this original righteousness and uprightness, but his soul was not actual righteousness.—Next God's property is to be essentially righteous and good, for God is actual goodness, integrity and righteousness: therefore if this original righteousness of the first man had been his substance, man would have been called righteousness itself: which could not be said without blaspheming God.—Now too the contrary of this original righteousness, original sin, is an accident, since it has entered man's nature. Since, moreover, the contraries are of the same genus, it follows that this original righteousness was not a substance but an accident.—Finally, since restoration of this image is nothing else than the restoration of fresh qualities (which takes place by regeneration), it follows that original righteousness was also a quality (by which the entire man was righteous and upright) and in fact separable; as was proved later by the lapse of man."

20.—It was merely loaned to human nature as such in the person of Adam.—MASTRICHT (III, ix, 33): "Original righteousness was conferred on Adam not as a private but as a public person, or what is the same thing, in Adam on the whole of human nature, whence it would have been transmitted to all his posterity.—But this original righteousness is not a substance as *Illyricus* used to rave, but a quality diffused as it were through all the substance, and so common to body and soul, to the mind, also to the will and the affections".

21.—Therefore, like all the original gifts and advantages of his likeness to God, Adam might have transmitted this righteousness to his successors, had he not fallen away from God, the prototype of his nature.—BUCAN (X, 7): "If Adam had persisted in this original righteousness, would it have been transmitted to posterity?—It would (1) because it was the righteousness of human nature, but not the righteousness of a private person; (2) because its contrary, original sin, was passed through Adam to all his posterity (Christ alone excepted); (3) because every like generates its like in nature and species; which, however, could not have been done by seminal power but by God's ordinance, as was previously said anent sin of origin".

22.—And that is why it is called "original righteousness".—Bucan (X, 6): "Why is it called original ?—Because it was natural and the first man was created in it and for it, not as a private person, but as the origin and root of the whole human genus".

23.—This original righteousness rested on the one hand upon Adam's *liberum arbitrium.*—Heidegger (VI, 98) : "The leader, companion and follower of the first man's original righteousness was *libertas* or *liberum arbitrium*".

24.—On the other hand it rests upon the help of the grace lent him. Man's *libertas arbitrii* (his αὐτεξούσιον) is generally "the faculty of mind by which freely, spontaneously, deliberately, after previous consideration and without external compulsion, he chooses what he first perceived, thought over and decided to be worthy of choice" (Heidegger VI, 98). Or "free will is volition inasmuch as it follows a judgment of the mind in choosing and preferring good without repugnance or difficulty" (Keckermann p. 222). *Liberum arbitrium* is thus the capacity of the will ("since *arbitrium* includes with will a judgment of the mind" *ibid.* 222) to take up a free attitude to the things presented to it by the power of knowing.

Liberum arbitrium is not the will, so far as it is freedom of action ; not an attribute of the power of knowing ; but the *facultas volendi*, which belongs to the personality over against the objects offered to it (through the understanding).—Hottinger (175) : " *Liberum arbitrium* is the faculty of willing or refusing, choosing or repudiating an object indicated by the understanding, by its own spontaneous and deliberate act ".—Bucan (XI, 2) : " Strictly *liberum arbitrium* does not signify the faculty of doing either good or evil or even freedom of judgment, but rather the faculty of willing or not willing a thing ; or the free resolve of the will, which follows the deliberation of the reason or mind and its consultation ; or free will, by which the will wills or does not will, elects or rejects the things presented by the mind or understanding ".—Mastricht (IV, iv, 10) : " Naturally considered then *arbitrium* (for the Greeks αὐτεξούσιον, a much too haughty word !) is the faculty of the mind and will, by which we do what we please, after counsel and judgment, in such a way that we are not determined by any other created cause. It belongs to the mind and will, so that the mind judges and indicates what is to be done, while the will commands what has been indicated and decided upon, and thereby radically it looks to the mind, but formally to the will.—More correctly therefore it is said to consist in the power of acting *ex consilio* and προαιρέσει (by plan and choice) or, which is the same thing, in the satisfaction of reason. Hence though it excludes any intrinsic necessity on the side of nature and an extrinsic one on the side of compulsion, it does not exclude the necessity of the divine dependence, infallibility and predetermination".

The relation of *liberum arbitrium* to the will and to the mind is aptly set forth by CALVIN (I, xv, 8) : " God equipped man's soul with a mind, with which to discern good from evil, righteous from unrighteous, and to see by the previous light of reason what must be followed or fled from : whence the philosophers have called this directing part τὸ ἡγεμονικόν. To this He joined the will, with which lies choice. The first condition of man excelled in these outstanding endowments, so that reason, intelligence, foresight, judgment might suffice, not only to govern earthly life but that by them men might rise to God and eternal felicity ; secondly, so that choice might be added, to direct appetite and control all organic movements, and so the will might completely assent to the control of reason. In such integrity man flourished by free *arbitrium*, by which if he were willing he might acquire eternal life."

25.—It should be noted in this connection that we can only speak of a true freedom of man's will, if it is capable of being defined in a way answering to the concept and definition of man—i.e. in a way pleasing to God—in other words if it can will what is good. For if a man wills sin, he is the servant of sin and is thereby not free.—HEIDEGGER (VI, 98) : " Before all we must grasp that freedom, or *liberum arbitrium*, if we prefer so to call it, is not the power of sinning and not sinning. For in that case it would not belong to God or the heavenly ones who are unchangeably good ".

26.—So *liberum arbitrium* is not essentially indifferent ; for since God could create man only good, He had also to bestow on him untrammeled freedom of the will to do good, together with knowledge of it.—HEIDEGGER starts (VI, 99) with the statement that : " In the difficult dispute over *liberum arbitrium* we must generally beware of the rocks both of the *Manichaeans* who deny the natural freedom of the *arbitrium* and of the *Pelagians* who so assert the free *arbitrium* of the will, that even in the state of sin they leave no room for the grace of God, and of the *Scholastics* who— place free *arbitrium* in indifference to good and evil " ; and from this standpoint fixes the doctrine of the *liberum arbitrium* as follows (VI, 100) : " Things being thus generally fixed we maintain that Adam was created not indifferent to good and evil but free, i.e. with a will not barred from doing what an upright mind dictated to be done ; not however thus free immutably or independently. He was not created indifferent by God because, although the election of will which he received from God was concerned with good and evil (in the way God's will also deals with good and evil, not by deliberating but by willing that and turning away from this), yet the will itself was so created by God, that, as good, upright, made in God's image and likeness it should have adhered to the Creator as its principle, and being ordained to Him as its final end should have had regard to Him only, not ambiguous or swithering whether it would adhere to God or revolt from Him to another principle and set up another final end for its desire and its action. Such indifference in a human being, lying as it were on the scales and fluctuating between right and wicked, is not only an imperfection, but also a flaw in the creature, the prime origin of sin and defection from God (since he who is not with Him is against Him, Mt. 12. 30) nor is it worthy of man fresh created by God nor of God the Creator, who cannot be the Author of any flaw or defect in the creature. And since doing well was for the first man according to his nature, doing ill outwith and counter to his nature, we may sufficiently gather that in that state there could have been no room for indifference to good and evil. Free therefore and not indifferent he was created by God, i.e. with a mind aware of right and good, and with a will not hindered beforehand from choosing and doing what the mind foresaw to be upright and good. For will without freedom is not will, but an impulse of other provenance, without true love of God as its principle and good, and so without the obedience and servitude appointed for God the One and Sole ; it is not a good, upright will and so neither is it a work of God. So it was necessary for man's will to be created such that it might love God in freedom and so be able to be happy by continuing in that love.".

Thus Adam's *liberum arbitrium* did not consist in his being able to obey and not to obey God, but in his being able to obey God perfectly. For says COCCEIUS on the *Heidelberg Catechism* qu. 7 : " True freedom is not to be hindered by any ignorance or difficulty from seeking and enjoying one's good, and to cling to it firmly and steadfastly ; and such is Christian freedom. In sinning therefore there is strictly no freedom, but whoso sins begins to be a slave."—It was even possible for Adam to persist in this freedom ; VOETIUS, I, 393 : " Perseverance in the state of innocence was possible for him ".

27.—But from the very beginning in Adam, *liberum arbitrium* is and was dependent upon God, since it was purely in dependence on God's will, counsel and providence that Adam had freedom of will to do good and was accordingly so free from any compulsion, that he was able by free judgment and self-determination, unhindered by any dominion of sin or earthly misery, to decide for what was well-pleasing to God.

In order to fix the doctrine of *liberum arbitrium* URSIN (*Loci.* p. 633) discusses the two questions "(1) What is common and what is different in the freedom of will in God and in creatures ? (2) What are the degrees

R

of freedom in the human will according to man's different states?"
To dispose of the first question URSIN first fixes the concept of freedom.
"Freedom is (p.634) the "faculty," "the right," or generally the "ordaining"
of a person or of a thing, whether done by someone's will or by nature,
to act, of its own (judgment) or motion in accordance with the order
congruent with its nature, and to enjoy the good things suited to it,
without prohibition or hindrance, and not to sustain defects or burdens
not proper to its nature". However, this concept of freedom does not
arise in the present discussion on *liberum arbitrium*. Man may will much
freely, which he yet cannot execute freely. Freedom of will described
"a natural potency in an intelligent nature together with a power that
wills", and is always related to an object offered to man's knowledge.
"Therefore *liberum arbitrium* is the faculty or power of willing or refusing
without compulsion, of its own motion and aptitude for either course,
that which the mind dictates as worthy of choice or rejection." This
capacity is called *arbitrium* in respect of the mind, indicating to the will
the object to be chosen or rejected". And it is called *liberum* "in respect
of the will freely and spontaneously following or rejecting the judgment
of the mind".

According to this God and the intelligent creatures, namely angels
and men, have it in common that they "(1) act as the result of deliberation
and counsel, and (2) will without compulsion what they have thought,
i.e. their will existing in a suitable nature for willing the opposite or
converse of what it wills or for delaying its action, inclines to one side
or the other spontaneously and by the force inherent in it".—635: On
the other hand God's freedom is distinguished from the creature's freedom
in that (1) as concerns *intellectus* God from eternity is aware of everything
most perfectly and He cannot err, whereas creatures "do not know of
themselves either everything or the same things at any time, but are
aware of God and His will and works as much and at the time, as and
when God wills to reveal it to them"; (2) as regards the *voluntas* God's
will is determined only by Himself, on the other hand the will of angels
and men is the cause of creaturely acts, in so far as it is none the less
directly or indirectly determined by God; 637: (3) as God knows
everything unchangeably, He "has also decreed everything which
happens from eternity and wills them immutably so far as they are good,
and permits them so far as they are sins".

HEIDEGGER (VI, 100): "Nor was the first man's freedom independent,
as God's is. It depended on God, His decree and providence, by which
man was bound to be predetermined in his action".—MARTINI
(*Gubernatio mundi* 251): "In every state the will by its nature is free from
compulsion; but in the state of innocence it was in addition free from

sin and from misery or punishment, but along with a changeable condition. Moreover man was not free from divine government or from obligation to obey."—RIISSEN (VII, 62): "Adam's freedom in the state of integrity was not that of independence, which belongs to God alone; nor freedom from mutability, for he was mutable. But his freedom was (1) freedom from compulsion, by which a man acts spontaneously and at pleasure, not under compulsion; (2) freedom from physical necessity, by which a man acts ἐκ προαιρέσεως, not by a brute instinct or blind impulse; (3) freedom from slavery, whereby a man is not liable to the yoke of any slavery or sin or misery."—RIISSEN (VII, 63) adduces the reasons: "Did Adam's freedom rest on indifference?—No; (1) because such ἰσορροπία or equal propension to good and evil is at variance with the nature of will, which necessarily follows the dictates of the mind; (2) at variance with the state of creation, in which the will was created very good; it would not be very good, if it had a propension to vice and virtue alike".

28.—[Adam, then, could decide for what was well-pleasing to God]. Since thereby, in virtue of his *liberum arbitrium* he was quite free from all compulsion, yet in the use of it—because in everything!—was utterly dependent upon God; in order to be able by means of *liberum arbitrium* really to do the good, he required God's gracious help, without which man can do nothing good. And Adam really rejoiced in this gracious help, since in regard to the fulfilment of His holy will God bestowed upon him the "possibility of not sinning if he wanted not to", but of course not "the willing of what he could", by which latter He would have been giving him the gift of unchangeable perseverance in good and making any lapse impossible.

POLAN (V, 34): As regards the actual manifestation of obedience to God Adam had received the *posse si vellet* but not the *velle quod posset*. To make this clear and to show that none the less Adam enjoyed *liberum arbitrium*, we must indicate the difference between the nature and the *vires* [powers?] of the *liberum arbitrium*; the result of which is that, in order really to manifest true obedience, Adam required God's gracious support. "The nature of man's *arbitrium* is that it is free, not in respect of the good or bad object, as though it might be equally strong both ways, as though it could equally choose and do good and bad, as though it could bend either way of itself, with the same facility and power.—But it is free as regards the efficient cause, because it accepts or rejects whatever it accepts or rejects μή ἀναγκαστῶς ἀλλ' ἑκουσίως, i.e. without any compulsion, (1 P. 5.2. . . . not of constraint, but willingly; Heb. 10. 26 if we sin wilfully after that we have received the knowledge of the truth, there remaineth no more sacrifice for sins). And that, both in this life, whether before or after the fall, and after this life.

"Powers of *liberum arbitrium* of themselves there are none without God's general or special aid, either in earthly or in heavenly things and actions; both in this life, whether before or after the fall; and after this life. General divine aid is the name for the general movement of divine providence, by which all things are governed and preserved Ac. 17. 28 (in him we live and move, etc.) Heb. 1. 3 (who being the effulgence of his glory and the very image of his substance and upholding all things by the word of his power, when he had made purification of sins, sat down on the right hand of the Majesty on high). Special divine aid is the name for the peculiar grace, moving, comforting and promoting to action, whether it be united with Christ's saving grace or the grace of regeneration, Jn. 15. 5 (I am the vine, ye are the branches . . . apart from me ye can do nothing) 1 Cor. 15. 10 (by the grace of God I am what I am : and his grace which was bestowed upon me was not found vain; but I laboured more abundantly than they all: yet not I, but the grace of God which was with me); or separated from it, by which of course God distributes moral gifts and moral virtues to whom he wills, even to the reprobate, 1 Cor. 12 (spiritual gifts),—Before the fall the powers of the *arbitrium* were of course suited to supplying everything according to their proportion: actually, however, they could not supply a single one of them without the help of the First Cause. Thus, by his natural powers, man was fit to love God, to trust Him, to obey His will, to do God's commands perfectly, but none of them could he actually accomplish without the help of God's grace. And that grace to accomplish all these things was available from the first creation to Adam's fall. But the grace to will beyond that and to persevere in perpetuity in obedience to God was not given to him, because not due. God is not bound to any man to give him more than He wished to *ex gratia*. None the less Adam had a free and good *arbitrium*; but changeable. Therefore he could incline as much to evil as to good: he could equally sin and not sin."

The teaching of the other dogmaticians is similar. At the same time it should be noted that the aid of grace here spoken of must not be confused with the gift of grace to persevere in the good, which would have made a falling away on Adam's part impossible. The help of grace meant is that which man requires for good as a being dependent on God. COCCEIUS (*De foed.* II, 56): "It was in keeping with God's constancy in offering Adam a covenant, to preserve the powers given him in creation and to increase them at his request, but not to fortify him behind them or to bring it about that he should not fall into temptation, whether by giving him *velle* because He had given him *posse*, or by not letting him lapse;

in that way He would have altered the nature and conditions of the covenant. What then ? Had He not given them to understand that life had been prepared for them in God, if they should abstain in faith from the forbidden fruit ?—HEIDEGGER (IX, 51): "And indeed the first man had need of assistance of the kind both to work and to persevere and to acquire merit. To work: without the stimulus of God moving before him, protecting and predetermining, man could not have wrought, as being essentially dependent upon God in works alike and in nature. To persevere: the will to persevere and to conquer temptation depends solely upon grace. As the event has shown. To acquire merit: finite obedience would not have availed ought in securing an eternal reward without God's gratuitous covenant".—BUCAN (XI, 7-8): "Did Adam in addition to the unimpaired powers in question also require the grace of God ? He did, in order of course to be preserved by it in the integrity of his nature and urged on to the acts in question", explaining that "just as a true and living vine endued with the natural powers of producing wine even so requires the outward aid both of rain and of sun, to preserve and move and promote its natural powers to effect their natural work, Jn. 15. 5 (I am the vine, ye are the branches . . . apart from me ye can do nothing) Ac. 17. 28 (in him we live, etc,).—But what is the nature of this grace ? Such that if he wishes man may live in holiness, but not such that he would wish to cling to God perpetually and stedfastly. Had he received such grace, he would have persevered altogether. Adam had received grace by which if he would he might not sin; but he had not received grace by which he refused and was unable to sin."—HOTTINGER (120-121): "In the state of innocence the first man needed the special help of God in order to work well always and to avoid sins stedfastly.—Yet there was no inclination to sin in unimpaired man".—BRAUN (I, iii, 3, 11-12): "As Adam was received by God into a covenant of works, he was also created with powers to keep the covenant.—But he had not sufficient strength not to be in need of God's further grace and help in order not to sin. *Augustine* in fact finely distinguishes between the *auxilium sine quo non* and *auxilium quo*. Adam had the aid without which he could not stand, but he had not the aid by which he would inevitably stand, so that he would not have needed God's further grace in order to stand".—MASTRICHT (III, ix, 337): "By this (original righteousness) man was born fit to submit to God and to continue in perfect obedience to Him, if of course he wished to; although the actual willing and the actual act of persistence required another additional and second sort of grace, by which the former would be excited and translated from potency into act and so preserved. For God works both to will and to do, Phil. 2. 13".

29.—Thus Adam's fall was possible because his free *arbitrium* was change-able.—CALVIN (I, xv, 8): "His will was flexible either way, nor was he given constancy to persevere".—COCCEIUS (*Summa de foedere* II, 52-53): The protoplasts had "uprightness with changeability, so that if God allowed and they were willing", since they were abandoned by the forti-fying grace of God, godlessness could gain ground in them.—The *liberum arbitrium* of the protoplasts was the "mutability linked in man with the faculty of reason and will, endowed with wisdom and uprightness, by God's grace, to choose the true good and to adhere to it and to avoid evil".—BUCAN (XI, 4): "Before the fall Adam has assigned him a *liberum arbi-trium* flexible alike for good and for evil, which distinction should by all means be noted."

30.—Analogously Adam's "bodiliness" was also changeable, in so far as it was essentially mortal, i.e. in so far as by its nature it could die. But by its original definition it was not subjected to the power of death. It rather possessed the *posse non mori,* as man in his will possessed the *posse non peccare*; and so it could become, of course, a blessed instrument of the soul and a fellow-heir of eternal life, if man did not surrender to the dominion of sin and death.

In the same sense in which Adam's *liberum arbitrium* was changeable originally, his bodily life was also changeable. As the former might enter into the slavery of sin, yet also if Adam withstood temptation, might be exalted to the higher state of perseverance, to real possession of eternal life, so too Adam's bodily nature might fall into the slavery of death and on the other hand achieve real possession of eternal life. Of course man's body was made of dust and therefore as such could not be incorruptible; on the contrary he needed it, in order to receive nourish-ment.

COCCEIUS indeed concedes "that no cause of death arose with man, and that God was not the cause of death". Yet he finds it beyond shadow of doubt, "that the first man could not have remained in the state in which he was created and at the same time approach ἀφθαρσία and ἀθανασία, the possession of the incorruptible and, of course, immortal life, which is in God's kingdom, 1 Cor. 15. 50 (flesh and blood cannot inherit the kingdom of God; neither doth corruption inherit incorruption), but requires to be changed into a better state". Adam's body required physical nourishment and was organised for generation, neither of which pertains to a spiritual body. Hence it is fixed "that the first man had not possessed ἀφθαρσία so that he could not suffer corruption and die, nor had he a spiritual body, i.e. one made alive by the power of the H. Spirit".

But God had impressed the image of His nature also upon man's corporeality in such wise, that if man had kept himself free from sin the latter might be immortal. This equipment, then, the *posse non mori*, was thus a special gift of grace. Bucan (XI, 12) asks, "Was man gifted by God with a mortal or an immortal body?—Partly mortal, because it might die, as the actual issue showed; partly immortal, because it might not have died; if it had obeyed God, that is.—The possibility of dying he had by the condition of his nature. The possibility of not dying was his, not by the constitution of nature but by the benefit of grace, because God had granted man this grace of being able not to die, if he obeyed His commands".—Hence although man's body might die, nevertheless, provided man had kept himself worthy of the grace bestowed on his corporeality, namely immunity from hypothetical death, it might have been transformed into an immortal body, permeated by the Spirit.

All dogmaticians express themselves in this sense. E.g. Ursin (*Loci* p. 560): "Not only in body but also in soul (Adam) had been meant to lead an immortal and perpetually blessed life, had he not brought death upon himself by sin".—Polan (V, 29): "Before sin Adam's body was mortal *per se*. But it was not meant to die, if he had not sinned, but by a most beautiful change it would without death have been transformed by God into eternal incorruptibility".—Heidegger (VI, 93): "Although the nature of the human body created by God was so far mortal, because were the power removed, man could die and be resolved into the elements of which he consisted; yet at the beginning of creation man was not by nature mortal as regards proximate power, nor had he need actually to die before sin, nor was he actually appointed to die. But this immortality was not absolute, like God's—but as man he could, by retaining his uprightness, not die".

31.—Thus in his original objectivity Adam had not been exalted to the proper perfection of his nature in the image of God, since the gift of unchangeability was still denied him. This he ought to have acquired for himself, by obedience to God, and thereby a goal was set him, for which it was his duty to strive after himself, in order to achieve the perfection of his nature. For this purpose God made His covenant with him.

It is one of the differences between Lutheran and Reformed doctrine, that according to the former, it is assumed that as Adam was called into existence, so he is the final goal of creation and the completely realised ideal of humanity, while on the other hand the Reformed system also recognises the full glory of Adam's *imago divina* (indeed more completely than is done on the *Lutheran* side) but stresses the thought that it is not the creation of man in God's image as such, but (1) the setting up of the *foedus* with him, and (2) the completion of man by the bestowal of the gift of persistent obedience of the will (perseverance) and of eternal life, that was God's real purpose and the end which man was to achieve here on earth.　Accordingly Adam's original condition was not the complete, ideal condition of man.　Man could only attain to his proper ideal in the possession of unchangeable righteousness, freedom and blessedness, and so to perfect likeness to God, if he should morally have merited the right to possess this ideal.—COCCEIUS (*De foed.* II, 31): "Although man was upright and happy in his own way, he was not yet a son and heir, in the way in which we have become by grace.　He was put in the position to acquire the right to eternal life, but he had not already become the heir".　Similarly CAT. PALAT. *qu.* 25: "Although God did not immediately make man perfected, as he is to be in the heavenly life, and put him in a state in which he might change and become bad and die, nevertheless, etc."—BRAUN (I, ii, 15, 21): "From these we shall have a ready answer to the question, whether Adam was also created righteous.　If righteousness be taken in place of actual holiness,—then truly he was also righteous.　But if we take righteousness to be a stedfast will to live rightly for ever, by which through fulfilling the law a man secures himself δικαίωμα and the right to ask for a reward, then Adam cannot be called righteous."

WENDELIN rightly says (*Collat.* p.161) that before the fall man had the *posse non peccare,* which belonged of course to his likeness to God.　But his *posse peccare* also given in this way did not belong to it [the likeness] till after the fall.　Thus Adam would have achieved complete likeness to God, if (as he might and ought to have merited it morally) he had been raised to the condition of *non posse peccare.*

CHAPTER XII

PROVIDENCE

1.—What God really intended by creating the world is set forth for us in the continuance of the world as God's Providence. There is a single divine act by which God creates the world and determines its government. That is why Providence may be conceived as a continuous world-creation. —The Reformed conception of the doctrine of Providence is characterised in the first instance by the fact, that in it the conception of Providence is validated as an element in the conception of creation or as the reverse side of it. The creation and government of the world constitute a single activity of God, which is shown first of all creatively and then as sustaining and governing. The government of the world is the proper purpose of creation. Hence, says Braun (I, ii, 12, 1): "God's providence is nothing else than that most effective volition of God, by which He willed from eternity that such should be the case, that it should exist so long and work in this way, which effective volition is God's *ipsissima creatio,* if the matter be regarded in its existence; it is *conservatio* or providence if regarded in its duration and operation. In respect of God the same action is creation *and* providence; God works all things by a single, most unifold will, that they exist, remain in existence and work."

In Reformed dogmatics, therefore, the conception of providence must be fixed on the one hand in relation to the conception of creation, and on the other to that of the eternal decree. In the first connection providence is described (Ursin *Expl. Catech.* 127) as the " continuation of creation". Says Heidegger (VII, 22) : " Preservation is not an act distinct from creation but is continued creation ". The reasons are the following : " If creation and preservation were two distinct actions, creation would first cease and preservation begin, either the same moment creation ceased or another succeeding moment. Yet (1) it would not begin the same moment ; because, since as regards God creation is an instantaneous action (for if it could last some time, it could last long enough for the thing to perish), so the thing would be said to be preserved at its own very first moment in which it is created, which is absurd. (2) Not at a moment following creation, because since time intervenes between any two moments, in the intervening time the thing would be neither created nor preserved. So just as creation is God's eternal and effective order that the thing exists, so preservation is the same order of God's that the thing previously ordered to exist exists forthwith. Both involve the same will and command of God and have the same end, namely that the actual *esse* of things, which is first produced in creation, continued when produced in preservation."—In any case MARCK (X, 6) correctly remarks that " here the difference between creation and providence should be noted, because the latter, as implying the existence of the creature does not exclude means subordinate to itself in all its actings ".

In another connection providence belongs to the " execution of the decree " (WOLLEB 29) (HEIDAN 347). It is the theistic conception of God which leads of itself to this conception of providence. URSIN (*Explic. Catech.* 101 ff.): " Creation is not to be feigned like the building of a ship, which after manufacture the architect hands over to the control of the navigator.—So we cannot rightly understand creation, unless we simultaneously embrace the doctrine of providence."—Hence CALVIN says (I, xvi, 4) : " First of all then readers should realise that providence is not that by which God idly views from heaven what is going on in the world, but that by which as if grasping the tiller He controls all events".— As regards the relation of providence to the decrees RIISSEN says (VIII, 3) : " The decrees are the norm of the whole of providence." Similarly as early as ZWINGLI (*De vera relig.* 282): " Providence is the kind of parent of predestination " ; (*ibid.* 283) : " Predestination is born, which is nothing else than if you should say that foreordination is out of providence, in fact is providence itself."—Hence BUCAN distinguishes two parts of Providence (XIV, 3) : " (1) One is a kind of eternal and unchangeable disposition, which has decreed to rule all things after their creation and to guide and lead them to their ends. (2) The second is the actual and temporal administration of the whole world by which God wisely, freely, powerfully and well steers, rules and controls the separate things created by Himself, and directs them to their ends ".—A DIEST 129 : " Providence is contemplated in the preceding decree and the subsequent execution " ; accordingly the " providence of the decree " and the " providence of execution" are distinguished. Similarly TRELCATIUS also p. 78.—At the same time providence is not to be confused with predestination. Says URSIN (*Explic. catech.* p. 129): " Providence strictly extends to all God's things and works, predestination to rational creatures ".

2.—Since God's will is the actual divine nature in its actuosity directed outwards, it is also just God's own nature by which He exercises His providence and not a force or activity distinct from it.—BRAUN (I, ii, 12, 7); " The act of God's providence by which He preserves things in their own being, moves and predetermines, governs and directs them to actions, in a word His whole influx and operation among creatures is not a sort of quality, virtue, act or movement distinct from God's essence, nor is it something created by God, to emanate from God and pass over into creatures and be injected into them.—Therefore the act of God's providence is the actual eternal and most effectual will of God, according to which God effects all things by command. Moreover since God's will is God's actual essence, it follows that He preserves, moves, predetermines, governs and rules all things by His essence."

3.—Hence the providential activity of God, in virtue of the divine essentiality, must be absolutely independent, omnipotent, holy, wise, etc. So RIJSSEN (VIII, 7) : " Which action, like all God's actions, ought to be almighty, holy, wise, independent etc.".

4.—" God's providence (πρόνοια) is His outward work, by which by the same His word He preserves all things created by His word, rules their movements, acts and passions, so wisely directs them all to their ends that He promotes all good things effectually and mercifully, the bad either severely restrains or holily permits, wisely orders, righteously punishes ; in a word, controls everything for the glory of His own name and the salvation of believers " (HEIDEGGER VII, 3). Or more briefly : " God's providence is God's transeunt action, by which He cares for and administers the world created by Him and all things that are and are made in it according to His own will for His own glory and the salvation of the elect ". POLAN (VI, 1).

Other dogmaticians define Providence similarly. For PEZEL, URSIN and ZANCHIUS see HEPPE (*Dogm. des deutschen Protest. Bd.* 1 pp. 319, 321, 324). KECKERMANN defines p.141 : " Providence is the efficacy of the divine volition in preserving, ordering and directing things (*res*) ".—The LEIDEN SYNOPSIS is fuller (XI, 3) : " In Providence we describe the actual and temporal preservation, direction and leading to the end determined by Himself and most wisely and righteously made for His own glory, of the things one and all which exist and are made, this in accordance with God's eternal, unchangeable and utterly free decree".—BEZA (III, p. 402): " Providence is our name in God for that most wise and excellent power of God, by which God resolved by Himself from eternity how, when and with what object He was to create things one and all and the way in which He was to govern them when created. On this efficacy of His all things both made and to be made depend and by it have been from the beginning of the world and are now being directed and will continue to be directed right to the consummation of the whole world, with the height alike of wisdom and of uprightness, to their own ends by the intervention of mediate causes ".—The distinction between πρόθεσις, πρόγνωσις and προορισμός, is valueless; wherefore BEZA continues: " Moreover in this providence we consider πρόθεσις, πρόγνωσις and προορισμός, which differ in manner rather than in substance, so that they are sometimes taken to be one and the same thing, namely God's eternal counsel preceding all mediate causes not only in time (for it is eternal and accordingly above all time), but also in the order of causes ". The name providence is traced back to Genesis 22.14 (יהוה יראה —God will provide), where already "care" is put forward as the most essential element in the concept.

Providence is thus not to be conceived as an inactive prescience; CALVIN (I, xvi, 4): "It follows that providence is to be located in action (*in actu*); for the trifling of many with bare prescience is excessively ignorant". URSIN stresses the difference between the two (*Explic. cat.* 127 ff; see HEPPE, *Dogm. des. deutschen Protest.* vol. 1, p. 319). But still less is the Christian concept of providence related to the heathen one of fate; as little too is the assumption of accident compatible with the former. Says HEIDAN p.367: "Above all we admit that His honour is incompatible with this effectual providence of God, if accident or fortune obtain in human affairs".

HEIDEGGER (VII, 15) explains the difference between providence and fate: "(1) Being His eternal and free counsel for preserving and governing all things outside Himself God's providence is in God Himself; the fate inherent in things is put in the actual causes and their series. (2) Next, providence does not tie God down to causes and to nature, but when acting shows Him to be most free. By the freest counsel He guards the order instituted in second causes and deliberately controls or even changes it, so that it acts either beyond or above or counter to nature, according to His pleasure. Fate on the contrary involves God Himself and so binds Him to the order of causes, that the Stoic *numen* could not act otherwise, "locked in the prison of the fates". (3) But also God's providence makes the actual series and connection of things freely set up by God's decree temporal, fate makes them eternal. (4) Besides, God's providence makes some causes which operate without counsel necessary and natural, others which act ἐκ προαιρέσεως voluntary and free. Fate makes them all necessary and determined, none of them free. (5) In short, God's providence so rules sin, that nevertheless it in no way makes God its author. Fate wildly raves that sin appears by necessity of nature and was implanted in matter by God."

5.—Faith in divine providence thus gives the Christian the comfortable assurance "that all things eventuate and happen by God's ordering and not by chance or luck or ill-luck. Therefore the Christian should direct his heart's gaze in all things straight upon God with whom he hath a covenant, as upon the prime source and cause of all things" (OLEVIAN, *Fester Grund*, p. 31). That God exercises a providential government over the world, which is therefore something quite different from the heathen fate—i.e. from "fate distinct from God" or "fatal causes inter-connected and acting by their own power" (HYPERIUS, 252)—and which equally excludes alike any chance or any mere necessity of nature (CALVIN I xvi, 2)—this may be demonstrated not only by statements of H. Scripture Ps. 14. 2 (the Lord looked down from heaven upon the children of men, to see if there were any that did understand, that did seek God) 33. 13-15 (the Lord looketh from heaven, He beholdeth all the sons of men; from the place of his habitation he looketh forth upon all the inhabitants of the earth; He that fashioneth the hearts of them all, that considereth all their works), 36. 6 (. . . O Lord, thou preservest man and beast) 104, 27-30 (these wait all upon thee, that thou mayest give them their meat in due season.   That thou givest unto them they gather; thou openest thine hand, they are satisfied with good.   Thou hidest thy face, they are troubled: Thou takest away their breath, they die, and return to their dust.   Thou sendest forth thy spirit, they are created; and thou renewest the face of the ground), Mt. 6. 26 (behold the birds of the heaven that they sow not, neither do they reap, nor gather into barns; and your heavenly Father feedeth them.   Are not ye of much more value than they?) 10. 29-30 (are not two sparrows sold for a farthing? and not one of them shall fall on the ground without your Father: but the very hairs of your head are all numbered) Jn. 5. 17 (My Father worketh hitherto, and I work), Ac. 17. 28 (in him we live etc.); but also by other proofs.   These proofs are derivable from 1) "God's nature": since God is absolute truth, wisdom, and power and the absolute good, it follows that God knows and can do everything and also wills it in His goodness; i.e. that He cares for everything: (2) "the condition of created things"; since all things are made of nothing, they cannot of themselves have the power of continuance and operation: (3) "the order and harmony of the creatures", which cannot be explained without assuming an absolutely intelligent government of the world: (4) "prophecy"; God has aroused as many witnesses to His foresight as He has sent prophets who foretold the future: (5) "the feeling of conscience"; the voice of conscience would have no meaning, were there not a divine providence which punishes evil and rewards good: (6) "the agreement of the saner nations and philosophers", which acknowledges the presence of a divine providence.

This is how the arguments for providence are set forth, especially by HEIDEGGER (VII, 5-8): "The same truth which is the Church's perquisite is powerfully confirmed by the nature of God as well as by the state of created things, by the order and harmony of the world, by prophecies, by revolutions in empires, by God's judgments and benefits, by the sense of conscience, by manifest types, by the agreement of nations and philosophers. To God's nature it belongs that He is, that He is the first cause of everything, is the highest truth and wisdom, the highest power, the highest good. These separate things establish the providence of God.—It is of the nature of the highest Truth to have all things within His view; of the nature of the highest Power to be quite able for all He has in view; of the nature of the highest Good to will also of His goodness the things He has had in view and is able for, and so to care for them all.— It is the condition of created things, that as they are partakers of nothingness, they have no power of subsistence or activity of themselves, and if the Hand by which they are sustained in being and activity be withdrawn they cannot subsist to do anything even for a moment.—Wherefore, how could this marvellous order and harmony in created things, alike in its incredible sympathies of conjunction and conspiracy and its inexplicable antipathies of distraction and discord—how could it be thought of without a godhead and higher ruler? The arrangement of parts, so mighty, varied, manifold, gorgeous; the movement of the heavenly bodies, their turning, fixity, concord, alternation; the change in weather, the riches in the bowels of the earth, the graces in plants, the multicoloured variety in animals, together with the multitude of members in individuals, their symmetry, relatedness, end in view, direction towards their goals, is the work not of nature (which as regards most of its parts betrays no traces of reason) but of supreme and inerrant Intelligence, as *Averroes* calls it.—Further too God's providence has as many witnesses as He has made prophets. Apart from it all predictions would be slippery and unsure, i.e. admittedly leaning on man's changeable will, not on God's disposing, on which alone it essentially depends, before all existing things.—But also the feeling of conscience, which the ancients declared to be like God in all mortals, supports divine providence. Naught is emptier than the consolation of its integrity or the terrors of its hurt, if human affairs do not interest God so that He cherishes the good, plagues the wicked, and fails to distinguish between godliness and ungodliness.—In short the consent of nations and philosophers supports this truth".

6.—Providence comprises a threefold activity, preservation (usually called *manutenentia* by the *Scholastics*), concurrence or co-operation with second causes, and government.—Many make this distinction. E.g. BRAUN (I, 12, 2): "The acts of providence are three: (1) He preserves all things in their being and duration; (2) He moves all things to their action by concurrence, in fact by precurrence; (3) He steers and guides all things to the desired end to which they were appointed from eternity". Others on the contrary assign "concurrence" (an expression which

Pictet (VII, iii, 9) uses with the remark: "if one may use the word although unsuitable") to "government" and distinguish in providence only "preservation" and *rectio* (direction) Keckermann (116) or "preservation" and "government" (Alting 78, Heidan 357) or "preservation" and "ordering" (Maresius 42).

7.—Preservation is that "by which God maintains and perpetuates the things made by Him as regards their existence, essence and natural faculties, whether in the species by the succession of individuals or in the individuals themselves" (Heidegger, VII, 20). That the world continues purely by divine preservation alone results from the fact that God is essentially absolute Spirit, the world essentially a dependent creature and therefore also dependent in its continuance, and that because the world is made out of nothing it cannot have the cause of its continuance in itself, but only in the omnipotence of the all-sufficient God.— Heidegger (VII, 20): "Right reason teaches the divine preservation of all things, whether we attend to God's or to the creatures' nature. (1) Since God is infinite, most perfect, independent and the first cause of all things, there is no creature which does not depend on Him, as in its being so also in continued being or duration of being and acting. Otherwise it would end in being independent, i.e. God Himself. But (2) since all creatures are *ex nihilo* and so partake *de nihilo,* they exist προσδεόμενοι in everything, in need of Another's strength at every moment, they must both exist and continue to exist by the strength of Him who alone is sufficient unto Himself and to all men."

8.—Hence *conservatio* is to be conceived as a *continuata creatio,* resting upon the same command of God as creation.—Cocceius (*Summ. theol* XXVIII, 9): "By reason of the things which have begun to be, preservation is a kind of creation continued." For "as often as things begin to be, they are in some fashion created", since "to create" is nothing but "to produce something new by a word". Hence e.g. God creates what parents beget.—v. Til: (*Comp.* II, p. 70): "Providence is the perpetual creation of God, differing only relatively from creation".— Amesius (I, ix, 18): "This preservation is actually the same as creation, differing solely in manner (*sola ratione*), because creation includes a certain newness which preservation excludes, and excludes a previous existence which preservation includes, so that this preservation is nothing else than a sort of *creatio continuata*".—Walaus: p. 292: "What is understood by this maintenance and preservation of all things?" Answer: "The continuation of the existence of the things themselves; and not only of their essence but also of all their natural strength and powers, whether these things (*res*) are stable or changeable".

At the same time preservation must not be conceived as a continued creation, as though by preservation the essential identity of the once created world were abolished. Hence WALAUS' remark p. 292: "The manner moreover in which this takes place is not to be grasped by man nor is it to be thought that new essences are always emanating from God, as light is perpetually emanating from the sun. The same essence always remains and is preserved by God".

9.—The second element in providence is the free concurrence of God in the series and concatenation of second causes, in which connection providence is called *mediata et ordinata* though not *conditionata* (indirect and ordered without being conditioned). "Concurrence or co-operation is the operation of God by which He co-operates directly with the second causes as depending upon Him alike in their essence as in their operation, so as to urge or move them to action and to operate along with them in a manner suitable to a first cause and adjusted to the nature of second causes" (HEIDEGGER VII, 28). God's "concurrence" does not therefore do away with the activity of second causes; on the contrary it is actually posited and sustained by the "concurrence".—HYPERIUS 249: "In no way do we remove second causes".—WOLLEB 30: "God's providence does not remove but posits second causes".

LEIDEN SYNOPSIS (XI, 13): "The creatures which God preserves in their nature and attributes He moves and applies to action according the measure of the nature of each and so concurs with them, that by His own action He inflows directly into the action of the creature so that one and the same action is said to start from a first and a second cause, according as one *opus* or ἀποτέλεσμα exists thereby. And if there is anything disorderly in it, it is not as the Creator's but as the creature's act; as in cutting some things happen through defect in the object or the instrument, and these are not to be imputed to the smith acting through the axe".—HYPERIUS p. 249: "In no way are we removing second causes, but our view is that they must be confined to the place to which they deserved to be confined according to their applicat ion. I.e., we admit their validity and advantage, but only when and so far as He orders and disposes, who is the First Cause and, as they say, the *Causa causarum*". This is how HYPERIUS explains this: "Thus food, drink, grass and the things doctors use are simple second causes appointed for preserving the body's health or restoring it if it shall have been lost. But they are useful at the time for which and for those whom and to the extent to which it has pleased God the all-wise to dispense them".

10.—But this co-operation of God must not be conceived as a mere maintenance of natural forces, or the mere setting up of a natural and moral law, or as the effecting of an indifferent, general movement, to be determined first of all by the creatures themselves, or as an activity of God different from the activity of the creatures and only coinciding temporally with it, working not upon the creatures themselves but only upon their activity. On the contrary it is an activity of God such that by it God directly and predeterminedly grasps the powers of the creatures and so arouses them to activity in their natural way that the activity of the creature is God's own action.

PICTET (VI, iii, 11): "Concurrence" is not "a virtue in God passed on to creatures", nor a "movement different from the movement of second causes", nor yet an "indifferent act" (as when the Sun with its heat bleaches one body and blackens another), nor does it do away with "a man's liberty"; "*concursus*" is simply the action of second causes produced in them, not by their own strength independently of God, but by dint of this act of will which is in God, by which He says, I will, in order that such an act may be done by such a creature etc." This "act of God's will precedes the act of our will", but "by no means" does away "with the man's freedom".—MARCK (X, 10): "This co-operation is not to be placed (1) either in sheer preservation of strength to work, (2) or in the giving of some law natural or moral, by which all things act *proprio motu*, (3) or in a general, indifferent movement, to be determined by the creatures, like the inflow of the sun, as is claimed by the *Jesuits, Socinians, Remonstrants*, (4) or in the simultaneous act of God distinguished really from the action of the creatures, by which God in no wise inflows into creatures, but only into their actions—but in all creatures' direct—as regards power and what underlies, by a previous, predetermining method not of time but of order—impulse and move to action, so that in this way the action of creator and creature is really the same, merely differently named."

Similarly the other dogmaticians, e.g. WITSIUS (I, VIII, 18): "Nor does God concur only in the actions of second causes when they work, He also inflows into the actual causes so that they may work. Because the beginning of an action depends, if not more at least not less on God than does its progress.—19 : Further, as a second cause cannot act unless led and first moved to action by the prevenient and predetermining influence of the first Cause, so too this influence of the first Cause is so effectual, that given it the second cause cannot act. To feign an indifferent concurrence of God, who is defined in the end by the co-operation of second causes, is unworthy of God ".—HEIDEGGER (VII, 30) : " (1) If two principal causes are both particular and not subordinate, they cannot at the same time directly concur in effecting the same thing. But God as a cause is not particular but universal, not only as regards things in common, in which second causes meet,—but also as regards the proper ways in which second causes distinct from one another in species and in number differ, and in which a second cause is subordinate to God in operation.—(2). Next, this co-operation by God is direct, not because He alone operates alone without the application of any second cause, but because between God's action and the result there is no intervention of creaturely efficacy, which touches the result more nearly than God. God does not merely so assign and preserve to the creature a faculty and power of action, that the creature meantime emits an action or produces an effect close at hand and directly, while God does so solely by the medium of the power which He gave and preserves to the creature ;—on account of the nature of the creature's dependence He attains to every action and result of the creature directly.—Hence " all things " are said to have been done " through Himself ", i.e. by this direct and proximate power as first cause Rom. 11. 36 (of him and through him and to him are all things).—(3) Besides, God's concurrence is both previous—whereby He inflows into the actual second cause, predetermines it to action and so precedes the creature's action not in time, but in order, dignity, and surpassingness—and simultaneous, as the barbarous expression is, i.e. by the method of conjoint action, by which He produces one and the same action along with the second cause, so that the action of first and second cause is one.—(4) Finally God concurs with creatures in the mode proper to the first cause and accommodated to the nature of second causes. It is proper to the first cause to operate independently and freely *ad extra*. Accordingly concurrence is God's free operation which He may apply or not apply. But since from eternity He decreed to create, sustain and govern the world, so also He set up in time the order of nature and resolved by a firm and adamantine law to endue separate creatures with their proper nature and character, to preserve and rule them and to concur accordingly with their operations ".

11.—Hence God avails Himself of "second causes" not of course as suitable tools, since He rather lets the force potentially immanent in them become active and issue in an action.—HEIDEGGER (VII, 27) : " But neither must it be thought that in such government second causes are simply and in themselves pure instruments of God and so in a state of passivity and not also of activity, as though God acts by second causes like a master tradesman with his tools, which do not act otherwise than as they are moved by the principal agent.—*At causae secundae propria et insita virtute operantur* (by their own ingrained power).—Otherwise all freedom would be destroyed in voluntary causes and so at once not the credit merely but also the defect and abuse in every human action, especially one which is intrinsically bad, would have to be assigned to God.—Finally neither does God act subjectively in second causes, because in that way every power with which the creatures are endued by God would be crushed, and they would have been created in vain, God being the sole operator.—He acts effectively, as the first cause, from which (second causes) have received the power to act and to cause, and by the concurrence of which they are singly urged and applied to action ".

CALVIN means exactly the same thing when he says (I, xvi, 2) : " Indeed of things inanimate we must hold that, although its attribute has been bestowed on the individual by nature, it does not however exert its strength, save in so far as it is directed by God's present hand. Therefore they are nothing else but instruments, into which God assiduously instils as much efficacy as He wants and bends and converts them to this or that action according to His own *arbitrium* ".

12.—So second causes are related to the governing activity of God not merely passively but also actively, since God is active in them not "subjectively" but "effectually", He being the *causa prima,* so that the activity of the second cause can never be regarded as anything else than an activity of God produced by it (HOTTINGER 133). But it does not follow that God needs the support for His activity which proceeds from second causes : God often acts without or against second causes (*providentia immediata*) and has ordained their activity only to glorify His mighty power and to warn man against false trust in divine providence, which despises the use of natural means.

HYPERIUS p. 250 ff: Second causes are for God not what we call instruments : God can effect all in all by Himself without second causes. Still, by wise and gracious purposes God has ordained " the *ordinaria ratio* of the *causae secundae* in which He Himself always acts by being present ". " Whence it follows that they gravely sin who despise second causes ". It is by second causes that God means to ensure to man the blessing of His providence. Only we must at the same time always be clear that God Himself works personally in second causes and that therefore the Christian has to put his trust not in them but solely in the living God.—HEIDEGGER (VII, 26) : " God uses second causes of this kind, not because He is lacking in or devoid of strength or afraid of fatigue or fond of leisure and relaxation, but partly in order to shew forth His power over His creatures and His royal dignity, based on the satellite position of His creatures or hosts, as well as His goodness in imparting to them power of action in a sort of co-operation with them, partly to shew man an example, not, in reliance on divine providence or even his own strength, to neglect the means and to dare tempt God ".

13.—The third element in providence is the government of the world in the narrower sense of the word. "Government is the work of divine providence, by which He directs to their mark all actions, corporeal as well as mental, or rather movements and thoughts along with their effects, so that there is nothing that does not respond to His purpose" (v. TIL *Hypotyposis*, p. 82). "God's government is the act of the same providence by which God ordains, directs and executes things all and individual of every kind to the end prescribed by Himself, both the intermediates and the final one" (HEIDEGGER VII, 24).—LEIDEN SYNOPSIS XI, 17). "We also subject to the providence of God the ordering of things to an end, especially a final one. For there not only belongs to it the ordering of means to an end, but also the achievement of the end".

14.—By government all things are so guided by God that they serve the purpose of the world whole and thereby achieve their own purpose.— LEIDEN SYNOPSIS (XI, 17-18): "Things which emerge among created things into the order of a particular cause, by another particular cause enter into the order of the first and universal cause.—Thus we shall be more correct in saying that it does not belong to Providence that by it each separate thing should be guided to the particular end suited to it, but absolutely to the end congruent with the whole work. As one who burns logs in a household does not ordain them to the use suited to logs, but takes care of one household. This will be more correct than if with some we declare σκληρῶς (not to say more weightily) that God's providence is sometimes frustrated in the attainment of an end, in whatever sense this is taken".

15.—All creatures, intelligent and unconscious alike, require the constant guidance of God to be able to reach the end appointed for them, for which they were ordained, but which they often fail to recognise.— HEIDEGGER (VII, 24): "Since nothing has been created by God or when created is preserved by Him save for a fixed end for which individual things exist and are moved, it is plain that without God's control creatures can in no wise achieve that end. Things deprived of *intellectus* are ignorant of their end and so cannot act in its interests or move towards it themselves. Indeed intelligent creatures neither themselves know their respective proximate and particular ends, as is clear from the various results which happen outwith their plan and purpose, with which nevertheless they unwittingly co-operate. And those who know their ends and act in furtherance of them, nevertheless do not act and move of themselves or independently of God."

16.—This supreme purpose is to glorify God by the blessing of the elect. "The end of providence is the glory of God and the salvation of the elect, which all subserve" (WENDELIN, *Systema* I,VI,12). In order then to let individual creatures attain to the purpose of their existence, God governs unconscious creatures by a legal order implanted in them, or rather by a certain constancy in the life of nature, which calls forth the eternal, unchangeable presence of God in nature; the intelligent creatures on the other hand (1) by the setting up of the moral law and (2) by its immediate effect on men, for what the law demands He either does or does not fulfil among men, and thereby (κατ εὐδοκίαν) does good among them and lets evil happen permissively (κατὰ συγχώρησιν) in order to lead even this to its goal.—HEIDEGGER (VII, 25): "One mode of government holds in natural things, another in things of the will. Natural things God governs both by a certain law stamped on nature or rather a force of God present in nature and urging it, according to which they do that for which they were created and individually keep the place and order appointed by God, and by the ῥοπή, instinct and inclination which God the Creator endued them with,—and by the power to obey, which all creatures possess, for doing as God tells them when He calls.—Voluntary things He governs by a peculiar method suited to their freedom, which is entirely moral and consists both in Him laying down what is to be done and forbidding what is to be left undone by the laws belonging to the nature in them born fit to serve God and His glory, and in Him personally fulfilling or not fulfilling in them by His movement, aid and grace according to His pleasure, what the law has ordered them to do or to omit. Nay there is yet another mode of His government, the *modus* κατ᾽ εὐδοκίαν, *secundum beneplacitum Dei*, which is that of the things good in themselves which God wills, effects and leads effectively to their goals, to which is also to be referred the mode κατ᾽ οἰκονομίαν or individual administration, which obtains in support of the sinners' nature and in the performance of miracles, another κατὰ συγχώρησιν, *secundum permissionem*, which is of things but such as God neither wills nor approves but allows, when allowed ordains to their end and upholds."

17.—The form of divine *gubernatio* in which God is active without second causes or uses them in a manner deviating from their orderly appointment and activity is God's performance of miracle.—HEIDEGGER (VII, 31): "Government is direct, when God either does not use second causes or uses them above, beyond and counter to their nature. He did not use second causes when He fecundated the earth without rain or cultivation Gen. 2. 5-6, when not with bread but with His word alone He sustained the life of Moses Ex. 34. 28 or of Elijah 1 K. 9. 8. But He is not said ever to have done anything contrary to universal nature, i.e. the order of the whole universe, to which He bound Himself of His own free will. But He frequently operated without means, beyond and counter to them, to show that all things are by Him or His proximate and direct goodness; nor does He lack or fail to use appropriately, as though lacking anything, any cause or instrument outwith Himself, by which He is made fit for the work ; lest of course there should seem to be anything which has a glory in common with Himself."

18.—"Miracles are works of God exceeding all the power and force of creatures of any kind" (HEIDEGGER VII, 32). That is not a miracle which surpasses the powers of individual intelligent creatures, but that which surpasses absolutely the power of all men and spirits, so that it can only be explained by the direct activity of God.—HEIDEGGER (VII, 32): "A miracle is not whatever exceeds the strength of this or that creature, but which outdoes the power of all, especially men and spirits. What a man cannot do an impure djinn might achieve: what an impure djinn cannot do a pure one might. But what no creature can do and what God without the operation of second causes thus does alone (in that no creature can be co-opted to accomplish His work, because of its impotence) is properly called a miracle".

As the most essential element in miracle the older Reformed theology emphasised its teleological character as a witness to revelation. Hence PETER MARTYR's definition: "A miracle is a difficult and unusual work of divine force, surpassing every power of created nature, made public in order to fill those who perceive it with astonishment and to confirm faith in the words of God". The end of miracle MARTYR describes as astonishment and the confirmation of faith and compares it, exactly as was the case in MELANCHTHON's dogmatics, with the sacraments (p.50); cf. HEPPE, *Dogm. des deutschen Protest.* vol. III, p. 28 ff. He says : " Miracles are in a certain sense like sacraments. Both are added to promises as a kind of sign. And as miracles are of no profit without the precious possession of doctrine, so sacraments are not advantageous but productive of much harm, unless they are apprehended in sincere faith. Both make for sincere faith, but neither of them are by themselves sufficient. Further those are blessed and truly praiseworthy who believe without the aid of miracles". In this sense MUSCULUS also (p. 317) speaks of miraculous signs. Among later dogmaticians RIISSEN represents this conception of miracle in his definition (VIII, 10): "Miracle is a singular work of God, beyond the order and above the power of creatures, for confirming divine truth Ps.72.18 (Blessed be the Lord God of Israel, who only doeth wondrous things)". Most dogmaticians however merely insist with HOTTINGER (p. 140) that "since miracles are powers which exceed the power of created nature, only God can perform them". ALSTED 291: "Miracles exceed the power of the whole of nature". WENDELIN (*Systema*, p. 1019) : " Miracle is defined as an unusual work, surpassing the created powers of the whole of nature, affecting the senses and hustling men into amazement, issued by God to build up faith in His word and to declare His power". ENDEMANN (I, p. 264): "A miracle is a supernatural effect, unusual, produced by no one save God".

Accordingly the signs of miracle are defined by HEIDEGGER (VII, 34): "The surer, clearer κριτήρια of miracles are those which are sought partly in the substance of the act, if the work perpetrated has never existed of the like in a nature retaining its movement, as when the sun's course is stayed; partly in the subject and principles of the act, the act itself perhaps existing quite frequently in the nature of things, but not in such a subject or on the basis of such principles, which are above and beyond natural principles and causes, as if a man were born of a virgin, or of a nonagenarian woman, if life were restored to a four-days corpse; finally, partly in the mode of operation, whereby either the forces of a natural cause are immensely magnified, as was done in the feeding of five thousand with the aid of five loaves and two small fishes; or that happens in an instant which usually takes place successively in nature, as if a fever or other most grave disease were cured in an instant, or a man smitten with a dizziness: where such things are produced, or a voice breaks forth from a devil's mouth against his will, here is the finger of God Ex. 8, 15 (one of the plagues of Egypt).—Apparent miracles are distinguished from miracles; VOETIUS treats them in a special essay, *De natura et operationibus daemonum* (vol. I, p. 906 f.).

For the rest OLEVIAN (*Substant. foederis* p. 171) notes, entirely in the sense of the Church conception of miracle and its value, that "the supreme miracle is the sending of the Gospel offering the Father's love, surpassing all the miracles from the beginning of the world, whereby He gives the Son as a λύτρον for us and the Head of the Church by faith in Himself. God so loved the world (says the Son Himself, Himself a remarkable miracle), that He gives His only-begotten Son, that everyone who believes him may not perish but have eternal life".

19.—As regards the objects of providence we have to distinguish general and special providence. "*General providence* is that by which God sustains and governs all things in the world by, as it were, a single yet common act. Special providence is that by which He cares for separate species and individuals singly and controls their issues separately" (HEIDEGGER VII, 36). Divine providence thus covers the whole of the world and every living element and member of the world, appear it to be ever so small, consciousless and intelligent creatures, angels and men, elect and non-elect, their good and bad actions, the contingent and the necessary. ("That is contingent", says PEZEL (*Arg. et object.* II, p. 191), "which when it takes place has a cause that could by its nature have acted differently"). —In the "Explanation of the Catechism" (p. 136 ff.) URSIN explains the concept of contingency and its compatibility with providence: "Contingency is the order between a cause and a changeable effect; necessity is the order between a cause and a necessary effect". Causes are of the same nature as their effects. The same effect may *diverso respectu* proceed from a variable and an invariable cause.—"In respect of God the order between cause and effect is unchangeable, but in respect of creatures the order is changeable between the cause and the same effect. Hence because of God there is necessity, because of the creatures there is contingency in the same effect. It is thus *not absurd* for the same effect to be called necessary and contingent in respect of different causes, i.e. necessary in respect of the first cause acting unchangeably, but contingent in respect of a proximate cause acting changeably". URSIN notes further that the concept of freedom is abolished only by the concept of *necessitas coactionis,* but not by that of *necessitas immutabilitatis*".

MASTRICHT (III, X, 30): "The Reformed are of opinion that all effects, whether they be contingent or necessary, happen surely and undeviatingly, provided their causes have been aroused and predetermined by the divine influx. From these they conclude that since on the one hand the predetermining influx of providence is necessary to operation—on the other hand many things turn up here and there, both in Scripture and in daily experience, which are truly contingent, this predetermining influx does not abolish contingency or import universal necessity. In fact they hold that this influx is the cause of all contingency, so far as it constructs such causes for such effects and predetermines the things that happen outwith the intention of the causes and which by their nature have no necessary nexus. I shall add that neither in respect of subordinate causes is it unusual for the same effect to be contingent and necessary in different respects. Suppose two servants sent out by one master to return by the same road by themselves: these servants will meet of necessity as regards the master who sends them out, but contingently as regards the servants".

20.—Although on the one hand in virtue of the decree of God or of the *causa prima* everything is immutably ordained and results infallibly, yet on the other hand everything occurs either necessarily or contingently or freely (*Conf. Westmon.* V, 2). That the conception of contingency is not abolished by that of a necessitating providence is clear, if a proper distinction is drawn between absolute (or simple) necessity and hypothetical necessity (the necessity of the consequence of an event, the necessity of infallibility). "Absolute necessity or simple necessity is of things whose opposites are simply impossible because of the nature of the cause or subject (e.g. the attributes of God). "Necessity of consequence or *necessitas ex hypothesi* is the unchangeableness of the effects which follow from things which being posited, it is necessary that the effect follow, but the causes themselves might not exist or be changed" (PEZEL *Argum. et object.* II, p. 196). To this belongs all that God in His eternal counsel does through second causes, and therefore all that must be regarded as contingent; because, if God so willed, the second causes in individual cases might also produce another effect. Since in this way contingent things are always necessary as regards the first cause (i.e. the divine activity), they are at the same time really contingent as regards second causes, and that in such a way, that the contingency is based upon and maintained by the first cause.

PEZEL (*Arg et object.* II, p. 191) : Contingency or " the mutability of effects, which depends upon the nature of second causes or upon divine power or freedom, is connected with the necessity or immutability of divine providence, which is a *necessitas consequentiae* or *ex hypothesi* ". " The work of divine providence " precisely is " to conserve the nature, order and mode of action instituted by God in second causes ". Whence it is clear that this does not exclude moral zeal in human plans and actions, but rather demands it. Besides, rejecting all fatalism PEZEL also insists that the concepts of a necessitating providence and of contingency may quite well be related ; " the same effect may have different causes by which it is effected and governed. And so in respect of some causes it is contingent, in respect of others necessary. Hence if we consider the nature of second causes, it is right to maintain contingency, against the *Stoics*. But it is also a right tradition among the orthodox, that contingent things are also necessary in respect of the first cause, since both as a whole and in detail they depend on the nod and will of God, even though the will of God concurs in one case in good, in another in evil human actions ".—So the other dogmaticians, e.g. ZANCHIUS p. 30 : saying " that all things happen necessarily in respect of God, but many contingently in respect of us ". ZANCHIUS explains this statement by examples. " What can be more contingent and so casual for a woodsman and a traveller, than if the one man's axe should fall from his hand and kill the other ? Yet the Lord says that it was the former who killed the traveller. And the Lord Jesus died voluntarily ; but he said that it behoved the Christ to suffer ".

WALAEUS 304-305 : " We admit that in one respect, namely in respect of divine providence, things are necessary which proceed from a free and from a contingent cause in respect of the proximate cause. But this necessity does not conflict with freedom. We must distinguish between absolute or simple necessity and hypothetical or relative necessity, which are called by others necessity of infallibility and of consequence, not of the consequent. This distinction is taken from the nature of the demonstrative syllogism. In every syllogism the middle term is always the cause of the conclusion, but it is not always the cause of what concludes, i.e. of the attribute of the conclusion, which in a syllogism has only the status of a διοτι, as is well known from logic. So then in different respects the same thing may be necessary and contingent. Just as in a common syllogism the form may be necessary, although the matter is only probable. It is also called a necessity of infallibility or of result, because given God's deter-mining the result will follow infallibly yet not directly from that determining, but through the medium of man's freedom, which God does not violate by His determining but includes and confirms. It is also called a necessity of infallibility in respect of foreknowledge, which penetrates both end and means and all the modes and connections of the means and cannot be deceived. It is also called *necessitas ex hypothesi* and relatively, i.e. to the decree which is presupposed to contain freedom in itself not to exclude it.—Thus absolute necessity of compulsion, also natural necessity, is opposed to freedom ; but not those kinds of necessity with which we have been dealing."—Similarly the *Bremen Confession* (cf. HEPPE, p. 171)—HYPERIUS declares himself very definitely (p. 249) against the distinction of *necessitas absoluta* and *consequentiae*.

21.—Since contingency may be based on and sustained by the first cause, it is in the final ordering which permeates contingent things that the effectiveness of divine providence is most clearly discernible.—HEIDEGGER (VII, 49) " All creaturely events, both the natural or necessary ones determined by God to unity, as well as the casual and fortuitous ones, are subject to divine Providence. That the natural ones as to the nature and order of action are based on God's providence, we have proved at length above. But God's providence is manifested particularly in things contingent. To discover order in things which are moved by the fixed order of nature is not so wonderful. But to discover order in things uncertain and casual belongs to God alone, by whom everything has not only been foreseen (*praevisa*), but also supplied (*provisa*) and whose eyes and ears nothing escapes ".

22.—God controls the free acts of men as well as unconscious things ; He completely determines man's will. Hence no creaturely freedom of the will is thinkable, which is not utter dependence upon God's absolute activity.—Cocceius (*Summ. th.* XXVIII. 19 ff.) : One element in *conservatio* is *concursus*, whereby " the dependence of second causes upon the first cause " is signified " in His actions ". The miracle here comes into the field, that something which at one time did not exist not only acts but also acts with freedom, so that it can do something contrary. How such beings which are free, and not only actuated but alive, at the same time live in essential dependence upon the first cause and upon the absolute will of God human reason cannot grasp. On the other hand for the glory of God man must admit, what is plain before his nose, that " the same act and the same work, since it comes from a second cause and is said so to come and bears that name, nevertheless also depends upon the first cause ; and not just remotely so far as the essence and efficacy of a second cause is derived from the first cause, but proximately and directly, in order that every motion of the creature may depend upon the first cause in particular Is. 26, 14 (they are dead, they shall not live ; they are deceased, they shall not rise : therefore hast thou visited and destroyed them, and made all their memory to perish) Rom. 8, 28 (we know that all things work together for good, even to them that are called according to his purpose) 1 Cor. 12. 6 (there are diversities of workings, but the same God, who worketh all things in all) Jer. 1. 5 (before I formed thee in the belly, I knew thee, and before thou camest out of the womb I sanctified thee ; I have appointed thee a prophet unto the nations). Every act of the creature thus presupposes a definite resolve of God, in accordance with which God concurs with it and preserves for the creatures not yet confirmed but liable to change the possibility of misusing the freedom accorded them. Thus the divine *concursus* precedes human action, since it accompanies the action of the creatures as the activity of the divine resolve in time, i.e. as the efficacy of the first cause.

23.—This is not to be thought of as though God leads man merely according to His foreknowledge of what man will do with his freedom. God's foreknowledge is not a mere knowing but an effective action.— Walaeus 303 : " Will determines itself by the judgment of practical reason, but subject to God's determination."—Leiden Synopsis (XI, 10) : " It follows therefore that there is in creatures no freedom of will not derived from participation in the highest increate freedom which is the first, proper and inmost cause of all created liberty and of all free actions, insofar as they are such ".—Heidegger (VII, 54) : " God's providence is not, either, the same as bare prescience but is care in action and will in operation, conjoined with the act of a knowing mind Ps. 115. 3 (our God is in the heavens : he hath done whatsoever he pleased) Is. 46. 10

(declaring the end from the beginning, and from ancient times things that are not yet done ; saying, My counsel shall stand, and I will do all my pleasure) Jn. 5. 17 (my Father worketh until now and I work) Eph. 1. 11 (in whom also we have been made an heritage, having been foreordained according to the purpose of him who worketh all things after the counsel of his will) ; and free causes are related to God's providence not only as being foreknown as future and destined to do this or that, but also as moved, roused and applied by God and ordained for their own acts and results, which we have proved above in many ways ; nor in short can prescience, which H. Scripture ascribes to God, be separated from His will".

24.—It is equally impermissible to think of providence merely as a general, in itself indifferent working of God upon the actions of the intelligent creation, which first receives its direction to a definite act by the free will of the latter.—HEIDEGGER (VII, 59) : " There remains a third mode of conciliation taken from the universal and indifferent influx upon the free actions of creatures. For *Pelagians* recent and ancient feel that God, or the first and universal cause of all things, so concurs with the free actions of second causes, that their concurrence is determined to a fixed sort of action good or bad by second causes or man's free will, plainly in such wise that subject to the general and indifferent influx towards the production of all things generable it so concurs, that this influx is determined to a fixed species by the generating particulars. In this way they think that man is left his freedom, through which this universal and indifferent influx may be determined or not determined, determined in this way or that. "—MASTRICHT (III, x, 10) : " An influx and *general and indifferent pre-motion* to action, determined by some creature like the sun, is not enough ; but one that predetermines the lot of them, one by one, to act thus and not otherwise 2 Sam. 16[10] (David on Shimei's curse). Otherwise there would still be a special independent predetermination over and above."

25.—For " God does not concur with human will only by a general and indifferent influx but by a special and determinative one " (HOTTINGER p. 135). Hence God governs man's will by determining it not merely morally (by His word, by attractive examples, by preparing opportunities), but also by direct action physically.

MASTRICHT (III, xi, 11) : " The Reformed—lay it down that in the matter of *liberum arbitrium* and its first determination God is not only occupied in advising and persuading by His moral providence but by a physical, by bending the will and that directly; not only by illuminating it intellectually, but also by infusing it through the will with a new

propension towards Himself and towards spiritual and saving benefits ".
—HEIDEGGER (VII, 63) : " Thus second causes are actuated by God
according to the nature outstanding in each, and that in part physically
by the movement of the nature suited to each, so far as God also rules
natural causes without any anxiety on their part ; and the free ones He
so controls that He moves the mind to know, the will to embrace or reject
an object, as He thinks good ; partly ethically or morally, not just by
moral suasion but by the movement of intelligent creatures according
to their qualities, and those opposite, good or bad ".—WALAEUS p. 310:
" The final question requiring treatment here is : whether the concurrence of divine providence with the will or *liberum arbitrium* of man is
physical or moral.—311 : By a physical cause they mean not that which
arises from nature or deals with nature ; but which acts truly and
effectively and really communicates its effectiveness to the effect, so that
in this cause it is preferably termed hyperphysical. It is called a moral
cause, if by merely persuading or dissuading, by proposing or removing
objects and occasions it is the cause of an effect.—First then we say that
there is a distinction between an act of God in which He operates on the
actual understanding, will and affections and an act or operation of God,
in which He operates with the same principles and faculties to elicit
further acts. In the first kind of act God of course operates ὄντως or
(as they put it) physically, as when He illumines the understanding or
blinds it and deprives it of light ; when He renews, regenerates, destroys
the will.—Moreover there is another sort of question *re* the concurrence
of divine providence, whether in the ordinary ruling of men or in the
operation of singular grace, in respect of the second acts or actions which
proceed therefrom ; for if you regard the actual entity of these actions,
there too is a physical concurrence.—But if you consider such actions
as are moral, it is not to be denied that in both ways God concurs
with man's *arbitrium,* as is quite clear from what was proved previously,
and that for the purpose of bending and directing it in the direction
pleasing to Himself. In this way He has often given warning Himself,
sometimes by angels, sometimes by particular men, that they should do
this or that, or not do this or that.—He has often bent men's wills this way
and that by objects or occasions offered or applied afresh ".

26.—Man's personal self-determination and freedom is not in this way
abolished but rather grounded and sustained. In being determined by
God man still always acts by his own deliberation and in the form of
spontaneity. Therefore divine determination as little excludes human
freedom, as man in determining his will himself thereby abolishes his
freedom. The conception of personally free determination does not

require that man should be the first cause of it. It is enough that he is the (second) cause of it at all ".—LEIDEN SYNOPSIS (XI, 11) : " So far is the operation of divine providence from destroying the freedom of the created will, that the latter without the former cannot exist at all. On the efficacy of God's will depends not only any act of the creature's but also the manner of the act. Hence it follows that the freedom of human acts is not destroyed but established through God's providence ".—WALAEUS p. 301: " When the will itself determines itself it is already acting freely ; why then should it not be acting freely when it is determined by God, since God moves it according to its nature ?—We admit that for freedom of *arbitrium* it is required that the free *arbitrium* should be the cause of its own movement, because by it man moves himself to action ; but it is not required that it should be the first cause of its movements ; just as a natural cause is the proximate cause of natural movements, but not the first cause. Therefore as in the action of His providence in natural causes God does not abolish nature from the natural cause or from its action, neither does He abolish freedom from a cause and from its free action.— Objection : This abolishes admonitions, fault-findings, prayers and other means. Answer : This is false ".

The question how man's personal self-determination is to be represented in conjunction with absolute divine determination was often discussed by the dogmaticians. E.g. MASTRICHT (III, X, 17): "How the freedom of our *arbitrium* consists with divine predetermination is not (in the opinion of many) so difficult to follow, if we reflect that the divine influx and its predetermination do not hinder man from acting on plan and rational satisfaction or from determining himself thereby, though otherwise undetermined and indeterminable by any created cause. Let me add that, if by determining the will and so producing a volition God were depriving the will of freedom, the will too by determining itself and achieving a volition would rob itself of freedom, which is a contradiction; or that if by determining itself the will does not deprive itself of freedom, neither does God by doing the same. Therefore by such determination God's providence neither abolishes nor harms the freedom of our *arbitrium* in any way by determining it".

But the explanations given of it are but descriptions of the two propositions which BRAUN (I, ii, 12, 17) sets side by side without mediation: " We admit that we cannot clearly and distinctly conceive, how the freedom of our will consists with the operation of God. Yet it is certain (1) that in all volitions our minds depend upon God. It is also certain (2) that our will always acts most freely ; no one has ever experienced compulsion of his will : so that if freedom were removed, will could be done away with too". Hence the will can never be thought of in a purely passive way. Braun says earlier (I, ii, 12, 11) : "From this it does not follow that wherever God acts upon our will, the will's attitude is purely passive, as though God should forestall it and determine it by physical praecursion and determination, in the same way as bodies and their determined by God, their attitude being merely passive, void of any movements are produced and natural actuosity and possessing nothing of its own. The nature of spirit is as different from the nature of body, as the operation of the former is ffrom the operation of the latter. As body by its nature has no actuosity, its attitude in any operation is merely passive. But since spirit is *actuosus,* and since its nature consists in *actus,* especially of the will, so that it cannot even be conceived without operation, its outlook cannot be purely passive, it must also be active. God in His divine providence so operates on it that it too acts and operates. God cannot act on the will without producing *velle* in it. But *velle* is not *pati* (like *moveri* in things physical or bodily) but is *agere.* If a man wills he also acts, is not acted upon (*patitur*). Therefore the outlook of his will also is active, not passive merely. God acts on anything in a way suited to the nature He gave it. The nature of bodies is such that they are only acted upon but do not operate. They are moved by blind impulse, compulsorily, without plan or freedom, according to their nature. So when God operates on bodies, the bodies' attitude is purely passive. But the will cannot be forced but always acts mostly freely, deliberately and spontaneously, in a matter suited to its nature, so that its whole nature would be destroyed, were it robbed of freedom. It follows that its attitude is always active, not passive, as regards either its volition or its operation. Thus all the physical determinations denoting an outward movement, like being acted on (passivity) and compulsion, such as we notice in bodies, should be sedulously removed from the will.

"So (Braun, 12. 17 again) although we cannot grasp τὸ πῶς or τὸ διότι i.e. the manner in which our will or freedom consists with God's eternal decree and act of providence, by which our will is determined, we yet gather that such is most clearly the state of affairs (a) by the supreme perfection of God, (β) by our dependence and imperfection, (γ) and at the same time by the nature of our will, which we know by practice acts most freely, never by compulsion".—For the rest Braun is also tempted to solve the problem by assuming that in every element of his being man is a new creature with a new installation of will, i.e. with a freedom newly given each moment, and that therefore in man's will absolute determination is identical with freeness (I, II, 12. 13). "Therefore we cannot better conceive the operations of God's providence as to our will, than by the mode of a new reproduction. As God preserves bodily things in so far as by a single eternal will He willed that they exist, exist so long with

their movements that at any time of their existence and movements there
is as it were a new reproduction by the might of that eternal volition of
God, so too mind by the same eternal volition of God was not only
created but is also at particular moments as it were reproduced *de novo*,
with its volitions and operations, so that the same eternal volition of God
is called creation, as regards the existence of the thing; as regards its
reproduction with the various movements of bodies and different modes
of thinking in minds is called providence".

27.—Divine providence governs the bad as well as the good actions of
men, the latter by an *actio efficax*, the former by a *permissio efficax*.—
WOLLEB p. 30: "By God's providence things good and bad are ruled.
Good things are ruled by effectual action, to which belong the prae-
currence, concurrence and succurrence of divine power. Bad things
are ruled by *actuosa permissio* and so by permission, determining and
direction".—POLAN distinguishes (VI, 17) two parts in "God's actual
providence", namely *actio* and *permissio*. "God's *actio*—is only one of the
good things which God effects right from the first creation of all things,
either by Himself or by others, in which also the punishment of evil is
counted, because it is of the nature of moral good.—Divine permission
is the act of the divine will by which God, in whose power it is to inhibit
the actions of others, if He willed, does not inhibit them, but according
to His eternal and righteous decree allows them to be done by the rational
creature".

28.—This *permissio* is not a moral one, by which God would approve of
sin, but a physical, by which He gives sin way, a *non-impeditio peccati*.—
BREMISCHE BEKENNTNIS (HEPPE, p. 169) : "Evil is partly *malum culpae*, partly
malum poenae. That "the evil with which God temporally and eternally
punishes and will punish the world is ordained by God, is undeniable.—
But that evil which is sin and which God neither creates nor causes, also
cannot be completely and in every way withdrawn from the eternal
ordering of God, even though it be said that God is such a controller of
the world that apart from and contrary to His ordering many a thing
happens in the world.—But God does not ordain evil as He does good,
i.e. as something that pleases Him, but as the sort of thing He hates,
nevertheless knowingly and willingly destines, lets be in the world and
uses wondrously for good".—RIISSEN (VIII, 12) : "Sin should not be
withdrawn from the providence of God. It falls under it as to start,
progress and finish.—13 : As to beginning God freely allows sin.—14 :
This permission is, however, not ethical, like a licence to sin, but physical,
a *non-impeditio* of sin.—The statement 'God wills to allow sin' thus does
not mean 'God wills to approve sin morally'". Hence KECKERMANN

(p. 115) says: "If willing to permit is the same as willing the permission of sin, we agree that God willingly permits it. If it is the same as permitting it approvingly or approving the thing permitted, we must not admit that God willingly permits sin".

29.—Moreover this permission is not a relation of indifference in God to man, but a positive act. By it God gives man opportunity to sin, withdraws His protecting grace from Him, and hands him over to the power of sin and the devil, so that in that case sin is the necessary result.—URSIN (*Explic. catech.* 131) : The word *permissio* is not to be rejected, since it is occasionally used in Scripture. This *permissio* is not "a cessation of divine providence and operation" but "a withdrawal of divine grace, by which God—either does not teach the acting creature what He Himself wishes done, or Himself does not bend its will to obedience. None the less meanwhile He rightly moves the creature thus deserted and sinning, and most excellently executes what He has decreed through it".—The later men (like RIJSSEN, VIII, 16-17) assign to *permissio peccati* (which is a positive act) (1) the "offering of occasions", (2) "handing over to Satan", (3) "desertion, by which God by withdrawing the grace that opposes sin deserts the man, or by not giving it in such sufficiency that he may thereby overcome the onrushing temptation". On this point the most explicit is HEIDAN (p. 374 ff.) who explains *permissio peccati* thus : "Sin is permitted (1) when God here and now suits His concurrence to the act of sin ; (2) when He does not remove occasions of sinning or does not supply contrary ones, but often offers them ; (3) when He does not supply the grace necessary to avoid sin or even withdraws it ; (4) when He does not illuminate and move mind and will by giving law and gospel; (5) when He allows a man to follow his own desires ; (6) when He lets him be corrupted by bad company and dirty talk; (7) when He hardens, blinds and hands him over to desires and lets in the effectiveness of error, 2 Th. 2. 11 (and for this cause God sendeth them a working of error, that they should believe a lie) ; (cf. the "lying spirit" to entice Ahab, 1 K. 22. 22 cf. Ezek. 14, 9 where God deceives the deceiving prophet: cf. also Rev. 17. 17 (God did put in their hearts . . . to give their kingdom unto the beast)): (8) when He hands him over to Satan". Hence HEIDAN's statement p. 380: "Given all these things they do them, so that sin is assuredly done, in fact cannot fail to be; so that given God's permission sin necessarily follows, at least *necessitate consequentiae* though not by causal nexus."

30.—As by God's active permission sin gains its beginning, so too the continuation and the end thereof are controlled by God. He determines the sin's compass to which it is raised in the heart of man and in its indications, bridles it and so guides it that it must serve the purpose of the world.—RIISSEN (VIII, 18): "As to the progress of sin divine providence is exercised by its potent ending, in setting limits to it both of intention that it may not expand infinitely, and of duration to prevent it lasting longer and so the sinner would do more harm to himself and to others. This it does either inwardly—by enlightening the mind—or by restraining and bridling wicked desires: or outwardly by repressing Satan's and the world's frenzies, by removing occasions of evil, etc.—19: As to the end of sin divine providence is revealed in a wise ordering and directing, by converting evil into good and leading it to a good end outwith the nature of sin and the will of the sinner".

31.—That God is not therefore the originator of sin becomes clear, if in the sinful act the act in and for itself, the material element in it, the physical action, and the formal element, the sinful outlook which man adopts in it are rightly distinguished. To the act in and for itself, i.e. to that which is the physical basis of man's sinful attitude man is literally driven by God. On the other hand the sinfulness of the mind proceeds so exclusively from man's own will, that because God does not hinder the awakening of sin in man's heart (in which He is perfectly justified) or purposely allows the wakening of sin to become an act, He may indeed be called the *causa deficiens*, but not in any sense the *causa efficiens* of sin.

BUCAN (XIX, 11): "God does not infuse malice into the wills of evil men, as He infuses goodness into the hearts of the godly.—In one and the same work of the godly what is a good and just action proper to God is to be distinguished from the defect and vice of the ungodly. The sin of the wicked is their own; their doing this or that by sinning is of God's power,—and so in the same work God is ascertained to be righteous, man to be guilty".—WOLLEB 30: "In evil actions two things must be looked to, the action itself and the ἀνομία of the action. The action itself as a natural movement takes place by God's effective operation: its ἀνομία however or its badness (*malitia*) becomes actual by God's permission".—WENDELIN (*Systema*, I, VI, 10) distinguishes in concrete sins (1) the natural underlying action; (2) the *vitium* or the ἀνομία, "sin as such"; (3) the possible and the actual ordering of the underlying action to a good end. Similarly HEIDAN p. 384 and HEIDEGGER (VII, 65): "In this sin there are three things which cannot be separated: (1) the nature or *actio* in which sin dwells as on someone else's estate; (2) the sin, viciousness or illegality, which inheres in such a subject; (3) the order which, sin once committed, God imposes by His rule. God operates the nature and the action while the freedom remains the same; which we showed above to obtain as regards the qualities and free actions physically considered. Viciousness and ἀνομία are effected not by God Himself but solely by the creatures; yet regarding God they work so variously, that it cannot be withdrawn from His providence. In short the order which by His ἡγεμονία, sin having already been committed, God imposes as Ruler and Lord of all creatures, looks up to Himself as none other than the actual and indeed the sole author".

MASTRICHT (III, X, 18): "We may fairly nicely come to an agreement, if we distinguish in sin its material part, the *habitus* or action underlying the badness, with which as being physically good God cannot fail to concur as efficient cause without loss of His independence, Ac. 17. 28 (In Him we live and move and are . . . for we are also His offspring), Rom. 11. 36 (of him and through him and to him are all things); and its formal part or ἀνομία, 1 Jn. 3. 4 (sin is ἀνομία), by which the act or *habitus* is sin. Of this He cannot be the author, because He cannot transgress the law, being placed above all law; nor by His providence does He become the author (of sin), because this ἀνομία is nothing but defect of operation, of which no author or efficient cause but only a deficient one can exist: for this reason alone the creature as such is the author of sin by transgression of the law".—BRAUN (I, II, 12. 27): "Sin (therefore) is not in the operation itself, but in the defect of the operation. So it has no efficient but rather a deficient cause. This apparently the Saviour had in view: on the last day he will convict the sinner not so much of actions as of defects of action, Mt. 25. 42-43 (I was an hungered, and ye gave me no meat; I was thirsty and ye gave me no drink; I was a stranger and ye took me not in; naked and ye clothed me not; sick and in prison, and ye visited me not).—MARCK (X, 21): "It must be said that here God's providence is clear (1) in the production of the actual act which is bad, since as an action it must be called metaphysically good. There is quite a difference between this action and the defect, not of God who is held by no law, but of man who is held by the divine law; just as between native corruption and vicious habit and the man, between a stench and water dissolved by heat, between lameness and the advance of an urged horse".

32.—It must also be noted on the one hand that God wills sin, not so far as it is sin but so far as it is the punishment of sin and of sinful inclination and hence as the righteous judge He determines the hardening of the godless, who are inexcusable in His sight.—WOLLEB 31 : " The hardening of the godless is ascribed to a most just judgment, so that no sin can be imputed to God nor can the godless be excused. The godless are inexcusable in respect that God only hardens those who harden themselves, and does not make them hard instead of soft but by a just judgment more hardened instead of hardened."—BUCAN (XIV, 14) : " In fact God punishes sins with sins. Hence He wills sin not as sin but as a punishment or act of justice, because all punishment of sin is just and thereby good."

MASTRICHT (III, x, 20): "God acts singularly in causing blindness Romans 1. 21 (... their foolish heart was darkened) Is. 6. 9-10 (hear but understand not, see but perceive not, make the heart of this people fat ... lest ... they ... convert and be healed) 2 Th. 2. 10-12 (with all deceit of unrighteousness for them that are perishing, because they received not the love of the truth, that they might be saved. And for this cause God sendeth them a working of error, that they should believe a lie ; that they all might be judged who believed not the truth, but had pleasure in unrighteousness) by which He hands over the will to its desires, Rom. 1, 24-27 (God gave them up in the lusts of their hearts to uncleanness that their bodies should be dishonoured among themselves—sodomy). These two things God does not actually effect nor does He infuse blindness or hardness into the sinner, Cf. Jas. 1. 13-15 (let no man say when he is tempted, I am tempted from God ; God cannot be tempted with evil, and he himself tempteth no man ; but each man is tempted by his own lust, being drawn away by it and enticed. Then the lust when it has conceived bears sin ; and the sin when it is fullgrown bringeth forth death); nor yet either does he just fail to remove blindness and hardness by not circumcising the heart Jer. 6. 10, 26 (to whom shall I speak and testify, that they may hear ? behold, their ear is uncircumcised and they cannot hearken ; behold the word of the Lord is become unto them a reproach— O daughter of my people, gird thee with sackcloth and wallow thyself in ashes ; make thee mourning as for an only son, most bitter lamentation ; for the spoiler shall come suddenly upon us), Ac. 7. 51 (Ye stiffnecked and uncircumcised in heart and ears, ye do always resist the Holy Ghost ; as your fathers did, so do ye), or by not conferring spiritual light upon the mind and softness and ductility on the heart Mt. 13. 14-15 citing Is. 6. 9-10 (hearing ye shall hear and in no wise understand ... lest haply (this people) should perceive etc. ... and should turn again and I should heal them) ; but over and above that (1) on account of previous crimes He removes or decreases in a just and holy manner what remains to the sinner of wisdom and moral goodness, and also increases and aggravates original blindness and hardness. And this is to make the heart fat (Is. 6. 9-10), to give itself over to its desires, Rom. 1, 24.28, to send effectiveness in error, 2 Th. 2. 10-11 (with all deceivableness of unrighteousness in them that perish, because they received not the love of the truth, that they might be saved. And for this cause God shall send them strong delusion, that they should believe a lie). (2) He so to speak gives Satan, the world, seductions the loose rein, 2 Th. 2. 9 (whose coming is according to the working of Satan with all power and signs and wonders of falsehood). His advent is κατ' ἐνέργειαν τοῦ σατανᾶ ἐν πάσῃ δυνάμει.　He sends a spirit of lying, 1 K. 22. 22-23 (. . . I will go forth and will be a lying spirit in the mouth of all his prophets. And He said, Thou shalt entice him and prevail also : go forth, and do so. Now therefore, behold, the Lord hath put a lying spirit on the mouth of all his prophets ; and the Lord hath spoken evil concerning thee). (3) He offers chances to convert, both outwardly by frequent exhortations, promises, threats, examples which they abuse, Ex. 5. 1 (Pharaoh besought to let the people go) Is. 6. 9 (hear, but understand not) ; whence the gospel becomes a savour unto death 2 Cor. 2. 16 ; and inwardly by instilling honest thoughts, remorses of conscience, by which they are withdrawn from wickedness and stimulated to good, which they refuse and quench, 1 Th. 5. 19 (quench not the spirit) Jude 10 (these rail at whatsoever things they know not : and what they understand naturally, like the creatures without reason, in these things are they destroyed), 2 P. 2, 12 (these as creatures without reason, born natural animals to be taken and destroyed, railing in matters whereof they are ignorant, shall in their destroying surely be destroyed). (4) He adds outward benefits, a wealth of kindness, tolerance and restraint of wrath, which in their hardness and unrepentant heart they reject, Rom. 2. 4-5 (or despisest thou the riches of his goodness and forbearance and long-suffering, not knowing that the goodness of God leadeth thee to repentance? but after thy hardness and impenitent heart treasurest up for thyself wrath in the day of wrath and revelation of the righteous judgment of God).　Likewise (5) outward punishments, Jer. 5. 3 (O Lord, thou smitest them, but they grieve not ; thou consumest them, but they refuse to receive instruction, they make their face harder than rock, they refuse to be converted) ".

By distinguishing between *velle malum* and *male velle* HEIDAN p. 383 seeks to prove that God is not to be regarded as the author of sin. The latter is " doing by willing, what God has forbidden ; or omitting by willing, what God has enjoined ". Of God of course we must predicate *velle malum* ; but " wishing evil to be done in a transeunt act of will, not for His own but for another's evil ".

33.—It is always a hardened man that God hardens and not something mild, then ; just as on the other hand God always uses sin, i.e. the act caused by Him in which the sinfulness of man is active, to achieve His holy purposes ; whereby the sinful nature of the means which are at His disposal and which He renders serviceable to Himself, cannot encroach upon the holiness of the divine acts themselves.

KECKERMANN 154 : " God can use ill instruments well, although beyond the intention and aim of the instruments ".—URSIN (*Loci* p. 575) : " It is by no means because of the goodness or badness of the instruments by which God executes the decrees of His will, that that will is more or less good ; whatever the nature of the instrument God's work through it is always most excellent, righteous and holy. The goodness or badness of the divine works depends not on the instrument's but on God's own goodness, wisdom, righteousness and uprightness.—It is absolutely necessary to admit that God does execute His righteous and holy works and judgments by bad and sinning instruments ; unless anyone cares to deny that the tests and punishments of the godly caused by wicked men, are both righteous and proceed from the divine will, power and effectiveness, then, likewise, that the virtues and deeds of the godly are God's salutary gifts and benefits to the human race and to the Church, i.e. that God is the effective and righteous judge of the world and the preserver and defender of His servants and the author and producer of all good things ".

CHAPTER XIII

THE COVENANT OF WORKS AND THE RIGHTEOUSNESS
OF THE LAW

1.—As God's creature man possessed nothing but the duty of obedience to God, without being able to raise any claim to enjoy blessed communion with Him. At the same time, as a creature in God's image man was made capable of and appointed to such communion by God Himself, since God wished to ensure this to him by entering into a covenant relation with man. Consequently man as a creature in God's image was created for covenant communion with God.

CONFESS. WESTMON. (VII, 1) : " So great is the distance between God and the creature, that though rational creatures owe Him obedience as their Creator, they yet would never have had any fruition of blessedness and its reward as their own, had there not been some voluntary condescension on God's part, which it pleased Him to express by making a covenant.—COCCEIUS (*Summ. Theol.* XXII, 1) : " Man who comes upon the stage of the world with the image of God, exists under a law and a covenant, and that a covenant of works ". Further on he says (17) : " We call that a covenant, or less fully a law, to which has been annexed a promise exciting one to expect good in the form of communion and friendship ; or more fully, the consummation of a pact of friendship ; or a right proceeding to communion and friendship in terms of a pact.—(18) : When further we say that he who bears the image of God given in creation was established under God's covenant, we do not mean that he has a right to the communion and friendship of God, but that he is in that state in which he ought to ask the right to the communion and friendship of God and to make it stable and so to have the offer of God's friendship, if he obeys His law ".

2.—The doctrine of God's covenant with man is thus the inmost heart and soul of the whole of revealed truth.—HEIDEGGER (IX, 4) : " Hence the marrow and as it were the sort of centre of the whole of Holy Scripture is the *berith,* the covenant and testament of God, to which as their single and most target-like target (*scopus unicus et σκοπιμώτατος*) everything comprised in them must be referred. Admittedly nothing else has been handed down to the saints of all ages through the entire Scripture, than what is contained in the covenant and testament of God and its chapters, save that in the flow and succession of times individual points have been expounded more lavishly and clearly ".

3.—Hence in all its peculiar elements, God's relation to man is necessarily to be considered in the light of the conception of covenant.—HEIDEGGER (IX, 5): "This being so, every intercourse of God with man and the marvellous kingship by which God the King of hosts has hitherto governed and will continue to govern man and the whole world for man's sake πολυμερῶς καὶ πολ υτρόπως to the world's end, is of course for eternity and is most clearly recognised as having the norm and form of a covenant. Thus if we are to continue and complete the sequence in our theology, we are bound, where we have reached God's business and intercourse with man, to speak of God's covenant and testament".

4.—"God's covenant is the pact or convention of God with man, by which in view of the eminent right He has and of His singular goodness God makes with man on fixed conditions a pact of eternal life in heaven and seals it with sure signs and pledges, as it were" (HEIDEGGER IX, 8). In virtue of His absolute right which He has as Creator over the creature God has appointed man to the fellowship of the covenant with Himself. —ib. 9: "This then is that eminent right, this is His singular goodness, that He alone as the Lord can make a covenant with man, and He alone as good wills to do so".

5.—This is why this covenant is primarily a one-way covenant (*foedus* μονόπλευρον). Since meanwhile man on his side must enter upon this covenant relation in free self-determination by promising God willing obedience and receiving in return from God the promise of eternal life, the covenant is further a relation between man and God which rests upon mutuality".—COCCEIUS (*De foed.* 5): God's covenant with man is made differently from men's covenants with each other. "Men make covenants for mutual benefits, God makes His covenant for His own benefit". God's covenant is nothing else than "a divine declaration of the way to perceive the love of God and to get possession of union and communion with Him". That is why God's covenant with man is a "one-way (μονόπλευρον) covenant".—HEIDEGGER (IX, 9): "Neither would children dare of right to make a pact or contract with their parents, nor subjects with their king, nor slaves bought with silver (ἀργυρώνητοι) with their owners, nor conquered with their conquerors, because the laws of prescribing for their superiors are voided of power. And much less can man, God's son, slave, dependent, subject bind Him (God) by his conditions by making a contract with God. To that extent God's covenant with men is not mutual but μονόπλευρον. It belongs to the one side or part. Nor is it simply μονόπλευρον, in the sense in which the covenant is so called which God is said to have made with day and night,

Jer. 33. 20.—It is not God alone who prescribes and promises something to man; man also passes over into God's covenant, Dt. 29. 12 (that thou shouldest enter into the covenant of the Lord thy God, and into His oath which the Lord thy God maketh with thee this day). He promises obedience to God, when He (God) imposes His conditions and he awaits a promise from Him. And so clinging to God in accordance with the terms of the Covenant he (man) so to speak binds Him (God) by his ὁμολογία or assent, with the force of a divine disposition, to bestow love and benefits upon him. So that in this way the conditions of man and God are distinct, their assent is distinct and in this sense the actual covenant is rightly termed mutual and two-way (δίπλευρον)".

6.—The covenant for which God had originally created man was a covenant of works. "The covenant of works is God's pact with Adam in his integrity, as the head of the whole human race, by which God requiring of man the perfect obedience of the law of works promised him if obedient eternal life in heaven, but threatened him if he transgressed with eternal death; and on his part man promised perfect obedience to God's requirement" (HEIDEGGER IX, 15), or: "The covenant of works is the agreement between God and Adam created in God's image to be the head and prince of the whole human race, by which God was promising him eternal life and felicity, should he obey all his precepts most perfectly, adding the threat of death, should he sin even in the least detail; while Adam was accepting this condition" (WITSIUS I, II, 1).

Since man as such was created for this covenant of works and since this determination of man is already based on his nature in the image of God, it may also be designated the covenant of nature.—EGLIN (De foedere gratiae, II, 10) "The legal covenant is the pact of works entered into freely with the human race, created from the beginning in God's image, holy, righteous and good in the protoplasts; and that as the declaration of His goodness and omnipotence; so that, as long as man persisted in obedience to the Creator, he should by this natural holiness, righteousness and goodness possess a blessed state of life. On the other hand if he transgressed God's commandment he should surely die, i.e., if he should with his entire posterity fall from that primaeval state of felicity, innocence and holiness, he would incur the penalty of present and eternal death for having violated the highest good. 11: This pact is called the covenant of works because it exacts from all the condition of works, i.e. the perfect obedience of original holiness and righteousness which the Creator of due right demands of us, as much as we by our own fault are unable of ourselves to pay. 12: It is also called the covenant of nature, because it was naturally inscribed from the beginning on men's hearts by God's saving finger.

Today only remorse of conscience remains of it, to render man ἀναπολόγητος, as being utterly denuded of all the true righteousness and holiness required to lead that life and as being dead in sins Eph. 1. 2:3:5 (grace to you and peace from God the Father and the Lord Jesus Christ. Blessed be the God and Father of our Lord Jesus Christ, who hath blessed us with every spiritual blessing in the heavenlies in Christ—having foreordained us unto adoption as sons through Jesus Christ unto Himself, according to the good pleasure of His will) 2 Cor. 3:5, 4:6 (not that we are sufficient of ourselves; our sufficiency is of God— (seeing) it is God that said, Light shall shine out of darkness, who hath shined in our hearts to give the illumination of the knowledge of the glory of God in the face of Jesus Christ)."

Cocceius (*De foed.* II, 22): " So far as the covenant of works rests upon the law of nature, it may be called the covenant of nature". For to man's nature belonged the *imago Dei*. But this comprised not only the original "uprightness of knowledge and will", but also, and for that very reason, the acknowledgment of the creature's dependence upon the Creator's absolute will. Accordingly (Cocceius says): "neither is it merely natural for a rational creature such as man to have the image of God; it also belongs to the created image of God to be subjected to the law of its Creator. Nothing is more natural than that the thing made should belong to its Maker and be subjected to Him in every way in which it may be subjected naturally to Him. Nothing is more at variance with nature and first truth, than that a rational being adorned with the image of its Maker should not be the servant of God as his Maker, should be outwith the law, should not be subject to Him, should not obey Him". Hence Cocceius concludes that the covenant of works is for man already founded upon his nature. " (Hence) it is plain that with the first men it was a covenant of works according as it is admitted to be natural, chiefly by the law enjoining love to God and by the obligation to be subject to it. Also by reason of the good to be looked for by the obedient it is rightly called natural; no one can εὐαρεστῆσαι God, that is, will to please Him, worship Him, seek Him, approach Him, walk with Him (for these phrases are used by St. Paul as equivalents), save one who believes that God is who both ought to be sought and may become the rewarder of them that seek Him, and does become the rewarder of them that seek Him Heb. 11. 6".

Cocceius defines the concept *foedus* (*Summ. de. foed.* 1, 2) as "a just agreement made on fair terms and on a sworn promise on both sides", adding that "it (the covenant) is declared in definite words, usually with the addition as well of notable signs suited to make it known, either generally as regards the covenant and its sanction (what sort of beast is to be struck, slain, etc.), or particularly, by its resemblance to the thing promised."

EGLIN (*De foed. grat.* II, 12): The "legal covenant" is also called the "covenant of nature" because "it has been naturally inscribed on men's hearts from the beginning by God's saving finger, the sole remnant of it still surviving being merely remorse of conscience".—MARTINI (*De gubern. mundi* p. 224): "Between Himself and men God set up in the beginning a covenant of natural religion, when He allowed them when placed in the garden of Eden to feed freely on all its trees; while He passed a law specifically on avoiding the tree of the knowledge of good and evil, under threat of death if they should eat of its fruit; whereby also was suggested the promise of a blessed life in perpetuity, if they persisted in obedience, by the addition of the sacrament of the tree of life".— Similarly MARESIUS, VIII, 3.

7.—Thus man is enabled to recognise from his own consciousness this appointment of himself to a covenant with God resting upon perfect fulfilment of the divine will.—HEIDEGGER (IX, 12): "It may also be recognised naturally, that there is a covenant intervening between God and man. Man's conscience keeps asserting that to God the Creator and Lord of man obedience on his part as a creature is bound to be enjoined and He must be loved singly as most excellent and the Author of all good.—In such obedience and love moreover consists the duty which God requires of man. Whence also there is ingrained in every man the faculty of realising what things are θεοπρεπῆ or worthy of God, and of praising and approving right things, of cursing what is wicked, of attesting the right and of condemning the wicked. This faculty has been obscured and corrupted by sin, although it has not perished altogether.—Then too man is naturally not ignorant of the promise of God in promising good to the obedient. Indeed he knows that God as the most excellent is not sought, looked up to, loved in vain, in fact that he who loves enjoys by love the God whom he loves; in which enjoyment of God man's blessedness consists.—And since man is not unaware of being God's creature and dependent (*cliens*), he is equally not unaware of the necessary requirement, that there should be friendship between himself and God, who offers it on terms. And no one can doubt the parallel requirement, that he in turn should expect from God the reward promised to the obedient and should be able to receive it because of God's truthfulness and faithfulness known by nature".

8.—By his conscience which teaches man to distinguish right and wrong he recognises not only the law of God, but also his own appointment

to a covenant of works, fellowship with God, since the consciousness also
is implanted in men along with the self-proclaiming power of conscience,
under which he certainly does desire to please God. Therefore about
himself man is sure that God has appointed him to seek His glory by
obedience and to live with Him in communion.—Cocceius (*Summ. theol.*
XXII, 2): "We here call the law knowledge of right and wrong, binding
us to do what is right and to avoid what is wrong.—(6) Moreover conscience is that light of the mind by which man distinguishes between
what is right and what is wrong, and knows the ways of doing and of
fleeing right and wrong, and likewise discerns true from false and grasps
the truth of connection and so judges of good and bad reasoning, of
wisdom and folly. In a word it is conscience by which it happens that
man is not in the dark as to his own past doings; and when he takes counsel
with himself as to whether he has done well or ill, he gives his answer as
his own readiest witness".

9.—Similarly man recognises from his own moral consciousness what
the purpose is of this covenant relation ordained by God. Conscience
attests to man that for him as a personal being in God's image God
and communion with God is the supreme essential good which God
Himself has granted him, which he must strive for according to God's
will and appropriate to himself by obedience to Him. Therefore by faithful fulfilment of God's law man sustains the certainty that fills his heart
with the holiest peace, the certainty that God loves him and that in virtue
of his obedience he possesses the righteousness that holds good with God.
    Cocceius (*Summ. theol.* XXII, 20-21) explains how man is taught by
his conscience about the covenant of works originally ordained by God.
Conscience witnesses to man that he "who has preserved the image of
God and has done righteously in accordance with it " has " a covenant
with God, provided that there is (1) " no offence between him and God
but (2) the peace by which benefits are possessed in security ; but also
(3) that he is righteous, i.e. has a right to God's friendship and communion
and to ask and expect of God what it is just, right and holy to expect of
God ". Conscience bears witness that " God cannot put off those who
seek Himself or refuse to satisfy and fulfil a right and holy desire ".
Could it be assumed that God wished not to be found of them for their
enjoyment, it would follow that it is wrong to seek and desire God. But if
it is wrong, God " is not man's good and cannot make man happy in
Himself." So it would have to be the case instead that " man's good "
and its " end " " are things created by God ; for man's good is man's
end ". Thus it follows (XII, 22) " that he who does what conscience
dictates has ἐξουσία and power to call God his God and to glory in

Him as his good ".—Similarly Cocceius shows in Scripture (*De foedere* I, 8) that a covenant of God with man is really ordained : (1) from the natural moral consciousness of man, from " the conscience or naturally inborn faculty of the soul to discern what things are θεοπρεπῆ and what things are unworthy of God, laudable or objectionable, licit or illicit ; and from that opinion which approves of the law of God and urges us to do the things that are right and laudable and to avoid the contrary, which attests things done righteously, condemning those done otherwise " Rom. 2. 15 (they shew the work of the law written in their hearts, their conscience bearing witness therewith, and their thoughts one with another accusing or else excusing them [difficult : see Moffat]); (2) from " man's will which seeks for the true good in which he can acquiesce (which is nothing but God) and longs for immortal life and flees death : which desire is not in him save of the Creator Himself " ; (3) and from the " daily and continual benefits by which man is urged to seek his Creator and Benefactor and to love, glorify and thank Him ; so that these things seem to proclaim aloud, Seek ye God, Ac. 17. 27 (they should seek God if haply they might feel after him and find him, though he is not far from each one of us) 14. 17 (he left not himself without witness, in that he did good and gave you from heaven rains and fruitful seasons, filling your hearts with food and gladness) Rom. 1. 21 ([the sin is that] knowing God they glorified him not as good, neither gave thanks ; but became vain in their reasonings, and their senseless heart was darkened)".

10.—Next man experiences in his own heart, that he can call upon God as his God, who lives in him and fills him with His truth, righteousness and blessedness, and that he may hope for the consummation of his communion with God in life eternal.—Cocceius (*Summ. theol.* XXII, 34) : " This communion arising out of the covenant is signified, when a man says " My God ".—(23) And this is the righteousness of the law, the right, to wit, of looking and asking for the greatest good, which consists in communion with God.—(35) Moreover in the consummation of it the Apostle says that we shall know even as also we are known, 1 Cor. 13. 12. It is called life and eternal at that.—*Communio Dei* thus consists of three parts : (31) " (1) that God is in him who loves God and dwells in him, i.e. gives him part in His life ;—(2) that God makes Himself manifest to him— and so the man never lacks God's word and counsel and the sign of His actual favour ; (3) that he has hope and the right to ask and expect the perception of God's pleasantness (*suavitas*) in the fullest degree ".—Marck (XIV, 24) : " So the Lord who was Adam's God by right of creation and preservation, likewise became so by dint of the covenant, by his submission to it and by the reward he expected of Him ".

11.—Man knows that God who is eternal truth, righteousness and love itself has bound Himself to him by the covenant for which He created man, and cannot therefore abandon him with His fellowship—because God cannot deny His own being.

Cocceius (*Summ. th.* XXII, 23-24, 27-28) most emphatically insists that God's *debitum* here is not to be connected with a *dignitas operum* in man. God could never become man's debtor : (1) Man as a creature is essentially the " slave of God " and himself owes everything to God ; (2) he has nothing which he has not received from God. A *debitum* on God's part only exists *ex pacto,* " and that by the single agreement by which works are exacted as the condition of righteousness ". But this *pactum* is worthy of God, " in so far as it cannot not intervene between God and man. And he who knows that man was made by God in His image, also realises, if he waits, that man is called by God to communion with God in life eternal and glorious through the accomplishment of works ".—Cocceius is therefore (XXII, 39) zealous against the *Scholastics*, who by an appeal to the " absolute lordship of God " assert, that if He willed God could abandon even a perfectly obedient man and the holy angels to eternal damnation. By this assertion the statement would have to be made that God not merely could do this, but also could will it, "and that there was no truth or decency in God which God might not deny, with which the statement is at war ". On the other hand Cocceius insisted that " as the method of creation is εὐδοκία alone, so it is not the only method of dealing with intelligent creatures in this or that way. For when an intelligent creature is made, it concerns God's truth that He should deal worthily and becomingly with it ".

12.—But as surely as conscience guarantees to man this comfortable circumstance, it also bears him witness that by disobedience to God's will expressed in his own inward part he loses the love of God and covenant fellowship with God.—Cocceius (*Summ. th.* XXII, 45) : " As conscience bears witness that he who has done the will of God cannot fail to possess God's friendship, it also bears witness that he falls out of God's friendship who has not performed all his dues or has failed in something, and that therefore there can be no other δικαίωμα Rom. 5. 16 18 (and as through one that sinned so is the gift : for the judgment came of one unto condemnation, but the free gift came of many trespasses unto justification . . . So then as through one trespass *the judgment came* unto all men to condemnation ; even so through one act of righteousness the free gift came unto all men to justification of life), i.e. merit or cause for a right to ask other reward than perfect obedience. Man is wholly God's, and unless he be wholly in accord with God in every thought, plan, judgment, desire, in words and deeds, he cannot genuinely call him Lord ".

13.—And conscience bears him witness that a single sin at once abolishes this covenant fellowship, since every sin is a denial of God's absolute authority at all.—COCCEIUS (*Summ. theol.* II, 13) : The covenant of works demands the observance of all commands. To transgress one command is to deny the authority of God in general. No man can love God if he hates his neighbour, nor love his neighbour, if he hates God. Love to God is not only " to rejoice in God the Creator and Benefactor, to find work worthy of God its actual exemplar, and to wish to be and to study to be to His glory as the end of all things and to affect and seek His good itself, to fear and justify His judgment ". But it is also a " recognition and celebration of the things which are God's, as being His very attributes ".

14.—What is thus guaranteed to man by the voice of his conscience is confirmed for him by the witness of H. Scripture—From H. Scripture the fact is proved as follows (MASTRICHT III, xii, 23), that God has made a covenant with Adam : "(1) It specifically ($\dot{\rho}\eta\tau\hat{\omega}s$) states in Hos. 6. 7 : ' they like Adam have transgressed the convenant ; there have they dealt treacherously against me ' ; cf. Job 31. 33 (if after the manner of Adam (man) I covered my transgressions by hiding mine iniquity in my bosom) where the best translators (*Vulgate, Tigurinus, Pagninus, Castalio, Belgae* and others) take כאדם *proprie,* not *appellative,* though I admit there are not wanting those who prefer the appellative sense. (2) The Apostle Gal. 4. 24. (which things contain an allegory : for these women are two covenants ; one from Mt. Sinai, bearing children unto bondage, which is Hagar . . . But the Jerusalem above is our mother) mentions a double covenant, the former of which is ' by works of the law ' 2.16, demanding most punctilious obedience 3. 10 (cursed is the man who does not give it), by means of which no one can ever obtain everlasting life 2. 16 (works do not justify) 3. 2 (Received ye the spirit by the works of the law or by the hearing of faith ?), under which we all were until the covenant of faith 3. 23 (Before faith came we were kept in wrath under the law, shut up unto the faith which should afterward be revealed), and are, as long as we live as children of the flesh 3. 22,29 (the scripture hath shut up all things under sin, that the promise by faith in Jesus Christ might be given to them that believe—if ye are Christ's, then are ye Abraham's seed, and heirs according to the promise), which only begets to slavery 3. 24 (the law hath been our tutor to bring us unto Christ, that we might be justified by faith) Heb. 2. 14-15 (since the children are sharers in blood and flesh, he also in like manner partook of the same ; that through death he might bring to nought him

that had the power of death, that is, the devil ; and might deliver all
them who through fear of death were all their lifetime subject to bondage).
And this is the very thing which we call the covenant of works, subsequently ; as the result of the faith of the Gospel. If you say the apostle is
speaking of a covenant not in Paradise, but the covenant at Sinai, the
answer is easy, that the Apostle is speaking of the covenant in Paradise so
far as it is re-enacted and renewed with Israel at Sinai in the Decalogue,
which contained the proof of the covenant of works. (3) Synonyms of the
covenant of works are extant in the NT Rom. 3. 27 (where is the glory? it
is excluded. By what manner of law ? Of works ? Nay : but by a law of
faith) Gal. 2. 16 (knowing that a man is not justified by the works of the
law save through faith in Jesus Christ, even we believed on Christ Jesus,
that we might be justified by faith in Christ, and not by the works of the
law ; because by the works of the law shall no flesh be justified). Moreover what is the law of works but the covenant of works ? What is law
simpliciter as opposed to grace ? Rom. 8. 3 (what the law could not do, in
that it was weak through the flesh, God, sending his own Son in the
likeness of sinful flesh and for sin, condemned sin in the flesh) ; what, I
say, if not the legal covenant ? Because we are said to be not under the
law but under grace Rom. 6.14-15 (sin shall not have dominion over you ;
for ye are not under law but under grace . . .) 4.16 (for this cause it is of
faith, that it may be according to grace ; to the end that the promise
may be sure to all the seed ; not to that only which is of the law, but to
that also which is of the faith of Abraham, who is the father of us all),
what is that but that we are not under the covenant of the law ? At least
for us these are plainly synonymous. (4) We have previously in the
exegetical section shewn that all the essentials of the covenant of works
are contained in the first publication of it Gen. 2. 17 (of the tree of the
knowledge of good and evil, thou shalt not eat of it ; for in the day that
thou eatest thereof thou shalt surely die). (5) To very many heads of the
Christian religion, e.g. the propagation of original corruption, the satisfaction of Christ and his subjection to divine law Rom. 8. 3-4 (what the
law could not do, in that it was weak through the flesh, God, sending his
own Son in the likeness of sinful flesh and for sin, condemned sin in the
flesh, that the requirement of the law might be fulfilled in us, who walk
not after the flesh, but after the spirit) Gal. 3.13 (Christ redeemed us from
the curse of the law, having become a curse for us : for it is written,
Cursed is everyone that hangeth on a tree, Dt. 21.23) 4. 4-5 (when the
fulness of time came, God sent forth his Son, born of a woman, born
under the law, that he might redeem them which were under the law,
that we might receive the adoption of sons), we can scarcely give suitable
satisfaction, if the covenant of works be denied ".

15.—God set up with Adam and in him (in virtue of the blessing pronounced upon nature) with Adam's entire succession a covenant of works, in the blessings of which every individual human was to participate not only with his spirit but also with his body.

COCCEIUS (*Summ. de foed.* II, 45) : " The covenant of works God made with Adam both on his own behalf and in him as stock, with the whole human race in virtue of the blessing on nature ".—WYTTENBACH (*Tent.* II, 574) : " The covenant which God fixed with the first man He made in his person with all his posterity : for the law of the covenant applies to all men whatsoever, and therefore God cannot avoid demanding the observation of it from all ; besides in Adam the first man, or the natural head of the whole human race, all men virtually existed already, and God foreknew who and how many would arise from it, so that all were really present in person at that time. Moreover, if the law of the covenant applied to all and God required the observance of it by Adam's posterity, who were all actually visualised as present, it follows no less that He wished the promise of the covenant to apply to all on condition of perfect keeping of the law. There is of course no reason for the law applying to all and not specifically the promise of the reward. Therefore God wished the whole covenant to apply to Adam's successors and so He made it in his person with all his descendants ".

Dogmaticians usually insist that as representing the human race Adam was a *persona publica,* and therefore entered as such into the covenant with God along with all who were represented by him, e.g. WITSIUS I, II, 14.— COCCEIUS (*Summ. de foed.* I, 9) : " God binds to Himself the whole man, i.e. his spirit and body 1 Cor. 6.19-20 (know ye not that your body is a temple of the H. Ghost which is in you, which ye have from God ? And ye are not your own ; for ye were bought with a price : glorify therefore God with your body), though the spirits are the prime parts, man offering himself and his whole body as a living victim ".

16.—Christ alone was not included in this covenant. —COCCEIUS (*Summ. de foed.* II, 46) : " Although he shall also have been a son of man, Christ under this covenant was not contained in Adam ".

17.—God founded His covenant with Adam in the first instance by setting up the law, inscribing in his inmost part, as man's ideal and as the norm he must follow, that which is the expression of His own holy nature. I.e. God revealed the law to man in the form of the *law of nature,* this revelation of the law being so vouchsafed to man, that he recognised it by his own self-consciousness. " The law of nature is defined as the divine law by which God first imbued Adam, and in him the common nature of rationally endowed men, with the knowledge of what is honourable and base, and bound it to do the former and leave the latter undone " (HEIDEGGER IX, 29).

WITSIUS (I, III, 2) thus defines: "The law of nature is the norm of good and evil inscribed by God on man's conscience right from creation and so binding man by divine authority. (7): It is further to be noted that this first-made law is the same substantially as that which has been expressed in the decalogue".—HEIDEGGER (IX, 27) divides the law into *lex archetypa* and *lex ectypa*. "*Lex archetypa* or *aeterna* is the actual sanctity of the divine nature so far as the rational creature can imitate and express it in its life.—(28): *Lex ectypa* is law which side by side with the eternal law is made and promulgated in time for existing rational creatures".— The law which Adam received in his conscience was thus not an arbitrary arrangement but the expression of the essential holiness of God ; HEIDEGGER IX, 37 : " The heads of natural law, especially those outstanding and universal, were not founded on God's sheer and indifferent decree as the result of His changeable *arbitrium*, but on His natural holiness. Love to God with the whole heart, in which neighbour love takes its rise, rests upon God's very nature, since He is the *summum bonum* and so lovable *per se*, and cannot be loved by any right (*ius*). Could God will that He be not loved, neither would He be the *summum bonum* equally able to enjoin hatred of Himself; which is a dreadful thing and involves a contradiction.—(38) From this it follows that the primaeval law of nature is quite unchangeable and indispensable". Compare with this what Cocceius (*Summ. foed.* II,13) says: The nature of the covenant of works along with the law pertaining to it, promise and threat included, is found expressed in Gal. 3.10-12 (as many as are of the works of the law are under a curse . . . and the law is not of faith, but, He that doeth them shall live in them). The law demands of man: "(1) that he do, i.e. fulfil by doing or omitting (2) all things that are written in the Book of the Law", and (3) "abide in them". Adam had not yet received the law in a law book, but it was "written on the tablets of his heart". Even now this is proved by the "testimony of conscience remaining in man even though fallen." Nothing else is contained in the "tables of the covenant and the books of the Law, save what the law of nature once demanded of man in his integrity; at least so far as it is the substance of worship and the spring as it were of a more particular injunction".

18.—At the same time Adam received a positive command of God that he should rule over all creatures, but of the fruit of one tree he was not to eat, of the tree of the knowledge of good and evil.—COCCEIUS (*Summ. de foed* II, 46): " The tree was called the tree of the knowledge of good and evil, "(1) Because it was πειραστικὴ or δοκιμαστικὴ of man whether he was to be good or evil; for man's goodness consisted in preservation of the likeness of God; (2) Because by this test, if he obeyed, he would arrive at a knowledge and sense of his own good, to which he was called and by a natural desire drawn, namely eternal life and perfected bliss as though righteous. On the other hand if he were disobedient, he was bound to rush headlong into evil, i.e. death, as unrighteous".—MARTINI (De gubern. mundi 228): "The tree of the knowledge of good and evil derives its appellation from the result, because of course it would turn out, that if man snatched to himself its fruit contrary to God's veto he would know by his actual trial how much good he would have lost and into how much evil he would have plunged himself."—MARCK notes in this connection that "The tree was good, but obedience was better".

19.—By conforming to this command Adam should have preserved his recognition of the absolute majesty of God; and besides, if he should be disobedient, he would come to know what sin in reality is.—BRAUN (I, III, 2, 9): "Besides the moral and natural law Adam was also given a positive law anent not eating the forbidden fruit. It is usually called probative and was given to Adam, because God wished thereby to prove man (1) whether he loved God perfectly and more than all the creatures; (2) whether he abstained from earthly delights, in order to delight in God alone; (3) whether he would subject his own dominion to that of God; (4) whether he would stay good or turn bad; (5) it was also given, that by sinning Adam might himself recognise the evil into which he hurled himself and the good from which he fell away; whence the tree was called that of the knowledge of good and evil.—COCCEIUS (Summ. theol. XXVI, 2) "It pleased God also to exercise and test him by an injunction, namely not to eat of a certain tree, which was called the tree of the knowledge of good and evil." This prohibition was purely an imperium dominicum and was only given to set forth outwardly to the protoplasts their dependence upon God, and to test their obedience. (3) "Who doubts that the eating of this tree might have been allowed man as well as of other trees and of itself did not make more for righteousness than not consuming all permitted foods? So this precept had to be obeyed from love for the rule of God." Cf. with this COCCEIUS (Summ. theol. XXVI, 4): The prohibition in paradise had a twofold purpose: "(1) It taught that men's good was not to be placed in things delightful to the senses; (2) That God is the Lord of man and of all his acts and movements; (3) That the dominion granted to man over the things of God is a stewardship, for which he must answer to God, and therefore a use of all things to be referred with thanksgiving to the glorifying and sanctifying of God."—Similarly speaks

OLEVIAN (*De subst. foed. grat.* p. 169): Already in his innate moral consciousness man was given the full content of the law given later in the decalogue. It commanded him, above all, Thou shalt love God thy Lord with the whole heart and thy neighbour as thyself; and to let men have practical proof of this love God had forbidden him to eat of the fruit of one tree and bidden him by obtempering this commandment to glorify Him as the Lord.—HEIDEGGER interprets in more detail (IX, 41) the purpose of this ban: "That interdict could have been neither one of natural law nor some sacrament of life, but only the divinely instituted sign of God's lordship and man's subservience, as well as the material means of finding Adam out. 42: Many things prove this decree of God to have been most wise. In forbidding a tree suitable for eating, desirable and pleasant to look at Gen. 3. 6., God has openly taught, that the highest good lies not in the things which delight the senses in this life, but in something more excellent, by which man's longing for eternal life is satisfied; that He is the supreme Lord of all things, particularly of man's acts; that the dominion given to man in creation was not a δεσποτεία but a pure οἰκονομία and stewardship; that the use of all things must be referred solely to the glory and hallowing of God; that life is not secured save as the reward of obedience; that it is bad to seek or attain to anything not in God or Godward; that the sole rule for seeking or shunning all things outside God is the will of God, as our Lord and Preserver; that man's obedience consists not in the soul's actions whether proper or only elicited, but in the right motion also and the commanded actions of all the members; that all transgression of God's will deserves death; that life is preferable to pleasure and that the preservation of God's image needs care; that contempt of it involves inevitable loss and attendant punishment; that although created upright by God man had not achieved the apex of his felicity and that it remained for him to prove his obedience by works also and at last to enjoy the true blessedness in heaven. Thus in the one precept of complete obedience in man God created peril in all parts of his duty."

Says LAMPE (*Einl. zum Gnadenbund* p. 25): " The law of the covenant of works was (1) generally, the law of love to God and neighbour ; (2) particularly, the test law, not to eat of the tree of the knowledge of good and evil ".

20.—On condition that Adam gave perfect obedience he was promised eternal life, i.e. not so much eternal continuance (which may also consist with eternal damnation and eternal death) nor yet merely unending earthly bliss in paradise, but rather after consistent faithful obedience the most blessed enjoyment of God's fellowship in heaven, which he was to merit for himself *ex pacto* (though not *ex congruo* or *ex condigno* BRAUN I, III, 2, 13).

FORM. CONS. HELV. 8 : " The promise annexed to the covenant of works was not just the continuation of earthly life and felicity, but primarily the possession of eternal heavenly life, in heaven of course, if it had finished a course of perfect obedience, to be passed in unspeakable joy in communion with God in both body and soul.—9 : Therefore we do not assent to any view of those who deny that any reward of heavenly obedience was propounded to Adam, if he should obey God, and do not recognise any other promise of the covenant of works than that of enjoying perpetual life overflowing with every kind of good things—and that in an earthly paradise ".—HEIDEGGER (IX, 53-54) : " The life promised to him that worketh is life both of body and of soul, because we established above that the covenant was made with man as a whole. But neither is this life simply survival or the persisting and interminable existence of both, both because in the actual creation man received a body and an immortal soul, as we asserted at length in the proper place, and so was not bound to merit or acquire such immortality by his works, and because such a persevering existence may also be death, as is proved by the immortality of bad angels and of men condemned to hell.—In short neither was the life promised to him that worketh a perpetual life rich in every sort of good things which might consist with both man's soul and body as constituted in the state of intact nature, and these to be enjoyed in an earthly paradise, as Cl. AMYRALDUS assumes ; but rather life in heaven after the course of obedience has been ended, to be enjoyed in mind and in body, through beatific communion with God, the supreme good."

According to this the covenant of works retained the following four connections (WYTTENBACH *Tent.* II, 571): " The act by which a first party demands something from a second is called *stipulatio* ; the act by which it assigns good to it, *promissio* ; while the act by which the second party takes upon itself to supply what the first had demanded is called *adstipulatio* and where it asks for the promise, *restipulatio*. Thus in any covenant there are four acts, two belonging to the party initiating the covenant, and two to that which accepts the covenant offered.—In God's covenant with the first man all four covenant acts are discernible. Whereas God has demanded of man perfect keeping of the law, we have discerned the *stipulatio* in it, and whereas He promised man life in heaven and has already conferred the greatest happiness in this world, we discern the *promissio*. On the other side as long as man studied to keep God's law, *adstipulatio* was being given by him to God's demand. Had he persisted therein vigorously and non-stop, he might in the end have asked a good promise of God and so *restipulatio* would have ensued."

21.—The promise.—WYTTENBACH (*Tent.* II, p. 568) : " By perfect obedience Adam could not have merited anything. God could rightly have demanded such obedience, being the Most High and Absolute Lord, and man owed such obedience, both on account of the divine perfections and for the sake of his own happiness and the tremendous benefits received from God, and so obedience, even the most perfect, would have been sheerly due to Him.—Eternal life was accordingly promised to man and represented in no sense as a reward.—(569) Adam could not have asked eternal life of God save in virtue of the pact ".

22.—God gave man this promise not arbitrarily but in accordance with His holiness and goodness, because of which God returns the love of the creature who loves Him with loyal obedience and blesses him with His full fellowship.—HEIDEGGER (IX, 57) : " The further question now arises as to the source from which flows the promise mentioned of eternal and heavenly life for man, if he fulfils the law. Is it of the sheer εὐδοκία and judgment (*arbitrium*) of the divine will, or of θεοπρέπεια of the virtues proper to God's nature, such as principally His goodness and holiness ? Those who affirm the former rely on the principle that God is free either to present the innocent creature with life or to annihilate, punish, torture it eternally. This is the hypothesis of most *Scholastics*.—Our view then must clearly be that it becomes God to return the love of the creature who loves Him, and that since a loving God cannot not wish and do well to one beloved, He must give and impart Himself entire to be enjoyed. Love is an affect of conjunction ; as proceeding from Himself, God cannot fail to approve it as good or to desert it as bad ".

23.—In paradise, in which Adam was made, and in the *tree of life* which was planted in it and which set forth not only life in and for itself but also Him by whom the fellowship of true life is communicated to man, namely Christ, God had depicted this promise *sacramentally*, and (24) thereby had taught man that true life was to be found outside himself, in God.

Most dogmaticians enumerate these two sacraments of the covenant of works, e.g. BRAUN (I, iii, 2,18) : " There were two sacraments of the covenant of works, (1) paradise and (2) the tree of life, which to Adam signified life eternal and heavenly." — COCCEIUS (*De foed.* II, § 32) : The " sacrament of the heavenly city and of eternal life " was paradise and the tree of life. Since then Christ alone is life, one must say (38) : " The tree of life signified him who is the life of men ".—(39). : At the same time the tree of life indicated the Son of God not so far as he is Christ, i.e. the Mediator of the covenant of Grace, but only so far as he is the Son of God.—(*Summ. theol.* XXIII, 7, 8): " That paradise was also a sacrament and pledge of that country in which righteousness and glory dwell, is to be gathered from the tree of life placed in the midst of paradise. If the tree in the midst of paradise is not so much nourishment (*alimentum*) as sacrament (as *Augustine* says), paradise itself, God's garden, is also undoubtedly a sacrament.—This tree received that name, not because there was in it power to reconcile eternal Power to man ; *—but because it had been given man, so long as he persevered in his uprightness, as a pledge that he had life as a reward to be counted on for obedience in God ".—HEIDEGGER (IX, 70) : " God sealed the covenant of works, particularly the promise annexed to it, by sustaining in man, by sure signs and sacraments, πληροφορίαν (and stability of hope) to which belonged both paradise and the tree of life.—(73) In paradise the tree of life stood out eminently Gen. 2. 9 ; 3. 22 as a splendid sacrament particularly of heavenly life and of Christ himself, the author of life.—(75) It was not only eternal life that the tree of life sealed, but it also signified the reconciling cause of eternal life, the Son of God ".—Similarly MARESIUS, VIII, 23ff.

Others on the contrary, deviating from the usual, describe the tree of life and the tree of knowledge as the two sacraments of the covenant of nature, e.g. MASTRICHT (III, XII, 20): "The covenant of nature—God confirmed by a twofold sacrament, one of which, the tree of life, sealed the reward of obedience, life most blessed in every way Gen. 2. 9-21: the second sacrament of the covenant of nature sealed to the transgressor the penalty of disobedience, the tree of the knowledge of good and evil Gen. 2. 16-17". So POLAN (VI, 50), WOLLEB (p. 35), AMESIUS (I. X. 33). RIISSEN (IX,14). Others speak of three or four sacraments, e.g. WITSIUS (I, VI, 2): "The symbols under the covenant of works were, if I mistake not, four in all, which I detail in this order (1) paradise, (2) the tree of life, (3) the tree of the knowledge of good and evil, (4) the Sabbath". AMESIUS describes the tree of life as the "sacrament of life", that of knowledge as the "sacrament of death". RIISSEN calls the former the "symbol of reward", the latter the "sacrament of discovery" (*exploratio*). In the institution of the sabbath WITSIUS (I, 7) sees a guaranteed copy of the perfect glorification of God in creation by means of His providence, and of the future rest and transfiguration of man in God. Against the designation of the tree of knowledge as a sacrament BRAUN however insists (I, III, 2, 20) that "It was not a sacrament (1) because the nature of sacraments consist in the natural use of the sign to denote a spiritual good: now the natural use of fruits is eating; but the use of the tree of the knowledge of good and

---

* In recognising this all dogmaticians are at one. But there was still a dispute, whether by the tree of life only one tree or a whole species of tree was meant. WITSIUS (I, VI, 11) describes the first view as a "*communis quidem opinio*, but not resting on any probable reason." BRAUN on the other hand says (p. 367): "It does not appear that this was a single tree only; it is more likely that it was a complete species".

evil, i.e. eating, was not conceded but prohibited; (2) sacraments signify spiritual benefits: but the tree of the knowledge of good and evil threatened and brought death; hence (3) man could not use a forbidden tree but only abuse it".

Later there was pretty much one usage only, to describe paradise and the tree of life as the sacraments of the covenant of works; e.g. WYTTEN-BACH (*Tent.* II, 573): "The covenant of works had its sacraments, paradise to wit and the tree of life; for paradise and the tree of life were signs of the life in heaven".—LAMPE (*Einl. in den. Gnadenbund* p. 25): "The sacraments of the covenant of works are paradise and the tree of life (*das Holz des Lebens*)".

24.—As to true life being found by man outside himself in God, here is COCCEIUS (*S. Theol.* XXIII, 13-14): "It was enough for Adam to be taught by such a symbol that that life was outside himself, the possession of which would exclude all death and make him ἄφθαρτος, to which he was invited and which he sought;—to us who are born in sin and have not only heard God's promise but also the Gospel, the indication is clear, that righteousness is given us in the same thing in which life had been offered to Adam, but on the condition of works. From this it is also clear that He Himself was despised for sin and that to Him we have become debtors, who has actually borne our sins and on whom they are bound to have imposed labour".

25.—On the other hand for the fall by his disobedience God threatened man with death, i.e. with his separation from holiness and from the fellowship of God and with the separation of his soul from his body; which threat however did not exclude the possibility of a revelation of the compassionate love of God to the disobedient.

HEIDEGGER (IX, 60-63): "First of all God threatened the sinner with his separation from God's holiness, through which man becomes dead in trespasses and sins Eph. 2 .1.—Secondly, with this death is very closely connected his separation from God, who as the highest good blesses and cheers man; this is the death of everlasting torture, by which the soul of the unexpiated sinner after this life and his body when raised from the dead are not admitted to the contemplation of God as their supreme good, but are spurned from God's face and transferred to the place of tortures, in which their worm dieth not and their fire is not extinguished Dan. 12. 2, 13 (many of them that sleep in the dust of the earth shall awake, some to everlasting life and some to shame and everlasting contempt—go thou thy way, till the end be: for thou shalt rest and shalt stand in thy lot at the end of the days) Mt. 10. 28 (be not afraid of them which kill the body, but are not able to kill the soul; but rather fear him which is able to destroy both soul and body in Gehenna) Mk. 9. 48-49 (their worm dieth not and their fire is not quenched. For everyone shall be salted with fire) Lk. 16. 23-24 (in Hades he lifted up his eyes, being in torments, and seeth Abraham afar off and Lazarus in his bosom. Father Abraham . . . send Lazarus . . . I am in anguish in this flame) 2 Cor. 5.10 (we must all be made manifest before the judgment seat of Christ; that each one may receive the things done in the body according to what he hath done, whether it be good or bad) Rev. 20.10 (And the devil that deceived them was cast into the lake of fire and brimstone, where are also the beast and the false prophet; and they shall be tormented day and night for ever and ever).—Thirdly the punishment of sin is the separation of soul from body, both as regards the uprightness of the body's members, their harmony and health as well as its conveniences for food and sustenance, its facility, and the rest of the earthly blessings ; lastly, as regards the actual body by the dissolution of the union.—The declaration of this threefold death was not so absolute as to exclude grace utterly. It could not be that it should cut off every chance and place of mercy, remission of sin and longsuffering inviting to repentance. This in fact is God's perfection, that He does good even to the evil Lk. 6. 35 (the Most High is kind to the unthankful and evil); this is the beneficence and the riches of His grace that He remits sins condoning the penalty of death".—COCCEIUS (*Summ. theol.* XXVI, 5): The transgression of the interdict God had threatened with death, in order to teach us: "(1) that by God's will life is not obtained by man, save as the reward of obedience; (2) that every transgression is worthy of the penalty of death, or that it is worthy of God to punish it with the penalty of death ; (3) that life is to be set above pleasure ; (4) that the preservation of God's image needs care and fear".—This threatening of death indicated not only the *placitum pungendi* (the decree to pierce) but also "the natural consequence of sin and death". Since then this natural result of death ensuing upon sin was founded upon the *decentia Dei* (what becomes God), in order to manifest God's "holiness", it is clear, that hereby the revelation of God's perfection, which consists in His *longanimitas* (longsuffering) and *misericordia* (mercy), was not excluded Mt. 5. 48 (Ye therefore shall be perfect, as your heavenly Father is perfect) Ps. 25. 8 (Good and upright is the LORD; therefore he shall instruct sinners in the way), "since the two things are natural to God, to be able both to prove His holiness and to exercise mercy". Further the " benefit " is not excluded, " by which it happens that man dead in sin may die in someone else, that free from the curse of the Law he may live unto God, that is, may be made alive by God (12)". God can reveal His holiness, in virtue of which he hates sin and can have no fellowship with the sinner, even if

He does not carry out the whole punishment at once upon the sinner and from compassion bears patiently with him and loads him with benefits, "that He may call him to repentance. For so even a threat might straightway become strong and yet the punishment be either reduced for a time or even be completely removed."

CHAPTER XIV

THE VIOLATION OF THE COVENANT OF WORKS

1.—To destroy the covenant which God had concluded with the man He had made in His likeness, the devil by means of the serpent misled man into disobeying God by availing himself of man's selection for a position of higher perfection, not yet bestowed upon him, to support the lie that by transgressing God's command, according to which he must not eat of the tree of the knowledge of good and evil planted in paradise, man would attain to the possession of godlike independence and knowledge, especially the possession of the attributes of divine majesty (OLEVIAN, *De subst. foed.* p.10).

CALVIN (II, i, 4): " This was the prodigious impiety that to a son of earth it seemed too little that he had been made for likeness (to God), unless equality (with Him) were added ".—BEZA I, 320 : " What are Adam and Eve thinking of, at the moment they have made themselves docile pupils of Satan ? Why, of convicting God of jealousy and lying, and of planting themselves against His will upon His throne ! "—WITSIUS (I, VIII, 7) : " (The devil) adds a promise of greater good : ' Your eyes shall be opened and ye shall be as God, knowing good and evil '. He presupposes, what was true and holy, that man's desire tends to some more perfect good. This he fixes in the fact that his is to be like God ;—further he asserts that this likeness goes hand in hand with the opening of their eyes and a greater light of knowledge.—And so far Satan might seem to have talked not so badly.—But the deception lurks in this (1) that he tells them not to wait for the time appointed by God, but with ill-advised precipitancy to seize the promised blissfulness ; (2) that he indicates a way to the goal that is no way—(II, I, 1) Listening to the devil's instigation and giving rein to his own reasonings he withdrew from God by a most unrighteous rape and resolved to be on his own, spurning his lawful subordination to God ".—KECKERMANN (p.234) : " To violation of the sacrament was added the detestable insolence and pride of the first humans ; not content forsooth with some likeness to God, whose sacrament the tree in question was, they began to affect divinity itself ; which may quite clearly be inferred from Gen. 3. 22: 'God said, behold the man is become as one of us '. Man acted thus, made this claim, to be made equal to one of the three persons of the Trinity : the kind of pride which previously had brought down some angels, who were afterwards the cause of this lapse in man ".

2.—Note on the ascription of this sin to Adam, LEIDEN SYNOPSIS (XIV, 5) : " Although this sin was committed by Adam and Eve, it is yet referred by the Apostle to Adam alone Rom. 5. 12 (as through one man . . .), as the head and universal beginning of the whole human race, from whom Eve herself was also created 1 Cor. 11. 8 (the man is not of the woman, but the woman of man) and in whom as in the primarius parent God assessed (censere) all men according to the nature of the pact entered into with him ".

3.—This Adam then let himself be deceived by this (devil's) lie and betrayed into disobedience to God. So it was first of all unbelief in the seriousness of the threat pronounced by God which awoke in his heart and led him astray into giving heed to the voice of the tempter and into such a craving to neglect the divine command, that (exactly as it is set forth in the account in Scripture, which is to be taken literally) he really ended in falling.

LEIDEN SYNOPSIS (XIV, 9) : " Regarding the species of this sin doctors' opinions are discrepant.—(12) : Most of ours assert that it was infidelity, by which they abrogated faith in this divine threat, ' In the day in which thou eatest of the tree of the knowledge of good and evil thou shalt surely die '.—(13) : We may accept this opinion, if we correctly balance what our parents first did, rather than the first direction in which they looked and directed their mind ".—RIISSEN (IX, 29) : " Our view is that we need not take anxious avizandum over the order of the actions in this sin or the first step in this sin, because it consists in a complication of actions. Meanwhile we may say that by thoughtlessness man had ceased to consider God's interdict and his own truthfulness and goodness. Hence flowed firstly incredulity or distrust, by which man had not the faith in God's word which he should have had, but cast it out first by hesitation, presently by denial, not believing that the fruit was seriously forbidden him or that he would die. Then we have the credulity with which he began to give ear to the devil's words and presently he made an error of judgment. From this his longing (appetitus) in will and his inclination to concupiscence existed to eat the fruit ; and lastly the overt action."

The opinion is rejected that the fall must be explained by an intemperies gulae.—CALVIN (II, i, 4) : " The common idea of greedy intemperance is childish. As though the sum and substance of all the virtues should consist in abstinence from one fruit only, amid a general abundance of every delicacy that could be desired, since in the blessed fertility of the soil there was not only plenty of everything to delight but variety as well. We must therefore look deeper. The forbidding of the tree of the knowledge of good and evil was a test of obedience, that by passing the test Adam might prove his willing submission to God's command ".—Similarly other dogmaticians.

4.—" Adam's transgression is his sin in which, upset by Eve who was seduced by the serpent, he ate along with her of the forbidden fruit of the tree of the knowledge of good and evil and so both broke God's universal law and the covenant made with him by God, rendering both himself (since he was a man) and the entire human race (since the first man was also the head of the human species) guilty of the death divinely threatened against the transgressor " (HEIDEGGER IX, 11). But by transgressing the one positive commandment given him Adam sinned against the whole moral law revealed to him in his conscience and made himself guilty of infringing all duties to God and to humankind.

WOLLEB (p. 39) : " Consider the parts of this lapse and you will rightly speak of transgression of the whole natural law ".—LEIDEN SYNOPSIS (XIV, 7-8) : " By the same disobedience he transgressed by inference the moral law, the express (model or) ὑποτύπωσις of the natural law imposed upon him by God. The first table of it he violated by his want of belief and his profanation of the divine numen, the second by his ingratitude to his heavenly Father, by his murder of himself and his descendants, by his unrestraint, theft and receiving of Another's goods, by assent to false evidence and by a wicked greed for higher knowledge and status ".— EILSHEMIUS (Ostfriessl. Kleinod p. 28) : " Tertullian explicitly proves that under the first law which God had given to Adam and Eve about the fruit of the tree all the commands of the following law of the Ten Commandments were included. As they transgressed this one command they sinned against all ten. This explanation of Tertullian's is worth reading. We therefore should not belittle this sin or blame God either, as though He had punished them much too severely ".

5.—This fall of Adam's was of course already foreseen by God in eternity and was ordained with a view to a more perfect and richer manifestation of the divine glory and grace, as well as to a richer blessing and a higher elevation of man by electing and redeeming grace. The Fall was therefore indeed introduced by God ex necessitate consequentiae sive eventus, not however so far as Adam's act was sin, but so far as God willed to use Adam's sinful action as a means to the revelation of His glory.

MUSCULUS (620-21) : "God's ways are not like men's ways, so that it must be thought that it happened to Him, as it usually comes to us every day: our plans and acts promptly fall out far otherwise than we had intended. He created man in His image, upright and unimpaired. Who so senseless as to say that He had not foreseen what would happen

to man by the serpent's persuasion? All therefore generally agree, and
rightly, in this, that Adam's sin had been foreseen and foreknown from
eternity. Thus the lapse of the human race did not so occur as to be
beyond the mind and intention of the Creator: which means that He is
a sham creator in His work, as though the thing happened otherwise
than He resolved; and as someone says, when He had begun a flagon
(*amphora*) a pitcher has issued from the flying wheel; just as it usually
comes to us mortals on account of our ignorance of things future, whereby
it happens that a father is in ignorance about his own son, what he is
to turn out, and although he hopes for the best and rightly trains him
with the greatest care, it yet frequently happens that contrary to expectation he experiences in him the very opposite of probity. Above all we
must insist that nothing such has happened to God. (2) In the next place,
to advance a little further, I also think that we must insist beyond shadow
of doubt that God's prescience of man's future lapse was not apart
from a fixed decree"—p. 21: "Since then this counsel and purpose which
has been manifested in Christ in the last times by the preaching of the
Gospel and the operation of the H. Spirit was not born in God until
after man's lapse, but before man had sinned, indeed before he had
been created, before the constitution of the world, it had been hidden
in Him from eternity: it is I think pretty clear that God refused to establish man's felicity and salvation upon his first state and constitution
such as it was, but established it on his (man's) restoration predestined
in Christ the Son, and He so arranged, that he should be redeemed and
preserved neither by his knowledge of Himself (whence He even forbade
him to eat of the tree of the knowledge of good and evil) nor by the
worthiness and merits of his own righteousness, but by the sole grace
and mercy of his free election, when otherwise ready to perish, by the
intervention of His Son. The universal fall of the human race served
to illustrate this grace of election. By the fall, before he had acquired
any offspring, Adam fell into sin; and the result is that no mortal can
be saved except by God's mercy. In the next place also the wretchedness,
corruption and perdition, which overtaking this lapse of our first parents
now holds the whole human race, renders the power and might of divine
providence much more splendid, while through Christ we are more
happily restored after the fall than we had been when created, before
we fell: just as on the day of resurrection, when we shall be raised from
the dust of the earth and the corruptible shall put on incorruption and
the mortal immortality, the might of God's power will be declared
much more gloriously, than if we were living for ever in this life devoid
of corruption and death."

WITSIUS (I, VIII, 10): "Undoubtedly God in His providence was occupied with this lapse of the protoplasts. Admittedly of course it had been foreknown from eternity, which nobody can deny.—(11): And if it was foreknown, it was also foreordained.—12: Hence by a plain inference we deduce that it could not have happened otherwise than that man should fall, because of the infallibility of God's foreknowledge, and of the *necessitas*, as they call it, *consequentiae*. The divine perfection does not allow of any decree of God being made, to which the issue does not correspond".—WOLLEB (p. 39): "The first sin God did not and did will. He did not will it so far as it is sin; He willed and decreed it, so far as it is the medium of revealing his glory, mercy and righteousness."

The question, how far Adam's fall was determined by God, is most adequately lit up by WITSIUS (I, VIII, 23-27). He begins with this proposition. "Neither does God merely excite and predetermine the will of men to vicious actions so far as they are actions. He also excites them so that it cannot but be that he should so act the acts. If given the influx of God it could be that the created will did not act, two absurdities would follow, (1) That human will could elude divine providence and could give or withhold its efficacy from the influx of God. (2) That there might be in a creature an act and that of such value as therewith to resist the divine influx, but which yet does not depend on God. For neither, methinks, will they say that God concurs in producing an action by which His influx is resisted. Moreover we refuted above a concurrence which is indifferent, determinable by the free judgment of creatures". Thereupon WITSIUS (24) composes the proposition: "Man's free judgment when excited to actions according to his physical being cannot give them moral and spiritual goodness save by the influx of divine Providence concurring in such goodness.—For since moral goodness is a higher, more perfect degree of entity than physical entity alone and man depends upon God for the physical entity of his actions, he is necessarily much more dependent upon God in producing the moral goodness in his actions; so that the glory of it should be refunded to God as the first cause". The two propositions now lead to the conclusion (25): "If in acting all creatures depend upon God; if He not only concurs with them when they act, but also urges them to action; if this urge is so powerful, that given it the effect cannot fail to follow; if God inflows with the same efficacy into vicious acts so far as they are acts; if the creature cannot without God give to his actions the moral goodness they require: it follows infallibly that if God moves Adam to know, will, emit, he cannot fail to know, will and emit, and if God does not give the goodness of the acts in question he will have been unable to know and will well". At the same time it does not follow that Adam is in an unfree state. Rather the freeness of his state is directly based upon divine providence (27): "For he sinned in judgment and in will, for which liberty, so far as opposed to compulsion, is so proper, nay essential, that they are neither judgment nor will, if they are not free. In addition, when we insist that God foreordained and infallibly foreknew, that man might sin freely, he could not in sinning do other than sin freely; unless we are content that the issue should not answer to God's fore-ordination and foreknowledge. And so far is anything taken from man's liberty in action by the decree of God, that on the contrary this freedom has no surer foundation than the aforesaid infallible decree of God in question."

6.—Hence God is in no way the cause of the fall; neither by His providence nor by His decree, nor by His permitting the fall, nor by His affecting the course of the actions in which Adam's fall was displayed, nor by His refusing Adam protective grace in the fall, so making the Fall not impossible and governing the Fall itself.

LEIDEN SYNOPSIS (XIV, 19-20): "The cause of this sin is either outward or inward. Its outward cause is not God's foreknowledge, nor His permission or impulsion, but the instigation of the devil".—WOLLEB (p. 38): "The cause of Adam's and Eve's transgression is neither God, nor God's decree, nor the refusal of special grace, nor permission to lapse, nor the arousing of natural movement, nor in short the government of the fall in question".—Particularly noteworthy is what WITSIUS says: (I, VIII, 28): "To make God the author of sin is such foul blasphemy, that it can never enter any Christian man's mind without a shudder. It is indeed true that God had made man mutably good, had infallibly foreseen his sin, had foreordained the permission of the sin and given man no doubt sufficient strength to shun sin, but inoperable without His influx; that meanwhile He had inflowed into man's faculties for natural actions, by not inflowing into the *moral* entity of such actions. All this we learn from the instruction of the upshot. But it is not less true, that God neither is nor could in any way become the author of sin. And although for us it might be difficult, indeed impossible to reconcile these truths with each other, what is plain should never be denied for the sake of what is obscure".

7.—On the contrary the sole *causa interna* of man's fall is man himself. He sinned in complete freedom in such a way that he willed disobedience towards God with full premeditaton .—COCCEIUS (*Summ. de foed.* III, 62): "Adam sinned voluntarily (i.e. willing the act which God had forbidden him) with God's perission, i.e. God not giving him grace to obey, by which he might surely will what he could; yet holily concurring with the act of sin, not however infusing the bad *habitus* or effecting sin in man. For God works good things in us, not bad."—MASTRICHT (IV, I, 20): "The Reformed insist that man had committed this first sin altogether freely, because (notwithstanding God's eternal decree, the predetermining influx of providence and the like) he committed it by reasonable counsel and satisfaction, in which alone the freedom of our judgment strictly consists." —LEIDEN SYNOPSIS (XIV, 30): "The inward cause of the lapse is the free will of each of our parents or rather the deflection of a will that listened to Satan rather than to God."

8.—The possibility of the Fall was of course given by God when He made man himself. Not as though God had made him in a state of conflict between spirit and flesh or had, by withdrawing the help of grace by which He empowered man's free will to morally good action, thrust him into this struggle before the temptation and left him to himself. But because He had made him in a state of moral changeability. Yet we should note that changeability is just the state which belongs and corresponds to creation as such. Therefore it is not to be regarded as itself the *causa peccati*.

HOTTINGER 159: "Mutability—was the cause of Adam's first sin, not indeed *per se* but still *per accidens*".—LEIDEN SYNOPSIS (XIV, 32): "Although God created both parents mutably good, this mutability in their intact state was neither a defect in the nature made in the image of God nor sin nor the cause of sin but a condition suited to the creature, from which the Creator is distinguished by this incommunicable mark of perfection, because *per se ac natura* He is unchangeably good".—WALAEUS (p. 263): "How could a mind holy and just revolt from justice and obedience? Here it is answered by some that God had deserted man and deprived him of His aid, in order to test his constancy. But I answer that we cannot prove this, because all desertion is the punishment of antecedent failure (*delictum*), as Paul bears witness R. 1. 24 (God gave them up to the lusts of their hearts . .) 2 Th. 2.11 (. . God sent them a working of error, that they should believe a lie), unless they say He had robbed man of the assistance by which he might infallibly persist and had left him in the hands of his own judgment (*arbitrium*), to test his constancy. But nevertheless it is always of necessity presupposed that he had as much grace in him as to be able to resist Satan's temptation. Otherwise he would also be a man to be excused in his lapse. His deprivation of a thing, the removal of which makes lapse inevitable, renders man excusable, unless it is done in the punishment of an antecedent fault, as we saw above. As a house cannot but collapse when its pillars are withdrawn! But how can man holy and just fall away? Answer: Although he was holy and just, yet he was not immutably holy and just. Accordingly, if he wished he could abuse his judgment and pervert his mind by neglect of it. But at that time he was left by God in the hands of his own judgment".—MASTRICHT (IV, I, 8): "If you ask how one blessed through original righteousness with perfect wisdom, holiness and righteousness could sin, I shall not answer with the PELAGIANS, JESUITS and REMONSTRANTS, because by creation there was in him a struggle of flesh and spirit; for I would be saying that God was the author of sin, because the concupiscence of flesh against spirit is by the pronouncement of God (Ex. 20.17, ixth Commandment) and of the Apostle (Rom. 7. 7. Is the law sin? God forbid. Howbeit, I had not known sin, except through the law . . .) undoubtedly sin. I shall rather say that he could sin although endowed with such wisdom, holiness and righteousness, because he was changeably endowed (since immutability is among the attributes of God; and the very prohibition of the covenant of works with the sanction annexed would likely have been superfluous if he could not have sinned at all), he was changed by the powerful assaults of temptations from his native rectitude, God's favourable confirming grace meanwhile ceasing, not being due at all".

Also God's relation to the fall of Adam is not that of an idle onlooker. He rather lets it take place according to His active *permissio* and *ordinatio*. I.e. God did not of course urge Adam to sin, nor did He withdraw his state of grace from him for the battle against sin; and just as little did He co-operate with Adam in the actual fall to consummate it. Rather God wrought upon Adam's fall as follows. He effected the outward, physical substratum of the action in which Adam sinned, exactly as He induces all other acts of men and generally every external living impulse in creation. He allowed the Devil to tempt man (who had the capacity to resist the Tempter) and allowed man in virtue of the liberty given him to acquiesce in the temptation, and ordained the fall thus brought to pass to be the means to a more perfect revelation of His own divine nature and of His higher claim and blessing upon a section of men.

9.—The consent to sin, in which Adam betrayed by the devil was brought to the fall, was thus altogether an exemplification of Adam's freedom, so that he became guilty in God's sight.

MASTRICHT (IV, I, 11) : " Although this violation was consummated by the skill of Satan and the seduction of the woman ; although too God was in no way the cause of it ; although further He in no wise forced man into this violation by His influx or government ; although before the commission of the crime He withdrew no grace or aid, so that willy nilly he had to lapse : nevertheless it is not to be thought that this happened completely without all inspiration (*numen*) or providence, or that God acted as an idle spectator of this struggle or of the whole upshot. In that case He would not be the absolutely first existent (*primum ens*) and so also not God ; and He whose care extends to everything down to sparrows, yea and even to our hairs, would have held the fates of the whole human race topsy turvy, quite apart from the objection that on this violation depends both the sending of the Mediator and the entire economy of redemption.—(IV, 1, 12) So without any doubt (1) He predetermined this violation by His eternal decree, by which He does all things according to the counsel of His will, no less than He predetermined all other crimes which were perpetrated by Herod, Pontius Pilate and the Jews concerning His Son Ac. 2. 23 (him being delivered up by the determinate counsel and foreknowledge of God, ye by the hand of lawless men did crucify and slay) 4. 26-27 (Why did the Gentiles rage and the peoples imagine a vain thing ? The kings of the earth set themselves in array, and the rulers were gathered together against the Lord and against his Anointed [Ps.2.1-2] : for of a truth in this city against thy holy Servant Jesus whom thou didst anoint, both Herod and Pontius Pilate, with the Gentiles and the peoples of Israel, were gathered together), since in particular the sending of the mediator, which presupposes a certain futurition of the lapse, is said to be foreknown and predetermined 1 Pet. 1. 20 (. . . foreknown indeed before the foundation of the world, but manifested at the end of the times for your sake). Then also (2) by His providence He no less effected the physical act underlying this sin than all other human acts whatsoever Acts 17. 28 (in him we live and etc.) Further (3) by permitting ἀνομία He denied the concurrence of grace and of confirming aid, as that without which the happening could in no wise have taken place. Neither was God held to bestow it, especially as man trusting in his own strength did not seek it. In fact (4) He tempted the protoplasts, not indeed like Satan to evil (Jas. 1. 13-14 let no man say when he is tempted, I am tempted of God : God cannot be tempted with evil, and himself tempteth no man. Each man is tempted, when he is drawn away by his own lust and enticed), but like Abraham later (Gen. 22. 1—God did prove Abraham) and the Israelites Ex. 20. 20 (God is come to prove you) ; Dt. 8. 2, 16 (remember God's leading in the wilderness to humble them— not to slay the nations will be a snare to them), that it may be manifest what is in man. Not to add (5) the entire government of this violation, by which He most holily directed it to the glory of His name, the redemption of His own and the just condemnation of the reprobate ".

God thus wrought in upon Adam's fall by His *permissio* and *ordinatio*. HOTTINGER (160-161) is the most adequate in making it clear, how this *permissio* and *ordinatio* is to be conceived. " Negatively : (1) God did not drive Adam to sin (a) because He severely forbade him, (b) in narrating the causes Moses makes no mention of God, (c) God made man upright, but he of his own motion forsooth, at the suasion and instigation of Satan, sought out a host of reasons. (2) God did not withdraw from him grace combatting sin, because (a) that followed him into the punishment of the sin, according as it is the deprivation of the image of God because of sin, (b) because otherwise He would have been driving man to sin : just as when a house necessarily collapses when the pillars are withdrawn. (3) Nor did He in any way co-operate with his sin. Affirmatively : (1) He did not confer on Adam the aid of new and special grace or help him with extraordinary aid, so that he might will to persevere. (2) Nor did He hinder Satan from tempting him and him from obeying the tempter. (3) He ordered and directed the fall to the ends which He had predetermined by his eternal counsel. Not the ends of sin, which of themselves are nil, but of the divine permission. Some ends are in respect of men, others in respect of God. As regards the former the proximate end was the manifestation of the creature's infirmity ; the remote major was the felicity and more perfect salvation in the second Adam, Christ. In respect of God : the proximate end is the beauty of the whole which arises out of this permission and consists in 'this, that in the world as in a great house there are various vessels ; the remote end is the revealing of His glory, primarily the display of His actual mercy in the salvation of the elect for Christ's sake ".—Hence above all it must be insisted that God effected Adam's fall not by withdrawing His common grace.—MARESIUS (VI, 29): " Much less must it be said that God positively withdrew His grace from man before the act of sin, because then God would be set up as the author of it ; but man freely sinning rejected and repudiated that aid ".—v. TIL (*Hypotyposis* p.122) : " God withdrew no strength from man before the sin ". But the *permissio peccati* was also not a mere *non-impeditio* of sin. As experience shows, God willed to let happen, what Adam willed to do. PICTET (VI, v, 6) : " If God wills not to prevent (sin), then that permission will not be just a mere *non-impeditio*, but God's effective volition. This permission includes preservation of the man's faculties and life and his strength, which God could remove, if He wished to hinder sin ".—MARTINI (*De gubern. mundi* 235) : " They had received sufficient grace both to do good and to beware of evil if they but willed, and theirs was the power and duty to obtain by prayer the necessary strengthening. Moreover it was lawfully required of them to will stedfastly what they could. Had they tested this at the right time which seemed good to God, they had the power to be confirmed indeed as angels.—In the actual temptation there arose a certain elation of mind, because of which God allowed man to be overcome in temptation. But. God did not do man wrong, in allowing him to be tempted of the devil

God had equipped him with sufficient strength to overcome the adversary easily, had he so wished, and suitably to implore God's assistance and to trust in Him. Nor did God do him wrong in allowing him to be overcome by temptation. He was not obliged to afford special assistance, especially when not called upon by man. Nay, secret elation deserved the humiliation of desertion ".—From this it follows (POLAN VI, 3) : " The first parents fell by divine providence and were deserted by God and necessarily, but nevertheless by their own free will, although with the devil as adviser and egger-on. They were endowed with their own judgment, which was free and could not be forced. Our first parents followed the advice and urge of the devil, but with the inclination of the proper motion of their own will. Adam of course was not seduced by the actual Serpent ; but a seduced woman was the cause of the transgression, 1 Tim. 2. 14 (Adam was not beguiled, but the woman being beguiled hath fallen into transgression) ".

10.—By this Adam lost God's respect and the hope of eternal life, as well as his righteousness and the grace which had strengthened him hitherto. He lost the perfection of lordship over the rest of the creatures and the enjoyment of the blessedness which thus far he ought to have been enjoying, i.e Adam did not lose the substance of his image of God, but God took away from him all the powers and advantages with which He had adorned it. Thus man was now a slave of sin and of the misery of sin and an object of God's displeasure, whose judicial verdict condemned him to eternal death.

COCCEIUS (*Summ. de foed.* III, 63): "By sin Adam became guilty, i.e., he fell from God's friendship, from the hope of eternal life, from the spiritual grace given him at creation, from uprightness, from his rights over the creatures subjected to him by God Himself, from life and the state of felicity; and he incurred God's indignation, wrath and judgment, being made liable to judgment and under a curse Rom. 3. 19 (. . . whatsoever things the law saith, it speaketh to them that are under the law, that every mouth may be stopped, and all the world may be brought under the judgment of God) Gal. 3. 10 (as many as are of the works of the law are under a curse: for it is written, Cursed is everyone that continueth not in all things that are written in the book of the law, to do them)".—In his *Summa theol.* (XXIX, 1, 2, 3, 18) COCCEIUS distinguishes the following "effects of Adam's disobedience": (1) "liability or *debitio poenae*", wherefore man is called ἀσεβής, "worthy of punishment"; (2) alienation from the life of God Eph. 4. 18 (darkened in their understanding, alienated from the life of God because of the ignorance that is in them, because of the hardening of their hearts) or "deprivation of sanctification, which comes from the Spirit of God"; whence man is called ψυχικός; (3) the resulting "impotence to submit himself to God's law and to know God, in such wise as to glorify Him and to render Him thanks", and "concupiscence reigning in his members"; (4) the "aversion" which makes "conversion" necessary for every man, since as the mother of the "infinite cornfield of actual sins" it brings it about that man "*nihil nisi peccat.*"

The utter seriousness of Reformed treatment of the misery that came upon humanity through the fall is thus expressed by OLEVIAN in the *Expos. Symb.* p. 7: "So great and mighty an evil is sin, that it merits the eternal destruction of man. Whence it follows that sin is a greater evil than the eternal damnation of man, since not even by eternal punishments can they expiate or overcome so great an evil. In short, so great an evil is it to have offended the majesty of God by even one sin, that the total destruction of all creatures would be a less evil. For not even the destruction of all creatures and their reduction to nothing would be an equivalent price to pay for expiating a single sin, which cannot be expiated save by the death of the Son of God."—Of the greatness and depth of the misery of sin in man the Reformed system speaks pretty much in the same way as the *Lutheran.* But the former never let itself be led astray into the error of *Flacius Illyricus* in *Lutheranism;* which appears in the *Lutheran* doctrine of the loss of the divine image. BOQUIN is already saying (*Exeg. div. et hum.* κοινωνίας, p. 109): "I am by no means displeased with what *Augustine* writes, "that that was not altogether destroyed in the heart of man by sin, which had been impressed upon it by the image of God when being created"; nor was it so destroyed by the defilement in question, that none, even the most extreme of its lineaments, has remained in the soul (there remained, of course, what could only be rational)". All later Reformed dogmaticians adhere to the distinction established in Melanchthonian theology between the substance and the *virtutes* of the divine image, and they accordingly teach that the original *virtus* and not the *imago* has been irretrievably lost. Cf. POLAN (VI, 5): "From this it is plain what of the divine image is left in corrupt man. There remained the substance of the soul; there remained the essential faculties of the soul, knowledge and will; there remained the essential attributes, as a kind of natural knowledge, reasoning power, judgment and thought, freedom from compulsion in the will; there remained natural life and the immortality of the soul. Therefore the image of the nature is not utterly destroyed by the sin of Adam and Eve; this must be credited to the mercy of God towards the human race. Nevertheless it has been lost in part and what is left is wretchedly corrupt and misshapen. Moreover all the rightness, i.e., the sanity and integrity of the perception and recognition of God and divine things, the original righteousness and holiness by which in particular man was a partner in the divine nature, has been completely destroyed, extinguished and left out" (see Ch. XI, 15 and quotations). Hence this point of doctrine also belonged to those who represented the difference between the *Reformed* and the *Lutheran* systems. So, e.g., WENDELIN (*Systema*, p. 508): "There remains in man corrupted by Adam's lapse a rational soul, which is an immortal spirit; there remain the faculties, thought and will; in thought there remain as though inborn the theoretical and practical principles of truth.—In short there is still some portion of dominion. Meanwhile none of these has been so acquired that by it fallen and corrupt man is able either to rise again or to prepare himself to receive the offer of grace, or to co-operate with God even when He is laying the first foundations of grace". Similarly in the *Collatio*, p. 125: "We assert that the principal part of the divine image, namely original righteousness, was plainly lost and abolished through the fall and sin of origin. Meanwhile we deny that the entire image of God in all its parts was utterly lost and abolished, which those will easily concede who recognise part of the divine image in the rational soul as an immortal spirit endowed with thought and will. By the fall man did not cease to be man, although he did cease to be righteous".

11.—In Adam then there fell not any single member of humanity but the genealogical head of the human race, representative of humanity; and in him fell not only his own person, but human nature as such fell also.

HEIDEGGER (X, 33): "We have clearly proved above (*Loc.* IX, 19, 20) that Adam in the covenant of works sustained a public character and represented the entire human race. Hence it is perfectly manifest that by sinning he sinned not for himself only, but for all likewise whom he represented; that indeed there sinned with him those whom he represented. One who is represented as doing or being acted upon may also be regarded as himself doing or being acted upon. To represent is with a certain force of law to exhibit the presence of that which is not present".—POLAN (VI, 3): "At first person infected nature, but afterwards nature infected person. Adam's sin was the sin of the actual nature: the sins of the lave are personal. Therefore his sin was transferred with nature, but not that of the rest. But why Adam by sinning destroyed not the person only but the nature, while other men injure their persons but do not worsen the nature, no other cause can be assigned than God's most righteous will. The infelicity which Adam voluntarily piled upon himself, God rightly inflicted upon the whole of his posterity. But why?

For so His will bears; and it is the norm of right and of righteousness".—
WITSIUS (I, VIII, 30): "Lastly it remains to be noted, that since Adam's
standing in this covenant was that of the head of the entire human race,
when he fell all his posterity are regarded as having lapsed with him and
having violated God's covenant".—WOLLEB (39-40): "In this business
Adam is to be regarded not as a private but as a public person and so
as the parent, head and root of the whole human race.—The first sin
then is not personal only, but natural as well. Therefore as person has
infected nature, so in turn the nature has infected persons. (Christ is
excepted from this liability etc.)".—RIISSEN (IX, 35): "We teach that
Adam's actual sin is actually so imputed to all descended from him in
the ordinary way, that for that reason they are all pronounced guilty
and either pay the penalty or are at least adjudged worthy of the penalty".

12.—Consequently all his posterity also fell with Adam. For they as
partakers in Adam's nature sinned in him. To them therefore (1) God
reckons Adam's guilt, and accordingly (2) as a righteous judge punishes
them with a heritable corruption.—*Form. Cons. Helv.* 10: "We are therefore of opinion that Adam's sin is imputed to his whole posterity by the
secret and just judgment of God Rom. 5.12,19 (through one man sin
entered into the world and death through sin: and death passed unto all
men, for that all sinned . . . through one man's disobedience the many
were made sinners . . .) 1 Cor. 15. 21, 22 (. . . by man came death . . . in
Adam all die).—Nor does any reason appear, as to how hereditary corruption can fall like a spiritual death upon the entire human race by the
just judgment of God, unless some fault of the same human race preceded,
inducing liability to such death, since God the most just judge of the
whole earth punishes none but the guilty person. 11: Thus on a double
count man after sin is by nature and so from his birth, before he admits
any actual sin unto himself, liable to the divine wrath and curse; first
because of the παράπτωμα and disobedience which he committed in
Adam's loins; secondly because of the consequent hereditary corruption
ingrained in his very conception, by which his whole nature is depraved
and spiritually dead, so much so, that rightly original sin is laid down as
twofold, namely imputed and inherent by heredity. 12: We cannot
preserve heavenly truth and straightway give assent to those who deny
that Adam represented his posterity and that by God's institution, and
that accordingly his sin is imputed to his posterity directly (ἀμέσως),
while on the pretext of indirect and consequent imputation they abolish
the non-imputation of the first sin only, but expose to serious danger the
assertion of hereditary corruption as well".—COCCEIUS (*Summ. de foedere*
III, 64): In and with Adam "by the law of the communication of the

same nature subjected to the curse, his successors also are guilty, i e. they have become such, that on them the same penalty may justly be imposed as on their parent, to whom God has also imputed this first sin by His rights and according to His holy law, i.e. He has marked out Adam's children as heirs to the evil patrimony, which their father had acquired for himself and has condemned them to the same punishments, Rom. 5. 16,18 (. . . the judgment of one came unto condemnation . . . through one trespass the judgment came unto all men to condemnation). —MASTRICHT (IV, I,13): "Already the violation, which was perpetrated by the protoplasts under the temptation by Satan seducing the woman under the direction of divine providence, concerned and implicated not themselves only, but also all their posterity".

13.—Thus Adam's fall is the cause of all the misery of humanity and of creation generally. On man's side it spells the abolition of the covenant of nature and is the root of all single sins; and with man God also subjected the rest of creation, which was created for man, to the misery incurred by man.—MASTRICHT (IV, I, 15): "This is a great and not sufficiently to be deplored violation of the covenant of nature, the chief crime of the human race and the supreme disaster of the age (*saeculum—αἰών*). In it we are to note, not this or that particular sin, whether of greed or pride or theft, as satisfies the *Papists*, but the seeds and the pathway of all sins.—CALVIN (II, i, 5): "Sin perverts the whole order of nature in heaven and on earth. All creatures groan in their subjection to corruption.—Above and below a curse has flowed, the result of man's fault, the depravation of nature.—(v.19) Let the truth stand—that man's mind is so alienated from God's righteousness, that it contrives nothing that is not ungodly, his heart is thoroughly imbued with the poison of sin".—HYPERIUS 223: "On account of the sin of the first parent the corruption has also passed over to the other creatures prepared for man's use, and those which of themselves were always to be salutary have become harmful *per accidens* (Gen. 3). The ground is cursed. The creature is subject to vanity ".—MARESIUS (V, 59) : " Without labour or trouble the earth would have produced its good things for him and the woman would have been sure to bring forth children without pain.— (VI, 33): The effects of the sin intensively considered were in common (1) the loss of original righteousness, (2) the feeling of nakedness, the feeling from shame, as the nakedness from sin, and when the Adamites and certain Anabaptists wished to lay the feeling aside, they were seen to have made war on nature herself; (3) the terror of conscience which accompanies sin; (4) ejection from paradise; (5) a host of every kind of toils and tortures; (6) death itself".

14.—Adam then by his disobedience had destroyed the covenant entered into with God. He was therefore liable to the punishment of eternal death threatened for this fall and was bound to bear the punishment willingly. For this reason God could as little forego His rights which were His as Creator and Lord over His creatures, as man could be relieved of his duty, binding upon him as a creature, over against his Creator and absolute Lord. I.e., after as well as before God was justified in demanding complete obedience from man; and man being covered by God's jurisdiction of punishment was none the less also further bound to give God complete obedience and thereby, if God should have mercy upon him, to accept with believing obedience the gracious salvation offered him.—Cocceius (*Summ. de foed.* IV, 71): Condemned by the covenant of nature and excluded from the benefits of it, man still remains bound to do all that the law of nature, as well as God with His rights as Lord, demands of man. Hence man is bound to two things: (1) "to the penalty for sin", and (2) "to obedience because of his subjection". Even if after the taking away of the promised reward and after the subsequent entry of *reatus poenae*, the latter boundenness had disappeared, man could only have been bound by a law voluntarily taken over by him from the very beginning. Also only in that case would Adam's fall be a real active sin; for *ubi obligatio non est, ibi nec peccatum est.*— (IV, 72): To that to which Adam as much as his entire posterity is also legally bound after the fall, belongs faith in "God the Saviour, if God proposed a sufficient ἱλαστήριον and invites them to grasp it and promises the gift of righteousness to everyone who embraces it". This boundenness already results "from the law of nature itself"; for even the angels, although the Mediator was not sent for them, are bound to give God the honour, that God alone can justify the godless, if He will.

15.—Now although man had infringed the covenant of God and had made all sorts of claim to the blessings of it, they were not yet on God's side absolutely abolished thereby. Of course, it was set aside so far as man could no longer be justified by God in conformity with the covenant of works by fulfilling the law. On the other hand the moral law remained. After as well as before it demanded perfect obedience from man, in the sense that God also threatened every further transgression with death, in order to express the divine nature itself in its immutable validity. Therefore if God wished grace to replace right and to set up thereby a covenant of grace with man by allowing the duty of perfect fulfilment of the law and of perfect atonement for the guilt of sin to be performed by a representative of men, it must be said that in that case this covenant of grace was not so much set up in room of the covenant of works, as added to it.

MASTRICHT (III, XII, 22): "That covenant was indeed broken by the transgression of the protoplasts Hos. 6. 7 (they like Adam have transgressed the covenant; there have they dealt treacherously against me). But it did not thereby either become altogether antiquated or remain intact. It was antiquated: (1) as regards power to justify (so far as by works of the law no flesh can now be justified R. 3. 20, Ps. 143, 2 (in thy sight shall no man living be justified), Gal. 3. 2 (. . . Received ye the Spirit by the works of the law or by the hearing of faith?) and to make alive (whence the letter is called dead and deadly) Gal. 3. 10 (as many as are of the works of the law are under a curse; for it is written Cursed is every one which continueth not in all things that are written in the book of the law to do them) 2 Cor. 3. 6, 7, 9 (. . . made us sufficient as ministers of a new covenant; not of the letter, but of the spirit; for the letter killeth, but the spirit giveth life. But the ministration of death, written and engraven on stones, came with glory, so that the children of Israel could not look stedfastly on the face of Moses for the glory of his face; which glory was passing away—if the ministration of death is glory, much rather doth the ministration of righteousness exceed in glory). It was antiquated (2) as regards strictness, so far as it now no longer requires fullness of obedience from the very elect under threat of death Rom. 8. 3 (what the law could not do, in that it was weak through the flesh, God sending his own Son in the likeness of sinful flesh and as an offering for sin condemned sin in the flesh) under the penalty of death, being content to be satisfied by a surety. It was further out of date (3) as regards power to curse the elect Gen. 3. 13ff. (what is this thou hast done? . . . the curse on the serpent and on the ground), so far as through the divine ἐπιείκεια He acquiesces in the transference of the curse from debtor to surety Is. 53. 3, 4, 6 (He was despised and rejected of men; a man of sorrows and acquainted with grief (sickness); and as one from whom men hide their face he was despised, and we esteemed him not. Surely he hath borne our griefs and carried our sorrows; yet we did esteem him stricken, smitten of God, and afflicted. . . . All we like sheep have gone astray; we have turned every one to his own way; and the Lord hath caused the iniquity of us all to light on him) 2 C. 5. 19, 21 (God was in Christ reconciling the world to himself, not reckoning unto them their trespasses, and having committed unto us the word of reconciliation. . . . Him who knew no sin he made to be sin on our behalf; that we might become the righteousness of God in him). These removed it is still in force as to these further stipulations, namely (1) supplying perfect obedience promptly to the moral law (Ex. 20), whereby we love God with the whole heart and our neighbour as ourselves Mt. 22. 37 and we are thus perfect as

our Father in heaven Himself is perfect Mt. 5. 48. Next (2) as regards
the penalty of the threat Dt. 27. 26 (Cursed be he that confirmeth not
the words of this law to do them), Gal. 3. 10 (as many as are of the works
of the law are under a curse . . .), R. 6. 23 (the wages of sin is death;
but the free gift of God is eternal life in Christ Jesus our Lord) Heb. 10. 27
((there remaineth) . . . a certain fearful expectation of judgment, and
a fierceness of fire which shall devour the adversaries); further (3) as
regards the power to curse the actual sinners also, those at all events
who have not been received into the covenant of grace, whom of course
Christ will not have freed from the curse of the law by becoming a curse
for them Gal. 3. 13 (Christ redeemed us from the law, having become
a curse for us . . .); in order that the covenant of grace (by which
what the law could not do, God sending his own Son conformed to
flesh liable to sin, condemned sin in the flesh, that the δικαίωμα τοῦ
νόμου might be fulfilled in us Rom. 8. 3-4) might not so much
have succeeded the covenant of nature, as have been added to it".—
WITSIUS (I, IX, 2): "This for us is certain, that many things in this
covenant are of immovable and eternal truth, which we recite in this
order: (1) the precepts of the covenant, barring the one πειραστικόν,
bind one and all in whatever state to perfect performance of duty;
(2) the life eternal promised by the covenant cannot be obtained on
any other condition than that of perfect obedience achieved in every
detail; (3) no disobedience escapes God's lash and always the punishment of sin is death. These axioms however do not exclude the sponsor,
who meets the pledge in man's place by paying the penalty and fulfilling the condition".—HEIDEGGER (XI, 1-2): "By man's sin the covenant
of works which God made with him while still intact, was broken off.—
But still the intact covenant of works could not have thus been broken
off and abolished. For since in that covenant, at least as regards God,
there was made both a stipulation of duty and a promise of life to the
obedient and a threat of death to the disobedient, the covenant as the
stipulation of a duty or an obedience could in no wise be broken off
by the sin of man. By man's sin God could not fall away any more
from His right to exact the duty and the obedience due by the benefit
of actual creation and bound up by the bond of the covenant. By sin
the creature did not cease to depend on God's dominion and His law.
Nay rather He was bound by the covenant of works to each of two
things, to obedience and if that was not provided to punishment at the
same time, as we have maintained above by several proofs. In fact
the obligation to obedience was prior to the covenant, and flowed from
man's state as created by God and lasts as long as man is God's creature
and depends upon Him, i.e. eternally".—BRAUN, p. 385: "Still the

covenant of works ought not to be regarded as so abrogated, as though no part of it had place today in the sinner. It is abrogated only as a benefit which can no longer justify or sanctify or glorify man, but it has not been abrogated as a duty and an obligation. Man should be bound to perfect observation of the natural law in this covenant to eternity ".—RIISSEN (IX, 26) : The question, turned controversial, as to " whether by committing sin man was bound not only to the penalty of of the first sin but also to the provision of a new obedience to the law and to punishment once more, should he sin ", is to be answered in the AFFIRMATIVE. RIISSEN adds the explanation: " The question as to the law's obligation, *whether it binds to obedience and to punishment alike,* arose on occasion of *Cargius'* view of the imputation of Christ's righteousness only in a passive sense, because, the law not having bound sinners to obedience but to punishment only, Christ as substitute in our place should have been due on our behalf the punishment only but not obedience. Now the question is not whether the law binds to obedience and to punishment ; for since it enjoins obedience and forbids disobedience under threat of punishment, clearly man was obligated both ways ; the question is *how ;* whether *it binds at once* or *successively, and whether man the sinner is bound both ways—which we assert* ".

CHAPTER XV

SIN, OR MAN'S STATE OF CORRUPTION AND MISERY

1.—The immediate fruit of the violation of the covenant of works is the introduction among men of the misery of sin.—MASTRICHT (IV, ii, 3). "The first origin of the Adamitic covenant-breaking was man's sin. As angelic sin did not enter the world of angels save by angelic transgression, so human sin did not enter the world of men save by Adam's covenant-breaking Rom. 5. 12 (. . . through one man sin entered into the world, and death through sin; and so death passed to all men, for that all sinned)."—It is to be noted that *Reformed* dogmatics conceives of sin preferably as the misery of sin, whereas the *Lutherans* regard it more as the guilt of sin, and that the former very specially appreciate man's abandonment by grace (*desertio a gratia divina*).

2. *Peccatum*.—LEIDEN SYNOPSIS XVI, 2: "*peccare*, ἁμαρτάνειν, is to wander from the road or mark, i.e., to decline from the prescript of the divine law".—COCCEIUS (*S. T.* XXIV, 2) enumerates the Biblical designations of sin חטאה, *peccatum*; עוון, עול, ἀδικία; בגד, מעל, פשע, ἀνομία; מרי, ἀπείθεια; עברה, παράβασις; מרד, רשע, ἀσέβεια; אשם, טמאה, παράπτωμα, ὀφείλημα, which the synagogue calls חובה ". [But consult Brown, Briggs and Driver].

3.—"Sin is ἀνομία or discrepancy from the law of God, i.e. the failure of nature and of the actions in intelligent natures, fighting with the law of God and involving them in punishment in accordance with the order of divine righteousness" (HEIDEGGER X, 4). Or, "Sin is evil at war with the law of God, taking its price in the will of the rational creature" (POLAN VI. 3). Hence it is not the act itself in which sin is committed, but the contradiction manifested in it to the law of God, that is sin. The outward action as caused by God is good in itself, so that if the man does it with an anti-God intention, it can only be designated sin in an improper sense.

In the earlier Reformed dogmatics it was regarded as quite permissible to describe sin as an *actio*, a *res*, etc. In time it was soon made clear that such a description did not really come to terms with the basic determinism of the system. If a man is determined to the *actio* as such, it cannot of course be said incontinently that "the actual sin is an *actio*", etc. Reformed dogmatics must rather insist that not the *actio* is the sinful deed proper, but the lack apparent in it of a God-given intention, i.e. "the defect consisting in the thing lacking that ought to inhere in it". Hence, e.g. WENDELIN says in the *Collatio*, p. 151, when opposing the *Lutheran* definition: "Sin called actual is not an *actio* formally, but the moral lack of *actio* or the absence of conformity with the law of God, which is called ἀνομία, whence the action is called ἄνομος". Therefore the sinful deed (*materialiter*) can only be called an *actio*, so far as the *actio* is the subject or the *materia in qua* of the sinful deed proper. "Hence the *actio qua actio* is attributed to God; on the other hand the lack inherent in the action belongs not to God but to man or to Satan".—Similarly KECKERMANN 269: "Since sin is not an *actus*, its cause too, properly and *per se*, will not be an *actus* but a *defectus alius*".—The act itself in which the sin is committed is "physically" good; and therefore only improperly can it be described as sin; LEIDEN SYNOPSIS (XVI, 9): "Now the adjacent subject of this sin with which we are dealing—the scholastics call it the material—is a *res* or an *actio* physically good, with which the *privatio* in question coheres as a sort of moral form or rather deformity; whence it happens that not only the actual viciousness but also the whole *actio* together with the viciousness is denominatively (as they say in schools) called sin and evil".—Hence says KECKERMANN, 268: "It is risky to define sin as an *actio*: because every second action is derived from the first Action, namely God. Therefore a thing (*res*) in and for itself is excellent, indeed is the actual perfection of the Actor. Everything is capable of what it does; therefore sin formally is not action itself, but the flaw or defect in an action". In the same sense VOETIUS (I, 1132): "The word *peccatum* may be taken in a double sense: "either abstractly for sin as such or for ἀνομία and defect in human action, speaking with such strictness and precision as to distinguish it from the substrate action or the act and motion itself regarded physically or metaphysically in the category of an *ens;* or concretely for the entire complex consisting of these three elements, (1) the substrate act in which ἀνομία inheres; (2) the actual ἀνομία or moral defect inherent in such act; (3) the ordainability and ordaining of such a sin-laden act to some good. If sin is taken in the first sense, we are now asserting that not a positive decree or volition to effect, but only one to permit, not a positive execution, determination and causality of real providence, but only a pure permission, can be attributed to God in the matter of sin. But if in the second sense we are maintaining that not just a bare permission is to be solely attributed to God, but in addition a real operation according to a positive and effectual decree of will with its adjunct or affect, necessity; not of course absolutely but in a sense confined to the substrate act and to its ordainability and ordaining for good; no one except an *Epicurean*, denies that this is effected by God, the supreme good and first cause."

4.—At the same time sin is not contradiction to the law of God, as though a man's actions in themselves were neutral, and only became sins if in them he acted contrary to an arbitrarily given commandment of God. On the contrary the contradiction to the law consists in contradiction to the holiness of God and to the essential demands of it, i.e. to the image of God in man and to the law of nature.—HEIDEGGER (X, 5): "We do not define sin in such a sense, as though all a man's actions, being by their own nature indifferent and free, were determined by the sole law of God in terms of the decree of His will and lordly command and not by a natural and called-for sanctity, and so nothing is base and ugly by nature in its inception but only by a law freely willed and enjoined.—At all events the fact that we must obey God when He wills and commands, is based not on arbitrary law but on nature, because otherwise all man's obedience would be unrestricted and free.—Alternatively then a thing is termed sin and evil not only by an ἀνομία or defection from a free and arbitrary law of God, but by ἀνομία resting upon defection from the law of nature and the holiness of God."—COCCEIUS (*S.T.* XXIV, 2): Sin is that, "in which the creature departs from God's likeness".

5.—This contradiction to the law man achieves by means of his will; at the same time it is not the spontaneity of the action as such, but the ἀνομία of it, that makes it sin (1 Jn. 3. 4.).—HEIDEGGER (X, 6): "The Scholastics are also very wicked in laying down three requisites of sin, which really dissolve its nature, namely τὸ ἄνομον, its illegality; τὸ ἑκούσιον, its spontaneity; and that, as sinning, it is a particular cause. For the formal nature of sin τὸ ἄνομον suffices; given that sin and everything connected with it is implied; remove it and you remove the sin".—BURMANN (II, vii, 9): "The *Papists* and the *Socinians* are wrong in insisting not upon τὸ ἄνομον only, but also upon τὸ ἑκούσιον in the formal nature of sin; and they will have nothing to be sin except what is equally voluntary, i.e. done knowingly and deliberately."— WENDELIN (I. *cp.* 10, *th.* 11, *expl.* 7): "Sin is not to be assessed by the will of man but by the law of God."—BULLINGER, III, 3: "The law says, Covet not. Therefore although you assent not to the covetousness which inflames you, the very impulse of your flesh is still sin".—MASTRICHT (IV, II, 22) in this connection makes the following distinction: "The Reformed recognise that the will is the direct [δεικτικός—direct as opposed to *reductio ad absurdum*] subject of all moral good and evil. They also recognise that the involuntary element, by which the will positively rejects all collusion, is not sin. But they distinguish between antecedent consent of the will, which is the cause and beginning of action, and concomitant, which applauds already existing sin. In this way they at least deny that previous or antecedent consent is necessarily required to constitute sin, considering that concomitant is sufficient."

6.—Essentially therefore sin in itself is not a negation, nor yet something properly positive or substantial. All positive being is created by God and therefore good as such. Rather sin is in the first instance a privative or *privatio iustitiae,* a lack of harmony in human being and action towards the holiness and law of God. But this lack is not a *mera privatio,* but simultaneously an active quality opposed to the good, an *actuosa privatio* or *vitiositas,* the absolute opposite of righteousness.—POLAN (VI, 3): "The form or formal nature of sin is deformity, i.e. aberration from the divine law, ἀνομία. Accordingly sin is nothing but what is committed against the law of God.—So it is not mere *privatio,* but also an evil quality inherent in a soul, contrary to the good quality which conforms with the law of God. Hence vices are opposed to virtues not just privately. They are contrary qualities".

HEIDEGGER (X, 8): "As to the formal nature of sin the question is, whether it is a *privatio* or something positive. Doctors' opinions vary on the point. But they perhaps admit of reconciliation, if the terms are duly understood and the opinion of certain *Papists* is rejected, who make it consist in the bare *privatio* of righteousness in the first man, as though righteousness had been conferred upon him *supra naturam.* Any sin whatsoever inheres in some habit or action, things which constitute a positive reality created by God, and it affects both habit and action with its ἀνομία and badness. Every evil is in a good and dwells in it as in another man's farm, so that it cannot be separated from it; and the cause and author of all good is God; but of evil as such the author could not be God. To this extent then theologians rightly opine that sin, i.e. the form of evil together with its subject, is something positive, because on the one hand the subject itself, the *habitus* or *actio,* is something positive and God-created, while badness or the form of sin itself affects its subject exactly like a positive thing, affecting as it does and distorting the mind and its actions. In fact it is predicated of the same subject, which it thus affects not only privatively (as they are all said to have turned aside, to have become unprofitable Rom. 3.12), but also positively (as when the law in their members is said to war against the law of the mind and to bring a man into captivity to the law of sin Rom. 7.23, and that every imagination of the thoughts of their heart is only evil continually Gen. 6. 5). So whether living and making its home in *habitus* or in *actio* sin is indeed a *privatio,* but not of any sort". —HEIDEGGER then draws the distinction used by *Thomas* between *privatio pura* and *non pura,* and that in habit and in action: (*privatio pura* in a habit is a deprivation of *esse,* without any of the thing being left, e.g. death, blindness; *privatio non pura* is a *privari* in which some of the *habitus* survives, e.g., sickness; *privatio pura in actione* is e.g., the inability to walk of one born lame, while a *privatio non pura* is the limping which has its cause in a bruised femur) : then he explains that " sin is a *privatio non pura*, because it leaves something original in the habit, namely a propension and proclivity to all evil, and the actual (sin) removes not action but rightness of action ". Only in this sense can we realise "that there is something positive in appearance in the nature of sin whether original or actual", since sin is a *privatio non pura* with a positive quality and action in which vitiosity inheres".— Similarly BUCAN (XV, 7): "Is sin something positive or privative ?— Sin is not a positive, i.e. an existent created by God. Nor is it simply nothing, or a simple pure privation, as death is the *privatio* of life or darkness the *privatio* of light. It is the defect or destruction of a positive entity, namely of the divine work and ordering in a subject, which takes the blame of its depravation, namely aversion from God; like collapse in a house, blindness or loss of vision in eyes. And Paul calls it a defect or privation when he says that "all fall short of the glory of God" (Rom. 3. 23), although outside movements are added, which are positive entities, but yet wandering and confused, as in Cain's murder the movement or raising of his hands is a positive thing. But sin itself is a defection from the law of God and an aberration from the will of God; it is an ἀταξία and a confusion of the divine order. In this sense *Thomas* declares that "sin is not a pure *privatio*, i.e. merely absence of good, but a sort of habit or act robbed of its due order, i.e. a tearing or disturbance of the order, by which all our powers and inclinations ought to be ruled."

LEIDEN SYNOPSIS (XVI, 4-9) : " Our men transmit a fuller definition, namely that it is an act against God's law, offending God and making the sinner liable to God's wrath and to death, except remission be made on account of Christ the mediator. This definition is drawn from 1 Jn. 3. 4 (every one that doeth sin doeth lawlessness : and sin is lawlessness) Gal. 3.10,13 (As many as are of the works of the law are under a curse : for it is written, Cursed is everyone that continueth not in all things that are written in the book of the law to do them (Dt. 27. 26) . . . Christ redeemed us from the curse of the law, having become a curse for us : for it is written, Cursed is everyone that hangeth on a tree (Dt. 21. 23)).— From this definition it is clear that the proper nature and form of this sin consists in the absence of the form of righteousness and holiness, which according to God's law should be in our actions inward or outward, whence too *Augustine's* excellent remark (*De civit. Dei lib.* 11, *c.* 9), that " evil has no nature ; the name of evil is given to the loss of good."— When therefore it is asserted by some writers of the Reformed Church that evil is not a pure privation, this is not to be understood as though evil possessed *per se* some truly positive or metaphysical nature. Every such entity is good and comes from God, alone the author of all good ; for in Him we live and move and are, Ac. 17. 28. This is understood by them of ineffective and otiose privation, such privations as absolutely remove a power, as blindness removes vision.—Now sin is an *actuosa privatio*, whereby the principle of action and the act itself proceeding therefrom is deprived of the only righteousness, by the corruption (not just the removal) of the principle itself, like the loosening of the legbone, from which movement is not taken away, only the ordering and correctness of movement. Whence it comes about that sin is enunciated by Scripture not only negatively but positively and an efficacy is assigned to it contrary and inimical to holiness and righteousness Rom. 8. 7 (the mind of the flesh is enmity against God ; it is not subject to the law of God, neither indeed can it be:) Gal. 5. 17 (the flesh lusteth against the Spirit, and the Spirit against the flesh ; these are contrary the one to the other ; that ye may not do the things that ye would) ; because the movement and action in which the *privatio* inheres, by dint of the inherent privation, opposes the holy and righteous movement and action and in consequence the law of God as well.—Moreover the proximate subject of this sin which we are dealing with (' material ' is the Scholastic term) is a thing or action physically good, in which the *privatio* inheres, like a moral form or rather deformity. Whence it happens that not only the badness itself, but also the whole act conjoined with the badness is called sin and the evil *denominative*, as the schoolmen say ".

7.—The direct effects of sin are defilement, *macula* in the soul (*pollutio spiritualis, difformitas naturae*), as a result of which the soul can no longer be an object of the divine good-pleasure (v. TIL) ; and the *reatus* which it brings upon man. In face of the judicial authority of God sin is essentially the causing of a relationship of guilt, since it makes man guilty and liable to punishment in God's sight.—RIISSEN (IX, 56) : " Two effects of sin are commonly cited, *macula* and *reatus*. *Macula* is the spiritual and moral defilement with which man's soul is infected. *Reatus* is liability to punishment for a previous fault. The latter corresponds to the benefit of justification, by which Christ removes liability from us by the imputation of his own righteousness. The former answers to the benefit of the sanctification of grace, by which the stain is washed out through the efficacy of the H. Spirit ".

8.—In face of God's judicial authority sin is essentially the establishment of a state of guilt, since it makes man guilty in God's sight and liable to punishment. " *Reatus* in a person sinning is obligation to penalties temporal and eternal ; which results from the ordering of the divine righteousness and will " (URSIN, *Loci*. p. 607).—AMESIUS (I, xii, 2) : " *Reatus* is the sinner's obligation to bear just punishment for a fault ".— A distinction is drawn between *reatus potentialis* and *actualis* ; on the other hand the scholastic distinction between *reatus culpae* and *poenae* is rejected. —RIISSEN (IX, 57) : " *Reatus* is potential, when it marks the intrinsic desert of penalty, which is inseparable from sin ; or actual, when it may be separated therefrom by God's mercy, i.e. by remission, which strictly is the removal of actual guilt. The former relates to the demerit of sin and τὸ κατακριτικὸν or its condemnability, which always adheres to sin. The latter belongs to the judgment or κατάκριμα or condemnation of demerit, which is abolished in those to whom forgiveness of sin has been accorded.—59 : But vile is the distinction by the *Papists* of *reatus* into lapse of fault and of punishment. They call it *reatus culpae,* by which of himself the sinner is unworthy of God's grace, deserving moreover of His wrath and damnation ; *reatus poenae,* by which he is exposed to damnation and bound thereto ".—Similarly BRAUN (I, iii, 3, 14) : " *Reatus* then is the state in which a man is liable (*reus*), until he is either acquitted or condemned. Or it is liability to punishment for sin. *Reatus* is distinguished into potential or actual. It is the former, which follows sin from the inner nature of the fault, so far as the sinner by his nature is worthy of punishment and is inseparable from sin. It is the latter, so far as by force of divine law man is ordained to punishment ; but it may by God's mercy be removed from the man, as it has been removed from the elect by the blood of Christ. So *reatus* is something midway between fault and punishment. It arises from fault and leads to punishment, so that there is but a single *reatus culpae* and *reatus poenae*. Therefore the PAPISTS make a foolish distinction between *reatus culpae* and *reatus poenae* ; as though Christ would have freed us from *culpa,* but in such wise that we should pay the *poena* ourselves, either in purgatory or elsewhere. This is most false. Where there is no *culpa,* no *reatus* and no *poena* is conceivable at all."

9.—The cause of sin is not God.—BEZA (I, 361) : " We have already shown that God righteously orders what men do unrighteously ; that God, I mean, makes good use of the sinning instrument. The Lord has one thing in view, His own glory, for which He made even the godless, as Solomon says (Prov. 16. 42). But the perverse will of Satan and wicked men proposes to itself something else. So it happens that in the same work God is righteous, Satan is unrighteous and so are men."

URSIN (*Loci,* p. 624) leads the following arguments to prove that "God is not the cause, effect or author of sin": (1) The express testimonies of

H. Scripture Gen. 1. 31 (God saw everything that he had made, and, behold, it was very good), Ps. 5. 4-6 (Thou art not God that hath pleasure in wickedness: the evil man shall not sojourn with thee. The arrogant shall not stand in thy sight: Thou hatest all workers of iniquity. Thou shalt destroy them that speak lies: the Lord abhorreth the bloodthirsty and deceitful man) Dt. 16. 12 (thou shalt remember that thou wast a bondman in Egypt: and thou shalt observe and do these statutes) 18. 12 (whosoever doeth these things is an abomination unto the Lord: and because of these abominations the Lord thy God doth drive them out from before thee) Lev. 18. 26-29 (Ye therefore shall keep my statutes and my judgments, and shall not do any of these abominations; neither the homeborn, nor the stranger that sojourneth among you: (for all these abominations have the men of the land done, which were before you, and the land is defiled;) that the land vomit not you out also, when ye defile it, as it vomited out the nation that was before you. For whosoever shall do any of these abominations, even the souls that do them shall be cut off from among their people) Prov. 15. 11-13, (Sheol and Abaddon are before the Lord: how much more then the hearts of the children of men! A scorner loveth not to be reproved: he will not go to the wise. A merry heart maketh a cheerful countenance: but by sorrow of heart the spirit is broken . . . Better is little with the fear of the Lord, than great treasure and trouble therewith) etc.; (2) God's absolute holiness, "on account of which it is impossible, that any effect of His should be bad"; (3) God's absolute truthfulness, which puts it beyond doubt "that there are no contradictory wills in Him." Since God attests that He hates sin, He cannot will it; (4) what anyone effects in another he cannot rightly punish. But since God is righteous in His punishment of all sins, He can neither wish nor effect sin.—Scripture teaches "that the efficient *per se* and proper cause of sin is the will of devils and men, by which they freely revolted from God and robbed themselves of God's image".— In addition the *causa peccati* can lie in naught else than in the (personal) will of angels and men (625) : "Sin can be nothing but the proper effect *per se* of that cause which can act against the law. Of this no nature is capable save the angelic and the human. God Himself is the law and cannot do or purpose anything contrary to His own law. Now since other creatures are not rational and so the law was not made for them, they cannot commit sin, since when the law has been removed no room is left for sin. Thus it necessarily follows that sin is such an effect as is competent only to the angels who have lapsed and to men.—P. 628: If it be objected that at least God is the "cause of the cause of sin" (for "God is the cause of the will, which is the cause of sin; therefore He is the cause of the effect of will, and so the cause of sin"), the reply is that "the remote cause (in this case God) is the cause now *per se*, now merely *per accidens*. It is *per se* the cause of an effect, if it not only calls the *causa propinqua* into existence, but also leads and determines it" in producing the effect which it intends— as when God moves the will of man, whom He has made, to good works. When on the other hand "the *causa remota* either does not move the adjacent cause or does not intend the effect of it",—it can only *per accidens* be called the cause of this effect. It is in this way that God creates and moves the will of man. "But because the will of men has been depraved by the devil and by itself, it effects sin, a thing which God neither in creating nor in moving the will intends or thinks to effect". [Cf. Ch. XIV, p. 305 ff. (WITSIUS I, VIII, 23-27)].

10.—The cause of sin is the changeability with which free will in rational creatures has been created. This liability to change is grounded in the fact that man possesses free will, good as such in and for itself, but still as a dependent creation not the absolute good, being incapable of having moral unchangeability in itself; and that he must therefore be able to turn aside from the good.

In order to prove that sin is not *ex Deo* COCCEIUS (*S.T.* XXV) recalls the purpose for which God created man. God created personal beings, because otherwise "all the other things which were made would be in vain; for there would not even be glorification of God or communication of blessedness". The creatures are not created for God's sake, in the sense that God requires them "to complete His beatitude", but "because God displays His perfections to them to be seen and glorified". This glorification of God in creation would still not be possible, were there in it only "a vision of the divine loftiness", were there not a "love" of it as well. God therefore willed to make known and to glorify His majesty precisely in the love which personal creatures have for it. Hence the human spirit had to be so created "as to have a *rectus appetitus*", since otherwise he would not have glorified God. Therefore according to God's eternal law the *mens* was given power over the *libidines*, the result of which was that the counter direction of man's *mens*, i.e. sin, cannot be caused by God. Now by many the possibility of sin is derived from man's freedom (*libertas*), but wrongly. Man's freedom consists in his loyalty to his limitations, to his original nature and to that which is his essential good. (XXV, 10): "It is indeed pre-eminently clear that if any mind persists in its beginning, it is truly free by willing and loving its good; it enjoys freely what it enjoys securely." Since then man in his essence is a creature made for the purpose of glorifying God, it follows all the more (XXV, 27) that "freedom of will is not independence of God." The ground and cause of Adam's sin was not his *libertas* but his mutability.

If merely by his own free will he could already change over to evil, then this very *mutari posse* was not *libertas* but the *libertatis imperfectio,* because it is the *possibilitas servitutis.* Hence we must distinguish between the concepts of *libertas* and *mutabilitas.* Of course it is true that "the election of the will is concerned with good and evil; but the result is not that freedom is indifference to good and evil, far less that mutability is present in freedom. Even God's will is concerned with good and evil not for deliberation, but to will the former and to hate the latter unchangeably. (XXV, 39): But it is just as definitely to be insisted that God has of course created for man freedom of will, but only an imperfect freedom, i.e. freedom and mutability of the will. That God could do this is explained by the οὐδένεια *creatae mentis* (the nothingness of the created mind) over against God. Although on the one hand it was worthy of God to make man in a condition of inclination to Himself the Creator, yet on the other hand man as a creature had no right to claim a permanent indwelling of God's holiness in him. Consequently it was in the creature's power so to turn away from God (XXV, 38), as to make itself, which is nothing, the measure of God's wisdom". Thus fell the Devil, since "the invention of false wisdom, i.e. of a lie, brought him down headlong", and similarly "the mind which was clothed by God with a body and to which He gave command over the bodily members, by gradually dropping God's mastery, while having of its own accord adjudged true the end of a tempting fruit, which was not its true end, fell from its own end and good and beauty".—HEIDEGGER (X, 10) thus replies to the question of the *causa mali*: "Either (1) there is no evil, or (2) it is originally derived from evil, or (3) it is derived from good," and reaches this decision: "If there is no evil, it was in vain the Lord bade us pray "Deliver us from the evil one".—If evil is originally derived from evil, the pestilence of the *Manichees* will triumph, who assert that sin comes of an evil God; thus even God will be evil, i.e. God will not be God.—Nor do those avoid the difficulty who with the *Jews* and the *Pelagians* summon evil from the state of matter, as though it could not have happened that something should be created of matter, which was not concupiscent and had not an evil desire". Hence the conclusion: "It remains that the cause of evil is good, not that supreme and immutable one which is God.—But a lower one, dependent on the supreme One, a rational creature, at once good and free, but, because of the imperfection of a nature made out of nothing and not rising to the perfection of God being created thus *changeably,* could exchange its goodness and freedom for wickedness and slavery.—A good tree can exchange its goodness for badness and thus changed bear evil fruits. The case is analogous of the good rational creature, which, as long as it is such, could not bear evil fruits; but by exchanging its good will for a bad by the conversion not of its nature but of its qualities could germinate none but evil fruits". Then follows the explanation: "This conversion of the will from a good into a bad one arose from the fact that the will, having a wider range than knowledge, fashioned happiness out of things unascertained and unknown and so having abandoned its guide with eyes and having adopted a blind one it fell with him into the pit".—In addition cf. Ch. XIV p. 305 ff.

11.—Since the sin of the entire human race originates in Adam's fall by sin it must be regarded primarily as inherited sin. Sin is so called because it is committed not through the power of bad example tempting to imitation, but through the nature and origin (descent) of man.—LEIDEN SYNOPSIS (XV, 16): "It is certain that sin did not pass into men by imitation but by propagation.—9: It is called original, because it has defiled our birth by hereditary propagation and has settled in us the moment we first became men, and has been canalised into us by the law of nature and of origin".—KECKERMANN, 251: "It is sin of origin or original sin that man drags with him from his first beginning".

12.—Hence sin appears as the natural sin of fallen men, according as man can be completely freed from it only in death. —POLAN (VI, 3): "Whence too sin is natural in us, i.e. because by nature it is in us and so in our nature, not as it was created from the beginning upright by God, but as it has now been depraved, not by a flaw in our common nature (which was common to Adam in his integrity and is common to Christ), but by a flaw in the instrument of primogeniture, through which we have all descended naturally Eph. 2. 3 (.. we also all once lived in the lusts of our flesh, doing the desires of the flesh and of the thoughts, and were by nature children of wrath, even as the rest) Col. 3. 6 (for these things' sake cometh the wrath of God upon the children of disobedience; among whom ye also walked aforetime, when ye lived in these things).—And because original sin is in us by nature, so it is in this life so completely inseparable, that it cannot be laid aside completely except at death".— From this however it follows also that we are not bound to transmit the sins of our other ancestors to our children, as we do the first sin of Adam; BUCAN (XVI, 27): "because that first sin was not so much a personal property of Adam as a natural one, i.e. a common one of the whole of human nature which was originally and naturally in his loins and therefore truly original. But Adam's other sins and those of the rest of humanity have been truly personal, for which see Ezek. 18. 20 (the soul that sinneth, it shall die: the son shall not bear the iniquity of the father, neither shall the father bear the iniquity of the son; the righteousness of the righteous shall be upon him, and the wickedness of the wicked shall be upon him."

13.—"Original sin is not only the absence of original righteousness, but both the depravity and corruption of human nature diffused through every part of the soul and communicated by Adam to his posterity, and the state of liability by which also the very babes at birth are on account of Adam's fall liable to the wrath of God and to eternal death, until remission is made" (BUCAN XVI, 34).—CALVIN (II, i, 8) is already insisting that the description of original sin as the "lack of original righteousness" is unsuitable. "Those who have defined original sin as the lack of the original righteousness which ought to inhere in us, although they include all that is in the matter, yet have not expressed with sufficient significance the force and energy of it. Our nature is not merely poor and empty of good, but so fertile and fruitful in all evils that it cannot be idle".— The later dogmaticians also usually repeat this remark, e.g. MARESIUS IV, 41: "It does not consist solely in the negation and lack of original righteousness, but also in a certain morbid and habitual quality of the soul".— a DIEST 82: "Original corruption consists of two parts, the deprivation of good and the inclination to evil".

14.—Inherited sin includes two things, imputed sin and inherent sin. Imputed sin consists in God's attributing Adam's guilt to all Adam's descendants, because of their natural descent from Adam (i.e. because of the natural unity of the human race in Adam), as their own guilt, as the guilt of their nature.

Original sin includes two things, imputed sin and inherent sin. Many dogmaticians do not use these terms. But they definitely enough describe the concepts expounded by them, usually by the application of the expressions *reatus* (inadequately *culpa*) and *corruptio*. E.g. POLAN (VI, 3), who reckons to original sin (1) "the fault of disobedience or defection from God in Adam's loins" and (2) the "corruption following upon Adam's defection in the whole nature of man". Similarly a DIEST p. 21: "Original sin is the liability and corruption of the whole human race inherent, as the result of the first fall, right from the origin of conception".—It was most usual to describe inherited sin as "imputed" and "original sin". Cf. KECKERMANN, 253: "(Original sin) is either imputed or inherent. Imputed original sin is the actual defection or first prevarication committed by Adam and Eve by the eating of the forbidden fruit, but imputed to the entire subsequent human race naturally produced by these two first persons". —BRAUN (I, iii, 3, 16): "Original sin is either imputed or inherent. Imputed sin is Adam's actual lapse according as all men are regarded as having sinned in Adam, and so are held worthy of the same punishment into which Adam hurled himself; (1) because Adam was the head of the whole human race and the first party to the covenant; (2) because all men were in the same covenant along with Adam, therefore they broke the covenant along with him; (3) all would have participated in the benefits, if Adam had stood out Gen. 1. 26-28 (And God said, Let us make man in our image, after our likeness: and let them have dominion over the fish of the sea, and over the fowl of the air, and over the cattle, and over all the earth, and over every creeping thing that creepeth upon the earth . . . and God blessed them: and God said unto them, Be fruitful, and multiply, and replenish the earth, and subdue it; and have dominion over the fish of the sea, and over the fowl of the air, and over every living thing that moveth upon the earth); (4) all to this day participate in the blessing, Increase and be multiplied; (5) All are under the same threat ; and so (6) under the effects of sin, under the curse and the same evils, pain, sweat, toil and death (Gen. 3. 16 etc. : Unto the woman he said, I will greatly multiply thy sorrow and thy conception; in sorrow thou shalt bring forth children ; and thy desire shall be to thy husband, and he shall rule over thee. And unto Adam he said, Because thou hast hearkened unto the voice of thy wife, and hast eaten of the tree, of which I commanded thee, saying, Thou shalt not eat of it : cursed is the ground for thy sake; in toil shalt thou eat of it all the days of thy life etc.); (7) our soul is produced devoid of original holiness; which cannot be, unless as a punishment for Adam's sin ; (8) in cited words we say that all have sinned in Adam Rom. 5. 12, that in Adam all die, that in Christ all may be made alive 1 Cor. 15. 22. Indeed death is said to reign even in those who did not sin after the likeness of Adam's transgression Rom. 5. 12, which ought to be understood of the very infants in their mother's womb or only just born".—God thus imputes Adam's guilt to all his successors because of their natural connection with him (Adam); RIISSEN (IX, 5): "We teach that Adam's actual sin is actually so imputed to all his descendants in the ordinary way, that on this account all are deemed criminals and either pay the penalty or are at least considered worthy of punishment".—And this is not done arbitrarily. As the result of our natural connection with Adam (BRAUN, I, iii, 3, 17) "we are born devoid of holiness on account of some sin": not on account of our own sin, since we could have committed no actual sin before we were born, therefore on account of another's sin, namely Adam's. Similarly LEYDECKER 165: "It would not have been fair and right for the crime of one angel to have been imputed to another, or one man's sin to be deemed another's, it being laid down that each of them separately had been created equal to the angels. Here therefore we must first regard the natural unity between

Adam and his posterity—upon which a covenanted unity was based. Our own CALVIN it is true fails to recall such a covenant in his eloquence, only the divine will and ordering by which it was ordained, so that the gifts which He had conferred on the first man he at once possessed and destroyed for himself and his heirs alike (*Instit.* II, 1).—171: Thus we have sin imputed; presently there follows sin as inherent".

HEIDEGGER (X, 32) explains what is meant by imputation: "To impute is not simply to think or simply to judge that some one has thought, willed or done what he has not actually thought, willed or done; it is to make the same judgment about one who has not done, as about another who has done a thing. In this sense Adam's sin by which he ate the fruit of the forbidden tree (not the rest of his sins committed after the fall when he no longer played the role of a public person) is imputed to all to be sprung naturally from Adam unto condemnation because of their connection with him; i.e., although Adam's sin was not actually committed by them, it is ascribed to them, so that because of it or in respect of it they may undergo liability and pay the penalty or at least be held worthy of all punishments. And in fact the hinge of the matter turns upon this imputation of Adam's sin, which is of the greatest importance".—Similarly MASTRICHT (IV, II, 10): "Imputation does not consist in a mere thought, by which God thinks that the covenant-breaking by the protoplasts had not only been perpetrated by them, but actually and personally by their posterity as well".—WOLLEB 41: "The proximate cause of original sin is liability for the first sin, in respect of which it is God's most just punishment".—For "although man's soul is breathed directly into him by God, it is nevertheless by its union with the body guilty of the first sin imputed to man as such, and so he is infected by that original defilement".

It was thus that predominant Church doctrine conceived the nature of the "imputation of Adam's sin", "direct imputation", as later Reformed dogmatics usually expressed it (cf. BURMANN p. 444), "imputed original sin", and its relation to "inherent sin". Of course objection was taken to this concession by the *Academy of Saumur*. But the *Form. Cons. Helv.* rejected this objection in article 10 [See Ch. XIV, 10]. The French Synod at Charenton had already in the year 1644 excluded all who denied this *imputatio* from participation in the Church's ministry. Among the later men WYTTENBACH (*Tent.* VII, 806ff, 812ff) still cling to the prevalent view. Its most famous opponent apart from *Joshua Placaeus* of Saumur was the Englishman named *Daniel Whitby* (*Tract. de imput. divina peccati Adami posteris eius universis in reatum ; Londini* 1711). ENDEMANN disassociated himself at least from the prevalent doctrine. As the customary proof of the latter he adduces the following arguments (*Instit.* I, p. 346 f.) : "(1)

Men are wretched the moment they are born; this misery is a divine punishment. It is only sinners God punishes; therefore men are sinners before they are born; which cannot happen, unless Adam's sin is considered to be their sin. (2) God foresaw that each of Adam's posterity put in his own place would sin and that then this world would not be very good, that therefore all might be justly punished: that God acted kindly in appointing Adam the first man, in allowing his fall and imputing it (p. 30) to his posterity. (3) Appeal is made to Rom. 5. 12ff, 1 Cor. 15. 21 (p. 332). (4) They teach that the thing is readily conceivable. Adam's posterity consented to the covenant of works and hence were also bound to consent to its results; hence by consent Adam's sin became sin shared in by his posterity, and so they were justly punished for Adam's sin. (5) They add that he who denies this direct imputation likewise denies the imputation of Christ's merit".—Against this proof, to establish a merely mediate imputation ENDEMANN validates the following arguments: (1) "God punishes no one with eternal punishments for Adam's fall alone; (2) argument No. 1 is void of proof, since the misery in which men are born is not a punishment strictly so called; (3) argument No. 2 is a sheer fiction: if God were for damning men for sins which they would have been sure to commit if placed in different circumstances, he would be damning them all; (4) the dicta appealed to in argument (3) obviously do not prove direct imputation; (5) argument 4 proves nothing, because there is no covenant of works, and even if there is one to the nth, tacit consent cannot be elicited from the idea of a covenant. To prove consent to Adam's sin from the sins that belong to his posterity is to be guilty of begging the question; our own sins arise from original sin, which does not depend upon us. (6) Argument 5 they plainly reject; the imputation of Christ's merit obviously does not depend upon the imputation of Adam's sin".

15.—Upon this attributed guilt of disobedience, as a just punishment of it, rests the corruption, or inherent original sin, with which God allows every descendant of Adam to enter life, and which at the root of all individual sins Rom. 6. 6 (our old man was crucified with Christ, that the body of sin might be done away, that so we should be no longer in bondage to sin) is also called the body of sin and is real sin.—HEIDEGGER (X, 39): "From the defection of Adam's heirs in his loins immediately flows the corruption of actual human nature or inherent original sin, which by impure generation is propagated into human individuals".—MASTRICHT (IV, II, 13): "From imputed sin, part one of original sin, also flows part two, inherent sin, when on account of the thing imputed God, to punish us, does not bestow upon us the original righteousness of His image, and in its absence nothing can possibly be there except complete unrighteousness".—KECKERMANN 254: "Inherent original sin is a disposition of the human faculties with a proclivity for evil, arising from the privation of those powers, which man used to possess for good before the Fall".—Many expressly insist that original sin, and imputed as well as inherent, had also existed in the mother of Christ; that on the other hand Christ himself was free from original sin, this resulting from the following reasons (BRAUN I, III, 3, 20), "(1) because he was not in Adam's covenant; (2) he was not born in virtue of the general blessing, Increase and be multiplied Gen. 1. 28, but in consequence of the special pact between Father and Son ; (3) he was conceived by the H. Spirit Lk. 1. 35. Therefore (4) the woman's, not the man's seed is mentioned Gen. 3. 15 ".—This *inherent original sin* is really sin : ZANCHIUS 37 : "Although this contagion, in order to punish the first transgression of the divine mandate, was inflicted not on Adam only but also on the whole of his posterity, yet it was not only the punishment of sin and the cause of all sins forthwith; it was also truly sin, so that even by itself it is sufficient for condemnation; of this we are as sure from the sacred books as of what is most sure."—CROCIUS 927: "The badness contrary to the image of God, which corrupts human nature, is evil concupiscence, which is both truly sin and the source of all sins.—Inherited sin, concupiscence, is thus already sin in and for itself. So it cannot be said that it only becomes sin, if man takes it up in his personal will and activates it thereby. On an adequate view even the very first impulses of concupiscence (i.e., the corruption clinging to the originally pure natural impulse) are never *involuntarii* ; which is why the view put forward by P. MARTYR among others is rejected, that in and by itself concupiscence is something intermediate. For this reason ZWINGLI's view also is naturally excluded: in original sin he saw merely an infirmity, a sickness, from which actual sins proceed, a punishment for the fall by sin, but not the individual's guilt and sin proper (cf. ZELLER, p. 59ff).—KECKERMANN 275: "(The Papists) declare that these first motions are involuntary and so are not sins. Ans. (1) The major is false. There is no involuntary sin. Sin of origin is truly sin, even if it does not include the assent of the will. (2) Moreover these motions are not altogether involuntary. We have attracted them by our will; and will, which is rational desire, is always conjoined with sense desire, even to the extent that the actual sense desire in man responds proportionally to the will. Be that as it may, these first movements we speak of are held by some theologians, particularly PETER MARTYR, to be something midway between original and actual sin, because the express and full will does not concur in such impulses, as it concurs in sins perpetrated with the assent of the will. But there is nothing to hinder us referring these motions also to original sin; concupiscence is of course actual sin; moreover these motions are either parts or first points, as we have said already, of concupiscence".

16.—This corruption is a twofold one, (1) "the defect of original good" and (2) "the succession of evil to the place of original good". The defect is a *privatio* of original righteousness and of the gifts and graces which man's spiritual and bodily nature originally enjoyed.—POLAN (VI, 3): "Defect of original good is the innate corruption or pravity by which our whole nature has been deprived of the original goodness or grace in which the first man had been created. This defect is in the whole man, both soul and body. Original sin is in the whole man, soul and body: in the soul strictly as in its proper subject, in the body as in an instrument through which the soul acts. In the soul the defect or vacuity is of original goodness and grace in every part, i.e. in the mind and in the will. The mind is robbed of the light and health of intelligence and reason. The will has been shorn of uprightness and freedom for good pleasing to God. Moreover the body has been robbed of conformity in affections and desires and locomotion with the law of God".

17.—The original condition has been replaced by evil concupiscence, that is, such depravity of the whole man, body and soul, that not only are the lower physical impulses thrown out of their usual order, but the will, the appetitive faculties and therewith the entire inner life of man, his very heart, have assumed an anti-god attitude and tendency, in fact a fleshly tendency; whence another name for concupiscence is the flesh lusting against the Spirit. In short the forces, attributes and organs of the body are filled and dominated by it.—POLAN (VI, 3): "The evil which has succeeded to the place of original good is that innate corruption or pravity, by which the whole nature is rendered unsuitable for good and merely prone to evil. It is called by the Apostle Paul Rom. 7. 7 coveting or cupidity, which is not the material or the matter in which or the subject of Original Sin; it is formally original sin itself, although original sin is situate in it by synecdoche. It is not just the disorder of lower forces in the soul, like sensuality or sensory and animal appetition, by the forceful assault of which we are forced into things sensory and carnal, which we deem desirable on account of something pleasant in them, shaking off the rule of reason; it is also the mad inclination and propensity of the very mind with which we think, ponder, contrive and will, and indeed even of the supreme and strongest part of the soul and its faculties for every impiety and unrighteousness. To put it more clearly it comprehends every disposition and every outlook opposed to the law of God, even in the higher part of the soul, in the most intimate recesses of the mind.—It is to be distinguished from natural concupiscence, that which God sowed in our nature, such as the concupiscence for food and drink, by which our bodies are nourished.—Evil concupiscence of itself is sin, even if the consent of the will be not added."

18.—Concupiscence is thus a fallibility in man's whole nature, caused by sin, which makes him guilty and so dominates all the impulses and utterances of his life, that he is not free of it until death.—LEIDEN SYNOPSIS (XV, 30-31) : " Those who taking the word in a wide sense have called this corrupt habit concupiscence have agreed with Scripture as to its general meaning. By the title flesh and concupiscence, which it attacks as evil and vicious, Scripture does not mean appetition in general, as embracing reason as well as sensibility, nor sensibility as a species, nor the appetition particularly called concupiscent, nor any other natural faculty or condition of human nature *per se*. These things were taken up into Adam at the beginning of creation, and by Christ along with the truth of his human nature. Concupiscence is the defect (*vitium*) in the nature, which wrought its way into it by sin and infected it guiltily, so to speak. Moreover it has to do with all those things which may be sought out evilly and inordinately by man. Thus after the apostle Gal. 5. 17 had said that the flesh lusteth against the Spirit, to show how widely such concupiscence extends, he appended a list of some works of the flesh, among which he enumerates not only fornication, uncleanness, etc., which are committed by sensory appetition and are called specifically carnal sins ; but also poisonings, enmities, contentions, murders, sects or heresies and the kind of things usually called spiritual sins. By calling them flesh and concupiscence the apostle indicated evil inciting to any sin ".—For not merely the lower sense faculties of man but also the higher spiritual ones are destroyed by original sin ; RIISSEN (X, 38) : " This hereditary defilement infected not the lower part of the soul only, τὸ αἰσθητικὸν and the senses, as the *Papists* would have it with their patronage of free will, but also the higher part, τὸ λογικόν, i.e. *intellectus* (knowledge) and will. Hence blindness and ignorance are assigned to the mind, rebellion and contumacy to the will ; and the whole man through and through is called corrupt, so that he can know nothing true and produce nothing good and requires regeneration and sanctification for both his parts ".

19.—The subject of original sin is thus the whole man, including body and soul.—BUCAN (XVI, 30) : " What then is the subject of original sin ? The whole man, body and soul, from head to foot, with all his forces and faculties of body and mind, higher and lower, mind, will, sensibility ; hence the Apostle Eph. 4. 17-18 contends that the mind is addicted to

vanity, the thoughts to blindness and the heart to wickedness. And Rom.
8. 7 τὸ φρόνημα τῆς σαρκὸς is enmity towards God. The same thing
is made clearer by the renewal, which the Apostle applies to mind, soul
and body ".

20.—Meantime concupiscence must not be confused with the natural
impulses, so far as God has created them and has willed their satisfaction.—
BUCAN (XVI, 31) : " Concupiscence is not, however, natural appetition
for food, drink, procreation, and delight in the senses ; in itself this is not
sin, provided it is ordered and seeks after what is lawful. Nor movements
of the heart so far as they are affections. Nor just ἀταξία of the
appetitions. It is the propension of all the forces to do what is prohibited
by the law of God, such as confusion or doubt in the mind about God and
His providence ; in the will and heart, contumacy against God ".—In
this way the erroneous dogmas of the Roman Church on concupiscence
are excluded, especially the opinion that it has its seat in man's physical
nature ; KECKERMANN, p. 274: " The *Papists* have some grave errors on the
doctrine of concupiscence. (1) They say that concupiscence resides only
in sensuality, as the barbarians say, i.e., in sensory appetition but not in
the will. (2) Concupiscence is the material of sin of origin, as BELLARMINE
lays down among others (V, 5), on the state of sin. But we showed
before that original sin resides in the faculties, but concupiscence in the
act of will and appetition. (3) It is wrong to say that concupiscence was
natural for man created *in puris naturalibus,* as *Bellarmine* asserts in the
passage quoted. Moreover man created *in puris naturalibus* is the
name for him considered before the fall, without the gift of the
divine image, equipped only with the powers of nature. But how,
I ask, can concupiscence be natural to man, when no vice is
natural but counter to nature ? And since natural things are
permanent, the defect of concupiscence would likely cease to adhere
to man in the second life. (4) The mistake which *Bellarmine* makes
there is that concupiscence consists of habits, not of acts ; since
linguistic use shows that concupiscence is one thing, the potentiality
of concupiscence another."

21.—Concupiscence then is not the substance of human nature but an
accident of it.—LEIDEN SYNOPSIS (XV, 23) : " It does not therefore follow
that concupiscence is the substance or the substantial image of the devil
in man or in man's actual soul or heart Rom. 7. 20-21 (if what I would not,
that I do, it is no more I that do it, but sin which dwelleth in me. I find
then the law, that, to me who would do good, evil is present), Heb. 12. 1
(let us . . . lay aside every weight and the sin which doth so easily beset

us).—It inheres in man like an accident in a subject. Although in corrupt man these things are not to be torn asunder, yet we claim that they must be distinguished. The Creator of all substances is God ; but sin was neither created by God, nor is it a creature or an essence at all. Even Adam after sin retained the essence of his nature the same as he had it before and was the same man. Moreover our nature is changed neither by sin nor by grace into a different essence, even if it is infected with evil or perfected by good."—BUCAN (XVI, 28) : " Is sin of origin a substance or an accident ? It is not a substance ; for it would be soul or body. Now as a substance body and soul are good creations of God, still being created by God. Therefore they are not sin. Nor is it a substantial attribute or something substantial in man. It is an adventitious quality, which is yet called natural, not because it has flowed from nature (inasmuch as it was created) but because, as the saying is, it holds its own in ward by a hereditary right and it inheres in human nature in its natural forces and faculties and is innate in man himself Eph. 2. 3 (. . . we also all once lived in the lusts of our flesh, doing the desires of the flesh and of the mind and were by nature children of wrath, even as the rest) Rom. 7, 17, 20, 21 (it is no more I that do it, but sin, which dwelleth in me . . . If what I would not, that I do, it is no more I that do it, but sin which dwelleth in me. I find then the law, that to me, who would do good, evil is present)." —LUD. CROCIUS 926 : " Original sin is not man's actual nature and substance, but is the inmost corruption of the entire human nature and substance, the result of evil which disturbs it on all sides ".—HEIDEGGER (X, 44) : " This corruption befalls the powers, the qualities and the organs of the human body. Powers are faculties implanted in man by nature, the principles of human actions. They are both higher and lower, and are so distinguished not by local distribution but by dignity of function and operation. The higher are mind and will, the lower the sensory and vegetative of which the former is seen partly in the outer and inner senses, partly in the affections; the latter is exercised in the faculty of generation and nutrition. In these severally the original defilement has its seat."–– CALVIN (IV, xv, 10-11) : " So these two points are strictly to be observed ; namely, that being thus vitiated and perverted in every part of our nature, already we are deservedly, merely for such corruption, held condemned and convicted in the sight of God, to whom nothing is acceptable except righteousness, innocence and purity. And thus even the very babes broadcast their own damnation from their mother's womb.—The second is, that this perversity never ceases in us, but steadily produces fresh fruits, those which we have previously described as the works of the flesh : exactly as a blazing furnace constantly gives off flame and sparks, or a spring puts forth water endlessly. Concupiscence plainly never perishes or is extinguished in men, until, delivered by death from the body of death, they forthwith put off themselves."

22.—Concupiscence is then the faulty condition of human nature, and is first of all a *privatio iustitiae originalis*. But it is not a mere *privatio* ; it is simultaneously a positive evil, since it evokes definite effects in man's inner and outer life, to wit, obscuration of the capacity for knowledge, alienation from God and weakness in the will, the enslavement of man by selfishness, generally speaking his spiritual death.—HEIDEGGER (X, 43) : " This corruption has affected the whole man consisting of soul and body ; although it is not the actual substance of man."—MASTRICHT (IV, II, 33) : " The *Reformed* believe that it (original defilement) is a sort of accident, intimately inhering in the whole substance ".—POLAN (VI, 3) explains more adequately : " Sin of origin is not the actual substance of man, as *Flacius Illyricus* would have it, but an accident, in fact a vicious habit ; nor is it the first man's liability to punishment for sin, as the *Scot* and *Gabriel Biel* have contended, nor is it sheer, naked privation ; it also includes positive elements, namely corrupt habit or positive corruption and a habitual disposition or ability, proneness and propension to evil, an impulse of nature counter to God's word and others of that kind. By a positive we mean not a subsistent thing created by God, but that which is not simply nothing or a simple privation, as death is the privation of life or darkness the privation of light ; but that which is at once the defect and destruction of a positive thing created by God and a vicious habit exciting and begetting inward and outward movements deviating from God's law and displeasing to God. None the less concupiscence is rightly called a privation, because it is an aberration from God's law ".

HEIDEGGER proceeds (X, 48) from the statement : " The formal reason of original sin consists neither in liability for another's sin, nor in concupiscence alone nor in the bare lack of righteousness, but in the active absence of righteousness and in lively evil," and he continues : " This sin is of course the lack of original righteousness, which was natural to the first man ; yet not bare lack, but such as places ignorance in the understanding, aversion from good in the will, and conversion to evil, rebellion in the will ; in all these spiritual death in what is good and the liveliest life in what is evil. It is not a privation void of all action or leaving no strength to act, like blindness. It is active, busy, maddened, abolishing the strength to act well, but for the rest inclining and distorting the faculties, affected so to speak by their own poison, to act evilly."—(RIISSEN IX, 36-37) : " Original inherent sin is that sinful disposition, by which man is inept for any good and inclined to all evil.—37. It is called a positive quality according as by it man is truly deprived of a good habit, which should be in him and is disposed and urged towards every evil. Here then we must hold that one thing is a positive physically, in the sense in which being and good are convertible and nothing is positive which is not from God ; another is a positive ethically and logically, which is affirmed of the subject in which it inheres, whether it be good or evil. Positive sin is taken not in the former sense, but in the latter ; and so it may have a positive cause not physically, because in this way it is only a deficient cause, but logically and ethically, because it induces a positive quality " (not a substance but a *virtus*).

23.—The transmission of sin is not to be explained by assuming a trans mission of souls by paternal seed affected by sin, nor by the sin-permeated act of begetting, nor above all *per traducem*, since rather for each new-begotten body God creates the soul and lets sin be so inherited in it, that He (1) attributes Adam's guilt to it (whereupon He fails to bestow on it the gift of *iustitia originalis*) and (2) imparts to it the state of corruption, to which man's nature has descended through Adam's fall.—What has just been imparted is to be regarded as the prevailing answer to the question as to the *propagatio peccati*. At the same time divergent views were also urged. On the content and compass of the *propagatio peccati* all were of course agreed. All teach like COCCEIUS (S.T. XXX), who distinguishes the following five points in the *propagatio peccati* : (1) The bodily successors (*ex coniunctione maris et feminae geniti*) received from Adam the *imputatio peccati actualis primi sive transgressionis Adami* ; (2) They received " the lack of righteousness, i.e. of the uprightness, with which man had been created, or of the divine image in the stricter sense of the word ; (3) perversion of the mind to creation and to sensible things ; (4) bad conscience, which frightens man away from God's judgment, so that he says to God : Turn from me (Job 21.14) ; and (5) increasing immersion in sin. On the other hand hesitations appear here and there, though quite isolated, in the conceiving of the question, how this *propagatio* is to be explained. Particularly teachers declare that the setting up of a definite theory is impossible, e.g. WITTACKER, *De pecc. orig.* I, 8 : " How sin was propagated from Adam to posterity ought rather to be believed than asked, and to be asked more easily than it can be understood and better understood than explained." Others, older dogmaticians, teach that sin is so propagated by generation, that the soul is infected and destroyed by the sin-dominated body, e.g. P. MARTYR 164 : " If it be asked, what is its seat, or, as is commonly said, what the subject is, we answer that it has its place in the flesh as in its root and principle : thereafter from that source it also seizes the soul and so spreads through the whole man. Therefore seed (*semen*) is the instrument by which this sin is transmitted from parents to sons—p. 178. "A fourth way is accepted with great agreement and seems very probable, namely that a soul is not created with sin but immediately contracts it the moment it is joined to a body derived from Adam. Since it lacks grace and the virtues with which the first soul of man was endued, and also acquires a body liable to a curse, and has unsuitable organs little fitted for spiritual works, when it ought to be ruling the body, it is weighed down and depressed by it and drawn to desires suited to the body. It is weakened on both sides, by the impurity of the body and by its own weakness, because it is destitute of the strength to overcome nature. From these two heads depend the depravity and corruption of the entire nature ".—Similarly POLAN (VI, 3) : " Query : how was original sin sidetracked on to us and contracted by us ? Ans. : Sin was transmitted by the paternal seed ; propagated in the paternal semen the corruption infected the soul, and as GERSON says in his 'Compend of Theology' on the flaws in nature, from its conjunction with the body it contracts the flaw in question ; as a man is filthed and spotted when he falls into slime. First of all person infected nature, but thereafter nature infects person, as theologians generally declare. If the person is infected by the nature, this must occur through the semen ".—ARETIUS expresses himself still more strongly (*Theol. probl.* VII, 2) : " Here the usual question is, how this evil is directed towards us. And what reaches the body is easily answered. We derive the body from Adam through generation ; there is no other way by which we are connected with him.—Further, the reason why impurity reaches us is more obscure. Some would say that souls were given at the same time as bodies, and to make this more probable they added that Eve had received both from Adam. Both statements are alike obscure and troublesome for an obvious reason. It is not clear that there is the same transmission of souls from Adam's soul, as may be readily gathered from the derivation of our bodies from his body, *per semen.* And our souls have no such seed ; nor do souls copulate like bodies to preserve the individuals of one species, man. Accordingly others preferred the fresh creation of souls daily, but corrupt, to be like the bodies also corrupt, like a bad guest assigned to a bad domicile. But a greater subsequent difficulty oppresses us. If God creates them bad, and that is the reason for damning them, since they were created thus, don't they seem to be throwing back the blame for sin upon God ? Away with them and their conjectures !—The received opinion is that they are created daily by infusion and infused by creation but in purity ; yet they contract defilement by union and inter-course with the body ".—Be that as it may, this view met with very lively contradiction. DANAEUS was already teaching (*Christ. isagoge ad locos communes* III, II, 18) thus : " *Augustine* teaches that the soul, which is created fresh by God and infused into the body, is not defiled by the flesh and he refutes those who think that it is infused into man by God in defilement. Strictly sin or *macula* is not in the body but in the soul. So it is not soul that is infected by the body but the body that is infected by the soul ". The earlier German-Reformed dogmatics also shows that no definite doctrinal conception on this point could be evolved for a longish time. PEZEL inclines to come down on the side of traducianism. At the same time he recognises that creatianism also has much in its favour. Hence PEZEL leaves the whole question unsolved and recommends us to be content with the truth adequately guaranteed in Scripture, that Adam lost the gifts imparted to him by God not merely for himself but also for all his successors.—On the other hand SOHNIUS (*Exeg. conf. Aug.* p. 606) expresses himself decidedly in favour of traducianism : " The whole man is suitably procreated from the whole man, body being roused out of body, soul kindled so to speak at soul ; thus sin also is propagated from man to man, so that like parents, also like offspring ". In confirmation SOHNIUS adduces the passage in which " Adam is said to have begotten son Seth in the image of himself, i.e. such as he was himself after the fall."—URSIN again already represents the later orthodox doctrine quite definitely (p. 53): " Original sin passes over neither through the body nor through the soul but through impure generation of the whole man on account of the first parent's fault, for which by a just judgment God in creating souls at the same time deprives them of their original righteousness and of the gifts which He had conferred on the parents, on the condition that they should confer them on their children or destroy them, if they should themselves refrain or lose them." With this URSIN also finds it compatible to recognise the truth of the proposition that the God-created soul is rendered corrupt by the perished body into which God pours it. For since one may speak of " an admixture of body vicious and prone to things evil," he may also allow himself to say that corrupted bodiliness corrupts " the soul not confirmed in righteousness ". HYPERIUS, who at the same time did obeisance to creatianism, quite definitely taught inheritance of sin, not " according to the soul " but " according to the flesh " (p. 447): " It is agreed of course that the soul does not arise by transmission, but that, as we showed above, the souls of individual men are created new by God and sent down into bodies, what time they are being shaped in the womb. Moreover men all receive from the first parent and so successively from the rest of their ancestors. Therefore, since this first flesh from being hale and unimpaired has become morbid and corrupt through sin, the necessary effect is that all men's flesh has been infected by the like flaw and corruption ". A modification of this, which aimed at being on terms with the prevailing creatianism, was expounded by KECKERMANN, who assumed that not sin itself, but its seed, principle or layout, was procreated by the physical route. Here is KECKERMANN's teaching (p. 257-258): " My view is that sin cannot be said to be propagated by the parent in the offspring, regarded *per se* and *secundum se*, as though the actual sin already constituted proceeds from the parents and infects the offspring, but a certain principle of this sin, i.e. the thing from which sin may arise, descends from parents to progeny, to wit, a disposition to an evil temperament of the kind of man who is near sin of origin, is propagated through seed. And while the infant is being formed in the mother's womb through the medium of things spiritual, vital and animal, a kind of impression of the mother herself is made on the infant, and from this impression this sin breeds, as fire is conceived from fuel, while the fuel is yet not the fire itself. Further the child as a whole draws into itself this fuel and impression, as it were, exactly as children usually derive from their parents not the identically same diseases, like gout, stone etc., but certain impressions and dispositions, which are the fixed principles of the diseases in question ".— BURMANN (p. 453) distinguishes a propagation of the first sin *quoad animam* and also one *quoad corpus* ; since in the first respect the soul " having been judged in Adam and found guilty of his lapse ", is created by God " bare and unclad, minus all spiritual grace and ornament ", which is nothing but the justest punishment of the fall of human nature; and since in a second respect the soul is corrupted immediately after the birth of man by the "contagion of the body".—In similar fashion other dogmaticians as well in manifold expressions stress *semen impurum* to explain the *propagatio peccati*, e.g. HEIDEGGER and HOTTINGER, the latter of whom (p.165) says : " The manner of the derivation of original sin is a combination of the imputation of Adam's sin and impure generation." In any case both recognise imputation as the most essential and insist upon creatianism. HEIDEGGER teaches (X, 54) : " Others when determining more accurately the first soul of sin and its principal seat assert that, being judged in Adam and by his lapse made guilty by God ; not just as the Creator in virtue of the blessing, Increase and be multiplied, Gen. 1. 28 (words which also contain the promise of divine concurrence to perfect or to form the body from semen and to supply what man cannot make by creating the soul), but chiefly by Him as judge ; the soul was produced lacking the image of God and original righteousness and united to the body it was inclined and converted to unrighteousness because of the lack of righteousness. They insist that this lack or deprivation of original righteousness from the point of view of God who deprives is a punishment and judgment for Adam's sin. This sin is imputed as a judgment of it, precisely because Adam's descendants, who consisted of body and soul, were in him when he sinned. But from the standpoint of the soul deprived it is a fault and sin, because it had become it to bear and preserve the image of God which it had received in Adam, and where it lost it in Adam it saddled itself with a serious sin. It is added that the soul thus sick and not knowing how to rule itself is not only received in that defiled bosom of a body and immersed in it, feeling and suffering the movements of its brother, the impulses and storminess of its blood and spirits which are the pullulations of sin ; but it is thrust into the world as a sort of common hospital, where driven into sinning by most potent enticements and being unwarlike and unfortified by garrisons it is open to rapers like a woman, and developing into greater ungodliness (2 Tim. 2. 16) it becomes the spoil and sport of all sinners ".

Most Church teachers express themselves like AMESIUS (I, XVII, 1): " (1) It is by this propagation that the whole posterity of man descended from Adam in the natural manner becomes a partaker in the same condition as himself Jn. 14. 4 (whither I go ye know the way) Ps. 51. 6 (thou desirest truth in the inward parts) Rom. 5.14 (death reigned from Adam until Moses, even over them that had not sinned after the likeness of Adam's transgression, who is a figure of him that was to come) Eph. 2. 3 (. . . we also all once lived in the lusts of our flesh, doing the desires of the flesh and of the thoughts, and were by nature children of wrath, even as the rest) ; and this by the just ordinance of God. (2) This propagation of sin consists of two parts, imputation and real communication.—(3) By imputation the same individual act of disobedience which was Adam's becomes ours also.—(4) By real communication ; not the same individual sin but the same in kind and like it in principle and in nature is turned on to us.—(6) Thus this *privatio* is transmitted by Adam by the scale of merit so far as it is a punishment, and by the scale of real effectiveness, so far as it has the nature of sin in addition. By the fact that a man is born the son of Adam he is rendered worthy of being deprived of the gift of righteousness ; since he ought to possess the latter and does not, the lack is sin for him ".—MASTRICHT's teaching is the same (IV, II, 19) : " This propagation does not take place by imitation alone ; even infants are propagated yet are incapable of imitation Rom. 5.15 (not as the trespass is the free gift. If by the trespass of one the many died, much more did the grace of God, and the gift by the grace of the one man, Jesus Christ, abound unto the many) ; nor by the female transmission, according to which the actual corruption passes with the soul from parents to off-spring, since not only his soul is " concreated " for a man by God Zech.12. 1 (the Lord . . . formeth the spirit of man within him) Eccl. 12. 7 (the dust returned to the earth as it was, and the spirit returned unto God who gave it) Heb. 12. 9 (fathers of our flesh . . . the Father of our spirits), but by the very transmission itself necessarily becomes material and composite and so dissoluble and mortal as well ; by the fact that the corruption-bearing soul cannot pass entire from parent to son, it accordingly remains for us to insist that a part only is transferred. Nor even separately : either through the body, since with the soul withdrawn it is a brute thing utterly incapable of good and evil ; or by the soul, since, as we said, it is concreated by God for each. Nothing then is left but to declare that it takes place (1) by imputation or by desert, so far as God adjudges the first covenant-breaking by the protoplasts to have been committed also by the entire human race Rom. 5. 12 (through one man sin entered into the world, and death through sin ; and so death passed unto all men, for that all sinned) 1 Cor. 15. 21-22 (by man came death, by man came also the resurrection of the dead. As in Adam all die, so also in Christ shall all be made alive) ; (2) by real communication, so far as God on account of the covenant-breaking committed in the protoplasts no longer confers on all their posterity the original righteousness of His image, i.e. wisdom on the mind, righteousness and holiness on the will, uprightness and submission on their affections."—In the same sense WOLLEB 41 : " Although the soul is breathed directly by God into man, yet when united with a body it is forthwith guilty of the first sin imputed to the whole of man and accordingly is infected also by that original defilement."—The " propagation of sin " thus takes place by the imputation of Adam's guilt and by the creation of souls in a condition of " lack of original righteousness ", whereby the " imputation of Adam's sin " is accomplished upon them. This imputation is justified by the natural connection of the individual with Adam and with the human nature which fell with him. This is why VOETIUS (I, 1096) says in an apparently quite traducian and quite illogical way, that " man deserved this death-dealing plague beforehand in the loins of Adam ". These words are explained by what follows (VOETIUS 1096) : " (Original sin) was propagated by generation, not contracted or acquired by imitation. That is, it was born in Titius from the first sin, i.e. because of the fault of the first parent, through generation and parallel to the natural generation and birth of Titius Gen. 5. 3 (Adam ... begat a *son* in his own likeness, after his own image ...) Jn. 14. 5 (we know not whither thou goest) Ps. 51. 7 (thou desirest truth in the inward parts) Jn. 3. 6 (that which is born of the flesh is flesh) Eph. 2. 3 (. . . we all once lived in the lusts of our flesh, doing the desires of the flesh and of the thoughts, and were by nature children of wrath, even as the rest)Rom. 5.12,19 (through one man sin entered into the world, and death through sin ; and so death passed unto all men, for that all sinned ... as through the one man's disobedience the many were made sinners, even so through obedience of the one shall the many be made righteous). Along with the *Reformed* who deny traducianism we add that it arises and exists in Titius by his defectibility, God most righteously as Judge, through

His providence according to the counsel of His will, not presenting Titius with His image but most justly withdrawing it ".

As regards the creation of the soul in the state of "lack of original righteousness" some assert with ZANCHIUS "that souls are created with original righteousness but are soon deprived of it in punishment of Adam's sin", while on the contrary the majority after the precedent of CALVIN and URSIN taught "that souls are created deprived of original righteousness for a punishment of the same sin". Cf. HOTTINGER (p. 166), who distinguishes three stages in the "propagation by successive generation": "the first is in the conception and generation of the body, which is begotten of impure, corrupt seed Job 14. 4 (who can bring a clean thing out of an unclean? no one), 1 Pet. 1. 23 (begotten again, not of corruptible seed) Jn. 1. 13 (born, not of blood, nor of the will of the flesh, nor of the will of man). The second is the creation of a rational soul, as to which however there are two opinions; one that of those who will have it that the soul is created together with original righteousness, but is soon deprived of it in punishment of Adam's sin, the view of the *Scholastics* and also of ZANCHIUS. The second is that of those who say that it is created minus this righteousness as a punishment of the same sin; this is the view of CALVIN, URSIN, and others. And the latter is truer (*a*) because in Adam all sinned and died; (*b*) because the image of God and original righteousness are not restored after the lapse save by regeneration; (*c*) because if they are created pure, entire, they will be righteous natures, then they become unrighteous. But there is none righteous, no not one. The third step consists in the animation of the body by the soul, or the union of body with soul to form one human person; by this step original sin is accomplished."

And the cause of this punishment is that the nature of all men has sinned in Adam. Therefore it is the convention in *Reformed* theology (according to the precedent of BEZA and COCCEIUS to translate the words Rom. 5. 12 ἐφ' ᾧ πάντες ἥμαρτον, "in whom all sinned". —HYPERIUS, it is true, had in his commentary on Romans (p. 366) translated these words "so far as (*quatenus*) we have all sinned". Others also represented this conception. On the other hand the later men taught the same as HEIDEGGER regarding this passage (X, 34): ἐφ' ᾧ πάντες ἥμαρτον, in whom, namely Adam, all sinned, so that ἐπί is used for ἐν, as also in other places—so that we do not translate ἐφ' ᾧ by "*eo quod, quia*" all sinned, as some think ἐφ' ᾧ must also be taken 2 Cor. 5. 4 (. . . we that are in this tabernacle do groan, being burdened; not for that we would be unclothed, but that we would be clothed upon, that what is mortal may be swallowed up of life) and Phil.

3. 12 (not that I have already obtained . . . but I press on), but perhaps less suitably". So also MARESIUS VI, 36, and others.

24.—In so far as this sin inherited by man is taken over by him into his will and manifested in a personal act, inward or outward, it appears as actual sin. "Actual sin is transgression of law, whether natural or revealed by the Word of God, actually committed by ourselves" (POLAN VI, 3). Or "Actual sin is ἀνομία injurious to the piety required in our actions in the law of God and inseparably pullulating like fruit from original sin" (v. TIL, *Hypotyposis*, p. 115). The essential course by which each individual actual sin comes into being is described in Jas. 1. 14-15 (each man is tempted, when he is drawn away by his own lust, and enticed. Then the lust, when it hath conceived, beareth sin: and the sin, when it is full-grown, bringeth forth death). Accordingly four stages are to be distinguished in it (HEIDEGGER, X, 62): (1) "temptation, not the one caused by God, Satan or the world, but the one caused by man's own concupiscence; (2) concupiscence conceiving; for it conceives and becomes pregnant, when sin insinuating itself in thought is not forthwith rejected but is admitted to the heart; (3) concupiscence giving birth by consent of the will; (4) the consummation of sin".— a DIEST 82: "Sin is the unrightness in inward and outward actions".

The relation between inherited and actual sin must therefore not be conceived as the relation in sinfulness *quoad potentiam* and *quoad actum*, which is already excluded by the distinction between the "substrate action" (in and for itself good) and the "malice of heart" in every sinful action, as well as by the recognition that original sin is real and makes man guilty in the sight of God. The two are more correctly distinguished as sin *quoad habitum* and *quoad actum*. Hence says MASTRICHT (IV, III, 5): "Sin is called actual, not because it is only sin by action, whereas original is not so save potentially, as *Pelagianisers* would like to have it, since even this is sin by action, in fact all sin is this ἐξοχῶς, indeed virtually: but because it is the deviation of action, under which however we also include habit, whereas original is the habitual duration of our whole nature".—POLAN (VI, 3): "Sin is called actual, not because sin is an *actio* or because an *actio* is sin, but because sin is in an *actio*, in which although it is good *qua actio*, there nevertheless adheres defect of moral goodness and wickedness; and that defect plus the wickedness is strictly sin, because committed by man, not by God. Yet it is figuratively, even metonymously, that sin is called an *actio* at variance with the law of God".—Besides this BUCAN (XVI, 36) calls attention to the distinction between original and actual sin: "In actual sin the *materia* does not persist. When a man has committed adultery or uttered blasphemy, once the thing is accomplished, these actions cease immediately, yet there remains over the offence against God and liability to punishment. In original sin the *materia* does not pass over; for we discover that the corruption of nature still remains. We still plunge into sin as before and are incapable body and soul of divine things".

25.—As regards distinction of sins that between mortal and venial is to be rejected. On the one hand every sin, even the one that seems most trifling, is in itself a deadly sin, rendering a man condemnable for eternity; although the comparative differences in the guilt and magnitude of sins among themselves is not done away with. On the other hand every sin of a person elect and born again is pardoned sin; that person can never fall away completely from grace or faith.

To begin with even Reformed dogmatics was inclined to recognise the distinction between venial and mortal sins as an essential one. Cf., e.g., BULLINGER (III, 3) : " All the sins of our thought, words and deeds are by no means equal to each other; they have their own degrees and are in fact some greater, some less than others. If inflamed by a bad desire a man yet represses it, so that he utters it neither in word nor in deed, he sins less than the man who loosens the reins of concupiscence and is completely carried away by cupidity. To sin against God is more serious than to be delinquent towards man. It is a grave sin to commit manslaughter but more serious to perpetrate parricide. He who commits adultery once, sins more lightly than if he should commit this same sin a second time. As the heap of sins increases, divine wrath and punishment are heaped up in the same degree. Differences in punishments are set up by the Lord; which otherwise would not be the case, were all sins equal.—Now the godly in all ages have unanimously transmitted it from Scripture, that certain sins are venial or daily; I mean the slips and errors done out of ignorance and weakness rather than of wickedness and committed by otherwise holy men, who daily pray for the remission of their debts.—Among capital crimes some are termed clamant (crying) as perpetually demanding divine vengeance, like the sin of the men of Sodom Gen. 18, of Cain Gen. 4; also defrauding poor hirelings of their profits and wrongs done to other poor men".—Meantime the polemic against the *Roman* theologians very early led to another and more adequate treatment of this article. The *Catholic* statement that certain sins are excusable by their nature was opposed by the *Reformed* Church with the dogma, that in and for itself even the seemingly very slight sin of men renders them liable in God's sight to eternal damnation; CALVIN (II, viii, 58): "The curse of God always rests upon transgression of His law. It is therefore impossible but that we visit the lightest cupidities with the sentence of death.—59: Every

sin is mortal".—MUSCULUS 31: "No sin in itself is so minute as not to
be worthy of death, if it be judged in the absence of mercy".—WOLLEB
44: "No sin is by its nature venial, or so light as not to deserve damnation". By this of course we recognise that compared not with the law
of God but with each other sins show a greater or less degree of guilt
and so also of condemnability, and that this is actually taken into consideration among unbelievers, but especially among believers; *Confess.
Helv.* II, 8: "We also confess that sins are not equal". As to how this
holds good of the sins of unbelievers PICTET e.g. says (XI, ii, 10): "We
do not confuse the continence of *Scipio* with the portentous lusts of
Nero, Fabricius and *Catiline;* not because the former was good, but because
he was less bad, as *Augustine* says".—VIRELLIUS (p. 86): "If then there
is no value in all the specious works emitted by unbelievers, will his
case be no better who bears himself with restraint and represses the
affections of his flesh, than his who spends all his life in unbridled fashion?
Not at all! God does reward such works; but only in this life. He even
frequently bestows generously the things that give occasion for exhibiting
them, good health, a quiet life, praise and popularity and the like.
Therefore Christ teaches that scribes and Pharisees who prayed and
fasted to obtain praise of men have received their reward. Besides that,
the state of men who have behaved modestly in this life will be more
tolerable in the day of judgment than that of others".—WALAEUS 250:
"We admit that a distinction must be made between daily, lighter sins
committed in infirmity or ignorance, and more serious ones committed
against conscience. We admit too that the latter incur a graver sense
of God's wrath than the former, and that of course the act of faith is not
so powerfully obscured and shattered in them as in the latter. We
admit thirdly that by penitence and the ordinary exercises of faith and
prayer lesser sins are purged through Christ, whereas more serious
ones are not purged without extraordinary penitence and heavier disciplines of faith, as examples of faith adduced earlier also teach. Nevertheless we also saw before that clearly not all grace or faith is extinguished
by them; and Paul also bears witness to the fact Rom. 8. 1 (no condemnation to them that are in Christ Jesus), and it is mentioned 1 Jn. 3. 9
(whosoever is begotten of God doeth no sin . . . he cannot sin, because
he is begotten of God) and 1 Jn. 5. 18 (we know that whosoever is begotten
of God sinneth not; but he that was Begotten of God keepeth him,
and the Evil One toucheth him not)."—It is emphasised that all sins
in believers are forgivable—not in and for themselves, but because
believers are never utterly abandoned by grace; CALVIN (II, viii, 59):
"The faults of saints are venial, not by their nature but because they
receive pardon by the mercy of God." Similarly WENDELIN, *Coll.* 155.

But when it is a question of assessing the nature of sin, everyone insists that every sin is a mortal sin. Cf. RISSEN IX, 54: "The question is simply as to the nature of sins in themselves and according to the rigour of the law, all of which we consider to be mortal, not one venial ".—WALAEUS p. 251: "The chief question between us and the *Papists* is this, whether certain sins are of themselves venial, i.e. deserving indeed of some temporary penalty or castigation in this world or after this life in purgatory, but not an eternal penalty. These they consider to be of two kinds; either because of imperfection in the cause, i.e. without full consent or will; or because of imperfection in the material or object, as if one were to steal a sixpence or a loaf in order to feed oneself, etc.— But we deny this and assert that all sin, if the man who sins is regarded as being outside Christ and faith in him, makes him liable to death and to cursing in time and in eternity."

Another distinction usual in Catholic dogmatics was also rejected in the same way by the Reformed theologians. The *Jesuits* were in the habit of distinguishing between theological and philosophical sin. E.g., according to MASTRICHT IV, III, 23, *Stephanus Bougot;* "Philosophical sin or moral sin is a human act unsuited to a rational nature and to right reason; while theological and moral sin is free transgression of the divine law. Philosophical sin, however grave in one who is ignorant of God or does not think of God in his action, is a grave sin but not an offence against God or a mortal sin dissolving the friendship of God or one worthy of eternal punishment".—The Reformed dogmaticians reject this distinction too, appealing to the Biblical statement that "every sin is mortal" (Rom. 6. 23 the wages of sin is death; Jas. 1. 15 sin when it is full grown bringeth forth death).

26.—It is better to use other divisions of sins: (1) inward sins or sins of the heart; and outward sins or sins of word and deed; (2) sins of omission, by which that which the law enjoins is omitted; and of commission, by which that is committed which the law forbids: (or it is a sin of omission where the act or the goodness of the act is lacking (BRAUN, 372)); (3) sins against God by which He is directly hurt (idolatry, blasphemy, etc.); against one's neighbour, by which the neighbour is hurt; and against ourselves, by which through his own fault a man does harm to himself or to his bodily or spiritual health; (4) sin *per se*, directly prohibited by the laws of God; and sin *per accidens*, not prohibited by the law of God but enjoined and so good in itself and by reason of the outward act, but lacking in some cause or circumstance: this may occur in four ways; (a) in its inception, if the act does not proceed from a good beginning; (b) in its upshot, if it is not referred to the glory of God or is referred to a bad end; (c) in its degree, as the faithful sin in those works of theirs which proceed from weak faith and love; (d) in its circumstances of place and time, whereby many things are done lawfully in and at one place and time, which would not be done lawfully in and at another place and time; (5) sins deliberate; and sins accidental where something turns out contrary to intention; (6) crying sins which call for the unique punishment of God for obvious reasons (shedding innocent blood, cheating fellow-workers, striking or oppression of widows, orphans, poor people, etc.); (7) spiritual sins, done within the spirit (heresy, pride, envy) and carnal sins (drunkenness, fornication).

With special emphasis the *Reformed* dogmaticians stress the sin of fornication, e.g. HEIDEGGER (X, 65): "A man sins in various ways with the body and its members and by some sin like greed or drunkenness attracts sin to his body and in a sense sins against his body. But the peculiar thing about fornication is, that the man who sins with his body indeed brings its members into obedience to sin but does not strictly make them the property of sin; but the fornicator strictly makes his members the property of sin and so of the devil, the author of lust and wantonness, because he makes over his rights and powers over his own body to the whore and to the devil himself, if not for good (as obtains in wedlock) at least for a time".

27.—(8) Sins of weakness, i.e. of ignorance (vincible or invincible), committed by ignorant people; sins of an erring conscience, committed by one who also commits an error of conscience; and sins of knowledge committed by those who know and see ahead; (9) besetting sins, which rule a man and which he perpetrates of free will and desire without any struggle or resistance against sin; and non-besetting sins, which are in the man in such a way that they do not beset him, but are committed by him not willingly but unwillingly; (10) remissible sins, for which there is remission, not of their own nature but because of Christ's satisfaction apprehended by faith; and irremissible: these latter are in part generally irremissible (in which all the reprobate perish without distinction), in part irremissible one by one, e.g. blasphemies against the Holy Spirit" (HEIDEGGER V, 61-71) [§§ 26-27]—Sin against the H. Spirit, or "blasphemy against the H. Spirit", is "the complete denial of evangelical truth thoroughly recognised, as well as hatred of it and attacks against it, proceeding not from common human infirmity but from singular malice and devilish hatred of it, wholly devoid of repentance or slackening" (HEIDEGGER X, 73). It is thus a peculiar, quite definite sin, differing in character from any other sin, termed the sin against the H. Spirit, because it is a sin against the gracious office of the

H. Spirit, who by His work of grace in the heart of man effects knowledge and experience of Christ as the sole Redeemer and Source of blessing.

HEIDEGGER (X, 72) : "Scripture Mt. 12. 31-32, Mk. 3. 28-29* (which compare and see 1 Jn. 5. 16 (the sin unto death)) both makes this one sin singular and eloquently opposes it to others for its singularity". The passage Heb. 6. 4-7 HEIDEGGER (X, 74) explains as follows: "It is impossible, says (Paul) [sic!], for those once illuminated (through Scripture and ἔλεγχος, through reproof and conviction, as a result of that which (Jn. 16. 8, 11 "he when he is come, will convict the world in respect of sin, and of righteousness and of judgment . . . of judgment, because the prince of this world is judged") is attributed to the H. Spirit, that through which those illuminated recognise that they are wandering in error and that the truth is contained in the Word of God), so that they have tasted the heavenly gift of God (Christ, that bread of life which is come down from heaven Jn. 6. 51 as the Saviour of the world, who came from heaven and rose again from the dead, him they have thoroughly realised and in a sense have already tasted his χρηστότης), and have become participants in the H. Spirit (meaning the gifts of the H. Spirit, which on Christ's ascension into heaven are communicated in His effusion by χειροθεσία, with the object of making Christ's kingdom glorious, and the Church's firstfruits to be planted) and have tasted the good Word of God (the gospel of the justification of the sinner by the sole grace of God through faith, which is *par excellence* the καλὸν θεοῦ ῥῆμα, the good word of God), and the power of the age to come (the good things, both of grace in the N.T. and of the glory which awaits in heaven those perfected in heaven, they realised not incidentally or by a certain sense and joy of the H. Spirit, but have rather in a way sipped that which is more carnal than spiritual) and if they have fallen away (i.e. lapsed not *simpliciter* but ἑκουσίως, willingly, as St. Paul explains himself Heb. 10. 26, "if we sin wilfully after that we have received the knowledge of the truth, there remaineth no more a sacrifice for sins", from maliginity, petulance, hatred, not from ignorance or fear, things which convict a man of doing something not ἕκων but ἄκων, not wishing to do it, having fallen away in revolt, both by resuming their whilom errors and the habits they had abandoned, by becoming hardened in them have sought a second death like a fresh hardening Rev. 9. 6, "in these days men shall seek death and shall in no wise find it; and they shall desire to die, and death fleeth from them"; and with devilish hatred have blasphemed the truth revealed to man by the

---

* Every sin and blasphemy forgiven, but not against the H. Spirit ; sin against the Son of man forgiven, but not against the H. Spirit.

H. Spirit, exactly as if it had proceeded from the devil), [it is impossible for them] to be renewed a second time to repentance (not because on a former occasion they were truly renewed within and endued with new faith and wisdom, but because they were retaining a certain resemblance to new wisdom, not without a certain joyfulness, but that carnal, appearing to themselves and to others renewed, quickened, enlightened and born again, whom the Apostle declares roundly to be incapable of being renewed again to repentance, as having fallen away voluntarily".

PoLAN (VI, 3): "It is called the sin against the H. Spirit, not in respect of the divine essence by which the H. Spirit is God, nor in respect of the person of the H. Spirit, whose dignity is not greater than that of the Father or of the Son; nor could one person of the Deity be offended without the insult recoiling upon the other persons too: but in respect of the benefit supplied directly by the Spirit, who teaches and reveals the truth in men's hearts and convinces them in their conscience that Jesus is that Christ and sole Saviour, by whom we must be saved."— WALAEUS (p. 285): "The question here therefore is, why this sin is so called. Ans.: It is thus called the sin *par excellence*, because it is committed against the proper office of the H. Spirit, which is to illumine our mind, engender faith, and sanctify us wholly to God. The other sins are also said to grieve the Spirit Eph. 4. 30, because though they do not quench the H. Spirit, they yet obscure and repress the Spirit's actions in us. Otherwise it is certain that all sins are committed against the common righteousness of Father, Son and H. Spirit".—BuCAN (XVII, 8): "This sin is said to be committed specially against the H. Spirit—in respect of grace and illumination, of which the H. Spirit is the proper agent in men's hearts, according as it is the proper and immediate office of the H. Spirit to illumine us and when brought into the light of the truth to open up for us the way to the Father, the Son and Himself. Although this work is common to the three persons, nevertheless the H. Spirit is peculiarly and principally the agent here, as is the Father in the work of creation and the Son in the work of redemption".

28.—The sin against the H. Spirit can never be incurred by an elect but only by a rejected person, and only by a rejected person who has experienced the effectiveness of God's means of grace through the Church. Hence we must add that that man is not guilty of the sin, who sins through any sort of blasphemy of the person of Father, Son or H. Spirit, or acts against conscience, or suppresses in passing the gracious visitation of the H. Spirit, or persecutes the Church of God.

MARESIUS (*De pecc. in Spir. S.* XXII): "This sin firstly does not fall upon God's elect and true believers,—secondly, although it is the sin of the reprobate only, it is not the sin of them all".—KECKERMANN, 278: "The sin against the H. Spirit falls only upon reprobate men [not angels?]. Not on all reprobate; only on those who placed within the visible Church have felt the grace of the H. Spirit and illumination by the ministry of the Word and sacraments in their consciences".—BUCAN (XII, 3): "I infer that the subject of this sin is not in all the reprobate, but only in those who have not recognised Christ and his truth; that the elect are not liable to this sin, since God's counsel to save them cannot be made of none effect".—MASTRICHT explains this more fully (IV, III, 17): "In order that we may arrive more accurately at the nature of this unforgivable blasphemy against the H. Spirit, it will be best on the one hand to mention what things do not cause this sin. It is not caused (1) by any blasphemy, suggestion or temptation insinuated by Satan against Father, Son and H. Spirit, which falls at times even upon the most sensitive believers to their extreme abomination, which fell even upon our Saviour himself, upon whom no sin falls, much less this outstanding one.—(2) It is not effected by any sin against the personality or deity of the Spirit.—(3) Nor is it effected by any sin committed against knowledge and conscience.—(4) Nor is it effected by any sin against the truth of Christ and the Gospel.—(5) Nor is it effected by any sin against the gracious movements and operations of the Spirit.—(6) Nor is it effected by any sin against grace restored. In truth believers very often experience in themselves their own invincible infirmities, their own doubts, terrors, distracting thoughts, inordinate passions, etc. Also in addition they sadden and extinguish the Spirit by choking the motions of the H. Spirit by declining from their first favour Rev. 2. 4 [thou didst leave thy first love 2. 4 ?], by falling into various crimes like drunkenness Gen. 9. 27 (Noah), incest Gen. 19. 33 (Lot), adultery and homicide 2 Sam. 11, Ps. 51 (David and Uriah, Bathsheba), by relapsing into former sins Gen. 27. 19-21 (Jacob personating Esau) Mt. 26. 32-34 (Peter's denial).—(7) Nor is it effected by any malicious persecution of the Church and truth Ac. 8. 1, 9. 1 (Saul), 26. 10-11 (Paul's account of it to Agrippa) 1 Tim. 1. 13-16 (Paul, though he was "a blasphemer and a persecutor and injurious", etc.) Ac. 2. 36 ("whom ye (Jews) crucified") many converted by Peter."—If we compare the passages of Scripture which have to do with the sin against the H. Spirit, the result is that "it is the universal and malicious apostasy of hypocritical professors from the truth and common gifts of the H. Spirit once received to blasphemous contempt of the Spirit of grace, also horrible contempt for the Son of God, and violent persecution of Christian truth".

29.—The only person guilty of this sin is the man who has known Christ through the gracious working of the H. Spirit and experienced His blessed fellowship, yet falls away from Christ and becomes the enemy of Christ and his kingdom.

The early-Protestant *Melanchthonian* dogmatics had generally with *Augustine* conceived the sin against the H. Spirit as "final impenitence". For the *Reformed* treatment of this doctrine CALVIN's exposition was *a priori* decisive. CALVIN says (III, iii, 22): "If *Augustine's* definition be correct, the sin is not committed unless persisted in till death". Then he continues: "But let us give the true definition, which when once it is established by sound evidence, will easily of itself overturn all the others. I say, then, that he sins against the H. Spirit who, while so constrained by the power of divine truth that he cannot plead ignorance, yet resists with dogged malice, merely for the sake of resisting". Hence URSIN says (*Loci*, 610): By the sin of the H. Spirit we cannot mean "final perseverance in any one sin", because in H. Scripture it is explained as "a fixed species of sin", while "perseverance in sins is nothing else than the sins themselves continued right to the end". As a closer clarification of CALVIN's view, we may content ourselves with what COCCEIUS says about the sin against the H. Spirit. By the sin against the H. Spirit COCCEIUS means the voluntary sin of the man who was already really in possession of the H. Spirit and had entered into the enjoyment of life eternal, i.e. man's resistance to the H. Spirit already imparted to him. Cf. *Summ. th.* XXIX, 48 : " But when a man has learned fundamental truth Heb. 10. 26 (if we sin wilfully, after we have received the knowledge of the truth, there remaineth no more a sacrifice for sins), having been convinced by H. Scripture, a conviction which takes place by the ἔλεγχος, *redargutio* or conviction of the H. Spirit Jn. 16. 8, 11 (he when he is come, will convict the world in respect of sin, and of righteousness and of judgment . . . of judgment, because the prince of this world is judged"), or as the Apostle says Heb. 6. 4-5, when a man has once been enlightened to know that he has been walking in error, that the truth is contained in the Word of God, and in such wise that he has tasted the heavenly gift, Christ given from heaven, and has become a participator in the H. Spirit, i.e. in the gifts with which the Church has been adorned and is edified, and has tasted the good word of God anent gratuitous justification by faith and the powers of the age to come, in the joy with which he received the word (for in these ways and excluding those which are κρείττονα and ἐχόμενα τῆς σωτηρίας, they may take place in the unregenerate) if then he sins voluntarily, i.e. returns to former errors and abandoned customs and blasphemes the truth out of hatred (seeking death Rev. 9. 6, i.e. his former induration), he blasphemes the H. Spirit, because Him whom he had formerly called the Spirit of truth and grace he calls a spirit of falsehood, and not Him alone, but also the Father and the Son ".

Similarly MARESIUS, who (*De pecc. in Sp. S.* VI) says: "For the formal constitution of the sin in question are required (1) sufficient knowledge of the divine truth and will by the irradiation, outward or inward, of the H. Spirit; (2) malicious rejection and impugning of known truth revealed by the H. Spirit; (3) stiffening of the mind and perseverance in wickedness right to the end".

Next the sin against the H. Spirit is committed by the man who has reached His gracious working in the same relation as the converted elect—only that he is not elect and therefore has only for a time and in passing entered into a relationship with the H. Spirit, out of which he betakes himself, now to live in conscious enmity to Him.—The definitions given by the other dogmaticians are in essential agreement with this. "Final impenitence" is more or less definitely described as just an accident of the sin against the H. Spirit. Cf. e.g. LUD. CROCIUS 937: "It is the sin against the H. Spirit, when with deliberate malice a man resists for the sake of resisting the divine truth revealed especially in the Gospel, in the light of which he is so bathed, that he cannot plead ignorance, yet loving his darkness better than the light of the gospel".—BUCAN (XVII, 3): "Sin against the H. Spirit is universally and with full assent to revolt from Christ truly discerned and known from the Gospel through the H. Spirit illuminating hearts, to deny Christ, to persecute his truth with deliberate malice by might and main and to cover him with insults by despising his offering of himself.—LEIDEN SYNOPSIS (XVI, 53): "We define sin against the H. Spirit as contempt of and malicious assault upon Christ and gospel grace known through outward hearing of the Word and brought convincingly home through the H. Spirit, whether He is in those who have not yet professed the doctrine of Christ, like the Pharisees Mt. 12, or have professed it and fallen away from it: concerning whom see Heb. 6 and 10". —RIISSEN (IX, 12): "We mean by it universal apostasy from true Christianity, whether it be total and persevering denial, detestation of and attack upon gospel truth of which a man has been convicted in his conscience, or the sophistical or the tyrannical kind, proceeding not from common human infirmity but from singular and deliberate malice and thoroughly diabolical hatred of it, conjoined with contempt of all the means of salvation and with final impenitence."—EILSHEMIUS (*Ostfriesl. Kleinod*, p. 37): "The sin against the H. Spirit is not a transgression of one or all of the commandments of the law proceeding from ignorance, inability or wantonness, nor yet a denial, blaspheming or persecution of Christ and his Gospel arising from fear or uncertainty. The sin against the H. Spirit is committed by those who have learned and understood the truth of the gospel through the illumination of the H. Spirit, and are so convinced by it that they cannot deny it and out of hostility and hatred as good as wickedly and obstinately renounce, blaspheme, damn and persecute such acknowledged truth against their own conscience. This sin is therefore punished by God with· persistent blindness, so that those who commit it cannot in this life attain to any repentance or forgiveness of it".

30.—So persistent is the blindness that even in death the sinner persists in conscious hostility to God's kingdom of grace.—KECKERMANN 278: "This sin has added to it final impenitence and the height of contumacy and hatred against heavenly truth".

31.—At the same time, apart from special illumination by the H. Spirit (as it happened in the Apostolic Age) it cannot be known who has really made himself guilty of the sin against the H. Spirit.—KECKERMANN 278: "This sin is not to be presumed or adjudged to be in any man save *a posteriori*, by the signs, that is, of despair appearing at the agony of death. Therefore a man will not immediately be regarded by us as having committed the sin against the H. Spirit if he denies and persecutes the truth recognised by himself, unless he concludes life in that contumacious apostasy".—BUCAN (XVII, 6): "How are we to pronounce in the matter of this sin? It is difficult to pronounce upon it, especially at this time, when the gift of διάκρισις πνευμάτων is not so strong in the Church as in the early Church.—In this matter therefore judgment ought not to be passed save *a posteriori* and as the result of final impenitence".

HEIDEGGER (X, 75): "It is undoubtedly rash to specify who have contracted liability for such a great sin. Who art thou that judgest another man's servant? To his own Lord he standeth or falleth (Rom. 14. 4). And since the persuasion and conviction of truth is inward, for it can make a conjecture of sorts by signs or images (εἰκόνες), it can by no means be proved and so be defined on account of the genius of charity; indeed that very hatred and blasphemy of the H. Spirit ought to be estimated rather from the mind into whose recesses no man can enter, than from words and deeds. So this sin cannot be shown up in any mortal without special divine revelation. In the apostolic age, so fruitful in *charismata*, it is usually inferred, that it might have been known by special revelation, from the words of St. John, when he forbids prayer for those who sin unto death 1 Jn. 5. 16 (.. not concerning this do I say that he should make request)."

32.—The reason for the irremissibility of this sin lies not in its objective character or in its nature, as though it made it impossible for the H.

Spirit to arouse again to repentance and conversion one who had known and experienced His grace and had subsequently made himself guilty of blasphemy against the H. Spirit. Rather, the irremissibility of the sin against the H. Spirit is founded on the fact that Father and Son from eternity had resolved not to allow the benefit of the work of redemption to those who committed this sin.

Many dogmaticians pronounced upon the reason for the irremissibility of the sin against the H. Spirit in a manner similar to HEIDEGGER (X, 77): "He who blasphemes the Son before the Spirit has been received to illumine and to convince of sin, blasphemes ignorantly about a thing of which he knows nothing. But the man who blasphemes the Son of God made known and in a measure received through the H. Spirit, nay even repudiates and pierces with threats his light-bearing and grace-enduing Spirit, what room for grace is left for such a one ? 1 Sam. 2. 25 (if one man sin against another, God shall judge him; but if a man sin against the Lord, who shall intreat for him ? Notwithstanding they hearkened not unto the voice of their father (Eli), because the Lord would slay them). It becomes not God to cast His pearls before dogs and swine Mt. 7. 6, or to squander Christ, the price of His grace, among those so hopelessly corrupt. Nor does it any more become the H. Spirit to breathe upon those who so wickedly possess His gifts and blaspheme Himself, the consummator of all grace. Thus both the righteousness of God, and the profanation of the entire H. Trinity accomplishing grace and salvation in the H. Spirit, and the principle of the dispensation of salvation, and the manner in which this sin is committed, all render it simply irremissible".—Still more decided is BURMANN (p. 459) in the view that the "sin against the H. Spirit" is irremissible "in and for itself."

More correct, however, i.e. more in correspondence with the Reformed system, is the teaching of MASTRICHT (IV, III, 17), who at the same time throws light in plenty upon the otherwise usual views as to the reason for the irremissibility of the sin against the H. Spirit: "There are those who look for it in the sin itself and its natural detestability, because in blaspheming the H. Spirit they are forsooth rejecting all the means by which He might bring them back to repentance and so to remission. I gladly admit that this (detestability) is outstanding. But whether the H. Spirit could not conquer and overcome it, for my part I should not dare to say ; especially as, where sin abounded, there would grace superabound Rom. 5. 20-21. Others look for irremissibility in the fact that it is repugnant to the separate *personae* of the Trinity, since the H. Spirit is sent by the Father and by the Son, to finish the business of redemption. But all sin is repugnant to the whole Trinity. In that case both to grieve the H. Spirit, to fight against the H. Spirit, to extinguish the H. Spirit are *ex hypothesi* irremissible sins; and on what principle, pray, can God, if He will, not remit a sin which strives against the whole Trinity?" Then MASTRICHT continues: "I should therefore think it the most correct thing to say that it is irremissible for the same divine cause and will by which all sins of the reprobate are irremissible, that of course it was not God's will that Christ should satisfy for them, neither did Christ will to expend his death on the remission of this sin. The apostle seems to suggest this reason, when he says that they crucify the Son of God afresh Heb. 6. 6., i.e. that they commit a sin such that if for it they had to be set free from it, Christ would have to be crucified afresh, since so far he has never been crucified for it. And even a little more clearly Heb. 10. 26, "There remaineth no more a sacrifice for that sin".—Similarly WENDELIN (*Collatio*, 159): "This sin is said to be irremissible, not because it simply cannot be remitted, but because by God's righteous judgment it is not remitted, since repentance never follows it, the just Judge denying the grace of repenting".— Similarly CROCIUS 937. Many dogmaticians unite the two views, like WALAEUS (p. 287): "The proper punishment of this sin is that it is irremissible. The reason for this fact is twofold. First, because by God's irrevocable judgment they cannot be recalled to repentance, as St. Paul says Heb. 6. 6. Next, because they pertinaciously reject all remedies against the sin, the gospel word, the operations of the H. Spirit and Christ's own merit, so that for them there remaineth no more a victim for sin, as the Apostle says Heb. 10. 26, and accordingly they are justly smitten by God with this stupor to the end of life".—Similar is the verdict of other dogmaticians who unite in stressing the "judgment" and the "ordering of God" as the main reason for the irremissibility and expressly contest the view that it is to be explained by "the difficulty of obtaining remission", e.g. BUCAN (XVII, 9): "Why is it called irremissible? Not because of the difficulty of obtaining remission, as some think; nor because it is too strong and great for the grace of God; for this rule of Paul stands Rom. 5. 20: "grace doth [*sic*] abound more exceedingly". But (1) because those who sin this sin have been smitten with eternal blindness for their ingratitude by the just judgment and ordinance of God, who does not suffer Himself to be mocked or His Spirit, who is the Spirit of truth, to be convicted of lying—(2) On account of their impenitence or the impossibility of their repentance, as says the Apostle Heb. 6. 6: "It is impossible for such to be renewed to repentance". For since true repentance proceeds from God's Spirit, and we obtain the Spirit of God in the one Christ by faith, they therefore can never repent who have sinned against the H. Spirit, and so can never obtain remission.—(3) Because there remains no other victim where men have departed from Christ's victim".

33.—The punishment—" punishment is evil inflicted upon the sinner because of sin " (AMESIUS I, xii, 10)—of the sin that has come upon humanity and of the guilt caused by it is death in the broadest sense of the word. " Death in the general sense is the wretched deprivation of life " (MASTRICHT IV, iv, 7). This death is of a threefold nature, spiritual, corporeal and eternal death.—Individual dogmaticians, like BULLINGER (III, 5) mention only a " double death ", namely eternal and temporal. The later men distinguish a threefold *mors*, whereby much already developed at an earlier stage must be repeated.—BUCAN (XV, 10) : " What is the fruit of sin ? Death, and that threefold. (1) The spiritual death of the soul, by which it comes about that the ungodly, deprived of the presence of the H. Spirit (which is the soul's soul), can do none of the things which are of God, and so being dead to God live unto Satan. (2) The death of the body, by which are also signified the miseries which harden it therefore. (3) The eternal death of soul and body, unless conversion to Christ takes place here Gen. 2. 17 (the threat upon eating of the tree of knowledge) Rom. 1. 18 (the wrath of God is revealed from heaven against all ungodliness and unrighteousness of men, who hold down the truth in unrighteousness) 6. 23 (the wages of sin is death) Jas. 5. 20 (let him know, that he which converteth a sinner from the error of his way shall save a soul from death and shall cover a multitude of sins) ". Similarly BURMANN (II, viii, 1) distinguishes : (1) spiritual death, by which man's life has become dried up by God " ; (2) " corporeal death " ; and (3) " eternal death, to which man became liable at the same time as he sinned ". Hence BURMANN remarks that spiritual is not essentially distinguished from eternal death, since the former by its nature is eternal and the latter but the " spiritual continuation of that death in hell ".

34.—" Spiritual death is spiritual impotence, arising out of the removal of original righteousness, to achieve spiritual good spiritually, conjoined with spiritual slavery " (MASTRICHT IV, iv, 9). This spiritual death is seen in the state of the divine image and of free will in fallen man. Of course man is still left with the substance of the divine image and of free will, but the original gifts of the divine image man has completely lost by the fall, and his *liberum arbitrium* is bereft of all force and effectiveness, since it is enslaved by the power of sin dominating man.—ZANCHIUS 40 : " We distinguish the question of the *vires* of the entire *liberum arbitrium* from the question of the nature of the human *voluntas*. By nature we mean the natural and essential property bestowed by God on the will, by which it happens that whatever it wills whether good or evil, it always wills it freely, spontaneously, unrestrainedly, always free from any compulsion. By the word *vires* we understand an innate or bestowed *potentia* by which we can both know with the mind what things are good and what bad, and choose with the will the former and reject the latter."—BUCAN (XVIII, 4) : " What then is your opinion of *liberum arbitrium* in the state of man before conversion ?—That it is throughly bad. The soul, it is true, with its faculties of knowledge (*intellectus*) and will has remained intact as an essence. But the powers of these faculties for spiritual good have been completely lost. Knowledge (*intellectus*) is thoroughly blind in things divine, lacking true awareness of God and saving understanding of His word, according to that of *David* in Ps. 14. 3 (they are all gone aside ; they are together become filthy ; there is none that doeth good, no, not one) and *Paul's* 1 Cor. 2. 14 (the natural man receiveth not the things of the Spirit of God : for they are foolishness unto him ; and he cannot know them, because they are spiritually judged), Rom. 8. 7 (the mind of the flesh is enmity against God ; it is not subject to the law of God, neither indeed can be). And Eph. 4. 23 bids us be "renewed in the spirit of our mind ", thus naming the inmost part of our mind, that which the philosophers call ἡγεμονικόν.—The will is completely turned away from God Ps. 5. 4 (evil shall not sojourn with thee). Powers and conations having plainly been removed have at the same time become useless 1 Cor, 12 .3 (no man speaking in the Spirit of God saith, Jesus is anathema ; and no man can say, Jesus is Lord, but in the Holy Spirit) 2 Cor.3.5 (not that we are sufficient of ourselves, to account anything as of ourselves ; but our sufficiency is of God) Phil. 2. 13 (it is God which worketh in you both to will and to work, for his good pleasure) ".—LUD. CROCIUS (p. 913) : " In order to the state of corruption man's *liberum arbitrium* is not only wounded, weakened and attenuated for true spiritual good, but also enslaved, destroyed, lost and its powers are not only weakened and broken unless assisted by grace, but even non-existent (*nullae*) unless excited and restored by grace ".— BURMANN (II, xi, 18) : " Scripture exhibits man as not only a slave but also dead in sins Eph. 2. 1-5 (you did he quicken, when ye were dead through your trespasses and sins . . . even when we were dead through our trespasses, he quickened us together with Christ (by grace have ye been saved)), 1 Tim. 5. 6 (she that giveth herself to pleasure is dead while she liveth) Jn. 5. 25 (verily, verily I say unto you, the hour cometh, and now is, when the dead shall hear the voice of the Son of God ; and they that hear shall live) ".

35.—Fallen man's will is thus indeed always a free will, so far as it is the " essential faculty of willing and of refusing " (HEIDEGGER X, 85), an " acting by design ", a *complacentia rationalis*, MASTRICHT (IV, iv, 10), i.e. moves in the forms of spontaneity, and is therefore never moved by compulsion.—MUSCULUS 23 : " It is not to be denied that there is in man a *liberum arbitrium* or free *voluntas,* although it is liable to the slavery both of sin and of Satan. Wherefore, that the Apostle writes of unbelievers 2 Tim. 2. 26, that they are held captive in the snares of the devil to do his will, is not so to be understood as that they serve the devil unwillingly, but that blinded partly by ignorance and foolishness, partly by the malice of a corrupt mind, they are held in the error and slavery of sin, and that not in spite of their own will but voluntarily and delightedly ".— HEIDEGGER (X, 85) : " There remains in the sinner the essential faculty of willing and refusing. There remain the accidental powers of the *arbitrium* in respect of outward good, natural, civil and moral, without detriment to the foreknowledge, decree and predetermination of God. But in things moral which the law prescribes, not only according to outward, but according also to inward rightness, things both superantural and spiritual, such as the spirit of God effects in man by regenerating him, there is as yet no faculty, no *arbitrium* in any man who is a sinner not yet regenerated ".

36.—It must also be recognised that, supported by the common grace of God fallen man is capable of producing an ordinary morality and of doing good in external and natural things, or at least of exercising himself in them. But even the goodness that man does in external, natural and ordinary things is not truly good and pleasing to God. He never achieves it entirely from the right motive, i.e., never from love and obedience to God alone. He always admits the joint influence of his concupiscence. As a result, it is true, the naturally and the ordinarily good works are rewarded by God with temporal benefits. But in truth they are sinful and condemnable. And in spiritual things man can do absolutely nothing good, since his spiritual eye is veiled from the knowledge of God that brings blessing and his will can do and achieve only what is contrary to God's good pleasure.

RIISSEN (IX, 45): "The question is not as to outward civil and moral good. We do not deny that some powers still survive in man after the lapse, as regards those outward works and civil goods, so that he exercises justice and temperance and emits an act of mercy and charity, so that he keeps his hands from theft and murder and emits operations of like virtues by the antecedent concurrence of God and His general assistance; this is the outlook of Gentile virtues, of which later. But the question is of spiritual and supernatural good which is pleasing and acceptable to God: whether man in the state of sin is so corrupt, that the power of his *liberum arbitrium* as regards the good in question are not only slipped and worn but quite perished, so that he cannot know anything truly saving or do anything good: which is what we affirm".—HOTTINGER 180:

"In fact even in civil items unregenerate man has no *arbitrium* free from God's special aid and motion or from the slavery of sin".

KECKERMANN (261-263): "Even without the special grace of the H. Spirit man can still through the remains of the divine image left after the fall effect the exercises of virtues ethical, economic and political. But there is the greatest difference between outward and incomplete virtues and complete virtues. By complete virtues I mean those which have their own perfection because of their perfect beginning and ultimate end. The perfect beginning of virtue is the true love of God, while the true and ultimate end is God's glory and our eternal salvation. Thus Gentiles without the special grace of the H. Spirit have through the remnants of *liberum arbitrium* been able to exercise incomplete virtues, complete ones never". Hence it must be maintained: "(1) That no man by the remains of *liberum arbitrium* can exercise perfect good or ethical, political or economic virtue without the special grace of the H. Spirit. (2) Whereas spiritual virtues, i.e., those which have both a true beginning and a perfect end and which thus perfect man for eternal salvation, those, I say, no man can in any wise exercise by the power of *liberum arbitrium*. (3) Therefore man cannot either know or love God savingly without the special grace of the H. Spirit".—This point is most adequately explained in the LEIDEN SYNOPSIS (XVII, 20-24): "With a view to definite action on our part, the will or *arbitrium* of a depraved man is not here uniform in the same way in every respect. In things which concern natural and civil life and which are subject to sense and reason and have in view outward discipline and carnal righteousness, determinable not only by outward actions but also by inward movement— in these the remnants and embers here survive, so that a man to a certain extent can not only appreciate them with his mind but love them with his will, seek them with affection and prosecute and do them with his might Rom. 1. 19, 32 (that which may be known of God is manifested in them: God manifested it unto them . . . knowing the ordinance of God, that they which practise such things are worthy of death, (they) not only do the same, but also consent with them that practise them) 2. 14-15 (when Gentiles which have no law do by nature the things of the law, these, having no law, are a law unto themselves; in that they shew the work of the law written in their hearts, their conscience bearing witness therewith, and their thoughts one with another accusing or else excusing them) 9. 31 (Israel, following after a law of righteousness, did not arrive at that law) Phil. 3. 6-9 (as touching zeal, persecuting the church; as touching the righteousness which is in the law, found blameless. Howbeit, what things were gain to me, these have I counted loss for Christ) Gal. 1. 13 (ye have heard of my manner of life in time past in the Jew's religion, how that beyond measure I persecuted the church of God, and made havoc of it.).—21. But though there is in man here a certain liberty and power of action, nevertheless there is great weakness on account of the strength of concupiscence, and the will often follows not the dictation of reason but the worse part, the movement and leading of the affections and desires. The devil also, who is effective among infidels, does not cease to jog and precipitate this tottering nature into various faults. Hence there also appears everywhere a mighty disturbance of this civil righteousness, and therefore it is also very rare among men.—22. Further this faculty, whatever its extent and although in appearance it is at times a distinguished righteousness, does not rise beyond the political and honourable and philosophical variety and is unable to rise to the true good pleasing to God. As regards the efficient cause persons of this kind are never pleasing to God at all. Nor do their actions rise from the pure spring, true recognition of God and faith and fear of Him. Nor are they undertaken, performed and directed with the end due to God's glory—by which things nevertheless a good work should be assessed.—23. And accordingly all such action here, although directed towards good and, if you look at the act itself, good in and for itself, yet because not well done, is turned into sin and is inflamed by sins Rom. 14. 23 (He that doubteth is condemned . . . whatsoever is not of faith is of sin) Heb. 11. 6 (without faith it is impossible to be well-pleasing; he that cometh to God must believe that he is, and that he is a rewarder of them that seek after him); and so the *arbitrium* and the action and work flowing therefrom are truly sin. However there is greater sin in the man who wills, desires and does evil things *in se* and *per se*, than in the man who acts morally and does badly things good in themselves. God even repays them with a corporeal reward 1 K. 21. 29 (Seest thou how Ahab humbleth himself before me? because he humbleth himself before me, I will not bring the evil in his day; but in his son's days will I bring the evil upon his house) Mt. 6. 2, 5, 26 (when thou doest alms, sound not a trumpet before thee, as the hypocrites do in the synagogues and in the streets, that they may have glory of men. Verily I say unto you they have received their reward . . . when ye pray, ye shall not be as the hypocrites: for they love to stand and pray in the synagogues and in the corners of the streets, that they may be seen of men. Verily I say unto you, they have received their reward. . . . Behold the birds of the heaven, that they sow not neither do they reap, nor gather into barns; and your heavenly Father feedeth them. Are ye not of much more value than they?).—But in spiritual and inward things the natural and unregenerate man's *arbitrium* is only free for evil things. For us knowledge (*intellectus*) is in great part ignorant of what belongs to the divine law, particularly of the things which are of the Gospel, plainly supernatural and so above reason and will and cannot without supernatural light and eyesight (i.e., faith) be known or grasped with a firm sense as they ought—so too the will fettered by wickedness wills, chooses and effects the opposite of them 1 Cor. 2. 14 (the natural man receiveth not the things of the Spirit of God: for they are foolishness unto him; and he cannot know them, because they are spiritually judged), Rom. 8. 6-7 (the mind of the flesh is death; but the mind of the Spirit is life and peace: because the mind of the flesh is enmity against God; it is not subject to the law of God, neither indeed can it be), etc."

37.—Hence fallen man enslaved by sin cannot in any way personally grasp gracious aid when offered to him, or rise to a positive non-resistance to it, or prepare in an external disciplinary or pedagogic way to receive a redemptive favour. POLAN (VI, 6): "The man who is not reborn has no strength or very little, by which in any way to respond to God if He called him, or to open the door to His knock, or to assent to His proposal of salvation, or in short to co-operate with Him, if He operated upon him".—MASTRICHT (IV, iv, 33): "Although the Reformed grant readily that man can non-resist in a negative way, as a man naturally dead can non-resist attempts to restore him to life, and although they concede that unregenerate man may frequent churches, pour forth prayers and other outward things, they deny that he can non-resist positively; they deny that an unregenerate can perform these outward good things by the sheer strength of their natural *arbitrium*, save by common grace; on which see Paul, Heb. 6, 4, 5, 6 (as touching those who were once enlightened and tasted of the heavenly gift, and were made partakers of the H. Ghost, and tasted the good word of God and the powers of the age to come, and then fall away, it is impossible to renew them again to repentance . . .)".—BURMANN (VI, ii, 19: "The previous dispositions of man have no place here".—PICTET (IX, iii, 5): "To all of which it must be added, that in that state man cannot dispose himself to receive grace or approach God in any way."

38.—The will of man then is only free for evil, which he always does freely and with pleasure. So our definition must be (POLAN VI, 6) that: "the will of corrupt man who has not been born again is a natural power without compulsion to choose or do anything but evil, which is proposed to the will by the reason, for choice and performance".— CALVIN II, ii, 7: "In this way man will be said to have *liberum arbitrium*, not because he has the free choice of good and evil alike, but because he acts badly, by his will, not by compulsion".—LEIDEN SYNOPSIS (XVII, 26): "In this case the *arbitrium* is free, where it is reduced to the other part, namely evil, and turns to sin not by a forced necessity but with gladness."

39.—Since then the enslavement by sin, from which man can never free himself, makes itself felt by him as a misery, it is at the same time the punishment for sin.—KECKERMANN 282: "Familiar is the axiom of the theologians, that 'God often punishes sins with sins'; This indeed is the severest punishment of all. There takes place in a sense a process *in infinitum*; for that by which the sin ought to be being expiated, is itself sin".—AMESIUS (I, ii, 46-47): "The sins ensuing have rather the nature of a punishment in respect of the first sin Rom. 1. 26 (God gave them up unto vile passions, etc.). This nature of a punishment is assigned to these sins firstly by reason of their effects or consequences; they promote man's death and increase his wretchedness. Secondly, they are also called punishments in respect of the inward suffering to which man is subjected in sinning, by which also his nature is depressed and rendered viler. Thirdly, they are called the punishment of former sin, because the preceding sin was the cause for which man is robbed of the righteousness and grace or divine aid, through the absence of which it comes about that man rushes into these sins. Fourthly, they may also to a certain extent be called the punishment of former sin, because the preceding cause disposed and prepared man to perpetrate the sins following and in that way brought on man all the sins and the evils whatsoever, which accompany and overtake him".

40.—Like this spiritual death corporeal death is also a punishment of God for the sin of man.—Nature herself does not involve death; since death is the destruction of nature. Moreover God is absolutely good, can as little will death for death's sake, as for the sake of anything else. God can only have ordained death to punish sin. At once, hereby, since by death man is depressed to the lot of the other creatures, man's original power over creation is broken and his whole corporeal glory and blessedness undermined.

MASTRICHT (IV, iv, 13): "Corporeal death is the second punishment of sin Ps. 90. 3, 5, 6, 8, 10 (Those turnest man to destruction, and sayest: Return, ye children of men. . . . Thou carriest them away as with a flood; they are as asleep: in the morning they are like the grass which groweth up. In the morning it flourisheth and groweth up; in the evening it is cut down and withereth. . . . Thou hast set our iniquities before thee, our secret sins are in the light of thy countenance. . . . The days of our years are three-score years and ten, or even by reason of strength four score years: yet is their pride but labour and sorrow; it is soon gone and we fly away) Heb. 9. 27 (. . . it is appointed unto men once to die, and after this cometh judgment). Death is not by nature; it is the destruction of nature, and cannot be sought *per se* by any good man, not to speak of the supremely good, nor sought and inflicted by God for any other reason than for sin, and as a compensation for that in which the nature of punishment consists. Nor is there only the punishment itself. There are all its appendages and preparatives, such as (*a*) loss of vivacity, sanity, strength Job 14. 1-2 (Man that is born of woman is of few days and full of trouble. He cometh forth like a flower and is cut down; he fleeth also as a shadow and continueth not) Ps. 90. 8-10 (above) by which the bond of soul and body is loosened and gradually dissolved; and (*b*) loss of dominion over the creatures, which because of sin shake off the yoke of man and become his enemies instead of his slaves (Job 5. 22-23 at destruction and death thou shalt laugh; neither shalt thou be afraid of the beasts of the earth. For thou shalt be in league with the stones of the field; and the beasts of the field shall be at peace with thee) Hos. 2. 18 (and in that day I will make a covenant for them with the beasts of the field, and with the fowls of heaven and with the creeping things of the earth); (*c*) loss of the honour and glory with which his life shone in the presence of God and men Rom. 3. 23 (all have sinned and fallen short of the glory of God); (*d*) loss of everything by which life is either supported or beautified, whence poverty, contempt and ignominy Dt. 28. 21, 22, 27, 28, 29 (pestilence; consumption and all fevers; boils, emerods, scurvy, itch incurable; madness, blindness, astonishment of heart; groping blind, misfortune, oppression) Prov. 6. 11 (thy poverty shall come as a robber, and thy want as an armed man)".

41.—But the peak of misery which overtakes man as a punishment for sin is eternal death, i.e. the eternal separation of man from the society and blessedness of God (*poena damni*) and the eternal suffering (*poena sensus*), which the sinner beyond the grave suffers in his conscience and on his body.

HOTTINGER 194 : " Eternal (death) is the eternal condemnation of the impious after this life in hell—where separated from God's blessed communion, in company with the devil and his angels, they will be subjected to infinite tortures in soul and body alike and will be tortured steadily and eternally ".—MASTRICHT (IV, iv, 16) : " This eternal death includes (1) total, final and eternal deprivation of all communion with God the highest good, and of every saving benefit Mt. 25. 41, 46 (Depart from me, ye cursed, into the eternal fire which is prepared for the devil and his angels . . . and these shall go away into eternal punishment . . .) ;

(2) horrible communion and society with the unclean spirits of hell to all eternity Mt. 25.41-3), incredible horrors and twists of conscience due to the recollections of sins, by which they spontaneously attracted these evils to themselves, and which arise from the sense of divine wrath and indignation Is. 66. 24 (And they shall go forth and look upon the carcases of the men that have transgressed against me ; for their worm shall not die, neither shall their fire be quenched ; and they shall be an abhorring unto all flesh) 30.33 (a Topheth is prepared of old ; yea, for the king it is made ready ; he hath made it deep and large : the pile thereof is fire and much wood ; the breath of the Lord, like a stream of brimstone, doth kindle it) Rom. 11. 8-9 (according as it is written, God gave them a spirit of stupor, eyes that they should not see, and ears that they should not hear, unto this very day. And David saith, Lo, their table is made a snare, and a trap, and a stumbling-block, and a recompense unto them) ; (4) ineffable tortures of the body and all its parts, Lk. 16. 23 (in Hades he lifteth up his eyes, being in torment), Mt. 25.41 (Depart from me ye cursed, into the eternal fire which is prepared for the devil and his angels) Rev. 3.18 (I counsel thee to buy of me gold refined by fire, that thou mayest become rich ; and white garments, that thou mayest clothe thyself, and that the shame of thy nakedness be not made manifest ; and eye salve to anoint thine eyes, that thou mayest see)".

HOTTINGER 194 : " The punishment of loss and the punishment of sense are truly inseparable in eternal death ".—LEIDEN SYNOPSIS XVI (25-26) : " The punishment due to sins is two-fold, either that of loss, or that of sense. By punishment of loss we mean (although some take this word in a slightly different sense) the harm which the soul that sins contracts inwardly in consequence of the act of sin, the greater or less removal of divine grace according as the indignity of the sin is greater or smaller ; also the spot (*macula*) as they call it, and defilement, which clings to the soul in consequence of the turning away.—Punishment of sense consists partly in the pangs of conscience, partly in other tortures of mind or body, which unrepentant men are sure to experience in this life or in the life to come Rom. 2. 8-9 (unto them that are factious and obey not the truth but obey unrighteousness, shall be wrath and indignation, tribulation and anguish, upon every soul of man that worketh evil) ".

42.—But since only the rejected are subjected to eternal death, for the elect temporal and corporeal death is not a real punishment. For them all God's punishments are but tests and exercises in humility and patience, and disciplines for divine blessedness.

KECKERMANN 290 ff : " By analogy the punishment in question is called by the theologians the δοκιμασία or the cross and affliction, by which the children of God in this world are exercised unto faith and patience. The reprobate are not capable of the ends of afflictions. Whatever the others suffer of the penalties and miseries, they suffer it all by the most just judgment of God, in order that the divine justice and law may be satisfied, although it cannot be satisfied for eternity. The Cross and affliction of the godly is properly not the punishment of sin, because Christ gave satisfaction for their sins with a sufficient satisfaction ".— ALSTED 448 : " Punishment is so called strictly or analogically—449 : It is παιδεία or castigation by which God instructs His own in the school of the Cross that they perish not.—Δοκιμασία is the divine searching or test, by which God proves the faith and obedience of the godly ".—MARESIUS (VI, 55) : " Whatever men suffer in the way of pain—belongs to the punishment of sin and results from the nature of the thing : although *per accidens* as regards persons the calamities of the godly, while penal in themselves and the fruit of sin (apart from which they would not be liable to them), are not for them—punishments in satisfaction—but only curative punishments or κολάσεις καὶ παιδεῖαι καὶ νουθεσίαι ordained for their amendment and correction ".

CHAPTER XVI

THE COVENANT OF GRACE

1.—After man had impaired the covenant entered into with God it was in God's power to punish him immediately with eternal damnation. God's object in creating the world was to make known the glory of His nature. This had not yet been manifested to man in its perfection. So God resolved not to let judgment take effect immediately, but to use Adam's fall as a means to a new and higher revelation of His nature, and to turn to the fallen world in the glory of His forgiving love and redeeming grace.—WITSIUS II, i, 3 : " It pleased God according to the unsearchable riches of His wisdom to make this violation of the legal covenant subservient as an ἀφορμὴ and occasion for His own stupendous works. By instituting a new covenant of grace in which to display the surpassing treasures of His all-sufficiency much more clearly than if everything had fallen out happily for man in accordance with the former covenant ; by thus revealing, just because it was incredible and ἀκατάληπτον, it appeared that the God of truth, righteousness and holiness could without diminution of these worshipful virtues, nay by their shining with far brighter light, become the God and the salvation of the sinner ".

2.—In and for itself then it was the entire fallen race of man which God made the object of His gracious revelation, when He resolved to present to humanity as a gift of grace the life which it had forfeited. This is the eternal testament of the Father, " the immutable will of God to give an inheritance to the believing ", and the eternal decree of the Father Himself, according to which He has promised the whole of humanity, so far as it accepts His grace with penitence and trust, righteousness and eternal life as an inalienable inheritance of grace.

Note the essentially universalistic basis upon which the idea of the covenant of grace rests. COCCEIUS introduces his exposition of the doctrine of the covenant of Grace (*De foed.* IV, 74), by declaring that of course God might at once have punished man with all evils. But the height of wisdom and power aided Him in His glorious plan for exercising mercy on man. Accordingly He resolved (1) to unfold His inexpressible mercy "in vessels of mercy", and (2) "to employ an ineffable kindness and long-suffering towards the entire human race".—Similarly EGLIN (*De foed. grat.* 40): The "impelling cause of the covenant of grace" is the "love of God for the world, i.e. for the whole human race, which by the act of Satan had fallen into misery". For this "common lapse" of the human race God had ordained in Christ a "common remedy." Now a distinction must be drawn between "God's general decree" and the "particular decree of election". The former is (43) the "covenant of grace including the whole human race and by the counsel of His will planning for all indefinitely in Adam, on condition that man should repent and believe." The latter on the contrary is the covenant according to which God "Himself graciously fulfils the condition required in those whom He has assigned to Christ from eternity". As regards the former (44) the "promise is general by an outward calling"; as regards the latter we can only speak of an "effective application of the promise in accordance with the special promise of grace".—Lud. Crocius 962: "The object of the grace of compassion is the whole human race as wretched and fouled with sin. This is what our Saviour teaches by the word "world" Jn. 3. 16 (God so loved the world . . .). It is certain that here by the word "world" is to be understood not the entire system of heaven and earth with all their denizens divinely produced out of nothing, but only the human race. —963: Nor yet does Christ here understand by the world the elect only, according as they have already been separated from the world, but the entire human race taken all together (*universe*), according as by nature it lies in sin and according as it is commonly called through the gospel to repentance and faith in Christ".

3.—Thus the direct effect of the covenant is withdrawal of the divine righteousness in punishing before the long-suffering of God.— Cocceius (*S.T.* XL, 3): "The first effect of the testament is ἀνοχή, tolerance".

4.—At the same time the absolute glory of God did not admit of God restoring the covenant broken by man by an immediate destruction of sin or by arbitrary forgiveness of the guilt of sin. Sin was in man, and if God's full glory was to be made known in it, the divine righteousness in punishment had also to be effective. And if God wished to forgive the guilt of sin, the sinner could not atone for himself. So the guilt had to be expiated by a Mediator and by him the righteousness had to be merited for man and bestowed upon him as another's merit (Olevian, p. 2 and 23. Thus God's holy love would only yield to the fallen human race by allowing a recompense to be given through a mediator, the value of which outweighed the guilt of entire humanity ; by announcing to one section of humanity the gravity of His punitive righteousness ; and by entering into a covenent of grace with the other section of it. This is why the Father's covenant, which was in and for itself universal, could only be effectual for one section of humanity.

Cocceius (*De foed.* IV, 78): Only by a mediator could God show Himself gracious to the world. Since the sinner cannot reconcile or justify himself, the sin must be atoned for by a mediator. If righteousness is to be restored to the sinner again, he must be made a present of it by God. "But to present righteousness can be nothing else than to condone sins and to accept the unjust as just".—Olevian (30 f.): "The heavenly Father resolved so to execute the decree of His love as to satisfy perfect justice. As it is essential to Himself, He can no more deny it than He can deny Himself. So in the actual execution of the righteousness the greatness and strength of His love in the Son and of His perpetual mercy sworn from the beginning had to shine forth". Even in the Redeemer's work of reconciliation its essentially universalistic side must be acknowledged. Hence Eglin (54) declares that it must not be said that God did not send His Son into the world "to be the common Saviour of the whole world, conditionally set forth". Only, the circumstance that not all attain to faith and blessedness must not give rise to the view, that "in proposing a common remedy" God had failed of His purpose (51): (1) "The things which He decreed *ex hypothesi* and conditionally must be estimated conditionally", and (2) "in those whom (the Father) willed to give to Christ, He Himself fulfilled the requisite condition gratuitously". But above all it must be insisted that it is not true to say that Christ accomplished nothing for the reprobate: "he broke and abolished the whole lapse of Adam, the whole curse of the whole law, in short, the one same enemy of all, Satan". Undoubtedly therefore we may say (63) with Scripture, that "as regards all-sufficiency of merit Christ made purchase even for the reprobate, and even for them paid the λύτρον of death in full considered by itself, although it is not applied to them by the saving attraction of faith".

5.—"Yet the covenant is a free disponing by God the Saviour concerning the inheritance of righteousness and heavenly life by fixed heirs in accordance with voluntary generation and nomination, a disponing to be approached beyond any danger of alienation" (Heidegger XI, 37).— Cocceius (*S. de foed.* IV, 86): The covenant of grace rests altogether upon the testament of God, "which is a free disposition by God the Saviour concerning His goods by His heir, to be possessed in accordance with voluntary generation and nomination beyond all danger of alienation Rom. 4. 14 (if they which are of the law be made heirs, faith is made void, and the promise is made of none effect) Gal. 3. 15-18 (. . Though it be but a man's covenant, yet when it hath been confirmed, no one maketh it void or addeth to it. Now to Abraham were the promises spoken to his seed. He saith not, And to seeds as of many: but as of one,

And to thy seed, which is Christ . . . A covenant confirmed beforehand
by God, the law, which came 430 years after, doth not disannul, so as to
make the promise of none effect. If the inheritance is of the law it is no
more of promise: but God hath granted it to Abraham by promise)
Heb. 8. 10 (this is the covenant . . . I will put my laws into their mind,
and on their heart also will I write them: and I will be to them a God,
and they shall be to me a people) 9. 16-18 (where a testament is, there
must of necessity be the death of him that made it. A testament is of
force where there hath been death: doth it ever avail where he that made
it liveth? Wherefore even the first covenant had not been dedicated
without blood, Ex. 26).—Nevertheless in this divine testament there is
a pact on which its fixity depends, a pact not with lapsed man but with
the Mediator".—BRAUN (I, iii, 4, 4): "The covenant of grace has chiefly
the nature of a testament and testamentary disposition. Hence it is
called a testament Gal. 3. 15 (*supra*). p. 373. To the testament of men
which has been ratified no one makes any addition. And Christ is called
the κρείττονος διαθήκης μεσίτης, Heb. 8. 6 (now hath he obtained a
ministry the more excellent, by how much also he is the mediator of a
better covenant, which hath been enacted upon better promises); cf. Mt.
26. 28 (this is my blood of the covenant which is shed for many unto the
remission of sins). Hence it is also called the eternal covenant Heb. 13. 20
(Now the God of peace . . . with the blood of the eternal covenant . . .)
because it is included in God's eternal decrees, whose will it is to give the
inheritance in this way. Hence everything that is required in a testament
is contained in the covenant of grace: (1) The testator who is God's
Son Heb. 9. 16-17 (where a testament is, there must of necessity be the
death of him that made it. A testament is of force where there hath been
death: doth it ever avail where he that made it liveth?) (2) The sanction
and ratification of the testament by the death of the testator Heb. 9.15-16
(for this reason he is the mediator of a new covenant, that a death having
taken place for the redemption of the transgressions that were under the
first covenant, they that have been called may receive the promise of
the eternal covenant), 16 (above), Ex. 24. 8 (behold the blood of the covenant which the Lord hath made with you) Mt. 26. 28 (above). (3) The
heirs of the testament, who are all the faithful, under the promise both of
OT and NT".

Similarly WITSIUS (II, ii, 5): "In Gal. 3. 17 Paul tells of a certain
διαθήκη προκεκυρωμένη ὑπὸ τοῦ θεοῦ εἰς Χριστόν, a pact or testament
ratified beforehand by God to Christ. The contracting parties are
indicated, on the one hand God, on the other Christ, and the convention
ratified between the two. And that none may think that Christ
comes into consideration here solely as the executor of a testament

disponed by God in our favour, the Apostle says twice, not that Christ was promised us or that salvation was promised us through Christ, although this also is true, but that the promises were made to Christ himself v.16, that Christ is that seed ᾧ ἐπήγγελτα to whom He had promised, or to whom the promise was made, i.e. concerning the inheritance of the world and the kingdom of grace and glory. Clearly therefore this διαθήκη, *pactum* or *testamentum* indicates something in virtue of which a promise is made by God to Christ".—WOLLEB 92 : "Hence the covenant is also termed a *testamentum*, διαθήκη, a disponing, because by it God appoints a heavenly inheritance for His children, to be acquired by the intervening death of Jesus Christ His Son". Whereas then the covenant of works was only a covenant and not a testament, the covenant of grace (BURMANN 478) "is at once a covenant and a testament, more properly a testament".

Of course this conception of a testament and its relation to the "covenant" was contested by many (e.g. MASTRICHT VII, I, 7), the idea being to base the testamentary character of the covenant of grace not upon the eternal decree but upon the death of the Mediator. Still COCCEIUS' manner of teaching was the prevalent one and was exclusively presented by WYTTENBACH, whose teaching is (*Tent.* II, p.817) that: "The covenant of grace is nothing but the execution of the eternal testament of grace. In the eternal testament the Father asked the Son to make a placation in time etc.,—Hence it follows that this covenant is in itself a testament and only a covenant in its execution". Hence since faith and holiness are the conditions of membership of the covenant, in and for themselves they are nothing else but the benefits and gifts of it. In fact (818): "so much more are they the good things and benefits of the covenant and so too of the testament, that on account of his corruption and slave *arbitrium* man cannot himself produce faith and holiness in himself".— It follows that "therefore the covenant of grace is and should be called a testament, not only for the reason that the death of the testator, namely Christ, had to be added, as also in a human testament the death of the testator must come first, if the transfer of ownership is to be made (which is the sole or chief reason why it wishes to go by the name of testament, CL. BUDDEUS, *Theol. dogm.* p. 712), but chiefly and principally because eternal goods have been bequeathed by the testator's wish, and because those very goods also which the testator demands flow from the same testament".

6.—If this reconciliation was to remove the guilt of Adam, it had to be the opposite of his sin, and so only the eternal son of the Father could achieve it. In Adam creation had fallen away from God, in order to be equal with God. Therefore this fall could only be atoned for by him who was equal to the Father assuming the nature of the creature, becoming the same as it, and so bearing the punishment out of free love. In order then to carry out the eternal testament the Father and the Son concluded a pact, in which the Son avowed to the Father that he would (1) satisfy for the sins of all those whom the Father had resolved to give him, in order to institute through him the covenant of grace with them, and (2) restore in them, by his merit and by his agency, the original image of God, obedience to God and enjoyment of blessed peace with God. Accordingly the Father declared the Son to be His Anointed, who as such was to come into the world in His name and by His commission, and who was promised that his sacrifice and his intercession would be accepted by the Father as a perfect satisfaction for the sins of the elect (OLEVIAN, p. 23). "The covenant of God the Father with the Son is a mutual agreement, by which God the Father exacted from the Son perfect obedience to the law unto the death which he must face on behalf of chosen seed to be given him; and promised him, if he gave the obedience, the seed in question as his own perquisite and inheritance; and in return the Son, in promising this obedience to God the Father and producing it in the literal act., demanded of Him in turn the right to demand this seed for himself as an inheritance and perquisite" (HEIDEGGER XI, 12).—BURMANN (II, 15, 2): "It is a mutual pact between Father and Son, by which the Father gives the Son as λυτρώτης and the head of a foreknown people and the Son in turn sets himself to complete that ἀπολύτρωσις."— HEIDEGGER adduces (XI, 12) the following evidences of H. Writ for the Trinitarian pact: Zech. 6. 12-13 (. . . Thus speaketh the LORD of Hosts, saying, Behold the man whose name is the Branch, and he shall grow up out of his place and he shall build the temple of the LORD . . . and he shall bear the glory, and shall sit and rule upon his throne; and he shall be a priest upon his throne; and the counsel of peace shall be between them both) Is. 53. 10-11 (it pleased the Lord to bruise him; he hath put him to grief; when thou shalt make his soul an offering for sin, he shall see his seed, he shall prolong his days, and the pleasure of the Lord shall prosper in his hand. He shall see of the travail of his soul, and shall be satisfied: by his knowledge shall my righteous servant justify many; and he shall bear their iniquities) Ps. 40. 7 (sacrifice and offering thou hast no delight in; ears hast thou opened for me; burnt offering and sin offering hast thou not required) Heb. 10. 10 (By which will we have been sanctified through the the offering of the body of Jesus Christ once for all) Jn. 6. 40 (This is the will of my Father, that everyone that beholdeth the Son, and believeth on him, should have eternal life; and I will raise him up at the last day) Ps. 2 .8 (Ask of me, and I will give thee the nations for thine inheritance, and the uttermost parts of the earth for thy possession) Heb. 7. 22 by so much also hath Jesus become the surety of a better covenant) Heb. 8. 6 (But now hath he obtained a ministry the more excellent, by how much also he is the mediator of a better covenant, which hath been enacted upon better promises).—WITSIUS (II, ii, 3) stresses Lk. 22. 29 (I appoint unto you a kingdom, even as my Father appointed unto me).—COCCEIUS (*De foed.* V, 90): " In consequence of this covenant Christ is called the second Adam. As with the first Adam God made a covenant of works concerned among other things with the inheritance of the image of God which was to be transmitted to his successors, should he maintain his stand (it actually fell out the opposite way), so He made one with the Son as the man to be concerned with the inheritance of righteousness and life for his seed through obedience to the law ".

To prove that the doctrine of the pact between Father and Son is no innovation WITSIUS (II, ii, 16) makes the following submission : " Since the doctrine of the pact between Father and Son has been handed down in sacred letters so often and so eloquently, it is wrongly traduced as being a new and recent εὕρημα. Although among the more ancient I shall find few who have professedly dealt with this material, I yet see that the most outstanding of theologians have made some mention of this pact. I say nothing for the moment of *Arminius* who discusses it not without assiduity in an oration he delivered *pro gradu* (for his degree ?), points from which are adduced and praised by the keen-witted *Amesius* in the *Rescriptio ad Grevinchovium c.*I. *Amesius* actually in the *Antisynodalia, De morte Christi c.* V, 5 ridiculously presses a distinction of the *Remonstrants* by denying that the covenant entered into with Christ (he shall see his seed, and the pleasure of the Lord shall prosper in his hand) was ever ratified. *Gomarus* in dealing with the baptism of Christ on Mt. 3.13 says that for Christ it was the signification and sealing of the covenant with God, to wit, that God was His God and the giver of salvation, while he himself was bound to produce to Him perpetual gratitude in obedience. Similarly on Luke 2. 21 on Christ's circumcision he says that it was the signification and sealing of the covenant with God. The covenant consisted in the fact, partly that God was Christ's God according to the general promise (Gen. 17. 7 I will establish my covenant between me and thee and thy seed after thee throughout their generations for an everlasting covenant, to be a God unto thee and to thy seed after thee) made to him also (as to the seed of Abraham Gal. 3.16. to Abraham were the promises spoken and to his seed . . .) and according to the unique view of him (Ps. 45. 8 . . . God thy God hath anointed thee with the oil of gladness above thy fellows ; and Heb. 1. 9 quotes it) ; partly that Christ was bound to obey God's will Jn. 6. 38 (I am come down from heaven, not to do my own will, but the will of him that sent me) ; Mt. 5.17 (. . . I came not to destroy, but to fulfil ; i.e. the law and the prophets) ; see also his disputation *De merito Christi* 1. The most learned *Cloppenburg, disp.* 3, *De foedere Dei,* does not merely touch upon this material, but treats it at length and with accuracy. Most famous is VOETIUS *disp.* 3, *vol.* 2 p. 266, (Christ) was subjected on our behalf to a special law for discharging our debt through adequate penalties, as our mediator and sponsor, according to the covenant entered into with the Father. His former pupil, later his colleague, *Essenius, De subjectione Christi ad legem, cap.* 10 §2. The sealing federally of the divine promise really takes place in Christ as well, according to Is. 53.10f. (it pleased the Lord to bruise him ; he hath put him to grief ; when thou shalt make his soul an offering for sin, he shall see his seed, he shall prolong his days, and the pleasure of the Lord shall prosper in his hand)." In addition *Owen* Hebrews, vol. II, exercise IV, p. 49 ; *Tirinus* on Is. 53. 2 (he grew up before him as a tender plant, and as a root out of a dry ground : he hath no form nor comeliness ; and when we see him, there is no beauty that we should desire him)".

7.—This *pactum* by which the Son, in order to become the mediator of the Father's testament, became its sponsor and the second Adam of the human race, is still not an event in the Trinity first produced temporally through the fall, different from the Father's eternal counsel. On the contrary it is essentially connected with the fallen human race and yet is an element in the eternal and unalterable decree of God Himself.—COCCEIUS (*S.T.* XXXIII, 1) : " The counsel of God is handled in more than one way in theology ". We speak of a *consilium Dei,* so far as it is the cause and goal of all things, so far as it deals not only with the good but also with the bad, and so far as it comes before us in the revelation of grace and of judgment. It is only of the latter that we speak here. Still it does not take place at this point, " as though God had taken this resolve on the spur of the moment, after sin had entered the world, and so these were second thoughts on God's part. The decree of God is one and eternal. Whence it is certain that what He decreed concerning human sinners in the way of grace and mercy, God had decreed before the foundations of the world were laid. Thus the very foundation of the earth and the propagation of the human race from one blood and the subjection of all creatures to vanity afford proof of eternal grace. And it would plainly be realised, that He who from the beginning made heaven and earth was He who wished to be called Israel's God. Even when He was creating them He saw that He was making the world the stage of His glory, namely of His grace, by which He triumphed so to speak with highest distinction. Yet we dealt with this counsel at this point, because it was at last revealed after the fall. Nor was it necessary, either that it should be revealed before the fall, or precognosced before it came up for review. On the contrary lapsed man is he in whom ultimately the execution of this counsel both could and was bound to take place ".—WYTTENBACH (*Tent.* II, p.819 : " Since the covenant of grace is the execution of the testament of grace, and this testament is identical with the decree of election, it is manifest that God's eternal election is the foundation of the covenant of grace".

8.—The pact thus rests essentially upon free mutuality (*foedus* δίπλευρον). —HEIDEGGER (XI, 15) : " While in respect of authority and power to make a pact the covenant of grace was μονόπλευρον, this one was plainly δίπλευρον, mutual, not only because of mutual terms but also because of the equal power and will of Father and Son ".

9.—At the same time, in virtue of the unity and unchangeability of the trinitarian will of God, once the Son had taken on the *sponsio* he could as little renounce it again, as the Father could ever again reject the Son's guarantee after He had accepted it, or drop His testament. Before the pact either *persona* was free not to enter it. Once made it had to stand.— HEIDEGGER (XI, 16) : " Not as it was open to Christ to promise and to the Father to receive him in his promise, was it also open to Christ to re- nounce his promise and desert his pledge, or for the Father to accept or reject the promise, the sponsor once received : which is the too crude paradox of the *Remonstrants* with their veil of free *arbitrium* ".—MASTRICHT (V, i, 35) : " The Reformed recognise both that God most freely demanded that the Son should take up the province of mediator, and that the Son had undertaken it with equal freedom, in that each acted on rational design and assent ; hence it is said that a *consilium pacis* had been entered into between the Lord and the man Zemach Zech. 6.13 (the man whose name is Branch shall build the temple of the Lord ; and he shall bear the glory, and shall rule and sit upon his throne ; and the counsel of peace shall be between them both) Ps.60 7-9 (6-8 God hath spoken in his holiness etc.) [the question is, who is " I " v. 6 ?]. They likewise acknow- ledge that as divine persons both Father and Son were *sui iuris* and to such an extent, that considered in Himself and in His nature the Father could not have demanded it, and to this extent too the Son might not have accepted what was demanded. Still given the Father's demand they think it harsh and boorish that the Son might not have obeyed and, after he had accepted the province, they further think it a treachery that he might have withdrawn from His burden, and that so the Son could not have resiled ".— [After all—the UNITY of God !].

10.—The Son's *sponsio* was not an *expromissio* (surety), such that the guilt of sin was transferred without further ado from the elect to the Son and they had already become guiltfree through the pact itself. Rather it was a real *fideiussio* (bail), a guarantee which was already effective from the start, even before the Son, in view of this merit of his in the future, had fulfilled his vow by completing the work of redemption. Although the Son had not yet plucked out the guilt of sin, it was no longer reckoned unto them.—COCCEIUS (*S.T.* XXXV, 1): "The effect of this *sponsio* is not, that the moment man had been created God's decree was adjudicated to him, whereby He decreed to justify the ungodly; it is agreed that even if His testament and the promise of the mediator were extant, God had yet none the less offered life to man as the reward of justifying work and a right thereto to be acquired by works. Nor did it mean that the sin which had been committed by man ceased to exist, i.e., could be said to have been destroyed, obliterated, expiated Rom. 4. 15 (the law worketh wrath: where there is no law, neither is there transgression) 5. 13 (until the law sin was in the world: but sin is not imputed when there is no law) Is. 43. 25 (I, even I, am he that blotteth out thy transgression for mine own sake) Zech. 3. 9 (. . . I will remove the iniquity of that land in one day) Dan. 9. 24 (Seventy weeks are decreed upon thy people and upon thy holy city, to finish transgression and to make an end of sins, and to make reconciliation for iniquity, and to bring in everlasting righteousness, and to seal up vision and prophecy, and to anoint the most holy). Nor is it in order that God's righteousness might be announced immediately after sin. For the announcement of it required an actual sacrifice according to a promise Ps. 40. 6-10 (Sacrifice and offering hast thou no delight in; mine ears hast thou opened; burnt offering and sin offering hast thou not required. Then said I, Lo, I am come; in the roll of the book it is prescribed to me; I delight to do thy will, O my God; Yea, thy law is within my heart. I have published righteousness in the great congregation; lo, I will not refrain my lips, O LORD, thou knowest. I have not hid thy righteousness within my heart; I have declared thy faithfulness and thy salvation: I have not concealed thy lovingkindness and thy truth from the great congregation). But the effect of the promise was this: (1) that after sin had been committed, it should not be imputed to the heirs written in the testament, i.e., that there could not be in God the will to punish their sins in particular persons, because it had been laid by agreement upon the sponsor and must be incurred by him and exacted from him Is. 53. 6-7 (He was oppressed, yet he humbled himself and opened not his mouth; as a lamb that is led to the slaughter and as a sheep that before her shearers is dumb; yea, he opened not his mouth (i.e., v. 6, he on whom the Lord hath laid the iniquity of us all)). —(2) That the advent of the sponsor (to provide the sacrifice and expiate all sin which God had resolved to remit) and the gospel of salvation and righteousness might be promised. In fact, that this promise might be propounded to the heirs of salvation and so God's testament be opened and published. And (3) that those who had believed the promise might be righteous in God's sight Gen. 15. 6 (he believed in the Lord; and he counted it to him for righteousness), and might be introduced into glory as righteous men and sons Heb. 2. 10 (it became him, for whom are all things and through whom are all things, in bringing many sons into glory, to make the author of their salvation perfect through sufferings) and in this life, even amid all miseries and in death itself, might be able to boast in God, who had already begun to deal with them as their God, by making a covenant with them; and that in future He might also be to them as God, through the redemption and the benefits thereto annexed; and that thus drawing nigh to God they might be ἅγιοι and δίκαιοι, holy and righteous, but should not in this life be τετελειωμένοι, perfected, as to the fruit of righteousness and the declaration of it, nor, even in glory, as to the perfect cause of it.—But this non-imputation of sin notwithstanding liability, as not yet abolished but outstanding, might none the less be charged and remembered, because till then the mediator had not yet offered the sacrifice Heb. 10. 3 (in those sacrifices there is a remembrance of sins made year by year).

This point of doctrine belongs to the controversies which arose from the time of COCCEIUS. On it MASTRICHT remarks (V, i, 34): "Those brethren who follow the famous COCCEIUS after his death, in order more conveniently to hold that in spite of the eternal promise the faithful of the O.T. were liable right up to the actual satisfaction, insist that the *sponsio* was a *fideiussio* by which the chief debtor remains under liability right up to the actual payment. The rest of the *Reformed* hold the view that by his eternal promise the Son had absolutely promised a payment or satisfaction without reservation of the benefits of order and quittance (*excussio?*) (which lawyers leave to their *fideiussio*), had taken upon himself once and for all the complete case of the elect sinner and his liability therewith and had undertaken them once for all and had thereby delivered those to be redeemed from all liability, although they incidentally add that this divine surety must not be exacted, in terms of some civil surety, with the same rigidity and universality."—At any rate HEIDEGGER (XI, 24) describes the prevailing view: "Let those who hold this opinion have joy of it. For me the reason for it does not hold. There is nothing to this effect in Scripture. Nor have theologians so far spoken to this effect. They regarded the *sponsio* as just a *fideiussio* (surety). By it Christ by going bail for the debtor and making himself the pledge promised payment of the obedience due, and in due course paid it by dying, and so as regards merit at least, freed the sinner who was the principal debtor, though not before his death; although the efficacy of this merit was exerted in many ways sufficient for salvation even before Christ's death. Indeed the final result of this *sponsio* or Christ, by the efficacy of a merit not present but future, was that man's sin could no more be imputed for condemnation: on the contrary faith was imputed unto righteousness and life."

11.—Upon the eternal testament of the Father, upon the likewise eternal vow of surety by the Son and upon the pact between Father and Son rests God's covenant of grace with the elect (*foedus gratiae gratuitum, evangelicum, novum*). "The covenant of grace is a gratuitous agreement between an offended God and certain offending men, in which of His grace and sheer good pleasure and to the same sobered believers God has assigned righteousness and life in the same Christ the Mediator, and these in turn, by promising to produce faith and sobriety to God through the grace of Christ, obtain from Him righteousness and the right to expect life" (HEIDEGGER XI, 8).—In the main these dogmaticians' definitions perfectly coincide. Here is URSIN's definition (*Explic. catech.* p. 99): "(God's covenant) is a mutual *pactio* between God and men, by which God assures men that He will be favourable to them, will remit sins, bestow new righteousness, the H. Spirit and life eternal through and because of the Son the Mediator. In turn men bind themselves to God to believe and to repent, i.e., to receive with true faith this sublime benefit and to afford God true obedience". This pact is called a covenant and a testament: covenant, "because God promises us definite benefits and bargains for obedience from us in turn, also adding solemn ceremonies to confirm it"; a testament "because by the intervention of Christ's death this reconciliation took place with a view to ratification."

EGLIN, 1 : "The covenant of grace is the gospel pact made in Christ after the fall with the first parents and their descendants. In his name it was renewed to the father of believers and to his posterity. And at length it was published to every nation, God fulfilling the condition required in the elect, in order that the credit for our salvation might be His entirely, and the inheritance of eternal life pass freely to those who walk according to the Spirit on account of the merit of the single Jesus Christ to display His glorious mercy."—COCCEIUS (*Summ. de foed*, 76): "The covenant of grace is an agreement between God and sinful man, God declaring His free good pleasure to give righteousness and an inheritance to a fixed seed in the Mediator by faith for the glory of His grace and through the promise of righteousness to be given to those that believe in Him who invites, man agreeing by faith of heart with what was contracted for peace and friendship and the right to expect an inheritance in good conscience Lk. 12. 32 (fear not, little flock: it is the Father's good pleasure to give you the kingdom).—MARESIUS (VIII, 4): "The covenant of grace is one by which God the Master of all freely promises remission of sin, redemption from all misery, life (in a word) and blessedness eternal and heavenly through Christ, upon condition of repentance and faith."—BURMANN 476: "The covenant of grace is a gratuitous agreement between God and the sinner, in which by His free good pleasure God assigns to a fixed seed through the injunction of repentance and faith, righteousness and an inheritance in the Mediator. Man moreover concurs in this promise and mandate through faith, and hence possesses the right to ask for the heavenly inheritance". —WITSIUS (II, i, 5): "The covenant of grace is an agreement between God and the elect sinner, God declaring His free good pleasure anent the free giving of eternal salvation and all the covenanted blessings pertaining thereto, through and because of Christ the Mediator, man moreover falling in with the decree in question by sheer faith".—HOT-TINGER 240: "The Gospel covenant is a free pact between an offended God and offending man, entered upon through the mediation of Christ the θεάνθρωπος. In him God for Christ's sake freely promises man remission of sins, regeneration by the Spirit and eternal life. In his turn relying on the same grace man accords faith and repentance to God who makes this the condition."—LAMPE asks (*Einleitung zum Geheimnis des Gnadenbundes*, p. 43): "What is the covenant of grace? The treaty between the triune God and the elect sinner, by which God promises the sinner everything for Christ's sake which he needs for his felicity, while the sinner agrees to these promises and thereby receives a right to demand them."

12.—The "contracting parties" to the covenant of grace are thus God (but not as the Creator and absolute Lord of the creature, nor yet as the holy Lawgiver, but as the merciful Father and Redeemer)—man, (not as the creature generally but as the sinful creature)—and Christ (as the Mediator between them).—RIJSSEN X, 11: "The contracting parties, or the subject of the covenant of grace, are three: (1) an offended God, who acts here, not as in the covenant of nature as the Creator and Lord, because He has abolished the natural intercourse which used to unite creature to Creator; nor as holding an infinite ὑπεροχή over created things, because in his guilt of sin and smitten by his sense of it

man could not have endured it; nor as the legislator and rigid exactor
of moral perfection, because this could not be expected from a corrupt
creature; but as the merciful Father and Redeemer: (2) offending man,
here regarded not as a creature simply, or as a creature intact and
righteous, as in the first covenant, but as a sinful creature giving offence,
as man dead in sins, the son of wrath: and this not simply; otherwise
this covenant should have coincided equally with sinners all and sundry;
but as a sinner conscious of his wretchedness, shattered by the sense
of it and so legally contrite: (3) the Mediator Christ here intercedes,
reconciling offending man to God. In the first covenant, because there
was as yet no discord between God and man, there was no need of any
Mediator. But in the subsequent one he was necessary, because on
account of His own righteousness God could not tolerate guilty man,
and because on account of his unrighteousness man had not the power
to approach God."—HOTTINGER, p. 244: "The matter consists of the
parties mutually covenanting by the mediator's intervention: an offended
God, offending man and a θεάνθρωπος mediator, reconciling the
Offended to the offender."

EGLIN (101): The "final cause" of the "covenant of grace entered
into with us in Christ" is a twofold one: "The supreme and primary
end is the manifestation of God's glory and mercy;—(102): the subordinate and secondary end is participation in eternal salvation conceded
through the merit of the one Christ Jesus to the repentant who grasp
Christ with true faith".—HOTTINGER (245): "The end is partly the
glory of God as well as of Christ the Mediator, through the declaration
of His wisdom, φιλανθρωπία and mercy, righteousness and truth;
partly in man's salvation and eternal bliss."

13.—The single ground of the covenant of grace is God's compassionate
love for all men and the free Trinitarian counsel of God.—EGLIN (*De
foed. grat.*, 40): "The impulsive cause of the covenant of grace has been
God's love for the world, that is, for the entire human race fallen into
misery by Satan's cunning".—HOTTINGER (242): "The efficient principal
cause of the Gospel covenant is God reconciling the world to Himself in
Christ and with Him the Son and the H. Spirit, or the whole sacrosanct
Trinity revealing itself most clearly in the three Persons. The subordinate
impelling causes are God's gratuitous φιλανθρωπία and compassion and
Christ the Mediator's outward satisfaction and intercession".—WOLLEB
92: "The efficient cause of it generally is the whole sacrosanct Trinity;
singly it is *Christus θεάνθρωπος*, the angel of the covenant."

And the purpose of the covenant of grace lies in the fact that God
would (1) be the cause of all salvation to His elect, in such wise

that the glory of the redemption belongs to Him alone and His absolute glory is made manifest; and (2) institute in His elect sure comfort in an eternal sonship to God that fadeth not away (OLEVIAN, p. 14).

14.—The covenant of grace is distinguished from the covenant of works first of all by being primarily connected not with Adam's but with Christ's person and heirs, i.e., with a definite number of sinners elected from eternity.—HEIDEGGER (XI, 11): "The second part of this covenant is man, not as such but as offending and sinful; and not any man, but man determined in eternity by God's decree; and not singly by himself, but in Christ as Mediator and sponsor".—RIISSEN (X, 14): "The covenant of grace differs from the former one (1) in the person with whom it is contracted: in the former case the first Adam, in the latter the second, Ps. 89. 4 (thy seed will I establish for ever, and build up thy throne to all generations); (2) in the persons for whom; in the earlier case all Adam's, in the latter all Christ's, 1 Cor. 15. 22 (as in Adam all die, so also in Christ shall all be made alive)".

15.—These persons God of His grace (not because or as though He had foreseen their faith) resolved to arouse to faith. The second difference is that it was based not upon a condition to be fulfilled by man but solely upon God's grace, and therefore it is unchanging and eternal. After the first covenant was broken by man, God resolved not to leave the new covenant exposed for a second time to the changeability of the human will. In order that the new covenant might not be imperilled again, God undertook the execution and maintenance of it entirely Himself ; and since He therefore claimed from man no other duty than that of faith in grace, He undertook to supply the elect with this faith Himself (OLEVIAN p.12).

The dogmaticians raise the question, whether the covenant of grace does or does not rest upon a condition. In general they express themselves in favour of its unconditionality. MASTRICHT here distinguishes between the *finis* and the *media* of the covenant of grace (V, i, 37) : " I think we must distinguish most carefully between those promises of the covenant of grace which are of the nature of means to an end, such as are the obtaining of redemption through Christ, regeneration, conversion, the conjunction of faith with purpose of amendment ; and those which are of the nature of an end, e.g. justification, adoption, glorification etc. If this is done, we seem bound to say that the promises of the covenant of grace of the first kind are plainly absolute. It involves a manifest contradiction to require of man dead in sins a preliminary condition for the redemption of Christ, like redemption etc. But promises of the second class, like justification, adoption etc. are altogether conditioned, yet in such a way that the satisfaction of conditions depends not upon the strength of *liberum arbitrium*, but on the absolute promises of this covenant.

That in the covenant of grace the fourfold relation of the covenant of works is also present is shown as follows by WYTTENBACH (II, 810) : " Since therefore God requires something in this covenant, a stipulation is made. And since He wishes to remit sins and to confer eternal life on the man who rejoices in faith and has a zeal for holiness, a promise is made. And where a man actually rejoices in such faith and holiness, an additional stipulation is then fulfilled. And thereupon moreover, he can ask for what is promised, the result being a counter-stipulation. So that in the covenant of grace there are four acts, as in the covenant of works ".— Similarly COCCEIUS (*S. T.* XLI, 2) : " The '*foedus* which God makes with the sinner' consists of four parts : (1) the *stipulatio, νομοθεσία* or *παραγγελία* ; (2) the 'conditioned promise persuading us to obey or assent' ; (3) the ' sinner's right to obtain or claim or expect the good promised, whereby ; (4) he is righteous and is so called ' ".

16.—So God set up the new covenant, which rests, not upon the commandment, " This do and thou shalt live ", or ' Thou shalt love God etc.", but on the promise, " God so loved the world that He gave His only-begotten Son, that all who believe in him should have everlasting life " (OLEVIAN, p. 270). The threats of eternal death, which are also announced in Scripture to the elect for his sins, belong therefore not to the covenant of grace but to that of works, in which all are born because of inherited sin.—WYTTENBACH (*Tent.* II, 822) : " To the covenant of grace and in it men come as sinners and in it God offers remission of sins with the right to eternal life and so therewith He offers deliverance from the penalty of which they rendered themselves worthy by having violated the covenant of works, expressly in order that the threat of the covenant of works may not be put into execution in their cases, which threat rests upon all. So if they do not accept the covenant of grace, they remain under the threat of the covenant of works, i.e. under eternal death. Thus the threat of eternal death does not take its rise in the covenant of grace but in the covenant of works, and the covenant of grace merely repeats the threats of the covenant of works.—(823) : Since the threats of the covenant of works rest upon all men, we can in a sense see the answer to the question, what covenant men are born under. Obviously because of the sin naturally inherent in and imputed to all the covenant of works can no longer have place, and so they are not born under it. At the same time, since the threat of this covenant has been left, they may, in this sense, be said to be born under it. Further the young children born to parents who have consented to the covenant of grace whether by word of mouth or from the heart, may, so far as they are represented by their parents, be said to be born under the covenant of grace."—LAMPE (*Einleit.*, p. 44) : " In the covenant of grace there are no threatenings because it can never be broken again ".

17.—In this covenant of grace are to be distinguished (1) the substance of the covenant itself or the gracious benefit promised by God, and (2) the dispensation of the covenant in the visible Church. The substance of the covenant of grace consists in God having vowed to be once more the God and Father of His elect, to adopt them in Christ as His children with whom He has ceased to be angry, and as heirs of eternal life to whom He has pardoned all sins, in order that He might be glorified in both lives by them for His merciful love (OLEVIAN, p. 2). Thus in the covenant of grace God puts forth a double blessing, the same eternal life which He had promised in the covenant of works, and, as the means to acquiring the same, the righteousness of Jesus Christ.—COCCEIUS (*S. de foed.* IV, 77) declares that the benefit which is received in the covenant of grace is finally and indirectly the same benefit as was promised in the covenant of works, namely eternal life : directly, it is the righteousness which holds with God.—HEIDEGGER (XI, 35) : " God has promised the believer in Christ who repents a twin boon, both a final and an intermediate one. The final one is heavenly life, the same of course as the covenant of works promised on condition of perfect and constant obedience. The intermediate one is perfect righteousness in the sight of God, which is acceptance of the covenanted person as righteous, i.e. as possessing through the obedience to the law and through the satisfaction made for his liability, the right to ask and to keep the inheritance of eternal life, from the hope of which man had fallen away through sin ".

18.—The administration then of the covenant of grace by the Word is the effectual calling of the elect from the misery of sin and death to the knowledge of the Son of God, to a hold upon his righteousness and upon eternal life and to the renewal of their original nature in the image of God. In order to testify to the *consensus mutuus* between God and us outwardly through the word and through visible signs (sacraments), God of His free grace makes this outward calling inwardly active and effective for the elect (but not for the ungodly, who always reject the proffered grace with wickedness and hardness of heart) (OLEVIAN, p. 3).— MARTINIUS (*Christ. doctr. summa capita*, p. 92) : " Because of our infirmity God deals with us by the word (as they say) audible and visible.— URSIN (*Explic. catech.* 197) : " This mutual paction between God and men is confirmed by outward signs, which we call sacraments, i.e. sacred signs testifying to this will of God towards us and to our gratitude and duties towards God."

19.—The adoption of the individual into the covenant of grace, or the arousing of the consciousness that he too belongs to the number of the elect, is effected and realised (since natural man is utterly incapable of raising himself to God), solely by the grace of the H. Spirit; and that, when on the one hand God by the grace of the H. Spirit seals in their hearts the promise made in the Gospel of forgiveness of sins and of reconciliation and begins the renewal to eternal life, in order to perfect them gradually—and when on the other hand man dead in sins receives the H. Spirit and by Him is so roused from death to life, that he not only can and wishes to believe in the forgiveness and renewal promised in Christ, but also really does believe and is accordingly inviolably sure that God has given Himself in Christ even to him as his reconciled Father (OLEVIAN, p. 18).—COCCEIUS (*S. de foed.* VII, 211): "Before grace supervenes, man has nothing by which to raise himself.—212: Hence it is clear that by grace alone is man drawn to the covenant and to the grace or friendship of God." 213-214: But this grace is not a mere "external illumination, by which the promise of heavenly blessings is clearly placed before his eyes". Rather, although clearly "no one is drawn to God by the use of reason without the revelation of the grace which is in Christ", it is worth noticing that the elect are introduced into the covenant of grace by two means:—(1) (215) by the *meritum Christi*, since Christ merits for believers not merely righteousness and eternal life, but has also secured that they should be reborn to faith; and (2) (223) by the "effectual regeneration of the Spirit of life in Christ, which is also called conversion".—OLEVIAN (p. 16): "In Jn. 6. 37 Christ does not say: "All that which the Father giveth me may come unto me", but: "cometh unto me" ".

20.—The effecting of an unshakeable certainty of salvation, on the basis of faith in the unchangeableness of grace, in the promise given to Christ that his seed shall never perish, and on the basis of faith that the salvation which Christ's seed receives is to be his personal and therefore inalienable possession, belongs essentially to the purpose for which the covenant of grace was ordained at all.—COCCEIUS (*Summ. de foed.* VIII, 245-248): The doctrine of "the fixity of the covenant of Grace" (*de constantia foederis gratiae*) belongs to the most fundamental propositions of H. Scripture. "In inculcating it Scripture scarcely satisfies itself in order to satisfy us". In this connection these points are to be distinguished (1) the immutability of grace; (2) the promise of seed which was given

Christ; and (3) the promise of salvation which was given the seed.—
The immutability of the covenant of grace is clear, (1) because, as in
Scripture ʼthe testament from which the covenant of grace proceeds
is called an eternal one, Heb. 13. 20 (the blood of the eternal covenant),
so too the covenant is called an eternal one, Is. 54. 10 (my covenant
of peace shall not be removed) Jer. 33. 20, 21, 25 (if ye can break my
covenant of the day, and my covenant of the night . . . then may also
my covenant be broken. . . . 25 recapitulates); (2) because it is a
testamentum ratificatum, "which cannot be rendered void by any disposition" Gal. 3. 15 (. . . though it be but a man's covenant, yet when
it hath been confirmed, no one maketh it void, or addeth thereto)
Heb. 9. 17-19 (a testament is of force where there hath been a death
. . . even the first covenant hath not been dedicated without blood
(Ex. 24. 6-8)); (3) because this testament disposes of a *gratia firma ac
constans* [διαθηκή is the word throughout, which R.V. always translates in all the passages by covenant and not by "testament"].

As to the second point [promise of seed] it distinctly is, that Christ
received from the Father a name and an inheritance. Thus it is impossible "that Abraham, Isaac, Jacob, David (who are types of believers)
should not have seed and an inheritance (250)". Similarly the last point
is also fixed; the *salus seminis* is absolutely sure. Salvation and eternal
life belong to each individual believer as a personal possession. It follows
that "this highest thing has been offered us in the Christian religion,
that we should have hope, to wit, of the manifestation of the divine
glory in us in its own time, and that we should be able to glory in it.
But to acquire this hope there is need of zeal in taking refuge (256)".

21.—The covenant of grace was already published in Paradise, after the
fall took place, Gen. 3. 15 (I will put enmity between thee and the woman
. . . it shall bruise thy head, and thou shalt bruise his heel). Subsequently this publication was frequently renewed in many ways, and
finally by the sending of the Son, was confirmed by God's strengthening
it with an oath and accredited by guaranteeing signs (*promulgatio, sanctio*
and *confirmatio foederis*).

"(The promise)" (Burmann, III, i, 6) "was first made in Paradise
itself, Gen. 3. 15. and this word has been the matrix and root of every
word of grace which has been heard subsequently and which ought
ever to have been heard in the Church, and the foundation of the faith
and salvation of Adam and of the Church which follows him into every
age".—Cocceius (*De foed.* VI, 198): To the "*declaratio* of God's good
pleasure or testament" there also belong the *sanctio* and *confirmatio* of it.
The *sanctio* is (1) "God's oath, by which God shows that this grace of

His is ἀμεταμέλητος", and (2) "His announcement of the stern
judgment in which all remain, who do not receive this grace, and of the
vengeance upon which they rush, who neglect and spurn so great a
salvation.—201: The confirmation of the testament lies in the signs
which . . . have usually been called sacraments". The latter are "signs
of the covenant or testimonies of God's friendship". In and for themselves (203) they are "earthly entities possessing an analogy with some
heavenly entity upon which God's blessings depend". They visibly set
forth "things heavenly, to spur consideration, to clear the mind compendiously and to aid the memory, what time God propounds a heavenly
entity under the likeness of an earthly entity".—HEIDEGGER (XI, 47-49):
"To the covenant of grace belongs its κύρωσις or sanction, which is absolved by the pact between God the Father and the Son and by the death
of the testator, by an oath and by intimation of judgment against the
unbelieving: (1) As regards the pact between God the Father and the
Son and the definite death of the testator the sanction of the covenant
is like that of a testament, since we have already said earlier that the
covenant is testamentary.—Gal. 3. 17 . . . A covenant (or testament)
confirmed beforehand by God, the law, which came 430 years after,
doth not disannul, so as to make the promise of none effect; Heb. 9. 16,
where a testament is, there must be the death of the testator; Mt. 26. 28,
this is my blood of the covenant, which is shed for many unto remission
of sins; Heb. 10. 29, of how much sorer punishment, think ye, shall he
be judged worthy, who . . . hath counted the blood of the covenant
wherewith he was sanctified, an unholy thing and hath done despite
unto the Spirit of grace?—(2) To this pact is added God's oath, by which
God willed to show that this grace of His was ἀμεταμέλητος, of which He
could not repent, Rom. 11. 26 ((Is. 59. 20f.) it is written, There shall come
out of Zion a Deliverer; He shall turn away ungodlinesses from Israel)
Gen. 22. 16f. (By myself I have sworn, saith the Lord, because thou
hast done this thing, and hast not withheld thy son, thine only son:
that in blessing I will bless thee and in multiplying I will multiply thy
seed as the stars of heaven, and as the sand which is upon the sea shore;
and thy seed shall possess the gate of his enemies) Heb. 6. 16-19 (Men
swear by the greater, and in every dispute of theirs the oath is final for
confirmation. Wherein God being minded to shew more abundantly
unto the heirs of the promise the immutability of His counsel, interposed
with an oath: that by two immutable things, in which it is impossible
for God to lie, we may have a strong encouragement, who have fled
for refuge to lay hold of the hope set before us; which we have as an
anchor of the soul, a hope both sure and steadfast and entering into that
which is within the veil),—(3) Finally God also sanctioned His covenant

by announcing severe judgment upon the unbelieving. How shall we excape, if we neglect so great a salvation? (Heb. 2. 3); Heb. 10. 26-28 (if we sin wilfully, after that we have received the knowledge of the truth, there remaineth no more a sacrifice for sins, but a certain fearful expectation of judgment, and a fierceness of fire which shall devour the adversaries. A man that hath set at nought Moses' law dieth without compassion on two or three witnesses, etc.) Rom. 2. 5 (after thy hard and impenitent heart treasurest up for thyself wrath in the day of wrath and revelation of the righteous judgment of God).—Nor are we to think either, that the guilt of the first sin and the judgment, which according to the covenant of works falls upon all Adam's children, is universally rescinded in the covenant of grace by Christ's death. Even the elect themselves are judged as ἀσεβεῖς, ungodly, sinners, enemies of God (Rom. 4. 5 to him that worketh not, but believeth on him that justifieth the ungodly, his faith is reckoned for righteousness) 5. 6, 8, 10, 11 (while we were yet weak, in due season Christ died for the ungodly . . . while we were yet sinners Christ died for us . . . while we were enemies, we were reconciled . . . we also rejoice in God through our Lord Jesus Christ, through whom we have now received the reconciliation). And those who do not believe in order that they may be justified by the grace of God, are equally called ἀσεβεῖς, ungodly and damned, in Scripture; and our sins are washed solely by the blood of Christ when we believe Eph. 5. 26 (. . . having cleansed (the Church) by the laver of water with the word) 1 Jn. 1, 7 . . . the blood of Christ cleanseth us from all sin) Rev. 7, 14 (. . . they washed their robes, and made them white in the blood of the Lamb). And so the sins of non-believers are not washed by the blood of Christ, but remain and are imputed to hem Jn. 3. 18, 36 (he that believeth not hath been judged already, oecause he hath not believed on the name of the only begotten Son of God . . . he that obeyeth not the Son shall not see life, but the wrath of God abideth on him) Heb. 2. 3 (how shall we escape, if we neglect so great salvation? . . .) 10. 26 ((Jer. 31. 33) . . . I will put my laws on their heart, and upon their mind also will I write them) Is. 27. 5 (or else let him take hold of my strength, that he may make peace with me; yea, let him make peace with me) Heb. 6. 4 (those whom it is impossible to renew unto repentance). The confirmation of the covenant of grace lies in the signs of grace, which because of the sacred use or mystery which they conceal, go by the name of sacraments".

22.—As regards substance the covenant of grace was at all times one and the same. Invariably the "covenanted parties" were the injured, merciful God and guilty man elected in the one mediator Christ.

Invariably it was faith and repentance that God demanded of man, and righteousness and eternal life that God promised him. Invariably it was the right of sonship to God that was bestowed on the partners in the covenant of grace. Invariably it was one and the same testament of God upon which the covenant rested. And invariably the substance of the sacraments was one and the same, namely the personal Christ and his gracious salvation, even though the form of the sacraments changed.—URSIN (*Explic. catech.* 99): "(God's covenant) is one in substance: (1) Because there is one God, one mediator of God and men, Christ Jesus, one mode of reconciliation, one faith, one way of salvation from the beginning for all who are being and have been saved. The great question is, whether the fathers of the old testament were saved in a different way from us. Unless it is correctly explained, great darkness is poured upon the gospel. The following sayings bear upon it: Heb. 13. 8 (Jesus Christ is the same yesterday, today and for ever) Eph. 1. 22 ((God) put all things in subjection under his feet, and gave him to be head of all things in the church which is his body, (to be) the fulness of him that filleth all in all) 4. 10 (he that descended is the same also that ascended far above all the heavens, that he might fill all things) Jn. 1. 18 (No man hath seen God at any time; God only begotten, which is in the bosom of the Father, he hath declared Him) Ac. 4. 12 (in none other is there salvation; for neither is there any other name under heaven, that is given among men, wherein we must be saved) Mt. 11. 27 (all things have been delivered unto me of my Father: and no one knoweth the Son save the Father; neither doth any know the Father save the Son, and he to whomsoever the Son willeth to reveal Him) Jn. 14. 26 (the Comforter, the H. Spirit, whom the Father will send in my name, he shall teach you all things, and bring to your remembrance all that I have said unto you) Lk. 10. 24 (I say unto you, that many prophets and kings desired to see the things which ye see, and saw them not; and to hear the things which ye hear, and heard them not) Jn. 8. 56 (your father Abraham rejoiced to see my day; and he saw it, and was glad). Thus all, under law as well as under gospel, who were to be saved, looked back in faith to the single mediator Christ, through whom alone they have been reconciled to God and saved.—(2) (The covenant) is one, because the principal conditions, which are called the substance of the covenant, are the same B.C. and A.D. In either testament before and after the manifestation of Christ God promises remission of sins to those who believe and act repentance, and men bind themselves to believe God and to act repentance (*agere poenitentiam*).

HEIDEGGER (XI, 74-82): "In fact and in substance the covenant of grace is one, perpetual and unchangeable right from the beginning of the

Church, starting with Adam's fall through all its ages (*aetates*) down to consummation of the *saeculum*.—In both cases the covenanted parties are the same: God, one in essence, trine in *personae*, offended at men's sins but reconcilable *ex gratia*; and likewise offending men in need of reconciliation to God.—Before and after the fall there was and is the same mediator, Jesus Christ, reconciling offending man to an offended God by his promise and his death, and by its efficacy even if not yet extant or by its actual merit if extant.—The actions of the covenant of grace, the stipulation of faith and repentance and the further stipulation answering to it, as well as the promise of righteousness and life and the corresponding restipulation to that, were imposed in common upon the whole Church before and after Christ.—Like the stipulation and astipulation of the covenant of grace the divine promise of it and its human restipulation, meaning the benefits of the covenant, namely Christ's righteousness together with the benefits annexed and life eternal and the right to both, competent for believers, by the ἐρώτησις or interrogation of a good conscience, agree in any state of the Church.—The adoption of the fathers in the OT to be sons was *sigillatim*.—In short these same fathers had both the promise and the supply of life, eternal and blessed, after this temporal one, both of the spirit of course after death and of the whole man after the resurrection from the dead.—As regards promise the testamentary nature of the covenant of grace is the same. For as a covenant which flows from a testament is one and the same and unchangeable, so also the testament or unchangeable decree, which God resolved to indicate more abundantly to the heirs of the promise is single and eternal, Heb. 6. 17 (God, being minded to shew more abundantly to the heirs of the promise the immutability of his counsel, interposed with an oath).—The sealing of the covenant of grace, while differing as to the seals and ceremonies of the Church before and after Christ, agrees as to the thing signified and sealed, namely, the covenant of grace, Christ and his benefits. This is quite agreed, whether the sacraments of the two testaments are viewed absolutely, as seals and by themselves, or are compared with each other ἀναλόγως, by comparative consideration".

23.—But although the substance of the covenant of grace was from the start an unchangeable, eternal ordinance, the manner and mode of proclaiming and appropriating it varied at different periods—HEIDEGGER (XI, 91): "Although however both covenant and testament of grace have been a single, immutable and eternal entity and the application of it as regards its substance the same at any one time, nevertheless its inward and outward mode of publication and of application by the same most wise decree and good pleasure of God is susceptible of a certain difference, which still does not derogate at all from the established unity of the covenant itself".

24.—We must distinguish the dispensation of the covenant of grace before and after the manifestation of Jesus Christ. Of course even before it Christ was the sole ground of all salvation of the elect, but still only in such wise that they also received salvation in the form of believing expectation and hope.—COCCEIUS (*Summ. de foed.* X, 277): The covenant of grace has "a twofold δικονομία" and "a twofold time", i.e. (1) "in expectation of Christ" and (2) "in faith in Christ revealed". Above all we must insist that "Jesus Christ is the same yesterday and today and for ever", Heb. 13. 8, i.e. that Christ has been and is the object of faith unto salvation in either period, Old or New Testament, and that all who are saved have been and will be saved for ever by his grace" (278).

25.—But in the kingdom of God before the manifestation of Christ the periods calling for special treatment are that of the patriarchs before the Law and that of the Mosaic law.—The threefold division of the *administratio foederis gratiae* favoured by some dogmaticians into (1) the non-legal evangelical period of the Protevangelium in Paradise up to the time of Moses, (2) a specifically OT period of the dominion of the Law from Moses to Christ, and (3) the evangelical period of the NT, was rejected by the majority of dogmaticians.—RIISSEN (X, 17): "There are some who are more attracted by the τριχοτομία of regarding the administration of the covenant of grace (1) under promise before the Law, from the protevangelium to Moses, which promise, they maintain, was of sheer grace and freedom without any yoke or kind of accusing law; (2) under law, from Moses to Christ; here they want the OT to begin, the inheritance of which is the land of Canaan; (3) under gospel; here the NT begins. But we do not think of resiling from the received view, which retains a διχοτομία, and describes the first dispensation before Christ by the notion of the OT, because by Scripture usage the promise is not only referred to the time before the Law but is extended to all the to centuries following under the law right up to Christ. Hence Peter says to the Jews of his time: The promise was made to you and to your children Ac. 2. 39, and the promises are said to belong to the Israelites Rom. 9. 4 (whose are promises).—The name OT is not restricted to the Mosaic dispensation but is extended to the entire dispensation which preceded Christ from the actual lapse of man and the promise given to him, 2 Cor. 3. 14 (Till this very day at the reading of the old covenant the same veil remaineth unlifted; which veil is done away in Christ). Hence Christ, Heb. 9. 15, is called the mediator appointed to expiate the transgressions committed under the former covenant; not, of course, just under the law, but right from the beginning of the world, and 8.13 (in that he saith, a new covenant, he hath made the first old), whatever is to be made old is called an old testament, not only the ceremonies first brought in by Moses, but the sacrifices and circumcision, which were already in vogue before the writing of the law. But if fixing of the OT is sometimes in a peculiar way attributed to the Mosaic dispensation, this is only in order more clearly to confirm it.—20: Those of course, like ROLLOCK, PISCATOR, TRELCA-TIUS etc., who make two substantially different covenants, take the old covenant strictly by not only separating the promise of grace from it but also by opposing it to it, so that the Old Covenant should be the covenant of works, the new covenant evangelical and to faith. But those who set up but one, like CALVIN, MARTYR, URSIN, take the word covenant more broadly to include also the promise of grace, although more ob-scurely. And because the promise was administered differently before and after Christ, they distinguish them into two, an old and a new, by a division not of genus into species, like the former lot, but of subject according to accidents, which others do not deny. So that the dissent is not only in a different use of terms but in the actual fact."

Consequently most teach like WOLLEB p. 23: "The administration of the covenant of grace is divided as to time into the old and the new testa-ment: the old testament is the covenant of grace administered in the time of Christ to be exhibited (*tempore Christi exhibendi*).—The form of this administration was threefold: the first from Adam to Abraham, the second from Abraham to Moses, the third from Moses to Christ.— Between the first and second forms of administration there is this difference (1) the former was made in the words of a promise, of the utmost brevity but of the utmost clarity. (2) The former has the rite of sacrifices only, the latter also has the rite of circumcision. (3) The former was propounded to the entire human race, the latter was restricted to Abraham's posterity. —Between the third and the two prior forms of administration there is this difference, that the third is proved perfect and truly testamentary, being enlarged not only by paschal types of Christ's death, but by any number of others. The NT is the covenant of grace administered after Christ had been exhibited".—Similarly HEIDEGGER (XII, 2): "There is a convenient distinction of twin periods of the Church preceding Christ and so a twofold economy of the covenant of grace administered in differ-ent ways, the earlier before the law and under the patriarchs, the later under the law handed down by Moses and in full operation right up to Christ." The types of these two economies are according to Gal. 4. 21-27 Hagar and Sarah and the sons born of them (XII, 5): "Hagar the bond-maid bore a son according to the flesh (Ishmael), Sarah the freewoman according to promise. The former St. Paul compares v.24 with the testament which is from Mt. Sinai and which begets into slavery.—Whence it is clear that by the former is not to be understood the covenant of works, since neither was it a διαθήκη or *testamentum* opposed to the NT nor had it its origin in Mt. Sinai nor did it *per se* beget into slavery, to mention only a very few points".

26.—Both the patriarchal and the Mosaic periods display the appropriate economy of the OT, by which expression is designated "the purpose of God to give His people their typical inheritance". This is called a "testament", because it is not merely a "pact" but also a "testamentary disposition", and is called the old testament, "not so much on account of its priority in time, as in respect of its being out of date and abrogated, whence its inevitable disappearance" (BURMANN IV, i, 7). The first proclamation of the Old Testament was imparted to Abraham. The real setting of it up with the people Israel first resulted through Moses on Mt. Sinai. And this is why both the OT periods are to be distinguished as economies proper of the Covenant of Grace (BURMANN 588). "(The economy under the patriarchs) is the free divine administration of a pure covenant of grace right from its beginning down to Moses, by which God notified the promise of a covenant to the first parents in Paradise, also published it abroad and explained it in the covenant entered into more solemnly with Noah and Abraham; in short by instituting the outward cultus of preaching the Word, of sacrifices and of sealing through certain sacraments He confirmed it to the heirs of a righteous seed and of eternal life" (HEIDEGGER XII, 7).—*Ibid.*: "We call it the administration of of a pure covenant of grace, because he obtained it not mixed with the law which calls to slavery, but unifold and pure. We call it free, because it was of God's mere εὐδοκία thus and not otherwise to rule the Church of the patriarchs, exactly as the head of the family is free to rule his family according to the different states and ages of the children in one way or in another, so long as it conduces to the family's interests."

27.—The sacramental signs of this economy were the rainbow and circumcision. The rainbow was a visible guarantee of the covenant of grace, since by it God sealed the promise that He would no longer destroy the earth, but would protect His elect on it for Himself and fulfil His promises. By circumcision God sealed the promise, that not Abraham's successors generally, but his chosen seed, purified from its fleshly nature, should be the heirs of the promise.—HEIDEGGER (XII, 75, 78) : " The economy of the covenant of grace had also its own σημεῖα, signs or sacraments, of which nature were the bow and circumcision. The bow was the sign of the covenant of grace, by which God signified and sealed by the bow set in the clouds the grace of the covenant and particularly of His long suffering, by which He fulfilled the promise on account of the woman's seed, no longer to destroy the world by flood, but while it still stood, to manifest the promised seed and in it to justify and save believers.—The second sacrament, circumcision, is the sign of God's covenant entered into with Abraham and his seed, wherein by the cutting of the foreskin in the males co-option into the covenant of grace as well as the cutting away of sins by blood and the Spirit of Christ to come was adumbrated and confirmed to him ".—COCCEIUS (*Summa theol.* LIII, 5) : " Abraham having been justified by faith God gave him the sign of circumcision as the seal of the righteousness of faith Rom. 4.11 (he received the sign of circumcision, a seal of the righteousness of the faith which he had while he was in uncircumcision : that he might be the father of all them that believe, though they be in uncircumcision ; that righteousness might be reckoned unto them) ; or, which is the same thing, the sign of the covenant between God and himself, by force of which Jehovah was to be his God and that of his seed, Gen. 17. 4, 6, 11 (as for me, my covenant is with thee, and thou shalt be the father of a multitude of nations . . . And I will make thee exceeding fruitful, and I will make nations out of thee, and kings shall come out of thee . . . And ye shall be circumcised in the flesh of your foreskin ; and it shall be a token of a covenant betwixt me and thee). (LIII, 6) : To understand the meaning of that sign it is necessary for us not to pass over the other parts of the promise which Abraham received. God promised Abraham that He would give to him, i.e. to his carnal seed, not all his sons but certain ones, those begotten of Isaac, all of whom did not actually exist yet as the heirs of this dignity, the land of Abraham's sojournings, and that sometime He would eventually multiply his seed as the stars of heaven which cannot be counted by man and are seen in the whole universe, so that Abraham's seed should likewise be seen in the whole universe as the stars of heaven are seen in the whole universe. The words point this way, which are read in Gen. 13.14-16 (lift up now thine eyes, and look from the place where thou art, northward and southward and eastward and westward : all the land which thou seest, to thee will I give it and to thy seed for ever. And I will make thy seed as the dust of the earth : so that if a man can number the dust of the earth, then shall thy seed also be numbered).—(7) : On this supposition we must consider what circumcision has come to mean. Generally, the removal of a particle of flesh means the removal of the flesh (in the sense of τὸ σαρκικόν or its state, in which man is and is called fleshly) and of that which is of the flesh. It is called by the Apostle περιτομὴ ἀχειροποίητος, the circumcision not made with hands, Col. 2 11-15 [*q.v.*] ".

POLAN (VI, 52) : " By God's command the foreskin was to be cut off as the sign that our nature was corrupt, that men in this fleshly generation are born guilty and so need regeneration and renewal, which was to be through that blessed seed, which was to crush the serpent's head and in which all nations were to be blessed ".

28.—The economy of the patriarchs was succeeded by that of the Mosaic law. " The law of the covenant of grace under Moses is the dispensation by which God determined so to propagate the grace of His promise right from Moses to Christ, that by the same covenant of grace which He had previously made with Abraham, renewed at Mt. Sinai, by the intermediacy of Moses, with the people Israel, who had been brought by a strong hand out of Egyptian slavery and was presently to be introduced into the promised inheritance in the land of Canaan, after making for them a law of faith and repentance and prescribing other aids to faith, and still more by the tutelage of a stricter law, donning the appearance of a law of works, He promised under the type of inheriting the land of Canaan a spiritual and heavenly inheritance and confirmed and sealed it by a host of revelations, types and sacraments " (HEIDEGGER XIII, 2). Even in this economy the sole true mediator was Christ, beside whom nevertheless Moses also was entrusted by God with the outward and typical mediatorship of the covenant.

HEIDEGGER (XIII, 9-10) : " The mediator of the Sinai covenant was twofold, a true and a typical. The same person was the true one, who is the mediator of every covenant of grace, Jesus Christ.—It pleased God also to make a pact with another mediator interceding, a typical one improperly so called, who was Moses ".—That is why during this period the heathen were excluded from the covenant of grace ; COCCEIUS (De foed. XI, 341) : " It is to be noted that du ing this first pact with Isreal the Gentiles (nations) were without Christ, alienated from the commonwealth of Israel, aliens from the testaments of promise, having no hope and without God in the world."—RIISSEN (X, 24, 6) : "We explicitly assert that Christ was not only foretold but was promised to the fathers and that they were no less saved by his grace in the OT than we are in the NT—Proofs : (1) Scripture teaches that the covenant of grace which God contracted with us was the same in the NT as the covenant formerly entered into with Abraham.—(2) The Mediator is the same in OT and NT—(3) The condition of the covenant is the same in both cases, namely faith, by which they obtained salvation.—(4) They were given the same promises as we.—(5) The sacraments which are the seals of the covenant were the same substantially under either covenant."—Hence *Amyrald's* distinction between a *foedus naturae* (with Adam before the fall), a *foedus gratiae* (with Adam after the fall) and a *foedus legale* (with the Israelites through Moses) is rejected. RIISSEN supplies the reasons (X, 10) : " It is to be observed that (1) Scripture mentions only two covenants, as St. Paul, Gal. 4. 24, under the allegory of Sarah and Hagar notes two covenants, the legal and the evangelical. In Heb. 8 based on Jer. 31 two covenants are likewise mentioned, the old which was broken and became void, the new which is eternal and immutable. (2) There may be as many covenants (and not more) as there are ways and means of obtaining blessedness and communion with God, who is the proper end of the institution of a covenant. But there are only two such means, either by inherent and proper obedience or by imputed, through *either* works *or* faith. (3) Although we admit that the covenant of Sinai differed as to mode of administration from the covenant of works and the covenant of grace, nevertheless as to substance and species we deny that it constituted a third covenant, and we insist that there was nothing else than a fresh administration of the covenant of grace, so that in actual substance it is the same as the covenant entered into with Abraham, but different as to accidents and circumstances ; that is, clothed as to outward administration in the form of a covenant of works, through a severe promulgation of law, but not with a view to exacting afresh a covenant of works with the sinner. That was impossible. The aim was to remember the violated covenant of works, and so to make the Israelites feel their sin and impending curse, and give them the more burning a thirst for the righteousness of redemption. So in it there was a mixture of law and gospel ; of the former, to strike terror into sinners, of the latter to raise up and comfort contrite consciences. Further, that the Sinaitic covenant was not different from the covenant of grace entered into prevoiusly with the patriarchs is clear : (a) on God's side, who makes a pact with the Israelites as their God and likewise as the God of Abraham, Isaac and Jacob (Ex. 3.6 ; Ac. 3. 13, in both of which passages the God of Israel is also the God of the fathers) ; (b) on the Israelites' side, who are viewed as God's people and Abraham's seed ; (c) on the side of the ceremonial law, the whole of which was typical etc."—*Confess. Westmonast* (VII, 6) : " There are therefore not two covenants of grace differing in substance (*re et natura*) but one and the same, although administered under more than one dispensation ".

29.—In this new economy of salvation the law was set up in Israel not to abolish once more the covenant of grace promised to the fathers and to institute a new covenant of law, but to prepare for its promised confirmation through the death of Christ. God through Moses published anew the law and the curse of the law, in order to arouse the consciousness of guilt in Israel, and to let them know that Christ, who as God's holy one was to be put under the law and to die, was to bear the curse of the law not for himself but for others, the believers. Hence since the law intervened in the time of the expectation of the Lord and announced the gravity of this expectation, it taught in the first instance that the promised atonement for the guilt of sin had not yet taken place, but that the promise remained in full force, that for those who believed in the promised Redeemer God would regard their guilt as though it were already purged.

OLEVIAN (p. 295-296) : " There was one eternal free covenant or gospel promised to the fathers from the beginning, Rom. 1. 2 (promised afore by his prophets in the H. Scripture), and of it only one confirmation had been promised having eternal force, namely the death of the testator *Λόγος*. The law moreover entered by the way, Gal. 3. 17 (. . . a covenant confirmed beforehand by God, the law . . . doth not disannul, so as to make the promise of none effect), not to abolish the promise or to alter the counsel of God, but to pave the way for the execution of the promise, i.e. to convince men of sin and so to turn them from itself to Christ and its types to bear witness to the confirmation to come, and so to lead the fathers to the foundation of the covenant of grace ; the death, I mean, of the testator, or the single victim offered once for all upon the cross, Jn. 3. 14 (as Moses lifted up the serpent in the wilderness, even so must the Son of man be lifted up), and brought to the sanctuary of heaven, in order that he might appear in perpetuity on our behalf Rom. 3. 24-25 (justified freely by his grace through the redemption that is in Christ Jesus, whom God set forth to be a propitiation, through faith, by his blood, to shew his righteousness, because of the passing over of the sins done aforetime, in the forbearance of God, Heb. 9. 10 (the law) being only . . . carnal ordinances, imposed until a time of reformation)."

So to the question, " if no one was made holy by the covenant of law, why did God renew it with the people of Israel through Moses on Mt. Sinai ? " This reply is given by RAVENSPERGER (*Wegweiser* p. 77) : " That the stiff-necked people might be brought to obedience, the whole world be made guilty before God, and many be attracted and driven to the covenant of grace."

30.—Thus the law given by Moses had an essentially evangelical character. It pointed to Christ as the fulfiller of the law and as the redeemer from the curse of the law.—HEIDEGGER (XIII, 32) : " St Paul in particular has portrayed this twofold aspect of the law thus introduced, Rom. 10.3-6. Moses, quotha, in v.3, describes the righteousness which is of the law, because if a man do the things he shall live in them.—The evangelical aspect of the law he explains by saying that the end of the law is Christ unto righteousness to everyone that believeth v.4. This is to be understood both of the end which is the aim and of the end which is the full stop, i.e. concerning Christ the end of the law both as to its intention and as to its termination, as well as concerning both the law or those precepts in doing which a man lives in them, and the law of carnal precepts. As to the former, so far as it was not the aim of God who gives it, that man should seek righteousness from it, but rather that, recognising therefrom his debt and sin as well as the impossibility of his own righteousness and the need for a mediator for righteousness who under the name of the Seed in which the nations are to be blessed had so far been set forth in the Church, he should look to Christ for righteousness of faith and receive it. As to the latter, so far as its carnal precepts as indicating the Isrealites' impurity or liability in many ways, nay even as imposing somewhat in expiation of sin, working wrath and imparting some kind of curse, had this chief aim, that they should sigh more ardently toward Christ, who should make a true purification and expiation for sins through himself, Heb. 1.3 (who being the effulgence of his glory and the very image of his substance, and upholding all things by the word of his power, when he had made purification of sins, sat down on the right hand of the Majesty on high) and should remove all impurity and curse, and that they should fix all their hope in him. In this way Christ was the aim of the law as regards intention. On that account he was bound also to be its end, i.e. its full stop aim as regards termination, so far as after Christ's manifestation there could be no room either for the outward scheme of the law of works or for those carnal precepts which contain the shadow of future benefits. Whence the law is termed a tutor given to a people in its minority, Gal. 3.24 (the law hath been our tutor to bring us unto Christ, that we might be justified by faith) 4.1-2 (. . . as long as the heir is a child, he differeth nothing from a bondservant though he is lord of all ; but is under guardians and stewards until the term appointed of the father), such as is given to νήπιοι, *pueri* ; but to grownups and men in the bloom of their foresight and strength one is no longer given."—RIISSEN (X, 24, 6) : "The very law of Moses, under which the fathers were, taught them about the covenant of grace; which it could not have done, unless the covenant of grace had already had a place. Hence the law is called the *paedagogus ad Christum* Gal. 3.24 and *Christus* the *finis legis* (Rom. 10.4 Christ is the end of the law unto righteousness to everyone that believeth)."— RAVENSPERGER (*Wegweiser*, p.79) : " The law covenant was abolished by the covenant of grace. But whether the law can manage the righteous and does not strictly compel them, by the force or power of the law covenant, much less condemn them, nevertheless it is incorporated in the covenant of grace, so far as it is an impulse to repentance and improvement, as well as the rule and plummet of a godly, virtuous and Christian life."

31.—Thereby the law established faith in the promise of grace. For the godly in Israel were justified not by the law which no one has fulfilled, but by faith in the promised Christ.—COCCEIUS (*Summ. theol.* LI, 13) : " Whence it is ocularly apparent that the ancients were not justified save in the faith of Christ, whom they believed to be the mediator with God of a testament, their Lord and vindicator, who would intervene on their behalf, and who would some day be manifested as a sufficient λύτρον to be given in their stead and fulfilling all the function of a saviour and priest and so justifying and attracting and announcing them."

32.—Thus justifying grace was one and the same before and after the manifestation of Christ.—COCCEIUS (*S.T.* LI, 2-3): "As regards the love of God with which He pursues believers, and His righteous will to justify them on account of the mediator there is no difference between the justified who hoped in Christ beforehand and those to whom the gospel was preached. (3) And so, too, before the Mediator appeared their sins were truly remitted to them and righteousness was imputed, if you keep in view this love and this judgment of God."

33.—Only the peace of heart, which believers in Israel enjoyed, still persisted to the consummation, which was first to be imparted by the appearance and saving work of the Lord and by the real uprooting of the guilt of sin.—COCCEIUS (*Ib.* 9-11): "As regards justification, which is the absolution of conscience and the consummation or consolation concerning the already existing cause of righteousness and prince of salvation already consummated, this did not exist before the law. If it had there would have been no transgression, sin and guilt, and so neither would Christ the promised seed have been looked for any more. (10): As regards this the Apostle says that sin was not imputed, Rom. 5.13, i.e. no account was taken of it.—(11) This phrase of the Apostle is comparable with another which he too uses. Rom. 3.25 he says concerning all the sins which took place before Christ our sacrifice was offered, that God in His forbearing patience exercised πάρεσις, i.e. praetermission and dissimulation."

34.—And now the meaning of the OT is clear. "The OT is the free disposition of God, by which at Mt. Sinai, when the children of Israel had been separated from the rest of the peoples and adopted as His peculiar people, He set aside the land of Canaan as their private inheritance and as the type of Christ who should be manifested in it and of the heavenly homeland, by fixed laws, not without a mediator who was

Moses, and by ratifying it through the blood of beasts: and exhibited it as presently to be possessed right up to Christ" (HEIDEGGER, XIII, 44).

The OT economy is particularly the period of types. "Generally speaking types are things which impinge upon the senses, ordered by God, to represent to the mind by some similitude a thing of greater moment pertaining to religion" (HEIDEGGER, XIII, 76). They are partly "personal types", which indicate and describe ahead people to come, partly "real types" which do the same for things to come. In judging of what is typical, we must proceed with the greatest care. Only by Scripture is it established, what must rank as a type. A thing or person is not yet a type, because it has actually become a pre-indication of a subsequent thing or person, but because it is recognised as a type by H. Scripture itself.—HEIDEGGER (XIII, 79): "Since H. Scripture has no mere types, it is not enough for a type, that some thing should be found in Scripture; but that it should be pronounced a type in Scripture."

35.—As regards their significance for the economy of salvation types are to be regarded as sacramental signs, which not only portrayed and guaranteed the promised salvation as a future one, but also—since every typical institution ordained by God was "a type of the Lamb slain from the foundation of the world, in whom alone the covenant was established" (EGLIN *De foed. grat.*)—sealed his sure inheritance in it to the believer.— HEIDEGGER (XIII, 79): "OT types might be, and not a few of them actually were, such as attested guiltiness and contained a certain typical expiation and absolution or cleansing; yet they were all the shadow of benefits to come. They did not represent the mystery of godliness only; they also sealed them to believing users. And to that extent they were also σφραγίδες, *seals of righteousness,* not only signifying a future actuality, but also supplying individuals faithful in their use of them with confidence in claiming the righteousness and in hoping for the benefit connected with the righteousness. Further there were also the sacraments, i.e. sacred signs indicating the sacrament or mystery of God, and sacred signs and seals of the covenant of grace so suited to the status of justified believers, as it existed before the actual reconciliation, that they at once witnessed to their righteousness and signified the future τελείωσις or consummation of the righteousness."

36.—To the sacraments which God had already ordained earlier there was further added in this dispensation a new sacrament, which like circumcision had essentially the same content of grace as the later sacraments of the N.T., namely Christ and Christ's mediating grace.—HEIDEGGER (XIII, 99): "These sacraments of the OT served solely to seal the covenant of grace, the nucleus of which was Christ together with his benefits, nor as to the thing signified and sealed did they present a greater deviation from the sacraments of the NT than the covenant of grace under the legal dispensation presented from the same covenant of grace under the dispensation of the gospel."

37.—The sacrament in question, peculiar to the OT in the Mosaic period, was the passover. "It was the *Pascha*, which is the ordinary and perpetual sacrament of the OT, by which in the slaying and chewing of a lamb there was signified and sealed to grownup Israelites of both sexes the deliverance from Egypt, but particularly the redemption through Christ as victim, and communion with him" (HEIDEGGER XIII, 80).—Individual dogmaticians, e.g. POLAN (VI, 52ff.), speak of ordinary and extraordinary sacraments of the OT. To the latter POLAN (XI, 54) assigns the following: "baptism in the cloud, and the sea, 1 Cor. 10. 1-2; the feast of manna and the water flowing from the rock 1 Cor. 10. 3-4; the shedding of the blood of victims slain by the will of God, Heb. 9.18-20 (15-17, ref. to the sprinkling with blood by Moses, Ex. 24. 6-8); the land of Canaan; the tabernacle, Is. 33.20 (Jerusalem . . . a tent that shall not be removed, the stakes whereof shall never be plucked up, neither shall any of the cords thereof be broken) Ezek. 37.27 (My tabernacle also shall be with them . . .) Rev. 13.6 (blasphemy of God's tabernacle) Lk. 16.9 (make friends of the mammon of unrighteousness, that they may invite you into eternal tabernacles) Heb. 8.2 (the true tabernacle which the Lord pitched, not man) 9.11 (Christ came . . . through a greater and more perfect tabernacle, not made with hands; i.e. not of this creation) Rev. 15.5 (the temple of the tabernacle of the testimony in heaven was opened) 21.3 (. . . the tabernacle of God is with men) the temple at Jerusalem Jn. 2.21 (but he spake of the temple of his body) Zech. 6. 12-15 (the building of the temple of the Lord) Mal. 3.1 (. . . the Lord whom ye seek shall come suddenly to his temple) Rev. 3.12 (He that overcometh, I will make him a pillar in the temple of my God . . .) 21.22 (I saw no temple therein: for the Lord God the Almighty, and the Lamb, are the temple thereof) the ark of the covenant (Ex. 2.5); the *propitiatorium*, ἱλαστήριον, Rom. 3.25 (whom God set forth to be a propitiation through faith by his blood etc.); the golden candlestick (*lychnuchus*) in God's sanctuary (*sacrarium*) 2 Cor. 2, Eph. 5. 8 (light in the Lord); the XII stones in the midst of Jordan and the same number set up in Gilgal ; the water of the pond of Bethesda Jn. 5.2-4."

38.—The OT ceased when the sacrifice of Christ was consummated and the joyful news of it proclaimed to the world and believed not merely by

Jews but also by Gentiles, since thereby the NT came into existence. What belonged to the substance of the covenant of grace hitherto manifested in the form of the OT passed over without change into the NT. On the other hand the type and shadow which the promised fulfilment of salvation had prophesied and veiled now ceased ; now the consummation of the revelation in Christ was given, and thereby all the elect were exalted to a perfect possession of salvation and of the knowledge of it— accordingly, too, in place of the OT sacraments new ones of greater clarity, quicker reality and unending duration had to come in—and to perfect, blessed enjoyment of sonship to God, of peace in God and of freedom from eternal death.

HEIDEGGER (XIII, 106) : " The OT—has been abolished and antiquated both *de iure*, the sacrifice of Christ having been offered at a time when it was wellnigh abolished, Heb. 8.13 (in that he saith, A new covenant, he hath made the first old. But that which is becoming old and waxeth aged is nigh unto vanishing away), because at that time it was sensibly approaching its end ; and *de facto*, by the preaching of the apostles and especially by the conversion of the Gentile Cornelius, who by being dipped in the sacred waves was the first to consecrate the salvation of the Gentiles Ac. 10. 44-48 ; and by the very recent destruction of the Levitical city, polity, temple, and rite whereby *the* hitherto sacred and hereditary *earth was smitten by a curse* Mal. 4. 6.—But the things which pertain to the οὐσία or substance of the eternal covenant of grace and of the testament remain the same in perpetuity without liability to change, alteration or abrogation and have passed over in succession untouched and without admixture into the NT."—According to COCCEIUS (*De foed.* XII, 355) the benefits of the NT are : (1) the *exhibitio perfectae iustitiae,* which righteousness is the obedience of the Son of God ; (2) the *notificatio clara nominis Dei,* given partly in Christ's preaching, partly in his obedience, his suffering and his resurrection ; (3) the *inscriptio legis Dei in corda* ; (4) *absolutio conscientiae,* also called τελείωσις, ἁγιασμός, etc. ; (5) *libertas,* i.e. the opposite of the fear of death.

The agreement and difference between the OT and the NT are given in more detail as follows (ALTING, p. 98): " *Things that agree in the OT and NT*: one God and one mediator 1 Tim. 2. 5-6 (there is one God, one mediator also between God and men, himself man, Christ Jesus, who gave himself a ransom for all; the testimony to be borne in its own times): Heb. 13. 8 (the same yesterday etc.) the one mercy of God Lk. 1. 54-55 (he hath holpen Israel his servant, that, as he said unto our fathers he might remember mercy towards Abraham and his seed for ever ; to show mercy towads our rfathers, and to remember his holy covenant, the oath which he sware to Abraham our father) ; the identical ransom of Christ

Ps. 40. 6ff. (sacrifice and offering thou hast no delight in ; mine ears hast thou opened : then said I, Lo I am come ; in the roll of the book it is written of me ; I delight to do thy will etc. ; Heb. 10. 9ff. quotes it) the same salvation and way of salvation Ac. 15. 11 (we believe that we shall be saved through the grace of the Lord Jesus in like manner as they (the converted Gentiles)) Ac. 4. 12 (in none other is there salvation: for neither is there any other name under heaven, that is given among men, wherein we must be saved). The double mode of dispensation in Old and New Heb. 8. 13 (p. 405) and Jer. 31. 31f., whence the difference, I—The old given to the people Israel only Gen. 17. 7 (between me and thee and thy seed) Ex. 19. 5-6 (if ye will obey my voice indeed, and keep my covenant, then shall ye be a peculiar treasure unto me . . . a kingdom of priests and an holy nation) Ps. 147. 19-20 (He sheweth his word unto Jacob, his statutes and his judgments unto Israel. He hath not dealt so with any nation, and as for his judgments they have not known them) Rom. 16. 25 (. . . the revelation of the mystery which hath been kept in silence through times eternal) : NT : to all Gentiles alike Mt. 28. 19-20 (Go ye therefore etc.) Mk. 16. 15-16 (. . . Go ye into all the world, and preach the gospel to the whole creation. He that believeth and is baptized shall be saved ; but he that disbelieveth shall be condemned) Ac. 10. 34 (. . God is no respecter of persons). II—OT more obscure because of figures and types Col. 2. 14-17 (having blotted out the bond written in ordinances that was against us, which was contrary true . . . which are a shadow of things to come . . .) Heb. 10. 1 (the law having a shadow of the good things to come, not the very image of the things, they can never with the same sacrifices year by year, which they offer continually, make perfect them that draw nigh) : the NT clearer by their removal Tit. 2. 11 (the Grace of God hath appeared, bringing salvation to all men. III—OT conjoined with less efficacy of the H. Spirit as regards knowledge of the mysteries and of the affections of the heart Gal. 3. 2-5 (This only would I learn of you, Received ye the Spirit by the works of the law or by the hearing of faith ? Are ye so foolish ? Having begun in the Spirit are ye now perfected in the flesh ? Did ye suffer so many things in vain ? if it be indeed in vain ! He therefore that supplieth you with the Spirit and worketh miracles among you, doeth he it by the works of the law, or by the hearing of faith ?) Jn. 7. 39 (But this spake he of the Spirit, which they that believed on him were to receive : for the spirit was not yet given ; because Jesus was not yet glorified) Dt. 18. 18 (I will raise them up a prophet from among their brethren, like unto thee ; and I will put my words in his mouth, and he shall speak unto them all that I shall command him. And it shall come to pass, that whosoever will not hearken unto my words which he shall speak in my name, I will require it of him) . . . 22 (When a prophet speaketh in the name of the Lord, if the thing follow not, nor come to pass, that is the thing which the Lord hath not spoken, the prophet hath spoken it presumptuously, thou shalt not be afraid of him). NT characterised by greater light and strength Jer. 31. 33-34 (I will put my law in their inwards parts, and in their heart will I write it : and I will be their God, and they will be my people : and they shall teach no more every man his neighbour, and every man his brother, saying, know ye the Lord : for they shall all know me, from the least of them unto the greatest of them, saith the Lord ; for I will forgive their iniquity, and their sin will I remember no more) Jn. 7. 38ff. (He that believeth on me, as the Scripture hath said, out of his belly shall flow rivers of living water (7.39 p. 406), Ac.2.17 (Joel 2.28f.) And it shall be in the last days, saith God, I will pour forth of my Spirit upon all flesh : and your sons and your daughters shall prophesy, and your young men shall see visions, and your old men shall dream dreams). Hence *the condition of believers in the NT is better than that of those in the OT* Mt. 13. 16-17 (Blessed are your eyes, for they see ; and your ears for they hear . . . many prophets and righteous men desired to see the things which ye see, and saw them not ; and to hear the things which ye hear and heard them not) Lk. 10. 23ff. (. . . Blessed are the eyes which see the things that ye see . . . many prophets and kings desired to see the things which ye see and saw them not ; and to hear the things which ye hear and heard them not) 1 Pet. 1. 10f. (concerning which salvation the prophets sought and searched diligently, who prophesied of the grace which should come unto you, searching what time or what manner of time the Spirit of Christ which was in them did point unto, when it testified beforehand the sufferings of Christ and the glories that should follow them. To whom it was revealed that not unto themselves, but unto you did they minister these things, which now have been announced unto you through them that preached the gospel unto you by the H. Ghost sent forth from heaven : which things angels desire to look into). Their condition is steadfast to the end of the world Mt. 28. 20 (lo, I am with you alway, even unto the end of the world) Jer. 32.40 (I will make an everlasting covenant with them, that I will not turn away from them, to do them good ; and I will put my fear in their hearts, that they shall not depart from me). But since the OT begins with Israel at Sinai Jer. 31. 31f (. . . a new covenant with the house of Israel and with Judah, not acc. to the covenant which I made with their fathers etc. . . but this is the covenant that I will make with the house of Israel after those days, saith the Lord : I will put my law in their inward parts, and in their heart will I write it ; and I will be their God, and they shall be my people): which covenant is yet said to be of grace (Gen. 17. 7 " between me and thee and thy seed") Ex. 19. 5-6 (p. 406) : it appears (1) that the covenant of

Sinai is of grace, the same as that with Abraham ; that is, as regards the evangelical σχέσις, or the conditions set forth by God ; (2) yet it must be out of date as regards the legalism of its σχέσις, which is also more covenantal as regards its manner of ratification, which being of works and not of faith (Ex. 24) had of course to be abolished and a new one substituted, and so it was said relatively to the old covenant of the same Israelites, but not to the older covenant with Abraham ; than which the Sinaitic is more recent, but it could not abolish the earlier one, Gal. 3.17 (A covenant confirmed beforehand by God the law . . . doth not annul, so as to make the promise of none effect), it is actually restored in the new one of the Israelites : for Gentiles who are called to the same covenant (to them first in Eph. 2. 12 (ye were at that time separate from Christ, alienated from the commonwealth of Israel, and strangers from the covenants of the promise, having no hope and without God in the world) now called to the covenant of Abraham Ps. 47. 10 (the princes of the people are gathered together to be the people of the God of Abraham : for the shields of the earth belong unto God ; he is greatly exalted) Rom. 4. 11f. (and he received the sign of circumcision, a seal of the righteousness of the faith which he had while he was in uncircumcision : that he might be the father of all them that believe, though they be in uncircumcision, that righteousness might be reckoned unto them ; and the father of circumcision to them who not only are of the circumcision, but who also walk in the steps of that faith of our father Abraham which he had in uncircumcision) Ac. 2. 25-26 [Ps. 16. 8f.] (I beheld the Lord always before my face ; for he is on my right hand that I should not be moved : therefore my heart was glad and my tongue rejoiced, moreover my flesh also shall dwell in hope : because thou wilt not leave my soul in Hades, neither wilt thou give thy Holy One to see corruption). And to the Israelites are applied the covenants Rom. 9. 3 (I could wish that I myself were anathema from Christ for thy brethren's sake, my kinsmen according to the flesh ; who are Israelites, whose is the adoption, and the glory, and the covenants, and the giving of the law, and the service of God, and the promises), which are said to have been denied to the Gentiles Eph. 2. 12 (ye were at that time separate from Christ, alienated from the commonwealth of Israel, and strangers from the covenants of the promise, having no hope and without God in the world) ; in any case if they had had only the Sinaitic, none of them could have been saved Gal. 2. 21 (I do not make void the grace of God : for if righteousness is through the law, then Christ died for nought) 3. 21-22 (Is the law against the promises of God ? God forbid : for if there had been a law given which could make alive, verily righteousness would have been of the law. Howbeit the scripture hath shut up all things under sin, that the promise by faith in Jesus Christ might be given to them that believe).

The relation between the OT and the NT sacraments is appropriately noted by WOLLEB (p. 106) : (1) "The sacraments of OT or NT agree in the things signified as regards the substance, viz. Christ with his benefits, who is the nucleus of all sacraments. The difference between the sacraments of OT and NT consists (1) in the external signs, (2) in the manner of signification : in the one case Christ was signified as about to be set forth, in the other as having been set forth ; (3) in number : besides circumcision and the paschal lamb they had others as well ; we have none apart from baptism and the H. Supper ; (4) in range : according as the NT does not extend to one nation only ; (5) in duration : the former last only till the coming of Christ, the latter till the end of the world ; (6) in clarity."—On the other hand the differences which the Papists would set up between OT and NT are rejected : " (1) that the sacraments of the OT were (merely) types of the sacraments of the NT ; (2) that the sacraments of the OT but adumbrated justifying grace, whereas ours really contain in themselves the very body of spiritual benefits ".

CHAPTER XVII

THE MEDIATOR OF THE COVENANT OF GRACE
or
THE PERSON OF CHRIST

1.—Consideration of God's covenant of grace leads directly to the exposition of that high and holy mystery beyond the grasp of human understanding, the mystery of God's Son becoming man to be the Mediator of this Covenant.—LEIDEN SYNOPSIS XXV, 2 : " After that of the Sacrosanct Trinity, of the three persons, that is, in the one essence, whereby the three persons really distinct from each other possess one and the same essence and are united in the numerically single essence, this mystery is the supreme one. In it two perfect natures are united in the one person of the Son of God. Whence the Apostle I Tim. 3. 16 calls this mystery, that God has been manifested in flesh, the great mystery of godliness.—3 : Whence also it cannot be taught or accepted by human reason, because in the whole of nature no perfect example exists which completely answers to it, although it is not at war with right reason. But it should be divinely taught and proved from Scripture and received with the eyes of faith ".

KECKERMANN 310 : " This is the nucleus of the whole of theology and this the supreme cause and the direct beginning of our deliverance from sin : I mean, the execution of the election administered through Christ's merit and efficacy, which the ancient, especially the Greek theologians, usually call the οἰκονομία, i.e. dispensation of the means leading to salvation ". Hence Christ is considered here (WOLLEB 61) not κατὰ θεολογίαν as the λόγος, but κατ' οἰκονομίαν as the θεάνθρωπος.

2.—To understand this mystery we must above all insist that the incarnation of the Father's eternal Son is purely the result of Adam's fall into sin, so that if the human race had not fallen, neither would the Son have come into the flesh.—To the question, "whether the Son of God would have been a man and come into the world, although Adam had not sinned" SOHNIUS (*Exeg. Conf. Aug. Art.* III, p. 216) gives the answer: "The question itself being vain and curious, affirmation of the question is accordingly false and everywhere exploded. Clearly Christ did not become man for any other reason than to redeem sinners; this is clear from the explanation of the previous question. Therefore as for the reasons there explained he had to become true man so if these causes had not existed by the fall of the first parents, there would have been no reason for his becoming man".—Similarly RIISSEN (XI, 41).

3.—Moreover only the eternal Son of the Father was by his humiliation to human form capable of consummating the work of redeeming the world and executing the counsel of grace. For (a) the covenant of grace rested sheerly on the twofold vow which the Son in eternity had promised to the Father and on the commission which accordingly the Father had imparted to the Son; consequently only the absolute love of the Father for the Son is the cause by which the Father also loves the elect and has resolved to redeem them (OLEVIAN, p. 26); (b) only the essential Son of God could offer the Father a perfect satisfaction for the sin of humanity, make effective intercession for it with the Father, conquer the power of sin, the Satan and death, restore in man the perfect image of God and righteousness, thereby remove misery from man and renew his lost blessed communion with God; and (c) on the other hand only if the Son adopted human nature could He complete the reconciliation of the world, because God's righteousness required that the punishment of sin should be borne by the same nature upon which the guilt of sin lay.

MARCK (XVIII, 19): "According to this eternal, immutable determination on the Father's part because of His oath, Ps. 110. 4 (the Lord hath sworn and will not repent: thou art priest forever . . .), and on the Son's part since on account of his steady love of God and the brethren the Son would not have fought against the promise propounded by the Father or have withdrawn from it afterwards, once he had voluntarily undertaken it, whatever the *Remonstrants* pretend to the contrary with their desire to assert a changeable predestination; according to that, I say, he was presently (a) manifested to man as the Mediator in the protevangelium which was more broadly explained through countless later promises, (β) delineated in types, etc."—TURRETIN (331): "The Son alone could duly have undertaken this office (1) as, being midway between Father and H. Spirit, to be the mediator between God and men; (2) it was fitting that he who was the Son by nature should make us adoptive sons by grace, that we might be the co-heirs of him who is the heir of all things; (3) it was his ἀνακτίζειν, to recreate, whose it was to create, so that the Word by whom all things were made in the first creation might reshape us to His own image in the second. The image of God obscured by sin and all but destroyed could not better have been restored in u. than through him who was the image of the invisible God; (4) no other was more fitted to make our reconciliation than he who was the Father's ἀγαπητός Son, in whom εὐδόκησεν (Mt. 3. 17)."

WOLLEB, p. 62: "That he should be God was required by the state of the parties, on the one hand the majesty of God, on the other our poverty and the magnitude of the evil to be removed and of the good to be restored. God's majesty is so great that no one save he who is one thing with the Father, could have interposed. Not even angels could have dared to do so; they themselves also have need of the Mediator Christ, Col. 1. 16–17 (in him were all things created, in the heavens and upon the earth, things visible and things invisible, whether thrones or dominions or principalities or powers; all things have been created through him, and unto him; and he is before all things, and in him all things consist), because compared with God not even they answer to his purity), Job. 15. 15 (Behold he putteth no trust in his holy ones; yea, the heavens are not clean in his sight), and therefore in God's presence they veil their faces), Is. 6. 2 (Above him stood the Seraphim; each one had six wings, with twain he covered his face, with twain he covered his feet and with twain he did fly). How much less therefore any human being, since not a single one has been righteous, Rom. 3. 10 (there is none righteous, no, not one)? The evil to be removed was sin and the consequences of sin, the wrath of God, the power of Satan and temporal and eternal death. I.—Now by whose passion would the offence against infinite majesty be expiated, save his who himself is also infinite? By whose intercession could the wrath of God be appeased save his, who is God's well-beloved Son? II.—By whose strength could Satan be conquered together with the entire power of darkness, save his who is stronger than all devils? Who in a word could have overcome death save him, who has power even over death Heb. 2. 15 (might deliver all them who through fear of death were all their lifetime subject to bondage)? III.—The benefits to be restored were perfect righteousness, υἰοθεσία (sonship), the image of God, the gifts of the H. Spirit, eternal life and the like. Who then could give us that righteousness save he who is righteousness itself? Who could better make us sons of God, save he who is himself the image of the invisible God? Who could more surely confer the H. Spirit upon us than he from whom He proceeds? In a word who would give us eternal life but he who is life itself Jn. 1. 4 (in him was life, and the life was the light of men)?—*That man should be God's was demanded by a righteousness which, as it does not leave sin unpunished, does not punish it save in the nature which sinned.*"

This then is the reason why the eternal Son of the Father entered the flesh. "Incarnation is the work of God by which according to the divine counsel of the Father, of Himself and of the H. Spirit the Son of God humbled himself and took unto himself true, entire, perfect and holy flesh of the V. Mary by the operation and effectuality of the H. Spirit in the unity of his person; so that the flesh should in no way have a subsistence of its own outwith the Son of God, but should be truly sustained and borne by him and in him: two perfect natures having been mutually united ἀτρέπτως καὶ ἀσυγχύτως, ἀδιαιρέτως καὶ ἀχωρίστως. Thereby is constituted the person of Christ the θεάνθρωπος (God-man), to the end that he might be able fully to perform the role of Mediator with God, to reconcile and unite men to God, and that he might reconcile and unite the elect to God, bestow on them righteousness, holiness and life eternal for proof of the righteousness of God and for the praise of His mercy" (LEIDEN SYNOPSIS XXV, 4).

4.—Thus the incarnation is an *opus oeconomicum,* a work of the triune God pertaining to the divine economy of salvation. In its actual execution it was wrought upon the Logos of the Father by the H. Spirit.— WOLLEB 61: "In its inception the incarnation of Christ is the work of the whole sacrosanct Trinity, but in its issue it is the work of the Son alone. The Son alone assumes the human nature, which the Father formed in the Son through the H. Spirit of the substance of the B. Virgin".

LEIDEN SYNOPSIS (XXV, 6-8): "If we accept the word incarnation, actively it is the work of God. Indeed, like every work and working of God outwards, as they call it, i.e., every work which has a relation extraneous to God, it is common to the whole Trinity, always provided that as in the divine persons so too in their actions order and subordination are preserved, so that the *fons actionis* is *a Patre* and so referred to the Father, the *medium* [*actionis*] in the Son, being the Wisdom of the Father, the *terminus* [*actionis*] in the H. Spirit as the strength and potency of God most high, through whom it is externalised. And this is to be understood by reason both of the decree and of the actual work. And yet as regards this *terminus* it is peculiarly appropriated to the H. Spirit Mt. 1. 18-20 ((Mary) was found with child of the H. Ghost . . . fear not to take unto thee Mary as thy wife; for that which is conceived in her is of the H. Ghost) Lk. 1. 35 (and the angel answered and said unto her, the H. Ghost shall come upon thee and the power of the Most High shall overshadow thee: wherefore also that which is to be born shall be called holy, the Son of God). Whence it says in the Creed: *conceptus de Spiritu sancto.*—7: Moreover it is an *opus oeconomicum,* i.e., a gracious action of the divine will, by a sure and wise counsel, suited to the order and action to be accomplished, to wit the restoration of our salvation.— 8: This *oeconomia* was referred to the Son (which is why, after the Apostle (Eph. 1), it is called the incarnation by the ancient fathers), or accepted by him passively and subjectively in the incarnation. And so not the Father or the H. Spirit but God's Son alone was incarnate or became man, as Scripture everywhere attests, Lk. 1. 35 (above) Jn. 1. 14 (the Word became flesh), Rom. 1. 3 (. . . born of the seed of David according to the flesh) Gal. 4. 4. (when the fulness of time came, God sent forth

His Son, born of a woman, born under the law . . .) Phil. 2, although he was incarnate by the will and good pleasure of the sacrosanct Trinity."

5.—But the incarnation is not to be conceived as though the divinity of the Son was turned into human nature or mingled with it.—CALVIN (II, xiv, 1): "That the Word became flesh Jn. 1. 14 is not to be understood as though it had been turned into flesh or confusedly mixed with flesh. But—he who was the Son of God became the Son of Man: not by confusion of essence but by the unity of the person."—ZANCHIUS p. 60: "We believe moreover that the Son of God became man, not by any change of him into flesh or by a change in the flesh or by a confusion of the divine nature with the human, but by the sole assumption of the human nature into the unity of the said person; and, as *Athanasius* says, not by conversion of the divinity into flesh but by the assumption of the humanity into God; so that in no way did it dismiss that which it was, but assumed that which it was not".—MASTRICHT (V, iv, 3): "*'Ο Λόγος* (the divine person) is said to have become flesh, not by change but by assumption, so that with it it should constitute one person."

6.—In particular the incarnation of the Logos is not to be thought of as though He had inwardly united Himself with a ready-made self-existent human being. Rather the person of the Logos of God took the nature of man or humanity up into its subsistence in such a way that without detriment to its divine existence it entered the human mode of being and condition.

In essentials all Reformed dogmaticians are agreed that the divinity of Christ is not really the divine nature (common to the three persons of the Trinity) but the person of the Logos, the Logos-determination of the Trinity, or the deity thought of under the personal determination of the Logos; and that the humanity of Christ is the human nature common to all human personalities, thought of in abstraction (and so not personally) but individually. Cf. e.g., POLAN (VI, 17): "When it is said that two natures, the divine and the human, have been personally united in Christ, the expression is figurative. It is not strictly the nature but the person or subsistence of the Word existing eternally in the form or nature of God, that has assumed the human nature and united it to itself. Exactly as Jn. 1. 14 does not say, The divine nature became flesh, but The Word became flesh. And Paul Phil. 2. 6–7 does not say, The form of God assumed the form of a slave, but Christ Jesus existing in the form of God assumed the form of a slave. Nor, as they insist, is it an objection that the divine nature and the subsistence of the Son do not actually differ but are one and the same. Although they do not actually differ, they are still distinguished in mode and manner so that the divine nature, while existing the same in all the persons yet has different modes of subsistence really distinct from each other. In the Father it exists ἀγεννήτως, in the Son γεννήτως, in the H. Spirit ἐκπορεύτως. So when the human nature is said to be united in Christ to the divine nature, we are not to understand the divine nature considered absolutely and as it is common to Father, Son and H. Spirit.—COCCEIUS (LVIII, 12 *S.T.*): "Τὸ πρόσλημμα, or that which is assumed, we must note, is not assumed into the nature but into the person of the Son.—Yet the Son it was who assumed it, the Father who prepared the body for the Son, and in that way sent him. The body made by the one divine will the Father willed to exist and to be recognised as the Son's body, while the Son willed it to be his own. So the Son is said to have assumed or taken it, not the Father. For to assume means to make one's own.— (LVIII, 13): And in fact every human nature or mind equipped with bodily organs is a person. It is created to be the basis of action and of being acted upon, not just the basis by which (as in the pretty eloquent talk of the schools), but also the basis which (*principium quo* and *principium quod*).—But the holy thing born of the virgin is called the Son of God, and that man's obedience and passion and glory is the obedience and passion and glory of the Son of God."—HEIDEGGER (XVII, 36): "This assumption took place not into the nature but into the person of the Son. Whence it was not Deity but the λόγος or *sermo* that is said to have become flesh, Jn. 1. 14, to be God manifested in the flesh, 1 Tim. 3. 16. He alone was manifested. Nor in consequence was anything added to the Son of God when assuming human nature, by which He was perfected, but rather something with which He might perfect others; nor was anything lacking in the human nature by the removal of which either its truth or its perfection might suffer loss."

SOHNIUS (*Exeg. Conf. Aug.* III, p. 20): "The Son alone became man, not the Father or the H. Spirit; and again the person of the Son, not the divine nature, if we would speak strictly. The person belongs to the Son or λόγος; but the divine nature is common and the same in him as in Father and H. Spirit."—HEIDAN 530: "It is the person that assumes. And it assumed not a person but a nature."

LEIDEN SYNOPSIS (XXV, 10): "Thus the Son of God, who was ὑφισταμένος from eternity, Prov. 8. 22–23: "The Logos possessed me at the beginning of His way, before His works of old: I was set up from everlasting, from the beginning, or ever the earth was . . . " the λόγος, *sermo*, who was from the beginning, who was with God and who was God, Jn. 1. 1, who was before Abraham was Jn. 8. 58, ὑπάρχων, existent, in the form of God Phil. 2. 6, He, I say, being ὁμοούσιος, 'ἴσος καὶ συναΐδιος with the Father, essential, equal and eternal, became flesh in time, Jn. 1. 14."

Thus the incarnation is not an *opus naturale*, but an *opus personale*. RIISSEN (XI, 8) : " Although the divine nature is well said to have been incarnate in the Son, it does not therefore follow that the entire Trinity was incarnate. The divine nature is said to have been incarnate not directly or considered absolutely and in itself, but indirectly in the person of the Son or under the double form as determined and characterised in the person of the Son, which culminates in the person and not in the nature. So it is quite well said that the entire divine nature was incarnate, not because it was incarnate in all three persons, but because the person of the Son of God lacks nothing as regards the perfection of the divine nature.—9 : If therefore our doctors have not admitted the LUTHERAN phraseology, which asserts the incarnation of the divine nature, it is not that they absolutely and out of hand deny the incarnation of the divine nature. They are merely criticising a less accurate manner of speaking."

7.—The humanity taken up into the personality of the Logos is, then, not a personal man but human nature without personal subsistence, yet thought of in its full spirit-body essentiality and individuality. This is why in the incarnation of the Logos it was not a new third thing that arose by the union of the divine and human natures. It was the human finite mode of being that was added to the eternal and infinite mode of being of the Logos, by the human nature being taken up into His personal subsistence. The Logos thus exists alike without and within the humanity of Christ. The Logos is still pre-existent, the Trinity is still complete. Christ's human nature had hypostatic subsistence only by its being taken up into the hypostasis of the Logos.

ALTING, p. 99f.: "The human nature was true and perfect, but devoid of an hypostasis of its own ... The mode (of assumption) is described (1) by the *terminus ad quem*, as into unity of the person, so that there is one and the same person of the assuming λόγος and of the human nature assumed; (2) by the extremely close and indissoluble conjunction resulting, so that outside the λόγος it never does or can subsist."—It is with quite special care that the dogmaticians seek to make this particular point clear.—Says TURRETIN (XIII, vi, 18-19) : Christ's human nature is of course a " prime intelligent substance perfect in the *esse* of its substance " (in scholastic terminology, an individual). But it is not yet a " person ", because it is not " incommunicable" and has not "a subsistence peculiarly its own ". The soul, too, is a " separate singular intelligent substance ".

But it is not a person, "because it is an *ens partiale*, incomplete, which does not subsist, but ought to be united to a second." Yet by the renunciation of personality nothing is abstracted from Christ's human nature as regards its truth and completeness. For the truth of the human nature is to be measured " by its matter, form and essential attributes ", and not " by its personality ". Christ's humanity is therefore to be regarded as a man not *suppositaliter* but specifically.—MARESIUS (IX, 23) expresses himself in exactly similar terms.

Hence Christ's humanity is of course an *individuum*, an exposition of human nature in individual form. It has real existence only in the person of the Logos, not in itself.—ZANCHIUS (*De incarnat. Filii Dei*, p. 152ff.) : " As a most perfect entity existent *per se* the person of the Son of God drew to itself a rather imperfect entity, lacking any subsistence of its own to make it self-existent ". The moment therefore " the Son of God assumed a true body with a true human soul, together with all the essential and natural attributes of both, and the defects as well, he is not therefore to be said to have assumed either a *persona* or an ὑφιστάμενον, but—a nature ἐν ἀτόμῳ, i.e. existing in a fixed *individuum*, which however has never existed anywhere of itself except in the assumer."

KECKERMANN 315 : " (Christ's human nature is) an *individuum* distinct from the divine nature, though not a distinct person. Concerning this thought we must first of all think accurately that person differs from nature, and so an *individuum* from a person, yet so that the human nature is not a person, but is meanwhile an *individuum*, or as the Logicians say a first substance. But some one may say : Every substantial *individuum* subsists *per se* ; if therefore considered by itself Christ's human nature is an *individuum*, it therefore subsists *per se*. Answer : Subsistence *per se* is sometimes opposed to what subsists in something else, and so human nature generally subsists *per se*, because it is a substance and not an accident, the property of which is to exist in something else. But if subsistence *per se* means the same as separate subsistence, outside the union and support of a second thing, then it is false to say that the human nature subsists *per se*. It is sustained by the λόγος to which it is united, so that apart from it it could not exist for a moment."—So it must be said (ALSTED 517) that : " He assumed not a person but a nature, and it considered as an *individuum*. The reason for the former statement is that Christ's human nature never subsisted *per se* but has always been an instrument ἐνυπόστατον ἐν τῷ λόγῳ."

So the Incarnation is not to be regarded as though by the union of two different essences a new third one had arisen, but in such wise that the human mode of being was added to the eternal mode of the Logos by the assumption of the human nature into its personality without altering the latter. ZANCHIUS (*De relig. Christiana*, p. 62) : "Although we recognise in Christ two natures, a divine and a human, we yet do not admit that the human was so assumed, either that out of the latter and the former, as out of parts, a new person was composed for Christ, or that the earlier and eternal person was perfected by the accession of the new nature ; but only that, when the latter was assumed into the unity of the former person existing in supreme perfection from eternity, the Son of God, abiding the same as he was, became what He was not and had something to offer to the Father on our behalf."—LEIDEN SYNOPSIS (XXV, 24-25) : " The manner in which the only-begotten Son of God became flesh is by the direct union of the person of the Son of God with the human nature or the assumption of the human nature into one and the same person, Phil. 2. 7; Heb. 2. 16 (. . . he taketh hold of the seed of Abraham) ; so that the Son of God, the second eternal person of the sacrosanct Trinity, assumed into the unity of his person right from the moment of conception not a pre-existent person but one ἀνυπόστατος of its own hypostasis or devoid of subsistence, and made it belong to himself. And so this flesh has no subsistence outside the Son of God, but exists, subsists in him and is borne and supported by him.—Whence in truth the Son of God began to be a son of man by remaining what he was and beginning to be what He was not ; not because something was added to him to perfect him. And the Son of Man became the Son of God ; i.e. what the Son of God was by nature, the Son of man became by the grace of union. And hence Mary is called *mater Domini* Lk. 1.35 and by the ancients θεότοκος, *deipara* ".—Hence too by his incarnation the Logos is enclosed neither in the assumed humanity nor in the manifestation of Christ. On the contrary even after the incarnation the Logos is absolute and infinite as the Second Person of the Trinity (as the λόγος ἄσαρκος); CALVIN (II, xiii, 4) : " Although the transcendent essence of the Word coalesced with the nature of man into one person, it is no inclusion of our inventing. The Son of God descended miraculously from heaven, so that he yet did not quit heaven. He willed to be borne miraculously in the Virgin's womb, to walk on earth and to hang on the Cross. Yet he always filled the world as from the beginning."—HEIDELBURG CATECHISM 48 : " Since the divinity cannot be comprehended and is present everywhere, it follows necessarily that it is actually outside the human nature which it assumed, but is none the less in it and continues in personal union with it ".—MARESIUS (IX, 30) : " Thus the Logos has united the human nature to itself, so as at the same time wholly to inhabit it and wholly to be outside it as being transcendent and infinite ".

Lutheran Christology rests upon the essentially *Nestorian* assumption, that the incarnation of the Logos was the union of the divine nature with the human nature to be conceived in a previous subsistence, and that in it the result is the deification of the human nature by the pouring into it of the divine attributes. In opposition to it Reformed dogmatics takes seriously the Biblical statement ὁ λόγος σὰρξ ἐγένετο. Hence MUSCULUS, supporting the generally customary terminology of the Reformed, remarks that it does not say, The Word took on flesh or united it to itself, but, The Word became flesh. For " there is something more in becoming flesh than in assuming it or uniting it to oneself."—ZANCHIUS (*De incarnat. Filii Dei*, p. 437) : " In the assumed form of a servant Christ emptied himself of all his divine glory, omnipotence, omnipresence, omniscience. He became from being very rich, very poor, from being almighty, weak, from being omniscient, ignorant, from being transcendent finite (p. 141) : The only-begotten Son of God did not dwell in a man formed as it were previously, but himself truly and essentially *became* man. I.e. he caused to subsist in his very own hypostasis flesh animated by a rational, intellectual soul.—The foundation of Nestorius' whole heresy was his thinking that outside the person of the λόγος a particular person had been created and conceived by the λόγος in the Virgin's womb and had been associated with the λόγος and joined to it ". Unfortunately Reformed dogmatics did not draw the full conclusion from this statement.

8.—Therefore as Christ is true God he is at the same time also a true and real man. He assumed not only a real human body and a real human soul, but (so as to be able to have a perfectly human development and feelings) the natural affections and weaknesses, though without sin, of man's bodily and spiritual nature. Because the eternal Son thus humbled himself not only to assume human nature but also to enter into the form of a servant which belongs to man's nature as a result of the Fall, just as *qua* Son of God he is perfectly like the Father in essence, so as a man Christ became perfectly like us in all respects, sin alone excepted. LEIDEN SYNOPSIS (XXV, 11-14) : " When he is said to have become flesh, not a phantasm of it is meant, but a true body consisting of flesh and bones and blood, Mt. 14.26 (when the disciples saw him walking on the sea, they were troubled, saying, It is an apparition ; and they cried out for fear. But straightway Jesus spake unto them, saying, Be of good cheer ; it is I ; be not afraid) Lk. 24.39 (See my hands and my feet, that it is I myself : handle me, and see ; for a spirit hath not flesh and bones, as ye behold me having) Heb. 2.14 (since the children are sharers in flesh and blood, he also in like manner partook of the same . . .) ; moreover, by synecdoche constituted a man complete in body and in rational soul, the essential parts of human nature—nay, a perfect man, endowed with the natural and indeed essential qualities which inhere necessarily and inseparably in him.—In addition there are accidental qualities which inhere separably and may be changed or abolished, like the increase of wisdom in the soul, Lk. 2.40, its passions like sorrow unto death, Mt. 26.38 etc., in the body increase of stature, Lk. 2. 40, hunger, thirst drink, weariness, sleep, bodily pains, tears, sweat of blood etc., Mt. 4.2 : Jn. 4.6 ; Mt. 11.19 (a gluttonous man and a wine-bibber) 8.14 (asleep in the storm) Mt. 26. 19 *(Eli, Eli . . .)*, Lk. 22. 44 (bloody sweat).—Altogether under the term flesh not only is a true upright and perfect man intended, ὁμοούσιος with us. There is also included a humble, wretched and weak state of man (which yet was in him for the time as compared with his first state) ; whence he is also said to have received the form of a servant, Phil. 2. 7, to have become a servant instead of a Master, Jn. 13. 13 (washing of feet), poor instead of rich, 2 Cor. 8. 9; ὁμοιοπαθής, similarly affected and like us in all things, Heb. 2. 17 ; 4.15 : all which things he indeed underwent gladly and willingly."—PICTET (VIII, 9, 3) : "The H. Spirit also ascribes to him a soul endowed with the faculty of knowing and willing, and all natural, blameless affections like joy, grief, anger, love, zeal, fear, Mt. 26. 8 (sorrow unto death). So Christ was a true man, not the empty simulacrum of a man."

With special emphasis it is insisted that Christ assumed human nature in its servant form with all its attendant weaknesses. Cf. MARESIUS, (IX, 20) : " He assumed certain penal infirmities of our nature and among others he was liable to a certain ignorance or rather lack of knowledge in respect of his humanity, which we teach against the *Papists* from Scripture which says that he increased in wisdom and in stature, and that as son of man he even knew not the day of the Judgment Mk. 13.22, that he was unaware that he would find nothing but leaves on the fig-tree, which he cursed Mk. 11.13. Not to mention the sorrowfulness, grief, fear to which he was liable, when his soul was exceeding sorrowful unto death Mt. 26.38 ; Mk. 14.32f. ; Heb. 5.7 (Gethsemane)."

In this connection it is naturally also noted that in Christ all these weaknesses were present in a sinless way. CALVIN (II, xvi, 6) : " Spotless of every flaw the Son of God yet donned the shame and disgrace of our iniquities and covered us with his own vicarious purity." Similarly POLAN (VI, 15) : " The difference in affections between us and Christ is mainly threefold. (1) It is derived from the differing principle of origin. Our affections proceed from corrupt flesh and forestall the judgment of reason and do not always obey reason. In Christ they did reside in sense appetition ; but because he was without sin and always obeyed right reason, they were roused by right reason rather than by sense appetition. Hence, as we read in Jn. 11.33, he groaned in spirit and was troubled, but with right reason and without sin. (2) It is derived from a diversity of objects. Our affections are mostly directed towards illicit and bad objects ; Christ's were never directed towards evil but always towards good. (3) It is derived from defect and repugnance. Our affections frequently revolt from right reason, fight against it and drag it down to their level ; in Christ they both are roused by and always obey right reason."

9.—But, let us repeat, as Christ is perfectly like the Father in essence as the Son of God, as a man he became perfectly like us in all respects, sin alone excepted.—HEIDEGGER (XVII, 16): "Just as according to the divine nature Christ is ὁμοούσιος with the Father, according to the human nature he is ὁμοούσιος with us, γενόμενος ἐν ὁμοιώματι ἀνθρώπου, exactly as in divinity he is ἴσα τῷ θεῷ and ἐν μορφῇ τοῦ θεοῦ Phil. 2. 6–7, ὁμοιωθεὶς κατὰ πάντα τοῖς ἀδελφοῖς Heb. 2. 17. Him the Sanctifier, to whom God gave the seed of Abraham to be defended, it behoved not only to be a brother, but also to die and so to be made like all his brethren and tempted, because it behoved him to be a priest both faithful and merciful."

10.—The union of the human nature with the person of the Logos is achieved in the conception of Christ. "It is the conception of Christ, by which without male action and with the sole blood of the Virgin Mary his human nature was formed, sanctified by the operation of the H. Spirit, assumed by the Son of God and united personally to himself" (a DIEST, p. 178). It could not be effected according to the order of nature but because of the pledge undertaken by the Son had to be effected by H. Spirit. (a) It was necessary that he who willed to satisfy for the sins of all elect should himself be thoroughly unspotted by original sin. Since then all those descended in the order of nature from Adam are by nature children of wrath, because they have all sinned in Adam, Christ had to be generated by the H. Spirit. (b) This was also necessary because the Mediator had to restore the elect to the image of God. He could not therefore be a child of Adam but had to be the divine Logos, the image of God Himself and had by the power of the H. Spirit to unite to himself in the Virgin's womb not a self-existent personal man, but human nature (OLEVIAN p. 39). But it was also just as necessary for Christ's human nature to originate not in the nature of the H. Spirit nor in the angels, but from the seed of Adam and David (to whom the promise was given). The righteousness and truth of God did not permit of Adam's fall and the sins consequent upon it being punished for the salvation of the elect in a nature other than the one descended from Adam (OLEVIAN, p. 40).

POLAN (VI, 13): "The reasons why Christ had to become man of a virgin only without a male are these: (1) He had to be wholly without sin; he had to deliver us from our sins. But those who proceed from male and female are not void of sin, as it says Jn. 3. 6: That which is born of the flesh is flesh. (2) Having a natural Father in heaven, he did not have to have a natural father on earth: as was announced in the type of Melchisedek whom Paul unfolds (Heb. 7. 3), where he says that Melchisedek was without father, and such Christ was bound to be: as man ἀπάτωρ, without father, ineffably conceived; as God ἀμήτωρ, without mother, ineffably begotten. (3) Christ had to be one person, not two; now he would have had to consist of two persons, if he had been begotten of two fathers. (4) As destruction was imported into the world through a virgin (for when Eve became the cause of transgression to her man, she was still a virgin, not yet known by Adam), so the salvation of the world had to be born by the ministry of a virgin."—COCCEIUS (De foed. IV, 79): The Mediator (1) could not be "of the number of those requiring redemption or subject to the same liability", and (2) yet he had to have part in humanity; he had "to be of the same seed which redeems and sanctifies".—KECKERMANN 323: "Christ's human nature had to be conceived and formed in the womb of a virgin and her one who had been born of the family of David. Christ had necessarily to be born of a virgin, both that his flesh might be pure and spotless, and that this person might be seen to be extraordinary. Moreover Christ had to be born of the family of David, both because of the promises made to David, and also that royal stock might add to him greater dignity and shadow forth his kingly office".

As regards the virginity of Christ's mother ZWINGLI of course held that even after the Lord's birth she remained unimpaired (Opp. III, 188: "she had—to be a virgin and perpetually a virgin, who brought forth him who could not have even the suspicion of defilement". Similarly WOLLEB 69: "We believe that after giving birth Mary also remained a virgin. Her marriage with Joseph consisted not in the begetting of the offspring, but in educating it and in a holy unity of life"—adding the remark that although three other brothers did not follow Christ, he is yet rightly called Mary's first-born". MARESIUS too (ix, 44) was of this opinion: "We recognise that even after the birth the B.V. was untouched by a male". On the contrary others taught like P. MARTYR: "We need believe nothing that is outside the Word of God. It is not necessary to believe that Mary remained a virgin, since the Scriptures do not assert it diserte. Augustine advises us not to believe either affirmation or denial in such cases." Similarly MARCK (XVIII, 11): "Mary's virginity did not flow from a vow, whether on the parents' part or on her own. With many other fairy tales contrary to the practice of the gens and the nature of wedlock she entered upon, this is a fiction of the *Papists*, using Lk. 1. 34 (How shall this be, seeing I know not a man?) for empty weaving of words, which, whether we translate them in the past with a frequent change of tense, or in the present or even, with reference to Isaiah's prophecy, in the future, establish not a prayer but only a particular fact. Nor does Christian faith demand that Mary's virginity be extended perpetually beyond the nativity of Jesus, as the *Papists* will again have it on the pretext of a vow and of the excellency of virginity and of the passage Ezek. 44. 2 dealt with allegorically with this in view (And the Lord said unto one, This gate shall be shut, it shall not be opened, neither shall any man enter in by it, for the Lord the God of Israel, hath entered in by it; therefore it shall be shut). But so far we agree with them against the *Helvidians* and the *Antidico-Marianites*, that we believe it more probable that Joseph abstained from conjugal contact with Mary even after the nativity of Jesus, because he sensed a gracious miracle."

HEIDEGGER may be regarded as representing the view that became dominant (XVII, 18): "When the ancients not a few and the monks in their train explain Mary's words as though she had intimated the taking of a resolve or vow of eternal virginity whether on her own or her parents' part, according to the story, or rather dream from the ivory gate, which *Gregory of Nyssa* relates under the title of A certain apocryphal Tale, they are quite mistaken, because if bound by a vow whether of her own or of others she would not have promised marriage to Joseph. At the time she was a virgin but betrothed to Joseph, Mt. 1. 18, with whom it is suggested in the same passage that she proposed to cohabit. Moreover God wished the most holy virgin to be betrothed, lest either the son as spurious, not being admissible to the congregation, Dt. 23. 3 (no bastard, unto the tenth generation) might be hindered in the administration of his office; or lest according to the law, Lev. 20. 10 (adulterer or adulteress put to death) a capital charge might be brought against Mary, as an adulteress. Those who adduce from *Epiphanius* that the virgin was ἐπίκληρος, we have shown earlier to be destitute of reason. Also the Church believes that she was always a virgin. Faith in Jesus bids us believe that both before and in parturition she was a virgin. Also that after an untainted parturition she retained the bloom of virginity is a pious belief of the Church, although it makes no difference to faith in Christ."

11.—The conception of Christ is thus a supernatural act which the H. Spirit so effected in the womb of the V. Mary, that while being altogether the *causa efficiens* He is not the *causa materialis* of it. The conception is produced not *de substantia* but *de potentia Spiritus S.*, and is not evoked by His *generatio* but by His *iussio* and *benedictio*.

RISSEN (XI, 25): "By the aid of the H. Spirit the Son assumed human nature from the blood of the V. Mary. And so in the conception of Jesus Christ a double principle is to be looked for, the active one of the H. Spirit, the passive one of the B.V.—The active principle is the H. Spirit, not to the exclusion of the other persons of the Trinity but in an appropriative sense, so far as the consummation and fecundation of things is usually assigned to the H. Spirit. Further, the Spirit's attitude here is not material but efficient only, δημιουργικὸς not σπερματικος; so that he might be conceived by the Spirit's power, not substance; not by generation but by benediction and consecration; so that the preposition ἐκ is the mark of efficient cause, as often elsewhere, Rom. 11. 36 (of him and through him and to him are all things), since all things are said to be of God and 1 Jn. 3. 9 the good are born ἐκ τοῦ θεοῦ. From this it is clear that the ἐκ in Mt. 1. 18, 20 is used for ἀπό" (Cf. ALTING, p. 996). In this sense must be answered the question raised by the *Socinians*, whether the H. Spirit is to be described as the Father of Jesus Christ. "For since the title of Father requires generation from the substance of Him who generates and the generation of a nature like itself and neither occurs here, it is evident that the H. Spirit cannot be called the Father of Christ".—WOLLEB 63: "The H. Spirit is not the material but the efficient cause of the conception of Christ. He was conceived not of His substance but of His power, not by generation but by command and blessing (*Aug.*)".

The effect of the supernatural conception is the birth of Christ, resulting in a genuinely human and natural way. "The conception of Christ was supernatural—but the nativity was natural" (ARETIUS, 32).

12.—In the conception of Christ itself are to be distinguished three acts of the H. Spirit: (1) the formation of the human nature, (2) the sanctification of it, and (3) the assumption of it into the person of the Son of God.

Cf. ALTING, 99a : "The conception of Christ is distinguished by three acts which are expressed by the one name *Incarnation*. These are (1) the formation, (2) the sanctification, (3) the assumption of the human nature."—WOLLEB 54: "The form of Christ's conception consists in the preparation and sanctification of the blood of the B.V. through the power of the H. Spirit; in the formation of the body, by which it was perfect once and for all, not successively as the bodies of other men; and in the inspiration of the rational soul. Whereas in ordinary generation the time of formation is fixed at forty days, Christ's body was absolute in a moment. Otherwise there would have been conceived not *Christus homo* but *Christus embryo*".—This latter statement by the way was only recognised by a few. E.g., MARESIUS says (IX, 31): "It is more probable that Christ's body just like ours was formed in stages, rather than that it was absolute in a moment."

Similarly KECKERMANN 323f.: (2) "Of the seed and blood of the V. Mary was formed Christ's flesh, the H. Spirit adding quickening force to this material. Of course the seed and blood of the V. Mary also possessed their own vital and animal spirits, as other men's seed usually has. But these were by no means sufficient for the plastic or formative force of the foetus in question. And so the H. Spirit's extraordinary shadowing and quickening were added: whence also it is said to have been conceived of the H. Spirit, a phrase and manner of speaking which is human and metaphorical, not strictly appropriate.—(3) Thus Christ's incarnation was at once ordinary and extraordinary: ordinary as regards the material supplied by the V. Mary, extraordinary as regards the formative force added to this material.—(4) The formation of the foetus in the Virgin's womb had its stages and processes, as is usual in the formation of other foetuses and which are usually completed in the space of 9 months. It was right that Christ should be made like us in this too, namely in not being formed and born in a moment, but being completed in a matrix suited to the order and processes of nature, the operation of the H. Spirit thus accommodating its process of quickening. —(5) The union of the divine nature with the human began the moment the formation of the human nature was completed, so that it would be said to have been composed of human matter and form".—RIISSEN (XI, 27): "Here the two chief operations of the H. Spirit were (1) the preparation of the material. First He had to prepare material taken from the substance of the V. Mary by a suitable sanctification, not only by imbuing it with force sufficient to beget without male seed, but also by cleansing it of all defilement of sin. (2) The formation of Christ's body, to which belongs its organisation, animation and the uniting of the two, body as well as soul, with the blood. 28: Query, Was Christ's body formed in a moment or successively? Answer: Three things occur here: (1) the preparation of the material of which Christ's body was formed; (2) the formation of the body out of the material duly prepared; (3) the completion of the same body brought gradually by its own increments to the proper stature. As regards (1) and (3) all are agreed that they were accomplished by degrees (*successive*). As regards (2) theologians disagree, some urging an instantaneous formation, others a successive, with the latter of whom we agree. Because: (1) the instantaneous and miraculous formation of Christ's complete body and its union with the soul is a fiction unsupported by Scripture; (2) in his assumption of human nature Christ is said to have been made like us, except for sin; (3) if

Christ's body was completed in a moment, it could equally have been born the same moment and the B.V. need not have suffered the inconveniences of ordinary gestation".

13.—The formation of the human nature is the act whereby it is formed by the power of the H. Spirit, without the intervention of a male, of the blood and substance of the V. Mary. Upon this ensued the " sanctification—consisting in the fact that by the same power of the H. Spirit the human nature of Christ is set apart and preserved from all defilement of sin " (HEIDEGGER XVII 26, 34). This sanctification, or the sinlessness of Christ's conception, had the result that on the one hand the H. Spirit keeps every speck of sin away from the humanity of Jesus in the Virgin's womb, and that on the other hand the sin of Adam was not reckoned to Jesus' humanity, because Jesus did not belong to the covenant of works and so had not sinned in Adam.

CALVIN (II, xiii, 4) : " It is childish trifling to say that if Christ is immune from all spot and was born by the secret operation of the Spirit from the seed of Mary, the female seed was therefore not impure, but only that of the male. We do not make Christ immune from all defilement, because he was begotten of his mother only without the co-operation of the male, but because he was hallowed by the Spirit, so that the generation might be pure and upright, as it was meant to be before Adam's fall. And let this be once for all fixed in our minds, as often as Scripture advises us of the purity of Christ, that the true nature of the man is indicated ; it would be superfluous to say that God is pure. Human generation is not unclean and vicious *per se* ? it is so by accident, the result of the fall."— HEIDEGGER (XVII, 34) : " The manner of sanctification is not so easy to explain. We dismiss the rash remarks of certain people, such as that of *Galatinus*, who (*Arc. cath. ver.* VII, 3) insists on the authority of *Rabbenu Hakkados*, that a part of Adam's flesh was preserved from the Fall, a portion of it was miraculously propagated down to the V. Mary and out of that Christ's human nature was formed. And that of the *Papists*, some of whom, the *Dominicans*, with inveterate disagreement, declare that while Mary was infected with original sin she was presently purged and hallowed from both the guilt and the defilement of it ; others, the *Franciscans* and the *Jesuits*, triflingly assert that preserved from all sin she also begot a holy offspring ; as though the coming, overshadowing and sanctification of the H. Spirit would have been neccessary, if when generating Christ the B.M. had been void of all spot and liability.—The manner of it is better explained by those who distinguish the proximate and remote causes of Christ's flesh. The proximate cause is the H. Spirit, who not only fertilised Mary's seed but also separated and preserved it from all the defilement with which it would equally have been defiled, if it had had to be the instrument of ordinary generation ; as we gather from Lk. 1.35; Mt. 1.20 (the part of the H. Spirit), where the nexus of cause and effect ought to be expected.—The remote cause of the same sanctification or immaculate conception is the non-imputation of Adam's sin. Though Adam's son and existing in Adam's loins when created Christ was not in him as sinning : he was not part of the covenant of works represented by Adam and so could refrain from sinning when Adam sinned. But he was also appointed mediator of the new covenant of grace (which he could not have been in Adam nor could he have been joined with him in contracting a covenant of works with God or in violating the covenant in and along with Adam). Therefore Adam's sin could in no wise be imputed to him."

The third act of the H. Spirit in the conception of Christ is the " assumption of the human nature into the person of the Son of God, whereby the Λόγος, the Son of God, in the very moment of formation and sanctification assumed the human nature void of an hypostasis of its own into the unity of its own person, in order that there might be one and the same ὑπόστασις of the λόγος assuming and of the human nature assumed, outside of which it neither ever subsists nor can subsist " (HEIDEGGER XVII, 36). And in fact Christ so assumed the human nature into the unity of his person, that since his incarnation, although as the Father's eternal Son he also exists in an infinite way outside the assumed humanity, his will personally is as Redeemer of the world never to be thought of, believed in or called upon apart from his humanity at all. Indeed even before his appearance in the flesh it was only possible to believe in him as one who intended to come in the flesh. So too the Father and the H. Spirit refused to be the object of faith and adoration save in the incarnate Son. Therefore because he wills never to be known apart from his assumed humanity, for his part the Son would never be acknowledged apart from the union of the elect with his person as the Head of his Kingdom ; which is why St. Paul calls the Church the πλήρωμα of his Body. The Son embraces the believers united to him with even stronger love than he does the body which he personally assumed. Only for love of us did he unite this body to himself, in order to offer it up to death for us. So far then from being able to think of or to acknowledge the Son of God apart from his flesh once he has assumed it, the Father Himself never knows the Son otherwise than as the Son who came in the flesh. So that it is only the spirit of antichrist that denies that the Son came in the flesh (OLEVIAN, p. 42).

14.—Thus (1) the assumption of the humanity into the person of the Son of God is not an assumption of it into the divine nature, but into the person of the Logos : yet the result of this assumption is such that there was as little an extension and completion thereby of the Logos-person, as the human nature was met with a diminution by receiving hypostatic existence (not in itself but only) in the Logos : (2) the result of the assumption is not that the hypostasis of the Logos subsists in the human nature, but that the latter subsists in the former.

Before dealing with (3) [§ 15] let us hear two voices on the first two. HEIDEGGER (XVII, 36) : "Since there is but one Christ, Gal.3. 16 (He saith not, And to seeds, as of many ; but as of one, And to thy seed, which is Christ), one Mediator, 1 Tim. 2. 5 (one God, one mediator also between God and man, himself man, Christ Jesus), one Lord, Eph. 4. 5, and since here and there things are predicated of Christ the man, which belong to God and *vice versa* ; assuredly there must of necessity be one hypostasis, one subsistent person. Either the divine nature subsists in the human, or the human in the divine. That the divine nature should subsist in and be sustained by the human is opposed to its infinite perfection. So the human is *per se* ἀνυπόστατος and becomes ἐνυπόστατος in the λόγος, who being pre-existent, in fact existent from eternity, has received in time the form of a servant Phil. 2. 7, and assumed the seed of Abraham, Heb. 2. 16 (he taketh hold of the seed of A.) as its shrine and instrument."—MASTRICHT (V, 4, 21) : " Query : whether the formal element in the union consists in the ὑπόστασις τοῦ λόγου having become the ὑπόστασις of the flesh ?—Scripture nowhere represents this union by such a communication but by a λαβὴ Phil, 2. 7 and an ἐπίληψις Heb. 2. 16, by which is signified the ineffable relation of the human nature to the divine person (an act, not a process ?). By this relation the former is not only inseparably conjoined with the latter, but is also maintained in existence by it, by the support not of common providence but of the person, whereby the former enters with the latter into the constitution of the one person, the θεάνθρωπος.

15.—And (3) the result of the assumption is that the humanity of Christ becomes not a part of his person but a serviceable instrument or tool, the medium of its effect upon life.—POLAN (VI, 16): "Christ's flesh is ἐνυπόστατος, subsistent in his person, not as a part adequate or analogous to the person, but as an instrument belonging to the unity of the hypostasis, or as a particular thing subsisting in its principle and ordered by its principle to its goal. Thus the composition of the person out of the natures is not a matter of parts but rather a matter of number, because the human nature subsists in the person of Christ."—HEIDEGGER (XVII, 36): "Whence the ancients call it an ἀνθρώπινον ὄργανον— and a πρόσλημμα, an assumpt or adjunct; the former as an operation, the latter as a state."—ZANCHIUS (*De relig. Christiana* p.64-65): "Therefore we acknowledge and confess in Christ, against NESTORIUS, only one person; and that eternal, most single and most perfect, as well as abiding for ever: the person, I mean, of the eternal Son of God. Next, to this eternal person there was added in time not another person but another nature, a human nature. And it not as a part of the person by which it was assumed, but a thing quite different from it, nevertheless assumed into its unity. And then, thirdly, we confess that in the one and same person of Christ there are two natures, the divine and a human, in which we do not doubt that it subsists, lives and works. So that we are not afraid to say, that Christ consists of a divine nature *and* a human taken up into the unity of the person, and that he is in a certain sense composed of them.—COCCEIUS (*S.T.* LVIII, 15): "By assuming our nature and making it a temple and bearer for himself the Son did not become more perfect, but he communicated his glory to the human nature. Nor did he become a composite or part of a composite; yet in consequence he was a man, as possessing both θεότης (divinity) φύσει (by nature), and humanity by grace and mercy."

16.—Upon this "assumption" of the human nature into the person of the Son of God rests the *unio* (περιχώρησις) of Christ's two natures. "The personal union (of the two natures in Christ) is the assumption not of a man but of a human nature into the unity of the person of the eternal Son of God, while the properties of each are preserved intact; in such wise that although these natures are most diverse and remain eternally distinct in their properties, since the Creator wishes to remain eternally distinct from all creatures, even from the *massa* which He assumed—yet they are so conjoined that they are both the one Christ" (OLEVIAN p. 38).

Definitions of the *unio personalis* agree completely in all dogmaticians. Cf. BUCAN (II, 15): "It is personal union in Christ by which the person of the Son of God, a person already existent from eternity, has assumed a most pure human nature devoid of a personality of its own into the unity of its person, and has made it its own, while preserving the attributes of both natures."—a DIEST (178): "The personal union of the two natures in Christ is that by which the person of the Son of God assumed a most pure human nature devoid of a personality or subsistence of its own and so united itself with the human nature, that there might be God and man in one person".—WENDELIN is the most precise (*Coll.* 63): "We agree (with the *Lutherans*)—that the personal union is a supreme communion, by which the divine and human natures in the one person of Christ have been so united, that they are the one person's two natures, which with all their attributes the person claims for itself, so that that same person is

God eternal, immense, omnipotent, omniscient and the creator of heaven and earth, in respect of the divine nature, and is at the same time a man, begotten in time of the V. Mary, and so a creature corporeal, finite, visible, once mortal, of finite knowledge and power, etc."

In the discussion of the nature of the *unio personalis* the question was usually discussed, whether it might be compared at all with any other relationship known to man: this gave rise to the stereotyped rebuttal of inapposite comparisons.—CALVIN (II, xiv, 1) had undoubtedly discovered the comparison between the relation of "body and mind in one man". The later dogmaticians on the other hand rejected it. Cf. ZANCHIUS (p.63-64): "We confess indeed with *Athanasius*, that as one man consists of a rational soul and flesh, so the one Christ is God and man; i.e. Christ is only one person although there are two natures in him: not that the person of Christ is made up of two natures as of parts (if we would speak strictly), in the way in which, to constitute the person of a man, the body as an essential part necessarily concurs with soul. Christ's person already existed entire and utterly perfect before his manifestations in the flesh. Person of man, say Adam, there was none, before soul was united to body. And since neither soul takes to itself a body nor body a soul, in the way in which the Son of God took to himself the seed of Abraham into union with the same person; and since further body and soul are also two ὑφιστάμενα, as is clear in the creation of Adam, the human nature never existed by itself but only in the person of God. Some people very evilly abuse this godly saying of a sainted man to prove their own dreams. It is altogether necessary that he who manifested himself (that is, the person of the Son of God) should differ from the flesh in which he manifested himself; and that not only before but also after the resurrection and session at the right hand of the Father; which (as *Augustine* says) brought glory to the flesh but did not abolish the nature".—Similarly RIISSEN (XI, 21); "The hypostatic union is not well explained by the simile of the conjunction of soul and body. They agree, it is true, in that as body and soul unite in one person, so do the divinity and the humanity; and as soul works through body as an instrument substantially united to it, so too the divinity through the humanity. But they differ, in that body and soul meet in a person as incomplete parts and natures. Divinity is strictly neither a part nor an incomplete nature. And secondly, from soul and body a third nature arises; but not from the divinity and the humanity". — BUCAN (II, 15) : " The union of body and soul is indeed a παράδειγμα of the *unio personalis*, but one which does not square every way. In man from the nature of soul and the nature of body a third nature arises composed of the two, called human nature. In Christ there is no construction of a single third nature out of divine and human;

each remains pure and unconfused."—Also the comparison was rejected between the *unio personalis* and glowing iron. BUCAN (*ibid.*): "Nor is the simile of glowing iron altogether suitable. Heat and glow in iron are qualities but not the actual substance of fire. Hence the Apostle calls [the *unio*] the great mystery of godliness, 1 Tim. 3. 16."—ZANCHIUS (p. 61-63), by the way, recommends comparing Christ's human nature to a garment: "We approve of the phrasing customary in the Church, that Christ clad himself or was clad in our flesh. Whence too *Augustine* says that Christ descended from heaven like a naked man descending from a mountain; but he ascended invested with our flesh as with a garment. Although not explaining the hypostatic union so perfectly, this phrasing yet shows the clear difference between the person of the Son of God which assumes and our nature which was assumed".—Still, ZANCHIUS himself finds even this comparison unsuitable, since he explains that "it cannot be denied that Christ is true man. Yet the man denies it who says, that the Son of God took upon himself the form of a servant exactly as man puts on a coat. He takes upon himself a human nature in which he subsists essentially. But a coat does not belong to the essence of a man". The usual designation of Christ's human nature is ὄργανον τοῦ λόγου, also *templum* or (RIISSEN XI, 23) "adjunct,—because it is conjoined in time in the unity of his person with the λόγος, who exists from eternity apart from the flesh."

Since God's covenant of grace holds eternally for the elect, it is clear that in Christ's person, as in the foundation of this covenant, the two natures are united for all eternity, that the full integrity of both natures and of their attributes continues in their union in the person, and neither can be absorbed by the other (OLEVIAN, p. 38).

17.—A distinction must be made between the *unio immediata* between the human nature and the person of the Logos, and the *unio mediata* of the two natures which is mediated by the H. Spirit. "Direct union is between the person of the λόγος and the human nature;—indirect is between the divine nature and the human" (WENDELIN, *Systema* I, xv, 3). The first is not an *unio* παραστατική or *per meram assistentiam*, as a sailor is in a ship he is navigating; not an *unio coessentialis,* as the persons of the Trinity are united by the essence; not an *unio essentialis et* δραστική, as the nature and power of the Logos are present in all things; not an *unio physica,* as form and matter are united; not an *unio* σχετική *s. consensus,* as friends are united; not an *unio mystica s. praesentia gratiae tantum* : not an *unio sacramentalis* : but an *unio personalis s.* ὑποστατική.—These analogies vary in detail in different writers. WOLLEB 65 : " For purposes of instruction it is advantageous to indicate how the human nature was and was not united to the Son of God. It was not united συνουσιαδῶς, as the divine persons are united ; not just οὐσιαδῶς καὶ δραστικῶς, in essence and in power (virtus), as Christ's essence is present to all; not παραστατικῶς or by the presence of grace only ; not φυσικῶς, as form and matter are united : not σχετικῶς, as friend to friend ; not just μυστικῶς, as Christ dwells in believers ; not sacramentally, as it is in the H. Supper ; but ὑποστατικῶς, personally."—RIJSSEN (XI, 20, 1) : " The question is not of a union, physical and essential, of two things to constitute one third nature, as soul is united to body to constitute a human being. Nor of an unio σχετικὴ et relativa, which consists in the union of minds, such as is the union of friends. Nor of an unio παραστατική, per meram assistentiam, like that of angels with assumed bodies.   Not of an unio δραστική, for general efficacy and sustainedness, by which all things are in God and we are, live and move in Him (Ac. 17.18). Nor of the union, mystical and gracious, of believers with Christ. Nor of the union, οὐσιαδής or essential, of the persons of the Trinity in one essence. But of the hypostatic union, by which nothing else is indicated but the intimate and perpetual conjunction of the two natures, divine and human, into unity with the person, by which the human nature, which was devoid of a personality of its own, was assumed into the person of the λόγος and conjoined with it into the unity of its person, so as to be now ἐνυπόστατος λόγῳ, so far as it is sustained by the λόγος ;   not by the general sustenance by which all creatures are sustained by God, but by a special and personal, inasmuch as it has coalesced into one person with the Word. Such a union is denied by the Socinians, who teach that in Christ there is only one nature, that he is not only true but also pure and unifold man, whose whole prerogative accordingly lay in the excellence of his attributes and office, not of his nature ; we affirm the point."

18.—As regards the indirect union of the natures, according to oecumenical teaching the two natures in Christ are so united to each other on the one hand ἀσυγχύτως and ἀτρέπτως (without confusion or change) on the other hand ἀδιαιρέτως καὶ ἀχωρίστως (indivisibly and inseparably), that the properties of the human and of the divine natures are present unmixed in the one person of Christ, i.e. that the divine nature preserves the attributes of deity and remains essentially infinite, whereas the human nature retains the creaturely human attributes in their complete integrity and, since finitum non capax infiniti, remains essentially finite.

ZANCHIUS 65f. : " We believe and confess these two natures to have been so truly and inseparably conjoined and united into the one person of

Christ, that we do not doubt that each nevertheless remains entire and unimpaired and truly distinct from the other, and retains its own essential properties and operations distinct, without the slightest trace of confusion ; so that as the divine, retaining its own properties, remained increate, infinite, immense, sheerly almighty, sheerly wise, so too the human, retaining its own, remains created, finite, bounded by fixed limits. And just as the divine has its own will and potency by which Christ as God wills and works the things that are God's, so the human has its, by which the same Christ as man wills and works the things that are man's ; to the extent that Christ according as he is God does not will or work by human will and potency, neither does he according as he is man will and work by divine will and potency, as it was wisely determined by the Fathers both against *Eutyches* and against *Macarius* ".

Polemically RIISSEN puts the matter still more clearly, (XI, 13ff.) : " In explaining this mystery two rocks must be avoided : *Nestorianism*, which divided the person, and *Eutychianism*, which confounded the natures.—14 : The first error is that of *Nestorius*, Patriarch of Constantinople, who out of the two natures of Christ was for fashioning two persons, and so denying that the B.V. can be called θεότοκος, *Deipara*, but was only χριστότοκος, while Christ was not θεὸς but only ἄνθρωπος θεόφορος, *homo Deifer*. And so he was for making two Christs, one of whom was crucified by the Jews, the other not. Hence his rather frequent groan, Whence boastest thou, O Jew ? Thou hast crucified a man, not God. Nor did he recognise any but an accidental union of the natures : κατὰ παράστασιν or by simple indwelling, according as the Word dwelt in the man Christ as in his temple : κατὰ χάριν καὶ εὐδοκίαν, according as God greatly acquiesced in this man ; κατ' ἐνέργειαν, by operation, according as he was God's instrument in those marvellous works which the Son of God produced : κατὰ ταὐτοβουλίαν et *effectum*, as regards the agreement of the wills of God and man in Christ : κατ' ἀξίαν et ἰσοτιμίαν, as regards the dignity conferred upon the assumed flesh. This view was condemned by the *Council of Ephesus*.— The second rock to be avoided here is *Eutychianism*, opposed to the former, named after *Eutyches*, archimandrite of Constantinople, who while quite heatedly opposing *Nestorius'* splitting of Christ's person into two, himself confounded the two natures into one and was condemned at the *Council of Chalcedon*. But Scripture witnesses contrariwise, where the opposition of the two natures in Christ is frequent, Rom. 1. 3 (born of the seed of David according to the flesh) 1 Pet. 3.18 (Christ also suffered for sins once . . . that he might bring us to God, being put to death in the flesh but made alive in the Spirit) Phil. 2. 6-7 [the exinanition].—In order to oppose this twofold error the Fathers of the *Synod of Chalcedon*, assembled in 451, declared that the union was made ἀδιαιρέτως καὶ ἀχωρίστως, *indivisibiliter et inseparabiliter* against *Nestorius*, and ἀτρέπτως καὶ ἀσυγχύτως, *sine mutatione et confusione* against *Eutyches*, because the two natures were so united in the one person that they could neither be converted the one into the other, nor confused so that a third should emerge from the two, but remained throughout unconfused with their respective attributes."

ALTING (p. 100) explains these definitions with more adequacy: "The *unio personalis* in Christ was made ἀδιαιρέτως, indivisibly, in respect of place, so that the human nature is nowhere unsupported by the λόγος, the λόγος nowhere fails to support the human nature, nor is it outside the λόγος or the λόγος apart from it: ἀχωρίστως, inseparably in respect of time, because this union is never dissolved but is perpetual, which was also seen in the death and burial: ἀτρέπτως, inconvertibly, so that the λόγος was not converted into the flesh nor nor the flesh into the λόγος: ἀσυγχύτως without confusion, so that no composite nature has issued from a mixture of λόγος and flesh, but in the union each nature has remained safe and sound with all the essential attributes proper to each".

19.—The effects of this *unio personalis* are a triple *communio* or *communicatio*, viz. (1) a sharing of graces or charisms to the human nature, (2) a sharing of the properties of both natures with the person, (3) a sharing of operations, in particular *communicatio* ἀποτελεσμάτων.—WOLLEB 66: "There are three effects of the personal union, the *communicatio idiomatum*, the excellence of the human nature, and the co-operation of both natures in the divine-human works."

20.—(1) *Communicatio gratiarum* is the work of the Logos-person, by which it imparts to the human nature (*a*) the grace of union with the person of the λόγος (since Christ's humanity is ἐνυπόστατος τῷ λόγῳ), the grace of eminence over all creatures, and as a result the honour of adoration; and (*b*) habitual graces or charisms. The latter are the gifts of the H. Spirit, especially those of knowledge, will and power, with which Christ's humanity is equipped above all other intelligent creatures. These *gratiae habituales*, of which impeccability or *non posse peccare* is one (since Christ could not sin), were of course imparted to the humanity of Christ without measure, since they are the highest gifts of the Spirit which a creature can receive at all; still they are essentially finite, created gifts. Moreover these gifts entered Christ exceptionally, not at once but during his humiliation, and only so as not to impair the natural development of his humanity. On the other hand, from the start of Christ's exaltation onwards they are exhibited in their complete perfection. The honour of worship naturally does not belong to Christ's humanity as such, but because the divine Logos has taken it up into his personality, which is worshipful by nature.

BURMANN (V, viii, 24): "The things communicated to the human nature as a result of this union are (1) the grace of union, by which assumed into society with the divine nature it constitutes with it the God-man.—(2) habitual grace and the communication of all gifts of the H. Spirit in such perfection and degree as created nature can receive."
—WOLLEB 67: "The excellence of Christ's human nature consists partly in the gifts which emanate from the grace of union, partly in the honour of adoration.—KECKERMANN among others insists, as a third effect of the personal union (321), upon "the supreme power of office given to Christ's flesh, that he might be the head of the Church".—BUCAN II, 23: "What is the effect of this personal union?—The conferring of gifts, by which the human nature in Christ's person was adorned and by which he excels all creatures in wisdom, goodness, holiness, power, majesty and glory; (615) which the *Fathers* call the deification of the flesh, the *Scholastics* habitual grace, quite distinct from the communion of ἰδιώματα which is alternate and is an ἀντίδοσις ὀνομάτων [a reciproca-tion of names or qualities?]".—KECKERMANN 321: "By the union Christ's human nature possesses the graces called habitual, i.e., most excellent good things, to wit, such complete knowledge as can befall a creature, and others of the kind. The gifts and powers of Christ's human nature are called habitual graces, i.e., infused habits or qualities implanted in Christ's flesh right from the first moment of his nativity; but with this distinction, that they increased in Christ with his growth, as Luke says in Ch. 2, not so much because of the actual quality considered by itself, as of its effectiveness in operation, which was less in Christ as an infant and a boy but greater in his man's estate, when he approached the execution of his ministry."—a DIEST 179: "The result of the personal union . . . is . . . the high excellency of the human nature.—181f. This high excellency of the human nature consists in the grace conferred on him alone above and beyond his fellows. It is fourfold : grace of union, habitual grace, grace of office, grace of honour. Grace of union is that by which Christ's human nature is raised to such dignity as achieves the stage next below divinity, so that being ἀνυπόστατος in itself it is ἐνυπόστατος in the λόγος.—Habitual graces are most excellent (but not infinite) endowments conferred on Christ's human nature beyond the measure of all other creatures."—Similarly TURRETIN (XIII, viii, 1):—WOLLEB 67: "First among the gifts must be considered his knowledge and power. Although the eternal knowledge which is the essential attribute of the divine nature was not transfused into the human

nature, yet the human nature also acquires a threefold knowledge, donative, infused and experimental.—Donative knowledge of good things is that by which in closest union with the divine nature the human nature sees, though it does not understand, what it knows. For the infinite cannot be grasped by the finite: (the human nature) sees God ὅλον, ἀλλ' οὐχ ὅλως, as a whole but not wholly.—Infused knowledge is knowledge by which anointed by the H. Spirit Christ knows whatever pertains to heavenly matters, yet cannot be seen at other times except by the light of grace. Experimental knowledge is knowledge by which Christ knows the things which are known by the light of nature, through understanding effects from causes, causes from effects, contraries from contraries. But although both donative and infused knowledge conquers angels no less than men it is nevertheless different from eternal knowledge or omniscience. Moreover to the experimental knowledge is opposed the ignorance attributed to Christ; in this kind of knowledge he is said to have advanced, Lk. 2. 52.—This power was given to the human nature in order that it might also be superior to angels and men; for it received the instrumental power of emitting miracles. But principal power or omnipotence is reserved for the λόγος, which uses the human nature as an instrument."—MAS-TRICHT (V, iv, 25): "The Reformed carefully distinguish the gifts from the divine attributes, effects from their causes; and they admit that gifts were communicated to Christ the Mediator according to his human nature of such magnitude and kind as may befall human nature, but neither infinite *simpliciter* nor once for all, but bound by lapse of time to advance gradually to their ἀκμή; and so Scripture makes him full of grace right from the womb, yet so that the gifts grow with his years. This is clear: (1) from the eloquent testimonies of Scripture, Lk. 2. 40, 52 (the child grew, and waxed strong, becoming full of wisdom: and the grace of God was upon him. . . . Jesus advanced in wisdom and stature, and in favour with God and man) Mk. 13. 32 (of that day or that hour knoweth no one, not even the angels in heaven, neither the Son, but the Father); (2) from the fuller outpouring of the H. Spirit, first made at the baptism, the symbol of which was the resting of the Spirit upon him, Mt. 3. 16, 17 (the dove at baptism and the voice out of heaven) Jn. 1. 32 (. . . I have beheld the Spirit descending as a dove out of heaven and it abode upon him) Is. 11. 1–2 (And there shall come forth a shoot out of the stock of Jesse, and a branch out of his roots shall bear fruit; and the spirit of the LORD shall rest upon him, the spirit of wisdom and understanding, the spirit of knowledge and of the fear of the LORD); (3) from the fact that he was in all things like us, sin excepted, Heb. 2. 17 (it behoved him in all things to be made like unto his brethren, that he might be a merciful and faithful high priest in things pertaining to God, to make propitiation for the sins of the people) 4. 15 (. . . we have not a high priest that cannot be touched with the feeling of our infirmities; but one that hath been in all points tempted like as *we are, yet* without sin). Nor does it help opponents, that God is said not to have given him the Spirit by measure, Jn. 3. 34. That does not completely exclude all measure, only that which is regularly applied to creatures, cf. Esth. 1. 8 (. . . none could compel . . .). If they add that all power in heaven and on earth was given him Mt. 28. 18, the answer will come easily, that we must not understand everything *simpliciter*, but all the things required for the government of the Church, as is clear from the verse following (Go ye therefore . . .).—RIISSEN XI, 34: "The plenitude is not infinite, because the humanity, which is finite, is not capable of the infinite. But this is to be understood *secundum quid* [relatively], because these graces are greater far than those which are communicated to angels or to men. In others there is the plenitude of sufficiency, whereby they obtain of God as much of the graces as suffices them for salvation. In Christ there is the plenitude of abundance, which suffices not for himself alone but for others also, which has all the degrees which can be possessed in accordance with God's law. Nothing equal to it can occur among men."—At this point *Scholasticism* usually closed the discussion of individual questions; e.g., whether Christ had faith and hope. VOETIUS did deal in a specific essay (II, 155ff.) with the question whether and what kind of faith Christ had and how he used the sacraments."—On this RIISSEN remarks (XI, 55): "Not a few condemn CALVIN, because he attributes faith to Christ. But that faith must not be denied *simpliciter* to Christ Scripture shows in more than one passage. It calls Christ faithful, Heb. 2. 17 (in all things like unto his brethren) 3. 2 (faithful unto him who appointed him) and Peter Ac. 2. 26 refers to Christ the words of Ps. 16. 9 "my flesh shall tabernacle in hope". And Mt. 27. 43 by calling the Father his God (he trusted in God) Christ witnesses to his faith in Him. Faith therefore is attributed to Christ, not so far as it is trustful apprehension of God's mercy, because so it is competent for sinners only; nor in a sense of a mode of knowing about the obscurity of the enigma, 2 Cor. 5. 7 (by faith, not by sight), which argues imperfection; but as regards the substance of knowing and assent to the thing known, i.e., the doctrine revealed by God and the trust which rests upon God's goodness providing all things needful for us. The same must be said of hope; whatever perfection there is in it as to the certainty by which we lean strongly on the divine promise for the future, is rightly assigned to Christ; but what involves defect and imperfection, so far as it is an obscure expectation of a thing not yet possessed, ought not to be ascribed to him."—In the same way the question is discussed, "whether Christ's soul was blessed from the beginning of his life, so that he knew everything and never felt pain." RIISSEN (IX, 39, 1) informs us in what sense the question was answered in the negative. "The question in this *locus* is not whether Christ laboured under crass ignorance of many things—a statement calumniously imputed to us— because he could not be exempted from sin. The question is whether Christ's soul was imbued with such knowledge from the beginning in virtue of the hypostatic union, that he was ignorant of nothing or could learn all over again. What the *Papists* affirm we deny. And while we acknowledge that Christ as God was omniscient, yet as a man we confess that he was endued with knowledge great above all others, but yet finite and created, to which something could be added and truly was added."—The question whether Christ was at once a *viator* and a *comprehensor* was negatived. On the other hand the question "whether Christ was so holy on account of the hypostatic union that he could not sin, was affirmed (RIISSEN, XI, 39, 4): "Proof: that if Christ could fail in the office of Mediator, the foundations of salvation could have been overturned." Against the objection that "he was free and so he could sin" it is insisted that the "freedom" did not consist in ability to sin.

The teaching of the others is similar. E.g., BURMANN (V, viii, 24): "With this is also connected the grace by which Christ could never sin, since in such great light of knowledge and perfect love of will and holy motions it was quite impossible for him to fall away."—MARESIUS (XI, 20); "Christ could never sin."—(21): Nor did Christ's impeccability stand in the way of his free judgment, since freedom of judgment—does not necessarily involve the faculty of sinning, i.e., of falling short of perfection."

21.—Naturally the honour of worship does not belong to Christ's humanity as such, but because the divine Logos has taken it up into his personality, which is by nature *adorabilis*.—WOLLEB 68: "The honour which results from the personal union is the adoration of the human nature; not however of the flesh *qua* flesh nor of the creature, but of God in the created flesh".—KECKERMANN 322: "It is because of the union that the whole person of Christ is worshipped, although the direct object of worship is the divinity alone."—ZANCHIUS 71: "The union of natures in the person of Christ brings it about that we cannot worship the Deity in Christ, unless at the same time we also worship the human nature in him, and that both the human and the divine nature in him must be worshipped by us altogether with the one worship only."—VOETIUS devoted an explicit section to the discussion of this doctrinal point

(I, 520–552), "anent the question whether Christ as the Mediator should be worshipped." VOETIUS distinguishes between "worship" and "worshipfulness". "Christ as mediator or under the formula *qua est mediator* is not worshipful"; for only God is "worshipful". But since Christ *qua* person is God it follows that "in and along with the flesh, in and along with the office of mediator Christ is to be worshipped, so that the object of our consideration is Christ's person, together with everything that is in it."

22.—(2): *Communicatio idiomatum* ("an *idioma* is a property of one nature which cannot be communicated to the other," WENDELIN, *Systema,* I, xvi, 2) is that effect of the *unio personalis,* "by which the attributes of each of the two natures coincide in one and the same person and are thereby also predicated of the person" (MASTRICHT V, iv, 12). For the attributes peculiar to either nature also belong to the person, because the natures have their substance in the person of Christ. Hence the attributes belong to the natures only *distincte,* whereas they belong to the person *indistincte.*

POLAN (VI, 16): The second "effect of the personal union in respect of Christ is that the attributes of either nature of Christ are communicated to the actual person. The things peculiar to the separate natures are common to Christ's person and are accordingly attributed to and true of the natures only distinctly, but of the person without distinction.— And this not merely verbally or by void titles, but most really.—For because the person embraces both natures, whatever participates in both natures or in one of them really belongs to it because of the hypostatic union of the natures. And what is proper to one nature is by no means common to the other one in it because of the essential and eternal difference between the natures, though it is common to the person or to one of the natures in the person.—Accordingly Christ is God not verbally but really. He is also man not verbally but really.—Hence whatever is predicted of Christ is affirmed of his whole, i.e. undivided person truly and really; and that with respect and regard to each or only one nature.— With respect and regard to both natures two things are assigned and belong to Christ : (1) the office of mediator [alone cited here], which was given Christ in time not only according to his humanity but also according to his Deity considered κατ' οἰκονομίαν. Whence it is plain that the pronouncement must be curbed, which is usually put out, that: Everything given to Christ in time was given him only according to his humanity. Nothing can be given to Deity considered singly and by itself. But according to that dispensation that brings us salvation there has been given to it and personally united to it human nature; as was said above, it was given the mediatorial office in time.—Accordingly the mediatorial office, while requiring two natures, also requires a conjoint but distinct operation of each of the natures.—In executing the office of mediator each nature in communion with the other effects what is proper to each, the Word, that is, effecting what belongs to the Word, and the flesh executing what belongs to the flesh: as even Leo teaches in the Epistle to Flavianus c.4.—Thus the whole Christ is according to his Deity and humanity our mediator, redeemer, intercessor and Saviour, King, priest and prophet; shepherd and head, and the vine of whom we are members and branches, Lord and judge of the world, knowing and willing his works and enacting them according to both natures.—As regards us there are also two effects of the personal union of the divine and the human natures in Christ, namely the union of us with God and our eternal salvation. The personal union of the two natures in Christ is the one medium of our union with God and of our eternal salvation. As God from the beginning of creation made the personal union of our soul and body to set up our common nature, so He provided the singular personal union of the two natures in Christ, by a singular grace admirable beyond any work of nature, for the restoration of our nature in the person of Christ. Things which were distinct, God and man, met together on the solution of their ancient disagreement and were united again, the mediator being Christ who bound the heights and depths together in himself. And because Christ personally united our nature to himself, we too have our being naturally in him, as *Hilary* says; naturally, I say, because in nature he is ὁμοούσιος with us; yet we are not in him carnally, but so far as we are inserted into his body by faith. We are made fellows of Christ through the Incarnation, says *Basilius, Ep. ad Caesarienses* 41."

BUCAN (II, 20): "Κοινωνία ἰδιωμάτων, also called ἐπίζευξις ὀνομάτων and κοινωτὴς and ἀντίδοσις or τρόπος ἀντιδόσεως, is not the effusion of the properties of one nature into the other or a mutual confusion of ἰδιώματα, but an attribution κατὰ συνεκδοχὴν or an alternative predication, by which (because there is in Christ one thing and another, ἄλλο καὶ ἄλλο, and not one man and another, but two natures in one person) what is proper to one nature in Christ is attributed not to the other nature but to the person named from the other nature, whether divine or human.— Or there is a manner of predication, by which to the one person of Christ are attributed in common the things which are proper to the natures, and this because Christ is both things in two perfect natures, i.e. perfect God and perfect man; to whom therefore are truly and actually assigned alike the things which are proper to God and those which are proper to man."—WENDELIN (*Collat.* 69f,): "We acknowledge that in Christ dwells the entire fulness of divinity σωματικῶς, provided the communication of the natures as well as of the properties is understood to have taken place in the person through union, not in the natures among themselves so that one nature has been communicated to the other along with its properties; namely to the human nature the divine nature and its properties, to the divine nature the human nature and its properties. Communication of this kind confuses or abolishes the natures and the attributes and is nowhere found in Scripture, and so it is ἄγραφος καὶ ἀντίγραφος."— BEZA (I, 658f.): "Yet he said he was in heaven, at the time he was addressing Nicodemus, Jn. 3. 13 (no man hath ascended into heaven, but he that descended out of heaven, even the Son of man, which is in heaven). This and other things of the kind are understandable through the κοινωνία ἰδιωμάτων.—God (meaning the λόγος) is this man and this man is God, and this because of the unity of the person, arising not as a result of the communication of the natures but of the union of the natures. Here God is not man so far as he is God but κατ' ἄλλο, i.e. so far as he is united to God.—God (meaning the λόγος) was conceived, born, suffered, was crucified, dead and buried and rose again, so far as he united man to himself, not so far as he is God. And likewise this man is the Son of God eternal, infinite, invisible, filling all things etc., not in himself, that is, so far as he is a man, nor by any communication of attributes, but so far as he has been assumed by the Son of God into the one person.—By communication of attributes we do not mean the personal union or the form of this union, but the predication, as the logicians say, which is made because of the personal union of the two natures, in which an essential attribute or operation appropriate to one nature is assigned to the person, in the concrete, not in the abstract. But since this predication is true, the truth must underlie it in the same respect, namely in respect of the whole person considered concretely."—PISCATOR (*Aphor.* p. 54): "The *communicatio idiomatum* is nothing else than a synecdoche, by which what is proper to one nature in Christ is attributed to the person itself, called by the name of the other nature".

23.—This *communicatio idiomatum* is *realis* as regards the divine-human person of Christ; in the strictest sense of the word we must say, that Christ the Son of David is omnipotent, omnipresent, omniscient. On the other hand as regards the natures the *communicatio* is a *communicatio verbalis* or a *praedicatio*. At the same time this *communicatio verbalis* is no empty *modus loquendi* with no real relation answering to it. It is a *praedicatio vera*. Between the two natures in and for themselves there is of course no possible community of *idiomata*; on being communicated to another nature the idiomata of a nature would cease to be idiomata; what is *proprium* cannot be called common. On the other hand it follows from the union of the natures in the person that, by synecdoche of course, the properties of the one nature may be predicated of the *concretum* of the other. The person embraces the two natures and their *idiomata*, in consequence of which Mary may with complete justification be called the Mother of God.

RIISSEN (XI, 39) : "This communication may be viewed either abstractly with respect to the nature, or concretely with respect to the person ; the words concrete and abstract not being taken in the abusive sense of the *Lutherans*, for whom abstract is the human nature abstracted from the Deity, concrete the human nature as united to the λόγος, but accepting the use of the schools, according as abstract is the name of a nature, as deity, humanity, while concrete is of the person or subject possessing the nature, as God, man. So we conclude that the attributes of one nature have not become those of the other nor can be predicated of it abstractly. Divinity did not suffer ; humanity is not eternal ".—WENDELIN (*Coll.* 70f.) : " Those of us who call the communication of attributes and natures a manner of speaking do not mean it as though the communication were only verbal but not real. We mean that this communication is expressed in certain formulae of expression, whereby concrete nouns derived from the natures and denoting the person (like God, man) are truly and really affirmed of them mutually, as that God is man, man is God ; because they could not truly be predicated and affirmed mutually of them by the abstract names of the natures, as that humanity or human nature is Deity or divine nature."—BUCAN (II, 21) : " Is *communicatio idiomatum* verbal merely, or also real ? It is a true and real manner of speaking because the person of which, by the figure of synecdoche, both divine and human names or properties and effects are commonly and equally predicated, truly and really contains in itself all things that belong to true God and to true man. The divine things, I mean, by which the same person is God, the human things by which he is man ; not however in respect of both natures but κατ' ἄλλο καὶ κατ' ἄλλο ; as *Cyril* teaches in the same passage. Otherwise the *Eutychian* heresy would be induced of the confusion of the natures or attributes, and it would cease to be a synecdochic manner of speaking."—COCCEIUS (*S.T.* LVIII, 17) : " With this wonderful union corresponds the manner of speaking of the person of Christ. In it we are considering the κοινωνία ἰδιωμάτων, commonly called the communication of properties or attributes. The communication of attributes is the truth (1) of calling the person by either nature, since it has them both and acts through them both ; (2) about the things which belong to either nature being predicated of the person called by the name of either nature.—Not that what belongs to one nature may be predicated of the other κατ' ἄλλο. Neither is the divinity mortal according to the flesh, nor the flesh omnipotent and present according to the divinity ; the person fills everything with its divinity. At one time it is in the Virgin's womb, at another on the Cross, at another in the lowest parts of the earth, at another in heaven according to the flesh. Nor has flesh a χρῆσις of omnipresence, because the divine person is not an ὄργανον τῆς σαρκός, an instrument of the flesh ; on the contrary the flesh is an ὄργανον of the divine person. And lest anyone think because the λόγος is omnipresent, that therefore the human nature also is omnipresent in order forsooth that the λόγος be not anywhere not united to the flesh, we must reflect that the λόγος is ἀμερής, without parts, and cannot be un-united to the flesh in heaven and on earth, although the flesh is hanging on the Cross and has not yet been borne to heaven ".—WENDELIN (Coll. 67) : " That the properties of the divine nature are omnipotence, eternity, infinity, ubiquity, omniscience we altogether concede, but in such a way that not only are they not and do not become the properties of the human nature, but also that they are not communicated to it with the divine nature. It is repugnant that anything should truly be a property of the divine nature and yet be common to it along with the human nature, whether by essence or by communication. When properties become common they cease to be properties. At the same time the properties of the divine nature also pertain to the person θεάνθρωπος, but according to the divine nature, not according to both ; because in the personal union the natures remain quite distinct. By a mutual communication of attributes, if the divine properties became common to the human nature and the human properties to the divine nature, they would be confused."—WOLLEB 66 : " We must here distinguish concrete vocables from abstract. The former belong to the person, the latter to either of the two natures. Thus I am right in saying that God is man and man is God, but not that Deity is humanity or humanity Deity. This difference also holds good in things natural. Many things are opposed abstractly, which concretely are diverse or subordinate. It is right to say that the bodily is animate and that anything bodily is animate. But not that soul is body or body soul. Thus totus Christus is everywhere, but not the totum Christi, i.e. both the natures."—POLAN (VI, 16) : " The word communication is used either for the personal union or for the real transfusion of the essential attributes of Deity into the flesh assumed by Deity. If it be taken in the sense of personal union, we admit that there are communicated, i.e. personally united to the flesh of Christ, omnipotence, omnipresence, omniscience: but not otherwise is Deity itself communicated, i.e. personally united, to it. But Deity is communicated, i.e. personally united to Christ's flesh, in such a way that the flesh itself does not on that account become Deity or God. Omnipence, to omnipresence, omniscience are likewise communicated, that is personally united to it, in such a way that the flesh does not itself on that account become omnipotent, omnipresent, omniscient. But if the word communication is used for the real transfusion of the essential attributes of Deity into the flesh assumed, the major premise is false and so also is the conclusion.   The hypostasis of the λόγος is so communicated to the flesh assumed, that it is nevertheless not on that account communicated or given over to the flesh, nor is omnipotence or any other essential attribute of Deity transfused into it."—HEIDEGGER (XVII, 48) : " This communication of attributes is real in respect of the person, verbal in respect of the natures. It is real in respect of the person, because the person claims the attributes of either nature for itself. Since the attributes really inhere in the respective natures, and each nature inheres in the person, it is necessary that the properties of both natures should really inhere in the whole person.—But in respect of the natures it is not real but verbal. One nature anything but transfers its properties to another. At some time properties would cease to be properties—what is proper cannot be made common."—WOLLEB 69 : " Accordingly Mary is to be called not only χριστότοκος (as the *Nestorians* wanted) but also θεότοκος."—RIISSEN (XI, 17) : " Concretely and specifically Mary is rightly called θεότοκος or *Deipara*, because she bore him who is also God ; but not *in abstracto* and *reduplicative* as God."

24.—Only in this there must be a proper distinction between the *concretum* and the *abstractum* of the natures. *Abstractum* is the name of the nature or form of one thing which inheres in a second either essentially or accidentally, like Deity or humanity. *Concretum* is the person or subject having the form or nature; this expressed by the concrete names God and man. The *abstracta* of the natures of Christ are not predicable of each other; we could not say, "The divinity is the humanity of Christ". Nor can the *abstractum* of one nature be attributed to the *concretum* of the other, or *vice versa*. For example it could not be said that "the divinity is man" or "the humanity is God". Only the *concreta* of the natures may be predicated of each other; "the man Jesus is God".—HEIDEGGER (XVII, 47): "The names of the natures abstracted from themselves are not predicable of each other. It is not a correct predication to say, Deity is humanity, and *vice versa*. Abstracts signify not so much what a thing is, as the way in which it is that thing; as whiteness does not signify a white wall, but the reason why the wall is white. Thus such things, if confused, without any essential and inward idea of the things mutually differentiated, cannot in any way be predicated of each other. Nor is it even right to predicate the abstract name of one nature of the concrete name of the other, and *vice versa*. As Deity cannot be called man, or humanity God, because in this way the opposite natures in Christ could not be distinguished. These apart, only the concrete names of the natures can be predicated of each other because of the hypostatic union, these alone signifying not precisely the formality of the essence but the essence itself, i.e. the formality plus all the adjuncts and circumstances by which the person is constituted and is distinguished from others."

25.—(3) The third effect of the *unio personalis* is "the *communicatio operationum*, especially the *communicatio apotelesmatum* i.e. the alliance of the two natures for the mediatorial operations, in such a way that these works proceed from the person of the God-man by the distinct effectiveness of both natures" (MASTRICHT V, iv, 13). In this connection it should therefore be noted that (1) the effective cause of the *apotelesmata* is the divine-human person of Christ; (2) the principles therein active are the two natures of Christ; (3) each of them produces its particular effect; (4) thereby the work so achieved, the *apotelesma*, is only a divine-human work.

Exactly like the *Lutheran* doctrine of the *unio personalis* and its meaning in the dogma of the *communicatio idiomatum*, the Reformed doctrine of the personal union was expressed in the dogma of the ἀποτελέσματα. In SOHNIUS, ZANCHIUS and KECKERMANN the concept of ἀποτέλεσμα is already completely fixed. It is the unitary action of the person of Christ in the work of redemption, in which both natures participate. SOHNIUS defines an apotelesm as "a single personal work, (in which) distinct acts of the two natures concur and unite", (*Exeg. Conf. Aug. p. 246*).—KECKERMANN (p. 331 f.) distinguishes thus:" An ἀποτέλεσμα is a work common to the two natures concerned with the function of the mediator. Ἐνέργεια is the proper action and operation of each nature, by which the ἀποτέλεσμα or *opus* in question is carried out in a way suitable to each nature".—ZANCHIUS 70: "We believe and confess that so great is the strength of the union of the (two) natures in the person of Christ, that first of all what Christ is or does according to the divine nature the whole Christ is said to be or do; and on the other hand what he is and does or has suffered according to the human nature the whole Christ, the Son of God, God, is said in the H. Scriptures to be, to do or to have suffered—since the natures too, although distinct, are yet joined in the one person of Christ. In fact Christ the Mediator never did or does anything according to his humanity, in which the divinity too did or does not co-operate, and achieved nothing according to his Deity, which his humanity did not subserve or agree to; so that rightly all the operations of Christ the Mediator are called θεανδρικαὶ by the Fathers."—LEIDEN SYNOPSIS (XXVI, 18-19): "In the work which exists because of the performance of this function each nature of Christ plays its part, not separately but unitedly, and not confusedly but in distinct fashion. In producing the common ἀποτέλεσμα θεανδρικὸν the divine nature enters into such an alliance with the human, that as the soul acts in bare man as the principal and the body as the instrument, so in the action of Christ the θεάνθρωπος the divine nature functions as the principal cause, the human as a less principal and assistant cause.—Hence it is that the same work in which the two natures in Christ concur the Scripture so attributes to the whole Christ, as entirely to attribute the infinite dignity and efficacy of the mediator's office to the power of Deity dwelling in him, which it denotes by the name of Spirit, Rom. 13. 4 (of the Seed of David . . . declared to be the Son of God . . . according to the Spirit of holiness) 1 Pet. 3.18 (put to death in the flesh, quickened in the Spirit) Mk. 2. 8 (perceiving in his Spirit) Heb. 9.14 (through the eternal Spirit offered himself".—MASTRICHT (V, iv, 13) says that in regard to the apotelesms the following four points should be observed: "(1) The producing cause, the θεάνθρωπος person ἐνεργῶν. (2) The two principles ἐνεργητικά of the producing cause, the two natures in the mediator. (3) The twofold efficacy of the divine and human natures, answering to the number of the two principles, or the twofold ἐνέργεια. Finally (4) the one work, the ἐνεργούμενον or ἀποτέλεσμα θεανδρικὸν, which the one mediator produces for the two natures through the efficacy peculiar to each. Thus for example the one mediating λυτρώτης—with the concurrence of the two natures as lutrotic principles by their twofold efficacy or λύτρωσις, the human by contributing the death, the divine by contributing value to the death—procured the one λύτρον or λύτρωμα."

26.—Thus a real communication of the divine attributes to the human nature can as little be assumed as a real communication of the human attributes to the divine nature, because in both cases the natures would lose their integrity and essentiality.—BEZA (Colloq. Mompelg. 265): "We also confess that the highest gifts of Deity which can fall upon the creature and of which human nature is capable, have been conferred on the humanity of Christ. But these gifts are not attributes of Deity, which are incommunicable, but habitual created gifts."—PEZEL (Arg. et resp. I, p.207-208): "Therefore the properties of the divine nature in the unio have not been transfused into the human nature, though κατ' οἰκονομίαν ἐνώσεως all the properties of Deity, including Deity itself, are rightly assigned to the Son of Man. Nor must the gifts, whether παραφυσικὰ or ὑπερφυσικὰ, in which by themselves human nature excels all other creatures, be confused with the properties or attributes of the divine nature. These cannot be separated from Deity itself, because it is necessary there should remain a perpetual difference between the infinite creative essence and the finite created essence."—HEIDEGGER (XVII, 60): "Specifically and properly speaking Scripture in talking of Christ nowhere attributes the divine properties to the human nature, much less the human to the divine. At different times it would put before us the deified humanity and an ἀνθρωπινὴ Deity. Since the divine *idiomata* are God Himself and the human ones are essentially indistinguishable from the humanity, the humanity could not be deified if the attributes of Deity were communicated to it, nor could the Deity be humanised if the *idiomata* of humanity were attributed to it. These are but fig leaves when they have ruled that Deity is called omnipotent, omnipresent, etc., κατ' αὐτὸ and οὐσιωδῶς, but the humanity κατ' ἄλλο and ὑποστατικῶς. To be omnipotent, omnipresent belongs to God alone. Moreover, as there is not one God κατ' αὐτὸ and οὐσιωδῶς, and another κατ' ἄλλο, there is not one omnipotent, omnipresent etc. *secundum se*, or essentially, and another *secundum aliud* and personally".

27.—In particular therefore the *Lutheran* doctrine of the omnipresence of the humanity of Christ is to be rejected.—ARETIUS (*Ex. theol.* 129) : " The trueness of the human body brooks not ubiquity ; Christ's body remains περιγραπτόν Mt. 28. 6 (he is risen ; . . . see the place where he lay) 26.11 (me ye have not always). It will come from heaven, therefore it is not yet here ".—KECKERMANN 320 : "When, engaged in rebutting the doctrine of ubiquity, people set forth the proposition : "where the presence of Christ is, there is all that is in the person or all that constitutes the person ; but the whole person is everywhere, therefore everything that constitutes the person of Christ will also be everywhere ", it must be insisted against this, that " the major would stand if the human nature were in the λόγος as in a subject or in a place ; both of which are most absurd. Therefore as the λόγος is infinite and everywhere whole and undivided, it carries and supports the human nature, even if it is not diffused beyond its place."—HEIDEGGER (XVII, 61) : " The Gospel story teaches very clearly, that Christ's human nature was conceived in the womb of the B. Virgin, formed in it, born of it, and so came into a light in which it was not ; and that the man Christ moved from place to place both before and after the resurrection and ascended from earth to heaven.—The presence of a visible, local body is nothing but a visible, local, circumscribed one ; and the opposite presence to that is the invisible, definitive and non-local presence of spirits."

CHAPTER XVIII

THE MEDIATORIAL OFFICE OF JESUS CHRIST

1.—The purpose of the manifestation of the eternal Logos in the flesh is in order that he may be a mediator between sinful man and the righteous and holy God. " The Mediator of reconciliation between God and fallen men is the *persona* who intervenes midway between a God angry at their sins and men the sinners, in order that by his own merit and satisfaction he may obtain from God for men and effectively bestow on them grace, remission of sins and all things necessary for salvation and also eternal salvation itself " (POLAN VI, 27). In conformity with the eternal pact between Father and Son the Son therefore became man to execute the office of Mediator, to which end the Father anointed him with the power of the H. Spirit, so that as God's Anointed, as the Christ, the Son is a mediator between God and man. This anointing Christ received when he was baptized. Of course the humanity of Jesus by its " personal union " with the Son was already filled with special gifts and graces of the Spirit, which nevertheless did not exclude Christ from developing gradually as a man and growing in wisdom and grace before God and men. At the baptism on the other hand Jesus' humanity received that spiritual anointing which it needed to execute the office of Mediator. This anointing of Christ was on the one hand " the solemn ordination or sealing of the whole *persona*, effected by the Father through the H. Spirit " and on the other hand " fulness of sanctification or equipment with spiritual gifts " (OLEVIAN p. 45).

COCCEIUS (*Summ. theol.* LIX, 2 & 3) : " Christ's anointing is either the commendation of the office, to which correspond the eternal promise and the demand for an inheritance ; or the indwelling of the divine *persona* in the human nature for the purpose of executing the office ; or the proof of the *persona* dwelling in the flesh and of the kingdom given him.—Moreover the kingly office is the consummation of the offices and leans upon the priesthood and is carried by the word which Christ spoke as prophet. For these three offices he was anointed.—Therefore (1) it was given to the Son to place many brethren to be filled with glory by the Father ; (2) for this reason it was given him to make salvation and to equip it unto righteousness ; and (3) to announce the salvation unto righteousness which is in himself, unto obedience of faith. But because these were interconnected, they were given together."—The excerpts here to be compared from OLEVIAN's work *De subst. foed.* see in HEPPE, *Dogmatik des deutschen Protest.* Bk. II, p. 166 ff.—In exactly the same sense URSIN (*Expl. catech.* p. 142) : " Christs' unction " consisted (1) in Christ's " having

been divinely ordained to the office of Mediator by the will of the Father :
(2) in his human nature having been adorned with gifts of the H. Spirit
without measure ".

2.—Thus " the office of Jesus Christ is that function of the Mediator
Jesus Christ, which he voluntarily undertook himself according to the
Father's will and the H. Spirit's unction, in order to reconcile to God and
to save the sinful men given to him ; which function he alone did and
does accomplish according to both natures " (HEIDEGGER, XIX, 2). Both
natures of Christ co-operate in executing his mediatorial activity, and each
of them in its peculiar way, the divine nature (person) not in the absolute
character of the divine nature but in conformity with its humiliation ;
the human nature on the other hand in an essentially human way.

The redemptive work is distinguished as the work of God and the work
of Christ ; a DIEST 162 : " Redemption is considered as God's and as
Christ's work. Redemption is God's work in the way in which He has
redeemed through Christ in time those whom He has elected to salvation
from eternity. Redemption is Christ's mediatorial work in the way in
which he has reconciled us to God through the satisfaction provided in
our stead." The object of Christ's mediation is sinful man considered as
elect. Hence this does not extend to the angels. Cf. e.g. MARESIUS,
X, 4 : " Moreover since the good angels have neither sinned ever nor
required to be reconciled to God, Christ can in no sense be called their
Mediator."

POLANUS (VI, 27) : " He is the mediator according to both natures,
the divine and the human : according to the divine nature considered not
absolutely and as it is common to Father, Son and H. Spirit but κατ'
οἰκονομίαν, i.e. so far as according to it Christ submitted by a
voluntary dispensation of grace, by receiving the form of a servant ;
according to the human nature absolutely, by providing all things, which
are proper in his mediatorial office."—HEIDEGGER (XIX, 15) : " Christ
undertook and fulfilled the office of mediator according to both natures.
As after the incarnation there are two natures in the Son of God, two
principles in the one substratum (suppositum), so the operations of the two
natures concur ad μεσιτείαν, and the ἀποτελέσματα produced
by these operations are refered to both natures. To announce the gospel,
pray, suffer, die is a human operation ; to declare the will of God from
the bosom of the Father and to reveal it directly Jn. 1. 18, to have power
to lay down his life and to take it again, 10, 18 ; to offer himself through
the eternal Spirit Heb. 9.14, to sanctify the sacrifice Mt. 23. 19, by his
strength to pass through the heavens, Heb. 4. 14, to hear the prayers and
groans of all, Rev. 8. 3, to protect the Church by his power, Jn. 10. 28,

Ut. 16. 18, is a divine operation."—WOLLEB (71): "The subject of this office is not only the whole Christ but also the whole of Christ and he is the mediator according to both natures."

3.—The mediation which Christ effects is the reconciliation of the world with God. Christ abolishes the enmity between the world and God and brings it to pass that by the bestowal of Christ's righteousness God forgives the elect their sins and imparts eternal life to them.— HEIDEGGER XIX, 22 : " Mediation itself consists in καταλλαγὴ of the dissident parts.—The actual mode of reconciliation consists in the fact that by his blood Christ has borne the enmity which in consequence of sin intervened between the two, God and man, restored amity and brought it about that from a condemning judge God became a judge who absolves and gives life as a gift, not imputing their sins to men but imputing to them the righteousness of Christ."

4.—Christ has effected this reconciliation *merito et efficacia*, by his merit and efficacy. " Merit is the work provided, to which a reward or retribution is due proportionate to the work " (VOETIUS II, 228). Such merit Christ acquired by his obedience. " The meritorious work of Christ is the voluntary and utterly perfect obedience, by which in human nature in our place he provided on our behalf as sponsor everything which God's law required of us " (VOETIUS, II, 229). Now the law made two demands on us, (1) perfect fulfilment of all God's commands, perfect holiness ; and (2) perfect repentance for our disobedience to God ; Christ did both for us and thereby acquired himself a merit, which justifies him in claiming a reward to be supplied by the Father.　This " reward " consists in the elect, for whom Christ offered his obedience to the Father, having through him two things : (1) " Liberty or immunity from the slavery or power of sin which condemns and masters them ", and (2) " the right, possession and enjoyment of eternal life " (VOETIUS *ibid.*). Hence Christ's merit (along with his efficacy) is so exclusively the means by which Christ has prepared salvation for the elect, that the teaching activity and the rest that Christ did to rouse the world to faith in redemption may be designated the cause of our redemption only in the more general sense of the word.　At the same time Christ's merit is not the ultimate ground of our salvation.　That rests rather upon the Father's decree and good pleasure, without which Christ could have merited nothing on our behalf.

What Christ secured by his merit for the elect (not for himself) he appropriates to them by his living efficacy. " Christ's efficacy is his virtue whereby he applies his merit to us and confers the benefits acquired for us by his merit, and he so conserves them for us that we persist in grace until the end " (POLAN VI, 27).

Here he is more fully. " He is our saviour in two ways, by merit and by efficacy. The merit of Christ the Saviour is the most perfect obedience by which he has fully satisfied the law of God in our place, being sufficient for all the men in the whole world, if they should all receive it in faith. And it (the merit) depends on and flows from the sheer good pleasure of God, because its (the merit's) efficient cause was the will of God the Father, i.e. His ordinance made from eternity, as we read Heb. 10. 10, " by which will we have been sanctified." Of course Christ could not have merited anything save by the eternal good pleasure of God. Secondly, the first beginning of our salvation is not fixed in Christ's merit, we must go back to the will and ordinance of God which is the first cause Heb. 10. 10, because by His mere good pleasure God made him mediator to acquire us salvation. Then the dignity and power of Christ's merit depends on the meriting *persona* which is divine or true God, and not only man ; had it been a bare creature, it could not have merited anything with God. The effects of Christ's merit are God's benefits which Christ obtained for us by his merit, namely reconciliation with God, faith, remission of sins, regeneration by the H. Spirit, salvation and eternal life."—HEIDEGGER : (XIX, 25) : " The Christian religion firmly and steadfastly holds as a κυρία δόξα (supreme opinion) and an everywhere controlling (βράβενον) dogma of the faith, that Christ is the mediator and saviour by merit of course and by efficacy, not in any old sense, certainly not in an impious and heterodox one, but actually in that eloquently handed down in the Scriptures, i.e. μόνως (solely or adequately), ἀδιαιρέτως or *indivise*, and ἐνεργητικῶς or effectually. He is the saviour by merit because he acquired salvation for us by his blood, Ac. 20. 28 (the church of God which he purchased with his blood) ; by efficacy, because he confers the salvation acquired and once acquired conserves it. In both ways he is the saviour μόνως, adequately, because there is no other parallel mode of mediation or salvation by which Christ may be called mediator or saviour κατ' ἐξοχήν. As for the assertion by some, that he reconciles and saves us in addition by teaching and performing miracles, they are considering the method and mode of reconciliation and salvation too generally; they are not looking at it in its propriety to Christ and in what distinguishes him not only from his servants the prophets and apostles, but also from the Father Himself and the H. Spirit. Moreover Scripture defines Christ as ἀδιαιρετῶς, indivisibly, the mediator and saviour by merit and efficacy, because it neither tears merit from efficacy nor separates it altogether from its subjects. The efficacy of merit is its end and its fruits."

5.—This mediatorship (we should add) Christ already exercised before his manifestation in the flesh. In conformity with the pact between him and the Father he was from eternity the λόγος *incarnandus ;* in the Father's eyes the sacrifice of Christ had been prepared from eternity. Therefore all the godly folk in Israel have attained bliss purely by his merit and by his efficacy.—So POLAN (VI, 27) : " Before the assumption of the human nature Christ was mediator according to both natures, because at that time he was mediator as being *incarnandus* (about to become flesh), just as he is now our mediator as being *incarnatus* (become flesh). In addition the two natures were regarded as being united in the knowledge and pre-destination and acceptance of God, since with Him things done and to be done, present and future are in the same place."—HEIDEGGER (XIX, 26) : " Christ's office of mediator is common to every state of the Church after the entry of sin. Christ Jesus is the same yesterday and today and for ever, Heb. 13. 8. But nevertheless he was mediator before the incarnation in one way, after it in another. Before the incarnation he was mediator both by future merit as the Lamb slain from the foundation of the world, Rev. 13. 8. and by the efficacy of the future merit which is always present, since through and because of it even the fathers redeemed B.C. were saved, Ac. 15. 2 (the necessity or not of circumcision) Heb. 2. 10 (It became him, for whom are all things, and through whom are all things, in bringing many sons unto glory, to make the author of their salvation perfect through sufferings."

6.—We have to distinguish three offices in the mediatorship of Christ, the prophetic, the high-priestly and the kingly; these are typically figured in the three OT offices of prophet, high-priest and king trans-mitted by unction; they are already indicated in Christ's name of Anointed; they are based on the world's need of divine illumination, reconciliation and guidance, a need caused by sin and satisfied by Christ; they are, finally, shown forth in the course of the activity of Christ, who came forward first as teacher, then consummated the high-priestly sacri-fice and is now active as king.—CALVIN (II, xv, 1): "It is admitted that the office enjoined by the Father was in three parts. He was given as both prophet and priest and king".—HEIDEGGER (XIX, 27): "It was unction that in the OT adumbrated Christ the true mediator. (1) Christ is the body of the shades, among whom there was no extreme unction, so that he is called Christus, Anointed, from unction. For the bodily unction of the anointed of old figured the spiritual unction of Jesus. Moreover we showed above that in olden times men of three classes were wont to be anointed, prophets, priests and kings. Since, then, the truth of ancient unction is to be sought in Christ, just as prophets, priests and kings were consecrated to their office by outward unctions, so Christ had to exist anointed by God Himself to be prophet, priest and king. (2) It is abundantly clear that both Moses the prophet bore the type of Christ the prophet, the Aaronic priests that of Christ the priest and the kings of the people Israel, above all David, that of Christ the King. (3) There was added the native condition and indigence of man corrupted by sin, to remove which Christ became mediator. By nature and by ignorance of spiritual things man was immersed in darkness and was alienated from God and was plainly incapable of returning to Him. Christ, therefore, who was come σῶσαι τό ἀπολωλός Mt. 18. 12 [See Lk. 19. 10, Mt. text doubtful] opposed a triple cure to sweep away this triple misery. As a prophet he ousted ignorance, Mt. 23. 10 (neither be ye called masters); as a priest he bore alienation from God and His life, Eph. 2. 13 (ye that were far off are made nigh in the blood of Christ); and as king he filled up the impotence to return to God, Ps. 23. 3–4 (restoreth, etc.: yea tho' I walk, etc.) 139. 24 (lead me in the way everlasting) Rev. 7. 17 (the Lamb shall guide them unto fountains of waters of life). (4) Moreover the method of conferring salvation upon us imposed the threefold office on Christ. He was bound both as prophet to instruct us by giving teaching anent salvation, in the fruition of which our felicity consists; and as priest to acquire the same through his blood by satisfying the law; and as king by his Spirit to confer the salvation acquired. (5) In a word, in this way he also executed his office. First as a prophet he taught the will of the Father and sealed his teaching by miracles; he bore himself as a priest by offering his own blood on earth and by entering therewith into the heavenly holy place and standing there before the Father's face; and at length in heaven as King he was crowned with glory and sat down at the right hand of the Father."

To see that and how the distribution of a threefold office of Christ was peculiar to Reformed theology (whereas Lutheran theologians up to the time of WENDELIN usually spoke of a *munus regium* and a *sacerdotale*) see HEPPE *Dogmatik des deutschen Protestantismus*, II, p. 222.

7.—At the same time, the order of Christ's offices in their intention is a different one from that in their execution. In the first respect the kingship comes first as the purpose of the other two offices, whereas the historical order of these activities is the reverse.—HEIDEGGER (XIX, 27): "There is a difference between the order of intention and that of execution. In the order of intention the kingship comes first as the goal of the mediation. Before all things God gave to the Son as king many brethren to be filled with eternal glory; he receives the priesthood as the means to this end, because that is why it was given to him to prepare righteousness; and prophecy follows last, because to him as a prophet it was given to proclaim righteousness, salvation and glory unto obedience of faith. The order of execution is plainly the opposite. There Christ existed first as the prophet of righteousness and the herald of salvation; then as a priest approaching the altar he offered himself as a victim to the Father; and lastly as King he sat down at God's right hand. These things however, as being connected, are given to Christ at once, and are so involved, that neither did the priest cease to be the prophet, nor did the king clearly put off the priesthood."

8.—"It is by his *prophetia* that Christ has fully and plainly revealed God's will for our salvation shown directly to himself" (HEIDEGGER XIX, 28). It includes (1) "the outward promulgation of divine truth" and (2) "the internal illumination of hearts by the H. Spirit" (POLANUS VI, 29). As regards the imparting of doctrine, Christ's "prophecy" is on the one hand a *prophetia legalis,* since Christ did not come forward at all as a new legislator. In order to found the true knowledge of the salvation of grace imparted through him he teaches us to recognise the true righteousness which the Law demands.—WOLLEB 72: "It is the prophetic office to instruct the elect in heavenly truth. The parts of it are the external promulgation of the divine counsel and the inward illumination of the mind."—LEIDEN SYNOPSIS: (XXVI, 39): "Prophecy is the function by which Christ instructs his people in the truth of doctrine legal and evangelical and, with the seal of miracles, cleanses both sections of it from the corruptions of false teachers, both by himself directly, and indirectly by other assistants of his Word equipped with the gifts necessary for that purpose; the earlier of whom are by synecdoche comprised under the name of prophets, the latter under that of apostles, Mt. 5. 25ff; Jn. 17. 8 (the words which thou gavest me I have given unto them; and they received them and knew of a truth that I came forth from thee, and they believed that thou didst send me)".—MARESIUS (X. 14): "Christ's prophetic office is that by which he deigns to reveal to his own the will of God fully and perfectly known to himself; not only outwardly, and that in part directly, through himself—in part indirectly, through his servants—but also inwardly, through the H. Spirit."—HEIDEGGER (XIX, 34): "Christ's legal prophecy consists in unfolding the true righteousness which the law requires. Apart from this and from firm realisation of it Christ could not be acknowledged as the true Saviour, because his whole salvation turned upon the exhibition of the true righteousness, which the law had exacted in the covenant of works. Therefore Christ had not brought a new lawgiver, but a teacher and prophet to prove the spiritual nature of the law once introduced by God through Moses Rom. 7. 14, and so the true righteousness of the law which he himself had entered flesh to fulfil."—The question "whether Christ as a prophet had corrected and enlarged the moral law by adding self-denial, cross-bearing, imitation of Christ and others" is answered in the negative by RIISSEN (XII, 3).

9.—On the other hand Christ's prophetic office is likewise a *prophetia evangelica*, since Christ arouses the most blessed knowledge of the gracious salvation extended to the world. The inward illumination of the heart by the H. Spirit is the other part of the prophetic office of Christ, since he "moves the faithful by the H. Spirit to receive the things taught with the mind and to will them heartily and to acquiesce in them" (POLAN VI, 29). This prophetic activity Christ already exercised right from eternity. As $\lambda \acute{o}\gamma os$ *incarnandus* he is from eternity as essentially prophet as high priest and king. But Christ prefers to exercise his prophetic office since he came in the flesh.—HEIDEGGER (XIX, 28): "He did this as God and the Son of God before the Incarnation, as the angel of the LORD, i.e. as he who was to be sent by the LORD to assert the seed of Abraham and to sponsor the testament. He who put enmity between the serpent and the woman already spoke in Paradise as the sanctifier of believers Gen. 3. 15.—(29): Christ was never not a prophet, as he was never not a saviour and mediator. But he was chiefly so when he appeared in the flesh."

10.—Hence from the very moment of his conception it was not the humanity but the divine $\lambda \acute{o}\gamma os$ of Christ that was prophetically active, since he mediated to angels and to men the knowledge that he was the promised Saviour.—HEIDEGGER (XIX, 30): "This office of a prophet was performed in the form of a servant by the same who before and after assuming the the form of a servant was and is $\acute{a}\tau\rho \acute{\epsilon}\pi\tau\omega s$ the one supreme teacher, together with the Father and the H. Spirit, and who has breathed with his Spirit upon all prophets whatsoever that have been in the world. From the first moment of conception the Son of God $\theta\epsilon\acute{a}\nu\theta\rho\omega\pi os$ performed the duty of a prophet, being $\acute{a}\delta\acute{\iota}\delta a\kappa\tau os$ according to the divine nature and through it dwelling in him $a\grave{\upsilon}\tau o\delta\acute{\iota}\delta a\kappa\tau os$ and instructed to shape human wisdom and made $\delta\iota\delta a\kappa\tau\iota\kappa\acute{o}s$ unto the opening of the human mouth. Immediately from the first moment of conception angels and men were the servants of this $\theta\epsilon a\nu\theta\rho\omega\pi\iota\kappa\acute{o}s$ mastery, preaching the gospel of Christ exhibited; like the angel Gabriel announcing his conception and nativity on Christ's own authority Lk. 1. 26, or Elizabeth carrying John in her womb going

on a congratulatory visit to Mary the mother of the Lord, Lk. 1. 41ff."
[only the visit was the other way on.]

11.—Christ's public prophetic function began with the full participation of his humanity in it, from the moment he was baptized by John and anointed by the Father as the only-begotten Son and proclaimed to the world.—HEIDEGGER (XIX, 33): "The public performance of the prophetic office Christ began to fulfil when baptized by John and commended by the heavenly voice of the Father: This is my son the beloved in whom I am pleased, αὐτοῦ ἀκούετε Mt. 3. 17, 17. 5 (the prayer for the resumption of heavenly glory)." [This was surely the revelation of eternal fact, not the beginning of the theanthropic miracle].

12.—In the broader sense of the word his miraculous activity also belongs to Christ's prophetic office, as well as his holy life and his death as a martyr, by which he confirmed and guaranteed his proclamation.— ALSTED 574: "The functions of the prophetic office are three in number, (1) the setting forth of teaching, (2) the confirmation of the doctrines set forth, and that through the Scriptures of the OT, by signs and miracles of every kind, e.g., the inspection (reading) of hearts, the revelation of things hidden, the foretelling of things to come, the healing of diseases, and in short by a most holy life and supreme endurance, (3) prayer."— a DIEST 206: "This training takes place both eternally, not only *viva voce* and that direct and indirect, but also by example and miracles; and internally, administered through the H. Spirit, both before and after the assumption of the flesh in a state partly of inanition and partly of exaltation."

13.—The manner and mode in which Christ exercises his prophetic office is twofold; partly direct, since without availing himself of human instruments Christ threw direct light upon particular patriarchs and prophets and spoke in the NT with his own lips; partly indirect, since Christ sent out apostles and still continues to call his servants with a view to instructing and illuminating the world through them.—LEIDEN SYNOPSIS (XXVI, 41): "We insist that the mode of prophetic instruction is twofold, direct and indirect. The former Christ usually employed either according to the divine nature only under the old covenant towards the prophets, or according to both natures towards the apostles. For both classes that Sun of righteousness illuminated with beams of the prophetic light he had in himself, by his own power. The latter he employed when ordering his servants the prophets and apostles to lay bare to his people in their addresses and writings all the mysteries of his wisdom necessary to be known for salvation. Moved by this consideration the Church of God repudiates all traditions which are not contained in the sacred codex. By the former mode of teaching both men's minds may be illumined inwardly without the aid of the latter and their hearts may be bent to the obedience of faith. By the latter neither of those effects can be produced without the aid of the former."—ALSTED 5 & 6: "The mode of Christ's prophetic office which he used under both covenants is direct; and while in the OT he taught the patriarchs and prophets by visions, oracles and dreams according to the divine nature, in the NT he taught his disciples fully and perfectly according to both natures.— For this reason he is called in Scripture the λόγος, the legate of Jehovah —the angel of the covenant—the supreme prophet.—The second mode is indirect, by which he taught the Church through his servants; formerly of course through the patriachs and prophets, then through the apostles, evangelists and all faithful teachers of the Word."

14.—"The *sacerdotium* or priestly office of Christ is that in which as a priest appointed by the Father he made perfect satisfaction to God the Father through the obedience of his exinanition even unto the death of the Cross on behalf of the sins of those given to him and intercedes with Him continually for us" (HEIDEGGER XIX, 55). Christ's priestly office comprises three things: (1) the voluntary undertaking of the commission received from the Father, or the voluntary self-offering of Christ to be an offering of reconciliation (*sacrificium propitiatorium*), (2) his death, and (3) his effective intercession for the acceptance of his sacrifice on behalf of the elect.—OLEVIAN (*De substant. foed.* I, 3 *passim*): Christ's sacrifice is a "propitiatory sacrifice offered along with intercession". To the "form of of the propitiatory sacrifice" belong (1) " a mandate imposed upon the *persona*, (2) spontaneous obedience to it, (3) along with intercession that this obedience might be accepted by the Father for us and the H. Spirit given." That all this is pertinent in Christ is clear from John 17 [the high-priestly prayer].

The dogmaticians insist that the type of Christ's priesthood is to be found less in the Aaronic and Levitical priesthood, and rather in that of *Melchizedek*.—BURMANN (V, xiv, 5): "He was a priest not according to the institution of the Aaronidae but according to the rite and order of Melchisedek Ps. 110. 4, who was older and greater than the priests of Aaron. Such as this Melchisedek meets us in the confines of Canaan a little after the beginning of the rebirth of the world after the flood, bearing among his fellows alike a kingship and a priesthood."—MARE-SIUS (X, 21): "He was the type of Christ, not, according to *Papist* trifling, in the sacrifice of bread and wine, since he did not offer these things to

God as a priest but to Abraham as a king, friend and benefactor and to his army as provisions; but (1) because he was called Melchi-sedek, the king of righteousness; (2) because at the same time he was *rex Salem*, i.e. the king of peace; (3) because his genealogy is not recorded, so that by this silence the eternity of Christ might be foreshadowed; (4) because he was at once king and priest; (5) because as a superior he blessed Abraham and received tithes from him, i.e. from Levi himself in his loins; (6) because he is said to have been given in the priesthood neither predecessors nor successors".

15.—Accordingly a distinction must be drawn in Christ's highpriesthood between his *satisfactio* and his *intercessio*.—a DIEST 200: "The sacerdotal office is that by which Christ as our sole and supreme priest reconciled us to God by the single offering of himself, and even now intercedes for us with Him. The two parts of it are oblation and intercession."— MARESIUS (X, 22): "The priesthood of Christ is fulfilled in two parts, satisfaction and intercession."—LEIDEN SYNOPSIS (XXVI, 42): "The priesthood of Christ is the function of Christ by which he appears before God (1) to keep the law accepted by himself in our name, to offer himself to Him as the sacrifice of reconciliation for our sins, (2) and by his intercession with Him to obtain us His everlasting help and the gift of the H. Spirit and to apply them effectively, Heb. 10. 7–8f. (Lo, I am come to do thy will)".—ALTING, p. 101: "The priesthood has a twofold action. I. Sacrifice, which belongs to the exinanition and is paid up by one with the voice of obedience.—II. Intercession, which belongs to the exaltation . . . as the priest, emerging after solemn expiation from the sanctuary where he had brought in the blood, began to don his golden vestments and to enter the holy place to make (*suffitum*) an offering of incense and to bless the people".—WOLLEB 72: "The priestly office is in order that he may appear in our room and intercede for us with fullest satisfaction before God. The parts of it are satisfaction and intercession."—BUCAN (II, 28): "How many parts are there of this office?— Two: satisfaction, by which he has fulfilled the law and paid up the ransom for the sins of the world; in respect of this part he is called redeemer and saviour and lamb or victim: and intercession, by which Christ solely desires that his sacrifice should avail for ever with God the Father for the reconciliation of his elect, brings our prayers to the Father and bestows upon us confidence to approach Him."

16.—The satisfaction rests entirely upon the voluntary obedience with which Christ gave himself up for the world, by his subjecting himself on the one hand to the will or *mandatum* of the Father for the elects' sake and on the other hand to punishment for the transgression of the law for them also, i.e., by his complete fulfilment of the law (his *oboedientia activa*); and his bearing on the Cross the full punishment for the transgression of the law (his *oboedientia passiva*).—CALVIN II, xvi, 5: "When it is asked how, after abolishing sins, Christ removed the discord between us and God and acquired us righteousness—it may be replied generally that he provided us with this by the whole course of his obedience. From the moment he put on the person of a servant, he began to pay the price of liberation for our redemption. In order however to define the manner of salvation more surely, Scripture ascribes it to Christ's death as its property and attribute.—Yet the remainder of obedience which he performed in life is not excluded.—And in fact—voluntary submission occupies the first place—discarding thought of himself in order to consult our interests."—ALSTED 714: "The entire obedience of Christ as the sponsor emptying himself to pay our debts—is the meritorious cause of our justification.—Christ obeyed the moral law on behalf of himself and his.—715: Therefore the satisfaction provided by Christ is not to be looked for only in the death of the Cross, although in this final act and completion of the satisfaction Scripture does place it by synedoche.—547: Every particle of Christ's sufferings belongs to the expiation of our sins, but particularly the one which is called *passio κατ᾽ ἐξαίρεσιν*".—WOLLEB 82: " The Father's behest which Christ obeyed was special and general; special in respect of the end, that he obeyed not on his own but on our behalf; general, in respect of the object. For he was subject to the same law prescribed for us and in everything to which the law has bound us. Those who wish only Christ's passive obedience to have the nature of merit, claim that Christ's obedience extended only to the special mandate of the Father that he should die for us. This would be not a special but a partial mandate: Christ's obedience extends just as widely as the law extends. Since therefore the law binds us both to punishment and to obedience, he satisfied both its requisitions."

17.—In Christ's active obedience a distinction must be drawn between natural and federal subjection to the law. Like any other creature Christ as a man was subjected to God and also like the angels and saints in heaven had to follow out the changeless canon of God's holiness. But since Christ's manhood was holy, he did not need first to fulfil the law for himself in order to merit thereby the reward of righteousness, eternal life. On the contrary he was justified by the essential holiness of his human nature in claiming this reward for himself beforehand. But as sponsor and mediator for the human race Christ on our behalf further added 'federal subjection' to this natural subjection to the law, i.e., in addition to his *subesse Deo,* he further undertook the *esse sub lege* by voluntarily, i.e., on our behalf, submitting himself to the law as a power demanding as the "condition of blessedness" the fulfilment of all its demands. Since Christ then in this sense entered upon a life of service to the law in order to merit righteousness for himself by the way of fulfilling the law, as our sponsor he produced this *oboedientia activa,* not for himself but purely as a mediator representing us, and secured once more by his merit the righteousness which we had lost in Adam.

The older German-Reformed theologians (chiefly those of Heidelberg, Herborn, Anhalt like URSIN, PISCATOR, SCULTETUS) had of course taught with apparent agreement, that Christ gave the "active obedience" purely for himself, in order to be able as the holy deliverer to offer the Father the only representative "passive obedience". Even later it was still pretty much admitted that this doctrine had once been acknowledged by the Church and WENDELIN was able to prove it to be quite simply the right doctrine (cf. HEPPE *Dogm. d. deutschen Prot.* II, p. 221). Anyhow, it was still generally the custom to brand as the peculiar heresy of PISCATOR the doctrine that Christ's *oboedientia passiva* only was imputed to us, and that Christ supplied his "active obedience" as a man purely for himself. It was generally taught concerning Christ's active obedience (VOETIUS II, 159) that "Christ was subject to active . . . obedience, i.e., to the law so far as it is the rule of life, in two ways, both as a man on his own behalf and as sponsor and mediator on ours." Similarly among others BURMANN (V, xvi, 4) and BEZA, the latter of whom (I, 670) expresses himself thus: "And yet Christ, so far as he became man, seems to have been obliged by nature—to produce the righteousness of the law— therefore he seems to have fulfilled the law not for us but for himself, that he might deserve life beforehand for himself; which cannot be said of the punishment of our sins to be dissolved by him! Answer: Although we say that Christ according to the flesh deserved eternal life beforehand by the fulfilling of the law—it nevertheless would not be absurd to say that, so great was the force of that merit, it is also outstanding for believers. But this cannot be said quite correctly. Since this humanity has been united to the λόγος by the personal union, and even in such a way as to be most holy, who would have thought that anything was wanting in the humanity assumed to prevent it from being even then most worthy to enjoy that eternal life from the very first moment of the union? Hence this obligation of the flesh to fulfil the law does not properly belong to the nature itself but to the will; and not simply because Christ was a man but because he became man for us, a condition which he voluntarily underwent and fulfilled, not for himself as one who already was most blessed by the fullest right, but for us, for whose sake he willed to be made under the law, that he might redeem those who were under the law, Gal. 4. 3ff."

Later this point of doctrine was more adequately fixed by distinguishing the concepts of "natural" and "federal subjection to the law". Cf. BURMANN (II, xv, 9): "In Christ obedience had strictly the appearance of subjection to the law. Such subjection is twofold; either natural, which is due by every rational creature; or the result of a peculiar covenant and pact. In the Scriptures this is strictly called subjection to the law and being under the law; and in this sense it is used of Christ. Although human nature, so far as it is a creature of God, ought always to be subject to God and cannot, unless holy and just, be pleasing to God, in the way in which both Christ's humanity in heaven and blessed souls are perpetually kept to the same law of holiness, yet properly and strictly that does not mean this subjection to the law; for although the blessed in heaven ought to be holy, they are no more subject to the law. And so apart from his promise Christ would have been bound to obey the law also, to love God and neighbour and to be a man holy and righteous; nevertheless he would not properly have been subject to the law. Subjection to the law means strictly to be under it as a mistress demanding obedience, as the condition of beatitude and not assigning it before the fulfilment of the condition. That is why neither the blessed in heaven nor Christ, although a man apart from his promise, would have been under the law on earth, since he could soon have been the comprehensor and the heir of bliss, and would not still have had to wait for it after a long course of obedience. And so since Christ of himself was not subject to the law nor held to the conditions in question, he subjected himself to the law with the freest will on our behalf through his promise and pact with the Father. This subjection was additional to that natural holiness, which also as a man he was bound to fulfil on his own behalf; and it demanded besides a certain course of obedience, before the implementing of which he could not hope for the reward; and it took its rise at the beginning of his nativity and ended with his death."

TURRETIN distinguishes a threefold subjection to the law, a natural, a federal and a penal subjection. (XIV, xiii, 15): "Natural subjection arises from the law, which is the rule of holiness and is suited to the creature *qua* creature; it is therefore eternal and indispensable;—federal depends on the law as prescribing the condition of acquiring beatitude and is suited to a creature fixed in a state of life in which God made a covenant with it and prescribed an office for it under promise of reward or punishment; penal belongs to the sinning, guilty creature."

18: From this it is clear, in what way Christ was *pro se* or *pro nobis* ὑπὸ νόμου. As a man he was indubitably "subject *pro se* to the law as the norm of holiness, by common and natural subjection, to which the angels themselves and the blessed in heaven are subject." But he was not yet subject to the law "as laying down the condition of beatitude, by economic and federal subjection, in order to merit life by working, when he was already getting it because of the hypostatic union being in force." And still less was he in a state of "penal subjection". Hence it follows that "if he took this double burden upon him of fulfilling the law in order to acquire life, as much by making precepts as by suffering a sanction, he had to undergo it all for us by a voluntary dispensation in consequence of the office of mediator and the force of the pact entered into with him by the Father."—WOLLEB 81: "As Christ's passion is necessary for the expiation of sins, so too are his active obedience and righteousness for the obtaining of eternal life." The reasons are as follows: "(1) Because the law binds us both to penalty and to obedience; to penalty because it pronounces him accursed who shall not have accomplished all the works of the law, Dt. 27. 26; to obedience, because it promises life to those only who shall have done everything, Lev. 18. 5; Lk. 10. 28 (this do and thou shalt live). Nor is there any difficulty in dividing righteousness into legal and evangelical, if the gospel in Christ exhibits the same righteousness which the law demands. (2) because this twofold satisfaction answers to our twofold wretchedness; the guilt of sin and damnation and the lack of righteousness through faith, Rom. 3. 22. (3) Because righteousness in the true and proper sense consists in actual obedience, Dt. 6. 25 (it shall be righteousness unto us, if we observe to do all this commandment of the Lord our God, as he hath commanded us). (4) Because he has provided the actual obedience either for himself or in our room. But not for himself; therefore in our room. That which is assumed is manifest from Christ's relation to us. Whatever he was and did in the whole course of obedience he was and did in our room." WOLLEB now goes into the usual objections to this doctrine: "Here those who recognise only passive obedience as satisfaction and merit, object that active obedience indeed makes for the redemption and salvation of us, but only as the necessary and requisite cause. It is required of us for two reasons; first, by right of creation; second, in order that his sacrifice may be pleasing to God and that he may be an holy priest. But the first part of this view is false, because in this Jesus cannot be compared with other men. As the Son of God became man and a creature not on his own behalf but on ours, he was subject to the law not on his own behalf but on ours. The second number confuses holiness and innocence with obedience or actual righteousness; which differ no less than a *privatio* and a *habitus* (habit). Innocence, it is true, is requisite for Christ's sacrifice; but actual obedience is not only requisite for Christ as priest, but is also part of satisfaction and merit. If Adam's actual disobedience is the meritorious cause of damnation, how should not the actual obedience of the Second Adam be the meritorious cause of salvation? Unless we say that the former Adam is stronger at damnation than the latter at salvation!"

As being the most essential interest in distinguishing between " active " and " passive obedience " and in the doctrine of the imputation of both it was generally insisted that Christ's merit was twofold, a positive (the imparting of the H. Spirit, of righteousness, of eternal life) and a negative (absolution of us from guilt and punishment), WOLLEB 82 : " Eternal life is considered either in itself according as it is fullest participation in heavenly delights, or as opposed to damnation according as it is deliverance from damnation. In the former sense the cause of eternal life is the perfect righteousness of Christ ; in the latter the cause of eternal life is the dissolution of penalties. It is one thing to describe eternal life privatively, another to do so positively. Strictly speaking the cause of eternal life is no other than perfect righteousness according to the law ; this do and thou shalt live. Yet Christ's death is called the cause of eternal life, so far as it is liberation from all evil. Nor are deliverance from damnation and heavenly joys parts of life, but merely different relations. From this it appears in what sense Christ promises that he will give his flesh for the life of the world, Jn. 6. 51." To contradict the two objections, " (1) that if Christ's active obedience is the cause of eternal life, then he suffered in vain ; (2) that if Christ has obeyed on our behalf, then we shall not have to obey," WOLLEB remarks that " in the first argument there is no conclusion ; the one end is common to both parts of the satisfaction, namely our salvation ; the other is proper to both. The end of the passion is deliverance from punishment ; but the end of righteousness is the acquisition of the right to life eternal. The second argument against the merit of active obedience is the same as *Socinus* forms against the merit of passive obedience. If Christ, quotha, died in our room, then we should not have to die. But in both cases there is no inference. Christ's death is one thing, that of the godly another. The former is linked with a curse, the latter with a blessing. Christ endured the former as the price of our sins ; we endure the latter, as the transition from this life to the heavenly. So Christ's obedience is one, ours another. The former is perfect righteousness which he provides in our room and in order to merit life. The latter is imperfect and is provided for the sake of testifying thankfulness for redemption."

18.—Christ's " passive obedience " is displayed principally in the suffering and death of Christ. Christ underwent this suffering before he ever made his sacrifice proper, and subsequently upon the cursed tree. He thus endured not merely the agony of body but also the agony of soul which men had merited. (a) He represented before his own holy soul as his own misery the entire abyss of sin and destruction in which the human race and every separate member of it had got lost and the magnitude of the curse which all had brought about, feeling it as his own misery. (b) Laden with the voluntarily undertaken guilt of all the elect who belonged to him from eternity, he was judged by the Father, in order that the Father might abandon him. But this feeling of the full wrath of God over sin, which rent Christ's soul and drove him to death, the Lord bore in full surrender to the Father, as is clear from the cry in which Christ complained that he was forsaken by his God (OLEVIAN 51-53).—VOETIUS (II, 167) : " This ' passion ' of Christ's soul consists in *poena damni* and *poena sensus*. The former is lack or loss of the joy and delight which the vision and fruition of God and the plenitude of grace would have brought him, and that by rejection from God's face, or dereliction.—This is both the tasting and the realisation of the divine wrath and of struggle with it,— and subjection to the power of darkness, at all events to vexation, though not to enslavement ;—and that curse by which he was bearing the full sense of the divine judgment on men's sins, the sign and symbol of which was the ignominy of the Cross."—WOLLEB 75 : " Christ endured various sufferings, of which there are three classes : those preceding death, death itself and those following death.—Those preceding death are inward and outward.—The inward are sorrowfulness, pangs and tortures arising from the fierceness of the divine wrath and from the conflict with temptation to object and desert, which forced from him both blood and sweat and the pitiable cry, *Eli, Eli, lama sabachthani*, My God, my God, why hast thou forsaken me ? Moreover although he struggled with the temptation to give in, yet he neither despaired nor succumbed to the temptation, but overcame it by firm trust in God. The undoubted proof of this victory is that at the height of his anguish he did not cease to call God his God.— The outward sufferings are tortures of the body which he bore practically with his separate limbs and senses, the head being torn with thorns and smitten with reeds, the face being defiled with spittle and bruised with slaps, his ears pierced with gibes and abuse, his eyes afflicted with the grief of his disciples and mother, his tongue parched with thirst and slaked with vinegar and gall, his body stripped and torn with blows, and himself fixed to the Cross by his pierced hands and feet and hung between thieves, his sinews strained and his side pierced by a spear."—KECKERMANN 346 : "The incalculable sorrow in Christ's soul, which he suffered towards the end of his life, arose from the magnitude of the sins committed or to be committed successively by the human race right from the world's beginning to the world's end, all of which the divinity set before the humanity at that very time for its contemplation as in a mirror, in order presumably that the humanity might know distinctly and specifically what the matter was for which ransom and satisfaction had to be paid. The second cause of this deadly sorrowfulness was the impression of the divine wrath against sin, the magnitude of which Christ's soul distinctly considered and felt in the highest degree. The pain . . . was ἀνάλογος and proportionate to this torture, which the damned will feel in hell and in eternal damnation. It arose from the fact that at that moment he did not perceive in himself the presence and strength of the divinity, the λόγος being quiescent, as *Irenaeus* 349 says : " The meaning then is, Why hast thou forsaken me ? i.e. why dost thou present me with such a horrible face and aspect of Thy wrath and indignation, as though that moment Thou wert about to desert me or such as is wont to belong to one who would desert ? Hence they are words of struggle and temptation, not the words of a desperate spirit ; so also the voice of faith rings at the same time in this utterance, while he calls God his God and perseveres in prayer."

The question " whether therefore Christ may truly be said to have borne in death the pains of hell (*infernum*) " is therefore answered in the affirmative (RIISSEN XII, 27).

19.—The subject or *subjectum quod* of this suffering was the *persona* of the Logos, in so far as it had become man, or in respect of its human nature. The humanity of Christ (*subjectum quo*) suffered, in that the Redeemer through his human nature took the sufferings upon himself. From this it is clear what it was, upon which the specifically redemptive value, the reconciling power of Christ's suffering rests. It was (1) not the suffering of a man but the suffering of the eternal Son of God and therefore it had an infinite value; it was (2) not indeed an eternal suffering: but still it was a suffering aroused by the same feeling as the eternal penal suffering of the damned; i.e. by the full feeling of the punitive wrath of God, so that in intensity and reality it was the same as the suffering of the damned; and finally (3) it was a suffering borne with perfect morality (i.e. free will), holiness and guiltlessness, so that for the holy love of the Father it would possess altogether the value of a full equivalent for the penal suffering incurred by humanity.—WENDELIN (*Collat.* p. 211): "Our righteousness and the satisfaction afforded us is not to be ascribed to the divine and human natures in the same way. It is Christ's human nature that suffered for us, not the divine which cannot suffer and die. But the divine nature added weight to the passion, which the human nature alone not personally united to the divine could not have effected. Hence blood could not have cleansed us from all sin, had it not been that of the Son of God. Therefore we ascribe the passion to the human nature, but the efficacy of the passion to the divine, because the Son of God suffered in the assumed and personally united human nature." —BUCAN (XXIII, 4): "What is the subject of this passion? The Lord himself, the Son of God made man.—But was the passion that of the *persona* or of either of the natures alone? The passion was that of the *persona* because the *persona* which suffered is God and man, but not in the divine [which is impossible!] but in the human nature assumed, which was capable of suffering".—BUCAN (XXIII, 21): "On what does the value and efficacy of Christ's death depend? On the dignity of the *persona*— because it is of infinite merit, that of the man who forsooth is God."— BURMANN (V, xvii, 8): "The subject of the sufferings, according to the varying manner of regarding them, is commonly called the *subjectum quod* or the *subjectum quo*. The former is the *persona* of Christ, the latter his human nature".—OLEVIAN (cf. HEPPE, *Dogmatik d. deutschen Protest.* Bk. II, p. 217): "The dignity of such a great humiliation and obedience depends upon the dignity of the *persona*, which alone had the right of presenting itself before the Father."—BURMANN (V, xvii, 8): "It must be held that although this passion of Christ practically exhausted the entire force of our punishments in intention, it did not however bear the eternity of them. The infinite dignity of the *persona* made up for the infinity of time". — WENDELIN (I 17, 5. 7. 5.): "Although he did not feel eternal death as regards duration, yet as regards intensity and quality he felt the torments of the damned."—WOLLEB 77: "As regards the form or mode of Christ's passion, he suffered (1) truly, (2) holily and innocently, (3) voluntarily. These three points must be honestly adhered to. Unless he truly suffered there would have been no satisfaction for our sins. Unless he had suffered holily and innocently, we would not have a perfect high priest, Heb. 7.26 (for such an high priest became us, holy, guileless, undefiled, separated from sinners and made higher than the heavens). Unless he had subjected himself willingly to the curse, his sacrifice would have been forced. Hence it says, Heb. 10. 7, "before Lo, I am come to do thy will, O God."

Since then Christ willingly bore the suffering undertaken in accordance with the eternal counsel of love to the point at which it became exhausted by itself, by being obedient to the Father unto the death on the Cross; and since the elect belong to Christ from eternity and are implanted in him, so that they were taken up by Christ with him on to the accursed tree; the elect are aware that in the Mediator God has really been mindful of all their sins and has punished them by the death of Christ in order to fulfill the covenant promise, that the remembrance of all the sins of the elect should be washed out (OLEVIAN p.55).

20.—Thus then Christ's active and passive obedience is the sole yet likewise the perfectly sure means of our renewal to righteousness and our redemption from eternal death. But they are not to be thought of as separate or distinctive manifestations in the life of the Lord. On the contrary both are set in mutual unity in the same Lord, since the active obedience by which Christ subjected himself to the law for sinners only was an *actio passiva* and his life and death a real action, a *passio activa*. The distinction between the active and suffering obedience of Christ is thus only to be understood from the double aspect of the *finis* of Christ's *oboedientia*, in that by the former Christ acquired thereby righteousness and eternal life, by the latter he freed us from the curse of the law.— BURMANN (V, xix, 20): "The satisfaction of the death and the obedience of the life are not to be torn apart, since you would not disjoin the one from the other without doing harm to both; and from the joining of the two full satisfaction arises at last."—BURMANN (V, xix, 3): "To satisfy is the same as τὸ ἱκανὸν ποιῆσαι Mk. 15. 15" [the words used of Pilate satisfying the mob by releasing Barabbas]. —WOLLEB 73: "It is the satisfaction of Christ, by which, subjected to the law in our room by undergoing the curse due to our sins and by most perfectly affording the obedience required of us by the law, he delivered us from the curse and restored to us eternal life. Therefore it consists in the full payment of the punishment and in perfect righteousness; in the former especially passive obedience, in the latter active obedience chiefly shines forth. Zealously I add the reservation, that we do not consider active and passive obedience to be so different, that the full payment of the punishment consists in passive obedience alone. They do not differ in time; both extend from the beginning of the incarnation to the death. Nor do they differ in subject; the same obedience is active and passive in a different respect, and so Christ's obedience exists as an *actio passiva* and a *passio activa*. So far as the suffering of penalty is a receiving, it is called passive obedience; so far as it is the testimony of utter love, it may be termed active. Nor is the division into active and passive a division into parts; it is only a distinction based on the ends in view, namely the double satisfaction, for the penalty and for eternal life. The threat of a curse made to transgressors, Dt. 27. 26 (cursed be he that confirmeth not the words of this law to do them) requires the former; the promise of life on condition of perfect obedience and righteousness, Lev. 18. 5 (ye shall therefore keep my statutes and my judgements, (sic) which if a man do, he shall live in them: I am the LORD) requires the latter. Analogically therefore we are said, by the unique and most perfect satisfaction of Christ, both to be freed from penalty because he bore the penalties on our behalf; and to be presented with the right to eternal life, because he fulfilled the law on our behalf."

21.—By this obedience of his Christ afforded the Father a perfect satisfaction. In general *satisfactio* is a *vera debiti solutio* (the true payment of
a debt) (v. TIL. *Hypotyposis,* 170) and the satisfaction afforded by Christ
is a representative one, a *satisfactio vicaria.* Accordingly the definition is
(LEIDEN SYNOPSIS XXIX, 4): "Satisfaction is an act of *Christus*
θεάνθρωπος, i.e., God and man, by which, in accordance with the divine,
benevolent and just decree for his obedience to the Father and love
towards men, putting himself freely and readily as a pledge and sponsor
in our place, i.e., in our place and for our good, Christ paid on our
behalf all the penalties due for our sins, and by enduring and exhausting
them he satisfied divine justice and by his merit delivered us from wrath,
the curse of God and eternal death, and acquired righteousness and
eternal life, so as to declare God's righteousness and mercy and to save
us." Hence H. Scripture says that Christ bore the punishment instead
of us, gave himself to death on our behalf as a reconciliation and became
a curse for us.—HEIDEGGER (XIX, 70): "No small emphasis on proving
Christ's satisfaction through the bearing of vicarious punishment is
contained in the utterances of Scripture, in which Christ's death is said
to have been sought ὑπέρ, on behalf of us, also ἀντι, *vice* us, in our
room. Mt. 26. 28 (this is my blood of the Covenant, which is shed for
many unto remission of sins) Rom. 5. 8 (God commendeth his own love
toward us, in that, while we were yet sinners, Christ died for us);
2 Cor. 5. 15, 21 (he died for all, that they which live should no longer
live unto themselves, but unto him who for their sakes died and rose
again—him who knew no sin he made to be sin on our behalf; that we
might become the righteousness of God in him): Gal. 3. 13 (Christ
redeemed us from the curse of the law, having become a curse for us):
1 Tim. 2. 6 (who gave himself a ransom for all; the testimony to be borne
in its own time): Heb. 2. 9 (. . . Jesus, because of the suffering of death
crowned with glory and honour, that by the grace of God he should
taste death for every man): 1 Pet. 3. 18 (Christ also suffered for sins once,
the righteous for the unrighteous, that he might bring us to God; being
put to death in the flesh, but quickened in the spirit): Jn. 10. 11, 15
(I am the good shepherd; the good shepherd layeth down his life for the
sheep; . . . I lay down my life for the sheep): Jn. 11, 50–51 (. . . it
is expedient for you that one man should die for the people, and that
the whole nation perish not (Caiaphas)): Rom. 14, 15 (. . . Destroy not
with thy meat him for whom Christ died): 1 Cor. 15, 3 (Christ died
for our sins according to the Scriptures): Eph. 5. 2 (And walk in love,
even as Christ also loved you, and gave himself up for us, an offering
and a sacrifice to God for an odour of a sweet smell): 1 Pet. 4. 1 (Forasmuch then as Christ suffered in the flesh, arm ye yourselves also with the

same mind; for he that hath suffered in the flesh hath ceased from sin)':
are outstanding.—The force of all these utterances is that for the man
for whom Christ is said to have died he is understood to have given
himself as an ἀντίλυτρον, the price of redemption on the analogy
of 1 Tim. 2. 6 (p. 468) and to have shed his blood for the remission of sins,
Christ himself being the indication of this, Mt. 26. 28. (p.468). In these
words such force is assigned by Christ and Paul to the death of Christ, as it
had in common with the expiatory victim bearing the vicarious punishment.
It is therefore beyond doubt that ὑπέρ signifies the place, representation
or substitution of Christ's death in place of our death which was due."

22.—In other words, if the elect were to be redeemed, this satisfaction
was absolutely necessary, not only because of God's righteousness which
must inevitably punish the sinner, but also because of the threat and
promise which God had linked up with the covenant of works and with
the law, and because of the powerlessness of the law, which cannot
abolish sin or the guilt of sin in man or justify it.

From the beginning of the seventeenth century recognition of "the
absolute necessity of the vicarious sacrifice" became predominant in
Reformed theology. Earlier many followed the precedent of CALVIN,
who taught (II, xii, 1) that: "If the question is as to its necessity, it was
indeed not a simple one (as the saying is) or an absolute one, but it
flowed from the eternal decree, upon which man's salvation depended".
Hence BEZA (I, 656) : "But could God not have preserved man by
some other method less remote from our feelings ?— Of course He could.
But this method was extremely suited to declare the height of both
that righteousness and that mercy of His."   The same sense was also
expressed by MUSCULUS (*De instit.* c. 3), ZANCHIUS (*De incarnat.* II,
cap. 3, *qu.* 1, *th.* 1) and others. Meantime, later on, BEZA was already
inclining to a stricter conception of this point of doctrine (according
to VOETIUS II, 240), and from the beginning of the seventeenth century
it was universally customary to recognise the absolute necessity of the
vicarious sacrifice of Christ. VOETIUS (II, 238) thus describes the dispute
in this connection: "Query, whether, given sin and the necessity for our
future deliverance from it, the satisfaction of Christ as sponsor was
necessary according to the essential and necessary righteousness of God,
and not only according to the decree and the verity of the law and
its threat?" (Similarly also, e.g., WITSIUS II, viii, 1). In opposition to
Socinianism which denied the necessity of satisfaction altogether, the
question was now emphatically answered by all in the affirmative, and
accordingly the earlier assumption of an hypothetical necessity, which
had usually intensified further into recognition of a "necessity of

congruence " (cf. TURRETIN XIV, x, 4), was rejected. Only it was insistec that this necessity was not a natural necessity *simpliciter,* such as in a fire to burn, but a moral and rational necessity which rested upon the holiness and righteousness of God and could only issue forth by a "free interceding will", so that it "might admit of modification varying according to the wisdom and ἐπιείκεια of God, provided His natural right remained to Him unimpaired" (TURRETIN XIV, x, 16).

Hence the teaching of dogmaticians like BURMANN (V. xix, 5-7): "Necessity is taught by (1) God's righteousness or His constant and eternal will, by which according to the immutable order fixed by Himself He renders each his due and so repays evil to the sinner who does evil; 6: (2) by the threats which God denounces;—(3) by the vaticinations of the prophets;—(4) by the sacrifices of the O.T.; 7: (5) by the law of works itself,—as one which could not be passed or ordered without the promise of life and the threat of death;—(6) the truth and necessity of this thing is accomplished by Christ's actual passion; indeed it were a crime unworthy of God to hand over to death an holy man worthy of God's supreme love, if the necessity did not compel."—Similarly COCCEIUS (*Summ. Th.* LXI, 5-10): "The necessity of satisfaction is proved (1) by God's righteousness"; for "God's righteousness (*iustitia*) requires satisfaction for sin, in the sense of His rightness (*rectitudo*), by which, as He cannot be like a sinner, so He cannot fail to judge the sinner and to manifest the baseness of sin by exclusion from His benefits and by the imposition of a penalty. (2) From the law of works, which was not passed apart from a promise of life and a threat of death. (3) By the impotence of the law. The impotence of the law is to be referred to this— that it was powerless through the flesh to condemn sin by accusing sinners and finding them guilty and to justify us, Rom. 8, 3-4 (what the law could not do, in that it was weak through the flesh, God!—sending his own son in the likeness of sinful flesh and as an offering for sin, con- demned sin in the flesh, that the ordinance of the law might be fulfilled in us who walk not after the flesh but after the spirit). (4) By the curse. The truth of satisfaction is especially proved by God's own words, God's curse upon hanging, which saying St. Paul does not cunningly abuse but solidly uses. In that saying it is plainly declared, that no man should be hung on the tree who was not guilty of sin or unless he was liable to sin on account of the curse. (5) From the type and commemoration of sin made through him. This is proved by every class of sacrifices and types. Amongst these shine forth the type of the Lamb—it is the hiero- glyphic for the sinner, Is. 53. 6 (all we like sheep have gone astray) 1 Pet. 2. 25 (ye were going astray like sheep; but are now returned to the shepherd and Bishop of your souls), bearing sin, Jn. 1. 29 (The Lamb of God. taketh away the sin of the world)—and that of the serpent, Jn. 3. 14 (as Moses lifted up the serpent in the wilderness, so must the Son of man be lifted up), in which nothing but the lying and guile or at least the imputation and curse of sin can be seen, and that of the priest who was said to bear the people's sin, when a part of that which was substituted for the body was being sacrificed, Lev. 10. 17 (wherefore have ye not eaten the sin offering in the place of the sanctuary, seeing it is most holy, and he hath given it you to take away the iniquity of the congregation, to make atonement for them before the Lord?). (6) From the pronouncements of Scripture signifying satisfaction. Nothing but satisfaction is signified by the words כפר—λύτρον, ἀντίλυτρον, λύτρωσις ; פִּדְיוֹן, i.e., by כפר—ἰλασμός, ἰλαστήριον, ἐξιλάσκεσθαι ἁμαρτίας ; also τιμή, ἐξαγοράζειν τοὺς ὑπὸ νόμου. Also αἴρειν ἁμαρτίαν, ἀνενεγκεῖν ἁμαρτίας ἐπὶ ξύλον—quae non rapui solvo also ἀποστέλλεσθαι περὶ ἁμαρτίας, to be sent as a sacrifice for sin, to become sin, ἀποθνήσκειν ὑπὲρ ἀνθρώπων, δί ἀνθρώπους and ἀντὶ πολλῶν."

Meantime BUCAN (V, xix, 11) insists that: "this necessity of satisfaction because of the vigour of righteousness nevertheless posits actual grace.— Therefore the righteousness was in the satisfaction itself and in Christ; the grace in the mode of dispensation and in us."

23.—That Christ could make satisfaction for us is clear from the facts (1) that he possessed our nature and could therefore do penance for guilty nature; (2) that he undertook his suffering voluntarily; (3) that even in the act he retained completely free disposal of himself; (4) that as the Son of God he was capable of bearing our guilt and bearing it away; and (5) that guiltless and holy as he was he had no need to do penance for himself. Hence the satisfaction provided for the Father by Christ is absolutely perfect, so that it does not hold merely *ex accepti-tatione*, i.e., because the Father regards it (*acceptum fert*) arbitrarily as a satisfaction given to Him, but because it is a real satisfaction and is acknowledged by the Father following upon merit and so is efficacious *ex acceptitatione.*—TURRETIN (XIV, x, 14): "In order that the substitution may be made known lawfully and without any unrighteousness, various conditions are required in the sponsor, all of which meet perfectly in Christ: (1) community of nature, in order that sin be punished in the nature that was guilty; (2) consent of will, so that he might take the burden on himself freely and voluntarily, no one forcing him; (3) power and control over his members, so that he is *sui iuris* and able to determine concerning himself; (4) power to bear and to bear away from himself as well as from us all the punishments due us; otherwise, if he could have been holden of death, he could have freed no one;—(5) spotless holiness and purity, so that undefiled by any sin he would have no need to offer for himself, but only for us.—15: These being the conditions laid down, it was not unrighteous that the righteous Christ should substitute for us the unrighteous".—Upon this the perfection and validity of Christ's satisfaction rests; MARESIUS (X, 35): "Now the nature of this satisfaction is plain on the face of it. It was most full and perfect, adequate to the demand of the law and equal to the evil merits and guilt of those for whose sake it was given. Not by favour of the acceptor from a desire to accept, which is an imaginary solution—but by sufficiency of merit and the worthiness of the work. Although he did not undergo eternity of punishment because he overcame and conquered it, yet he suffered that extreme penalty which is eternal for the reprobate—both in loss and in sensation."

TURRETIN (XIV, xi, 8): "Hence it is clear that this redemption was neither made simply by manumission, like that of slaves who are liberated by their owners; nor by sheer courage and power, as prisoners are snatched from the hands of enemies; not by bare exchange, as is usually done in war; but by just satisfaction, as the sponsor pays for the debtor. Although gratuitous deliverance has a place so far as we are concerned— and deliverance by power obtains here, so far as the devil is concerned —and the exchange so far as Christ is concerned—yet as regards God the judge a just satisfaction must intervene.—9: This is an inference from the passages where Christ is said to have died for us, not only for our convenience and good, but also in our room, by substitution strictly so called, Rom. 5. 6–7 (while we were yet weak, in due season Christ died for the ungodly. For scarcely for a righteous man will one die: for peradventure for the good man someone would even dare to die. But God commendeth his love for us, in that, while we were yet sinners Christ died for us) 8. 32 (. . . spared not his own Son but delivered him up for us all) 1 Pet. 3. 18 (Christ also suffered for sins once, the righteous for the unrighteous, that he might bring us to God; being put to death in the flesh, but quickened in the spirit). The *Arminian* theory of *Hugo Grotius*, according to which Christ offered only a "hypothetical sacrifice" and satisfied "vindictive justice", not really, but only so far as God allows this satisfaction to hold, from a desire to accept, so that Christ did atone completely, not in our room, but only suffered in a manner profitable to us (because the Father was content to be satisfied with this "single victim", in which he who is "equal to anything" set up a pattern, in order to show how He could really deal with all men), is accordingly rejected unanimously by the Reformed dogmaticians.

24.—At the same time Christ's satisfaction is not to be understood as though God who is unchangeable in His nature and will was first caused or determined by the sacrifice of Christ to let grace pass for justice, or as though He was thereby transformed from an angry to a reconciled God. On the contrary Christ's work of redemption rested upon the eternal counsel of God and upon the commission imposed in consequence upon the Son, according to which He had resolved from eternity in this manner, which accords with His holiness, to have the redemption of the elect through the Son prepared in time.—MARESIUS (X, 41): "Christ's satisfaction was not only in full payment of all our debts, but also in reconciliation of us to God, so far as for us who were already beloved he [Christ] reconciled His [God's] love in the eternal decree with God's love of benevolence,—but not that he transformed God from one who refused to one who wanted to save us, from one who hated us to one who loved us, as certain *Remonstrants* say. This is too foreign to God's unchangeableness. Nothing in fact is falser than their dogma that no one is loved by God except in Christ through existing faith, Scripture teaching the opposite, Jn. 3. 16 (. . . that whosoever believeth) Rom. 5. 8 (. . . while we were yet sinners . . .). 42: Nor moreover are the giving of Christ to be Redeemer and his satisfaction ordained before eternal election, as the same *Remonstrants* falsely assert and those who ride their hobby, being ready to do battle for universal or at least objective grace, as they love to say, but it is subordinate to it [eternal election], as completing it and carrying it out."—ALSTED (548): "The principal cause of Christ's sufferings is God's eternal decree for redeeming the human race in this way, which seemed most suitable to the divine wisdom. God decreed from eternity (1) to reveal in time His immense love for man and (2) to declare in time His hatred of sin; (3) to set before us as clearly as possible for our imitation examples of obedience, humility, constancy and other virtues, which supported all men in the suffering Christ, and therefore He decreed to deliver up His Son into the hands of sinners, in order that this might be the means of reaching the pre-established end."

25.—The effect of the satisfaction offered by Christ to the Father for the elect (or his obedience) is on the one hand the expiation of the elect and the reconciliation of God to them, and on the other hand the merit which Christ has acquired for himself, in virtue of which on the basis of his eternal pact with the Father he can demand of Him the pardon of the elect. And of course this merit is a merit not merely *ex pacto* but also *ex condigno*.—BURMANN (V, xix, 18): "That by Christ's death our sins have been expiated is clear from the passages Rom. 5. 9–10 (. . . being justified by his blood we shall be saved from the wrath of God through him . . .), 2 Cor. 5. 19 (. . . God was in Christ reconciling the world unto himself, not reckoning unto them their trespasses, and having

committed unto us the word of reconciliation), 1 Jn. 2. 2 (he is the propitiation for our sins; and not for ours only, but also for the whole world)."
—Cocceius (*Summ. theol.* LIX, 10): "This obedience of Christ belongs
to the priestly office, not only because it was necessary for Christ to
offer himself a pure and immaculate victim to God (as some will have
it), but also because the obedience itself is a δικαίωμα or merit by
which many are made righteous, Rom. 5. 18–19 (if by the trespass of
the one death reigned through the one; much more shall they that
receive the abundance of grace and of the gift of righteousness reign in
life through the one, even Jesus Christ. So then as through one trespass
the judgment came unto all men to condemnation; even so through
one act of righteousness the free gift came unto all men to justification
of life). It is the cause of the right to ask for life and is therefore truly
a θυσία or sacrifice, Eph. 5. 2 (. . . gave himself up for us, an offering
and a sacrifice to God for an odour of a sweet smell)."—Cocceius (*De foed.*
V, 31) holds that Christ's obedience had a real and proper "quality of
merit" for all that the Father had vowed to him in the eternal pact,
namely (1) that in his humanity he was proved and glorified as the Son
of God, which was why he could not be holden of death; (2) that he was
given to the Church to be King and head; (3) that the world is his
heritage; and (4) that all his enemies must be subdued to him (103).
This merit accrues to him not solely *ex pacto* but also *ex condigno*, "because
such humiliation of such a person is altogether proportionate to such
exaltation and glory".

26.—By his representative obedience Christ has brought it about that
without injury to His holiness God can justify the godless; that the
commandment to believe in the Redeemer is perfectly established, since
all elect now see in him the way prepared to the Father; that those who
belong to Christ are now really reconciled and freed from all accusation
by the law; that all nations now have peace in Christ, since Christ is
promised the kingdom over all nations; and that the fidelity and divine
glory of Christ are proved.—Cocceius (*Summ. theol.* LXI, 18): "The
effects of the satisfaction are to be expected; they are an outstanding
proof of its truth. First, by it God is sanctified as the justifier of the
godless so that he is without spot, Rom. 3, 25–26 (. . . that he might
himself be just and the justifier of him that hath faith in Jesus). (19):
Second, by it are founded the precept of faith towards Christ and the
promise of righteousness by faith. Because the Father gave up the Son
and the Son offered himself to the Father, it follows therefrom that (1)
all men whatsoever may be commanded to recognise in Christ the true
and only Saviour and to be fully persuaded in themselves, that blessed

are all they that take refuge in him; (2) that all who believe in him in this way do not perish but have everlasting life (Jn. 3, 14, 15, 16)—20: Third, by the satisfaction the reconciliation has been effected of those who were given to Christ.—(21): Fourth, Christ's satisfaction, now no longer promised but also provided, brings to believers freedom from the accusation of sin.—(22): Fifth, the satisfaction makes peace for the Gentiles; Christ has been promised the kingship among the Gentiles.—(23): Sixth, in Christ's obedience lies the merit of the glory and blessedness of his humanity, his translation into which is Christ's justification both from the accusation of falsehood and blasphemy made by the Jews, and from the debt of satisfaction, and so Christ is blessed in the flesh, not only as the Son but also as a righteous servant.—(24): In short, by satisfying the Son of God proved himself a πιστὸς κτιστής, a faithful creator, and built up the whole glory of the divine virtues by his deeds, that we might honour him as the Father, and the Father in him."

27.—In particular it is further to be emphasised that Christ merited and secured for those for whom he made satisfaction to the Father the H. Spirit and His gift, regeneration to faith.—HEIDEGGER (XIX, 88): "Principally we must guard and firmly grasp the fact that for those on whose behalf he satisfied to God his Father by his death Christ has merited and obtained the H. Spirit and His peerless gift, so uniquely essential to salvation, regeneration to faith."

28.—But of course it still holds that not for all men did Christ secure satisfaction and merit the imparting of the H. Spirit, but only for those for whom he interceded as surety with the Father's consent. Although Christ died *sufficienter* for all men, and although Christ's obedience and suffering are so absolutely perfect that for this satisfaction the Father might have forgiven the sins of the whole human race, the merit of Christ can really hold *efficaciter* only for those whom the Father has given him, for whom the Father has accepted the dedication and surety of the Son, and for whom Christ in accordance with his own intention was ready to die and did die.
OLEVIAN (pp. 67–68): The sacrifice of Christ, so perfect in itself, is, both by the eternal counsel of God and by the high-priestly intercession of Christ himself, appointed only for those whom the Son of God has awakened to faith; sacrifice and intercession belong to each other. Hence although Christ has suffered *sufficienter* for all, he has done so *efficaciter* only for the elect. Had he also prayed for the rejected and sacrificed himself for them, they too would have had to be blessed and roused

by the H. Spirit to faith (p. 69): "He offered himself for those whom he knew the Father had given him, but never by chance or accident—as some imagine that the grace of sacrifice has been scattered in the air, in order that he who would might snatch it for himself."—v. TIL 175: "As to the wideness of this grace we declare that the obtaining of this salvation was not achieved for men one and all but solely for the elect destined to Christ for a peculiar possession by the eternal testament".—COCCEIUS (*Summ. de foed.* V. 108): "Where we are dealing with the pact between God and the Mediator, we must not omit to ask, whom he stood sponsor for and ought to have stood. And first it is plain, that for those whom he sponsored he also obtained; that the merit was for them; that their sins had been injected into him and condemned in him; that he had sacrificed himself for them, prayed for them." Hence it is quite right to teach that "Christ did not go bail for all without exception, or even for those who are not saved." To this it is objected that Christ as a man loved all men and therefore must also give himself for all men. (109): To this we must reply, that Christ had also really loved all men, even his enemies, and e.g., had a heartfelt compassion for Judas. But if Christ were to be a mediator for all, there would have had to be added to this love of Christ for men and to the value of his sacrifice, which of course could atone for the sins of all, "the will of the Father, without which no sponsorship can stand".—It cannot be said, says COCCEIUS (V, 110) later, "that those in whose flesh and blood Christ participates are his brethren and children," but on the contrary "that because brethren and children are given him as ἐπιλήπτωρ and participate in flesh and blood, he too in like manner has the same things in common or ought himself to be made like unto his brethren in all things."

The reason for assuming the particularity of Christ's sacrifice is given by COCCEIUS (V, 120–150): (1) In the passage 2 Cor. 5. 15, where St. Paul says that Christ died for all, he understands this "of the surrogation of the sponsor offering the sacrifice which involves regarding the guilty as dead." (2) Also on this passage he entertains no doubts about saying that all is become new, whereas shortly before he said: if any man be in Christ he is a new creature. (3) Similarly it says in v. 18, "all things are of God which reconcileth." (4) H. Scripture often uses the expressions πᾶς, πάντες, πάντα not as "excluding exceptions" but as "excluding distinctions", e.g., Rom. 10, 11–12 (the Scripture saith, Whosoever believeth on him shall not be put to shame. For there is no distinction between Jew and Greek: for the same LORD is Lord of all and is rich unto all that call upon him), Gal. 3. 26–28 (Ye are all sons of God, through faith, in Christ Jesus. As many of you as were baptized into Christ did put on Christ . . . ye are all one in Christ

Jesus), Col. 1. 20–28 (through him to reconcile all things unto himself . . . whether things upon earth or things in the heavens . . . that we may present every man perfect in Christ). (5) The Apostle also uses these expressions to indicate things opposed, e.g., Rom. 11, 32 (God hath shut up all unto disobedience, that he might have mercy upon all). (6) "In some places actual quickening is predicated of all", e.g., 1 Cor. 15, 22 (as in Adam all die, so also in Christ shall all be made alive); here it says that in Christ all shall be made alive, which however is at once explained by 'those who belong to Christ'. (7) As often as it is said of Christ that he died for all or for the world, this refers to the promise which Abraham had received, that in his name, i.e., in Christ, all nations should be blessed, which promise means that God would redeem the Gentiles by faith in Christ. Hence COCCEIUS (V, 149) expresses the wish that no learned, peaceable man, busied with the Church should ever use the unsuitable expression that "Christ died for all without exception", but should invariably stick to the two propositions, (1) that by the Father's decree according to his eternal promise Christ became a victim to secure the inheritance of a peculiar people from Jews and Gentiles, to which in virtue of his own merit and the Father's gift he disponed by testament an eternal communion in his benefits, Jn. 7, 39, 37 (This he spake of the Spirit, which they that believed on him were to receive. . . . If any man thirst, let him come unto me, and drink); (2) that this offering of Christ is truly of such value and sufficiency that the whole world and all men without exception coming to him may discover in him sure and perfect salvation; and God has willed that this sacrifice offered for the Church is set forth by a miraculous dispensation ἰδίοις καιροῖς, but without distinction between those to be saved and those destined to perish, with the behest not to neglect this great salvation but to lay hold of God's citadel, Is. 27, 5 (let him take hold of my strength that he may make peace with me . . .) in true conversion of the heart to God and with the most sure declaration that all who came to him shall find salvation in him, Jn. 6, 40 (for this is the will of my Father, that every one that beholdeth the Son, and believeth on him, should have eternal life; and I will raise him up at the last day).

That the satisfaction of Christ would be sufficient to atone for sin-guilt in all men, if the Father would let it benefit them all, is generally recognised. Cf., e.g., RIISSEN (XII, 11): ". . . the satisfaction of Christ might be said to be sufficient for the sins of one and all, if so it had seemed good to God; for since it was of infinite value, it was quite sufficient for the redemption of one and all, if it had seemed good to God to extend it to the whole world. And here belongs a distinction used by the Fathers and retained by various theologians, that Christ died sufficiently for all, but effectually only for the elect; which phrase, understood of the worthiness of Christ's death, is very true, although it is less accurate if referred to the will and counsel of Christ. For the Son gave himself to death, not with the purpose and intention of acting personal substitute in the room of one and all, to give satisfaction for them and secure them salvation; but for the elect only, who were given him by the Father to be redeemed and whose head he was to be, he was willing to give himself up."

Towards a more adequate definition and explanation of the question RIISSEN remarks as follows: "Point in dispute: Whether by his obedience Christ has satisfied for all the sins of men one and all?—Negative, against *Papists* and *Remonstrants*:—Now the question is not as to the fruit and efficacy of the death of Christ, whether one and all participate in this act, as *Puccius* and *Huberus* once wished. But the question is of the counsel of God in sending the Son into the world and of the intention of Christ in dying; whether it had respect to men one and all, that Christ put himself in their place and satisfied for them and obtained remission of sins and salvation; or only to the elect. The former they affirm, the latter we.—Proofs: (1) Christ's mission and his death are straightway restricted to particular men, the people of Christ, his sheep, his friends, his Church and his body.—(2) From the connection between the satisfaction and the intercession of Christ. The same person must be the object both of ἱλασμός and of ἐμφανισμός, as they are connected by an indissoluble bond by Paul and John, 1 Jn. 2, 1–2 (My little children, these things write I unto you, that ye may not sin. And if any man do sin, we have an Advocate with the Father, Jesus Christ the righteous; and he is the propitiation for our sins; and not for ours only, but also for the whole world) Rom. 8, 34 (Who is he that shall condemn? It is Christ Jesus that died . . . who also maketh intercession for us). But Christ himself bears witness that he does not intercede for one and all, but for those only who were given him by the Father, Jn. 17, 9 (I pray for them: I pray not for the world but for those whom thou hast given me; for they are thine).—(3) From the supreme love of Christ. Those for whom Christ died he loved so greatly that a greater love can not be given: Greater love hath no man than this, that a man lay down his life for his friends, Jn. 15, 13.—(4) For those only Christ died, to whom he applied the salvation obtained. Christ's death is destined by Christ on our behalf to obtain us salvation, and the end of obtaining it is none other than the application of it, and it would be obtained in vain if it were never to be applied. Whence it follows, that if salvation was obtained for all, it ought to be applied to all alike. But it is not applied to all, since many know nothing about Christ. But then Christ would have set himself an empty aim in a matter which was not only not to be, but which also could not be given without his gift. He would have willed to obtain redemption for all without the aim of its being applied to all, if only they believe; and yet he would have willed neither to reveal redemption to countless people, nor to give to the countless people to whom it was revealed the condition without which it could not possibly be applied to them for eternity.—(5) From other absurdities. If Christ died for one and all it follows (i) that Christ died for countless on condition that they believe, to whom neither Christ nor his death was ever known and who therefore could not believe it; (ii) that he died for those whom Christ knew to be sons of perdition, passed over by God, held in the greatest hatred by God, etc.; (iii) that he died for those already being tortured in hell and who had actually been damned already; (iv) Christ will be called the Saviour and Redeemer of those who not only were never saved but who even can never be saved; or else an imperfect partial Saviour who by his satisfaction was the author of obtaining but not of applying, since he can only be called the Saviour truly in the case of those whom he makes sharers in salvation and who actually are saved."

29.—For those who hear God's call outwardly but are not elected this outward apprehension of the divine grace therefore only means that they are the more inexcusable.—HEIDEGGER (XIX, 91): "Although certain benefits do also redound to some, who are actually perishing, being called outwardly because of Christ's death and the preaching of the Gospel consequent thereon, but tend rather to ἀναπολόγησις and increase in damnation than to their salvation, Heb. 6. 4-5 (As touching those who were once enlightened and tasted of the heavenly gift, and were made partakers of the Holy Ghost, and tasted the good word of God, and the powers of the age to come, and then fall away, it is impossible to renew them again to repentance). 2 Pet. 2, 20 (if after they have escaped the defilement of the world through the knowledge of the Lord and Saviour Jesus Christ they are again entangled therein and overcome, the last state is become worse than the first) Christ none the less laid down his life as the price and sacrifice of satisfaction not for them but for the elect alone. For them alone he offered himself, them alone he redeemed by the price of his blood."

30.—After his exaltation Christ exercises the high-priestly office. In continuation of the intercession offered to the Father in his immolation of himself, he appears before the Father as he who has consummated the sacrifice for the guilt of the world; and in virtue of the satisfaction accepted by the Father he mediates and effects the appropriation of his merit by the elect, as a gift of grace to be lavished by the Father, he protects and advances the faithful in the enjoyment of the salvation of grace, and he offers their prayers to the Father: this is why the faithful may call upon the Father only in the name of Christ.—LEIDEN SYNOPSIS (XXVI, 48): "Christ's intercession is the function by which, placing himself in the heavenly holy place, he importunes from God the Father in our name both His mercy and the remission of sins obtained by the merit of his expiatory sacrifice and its riches and the gifts of the Holy Spirit, by which we are daily made readier and readier for all the duties of obedience and εὐχαριστία".—MARESIUS (X, 53): "Intercession means that by which after the expiatory oblation he stands before God the Father, to represent the efficacy of his oblation and to obtain thereby the application of the redemption secured for us, the grace of the Holy Spirit and the hearing of our prayers.—Relying upon this intercession of the one Christ, true Christians ask nothing of the Father except in the Son's name."—a DIEST (207): "The intercession is twofold, the one humble in the state of exinanition, the other glorious, which is Christ's compearance in heaven before the Father in the state of exaltation".—BEZA (I, 659): "He intercedes (1) by the perpetual vigour of his integrity and obedience which appeases the Father in our favour, (2) next, since we cannot duly approach the Father except in his name, by always intervening between us and the Father as a midway conciliator, whereby whatever we offer is pleasing to the Father. But as for some who talk moonshine about Christ's supplication and his casting Himself at the Father's knees, it is an empty lie of those fellows who cannot distinguish Christ weak from Christ glorious, heavenly things from earthly" [sic]—TURRETIN (XIV, xv, 13): "This intercession is made—rather in things than in words by the representation of his death in heaven."

Essentially therefore Christ's intercession is the *vigor* of his redemptive work in eternity, in virtue of the abiding "personal union" of the λόγος with the assumed humanity, and in virtue of the abiding validity of the "obedience" afforded by him, and, in fact, so far as Christ's mediation is considered in relation to the connection between the individual elect person and the Father.

That Christ already exercised this intercession here on earth is expressly stressed and not merely by RIISSEN. BURMANN (V, xiv, 14): "The second function of Christ's priesthood is intercession. This is not private prayers—but public, such as he pours forth both once upon a time in Jn. 17, and especially now in heaven."—MARESIUS (X, 54): "Although all Christ's prayers were not intercessory—most of them were, and particularly those which are recited entire, Jn. 17, in which he revealed a lively image of his intercession in heaven for the Church. Wherefore Christ's

intercession does not begin *simpliciter* after his ascension into heaven".
Similarly WOLLEB (p. 83) expressly stresses Christ's intercession in the
state of humiliation".

31.—Further this intercession of Christ can only hold for those who according to the Father's eternal counsel of grace are assumed into the eternal
covenant of grace, and for whom therefore the Son has given his eternal
sponsio.—HEIDEGGER (XIX, 95): "Therefore the intercession and inter-
pellation of Christ the high priest, who has entered heaven and compears
before the Father's face with his own blood shed for us, accomplishes this
for those for whom he offered himself unto death to the Father and did die."

32.—The third office of Christ is his *regium munus*, whereby he rules by
his word and Spirit and guards and preserves it against all enemies" (HEI-
DEGGER XIX, 98). To be distinguished are the *regnum Christi* in the more
general sense of the word, the *regnum essentiale, naturale* or *universale,*
which as the eternal Son of the Father he exercises over the world with
Him and the H. Spirit, and the *regnum personale* or *oeconomicum*, the kingdom of grace which accrues to Christ as the God-man.—ALSTED 587:
"Christ's kingship is twofold, essential and personal; the essential, which
is also called natural and universal, Christ holds with a glory and majesty
equal to the Father and the H. Spirit; the personal, which is also called
the donative, the economic and the dispensative, Christ administers as the
$\theta\epsilon\acute{a}\nu\theta\rho\omega\pi o\varsigma$ in a single mode; and it is of grace or of glory; the former
is the Church militant, the latter the Church triumphant."—MARESIUS
143: "The kingly dignity in Christ is twofold, the natural which belongs
to him as God, the second, the economic, which is his as the $\theta\epsilon\acute{a}\nu\theta\rho\omega\pi o\varsigma$".
—For the conception of the *regnum Christi* in the earlier German Reformed
dogmaticians cf. HEPPE *Dogm. d.d. Prot.* Bk. II, p. 222-223.

33.—This mediatorial kingship is assigned to Christ, because by his
propitiatory sacrifice he has prepared for himself a people which is his
peculiar possession, and which he therefore guides and rules and guards
against all attacks. Of course the power of Christ does not extend merely
to the community of believers, but also to their enemies, in fact, to all
creatures generally in heaven and on earth, since Christ makes them
serviceable to himself for the benefit of his kingdom. But the *regnum
Christi* itself is only the kingdom of grace, the Church, and comprises
(1) the *gubernatio* and (2) the *defensio* of it.—HEIDEGGER (XIX, 99):
"Kingly power was bound to be conferred on Christ, because he acquired
it by his death and secured for himself, as his perquisite or substance, a
$\lambda\hat{a}o\varsigma$ $\pi\epsilon\rho\iota o\acute{u}\sigma\iota o\varsigma$, a people of his very own, Tit. 2, 14, i.e. as a treasure

set apart, preserved, guarded, so that by it he might be reckoned wealthy as its possessor and might display his magnificence."—ALTING 102: "Christ's kingship is that by which as head of the Church he rules it by his word and spirit and guards it against enemies".—WOLLEB 72: "The kingly office is to govern and preserve the Church. The divisions of it are the government of the Church and the defeat of its enemies."—RIISSEN (XII, 15): "Christ's kingly office is the power of applying everything which he has merited to the salvation of those for whom he merited and of warding off what is contrary."—BURMANN (V, xv, 3): "Christ's kingly office is the power and authority of the mediator, by which being constituted king and head of the Church he flourishes with supreme power in heaven and on earth and governs all things concerned with the Church with full rights and rules and perfects it both by the word and by the interior power of his Spirit; and guards it against the assaults and power of all sorts of enemies; and will at last crown it victor in heaven for ever, perfect in body and mind."—Hence it is not right, when it is said that according to Reformed doctrine the kingship of Christ also extends over the extra-Church sphere (of nature). Of course Christ has power over this also, but only for the purpose of exercising his mediating Kingship over the Church. Hence BURMANN of course says (and quite correctly) (V, xv, 29): "(But) just as the spiritual, so also the universal kingdom of the Messiah is the faithful of all ages and all lands, nay embracing also in its ambit the power of universal nature."—Hence (10): "All things are subdued to this kingship and all creatures are its servants";—meantime be it noted, "not because all men properly belong to that Kingdom, but because it could not be administered without that infinite power".

34.—Christ's kingdom is essentially of a spiritual kind; only all those belong to it who are spiritually born again, i.e., are members of the Church, and therefore it is essentially manifested in the state of the redemption of Christ.—CALVIN (II, xv, 3): "I come to (Christ's) Kingship, concerning which words would be in vain, unless readers were at first advised that its nature is spiritual; because therefrom we gather what its value is and what good it does us and its entire strength and eternity".—BURMANN V, xv, 5): "This Kingship is moreover spiritual and eternal, not like the kingdoms and principates we see among men, resting upon outward force and power, and setting forth much of human splendour, but clearly of a different kind. For its seat is in the minds of men and in the hearts of those who love God."—KECKERMANN 358: "As the prophetic and priestly function belongs principally to the state of humiliation, so the kingly function embraces the state of exaltation particularly, although in the state of humiliation it has shown some instances of its royal dignity and power."

35.— But if this mediating kingship of Christ is already to be distinguished from its participation in the general government of the world, Christ rules even the former at all only by the will of the Father, since the Son only wills what is of the Father's good pleasure.—HEIDEGGER (XIX, 102): "Even as God Christ wields this personal kingship not beyond or short of the Father's will, but according to it ; as God and mediator he is able for all he wills. But he wills nothing that is not pleasing and acceptable to God the Father. He wills everything of that nature. It is moreover pleasing and acceptable to God, that Jesus Christ, whom He Himself appointed to be the μεσίτης of man with Himself and of Himself with man, should not only teach the people truth, restrain them by law, sanctify them by the Spirit, raise them to eternal life, but also commend them to himself as their *patronus*. All this belongs to the honour of God and is glorious to Him. God therefore did not retire from the throne of His majesty because Christ was King, nor so made over the Kingship to Jesus Christ as Mediator, as to abrogate it from Himself or subject Himself to Christ."

36.—As regards the exercise of Christ's kingly rule, it is on the one hand a *vocatio*, on the other a *judicium*. The former is partly a general calling mediated by the outward proclamation of the word, partly a special calling since Christ makes the proclamation of the word effective in the hearts of believers through the H. Spirit. Christ exercises judgment here on earth upon the elect, since he aquits them of their sins and shields them against all hostility; upon the rejected and godless, since he disciplines them with temporal punishments and since he sets bounds to the effectiveness of their godless nature. In eternity Christ exercises his kingship, since he perfects and transfigures believers; but he punishes the godless with eternal damnation.

Many dogmaticians make still fuller distinctions, e.g., CROCIUS, p. 1003: "To the kingly office belong (1) *vocatio* to participation in Christ's Kingship; (2) *legislatio;* (3) bestowal of the good things necessary in this life for salvation; (4) sweeping away the evils the opposite of these; (5) judgment together with the things annexed."

37.—As in the other offices, so too in the exercise of the kingly rule of Christ his two natures are active, since the divine Logos is in this active αὐτοκρατορικῶς, the human nature on the contrary as the finite and conditioned organ of Deity.—HEIDEGGER (XIX, 103): "Christ the θεάνθρωπος performs this kingly function as God and man: God reigning αὐτοκρατορικῶς in the edifying, guarding and glorification of the Church; man, not as the Lord of the universe, but as mandatory of the Father, using finite and dependent power. As for the priestly inter-cession the bowels and compassion of the human nature are required, so for the administration of this kingdom his care and pains are also required".

38.—This kingship of Christ shall endure for ever, since his meritorious activity for the elect must one day cease, because otherwise it would be imperfect; so Christ will be for ever the heir of his own, whom he can no longer leave apart from himself.—HEIDEGGER (XIX, 112): "And not even in heaven after the end of the world will Christ abdicate his mediatorial Kingship nor himself be divested of that kingship by God the Father. That his Kingdom is eternal we have proved above. Christ will of course sit at the right hand of God εἰς τὸ διηνεκές (for ever), Heb. 10. 12 (when he had offered one sacrifice for sins for ever, sat down [sic] on the right hand of God), and so he will be king to eternity; because the session of the mediator at the right hand of God is the function of the mediatorial kingship in glory. And he also performs the same in eternity. Although the meritorious action of the mediator ceases and ought to cease, because otherwise it would be imperfect and so not meritorious, yet his will by which he demands the inheritance and the good of his inheritance will not cease. The tranquillity and glory of it shall ever be consummated over all the profligate enemies of the Kingship and ever be imperturbable by any hostile power. The Kingship will be the same, but its appearance and government will not again be disturbed and picked out by vicissitudes, but will be pacified, glorious, equable and changeless."

39.—The administration and government of this eternal kingdom upon earth has nevertheless not been the same always. In the OT Christ had according to the counsel of the Father chosen for himself the people of Israel to be the people of his possession, in order so completely to rule over them, as himself also to determine even the civic commonweal of the people. Accordingly Christ ordained kings and prophets in Israel, in order to exercise his Kingship through them. But as these institutions were only an indication of the true glory of Christ's Kingdom, which could not yet be perfectly manifested in them, the OT economy could not yet call to life the true joyfulness and blessedness of the Kingdom of Christ. This first occurred at the time it was proclaimed to Jews and heathen alike, that the Kingdom of Christ is in no wise of this world, that it is purely heavenly and in the souls of believers.—HEIDEGGER (XIX, 110–111): "As Jesus Christ is the same yesterday, today and forever, so also he is and shall be the everlasting King and his Kingdom is eternal.—Yet the economy and administration of the Kingdom, eternal though it be, admits of difference. In the OT he chose the people of Israel from all the peoples as his own possession, to which He should be known, which he should keep under carnal discipline and whose elect, he should sanctify, along with a few proselytes. "Ye shall be unto me a kingdom of priests and an holy nation," Ex. 19. 6. But plainly Christ regulated this Kingship in an unique way. Besides the fact that as God he was head of that people in the civil power also, and, as we showed above (Ch. 16, § 7), in the matter of his spiritual Kingship he wielded it according to the type of the OT Also in the Kingship of the Church in the OT he obtained a peculiar and unique thing, in that in it he associated with himself the chiefs and those with power, to subdue the same people, in which the seed of God was contained, to the elements of the world, and to see to it that the law of the carnal precept should remain in force, and to exercise judgments within the bounds. Next he set up priests to offer money and an ἄλογος victim for the people, the type and shadow of a better sacrifice. These he installed for a time veiled as it were. But this was not merely and sheerly the Kingdom of God, nor, while in this guise Christ offered himself to the men of one people and ruled over them, was it a δεσποτεία of God, because Christ was not the only king and prince nor was there true liberty to serve him alone without princes, servants and earthly interests. Nor yet was there love, joy and thanksgiving as great as there could be in the Kingdom of God in the highest sense, since there were wanting the things referable to severity rather than to grace. So this outward face of Christ's Kingdom and the princes and the powers allied to it were bound to be put off at Christ's advent into the flesh, Col. 2. 15 (having put off from himself the principalities and the powers, he made a show of them openly, triumphing over them in it). The herald of this was John Baptist when he said, Repent ye, etc., Mt. 3. 2, where Christ's Kingdom is called the Kingdom of heaven, not only as in Dan. 4. 34 because God has his throne in heaven and so he is not on earth as a man (And at the end of the days I Nebuchadnezzar lifted up mine eyes to heaven, and mine understanding returned unto me, and I blessed the Most High, and I praised and honoured him that liveth for ever; for his dominion is an everlasting dominion, and his kingdom from genera- tion to generation), but much more because the Kingdom of God is heavenly and not earthly."

40.—In eternity, where the Church must be raised from the state of grace to the state of glory, the Kingdom of Christ will also appear in its completeness, and this Kingdom will have no end. Then Christ will exercise his power no longer as it is exercised here on earth, through outward instruments (through the messengers of the Gospel, through godly governments, etc.), but directly through himself. And although as the Redeemer, as the Word made man, Christ will throw himself at the Father's feet, yet his Kingdom remains always and for ever the kingdom of redemption and of salvation (*regnum oeconomicum*) as regards the dignity of his person, as regards his power over the angels and believers and as regards the glory which he receives from them.—LEIDEN SYNOPSIS (XXVI, 52): "As the state of Christ's Church is twofold, one of grace in this world, the other of glory in the world to come, so the present government of the Church is to be distinguished from the future. In this life Christ rules his Church indirectly through the ecclesiastical administration of faithful pastors and protects it by the political administration of godly magistrates. In the second life he will rule it directly without such outward aids according to the Deity which he shares with the Father and the H. Spirit, so that he is all things in both respects among all of the household of faith, whom he will bless with the closest, sweetest vision and communion with himself in heaven, 1 Cor. 15. 25 (he must reign till he hath put all his enemies under his feet) Rev. 21. 22–23 (And I saw no temple therein: for the Lord God the Almighty and the Lamb are the temple thereof. And the city hath no need of the sun neither of the moon to shine upon it: for the Glory of God did lighten it, and the lamp thereof is the Lamb)."—RIISSEN (XII, 19): "Therefore Christ's Kingdom will abide for ever (1) by reason of the dignity of Christ's person; (2) by reason of his power over the angels and the faithful; (3) by reason of his receiving honour from them, Rev. 22. 3 (there shall be no curse any more, and the throne of God and of the Lamb shall be therein: and his servants shall do him service). Among the orthodox there are some who, although with unlike intention, even lay it down that Christ's mediatorial kingship will end with the world, in order that room may be made for the essential kingship alone, through which God will be all in all. But although we admit that this Kingship may be changed in form and manner of administration, we lay it down that the substance of the Kingship will abide for ever."—WOLLEB (VIII, 80): "This economic Kingship he will exercise for eternity."— ALTING (p. 102) indeed says that "in the consummation of the *saeculum* 1 Cor. 15. 24–25 (then cometh the end when he shall deliver up the kingdom of God, even the Father; when he shall have abolished all rule and all authority and power. For he must reign, till he hath put all his enemies under his feet) the *regnum mediatorium* will cease and with it the prophetic office, 1 Cor. 13. 8 (whether there be prophecies they shall be done away: tongues, they shall cease; knowledge, it shall be done away) and the priestly also as regards intervention (for he completed the satisfaction once for all), the Church being glorious and purged of all defilement, Eph. 5. 26–27 (that he might sanctify it, having cleansed it by the washing of water with the word; that he might present the church to himself a glorious church, not having spot or wrinkle or any such thing; but that it should be holy and without blemish) and most fully vindicated from all enemies, 1 Cor. 15. 25–26 (the last enemy that shall be abolished is death)." Meanwhile he continues: "although even then the Lamb will still be there, Rev. 21. 22–23 (p. 486) 27 (and there shall in no wise enter into it anything unclean, or he that maketh an abomination and a lie; but only they which are written in the Lamb's book of life) 22. 1, 3 (and he shewed me a river of water of life, bright as crystal, proceeding out of the throne of God and of the Lamb . . . and there shall be no curse any more, and the throne of God and of the Lamb shall be therein: and his servants shall do him service), the memory and glory of the benefit afforded abiding to eternity."

CHAPTER XIX

CHRIST'S STATES OF EXINANITION AND EXALTATION

1.—In the manifestation and activity of the Logos made man there are two states of it to be distinguished, a state of humiliation and a state of exaltation; the Logos became man in the state of humiliation and from that passed over into the state of exaltation, in such a way that in the former he predominantly executed his highpriestly, work in the latter predominantly his kingly office.—a DIEST (208): "His state in the assumed flesh is that in which Christ executed his mediatorial office as the θεάνθρωπος. Christ's state in the assumed flesh is twofold, either of exinanition or of exaltation. The state of exinanition is that in which Christ as it were has divested himself of divinity, the same being hidden and has appeared in the form of a servant [κένωσις]. 210: The state of exaltation is that in which, redemption accomplished, Christ was borne to the height of glory, the human nature being glorified, whereas the divine glory was manifested a second time."

2.—"The state of humiliation is that in which as regards the divine nature the mediator deprived himself of the use and display of the glory otherwise belonging to him, and as regards the human nature was subjected in extreme humility to the divine law for the accomplishment and performance of all that was required to restore the sinner" (MASTRICHT V, ix, 4). Christ's humiliation—the subject of which is not the Logos in and for himself, and still less the human nature adopted by him, but the Logos become man—therefore consists not in his becoming man as such. The Son of God could adopt the human nature and in it let his full divine majesty shine. But Christ rather humbled himself by assuming the servant-form of man (living in the state of sinful misery) and therefore on the one hand divested himself of his divine glory by concealing the divine nature of his person beneath the assumed slave-form of the human nature, and on the other hand subjected himself as mediator to the Father and to the Father's law, in order to fulfil it with perfect obedience on our behalf and to bear the curse of the law for us who had transgressed it. So we must distinguish between the *exinanitio* (κένωσις) and the *humiliatio* (ταπείνωσις) in the stricter sense of the word, so that the former denotes the slave-form of Christ's whole life, assumed in becoming man, and the latter on the contrary (which consequently presupposes the "exinanition" of Christ's person) the subjection of it to the power of death.— COCCEJUS (*Summ. theol.* LX, 3; "On Christ's humiliation and sufferings)" "Christ's humiliation does not consist in the fact that he was born a man. Even in the state of ὕψωσις (exaltation) he is the Son of man and so even in glory has the slave nature in which he does the will of God. Indeed all God's works are subject to the Son of man, even the angels themselves Ps. 8. 7 (6) (thou mad'st him to have dominion over the works of thy hand: thou hast put all things under his feet) Heb. 2. 5–9 (quoting Ps. 8). 4: The first element in the humiliation is κένωσις, which is not ἐνσάρκωσις simpliciter—but ἐνσάρκωσις such that in it he was not equal to God (Dei instar) even as it is right for him to be God or to be equal to God ἐν μορφῇ (in fashion) among men, for in it [ἐνσάρκωσις] he received the μορφὴ δούλου, ἐν ὁμοιώματι ἀνθρώπων γενόμενος ; i.e., took upon himself the state of a slave, μορφὴ δούλου, made under the law, while he was made like unto men as a brother Phil. 2. 7. Whence he could indeed be recognised as the Son of God or him whom the Father had sent, and in fact he could be recognised by clear facts and proofs, so that those who beheld him were truly beholding the glory as of the only-begotten of the Father, but only in the case of those who believed Moses and the prophets, so that the Word of God was abiding in them Jn. 5. 38, 46 (whom he sent, him ye believe not: . . . if ye believed Moses, ye would have believed me; for he wrote of me), i.e., so that they perceived the drift of God's words by Moses and received it by faith. For though the proofs, by which his glory might be displayed were evident, it was still evident only to the faithful that they were proofs of the glory of the only-begotten Son of God; the rest could be offended in him."—LEIDEN SYNOPSIS (XXVII, 3): "The nature of order demands that we should now speak of this state of humiliation. By this name is generally meant the whole economy by which, accepting the form of a servant, Christ was obedient to the Father unto death, even the death of the cross Phil. 2. 7. And in a broad sense it includes the whole humility of the incarnate Son and all its degrees; but strictly the extreme submission or final act of life until his death, which is also commonly called the passion κατ' ἐξοχήν in the received sense of Scripture."—BURMANN (V, xvii, 1): "Christ's state of humiliation presents itself to our contemplation in a twofold aspect and a twofold degree, of which the one aspect is called κένωσις or exinanitio and evacuatio, which consists in the acceptance of incarnation and the form of a servant,—the second aspect, called ταπείνωσις, was a sort of depression of the now voided Deity and of the whole persona . . ." (V, x, 1): "Christ's humiliation is to be seen both in his life and in his death. In Phil. 2 the apostle particularly designates the one by the name of κένωσις, exinanitio, and the other by that of ταπείνωσις, humiliatio."

3.—The four most essential states to be distinguished in Christ's humiliation are his birth, burdensome life, death and descent into hell, the two latter of which require special treatment. In the death of Christ, in which the work of atonement for the sin-guilt of the elect is completed, Christ's body and soul were separated. In order that the power for a while given to death over the Son of God might be completely manifest and that his humiliation might be complete, Christ's body was buried, whereas his soul descended into Hades. But even in this separation of soul from body the person of the Logos remained in its "personal union" with the assumed humanity. Had this personal union been dissolved, the testament in the sense in which the Father had decreed it would not be observed and we should still be in our sins (OLEVIAN, pp. 58–59). The *descensus ad inferos* or descent into hell itself is not to be thought of as a spatial event.— ALTING, p. 100: "In no sense (in H. Scripture) is there indicated a local descent into hell to conquer the devil there, whom he had no call to be seeking for there, since the devil attacked him Jn. 14. 30 (the prince of the world hath nothing in me)."—MASTRICHT (V, xiii, 12): "The Reformed deny all local descent, because (1) neither would he have descended according to the divine nature (which by its omnipresence rejects all local movement), nor according to the human, which once more neither descends as regards the body (which throughout the three days partly hung on the Cross, partly lay in the tomb), nor according to the soul, since when at the point of death he commended it into his Father's hands, and since it ascended that very day to Paradise Lk. 23. 43, as Adam on the very day of his sin was ejected and carried away from Paradise Gen. 3. 23–24. (2) Because a local descent is quite useless and superfluous. He did not descend into hell to suffer for us there: that had already been finished on the cross Jn. 19. 20. Nor to satisfy for our sins by such a descent; this was already provided for by his death Heb. 2. 14 (that through death he might bring to naught him that had the power of death, that is, the devil) 9. 12 (through his own blood entered in once for all into the holy place, having obtained eternal redemption) 1 Thess. 1. 10 (Jesus, which delivereth us from the wrath to come). Nor to bring the patriarchs of the OT out of hell, since they never were in hell, as is clear from Enoch's case Heb. 11. 5 (God translated him) (he did not see death) and Elijah's 2 Kings, 2. 11 (a chariot of fire and horses of fire took him by a whirlwind into heaven). Nor to triumph over the devils; that was already done on the cross Heb. 2. 14. (above) 15 (might deliver all them who through fear of death were all their lifetime subject to bondage) Col. 2. 14–15 (he triumphed over principalities and powers on the cross) and afterwards also in the ascension Eph. 4. 8–12 (when he ascended he led captivity captive and gave gifts to men).

I shall add (3) because the *Papists'* limbo is nothing but a superfluous fiction devoid of all Scripture and reason."

4.—The descent then was but the reverse side of this most profound humiliation, in which Christ was abandoned by the Father to the power and dominion of death. Like all human souls which separate from their bodies, even Christ's soul had to descend into Hades, because his whole divine-human person was punished with real death, in order that sin might be atoned for and the covenant of grace consummated. In any case the power, which death held over the Son in passing, had already begun with the agony of death on the Cross, where the Father forsook him and gave him up to death; the descent into hell is also to be connected with these hell-throes which Christ felt upon the Cross (OLEVIAN, pp. 60–61). Christ's descent thus signifies on the one hand ("strictly") the reality of Christ's human death and of his burial, and on the other hand ("figuratively") the pang which Christ suffered in his soul, when he felt the punitive judgment of God, and especially the abyss of humiliation which met the Redeemer, by the Father's abandonment of his whole divine-human person for a time to the power of death.

What has just been given above is to be regarded as the conception of "Christ's descent" which gradually became the dominant one in the Reformed Church, as may be seen from what follows: POLANUS (VI, 21): "Christ descended into hell the moment when in the garden he struggled with the judgment and wrath of God and the horror of eternal death and ran the whole of him with bloody sweat; and was made a curse for us on the cross. And accordingly he descended living into hell and tasted the tortures of gehenna, though not however dead. Whence we understand that Christ descended into hell not locally, i.e., by quitting the body with the substance of the soul for the place appointed for the damned, because with it he entered paradise, it he committed into the Father's hands; but virtually, *secundum virtutem,* by the strength by which he conquered hell and its pains in himself for our good. True, in the *Apostolic Symbol* the article on Christ's descent into hell is placed after the article on the burial. But this is done in order that the things which happened outwardly to Christ, expressly in his body, might be recounted first, and only then the inward happenings to his soul."—MARCKIUS (XXI, 15): "We adopt the view which refers this article to the pains of hell (*a*) because it is fitting that more explicit mention should also be made of these also in the symbol, since they were truly borne by Christ; (*b*) they are correctly described in this phraseology Ps. 18, 5 (the cords of Sheol were round about me; the snares of death came upon me) 116, 3 (the cords of death compassed me and the pains of Sheol

gat hold upon me: I found trouble and sorrow) 1 Sam. 2, 6ff. (Hannah's
song); (c) and very trifling is the objection taken from the descent only
being recounted after the death and burial, since the pains preceded
them; neither ought we to be as anxious about the order of the Symbol,
which arose *successive* (in bits), as about its perfection; nor can these pains
be put anywhere better than in the last place, so that there may be an
advance from bodily evils to spiritual, from lighter to heavier, from those
in a word which followed each other in turn to those which intertwine
continuously."—COCCEIUS (*Summa. theol.* LX, 35): "Even although the
soul, by which the body was quickened, is said to be in Sheol as long
as the body, yet Christ's soul which is called πνεῦμα, spirit, was not
anywhere after death except in paradise as a deposit commended to God.
Nor did it depart into the gehenna promised to the wicked, nor to a
limbo to bring the patriarchs from it (for they too were in paradise),
nor yet to suffer in gehenna. For all things are consummated by the
death.—When it is said of Christ that he had descended into the lower
parts of the earth, it is enough to understand this both strictly of the
burial, and allegorically of his own sorrowfulness and agony."—Similarly HEIDEGGER (XVIII, 32): The words "he descended into hell"
have "either a strict or an analogical sense of the highest significance,
analogous to the Scriptures. Strictly Christ in his burial descended
truly into hell, since in Hebrew שׁאל signifies hell, i.e., the place to
look for one who is not visible, in Greek ᾅδης. However, according
to the usage of Scripture descent into hell means more even than burial,
since burial signifies the act of burying or funeration, descent into hell
the state of perseverance in that state under the lordship of death, in
which one removed by death can be seen. So Christ strictly descended
into hell, when he not only was buried but continued three days in the
sepulchre, so that by his death he exhibited the likeness of himself subdued
and triumphed over.—(34) Nor did the body suffer death only, but
still graver torments, those of hell, as due for sin, his soul endured:
without the endurance (*exantlatio*) of which our deliverance from the
power of the devil and hell would not have stood, as is proved by what
we said of his agonies in the garden and on the cross."—BURMANN (V,
xxi, 13–14): "The due meaning of these words may be laid down as
either literal or metaphorical; the literal denotes Christ's descent into
the grave or his three days' continuance in that state under the lordship
of death. 14: Analogically also and metaphorically by these words may
be denoted the tortures and pains of Christ borne both in the garden and
on the cross, by which in an improper sense, he descended into hell."

The LEIDEN SYNOPSIS (XXVII, 25–32) summarises the manifold conceptions of the dogma peculiar to the Reformed Church and notes

in regard to them: "30:—Some would have it that in this article is contained an ἀνακεφαλαίωσις (recapitulation) of everything that is told about Christ's outward humiliation: what had previously been put in separate articles is so to speak compressed into a strait at the outlet, in order that the whole state of humiliation may be indicated from the first step to the last. This same interpretation is embraced by those who take hell to mean death and descent into hell to mean descent into death. 31.—others sic! understand by hell the state of death and by the article on the descent that by which Christ underwent the state of death, and therefore they note that Scripture never asserts that Christ rose from the grave but ἐκ νεκροῦ, to signify that he who had formerly been among the dead had not always been in the state of the dead, but had at some time ceased to be dead. Nor far removed from their meaning are those who refer this article to the three days' sojourn, which, they insist, differs from the burial and contributed a separate benefit and so has deserved a separate article in the symbol, in which Christ had a full taste of the baseness of our bodies (St. Paul calls it a sowing 1 Cor. 15. 43), unless the difference is insisted upon, that the state of the dead is referred to the body and to the soul so far as it has been separated from the body, but the sojourn in the grave to the body only. 32: If the coherence of the articles be considered and if the order of events is recounted exactly as in the Gospel narrative, these latter senses have very great probability, especially as amongst the first and strict meanings of this phrase is that of the state of death, as was said at the beginning. But neither is the interpretation commonly received in public catechisms less true or apt, by which by the descent into hell are understood the pangs of hell and the gravity of God's wrath and, as it were, the desertion which Christ experienced in his soul, as we have expounded above. Nor is it inappropriate to unite these two descents, as some do: each of them belongs to Christ's extreme humiliation and has a foundation in language; also the doctrine of each is true and necessary, as is abundantly clear from what has been said."

Similarly MASTRICHT (V, xiii, 5): "What pray is this descent? Setting aside in their own place the opinions of the heterodox, there are among the orthodox (1) those who restrict it to burial, so that in the symbol it may be the exegesis of the article on burial; so our BEZA on Ac. 2. 26-27 (Therefore my heart was glad and my tongue rejoiced; moreover my soul shall dwell in hope: because thou wilt not leave my soul in Hades neither wilt thou give up thy Holy One to see corruption Ps. 16). This does not satisfy others (a) because not only does it import a tautology into the very accurate brevity of the symbol, but it also (b) tries to explain what is clear by the more obscure. (2) Others restrict it to the sufferings of Christ's soul, like CALVIN, with several of the Reformed: this does not please others for this twofold reason (1) because these sufferings of soul point to his death, which had been dealt with in preceding parts of the symbol and so weighs down the symbol with a tautology, (b) because it puts the sufferings of the soul after the burial and thereby upsets the order of the symbol. Hence others (3) will not have the burial of the pains of mind signified by this descent, but the state and lordship of death, under which he was during the three days of burial. So SOHNIUS on the Augsburg, PERKINS on the Symbol, AMESIUS, the two Catechisms, larger and shorter, of the WESTMINSTER SYNOD and others. What if, to reconcile the apparently dissident opinions of the orthodox we conjoin the subordinates or co-ordinates and count a threefold descent of Christ, of the body into the grave, of the soul into the state of hell, of the whole Christ into the power and lordship of death ? (1) Scripture by the word descent is not only wont to designate three things, but distinctly assigns them to Christ, as will be shown more clearly by what is to follow. (2) In this way also the descent and the profundity of the humiliation will thereby receive more ampli-fication and recognition; and (3) the symbol itself will be more conven-iently cleared of ταυτολογία and ἀμεθοδία (tautology and lack of method)." For the conceptions of the *descensus* given in the older Ger-man-Reformed theology cf. HEPPE, *Dogmatik des deutschen Protest.* II, p. 175-177.

5.—From the state of humiliation Christ passed to that of exaltation, and in such wise that the humiliation which Christ had voluntarily undertaken was the reason for his subsequent exaltation. —HEIDEGGER (XVIII, 39): "The emptying and humiliation unto the Cross was produced for the sake of the loftiness and glory of the name given." WOLLEB of course (85) is of the mind that "Christ obtained this exaltation by his obedience not as by merit but as by a way and means".—On the other hand most say like BURMANN (II, xv, 14) that: "since this exaltation was due the Son in terms of the pact, his obedience and submission was of the nature of true merit strictly so called, and it came first for his own glory not only ante-cedently, as some would have it, but also meritoriously."

6.—Christ's exaltation is his state in which after his humiliation he is raised up to the highest ineffable glory, that we might be exalted in him" (POLAN VI, 22). Like the humiliation the exaltation of Christ's whole person also belongs to the Logos made man. Christ's divinity was not glorified by an essential exaltation imparted to it, but only so far as ("by the disclosure of majesty") it laid aside the assumed servant-form and made its full majesty known. And the human nature was exalted

" by the laying aside of the infirmities assumed"), it not only became free of all infirmities which belonged to it previously, but ("by glorification, by the taking up of gifts or charisms") also gained the highest glorification in body and soul of which the creature is capable at all. Christ's body became immortal, free from suffering and equipped with divine glory, and Christ's soul received gifts of knowledge and will, which indeed thoroughly possess the character of creaturely gifts (so that e.g. the all-knowledge of Christ's humanity was exercised only in the form of discursive thinking), but which are quite incapable of higher perfecting.

WOLLEB 85 : "The exaltation of the person of Christ the God-man belongs to both natures.—According to the human nature he was exalted by the laying aside of the infirmities he had assumed and by the securing of gifts which he had not possessed previously: for he attained to such perfection of body and soul as the creature could contain at its height.— According to the divine nature he was exalted not by the accession of any dignity belonging to it by itself, $\kappa\alpha\theta$' $\dot{\epsilon}\alpha\nu\tau\dot{o}\nu$, but by the manifestation of his majesty which was formerly shut up under the form of a servant".—LEIDEN SYNOPSIS ((XXVIII, 4-6): "The infirmities which Christ laid aside by rising again are of two kinds, both those to which human nature was subject from the first creation down to this animal life, with which the Apostle deals 1 Cor. 15. 44 (it is sown a natural body; it is raised a spiritual body. If there is a natural body, there is also a spiritual body) and Scripture elsewhere, and those by which as our sponsor on account of our sins he submitted himself in a peculiar sense, tempted in all things like us, yet without sin, Heb. 4. 15. Nevertheless that is why we deny that Christ laid aside either the essence or the essential properties of human nature by his resurrection, any more than we shall lay them aside after this life, when our bodies shall be conform to his glorious body Phil. 3. 21. After the resurrection Christ himself also testified to his disciples that his body consisted of flesh and bones and was exposed to sight and touch Lk. 24. 39. So we see how seriously they err, who state that after his resurrection Christ resumed a body lacking all quantity and dimension and passing like a spirit through other bodies without them yielding or opening up. And how much more gravely do they err, who claim that it is present in many places simultaneously (a thing not conceded even to spirits) by reproduction. So our latter-day *Jesuits* talk."—POLANUS (VI, 22 : "As regards his human nature Christ's exaltation has two parts. The first is the laying aside of all infirmities, all of which Christ has assumed with the human nature (sin excepted), as his office demanded. Such infirmities are hunger and thirst, weariness, pain, disgrace, negative ignorance of the last day and of other matters, passiblity, mortality, etc. All these he simply set aside, so that now he is no longer liable to them. The second part is the glorification of the human nature in both body and soul. Christ's body is rendered glorious, so that it is and remains eternally incorruptible, impassible, immortal, increased in strength and agility, glowing with brightness and glory heavenly and divine, i.e. with the appropriate body of God. But the endowments of its soul are increased and perfected to the utmost perfection which can befall a created nature, whether we regard reason or will. As for reason, Christ in glory already knows with his human mind all that in his humility for our sakes he was ignorant of. He now knows the moment of the last judgment. There is nothing so difficult, so minute in all the works of God, i.e. his own works, past, present or future, which is not to hand any moment he wishes, and as often as he wishes, to know and think with his human reason, as if it had been offered to his eyes and bodily senses. But all this and anything else that can be mentioned he knows and thinks in distinct and successive acts of thought, whether ideas or intelligible species, according to the essential character of a created mind. But this omniscience is vastly different from the increate wisdom of God, by which God views Himself and all His works and those of others by one eternal, immutable act of His own accord. As to will, all virtues have received such increase in it as can enter into a creature.— Briefly, the endowments of both Christ's body and his soul are more numerous and greater and more perfect than all other creatures could receive. But although they are above nature they yet are not counter to nature, and they do not remove or destroy the attributes and essentials of human and created nature, in order that our flesh and David's seed may reign in heavenly glory for ever".

7.—This exaltation did not at once make itself known in Christ's body, but was first completed after his return home to the Father.—BUCAN (XXVI, 18): "How did Christ rise?—Wholly glorious (1) in respect of divinity, because formerly concealed in Christ it manifested itself and was fully revealed; (2) in respect of humanity, because, having laid aside the infirmities and accidental attributes with which Christ had been born, adversities and all wretchedness, needs for food and drink, sleep and the like, it was adorned to the degree of perfection with new qualities but created, over and above the common order of nature, such as in the soul wisdom, joy, i.e., in the body incorruptibility, refinement, agility, clarity and glow thanks to the power of indwelling Deity, and was exalted far above all creatures, while preserving the essential attributes, so that his body even now in glory is according to the ordinary dispensation visible, palpable, organic, finite and circumscribed, as Christ himself teaches after the resurrection (Lk. 24, 39).—HEIDEGGER (XVIII, 47): "Nor was that glory with which Christ endued his body when it was made alive by the resurrection from the dead, consummated on earth in order that he might be called glorious in the same sense in which he has been carried above the heavens as σῶμα δόξης Phil, 3. 21. For although Christ could not die any more, being justified from sin, having died once for sin and being now alive to God (on account of the life, will and glory of God) Rom. 6. 7, 9, 10 (he that hath died is justified from sin in knowing that Christ being raised from the dead dieth no more; death hath no more dominion over him. The death that he died, he died unto sin once (for all), but the life that he liveth he liveth unto God), and having been raised by the Father from the dead, he was no longer to return gravewards to corruption Ac. 13. 34 (as concerning that he raised him up from the dead, now no more to return from corruption, he hath spoken on this wise, I will give you the holy and sure blessings of David) and had no further need to be offered for sin Heb. 9. 26 (else must he often have suffered since the foundation of the world; but now once at the end of the ages hath he been manifested to put away sin by the sacrifice of himself) 10. 18 (where remission of (sins) is, there is no more offering for sin) — Yet the glorification of Christ's body made immortal and incorruptible, began in the resurrection, made progress in the ascension, but reached its peak and crown at length in the session at God's right hand in heaven. As long as Christ moved about on earth after the resurrection and held intercourse with his most beloved, God was so far indulgent to the frailties of his disciples, that the glory of the body did not radiate visibly."

8.—The three stages of Christ's exaltation are the resurrection from the dead, the ascension into heaven and the session at the Father's right hand. This triple exaltation was imparted to Christ not to complete his work of redemption (which did not need fulfilment), but in order that it might be revealed, glorified and appropriated to the elect, and in order to uphold Christ's name thereby, which is above every name, so that all lips should confess that he is the Lord to the glory of God the Father.

The resurrection is the first stage of Christ's exaltation. The Son by his own divine power requickened his body, which in death he had not abandoned, but of which he had not availed himself while it lay in the grave, in order to be active through it as through his instrument.— COCCEIUS (*Summ. Theol.* LXII, 11): "The first stage in exaltation is the resurrection of the body, not the descent into gehenna to triumph there or to the subterranean limbo of gehenna, in which the souls of the patriarchs were, to bring them out.—12. Moreover he rose according to the body. He had also been dead and buried in the body alone. The soul was alive in Paradise.—13: On rising he resumed the body, not because he had ceased to have it united to himself, but because he had ceased to act through it as through an instrument. For even while the body lay in the tomb he was actually said to have been buried.—14: Moreover he resumed it by power Jn. 10, 18 (No one taketh it away from me, but I have laid it down of myself. I have power to lay it down, and I have power to take it again. This commandment received I of the Father), namely by his own power.—15: None the less it is often said that the Father raised him, not because the power by which he rose was not the Son's, but because the resurrection of the Son is (1) the proof by which that dead man was proved to be God's Son and was justified—(2) the proof of the judicial pronouncement by which the redeemed are acquitted in him."

Reformed dogmaticians toy with the thought that the raising from the dead of the Logos really become man is to be thought of pretty much in the same way as the rousing of man dead in sins to spiritual life. This is why they regard the former as also the common work of the persons of the Trinity. A real cause of the polemic against the *Socinians* and against their contesting the essential deity of Christ was that they preferred to prove that the *causa resurrectionis* was the almighty will of the Logos, and that accordingly the resurrection of Christ was a self-arousing. Hence they all teach like Cocceius, e.g. Bucan (XXVI, 3-4): "By what power did Christ rise ?—Not by any precarious power or power of created nature, but by his own proper power of Deity Jn. 10. 18. Hence his own true Deity is proved by his own resurrection Rom. 1. 4, (declared to be the Son of God with power, according to the spirit of holiness, by the resurrection of the dead). Nevertheless because the *opera ad extra Trinitatis sunt indivisa*, this resurrection taken in an active sense is attributed both to Christ, and to Father and H. Spirit, Eph. 1. 20 (which he wrought in Christ, when he raised him from the dead, and made him to sit at his right hand in the heavenly places). —Did Christ's humanity co-operate in the resurrection ?—According to his divine nature Christ brought about his own resurrection. He suffered because of the infirmity of the flesh. And he lives because of the power of God. But he rose strictly according to the human nature, which obeyed the resuscitating of Deity and moved according to His will and power. Hence there exists a common ἀποτέλεσμα or thing effected on the part of both natures, namely death swallowed up in victory, 1 Cor. 15. 55, and the resurrection is assigned to the whole Christ; but in the active sense according to the Spirit of sanctification, in the passive sense according to the flesh."

9.—By this first exaltation of Christ (i.e., the resurrection), (1) the certainty and glory of the satisfaction provided by him is attested, and (2) it is itself a practical declaring righteous of all those who are aroused to faith in Christ. Just as by giving the Son to death the Father actually condemned all our sins in him, the Father also by raising Christ up from the dead, acquitted Christ of our sin-guilt and us in Christ (OLEVIAN, pp. 76–77). So Christ's resurrection is our righteousness, because God further regards us in the perfection in which Christ rose. Whereas the Father regarded us previously in the dying Son as sinners, He sees us now in the resurrected Son as righteous; or rather; whereas previously He regarded the Son in our sins as a sinner, He regards Him now, and us in Him, as the person which He is, and which He is not for Himself but for us (OLEVIAN, p. 80). At the same time the fulfilment of the first vow undertaken by Christ is guaranteed by his resurrection, and likewise also the fulfilment of the second vow, that he would renew in us the complete glory and blessedness in the divine image. As Christ rose not only from death but also from the pangs of death, and thereby attested that death and the punishment merited by us of God-forsaken-ness was conquered by him, he also makes those whose sins he has atoned for free from the wages of sins, and gives them the achieved victory of life and the gifts of perfect communion with God (OLEVIAN, p. 87). At the same time we are assured by the resurrection of Christ, that we may likewise hope for our bodily resurrection, in the same way as we have received in Christ spiritual resurrection from the death of sins.

LEIDEN SYNOPSIS (XXVIII, 8): "The ends of Christ's resurrection—they may also be called its effects and fruits—are many and various. (1) In order that the very full satisfaction achieved for our sins and the restoration of eternal righteousness might be attested by this victory of his over death Rom. 4. 25 (delivered up for our trespasses, raised for our justification) 1 Cor. 15. 17, 57. ("if Christ hath not been raised . . . ye are yet in your sins . . . But thanks be to God which giveth us the victory . . . ") ; (2) In order that as by the power of his death our old man has been mortified, so too by the power of his resurrection the new man might live again in us and the image of God be restored Rom. 6. 4 (buried . . . into death; that like as Christ was raised . . . so we also might walk in newness of life). (3) In order that his resurrection might be the most sure pledge and cause of our future resurrection 1 Cor. 15. 22 (in Christ shall all be made alive). In short, in order that by his resurrection he might open up access to himself and to the rest of the offices to be performed on our behalf, by which as our prophet, intercessor and king he might apply the energy of his death and sacrifice to us for ever Rom. 14. 9 (that he might be Lord of both the dead and the living.—(XXVII, 22): Hence it is easy to differentiate on the end of Christ's death. It is twofold in constitution. (1) The

expiation of our sins by a satisfaction of infinite value and cost; (2) the
mortification and abolition of the body of sin which is signified by his
burial, made partakers in which believers dead in sin are buried along
with Christ, that they may rise again to new life Rom. 6. 4 (buried
unto death; that like as Christ was raised—so we also might walk in
newness of life) Col. 2. 12 (having been buried with him in baptism,
wherein we were also raised with him through faith in the working of
God, who raised him from the dead".—WOLLEB 36: "Apart from the
general one mentioned above the aim of the resurrection is the certainty
of our resurrection too, both from the death of sin and from bodily
death."

10.—The second stage in the exaltation of the Redeemer is his ascension
into heaven. The Son of course had lived in heaven from eternity.
Hence we must insist that the ascension is not to be asserted of the Son
in and for himself, but of the Son become flesh. The Son of God become
man was raised up in the ascension, after he had conquered sin and
death, to the place where as man he had not yet previously been (OLEVIAN,
p. 109). And the ascension in the strictest sense of the word is to be
thought of as a spatial bodily event, as the raising of the God-man from
a lower to a higher place, so that from the ascension of the Lord onward
until his return to earth Christ's humanity is no longer present [i.e.,
on earth].

BUCAN (XXVII, 2–3): "What is to be understood by the ascension?—Not
the change or μεταβολή of one condition into another or its disappearance,
but strictly a φορά, i.e., a movement from place to place, and in fact from a
lower to a higher; for those who move from a lower place to a higher are said
to ascend.—Is this usage strict or figurative?—Strict of course; this is plainly
assured by the different phrases used by the evangelists by way of ἐξήγησι:
Mk. 16. 19 (was received up and sat down) Lk. 24. 51 (was carried
up)".—RIISSEN (XII, 34, 1): "Did Christ's ascension take place strictly
by a local movement from lower places to the highest heaven of the
blessed or metaphorically by disappearing? The former is affirmed, the
latter denied, against the *Lutherans*.—Those among the *Lutherans* who
assign ubiquity to Christ's body, in order that they may more easily
raise the proof they seek from Christ's ascension to prove the circumscription of Christ's body, say that Christ did not truly and strictly ascend
but only figuratively, inasmuch as he withdrew his visible presence from
the world, although it still remains invisibly in the world. And the
heaven to which he ascended, they maintain, is not the highest or third
heaven, but the blessedness and kingship of God which is everywhere.
So their idea is that the heaven to which he ascended was not a

particular bodily place set above the visible heavens and separated from this earth by local distance and is defined not so much by any local situation as by joy and glory from the H. Spirit. We insist that Christ was borne locally, visibly and bodily from earth to the third heaven above the visible heavens; not by the mere withdrawal of his visible presence and familiar way of life, but by a true and local translation of his human nature, where it is to dwell until the day of judgment: so that although he is always present with us by his grace and Spirit and divinity, he is no longer with us by the bodily presence of his flesh".— LEIDEN SYNOPSIS (XXVIII, 14): "The manner of this ascent was true and bodily."—TURRETIN (XXIII, xviii): "Was Christ's ascension made strictly by local movement from lower places to the highest heaven of the blessed, or metaphorically by disappearance? The former is affirmed, the latter denied, against the *Lutherans*".—BUCAN (XXVII, 5): "The whole Christ, then, really ascended, because the same Christ is true God and true man; but in respect of his humanity he ascended strictly and locally with his own body from earth to heaven, just as he had truly and by local movement (and not more miraculously) previously ascended from the grave to the land of the living."

11.—By the heaven into which Christ has gone up is to be understood the place of the highest and loftiest glory of God, which (above the air-layer enveloping the earth, as well as above the sphere of the heavenly world-bodies) is the dwelling-place of the blessed spirits, the highest (third) heaven: but not a mere condition (*status gloriosus, coelestis*) or the nature of the divine majesty, which must therefore be conceived of as a spatiality distinct from the state of faulty revelation of the glory of God. —HEIDEGGER (XVIII, 59): "The heaven to which Christ ascended is not that lower one which surrounds our heads, but the highest one, the heaven of heavens, which for St. Paul is called third 2 Cor. 12. 2, for the prophets the throne of God Is. 66. 1 (the heaven is my throne); in which is our Father Mt. 6. 9. He crossed the heavens; the first, in which the air is, and the second in which the stars, sun and planets are Heb. 4. 15 (who hath passed through the heavens), and so was made higher than the lower heavens which we can behold Heb. 7. 26 (made higher than the heavens). And this highest heaven is the place and dwelling of Christ and the blessed." "In my Father's house are many mansions".—Further, that the heaven to which Christ ascended is a place is also proved by other things. "Ἄνω is *sursum* Jn. 11. 41 (lifted up his eyes) Ac. 2. 19 (the heaven above . . . the earth beneath) [from Joel 2], Col. 3. 2 (the things that are above: the things that are on the earth). Consequently ascension is called ἀνάστασις, ἀνάληψις.

And this heaven receives Christ as a throne a king, till the time of the restoration of all things (Ac. 3, 21). For he was made higher, higher than the visible heavens Heb. 4. 14; 7. 26; Eph, 4, 10 (far above all the heavens)."—MASTRICHT (V, xvi, 13) adduces the following proofs. "(1) Scripture always speaks of heaven as a certain fixed place Dt. 26. 15 (look down from thy holy habitation) Ps. 2. 4 (sitteth in the heavens) 33. 13 (the Lord looketh down) Is. 66. 1ff. (heaven is my throne), clearly distinguished from the earth and other places. (2) The heaven to which Christ ascended is marked as a definite place, which Christ should occupy Ac. 3. 21, whence he is said to have ascended ὑπεράνω πάντων οὐρανῶν Eph. 4. 10; he was made ὑψηλότερος τῶν οὐράνων, i.e., the lower ones Heb. 7. 26, διεληλυθὼς τοὺς οὐράνους, Heb. 4. 14; (3) This same heaven of Christ's is designated by such synonyms as could not fail to denote some particular place distinct from all others, e.g., it is called the Father's house Jn. 14. 2, highest heaven Heb. 1. 3, the heaven of heavens 1 Kings 8. 27, the third heaven 2 Cor. 12. 2, the heavenly Jerusalem Gal. 4. 26, paradise Lk. 23. 43, the place of angels Mt. 6. 9–10, from which we look for Christ Phil. 3. 20: (4) the hypothesis on which our adversaries' error is built or claims to be fixed, viz., the essential presence of Christ's flesh in the symbols of the H. Supper, the omnipresence conferred by the human nature's *communicatio idiomatum* have been or need to be refuted elsewhere: (5) especially: the distinction between κλῆσις and χρῆσις in omnipresence, by which he could be present or not present at his whim, since the omnipresence of God and Christ is the same. I shall add that (6) Scripture nowhere records that Christ ascended visibly and locally only as far as the clouds: it rather definitely attests the opposite in all the passages adduced for the 2nd and 3rd reasons".—PICTET (VIII, xviii, 6): "The heaven to which he was borne is not God Himself nor heavenly glory and beatitude, but is that third heaven, the abode of the blessed, the holy place not made with hands, Heb. 9. 24."

12.—Christ's ascension is also a confirmation of the covenant of grace, since Christ (as the Logos become flesh) has thereby entered upon the heavenly heritage in his brethren's name, in order to impart to his elect from heaven itself the first fruits of the Spirit, as the sure pledge of their future inheritance.—LEIDEN SYNOPSIS (XXVIII, 20): "The fruits of Christ's ascension are many and great. By his entry the heavenly holy place was opened to us Jn. 14. 2 ("many mansions"); Heb. 9. 8. ("holy, heavenly place.") The hope of our future inheritance was most fully confirmed upon our heads and we were placed with him in heaven Eph. 2. 6 (raise us up . . . to sit with Him in the heavenly places). The outpouring of the H. Spirit was obtained for us Jn. 16, 7, and in short by his power our hearts and affections were borne upwards to heaven, so that we should no more seek the things that are on earth, but the things that are in heaven Col. 3. 1–3."—KECKERMANN 363: "It was thereupon necessary for Christ too to ascend into heaven, that he might inform the Church with the necessary gifts through the H. Spirit."

13.—The third stage in Christ's glorification is his exaltation to the right hand of the Father. "Christ's session at the Father's right hand is not the equation of Christ's human nature with the Father in reigning, really communicated to it with equal power and majesty. It is the highest stage of the exaltation of Christ the God-man, since he has been placed in the heavens above all angels and so above all creatures, in order that he may now perform in glory the office of prophet, priest and king" (POLANUS VI, 26). The figurative expression of "sitting at the right hand of the Father" denotes exaltation to participation in God's majesty, i.e., Christ's exaltation to participation in the glory and honour and in the power and might of the Father.—LEIDEN SYNOPSIS (XXVIII, 22–23): "Strictly he could not be received at God's right hand in this place, since God is Spirit and consequently does not have flesh and bones. But is it taken metaphorically for that highest degree of glorification to which Christ was raised by the Father after his passion and ascension into heaven.—Moreover this metaphor is taken from the custom of kings and princes, who when sitting on their thrones or giving law before their judgment seats, are wont to place on their right hand those whom they give the highest honour after themselves or whom they make sharers in their kingship as is customary in all princedoms."—BUCAN (XXVIII, 5): "Is it strictly or metaphorically that Christ is said to sit at the Father's right hand?—Not strictly. It by no means suits His Deity, and although it may be accommodated to the second bodily nature with a strict meaning, the glorious body in heaven is not to be thought of as constantly sitting or moving or standing, although it is truly circumscribed and local. And God's right hand must be taken much less strictly, since God is incorporeal, as was said."—RIISSEN (XII, 31): "Session at God's right hand may be understood not strictly and literally, but figuratively and metaphorically, to indicate the supreme dignity and command of Christ; the metaphor being taken from the custom of kings and magnates who are wont to place on their right hands those to whom they grant the degree of government nearest to themselves both in honour and in power. As to the nearest degree of honour, this phrase is understandable 1 Kings, 2. 19, where Solomon when about to do his mother singular honour places her on his right. As to the *imperium* or administration of the kingship it is used in Mt. 20, 21, where the mother of the sons of Zebedee asks that her sons may sit on the right and left of Christ in his kingdom, i.e., perform the chief functions (*munia*). Hence by session at the right hand two things chiefly are indicated: (1) the height of majesty and glory, by which he is highly exalted by God and has received a name above every name Phil. 2. 9–10; (2) the height of rule, which he exercises powerfully over all creatures and which he shows especially in the government and defence of the Church."—HEIDEGGER (XVIII, 63): "To sit here is the sign of honour and power; and session at the right hand denotes the honour and power by which a man rejoices in his degree of order or in communion with someone else." HEIDEGGER gives the following references for Christ's session on God's right hand: Phil. 2. 9 (wherefore also God highly exalted him, and gave unto him the name which is above every name) Mt. 28. 18 (all authority hath been given me in heaven and on earth) Ac. 2. 33 (being therefore by the right hand of God exalted and having received of the Father the promise of the H. Ghost, he hath poured forth this which ye see and hear) Jn. 17. 5 (glorify thou me with thine own self with the glory which I had with thee before the world was) Lk. 24. 26 (Behoved it not the Christ to suffer these things and to enter into the glory?) Ac. 2. 36 (let all the house of Israel therefore know assuredly, that God hath made him both Lord and Christ, this Jesus whom ye crucified) Eph. 1. 20–22 (which God wrought in Christ when He raised him from the dead, and made him to sit at his right hand in the heavenly places, far above all rule and authority and power and dominion and every name that is named, not only in this world but also in that which is to come; and he put all things in subjection under his feet, and gave him to be head over all things in the Church)."

14.—This exaltation was of course only improperly assigned to Christ's divine nature; it possessed this from eternity, and only now manifests it perfectly. On the other hand the majesty was quite properly given to Christ's humanity now for the first time, since it was exalted above all creation eternally. As hitherto the Logos as such was equal to the Father from eternity in majesty and glory, so now his humanity also entered into real possession of this divine majesty. And just as the Logos as such exercises "natural kingship" from eternity along with the Father and the H. Spirit, so now the Logos become man administers "economic kingship" with divine majesty and power.

LEIDEN SYNOPSIS (XXVIII, 24-25) : "Thus this session of Christ at the right hand of the Father does not signify strictly that glory and natural kingship which was common to the Son with the Father from eternity (on these terms the H. Spirit also would sit at God's right hand), but the economic and voluntary kingship, in which as the God-man and our Mediator he is appointed by the Father to gather his Church and to defend it. Hence the apostle Paul asserts that all things were put in subjection to him by the Father, except him who did subject all things unto him, 1 Cor. 15. 27. Therefore Christ's session at the Father's right hand embraces these two points : first, the glory and supreme honour with which he received the name above every name, and was borne far above angels or any other creatures and became their heir and head, as the Apostle clearly explains this Eph. 1. 20-22 (504) Phil. 2. 9-11 ; Heb. 2. 7-8 (Ps. 8. 5-6) and elsewhere ; whence it is called Heb. 1. 3 the right hand of the μεγαλοσύνη or majesty, Heb. 8. 1 the right hand of the throne of the μεγαλοσύνη) and Heb. 12. 2 (the right hand of the throne of God)".—BUCAN (XXVIII, 13) : " But did he always reign with the Father and so sit perpetually at the Father's right hand ?—Reign He did, but as God, bare, without flesh, clothed upon with only his own glory, before He began to assume humanity. But afterwards in time as God clothed in flesh, after the completion of the time of exinanition, he began to sit at the Father's right hand, i.e. to reign in heaven and on earth. So he accepted the kingship which he had before, accepted it (I say) in respect of manifestation, as in Scripture a thing is said to happen when it is manifested."—Observe the following question and answer : " When he did begin to sit at the Father's right hand ?—By rights from the very first moment of the hypostatic union, actually or *de facto* (as they say) after his suffering, resurrection and ascension. Scripture and the Apostles' Creed so distinguish these articles that the resurrection and ascension into heaven are followed by the session at the Father's right hand."

15.—Hence the expression "session at the Father's right hand" signifies pre-eminently that the Logos become man now rules as eternal high-priest and king of his kingdom everything in heaven and on earth before the Father's face (OLEVIAN p. 122). Only by Christ's unceasing activity in his high-priestly intercession before the Father's face have the elect the comfort, that Christ's sacrifice has for them an eternal validity and effectiveness, and that their prayers are heard by the Father.—LEIDEN SYNOPSIS (XXVIII, 33-34) : " This intercession of Christ in heaven at God's right hand is not the one and only act of Christ the priest, as the godless *Socinus* lyingly suggests, but one of the priestly acts by which, after offering himself on earth as a propitiatory victim for our sins outside the heavenly holy-place, he intervenes in heaven itself before the Father's face, and that against Satan and his tools and on behalf of the Church and her members, according to the distinct type of each as set before us Zech. 3. 2ff. (the Branch passage).—This intercession or intervention consists moreover of three parts : (1) Christ brought his own propitiatory offering into the very holy-place of heaven, to sanctify it for us, and there he appears before the face of God on our behalf Heb. 9. 23-24 (It was necessary that the copies of the things in the heavens should be cleansed with these ; but the heavenly things themselves with better sacrifices than these. For Christ entered not into a holy place made with hands, like in pattern to the true ; but into heaven itself, now to appear before the face of God for us) ; (2) by his burning will and desire as he had done before on earth Jn. 17. 11,15,24 (And I am no more in the world, and these are in the world, and I come to Thee . . . Holy Father, keep them in thy name which thou hast given me, that they may be one even as we are.— I pray not that thou shouldest take them from the world, but that thou shouldest keep them from the evil one.—Father, that which thou hast given me, I will that where I am, there they also may be with me ; that they may behold my Glory, which thou hast given me ; for thou lovedst me before the foundation of the world), so also in heaven with the Father he demands the application of the power and efficacy of his death to us for salvation, as may be seen Zech. 1. 12 (O Lord of hosts, how long wilt thou not have mercy on Jerusalem and on the cities of Judah, against which thou hast had indignation these three score and ten years ?) Jn. 14. 16 (And I will pray the Father, and he shall give you another Comforter, that he may be with you for ever) also Ac. 2. 33 (Being therefore by the right hand of God exalted, and having received of the Father the promise of the H. Ghost, he hath poured forth this which ye see and hear). In short by his merit and longing he renders our prayers poured forth in his name pleasing and acceptable to God the Father Jn. 14. 6, 13 (I am the way, the truth and the life : no man cometh unto the Father, but by me—whatsoever ye shall ask in my name, that will I do, that the Father may be glorified in the Son) 1 Jn. 2. 1-2 (My little children, these things write I unto you, that ye may not sin. And if any man sin, we have an Advocate (Comforter) with the Father, Jesus Christ the righteous, and he is the propitiation for our sins, and not only for ours but also for the whole world.)".

16.—Otherwise [i.e. failing this intercession and demand] even the elect with their sins would have had to become liable to eternal damnation. Only because Christ rules his Church by his H. Spirit and everything is subject to him in heaven and on earth, are believers sure that they are kept in faith and in grace to the end (OLEVIAN, p. 124), and that Christ not only supplies the entire Church with the manifold gifts of his Spirit, but also imparts to each separate member as many gifts as are necessary for the glorification of the Head of the Church, for the edification of the whole Body and for the edification of the actual individual member (OLEVIAN p. 139).

To be rejected are all sorts of false conceptions of the exaltation of Christ to the Father's right hand, which for the believer essentially burden the faithful trust which reposes on this fact. Above all it must not be assumed that in heaven Christ is bound to the limitations of space. Of course Christ exists in heaven spatially in a circumscribed way, since a corporeality cannot be thought of non-spatially ; by this however he is not prevented from filling heaven and earth with his divine power.— BUCAN (XXVII, 15) : " If Christ ascended above all mundane heavens, is his body no longer in a place because (as *Aristotle* proves in *De coelo* I) there is no place above all the heavens ?—Although not every place is of the same kind and such as is described by *Aristotle* in the Physics, yet where there is a body there is space by which the body is necessarily contained, according to *Augustine's* famous saying: " Remove the spaces of places from bodies and they will be nowhere, and because they will be nowhere, they will cease to exist." Therefore this space Scripture calls a place Jn. 14. 2, I go to prepare a place for you. But even to Aristotle we oppose the authority of Christ.—16 : Then is Christ's ascension at variance with what he says Mt. 28. 20 : I shall be with you even unto the consummation of the age ?—It is not. *Augustine* says : " He both departed and is here ; he will come again and has not deserted us ; for he bore his body in heaven, he laid not his majesty aside in the world." Hence Christ's words are to be understood of his divinity, which is always present everywhere, and cannot be contained in any fixed local spot, since it always contains everything itself, but particularly in the matter of his *praesentia* ἐνεργητική in the minds of believers, but not by the presence of the humanity which is finite and circumscribed, according to which he says Jn. 12. 8 : "The poor ye have always with you, but me ye shall not have always." And Mt. 24. 23 he foretold that antichrists would say, Lo here, and Lo there. And Paul bids us shew forth the Lord's death, till he come 1 Cor. 11. 26.—What then is the meaning of Paul's statement Eph. 4. 10, that Christ ascended above all heavens, that he might fill all things?—that by pouring forth his gifts and benefits he might gather the whole Church consisting of Jews and Gentiles. For such is the meaning of the word "fill". And this answers to what I said before from Ps. 68. 19, he ascended and gave gifts unto men, the figure being derived from princes, who after gaining a victory testify their generosity to the whole nation either by a solemn banquet or by largesse. Or understand it in the way *Bernard* translates it, That he might fill up all things, which of course were foretold and were required for our salvation."

17.—Besides, space is not a limitation for him, by which he would be fettered, since on the contrary he can be where he likes at any moment. —POLAN (VI, 26) : " Christ's session at the right hand of God the Father is not his being shut up in heaven and tied down to a fixed place. Christ moves most freely and by will in heaven and rules in the fatherly name, being raised above all other creatures. Nor is he enclosed in a certain place or places or as if within barriers (*in cancellis*) : at any moment he is everywhere and in the way it pleases him according to his majesty."

18.—But just as definitely the view is to be rejected, that by Christ's exaltation to the right hand of the Father his human nature is simply extended over space and has become omnipresent. On the one hand on this assumption the essential bodiliness of Christ's humanity is abolished ; a spaceless, omnipresent, infinite body is not a body at all. And so Christ's return to earth, which is promised us, is hereby reduced to a merely apparent fact and to a completely meaningless event.—HEIDEGGER (XVIII, 70) : " Nor must we conceal the errors of those who defend the omnipresence of Christ's flesh against even his session at God's right hand, at least so far as they make its χρῆσις of none effect.—The honour, the dignity of Christ's person and natures is not the same as ubiquity, since the former is an axiom of the person and natures, the latter the attribute of essential Deity. And since omnipresence destroys flesh and so is also derogatory to the honour of the flesh, which is not changed in the session at God's right hand, it cannot belong to the honour and glory of Christ. If God's right hand is also flesh, because he sits at His right hand, it is rendered omnipresent. Besides, too, we have already affirmed that Christ sits at God's right hand according to his humanity. So God's right hand is not simply Deity. And so neither does sitting at God's right hand impart anything divine as regards His nature and attributes. Further Scripture eloquently testifies that Christ sits at God's right hand, not everywhere but only in heaven and that it was also for this that he ascended into heaven Eph. 1. 20 (... made him to sit at his right hand in the heavenly *places*) Heb. 8. 1 (we have such an high priest, who sat down on the right hand of the throne of the Majesty in the heavens) Jn. 14. 3 (and if I go and prepare a place for you, I come again, and will receive you unto myself ; that where I am, there ye may be also)."—MARESIUS (IX, 59) : " Nor has Christ's session at God's right hand to do with position and whereness (*ubietas*), as ubiquitarians would vainly infer πανταχουσίαν (everywhereness) from it. By it is signified the

height of his glory, the metaphor being taken from kings, who place at their right hand those whom they honour most highly after themselves."
—LEIDEN SYNOPSIS (XXVIII, 30) : "As for the fact that certain ubiquitarians contend that by this session at God's right hand Christ's body becomes present in all places in heaven and on earth, besides the fact that it overturns the foundations of those who derive this alleged omnipresence from the hypostatic union, they contradict different and clear passages of H. Scripture, which make mention of only one return of Christ to this world, when at the end of the world he will appear in his glory."

CHAPTER XX

CALLING

1.—The merit which Christ acquired for himself by his humiliation and obedience is made effective for the elect and for them alone by their appropriation of the benefits and promises of the covenant of grace, namely Christ and his benefits, and by God's institution in them thereby of real communion in the covenant of grace. Meanwhile this appropriation is not to be conceived as though before that Christ's merit had been completely alien to the elect. On the contrary the objective appropriation of salvation to the elect, which followed from the work of Christ's deliverance itself (since Christ instituted it with the intent that his merit should be let stand for their benefit) is only subjectively realised in the *applicatio salutis,* so that the latter is based essentially on the former. Such *applicatio salutis* is the result of the calling of the elect. "*Vocatio,* which broadly is derived from *vox,* is the act of God by which through the preaching of the Word and the power of the H. Spirit He brings man from the state of sin to the state of grace " (RIISSEN XIII, 3). Or better : " Calling (is the act of God) by which we are transferred from the first Adam to the second, from death, darkness and the state of sin to life, light and the covenant of grace, in order that being planted in Christ the Head and Root we may live and bring forth good fruits" (MARESIUS XI, 2). Hence as a *vocatio specialis, supranaturalis* and *evangelica* the calling of the elect is to be distinguished from *vocatio universalis* and *naturalis.* By the latter God as the Creator calls all men, to whom He has attested Himself in nature and in their conscience, to Himself and to His fellowship ; whereas the former is the calling of individuals to the fellowship of the Redeemer and to the enjoyment of the covenant of grace.

MASTRICHT (VI, i, 4) : " The application of redemption is—the appropriation of Christ and his benefits, whereby all the things which Christ as mediator suffered and did, are rendered effectual in act in certain particular men".—LEIDEN SYNOPSIS (XXX, 2-5) : "This special calling of men to Jesus Christ the Redeemer of the world is to be distinguished from the universal calling of them to God their Creator. Universal calling is that by which men one and all are invited by the common proofs of nature to the knowledge and worship of God their Creator Ac. 17. 27 (that they should seek God, if haply they might feel after him, and find him, though he is not far from each one of us) Rom. 1. 20 (the invisible things of him from the creation of the world are clearly seen, being perceived through the things that are made, even his everlasting power and divinity). This may therefore be called natural calling.

These common proofs of nature are partly internal and inscribed on the hearts of all men, partly outward and graven on the things created by God Rom. 2. 14 (when Gentiles which have no law do by nature the things of the law, these, having no law, are a law unto themselves) : the latter are distinguished by the title of speeches pronouncing the glory of God. Ps. 19. 5 (their line is gone out through all the earth, and their works to the end of the world . . .). Special calling is that by which God calls some out of the entire human race from the defilements of this world to supernatural knowledge of Jesus Christ our Redeemer and to saving participation in his benefits by the ministry of the Gospel and the power of the H. Spirit ; and therefore it may be called supernatural and evangelical calling."—For the rest it is noteworthy that the preparation for and appropriation of salvation are not to be kept abstractly separate, since the former already has its actual source in the latter. For, says OLEVIAN (p. 69) the atonement offered in intercession for particular elect is already the imparting of it to believers. Yet this imparting results subjectively in us, when Christ allows the word of reconciliation to be proclaimed effectually and the peace of God to be borne into our hearts.

2.—According to its real nature the calling of the elect is thus an *insitio in Christum* or *unio cum Christo,* a real, wholesale, spiritual and indissoluble union of the person of the elect with the divine-human person of the Redeemer, so that for the former the latter is exactly the same as soul is for body. The implanting of the elect into Christ is thus the beginning of all appropriation of salvation, of all fellowship in salvation (*gratia*) and in glory (*gloria*).

At the root of the whole doctrine of the appropriation of salvation lies the doctrine of *insitio* or *insertio in Christum,* through which we live in him and he in us. So the dogmaticians discuss it with special emphasis. (For the discussions of BOQUIN, ZANCHIUS and OLEVIAN, see HEPPE *Dogm. d.d. Prot.* II, pp. 312-315). They all have the conception of *unio cum Christo.* E.g. WITSIUS (III, v, 3-6) : " The goal to which we are called is Christ and communion with himself.—4 : The result of this communion is communion in all the benefits of Christ, in grace as well as in glory, to both of which alike we are called.—5 : And since Christ cannot be separated from the Father and his Spirit, we are at the same time called to communion with the single (*individua*) Trinity.—6 : Further, since all elect partake of one and the same grace, they are all likewise called to mutual communion with each other."—WITSIUS goes on to explain (III, xiii, 31) how far this *unio cum Christo* is the basis of all appropriation of salvation to believers : " It should be noted that not only has Christ in accordance with the eternal counsel of the Father promised all these things on behalf of the elect and fulfilled them in accordance with the promise, but also, before Christ's righteousness is fulfilled to the elect for justification of life, they are so closely united to him by faith that they are one body 1 Cor. 12. 13 (in one Spirit we were all baptized into one body) and, what is still more indivisible, one spirit with him 1 Cor. 6. 17 (he that is joined with the Lord is one spirit) ; and not merely united to him but one with him, and that in such a unity, that in it in a sense there is a certain shadowing forth of that most single unity, in which the divine persons are a single entity among themselves."—MASTRICHT (VI, v, 10-13) gives the attributes of this *unio* ? it is (1) real, not imaginary or in intention only— —or accidental merely—but in its own way substantial ; (2) total, (as) the whole Christian is united to the whole Christ, body and soul with Christ's natures, the human and the divine ; (3) indissoluble and eternal ; (4) spiritual, being wrought by the one Spirit who is in Christ and Christians Rom. 8. 11 (if the Spirit of him that raised up Jesus from the dead dwelleth in you, he that raised up Christ Jesus from the dead shall quicken also your mortal bodies through his Spirit that dwelleth in you), in Christ of course as the head, but in Christians as the members ; and also (5) mystical, so far as it tends to a body not natural but mystical."

3.—This calling is imparted only to the elect ; God not only has His word proclaimed to them through man (*vocatio externa*), but also introduces it by the H. Spirit into their hearts and there sets up living communion with Christ (*vocatio interna*).—HEIDEGGER (XXI, 8) : "Calling is of those elect and redeemed through Christ. These alone are so called that they are also attracted and created new and begotten. They alone are those for whom God not only strikes their ears by His word preached through men, but also attacks their hearts, opening them, writing His law in them, changing them and inflaming them to love him."

4.—On the other hand the rest who are not elect in accordance with the counsel and covenant of God are also called, not according to this but according to the judgment of God. Accordingly God only allows the call of the word proclaimed by men to be imparted to them and suffers them in the outward fellowship of the elect, even frequently assures them a rich outward knowledge and in passing even inward assurance of salvation, so as thereby to deprive them of all excuses for their hardness of heart.— HEIDEGGER (XXI, 9) : "Clearly of another sort is the calling of those who are left non-elect and rejected. The non-elect called are not called according to the purpose and covenant of God, as heirs entered therein, but according to God's judgment and dispensation, whereby He suffers them in the outward communion of the elect through the Word of His goodness, convicts them of their wickedness and cuts short their excuse for not coming to the wedding of the King's Son. Also they are not called so directly by God affecting, changing and regenerating the heart, as indirectly through men, who may strike their ears but cannot get through to their hearts. And so they are called by the Word preached by men ; yet so that they are not brought by the Spirit of God to communion with God."—So there must be a distinction between *vocatio externa* and *interna*. RIISSEN (XIII, 4) : "Calling is either outward or inward : the former, which takes place only by the ministry of the Word and sacraments, which are outward means of applying it ; the latter over and above this, by inward power and the almighty H. Spirit : the former which beats only upon the body's ears ; the latter which also opens the heart : the former advises morally ; the latter also persuades and draws effectually."

5.—Moreover outward Church calling is not imparted to the non-elect in such wise that God wished to present them with faith, should they refrain from resisting the activity of the H. Spirit. Otherwise the possibility would arise of a counsel of God being perhaps rendered futile by man. Besides it is to he noted that man can only resist the H. Spirit.—HEIDEGGER (XXI, 10) : " Nor does God altogether call particular reprobate in such wise that He has decreed and wills to give them faith and repentance just like the elect, provided only they do not resist the H. Spirit's call, as is the λεπτολογία (frivolity) of some. There are no decrees of God which men or any creature can frustrate. They are altogether effectual and have a most definite outcome. If He has decreed to give to some faith and repentance, He bestows them in time through the Word and the H. Spirit. In that case all men of themselves and by their nature resist the H.Spirit : Rom. 8, 7 (the mind of the flesh is enmity against God ; it is not subject to the law of God, neither indeed can it be).

6.—God, it is true, does not always rouse his elect to faith in one and the same way. At the same time God so deals with them all, that He first prepares the hearts of the elect for faith, whereas from the rest who are not aroused to faith He takes away every ground for excuse, by holding before them as His creatures their boundenness to fulfil the covenant of works and the law attested in conscience as well as in the tables of the law, and making them realise their righteous condemnation by their transgression of the law. The horrors of conscience which proceed from this knowledge are for the rejected a foretaste of the future judgment. For the elect on the other hand, who in view of the law and the covenant of works see themselves in the first instance in the same situation as the rejected, they are a preparation for faith, since by His prevenient grace God leads the elect out of darkness into light by causing a serious longing for redemption to proceed from these terrors of conscience, and then holding before them the promise of grace in the Gospel and causing what is offered them from without to be brought into their hearts by the H. Spirit (OLEVIAN, p. 252).

Since then in accordance with His eternal counsel and covenant God draws only the elect to Himself by such efficacy of His grace, their calling is an absolute one, but is at the same time the result of means, which yet are not conditions secretly imposed on man's freewill but free benefits of God's grace.—HEIDEGGER (XXI, 12): "Quite otherwise than the reprobate the elect are called to salvation in such a way that when called they are also affected, drawn and led, and that according to the eternal purpose and testament; and absolutely, although not without means, which however as regards the called are not conditions within their sphere of choice, but God's free benefits."

7.—These means are first of all the revelation of the kindness and the love of God in the works of creation, which cannot assure a permanent and living hope in God, because to the sin-conscious heart they cannot give the comfort of the forgiveness of sin and because man blinded by sin is all too prone to misunderstand and misuse God's revelation in nature. The proper means of calling (which in time does not coincide with baptism) is the Word by which God proclaims His eternal counsel and His eternal covenant, that He will redeem, sanctify and restore to Himself the sinner on whom He has had mercy for Christ's sake.— HEIDEGGER (XXI, 13): "Like all men generally the elect also are thus called by God's works and His longsuffering and kindness in some way to seek God and His communion. Nature herself is not dumb, but calls to man in many ways not to acquiesce in earthly things, but to ascend by this ladder, as it were, to better, heavenly and eternal things. For what else are the works of God that announce themselves in nature, but a sort of figures and symbols of things heavenly?—14: Be that as it may, although this calling through nature may excite conscience to think that God can justify impious man and to seek him and the knowledge of His will, it does not supply true hope which is living and which can never be put to shame, because neither by its sign does the righteousness of God and the justification of the ungodly become known nor on account of his blindness and folly can man deserted by God fail to abuse God's tolerance.—15: The elect are called by another more potent means, the Word of God; not any word, but that one by which God becomes lovable to man the sinner. This word is the notification of the eternal testament or purpose of God, which He decreed to redeem the sinner in Christ."

8.—This word is of three kinds: (1) witness or proclamation, that God in Christ has given the world new salvation and life; (2) the command that those who hear this proclamation believe it with remorseful and penitent hearts; and (3) the promise that those who believe this proclamation with upright hearts really attain to the salvation prepared in Christ.—HEIDEGGER (XXI, 6): "Three things are contained in this Word by which the elect are called: testimony, command and promise. Testimony has to do with the salvation given in Christ.—This testimony is called the Gospel, because first there comes the promise of the salvation to be prepared through Christ.—The command is to repent and believe the gospel. On the presupposition of God's witness to the salvation given to the elect in Christ, the command is part of the law, bidding us believe every testimony of God and fulfil every revealed wish of His. Also this law, when preached to him who is called, not only leads to recognition of sin Rom. 3. 20 (. . . by the law cometh the knowledge of sin), 7. 7 (I had not known sin, except through the law; for I had not known coveting, except the law had said, Thou shalt not covet) and shows up the defects and the depravity of nature and its manifold ἀνομία in actions, but also threatens a curse; and by both these acts prepares for the grace appointed for labouring and burdened sinners. In short the promise concerning the salvation to be presented to every believer— is preached in the same Word."—WOLLEB 90: "The form of this calling consists partly in the offer of the benefit of redemption, partly in the injunction to accept it."—WOLLEB 136: "The time of calling is not confined to baptism. Some God calls before, others in, others after baptism.—As Abraham was called and justified even before circumcision Rom. 4."

9.—Without the Word God calls man only in unusual ways, unfamiliar to us.—LEIDEN SYNOPSIS (XXX, 33): "God does not always apply the two methods of calling possible to Himself (i.e., outward and inward calling), but calls some to Him only by the inner light and leading of the H. Spirit without the ministry of His outward Word. This method of calling is of course per se sufficient for salvation, but very rare, extraordinary and unknown to us."

10.—Since the covenant of God is proclaimed in the Church by man, all are called outwardly who hear the proclamation of the Gospel. But when the H. Spirit calls inwardly and effectively, it is never promiscuously but always individually and personally; He realises their calling in the individual elect at the time which God has ordained for each individual. —HEIDEGGER (XXI, 19): "Although by a sort of alien power outward calling is directed to reprobate as well, yet it never is nor has been directed to all promiscuously. Since God's Word is preached to all the elect alone, it is pretty clear that the elect have not existed nor do exist in all parts of the world at any one time. So calling by hearing has its ἰδίους καιρούς 1 Tim. 2. 6, and a fixed μέτρον κανόνος (measure of the limit 2 Cor. 10. 13, 15) of its sending, so that neither has it reached one and all at one time nor has it so far reached all at different times, the sure sign being that both calling and salvation are given only *ex testamento*, and the notification of this is the actual calling."

11.—This personal calling of God is experienced by the individual who asks himself with a heart full of anxiety whether Christ's salvation was prepared for him too. He experiences it in his heart through the H. Spirit, who accords him the imperishable confidence, that he too is really called to inherit eternal life.—COCCEIUS (*Summ. de foedere* VI, 180): "Query, whether all and sundry are commanded to believe that Christ died for them? Answer: that this is really the consolation which is the fruit of righteousness and belongs to none but the contrite consciences and souls hungering and thirsting after righteousness. This consolation is the believing affirmation of God's address to our soul, by which He attests that He is God and our salvation Ps. 35. 3 (say unto my soul, I am thy salvation) and of the witness of the H. Spirit to our hearts, that we are the sons of God, so that our answer to God is Abba, Father."

12.—Hence we are not to fear that the elect who have not yet attained to conversion may never appropriate the call of grace or that the converted may fall from grace and the consciousness of the state of grace in the hour of temptation. The elect not yet converted become believing when the hour of their calling sounds; and the converted who fall into temptation issue from it with fresh certainty of their election, which rests upon God's word and their own conscience.— HEIDEGGER (XXI, 18): "There is no danger that the not yet converted may not be able to apply the Gospel promise to themselves or that the converted but tempted may not be able to make a sufficient struggle out of the whirlpool of temptations; a fear which some try to strike into our hearts when we restrict calling by the Word of the Gospel to the elect alone. The not yet converted are either elect or reprobate. The former by the grace of calling surely apply the promise of the gospel to themselves, when the hour of their calling is at hand.—As for the converted who are tempted, they ought to be set free from the billows of temptations— by the guardianship of their election confirmed by the surest criteria revealed in the Word of God and in the feeling of conscience."

13.—In the same way too it cannot be concluded that because the outward calling of the rejected is ineffectual it is therefore not seriously meant by God. Outward calling is always *per se* a real calling to salvation, since everyone who follows it up thereby gains righteousness in Christ and eternal life: only, in the case of the godless, it is ineffectual because of their hardness of heart. Similarly, the calling from God's side is always seriously intended, since God promises grace even to the rejected upon condition of faith, and makes faith for them a duty. But of course God omits to give faith to the rejected, because He is not bound to do so in the case of any man.—POLAN (VI, 32): "Ineffectual calling is of the reprobate.—It is called ineffectual not *per se* but *per accidens,* not in respect of God who calls, but in respect of men who have deaf ears of the heart. In itself calling is always effectual, although it is not so in those who are perishing, as the sun is effective by his light in itself, although it by no means illumines the blind."—From this it follows that even the calling of the godless is on God's side "sincere and serious" (HEIDEGGER XXI, 11): "Whether the serious is opposed to a joke, God in no way plays in the business of calling; or to pretence, He likewise does not simulate, because He does not profess one thing outwardly in words, concealing something else inwardly in His mind, but declares to men by calling His plain, open and steadfast will. And since the parts of calling are commands and promises, as often as He calls He commands and orders them seriously to repent and believe. For He wills that they repent and believe by His preceptive and·approving will, although He does not will by His decerning will, effectual to the giving of faith and repentance. He has the right to demand both.—Moreover calling promises salvation, but not to anyone promiscuously or without condition, only to the believing and repentant person". —Similarly WOLLEB 91.

14.—Thus in the calling of the elect man's proclamation is essentially combined with the inward efficacy of the H. Spirit. Without this activity of the H. Spirit, who writes the Word in man's heart, God's Word itself is but an empty letter, slaying the sinner and enticing him into fresh service of sin.—COCCEIUS (*Summ. theol.* XLII, 13): "This calling takes place through the word heard Rom. 10. 14f. (how shall they call on him in whom they have not believed ? and how shall they believe in him whom they have not heard ? and how shall they hear without a preacher ? and how shall they preach, except they be sent ?)".—HEIDEGGER (XXI, 21): "The outward calling of the elect through the word preached by men is very closely connected with inward accosting by the H. Spirit. Were it separate from this it would be of no avail. For the word preached by men strikes the ears of natural man, dead in sins.—Any word, however divine, most true, most wise, most pleasant in itself and thoroughly lovable, when addressed to a sinner still dead in sin, whose heart has not been inscribed by the H. Spirit, remains but a letter, slays the sinner and provokes him to sin 2 Cor. 3. 6 (. . . a new covenant; not of the letter, but of the spirit; for the letter killeth, but the spirit giveth life) Rom. 5. 20 (the law came in beside, that trespass might abound; but where sin abounded grace did abound more exceedingly) 7. 8 (sin, finding occasion, wrought in me through the commandment all manner of coveting: for apart from the law sin is dead)."

15.—Therefore we must insist that the word by which the H. Spirit effects calling is the same word by which God's call to grace is outwardly proclaimed to man.—HEIDEGGER (XXI, 22): "The word is the same which man preaches and which the Spirit writes on the heart. There is strictly one calling, but its cause and medium is twofold: instrumental, man preaching the word outwardly; principal, the H. Spirit writing it inwardly in the heart."

16.—Calling is therefore the act of the H. Spirit, by which out of the old sin-serving man He creates a new man serving God in Christ.—HEIDEGGER (XXI, 23): "Thus completed calling, fulfilling the whole measure and emphasis of the word, is that by which, the Spirit inwardly renewing, enlightening, bending, drawing, founding, consolidating, strengthening, sealing, man becomes a new creature in the realm of grace."—BURMANN (VI, iii, 1): "The first effect of calling is regeneration".—HEIDEGGER (XXI, 62): "The work of divine calling is ἀναγέννησις,, regeneration, or δευτέρα γέννησις."

17.—The direct effect of such a calling is thus the regeneration of human nature. "Regeneration is the hyperphysical act of God, by which the elect man who is spiritually dead is imbued with new, divine life, and that from the incorruptible seed of God's Word, fecundated by the transcendent power of the Spirit" (WITSIUS III, vi, 4): Or: "Regeneration is God's action in elect sinners, redeemed, actively justified and called through Christ, by which He substantially (realiter) turns them from corruption to new life (or holiness), that they may henceforth live unto God" (VOETIUS II, 436). Or: "Regeneration is God's beneficium, by which our corrupt nature is begotten and renewed a second time in God's image through the H. Spirit by the incorrupt seed of God's Word" (POLAN VI, 37). By regeneration, then, man's sin-corrupted nature is so transformed, that in virtue of the new divine life imparted the old sinful kind dies out in him; and this takes place the moment the H. Spirit by His effective calling implants a man in Christ, so that rebirth is accomplished by the fact and to the extent that the state of the regenerated man constitutes a specific and insuperable contrast to that of the natural man.—WITSIUS (III, vi, 7-8): "By regeneration moreover new life is put into them (the elect), as the result of gracious union with God and His Spirit. What soul is to body, God is to the soul.—8: Undoubtedly regeneration takes place in a moment. The passage from death to life admits of no delay. As long as man is in the state of spiritual death, he is not yet regenerate. But the very moment he begins to live, he is begotten again. Therefore no intermediate state between regenerate and unregenerate can even be feigned in thought, if we are thinking of regeneration in its first action".—BURMANN (VI, iii, 8): "All regeneration is consummated in a single moment."—VOETIUS (II, 449): "Regeneration is instantaneous, or happens in an instant. When it is termed successive by some, this is to be understood of the whole complex or collection of the term in the first few moments. Here we are dealing with the term regeneration in its first moment."—The majority of dogmaticians deal with the doctrines of calling, regeneration, conversion, faith, justification and sanctification in the order given here. This MASTRICHT e.g. (VI, viii, 7) indicates as follows: "The Reformed hold the view that in the elect (1) spiritual life is restored by regeneration; (2) this is stimulated and extended into action, so that the man grasps God and the mediator with true faith and conceives a serious purpose of abandoning sins and showing zeal for good works: this happens by conversion; finally (3) good habits or virtues are infused into the converted man and his will and these are advanced to all kinds of good works by sanctification."

18.—The "meritorious and exemplary cause" of this activity of the H. Spirit is Christ alone. On the one hand by his merit he has acquired the elect to be the people of his possession; and on the other hand in his action and suffering he is the pattern by which the nature of the elect is renewed.—VOETIUS (II, 440): "Christ is (1) the directly and physically efficient cause of regeneration—by supreme right and the original power which he shares with the Father and the H. Spirit. (2) He is the cause that effects it—by grace—by an inferior right or power, dependent, subordinate, which arose or was produced in time and was granted to him as the Son of man and the Mediator. (3) He is the subordinate, meritorious-administrative cause. (4) He is the exemplary cause".—WITSIUS III, vi, 23): "Christ theologically considered is along with the Father and the Spirit the principal cause of our regeneration. But administratively considered he is the meritorious and exemplary cause of the same regeneration."

19.—In this matter the H. Spirit so works upon man as to bring his will to observe the Word of God, to arouse his understanding to cognisance of it, to redetermine man's will to love God's known will and to surrender to it and so to control and guide man's affections.—WOLLEB 135: "The form consists in the gracious change in man, primarily in mind and heart, by which not only is the mind irradiated but our hearts also of stone are turned into flesh or bent to obedience."—HEIDEGGER (XXI, 27): "In calling, drawing, leading and converting by His Word and Spirit, God both moves the will to attend to the proof, truth and goodness of the word announced; illumines the reason to conviction of the truth and healthfulness of the Gospel to which it thus attends, and to assent to it; and in a word bends and determines the same will, so that we love the true and good word, to which we attend and assent."

20.—In this way is displayed the regeneration of man's nature effected by *insitio in Christum*, which is predominantly liberation of it from the misery of sin and restoration of it to true likeness to God's image, in the form of conversion of life to God and liberation of it from the service of sin. Conversion is thus purely the work of the H. Spirit. Man dead in sin is only passively related to the activity of the H. Spirit in grace, and so far as he is self-active, can only resist it, so that grace must literally break the man's natural anti-God will, in order to convert him to itself:—LUD. CROCIUS p. 918: "(1) As regards the start towards good, or the first act of reparation and conversion, because of the *liberum arbitrium's* nature (which as regards things spiritual is truly corrupt, in fact dead, yet able to be stimulated and corrected by God) it does not co-operate with God, but remains passive in its attitude towards God's action. (2) Yet here with his *liberum arbitrium* man does not behave like a log or stone. God acts on man the subject by His Word, as on one endowed with the faculty to think and will. (3) Nor is it as though natural man himself allows God to act. This too is an act of good will. And when God uses His word outwardly, by promise and threat and other persuasions, human nature resists God. (4) But he is like one wholly affected and enslaved by an evil quality and affection. (5) So here God acts in a divine way, and with such grace, power and effectiveness, that in the issue He removes wickedness from the will and inserts righteousness and so makes the man free instead of a slave, willing in place of unwilling, obedient instead of resistent".—KECKERMANN 263-264: "In the conversion of a man there is no concurrence of the powers of free *arbitrium*. But at the first moment of it man and his will act in a purely passive state. Here we are speaking of the first impulse and moment of conversion, or the first beginning of this movement, in which acknowledging his sins man turns to God. And this first beginning, we assert, does not depend on the natural strength of the will, but is the beginning of grace alone, according to the express testimonies of Scripture Col. 2. 13 (and you being dead through your trespasses and the uncircumcision of your flesh, you, I say, he did quicken together with him, having forgiven us all our trespasses), where it is said that men are dead in sins . . . Yet at the very moment in which God effects in us the grace of conversion He also bends man's will to desire and seek for that grace, and so in the progress of conversion the will co-operates with divine grace".—RIISSEN (XIII, 18, (3): "Does man then hold a purely passive attitude in the first regeneration? Yes, against the *Synergists*". —BUCAN (XVIII, 10): "What is the state of man's will in conversion, active or purely passive? As regards the approach of prevenient grace from without, so far as it is not yet beginning to be regenerate, the will is in a purely passive state. But as regards the time at which the conversion actually takes place the will is not like a log, but when healed by the H. Spirit it also is in an active state ; i.e. the will in conversion is not idle or motionless or insensible (like a statue), but follows the Spirit who draws it. God brings it about at the same moment, that by grace we will and really will, that is, He moves and bends our will and secures that we really will: yet in such wise that the whole effectiveness of the action is and remains with God's Spirit."

This is the sense in which all Reformed dogmaticians speak about conversion, excepting the earlier German-Reformed teachers of Melanchthon's school, HEMMING, SOHN, URSIN, PEZEL and others, who like the Reformed Confessions of *Anhalt* and *Nassau* represented the Melanchthonian doctrine of conversion, at first in its entire peculiarity, though later with essential modifications.

21.—In any case the H. Spirit so works upon man as to esteem him a personal creature and so does not regard him as a clod or a stone, but acts so that enlightened by the Word and impelled by grace man receives in conversion the will to convert to God and so his conversion takes the form of spontaneity. Yet since in conversion every sort of co-operation of man's will with the H. Spirit is completely excluded, the activity therein exercised by the H. Spirit is no merely natural, merely moral or mediate activity (no mere *suasio per verbum*), but at the same time and pre-eminently an immediate, supernatural one, in which the H. Spirit avails itself of the Word as its means, yet, in a way completely independent of the natural activity of the Word, works essentially and irresistibly [? *finaliter*] upon the thought, will and life of man.

MASTRICHT (VI, iv, 8–9): "The act of being converted, or conversion, is twofold, (1) moral, (2) physical. Moral conversion is achieved by the

mediation of the Word Is. 59. 21 (as for me, this is my covenant with
them, said the Lord: my spirit that is upon thee and my words which
I have put in thy mouth, shall not depart out of thy mouth, nor out
of the mouth of thy seed, nor out of the mouth of thy seed's seed, saith
the Lord, from henceforth and for ever) Rom. 1. 16 (I am not ashamed
of the gospel: for it is the power of God unto salvation to the Jew first,
and also to the Greek) 10. 17 (belief cometh of hearing, and hearing by
the Word of God) Ps. 19, 8 (the precepts of the Lord are right, rejoicing
the heart: the commandment of the Lord is pure, enlightening the eyes),
read, heard and pondered, which, in calling at least, resembles scattered
seed, in conversion an instrument by which God indicates this duty
to the convertends and attracts them into fulfilling it. But while the
Word is called the instrument it is well enough understood that it does
not act in conversion by its own strength, but in that of the principle
cause (see above). The second act of conversion is physical, whereby it
powerfully draws the convertend and opens his heart, creates in him
a new heart, accomplishes it in him to will and to do, and so converts
him that he is converted."—WALAEUS 815: "We have shown that in the
conversion and regeneration of man there has not only been applied by
God a sort of moral or gentle suasion by the outward word of law and
gospel, but that there is besides a work by a different operation of the
H. Spirit, linked with the Word yet distinct from the Word, by which
actual regeneration and conversion are effected."—RIJSSEN (XIII, 18):
"Is the whole act of God in converting a man nothing more than a moral
one, namely illumination and persuasion by the Word? No! Does God
infuse new life by a physical action of the Spirit? Yes, against the *Remonstrants* and *Socinians*. The view of the orthodox on this question is that the
movement of effectual grace is strictly speaking to be called neither
physical nor ethical, but supernatural and divine, which practically
includes each σχέσις. It is not simply physical, because the moral
faculty is involved, which must be moved in accordance with its nature;
nor simply ethical, because God would be acting only in an objective
way and using gentle persuasion, as the *Pelagians* used to insist; but
it is supernatural and divine, transcending all these categories. Meantime it has some part in the ethical and the physical. It belongs to the
physical mode, because God creates us by His Spirit, regenerates us,
gives us a heart of flesh, etc. It belongs to the moral, because it teaches,
bends, persuades, etc., us by the Word. The question thus is, whether
in addition to the objective and mediate grace by which the Spirit acts
upon our minds by the Word preached at every opportunity and upheld
by particular circumstances and aids, there is required another subjective
and immediate grace, whereby it works directly upon the faculties

themselves, to dispose them to a saving reception of the Word and by the efficacy of which conversion is necessarily and infallibly produced. This we maintain".—TURRETIN (XV, vi, 7) explains the sense in which irresistibility of grace is to be conceived. "The question comes back to this, whether the manner of the operation of effectual grace is always resistible, i.e., whether, given all the effects of grace which God uses to effect grace in us, conversion still so remains in man's power, that he can raise or not raise an obstacle, i.e., receive it or reject it and so convert or not convert. Which is what our opponents want but we deny, insisting that effectual grace so works upon a man, that although he cannot avoid resisting it from the start, yet he never resists it to the extent of finally overcoming it and hindering the work of conversion."

22.—Thus neither can it be said that in the hearts of the elect before their conversion there is a seed of election present in virtue of which calling becomes native to them. Before their conversion the elect are in the same condition in this respect as the rejected, only with the difference, that by God's grace they are saved from complete collapse in destruction.— CALVIN (III, xxiv, 10): "Ere the elect are gathered to the Chief Shepherd, they wander scattered in the common desert and are no different from others, except that they are protected by the singular mercy of God from rushing over the final precipice of death. So if you have regard to them, you will see Adam's progeny rank with the corruption common to the mass. That they are not borne off into extreme and desperate impiety is not the result of any goodness inborn in them, but is because God's eye watches over their salvation and His hand is stretched out still. Those who delude themselves that from very birth some strange seed is sown in their hearts, in virtue of which they are always inclined to piety and the fear of God, are not even aided by the authority of Scripture and are refuted by actual experience."—Similarly HEIDEGGER (XXI, 28).

23.—It is thus not excluded that in many a case the H. Spirit works in the elect before regeneration the same gradually preparatory acts, since He urges them, e.g., to read and listen to His Word, to recognise His will, to bewail their miserable sin, etc., all of which ought to bear fruit, should the hour of rebirth come; wherefore too the omission of this "precedent act", when the H. Spirit rouses man to it, makes him still more liable to punishment.—LUD. CROCIUS 919: "Wherefore no one contributes anything to this grace, or can prepare, dispose and apply himself to it, even by the boon of universal grace and natural light or of the more special grace, i.e., the Law (which is given the name of grace improperly and by misuse), any more than anyone can contribute anything to his generation and quickening. Yet we admit that God uses here certain antecedent circumstances like nature or law, led by which to despair of himself, the sinner is brought to the consolation of the Gospel and hope in God."—HEIDEGGER (XXI, 70): "Although in those whom God wishes to regenerate he previously produces certain effects, usually called precedent acts, in a variety of ways, e.g., their hearing of His Word, realisation of His will, acknowledgement of their own wretched state with a certain grief, etc.—things which later, when their hour of salvation is upon them, are not received in vain in the case of one who is regenerated 2 Cor. 6. 1 (receive not the grace of God in vain), but become clearly useful and profitable—yet no disposition or preparation or congruence or sufficient grace can be recognised as effective in him who is not yet regenerate."—LEIDEN SYNOPSIS (XXXII, 8): "Meantime, however, we also affirm that those who resist the proofs of nature or law or gospel which call them to repentance, or hold them in unrighteousness, by this act of theirs amass for themselves fresh guiltiness and higher condemnation and so become more and more inexcusable in the judgment of God, as the Apostle also teaches Rom. 1. 20 (the invisible things of him are clearly seen) 2. 1 (wherefore thou art without excuse, O man) cf. Jn. 15. 22 (if I had not come and spoken unto them, they had not had sin: but now they have no excuse for their sin)".

For a considerable time of course the proposition was defended by individuals, chiefly English dogmaticians, that a real *praeparatio ad conversionem* was possible for man. Here is WITSIUS' account of it (III, vi, 11): "There were also some of ours who spoke of preparation for regeneration and conversion, but in quite a different sense from the *Pelagianisers*. They laid down in those to be regenerated (1) the breaking of natural contumacy and flexibility of will, (2) serious consideration of the law, (3) consideration of their own sins and offences against God, (4) lawful fear of punishments and terror of hell and so despair of their salvation on the score of anything in themselves. This is the order in which *Perkins* recounts these preparations in his 'Cases of Conscience', V qu. 1 sect. 1. Nor is AMESIUS any different, 'Cases of Conscience' II ch. 4. In almost the same sense the British theologians explained themselves at the SYNOD of DORT. (p. 139 Edn. Dordrac. A. 1620 in folio). "In any case" WITSIUS continues, "we think those more accurate in their philosophising, who lay it down that these things and such as these in elect persons are not preparations for regeneration but the fruits and effects of initial regeneration and yet preparations for subsequent and more perfect operations of a more generous Spirit".—And so later, in place of the expression *actus preparatorius* which was the earlier use, the expression exclusively employed came to be *actus praecedaneus*".—URSIN on the same matter (*Loci*, p. 650):

"If they insist that the H. Spirit is not effectual in those who do not hear the word and persevere in their sins against conscience, that therefore for hearing the word and dropping sins it is necessary for them, being unconverted, to prepare themselves for conversion—we reply that this may be conceded as a whole, but that the two points do not follow. First: that the works in question are pleasing to God. Although God uses not only these but also other works of the non-reborn (like acknowledgement of sins and fears of conscience, association with the godly who attract them to godliness or with the ungodly who deter them from ungodliness, their own crimes and punishments), to prepare men for conversion and salvation, nevertheless so far as the men themselves are concerned, all these things are sins prior to conversion. Second: that such morally good works are due by the non-reborn without divine providence and suggestion governing their minds, so that at last they might be gathered as elect into the Church. Even in the non-reborn nothing good can be done, which God does not effect so far as it is good."

24.—Meanwhile it is clear that before his rebirth there is no real disposition to it at all to be found in man.—VOETIUS (III, 443): "In all or some potential converts are there preparatory dispositions, which contribute to regeneration by a causality of their own? We absolutely deny it."

25.—Since then in regeneration and conversion the new man replaces the old, this does not occur in such a way that first of all the old sin-stained life ceases and then the new life upheld by God's will begins. On the contrary the old life is buried by the power of the new life which fills man.—HEIDEGGER (XXI, 63): "In regeneration both the old man —is discarded—and then the new man—is put on. Not that the discarding of the old condition precedes the assumption of the new. The old man is dispelled only by warmth, hatred only by love. There is no intermediate state."

26.—Of course man's regeneration never reaches completion here on earth. Even after the ensual of regeneration sin continues to work in man although no longer as a dominant force. Thus life advances from rebirth with greater or less variations.—HEIDEGGER (XXI, 73): "Neither is either regeneration perfect in this life or the regenerate man perfect. As long as men are sojourners in this mortal flesh, they are at war with the relics of the old Adam, which are not extinguished either at the beginning or during the progress of regeneration in this life; and regeneration actually experiences frequent vicissitudes, according as the working of its progress is now greater, now less."

27.—The object is, that the glory of grace may appear to men in all the clearer light.—HEIDEGGER (XXI, 75): "Nor is regeneration left imperfect in this life without grave reason and the struggle with sin and the remnant of the old Adam sternly shewn to man. It concerns God's glory not only that His autocracy in lordship and liberty should be displayed in the struggle appointed to man in accordance with His will, but also that the potency of His grace should be made perfect in our weakness. So He allows the saintliest to be preoccupied with lapses Gal. 6. 1 (Brethren, even if a man be overtaken in any trespass, ye which are spiritual, restore such a man in a spirit of meekness; looking to thyself, lest thou also be tempted); partly that they be not carried away, but humble themselves in the sight of God; partly that they be not held by others in excessive esteem to the detriment of God's honour; partly that others terrified by their example may be afraid and serve God with fear and exult with trembling. In short (it becomes God's glory) that progressive corruption of the outward man and renewal of the inward man should bring in its train both contempt of the world and of the things which are seen, and the longing for the heavenly and divine home, and for not just the enduring of Christ's righteousness but also for the superenduing of heavenly glory and faith in God the Father, spiritual joy by the increase of renewal and ardour in pleasing God, things which St. Paul most amply confirms 2 Cor. 4. 16 (wherefore we faint not, but though our outer man is decaying, yet our inward man is renewed day by day), 5. 1-2 (We know that if the earthly house of our tabernacle be dissolved, we have a building of God, a house not made with hands, eternal, in the heavens. For verily in this we groan, longing to be clothed upon with our habitation which is in heaven)."

28.—Regeneration and conversion are manifested in the elect person as faith. Faith is the direct effect of regeneration.—BURMANN (VI, iv, 1): "The first act of regeneration and the first movement of the new man is faith."

Not all Reformed dogmaticians expound the concept of calling, regeneration, conversion and faith in the mutual relationship here set forth. Many indeed use these expressions as synonymous descriptions, as WYTTENBACH, e.g. (II, 858), remarks. For the exposition given here the greatest weight was assigned on the one hand to the authority of the most distinguished teachers of the golden age of Church orthodoxy, and on the other hand to the implications of the Reformed doctrinal principle.

WITSIUS (III, vii, 1): "The principal act of the spiritual life implanted in the elect by regeneration and the true source of the consequent vital operations is faith in God through Christ.—"Faith" is thus not the 'cause' but the direct "effect of regeneration". See Voetius (II, 42): "Is faith the cause of regeneration or its inward instrument? Answer in the negative, because faith is its goal and effect".—Wyttenbach (II, 871): "Faith is produced by effectual calling or regeneration. Or, which is the same thing, it may be said that in the effectual calling or regeneration of a man faith is produced in him." This Wyttenbach explains thus: "This calling taken on God's side or actively is the act by which God impresses this conation on man (i.e., on faith): on man's side or passively taken it is the change made in man and the mere beginning indeed of the change for the better, which if continued constitutes faith. And so faith is the continuation of the change made in man by God's calling, while the calling of man is the beginning of faith."

29.—Faith is, generally, a conviction resting not upon sensible apprehension but upon witness to God's revelation.—Heidegger (XXI, 82): "Generally, therefore, faith is πεισμονή Gal. 5. 8 (This persuasion (to turn aside) came not of him that calleth you), or persuasion of the truth removed from the senses by the witness of God revealing."

30.—Faith is based upon a witnesser who is infallible, and can therefore be founded only upon God.—"Faith regards the witness and His veracity", says Heidegger (XXI, 83), "infallible knowledge and evidence, who cannot be other than God, as alone being ἀληθής Rom. 3. 4 (let God be found true, and every man a liar), σοφός 1 Tim. 1. 17 [textually Rom. 16. 27] (the only wise God), ἀψευδής Tit. 1. 2 (who cannot lie) and needing no other witness Jn. 5. 34 (the witness which I receive is not from man)."

31.—Hence *fides* is essentially distinct from *opinio,* which lacks all inward certainty, and from *scientia,* which is based upon reasoning and proof.— Bucan (XXIX, 2): "What is the difference between opinion and knowledge? That is called opinion, which tends to either side not without fear or hesitation as to the truth on the other side. Knowledge begets firm assent, but by the operation of proofs, because proof is a syllogism causing us to know. But faith rests on authority and according as it affects our affairs through the afflatus of the H. Spirit, it affords firm assent to the Word of God and rests on the authority of God Himself."

32.—But since faith is only thinkable in relation to its object, the self-revealing God, there are accordingly various relations of the concept faith. From the standpoint of the object faith may be distinguished as *fides quae creditur* and from the standpoint of the believing as *fides qua creditur.* A further difference in *fides* results from the inner nature of the object. Faith may be legal or evangelical, according as it relates either to the revelation of the divine will of God or to God's revelation of grace in Christ. Particularly as regards the latter the question arises as to the relation of the subject to it. Faith in God's revelation of grace in Christ may be related to the subject as the mere object of knowledge, so that faith is merely a conviction, based on the witness of faith, as to the truth of the facts of revelation, but for that reason cannot have the liveliness to renew man, because it regards the truth of revelation as something indifferent to its really-personal interests: this is *fides historica,* "bare assent to truth revealed and apprehended" (TURRETIN XV, xvii, 4). But man may also recognise the facts of revelation as a truth valid for him and for his personal interest in blessedness, so that his acknowledgement of its truth becomes more than mere conviction, namely personal possession of revelation. But even here two possibilities are open. Faith which includes the comfort of revelation may be transitory or non-transitory. In the first case it is the faith merely of man's enlightenment, not of his renewal, is not rooted in the deepest soil of life, in his heart, is not a proper, direct gift of the H. Spirit and so does not assure the blessed comfort of true sonship to God. So that such faith, not containing in and for itself the guarantee of permanency, is essentially *fides temporaria,* and but a fading copy of the true, unfading *fides salutaris or salvifica* (and so specifically different from it) which alone can be spoken of here.

WOLLEB 137: "Faith has five meanings in Scripture. Either it is taken in a transferred sense as meaning sound doctrine, which is not *fides qua credimus,* but that *quam credimus,* 1 Tim. 3. 9 (holding the mystery of the faith in a pure conscience); or *fides historica* Jas. 2. 19 (Thou believest that God is one; thou doest well: the devils also believe, and shudder); or *fides temporaria* Mt. 3. 20 (heareth the word and straightway with joy receiveth it; yet hath not root in himself, but endureth for a while; and when tribulation or persecution ariseth because of the word, straightway he stumbleth); or *fides miraculorum* Mt. 17. 20 (. . . your little faith . . . if ye have faith as a grain of mustard seed, ye shall say unto this mountain, Remove hence to yonder place; and it shall remove; and nothing shall be impossible unto you); or *fides salvifica* Mt. 10. 8 is understood (Heal the sick, raise the dead, cleanse the lepers, cast out devils; freely ye have received, freely give)."—HEIDEGGER (XXI, 84-85): "Faith is legal or evangelical. The former is persuasion of the truth of some witness divinely revealed, the latter the truth of the particular believing witness to Christ the Saviour revealed not in the law but in the gospel alone." At the same time legal and evangelical faith have also an element in common. "Granted the revelation of Jesus Christ the Saviour of believers, evangelical (faith) binds by the very force of the law which orders us to believe any revelation of the divine witness". Evangelical faith is either *communis or propria*. "Common faith also falls upon the reprobate and those not yet regenerate; strict faith falls upon the elect alone."—WYTTENBACH (II, 890): "If anyone gives assent to the truths necessary to be apprehended merely as matters which he does not greatly long to have for his own and which do not much interest him, i.e. without emotion, it is called *fides historica*. 891: When assent is given to evangelical truths as directed to a man's self and desirable, but in no other way or respect save that they bring a temporal convenience or commend themselves by their beauty and excellence, it is *fides temporaria* that gives ear.—Temporary faith thus proceeds from the fact that it does not embrace evangelical truths for the special end to which they point, deliverance from wretchedness."— TURRETIN (XV, xv, 1): "Does temporary faith differ from justifying faith only in degree and duration or in kind ? The former is denied and the latter affirmed against the *Remonstrants*". The main reason lies in the *principium internum* and the *modus radicationis*. "The principle of saving faith is the Spirit of regeneration and adoption Jn. 3. 5 (except a man be born of water and the Spirit, he cannot enter into the kingdom of God) Rom. 8. 15 (ye received not the spirit of bondage unto fear; but ye received the spirit of adoption, whereby we cry Abba, Father); that of temporary faith is the spirit of illumination Heb. 6. 9 (we are persuaded better things of you and things that accompany salvation, though we thus speak). The manner of radication is deep in the former and superficial in the latter. Justifying faith is rooted intimately in the heart, consisting in the deep, most inward, vital and loving, and effectual impression by which the Word becomes ἔμφυτον and tempered by faith Jas. 1. 21 (putting away all filthiness etc., receive with meekness the implanted word which is able to save your souls) Heb. 4. 2 (. . . we have had the good tidings preached unto us, even as also they; but the word of hearing did not profit them, because they were not united by faith with them that heard). And the faithful are ἐρριζωμένοι ἐν ἀγάπῃ Eph. 3. 17, rooted in Christ and stablished in faith Col. 2. 7. But *fides πρόσκαιρος* has no root Mt. 13. 21, i.e. clings to the utmost surface of the soul, namely to the reason, but does not reach to the heart."

Temporary faith is thus distinguished essentially from justifying faith in that (1) it is not the regeneration of the whole man but only illumination of the reason (*intellectus*), and (2) it does not assure the certainty of sonship to God.—CALVIN (III, ii, 11): "I am aware it seems hard to some, when faith is assigned to the reprobate, seeing that Paul declares it to be the fruit of election and yet the knot is easily untied, for although none are enlightened unto faith or truly feel the effectiveness of the gospel

except those ordained to salvation, experience yet shows that the reprobate are sometimes affected in almost the same way as the elect—the
Lord, the better to convict them and leave them without excuse, worms
His way into their minds (*se insinuat in mentes eorum*), so far as His goodness
may be savoured without the Spirit of adoption.—They are presented
with halting faith for a season, but only in the elect is the trust of adoption strong, extolled by Paul, so that with a loud voice they exclaim
Abba, Father. Therefore . . . it is only the elect whom God regenerates
for ever of incorruptible seed. . . . But there is nothing to prevent the
lower operation of the Spirit having its course in the reprobate also. . . .
They never have any but a confused sense of grace, so that they grasp
the shadow rather than the solid substance. . . . (12): Nor can it be
said that the Spirit deceives, because he does not quicken the seed which
he casts in their hearts, so that it may always abide incorruptible as in
the elect."

Dogmaticians also discuss a further *fides miraculosa* (HEIDEGGER XXI,
85): "Miraculous faith is the heart's conviction of the emission of a
miracle proceeding from the singular and hidden divine revelation".
For this the *verbum Dei generale* is not enough; "there is required a special
revelation and promise, such as God made to Gideon."

33.—"*Fides propria* is a supernatural virtue poured into man by God,
by which he is not only surely aware of Christ the Redeemer and his
saving benefits as these are offered in the word of the gospel and sealed
in the sacraments and assents to them, but also grasps them trustingly
and assigns them like a seal to himself and affixes them" (HEIDEGGER
XXI, 86). In this true personal faith (*fides propria*), by which the Gospel
eternally remains the personal possession of the elect person, three distinctions must be made between *notitia, assensus* (both these belong to
intellectus) and *fiducia* (which rests upon *voluntas*). "*Notitia* is the apprehension of the things which are necessary to salvation. *Assensus* is that
by which it is firmly believed, that the things transmitted by the Word
of God are true. *Fiducia*, called πεπόιθησις and πληροφορία by
the Apostle Eph. 3. 12 (boldness and access in confidence through
our faith in him) 1 Th. 1. 5 (our gospel came not unto you in word only,
but in power and in the H. Ghost and in much assurance), "is that by
which each of the faithful applies the promises of the Gospel to himself"
(WOLLEB, 139). Since faith then is above all *notitia*, it cannot be *fides
implicita* ("by which we believe what the Church believes, without knowledge of the object of faith").

ALTING 113a: "In form the acts of faith in an object are two in number,
the first of which however has two parts, so that it may be said that there

are three. I: *Cognitio certa,* embracing (1) *notitia,* by which the Word of God is known, especially that of the gospel and its promises, and through which it is known what we believe: (2) *assensus,* by which God's Word, including especially the promises of the Gospel, are approved as true, unshakable and sure.—II: *Fiducialis apprehensio,* whereby the promise of the gospel concerning Christ with all his benefits, made to all who repent and believe, realised from the Word and approved by assent as true and good, is assigned to himself by each repentant believer as a seal, put into practice, sought, applied, appropriated as being addressed to himself, and he rests wholly upon it and so leans upon it, that by its formula he is ready to live; and because of his firm conviction of the truth and power of Him that promiseth, he ventures to risk his life and soul and salvation in every kind of way".—BUCAN (XXIX, 7): "Faith is knowledge of, assent to and seeking for the grace promised in the Word, and so a firm trust and grasp of the salvation to be obtained for Christ's sake. Or, faith is the firm and sure recognition of the divine benevolence towards us, which, founded on the free promise of Christ, is revealed through the H. Spirit, sealed in our minds and hearts. Or, faith is the longing and apprehension of the will or heart, in consequence of the knowledge and approbation and special judgment of the mind, by which *singuli κατ' ἰδίαν* we apply to ourselves Christ crucified, offered along with his benefits in the word and sacraments. Or, faith is that tool, instrument and means by which *homo peccator* embraces the whole of Christ with all his benefits, applies them to himself and is united to Christ and lives".—BUCAN hereupon (XXIX, 8) raises the question, whether this definition of faith does not stand in contradiction to Heb. 11, 1 (faith is the assurance of—or giving substance to—things hoped for, the proving —or test—of things not seen), and his answer to it is: "No, since in it accurate mention is made both of the form of faith stated in the terms *ὑπόστασις* and *ἔλεγχος* and of its objects, namely things hoped for and things invisible. By *ὑπόστασις* he means not *persona* as in the article on the Trinity, but the basis and even lever on which the mind pushes and rests, to signify that faith is a certain sure and secure possession of the things which are promised us by God".—LEIDEN SYNOPSIS (XXXI, 14): "The proper and special object of justifying faith in man is not only reason (*intellectus*) but also will. Knowledge and assent belong to reason, *fiducia* to *voluntas*. Nor is it enough for justifying faith, that reason should grasp the things which are of God, unless the will also apprehends and embraces them".—The result of which (WOLLEB 139): "Implicit faith which is believed by blind assent, as the Roman Church believes, is no faith. There cannot be faith without knowledge, (1) because it comes by hearing; and hearing is by the Word of God Rom.

10, 17 (belief cometh of hearing, and hearing by the word of Christ);
(2) because it is wisdom by which God is known Is. 51. 13 (. . . the Lord
thy Maker, that stretched forth the heavens, and laid the foundations
of the earth . . .) Jer. 31. 34 (they shall teach no more every man his
neighbour, saying, know the Lord; for they shall all know me: for I will
forgive their iniquity, and their sin will I remember no more) Jn. 6. 69
(We have believed and known that thou art the Holy One of God)
17. 3 (and this is life eternal, that they should know thee, the only true
God, and him whom thou didst send, even Jesus Christ) 1 Cor. 1. 21
(seeing that in the wisdom of God the world through its wisdom knew
not God, it was God's good pleasure through the foolishness of preaching
to save them that believe).—Nor is the faith which is not conjoined with
firm trust any better than historical faith."—COCCEIUS (*Summ. theol.*
XLVI, 33): "Since faith is known to express assent, the question is, how
a believer assents to the Word of God and to certain truths. The *Papists*
here thrust upon us a sort of implicit faith—by which one induces the
mind to believe what the Church believes; which is nothing else than
the willing surrender of one's soul to the Pope, without any scrutiny
of what he enjoins by the word of Scripture. In fact, to speak plainly,
it is nothing less than to choose, say and do what the Pope says and does
with the crowd that obeys him".—35: Revelation contains the core
"which cannot be ignored without loss." As regards what does not belong
to this inmost substance of revealed truth, man may of course, without
detriment to his soul, remain in ignorance or even in error. "Those who
hold the rule and foundation may be ignorant of certain things which
make for the adornment of the foundation and are contained in Scripture.
They may even err in certain points or hold a false position without
divine authority, yet not attending to the rule and to the wiles of Satan,
as we see that Christ's disciples departed in many ways from the truth. So
the man who is otherwise prepared to believe the word of God and cannot
be led at once to all knowledge, or cannot at once be led away from all
opinions, is not on that account to be immediately condemned and avoided."

34.—Meanwhile the essence of *fides* is *fiducia*. Hence *assensus* is not a
theoretical but a practical assent, i.e., an *apprehensio fiducialis*. For faith
is a trust which rests essentially upon the Gospel, that the promise of God
has the full value of visible possession of the benefits promised. In faith
the believer is aware of the gracious salvation proclaimed in the Gospel
as God's gift belonging to him personally, with which he comforts himself and rejoices with all his heart.

In later Reformed dogmatics a difference in the conception of the
idea of *fides* appears, which is worth looking at. At first it was generally

usual to describe the nature of *fides* as being *fiducia* or *assensus fiducialis*. This is also particularly the case in CONF. HELV. II, 16; "Faith is not opinion or human conviction but the firmest trust and manifest and fixed assent of mind; in short, a most assured grasp of God's truth—and especially of the divine promise and of Christ"; and in HEIDELBERG CATECHISM Q. 21. Later, on the other hand, this conception was rejected by many, on the assumption that faith as a living force poured into man by God was in and by itself not yet *fiducia* but first led to *fiducia,* and that consequently faith might actually be present in men without *fiducia.* MARCK describes the question in dispute (XXII, 33): "It must be openly admitted that on the actual application of trust our theologians too hold diverse views. (1) The older men in accordance with our catechism make this act of faith essential, but not to be conceived of apart from a previous embracing of it and the repentance involved in that. (2) Several of the more recent men will rather have it that it is the result of faith itself and of justification, which may be absent from faith and abiding salvation."—According to this view which MARCK describes as the more universal, faith is an act by which man adopts God and Christ into himself. The clearest expression of this view is to be found in MASTRICHT (II, i, 6). He defines saving faith as an act of a rational soul, which consists in receiving God as the end and Christ as the Mediator; the manner of which consists in the ὑπεροχή, by which we receive God as the supreme end and Christ as the sole Mediator". Faith is thus an "act" and an "act of a reasonable soul, which consists in receiving God and the Mediator" and in "receiving God as the supreme end and Christ as the sole mediator." This act of the soul demands (II, i, 8–10) "in the reason (1) knowledge of the evangelical promises and (2) explicit assent; in the will consent, by which we receive . . . God and the mediator; in the emotions (1) love to God and the mediator, (2) longing for them, (3) joy, (4) hatred and detestation of the things which are contrary to them." The "end and fruit of faith" is "union with Christ" and "participation in his benefits". According to this, then, the personal trust by which man relies upon Christ's merit as upon his own merit (what MASTRICHT calls *persuasio*), does not belong to the nature of faith but is an effect of the act of faith.—At the same time the majority of dogmaticians hold to the proposition, that "fiducial assent is the form of faith."

As regards the attitude of the various Church groups to the dispute in this connection MASTRICHT's account is (VI, vi, 27) that the *Lutherans* of course, in conformity with their doctrine of the universality of grace, assume that "if only a man believe that Christ died for him and acquired him remission of sin, he has thereby been justified." Among the Reformed

MASTRICHT distinguishes. "Most of the Reformed, at least of the *Germans,* to whom are to be added some of the *English* and *French* and others, do not indeed insist that Christ died for one and all. But they consider that he died for all those who are persuaded that Christ died for them, and so in such persuasion they put the nature of saving faith". As regards the rest of the Reformed MASTRICHT remarks that "Most of the Reformed, at least of the more recent men, gladly acknowledge that this sure persuasion may be obtained by ordinary means, though there must be an effort after it on the part of each true believer, 2 Pet. 1. 10 (give the more diligence to make your calling and election sure: for if ye do these things, ye shall never stumble) Gal. 2. 20 (I have been crucified with Christ; yet I live; and yet no longer I, but Christ liveth in me: and that life which I now live in the flesh I live in faith, the faith which is in the Son of God, who loved me and gave himself up for me),—yet they deny that the actual essence of saving faith consists in such persuasion, or pertains to it to such an extent, that he who is devoid of such persuasion does not possess saving faith."

WALAEUS (759) expresses himself in the most opposite sense: "The question on which there is disagreement among certain orthodox writers is, whether trust in God's mercy is a part of faith, or its form, or its consequent and effect. Some think, among them BEZA and ZANCHIUS, that this trust is rather hope and the result and effect of faith rather than the form of faith itself or a part of it. We, however, with all respect to the judgment of these gentlemen, feel together with most writers of the Reformed Church and among them CALVIN and LUTHER along with all Luther's disciples, that trust is the very form of faith as justifying and its noblest part, or at least that it is included in justifying faith."—The majority of dogmaticians declare in the same fashion, e.g., HEIDEGGER (XXIV, 82): "Justifying faith involves trust, and that in the threefold form of practical assent, laying hold of Christ as our saviour and confidence or acquiescence and the consolation, arising from the soul's καταφυγή to Christ."—MARESIUS (XI, 43): "Therefore the formal nature of justifying faith should consist in firm, sure and trustful assent, which lays hold of and applies to itself the merit of Christ and the promises of free salvation through himself."

35.—And faith is so thoroughly reliance upon grace, that the believer can never desire a feeling of grace, since he clings not to the feeling but only to the promise.—OLEVIAN (p. 302-303): "So far is it from being true that the promises of the gospel are separable from Christ or Christ from the promises—that on the contrary, since the Lord does not wish the things promised to be completed in us for as long as we live on earth, it is the highest proof of obedience of faith, and the Lord wishes the faithful to exercise themselves steadfastly in the thought, that their faith does not depend upon the fruition and sense of the things promised, but is content with the bare promises, although in reality they are not bare, but He seems to withdraw the sense of His benefits from us. For then in truth the honour due is paid to God's true form and so to His majesty, when His promise put forth in but a single word is of such high repute with us, that we have no doubt of the fulfilment.—We feel sin in ourselves; we are bidden believe that Christ was made sin on our behalf and that we are the righteousness of God in him Rom. 7 and 8; 2 Cor. 5. It becomes us to rest content with this word and not doubt our righteousness in Christ, whatever is actually dinned into us by the sense of sin or the slenderness of the fruition of grace.—We see ourselves hedged in by many perils; no desertion is to be dreaded on the score of their number. The promise is sure to Joshua, I will not fail thee, nor will I forsake thee Heb. 13. 5. So let us be satisfied with this word, that God will never fail us at any moment, however much to the contrary the flesh may seem to feel and to be aware of. He does not even fail us when we seem to be stripped of the sense of His present help. Faith rests not upon feeling but upon the promise."

36.—Faith is always bound up with love (*caritas*): yet it is not *caritas* but *fiducia*, which is characteristic of faith.—URSIN (*Explic. catech.* p.59): "Love of neighbour should proceed from love of God".—BURMANN (VI, iv, 14): "Love always accompanies this trust (*fiducia*)".

37.—The object of faith is God in Christ, i.e. the salvation by grace promised in the Gospel, God's covenant of grace. And the inmost core of the object of faith is the death of Christ. Since the covenant of grace rests altogether upon the death of Christ, the minute the eye loses sight of Christ's death, faith must inevitably go to pieces: on the one hand because of God's unchangeable righteousness which can only forgive sin for the sake of the Son's death, and because of God's unchangeable truthfulness who has given His promises only to believers; on the other hand because of the way we are made. The consciousness of law created in man tells him that God punishes sin. This voice of the law, which finds expression in conscience and lets man feel the wrath of God, can only be silenced if it be certain that the Son of God by his death has given complete satisfaction to the Father's righteousness for the sins of man. The foundation of the covenant of grace is thus the death of the Son of God (OLEVIAN p. 297). Since then the believer puts his unconditional trust in Christ's death and merit, he is by faith immovably sure that God in Christ is his God and Father, his real property, that Christ is also his redeemer, that Christ's merit is also his.

BURMANN (VI, iv, 11-12): "And first of all this act of faith seeks and beholds God Himself and Christ and at last settles in His bosom the soul aweary of its tedious wanderings and soothingly makes it lie down and be at rest.— 12: Hence this trust is directed to the thing promised and to it as its own special perquisite it inseparably clings."—TURRETIN (XV, xii, 1): "Whether the proper or specific object of justifying faith is the promise of special mercy in Christ? Answer, yes, against the *Papists*."—WOLLEB 138: "The matter (*materia*) which has the nature of the object (of faiths is commonly the Word of God, though strictly it is the free promise) founded on Christ."

38.—Finally the believer is immovably sure that further thereby he is really taken up by God into the covenant of grace.—WYTTENBACH (II, 908): "By faith the covenant of grace is set up; in other words, where man rejoices in saving faith, he assents to the covenant of grace."

39.—Thus certainty of salvation and assurance of the state of grace is the most essential sign of faith and the most direct effect produced by it in the consciousness of the elect person. And this certainty of salvation (which excludes fleshly certainty exactly as it includes childlike fear) is not a conviction based upon reflection (not a *certitudo coniecturalis, moralis*), but a direct *certitudo absoluta* given with faith itself. The believer is certain not only of the truth of the object of faith, but also of the fact that his subjective faith is real faith and that by it he really possesses salvation and enjoyment of the covenant of grace.

TURRETIN (XV, xvii, 6): "The view of the orthodox is that the faithful may not only be certain of their faith and of its truth and sincerity, a certainty not human and fallible but divine and infallible, which is yet greater or less according as faith itself is found to be firmer or laxer; but both may and ought to be certain of the grace of God and remission of sins, so far as in serious contrition for sins they do with true faith grasp the promise of free mercy in Christ, rest in it confidently and so render their hearts carefree. Yet this security neither induces carnal confidence nor excludes filial fear and godly anxiety, nor is it always placed beyond the wing of temptation or the fear of what is contrary. The foundation of it is partly the infallible promise of the Gospel Jn. 3. 14-16 (as Moses lifted up the serpent in the wilderness, even so must the Son of man be lifted up; that whosoever believeth may in him have eternal life. For God so loved the world, that he gave his only begotten Son, that whosoever believeth on him should not perish but have eternal life) 1 Tim. 1. 15

(faithful is the saying, and worthy of all acceptation, that Christ Jesus came into the world to save sinners; of whom I am chief); partly the infallible witness of the H. Spirit in the individual conscience Rom. 8. 16 (the Spirit himself beareth witness with our spirit, that we are children of God)."—MARESIUS (XI, 38): "Since this is so, the believer should be sure that his sins have been remitted and that salvation is to be conferred through Christ; and that not by a moral certainty only or a conjectural—but by an absolute one and to divine faith, i.e. within the special revelation, by the intrinsic nature of faith itself. Faith imports not only objective certainty of the things believed, but also subjective in the believer himself, who is not only persuaded that what he believes is sure and undoubted, but also that this faith of his by which he believes these things is true and sure."

40.—Doubts of course frequently invade the believer's certainty of salvation, so that he has to ask himself whether he really can take comfort in the grace of God and regard himself as elect. But these doubts are never such that the comfort of faith is utterly overcome. On the contrary in every elect person they lead conclusively to the certainty of his peace with God.

CALVIN III, ii, 17: "When we teach that faith should be certain and secure, we are certainly not speaking of an assurance untouched by any doubt or of a security unassailed by any anxiety. We rather maintain that believers have a continual struggle with their own distrust and are far from situating their consciences in a placid calm unruffled at all by any disturbances. On the other hand, however they are afflicted, we deny that they fall away and defect from that sure trust which they have conceived concerning the mercy of God."—WOLLEB 139: "We do not teach a firmness of trust which has no struggle with doubts, but one which does not finally succumb to doubts."—BUCAN (XXIX, 27): "May this faith not fail? As faith receives increase according to "Increase our faith" Lk. 17. 5, it may also suffer decrease and endure a lack, as it is smitten, darkened, uprooted, made slack sometimes by the blasts of manifold temptations; yes, even in saints, exactly as in drunk men and in children, reason is lulled and buried, as in David when he allowed adultery, and in Peter when he denied Christ thrice. But it is never struck out or extinguished altogether.—28. But is faith likely to cease at any time? As regards the object, Christ, as he is offered in the word and sacraments, faith will disappear when we have Christ in heaven: as the Apostle says, 1 Cor. 13. 8-10 (but even prophecies shall be done away . . . and knowledge . . . and that which is in part). Moreover there will be no use for faith, when the things which we believe in and hope are to be given us in this life are provided and most fully exhibited to us. But if we are speaking of Christ absolutely, without the wrappings of Word and sacraments, then faith in him, or, if you prefer, the actual thing called by that name, i.e. knowledge and grasp of Christ, is never likely to cease at any time, but will be at the height of perfection in heaven because of the sight and contemplation of Christ and no longer because of the ministry of the word. Actual knowledge, I say, will not be abolished, it will indeed be perfected. But the manner of knowing will give way to contemplation of God Himself. This is what the Apostle calls perfect 1 Cor. 13. 10 (after that which is perfect is come)."

41.—This *certitudo salutis*, which blessed faith guarantees, rests upon its being altogether the gift of God. Of His free grace God infuses into the elect the spirit of faith by arousing the man's knowledge and will to faith: whereupon as the peculiar, supernatural new principle of life in the converted man, faith is describable not strictly as an act but rather as a habit in him.—WOLLEB 138: "Faith is a gracious gift, not only because we have not deserved it, but also because it is poured into us through the H. Spirit."—LEIDEN SYNOPSIS (XXXI, 9): "The efficient cause of this faith is God the Father in the Son through the H. Spirit, who illumines the mind and moves and bends the will otherwise averse to God. And that not only by a metaphorical manner and act of causation, which the SCHOOLMEN call moral, the goodness and meetness of the object being set forth by the measure of the end, as they say; propounding through the illuminated, practical intellect His final judgment, which the will necessarily follows: but also by His action directly affecting the will and inflowing upon the man's movement and action, while (if I may use AUGUSTINE's words *De grat. Christi* 14) by an inward and hidden miraculous and unspeakable power He effects in men's hearts not only true revelations but also good volitions. These words do indeed indicate a real and proper efficacy. Hence for a reason of its own faith is called the gift of God and its author the Spirit, the Spirit of faith 1 Cor. 12. 9 (to another faith, in the same Spirit) 2 Cor. 4. 13 (having the same spirit of faith according to that which is written, I believed, therefore did I speak: we also believe, and therefore also we speak) Ac. 16. 14 (Lydia . . . whose heart the Lord opened, to give heed unto the things which were spoken by Paul) Phil. 1. 29 (to you it hath been granted in the behalf of Christ, not only to believe in him, but also to suffer in his behalf) Col. 2. 12 (buried with him in baptism, . . . raised with him through faith in the working of God, who raised him from the dead) Heb. 12. 2 (Jesus the author and perfecter of our faith)".—HEIDEGGER (XXI, 88-89): "We define this justifying faith as not so much an act as a habit, supernatural and infused by God.—Moreover Scripture attests that faith is not an acquired habit, such as, though with difficulty, may be lost as it is acquired, but an infused one, such as lasts for ever. It is generally taught concerning all gifts of saving grace, that they are poured out upon us, and that through their effusion upon us we operate as initiators of actions." —WYTTENBACH (II, 895): "Saving faith is not so much an act as a habit of soul infused by God. It is the continuation of regeneration: accordingly not something transient, but something permanent.

42.—God gives this faith to the elect not of course in one moment in entire perfection; it is rather bestowed on individuals in varying measure. —BUCAN (XXIX, 12): "Does God create full and perfect faith in our hearts in one moment? By no means, but by increases and sure stages, in the measure and at the time He pleases, and by the means by which He plants it in our hearts (just as the philosophers say that we exist and are nourished on the same things and as an infant is brought up and developed by the same blood turned into milk from which he was born) He cherishes and confirms it by frequent hearing, i.e. of the word of God.—13: Is faith given in like measure to all believers? No : but to some greater, to others less; but no one is given less than suffices for salvation".

43.—But the ground on which God gives faith at all to the elect through the H. Spirit is the same in every case, namely the merit of Jesus Christ:— HEIDEGGER (XXI, 91): "God the Father infuses faith and gives it for the Son's sake by the H. Spirit. We have more than once shown that the Son merited faith in advance by his death; and to him as its author the saints refer the receipt of faith."

44.—Similarly the means by which God pours faith into us is the same in every case, namely the word which God makes effectual in our hearts through the H. Spirit.—WOLLEB 138: "The instrumental cause by which faith is given us is usually in adults the Word of God.—But the preaching of the Gospel alone is not the cause of faith, but only as it is conjoined with the effectuality of the H. Spirit."

45.—Of course by the gracious working of the H. Spirit God may also bestow faith without the word. But this happens only exceptionally. Which is why such a direct infusion of faith must not be expected by anyone.—URSIN (*Explic. catech.*, p. 108): "Justifying faith—is given to all the elect and to them alone, even, by inclination, to infants".— BUCAN (XXIX, 11): "Apart from the preaching of the word or the ministry of the Church can God create faith in His own by an inward afflatus? He can, as formerly in St. Paul, but not usually and very seldom; and we must not look for it, nor must it be rashly admitted. Moreover in diagnosing whether faith is from God the unchanging principle is, that it must always agree with the written prophetic and apostolic word."

46.—Only in regard to elect children must it be acknowledged that God imparts to them as heirs of His testament and partners in His covenant of grace, not "actual faith" but still the "seed of faith", the "inclination of regeneration" by the H. Spirit: but not by the act of baptism, by exorcism or in answer to Church intercession.

CALVIN (IV, xvi, 17): "But how, say they, are infants regenerated, since they are not endowed with the knowledge of good and evil? We reply that, though God's work is not subject to our capacity, it is not therefore nothing. Further infants who are to be saved (as assuredly some are saved at that age) are obviously first regenerated by the Lord."
—POLANUS (VI, 37): "Spiritual regeneration does not pertain to all men but only to those elected to eternal life. But it belongs not only to grown-ups, but also to infants.—Infants who are to be saved—especially if they die in infancy or in their mothers' wombs, must be regenerated and sanctified, (1) because none of the elect is summoned from the present life to eternal life, unless he is first sanctified and regenerated by the Spirit of God;—(2) because Christ was sanctified from his early infancy, in order that he might sanctify his own elect in himself without distinction at any age;—(3) because the prophet Jeremiah and John the Baptist were sanctified in their mothers' wombs".

Of course this belief is contested by individual dogmaticians, e.g., by MARCK (XX, 12); but the overwhelming majority of dogmaticians teach like RIISSEN (XIII, 29–31): "The question is, whether infants have faith. I answer that on this topic the *Anabaptists* err in defect. They deny all faith to infants and on this pretext exclude them from baptism. There is error in excess on the part of the *Lutherans*. In order to oppose the *Anabaptists*, they fall to the other extreme, insisting that infants are regenerated in baptism and presented with actual faith. The orthodox hold the mean, as will be apparent in what follows.—30: Upon infants no actual faith falls. (1) They are not capable of acts of faith or of knowledge, because it is not given without the action of reason, whence they are said not to know good or evil or to be able to distinguish between their right hand and their left, Deut. 1. 39 (your little ones, which ye said should be a prey and your children which this day have no knowledge of good or evil, they shall go in thither, and unto them will I give it, and they shall possess it) Is. 7. 16 (before the child shall know to refuse the evil, and to choose the good, the land, etc.) Jonah 4. 11 (six score

thousand people that cannot discern their right hand from their left);
nor of assent, which must be conveyed to the object known; nor of trust,
which has play in the special application of the promise of grace.—(2)
They are not capable of hearing the word, of which faith is conceived;
for faith is by hearing Rom. 10. 17 (belief cometh of hearing and hearing
by the word of Christ).—31: Although actual faith does not befall infants,
the seed or root of faith cannot be denied them, i.e., the beginnings
of regeneration and holy inclinations which are begotten in them by the
H. Spirit from a tender age in a manner for us indescribable and in their
own time issue in action, with the addition of the human institution
without and the greater effectuality of the H. Spirit within. For (1) the
promise of the covenant was also made to the children Ac. 2. 39 (to you
is the promise, and to your children and to all that are afar off, even
as many as the Lord our God shall call unto him); therefore so also the
benefits of the covenant, remission of sins and sanctification. (2) To
children belongs the kingdom of heaven Mt. 19. 14 (for of such, etc.);
therefore so also does regeneration, without which there is no entry
into it (the kingdom) Jn. 3. 3-5 (except a man be born anew, he cannot
see the kingdom of God. How can a man be born when he is old, etc.
. . . Except a man be born of water and the Spirit, he cannot enter . . .).
Examples are given of various infants who were sanctified from the womb,
as is admitted in Jeremiah, who is said to have been sanctified from the
womb Jer. 1. 5 (before I formed thee in the belly I knew thee, and before
thou camest forth out of the womb I sanctified thee . . .), and John
who leaped in his mother's womb Lk. 1. 15 (the angel to Zachariah)
1. 80 (and the child grew and waxed strong in spirit, and was in the
desert until the day of his showing unto Israel). (4) As before the use
of reason men are well called rational, who possess the beginnings of
reason in a reasonable soul, so nothing prevents the faithful from being
called before actual faith, because the seed which is given them is the
beginning of faith, in consequence of which they are rightly so called,
just as they are rightly called sinners, although they cannot yet perform
acts of sin." Similarly many others, e.g., PICTET (IX, iii, 18).

Decisively rejected is the view that faith can be aroused in children
by exorcism or by the baptismal act or by Church intercession. Cf., e.g.,
BRAUN (I, iii, 8, 24): "But this faith cannot be said to have been produced
in infants by exorcism or by the prayers of the Church in baptism, as
the *Lutherans* would have it; nor because they believe in act by the faith
of sponsors or of the Church; nor because in baptism there is infused
the habit of faith, as the PAPISTS teach".—VOETIUS (II, 142): "The
opinion of this author (Cornelius BURGESS, *Tract. de baptismali regeneratione
electorum infantium, Oxoniae,* 1629) pleases me, to the extent that he insists

that in elect and covenanted infants there is room for the initial regeneration of the H. Spirit, by which is impressed the beginning and seed of actual conversion or renovation which is to follow in its own time. But as for his putting this regeneration after baptism and linking it to it as the indispensable cause and moral instrument upon which it follows, this is not proved from the Reformed theologians just quoted. Their opinion is well known, that baptism is effective not in producing regeneration, but in sealing it when already produced. So its whole and entire effectuality is the exhibition and conferring of it by means of sign and seal."

CHAPTER XXI

JUSTIFICATION

1.—As regards the relationship of man to God the immediate effect of the calling of the elect person is his justification in God's sight. Those whom God has implanted in Christ are regarded by the Father as though they possessed all that Christ had done and suffered.—HEIDEGGER (XXII, 1): "The grace of justification is closely connected with the grace of calling. Those whom God calls he gives to Christ and thereby wishes them to come to Christ, in fact He draws and leads them to him, Jn. 6. 37 (all that which the Father giveth me shall come unto me; and him that cometh to me I will in no wise cast out). Those who thus called, drawn and led come to Christ are joined and united to him, to the end that they may have communion with him 1 Cor. 1. 9 (God is faithful, through whom ye were called into the fellowship of his Son Jesus Christ our Lord). This communion—makes them partakers in that righteousness—which Christ secured by his blood."—MASTRICHT (VI, vi, 3): "Therefore being united by faith with Christ in his blood or reconciling righteousness they are regarded as righteous by God unto the remission of sins and, as a result, possession of eternal life. Hence to those who are in Christ, Christ is said to have been made δικαιοσύνη by God 1 Cor. 1. 30 (of him are ye in Christ Jesus, who was made unto us wisdom from God, and righteousness and sanctification and redemption)."—BOQUIN insists that by the *unitio* of the believer with Christ the eternal *pactum salutis* between Father and Son is in a measure transferred to the believer and he is justified by it.

2.—Thus the whole evangelical doctrine of salvation stands or falls with the doctrine of justification, as being the inmost core of the doctrine of redemption.—LEIDEN SYNOPSIS (XXXIII, 1): "The topic of justification in theology is easily foremost and for us the most saving. If it be obscured, adulterated or overturned, it is impossible for purity of doctrine to be retained in other *loci* or for the true Church to exist."—WALAEUS p. 746: "This article is of such high moment, that *Luther* himself, *Chemnitz* and all the writers of the Reformed Church were always of the opinion that it is the foundation of the whole Reformation and the source of all our true consolation and gratitude."

3.—By the justification of man H. Scripture thinks not of an inpouring of God's righteousness into him (i.e. not of an *actus physicus*), but of a judicial declaratory act (*actus forensis*) by which God declares man righteous, i.e. to be an object of His good pleasure. Hence justification is

an exterior but not an interior change in man.—Riissen (XIV, 3):
(1) Justification is a forensic act of God, not as a creditor and private
person but as a ruler and judge pronouncing sentence upon us in front
of the tribunal. (2) It is the act not of a subordinate judge who is confined
to the formula of the law, but of the supreme magistrate and prince to
whom alone it belongs, in virtue of His "autocratic" right, to show grace
to the guilty and to relax the vigour of the laws laid down. (3) Moreover
God here does not sit upon the throne of righteousness, in order to act
κατὰ τὸ ἀκριβοδίκαιον νόμου, but upon the throne of grace, in order to
act according to gospel ἐπιείκεια. (4) He acts from pity, so that this may
be done without detriment to righteousness, which since it cannot suffer
its laws to be violated with impunity, of necessity requires some λύτρον,
by which He may be satisfied Himself. (5) Whence it follows that God
cannot show grace to anyone or justify anyone without perfect righteousness. Since God's judgment is according to truth, He cannot pronounce
anyone just who is not truly just. But since after sin no mortal has such
righteousness in himself, indeed by sin he has become a child of wrath and
liable to death, it had to be looked for outwith us in another, by whose
intervention *homo peccator* might be justified without righteousness of his
own".—Mastricht (VI, vi, 19): *Protestants* never think that justification
denotes an inward change in man, but always an outward one procured
by declaration."

4.—We have to distinguish in justification between that of the sinner,
and that of the righteous.—Heidegger (XXII, 6): "Evangelical justification with which we are dealing at the moment is twofold, one of the
sinner, the other of the righteous."

5.—Man is convicted of sin and liable to eternal death, but is yet elect
from eternity and called in time on account of the pledge of Christ's
dying in time and of his obedience and righteousness freely given and
imputed to man and apprehended and applied solely by faith in him;
for even in the judgment of God Christ was absolved and justified of the
debt which he freely and willingly took upon himself. Hence justification of
the sinner is a judicial act by which man is pronounced righteous by God
the judge, absolved from sin and its condemnation and made a partaker
in eternal life, to the glory of God's righteousness and mercy and to man's
eternal salvation" (Heidegger XXII, 7). Therefore since man to be
justified is man the elected, redeemed and called sinner, we must distinguish in him an inward and an outward state. As regards the former man
to be justified is a sinner given over to his godlessness and to his guilt and
liable to eternal damnation. As regards the latter he is elected from

eternity and called in time.—MASTRICHT (VI, vi, 8): "The object of justifying action is—men who are (1) elect, (2) sinners, (3) redeemed, (4) called, (5) begotten again and quickened, illumined in mind, renewed in heart (or will), (6) converted, so that by the strength of regeneration accepted by faith they may actually receive God and the Mediator and be turned from sins unto righteousness, (7) united to Christ, so that in none save Christ they may get possession of a righteousness, not their own but Christ's, which is by faith."

6.—The inward cause by which God justifies elect and called sinners is simply and solely His free grace, by which He wills the redemption of the elect.—LEIDEN SYNOPSIS (XXXIII, 11): "The inward impulsive cause by which God the Father was self-moved to justify us is God's peculiar grace, mercy, φιλανθρωπία, God's charity of love, both by which He gave the Redeemer Jn. 3. 16 (God so loved the world etc.) Rom. 5. 8-9 (God commendeth his own love toward us, in that, while we were yet sinners, Christ died for us. Much more then, being now justified by his blood, shall we be saved from the wrath of God through him) Tit. 2. 4 (the grace of God hath appeared, bringing salvation to all men) 3. 4 (the kindness of God our Saviour, and his love toward man appeared) and handed him over to death for our righteousness and justification Rom. 4. 25 (delivered up for our trespasses … raised for our justification) and by which he was graciously pleased to ratify that obedience of His Son, supplied outwith us indeed, but on our behalf Eph. 5. 2 (… gave himself up for us, an offering and a sacrifice to God for an odour of a sweet smell); in both of which respects he is said to have reconciled us to Himself in Christ 2 Cor. 5. 18 (God reconciled us to Himself through Christ); and finally by which He appointed it [the obedience] according to His eternal decree and applies it by His own Spirit to His own elect Rom. 8. 30 (whom he foreordained, them he also called; and whom he called, them he also justified; and whom he justified, them he also glorified)."

7.—Hence the 'justification' is essentially 'gratuitous', 'given gratis'. To this inward cause must also be added an outward motive on account of which God accomplishes justification. Since the holy and unchangeable God cannot put His own law out of force and so in conformity with law can only declare him righteous who has satisfied the law, the elect and called sinner must have to point to a righteousness that is his, which belongs to another, i.e., to a work belonging to himself, by which the law is fulfilled and his guilt atoned for, so that God may declare him righteous because of this work.

HEIDEGGER (XXII, 15): "In this judgment there is required outside God a cause by and because of which God absolves the sinner and presents him with the right to eternal life, which must be some δικαίωμα or *opus perfectum*, which God's law exacts from him who should be declared just, and without which neither an untainted man nor a sinner can be justified. Because He Himself prescribed no other cause of the right to ask for life, than the doing of that which the law prescribes and threatened death and damnation for him who failed to do it, it was not in such wise that He should justify any without it, as one just, holy and truthful may lose that cause or postulate of the δικαίωμα in judgment, in order to justify the sinner. Otherwise he could not deliver a right judgment. In fact He Himself—a blasphemy to think!—would be taking darkness for light, bitter for sweet and compensating deliquences with a reward." —MASTRICHT (VI, vi, 10): "The outwardly moving cause for justifying is a righteousness, by justifying on account of which He pronounces men just. Since He is a just judge and also truthful, whose judgments are at once both just and true, He cannot declare righteous one who has no righteousness."

8.—This work and this righteousness is the redeeming work of Christ which he has consummated for the elect and which therefore in virtue of its objective value is a 'meritorious and material cause of justification', because, purely for the sake of this work which He assigns and appropriates to the elect Himself, God acquits him of his sins and institutes him heir of eternal life.—BUCAN (XXXI, 11): "The material cause of our justification, that on account of which we are justified, is not faith or love or works or our merits or those of the saints or sufferings or sacraments, but Christ with his righteousness. And not a man's works principally or his merits in a less degree, but Christ alone completely and that according as he is apprehended by faith Rom. 3. 24 (being justified freely by his grace through the redemption that is in Christ Jesus) 1 Pet. 1. 18–19 (redeemed, not with corruptible things . . . from your vain manner of life handed down from your fathers, but with precious blood as of a lamb without blemish, and without spot, even the blood of Christ) Ezek. 20. 18 (walk ye not in the statutes of your fathers . . . I am the Lord your God: walk ye in my statutes)."—HEIDEGGER (XXII, 16): "This cause of justification outside God some call the meritorious, others the material cause in the same sense: meritorious, because it is that by which strictly speaking he merited justification beforehand; material, because it is the thing which in the judgment of God is reckoned unto us for righteousness."

9.—Gospel justification is thus distinguished from the legal kind not *quoad essentiam* but solely *quoad circumstantias,* since Christ takes the place of the sinner.—LEIDEN SYNOPSIS (XXXIII, 5): "Justification is of two kinds, legal and gospel; the former by the law and its works, the latter by faith Ac. 13. 38–39 (. . . through this man is proclaimed unto you remission of sins, and by him every one that believeth is justified from all things, from which ye could not be justified by the law of Moses) Rom. 3. 20–21, 28 (by the works of the law shall no flesh be justified in his sight: for through the law cometh the knowledge of sin. But now apart from the law a righteousness of God hath been manifested, being witnessed by the law and the prophets: even the righteousness of God through faith in Jesus Christ unto all them that believe: for there is no distinction—a man is justified by faith apart from the works of the law) Gal. 3. 11–12 (that no man is justified by the law in the sight of God is evident; for the righteous shall live by faith and the law is not of faith); the one inherent, the other by imputation of another's righteousness Rom. 4. 4–6 (to him that worketh the reward is not reckoned as of grace, but as of debt. But to him that worketh not, but believeth in him that justifieth the ungodly, his faith is reckoned for righteousness. Even as David also pronounceth blessing upon the man, unto whom God reckoneth righteousness apart from works Ps. 32, 1–2 : (Blessed, he . . .whose sin is covered . . . unto whom the LORD imputeth not iniquities) Rom. 10. 3, 5–6 (being ignorant of God's righteousness and seeking to establish their own, they did not subject themselves to the righteousness of God. . . . For Moses writeth that the man that doeth the righteousness which is of the law shall live thereby. But the righteousness which is of faith saith thus, Say not in thy heart, etc. But what saith it? The word is nigh thee, in thy mouth and in thy heart); by the former after the fall no one is justified, by the latter everyone endued with the true faith in Christ Rom. 3. 20-26. 30 (sic) (by the works of the law shall no flesh be justified in his sight . . . (Christ) for the shewing of his righteousness at this present season; that he might himself be just and the justifier of him that hath faith in Jesus . . . he shall justify the circumcision out of faith" and the uncircumcision through faith."—20: "Nevertheless the law or righteousness legal and of works is not simply opposed to God's righteousness in Christ or to Christ's. We are not justified contrary to the law, as that which Christ fulfilled both by suffering the punishment due to our sins, thereby destroying guilt, and by displaying all righteousness and obedience to the law, by which he laid down the condition of eternal life; but in a certain sense because it was full obedience to it by the Son of God on our behalf, not on our part, because the law demanded this fulfilment in addition Rom. 8. 3–4 (what the law could not do. . . . God sending his own

Son . . . condemned sin in the flesh; that the ordinance of the law might be fulfilled in us who walk after the Spirit) Gal. 3. 13 (Christ redeemed us from the curse of the law) 4. 4-5 (God sent forth his Son . . . born under the law, that he might redeem them which were under the law, that we might receive the adoption of sons)."—HEIDEGGER (XXII, 15): "And to this extent it does not cease to be legal righteousness, since [it differs] from evangelical not essentially, which consists in looking to the cause or δικαίωμα, but as regards the circumstances alone, Christ being put in the sinners' place, fulfilling the δικαίωμα of the law."

10.—Christ's righteousness becomes our righteousness (and only as our righteousness can it avail anything), since the law which is fulfilled by Christ as our guarantor acquits us, and the Father so accounts the righteousness of Christ to us, that the same righteousness which belongs to Christ *inhaesive* (inherently) is in us *imputative* (by imputation).— MASTRICHT (VI, vi, 12, 13): "The nature and amount of righteousness does not matter, if it is quite foreign to us. Hence those who without Christ are alienated from the commonwealth of Israel, being outside the pacts of the promise, are pronounced ἄθεοι. And if no appropriation at all were exacted (since Christ's righteousness is of infinite worth), one and all would of course be justified and saved. Moreover this appropriation depends partly, us apart, (1) upon the divine giving, (2) upon the divine imputation and partly, us included, (3) upon faith."—HEIDEGGER XXII, 31): "God's righteousness acquired by Christ's merit should in a certain sense be ours, nor does anything not ours avail in the judgment of God for our justification.—Although the sponsor's righteousness is foreign in quality, because it belongs to him and was acquired by him alone, yet it is ours by the law according to the righteousness supplied by the surety who absolves and by the judgment of God, by which sin is not imputed to us; but there is imputed to us and thus presented to us the righteousness of Christ."—BURMANN (VI, v, 9): "The righteousness which is valid in this justification is none other than the righteousness of Christ imputed to us. This is readily evident, since there are but two kinds of righteousness, our own or someone else's, and according to that a twofold nature of justification Rom. 4. 4-5 (to him that worketh the reward is reckoned . . . as of debt; but to him that worketh not, but believeth on him that justifieth the ungodly, his faith is reckoned for righteousness). Scripture (1) openly sets aside our own righteousness, since it claims to deal with man the guilty sinner Rom. 3. 23 (all have sinned and fallen short of the glory of God) 4. 4-5 [§ 9, p. 547] ; and (2) constantly insists upon and teaches the second righteousness and calls it the righteousness of God and Christ and attributes it solely to grace Phil. 3. 9 (not having a righteousness of my own . . . but that which is through faith in Christ, the righteousness which is of God by faith) Is. 46. 13 (I bring man my righteousness, it shall not be far off, and my salvation shall not tarry; and I will place salvation in Zion for Israel my glory) Jer. 23. 6 (. . . this is his name whereby he shall be called, The Lord is our righteousness) 1 Cor. 1. 30 (of him are ye in Christ Jesus, who was made unto us wisdom from God, and righteousness, and sanctification and redemption); (3) and since that cannot become ours save by imputation, and there is no other way of obtaining it, [Scripture] says in a word that it must plainly be imputed to us, using the word λογίζεσθαι, which, taken from merchants' columns, is frequently used by the Apostle on this topic Rom. 4: 5. 15 (. . . much more did the grace of God, and the gift by the grace of the one man Jesus Christ, abound unto the many) 2 Cor. 5. 21 (him who knew no sin he made to be sin on our behalf; that we might become the righteousness of God in him)."—WOLLEB (142): "The form of justification discerned actively is the imputation of the whole satisfaction of Christ, by which it is wholly ours, just as if we ourselves had provided it. The righteousness imputed to the believer is inherently in Christ, imputedly in us."— WALAEUS 791: "By imputation we mean not *insitio* or infusion, as certain *Papists* wrongly infer from the rural use of this word, but acceptance of Christ's righteousness in place of our own, as is plain from the force of the word λογίζεσθαι, which is taken from the accountants (*rationarii*). Moreover, the basis of the imputation is either the dignity of the person to whom something is imputed, or the sole grace and mercy of the imputer, as is clear from Rom. 4. 4 (to him that worketh the reward is not reckoned as of grace, but as of debt. But to him that worketh not, but believeth on him that justifieth the ungodly, his faith is reckoned for righteousness). In the latter way Christ's merit is imputed to us; for there is imputed to us a righteousness which we do not possess in ourselves Rom. 4. 11 (he received the sign of circumcision, a seal of the righteousness of the faith which he had, while he was in uncircumcision: that he might be the father of all them that believe, though they be in uncircumcision, that righteousness might be reckoned unto them), and sin is not imputed to us, which we do possess in ourselves Mt. 15. 28 (great is thy faith; be it done unto thee even as thou wilt. And her daughter was healed . . .) Philemon 18 (if he hath wronged thee at all, or oweth thee aught, put that to my account) Rom. 2. 26 (if the uncircumcision keep the ordinances of the law, shall not his uncircumcision be reckoned for circumcision?)."—LEIDEN SYNOPSIS (XXXIII, 22): "This imputation is not a fiction but has a place in equity and civil law, as laying it down that the one creditor has rights over sponsor and debtor."

11.—H. Scripture expressly attests that Christ's righteousness is given us by attribution, and so becomes our righteousness.—COCCEIUS. *Summ. theol.* XLVIII, 28): "And yet, say they, we nowhere read that Christ's righteousness is imputed to us. Answer: It reads, which is more, that it is gifted to us Rom. 5. 15–17 (not as the trespass, so also is the free gift. For if by the trespass of the one many died, much more did the grace of God, and the gift by the grace of the one man Jesus Christ, abound unto the many. And not as through one that had sinned, *so* is the gift; for the judgment came of one unto condemnation, but the free gift came of many trespasses unto justification. For if, by the trespass of one, death reigned through the one; much more shall they that receive the abundance of grace and (of the gift) of righteousness reign in life through the one, even Jesus Christ), so that we may become the righteousness of God in Christ 2 Cor. 5. 21 [p. 549] who became righteousness for us 1 Cor. 1. 30 (*ib.*); that we are sprinkled with the blood of Christ 1 Pet. 1. 2 (elect . . . unto obedience and sprinkling of the blood of Christ), washed in him 1 Cor. 6. 11 (. . . but ye were washed . . . in the name of the Lord Jesus Christ and in the Spirit of our God), purified Rev. 7. 14 (. . . washed their robes and made them white in the blood of the Lamb) Heb. 1. 3 (. . . when he has made purification for sins . . .) 1 Jn. 1. 7 (. . . and the blood of Jesus his Son cleanseth us from all sin)."

12.—But this righteousness is not the essential righteousness of God, which is identical with God's nature and cannot therefore be imparted to man; it is the righteousness of the Law, upon which God had concluded His first covenant with man, and which Christ as man had acquired for himself by his active and passive obedience.—OLEVIAN (p. 85): "It is therefore not the essential righteousness of Jehovah or of the Son who is Jehovah, that is imputed to us, but the fact that he submitted himself in his whole person, i.e., not only as he is a man, but also as he is the Son from eternity—in order that the submission once made might be perpetually strong and might be steadily imputed by the head to the members."—HEIDEGGER (XXII, 45): "Christ's righteousness which is imputed to those to be justified is not the essential or eternal and infinite righteousness of Christ's deity.—Through the singleness of the divine essence this is Deity itself; it cannot enter into the accountancy (*rationes*) of the righteousness imputed to man, short of a monstrous deification of it. It is therefore legal or exact by the measure of that law, on con-condition of which God made the covenant of works with man in his integrity."—WITSIUS (III, viii, 37): "The thing on account of which we are justified (some call it the matter (*materia*) of our justification), is the sole perfect righteousness of Christ".—MASTRICHT (VI, vi, 11): "Christ's sole righteousness acquired provides the δικαίωμα on account of which we are justified by God."—HEIDEGGER (XXII, 45): "Since man has transgressed (the law) and by his transgression has merited death, yet so that as an abiding creature of God he has been anything but absolved from the duty to obey and fulfil the law—it becomes clear that Christ who took the sinner's place in the covenant of grace, not only had to suffer death on our behalf and to become a curse, but also had to fulfil all righteousness."

13.—The fruit of the divine attribution of Jesus Christ's righteousness is not the plucking out of the sin (*peccatum inhaerens*) in man's heart.— WENDELIN (*Collat.*, p. 205): "Strictly however by justification it is not the sins inherent in us that are removed so that we are plainly cleansed again from sins, but our liability or obligation to punishment, when sins inherent in us are no more imputed unto damnation but are condoned; and so by justification the righteousness of Christ is imputed to us, which does not inhere in us."—RIISSEN (XIV, 11): "We lay it down that remission of sin does not consist in the abolition of spot or vicious quality, but in the free condonation of the fault arising from it" (the *macula*).

14.—What we receive is (1) the forgiveness of sins or the removal of the guilt of the sins, (2) assurance of eternal life. The latter also belongs to the nature of justification; the law itself promises eternal life, on the condition fulfilled by Christ that it should be fulfilled completely.—BURMANN ((VI, v, 18): "The imputation of Christ's righteousness consists of two parts: (1) remission of sins, (2) the adjudgement of eternal life. It is not merely pardon that is here involved."—LEIDEN SYNOPSIS (XXXIII, 8): "There are two parts in justification : the imputation of passive righteousness or absolution from sins, and the imputation of active righteousness. By the former of these we are delivered from liability and condemnation, and exempted from eternal death. By the latter we are also deemed worthy of a reward and receive the right to eternal life and it is adjudged to us, Rom. 5. 17 [p. 550], 18 (as through one trespass the judgement came unto all men to condemnation, even so through one act of righteousness the free gift came unto all men to justification of life) 8. 3-4 (what the law could not do in that it was weak through the flesh, God [did;] sending his own Son in the likeness of sinful flesh and as an offering for sin [He] condemned sin in the flesh, that the ordinance of the law might be fulfilled in us, who walk not after the flesh, but after the spirit)".

15.—Moreover the sins which God forgives men in justification are not merely past sins but man's generally, since by justification God declares

the sinner to be one who has a right to the inheritance of eternal life.—
HEIDEGGER (XXII, 49): "When the Apostle Rom. 4. 5 [p. 549] said that
faith is imputed unto righteousness, it is not only faith by which remission
of past sins is believed in, but also the faith by which it is believed that God
justifies the ungodly. Now to justify is to regard a man as one who may
rightly ask and look for the reward of eternal life."

16.—Hence since by justification God enters into the relationship of a
father with the sinner, the assurance of eternal life guaranteed in it is to be
regarded as the adoption of the sinner. "Adoption is the gracious sentence
of God—by which those justified by faith and reconciled to God through
and on account of the same Christ are in addition also assumed as sons and
heirs, and co-heirs with Christ" (HEIDEGGER XXII, 86), who also says
earlier (XXII, 62): "The second part of justification is the adjudgement
of life or inheritance. On account of Christ's righteousness and obedience
not only are his sins condoned in a man, but the right to ask for heavenly
and eternal life is also assigned to him. This concession of the right to life
really coincides with adoption and is none otherwise distinguished from
it than that in justification eternal life is viewed as a due, in adoption
as an inheritance; and in the former case God sustains the role of a judge
in the latter that of a Father."

17.—Of this adoption the person justified becomes certain by the seal of
the H. Spirit given in faith itself.—BURMANN (VI, vi, 1 : "The result of
justification is adoption, which is that lofty dignity of the faithful, by
which they are received for Christ's sake into the family of God and constitute a part of His house and in short become partakers in the heavenly
inheritance.—5: The sign and seal of that gracious title is the H. Spirit,
who is called the Spirit of adoption Rom. 8, Gal. 4, who by that inward
commerce and address softens our soul and causes it to approach God
with confidence as Father. So that we may now call Him "Father",
by which name and sound as of nature itself those formerly sought the
Father who were to be added to a strange household. Whence Christ too
is said Mk. 14. 36 to have used it of his own Father (Father . . . remove
this cup from me).—6: But this witness is not to be located in some unusual
address within or a peculiar reply of the *numen*, as it were, and is not to
be over nicely distinguished from faith and other affections of the Christian
soul, as though we believed it was insinuated into us by another Spirit's act
and a direct address by Him; as opponents are wont to accuse the Spirit
of adoption and to compare it with an empty and deceitful sort of echo.
As soon as we believe and by the very fact that we believe, we are sealed;
and this is the very mark and impress of the Spirit, and faith is its only

sign."—HYPERIUS (p. 409) aptly describes adoption as the equation of the believer *qua* 'son of adoption' with the 'natural son of God' in the sight of the Father."

18.—By the seal of the H. Spirit given in faith the believer gains Christian freedom, or the freedom of the children of God, i.e. freedom from captivity to sin and the law.—RIJSSEN (XIV, 11): "From this adoption arises Christian freedom, which is not immunity from all laws, which pleases the libertine; not exemption from the jurisdiction of the magistrates, such as the *Anabaptists* are keen on and the priest of *Rome* claims for himself. But it is spiritual manumission acquired for us by the blood of Christ, by which we are claimed from spiritual servitude to the law, sin, the world and Satan for the liberty of the sons of God."—BURMANN (VI, vi, 9): "The fruits of adoption are (1) freedom from slavery to sin and the law, which was continual in the Church under both the Old and the New Testaments Rom. 6. 22 (. . . being made free from sin, and become servants to God, ye have your fruits unto sanctification and the end eternal life) Jn. 8. 36 (if therefore the Son shall make you free, ye shall be free indeed), although a greater degree of it was notable under the New; (2) the inheritance of believers and dominion over all the creatures, now allowed us and pure 1 Cor. 3. 21-22 (let no one glory in men. All things are yours, whether Paul, or Apollos, or Cephas, or the world or life or death, or things present, things to come, all are yours); Tit. 1. 15 (to the pure all things are pure: but to them that are defiled and unbelieving nothing is pure . . .)".

19.—The condition to which the attribution of Christ's righteousness is attached is not the performance of a work (for by works fallen man can merit nothing nor satisfy God in any way), but only faith in Christ and his work of redemption. But this faith effects justification not as a meritorious work or as the root of good works, but purely as a *causa instrumentalis*, not for one moment as a condition fulfillable by man,— for a condition of justification can only be laid down by the law, but not by free grace, and the single real condition of justification is perfect obedience to the law.—MASTRICHT (VI, vi, 14): "It is worth while inquiring how faith inflows into justification.—(1) It does not do so as the meritorious cause of it.—Nor (2) because of faith;—but we are justified through faith".—WITSIUS (III, viii, 52): "Nor does it seem to me an accurate statement, that faith is the condition which the gospel demands of us, that we may be held righteous and innocent with God. Strictly speaking the condition of justification is nothing but perfect obedience. — This the law enacted. Nor did the gospel substitute another; it teaches that the law has been satisfied by our sponsor Christ. It is at once the duty of faith

to accept and by accepting to make its own satisfaction offered for it."—
CROCIUS 1223: "So not only are those works excluded from the act of
justification, which are emitted by a man before faith and conversion, but
also those which proceed from faith."—BURMANN (VI, v, 25): "Indeed
faith is so opposed to works in this matter that it even excludes itself,
if it is considered as a work. Although regarded by itself it is a work,
in justification it is not regarded after this manner but purely as an instrumental work"—BUCAN (XXXI, 34): "In what sense are we said to be
justified by faith? It is not regarded in its own intrinsic dignity or merit,
nor as a work or a new quality in us, nor in its force and efficacy minus
love; nor because it has love added to it or works through love; nor
because faith imparts the Spirit of Christ, by whom the believer is rendered
just because we are bidden seek righteousness not in ourselves but in
Christ; but because it seeks and embraces the righteousness offered in the
Gospel Rom. 1. 16:17 (I am not ashamed of the gospel of Christ: for it is
the power of God unto salvation to everyone that believeth, . . . therein
is revealed a righteousness of God by faith unto faith: as it is written,
But the righteous shall live by faith). As regards justification faith is a
purely passive thing, bringing nothing of ours to conciliate God, but
receiving from Christ what we lack."

20.—Faith therefore justifies purely because the sinner by faith so grasps
the righteousness of faith offered him from without in the Gospel, that
that can be produced by faith which is itself the merit of Christ, (who is)
the object of faith. In truth not faith but the righteousness of Christ is
the δικαίωμα that justifies the sinner, whence also the justification of the
elect is determined by God, not according to ever imperfect faith, but
according to the ever perfect righteousness of Christ. Since therefore
faith can only be described in an improper sense as the *instrumentum
justificationis*, it is better to say that faith itself is man's being justified.—
—WALAEUS p. 782: "So far the errors concerning the way in which faith
justifies have been refuted. It follows that we reveal the view which is
that of the Reformed Catholic Church.—Namely that faith justifies or
that we are justified by faith, because it grasps Christ's righteousness
offered us in the Gospel, or so far as it is considered relatively and with
respect to Christ's merit."—WOLLEB 141: "This phrase "we are justified
by faith" is metaphorical, and is equivalent to saying that we are justified
by the merit of Christ grasped by faith".—CALVIN (III, xi, 7): "Did
faith justify of itself or, as they say, by its own intrinsic merit. Since it is
always weak and imperfect, its efficacy would only be partial. Thus
righteousness would be maimed and would bestow on us but a morsel of
salvation. We indeed imagine nothing of the kind, but speaking strictly,

we say that God alone justifies—we compare faith to a kind of vessel."

Hence Reformed dogmaticians usually insist that we are not really justified by faith, since we can only be justified by Christ, and would therefore only allow faith to be described with reserve as the *instrumentum justificationis*. The interest by which dogmaticians are here led is described by MASTRICHT (VI, vi, 28): "so that this faith of ours may in no sense be our δικαίωμα or part of it or depend on our strength." Of course what WITSIUS (III, viii, 56) says is correct, that "The genuine view of the Reformed is that faith justifies, so far as it is the bond of our closest union with Christ, by which all things which are Christ's become ours also, or, which is meant in the same sense, so far as it is an acceptance of the gift offered, making the donation settled and irrevocable." But withal the dogmaticians invariably come back to the thought that we are not justified *per fidem*, but that faith is already justification in and for itself. To believe in Christ is essentially='grasping Christ', and so essentially and directly= 'being justified'. This view is represented as early as URSIN (1612) (Cf. HEPPE *Dogm. d. deutsch. Protest.* p. 310).

21.—Man is not justified, because to achieve justification he uses the means of faith in Christ. God justifies man by making him a present of the righteousness of Christ in the form of faith. Hence the distinction between active and passive justification. 'Active justification' must not be confused with God's eternal counsel of grace; the decree of justification is one thing and justification another. It rather results in time, on the one hand in the person of Christ, since Christ accomplished his work of reconciliation on earth and is now effectual at the Father's side as the representative of the elect; on the other hand in the person of the individual elect, as soon as God calls him effectually by the H. Spirit and effectually imparts His grace to him by the infusion of faith. 'Passive justification' is the subjective feeling of grace in the consciousness of the man justified by faith. In the former case justification of the elect results in a complete 'single act' once and for all (KECKERMANN 415), the moment faith awakes in his heart: therefore justification of the sinner happens only once, repetition is excluded. In the latter respect on the contrary, so far as justification is the blessed consciousness of the state of grace, or the absolutely comfortable feeling of the grace of God in a man's own heart variations in justification are possible, for this passive justification remains at the best of times so imperfect here on earth, that the believer must cry to God daily for forgiveness of his past and his future sins.

The distinction between 'active' and 'passive' justification is immovably fixed in Reformed dogmatics, and in it the latter is given a special significance, because the elect implanted from eternity in Christ have really shared already in experience of the whole work of redemption in Christ, so that the whole *applicatio salutis* in this connection can only consist in what already belongs objectively to the elect, being also made subjectively alive in them. Meanwhile the distinction between active and passive justification is not perfectly and adequately expounded by all dogmaticians.—HEIDEGGER (XXII, 78) speaks thus: "Although in itself an undivided act in terms of the sense of receiving remission of sins, justification is yet divided and imperfect. Justification is considered in two ways: so far as it is God's love and judgment upon those whom He finds existing through faith in Christ Phil. 3. 9 (found in Christ, not having a righteousness of my own, even that which is of the law, but that which is through faith in Christ, the righteousness which is of God by faith), absolves from sin and presents with the right to ask for life; and so far as it is the pronouncement and deliverance of that divine love and judgment, on the announcement of which to the soul or heart of the believer they themselves realise and feel in themselves that they are loved as righteous men by God in Christ the mediator and are entered as heirs of life. In the former way it is usually called 'active justification', in the latter 'passive'.—(79): The active justification of all faithful justified is uniform and clearly undivided, perfect and as it were placed in an indivisible atom, and admits of no difference at all among the justified before and after Christ. Nor is it in the strict sense accomplished from eternity, because God does not execute the eternal decree to justify before faith, but in time, partly in heaven, after Christ's sufferings on the Cross were accomplished, when Christ our advocate—pleads our cause and the Father absolves us; partly in conscience, as soon as we believe in Christ and sentence of absolution is pronounced as to our faith.— The passive is unequal, imperfect, divided, varies and differs both as regards the justified of OT and NT— and as regards individual justified. It consists in the sense or taste of the sentence pronounced and in joy over the accepted absolution and particularly in the ensuing and consolatory act of faith it is absolved by the sealing of the H. Spirit.—For although active and passive justification coexist simultaneously as a formally justificatory act, as a feeling and consolation of the soul, particularly as a reflex and final act of faith, as well as that sweetness of soul arising from justification, the latter turns up often only a long time after and is not seldom broken into and interrupted. In graver sins against conscience, also in more trying temptations, there is no sense of the grace of a propitious God, though by the victory of the Spirit the grace returns and is renewed.—And for the same reason it is imperfect also.—Whence believers already justified by faith are bidden seek daily remission of their sins both past and future".—Similarly BURMANN (VI, v, 28-29).

But otherwise on the contrary Rᴜssᴇɴ (XIV, 5): "Justification is distinguished by healthy sense into active and passive. Active is the general pronouncement of God by which He at the same time absolves all believers for Christ's sake. And that (1) in Paradise and in the promise Gen. 3. 15 (I will put enmity between thee and the woman, and between thy seed and her seed; it shall bruise thy head, and thou shalt bruise his heel); (2) in Christ the Head 2 Cor. 5. 19 (God was in Christ reconciling . . .); (3) in His word Rom. 8. 1 (now no condemnation to them that are in Christ Jesus). Passive belongs to each separate believer (1) in his person, when Christ is being given to him; (2) in conscience after the act of faith Rom. 5. 1 (being justified by faith let us have peace with God through our Lord Jesus Christ), which is also often repeated. Active justification precedes our faith and sanctification, passive follows them; and so the will not to punish the sins, e.g., of Paul, exists in God before his faith; but as regards his person the believer remains under liability until he has received Christ by faith."—Rᴜssᴇɴ (XIV, 13) proves that active justification is not to be confused with the eternal decree of God. "Query: Has justification been made from eternity? Answer: There are some who wish justification to have been made from eternity. They conceive of it as an act immanent in God. As nothing new can be added to God in time, they think that it was already made in Him from eternity and is assigned to faith only as regards knowledge and the feeling which leads us into knowledge and makes us sure of it. But although our justification was already decreed from eternity, we are not thinking accurately when we say that justification itself could be called eternal. (1) The decree of justification is one thing, justification itself is another. (2) If this were the case, Paul could not have put calling before justification in the chain of salvation Rom. 8, 30 (foreordination, foreknowledge, calling, justification, glorification), nor could we be said to be justified through faith and by faith, because faith is something prerequisite to justification. (3) Since justification or the remission of sins necessarily involves deliverance from liability to punishment, no one can obtain this without positing faith and repentance; it is clear that such justification could not have been made from eternity, but only in time, the time a man actively believes and shows repentance. (4) Since justification is God's benefit, and the benefit cannot be passed to us and actually conferred on us except in time, clearly it must not be conceived after the measure of an act immanent and inward in God.—15: We embrace the middle view which lays it down that justification is made in this life, in the moment of effectual calling, and by it man the sinner is transferred from the state of sin to the state of grace and is united to Christ his head by faith. Hence it comes about that Christ's righteousness is imputed to him by God, for by his merit grasped through faith he is absolved from his sins and obtains the right to life. This absolute pronouncement the Spirit makes in his heart when he says, Son, be of good cheer; thy sins have been remitted thee."

MARESIUS again (XI, 58) is different: "Our justification may be considered (1) actively and from God's side, not only in His counsel and where it was provided by His act of admitting Christ's satisfaction for our sins and resolving in Himself not to impute them to us for punishment but fairly and fully to condone them; but also, for the actual execution of the purpose, intimating this decree and counsel of his to us through the H. Spirit, and truly pronouncing over and to us, as it says in Heb. 4. 16 (draw near with boldness unto the throne of Grace, that we may receive mercy and may find grace to help us in time of need) from the throne of grace, judicially, a true sentence of justification and absolution, practically in the words, Be of good courage, my Son, thy sins are forgiven thee Mt. 9. 2.—(2) Passively and from our side, so far as with faith, joy and protestation of thankfulness we admit and take upon us this decree and counsel of God, intimated in the court of conscience by the H. Spirit and the absolute sentence resulting from Christ's obedience and satisfaction admissible in God's eyes on our behalf. In the former sense justification is in a way prior to faith and at least to nature, as being its justificatory act: for object is prior to the operation which deals with it. In time it is scarcely prior, since hardly any interval is conceivable between the pronouncement and formulation, through the Spirit of adoption, of the sentence of justification and the apprehension and admission of it with firm confidence. So far is our active justification from preceding our birth, as some dream, or from being before our calling, to which it is so expressly put in reserve Rom. 8. 30 (p. 557): whom he called them also he justified. In the second sense faith might apparently be said to be a prior nature to justification, as recipient is prior to the thing received and instrument to sensation; and also faith is exacted from man the sinner, so that he receives remission of sin passively considered. But really they are simultaneous, because the actual publication and intimation of our absolution with God and reconciliation through Christ is the illumination to formally justifying faith, from which it is only distinguished by method and in the light of our mode of conceiving, and to which from the very outset our attitude is purely passive; although afterwards from that very light of faith already flooding our minds we at once elicit various acts of faith for our consolation and the determination, application and extension to our daily sins of the judicial absolution and justification in question by looking back to the merit of Christ and to the reconciliation required and offered us in him."

Later dogmaticians like WYTTENBACH (II, 939) and others call active and passive justification first and second justification and identify it with the justification of the sinner and that of the righteous.

22.—As regards the subjective side of justification there arise in consequence three different acts of faith, namely (1) an *actus dispositivus sive praeparatorius*, i.e., the knowledge of the righteousness prepared in Christ for believers and desire for the same; (2) an *actus iustificatorius*, i.e., the consciousness of received fellowship with Christ and of his received righteousness; and (3) consciousness of blessed peace with God abidingly gained thereby.—MARESIUS (XI, 57): "A threefold act of faith comes up for consideration and distinction in justification: (1) dispositive, by which I believe that Christ merited for his own the remission of sins according to the teaching of the Gospel, and that therefore my sins will be remitted, if I have repented and rested in true confidence in the merit of Christ.—Wherefore since faith, as regards this act, precedes the actual remission of sins in the court of heaven and our conscience, so is it also required beforehand in the word, if remission is to be obtained: (2) justificatory in the formal sense, by which, when the actual sentence of justification and absolution is proclaimed and intimated to me by the Spirit of adoption, I at once believe that if I am sorry for my sins and promise God accordingly serious zeal in emendation, all my sins have been remitted in Christ, both those which I have hitherto committed and those into which I may subsequently slip through infirmity, and that God will never impute them to me unto condemnation, but by the imputed righteousness of my Saviour He will hold me innocent and will surely give me eternal life; and this act is simultaneous with actual justification and the remission of sins: (3) consolatory, by which I believe that all my sins have already been remitted to me in the past and that I am no longer subject to any condemnation, as says St. Paul, Rom. 8. 1, and I trust in the absolute sentence previously intimated to me, that mercy will be extended and applied to me by God's mercy for the sins incurred daily, for which actually every day I ask remission in that sense in the Lord's Prayer; and this act of faith follows justification and remission of sins. Whence it is clear, in what sense and to what extent faith is a condition prerequisite to it. In the first respect the relation of faith to justification is antecedent, in the second simultaneous, in the third consequent."—Similarly BURMANN (VI, v, 26).

23.—That faith in this sense is man's justification is attested by H. Scripture, which altogether promises surely to faith, excluding any meritoriousness of works, the comfort of justification, fellowship with

Christ and eternal life.—HEIDEGGER *Medull.* XXII, 37): "Thus in this sense it is a truth well attested in Scripture, that faith alone justifies. (1) Everywhere Scripture assigns to faith justification, life and communion with Christ, Rom. 1. 17 (in the gospel is revealed a righteousness of God by faith unto faith: as it is written, But the righteous shall live by faith), 3. 26–28 (for the showing of his righteousness at this present season; that he might himself be just and the justifier of him that hath faith in Jesus Christ. Where then is the glorying? It is excluded. By what manner of law? of works? Nay; but by a law of faith. We reckon therefore that a man is justified by faith apart from the works of the law), Gal. 2. 16, 20 (knowing that a man is not justified by works of the law, save through faith in Jesus Christ, even we believed on Jesus Christ, that we might be justified by faith in Christ, and not by works of the law: because by the works of the law shall no flesh be justified ... I have been crucified with Christ, yet I live; and yet no longer I, but Christ liveth in me; and the life which I now live in the flesh I live in faith, *the faith* which is in the Son of God, who loved me and gave himself up for me), Hab. 2. 4 (the just shall live by his faith), Eph. 3. 17 (that Christ may dwell in your hearts through faith; to the end that ye being rooted and grounded in faith, etc.).—Then (2) works as causes are excluded from justification, life and communion with Christ and are opposed to faith, Rom. 3. 28 [above] 4. 4–5 (to him that worketh the reward is not reckoned as of grace, but as of debt. But to him that worketh not, but believeth on him that justifieth the ungodly, his faith is reckoned for righteousness), etc."—LEIDEN SYNOPSIS (XXXIII, 25): "On our side then we are justified by our faith, Rom. 5. 2 (through whom also we have had our access by faith into this grace in which we stand) Ac. 26. 17 (delivering thee from the people, and from the Gentiles, unto whom I (Jesus) send thee); and *ex fide* and *per fidem* Rom. 3. 30 (God shall justify the circumcision by faith and the uncircumcision through faith); and so God justifies us; by faith, I say, in God and in Jesus Christ our Lord Ac. 26. 18 (to open their eyes, that they may turn from darkness to light, and from the power of Satan unto God, that they may receive remission of sins and an inheritance among them that are sanctified by faith in me), *ex fide in fidem,* Rom. 1. 17 [above], and in fact *fide sine operibus;* in an opposed sense *fide* and not *operibus legis;* and *nonnisi ex fide* and *tantum fide,* i.e., *sola fide,* Rom. 3. 28–30, Gal. 2. 16 [both above] Lk. 8. 5 (the Sower). Whence also this righteousness is called the *iustitia fidei,* Rom. 4. 11–13 (and he received the sign of circumcision, a seal of the righteousness of the faith which he had while he was in uncircumcision: that he might be the father of all them that believe, though they be in uncircumcision, that righteousness might be reckoned unto them: and the father of circumcision to them who not only are of the circumcision, but who also walk in the steps of that faith of our father Abraham which he had in uncircumcision. For not through the law was the promise to Abraham or to his seed, that he should be the heir of the world, but through the righteousness of faith)."

24.—Hence although the little word *sola* (*fide*) is not found in use where it speaks of justifying faith, and although in relation to good works faith is never solitary but always "effectual through love" and essentially "living faith", the meaning of Scripture teaching yet is most adequately expressed by saying that man is justified *sola fide*.—Crocius, p. 1,222: "Even if faith is never alone but is supported by good works as its fruits, yet it alone grasps Christ's merit and so alone justifies, even without the concurrence and assistance of works."—Walaeus, p. 776: "When we say that we are justified *per solam fidem*, by that we do not mean empty faith:—but we are dealing with living faith effectual through love, although it does not borrow from love the power to justify."—Rijssen (XIV, xi, 1): "The question is, not whether solitary faith justifies, i.e., faith separated from the other virtues ; which we agree cannot easily be the case, since it is not even true of living faith; but whether it alone concurs in the act of justification—our own claim!—as the eye alone sees but not plucked away from the body. The particle alone determines, then, not the subject but the predicate. Thus faith *alone* does not justify, but faith alone *does* justify. The co-existence of love with faith in him who is justified is not denied, but its co-effectuality or co-operation in justification. Nor is the question whether faith which justifies is active in love, because at other times it is not alive but dead; but whether as justifying or in the very act of justification it must be viewed under such a σχέσις. To which we say No."

25.—Only to the elect but—in spite of all waverings and graduations of faith—to each one of them justification is imparted in full, and—in spite of the difference in the dispensations of the covenant of grace before and after Christ's manifestation—at all times in the same way. For in its nature justification of the sinner is "one and unique, equal, absolute, perfect," and "immune from loss."—Maresius (XI, 60–62): As saving faith is only for the elect, so only the elect but they all and entirely—are justified by God.—Now various properties of this justification should be observed. (1) It is unique, executed on God's part by a unique act and once only, then presently by a saving *vocatio*.—61: (2) It is perfect, intrinsically free from increase or decrease, although as regards the grasping and the certainty of it our faith so advances by steps, as sometimes to its troubles, like the moon.—62: (3) Finally, as there is absolute remission of sins in those once justified, justification itself is also absolute, not dependent on any uncertain or potential factor: although God requires faith and repentance; but God surely effects these in His own."— WOLLEB 146: "The righteousness imputed to us is perfect and equal in all believers. Imperfection is no barrier to faith. As the strong and the weak hand grasps the same jewel, so strong and weak men obtain the same righteousness of Christ.—When it exists, it cannot be lost. The gifts of the divine calling are ἀμεταμέλητα Rom. 11. 29 (the gifts and the calling of God are without repentance).—It is also unique. When therefore saints already justified ask for their sins to be condoned, they have regard not so much to the act of justification, as to its fruits, confirmation and certification."

29.—"Justification of the just", of which we have still to speak, is the certainty which the justified person receives as to the sincerity of his faith and the reality of his position under grace by the testimony of his conversation and works. — HEIDEGGER (XXII, 80): "The sinner's justification is of the past. There is also justification of a second kind, viz. of him who by faith is already just and justified. This justification is the indication of the just man or the declaration of the receipt of the righteousness of faith, by which a man who has been justified by faith, in proving by works in the sight of God receipt of the same righteousness of faith and so the real sincerity of his faith, is truly justified by faith in conscience and in the sight of men, is declared and pronounced to be truly a believer, not a hypocrite but upright and a walker in God's sight, Rom. 4. 2 (If Abraham was justified by works, he hath whereof to glory, but not toward God), Jas. 2. 21-24 (Was not Abraham our father justified by works, in that he offered up Isaac his son upon the altar? Thou seest that faith wrought with his works, and by works was faith made perfect; and the scripture was fulfilled which saith, And Abraham believed God, and it was reckoned unto him for righteousness, (Gen. 15. 6); and he was called the friend of God (2 Chron. 20. 7; Is. 41. 8 (seed of Abraham) ; Wisdom 7. 27 (Ye see that by works a man is justified and not only by faith) Rev. 22. 11 (. . . he that is righteous, let him do righteousness still)."—BURMANN (VI, v, 34-35): "Lastly there remains to be dealt with a third state of man, as from being a sinner he has become regenerate, and in view of this state of his a different manner and type of justification must be considered, the justification not of the sinner but of the righteous. This takes place not only by faith but also by works, which the Apostle, Rom. 8. 3 implies, when he maintains that every δικαίωμα of the law must be fulfilled in us. This is never done completely so long as it rules over the corrupt sinner and as the δύναμις ἁμαρτίας rather calls forth and stimulates sin. So that he must not only be endued with the righteousness of Christ the Head and covered with that garment he must also be seemly in a holiness of his own and conform to the law. In a word, with its consent, he must be righteous and blameless.—35: For as man may be accused on two counts, either liability or hypocrisy, and as righteousness is twofold, one imputed, to meet the first charge, the other inherent, to purge him of hypocrisy; so there is also a twofold justification of man, and in both ways he may rightly be called righteous. No use floundering in verbal superstition. The former may be called first, the latter second justification. The former rests upon the imputed righteousness of Christ, the latter upon the inherent holiness of a man: the former is that of the godless, the latter that of the righteous. The former consists in the remission of sins, the latter in the recognition of inherent righteousness by no means perfect but nevertheless genuine. The former is perfect, the latter imperfect. The former in short is achieved by faith, the latter proceeds from works. But both rest upon the righteousness of Christ, since the works of the regenerate emanate not from law but from grace and the Spirit of Christ. The result is that though the works are imperfect, yet they get credit from God. And in this sense everything seems most rightly understood which occurs *passim* in Scripture, especially the N.T., on the justification of us by works of grace, faith and the gospel and their need of and concurrence in justification".—Similarly COCCEIUS (*Summ. theol.* XLVIII, 39). WENDELIN *Coll.* p. 189: "True justification is not without inherent holiness."—Reformed dogmaticians also speak in the same sense of a growth in justification, e.g. PISCATOR (*Aphorism.* p. 74) who says that "not only the start of justification but also its progress is purely of grace."

27.—The judicial voice which hereby guarantees to the believer the sincerity of his faith is his own conscience, i.e. the voice of God in his own heart. Through his conscience the believer is aware that Christ's righteousness is not merely imputed to him (*iustitia imputata*), but also really indwells through the H. Spirit (*iustitia inhaerens*), and that he thereby grows in righteousness, i.e. in the *iustificatio iusti* not *peccatoris*. But although *iustificatio iusti* is recognised from his works, it still no less than *iustificatio peccatoris* rests solely upon the grace of Christ, because the works of a regenerate man are not works of the law but of redeeming grace and the Spirit of Christ, and so alone—in spite of defectiveness—well-pleasing to God.—HEIDEGGER (XXII, 81): "A man's conscience making trial of his faith in Christ stands or falls not otherwise than by works which prove faith, he himself being the judge. So he is held to be either δόκιμος or ἀδόκιμος, he is either acquitted and justified or he is condemned. And since conscience is nothing else than God himself speaking in the heart, absolving or convicting, so this divine tribunal is regarded as at the same time sojourning, but privately and in the inmost heart. (32):—Thus explained these things display a very complete agreement on justification between St. Paul and St. James.—The simplest and truest reconciliation is that St. Paul treating of the justification of the sinner *a priori* or by its causes and St. James treating of the justification of the righteous *a posteriori* and by signs or effects, both deal by proof and assertion with the signs, evidences and effects of the same righteousness accepted by faith."—COCCEIUS (*Summ. theol.* XLVIII, 39) insists that, James 2. 2 4 (p. 562), does not deny man's justification by faith, but denies that the man who declares that he has faith and no works can be told, 'Η πίστις σοῦ σέσωκέ σε. Further, that James understands by works not works of the law but good works upon which we are founded, Eph. 2. 10 (ye are his workmanship, created in Christ Jesus for good works, which God afore prepared that we should walk in them). James is said not to ascribe τὸ σώζειν ἡμᾶς to these works in the way in which faith and grace make man blessed, but to teach that "if faith is without works it is dead, i.e. is not the faith which saves."

28.—In this way it is possible for the Christian to become certain of his faith and of its sincerity and so of his state of grace. And that is why it is the Christian's duty to test himself and find out whether he is really living in faith and whether he really has the righteousness that stands with God.—WYTTENBACH (II, 995): "Hence it follows that a man may know whether or not he rejoices in faith, or, that consciousness of faith is strictly possible. Hence because this consciousness is possible, a man is bidden try himself as to his faith."

29.—The chief purpose of justification is the glorification of God, i.e. above all, the manifestation of the absolute mercy and righteousness of God, wherein in a subordinate way is united the purpose of blessing the elect in time and eternity.—HEIDEGGER (XXII, 75): "The supreme end of justification is the ἔπαινος δόξης gratiae Eph. 1. 6, or the glory and recognition of God and of His virtues, such as are primarily mercy and righteousness.—After this supreme end a subordinate one is the salvation of the elect and their most firm consolation in life and death."

CHAPTER XXII

SANCTIFICATION

1.—When the elect and called sinner is justified, sanctification thereby begins in him. "Sanctification is the gratuitous act of God by which He delivers believers, ingrafted in Christ by faith and justified by the H. Spirit, more and more from their native viciousness and renews them after His own image, in order that they may be rendered fit to glorify Him by good works."—(WOLLEB 144). It is not just a moral but a physical effect of the H. Spirit, by which God infuses into man the Spirit of holiness, i.e., horror of what is displeasing to God and striving after what is well-pleasing to God, and accordingly urges man to actions well-pleasing to Him.—COCCEIUS (*Summa de foed.* XV, 539): "Reconciliation and regeneration and justification cannot exist without the benefit of sanctification. Here I mean not, as this word is widely used elsewhere, actual regeneration and justification, but ἀνακαίνωσις, renewal or continued purification from vices and the inauguration of virtues."— MASTRICHT (VI, viii, 7): "By sanctification we mean the physical operation of God, by which He infuses holiness into His own and secures its exercise." Hence two things must be distinguished: (1) what "holiness" is, and (2) the nature of the "sanctifying operation." Holiness is "the disposition of heart, by which it tends to avoid what is adverse to God and to seek what is acceptable to Him." The "sanctifying operation" is not merely a moral but also a "physical" one, or an "intrinsic change of being sanctified, by which (God) (1) infuses into the heart a disposition suited to God, then (2) urges it when infused into exercise, into actions." —BRAUN (I, iii, 10, 10): "Sanctification" is a "change in man", the "*terminus a quo* of which is the corruption of the image of God", of which the *terminus ad quem* is the "restoration of that image".

2.—Of course sanctification is involved in justification, so far as the latter is the real and essential beginning of sanctification. Nevertheless sanctification is to be distinguished as well from justification as from vocation; for vocation is the beginning of regeneration, whereas sanctification is the continuation of it to gradual completion; and justification is an act of God resulting outwith man, by which God assigns to him an alien righteousness; whereas sanctification is an activity of God in man's inward part. The former rests directly upon the sacrificial death and merit of Christ, the latter on the contrary is an effect which the death and life of Christ produce indirectly in the person called. The former is a once-for-all act of God imparted in the same way; the latter is a gradual process variously completed according to the varying measure of the Spirit which the individual receives. In the former man's relation to the grace that sanctifies him is purely passive; in the latter he co-operates with it.

URSIN (*Explic. Catech.* p. 315): "We know that we have received justification in Christ by faith; although it is never given to the elect without sanctification."—TURRETIN (XVII, i, 15): "Although we may be of opinion that these two benefits must be distinguished and never confused, yet they are connected by the ordinance of God and the nature of the thing, so that they are never to be torn asunder."—RIISSEN (XV, 2): "Sanctification differs from justification: (1) justification is a forensic action; sanctification is physical and real; (2) justification takes place to a great extent outside a man in the word of God and in Christ; sanctification takes place in a man; (3) justification involves no more than a moral change and one of status; sanctification imports a real and new creation (*creatura*); (4) justification takes place perfectly once for all; sanctification is gradual."—WOLLEB 149: "Sanctification differs from justification (1) in *genus;* the righteousness of the former belongs to the category of quality, that of the latter to the category of relation; (2) in form; (a) in justification faith is regarded as a hand grasping the righteousness of Christ, in sanctification faith is regarded as the principle and root of good works; (b) in justification sin is removed only as regards liability and punishment, in sanctification it is gradually abolished as regards existence; (c) in justification Christ's righteousness is imputed to us, in sanctification a new righteousness inherent in us is infused into us; (3) in degrees: for justification is an acting, one, individual, perfect, happening alike to all; but sanctification is a successive act, gradually tending to perfection and, according to the variety in the gifts of the H. Spirit, more shining in some, less so in others.—148: In the first regeneration or calling man is already in a παθητικὸς (passive) state: in sanctification once he has been presented with saving faith, he is also the acting (active?) principle of his actions, though not without the special grace and impulse of the H. Spirit."

3.—Man needs this sanctification exactly as he does justification. The elect are called not only to redemption from the curse of sins, but also to the serious purpose of the sanctification of their hearts, since those who have found in Christ the atonement for the guilt of their sins ought also to rise with Christ to a new, holy life. Therefore no one can be confident of the forgiveness of his sins, who does not apply himself to sanctification. —COCCEIUS (*Summa de foed.* XV, 47): "Where the Spirit of sanctification is absent, darkness must be present in the understanding and wickedness in the will."—HEIDEGGER (XXIII, 7): "The greatest need is for sanctification.—We are not elected merely to be purged of sins by the blood of Christ and regenerated to faith,—but also to a serious purpose out of a pure heart.—Those who have been given to Christ and for whom he died, just as they have died with him to sin 2 Cor. 5. 15 (he died for all, that they which live should no longer live unto themselves, but unto him who for their sakes died and rose again) have a reason in Christ why their flesh and its desires must be abolished and have already begun to crucify the flesh and its desires. If therefore the efficacy of Christ's death is, that in the redeemed their flesh or old man is abolished, it follows that redemption and consolation concerning it belong to no one, so long as he lives in sin and does not crucify his flesh with its desires."

4.—In no way is the believer thereby subjected anew to the yoke of the law; he rather lives in favour with God, precisely because he lives no longer under the law but in the grace, which has imprinted the law on his heart by the H. Spirit and renews him to the true likeness to God.— COCCEIUS (*Summa de foed.* XV, 542): "But although, as has been said, it is impossible without sanctification to see God and all holiness has the law of the decalogue as its measure, none the less we are not under law but under grace. In fact, because we are not under law but under grace, we therefore serve God's law and righteousness, Rom. 6. 14 (sin shall have no dominion over you: for ye are not under law but under grace).—544: Those therefore who are sanctified by the Spirit of Christ are not under law, as they were formerly under the law as miserable sinners. They are freed by the law of the Spirit of life in Christ from the dominion of sin and death, Rom. 8. 2 (the law of the Spirit of life in Christ Jesus made me free from the law of sin and death), i.e., from the dominion of sin and death, which according to the law's sentence follows sin".—HEIDEGGER (XXIII, 9): "It is idle to fear lest men should be subjected once more to law and suffer loss of God's grace. Nay rather, because we are not under law but under grace, we are slaves to God's law and righteousness, Rom. 6. 14 (dominion (above)).—It is one thing to be under a law which prescribes the conditions of righteousness and life, another to be in Christ Jesus under the law of the Spirit of life, who writes the law in man's heart and renews man's heart to the image of God."

5.—God gives the power of sanctification only to those who are elected to the fellowship of the covenant of grace, implanted in Christ, called and justified. But (since sanctification is more than improvement of human actions, namely improvement of the whole man) these are sanctified by Him in their whole man, body, soul and spirit, because body, soul and spirit are on the one hand destroyed by sin and on the other are three distinguishable agents of human actions.—LEIDEN SYNOPSIS (XXXII, 18): "The subject of regeneration is the whole man inserted or to be inserted into Christ by faith, Ac. 15. 9 (and (God) made no distinction between them and us, cleansing their hearts by faith)."— HEIDEGGER (XXIII, 11): "God sanctifies man and man's corrupt nature: but not any man; the elect, called and justified only.—And God thus sanctifies the elect and justified man whole and entire, spirit, soul and body. All these parts being corrupted by sin need sanctification. Nor is man just body, but also spirit and soul, which are so many principles of operation.—BRAUN 453: "The *Socinians* therefore teach very badly, that sanctification consists solely in amending actions, if a man but repents of the sins to which he is most addicted. It really consists in the cleansing of the whole nature."

6.—And God so effects man's sanctification, that in the first instance He fills his understanding with the light of His truth, thence He hallows man's will and inclination, next lays hold of man's bodily life, and makes it serviceable to the power of His Spirit, and so also drives man, thus sanctified in all his organs by the direct inworking of the H. Spirit, to holy action also.

HEIDEGGER (XXIII, 11): "Because the spirit or mind is the principle of our actions, which are completed by the body as instrument, holiness begins in the mind, which ought to be renewed in God the Creator's image.—Instead of it being a profligate mind in gross darkness He brings it into the same light of knowledge and wisdom.—From the mind sanctification proceeds to will and desire.—In fact even members which hitherto have been members of unrighteousness (sanctification) constitutes instruments of righteousness unto God, Rom. 6. 12–13 (Let not sin therefore reign in your mortal body, that ye should obey the lusts thereof: neither present your members unto sin as instruments of unrighteousness; but present yourselves unto God as alive from the dead, and your members as instruments of righteousness unto God).—There is great reason for the sanctification of the body and members. In them is the seat of concupiscence and of the law of sin, which produces strife and war with God's Spirit even in the very soul."—LEIDEN SYNOPSIS (XXXII, 18): "In true and saving regeneration and repentance all the faculties are more and more affected by supernatural and inherent grace on the part of God through the Spirit, and that by direct action."— 23: It must in particular be acknowledged that, when God has already illumined man's "understanding", his will also is regenerated, not by this but by a fresh, direct act of God.—"It cannot be that the will, equipped by mere natural powers, should of itself follow an understanding already affected by a supernatural gift or that the understanding should of itself impress on the will a supernatural quality inherent in itself; since this, as Scripture everywhere asserts, belongs solely to the Spirit of God.—As God created in man the faculty as well of understanding as of will, so by His new creation He superadds supernatural gifts as well to the former as to the latter."—24: It must also be observed that, when the will is sanctified by grace, it still needs the further help of grace, since it is only by it that it can achieve any action pleasing to God. "Nor for producing spiritual actions from this spiritual habit is it enough that this initial gift has been conferred or been made an habitual possession. As prevenient and effective grace first achieved this gift in us, it is necessary that concomitant and co-operant grace should stimulate it to acts worthy of repentance and perfect it daily more and more."

7.—The norm of man's sanctification is the word of God, and Law as well as gospel; whereby the activity of both comes under consideration. The law demands obedience, the gospel causes man to obey. The law requires obedience to God as Creator, the gospel urges the same obedience to God as Redeemer. The law knows only one sanctification which is the condition of participation in eternal life; the gospel's intention is to manifest in man's sanctification thankfulness for the saved life bestowed upon him.

HEIDEGGER (XXIII, 14): "The word of God, the rule of our sanctification, belongs to both law and gospel.—As the law exacts obedience from man, the gospel directs man in affording that obedience.—But here lies the broad difference between gospel and law, whether we regard the manner or the end of the operation of each. As to the manner in which law and gospel enjoin sanctification, the former sets God forth to be worshipped as the Creator, the latter the same God, especially in Christ, as the Redeemer.—As to the end, because the law enjoins sanctification for the sake of acquiring life, the gospel enjoins it as a duty of gratitude for life and salvation acquired.—Finally as to operation, because the law demands obedience but does not provide strength to obey, since it has single regard to man as God's creature to whom in the beginning God gave strength to obey, He enjoins the Gospel and sanctification and effects it in the regenerate by the Spirit of God.—LEIDEN SYNOPSIS (XXXII, 10–12): "The instrumental cause of this benefit is the Word of God, both law and gospel.—By the law both inscribed on nature, Rom. 1, and renewed on the tables of stone, 2 Cor. 3. man is led

to a true acknowledgement of his condemnation and wretchedness.—
But through the Gospel and its promises is conceived grief according
to God, the afflicted conscience is roused to hope of pardon, Christ is
at last laid hold of, not only for the remission of previous sins but also
for the abolition of the old man and the resuscitation of the new."—
RIJSSEN (XV, 10–12): "The norm to which good works ought to be
directed is the moral law of God contained in the decalogue.—11:
Concerning the first law it is first asked, whether the decalogue promulgated on Mt. Sinai did nothing but continue the covenant of grace
and its pure demands. Answer: The law of works contained in the
decalogue is distinguished from the law of faith and the promise of grace
in Paul, Rom. 3. 27 (where then is the glorying? It is excluded. By what
manner of law? of works? Nay, but by a law of faith), Gal. 3. 17–18
(A covenant confirmed beforehand by God, the law which came 430
years after, doth not discount, so as to make the promise of none effect.
If the inheritance is of the law, it is no more of promise. But God hath
granted it to Abraham by promise).—12: But we do not say this as though
we would deny that a covenant of grace was then made with the Israelites;
this is sufficiently to be inferred from the sanctioning of it, Ex. 19. 5
(if ye will obey my voice indeed, and keep my Covenant, then shall ye
be a peculiar treasure unto me from among all peoples . . . ye shall
be unto me as a kingdom of priests and an holy nation), where God
adopts the Jews [sic] as His peculiar people, and from his solemn confirmation of it given in, Ex. 24, where mention is made of the sprinkling
of the blood of victims and of the access of the elders to God; or as though
we thought that the decalogue had nothing in common with a covenant
of grace and was nothing else than the covenant of works itself, renewed
for the purpose of recalling the people to it, that they might seek life
from it. Since the law became weak in the flesh after sin Rom. 8. 3
(what the law could not do . . . God . . .) man's way to life by it
became impossible. Hence God willed that there should be strictures
of the covenant of grace in the decalogue, as is pretty openly shown
by the preface annexed to it, where He professes Himself His people's
God, who brought them out of the Egyptian bondage, and by the promises
annexed to the second and fifth commandments."

8.—Subjectively considered the nature of sanctification is man's effort,
lasting his whole life, to live in thought, word and action solely according
to God's good pleasure and for His glory.—HEIDEGGER (XXIII, 18):
"Sanctification involves continual praxis and action.—This exercise consists in the faithful attending to themselves, applying all care and zeal
to doing things that belong to godliness and in receding from all evil and

so by God's grace contracting the habit, enduing the custom (and becoming apt and fit therein) of thinking, speaking and doing the things that are best, most glorious for God and most useful for their neighbour."

9.—Sanctification is then on the one hand repentance or improvement, on the other hand new obedience.—HEIDEGGER (XXIII, 19): "The exercise of sanctification and of godliness consists in repentance and new obedience. Repentance—signifies conversion from Satan to God and more agreeably μετάνοια or a counsel of amendment conjoined to μεταμέλεια, anguish, anxiety and as it were mental torture over the admission of sin." The expressions μετάνοια and μεταμέλεια are of course used promiscuously. But strictly μετάνοια means renewal and change of mind and counsel, retreat from κακία, and belongs to believers alone. Μεταμέλεια is anguish and anxiety over the admission of sin, which united to faith is saving, but separated from it belongs also to unbelievers and hypocrites."

10.—"Repentance is the change of mind, proceeding from the H. Spirit, from natural pravity to serious and filial fear of God, which arises partly from a recognition and sense of the righteous divine judgment against sins and of its holiness, partly from the taste of the sworn eternal mercy in Christ" (OLEVIAN, p. 268). Repentance is thus a gracious power, bestowed only on the elect, by which they lay aside the life of sin and busy themselves with righteousness.—BRAUN (I, iii, 12, 15): "Repentance is a kind of evangelical virtue given by God to the elect alone, by which they acknowledge their sins, shudder at them and flee from them; after serious grief over evil things previously done they love and practise the good."

11.—It therefore includes two elements, namely the "mortification" and the "quickening" of man. "It is mortification of the old man, by which the corruption of nature from sin is gradually lessened in them and abolished.—Quickening of the new man it is, by which the same corrupt nature is more and more renewed to the image of God in Christ" (HOT- TINGER 473). But the two, mortification and quickening, do not follow each other as two different events. The two are so involved mutually that (1) quickening is just the obverse of mortification, and that (2) by the former the old man is not repressed but gradually and literally slain.

POLAN (VI, 37) develops the doctrine of sanctification in connection with the doctrine of the "soul's regeneration". The latter according to him includes "illumination" and the "gift of repentance." To repentance belongs "mortification of the old man" and "quickening of the new man".

"Mortification" consists in "acknowledgement of sin" and "saving contrition". "Quickening" includes "joy of conscience through Christ" and "new obedience".

As regards the main point repentance is also similarly conceived by the other Reformed dogmaticians. (How even in German Reformed theology it took the place of the *Melanchthonian* conception, originally held, of *poenitentia* (consisting of *contritio, fides* and *nova oboedientia*), see HEPPE, (*Dogm. d.d. Prot.* II, p. 370). On URSIN, OLEVIAN and EGLIN see also HEPPE *ibid.*, p. 371ff. COCCEIUS says (*Summ. theol.* XIV, 6–7): "There are two parts of conversion answering to the two ends. The man who is converted is converted from bad to good, from darkness to light, from the slavery of Satan to God, 1 K. 8. 35 (Solomon's prayer: When the heaven is shut up and there is no rain, because they have sinned against thee; if they confess thy name and turn from their sin, when thou dost afflict them, then hear thou in heaven, etc.) Is. 59. 20 (a redeemer shall come to Zion, and to them that return from transgression in Jacob, saith the Lord), Jer. 15. 19 (. . . if thou return, I will bring thee again . . .) Ac. 26. 18 (. . . to open their eyes, that they may turn from darkness to light and from the power of Satan unto God, that they may receive remission of sins and an inheritance among them that are sanctified by faith in me). These parts are called in Scripture νέκρωσις, the mortification, or ἔκδοσις, the putting off of the old man; and ζωοποίησις, quickening and ἔνδυσις, putting on of the new man, Col. 3, 9–10 (. . . seeing that ye have put off the old man with his doings, and have put on the new man, which is being renewed unto knowledge after the image of him that created him).—(XIV, 8) These parts go together. But, as regards the order of nature, although newness is subsequent to oldness,—yet the newness of the love of God is the cause of abolishing the oldness of the enmity of God. Darkness is not removed save by light; nor death save by life; nor poverty save by riches; nor nakedness save by being clothed; nor ugliness save by beauty; nor vice save by virtue; and so neither hate save by love."—VOETIUS (II, 464): "Regeneration is divided by reason of its effects into mortification and quickening of the new man. Not because there are two *actus* substantially distinct, but because one and the same *actus* is called mortification by reason of the *terminus a quo*, which is rejected, and quickening by reason of the *terminus ad quem*. No peculiar positive *actio* is required, distinct from quickening, to abolish sin. He who imports the light at the same time expels the darkness."—WOLLEB 148: "The form is expressed in two *actus*, aversion from bad and turning towards good. The former is mortification of the old man, the latter quickening of the new man."
—LEIDEN SYNOPSIS (XXXII, 13): "Sanctification does not merely repress

nature, as some wrongly opine; it abolishes it, and puts true holiness and righteousness in its place, which also shine in the actual fruits of repentance."

12.—Therefore quickening can only be present truly, where true mortification pleasing to God is really present in man's heart. But this is no "sadness or sorrow of this world," a wordly self-seeking pain at the consequences of sin, which only leads deeper into eternal death, but a "sorrow according to God", a spiritual pain which man feels because in sin he has offended God, abandoned God. Hence in this genuine pain of repentance there is also invariably bound up a serious horror of sin, joy in the law of the Lord, trust in Him and His gracious promises and a serious resolve after new obedience to Him.

COCCEIUS (*Summ. theol* XLV 13-14): "There is further in conversion displeasure with sin, Ps. 34. 13f. (keep thy tongue from evil, and thy lips from speaking guile; depart from evil and do good, seek peace and pursue it) 97. 10 (O ye that love the Lord hate evil . . .); hatred of Satan and his works, Gen. 3. 15 (I will put enmity between thee and the woman and between thy seed and her seed; it shall bruise thy head, and thou shalt bruise his heel), grief over the desecration of God's name and glory Mt. 5. 4 (they that mourn), Is. 61. 2 (to comfort all that mourn), denial of one's own wisdom and righteousness and power, Is. 55. 7 (let the wicked forsake his way and the unrighteousness man his thought and let him return . . .). So on the other hand it includes delight (*condelectatio s. deliciatio*) in the law of God, Rom. 7.22 (I delight in the law of God after the inward man) Ps. 1. 2 (his delight is in the law of the Lord, and in his law doth he meditate day and night) and hunger and thirst after righteousness to the glory of God, Mt. 5. 6 (. . . for they shall be filled), with the prayer, purpose and serious zeal of advancing to ἐπίγνωσις full of knowledge worthy of the image of the creator Col. 3. 10 (and have put on the new man, which is being renewed unto knowledge after the image of him that created him), and to πληροφορία τῆς ἐλπίδος, fulness of hope, 6. 11 (we desire that each one of you may shew the same diligence unto the fulness of hope even unto the end)."—HEIDEGGER (XXIII, 26): "A twofold sorrow and sadness is conceived by the sense of sin, one of the world, the other according to God."—LEIDEN SYNOPSIS (XXXII, 38): "Sorrow according to God is distinguished from sorrow of the world not only by results but also by nature. Not only is it born of a man's own charity and fear of punishment. It is united to hatred of and displeasure at actual sin and with shame at offending God.—39: United to conversion to God is approval of the divine law, Rom. 6. 16 (. . . to whom ye present your selves as servants unto obedience, his servants ye are whom ye obey,

whether of sin unto death, or of obedience unto righteousness) and
delight in the study of it Pss. 1. 119, hope of pardon conceived by the
promises grasped through faith 130. 4 (there is forgiveness with thee,
that thou mayest be feared) and in a word spiritual consolation and joy,
Rom. 5. 2, 3, 5 (through whom also we have had our access by faith into
this grace wherein we stand . . . and let us rejoice in our tribulations . . .
hope putteth not to shame; because the love of God hath been shed
abroad in our hearts through the Holy Ghost which was given unto
us) 14. 17 (the kingdom of God is not eating and drinking, but
righteousness and peace and joy in the Holy Ghost)."

13.—Faith is always bound up with repentance, but it is not a part of it.
Faith is primarily a relation of man to Christ. Repentance on the other
hand is a relation, resting on faith in Christ, of man to God and to God's
will. Therefore repentance can only enter in, where faith is already
present as its presupposition.

OLEVIAN p. 267: Repentance so grows out of faith, that faith, as including
the Christ offered in the Gospel, not only gains Christ's righteousness, but
also renews us to repentance, which is thus a work of Christ received
in faith. The Greeks rightly call it repentance, μετάνοια, i.e. change
of mind, in contrast to which μεταμέλεια (in German "Strafreue",
punitive repentance?) is the effect of sin on conscience. "But μετάνοια
is not the wages of sin but the gift of God emanating from His true
grace, changing the mind for the better.—Repentance is of the
mind, etc." (See §10 of this Chapter).—LEIDEN SYNOPSIS (XXXII, 40):
"From what has been said so far, the solution of a difficult question is
clear, in the explanation of which some great authors of the Reformed
Church seem to disagree, whether faith is a part of repentance. If the
word repentance is taken in the broad sense of the whole work of our
conversion, as it is sometimes used in Scripture, Ac. 3. 19 (repent ye therefore and turn again that your sins may be blotted out, that so there may
come seasons of refreshing from the presence of the Lord) 11. 18 (. . . to
the Gentiles also God hath granted repentance unto life), there is assuredly
also our faith in it, exactly as infidelity is understood by the apostle as
contrary to it beneath an ἀμετανόητος (impenitent) heart, Rom. 2. 5
(after thy hard and impenitent heart treasurest up for thyself wrath in
the day of wrath and revelation of the righteous judgment of God).—
41: But if the word repentance is taken strictly, as previously defined by us,
then it is usually distinguished from faith, as are cause and its proper effect
and fruit, and so Scripture distinguishes it in different passages, see Mk.
1. 15 (repent ye and believe the Gospel), Ac. 20. 21 (. . . testifying . . .
repentance towards God and faith toward our Lord Jesus Christ) etc."

—Braun (I, iii, 12, 7): "Repentance differs from faith (a) because faith looks back to Christ as the source of salvation, but repentance to a lovable God; (b) because faith deals with remission of sins, but repentance with amendment of life."

14.—So long as man's earthly life continues, he must also work for the improvement of himself, especially if he has fallen into serious sins, or if God visits him with affliction.—Heidegger (XXIII, 37): "Man must repent throughout the whole course of life.—None the less certain cases and times exact a singular repentance and as it were its παράδειγμα, as when believers fall into grave sins that lay conscience waste or singular judgments of God—fall upon them etc."

15.—The whole life of the regenerate man is a continual fight of spirit against flesh, of the new against the old man: whereas in the unregenerate only one desire fights with another and evil consupiscence generally against conscience and against the voice of God in conscience.—Braun (I, iii, 10, 17): "There is thus a continual struggle between Spirit and flesh, between the old and the new man, Gal. 5. 17 (flesh . . . against Spirit and Spirit against flesh), Rom. 7. 23 (I see a different law in my members, warring against the law of my mind and bringing me into captivity under the law of sin which is in my members) 8. 2 (the law of the Spirit of life in Christ Jesus made me free from the law of sin and death). And although struggle is found in the regenerate, none the less there is a great difference in the struggles of regenerate and unregenerate. (1) In the regenerate it is a struggle between the Spirit and flesh; in the unregenerate there is no struggle with the Spirit, since they do not have the Spirit but are carnal and animal. So the struggle in them is only between flesh and reason, then between the various desires, e.g. between greed and luxury. (2) The unregenerate are at war only with the graver sins, and the regenerate with the lighter and slight ones. (3) The unregenerate rush at once into grave crimes; the regenerate, where they have come off victorious, crush down the flesh more and more, Gal. 5. 24 (they that are of Christ Jesus have crucified the flesh with the passions and lusts thereof), Rom. 8. 2 (the law of the Spirit of life in Christ Jesus made me free from the law of sin and death). (4) The unregenerate suppress the desires of the flesh from fear of punishment, the regenerate from the love of God and virtue".—Cocceius (*Summ. theol.* XCIV, 5): "This struggle is not found in carnal men, because they are carnal and animal and lack the Spirit of God. They have in them, true, the war of concupiscence with conscience, as the poet says: "*Video meliora proboque, deteriora sequor.*"—But this war is not against the old man. It is the old man's war against the light of

God which shines in the soul of man, Prov. 20, 27 (the spirit of man is the the lamp of the Lord, searching all the innermost parts of the belly), which he attacks with reasonings, murmurings, in a word, with pagan effrontery."

16.—So even the repentance of the regenerate is never complete. It must rather grow by slow degrees.—LEIDEN SYNOPSIS: (XXXII, 14): "But if you look to its final perfection, this form (of regeneration and repentance) is not introduced once and for all but by degrees; this is why some regenerate are compared with children, some with grown and perfect men, Heb. 5; Eph. 4.—15: Just as children, although they display it imperfectly, yet have the unimpaired form of a man constant in all its parts, so we recognise none as truly regenerate, unless he possesses the unimpaired form of regeneration, with, as they say, perfection of parts, although he must advance daily in perfection of degrees."

17.—That is why even at the last moment of life repentance, if it is but honest and serious, does not come in too late. But it must not be concluded from this that one ought to put it off.—HEIDEGGER (XXXIII, 38): "Repentance which is genuine is never too late. It is genuine, if it has a combination of hatred for sin and flight from it, Ps. 119. 128 (I esteem all thy precepts concerning all things to be right, And I hate every false way), which warms to love of good and zeal to do one's duty without exception.—But neither does it follow from this doctrine that repentance can safely be put off."

18.—The fruit of repentance is the Christian life of the regenerate, which differs from natural life in its whole character. "It is Christian life by which the sanctified, imitating Christ, are eager through him to give new obedience to God, especially by denying themselves, by bearing their cross and by doing all things proper to their vocation" (HEIDEGGER XXIII, 75). The distinguishing thing in Christian life is above all new obedience to God. "Repentance", says HEIDEGGER (XXIII, 45) "is followed by new obedience, which is exercised through good works."

19.—Here the specific difference of Christian from natural life comes out, and proves itself above all by good works.—"Good works are the actions of the regenerate, which are done according to the prescript of divine law by faith through love for the confirmation of our election and calling and the edification of our neighbour and God's glory" (LEIDEN SYNOPSIS XXXIV, 2).—Good works generally are such works as (1) are commanded by God, (2) are done with true faith in Christ, so that because of this faith the person and his work are well-pleasing to God and (3) are done for the glorification of God.—URSIN (*Explic. catech.* p. 313-314): There are three things about a good work: "(1) that it should be commanded by God, (2) that it should be done of true faith that leans on the mediator's merit and intercession, and by which one is sure that person and work please God for the mediator's sake, (3) that it refers mainly to the honour and glory of God."—BRAUN (I, iii, 113): "Now good works are virtues according to God's law, out of a heart purified by faith, to the glory of God."—Hence it follows that the *Papists' consilia evangelica*, enjoined not by God but by the Church, are not to be reckoned among good works.—BRAUN (I, iii, 114): "Whence it appears that the evangelical counsels of the *Papists* are inept, which are good works not commanded by God's law, but propounded as though saving by the Church; like their celibacy, mendicity, blind obedience and other monastic vows."

20.—Therefore all works done by heathen and unregenerate generally are sins, not in and for themselves, not *materialiter,* but so far as they proceed from an impure mind.—HEIDEGGER (XXIII, 55): "No work of Gentiles and unregenerate, whatever its outward show, can be truly and morally adjudged good by the judgment whether of God or of man."—LEIDEN SYNOPSIS (XXXIV, 20): "Still, the virtues of unbelievers are not bad absolutely or *per se,* but relatively or *per accidens.* They are good considered materially and nakedly. They are radically bad, as issuing from an impure heart and formally so, as being done otherwise than as they ought to have been done."

21.—And that is why even the works of the regenerate, when tested before the judgment seat of God, are bad, not in and for themselves, but in view of the lack present in them.—HEIDEGGER (XXIII, 58): "Not even the good works of believers tried by the measure of divine law so fulfil all the elements of goodness that no flaw can be said to inhere in them." For "legally considered" i.e., "in the court of divine justice" they are "sins; not *per se,* because what is good in them ought not to be put out of count by a defect; but accidentally, because they labour under defects."

22.—Thus no regenerate man's work establishes for him a claim of merit. —TURRETIN presents what belongs to the concept of merit (XVI, v, 6): "For true merit these five conditions are exacted (1) that it should not be due, for no one merits by paying what he owes, Lk. 17. 10 (Even so ye also, when ye shall have done all the things that are commanded you, say, We are unprofitable servants; we have done that which it was our duty to do) but merely satisfies; (2) that it should be ours, for no one can be said to merit by the act of another; (3) that it should be perfect in every detail and lacking in any blemish, for where there is sin there cannot be merit; (4) that it should be equal and proportioned to the reward and profit, otherwise it will have been a gift and not merit; (5) that a reward should be due such a work in justice.—Hence it is commonly defined as a work not due, making due instead of not due the reward in the order of justice. —7: From which we easily gather, that there cannot be found in man any merit with God in any works whatsoever, either *de congruo*—or *de condigno*.

23.—And yet for the regenerate the doing of good works is a duty.— HEIDEGGER (XXIII, 60): "Good works are no less necessary than actual sanctifications."

24.—Why? Because the regenerate can do works which are not good *bonitate graduum*, i.e., perfectly good, but which are good *bonitate essentiali*, i.e., essentially good. As right faith, however weak it may be, is yet real faith, so the works which the Christian does with believing heart, be they never so defective, are yet really works of faith and are therefore essentially good and well-pleasing to God.

BRAUN (I, iii, 11, 5): "Works are called good or of a perfect goodness, and of a perfection essential or graduated (*graduum*). Those works are said to have goodness or essential perfection, which are done (a) according to God's command, (b) out of a heart purified by faith, and (c) for the glory of God, i.e., those which fulfil the three conditions of which we have just been speaking. These are not found in the unregenerate, but in the regenerate only. Works which are good or perfect in goodness or in perfection of degrees, are those in which the three conditions are found in perfection, where nothing is done except as prescribed in the law of God; out of a heart which has been perfectly purified by perfect faith and which acts solely for the glory of God. In this sense only the blessed in heaven emit good works, not believers on earth.—6: None the less works of the regenerate may be called virtues and good works. Not because they are good by goodness of degree, but by essential goodness; so that, although they are not perfectly good, they are yet truly good, as heat in the fourth degree is true heat no less than in the eighth, although not so strong. As therefore our faith however imperfect is none the less faith if it be sincere, so too with our works which proceed from it. In one word, our works are pleasing to God in the same sense in which we ourselves are pleasing to Him. We are pleasing to God **through faith in Jesus Christ**; then so are our works."

25.—The purposes of good works are the following. By them the Christian should above all glorify God, whose gracious Spirit effects the good works in him; he should next by them offer God thanks for grace received, attest his faith before the world, assure himself thereby of his position in grace and further the edification of his neighbour. In fact even for the attainment of everlasting life the performance of good works is necessary.

URSIN (*Explic. catech.*, pp. 314–315, *conf.* p. 307): The *causae impulsivae* of good works are: "(1) regeneration, necessarily involving justification; (2) gratitude for redemption; (3) making God famous; (4) confirmation of our faith and election, and (5) a good example by which others may become profitable to Christ."—LEIDEN SYNOPSIS (XXV, 16–18): "The ends of good works are three, of which (1) the first has regard to us, testification of our gratitude to God;—(2) the second end is the edification of our neighbour, whether believer or unbeliever;—(3) the third end, to which the two preceding ones are subordinate, is the glory of God." —BRAUN (I, iii, 11, 14): "That good works are alike profitable and necessary for believers is proved by many reasons: (1) because they are commanded by God, Mt. 5. 16 (Even so let your light shine before men, that they may see your good works and glorify your Father which is in heaven) Is. 1. 20 (if ye be willing and obedient—but if ye refuse and rebel), Ps. 34. 14 (Depart from evil and do good, seek peace and pursue it); (2) because they are necessarily conjoined with faith (faith without works is dead, i.e., is null, Jas. 2. 20): (3) because by good works God is glorified and our neighbour edified; (4) because He bears witness that we are justified by faith; (5) we ought to witness to God a grateful mind, which cannot be done otherwise than by good works; (6) they confirm our calling and surrender, i.e., by good works we avoid sins for ourselves and become surer of our election, 2 Pet. 1. 10 (give the more diligence to make your calling and election sure . . .); (7) they are our roads of approach to the eternal inheritance; for "we are created in Christ Jesus for good works, which God afore prepared that we should walk in them", Eph. 2. 10."

26.—Of course no one by good works can merit righteousness and the prospect of eternal life. So good works are necessary for attaining to salvation not "by the necessity of merit" or "of efficient cause".—RIISSEN (XV, 8): "Good works, then, are not necessary for salvation by necessity either of merit or of efficient cause, whether principal or instrumental properly so called and contributory to salvation.—Controversy: whether man by his own good works can merit grace or glory. Answer, No: against the *Papists*."

27.—But of course good works are necessary as the God-appointed road, on which by grace we are to attain to the possession of eternal life. This naturally can hold not for those elect who die at an age of minority or at the beginning of their rebirth, but only for those who have time and opportunity for good works.

MASTRICHT (VI, viii, 27): "The Reformed—deny the necessity of good works for obtaining the right to eternal life. Indeed if done with this intention they say that in consequence they are actually evil and pernicious. But they declare that they are necessary by divine prescript for receiving possession of life, as conditions without which God refuses to bestow salvation upon us."—HEIDEGGER (XXIII, 62): "The *Helvetic Confession* ch. 16 denies that good works are so necessary to salvation, that apart from them no one has ever been saved. And yet both infants are saved without good works and adults dying amid the actual beginnings of regeneration may be robbed of the time and occasion, at least as regards the outward act, of emitting good works; for them the grace of God suffices. As to the great agreement otherwise we teach that for all adults who receive time and opportunity for it good works are so necessary, that those who despise them, turn up their noses and plainly and wantonly neglect them, have no hope of salvation." In this sense the proposition is recognised, "that good works are necessary to salvation." We must say more fully "that good works are necessary for obtaining salvation through grace and faith, a phrase applied to this controversy by the most learned *Horneius*."—RIISSEN (XV, 8, 1): "We agree that good works are pleasing to God, that we may work with the thought of profit, if it but be a thought of profit as a free reward and does not in principle look past the glory of God; that works have some relation of order and connection with eternal life, as between means and ends, the relation of way to goal, of competition to prize, of antecedent to consequent. Finally, that God by agreement ought to pay the reward for good works, so that in this way He is somehow a debtor, not to us but to Himself and to His faithfulness. But that good works are related to eternal life as a cause in the strict sense and by intrinsic worth and worthiness deserve a reward from God and effect salvation, we deny."

CHAPTER XXIII

THE FIXITY OF THE COVENANT OF GRACE

or, The Perseverance and Assurance of the Saints

1.—The state of the elect in grace receives its completion and sealing through divine preservation in it.—LAMPE (*Einl.* p. 66): "What is the highest good of the covenant of grace? Sealing or the work of God's Spirit, by which believers are continually preserved in the state of grace and from this preservation experience in their souls a sweet assurance."— WITSIUS (III, xiii, 1): "Those whom God has presented with true faith and holiness He also guards with such solicitous care, that it is ἐκ τῶν ἀδυνάτων for any of the truly faithful to revolt totally and finally from holiness once begun and so to fall from the salvation appointed for them, 1 Thess. 3. 3 (that no man be moved by these afflictions: for yourselves know that hereunto we are appointed)."

2.—"Preservation is that gracious action of God, by which He so guards the elect, redeemed, regenerated believers and sanctified, as being weak in themselves and liable to fall away, inwardly by the most potent power of His Spirit, outwardly by means wisely ordained thereto, that they never altogether lose the habits of the virtues impregnated in them, but by steady perseverance are surely led to eternal salvation" (WITSIUS III, xiii, 2). On this rests the essential unchangeability of the covenant of grace, which includes two things, namely the gracious gift of persisting in faith and that of the certainty of the elect as to their own state of grace.—HEIDEGGER (XXIV, 1-2): "There are two heads of the fixity of the covenant of grace, the grace of the perseverance of the saints right to the end in the grace once conferred, and the grace of the certainty of grace, by which the covenanted are sure of the love and grace of God and of obtaining his salvation. Apart from the perseverance of the saints all the grace that is left—is vain and profits not for salvation, Mt. 24. 13 (he that endureth to the end shall be saved), Rev. 3. 5 (he that overcometh shall thus be arrayed in white garments: and I will in no wise blot his name out of the book of life) 2. 10 (. . . Be thou faithful unto death and I will give thee the crown of life). He is neither elect nor believing nor holy, who does not persevere.—And on a par with the certainty of grace and salvation is the reason why persevering unto the end they have a sure trust and hope of both. He who approaches God should know above all, that those who do approach may be certain of the grace and salvation of God."

3.—But the real heart of the doctrine of the immutability of the covenant of grace and so the more distinctive mark of correct confession is the doctrine of the persistence of the believer in obedience of faith.—WYT-TENBACH (II, 1,000): "The fixity of the benefits of the covenant of grace is also called by another name, the perseverance of the saints."—HEIDEGGER (XXIV, 3): "First of the firmness of the object or the perseverance of the saints, which as it were is the basis of the firmness or certainty of the subject.—In itself the former is always unmoved and always equal and does not admit of degrees, because it rests upon unchangeable and perpetual causes; the latter suffers changes and is not always the same in fidelity of mind. And the more accurate the treatment the doctrine of perseverance deserves, the more strongly it is attacked by almost all the enemies of the Reformed. Truly it is the stamp of the purity of Reformed religion above all the many sects of the Christian religion and is a kind of πλεονέκτημα."

4.—"The perseverance of the saints is the gift of God, by which Christ's grace is sealed through the Spirit to the elect who are justified and sanctified, so that they never fall away completely" (WOLLEB, p. 150). Or "The gift of perseverance is God's benefit, by which He seals Christ's saving grace through the H. Spirit in the regenerate elect, so that they persist in it to the end and can never fall away from it at all" (POLANUS VI, 43). At times of course regenerate man becomes weak in faith and love, and even falls into the greatest sins. But each time he sins as a child, not as an enemy of God, since he sins never from really wicked, anti-God design and with a completely bad conscience, but only from weakness.—LEIDEN SYNOPSIS (XXXI, 38): "We do not deny that saints may sometimes slip and actually do slip through weakness of the flesh into sins not only light but even most grave; and that they cannot be hindered by any absolute abstract impossibility from perhaps losing faith we affirm, but only in a limited way as regards Christ's gracious promises, the faithful guardianship of the H. Spirit and God's unchangeable counsel to save them."—BREMEN CONFESSION (IX, 5): "Although even believers sin at times, there is still a great difference between the sins of the elect and those of the wicked.—The former sin from weakness and return to conversion; the latter from the whole of their character, and they remain without conversion.—(IX, 9): And this whole business cannot be made plainer or clearer than by keeping the parable of the parents and the children before one's eyes. Because believers are God's elect children and God for them is eternally their Father in Christ, they also sin as children, not as enemies, and it is with them also with God the Father as with children, when they anger Him by disobedience. Children commonly sin from childish folly—but never from hate or envy of their father—the child's love remains in them, although the appearance is otherwise.—So the saints in their fall never fall away completely from God."—Wolleb, p. 150: "Although faith is last in respect of the act following, it is never lost as regards the habit and the first act in which it grasps Christ."

5.—Regeneration is so guarded by the Spirit of grace, that in virtue of the Father's eternal counsel of grace, in virtue of his living connection with Christ (into which the regenerate is so implanted, that Christ's merit and eternal intercession are in his favour) and in virtue of the activity of the H. Spirit he can neither "totally" nor "finally" fall from grace.

BREMEN CONFESSION (IX, 3): "H. Scripture in addition against the fear of despair and eternal rejection for the sin committed by us erects for faith four immovable pillars upon which faith takes free and sure stand right to the end. (1) The first is the effect and attribution of Christ Jesus' most holy sacrifice.—(2) The second is the aye enduring power of Jesus Christ's intercession for all believers.—(3) The third is the almighty power and government of Christ Jesus at the right hand of God's majesty, by which he rules mightily over sin, death, the devil and hell and suffers not his sheep to be snatched from his hands.—(4) The fourth immovable pillar is God's eternal love and gracious choice, whereby He has loved and elected us in Christ, before the foundation of the world was laid, and never changes this love and gracious choice of His in eternity."—WITSIUS (III, xiii, 25): "Christ so joins believers to himself, that he himself is the head. They at the same time are assumed as the body, individuals as members of the body, Eph. 5. 23 (Christ also is the head of the Church, being himself also the saviour of the body). Whence once more arises the twofold proof: (1) As it is impossible for any member to be torn from Christ's natural body now glorified, it is no less impossible for this to happen in Christ's mystical body. Because as Christ by the merit of his humiliation secured that he should be immune from all hurt for ever in glory, so too by the same merit he secured that he should present his entire mystical body (i.e., the true Church and its spiritual members severally) to himself a glorious body, Eph. 5. 27. But he could not do this if any members of it were torn off. (2) As the spirits which rouse movements in the limbs move continually through the medium of the nerves from the head to the lower parts, so the strength and efficiency by which spiritual life is both controlled and exercised are continually instilled by Christ into the faithful; although he moves them unequally to emit spiritual actions, he at least preserves that life and does not suffer it to be choked altogether."—COCCEIUS (*Summ. theol.* XLIX,

17): "Those who deny perseverance remove hope, the incentive and nurse of godliness, and make men either despair or at least always be struggling with despair or carelessly neglecting salvation, and they have necessarily to make persevering faith not altogether God's gift, requiring to be compassed by constant prayers, lest it remain true that he that glorieth let him glory in the Lord. In short faith which has no root and therefore may fail—does not save. It is hypocrisy."—HEIDEGGER (XXIV, 5): "This is the sum of the Catholic doctrine of the perseverance of the saints; that those elect, called and faithful cannot so fall away from the grace of election, vocation, justification and sanctification once conferred (whether totally, so that a new infusion is needed, or finally, by reason not of nature but of grace, or by reason not of self but of God and the issue), as obviously to disturb the Spirit of God and His grace and lose them and perish eternally."

6.—This perseverance is thus not an advantage which the believer might appropriate to himself by moral effort and exercise, but a supernatural gift which proceeds solely from God's free grace.—COCCEIUS (*Summ. theol.* XLIX, 1): "Along with Scripture and the first doctors of the Church the Reformed Church teaches the perseverance of a faith not superficial but true and justifying, not because of faith's power or strength or dignity." —HEIDEGGER (XXIV, 6): "Such perseverance is God's liberal gift 1 Cor. 1, 8 (. . . that ye be unreprovable in the day of our Lord Jesus Christ): and it is God's gift in such a way, that it is not in man like a moral or ethical habit acquired by frequent acts of faith and obedience— but supernatural, spiritual and theological, produced in the perseverer by the power of the H. Spirit."

7.—And indeed the deepest ground for the perseverance of believers is the activity of the Father, who has loved and elected believers from eternity,—and next, the Son's activity in dispensing salvation, since to those whom the Father has elected in him He (the Father) has promised, on condition of the redemptive work carried out by the Son, not only faith but also persistence in faith, and since Christ has really carried out this redemptive work for those given him by election. What then the Father's will is with the Son's merit is made real by the H. Spirit, who with divine omnipotence implants the elect person in Christ, turns him thereby into a new man and preserves him in Christ.

WYTTENBACH (II, 1001-1002): "The reason for perseverance is the guardianship of God,—the Son's intercession—and the continued working of the H. Spirit."—HEIDEGGER (XXIV, 9): "The first foundation of perseverance is the operation of God the Father who loves and elect us from eternity.—12: The second foundation of perseverance is the dispensatory work of the Son in himself as mediator—in redeeming in time those elected by God the Father and loved from eternity. Scripture teaches that when the covenant of works was broken—God made a new covenant of grace in and with the second Adam, Christ, and those who were to have fellowship with him, in which He promised to those whose person He sustained not righteousness only and salvation but also faith and perseverance in faith, Christ promising vicariously and supplying to God the Father the redemption of his own or those given to him through the merit of his death.—44: The work and sanctification of the H. Spirit governing, completing and sealing everything powerfully, confirms it.— —46: The Spirit, who is the seal or mark of God and the earnest or pledge is also the same Spirit of power or powerfully working, 2 Tim. i. 7 (God gave us not a spirit of fearfulness, but of power and love and discipline). Our Creator is also the mighty creator of the new man, through whom we are inserted into Christ who preserves us and makes us all partakers in God's grace, and, in a word, He brings it about that God's benefits acquired through Christ are bestowed on believers, and are not bestowed merely, but also abide even unto the end."

8.—The other side of this perseverence of believers is the "certainty (assurance) of salvation" on the believer's part. God wills that the salvation of the elect should be direct; He also wills that believers should be certain of the security of their state in grace and should feel assured of it. —BURMANN (VI, x, 17): "Upon certainty of perseverance follows certainty of salvation, the latter does not exist without the former; unless he persevere no one is saved. Some wickedly tear them apart and while upholding the certainty of salvation deny that of perseverance. This is a claim to assert subjective certainty without objective certainty, as is commonly said, though not quite correctly; strictly, all certainty is subjective, since it is an attribute of the mind and its assent. But we must see (1) the nature of this certainty of salvation, and (2) what its foundations are."

9.—Believers' certainty of faith then is the consciousness, based on the witness of the H. Spirit and on experience of the grace working in them, that not in virtue of their worthiness but in virtue of the Spirit of Jesus Christ, in spite of any temptation of the flesh and of the world, they will persist in faith not only now but also in the future and surely receive the inheritance of eternal life.—HEIDEGGER (XXIV, 72): "The certainty of grace and salvation is the conviction of the elect and believers, by which leaning on divine faith, through the witness of the H. Spirit and the sense and experience of grace working in them (not as a continued act but as the foundation and habit of faith) they can surely trust according to the measure of their faith and of the H. Spirit; and they trust that they are in a state of grace, not because of a deliberate intuition of their own dignity but of the divine conferring of it and guardianship of it not just for the present, but certain they will also persevere in the same, though not without a struggle combined with hesitancy and temptation, right to life's end, and so are infallibly salvable to the praise of the glory of God's grace and their own consolation amid the perpetual misery of this life."

10.—This certainty of its own state belongs to the most essential characteristics of the believing consciousness.—OLEVIAN p. 257: "We see first how great is the certainty of faith, which is as it were its essential attribute. It is a light created by the H. Spirit in man's mind, such that by it in the witness or promise of the gospel it not only sees God's will in Christ toward us with certainty as eternally benevolent and never likely to be angry with us or to inveigh against us, but also such that by it the heart is confirmed by the H. Spirit, because Himself is our God according to the entire substance of the covenant expounded above, Is. 53, 54. 5-8-9 (the Holy One . . . is thy redeemer; the God of the whole earth shall he be called . . . In overflowing wrath I hid my face from you for a moment; but with everlasting kindness will I have mercy upon thee, saith the Lord thy redeemer. For this is as the waters of Noah unto me: for as I have sworn that the waters of Noah should no more go over the earth, so have I sworn that I would not be wroth with thee, nor rebuke thee). That substance is allowed by undoubted testimony by Him who is truthful and mighty, who actually provides what He promises. This certainty of God's good will is so linked with faith and proper to it that faith never allows itself to be bereft of this certainty, leaning on the infallible witness of the gospel, by the might of the H. Spirit who is the author of faith."

11.—This certainty is guaranteed on the one hand indirectly, as well by experience of its fellowship, its intercourse with God, as by its own industry in sanctification, by the blessing of prayer life and by use of the sacraments; on the other hand directly by the received first fruits of the H. Spirit in the consciousness of faith itself.—WYTTENBACH (II, 999): "Consciousness of salvation which is held because of serious self-investigation in the matter of holiness and certainty of faith, causes indirect certainty of salvation. When, next, it is confirmed by the H. Spirit, Rom. 8, 16 (the Spirit himself beareth witness with our spirit, that we are children of God), as saving truths are confirmed by Him, direct certainty arises.—Indirect certainty therefore ought always to be there first, unless the second is bound to be an illusion, as also the outward word precedes the inward working of the H. Spirit. To direct certainty theologians refer the pretaste of future life designated by the name of firstfruits of the Spirit, Rom. 8. 23; also a lively comprehension of the surpassing excellence and benefits of God (which belong to illumination, and the latter does not differ much from spiritual taste); also a great measure of love to God, which God imparts in certain circumstances."—LAMPE (*Einl.* 68): "How manifold is assurance?—Indirectly, when one finds in oneself faith and the fruits of the Spirit, from that concludes that he has an inheritance in heaven;—directly, in the first fruits of the Spirit, which are imparted to believers for their comfort and encouragement."—HEIDEGGER (XXIV, 89-90): "Union and communion with God and holy agreement and familiar intercourse with Him are a greater witness to this certainty than any exception.—But also zeal to make our calling and election sure shows the certainty of grace and salvation.—There is in addition the efficacy and privilege of prayer. What we seek and are bound to seek from God in prayer, we believe to belong to us deservedly, and it cannot be doubted that we are rendered more certain of it when it is to be or has been obtained.—Finally, the sealing of the sacraments also evinces this certainty. They are signs and seals of the covenant, of righteousness and of salvation."

12.—And that is why believers are sure of the immutability of their state of grace not only for the present, but also for the future, since believers' certainty of salvation rests on the gift of perseverance bestowed on them in faith itself.—HEIDEGGER (XXIV, 94): "Believers may not for the moment be certain, but remain uncertain and wavering about the future. For it is sufficiently clear from what we have adduced, namely the foundations of certainty and the acquisition of grace and salvation, that certainty of grace which persists to the end is promised and is bestowed.

13.—Of course the Christian does not at all times enjoy the same conviction of the certainty of his state of grace. The believing life moves forward with variations. Faith is now more, now less living and strong. But here it should be noted that in God's sight it is not a question of whether faith is greater or less, but whether it is sincere.

COCCEIUS (*Summ. theol.* XLIX, 15): "We do not deny meantime that faith is both disturbed and in a way sifted and assailed and darkened as regards the joy of salvation, when the spirit is grieved at sins of the flesh Eph. 4. 30 (grieve not the H. Spirit . . .). But believers never cast away the ὁμολογία τῆς ἐλπίδος Heb. 10. 23 (let us hold fast

the confession of our hope that it waver not; for he is faithful that promised), i.e., the assent which is the fuel of hope or the hope which is
assent. Nor do they lose the Spirit, who for a season works in them
godly sorrow, 2 Cor. 7. 10 (godly sorrow worketh repentance unto salvation, a repentance which bringeth no regret), that by it they may be
restored to the joy of salvation, Ps. 51. 12 (restore unto me the joy of thy
salvation)."—HEIDEGGER (XXIV, 96): "The faith even of the best—
struggles on earth, but in heaven it at last struggles out. Sometimes
it is lively, sometimes languid, sometimes, as in temptations, nil. For
in the spiritual gifts with which we are imbued in this life, sincerity
is what is looked for, not perfection in degree.—Even the actual principles
of the Catholic faith, however clear in themselves by revelation, being
made known to us by certainty not of evidence but of adherence, are not
issued to believers with such even fixity of assent as is possessed by
mathematical proofs and common ideas. When they are reviewed
by the remains of carnal distrust, mists promptly envelope them by
which the light of changeless divine truth seems in a measure to be
obscured for us.—97: In particular the certainty of experimental signs
and conviction of God's grace are occulted by a sort of cloud of
temptations."

14.—But although at times the believer's heart is visited by doubts of the
certainty of its election, he does not use them to despair. God permits
such visitations of the believer, not to destroy him but to exercise him
and to keep him in sanctification.—HEIDEGGER (XXIV, 98): "Nor does
anxious and wellnigh desperate sorrow conflict with the assurance and
salvation of God's children. These things are visited upon them not to
destroy but to save them. It pleases God's wisdom to lead them thuswise
into knowledge of Himself, to exercise and prove their faith, patience,
humility, longing for grace; and also by the same care in relating this
faith to set an example to those who know, seeing which they may learn
to fear the weapons of almighty God, to shudder at sins, to sigh for grace
and the friendship of God and to believe what is read in Scripture concerning the eternal pangs of the godless."

15.—Although in the regenerate flesh still fights continually with the
Spirit and visits the believer with thoughts of doubt as to his belonging
to God's gracious covenant, this doubt belongs only to the flesh, not
to faith itself, which rather causes the regenerate to raise himself continually anew and with ever greater certainty above the temptations
of the flesh (OLEVIAN, p. 258). For when the believer sees the remnants
of sin in himself, he sees them, in virtue of the consciousness of his fellow-

ship with Christ, transferred to Christ and is therefore sure of eternal blessedness (OLEVIAN, p. 263).

The condition into which man is transposed by rebirth and sanctification is incomparably more glorious than the condition of man's primal likeness to God. By faith he is also raised to knowledge of God's redeeming grace and so to a perfect knowledge of God; and by the gift of perseverance he is guarded once for all against the danger of a real falling away (OLEVIAN, p. 93).

CHAPTER XXIV

SACRAMENTS IN GENERAL

1.—To assure the individual elect, who because of the natural timidity of his heart towards the Word of God preached to him cannot with proper confidence believe in his election and justification—to assure him that he too is really adopted into the covenant of grace and to remind him at the same time personally of the duties which, as God's child in the fellowship of the covenant of grace, he has to fulfil, God has also ordained alongside the Word visible signs, by which He offers the Word and the promise of grace in a sensible form and seals to the elect possession of the covenant of grace.

COCCEIUS (*Summ. theol.* LII, 1): "God wished to offer the covenant of grace to man and to call him to peace and friendship and the right to expect an inheritance, not in word only; He also wished by signs to make believers sure about the covenant and its benefits."—"*Express Account of what the Reformed Churches in Germany believe or do not believe*" (HEPPE, *Bekenntrisschr.* p. 258): "As men are wont to deal with each other by making their covenants and treaties not only in words, but also confirm them by letter and seals or other public declarations, usages and ceremonies, so too God deals with us. He has His gracious covenant with us set forth not in words only, has even composed it not in writing only, but has also ordained certain ceremonies by which His covenant between Him and us is to be confirmed, strengthened and, as it were, sealed before the eyes of the whole world."—Similarly BULLINGER, p. 116, and others; CALVIN (IV, xiv, 1): "It seems to me this will be a simple and appropriate definition of sacrament, if we say that it is an outward symbol by which the Lord seals in our consciences the promises of His good will towards us, to sustain the weakness of our faith. And we in turn attest our godly duty to Him alike in presence of Himself and the angels and before men. It may also be defined otherwise with greater compression. It may be called the witness of divine grace to usward, confirmed by an outward sign, together with mutual testimony to our godly duty to Him."—OLEVIAN (pp. 320–322): "The sacraments are called visible seals of the covenant of grace, because they seal the witness of the gracious promises. God has added them to the Word (1) because He wished to offer the glory of His grace not only to hearing but also to the eye, to authenticate the unchanging nature of His promise before all the world and to come to the aid of our weak faith; (2) because man better realises what is set forth with manifold obviousness; so God wished to display to man as in a picture the grace attested by the Word; (3)

because we more surely and confidently believe what can be apprehended by the eye and touched by the hands; and (4) we also preserve it more faithfully in memory. So to remove any doubt as to the covenant of grace established to all eternity in Christ's death and as to our union with Christ, God willed that we should be so exhorted by visible evidences of His covenant and so fortified by the use of them, as though we had seen the attested grace with our own eyes and touched it with our own hands.—CALVIN (IV, xiv, 3): "From this definition which we have laid down we understand that there is never a sacrament without a preceding promise, but that it is rather added to it as a sort of appendix, to the end that it might confirm and seal the actual promise, and make it for us more attested or in a sense ratified, as God foresees the need of it for our ignorance and slowness first of all, then for our weakness; but (strictly speaking) not so much to strengthen His holy Word as to establish us in faith in Himself."—On the expositions of URSIN, BOQUIN, SOHNIUS and ZANCHIUS, which agree completely with the doctrine of sacrament given or indicated here, cf. HEPPE *Dogm. d.d. Protestantismus,* vol. III, where in addition excerpts from OLEVIANS' writings are to be found.

2.—These visible signs are called the sacraments of the covenant of grace (AMESIUS I, xxxvi, 10): "The seal of God's signing the covenant is called a sacrament, Rom. 4. 11 (the sign of circumcision "was a seal of the righteousness of the faith which he had while he was in uncircumcision"). —Since all substantives ending in-*entum* have not a passive but an active meaning, *sacramentum* is not a *res sacra* but a *res sacrans* (cf. *alimentum*).— RIJSSEN (XVII, 3): "*Sacramentum* is derived from *sacrare* and in the ancient authors of the Latin tongue signifies two things: (1) the money or pledge deposited by litigants with the priests in a holy place, from which the loser in a case was fined as a penalty for unjust litigation; (2) the oath which was taken only after invocation of some sacred numen. But in a special sense it is applied to denote the military oath, by which soldiers used to be bound to the magistrate to do vigorously everything the general ordered and not to desert the military standards. The word was transferred from the military business to sacred uses by ecclesiastical writers and was used to signify a mystery. More strictly it is taken to be a sacred sign or outward symbol, which exhibits one thing to the senses, another to the mind. Only it consisted in the fact that it denoted the sign and seal of the covenant in Christ instituted by God in the Church."

As to the other descriptions of sacrament to be found in H. Scripture RIJSSEN remarks (XVII, 4): "Scripture more correctly calls them signs of the covenant, Gen. 9. 12-13 (this is the token of the covenant which I make between me and you . . . for perpetual generations; I do set

my bow in the clouds, and it shall be for a token of a covenant between
me and the earth) 17. 11 (circumcision—shall be a token of a covenant
between me and you), signs and seals of the righteousness of faith, Rom.
4. 11 (p. 591) and signs simply, Ex. 12, 13 (the blood shall be to you for
a token upon the houses where ye are; and when I see the blood I will
pass over you . . .), ὑποδείγματα, copies Heb. 8. 5 ("a copy and
shadow of the heavenly things," of the making of the tabernacle) 9, 23
(It was necessary that the copies of the things in the heavens should be
cleansed with these (cf. the setting apart of the elements with us); but
the heavenly things with better sacrifices than these), and ἀντίτυπα,
likenesses, 1 Pet. 3. 21 (through water (ark); which now after a true
likeness doth now save you, even baptism, not the putting away of the
filth of the flesh, but the interrogation of a good conscience towards God
through the resurrection of Jesus Christ); in the OT the word אות
occurs, Gen. 17, Ex. 31, Ezek. 20, which denotes a sign and is applied
to the sacraments."—WOLLEB 95: "It is also called *mysterium*, so far
as it signifies a secret and divine matter set forth by signs and types. But
the word mystery is broader than sacrament: every sacrament is a
mystery, but not every mystery is a sacrament."

3.—A sacrament is a sacred action divinely instituted, in which the grace
promised to the covenanted through Christ is sealed to them by God
with visible signs and they in turn are led to obey Him" (WOLLEB 95).
Or "A sacrament of the covenant of grace is a sacrament by which
(I) God renders the individual believers using the sacrament (i) both
certain that the covenant of grace and all the benefits promised in it
belong not to others but also to themselves individually, who use the
sacrament according to the divine institution; (ii) and admonishes them
of their obligation by which they are bound; (II) the faithful themselves
attest their piety as well in the presence of God and the angels as before
men" (POLAN VI, 5).

The sacrament thus consists (*a*) of a visible element (water, bread,
wine), which has the significance of a sign, seal and pledge; (*b*) of a definite
action ordained by God (*actio ritualis*), and in according to which the
element is to be used (COCCEIUS, *Summ. theol.* LII, 9): "To the earthly
element there also belongs an *actio ritualis*, whereby it is treated in a
fixed way with a fuller meaning," and (*c*) of the saving benefit of the
covenant of grace, which God has promised to the elect in the Gospel.

4.—The nature of the outward *actio ritualis* of the sacrament consists
in the *verbum institutionis* or *consecratorium*, i.e., in the recital of the words
of the institution of the sacrament. The consecration, hereby carried

out, of the elements to be used in administering the sacrament is nevertheless (because no *virtus operativa* at all resides in the word of institution) not a change in the use and destination of them. "God effects the sacrament by the word of institution, which being added to the element it becomes a sacrament, not by the infusion of a new quality but by change of use" (TRELCATIUS, p. 190). By consecration the element is set apart from the natural to the spiritual use; from the natural to the spiritual destination, so that the element, i.e., water, bread, wine, comes to be regarded no longer as such, no longer as a means which cleanses and/or nourishes the body, but as a sign of covenant grace. To "consecrate" or to "sanctify" "is to dedicate to God and to sacred uses, that is, to set apart from common use and in accordance with God's ordinance to destine and assign to a single and sacred use" (BULLINGER VIII, 12). This consecration of the elements (which naturally holds only for the duration of the sacramental action, for "apart from the use instituted by Christ it has no standing as a sacrament") is consummated not for the sake of the elements themselves but for the sake of the believers who come to the sacrament. Since then the real purpose of the consecration is the edification of those who wish to receive the sacrament, the "words of institution" should be given out in a distinct voice and listened to with a believing heart, in order that each may be assured that the proposed action is the same as Christ instituted and blessed with his promise.

RIISSEN (XVII, 15, 2): "The question is not whether there is a sacramental word that consecrates, which we do not deny; but whether it consecrates in such a way that it is operative, which we do deny: not whether a word is to be emitted over the signs, [but] whether it is to be enunciated in a deep and intelligible voice, so that it may be understood by those to whom the sacrament is to be administered, or can be called a word to be spoken in that way; or whether it is put in a fixed formula which does not edify those about to communicate, but consecrates by a certain power put into the actual words, which words are to be muttered in a low voice over the elements. The *Papists* deny the former, affirm the latter.—We on the contrary."—WOLLEB 96: "The instrument by which the sacraments are effected or by which the signs are consecrated, is the word of institution consisting of two chief parts: the instruction concerning the lawful administration of the sacrament and the perception and promise of its fruit and efficacy.—The word of institution changes not the substance or quality, but only the use of the elements; and that not by a secret power inherent in the actual words, as the *Papists* pretend, but by the ordinance of God.—As a stone by a magistrate's decree is changed into a boundary mark, its substance and qualities remaining, so by the addition of the words to the element (as *Augustine* says) it becomes a sacrament, the substance and quality of the element remaining, the common use only being transformed into the sacred.— A foolish opposition is made between the *verbum concionale* and the *verbum institutionis*. They do not differ really, only technically. *Concio* is nothing else than the explanation of the words. Therefore the words of institution belong to the essence of the sacrament, the *verbum concionale* to the manner of institution."—RIISSEN (XVII, 16, 2): "Necessary to the constitution of a sacrament are the word(s) of institution, which consist of an injunction and a promise. This we call the *verbum sacramentale seu concionale et praedicatum*, not so much because it is taught and preached as because it is put forth in a clear high voice at the instituting of the sacrament for the information of believers present. We must hold well to this point, because most arguments of our opponents sin from ignorance of the thing in dispute; as though by the spoken word (*concionale verbum*) we meant a public address by the minister to explain a passage of scripture in an ecclesiastical gathering."—BULLINGER (VIII, 2): "When water, bread and wine are used in the sacraments and the prayers of believers are rightly and orderly made, they retire from common use and by God's institution and behest are transferred to another singular use and so become other in mode than they were before. Before they were ordinary common water, bread and wine, in the daily or common or profane use of men, whereby men wash and cleanse themselves outwardly with water, while they use bread and wine to nourish the body. From this use they depart when they become sacraments.—Baptism is not now a washing of the body, but the sacrament of regeneration and of the condonation of sins."—BEZA (*Opp.* I, p. 207): "The signs are not changed in the actual nature or substance of them but only as regards their use, and that only so long as the action is proceeding to which they are subservient. In the sacred mysteries we have not simply water as water or bread as bread or wine as wine, but as sure and true symbols and pledges of those things which God gives indeed in another way, but yet most truly and surely."—BUCAN (XLVI, 22): "Is this change in the use of the elements perpetual? By no means. It has regard only to the use in Church and that a public use. So that apart from the action of the mysteries of the administration of the sacraments no room is left for them. Nothing has the nature of a sacrament apart from the use instituted by Christ."— For the rest WENDELIN (*Coll.*, p. 421) remarks that the Reformed avoid the designation "words of consecration" and instead of them use the expressions *verba ordinationis* and *verba promissionis*".

5.—The invisible benefit of grace in the sacrament is the salvation of the gospel promised in the covenant of grace and mediated by the H.

Spirit, namely the living Christ with his merit and his gifts of salvation. —RIJSSEN (XVII, 5): "The inward (matter of the sacrament) is the covenant of grace or the gospel promise of the remission of sins, regeneration of the spirit and life eternal through and for the sake of Christ, which is called the thing signified."—WOLLEB 97: "The inward and heavenly matter is the thing signified, Christ of course with all his benefits."— LEIDEN SYNOPSIS (XLIII, 20–21): "The signs which meet the outward sense import into our minds other things plainly spiritual and heavenly, and set them forth to be understood and to be sealed through faith.— These things are Christ with all his benefits to be applied to us through faith. Christ generally is the *res sacramenti;* by reason of his person, because he is exhibited entire to the believing soul for spiritual κοινωνία; and by reason of his merit, because in the sacraments the truth and efficacy of Christ's death are set forth and confirmed, by which he secured life for us."—TRELCATIUS, p. 193: "The *res sacramenti* is Christ himself in respect of both person and merit and benefits."—AMESIUS (I, xxxvi, 23): "The spiritual thing which is signified in the sacraments of the new covenant is the new covenant itself, i.e., Christ with all the benefits which are prepared in him for believers."

6.—The sacrament thus has no other content of grace than the word, since the saving benefit given in the word is identical in substance with the grace sealed by the sacrament and differs only in respect of the form of manifestation and of the effectiveness of the grace. The word is apprehended by hearing, the sacrament by the eye, so the latter is also called the "word visible". The word proclaims salvation to all who hear it, the sacrament appropriates it only to believers. The word is meant to arouse faith in itself, the sacrament is meant to fortify faith in the word. CALVIN (IV, xiv, 4): "He is deceived who thinks that anything more is conferred on him through the sacraments, than what he perceives by true faith when offered in God's word."—POLAN VI, 51: "Perception of Christ, whether in the bare word—or in the sacraments, is the same, namely spiritual, i.e., perception accomplished by the H. Spirit's power, with the single instrument of faith. Perception of Christ in the word and perception of him in the sacraments do not differ actually. In both cases there is the same thing, the same substance, namely Christ with his benefits. They do not differ in manner; in both cases it is spiritual. They do not differ in the instrument of perception; in both cases the instrument of perception is faith. How then does perception of Christ differ in the simple word and in the sacraments? Only in the outward form."—WOLLEB 100: "Word and sacraments agree in substance: the seals stamp the same thing as is promised in the testament. They differ

(1) because the word is perceived by hearing, the sacraments by sight; and so a sacrament is the word visible: (2) because the word of the gospel is general; in a sacrament the gospel promises are applied to each of the faithful: (3) because usually faith is roused by the word, confirmed by the sacrament."

7.—The outward element in the sacrament is a visible exposition and portrayal of the promised invisible grace, and at the same time a sealing of the real impartation of the promised gracious benefit to the believer, so that it assures him that he as certainly has and receives the invisible gracious benefit, as the visible guaranteeing sign is imparted to him.— POLAN (VI, 51): "The earthly part in the sacrament is the sign or symbol, by which the heavenly part promised to believers is not only represented and signified by a sort of likeness, but is also exhibited along with it, so that believers are assured that the heavenly part is present spiritually and given to them, as surely as they see the earthly part present in bodily form before their eyes."

8.—But the elements have the guaranteeing significance of sign and seal only because they are ordained and destined thereto by God.—BULLINGER (VIII, 1): "Believers must know that the sacraments of Christ and his Church have no other principle, no other origin and cause than God Himself, and that therefore we have the sacraments only from God since besides God no one can or ought to institute a sacrament."—COCCEIUS (*Summ. theol.* LII, 8): "The word by which the element or visible species (for so the *Latins* called the actually earthly bodies of the sacraments) is changed into a sacrament, is that by which the Author of the Covenant substituted for the spiritual, heavenly, invisible part, as a seal, earnest and pledge, the earthly, bodily visible part, in some way analogous to it by nature; and transmits it as a sign of the covenant, and bids it be received faithfully and worthily as the sign of the covenant."—CROCIUS, p. 1,132: "Only the divine institution effects the sacrament. Remove it and the sacrament is removed, change it and the sacrament is changed."

9.—In virtue of this divine ordering, according to which there takes place in the sacrament for the outward apprehension a "substitution of the sign for the heavenly fact," the signs in the sacramental action have the meaning of the gracious benefit itself.—COCCEIUS (*Summ. de foed.* 204): In the sacrament we thus have a "substitution of the sign for the heavenly part in the perception of each believer through the word of the promise and sacramental praise. By this sign the name of the analogue is given to it, to represent the equivalence possessed by the earthly application to the sensual perception and presence of the heavenly part in accordance with the will and declaration of God—to create certainty about the heavenly part and the benefits connected with it."

10.—This is the "sacramental union" of sign and thing signified, which is to be regarded as the "essential form of the sacraments" and to be conceived in accordance with what had been expounded so far. On the one hand the signs are not "bare signs" or signs of absent things, so not merely memorial signs, since rather as "significant, exhibiting, applying and sealing signs" they not only portray and seal the promised gracious benefit but also mediate it.—CROCIUS (p. 1133): "Although the sacraments are signs they are not empty signs, but exhibitive of the thing signified, to wit spiritual grace, as being related to them [the signs]".— LEIDEN SYNOPSIS (XLIII, 29): "We suffer the calumny that we would be setting up bare, empty and therefore ineffectual signs, because in addition to their significance according to God's institution we also attribute to them the exhibition (but in a manner suited to a sacrament) and sealing of the divine promises; including the various expressions figured both in Scripture and in the Church's common use, when the name of the thing signified is attributed to the sign or the attribute of the thing is attributed along with the sign."— RIISSEN (XVII, 16, 1): "The orthodox do not deny that sacraments are signs distinctive of Christians and the tickets or labels (tesserae) of their profession. But against the Socinians they deny that they are confined to that. But apart from this less fundamental use they are of opinion that it is primary that they are seals of God's grace, which He willed to join to the word of the promise, as the seals of princes are attached to documents to certify them."—WOLLEB 97: "Nor are the sacraments empty signs because sign and thing signified are not united locally. They remain none the less (i) significant (ii) exhibiting (iii) applying, (iv) sealing signs.—Firstly, the outward symbols signify and represent Christ's body and blood. Secondly, along with the sign is also exhibited the thing signified, though not in the sign but in the sacramental act when the minister exhibits the sign, Christ the Lord being the giver of the thing signified. Thirdly, the thing signified having been promised generally to believers by the word of the Gospel is applied to each believer when the sign is exhibited. Fourthly, the same promise is sealed in the sacrament; whence they are called not signs only but seals, Rom. 4. 11 (circumcision).".

11.—On the other hand they are in no wise bearers, vehicles or channels, which enclose and mediate the gracious salvation physically.—AMESIUS (I, xxxvi, 18): "The sacramental signs do not contain the spiritual part to which they refer by physical inherence or adherence; so they would be at once signs and things signified."—HEIDEGGER (XI, 60): "Generally the sacraments of the covenant of grace are neither miracles nor drugs nor causes nor conditions nor σχήματα, vehicles and channels of justifying and sanctifying grace, but signs of it conferred and so signs of the righteousness of faith."—LEIDEN SYNOPSIS (XLIII, 25): ". . . sacraments are not the causes of grace, physical or primary or even instrumental; whether by some inherent quality or by the motion of God raising the sacrament to such effect as it attains."

12.—The "sacramental union" is thus not to be conceived as a "local, physical or spiritual union (as though the *vis iustificandi* inhered in the sign itself, so that sign and thing signified inhered in real unity of "inexistence"); but as an *"unio relativa, significativa" or "moralis"*; because he who receives the sign in the right way at the same time becomes a participator in the thing itself also.—MASTRICHT (VII, iii, 8): "The form is the union of sign with thing signified, not (a) a corporeal form achieved by contact and co-existence, as between two boards held together by glue, nor (b) imaginary, as between seeing eye and thing seen, nor (c) strictly spiritual, as between Christ and the believer, but (d) sacramental, by which although the thing signified is not contained in the sign or, much less, is the sign by nature; but in virtue of the divine institution and promise there is such a moral nexus between thing and thing signified, that he who accepts the signs in the way appropriate to the divine institution, at the same time receives the thing signified."—RIISSEN (XVII, 13): "The sacramental union of sign with thing signified is neither physical, like that of matter and form, subject and accident; nor local, by contact and absence of distance ; nor spiritual, so that power to justify is directly instilled into the actual signs, which must be upheld against *Papists* and *Lutherans*; but is entirely σχετική and relative or moral, as between pledge and the thing signified by the pledge." — WOLLEB 97: "The union of sign and thing signified is not φυσική or local, but σχετική, so far as sign represents thing signified; and on the sign being exhibited by the minister, the thing signified is also given to the faithful by Christ."— LEIDEN SYNOPSIS (XLIII, 24): "From what has been said it is fairly gathered that in the sacraments we are not laying down any union or connection between signs and things signified; whether physical, as of matter and form, or of subject and accident by inexistence; or local by absence of distance; or even spiritual, by infusion of some power latent in the sign itself; but relative and sacramental, by which yet the things themselves are truly exhibited and sealed to the faithful, but are to be perceived in a spiritual manner."—TRELCATIUS (p. 195): "This conjunction of signs and things signified is not natural, by substantial contact and connection; not local; not even spiritual, directly quickening the actual signs; but entirely relative and sacramental, consisting chiefly in three things: signification, sealing and the provision of the thing signified." —BUCAN (XLVI, 12): "It is true that the sacramental conjunction in respect of us and of the things signified is not essential and personal, but mystical. Yet in its own class it is real, indeed spiritual, solely by the power and virtue of the H. Spirit."

13.—Therefore in the well-grounded usage of H. Scripture and the Church (in the *phraseologia sacramentalis*) the sign quite usually bears the name of the thing set forth by it.—POLAN (VI, 51) "Therefore, after the trite and clear manner of speech in Scripture and the Church, the earthly thing is often called by the name of the heavenly, because the heavenly thing is signified, understood and sealed through the earthly thing. The blood of victims is called the blood of the covenant, Ex. 24. 8. Circumcision is called the covenant, Gen. 17. 10. The paschal lamb is called the passover, Ex. 12. 11. Baptism is called the laver of regeneration, Tit. 3. 5."— HEIDEGGER (XI, 62): "The sealing of the covenant of grace through the sacraments depends on the truth of the divine promise and of the substitution of one for another. But since because of the fixity of God's word this truth also is fixed and infallible, hence the fact that the names for signs and things signified are interchanged in Scripture, and one is said to be the other. Accordingly sacramental phraseology in Scripture will be found to be twofold, one strict, the other improper [i.e., not strict] and figurative. It is strict phraseology, when what belongs to the sign is attributed to the sign, and what belongs to the thing signified is attributed to the thing signified. As when circumcision is called the sign of the covenant, Gen. 17. 11, the seal of righteousness, Rom. 4. 11, and the blood of Christ is said to cleanse from all sin, 1 Jn. 17. It is improper or figurative, when what belongs to the sign is attributed to the thing signified, and what belongs to the thing signified is attributed to the sign."—MASTRICHT (VII, iii, 8) discusses the "sacramental phraseology" based on the "sacramental union". "Upon this sacramental union is based the sacramental phraseology by which (1) the sign is predicated of the thing signified, as when sanctification of the heart is called circumcision Rom. 2. 29; (2) the thing signified is predicated of the sign, as when e.g., circumcision is called the covenant, Gen. 17. 11, bread the body of Christ, Mt. 26. 26 ; (3) the thing effected by the thing signified is set forth in terms of the sign e.g., when regeneration is attributed to baptism, Tit. 3. 5; (4) the attribute of the sign is attributed to the thing signified, as when fraction which is appropriate to bread is attributed to the body of Christ, 1 Cor. 11. 24; (5)

the attribute of the thing signified is attributed to the sign, as when remission of sins is attributed to external baptism Ac. 22, 16."—WOLLEB 98: "From the union and relation of the thing signified with and to the sign flows the sacramental locution or phrase, by which the thing signified is predicated of the sign. In this manner of speaking there is expressed, not so much what the outward signs are in themselves and by their nature, as what they signify.—99: This manner of speaking is termed sacramental metonymy, putting the thing signified for the sign. It does not make much difference whether the trope is said to be in the attribute or in the copula. Although the trope is placed in the attribute, yet the cause or foundation of the trope is in the copula."—"It is sacramental phraseology by which the name or attribute of the thing signified is by a metonymy customary in Scripture attributed to the sign" (HOTTINGER 346, ALTING, *Opp.* V, p. 106).

14.—The efficacy of the sacrament rests not upon the power of the signs, (in which no peculiar power of grace is immanent), but solely upon the efficacy of the H. Spirit, who is active in such a way in the outward sacramental action (since He lets it work upon the heart of man at His own will), that a distinction must be made between the latter and the invisible action of the H. Spirit.—BEZA (*Opp.* I, p. 209): "Whence the efficacy of the sacraments ?—From the operation of the H. Spirit entirely, not however from the signs, except so far as the inward feelings are moved by these outward objects. Now these movements the H. Spirit, using those aids to our weakness, renders effective in the degree and at the moment that it pleases Him."—*Conf. Helv.* (II, 19): "Whence also the faithful discriminate openly in the administration of the sacraments between the Lord Himself and the Lord's minister, confessing that the matter of the sacraments is given by the Lord Himself, but the symbols by the Lord's ministers."—MARESIUS (XVIII, 25): "Hence it is that the outward sign is extended by the minister, the thing signified is extended inwardly by the H. Spirit."

15.—The eye of faith has therefore to fasten not on the outward aspect of the sacrament. Instead the sacrament, which as a sign and witness witnesses not to itself but to the crucified and risen Christ, is meant to lead faith to Christ's death and merit and to the gracious benefits mediated by the H. Spirit.—OLEVIAN (p. 303): "The aim of the sacraments or visible testimonies is not that they should confine us to themselves, but that they should direct faith to the victim Christ, i.e., to the thing testified. —309-310: As the witness to the covenant, which rings in our ears through the preaching of the Gospel, leads us along with our lost offspring to Christ's death, in which the eternal covenant acquires confirmation;

so too the visible seals of that testimony lead us as though our hands were taken to the same death of the Son: those of the ancients in such wise that blood was shed in the actual testimonies, by which it was shown that the debt was not paid,—ours without any shedding of blood attest—that the single shedding of the blood of God's Son—has confirmed the covenant of grace for ever.—333: The word of the promise and the seal annexed are testimonies bearing witness not to themselves, but to Christ crucified and risen again."

16.—Also the sacrament is meant to be not the cause of justification, but a guaranteeing sign of the righteousness which is given to faith.—CALVIN (IV, xiv, 14): "With great consent the sophistic schools handed it down, that the sacraments of the new law, i.e., those now in use in the Christian Church, justify and confer grace, provided we do not set up the obstacle of mortal sin. It is impossible to say how pernicious and pestilent this opinion is, and the more so as it held for many centuries before, to the Church's great loss in a good part of the world. It is of course assuredly of the devil. For while righteousness is promised apart from faith, it leads souls headlong to destruction. Then because it derives the cause of righteousness from the sacraments, it ties men's wretched minds down to earth by this superstition, though more than sufficiently inclined thereto of their own will, so that they acquiesce in the spectacle of a thing corporeal, rather than in God Himself."—PISCATOR p. 132: "(They err) who attribute to the signs the power of conferring the grace to which they testify."—COCCEIUS (*Summ. theol.* LII, 17): "Sacraments are neither the causes of justification and sanctification nor the conditions of them, but the signs of the covenant, partly inviting us by the Spirit's grace to faith whereby we flee to Christ, and working morally upon faith for communion with him."—POLAN (VI, 51): "Hence also we see how the sacraments save us, not of course as efficient causes or instruments conferring grace and salvation and that *ex opere operato*, apart from any good motion in the user, as the *Papists* impiously taught, but as signs and seals sealing to believers grace and salvation, which are conferred by God Himself."

17.—Hence the sacraments are designed absolutely for believers who really have part in the covenant of grace. For the unbeliever they are completely meaningless, because the unbeliever has no connection with the covenant of grace.—WOLLEB 100: "The sacraments are common to all covenanted people as signs, but peculiar to the elect as the thing signified."—POLAN (VI, 51): "The legitimate use of a sacrament of the covenant of grace is not just the outward observance of the rite, without the faith to refer the

rite to any end, by the grace of which it was instituted by God."—
COCCEIUS (*Summ. de foed.* 209): "The sacraments were instituted strictly
for believers and were given to them."—HEIDEGGER (XI, 65): "The
sacraments belong to the same whose is the covenant of grace of which
alone they are the signs and seals; and so to the Church of elect believers.
As to them alone as by a covenant He promises His grace in the word,
so He seals the same through the sacraments. But for the reprobate and
unbelieving as aliens to the testament and covenant of God, as nothing is
promised them by God nothing is sealed. Sacraments are the seals of the
righteousness of faith."—POLAN (VI, 51): "The sacraments of the covenant of grace were instituted for the faithful alone by God. As the word
not accepted by faith is an empty sound, so the sacrament not accepted
by faith which believes what the rite signifies is a useless ceremony and an
empty show. Therefore to the godless and unbelieving sacraments are
not sacraments so far as concerns them, because to them they are not the
seals of the righteousness of faith. Nor is the external perception of them
of any advantage to those who remain destitute and void of their inward
truth. The sacraments of course remain sacraments so far as God is
concerned. Sacraments are signs of grace to the converted. But they lose
the force and reason of a sacrament, as far as infidels who abuse them are
concerned."

18.—Of course God also offers unbelievers the grace promised in the
sacrament. But these shut themselves against it and reject it.— CALVIN
(IV, xiv, 6): "As God calls His promises covenants and His sacraments
symbols of the covenants, the like may be adduced from the actual
covenants of men. Nor is their reasoning much to the point who contend,
that there are no testimonies to the grace of God, because they are extended
to the godless as well; these still do not feel that God is any the more
favourable to them for that, but rather incur a graver condemnation."
CALVIN compares unbelievers receiving a sacrament to a (sealed) vessel
which, overflowed ever so richly by a fluid, yet remains empty; (IV, xiv,
17): "Wherefore let it be a fixed point, that the part of a sacrament does
not differ from that of God's word: which is to offer and hold forth to us
Christ and, in him, the heavenly treasures of grace. But they confer
nothing and avail nothing, if not received in faith. Just as wine or oil or
other liquid, however generously you pour them in, will nevertheless run
away and perish, unless the mouth of the jar is open. While the jar itself,
though poured upon from all sides, will none the less remain void and
empty."—BEZA (*Opp.* III, p. 173): "Christ is true, therefore he never
offers sacred signs, unless he is also truly offering what he signifies by them.
And further they are always true and straightforward sacraments

because of God's word. But since the symbols are supplied for hand and mouth, and the things signified, i.e., Christ's very self, are supplied to the believing mind, therefore all who apply hand and mouth perceive the symbols, but the mind unendued with faith rejects the matter of the sacrament.—p. 171 We confess that full sacraments, i.e., both the outward and earthly and the things signified and heavenly are truly offered by the Lord Himself, who is the one Giver of them, to both worthy and unworthy."—*Conf. Helv.* (II, 19): "We acknowledge that the integrity of the sacraments depends upon faith or the truth and sheer goodness of God. As the word of God remains the true word of God, whereby not only are bare words recited in preaching, but at the same time there are offered by God the things signified or announced by the words, although the godless and unbelieving hear and understand the words, yet do not enjoy the things signified, because they do not receive with true faith: so the sacraments remain—true and unimpaired sacraments, not only signifying the sacred things, but God also offering the things signified, although unbelievers do not discern the things offered."—CROCIUS (p. 1133): "By the sacraments as instruments God exerts His power to apply and seal grace; not to any, but only to those who grasp what is offered with true faith."—BUCAN (XLVI, 13): "Are both conjointly, thing and signs, offered to us by God? Yes, conjointly, truly and without deception as regards God who promised: but nevertheless distinctly, so that frequently he that receives the signs receives nothing less than the thing itself."

19.—For the nature of the sacrament is independent of the faith of the recipient, because not faith but the divine institution makes the sacrament, and because not faith but the *unio sacramentalis* is the *forma sacramenti*. Thus in consequence the sacraments are in and for themselves always a real and objective offering of divine grace.—BUCAN (XLVI, 18): "Does faith belong to the substance and integrity of the sacrament?—By no means, because it is not faith that effects the sacrament but the divine institution. Faith indeed is necessary to appropriating the matter of the sacrament; by faith Christ dwells in our hearts. But whether a man does or does not believe, if the sacrament be lawfully administered, he receives the true sacrament, i.e., as regards God."—HOTTINGER p. 347: "It is not true that the Reformed teach that faith is the form of the sacrament."

20.—Yet in their effect the sacraments are, only for the believer, a true seal of the covenant of grace, by the bestowal of which God attests the certainty of His grace, by the use of which the believer attests his appurtenance to the covenant of grace and his recognition of the duty thereby undertaken (i.e., his conscience). Hence for the believer receipt of the sacrament is (1) a real receipt of the substance of the covenant of grace; (2) a new binding of his conscience to loyal persistence in it; and (3) a new attestation by God, that He will eternally keep His covenant with the conscience surrendered to Him and maintain it in being.—OLEVIAN p. 329: "Thus as seals to the free covenant between God and us we have the visible public testifications (between God and man's conscience), through which God binds the conscience to Himself by insisting that he consent by God's grace to the free covenant offered in the promulgation of the Gospel and to its whole substance, and be content to live and bring up his household in such recognition and celebration, so that the covenant may be propagated in an unbroken succession to the glory of God, Gen. 17. 18 ("Oh that Ishmael might live before Thee!" And God said, "Nay, but Sarah . . . shall bear thee a son"). In turn God binds Himself to the conscience, that the oath taken by Him once for all and the whole substance of the free covenant comprised in the articles of faith shall be firm and ratified for those who feel in their conscience that they have been animated as was said.—So there are three degrees in the administration of the seals: (1) the offering of the entire covenant and of its entire substance contained in the articles of faith through the preaching of the gospel;—(2) an obligation on the conscience which consents through God's grace, or stipulation of conscience's assent to the offered covenant and to its whole substance in Christ ; or if it lies, that it is rightly excluded from the whole substance of the covenant and condemned; (3) an obligation on God's part towards the conscience thus affected by His grace, that the sworn covenant and its whole substance will be ratified for ever and that there is no danger of any change of view; or if He shall not prove mindful of it, He will not be the Holy God."

21.—Since the gracious benefit of the sacrament, to wit the personal Christ with his benefits, is of a spiritual nature, it can be received only with the instrument of spiritual life, the heart, i.e., with the believing heart or with faith.—ALSTED, p. 822: "Christ is touched by faith, not by the body,"—BUCAN (XLVI, 14): "What is the method of discerning signs and things signified?—The actual things signified are imparted with respect to God through the H. Spirit, with respect to us through faith, through which alone Christ with all his benefits is apprehended by us. An intelligible thing spiritually set forth cannot be discerned save in a spiritual manner."

22.—The sacraments bring their blessing not *ex opere operato*, i.e., by a saving power dwelling objectively in them, but purely because of the promise, which Christ fulfils directly and personally in believing reception of the sacrament by the power of the H. Spirit.—POLAN (VI, 51):

"Sacraments are advantageous, i.e., exhibit grace in the true use (1) not *ex opere operato*, i.e., by the natural suitability and power of the actual work done—or as others will have it, by way of the presence of the divine power assigned, because of the pact, even without faith and the inward motion of the user. It is a false lie of the *Scholastics* that sacraments justify *ex opere operato*. Neither do sacraments infuse righteousness into the users, as when a pitcher is poured into a vessel. Nor do they impress grace by a power put into them, as a nail is driven by a hammer into a board, or some sign stamped on metal. (2) Nor *ex opere operantis*, i.e., because of the devotion or merit of the user. But (3) because of God's promise who institutes the sacrament and because of living faith in the man using the sacrament."—CROCIUS, p. 1133: "The fruit of the sacrament is from the sole power of God as principal cause. But the sacraments themselves are nothing else than means and instruments of this power.— In the sacraments no other sort of inherent quality is to be looked for, which is communicable to the users."

23.—Only preachers of the Gospel called by the Church are entitled to administer the sacraments, but not lay men or women. To these falls the administration of the sacraments orderly. And in the Kingdom of God there can be no instance to entitle a Christian to infringe the order of it.—BUCAN (LXVI, 62): The sacrament is to be administered "by a public person or one duly called or at least" (which is worth noting!) "by a common error performing a public function." Even in this latter case the action is a "true" and "effectual sacrament!"—LEIDEN SYNOPSIS (XLIII, 12): "Hence it is that Christ unites a command about administering sacraments with a command to "preach" and "teach", Mt. 28, 19, which command was committed to "stewards of the mysteries of God", 1 Cor. 4. 1, who are also called θεοῦ σύνεργοι 1 Cor. 3. 9, not of course in the institution of them, which is most directly from God, but in their administration, to which under the pretext of a case of necessity no one is to be admitted who is not lawfully called thereto, and it follows that the custom is to be rejected of those, who also give the power of administering certain sacraments either to laymen or to women."

24.—But it should be noted that what is involved is only the Church's calling of the minister and not his moral worthiness. Even if the sacrament is administered by an unworthy minister, it is still a guarantee and seal of the covenant of grace.—BEZA (*Opp.* III, 71): "We assert that sacraments do not depend on the faith or unbelief of the minister distributing."—LEIDEN SYNOPSIS (XLIII, 12): "Although for the due administration of a sacrament a call in the sense of an office is necessary, we do not think that personal holiness is essential. Because a minister acts in this administration in God's name, not his own, we deny that worthiness or unworthiness in the minister can add anything to or take away anything from the integrity or effectiveness of sacraments."— *Couf. Helv.* (II, 19): "Let believers—recognise for themselves, that if a minister has a striking defect, it is no obstacle, since they recognise that the integrity of the sacraments depends on the Lord's institution."

25.—As little does the efficacy of the sacrament depend on the intention with which the preacher administers it. If the preacher administers the sacrament not in the sense intended by Christ, he invites great guilt upon his own head, but does not thereby deprive the believing recipient of the sacrament of the grace of the sacrament. Its efficacy rests purely upon Christ's institution, not upon the ministrant's intention, and has an absolutely certain efficacy, because one may be absolutely sure of the reliability of Christ's promise, but not of the purpose of the ministrant.— LEIDEN SYNOPSIS (XLIII, 13): "That the intention to do what God enjoined to be done in the Church is necessary for a minister when administering a sacrament, to avoid incurring sin, we affirm. But that intention belongs to the *raison d'etre* and essence of the sacrament, so that it is not valid without the intention of the minister, even if Christ's institution and other things necessary in a sacrament are observed, we regard as a sacrilegious dogma, by which certainty of consolation is imperilled, which we hope for from discernment of the sacraments."—WOLLEB 96: "Unless a sacrament depends rather on God's institution than on the minister's intention, all consolation will be reft from wretched consciences, to which the thoughts of the minister administering the sacred rite are unknown."—Similarly TURRETIN (IX, 7) and all other dogmaticians.

26.—The most essential purpose of a sacrament is, that for the elect person it is a sealing divine of his fellowship in the covenant of grace. Hence the sacrament must (*a*) confirm in the elect faith in his belonging to the covenant of grace and so rouse him to faith in the grace of election which pertains also to him personally; so enjoyment of the sacrament cannot be made dependent on the certainty of an election previously and otherwise fixable, since rather enjoyment of the sacrament ought to establish this comfort precisely in the feebly believing heart of the elect person. Then as the seal of the covenant of grace the sacrament should (*b*) be a powerful exhortation to our duty to God undertaken when we entered into the covenant of grace.

OLEVIAN, p. 327: "Nor is it right to bind men to the state of election by the sacraments. In this way they would depart from the sacraments more uncertain than they had come. It is at variance with the aim of the sacraments, that through them sensibly the disclosure of election should descend to us and we ascend from them to election; so far, of course, as we rise from the believing sense of conscience, confirmed by use of the sacraments and bound to God, to effectual calling and thence to unchangeable election. So far is it from being the case that the seals hang our faith upon the condition of secret election in the use of them. This would necessarily be the case, if certainty of salvation were first of all estimated from the certainty of the outward sealing which is common to elect and reprobate; and not rather upon the effect of the gospel calling in the believing conscience (in confirmation of which is added God's visible sealing), whence later advance is made in safer security to the immutable decree of election, Rom. 8. 30 (" called, justified, glorified "), 2 Cor. 13. 5 (Try your own selves, whether ye be in the faith; prove your own selves. Or know ye not as to your own selves, that Jesus Christ is in you? Unless indeed ye be reprobate)."—WOLLEB 99: "The aim of the sacraments is the sealing of the covenant of grace."—LEIDEN SYNOPSIS (XLIII, 30): "The proper end of sacraments is to seal to believers the gospel promise and to confirm faith, since like the word the sacraments are instruments by which God operates and moves the hearts of believers. An incidental and less proper end is to be a testification of piety towards God, of love to neighbour and tokens of public profession, distinguishing the Church from unbelievers."

From this it is clear that the sealing of the promise of grace is the first purpose of the sacrament. Meanwhile the dogmaticians like the confessions of the Reformed Church recognise that the attestation of duty to the covenant on the believer's part is just as essentially the purpose for which Christ founded the sacraments. Cf., e.g., the *East Frisian Confession* of 1554, Qu. 54: "To what end are the sacraments?—Firstly, to set most clearly before our eyes, to attest and to seal the promises of the holy gospel of the unmerited forgiveness of sins and of fellowship in Christ's righteousness; secondly, to exhort us once more to our duty towards God and our neighbour and to move us to gratitude, love, fidelity and obedience to His will."—Similarly, *"What the Reformed Churches of Germany Believe or do not Believe"* (HEPPE, p. 257): "We believe that, to preserve and strengthen us in faith, God has also ordained the holy sacraments—so that we might not only hear but also see, feel and grasp how He is minded towards us, namely that He would forgive us our sins, send the H. Spirit and eternal life for the sake of the shedding of blood by Christ.—But once more by use of the sacraments we should also bind ourselves to God, to believe stedfastly in Christ and desire to lead a blameless life in his honour." As a rule, therefore, both chief aims are already stressed in the definition of the concept of a sacrament, e.g., by TRELCATIUS, p. 189: "A sacrament is a sacred action divinely instituted, in which God according to promise seals His grace in Christ and we in turn attest our faith and godliness towards Him."—ALTING (*Opp.* V, p. 105): "Sacraments (1) illustrate the will and promise of God who calls; (2) apply the same specifically; (3) bind the called to repentance and faith according to the tenor of the word or the conditions of the covenant."

27.—In this connection the sacrament has the further purpose of a public profession of faith on the believer's part and of an active confirmation of mutual love and fellowship.—COCCEIUS (*Summ. theol.* LII, 20): "Sacraments further have an important use in (1) provoking the confession of individuals; (2) unifying brotherliness; (3) spreading Christian doctrine and both spreading the story of its traditions and putting it beyond doubt;—(4) displaying the nucleus of its teaching and the foundation upon which everything is concentrated, without which everything collapses and empties. Wherefore, as in the holy use of them there is a salutary exercise of faith and invocation and glorification and love and repentance, so in careless contempt and neglect of the divine covenant there is ἀθέτησις, rejection."—POLAN (VI, 51): "These ends of a sacrament of the covenant of grace are common to all kinds of federal sacrament: (1) to be a monument, sign and seal of the covenant of grace and of the communion with Christ promised in the covenant and so of the benefits of God both exhibited and to be exhibited, i.e., to warn, re-assure and seal believers concerning the benefits conferred or to be conferred on them; (2) to admonish us of the obligation, by which we have bound ourselves to God, that we will be His people, and accordingly to secure the exercise, increase and confirmation of our faith in that direction; (3) to excite us to remember Christ and to thank him for the benefits of redemption; (4) to be the bond of mutual love and concord in the Church, i.e., so that by communion with him we may more and more be conquered by mutual love: (we being many are one bread, one body, 1 Cor. 10, 17); (5) to make it the nerve of public assemblies and of the preservation of the ecclesiastical ministry, Ex. 12. 17 (and ye shall observe the feast of the unleavened bread: for in this selfsame day have I brought your hosts out of the land of Egypt: therefore shall ye observe this day throughout your generations by an ordinance for ever), 1 Cor. 11. 26 (as often as ye eat this bread and drink this cup, ye do shew the Lord's death till he come); (6) to make it the mark of profession, by which as by a label the Church is distinguished from unbelievers, Ex. 12. 43 (there shall be no alien eater of it (passover)); in this way circumcision

distinguished Jews from other nations; (7) to be a witness of confession
and alliance with the Church ; (6) refers to the whole Church, (7) to
individual believers); (8) to afford opportunity for children to ask and
learn about God's benefits, and for parents and others to explain them,
Ex. 13. 14."

28.—An absolute necessity for the sacrament cannot be asserted, since
it is but the Word supplied with a guaranteeing sign. Faith may completely gain the covenant of grace in the word also. Hence a man who
is so strong in faith, that he can be joyfully confident of his state of grace
can do without the sacraments. But a relative necessity for the sacrament
results (1) subjectively, from the despair and little faith of the human
heart, which so often only rises to joyful faith, when it sees the promise
given to it before its eyes, and (2) objectively, in so far as the use of
sacrament is commanded by God and so is a duty.—Riissen (XVII, 10):
"Sacraments are not necessary by a necessity in the means. Although
they are means instituted by God for salvation, they do not therefore
possess necessity as a means without which salvation cannot be obtained.
—They are necessary, then, by a necessity of precept, in accordance
with God's command."—Olevian, p. 309: "Deprivation of the sign
attached without contempt does not import or result in denial of the
covenant or promise as a result of the thing promised, because seals
being accessories are not on a par with the covenant which is principal."
—Olevian 313: "By enjoining upon us the use of the sacraments God
wishes us to testify, that having been convicted by God's law we have
rebelled against Creator and law of creation and with our offering take
refuge with the Redeemer whom the Gospel offers free, to wit, Christ
clothed in a free covenant."

29.—From this it follows that it is contempt of the sacrament, not dispensing with it in and for itself, that involves liability to condemnation.
—Leiden Synopsis (XLIII, *Corollaria* 2 and 3): "No sacraments are
absolutely necessary to salvation. Moreover on the hypothesis of divine
injunction none are so necessary by a necessity in the means, that if
contempt was absent and impossibility was the cause of deprivation,
a man could or ought to be barred from participation in salvation, who
could not use the visible element."

30.—Regarding the number of the sacraments H. Scripture teaches, that
Christ ordained only two actions as seals of the covenant of grace, namely
baptism and the Lord's Supper. (These answer to Paradise and the
Tree of Knowledge in the original state, to Circumcision and the Passover

under the Mosaic dispensation: man at any stage being dependent upon grace for receipt of God's word, and so requiring in addition the support of visible signs which are also seals of the invisible benefits).—RIISSEN (XVII, 24): "The bases of the number two in the sacraments are: (1) Christ's institution, because no others are said to have been instituted by Christ except baptism and the Supper. (2) The nature of the sacraments, because to them alone belong the essential attributes previously listed as constituting a sacrament. (3) St. Paul's testimony, who only remembers these two, whether in comparison with the extra-ordinary sacraments of the Israelites in the desert, 1 Cor. 10. 1–2–3 (. . . our fathers were all under the cloud and all passed through the sea; and were all baptized into Moses in the cloud and in the sea; and did all eat the same spiritual meat [manna] and did all drink the same spiritual drink [when Moses smote the rock]: for they drank of a spiritual rock that followed them: and the rock was Christ), or in relation to the thing signified, 1 Cor. 12. 13 (in one Spirit were we all baptized into the one body, whether Jews or Greeks, whether bond or free; and were all made to drink of one Spirit). (4) The analogy of the ordinary OT sacraments, such that they were only two, circumcision and the passover: the former answers to baptism, the latter to the Supper. (5) The need for grace, which is required for spiritual life and which God wishes to seal to us through the sacraments. Two things are necessary, first that life should be given us, then that when given it should be preserved and nourished. Birth is foreshadowed in baptism, nourishment in the Supper. Hence the former is called the sacrament of initiation and the laver of regeneration: the latter the sacrament of confirmation and nourishment."

CHAPTER XXV

BAPTISM

1.—Baptism is the action instituted by Christ, Mt. 28. 19, by which God sealed in pledge to the elect their participation in the covenant of grace and binds them to a life sanctified by the believing consciousness of fellowship in the covenant. The visible sign with which this pledged sealing is given is water and dipping in it, by which the dipping of the elect person into the name of the triune God is figured and sealed. From this the full concept of baptism (POLAN VI, 55): "Baptism is the first sacrament of the NT, in which those to whom the covenant of grace belongs are according to Christ's command dipped or washed in water into the name of the Father, Son and H. Spirit, i.e., so that it may be signified and sealed to those who are baptized, that they have been taken up into the communion of the covenant of grace and inserted into his mystical body of the Church, are justified on account of the shedding of Christ's blood on our behalf and are regenerated through the Spirit of Christ; and in turn are obligated to worship in faith and good conscience and to call upon this only God the Father, Son and H. Spirit, Mt. 28. 19: Ac. 2. 38 (repent ye, and be baptized every one of you in the name of Jesus Christ unto the remission of sins; and ye shall receive the gift of the H. Ghost), Mt. 3. 11 (John and Jesus contrasted), Mk. 16. 16 (he that believeth and is baptized shall be saved), Lk. 3. 3 (John's baptism of repentance) cf. Mk. 1. 4, (John's Baptism), Rom. 6. 3 (all we who were baptized into Christ were baptized into his death), 1 Pet. 3. 21 (which... doth now save you, even baptism . . . the interrogation of a good conscience toward God through the resurrection of Jesus Christ). Or WOLLEB 104: "Baptism is the first sacrament of the new covenant, in which to the elect received into God's family by outward sprinkling with water are sealed remission of sins and regeneration by Christ's blood and the H. Spirit."—HEIDEGGER (XXV, 21) thus defines: "Baptism is the sacrament of regeneration, in which by sprinkling and dipping in water inward ablution from sins through the blood and Spirit of Christ is declared and sealed to one and all of God's covenanted."—HEIDEGGER thereupon discusses the proper meaning of the word βαπτισμός (really—"immersion" and only improperly— "ablution", as *taugen — tauchen*), and touches on the mediaeval distinction of a baptism *fluminis sive aquae, flaminis sive Spiritus* and *sanguinis sive martyrii.*—For definitions of baptism set out by URSIN, OLEVIAN and PISCATOR, cf. HEPPE *Dogm. des deutschen Protest.* III, 102–123.

2.—To carry out the baptismal action only those are entitled whom the Church has orderly called to the preaching office—so not laymen, not unbelievers, not women.—POLAN (VI, 55): "Only ministers of the Word who have been lawfully called ought to baptize. No women, no others, because only those to whom the office of preaching the word of God has been committed by God can legally confer baptism. Christ spoke to ministers of the word appointed by himself, but not to women or to anyone else, Mk. 16. 15–16 (. . . blessed art thou, Simon bar-Jonah . . . etc.); Mt. 28. 19, etc."—HEIDEGGER (XXV, 27): "It follows that the administration of baptism demands a mission and a vocation. Nor does it belong to others than those who are actually called to preach and to evangelise.—Then Christ combined the office of baptizing with the office of preaching the Gospel, bidding them teach, preach the gospel and baptize. Now none but a man called and sent may preach, Rom. 10. 15 (how can they preach except they be sent?).—It is a silly way out (κρησφύγετον) that men and women may teach, not of course publicly and solemnly but solemnity apart and privately; and so they may also baptize. Christ combined the power of baptizing with the public office of preaching the gospel, not with any old act of teaching."

3.—This holds also of so-called urgent cases, since there can be no urgency to justify an infringement of God's ordinance.—POLAN (VI, 55): "The urgency of a case is put forward in vain, since there is no necessity which can compel us to violate an ordinance prescribed by God. Paul does not write, 1 Cor. 1. 17, that he was not sent to baptize, i.e., principally, because sacraments are but appendages of the word of God; and they could be administered even by those who were not apostles, but yet were lawfully called to the function of preaching the word of God, Ac. 10. 48 (Peter commanded them to be baptized in the name of Jesus Christ)."— WOLLEB 104: "We do not hold allowable baptism administered by a private individual or a woman. If it is never found anywhere in an earthly state that a private individual acts contrary to injunction, how much the less will such a corruption please Christ in his Church!"— HEIDEGGER (XXV, 29): "Our opponents as a rule centre their single defence in the absolute necessity to baptize. But we will prove below that it is not absolute. If it were necessary, what temerity it would be for that reason to overthrow the divine ordinance and for men to want to save it by man's foresight against the will and pleasure of God? Or shall a woman, a pagan, a heretic in this way render God's purpose vain?" HEIDEGGER (XXV, 30) further insists that in the dispenser of baptism there must also be, apart from orderly calling, right faith and moral integrity, if baptism is to be administered orderly. "In the baptizer

are required lawful calling, right faith concerning baptism and uprightness of life; lawful calling to the ministry, because, as we said, it is not
lawful for anyone to baptize unless called to the ministry; right belief
regarding baptism, at least as regards essentials, because one who denies
the essence of baptism cannot be regarded as a minister of God's word
and sacraments; uprightness of life, because any minister and dispenser
of God's word and so also sacraments ought to be ἀνεπίλημπτος
1 Tim. 3. 2–3." At the same time HEIDEGGER adds: "The first points
are required both for the person and for the efficacy and validity of the
sacrament; the last is required for the person of the baptizer, not for the
efficacy of the sacrament."

4.—The outward act of baptism then consists first of all in the person to
be baptized being washed with water, while the dispenser of baptism
applies to this washing Christ's command and word of institution and
intends baptism into the name of the triune God, i.e., in Christ's sense.—
HEIDEGGER (XXV, 34): "To the element Scripture joins the word.
Christ gave himself for the Church, that he might sanctify it, when
cleansed, by the washing of water in the word, Eph. 5. 26. Washing with
water is the basis in Christ's word of institution, Mt. 28. 19. This word
is added to the element and it becomes a sacrament. The baptizer must
therefore repeat the words of Christ's institution, and the doctrine
concerning the mystery and essence of baptism which it seals."—BUCAN
(XLVII, 20): "The word of the Gospel—the sum of which is embraced
by Jesus Christ's institution together with the promise of eternal life,
Mt. 28. 19 and the clear utterance of this formula in vernacular speech
so that all may understand : "I baptize thee in the name or into the
name of Father, Son and H. Spirit"—is the word in baptism.—When
Ac. 2. 38 the apostles are said to have baptized in the name or into the
name of the Lord and Christ, it is either said synecdochically, as AMBROSE
maintains, and has the same sense as the above formula, because in
Christ are Father and H. Spirit, and whoso believes on the Son believes
also on Father and H. Spirit : or in Christ's name, i.e., in accordance
with the name and command of Christ."

5.—Upon the application of this rite the validity of baptism depends
absolutely. Hence that of such heretics as do not acknowledge the basic
dogmas of the Church, especially the doctrine of the triunity of God, is
to be as emphatically rejected and regarded as null, as the baptism of
those heretics who confess these dogmas (and so also the baptism dispensed in the Romish Church) must be considered as real baptism.—
RIISSEN (XVII, 33): "Query: whether baptism administered by heretics

is lawful? Ans: The question had been discussed in earlier days in the
time of CYPRIAN and of STEPHEN the Roman bishop. The former, with
his fellow-bishops of Africa, wished those baptized by certain heretics to
be rebaptized. The latter was of opinion that none of them needed re-
baptism. The query is solved by a distinction. There are some heretics
who corrupt the substance of baptism and omit and change the form of
institution, such as were the early *Arians* who denied a trinity of persons in
the unity of the essence, and such as are the *Socinians* today. There are
others who, while retaining the substantial points and observing the
true doctrine of the Trinity, which is contained in the formula of baptism,
err in other heads of doctrine, like the early *Novatians* and *Donatists* and
today the *Romans* and *Arminians*. As regards the former lot we are of
opinion that baptism administered by them is null, because they clearly
corrupt the essential form of baptism, to which the invocation of the
Trinity belongs. For that reason in early days the baptism of *Arians*
was rejected at the *Council of Nicaea*. But again some distinctions ought to
be observed here. Either the minister alone is infected with this heresy, or
with him the whole Church. If the latter, we deny that it is true baptism;
if the former, we believe that the baptism is in order, because the sacrament is the *peculium* of the Church, as it is dispensed in the name of the
Church and in her faith; therefore a hidden error in the minister of
baptism in no way detracts from its integrity, provided the essentials are
observed. If heretics retain the fundamentals of baptism which constitute
its essence, and do not change or corrupt the form, we lay it down that
baptism administered by such is in order, although in various heads they
err against the faith and their baptism is spoiled by various accidental
foreign rites."—WOLLEB 106: "If the essentials of baptism are observed,
baptism once received is not to be repeated. For this reason our Church
regards baptism administered in the *Papacy* as in order; not as regards
the abuse mixed up in it, but because the child has been baptized into
name of the H. Trinity.

6.—Baptism then may be administered in the form of a single or threefold
dipping into water as well as in that of a single or threefold sprinkling
with water.—LEIDEN SYNOPSIS (XLIV, 19): "Whether baptism must be
in a single or threefold dipping has always been considered indifferent
in the Christian Church. Similarly whether immersion or aspersion is
to be used, since no express command of the former is extant and examples
of sprinkling as well as of dipping may be gathered in the Scriptures.
While, Mt. 3, Christ entered the water and came out of it and so did the
Ethiopian, Ac. 8, so many thousands are said to have been baptized in
Jerusalem in one day, Ac. 2, also many in private houses, Ac. *cc.* 16, 18 ;

1 Cor. 1. 16 (Stephanas' household), where such entry into the water there could scarcely have been. This rite is also supported by the baptism in the cloud and in the sea, with which Paul deals 1 Cor. 10, and the word ῥαντισμός, i.e., sprinkling, is used of the blood of Christ for the doing away of our sins, Heb. 9, 14."—MARK (XXX, 10): "As to the number of the ablutions it is asked, whether it should be done once or thrice.—This of course is a matter of indifference (1) since it has not been determined by divine command, the passages, Eph. 4. 5 (one baptism) Heb. 6. 2 (the teaching of baptisms) being wrongly adduced on behalf of one or the other; (2) since there are also representations in favour of both, on the one hand those of the unity of the divine essence, of the mediator, of the death of Christ and of the washing from sins, on the other those of the trinity of the persons, of Christ's three days' sepulture, of the multitude of sins and of the perfection of our cleansing. So we think it safest that the varying practice to date be retained in the various Churches."

7.—The symbolic sense of this action is that the person baptized is implanted into the triune God as His property to His service and praise, as surely as the dispenser of baptism accomplishes the outward action upon him.—HEIDEGGER (XXV, 36):—"The formula of baptism is that by which the baptizer witnesses that he is baptizing into the name of the Father and the Son and the H. Spirit.—The formula—has the meaning, that those baptized into Father, Son and H. Spirit as three witnesses witnessing in heaven and on earth, 1 Jn. 5. 7-8 (it is the Spirit that beareth witness, because the Spirit is truth. For these are three who bear witness, the Spirit and the water and the blood; and the three agree in one) —call the Father God and the Father of the Son and our Father, call the Son the Redeemer, call the H. Spirit the sanctifier, paraclete and earnest, in all glorying, glorification and giving of thanks, and to these persons they consecrate themselves as a peculiar people.—Baptism εἰς ὄνομα Ἰησοῦ Χριστοῦ is equivalent to this formula".—RIISSEN (XVII, 35): "The formula briefly embraces all that is sealed to us in this sacrament. These may be referred to under three heads; God's institution, the promise of grace and the stipulation of faithful duty. Therefore when the pastor says, I baptize thee, it is the same as if he were saying, I declare in God's name that this water in which I wash you is a symbol of your admission into God's covenant and His Church; that the Father accepts you as a son, the Son as a member of his body and a brother, and the H. Spirit as a host with whom He is willing to dwell for ever; and that you worship Father, Son and H. Spirit, in virtue of the terms of your duty to the triune God, with worship and obedience, and consecrate yourself wholly to the worship of the Trinity for ever."

8.—The nature of baptism which is thus set forth by the outward action is thus the divine sealing of the adoption of the person baptized into the covenant of grace, of his death in Christ according to his old man and of his resurrection as a new man of a righteousness which holds in God's sight, and of his boundenness to a new life dominated by the Spirit of Christ and his sole appurtenance to the covenant of grace. Hence, 1 Pet. 3. 21, baptism is also described as the covenant (interrogation!) of a good conscience with God.—CALVIN (IV, xv, 1): "Baptism brings three things to our faith.—The first is that it is set before us by the Lord, to be the symbol and proof of our purgation, or (to explain better what I mean) to be like a sealed document by which He confirms to us, that all our sins have been destroyed, cured, obliterated, so that they never meet His eye, are not remembered or imputed.—5: It brings a second result, by showing us our mortification in Christ and new life in him.—6: Lastly our faith also brings the boon from baptism, that we have sure testimony not only that we are implanted into Christ's death and life, but that we are so united to Christ, that we are participants in all his benefits."—OLEVIAN p. 530-531: In baptism three distinctions have to be made: (1) God exhorts us faithfully to assume His grace in Christ; (2) God bids us have ourselves (and our children) baptized, in order that we may bear witness, that we gratefully assume God's covenant promise for ourselves (and our children), that we take upon ourselves the vow of sanctification and that we vow to God to baptize our children also and train them up to repentance, and (3) God seals to those so minded fellowship with Christ, participation in the covenant of grace and enjoyment of the benefits of it, forgiveness of sins, adoption and sanctification.— MASTRICHT (VII, iv, 10) : "The thing signified was generally the covenant of grace."—HEIDEGGER (XXV, 38): "The thing signified and sealed by the element of water and sprinkling of it by the baptizing minister is generally the whole gospel, but as a seal it is regeneration through Christ and the H. Spirit."—BUCAN (XLVII, 56): "The effect of baptism is the sealing of Christ's saving gifts and of our righteousness before God, and the stipulation of a good conscience towards God, God offering and promising free salvation for Christ's sake, conscience replying and receiving the promised grace by faith, whence arises tranquillity of conscience towards God."

9.—The benefits of grace are set forth and sealed by baptism, not just sensibly but also in pledge, to the man to whom it is orderly dispensed. Therefore the meaning and efficacy of baptism must be derived, not from the power of the H. Spirit, essentially inherent in it or in the baptismal water, and of magical effect—for grace is not tied essentially to the sacrament—but solely from the promise lent by God to the baptismal act, according to which it is to be a visible seal and pledge of NT imparting of grace. This promise Christ so fulfils, that in the outward act of baptism he is inwardly active himself through the H. Spirit and pours the grace of baptism directly on the believer.

LEIDEN SYNOPSIS (XLIV, 32): "We agree that the sacrament like everything else is also exhibitive of the thing promised, in respect that in the lawful and worthy use of this sacrament the things promised are by the H. Spirit not only offered to believers but also actually exhibited and conferred; God is true in sealing His promises and our sacraments are not affixes of a dying letter but those of a quickening spirit."—HEIDEGGER (XXV, 42): "These most outstanding benefits of the Gospel baptism does not just barely represent. Legitimately used it seals and exhibits to those baptized the things pertaining to them in terms of the promise of the covenant of grace. Not however as efficient by an inherent cause or present power, but as a seal, earnest and most sure pledge, creating faith in the things received or to be received.—Like all sacraments— neither does baptism produce grace *ex opere operato,* by a power whether inherent and physical (as *Thomas of Aquino* and the school of the *Dominicans* who follow him), or assisting (as the *Scot* and the school of *Franciscans* who agree with him assert). By making elements of the world and creatures the causes of grace this error transforms the sacraments into idols and a kind of magical chants. Would that the *Augustans* [Augsburg] (i.e., *Lutherans*) would proclaim the news bluntly, by laying it down that the sacraments are ὀχήματα (vehicles) of grace and a sort of hand by which God presents His grace." The chief objection to LUTHERAN sacramentalism is this: "The apostle, Rom. 8. 29-30 (whom he foreknew etc.) expatiating on the causes of salvation, mentions neither baptism nor any other sacrament. He asserts that the elect are glorified. And yet it is admitted that many baptized persons are neither elect nor glorified, as many unbaptized persons are both elect and glorified.—The causes and means of salvation are far deeper than earthly things and elements, namely eternal foreknowledge, predestination etc."

Explaining the efficacy of baptism HEIDEGGER incidentally recalls the thought already expressed by others, that the one baptism with which all would be baptized, since even Christ was baptized with it, includes and involves contact with Christ's baptism and Christ's actual person. "The Fathers rather aptly declared that our baptism derived its power and efficacy from contact with the Christ baptized by John"—WALAEUS 939: "These views then being rejected as manifestly erroneous, we must examine the opinion of the *Lutherans* and of certain *Papists*, who feel that, while the H. Spirit always exercises His efficacy in the baptized at the

same moment, not indeed *ex opere operato* but as the result of the administration of baptism plus the baptism, He does it in such a way that as the
H. Spirit works with the Word, so He works with outward baptism. So
they lay it down that baptism is both the ordinary means of regeneration
for children and accordingly necessary in the same way. We too admit
that the H. Spirit ordinarily effects by baptism the things sealed in baptism. Yet we deny that the action of the H. Spirit is always tied to the
act of baptism, in a way in which the virtue of the word is not always
tied to the word of preaching. And as seeds sown in the ground, do not
always grow at the time they are committed to the ground, but at
the time the rains water them from heaven and make them fertile;
so also when it seems good to God in baptism. The Spirit works where and
when it listeth, Jn. 3."

LEIDEN SYNOPSIS (XLIV, 24-25): "This union of sacramental sign and
thing signified is not a real and subjective conjunction, as some imagine,
but σχετική merely or *relativa*, consisting in the mutual respect in which
sign places and seals the thing signified for the believer before his eyes
and the thing signified is supplied and offered by the principal cause on
condition of faith and repentance. Neither is Christ's blood really and
carnally in the water of baptism, nor is Christ's Spirit, although by its
nature omnipresent, subjectively inherent in it. Nor is purification from
sins effectually accomplished by outward washing with water, since
such power is purely divine, of which no creature is capable *per se;*
but Christ himself unites us more to himself by the efficacy of his Spirit
and communicates his benefits secured for us by the power of his death,
just as usually happens with the simple word. But he does this so much
the more effectually in the lawful use of this sacrament, the more singularly
(and that by the two senses of hearing and sight) the things signified
are here set forth, and in consequence our faith is both more strongly
roused and rendered active. And so it also happens, that in this operation
outward baptism is clearly distinguished from inward, and the administrative cause from the principal, as may be seen in Mt. 3. 11 (John and
Jesus) Col. 2. 11 (a circumcision not made with hands), 1 Pet. 3. 21 (the
interrogation of a good conscience with God)."

10.—Meanwhile the receipt of grace, the imparting of which is attested
and sealed by baptism, is not tied to the outward act and to the moment
of the act of baptism. The efficacy of baptism rather presupposes the
faith and conversion of a man—both at least at heart.—LEIDEN SYNOPSIS
(XLIV, 29): "The efficacy of baptism we do not tie to the moment at
which the body is wet with outward water, but in all who are to be baptized we require with Scripture faith and repentance, at least according

to the judgment of love. And this as well in covenanted children, in whom, we maintain, must be placed, by the power of the divine blessing and the Gospel covenant, the seed and spirit of faith and repentance, as in adults in whom the profession of actual faith and repentance is necessary. Then, as seed cast upon the ground does not always germinate at the same moment, but when rain and warmth supervene from heaven, so neither word nor sign of sacrament is always effectual at its first moment, but only at the time when the blessing of the H. Spirit is added."

11.—Therefore since baptism in no way exercises a magical efficacy—which is why many baptized do not receive salvation—the washing away of sins attested by it is not a plucking out of sin itself, but an abolition of guilt and of the power of sin. *Reatus* is completely removed from the man and concupiscence ceases to be the power that enslaves him; in consequence as *concupiscentia mala* it still continues to live in man as real, proper sin, only challenged and more or less held down by the Spirit of grace.—RIISSEN (XVII, 40, 1): "The question is not, whether the efficacy of baptism extends only so far as sin is not imputed but not really removed, but whether it is so fully and perfectly removed as not to be imputed or to be mastered and also so as not to cease existing. We therefore lay it down that *reatus* (liability) is fully removed, but the stain only in a preliminary or partial way."—POLAN (VI, 55): "In baptism original sin is not radically removed as an *actus*, but it is washed away and abolished as regards *reatus*, that is, fault and punishment, the actual defect and disease remaining, namely wicked concupiscence and inclination towards evil. And this to the end that, throughout life we may fight with sin and the devil, the author of sin, meanwhile incessantly beseeching the Lord and clinging perseveringly to him.—The residual evil concupiscence after baptism in the regenerate is truly and strictly sin."

12.—To the individual man baptism can be imparted only once,—not as though it bestowed an indelible impress, but because God makes His covenant of grace only once with the individual elect, who in that case can never fall away again, and because a repetition of the act of baptism would set forth the objectionable view, that what should be sealed through the first act of baptism in virtue of divine appointment—namely the implanting of the individual in the mystical body of Christ and his adoption into the covenant of grace—was not true. If anyone has received baptism without faith, the receipt of baptism has not of course for him been unto salvation. But if the baptized person converts, there is no need to repeat baptism, because for repentance the road to grace lies open all the time.—COCCEIUS (*De foed*). XIII, 449): "The reason why baptism is not repeated is to be sought not in the impression but in the thing signified. Since baptism and the H. Supper signify the κοινωνία of Christ, baptism has the characteristic of signifying ingrafting into Christ by regeneration and its result, eternal righteousness. So if it were repeated, either it would not be teaching ingrafting into Christ for communion, or it would be teaching the imperfection and weakness of the first ingrafting, as if communion with Christ might be rescinded and begun afresh. But as Christ cannot die a second time, so if, once a man has been united to Christ, he could not be separated from him, there could be no reparation, Heb, 10. 26 (if we sin wilfully, after that we have received the knowledge of the truth, there remaineth no more sacrifice for sins)."—POLAN (VI, 55): "Each believer should be baptized only once", mainly "because God enters upon and concludes the covenant of grace with each of us once only. The first agreement once made with God cannot be undone." —WENDELIN (*Coll.* p. 365): "So far as baptism is administered according to God's institution by suitable ministers of the word—and applied to suitable persons, it is true baptism, even though by the fault and defect of the recipients it is not saving.—Whence also if this defect is removed and altered, the actual ceremony once lawfully administered and applied is not to be repeated.—Return to grace lies open through repentance without repeating baptism."

13.—Therefore also by baptism forgiveness is sealed to the person baptized not only of past sins but of all the sins of his life whatever.—CALVIN (IV, xiv, 3): "Nor must it be thought that baptism is to be conferred only for time past, so that for new lapses into which we fall from baptism other new means of expiation must be sought."—POLAN (VI, 55): "Although we are baptized once only, baptism is for us the perpetual sacrament of washing from sins and of regeneration, i.e., baptism not only clears out and washes away original sin, but all sins whatsoever, past or present. Those who are baptized are baptized into Christ's death."

14.—All are entitled to receive baptism who belong to God's covenant of grace, i.e., all who confess Christ and who therefore are to be regarded by the Church (which cannot of course search hearts) as belonging to God's covenant of grace according to the verdict of love.—WOLLEB 105: "All covenanted persons are the subject of baptism, even their children, who are reckoned in the number of the covenanted."—HEIDEGGER (XXV, 53): "The subject of baptism is God's faithful people, whether they are truly so or reckoned so because of outward profession of faith and communion with believers apart from any distinctions of race, sex and age."— RIISSEN (XVII, 41): "Grownups of the Gentiles ought to be baptized

when they give their name to Christ, and the children of Christians."—
MASTRICHT (VII, iv, 13): "Only the covenanted are to be baptized. As
many therefore as the Church by the judgment of love, if it but rest on a
just foundation, can regard as covenanted must be baptized."—LEIDEN
SYNOPSIS (XLIV, 44-45): "However not all men living in the world are
capable of baptism, but only those who may be regarded by us as being
covenanted and heirs of the NT, of which this sacrament is the seal and
pledge. Such are firstly all adults and only those who profess faith in
Christ and true repentance, of whatever race, condition or sex.'

15.—But since the promises which God has made to believers hold not
only for them but also for their seed, the Church is bound to baptize not
only confessors of the name of Christ but also their infants, the children
of Christians, exactly as the children of Israel were circumcised. On the
other hand children of such parents as do not belong to the Church
should not be baptized until they have been instructed in the faith and
aroused to faith.—KECKERMANN 453: "The children of Christians, whether
born Christians of both parents or only of one, ought to be baptized."—
LEIDEN SYNOPSIS (XLIV, 44-45): "Secondly we regard as such children
who are born of believing and covenanted parents, according to God's
promise, Gen. 17 (I will be a God unto thee and to thy seed). And this
not only from the example of circumcision, which was a seal of the
same covenant and to the place of which baptism succeeded, Col. 2. 11
(the circumcision not made with hands), but because the actual sign
cannot be denied to those to whom the thing signified belongs, as the
apostle Peter eloquently testifies, Ac. 10. 47; 11. 17 (Cornelius of Caesarea).
But now no one can deny that the benefits of Christ's blood and Spirit
belong to the children of believers, except one who wants them excluded
from salvation. For as no one may enter the kingdom of God save he
who has been born again of water and the Spirit, Jn. 3. 5, so no one is
Christ's who has not Christ's Spirit, Rom. 8. 9 (if any man have not the
Spirit of Christ he is none of his)."—But now it is also expressly insisted,
that also the children of such parents as belong outwardly to the Church
but "because of impurity of life declare that they are not truly of the
Church", should be baptized. For, says BUCAN (XLVII, 33), "the godlessness of the parents should not mean loss to their children born in the
Church."—RIISSEN (XVII, 41, 1): "The question is not of any children,
even of unbelievers, but only of those of covenanted Christians. As
regards the former we agree that they cannot and ought not to be baptized
without previous training and at an adult age, when, i.e., they can give
a reason for their faith."—WOLLEB 106: "There is another way with
unbelievers and their children, who are not even born of one believing

parent. These must not be baptized until they have reached years of discretion and have testified to their faith."—WALAEUS 950: "We make a distinction between children of unbelievers and the children of believers and those born in the lap of the Church. As for the children of unbelievers and their parents, who are plainly alien to the Church, as Jews, Turks, Gentiles, we do not admit their children to baptism; (1) Neither command nor promise nor example of such a thing is extant in the whole NT or in the whole of Scripture, but on the contrary "the promise is to you and to your children and to as many as God shall call", as Peter says, Ac. 2 [39].—(2) We are to judge only those who are within the Church, those who are outside God will judge, 1 Cor. 5. 12–13 (what have I to do with judging them that are without? Do not ye judge them that are within, whereas them that are without God judgeth? Put away the wicked from among yourselves.)—(3) The apostle, 1 Cor. 7. 14 says expressly that the children of unbelievers are unclean; only those of believers are holy.— (4) Baptism is a sacrament of the Church, not of those who are outside the Church: Eph. 5 [26], Christ cleanses the Church with the washing of water in the word; and 1 Cor. 12. 10 we are baptized by the one Spirit into the one body."

OLEVIAN infers from this that the Church is not allowed forcibly to baptize the children of Jews and heathen (p. 307): "How happens it that we do not snatch their children from Jews by force and restore them after being baptized, in order that being baptized they might become saved, except that the Gospel offers the grace of the covenant conjointly to parents along with their children unto the thousandth generation? So when parents reject the offered covenant, their children are in no wise received into the covenant. And if children snatched from Jews were baptized it would be nothing but an ugly desecration of H. Baptism; the seal of the covenant would not be stamped on one to whom the covenant did not belong, and so there would be neither obedience to a commandment nor the sealing of a promise: commandment, because God commands, in order that the elect may be seen in the assembly and in the visible communion of saints."

HEIDEGGER adds to the usual exposition of this doctrinal point a further series of explanatory distinctions (XXV, 50): "Adults and children are baptized: those adults who—publicly confess faith in him (Christ), and those children who born in the Church's lap to believing parents rejoice in the covenant of grace and likewise rightly rejoice in the seals of it. As for the adults, outward baptism does not seal inward grace for all of them, but for those alone who bear in their hearts a faith the reverse of feigned and confess it in words. Nor yet for the children of believing parents one and all, but only for the elect is baptism the sign of regeneration and universal spiritual grace. Although it is right and godly in the case of individual children of the kind to have good hopes of the judgment in love, in the case of them all it is not so." As regards *infantes* the following distinction is to be kept fixed: "There is one way with elect who die in infancy, another with those who put off life until they have the use of reason and beyond it."—"For those who die in infancy baptism is as surely the sign of regeneration and of ingrafting into Christ, as their body is surely sprinkled with water." As regards them it may be assumed that they "are so regenerated and sanctified even in their mother's womb, and therefore baptism is presently the sign of a regeneration already made and persevering right up to death." That children can neither hear nor believe the gospel, does not contradict this assumption, "because even without these the H. Spirit can apply Christ's righteousness and death to them." Of course our faith is the "hand grasping the gifted grace of Christ." But "the Spirit may also give it not grasped by the hand."—Any deficiency in faith God supplies by the sanctifying of His H. Spirit and the things of faith by His provision in a loftier way, because it is principally clear from the soul of the infant Christ, sanctified through conception by the H. Spirit, even without faith such as adults have." (Cocceius *De foed.* XIII, 459, proves this by the example of the Baptist, "who being not yet born saluted the Lord conceived with a leap"). On the other hand it is different with the children of believing parents who live to the use of their reason and still further, "Some lay down for all of these promiscuously, that by baptism comes the sign of grace and regeneration present, not without rashness, certainly without solid reason." "If by baptism the 'habit' of grace were either infused into or sealed to them, it would pretty quickly betray itself, nor would the fire of the H. Spirit remain too long lulled beneath the ashes of the flesh. Nor in such cases does God seem to desert His order, which consists in faith being begotten by hearing." But further Heidegger still recognises the essential prerogatives of the "baptized non-elect over the unbaptized" (XXV, 49): "Even in early times circumcision also conferred upon the circumcised among the non-elect a privilege above the non-circumcised. To them were entrusted the oracles of God Rom. 3. 1–2.—By a like reasoning there is a common grace and favour of God, which all baptized persons possess, even the non-elect, viz., initiation and ingrafting into the outward body of the Church, in virtue of which even though perishing they have a right to the name of υἱεῖς βασιλείας and enjoy the outward privileges of God's covenanted.—But this is the mere court-yard, shell and surface of baptism."

The two most essential grounds to which baptism of Christians' children can be referred to are thus (Polan VI, 55): "(1) All covenanted with

God are to be baptized. But the children too are included in the covenant of grace, 1 Cor. 7. 14 (the unbelieving husband is sanctified in the wife, and the unbelieving wife is sanctified in the brother: else were your children unclean; but now are they holy). The universal command to baptize all those covenanted with God includes the particular command regarding the baptism of children who are within the covenant. What belongs equally to all is not to be restricted to the adult part of the seed; —and (2) even under the old covenant children were circumcised."

16.—Since baptism is not a means and source of salvation but only a sealing of it and a means of fortifying (men) in the possession of salvation, we cannot speak of an absolute necessity for it. It is necessary for the believer only so far as he is bound to carry out the commands of the Lord, and hence must also receive the baptism which the Lord has ordained, or at least, if he cannot receive it because of an external compulsion under which he finds himself, must seriously desire it.

WENDELIN (*Coll.*, p. 352): "We agree to the necessity for baptism, given the divine injunction. Baptism cannot be despised with impunity. Hence the received view that "not deprivation but contempt of the sacrament damns." Meantime baptism is not absolutely necessary to salvation. Many are saved even without baptism, both children and grownups, those of course who are deprived of baptism without fault of their own." —WOLLEB 106: "Baptism is necessary, not absolutely but in accordance with Christ's precept. Nor can such necessity be feigned, as a result of which either children ought to be baptized by other than a minister or if they die without baptism, they must be excluded from the number of the elect."—RIISSEN (XVII, 32, 2): "Our view is that baptism is a necessary thing because of its divine institution as an outward means of salvation through which God is effective in the lawful use of it, so that he who despises it is liable to a serious accusation and incurs eternal punishment. But we do not believe that it is so necessary absolutely that a man deprived of it without fault of his own is to be excluded from the kingdom of heaven forthwith, or that salvation cannot be obtained without it."—POLAN distinguishes (VI, 55) between "absolute" and "conditional necessity", and in the latter between a "condition of the divine institution" and a "condition of those to be baptized." As regards baptism it is not the "aim of the divine institution" either to tie the thing signified to the signs, or men to the sacraments by "an absolute necessity." If "the state of those to be baptized" is to be considered, these are either "adults" or "children". "For adults baptism is necessary for salvation in two ways, either by prayer and will, if opportunity of receiving the washing of water is not vouchsafed, or actually and in fact, if opportunity is granted. Faith always has joined to it zeal to obey Christ's command."

By an appeal to 1 Cor. 1. 17 (Christ sent me not to baptize but to preach the gospel) it is frequently insisted, for example by BUCAN (XLVII, 50), that the word stands higher than the sacrament and that the "function of teaching the gospel is greater than the function of baptizing."

17.—As the covenant of grace which God has set up with us lasts for ever, the Church has to administer the sacrament of baptism right to the end of time and with it to seal adoption into the covenant of grace.—RIISSEN (XVII, 32, 1): "Our view is that baptism is a sacrament divinely instituted and administered by the apostles at Christ's command, to be perpetually used in the Church to seal remission of sins and regeneration."—LEIDEN SYNOPSIS (XLIV, 38): "This perpetual efficacy of baptism is attested for us not only by the nature and perpetuity of the new covenant sanctified by baptism, described for us Is. 54. 10 (the mountains shall depart and the hills be removed; but my kindness shall not depart from thee, neither shall my covenant of peace be removed, saith the LORD that hath mercy on thee), Heb. 8. 12 (I will be merciful to their iniquities and their sins will I remember no more—Jer. 31. 34. "they shall all know me") and *passim* elsewhere, but also by the example of circumcision, by which if you look to its substance the same covenant was confirmed, and yet at that date penitence, even on the admission of the *Papists*, was not a sacrament of the remission of sins that followed afterwards, but the single seal of circumcision sufficed for sealing to the penitent perpetual righteousness of faith and circumcision of heart.".

18.—Note: The baptism of John was essentially like the baptism founded by Christ. Of course it could not be a proclamation of already consummated work of redemption, because Christ had still to finish it, and so John's baptism could not dispense so many gifts of new life as Christian baptism. But what was the proper nature of the latter was also the nature of John's baptism, since above all it was a sealing of the forgiveness of sin ordained by God and of rebirth by dipping into water.—CALVIN (VI, xv, 7): "Further, that John's ministry was the same as was afterwards delegated to the apostles. The different hands by which it is administered do not make it a different baptism. The same doctrine shows that it is the same. John and the apostles agreed on one doctrine. Both baptized unto repentance, both unto remission of sins, both also into the name of Christ, of whom is repentance and remission of sins.— That more shining graces of the Spirit were poured forth by Christ's resurrection has nought to do with setting up a different baptism."—

COCCEIUS (*Summ. de foed.* 462): "John's baptism was the same as Christ's baptism, who administered it by disciples. The divine command, the matter, the significance, the grace is the same in both cases. The preaching is the same, Mt. 3. 2; 4. 17 (prepare ye the ways of the Lord—the kingdom of heaven is at hand). The name is the same, Jn. 1. 32–33 (John: "I have beheld the Spirit descending as a dove out of heaven and it rested upon him": both baptize). As the apostles also declare, Ac. 19. 3–4, where it sufficiently shows that John had not only baptized into the name of the Father who had sent him to baptize, but also into the name and faith of Jesus, and him as the Christ, whose of course it was to baptize them with the H. Spirit (Paul: Into what baptism were ye baptized? Into John's baptism. John baptized with the baptism of repentance, saying that they should believe on him that should come after him, that is, Jesus. Then baptized into the name·of the Lord Jesus) Ac. 19. 3-5." —HEIDEGGER (XXV, 24): "Therefore although his (John's) baptism was different from Christ's baptism; both in the manner of disclosure : it signified Christ neither absent afar nor present and dead but presently to suffer, while Christ's baptism, which—his disciples administered, signified Christ as having already suffered, died and been perfected : and in the conferring of gifts; with Christ not yet glorified John—could not seal such a present supply of gifts—as the baptism of Christ's disciples ; yet in the substance of the matter and in the sealing of regenerating grace and remission of sins—the power of each was exactly the same." The agreement between John's baptism and that of Christ's disciples lies in the following points. "The causes and effects of both baptisms agree. The efficient cause of John's as well as of Christ's baptism was God effecting; outward matter—water; inward—the promise of the grace of remission of sins and of regeneration by the Spirit; form: testification and healing of the same grace by water and the rite of ablution, likewise the linking of the promise with this element and its rite; end: both repentance and remission of sins and faith in Christ and the presence of God's Spirit as regards ordinary gifts—as regards extraordinary ones, adoption also after Christ's coming ascension; all which John's baptism sealed."

CHAPTER XXVI

THE LORD'S SUPPER

1.—As baptism is the sacrament of rebirth and of implanting into the covenant of grace, the H. Supper is the sacrament of continuing nourishment by the gifts of it.—CALVIN (IV, xvii, 1): "Once God has received us into His family, it is to keep us in the place not of servants only but of sons. That He may fill the part of an excellent Father, anxious for His offspring, He forthwith provides also for our maintenance throughout the whole course of our lives. Not content with this, having given His pledge He has willed to assure us of this continuous liberality. To this end therefore He has given His Church the second sacrament by the hand of the only-begotten Son, namely a spiritual feast, at which Christ attests that he is the living bread Jn. 6. 5, on which our souls feed unto true and blessed immortality."—The relation of the two sacraments to each other is described by the dogmaticians in the expressions *sacramenta regenerationis et nutritionis, initiationis et confirmationis, ablutionis et alimoniae, nasci et pasci,* and the like.

2.—"The Lord's Supper is the second sacrament of the NT, by which through the distribution and discernment of bread broken and of wine poured forth the communion of the body of Christ broken for (believers) on the Cross and of his blood shed for them for the remission of sins and eternal salvation is declared and sealed." (HEIDEGGER XXV, 72).

The dogmaticians' definitions are in essentials in thorough agreement. —MARESIUS (XVIII, 61): "The second NT sacrament—is the H. Supper, in which spiritual participation in the body and blood of Christ to life eternal is signified, offered and sealed to adult Christians in the use of the bread and cup commanded by Christ."—RIISSEN (XVII, 42): "The H. Supper is the sacrament of nutrition, in which by the distribution and discernment of bread broken and wine poured out is declared and sealed to adult believers the communion of the body and blood of Christ as spiritual food and drink unto life eternal."—TURRETIN (XIX, xxi, 1): "The second NT sacrament is the H. Supper in which by the distribution and discernment of bread broken and wine poured forth is declared and sealed to believers the communion of Christ's body broken on the Cross for them and of his blood shed for them unto life eternal."—CROCIUS (p. 1154): "The Lord's Supper is the NT sacrament directly instituted by Christ himself for the use of the Church till the end of the world, in which by the lawful outward administration of bread

627

and wine and their reception, eating and drinking the Lord's death is proclaimed, the taking and enjoyment of Christ's body and blood is inwardly exhibited, and that most close union or κοινωνία by which we are united with Christ our Head is sealed and confirmed, while believers profess their gratitude and indebtedness to God, fellowhip with one another and separation from all others."—LEIDEN SYNOPSIS (XLV, 6): "The Lord's Supper is the second sacrament of the New Covenant or Testament, i.e., of spiritual nourishment, instituted by Christ our Lord for believers, by which with bread broken and wine poured out Christ is signified as having suffered and died or His body broken and blood shed for the remission of sins, and by participation and communion in them He is offered to those receiving as spiritual food and drink and conferred upon believers; to be used in remembrance of Christ as well as to proclaim His death, and for union and communion with Christ as Head into a true mystical body, proceeding for believers to certification of life eternal and the glory of God's grace."

RIISSEN (XVII, 43) recounts the various relationships of the Supper: "(The Holy Supper) is marked by various names both in Scripture and among writers early and late. Scripture calls it δεῖπνον κυριακόν, the *coena dominica*, 1 Cor. 11. 20. It is called εὐλογία and εὐχαριστία by Paul, 1 Cor. 10. 16; τραπεζὰ κυρίου (1 Cor. 10. 21), κοινωνία 10. 16; κλάσις ἄρτου, fraction of bread, Ac. 2. 42; 20. 7.—By the Fathers it is also called σύναξις, because this sacrament is ordinarily administered in public assemblies of the Church; λειτουργία, because it is the part, by no means the last, of an holy public ministry. Λειτουργία in general is a public work; λειτουργεῖν is to provide work publicly. From this in accordance with Church use the common word is transferred to things divine, and has now the wider meaning of some office of godliness, as Rom. 15. 27 λειτουργεῖν τοῖς σαρκικοῖς, to minister in carnal things, i.e., to dispense help to the poor, and 2 Cor. 9. 12 (the ministration of this service not only filleth up the measure of the wants of the saints, but aboundeth also through many thanksgivings to God) kindness to the poor is meant. In the narrower sense it is taken generally as intended to fulfil a sacred office in the Church, as it is taken Heb. 10. 11 of the priests of the OT who are said λειτουργεῖν (to minister). So Christ is called λειτουργὸς τῶ ἁγίων Heb. 8. 2 (a minister of holy things). In this sense preaching the Gospel is called by Paul a λειτουργία Rom. 15. 16 (. . . a minister of Christ Jesus unto the Gentiles, ministering the Gospel of God). Hence among early writers λειτουργίαι meant certain descriptions of the order to be observed in celebrating in things holy. Specifically in later times the word is used to denote every ministry carried out in connection with the H. Supper."—In addition we find the expressions μυστήριον, θυσία, ἀγάπη. "*Agapae* were fraternal feasts at an ecclesiastical assembly, the aim of which was either general, that by them mutual affection might be nourished among Christians; or special, in order that the poor might be helped by that refreshment. Because with them was coupled the celebration of the H. Supper, the name *agape* was given to the Supper in consequence."

3.—The Supper is thus appointed only for the real partners in the covenant of grace, only for believers. This is why the promises attached to enjoyment of the Supper are also to be considered only in relation to them.—BUCAN (XLVIII, 8): "For whom was the Lord's Supper instituted? Not for all promiscuously; Mt. 7. 6 forbids that which is holy being set before profane persons and dogs and those alien to Christ. It is for those who have been regenerated by water and the Spirit, i.e., for Christ's disciples; to these alone he has promised, as he also supplies, the nourishment of his life-giving flesh and his blood. And the sacrament belongs to those to whom the promise belongs."

4.—As regards the outward administration of the Supper it can only be dispensed by an orderly occupant of the preaching office, in company with whom, chiefly for distributing the cup, there may also be other servants of the Church, elders and deacons, at his side to help him.—POLAN (VI, 56): "Ministers of the Church, and these include pastors, and presbyters or elders (*seniores*) added to the pastors for the government of the Church and deacons lawfully called, ought to preside at the administration of the Eucharist, no others. If the pastors alone can carry through the administration, as in small gatherings, then the help of others is not required, as TERTULLIAN writes (*De corona* 3): "We do not take the sacrament of the Eucharist from the hands of others than those presiding." But if the gatherings are large and the pastors are not sufficient to perform the administration of the Supper alone, they may co-opt elders and deacons to help them, especially in the distribution of the cup."—HEIDEGGER (XXV, 73): "The first to administer was the same as he who instituted it, Christ.—By Christ's authority and orders the apostles in succession and those who followed them, the pastors and rulers of the Church (*rectores*) did and do administer it. No more than baptism or the preaching of God's word can it be administered by private persons or by any private person at a banquet."

5.—The outward means for administering the Supper are real ordinary eating bread (*panis cibarius*) and wine. The fact that in founding the

Supper the Lord used unleavened bread, was only because it happened
to be at hand.   Therefore it is a matter of complete indifference, whether
the Supper is dispensed in leavened or in unleavened bread, if only in the
choice of one or the other bread any sort of superstition is kept apart,
which attributes to either a special religious value.—MASTRICHT (VII,
v, 16): "Rejecting hosts the Reformed teach the use of ordinary bread
suitable for nourishment, but not precisely unleavened or fermented
either; provided it be true bread and superstition absent either way,
they think that enough."—Similarly also the other dogmaticians declare
still more definitely, that the use of unleavened bread at the institution of
the Supper was something purely accidental, and that therefore normally
the usual, i.e., leavened eating bread is to be used. E.g. BUCAN (VII, x, 16):
"The bread which Christ used in the first Supper was unleavened. This
was accidental, because of the law of the passover which commands
abstinence from all yeast during those days. Whence the early Church
used daily eating bread, plainly in accord with Christ's meaning, who for
the more appropriate signification of the mystery did not institute a bread
other than that on which we feed at common feasts."—Similarly BRAUN
p. 836, and others.

6.—Only the use of so called hosts (*placentulae orbiculares*, circular cakelets)
is inadmissible, since the distribution and enjoyment of them does not at
all expound the meaning and nature of the Supper, viz., a real feeding.—
HEIDEGGER XXV, 79: "Christ did not use penny-shaped hosts of this
kind, nor do they deserve the name of bread but rather of glue and assuredly possess either simply no analogy or an obscure one between sign and
thing signified; and at the same time they abolish the rite and mystery of
breaking, and the significance of the unity of many, which the apostle 1
Cor. 10. 17 insists that they abolish, and the use of them did not creep
into the Church earlier than the weakening caused by the doctrine of
transsubstantiation, to the nourishment of which monstrosity they seemed
to help not a little."—RIJSSEN (XVII, 51, 3): "Are circular hosts to be
used and these to be put into men's mouths?—No, against *Papists* and
Lutherans."—Generally most of them describe the genuinely Reformed
point of view, in accordance with which these and similar questions are
to be conceived, just as does CROCIUS (p. 1163): "If the substance of bread
and wine be retained in the Supper, it is all the same whether the bread
is unleavened or fermented, round or oblong, thin or thick and likewise
the wine red or white." [But it must be wine!?].

7.—On the contrary it is where real bread and wine are not to be had,
that it is quite permissible to use in the administration of the Supper such

foods as are locally used in ordinary life instead of bread and wine.—
WITSIUS IV, xvii, 12): "But since it may happen, as it frequently does,
that in some regions there is no use of bread and wine, as in America
and other parts of the world where in place of bread they have food made
of vegetables or herbs or tree-fruits or even barks; and drink of honey or
sugar or other spices or even from cocos trees in place of wine: the not un-
warranted question arises, whether in these regions they must simply abstain
from the Lord's Supper, or whether it is lawful to use in the Supper, in place
of bread and wine, the food which sustains instead of bread and wine
and is suitable for strengthening the body and stimulating the heart[!].
Now in the use of the sacraments we think that there should be no rash
innovations. But necessity is above law. And it seems altogether harsh
to order such wide tracts of earth with their inhabitants and incomers to
do without the Lord's Supper and their Christianity to be mutilated for
want of sacramental mastication. Chiefly because what is important in the
analogy is retained by the using of food and drink, with which the body
may be fittingly nourished and the mind made joyful[!]. —Similarly
BRAUN (p. 593): "Should there be a gathering destitute of bread and
wine, as perchance among the Indians, who for bread use the baked
marrow of a certain tree, or a fixed root, or rice, or such other things,
the gathering may—if, I say, there is no bread of corn—safely use what it
is accustomed to use in place of bread. It is not so much the outward
form and kind of corn that ought to be regarded, as the nourishment and
what chiefly nourishes.—The same must be said if wine is lacking.
Something else might be applied, in place of wine, as scarcely any nation
is discoverable, which has not some beverage which it uses to restore the
spirits [!] in place of wine."—Similarly, too, BUCAN (XL, 21) and others.

8—And they are in accord with the Lord's behest who commanded the
use of both elements by the whole Church, and so by all the members of it,
and according to the precedent of the apostolic Church in solemnising
the Supper (commanded) the dispensation of both elements and the enjoyment of them by each communicant.—WENDELIN (*Coll.* p. 425):
"By what arguments can the need for both symbols or kinds be proved?"
Lutheran answer: "By three in particular. The first is, because Christ
instituted both parts and did so not just for one part of the Church but
for the whole Church. But if for the whole Church, why is one kind
taken from a part of the Church, and Christ's ordinance thus changed?
(2) Because Christ clearly bade all drink of the cup Mt. 26. 27 (drink
ye all of it). (3) Because according to the apostle Paul 1 Cor. 11. 24-25
it is obvious that the whole Church used the two kinds." Reformed view:
"We agree."

9.—It belongs to the outward use of the bread (or wine) that it is blessed, broken, distributed and enjoyed.—BRAUN 594: "Four principal rites are to be observed in this sacrament: (1) The breaking of the bread, (2) the blessing, (3) the distribution, (4) the mastication. For Christ took bread, (1) blessed (2) broke (3) gave it to the apostles, and (4) said, Eat Mt. 26. 26 (Take, eat, this is my body) Lk. 22. 19 (This is my body—this do in remembrance).—HEIDEGGER (XXV, 80): "The rites anent the bread are the taking of it in the hands, the blessing or sanctification of it, the breaking, the distribution, the acceptance and the chewing of it."

10.—The blessing of the bread and wine, by which they become sacraments of Christ's body and blood, is not a power to be imparted magically by the administrant to the elements in solemnising the Supper, but it is the putting of them under the perpetually enduring blessing of the thanksgiving prayer, which Christ uttered when instituting the Supper, so that the bread and wine are withdrawn from their natural signification and in virtue of Christ's appointment become sacraments of his body and blood.

Regarding the consecration of the Supper Reformed dogmaticians teach as follows. When Christ wished to solemnise the Supper, he uttered the thanksgiving prayer, in which he thanked the Father for all he had received from Him for carrying out the work of redemption in his humiliation, and by which he set apart from profane use the elements to be used for the celebration of the Supper.—BUCAN (XLVIII, 25): "By prayer to God he prepared, appointed and sanctified the bread and wine for sacred use."—PICTET (XIV, iv, 9): "By this blessing the symbols are consecrated; for in this blessing were contained thanksgiving to God for benefits received and a petition that the symbols might be rendered effective for the spiritual use and benefit of the recipients. And so the ancients were wont to consecrate with prayer, as is clear from their liturgies and writings, and all these things were done not in a quiet whisper but in a loud voice, so that the people might groan (*ingeminare*) Amen."—That in this thanksgiving, by which he consecrated the elements of his Supper, Christ availed himself of the customary liturgical formula is probable. At the same time we do not know what prayer formula it was.—LEIDEN SYNOPSIS (XLV, 27): "What formula of blessing and thanksgiving Christ here used is not explained. But Christ here adopted the solemn rite of the old synagogue in the eating of the passover. And the ancient liturgies prove that the early Church had its own prayers in consecration."—Similarly WITSIUS (X, xvii, 15).—This consecration carried out by Christ is the consecration of the Supper celebration generally, so that in virtue of the εὐχαριστία or εὐλογία spoken by Christ at the institution of the Supper, which was naturally heard by the Father, at every Supper celebration bread and wine are from now to the end of time the sacrament of the body and blood of Christ.— POLAN (VI, 56): "Nor is the bread the sacrament of Christ's body by magic consecration in a subdued whispering of the five words "*hoc est enim corpus meum*", made by the priest with a breath or panting towards the bread.—Nor by the recitation of Christ's words over the bread. But by Christ's first consecration made at the institution of the Supper, at which it became a sacrament when the word was added to the element." —HEIDEGGER appositely demonstrates that consecration cannot possibly be assumed in the recitation of the words *hoc est corpus meum* (XXV, 80–81): "As Christ at other times by blessing and thanksgiving sanctified loaves and other foods to a natural use, Mt. 14. 19 (loaves and fishes) Lk. 9. 16 (ditto)—so Christ by this blessing and thanksgiving set bread apart from a natural to a sacred use, that there might exist a sacrament of his body.— This original blessing and sanctification of the bread (and the like blessing also of the cup) conferred by Christ, the Lord and Author of the Eucharist, is so important, that by it the eucharist observed everywhere according to its institution is effective to the end of the world. What an immense gap between this and the Mass priests' consecration of Christ's words *hoc enim est corpus meum,* by a recitation made over the bread by which both because of the hidden power of these words and because of the peculiar virtue in the priestly order they declare that the bread is really and substantially transmuted into the body of Christ! That Christ had blessed and consecrated by these words is utterly absurd, since before he had uttered these words he has already blessed, given thanks and by blessing and giving thanks has consecrated the elements. He was undoubtedly heard when blessing bread and cup, and so made the bread blessed by the blessing and the cup likewise previously to his pronouncing the words *hoc est corpus meum.* And as he pronounced the words the bread was already body and did not just become it, because he did not say *hoc fiat* but *hoc est corpus meum,* and our opponents themselves understand by the pronoun *hoc* Christ's body. And since blessing and consecration are a kind of prayer, there is assuredly no sort of praying in the words *hoc enim est corpus meum.* Besides, to count certain words and ends of syllables and to assign effect to them when muttered in a secret whisper, is little removed from the mysteries of magicians and the profane potency of words. To this it is also relevant, that by the same low whisper they usually address neither God nor man but the sacred signs, and these they assert, are changed by such imperious words from a crust into the body of Christ."

From this it is clear that alongside the recitation of the words of instition,

by which the identity of every Supper action with the foundation
of Christ is set forth and every Supper celebration is set under the blessing
of Christ's εὐλογία, no other sort of consecration has any place. The
actual celebration of the Supper founded by Christ is the consecration
of the elements used for the purpose.—TRELCATIUS, p. 230: "By prayer
to God, thanksgiving and the whole sacred action Christ prepared,
appointed and sanctified the bread and wine for sacred use, that they
might be the sacrament of his own body and blood, not by their own
nature but by divine institution."—RIJSSEN (XVII, 51, 1): "We deny
that consecration must be attached to the pronouncement of the sacramental words. It must be placed in Christ's entire action and especially
in the blessing, by which the elements are transferred from a common
and natural use and applied to a holy use, since Christ is said by the
evangelist to have blessed and given thanks after the bread was accepted."
—BUCAN (XLVIII, 25): "It is consecration, or sanctification and blessing,
by which not merely by historical reading of the text (the Epistle to the
Corinthians or the Gospel) but by prayers, thanksgiving, clear and
faithful repetition of the words of Christ's institution and promise which
is always effectual and lively, significant exposition of them, and by the
whole λειτουργία or sacred action which Christ commanded us
to make as he actually made it, in which God is effectual, things which
were vulgar and common aids to nourishing the body become sacraments
of Christ's body and blood appointed and set forth for us as quickening
food and drink, and thus are transferred from common and physical
food into holy and spiritual food, in fact destined for the use and office
of being Christ's body and blood, not by their nature but by divine
institution, which ought to be recited and explained."

11.—The breaking of the bread is not to be regarded as an indifferent
use, but is necessarily to be used in solemnising the Supper as a symbol
ordained by Christ of his broken body and of the communion which the
many believers have in the one Christ. At the same time Church fellowship is not to be refused to those Churches which reject the rite of breaking
the bread.—BUCAN (XLVIII, 27): "Is the breaking of bread a midway
i.e., indifferent ceremony? It is not, but an essential and sacramental
one altogether belonging to faith or to the aim and so to the form of the
sacred Supper; just as also the pouring of the wine into a cup: things by
which believers behold with the eyes of the mind Christ not only hanging
for us, but as it were torn, bruised, broken on the Cross by unspeakable
tortures of mind and body and dispersed into most violent separation
of soul from body and torn so to speak into two parts according to the
human nature and as if still dropping clots of blood for the sake of our

salvation."—RIISSEN (XVII, 51, 4): "The orthodox retain fraction which was used by the Lord and which breaks up as many loaves as suffice to communicate the people into various morsels to be distributed to many. They are of opinion that the ceremony is not indifferent, but in accordance with Christ's institution no less necessary than receiving into the hand, passing it on and communicating. Nor would they contend so rigidly over it, as that no fellowship could be retained with those who omit it. But they think such defect to be not of a small matter and not to be conceal- ed or tolerated if it could be abolished, and that therefore those who thus lay it down are to be found fault with, though not absolutely con- demned."—WOLLEB 108: "The breaking of the bread is not a matter of indifference. Christ himself used it, ordered its use, saying: This do; he himself explained it, adding: This is my body, which is broken for you. From it the Holy Supper takes its name. By it in short the unity of the Church is designed 1 Cor. 10. 17 (seeing that we who are many, are one bread, one body; for we all partake of the one bread)."

12.—The third part of the outward action is the distribution of the broken bread and of the cup, at which Christ's words of institution, or the words of the Apostle 1 Cor. 10. 16 (the cup of blessing which we bless, is it not a communion of the blood of Christ. The bread which we break, is it not a communion of the body of Christ ?) are to be spoken.—" Distribution" is followed by discernment, since the communicants take in their hands and enjoy the bread and the cup.—BUCAN (XLVIII, 30): "(Christ) bids his apostles or ministers when λειτουργοῦντες to take the bread and wine, to give thanks to God the Father, to break the bread and to distribute it.— 33 : λαβεῖν or λαμβάνειν is understood strictly of the hand.— It is therefore superstitious to prevent communicants receiving the eucharistic bread or cup with the hand."

13.—Since the Supper is a feast of the fellowship of the covenant of grace, it must also be celebrated in fellowship in the house of the Lord. Hence the offering of the Supper to individuals, who wish to receive it by them- selves in God's house separated from the congregation, as well as to sick persons in private houses. must rank as illegal.—BUCAN (XLVIII, 125): "In what place is (the H. Supper) to be administered ?—In public assem- bly, not to individuals privately or to those ill in bed at home or about to die outwith the congregation of the faithful and their participation. Communication should be ecclesiastical and public, not an ἴδιον δεῖπνον. And the Supper is a symbol of the communion of saints and access should not be opened to the opinion of *opus operatum* and preposterous *fiducia* as it is in the *Papist* communion." —BEZA (III, 364): "The Lord's Supper is not the private act of a family but purely ecclesiastical."—POLAN (VI, 56): "They do ill who make of the public and common feast of the whole believing gathering a private supper of their own, in which only certain people, and those the richer and more powerful in this world, eat of the Lord's bread and drink of his cup, others not being expected or not admitted.—These do much worse, who administer the H. supper publicly or in private houses to one person only, whether averse from unaccustomedness to communion with others and demanding a single supper for himself alone, or sick at his home and, when properly well, wantonly neglectful of the use of the Lord's Supper in public assembly or caring little for it."

14.—And since further the Supper is not a sacrificial action but a community festival, resting upon the sacrifice of Christ himself, it is not to be celebrated on an altar but at a table, the Lord's Table.—BURMANN (VII, x, 45): "The first supper was carried out at a common table Mt. 26. 20 (sitting at meat with the twelve) 1 Cor. 11. 20 (assemble yourselves together . . . to eat the Lord's supper).—It was very bad of the *Papists* to revive again altars in the strict sense in the Church. To wish to restore them after the offering of Christ's sacrifice is the corruption and poison of Christianity Heb. 13. 10 (we have an altar whereof they have no right to eat which serve the tabernacle [and the contrast with a real altar is brought out]). Nor is it free from all leaven, that the *Lutherans* are so in love with forms of altars and celebrate their Supper at them, while yet they hate the sacrifice of the *Papists*. What is an altar without a victim ?".

15.—The invisible saving benefit, the "inward matter" of the Supper is the personal divine-human Christ, with the gracious benefits which he has acquired for himself through his obedience and his merit. Thus Christ is the saving benefit of the sacrament, not merely according to his divinity but also according to his humanity, meaning the humanity in its humiliation unto death. This is why we have "really" present in the Supper not merely Christ's merit, power and efficacy but the substance of his body and blood, i.e. the Son of God made man, and not as Christ's body and blood generally but as Christ's broken body and shed blood, by which the whole Christ is described by synecdoche.

MASTRICHT (VII, x, 45): "The elements, bread and wine, represent Christ's body and blood, i.e. the whole Christ, in body as well as in soul, in his divine as in his human attributes, in short as regards all his riches and benefits, so far as he is not only spiritual food and drink but also the sacrifice for our sins."—WOLLEB 108: "The inward matter (of the Lord's Supper) is Christ with the whole of his satisfaction and merit."—BUCAN

(XLVIII, 81): "(The thing signified in the Lord's Supper) is Christ himself with all his benefits, offering himself to be grasped spiritually through faith with our minds. In the Lord's Supper we are rendered participant not only in the ἐνέργεια or the benefits and gifts of Christ, but in the οὐσία of Christ's quickening body."—RIISSEN (XVII, 49): "The inward matter is Christ with his entire satisfaction and merit."—MARESIUS (XVIII, 65): "Christ's blood is offered there, not as it is in his veins but as poured out for us and separate from his body.—BRAUN p. 597: "The thing signified is the body and blood of Jesus Christ broken and shed for the remission of sins."—BUCAN (XLVIII, 82): "By synecdoche Christ's whole humanity both ὅλως and κατὰ μέρη, the true and natural body of Christ given, crucified and buried for us, and his true blood shed for us and his true soul, in fact Christ's entire person (is given us). Not just his humanity without the verity of the λόγος, who is life itself and the fountain of life, can be to us the bread of life, nor can the humanity be separated from the Word."—LEIDEN SYNOPSIS (XLV, 55): "Christ then is considered not simply and absolutely as a man and the θεάνρθωπος at that, but—as man lowly, crucified and dead.—58: In a word Christ himself is perceived in this way and in humiliation at that and dead, so that along with himself are included the merits of his death and his benefits and gifts, strength, efficacy, remission of sins of course, righteousness and eternal life. These things must be joined inseparably, Christ, his death and the benefits so acquired and their efficacy. Hence those who by body and blood explain the merit and efficacy only, do not transmit the truth with sufficient fulness."

Against objection that the latter is the real meaning of the Reformed Church doctrine all dogmaticians protest. E.g. POLAN (VI, 56): "Christ's body is in heaven corporeally but is present to us who exist on earth not corporeally but spiritually; i.e. by the mediation of his Spirit in him and dwelling in us he is united as the Head to us his members.—Christ's body is absent from us locally. But he is most present to us by our union with him, through Christ's Spirit dwelling in him and in us. So there is present in the Supper not only bread and wine and not only Christ's deity and not only Christ's power and efficacy but also his actual body and actual blood are there in the H. Supper."—Conf. Gall. 36: "Although Christ is now also to remain there in heaven until he comes to judge the world, yet we believe that by the secret and incomprehensible power of his Spirit he flourishes and quickens us by the substance of his body and blood apprehended by faith."—TRELCATIUS p. 240 : "We do not exclude the entire actual Christ from the Supper, since when we say body and blood we understand by synecdoche Christ's entire humanity, indeed his entire *persona*. Neither the humanity without the divinity nor the divinity without the humanity could mediate without the common substratum. The reason for the synedoche is that, although Christ, God and man, who suffered for us, is one and the same, he did not suffer in his actual divinity but in the flesh."—ALSTED 737: "The entire Christ is the thing signified, inasmuch as he was crucified for us."

16.—To this invisible saving benefit the visible elements are related as representative signs and guaranteeing seals of his presence, his being offered and his being received. Here where they are used in a sacramental action, the words "This is my body" have the sense of "This is sacramentally my body". Since then the real *forma sacramenti* is the *unio sacramentalis* of the *signum* and the *res signata* [see c. xxiv, 10] these words must be regarded as meaning: "the true, real bread is the sacrament of the true, real body of Christ, i.e. the copy and pledge of his real presence." This is why bread and wine, in the *phraseologia sacramentalis*, are called by metonymy Christ's body and blood.—POLAN (VI, 55): "Now the bread is Christ's body by a sacramental metonymy which does not inhere in the subject. By it is understood the true and natural bread. Nor does it inhere in the predicate. By the former is understood Christ's true and natural body, retaining its former, natural form, appearance, circumscription and essence, although by the resurrection it became immortal and was set down at God's right hand and is adored by everything created." Hence it follows that "it is genuinely and not falsely genuine, it is Christ's genuine body; not the mystical one which is the Church, but Christ's proper, real, natural and substantial body—but not properly, really, naturally and substantially, because the adjectives in question determine the predicate, but the adverbs the copula; and the true [genuine] is not opposed to the figurative but to the false, and they are not opposed truly and figuratively, but they are truly and falsely contrary." The metonymy resides rather in the copula "is", "whereby the predicate is attributed to the subject. *Esse* in this statement has not the same force as existing substantially, as when it is said that Christ is God; not the same force as becoming substantial. It merely has the same force as signify, or represent sacramentally." Hence it follows that " the bread is sacramentally Christ's body; or it is the sacrament of Christ's body given to death for us."—ALSTED 822: "Sacramentally, i.e. relatively, he is in the signs by reason of the promise or of the union in the pact, as the promise to marry is in the ring." At the same time it is insisted that (ZANCHIUS p.133): "the true and substantial body of Christ is predicated of the bread, but loosely and figuratively."—HEIDEGGER (XXV, 103): "It is clear that strictly neither is the bread the body of Christ given for us nor the cup Christ's blood shed for many. Nor are the bread and the cup the communion of Christ's body broken and his blood shed. Since all these things are disparate, they cannot strictly be predicated of each other. Nor likewise is the bread the cause of the κοινωνία of Christ's body ; the Spirit is life, and not even Christ's flesh chewed in the mouth, still less the bread, avails unto life Jn. 6. 23 (the place where they ate the bread after the Lord had given thanks). Otherwise the words of the Supper would have to be explained similarly ; *hoc est corpus*: this is the cause of the body, which assuredly will be absurd. Since then the bread and the cup are not the cause of the communion of Christ's body and blood, it follows that they are the sign, pledge, earnest or (as Paul calls it 1 Cor. 11. 25) the commemoration of Christ and also of the communion of Christ's body and blood."

Similarly RIISSEN (XVII, 51, 7) shows that the words of institution must be conceived metaphorically. "The proofs: From the actual words of the promise, where there occurs (1) the subject expressed by the demonstrative pronoun *hoc*, which is necessarily to be referred to the bread, because it is the demonstrative pronoun pointing to the thing present. Now so far nothing was there save the substance bread, which he had received, broken and was offering to the disciples etc. (2) The predicate of the statement is Christ's body, not living but dead or shortly to die, given, i.e. exposed to death, or certainly very soon to be exposed on our behalf; and his blood, not that which is still in his veins, but as shed and scattered beyond his body. (3) The copula *est*, which cannot strictly unite subject to predicate, because a disparate cannot strictly be predicated of a disparate. But it is agreed that the bread, indicated by *hoc*, and Christ's body are disparates. The substance of bread neither is nor can be called the substance of Christ's body, nor can the substance of the cup be called the substance of Christ's blood; they truly differ from each other in number, definition, essence and adjuncts. This is also confirmed from the fact that by body is meant here not the living but the dead and crucified one. It is already impossible and contradictory that bread or any other substance should be strictly and without figure the dead body of Christ, at the very time when Christ is not dead. Further if the bread is strictly called the body of Christ, it would follow that all Christ's attributes would strictly belong to the bread, like being born, dying, rising again etc. and all the attributes of the bread to the body, as being sown, reaped, ground, cooked etc. It would also follow, that when Christ was taking the bread from the table and breaking it, he had taken his body and broken it and shed his blood before he had been crucified and that we are now breaking Christ's body and shedding his blood today, after Christ has risen and is in the state of glory, where he cannot die any more. So it follows that the propositions *hoc est corpus meum, hic est sanguis meus* are tropical and figurative, a mode of speaking which is very usual in every language, whereby the thing signified is predicated of the sign and the former's name is given to the latter: e.g., the seven kine are called seven years, Gen. 41. 26, the bones are called the house of Israel, Ezek. 37. 11, the four beasts are four kings and the ten horns are ten kings, Dan. 7. 17-23-24; 8 20-21.—So Mt. 13. 38-39 the field is the world, the good seed is the sons of the kingdom, the enemy is the devil, the harvest is the end of the world, the reapers are the angels etc. And, Rev. 1. 20 the seven stars are seven angels, the seven candlesticks are the seven churches, and 17. 9 the seven heads are seven mountains, the ten horns are ten kings 17. 12, the woman whom thou sawest is the great city 17. 18 etc."

That the trope lies in the word '*est*' but not in '*corpus*' is therefore (at least later) generally recognised, e.g. by BEZA (III, 357): "Let the trope be placed neither in the subject nor in the attribute but in the copula or genus of attribution."—Similarly TRELCATIUS p. 234: "The copula, by which attribute is tied to subject, is the substantive word *est*, which neither ought to nor can be taken ὑπαρκτικῶς and substantially, since for no reason at all may a disparate be strictly and essentially predicated of a disparate; but in a figure, in view of the mystical and sacramental *esse*, by which the thing that signifies receives the name of the thing it signifies. By that expression Christ did not teach what bread and wine are in nature and substance but what they are in signification, office and use."—As to how PISCATOR bases the symbolical exposition of the words of institution, cf. HEPPE *Dogm. d.d. Protest.* III 220f.—The varying views of the older Reformed dogmaticians regarding the *sedes tropi* (the seat of the metaphor) in the words of institution are recounted in the LEIDEN SYNOPSIS (XLV, 58-61).

In this connection it is as a rule insisted that the *est* has not a mere significative meaning, e.g. by WENDELIN (*Coll.* p. 375): "We deny that the word *est* is expounded by the Reformed as bare signification. With signification we unite sealing and exhibition. The eucharistic bread is such a sign as not only signifies but both seals and exhibits the fact that Christ's body is to be grasped by faith."—POLAN makes the real point when (VI, 56) to the question, "why Christ did not say, This is the sign of my body,"—he replies: "The reason is that this phrase is not sacramental and mystical but literal *(propria)*, that in the common and literal sense there inheres and is contained no promise of the thing signified nor the power or energy of the mystery, but a simple bare adumbration merely of the thing signified. But because our Lord wished these mysteries to be instituted and handed down not only to signify things spiritual and divine but also to communicate them, he said, This is my body, in order that by this mystical form of expression, as by the promise of grace, he might the more significantly express the power and efficacy of the sacrament resulting from the actual use and aim of his institution in the secret and spiritual dispensation of the things along with the signs."—The inner contradictions of the *Roman* and *Lutheran* exposition of the words of institution are very clearly expounded, especially by KECKERMANN, pp.457-463.

17.—This does not mean that Christ's body and blood in the Supper are only subjectively present in the idea of the communicants, and that the bread and wine are in truth but empty signs. Although Christ is not in the substance of the bread and wine, he is in the action of the Supper, present not merely according to his divinity, but also according to his humanity in his body and blood, not of course *corporaliter* or *localiter* but *sacramentaliter*, i.e. Christ is present in the solemnisation of the Supper, in such wise that (*symbolice*) the believer sees in the elements Christ's body and blood in a picture, and that (*spiritualiter*) by the enjoyment of it he participates not only in the body and blood of Christ, i.e., in the divine-human person and the merit of Christ, but also in the fruits thereof.

HEIDEGGER (XXV, 111): "To start with there is not in the eucharist of Christ's body and blood as they say any presence and communion that is imaginary and of intention, because it is not corporeal. Nor does this mystical feast promise bark without core, i.e., bare and empty signs without Christ. Not even the OT sacraments, in which Christ's bodily presence cannot even be thought of, were void of Christ, 1 Cor. 10. 3-5 (the cloud, the sea, the spiritual rock that followed them). And how much less are our sacraments void of Christ!"—WOLLEB 97: "We do not deny the presence of Christ and his body and blood in the sacramental action. Apart from the fact that his divine person is present also by his H. Spirit, it is also present in his body and blood, not locally but sacramentally.— Besides the local presence another threefold presence is given: (1) symbolic, when a thing is represented to the human mind by some symbol, as a thing by a word or sound, a man by an image; (2) spiritual presence, when we represent to ourselves by faith a spiritual thing not present to us, as Abraham made Christ's day present to himself and saw it Jn. 8. 56; (3) a presence of power, when what is remote spatially is present in efficacy, as the sun. These three modes of being present concur in the sacraments. The body and blood of Christ are present to us (1) symbolically, so far as represented by the outward symbol ; (2) spiritually so far as we apply to ourselves by faith Christ's body and blood together with his merit; (3) in power, so far as we perceive his fruit in our hearts by faith. The first stage of sacramental presence belongs even to unbelievers, the second and third only to believers. Thus although Christ's body in local presence is as remote from the sign as heaven from earth, yet the sacramental presence remains. The presence is opposed not to distance but to absence." —POLAN (VI, 56): "The mode of the presence of Christ's body and blood in the H. Supper is sacramental and spiritual. Sacramental, because, as the nature of sacraments bears out, Christ exhibits along with the signs the things signified. Spiritual, because Christ's body and blood are to be considered intellectually, as mystical things are set forth and presented to mind, not body, to faith, not the senses, to be grasped moreover by the mind and by faith alone."

CROCIUS 1164 : " Christ's body and blood are things present in the Supper neither locally nor in any physical way, but truly and really, without any fiction, united with the bread and wine by a sacramental union, on a mystical analogy and relation which is not fictitious but the true and real conjunction of the pact."—BUCAN (XLVIII, 76) : " If Christ's body is said not to be in the bread of the Supper, whether Christ himself is said to be completely absent from the Supper ?—No ; but in such wise that he is present *totus* (whole), not as a *totum* (whole thing)".— WOLLEB p. 109: "It is one thing to say that Christ is present in the bread, another to assert the presence in the H. Supper. Christ is present in his deity and in his Spirit. He is also present in his body and blood by a sacramental presence. This is (1) that of the sign, not because he is present in the bread, but because he is represented by the to bread as a sign; (2) that of faith, by which we apply Christ ourselves together with his merit; (3) that of power and fruits."— WENDELIN (*Coll.* p. 570) : "There is no local and corporeal presence of Christ's body and blood in the bread and wine. Meantime we admit the sacramental union of the bread and wine with Christ's body and blood, and we say that the bread is truly Christ's body and the wine truly Christ's blood, although not strictly so. There is moreover a sacramental union and presence of signs and things signified, i.e. of bread and Christ's body, or wine and Christ's blood, whereby through the bread Christ's body and through the wine Christ's blood are signified and offered to the apprehension of faith. This may happen without the local and corporeal presence of signs and of things signified, apart from bodily existence in, with and under the signs, without hindrance from spatial separation. And this presence, union and apprehension, although not local and corporeal, is most true and real."—HEIDEGGER distinguishes (XXV, 112-113) (1) a relative, i.e. symbolic or sacramental and (2) a spiritual presence and fellowship of Christ's body and blood in the Supper. The former is "the way in which according to the Lord's institution bread and wine and the simultaneous breaking and eating of the former and the pouring and drinking of the latter are ordained and consecrated to seal the word of the promise and to signify and exhibit the benefits promised (the Lord's body given up for us and his blood shed for us)." Here it must not be inferred from the circumstances, that the relation of the bread and wine to the promised benefits is a relative and symbolic one, that the "presence of Christ's body and blood" in the Supper is an imaginary one. Rather "the bread and wine taken according to the Lord's institution exhibit and seal the Lord's body and blood, and the word of promise to us; relatively, it is true; but, in accordance with the character of the related things instituted by the Lord himself in the first instance, so powerfully, that this sacrament far more surely puts into our hands the benefits promised, the Lord's body and blood, than a will · exhibits and seals bequests or letters and stamps seal the annual revenues to the heirs and possessors."—But in order that this objectively symbolic offering of Christ's body and blood may not be purposeless, there is further added to it a "spiritual mode of the presence of the two", "by which the H. Spirit offers, donates and applies to believers the soil and fruits, i.e. the Lord's body betrayed and his blood poured forth for us, all the benefits in detail, which by his death he acquired for us, through the outward signs and the word of promise."

The proper and true sense of Christ's words, *hoc est corpus meum* is therefore this (BUCAN XLVIII. 74): "This, i.e. the bread, is that actual body of mine ; not substantially or essentially or naturally and in itself, but mystically and by sacramental promise; not by a single bare significance, but by a real though spiritual exhibition; that is, true and not imaginary; nothing happens so truly as that which the H. Spirit does on the condition of faith; or, as St. Paul explains, 1 Cor. 10, 16, the bread is the κοινωνία of Christ's body, i.e. the seal and effective tally or instrument or means of the communion of the body of Christ."

18.—The bread and the wine, which sacramentally are Christ's body and blood, impart Christ to us in the Supper to eat and to drink. Therefore since in the enjoyment of the bread and wine we eat and drink Christ's body and blood, this eating and drinking is not faith in Christ in and for itself, but the fruit of faith. Since in the Supper Christ lets us receive his body and blood sacramentally, we thereby receive the broken body and the shed blood, i.e. Christ with his reconciling death and merit, as our possession. And since Christ lets us eat and drink both, we thereby receive Christ the redeemer and quickener as our nourishment, so that he becomes our own living substance.—CALVIN (IV, xvii, 3): "What he bids us receive he signifies to be ours; what he bids us eat he signifies as becoming one substance with us."—BUCAN (XLVIII, 39) : "(To chew the body and drink the blood of Christ) is not only to believe in the divine promise,—that Christ's flesh was crucified for us etc.—but by the communion of Christ's body to be restored spiritually as by nourishment and to receive spiritual life and vigour—and to embrace Christ by faith, who does not appear afar but so unites himself to us and pervades us, that he himself is our Head and we are his limbs."—WENDELIN (*Coll.* p. 373): "We deny that for the Reformed eating Christ's body has no other significance than to believe in Christ."—CALVIN (IV, xvii, 5): "There are those who define chewing Christ's flesh and drinking his blood, in one word, as nothing else than believing in Christ himself. Christ seems to me to have wished to teach something more definite and sublime in that outstanding address, Jn. 6. 51, namely that by true participation in himself we should be quickened. This he described by the words chewing and drinking, to prevent anyone thinking that the life we receive from him is apprehended by simple cognition.—In short, our souls do not feed on the flesh and blood of Christ, otherwise than as bread and wine preserve and sustain bodily life."—BUCAN (XLVIII, 39): "Eating Christ's flesh and drinking his blood is not only faith but a consequent and effect of faith, the intimate union of us with Christ."

Besides, we should here observe that we can only enjoy Christ as the bread of our life, so far as he is our atoning sacrifice. So that Christ's self-impartation for our enjoyment has its source in his offering of himself up. Hence OLEVIAN's remark (p. 345) that we must receive Christ as our food, as the word promises: "Now he promises it as food on our behalf by giving himself up for us and so removing sin, the cause of *inedia* (starvation) and death. And by uniting himself entirely to us by faith and the H. Spirit, as Head to his limbs, in order that his life may be shared by us."

19.—In fact, in this enjoyment there takes place not only a union of our spirit with the Spirit of Christ, but the union of our whole spirit-body person with Christ's divine-human person, so that first of all, and that in body and soul, we become participant in the flesh or humanity of the Lord, and thereby also in his divinity.—BUCAN (XLVIII, 110-111): "Is our soul merely without the body, united to Christ's soul only, or our flesh also with Christ's flesh? Indeed the whole person of each believer, in soul and body, is truly joined to the whole person of Christ.— To what first is our mind and in consequence our flesh attached, the word or the flesh? We are united first to the flesh by faith, then through the flesh to Deity itself; (1) Because as Scripture sets Christ forth first as man, then as God, so we know, grasp and perceive him earlier and sooner as a man than as God.—(2) Because, as we are not united to God save through the Mediator, so neither to the Deity of Christ save through his flesh, in which he achieved the principal offices of a mediator. In his flesh redemption was made, sin destroyed, the devil mastered, death conquered, eternal life and salvation obtained, and the life which flowed entirely from the fulness of Christ's deity as from a spring is connected up to us only in and through Christ's flesh as channel or instrument but inseparably, through the unity of the person derived from the Deity Rom. 5. 10 (reconciled . . . through His son . . . saved by his life) 11. 17 (grafted in among them, didst become partaker of the root of the fatness of the olive tree) Jn. 6. 58 (. . . he that eateth this bread (from heaven) shall live for ever). So unless a man grasps this channel and is united to it, he assuredly cannot become a partaker of the waters which flow from the spring. Hence in the exercise of faith and godliness we must immediately and first of all fix the eyes of our mind on Jesus Christ's human flesh as on a veil, through which entry was being made into the holy of holies; next to make our way to contemplation of his Deity or to the actual holy place."—BEZA (III, 337): "In it I follow Christ the Master, who eloquently insists upon the names of his flesh and blood in this mystery of our union with Him. Because of course we cannot be connected with Him, save by the intervention of His actual human nature and so far as He is our brother."

20.—This union, then, with Christ or the taking up of the divine-human person of Christ into our own life as its food and substance is as regards the objects of the union an *unio essentialis*, as regards its truth an *unio realis*, and as regards the manner and mode in which it results an *unio spiritualis*—but not an *unio localis, naturalis, corporalis*.—BUCAN (XLVIII, 103): "How does this union take place? By the real, actual and corporeal, invisible descent of Christ's flesh into us and by a natural contact with ours, whether by συναφή, contiguity, absence of local distance, by oral perception, by an essential mingling of Christ's flesh with ours, or by the bodily entry and union of His body with our body and soul?— Not at all. The trueness of Christ's flesh and its ascension into heaven does not admit of this. Besides, from the substance of such a variety of bodies there would be born a most monstrous body. It is by a connection or συναφή plainly spiritual and supernatural, yet real and true: clearly in a divine and heavenly fashion. If we regard the things united, it is an essential union, if the trueness of the union, it is a real one; but if the manner in which the union takes place, it is a spiritual one."

21.—Consequently to enjoy Christ (*communicare Christo, manducare corpus, libare sanguinem Christi*) means not simply to confess and love Christ and lay hold of his merit, but by the H. Spirit who dwells in him and in us to be so incorporated in him as members, that really and essentially he dwells in us and we are in him, and so we not only become participant in his righteousness but also "are united more and more with his blessed body, so that, although he is in heaven and we on earth, we are nevertheless flesh of his flesh and bone of his bone and eternally live and are ruled by one flesh, as the members of our body by one soul" (*Catech. Palat.* 76).— POLAN (VI, 56): "To eat Christ's body and to drink his blood is to have communion with Christ's true flesh and blood and to have part in his reconciliation, justification, regeneration; and, to put it still more clearly, it is by the H. Spirit who dwells in Christ and believers to be inserted and incorporated into Christ as his members and to become partakers of his eternal righteousness and life and glory which are in himself, and to contact this communion of Christ himself and of his benefits as truly as the outward words of the promise and the outward symbols, bread of course and wine, are perceived truly."—BUCAN (XLVIII, 101): "To communicate with Christ is not only to confess Christ or merely to communicate with his ἐνσάρκωσις, by which he became in species a single unit with the entire human species (although this ἐνσάρκωσις is the basis of the uniting we are dealing with). Nor is it to be united to Christ merely by affection, love, agreement and concord, nor to communicate merely in Christ's merits. It is to have Christ abiding and living in us and for us to abide and live in Christ. And that actually (*reipsa*), as *Chrysostom* says, and naturally, as *Cyril* says. That is, to be united and joined to Christ also by the actual communication of Christ's human nature: we to stick to him (Christ) and Christ to become ours and we in turn to become Christ's and so to be nourished on Christ or joined to and inserted into him. So that merging more and more into his mystical body, into his one Spirit, we are his members, of his flesh and of his bones, and we all issue into the unity of the faith and the acknowledgment of the Son of God, into a grown man, by the measure of the stature of the full Christ [the full scale of Christ] Eph. 5. 30 (because we are members of his body) 4. 13 (unto the measure of the stature, etc.).—ALSTED 821: "We become partakers in Christ's divine person, also in Christ's flesh and blood in the H. Supper, in fact so that Christ dwells in us and we are united to him, by a like bond as exists between the head and limbs of the same body. Then we become partakers of all the fruits of Christ's death and resurrection."

22.—To this spiritual and personal enjoyment of Christ's divine-human person is related the bodily enjoyment of the bread and wine as the illustrative sign and guaranteeing seal of it. Through the enjoyment of the broken bread and the wine in the Supper, it is sensibly set forth to the believer and certified in pledge, that Christ's death and life are as surely his personal property as the bread and wine he receives, and that Christ as surely died also on his (the believer's) behalf for the forgiveness of sins and is as surely his (the believer's) nourishment and food unto life eternal as he enjoys the outward food of bread and wine.

OLEVIAN p. 394: "That we may be certain of this union, namely that our bodies also are united through the Spirit with Christ's body to be flesh of his flesh, bone of his bones, without mixture, through the secret bond of the Spirit, Christ willed that our bodies feed on the evidence of his body of bones and be given to drink of the testimony of his actual blood, that in accordance with the testimony made along with us and reduced to our substance by natural conjunction and digestion, we may confidently assert that by the secret bond of the Spirit beyond nature Eph. 5 (short however of the confusion or mixture of his flesh with ours, since even in Christ's actual person the natures must not be mixed or confused) our bodies have been united to his body and to be stimulated or quickened unto life eternal by the same Spirit by which his own body has been quickened Jn. 6."—POLAN (VI, 56): "The distribution of the bread is the minister's action, by which it is signified and sealed to us, that Christ's body is as surely offered to us and bestowed upon us, as the bread is offered and bestowed upon us."—*Basic Account of what the Reformed Churches in Germany believe* (HEPPE Bekenntnisschriften p. 259) : "The meaning, when he takes the bread and breaks it and says etc., is as though he said to each individual specially, Behold, dear man, I am quite aware that you are troubled about your sins. But be comforted. As surely as the bread is broken before thine eyes and the wine separated from the bread, so surely was my body broken for thee on the upright of the Cross, etc.—Also, as surely as I give thee the holy tokens of my body and blood to eat and to drink,—so surely thou shalt also have part and fellowship in my body and blood, as I gave them to death on the upright of the Cross."—Since then outward enjoyment is a pledge of the reality of the inward, it follows that the latter takes place not in the former but contemporaneously with it; POLAN (VI, 56): "Thus with the bread and wine Christ's body and blood are exhibited by Christ and discerned by true believers. These must not be understood ὁμοῦ, i.e., simultaneously in place, as though the body were in or under the bread, or Christ's blood in or under the wine, in the same place on earth, but ἅμα, i.e., simultaneously in time. The meaning then is: When a believer eats the Lord's bread and drinks the Lord's wine with the bodily mouth, then simultaneously he eats the body and drinks the blood of Christ with the soul's mouth."

23.—Only we must distinguish in the Supper between the thing and the guaranteeing sign. If this is not done, the one tends to be identified with the other; alongside the true bread and the true and risen Christ exalted to heaven yet a third is assumed, which is not the Christ come in the flesh, but a Christ come in the bread and so a false Christ. At the same time in consequence an essential distinction would be set up between our Supper celebration and the institution of it, in which even before he had consummated the sacrifice Christ was able to give the disciples the pledge of his broken body, but not the broken body itself.—OLEVIAN p. 335f.: In the supper two things fall to be considered, the *testimonium* and the *res testata*. The former is "the bread and wine along with the promise, the *res testata* was the true body which spoke with the disciples;" i.e., (362) "(1) the victim of Christ's true and natural body and blood once offered on the Cross for our sins, and (2) union with that victim through faith and the H. Spirit". (363) Thus in the doctrine of the Supper all we have to consider is just bread and wine and Christ's true body speaking at the time with the disciples, i.e., the *logos incarnatus*, and not "transubstantiated bread", or some third thing which would be neither bread nor the incarnate word.—"Certain it is that those who will have it that at the first institution of the Eucharist Christ handed out his body in the bread to be eaten by the disciples, are insisting on a different food from the unique blood victim of the Son of God offered once for all. They themselves admit that at the time he was not in the bread: eventually he was offered on the Cross. And they must confess now that that is true, because we have no other Supper than the first one instituted by Christ."

24.—The sacrament is not meant to tie the eye of faith to itself, but is meant to lead and raise it to the Christ hanging on the Cross and thereafter exalted to the Father's right hand, who as the crucified, risen and exalted Christ is the sole saving benefit of the Supper, and who founded the Supper for the very purpose, that we might know that he gave his body to death for us, and that he himself with his merit is our property.—POLAN (VI, 56): "So, when, approaching the H. Supper, believers look upon the sacramental bread with the eyes of the body, they are exhorted by that visible sign at the same time to behold and embrace with the eyes of faith Christ's body broken for us on the Cross or crucified. The bread has the name of body, to prevent believers from sticking at the bread, from looking for Christ's body in the earthly elements, to make them raise their hearts by faith to heaven, whither he ascended and where he is, and behold him with the eyes of faith and join in eating at the heavenly table the spotless lamb slain for them. As the Church sings: "*Sursum corda!*" "—OLEVIAN p. 390: "Both for the disciples' sakes and ours there was also need of a promise anent the actual body and the visible witness. Neither the sight of Christ's body would have advantaged them, nor even his actual immolation on the Cross, without the promise that he was to be immolated on their behalf. Nor would they have applied to themselves a victim-to-be not yet offered if faith did not view the promise, which as it is begotten of the Spirit's secret power as from the actual promise, so also leans upon the same promise, is cherished and preserved by it. It would have done them no good, I repeat, to behold the body with their bodily eyes, unless they beheld it by faith as about to be offered up on the cross and united to them more and more by the Spirit; which accords with the nature of faith Heb. 11. 1 (faith is the giving substance to things hoped for, the proving of things unseen)."

25.—In the action of the Supper then we must distinguish between a visible, bodily and an invisible spiritual dispensation, the one of which has of course the same reality as the other, which is yet of a different kind. The outward elements are dispensed by the minister of the Church, the invisible benefit on the contrary by the H. Spirit, so that Christ dispenses himself personally to us in it. Not as though Christ betook himself to the limitations of our corporeal existence, but because although he is infinitely exalted above us and will only return to us at the end of the days, he so unites us as his members to himself by the H. Spirit, that he is literally our life, and that we are bound far more closely and nearly to him, than the binding that permeates the separate limbs of our bodies. —CALVIN (IV, xvii, 10): "Although it seems to us incredible that Christ's flesh should get through to us where the live places are so far apart, as to be to us for a food, we should remember how far the secret power of the H. Spirit transcends all our senses, and how foolish it is to think of measuring His transcendence by our scale. So what our mind fails to understand let faith conceive, that the Spirit does truly bring together things which spatially are disjoined."—Conf. Gall. 36: "Although Christ is now in the heavens, destined also to remain there until he comes to judge the world, yet we believe that by the secret and incomprehensible power of his Spirit apprehended by faith, he feeds and quickens us with the substance of his body and blood".—Gründl. Bericht der Heidelberg. Theologen vom heil. Abendmahl, 1574; "Christ is not within our body. As the head in our body is not in the arm or in the foot, or the arm in the head, or as the vine is not inside the tendril or the tendril inside the vine, but all members depend from the head and all tendrils from the vine by their veins and ligaments and joints and grow by them because they live on them, whether locally they stand near the head or vine or far away, it matters not: so too Christ's body is not in our body as our body is not in Christ's body. The H. Spirit who dwells in him and in us is the living, eternal, inconceivable bond between him and us, by which our mortal flesh is many thousand times more adequately, fixedly and strongly incorporated and fixed in Christ's. living flesh, than all the limbs of our body are connected by their veins. and bodily ligaments to our head, and we become members of his flesh and bones, no matter whether we are near or far from Christ's body positionally or locally."

26.—Bread and wine are enjoyed by the bodily mouth and so by believers and unbelievers alike. Christ's body and blood are enjoyed by the mouth of the believing soul with faith, and so only by believers, but not by un-believers.—Not as though faith effected the presence of these benefits (which Christ himself offers, wherever his Supper is celebrated at all), but because faith alone can accept and receive what is objectively offered to all by the H. Spirit. If anyone without faith and so with his bodily mouth receive the God-man to himself as the nurture of his own existence and nature, anyone even without faith might by outward parti-cipation in the Supper enter into personal possession of righteousness and eternal life. But faith which enjoys Christ's body and blood, is not such a faith in bread and wine, as regards these as essential manifestations, bearers and coverings of Christ's body and blood, but faith in Christ's person and merit, i.e., true evangelical faith.—HEIDEGGER (XXV, 104): "Thus at once the food and drink at the Eucharistic feast are twofold, one symbolical, corporeal and visible, bread and wine; the other real, spiritual and invisible, Christ's body broken for us and his blood shed for us for the remission of sins."—BUCAN (XLVIII, 114): "Since Christ's body is in heaven and not to return therefrom until the last day, how can he be really and truly united to us?—Because the H. Spirit works in us, and faith. If our vision in a moment of time visually touches the very stars, saith *Augustine*, much more doth faith unite us to Christ himself and so to his human nature situated in heaven. Send, quotha, thy faith heavenward, and thou hast laid hold of him as though he were present on earth."—POLAN (VI, 56): "This presence our faith does not effect; Christ himself by his Spirit causes the presence to us of his own body and blood."—POLAN (VI, 56): "Bread and wine are taken with the bodily mouth, the body and blood of Christ with the soul's mouth, i.e., by true faith. By true faith, I repeat. Not that by which Christ's body is believed to exist in the bread and to be eaten by the bodily mouth,—but that by which we believe that for our sakes Christ surrendered his body to death and shed his blood for the remission of sins and by which believing this we are incorporated in Christ and become partakers of him.—Thus Christ's body and blood are not received by the bodily mouth, because neither were they received by the apostles with the bodily mouth at the first Supper.—The bread and wine are taken by the outward man,

Christ's body and blood only by believers.—The bread and wine are taken corporeally, Christ's body and blood spiritually.—And as the broken bread is taken into the mouth and the poured out wine, so Christ's body is eaten, not so far as it is glorious, just as neither did the disciples at the first Supper eat the glorious one; but as it was slain and dead for our sakes. And Christ's blood is drunk, not as it is contained in his veins, but as it was shed on the Cross."—BEZA (I, 30): "The instrument by which we receive heavenly things is faith. Wherefore, as *Augustine* says, he who is not in Christ's body doth not eat Christ's body."

Christ's body and blood in the Supper are thus offered to all believers and unbelievers alike. But only believers can receive him. CALVIN (IV, xvii, 10): "Of course he offers and exhibits the thing there signified to all who assist at this spiritual banquet, although it is perceived fruitfully only by the faithful.—Unless a man would call God a deceiver, let him never dare to say that an empty sign is put forth by Him."—ZANCHIUS p. 136: "Although Christ's flesh is offered to all for the eating in the Supper, we believe that it is truly eaten by believers only, both because they only already have communion with Christ and so with his body and blood—and because they alone have the Spirit of Christ, by whose power alone Christ's flesh is truly communicated."—ZANCHIUS: p. 138: "Since we say that Christ's true body is taken not only sacramentally but also truly by believers alone, we mean that it is eaten not with the bodily mouth but with that of the mind and spirit endued with faith, and that by the work of the H. Spirit working effectually in us and applying the entire Christ to us.—(139) Just as all true union with Christ takes place through the H. Spirit, even though he remains in heaven, we on earth, it is also necessary that the eating should take place in the same way."—HEIDEG-GER (XXV, 128): "Since then neither is Christ's body contained in, with and under the substance of bread, nor is the eating of it by mouth, it follows at once that his body and blood are not perceived by unbelievers and unworthy persons who eat the bread. They eat nothing but bread and drink nothing but wine, thus perceiving the bare symbols, but not the thing signified by the symbols."

The *Lutheran* doctrine of the (oral) enjoyment of the body of Christ on the part of unbelievers is rejected by pointing to the blasphemy involved in it. Says e.g. OLEVIAN p. 371: The question is (1) whether we are not putting a false Christ in place of the true, and (2) whether too we are receiving the true Christ as our food, in the way the Word promises him. Now the true Christ is the incarnate Word of the Father, which is itself eternal life. Hence the doctrine implies that in the Supper Christ is also enjoyed by the godless: a blasphemy, since here in place of the true Christ, who is essentially eternal life, a false Christ is set up who may also be eternal death.—We must still further insist that in the *Lutheran* doctrine, if it is not to contain an idle dishonouring of "Christ's body and blood", there must necessarily be involved injury to the concept of "eating and drinking." "Eating and drinking" means receiving a thing to oneself not as an object indifferent or alien to one's own existence and life, but in such wise that it becomes part of one's own living substance and the food of one's own existence. Hence the man who enjoys Christ's body and blood, must take eternal life up into himself, and so cannot be unbelieving".—Besides this the dogmaticians stress what e.g. the General *German-Reformed Confession* (18; HEPPE p. 281) says: "So long as the article remains true, that Christ ascended to heaven, so long it remains true, that we may not seize and eat him with our mouths."

27.—Believing enjoyment of the sacrament is at once the proper memorial solemnisation of Christ's death, for which Christ founded his Supper and which he commanded. It is therefore not an idle, outward remembrance of Christ, but a living grasp of his person and of his merit,—BUCAN (XLVIII, 93): "This ἀνάμνησις should not be a bare and idle recollection of a past fact which has nothing to do with us, but an ἐνεργητικὴ one, such that by it a believing mind in using this sacrament may grasp Christ by faith with all his benefits, apply them individually to itself, and so recollect the past sacrifice once accomplished in the flesh, that from it it may feel present consolation, mental joy, peace of conscience, increase of faith and charity, and above all conceive the surest hope of life and blessedness on account of that sacrifice; in short be aroused to a mighty outpouring of love to Christ and the offering of a sacrifice of praise by faith to him and the rendering of thanksgiving."

28.—Accordingly in the enjoyment of the Supper we must distinguish a twofold enjoyment: (1) an enjoyment of the outward elements, which is a sheer *manducatio externa, sacramentalis* and *symbolica*, and is imparted to unbelievers and believers alike,—and (2) an enjoyment of the invisible benefits, a *manducatio spiritualis*, which is imparted to believing communicants—but only to them—along with the *manducatio symbolica*. On the other hand, the assumption of a third enjoyment, a *manducatio oralis*, by which Christ's body and blood would be enjoyed even by unbelievers and godless, is to be rejected as contrary to Scripture.—BUCAN (XLVIII, 41): "Because the sacrament is not universally taken as the whole action of the Lord's Supper and as the actual perception of both sign and thing signified,—there is one outward eating, sacramental, symbolical or ceremonial merely, that of those who in the Lord's Supper eat the sacred sign of Christ's body with the bodily mouth, but which apart from faith is of no moment for salvation. Another is mental or spiritual eating only, of the thing signified of course, which takes place *sola fide,* from hearing, reading and meditating on God's word, on which Jn. 6. 53-55, 63 (Except ye eat the flesh of the Son of man and drink his blood, ye have not life in yourselves. He that eateth my flesh and drinketh my blood hath eternal life and I will raise him up at the last day. For my flesh is meat indeed and my blood is drink indeed . . . It is the spirit that quickeneth; the flesh profiteth nothing; the words that I have spoken unto you are spirit and are life) : (it also belongs to all times but only for believing men and formerly was also common to the patriarchs). And in short there is another eating alike spiritual and sacramental in the lawful use of the Lord's Supper, that of those who in the Lord's Supper both eat the sign of Christ's body with the bodily mouth and discern Christ's body with the actual soul's mouth, i.e. by true faith, and are truly made participators in it by the efficacy of the H. Spirit, eating not only the Lord's bread but the Lord the Bread, as *Augustine* once said.—But carnal or oral eating, by which Christ's body is received by the mouth and transferred to the stomach, there is none. Because it is not consistent with spiritual eating and with the Ascension. And because carnal eating is not only useless but of Capernaum, while spiritual eating quickens."

The other dogmaticians express themselves quite similarly, and so do the confessional writings of the Reformed Church, e.g. the *Hessian Confession* 1607, in which it says in closing: "These two kinds of eating, oral eating of the sacrament and then spiritual eating of Christ's body Scripture contains in clear distinct letters. But that over and above this there is a third eating, since Christ's body is eaten by the bodily mouth even of blasphemers, sorcerers and other unbelievers in an unsearchable and unfeelable way but without any profit or fruit, this is not to be found in the institution of the Supper or in H. Scripture. Therefore we hold to the above-mentioned two kinds of eating expressly laid down in God's word, and the third which hath neither command nor promise in Scripture we consign to its appropriate quarters, but have no desire to fight with any Church because it believes in it or holds it, or to condemn it."

29.—The Lord's Supper is ordained only for those who have knowledge of the Lord and faith in the Lord. Wherefore only true believers who have previously examined themselves earnestly are entitled to enjoy the Supper—but not children who are not yet capable of self-testing, or insane persons, or unrepentant sinners. The Apostle, 1 Cor. 11.28, commands everyone before proceeding to the Lord's Table, to examine himself, in order that he may come to it worthily and not eat and drink judgment to himself, because with unrepentant and unbelieving heart

he rejects the gifts of salvation offered him.— CROCIUS p. 1167: "While
Christians alone are to be admitted to the H. Supper, not all of them
promiscuously. Only those who are able and willing to test themselves,
to discern the Lord's body rightly and to celebrate this sacrament in
remembrance of Christ's death."—HEIDEGGER (XXV, 75): "After the
first Supper all believers and true Christians are added to the number
of communicants who have duly examined themselves and have learned
these mysteries and shewn themselves to be clean and upright in life.
Let each one examine himself and so let him eat of that bread and drink
of that cup, 1 Cor. 11. 28. In the number of these infants are not included.
—From the same feast are to be barred *furiosi* (madmen), so long as they
are mad. Then open criminals and the unrepentant; since their sins
cannot be remitted but ought to be retained, it is neither right nor godly
that they should be offered pledges of remission. Then catechumens,
who inexperienced in the mysteries cannot yet profess faith with appropriate reasons. As to the deaf and weak-minded (*amentes*) judgment
must be formed on outstanding signs of faith and on better intervals,
in accordance with the rule of charity. Nor are favours to be restricted at
all but are even to be increased".—BUCAN (XLVIII, 131): "What advice
does the apostle give those approaching the Supper? Let every man
prove himself and so—let him eat of that bread and drink of that cup, 1
Cor. 11. 28.—132: What must he prove?—This Paul, 2 Cor. 13. 5, explains by saying: "Try your own selves, whether ye be in the faith;
prove yourselves. Or know ye not as to your own selves, that Christ is
in you? Unless indeed ye be reprobate!" Yet neither are they at once to
be adjudged reprobate, who have not yet been effectively called, or
who still after calling fall into grave lapses. Wherefore a just proof and
examination consists in each one descending into himself and holding
a thorough examination and search (1) as to whether he is truly sorry
for admitted sins; (2) whether he believes in Christ the expiator of sins;
(3) whether he has a serious purpose of fleeing sins henceforth, hatred,
lust, drunkenness, and the like and of living in righteousness and
holiness, in order thus to display his gratitude to God."

30.—But those are not to be regarded as unworthy participants in the
Supper, who are still struggling with grievous temptation and even
succumb to them in passing and who are still weak in faith—for Christ
instituted the Supper precisely in order to strengthen weak faith—but
those who still serve sin in their hearts and cling with heart's desire to
the service of sin.

    BUCAN (XLVIII, 135): "Who approach the Lord's Supper unworthily?
Not those who are simply susceptible to sins or weak in faith. It was

especially for the weak that the Supper was instituted, and the Centurion rightly said, Lord, I am not worthy that thou shouldst come under my roof, Mt. 8. 8. But those who are ignorant as to what it is all about and are completely lacking in the fear of God or repentance or faith, persevere in faults against conscience, also those who nourish confidence in their own virtues, in superstition and hypocrisy and false worships (*cultus*), who look upon manifest errors or work amid discords, retain an evil purpose of giving way to wrath, lust and other wicked affections or despise the poor, and approach not as to a mystical but as to a common or profane table."

31.—The purpose of the Supper celebrations is first of all to preserve the memory of Christ's death, to refresh the consciousness of covenant fellowship with God and to seal spiritual communion with Christ, which believers so enjoy, that Christ is literally the foundation of their life. Further, to practise the inward living communion, by which all believers are united, to attest thankfulness to God as the Giver of covenant grace, and to be the ground of the hope of resurrection in believers' hearts.

On the purpose of the Supper dogmaticians express themselves in anything but a regular manner. At the same time all agree in recognising the points that have already been made. Cf. *General German-Reformed Confession* (HEPPE p. 279): Thus "the Supper is strictly speaking the memorial of Christ's death and the refreshment of God's covenant with us men."—TURRETIN (XIX, xxii, 3): "The aim of the whole institution may be threefold: (1) commemoration of Christ's death;—(2) the union of us with Christ and so communion in his benefits;—(3) certainty of the remission of sins and of the eternal life acquired for us through Christ's death."—MARESIUS (XVIII, 74): "It is clear from this, what end the H. Supper was particularly instituted for, namely to signify our spiritual nourishment in Christ; for which it is necessary that with true faith we should eat his flesh and drink his blood; i.e. as *Augustine* explains, that we should communicate in his passion and with holiness and utility keep in mind, that it was for us that his flesh was crucified and wounded.— It further serves to signify and to promote the unity of the Church, 1 Cor. 10. 17 (we who are many are one bread, one body; for we all partake of one bread) 12. 13-14 (in one Spirit we were all baptized into one body . . . and were all made to drink of one Spirit. For the body is not one member but many), as well as to bind us more and more to God and to arouse in us the offices of godliness and gratitude."—BEZA (III 252): "Thus I define the Lord's Supper as a sacred action enjoined by Christ upon all adult believers in the Church till the consummation of the age: in which by the fitting analogy of elements and rites both the memory of his death is represented and our incorporation in him spiritually sealed, our mutual union in him consecrated and thereupon solemn giving of thanks paid to him."—TRELCATIUS (p. 239): "The end of the sacrament is to seal our perfect renewal in Christ.—244: The end of the Lord's Supper is twofold. The primary one is that, celebrating in the lawful use of signs the memory of Christ's death, we are assured concerning our communion with him and our nourishment in him to eternal life. The secondary one is, that it may be a symbol of our resurrection, a testimony of gratitude, a pledge of mutual love, and finally a public mark of setting apart and profession."—ZANCHIUS declares p. 131 that "increase of κοινωνία with Christ is the chief end of the Supper. There are also other ends of the Lord's Supper as instituted: namely that reminded by both words and symbols which represent Christ's death and his blood shed for us we should mentally dwell upon the benefit of redemption;—and further the end is, that we should be confirmed in faith in the remission of sins, nourished into hope of a blessed resurrection, should thank him for so great a benefit, should be roused to repentance, in short should renew in the presence of the whole Church the covenant entered into with God. But since all these things have in view that we should be united more and more to Christ and become one with himself,—therefore we do not doubt that the Supper was above all instituted to increase this union ("unition") and communion with Christ."

32.—Hence whereas baptism, being the sacrament of implanting into the covenant of grace, can only be received once by the believer, it is his duty to appropriate with ardent longing the comfort and blessing of the Supper by more frequent enjoyment of it.—CALVIN (VI, xvii, 44): "Our discussions on this sacrament so far abundantly show, that it was not instituted in order to be received once a year and that perfunctorily (as the common custom is today), but that it might be used frequently by all Christians".—CROCIUS (p. 1171): "True Christians do not use the H. Supper out of habit or custom, but readily and religiously from a burning desire for Christ, in order to obtemper his injunction with love and goodness and enjoy that most abundant treasure; then they also do so frequently because of their own need, in order to strengthen weak faith and nourish it and to make further greater advances in zeal for Christian godliness."

CHAPTER XXVII

THE CHURCH

1.—In His gracious counsel God calls all elect people to the enjoyment of one grace, and in virtue of His eternal gracious counsel He does not isolate them but assumes them as a community into the covenant of grace and implants them in Christ. Hence all who belong to the covenant of grace as members of the one mystical body of Christ constitute one Church which, because it is "called out" of the world to enjoy the salvation in Christ, is termed ἐκκλησία, the Church.—WITSIUS (II, v, 6): "Since all the elect participate in one and the same grace, they are also called to mutual communion with each other."—HEIDEGGER (XXVI, 1) "The subject of the covenant of grace and its benefits under any administration of the covenant of grace, as well as of the sealing of the same, includes the elect, called and believing, individually, but also bound to each other in close communion. When they are thus bound together Scripture gives them the name of the Church Eph. 5. 25 (Christ loved the church) Ac. 20. 28 (. . . feed the church of God which he acquired by his own blood) Eph. 5. 23 (Christ the head of the Church) 26 (sanctifies it, having cleansed it by the laver of water with the word) 27 (that he might present the church to himself a glorious church etc.) Mt. 16. 18 (upon this rock I will build my Church, etc.). Even from eternity God did not elect individuals rent from each other but joined together. He chose us all united as one body in Christ the head."—LEIDEN SYNOPSIS (XL, 29): "With Scripture we call this multitude the Church, because through the word and Spirit of God they are called out of the world to this faith and holiness, and because they have pure and inward communion and society with Christ and all true believers."

2.—"The Church is the assembly or collection of the elect, called and believing, whom God by the word and Spirit calls from the state of sin to the state of grace for eternal glory" (HEIDEGGER XXVI, 6).—MASTRICHT (VII, i. 4): "The Church is the gathering of men effectually called in Christ".—HEIDEGGER (XXVI, 4): "The word Church in the NT denotes the sacred gathering of called (ἐκκληθέντες) men. In the word ἐκκλησία generally there is the idea of κλῆσις, as is clear from Ac. 2. 39 (as many as the Lord our God shall call unto him) 47 (. . . the Lord added to them day by day those that were being saved).—Thus the Church is the gathering of those called by the Lord".—a DIEST (p. 405): "The ecclesia of men is the gathering of God's elect effectively called by God from a state of wretchedness to a state of grace and collected under one head, Christ, both adults and children."—As for the *German-Reformed* dogmaticians PEZEL, SOHNIUS, URSIN, HYPERIUS, OLEVIAN, PISCATOR on the idea and nature of the Church, see HEPPE, *Dogm. d.d. Protest.* III, 320-323.

3.—The Church is thus not the community of the elect generally, but the community of those elect whom God has called effectually, and to whom for the sake of Christ's mediatorship He has not only promised His testament but has also really given it.—HEIDEGGER (XXVI, 6): "The Church is not simply the assemblage of the called and elect. Neither those called outwardly only and not also inwardly, nor those elect but not yet called and faithful are the Church or its members. It is the assemblage of the called, the elect, i.e. those called in accordance with election by the word and Spirit of God in time, and at the same time believers or inserted into Christ by faith as members in the Head. All *cives* of the Church are elect, but not all elect are *cives* of the Church, unless by being appointed and given a testament, in which they are entered as Christ's inheritance, and by being demanded by the Redeemer."—Similarly MASTRICHT (VII, i, 5).

Dogmaticians are busied throughout with the question whether angels, the unbaptized children of the elect, the ex-communicated and schismatics belong to the Church. POLAN regards all intelligent creatures ("the multitude of rational creatures, angels and men") and therefore angels [they rejoice over one sinner that repenteth] too as essentially belonging to the Church. On the other hand all other dogmaticians (with whom at the close of his reasoning even POLAN is in a measure of agreement) teach unanimously, that the angels cannot be regarded as members of the Church, because the Church is essentially the fellowship of those called out of the misery of sin into the state of grace. Cf. e.g. MARCK (XXII, 6), BRAUN (II, iv, 24, 20), BUCAN (XLI, 16) etc.—The *infantes fidelium* are to be regarded as members of the Church because of the claim granted by God (BRAUN. *ibid.* 11).—Apart from this all dogmaticians are unanimous in their teaching, like TURRETIN (XVIII, iv, 1): "Whether catechumens, unbaptized, excommunicates and schismatics belong to the Church?" —3: "We think that the question may be solved by a twofold distinction. Firstly, if the non-baptized who are alien to faith and religion, whom Paul calls τοὺς ἔξω 1 Cor. 5. 12, are distinguished from unbaptized believers or people already disposed towards faith, although they have not yet received the outward sacrament of baptism; the latter only, not the former we consider to belong to the Church. Secondly, the Church may be looked at in two ways, either as to its outward state and visible form or as to its inward and invisible form. Catechumens and unbaptized are said to belong to the Church, not in the former sense as to their outward state, but only in the latter as they belong to Christ's mystical body, although they have not yet been called outwardly to outward and visible communion, nor have they the right to things sacred.—11: As to excommunication—we say that excommunication is unjust, which is perpetrated when the keys make a mistake; and that such excommunication is not ratified by God and cannot cut off from the body of Christ and the communion of the Church which Christ has not abandoned; such as was the excommunication carried out against Christ and those who followed him, who were made ἀποσυνάγωγοι. Or it is just and lawful, being either partial and relative in a fixed degree, by which the excommunicate is barred the Lord's table, prayers and assemblies; or absolute and total, called major, by which the excommunicate is cut off from the very society of the Church. —12: This being laid down, those excommunicates are outside the Church, who content with outward profession have for some time had no communion of faith and love with Christ and believers, of whom it must be said at their excommunication, what John said of the apostates 1 Jn. 2, 19: they went out from us, but they were not of us. But others, who although ejected from the outward communion retain the inward and do not cast away the seed of faith and repentance, are said to be of the Church, although it may happen that before their decease they are not admitted to the peace of the Church, having experience of harsh pastors; because God does not favour human vices, nor can it be that a man who has once been admitted by faith to the body of the Church should be ejected by Him.—18: As to schismatics, to be brief, we readily grant that those who rashly and wrongly recede from the true Church by rending its unity, do not belong to the Church. But we deny that those who are falsely traduced on this odious count of refusing to submit to the Roman pontiff, as *Bellarmine* gabbles, must be excluded from it."

4.—Therefore the Church is called the community of the saints; on the one hand Christ is their sole salvation and the sole cause of their joyfulness to God; on the other hand living believers and those asleep are aware of being purified in the community of their hope in the Lord, in the community of intercession for all members of the Church and in the community of the same gifts of the H. Spirit.—HEIDEGGER (*Med.* XXVI, 7): "The Church—is the communion of saints, which is the union, society and assembly of all believers who have something in common with each other. Now this common thing is Christ the Head of the Church, as well as the gifts which flow down from Him as Head to the Body. It is accordingly bipartite, being mutual between Christ the Head and the members. In it Christ imparts to the Church everything for life and salvation, and the Church in turn imparts gifts to Christ who receives in her love, worship, praise, thanksgiving. In it the living saints communicate with those living or with those dead. The communion of living with living consists in the mutual and even affection formed by one and the same Spirit, as well as in the imparting of the gifts of the H. Spirit, and also of those of the body for the use and honour of the whole body. Nor does communion with the dead cease, because both the dead of the Church militant commend their salvation to God, Rev. 6. 10 (How long, O Master, holy and true, dost thou not judge and avenge our blood on them that dwell upon the earth?) and the living share with the dead the common πολίτευμα in heaven, as far as προθυμία goes, aspire to union with them, praise their virtues and strive to imitate them. The bonds of this communion the Apostle prosecutes, Eph. 4. 3-4 (giving diligence to keep the unity of the spirit in the bond of peace. There is one body, and one Spirit, even as also ye were called in one hope of your calling)."

5.—Since accordingly the continuance of the Church rests solely upon the gracious operation of the H. Spirit, in and for herself she is not visible and not the object of vision, but invisible and the object of faith.— HEIDEGGER (*Med.* XXVI, 8): "The Church is strictly called invisible, because we do not feel and see it as an earthly kingdom but we believe in it."—MARESIUS (XV, 14): "I am not unaware that some of our opponents seriously inveigh against the Church of the elect or against the primary acceptance of the name of Church, by which it is taken as the sole mystical body of Christ of which none but the elect are members. This, because they see that at least in this sense they must recognise an invisible Church of which the Pope cannot be the Head. But it is clear that they do so vainly.—The name Church is of course derived from calling, the calling however which flows from predestination."—BUCAN (XLI, 8): "What it says in the Creed is understood not of this or that one Church, but of the Catholic Church, i.e. of the whole body of the Church, at whatever time it ever existed on earth. And since it consists of the godly and elect who have once existed from the foundation of the world, exist now and are to exist till the end of the world, all gathered together, whom no man can ever see with his eyes, assuredly the Church is believed in and is not seen."—OLEVIAN p. 215 expresses this so : "Of course God could not have given anyone His grace, if any worthiness had pertained to man at his assumption into the covenant of grace. Just because in His free compassion God implants His grace in the hearts of those who have merited nought but eternal death, the existence of the

Church is an article of faith." "If the substance of the covenant is imparted to those who of their own strength can contribute something, even a good thought, then it will be imparted to no one. Hence it follows: I believe in the holy, universal Church.—Since therefore he has presented me with most holy faith, I believe that I also am freely elected and presented to His Son and so I cannot perish. By the Gospel he executes the immutable decree of His election, when by the preaching or ministry of it as by an instrument He gives the H. Spirit, who effects faith when and in whom He wills, i.e. in all the elect and in them alone—at the time that has seemed good to Himself."

6.—"I believe in the Church" therefore means, "I believe that from eternity God has preserved and will preserve to Himself for eternity a congregation of those, with whom He has set up His covenant of grace in Christ, and whom he has awakened to faith in their belonging to that covenant; and that I too by God's grace am and shall eternally remain a member of this congregation" (OLEVIAN p. 215). To this community of the Church (*ecclesia universalis*) belong the believers of all places and of all times, since all are implanted in Christ by the H. Spirit and by Him are eternally preserved in the community of Jesus Christ. Thereby the Church embraces both the believers blessedly at rest and those alive on earth. So *ratione status ecclesiae* (from the nature of the Church's status) there belongs essentially to the concept of the Church the distinction between the *ecclesia triumphans* and the *ecclesia militans*. The former is the community of those who have fallen asleep in true faith here on earth and have now entered upon the condition of perfect freedom from sin and death, upon God's perfect peace and upon perfect blessedness. The latter, of which we have to speak particularly here, is the community of believers here on earth.—RIJSSEN (XVI, 6): "The Church is commonly divided *inter alia* into militant, which is still on active service on earth, and triumphant, which triumphs and reigns in heaven. This distinction is not essential and specific by nature, but only accidental, a matter of state and degree. Nor must we listen to the *Papists*, who invent a third, to wit the sleeping or toiling Church in purgatory. This deception we shall refute later."—As to the interest validated in the distinction between the triumphant and the militant Church cf. MASTRICHT (VII, i. 23) "Query, whether the Church universal is with sufficient accuracy divided into triumphant and militant. The *Socinians* deny the Church triumphant, because they say that after death man ceases to exist either in soul or in body. Although the *Anabaptists* admit that the soul survives death, they insist that it is asleep without any sensation of joy, while with the *Socinians* they declare that there is no triumph in heaven. On the other hand by fashioning, in addition to the triumphant in heaven and the militant on earth, those who toil in purgatory for excessive sinning, the *Papists* divide the Church into three analogous parts. Because they insist that after death the souls of the godly do not merely survive but also experience delights in heaven, the *Reformed* teach the Church triumphant."

7.—Like the Church generally the Church militant possesses the attributes of unity, holiness, infallibility, universality, imperishability.—The Church has the character of unity (*unitas essentialis*), in so far as she rests on Christ as the cause of life in all believers, in so far as she is single in kind (*unica* and so *una*), and in so far as being an essentially spiritual community she is in no wise touched by the limitations natural to humanity.— HEIDEGGER (*Med.* XXVI, 9): "The Church is one, holy and catholic. It is one, not as a worldly kingdom but in a spiritual and catholic way and with a numerical unity, and is one (*una*) in the sense of being single (*unica*)."—RIISSEN (XVI, 7): "Although in the outward and accidental state of place or time or rites or age the Church is diverse, it is yet one with an essential unity: (1) unity of body; although consisting of various parts, as in the actual number of members living in different places and at different times, it is yet a single body, 1 Cor. 12. 12 (as the body is one and hath many members, and all the members of the body, being many, are one body, so also is Christ); (2) unity of head, Eph. 1. 10 (purposed . . to sum up all things in Christ . . . in the heavens and . . . upon the earth); (3) unity of the Spirit, Eph. 4. 4 (one Spirit) 1 Cor. 6. 17 (he that is joined to the Lord is one spirit); (4) unity of faith; there is "one faith," Eph, 4. 5, but faith *quae creditur* as well as *qua creditur*, i.e. one doctrine of salvation set forth in the Gospel and embraced by faith, which both subjectively because of them that believe and objectively because of the object to which it is directed, always has been and always will be one both before and after Christ, Heb. 13. 8 (Jesus Christ is the same yesterday, today and for ever) 15 (through him let us offer up a sacrifice of praise to God continually . . .); (5) unity of love: believers united to Christ through faith should be bound together mutually by love; (6) unity of hope, Eph. 4. 4, i.e. unity of the thing hoped for and of the heavenly inheritance to which we are all equally called, and of which we shall all come to partake in our time."

8.—The Church is holy and infallible, i.e. she is established in the life and knowledge of faith, in the same way as her members, the elect and called believers, who cannot fall into deadly sins or deviate from the sanctifying basis of truth. Consequently, while the Church is indeed not without lack of knowledge and of life, still, preserved by grace she cannot completely lose the righteousness of Christ bestowed on her, deny the basic doctrines of the Gospel and sin against God with really deliberate disobedience and persistently; so that at any time she therefore remains in essential possession of grace and of sanctifying knowledge.—WENDELIN (*Coll.* p. 313): "(The holiness of the Church consists) partly in the holiness and righteousness of Christ acquired through faith, partly in the renewal and sanctification of hearts."—HEIDEGGER (*Med.* XXVI, 10): "So then as regards inherent holiness it [she!] is holy, though yet while militant on earth not devoid of all ignorance and error in mind, of defect and flaw in will, nor infallible nor ἀναμάρτητος. As is the *ratio* of individuals, the same is that of the whole Church. And as in her life as regards individuals she may lapse, so also she may err in understanding. Yet as individual believers cannot sin voluntarily, so neither can they err pertinaciously and in a fundamental of the faith. And since the Church does not regard herself as like an idea or a Platonic republic which subsists outwith the individuals, but subsists in her individual elect, called and faithful of whom she is the collection, she cannot have a different and more perfect nature than the individuals, and they the best, possess."—CALVIN (IV, viii, 13): "If we concede the first point, that the Church cannot err in things necessary to salvation, our meaning is that this is so, because abandoning all her own wisdom she lets herself be taught by the H. Spirit through the Word of God."—In the first instance of course infallibility is to be predicated of the invisible Church of the regenerate; BURMANN VIII, i, 25): "(The attribute of infallibility) is to be understood of the Church, not so far as she is public but so far as she stands for the assembly of the elect. This she is by the guardianship of the H. Spirit, so that they cannot wholly wander away or fall from salvation." On the other hand 36: "particular assemblies may not only err but radically lapse and be extinguished." Hence infallibility is rightly predicated of the visible universal Church, in which the invisible is concealed; WENDELIN (*Coll.* p. 316): "As to the Church catholic and invisible—it is beyond controversy that she cannot err in a fundamental".—To the question discussed almost in all Reformed compendia, "why the whole Church is said to be incapable of erring at the same time", the dogmaticians make the reply, that in Paradise the whole Church consisting of Adam and Eve did fall, but that after the fall a complete collapse of the Church is impossible in virtue of the ordering of the covenant of grace.

9.—The Church is universal or catholic, because she is not bound to places or times or limited to them, because the one Church that exists has the qualification of being the sole Church on the whole earth.—RIISSEN (XVI, 8): "The Church is also called catholic,—(1) as regards places, because she is not confined specifically to any region, city or place, Jn. 4. 23 (the hour cometh and now is, when the true worshippers shall worship the Father in spirit and in truth: for such doth the Father seek to be his worshippers); (2) as regards persons, because she is not tied to any one age or condition, Ac. 10. 34 (God is no respecter of persons, 35: but in every nation he that feareth him and worketh righteousness is acceptable to him); (3) as regards time, since she embraces all ages of the world indiscriminately, 1 Jn. 1 .1-3 (that which was from the beginning, that which we have heard etc. declare we unto you also, that ye may have fellowship with us, yea and our fellowship is with the Father, and with his Son Jesus Christ);—(4) as regards parts, because all the particular Churches which have ever existed or are to be, although some are purer than others, belong to her [literally "are her", i.e. the Church] as long as and so far as they are Christian."—HEIDEGGER (*Med.* XXVI, 11): "The Church is also catholic or universal. This word has been adopted by the Church to distinguish herself from the conventicles of heretics severally contained within her various provinces. It is the same as one, except that it denotes the extension of the unity."

10.—This one, holy and universal Church has an imperishable continuance. Her existence rests, not on any chance but on God's counsel and on the activity of the H. Spirit. Therefore although particular parts of the visible Church may disappear, a congregation of elect and called will always be preserved on earth.—HEIDEGGER (*Med.* XXVI, 11): "Christ's Church in the strict sense is of necessity in possession of constant existence in the world, and that not contingent but based on the hypothesis both of the first efficient cause which is the changeless will of God, and the second, which is the word of God and the H. Spirit made effective through the word."—RISSEN (XVI, 10): "In this way God keeps the Church (1) always universal, invisible; (2) He also always reserves a particular instituted Church for Himself in some part of the world; (3) but this not constantly in the same place, but now here, now there."

11.—The adherence of individuals to the Church rests upon their calling through the H. Spirit. But since the calling of the H. Spirit is mediated through the outward word, which He makes effectual in the hearts of the elect, whereas for the rejected He is completely ineffective, it follows (1) that the community of the Church—invisible in and for itself because mediated only through the H. Spirit and guaranteed to individual believers only in their personal consciousness of faith—has also its visible side, namely, the sphere of proclamation and of the outward lordship of the Word; and therefore [it follows] (2) that the Church so far as she takes outward form also includes hypocrites and dead members, who do not belong to the community of the covenant of grace. Hence in the *ecclesia militans* we distinguish the *ecclesia visibilis* and the *ecclesia invisibilis*. The invisible is the community of the elect effectually called by the word and by the H. Spirit; the visible is the community of those called by the word.—MARESIUS (XVI, 51-52): "Visibility and invisibility belong to the Church, not because we make the Church twofold according to the *Papist* calumny, but because these two things belong to the Church in different respects. Election, faith and love, which are the formal elements of the true Church, are invisible; and so no marks can be given by which it is distinctly and surely fixed, what she is. The marks assigned merely give a confused and probable indication of its localisation. Yet it is made visible and knowable in the two respects in individual assemblages, regarding which it is one thing to see the Church, another to see that she is the true Church."—v. TIL (*Hypotyposis*, p. 218): "The invisible Church is the multitude of the elect in spiritual communion with Christ. The visible Church is the assembly of those who coalesce into an outward association under the dispensation of the word, sacraments and discipline." Similarly the rest.

12.—But the two are not two Churches but only one, which is called invisible "in respect of inward communion with Christ", visible "in respect of outward profession or of sacred rule and government" (PICTET XIII, i, 7). The distinction into the visible and the invisible Church is thus not the difference between two species of a genus, but a defining of one and the same subject according to the different relations in its composition,—RIISSEN (XVI, 9, 1): "When we distinguish the Church as visible and invisible, the division is not one of genus into species, as though we were fashioning two mutually opposed species of Church, as our opponents charge us with doing, but is only the limitation of the subject according to its various σχέσεις. And although the Church may be called visible in many ways, as we have indicated above, in this place it is rightly called invisible as regards its inward form, i.e. true faith, so far as it is deemed to be Christ's mystical body."

13.—"The visible Church is the assemblage of those who through the outward word, the use of the sacraments and ecclesiastical discipline coalesce into one outward body and society"—(LEIDEN SYNOPSIS XL, 32). And the Church is visible either as a territorial Church through the unity of outward ruling and worship, or as a confessional Church through the unity of the outward confession. The latter may include a complex of territorial Churches.—LEIDEN SYNOPSIS (XL, 33): "This visible Church is regarded in two ways, either as a particular assembly in one village, city or province, of those united to each other not only by community in faith and sacraments, but also in the form of outward government and ecclesiastical rites; or as an oecumenical and universal assemblage scattered throughout the whole world in different places, but though often differing considerably from each other in the actual form of outward government and in the detail of rites, yet come together in an essential community in faith and in sacraments."

14.—Within the realm of the visible Church are also to be found unbelievers and hypocrites, who are nevertheless not to be regarded as members of the Church. Although outwardly they represent the confession of the Church, participate in her sacraments, and fit outwardly into the Church order, their godlessness is decisive that they are merely associates of the outward institutions but not real members of the Church. —RIISSEN (XVI, 8, 1): "We admit that it is also possible for reprobates to belong to the outward State of the Church, which consists in the profession of faith or in the outward and perceptible participation in the same sacred things. But we deny that they belong to her inward state, which consists in inward and effectual calling through the word and Spirit.—So the question comes back to this, whether the essential form of the Church consists in the sole outward profession of faith, or is to be found in the inward genuineness of faith; whether if the godless and impenitent but outwardly unite themselves to the fellowship which professes Christ's teaching, although otherwise they are devoid of faith or holiness, they may be said to constitute the Church; whether it is not solely the godly and believing who not only profess faith but truly believe and are regenerate, who are presented with this title and enjoy this privilege. The former is the *Papist* claim, the latter our own."— WENDELIN (*Coll.* p. 308): "The reason why the godless are not true members of the true Church lies in the actual ungodliness, through which they are separated from the Head of the Church, so that they are not his members, not being joined to him either by the H. Spirit or by faith, although they seem to be so intermittently and are regarded as members of the Church as long as they simulate faith by outward profession of the word and by use of the sacraments."—MARESIUS (XV, 12): "It is most true—that the elect alone are true and genuine members of the Church."—TURRETIN (XVIII, iii, 1): "Over and above the elect who are called are reprobate and unbelievers, whether hidden or plain to see, also true members of Christ's Church? No, against the *Papists*."

15.—Therefore the duty is laid upon the Church to cleanse herself, by means of Church discipline, from the society of the godless and hypocritical, if they are known to be such.—LEIDEN SYNOPSIS (XL, 36): "Although this Church is never completely free from hypocrites and godless, yet she is bound both to unmask hypocrites so far as she can and by the keys committed to her by Christ to exclude the godless from her company according to Christ's prescription, Mt. 18. 17 (if he refuse to hear witnesses, tell it unto the church; and if he refuse to hear the church also, let him be unto thee as the Gentile and the publican), Rev. 2. 2 (. . . that thou canst not bear evil men, and didst try them which call themselves apostles, and they are not, and didst find them false) 14 (I have a few things against thee, because thou hast there some that hold the teaching of Balaam, who taught Balak to cast a stumbling-block before the children of Israel, to eat things sacrificed to idols, and to commit fornication); but powerfully to recall actual believers, who have relapsed into defection of life or faith, to serious repentance through the same discipline, as St. Paul advises, 1 Cor. 5. 5 (deliver such a one unto Satan for the destruction of the flesh, that the spirit may be saved in the day of the Lord Jesus)."

16.—The invisible Church is the communion of the elect who are reborn and converted by effectual calling. This communion is called the invisible Church, because the inward and essential form of adherence to it, true faith and life in the H. Spirit, is essentially of an invisible kind.— The effects of rebirth, outward confession of faith and good works may also be deceptively imitated by unbelievers—and only God's eye can unerringly distinguish between reborn and hypocrites.—LEIDEN SYNOPSIS (XL, 27): "This Church militant is divided by our men into the Church visible and invisible. The invisible Church is the name given to the multitude of believers and elect discerned by God's eye as well in particular assemblages as in all the Churches and places in the whole world. She is called invisible, because her actual inward and essential form, to wit, true faith and holiness, is invisible to men. Though we do not deny that actual inward faith and holiness are also manifested by confession and good works, nevertheless, since hypocrites may imitate all these things for a time, no infallible judgment can be formed on these grounds alone concerning others."—WOLLEB III: "The invisible Church is the assemblage of the elect only.—It is called invisible, not because the men belonging to it are not visible as men, but because they are not discernible as the elect. God alone is aware, who are His own, 2. Tim. 2. 19 (the firm foundation of God standeth, having this seal,

the Lord knoweth them that are his: and, let every one that nameth
the name of the Lord depart from unrighteousness)."

17.—As, now, the distinction between the visible and the invisible Church
holds in the first instance of the whole Church, it is to be applied also to
every individual part of it.—BRAUN (II, iv, 24, 22, 7): "One and the
same Church may be called visible and invisible, but for a different
reason. It is to be called visible, not only because the men as men are
visible, but because outwardly they profess Gospel truth and celebrate
the sacraments according to the lawful use for which they were instituted
by God. It ought to be called invisible because of the Spirit and true
faith, which reside in the mind alone, which no man can see, which God
alone knows."

18.—Since the Church *qua* invisible Church has taken form as separate,
definitely circumscribed and individually characterised, individual
Churches, the question is, by what signs (*notae*, γνωρίσματα) the
purity of the separate Church communions is to be tested, and the true
Church to be distinguished from the false.
    RIISSEN (XVI, 13): "The true Church is recognised by its marks,
which are outward signs indicating clearly and surely what the true
Church is".—PICTET explains how this is to be taken (XIII, vi, 1):
"The marks of this Church are to be investigated and that after we
have observed—(3) that it is not a question of marks by which believers
can be distinguished from hypocrites, but of marks from which we may
discern whether a communion is true, so that we may join it; and that
it is not a question of the marks of the Christian Church generally—the
profession of Christianity suffices to distinguish it from others—but of the
marks of the true Church among those assemblages which call themselves
Christian."—TURRETIN (XVIII, xii, 5): "It is a question of the marks of
a particular visible Church, so that we may distinguish the orthodox and
purer Church from the heterodox." Similarly, too, other dogmaticians
e.g. MARESIUS (XVI, 20). It is to be noted that whereas almost all other
dogmaticians also (cf. para. 19 below) speak of the "true marks of the
Church," MARESIUS and POLAN speak more adequately of the "orthodox
and purer Church to be distinguished from the heterodox and more
impure" and of the "marks of the pure and orthodox Church." "Every
pure Church of God is also true, but not every true Church is continuously pure." Hence POLAN recognises, what others deny, that the
Roman Church is a "true Church"; he only disputes the possibility of it
being described as a pure Church.—As regards the Roman Church it is

regularly explained e.g. by TURRETIN (XVIII, 14): "Surely the Church of Rome of today cannot be called a true Church of Christ ! *Negatur.*"

In spite of its *"naevus"* (blemish) the *Lutheran* Church was invariably acknowledged by the Reformed to be allied in faith and it invariably received free access to the Supper celebration of the Reformed. The French General *Synod of Charenton* e.g. resolved A.D. 1631 that even without transfer to the Reformed Church *Lutherans* might participate in the sacraments in it, "because the Churches of the *Augsburg* Confession agree with the other Reformed Churches in the fundamental points of the true religion, and because there was neither superstition nor idolatry in their worship" (AYMON, *Synodes nationaux,* II, p. 501). Even though the *Lutheran* Church was designated schismatic by Reformed dogmaticians, yet the kinship in faith of the two Protestant confessions was acknowledged. For (a DIEST p. 429) "a schismatic is one who while preserving faith's foundation departs from some rite of the Church or from a received doctrine or, for some other reason, from the Church. A heretic is one, who convulsing the foundations of faith either directly or by inevitable inference gives persistent battle on behalf of his heresy.—ALSTED 689: "A heretic differs from a schismatic.—The former errs in the doctrine and substance of faith, the schismatic in accessories.—The heretic corrupts the purity of faith by false dogma, the schismatic disrupts the bond of fraternal association."

19.—The distinguishing marks of the true Church are (a) the pure preaching of God's Word, (b) the use of the sacraments in accordance with their institution and (c) the serious and zealous practice of disciplined Christian life. Where these three *notae verae ecclesiae* admit of being perceived, there the true Church is certainly present.—HYPERIUS 552: "(1) The first sign of the true Church is pure doctrine and agreement upon it. (2) The second sign of the true Church is the dispensation of the sacraments as they were instituted by God and their lawful use. (3) The third sign is the obedient answering to doctrine and sacraments."— CALVIN (IV, i, (10): "We have laid down, as the signs for discerning the Church, preaching of the word and observance of the sacraments."— URSIN (*Explic. catech.* Ed. 1598, p. 393): "There are three marks of the true Church: (1) profession of the true, uncorrupted and rightly understood doctrine of law and gospel, i.e. the doctrine of the prophets and apostles; (2) the right and lawful use of sacraments; (3) profession of obedience to the doctrine or ministry."—POLAN (VII, 8): "Two marks of the pure and orthodox Church are essential: divine doctrine sound and uncorrupted;—and divine discipline;" which latter consists on the one hand "in the lawful administration of the sacraments", on the other "in obedience to the divine commands as to sincere religious worship of God alone and as to holiness of life."—MASTRICHT (VII, i, 20): "Some of the orthodox admit of only one mark of the true Church, profession of the true faith, in which everything is included. But since the true communion of saints is exercised in the common use of the divine word, of ecclesiastical seals and of ecclesiastical discipline, some desire a little more distinctly three true marks of the Church: profession of the true faith, lawful administration of the sacraments and prudent exercise of ecclesiastical discipline."—MARCK adduces (XXXII, 10) two marks of the true Church, namely "purity of fundamental doctrine" and "holiness of life."—LEIDEN SYNOPSIS: (XL, 45): "The true and essential and visible marks of this pure Church are the pure preaching and reception of the word, sealed through the lawful use of the sacraments and maintained by the use of the keys or ecclesiastical discipline, according to Christ's institution."— WENDELIN in consequence describes it as a difference between the *Lutheran* and the *Reformed* conception of the doctrine, that the former describes only the dispensation of word and sacrament according to Scripture as "the marks of the Church", whereas the latter further adds to it a believing life (*Collat.* p. 321): "Indisputably the marks of the true Church are purity of heavenly doctrine and lawful use of the sacraments. But the Reformed rightly deny that these two are the marks and that there is not a third besides them. Whence we add a third, holiness of life, or zeal for good works that meet the senses [that men may see your good works and glorify the Father]. This is called the obedience due to the ministry of the Word according to the prescription of the Word."

Meantime the dogmaticians as a rule insist upon the greater significance of the first two compared with "discipline". Whereupon BUCAN e.g. (XLI, 20) remarks that "although in God's H. Church discipline too is required, yet if the rulers of the Church should cease in office, the Church must not immediately be denied, provided that these two fundamental and essential visible marks of the Church are present."

20.—Naturally these attributes do not attach to all separate Churches in the same perfection, yet that is why the Christian must not forthwith separate himself from the communion to which he belongs when he notices in it errors and lacks of minor importance. All that matters is that everything that belongs to the saving nature of revelation is preserved in complete purity.—CALVIN (IV, i, 12): "When we say that pure ministry of the word and pure rite in celebrating the sacraments is a fitting pledge and earnest, that we may safely embrace as the Church a society in which both exist, it holds to the extent that it is nowhere to be rejected, so long as it persists in these things, although it is otherwise rife in many defects."

—WOLLEB p. 115: "These marks belong to all Churches alike as regards the foundation of religion. But as regards the accidents they belong more to one Church, less to another. So we must not straightway hesitate over the truth of a particular Church because of some error or abuse. Such purity is not required, whereby there is no error in a single article, or no abuse creeps into the administration of the sacraments, provided there is no retreat from the pivot of salvation, namely the two tables of the law and faith in Christ, 1 Cor. 1. 11-12 (the divisions at Corinth)."

21.—Still less is it permitted to a Christian to withdraw in an *Independent* and *Libertine* manner from all fellowship in Church life. God bestows His saving grace on us through the Church, so that we have to regard her as the mother of our spiritual life (*mater fidelium*), and so precisely in the fellowship of Church life we ought on the one hand to grow conscious of our state of grace and on the other hand to maintain ourselves as confessors of the Lord to our own and our neighbour's edification. So it is God's will that we should connect ourselves as living members with the Church fellowship which we recognise as the true or as the purest Church. —OLEVIAN p. 222: "When God provides our eyes with the sight of an assemblage which is a member of the H. Catholic Church, the mark having been shown of true prophetic and apostolic doctrine (under which are embraced lawful administration of the sacraments and training in all godliness, Mt. 28. 20 (teaching them to observe all things whatsoever I have commanded you)), we ought to unite with that assemblage. For as He is Himself our Father, it is His pleasure that the Church be our mother, Is. 54. 1-2 (Sing, o barren . . .), Gal. 4. 27 (Is. 54. 1-2) 28 (Now we are children of promise) 31 (we are not children of a handmaid, but of the freewoman). In her we are both born and brought up right to the end of our lives. God is pleased by the Church's ministry to quicken us by His Spirit, stamp remission of sins on our hearts and reshape us daily in the same unto His own image. On the other hand he who despises such an assemblage possessing the mark of a true Church, to wit truth of prophetic and apostolic doctrine—which happens when a man does not communicate in sound doctrine and in prayers and when he does not attach himself to the communion of saints through the visible witnesses of the Covenant, baptism and the sacred eucharist—cannot be sure of his own salvation. And he who persists in such contempt is not elect Ac. 2. 47 (. . . and the Lord added to them day by day those that were being saved)." —MASTRICHT (VIII, i, 31): "Query, whether any Christian, if he can, is bound to associate himself with any particular, fixed true Church. The *Schwenkfeldians, Libertines, Enthusiasts* and other fanatics, with whom also act the *Socinians*, say No. The Reformed recognise that there may be a hidden Church, since you cannot join any Church. But where you can, they lay it down that you simply must."

22.—On the other hand it is just as sure a duty of the Christian to separate himself outright from a fellowship, in which the basis of the covenant of grace is denied. Although in this respect we must distinguish between crucial doctrine and a manner of life which may be corrupt and still does not justify us in walking out of the fellowship! Just as in the matter of doctrine itself errors of minor significance must not be regarded like an error which upsets the foundation of doctrine (OLEVIAN p. 223).

Since then at all times the Church takes form as a visible communion or *coetus,* and thereby aims at achieving her purpose of being the *mater fidelium,* it follows that, in order to achieve her purpose, she requires a definite organisation and government.   Thus *gubernatio ecclesiae* is of course exercised in the first instance invisibly by him who is the sole Head and Lord of the Church, by Christ (*regimen principale*).—HEIDEGGER (*Med.* XXVII, 2): "The principal outward rule of the Church belongs to God and Christ alone; by it He alone rules and controls the Church with principal power, according not only to its invisible form but also to its outward and visible condition."

23.—In order to exercise this kingship of his over the Church Christ avails himself of human instruments.   This is why in every separate Church communion cut off by human and natural conditions—in every separate Church—a Church government (*regimen ministeriale*) must be organised.   On the one hand it is a *regimen ecclesiasticum* exercised by the individual instruments of the Church, and on the other a *regimen civile,* exercised by the (Christian) State government.—HEIDEGGER (*Med.* XXVII, 3): "The ministerial rule of the Church is that by which God guards and rules a Church gathered out of the world by the ministry of men.   And this (ministry) is either ecclesiastical or civil.   That is ecclesiastical, by which He governs the Church through ecclesiastical persons, minsters of God and Christ according to His Word, and through canons of the Church congruent with the same Word."

24.—The basis and root from which the *regimen ecclesiasticum* is formed is the *ministerium ecclesiasticum* ordained by Christ.   This is necessary for the Church, though not by an "absolute necessity."   God could also have imparted His salvation directly by the omnipotent operation of His H. Spirit.   But by a "hypothetical necessity."   It is God's good pleasure that the individual should attain possession of the N.T. covenant of grace by man's proclamation of the Word, especially by Church ministry.—

RIISSEN (XVI, 19, 1): "Is it necessary that there should be a public ministry and a calling to it in the Church? Yes, against fanatics and enthusiasts.—The question is not(1) of the usefulness of the ministry, or of its dignity, but of its necessity; whether it was necessary for some such office to be constituted in the Church, which our adversaries deny and we affirm. Nor is the question (2) of the absolute and unifold (*simplex*) necessity for it. We do not deny that if God had willed He might have converted and saved men directly through Himself apart from the ministry of men. But it is a question of hypothetical necessity in relation to God's actual εὐδοκία and decree, which we assert against present-day *Enthusiasts* and *Schwenkenfeldians* and other fanatics of that ilk, who boast of nothing but divine *afflatus* and ἐνθυσιασμοί".

25.—In fact this God-ordained human mediation of salvation is called a "ministry", because it does not consist in a lordship over souls, but is a service which a man offers to brethren according to God's will. So the "ministry" is not a "priesthood", with such a power over souls that without it no one can enter into possession of saving grace; and so in the Church of the NT there is no opposition between priests and laymen. Believer are together a priestly nation.—BUCAN (XLII, 2): "Why do you call it a ministry"? Because it is not an ἀρχή, principate, lordship, magistracy or imperial office, but an ἐπιμέλεια καὶ διακονία, which asserts the same thing as λειτουργία or *ministerium*. Nor are ministers of the Church ἄρχοντες κύριοι, or lords who must lord it over clerics or consciences or members of the Church, or arrogate to themselves the power of making laws and transferring kingdoms. But they are slaves or ministers of one emperor or Lord of lords. Christ specifically forbade ministers lordship, both by word Lk. 22. 25-26 saying, "The kings of the Gentiles lord it over them, but ye are not so", and by example v. 27 (I am in the midst of you as he that serveth). And so Peter himself says, 1 Pet. 5. 3: "not lording over the *cleri* [*sic*] but being ensamples of the flock."—*Conf. Helv.* (II, 18): "Priesthood and ministry are things very different from each other."—TURRETIN (XVI, 20): "The difference between clerics and laymen is a *Papist* fiction."—CALVIN (IV, xix, 28): "To start with it ought to be admitted that all are insulting to Christ who call themselves priests to offer the victim of appeasement. He was constituted and consecrated priest by the Father—in him we are all priests."

26—Since then the ministry is a service by which God's gracious will to man should be realised, this necessarily presupposes in the man who proposes to undertake and exercise the ministry a commission imparted to him or a call, by which it is attested to him and to the Church, that

God wishes to avail Himself of him as His instrument, in order to make His grace effective through him. This calling may be an inward one, by the man's experiencing through the mysterious activity of the H. Spirit, that God wishes to use him as His servant; and an outward one, which in order is a ' mediate calling ', i.e., a calling mediated through human instruments.— CALVIN (IV, iii, 10): "Care must be taken that no one assume public office to himself in the Church without a call, Heb. 5. 4 (no man taketh the honour unto himself, but when he is called of God, even as was Aaron) cf. also Jer. 17. 16 (As for me, I have not hastened from being a shepherd after thee; neither have I desired this woeful day; thou knowest: that which came out of my lips was before thy face). So in order that a man may be accounted a true minister of the Church, he must first be duly called. Then he must answer the call."— HEIDEGGER (*Med.* XXVII, 8, ii, 10): "In order to a lawful undertaking of the ministry *vocatio* is required, Heb. 5. 4 *supra* [CALVIN], Rom. 10. 15 (how shall any preach, except they be sent ? How beautiful are the feet, etc.) The chief author of the calling of ministers is Christ who gives some pastors and teachers, Eph. 4. 11.— The right of thus calling rests with the entire Church, shepherds and sheep.— It is to the whole Church that the power of the keys was given, no least part of which is the right to call ministers."— BUCAN (XLII, 35) : "Lawful calling is twofold : Inward or secret, which takes place through the H. Spirit ; and every minister should be conscious of it before God, that he receives the offered office neither from ambition nor from greed nor from any other cupidity, but from sincere fear of God and zeal to edify the Church. It is outward and solemn as it regards public order ; and this once more is twofold : indirect, also called ordinary; direct, called extraordinary and special."

27.— For this three things are required. The person to be called must (1) be suited to take over the ministry, (2) be called by the whole Church or by her legal representatives, and (3) be convinced of his own usefulness and be willing and ready to undertake the ministry.— BRAUN (II, iv, 26, 22, 24): " These three things in particular are therefore required for a lawful call. (1) He who is called must be suited for exercising the office in question. (2) He must be called by the whole assemblage or by those to whom that power has been granted by the whole assemblage. (3) The man called must be convinced of his own suitability and be willing to enter upon the office in question." The subject who calls is according to order not the civil government but the Church; MASTRICHT (VII, ii, 32): "Query, whether the ministerial calling of ministers be competent for anyone except the Church ? *Thomas Erastus* the physician and after him the *Remonstrants Grotius* and *Utenbogardus* refer the power to call to the magistrate, declaring that the Church does not call save by power delegated to her by him. *English Independents* refer the right of calling to the whole congregation and its individual members. Some politicals refer to patrons the right of nominating or electing or both, whether these patrons are ecclesiastics as among the *Papists*, or seculars as among *Protestants*. The *Papists*, with whom certain hierarchs act in their own way, refer the right of calling to bishops, except that with the agreement and connivance of the Roman pontiff they also leave the election to others. The Reformed assign the divine right of calling to the Church alone, so far as this does not denote the members of a particular Church one and all, but the representative Church or Presbytery, except that, so far as those to be called become citizens and are supported publicly, they leave to the believing magistrate the right of approach and confirmation. But in unusual cases where there is either no Presbytery, so far as the man called is destined to a clandestine Church (and these therefore cannot call), they refer it to the *classis* or Synod."

28.—"The calling of ministers is that by which after examining their life and doctrine the Church elects men to the ministry and inducts them by solemn rite into possession of office" (WOLLEB p. 119). The outward form in which the call is consummated is generally unessential. All that matters is that each is called as demanded by the order existing in the congregation concerned.—BRAUN (II, iv, 25, 2, 32): "Any order which is received in a Church for propagating the truth, for preserving peace and by which no violence is inflicted upon Christian liberty, should be preserved. Anyone called and consecrated in accordance with such an order is beyond doubt a lawful minister of Jesus Christ."

29.—Orderly calling of the minister is to be insisted on as the basis of the entire Church organisation, so long as the Church order itself has standing —BUCAN (XLII, 41): "How long must we adhere to the visible and ordinary calling and succession of pastors ? As long as order and legal statu- in the Church are fixed and plain, so that people are not permitted anyhow, without ordinary lawful calling, to foist themselves into a Church ministry. Once the actual order and status have collapsed or been interrupted God Himself institutes order for the Church outwith order, or rather outwith wonted custom, through those whom by His unsearchable counsel He has chosen for and urges to that work."

30.—Only where it collapses and cannot be restored to wonted ways, may the activity of an extraordinarily called minister be considered, an activity which God directly arouses and calls, in order to institute a new

Church order, or to restore an old one that has collapsed.—WOLLEB 118: "Extraordinary ministers are those whom God raises up outwith order, either to set up a new regime in the Church or to restore one that has collapsed."—BUCAN (XLII, 42): "An extraordinary call is one made by God Himself or God's Son ἀμέσως *et proxime* without the help or ministry of men, one by which of Himself God actually gives a call to some ecclesiastical office. This makes calling threefold. (1) Where no human vote has been applied, by His own voice, as was the calling of Abraham, Moses, the prophets under the Law, of John Baptist and the apostles. (2) Where some votes were exercised, but merely as intermediaries announcing God's call and command, like Aaron and the tribe of Levi by Moses' intervention. (3) He sends it hither and thither by His own intrinsic afflatus, like Philip the deacon's calling before and hi s going after the dispersion of the Jerusalem Church to the city of Samaria unknown to the apostles."

31.—Whether a man who emerges in the Church as God's servant extraordinary is really called by God, is recognised if he proclaims the pure word of revelation, if he reveals an unusual equipment such as is required for the exercise of an unusual calling, and likewise special gracious help from God which blesses his work and which despite all the temptation in the world guides him to the goal.—BUCAN (XLII, 45): "There are three signs of a lawful extraordinary calling: (1) that he who alleges it, purely preaches the word of God; (2) that he who is sent extraordinarily by God, possesses the gifts of the H. Spirit necessary for executing that office of his and plainly extraordinary: as principally those of the true wisdom of God and knowledge of heavenly doctrine: (a) the gift of uttering and teaching it; (b) and the gift of unafraid constancy in the true doctrine of the true God, after the example of Isaiah and Christ and Paul; (3) an incredible and unexpected and quite amazing blessing of God on the labours of such a calling, success and its fruits and effects resplendent in the miraculous reformation of life, a rich sowing of churches and propagation of them increasing daily, although the devil and even the whole world was in opposition."

32.—The ministry comprises two offices, those of "ministering ministers" and "teaching ministers". These are the pastors and the doctors of the Church. The pastors or shepherds of the congregation are given the duty of proclaiming God's word, administering the sacraments, laying all their congregations' needs before God in prayer and dealing with discipline. - WOLLEB 118: "Pastors are those who are at the head of a definite flock for teaching, administering the sacraments and exercising oversight.—BRAUN (II, iv, 26, 22, 19): "The office of ministers of the Church under the New Covenant is (1) to preach the word; (2) to administer the sacraments; (3) publicly to offer prayers in Church for people; and (4) to exercise ecclesiastical discipline and preserve all seemliness in the Church."

33.—For their orderly calling it is required that before the ministry is handed over to them they should be tested in life and doctrine, elected by the representatives of the Church with an appeal to God, and then solemnly ordained and confirmed as *ministri ecclesiae.*—SOHNIUS (*Method. theol. Opp.* 1, 209): "The parts (of the mediated calling made by men) are (1) an examination or test of doctrine and life; (2) election and (3) ordination." Ordination is the act "by which the elect are installed with solemn ritual and pious prayers and as it were sent to their office. The ceremony applied here as a rule is the imposition of hands."—WOLLEB p. 120: "To lawful calling three things belong: investigation, election and confirmation. Investigation is both of life and doctrine. But life must be investigated before doctrine. If a man's morals are not tolerable, he should not be admitted to the test of doctrine."—(Cf. POLAN's "test of life and test of doctrine" VII, 15).—"The process of election is that after the offering of ardent prayers to God, and persons having been nominated from whose number someone is to be elected, one individual is elected by the votes of all, or of the majority, the votes being indicated by voice or by χειροτονία (show of hands).—Confirmation is the introduction of the person elected, in which after public prayers he is commended to the Church and his calling confirmed to him by the laying on of hands."

34.—This ordination may be imparted by the laying on of hands. At the same time this rite does not belong to the essence of ordination. It is rather an absolutely free usage of purely symbolic significance.— COCCEIUS (*Summ. theol.* LXXVII, 27): "χειροθεσία or laying on of hands was used by the apostles and the presbytery in ordaining ministers of the Church, so that being placed in sight of the Church as approved by it they were commended to her and thus in doing their duty they were outwith the reproach of ἀλλοτριοεπισκοπία and unlawful calling."— BRAUN (II, iv, 26, 22, 21) "Hands were usually laid on by the apostles as a sign that they conferred the gifts of the H. Spirit, and greater fitness to perform the office, Ac. 8. 17-18-19 (they laid their hands on them and they received the H. Ghost. Then the "simony" incident) 19. 6 (when Paul had laid his hands upon them, the H. Ghost came on them; and they spake with tongues and prophesied), 1 Tim. 4. 14 (. . . the gift that is in thee, which was given thee by prophecy, with the laying on of the hands of the presbytery) 2 Tim. 1. 6 (the gift of God which is in thee by the laying on of my hands), as χειροθεία was the sign and symbol of the conferring of gifts of the H. Spirit. But since today the gift of miracles ceases and gifts of the H. Spirit cannot be bestowed by us on anyone, it follows that for the same end hands are no longer to be laid on on ministers of the Church. So they are laid on only in the received manner, as a sign of confirmation, and because we seek the gifts of the H. Spirit and His aid to be confirmed in addition from God, in order that the minister may be able to cope with so holy and so difficult an office. Whence it follows that the imposition of hands for confirmation is not absolutely necessary and is not of the essence of the ministry."

35.—Next it should be noted that the act of ordination generally is just a solemn and confirmatory authentication of that ordination which the individual has already received in essence by election itself.—HEIDEGGER (*Med.* XXVII, 12) : "The complement of actual ecclesiastical calling and ordination consists in the confirmation and inauguration of it. By it the man elected and proved and so already ordained by appointment (*destinatione*) is by solemn rite put in possession of his office and as it were espoused to the Church for which he was destined. In fact in this inauguration, which comes by the name of ordination from the final act and so by synecdoche, the apostles called the Church to fastings and prayers and entrusted the elect with Churches by the laying-on of hands.— Nevertheless this rite is not of the essence of ordination, but is a more solemn declaration of it, which if a man lacks he need not therefore be adjudged unordained, just as a king lawfully elected does not cease to be a king before he is crowned or if he is not crowned."

36.—Only genuine ordained preachers are entitled to impart ordination since obviously no one can give what he does not possess himself.— MARESIUS (XV, 63): "Ministers of the Church should be ordained by those already in the same degree, since none can give what he does not possess. But that the rights of ordaining are claimed for bishops alone, as is the case with *Papists* and their apes, no reason persuades us. It is assigned to the whole presbytery by Paul, as it seemed good to its own locality. Nor could it be done canonically by one alone [Paul!?] and ordination makes all equal in office and dignity."

37.—The spiritual authentication of office which is transmitted by ordination is invariably one and the same. Therefore among bearers of the office of preacher there may be a difference between superiors and inferiors. There can be no difference of unequal "orders".—BUCAN

(XLII, 51): "Because of the order and position (*politia*) of those on whom the office of teaching is enjoined, one may take precedence of others who is first among his colleagues not in rank (for among parsons there is a common, equal authority) but in order.—But we deny that there is any degree or ὑπεροχή of power among ministers."—TURRETIN (XVIII, 21): "Is episcopacy an order or a grade of the ecclesiastical hierarchy distinct from the presbyterate and superior to it by divine right?—No!"

38.—The second teaching office of the Church is that of the "Church doctors" proper, whose duty it is to care for the maintenance of pure doctrine, for the spread of it among the young and particularly for the education of the future servants of the Church. —WOLLEB p. 118: "Doctors are those who in schools are intent that truth of doctrine should be instilled in the young and obtain also in the Church."—HEIDEGGER (*Med.* XXVII, 17): "Next is the office of the doctors.—Christ also gave διδάσκαλοι, i.e., those who only teach, Eph. 4. 11.—It is theirs to transmit sound doctrine which is according to godliness, whether by instilling into catechumens the foundations of faith or by shaping the catechists and pastors of tomorrow not without ἑρμήνεια γλωσσῶν (1 Cor. 12. 10) or by refuting errors opposed to the truth or by setting their face against wanderers and by securing that the Church stand on a firm step and advance in zeal for the truth."

Generally dogmaticians hold a variety of views in their conception of the office of doctor. BUCAN (XLII, 22) gives to the question, whether those who have obtained the degree of the doctorate in the Universities, as they call it, ought lawfully to be called doctors of the Church, the answer "No, because the right of election which belongs to the whole Church and by which approach if a man does not enter the Church he is a thief and a robber (saith Christ, John 10), was not conferred by the Church upon the Masters of Universities. So by all means let them render to sedulous pupils what they deserve, a token of godliness and learning. But the right to teach and the authority for actual teaching let the Church alone concede to them by lawful order in a fixed place, if they wish to be and be considered teachers."

On the other hand MARESIUS says (XV, 53) anent doctors that "they are those who in schools are free to explain H. Scripture, to defend truth against heterodoxy, to shape and prepare youth for the H. ministry. Nor must we listen to those who superciliously belittle their office and would have left it far behind the pastoral dignity, because schools are merely appendages to the Church. Pastors themselves are no less for the sake of the Church than schoolmen and academics. And since universities are workshops in which the actual ordinary pastors are made and shaped beforehand for their duties, the doctor is as much supreme in the Universities (—y) over the pastor in the flock, as father excels son or teacher pupil."—Reformed dogmatics was never quite clear as to where they really had to demonstrate the doctoral office proper in the Church herself.—MASTRICHT (VII, ii, 20): "(The Church has) doctors, Eph. 4. 11, whom others nevertheless confuse with pastors, because in the passage quoted they do not seem to be distinguished; and elsewhere, 1 Cor. 12. 28-29 (apostles, prophets, teachers) they are mentioned alone to the exclusion of pastors ; and so from the double function of their ministry they are called from government ποιμένες καὶ ἐπίσκοποι, while institutionally owing to their νουθεσία καὶ παράκλησις they are termed *doctores*. Others refer the doctorate to extraordinary men. The grades, which obtain among us, of doctors and professors in the schools, are too recent to occur in apostolic writings. Nevertheless if you look to the actual substance, they were as different from extraordinary ministers as from pastors. In the Church there have never been lacking such doctors or καταχρησεῶν *magistri,* who transmitted doctrine not to the promiscuous herd of believers, but to others particularly who were themselves to become pastors or masters (*magistri*)."

39.—Among *ministri ministrantes* are to be distinguished the *presbyteri* or *seniores* and the *diaconi,* both of whom are generally appointed to supplement and support the official activity of a pastor. Hence with the pastor they constitute the Church Council (*presbyterium, senatus ecclesiasticus, ecclesia representativa* (kirk session). The seniors or elders have the special duty to look after Christian discipline and order in the congregation and hence to support the pastor in handling Church discipline with all their power.—MARESIUS (XV, 75): "So much in a slightly fuller way for those who teach in the Church. I mean now those who *speciatim* are called presbyters or elders, as opposed to ministers of the gospel or pastors, and deacons. Elders is our name for those who along with the pastors, as their assessors or like the Levites of old along with the priests, are at the head of the Church's government in the censorship of morals, except that they do not labour in the word and teaching. Of their joint session with the pastors (some Churches summon the deacons to it, others entrust the diaconate as well to the elders) is composed the *synedrium* or Church representative as it is commonly and usually called, or the *senatus ecclesiasticus.*"—WOLLEB 119: "Elders are godly men of weight, joined to the pastors to help them in matters pertaining to the συνταξία of the Church, in visiting the sick, in keeping an eye upon inordinate livers and other like matters."—HEIDEGGER (*Med.* XXVII, 15): "From pastors or teaching elders are to be distinguished non-teaching but ruling elders. Their institution is divine, because if by Christ's precept one or two more prudent men may be summoned to confute a sinning brother, Mt. 18. 16, rulers may also be appointed by the Church and when appointed according to Christ's precept may be called, approached by the Church and may maintain discipline *communi* ἐλέγχῳ.—Above all St. Paul says eloquently that "presbyters who do well are given double honour, particularly those who labour in preaching and doctrine" 1 Tim. 5. 17. Therefore some labour in preaching and doctrine, others do not. *Κοπιᾶν* does not denote degree of labour, as the *Remonstrants* mistakenly make out, but specifically the thing itself."

40.—The office of elder is distinguished from that of pastor. The former is not undertaken as a life-long calling [?] and does not entitle to preach and to administer the sacraments. Since then elders have the character of the pastor's assistants, they are never entitled to make onesided regulations in Church matters without the pastors.—MARESIUS (XV, 77): "This may be added to the differences between pastors and these elders that the latter may bind themselves only for a time, but the former have devoted and bound themselves to God for life. The former also have the right to preach and to dispense the sacraments, the latter not. Therefore if the pastor be absent, the elders alone cannot depose, suspend, excommunicate anyone, or perform any other act which belongs directly to the power of the keys."

41.—Deacons are the managers of the Church who control the external goods and management of the Church in accordance with the order prescribed for them and in particular exercise the Church's care of the poor.—HEIDEGGER (*Med.* XXVI, 20): "There remains the order of deacons, a title which though belonging to any Church duties was yet, when the Church had grown, applied to the assistants of the sacred treasury and consecrated by the apostles themselves under the name of διακονία καθημερινὴ and τραπεζῶν, Ac. 6. 1-2. Thus according to this idea deacons are the guardians and dispensers of the sacred treasury of bodily things, called to this office by God through the Church."—BUCAN (XLI1 26): "Who are the deacons?" "Stewards of God's House, lawfully chosen from the assemblage of the Church, peculiarly so called since they preside over the ecclesiastical treasury or the *manus opitulationum*, i.e., both for receiving and for disbursing and distributing in fixed order the holy alms and collections and other goods of the Church according to their own judgment and that of the pastors and eldership, and are in charge of the sacred uses of the poor, orphans, widows and strangers but chiefly their own believers, and such like uses." —MARESIUS (XV, 78): "We call those deacons who supervise the collection and disbursement of means of aid for the poor."—By these four ministries the Church exercises the power proper to her, the *potestas ecclesiastica*. "(The ecclesiastical power) is the faculty given the Church by God, to be exercised by the actual heads of the Church, in order to create and perpetuate purity of doctrine and worship, seemly order, sanctity in morals and honesty both public and private in the Church and her members, and that not with licence to order anything or arbitrarily, but according to the prescription and mind of God's written word, for the salvation and edification of the Church" (BUCAN XLIII, 3).

42.—The one source of the Church's power is Christ, who is the invisible Head of the Church and alone rules it by the H. Spirit. Hence the inner spiritual rule (Christ's autocratic *potestas dominica*) by which the Church is led, is a purely monarchical one. On the other hand the 'ministerial power', by which the Church rules herself according to the order given by Christ, is as little monarchical as democratic, but is aristocratic in nature, since it was handed over by Christ not to the mass of Church members, but to individuals called thereto.—MARESIUS (XVI, 12): "Christ is the sole head and foundation, the sole spouse, monarch and ἀρχιποίμην of his Church."—WOLLEB p. 123: "The author and founder of this power is Christ."—MARESIUS (XVI, 4): "It is agreed between us and our opponents that the inward and spiritual rule of the Church is always monarchical and belongs alone to Christ the Head ;— but the Church's outward rule, by which through external means she strives to her end, we freely recognise to be not democratic purely, as some *Fanatics* and *Anabaptists* have dreamed and the *Independents* and *Brownists* of today seem to insist.—Strictly speaking the rule of the several Churches is nothing but aristocratic, as it was from the beginning through the college of apostles and afterwards through synods and councils; as that of individual Churches was by presbyteries and synedria."—HEIDEGGER (*Med.* XXVII, 22): "From these it is easy to judge of the form of ecclesiastical ministerial rule. It is not strictly monarchic, aristocratic or democratic. Κράτος, dominating power as in these forms, belongs neither to the Church nor to her ministers, but pure διακονία and οἰκονομία. Analogically however, it may be called aristocratic, because Christ committed the gathering, government and propagation of the Church neither to one nor to all nor to individuals, but to a few apostles and those chosen singly, and to seventy disciples."—TURRETIN

(XVIII, xxix) : "Does the Church possess a spiritual power distinct from the political ? Yes.—1 : The *Papists* sin in excess. They convert that power into a domination and tyranny intolerable to consciences. And this supreme and absolute authority they confer on the Roman Pope, as Christ's vicar and Peter's successor. *Erastians* and *Libertines* and other disturbers of that kind sin in defect. They admit that no spiritual power was given to the Church, but that pure preaching and persuasion was left to pastors and that, if any power belongs to them, it is derived entirely from the magistracy; while all other power, they maintain, is thus part of the mystery of iniquity.—3 : Holding the mean between the two extremes the orthodox recognise that a power and authority was given to the Church distinct from the political. But it is merely ministerial and subaltern, not supreme and αὐτοκρατική. And as they admit that the tyrannical power of the *Papacy*, humanly introduced, was deservedly abolished, they are of opinion that the ecclesiastical order divinely sanctioned is to be retained in accordance with the word of God, against the ἀταξία of the *Anabaptists* and *Libertines*."

43.—This power is exercised by a representation of the Church (the *ecclesia representativa*) consisting of Presbyteries and Synods.—MARESIUS (XVI, 17): "Both of these powers are exercised in particular churches by their pastors and the eldership, in several churches of the same province or nation or kingdom by synods and councils, provincial or national, or even of several nations together, such as existed formerly, which were called oecumenical or universal, because they assembled from the whole empire, not absolutely, but in the sense of the Roman Empire."— MASTRICHT (VII, ii, 25) : "Under the NT there is counted a threefold joint session of Church ministers, presbyterial, diocesan or classical, and synodal. Firstly, I say, Presbyterial, in which the presbyters, both teaching and ruling, of this or that particular Church assemble to attend to the matters peculiar to their Church.—26: Secondly diocesan, which we here call classical, at which fixed προϊστάμενοι, not of one particular Church but of several Churches in some fixed district, who have made a peculiar union for common edification, assemble to attend to what pertains to that district. 27: Thirdly synodal or provincial or national or oecumenical, according to the nature of the cause which happens to need determination."

44.—In all essential parts prescribed by the gospel, i.e., in the general arrangements of the Church, Church government must naturally arrange and demand one and the same thing in all individual Churches. On the other hand as regards the special forms not prescribed by the word of God, by which it realises the universal and essential, it has its freedom whereby with wise love it must consider in particular the peculiarities to be found in the natural character and customs of individual national fellowships.— HEIDEGGER (*Med*. XXVII, 23): "This rule of the Church in things general, the preaching of the word, the administration of the sacraments, the exercise of discipline and the care of the poor, is uniform and immutable. In particular things, ceremonies not defined in the word of God, the order suited to persons and places and the peculiar way of doing in particular Churches may be changeable and various. Although harmony even in these things is desirable, it is not sheerly necessary, nor should it be exacted in a quarrelsome, morose manner, lest for the sake of the straw we imperil the wheat. Many things have not been defined in the word of God; and those which have been have not all been defined in perpetuity.—And since the Church is in a State and the gospel does not abolish States, we are bound to follow their genius, nature and condition in many things."

45.—The Church's authority is a threefold one, the *potestas ministerii, ordinis* and *correptionis* or *disciplinae*.—MARESIUS (XVI, 70): "The power (of the Church or of the keys) should be laid down as threefold, of ministry, of order and of discipline (*correptio*). The power of the ministry, consists in the proclamation of God's word, and the administration of the sacraments, upon which no one ought to presume, unless he has been authorised and called by God."

46.—"*Potestas ministerii* is the authority and right to teach not anything, but the one thing which the Lord enjoined by His prophets and apostles, and to administer those sacraments which he instituted according to his own ordinance and to bless wedlock in accordance with the Church's perpetual use" (BUCAN XLIII, 7). This is also called *potestas clavium*, the power of the keys, since to pastors is delivered the right of proclaiming the word of God, with authority to announce in the name and by the commission of God to those who hear the word in repentance and faith the *solutio* or forgiveness of sins, which has indubitably been imparted to them individually (i.e., by God): but to unbelievers the retention of their sins. Hence since the power of the keys comprises the keys of loosing and binding, really only the former belongs to the *potestas ministerii*, since the latter is rather the *potestas disciplinae*.—HEIDEGGER (*Med.* XXVII, 21): "Therefore it is general, this power of the keys and the power of preaching the Gospel to Jews and Gentiles, and so of teaching, advising, convicting, consoling, judging and in these ways of binding (retaining sins in unbelievers) and loosing (remitting sins to believers) with the consent of the Church, to which (and in her to the apostles and pastors, particularly in Peter as an example) this power was given by Christ. And this power given to all ministers of the Church is one and equal, because no one person has been endowed with greater power than all the rest."

47.—But the power of the keys is not a judicial warrant, but only authority to proclaim the divine will revealed with indubitable certainty in the Gospel, in its relation and application to the individual. Hence the sinner receives absolution, i.e., the comfort of the forgiveness of sins, proclaimed indeed by the preacher but imparted by God. And as therefore every imparting of absolution to a godless hypocrite is empty and meaningless, so the condition of the validity of absolution is not faith in the absolute authority of the preacher, who could arbitrarily and *ex opere operato* remit and retain sins, but solely saving faith in Christ.

The main propositions in connection with fixing the doctrine of absolution are expounded by all dogmaticians pretty much as by OLEVIAN p. 282: "Moreover as the ambassador himself gives neither repentance nor faith, 2 Tim. 2. 19-20 (the Lord knoweth them that are his, etc.), so neither does he justify or absolve sinners himself, but is a witness and appointed herald of so great a matter belonging to the divine majesty; not in his own but in Christ's name, Christ meanwhile freely using this preaching or instrument and opening the hearts of those he wishes to attend to what is said, and in this way by faith to receive the remission of sins inspired by Christ himself, with the interposition of the minister's labours to lead them to repentance and faith as is seen in the case of Lydia the purple seller, Ac. 16. 14-15."—p. 283: We must also consider that the promise of forgiveness of sins and the authority, which God's servant has, to impart absolution, refers only to believers and holds only for them.

"This remission of sins or reconciliation to God and life eternal as the result is not promised in God's name to others than believers in the Son of God. And this is so because the promise of the Gospel belongs to them all and to them only. Jn. 3.—Therefore if the minister absolve one who does not believe in the Son of God, the absolution is void. Christ says that he who believes in the Son of God has everlasting life; he who does not believe, the wrath of God abides on him.—p.284: The condition of the validity of absolution is thus not the mighty perfection of God's servant, who can arbitrarily remit and retain sins, but faith in Christ."

48.—The subject to whom God has transferred the power of the keys is the whole Church, the communion of believers, which may allow it to be used orderly only through its ordinary servants.—MARESIUS (XVI, 70): "While these keys were assigned to the whole Church for her edification, strictly speaking they must be handled by her ministers only."

49.—The second part of the Church's power is the *potestas ordinis*, i.e., "the faculty of the Church by which she deals with the establishment both of doctrine and of the dogmas of faith, and of the laws of outward polity in the Church" (BUCAN XLIII, 12). This is not so to be regarded, as though by her own judicial authority the Church might prove that of the word of God or create new dogmas or set up an infallible interpretation of Scripture. The *potestas ordinis* rather consists in the Church preserving H. Scripture and expounding it in accordance with the norms given in Scripture, and setting up Church confessional writings, the repute of which must not in any way be compared with that of H. Scripture. The authority of Church confessional documents rests entirely on the authority of H. Scripture, which is the exclusive *norma veritatis*, whereas they are only the "norm of the doctrine received in a particular Church." Hence while H. Scripture binds the Christian in his conscience and before God, confessional documents can only obligate him before the forum of the outward Church fellowship, but in his conscience only so far as they are discovered to be in agreement with the Word of God.— The Church possesses no real power by which she might bind consciences. MARESIUS (XVI, 71-72): "The *potestas ordinis*, the constant rule of which is the word of God, is twofold, according as it is concerned either with doctrine or with εὐταξία. As regards doctrine the Church does not give an authority to the word of God which it does not possess; does not make non-canonical books canonical; does not strike out new articles of faith as the *Papists* imagine. But she defends the truth accredited by Scripture and clears it of heretical twists and formulae of consent forced upon Scripture, and those within which her own people are contained she is eager to fortify.—72: As regards εὐταξία in matters naturally outward and indifferent she sets up those she thinks most likely to further edification, not in order that, as is the vicious way in the *Papacy*, they may become an essential part of divine worship, the norm of which is to be sought in God's word alone; but in order that they may be its supports and instruments suited to persons, times and places, as things concerned solely with the determination of outward circumstances, which may be altered in various ways to meet the exigencies of public edification."—RIISSEN (XVI, 29): "The power of the Church concerning dogmas does not consist in the Church winning authority for the word or creating new dogmas of faith, or in interpreting Scripture αὐτοκρατορικῶς and infallibly at her pleasure, or in being the supreme judge in controversies, of which we have already spoken earlier. But it consists (1) in the guarding and expounding of Scripture; (2) in judging what the Church ought to do in the matter of doctrine and in the symbols and confessions which she is bound to construct, in order to preserve doctrine and to bind the Church fellowship together. This authority ought indeed to be great in the Churches. But it still falls below the authority of Scripture. And they are at most secondary norms not of truth but of the doctrine received in a particular Church, since by them may be perceived and discerned what accords with the Church's doctrine and what disagrees with it. Thus they are obligatory in the court of the outward fellowship, not in the inward court of conscience, except so far as they are realised to be suitable to the word of God."—TURRETIN explains this more fully (XVIII, xxx, 9-10): "The authority of these (public confessions of the Church) should be great in the Churches among the godly, yet it falls below the authority of Scripture. The latter is the rule, the former is the thing regulated. The latter alone is αὐτόπιστος and both in words and in matter is divine and infallible. The former, as in matter they are divine, yet in language and in mode of treatment are human documents. To the latter faith is due directly and absolutely; the former must be judged, and by such mediation be believed, if they agree with the word. The latter is the fixed and unchangeable rule of faith, but the former are liable to fresh revision and examination, in which it is right not only to explain and expand them, but also to correct any flaw noticed in them and to reform them by the norm of the word. Whence it is clear that they err in excess here, who make such confessions replace the norm of actual truth and equate them with the word of God, since at most they are but secondary norms, not of truth but of the doctrine received in a particular Church, since by them may be perceived and discerned, what agrees with the Church's doctrine or what disagrees with it.—10: Thus their true authority is to be found in the fact that they are binding on those who are liable to them in the forum of the outward fellowship, because written by the Churches or in the name of the Churches. by which the individual members in the outward communion are bound, 1 Cor. 14 32 (the spirits of the prophets are subject to the prophets). Accordingly if they think they see in them anything worth correcting, they should undertake nothing rashly or ἀτάκτως and unseasonably, so as vitally to disturb their mother's innards, as schismatics do, but should commend the difficulties they have to their Church; or either put her public opinion before their own private judgment, or break away from her communion, if conscience cannot acquiesce in her judgment. Thus they cannot bind in the inward court of conscience, except so far as they are found to agree with the Word of God, which alone has the power to bind conscience."—TURRETIN

(XVIII, xxxi, 1): "Does the Church possess legislative power in the strict sense to pass laws binding *per se* on conscience, or only a διαλεκτική power of sanctioning constitutions and canons *ad εὐταξίαν*? The former is denied, the latter affirmed, against the *Papists*."

50.—To the *potestas ordinis* there also belongs in addition the Church's right to ordain ceremonies for the worthy observance of divine worship, which yet must always be regarded as a matter of Christian freedom without any religious or essential value.—HEIDEGGER (*Med.* XXVII, 29): "Rule is also in vogue as to the ceremonies of the Church. Such is man's infirmity that without outward and visible supports he can scarce be suitably instructed in the doctrine of the Word of God or built up in faith in Christ and his Kingdom. Of these there are two kinds divinely instituted, to which first of all the sacraments are referred—and (ceremonies) of εὐταξία, which deal with administrations of sacraments and the order and seemliness of all outward worship. Of them it must be held generally that in them we have not a part of the divine service, but the exercise of ecclesiastical order, foresight and the defining power left to the Church."

A peculiar contrast between *Reformed* and *Lutheran* doctrinal fashion became fixed in the doctrine of things indifferent. *Lutheran* dogmaticians insisted that under no circumstances is it permissible "to take opponents' *adiaphora* into favour or to put ancient ones out of vogue." Against this the *Reformed* teach (WENDELIN *Coll.* p. 331) that "if with opponents' consent ceremonies are indisputably indifferent and yet some section persists rather stubbornly in its custom, and there is a risk of greater and more dangerous discord and confusion, some indulgence and concession may be made without danger."

51.—The third part of the Church's power (*potestas*) is Church discipline. "Ecclesiastica l discipline is the ecclesiastical pedagogy instituted by auththority of the Word of God, by which men received into the family of Christ are guided and constrained towards godliness, so as to commit nothing unworthy of the Christian profession; but if they sin they are convicted, adjured and corrected, that they may return to the Way and individually do their duty according to the prescript of evangelical doctrine." (BUCAN XLIV, 2). It is concerned with those sins by which the Church is given public offence. The most essential rules in accordance with which Church discipline should be handled, Christ has described himself, Mt. 18. 15 (if thy brother sin against thee etc., etc.) Hence if the means for improving the sinner, which brotherly love puts into one's hands, are exhausted to no purpose, the Church has to proceed against him in such a way, that if he does not listen to her exhortation, she excludes him from the communion of the Supper, (minor excommunication, lesser ban); and, if this also remains without effect, from Church fellowship generally (major excommunication, greater ban). But like Church discipline generally the ban also must invariably be handled in the spirit of ministering love, which is why even the greater ban is to be proclaimed never in the form of a curse on the sinner, but so that the person excommunicated is assured, in case of his conversion, of re-assumption into the bosom of the Kirk.

PICTET, (XIII, xi, 6): "This power is concerned with the exercise of discipline. Public sinners are thereby corrected, convicted of impurity in doctrine of life, and after the rejection and contempt of the private and public admonitions or the Church, they are debarred by the order and authority of the Presbytery from the signs of divine grace and, if they persevere in such contumacy, they finally pronounce them excluded in the name of God from the communion of the Church until reconciled by true repentance to God and the Church."—BURMANN (VIII, v. 25): "The parts of discipline are brotherly *correptio* and excommunication. *Correptio* is either private or public. The degrees of it are expressed by Christ, Mt. 18. 15. [P,688]"—BRAUN (II, iv, 28, 10): "This is the way and procedure in brotherly censure and *correptio*. (1) He who has sinned against us ought to be *corripi* and exhorted as to his duty: he is to be *corripi* privately. If he hear thee not, (2) one or two brethren must be co-opted, in order that he may be *corripi* in their presence. If he hear not these, (3) either the Church must be told or those who are called by the Church to the public ministry. If he hear not the Church either, (4) he is to be separated from the Church, as though infected with scabies and regarded as a publican and a heathen; i.e., one who lacks faith and so who is not a member of the Church and with whom no fraternal dealings are to be held on Christ's advice, Mt. 18. 15 and on Paul's, Tit. 3. 10-11 (a man that is heretical (*or* factious) after a first and second admonition refuse (*or* avoid); knowing that such a one is perverted and sinneth, being self-condemned). See Rom. 16. 17 (mark them which are causing the divisions and occasions of stumbling, contrary to the doctrine which ye learned: and turn away from them) 2 Cor. 2. 9 (you should rather forgive him and comfort him, lest by any means such a one should be swallowed up by overmuch sorrow) 1 Cor. 5. 11-13 (Put away the wicked man from among yourselves) 2 Jn. 10 (If anyone cometh to you, and bringeth not this teaching, receive him not into your house and give him no greeting: for he that giveth him greeting partaketh in his evil works) 2 Th. 3. 14-15 (if any man obeyeth not our word by this epistle, note that man, that ye have no company with him, to the end that he may be ashamed.

And yet count him not as an enemy, but admonish him as a brother).
For such a fellow prayer should be made, that God would bring him
back to the duties of godliness and love. Nor is he plainly to be ejected
from the society of the brethren, but to be separated for a time, not to
be regarded as an enemy, but as a brother to be warned, 2 Th. 3. 14-15
supra. This is called minor excommunication or suspension from things
sacred. If he is not yet converted to all these but ultimately persists in sin,
then (5) as a rotten limb which would corrupt the whole body he is to be
cut off. And this is called major excommunication strictly so called,
in fact even ἀνάθεμα [?].—(23): No one should be excommunicated
to the accompaniment of dire execrations. Nor should anathema or
maranatha be addressed to him. Such judgment should be left to God.
For God alone knows who are His."—BUCAN (XLIV, 16): "The person
excommunicated is excluded not only from participation in sacraments—
this is merely suspension—but from the entire body and benefits of the
Church and from ordinary preservation, conversations, dwelling, intercourse of life with the rest of the members of the Church. We ought to
have no voluntary, familiar commingling with the excommunicate, or
association or communication, 2 Thess. 3. 10 (even when we were with
you, this we commanded you, if any will not work, neither let him eat)
1 Cor. 5. 2 (ye are puffed up and did not rather mourn, that he that had
done this deed might be taken away from among you); but he ought to
be to us as an *ethnicus* [Gentile]".

52.—The purpose of Church discipline is to keep the Church pure and to
edify her and to save the sinner.—WOLLEB 123: "The aim of this power
is to preserve the Church's polish and seemliness (*nitor et decus*) and to
bring back the godless to repentance."—MARESIUS (XVI, 83): "Since
the aim of this discipline is both the edification of the Church and the
salvation of him against whom it is exercised by name, etc."—HEIDEGGER
(*Med.* XXVII, 35) relates concerning the disputed question ventilated
in the Reformed Church, as to whether Church discipline is to be
exercised by the Church or the civic authority, and whether accordingly
the secular government is subject or not to Church discipline, that "this
is the capital reason for ecclesiastical discipline, which ought to be
vigorous and not frigid in the separate Churches. But a controversy
against it was raised by *Thomas Erastus*, a Heidelberg doctor, and after
him in England by *Coleman*, a London minister, who both thought that
the Church was destitute of all power to apply the word of God by way of
censures, particularly excommunication, and that authority for such
discipline as the Church uses depends upon the mere delegation of the
magistrate, and that consequently the magistrate himself is not liable

to the censures of the Church, because nothing more than the public preaching of the word and the administration of the sacraments is competent in her case, since in them all the power of the keys is contained. But Christ openly taught that the power of the keys consists not in preaching alone but also in the rebuke and censures of the Church, Mt. 18. 1-2 [the "classical" chapter]." Fuller discussions on this point in BURMANN (VIII, v, 18).

A second dispute concerned the handling of the great excommunication. HEIDEGGER relates in this connection (*Med.* XXVII, 36): "As to excommunication, which is the extremity of Church judgment the opinion and practice of the Reformed Church varies. Some suspend the excommunicate and those regarded as publicans and Gentiles from the use of the seals of grace and other benefits of the Church, and if the ground of contumacy requires it, they debar them by severe denunciation and threats from all communion proper to saints. Others enacting in the first instance a solemn removal from use of the Supper, which they call the greater excommunication, commit the scandalous and contumacious to the civil power (believing), to be coerced by laws not civil merely but Christian as well. The former, particularly OECOLAMPADIUS, BUCER, CAPITO, CALVIN, were preceded by the old Church, still quite holy and chaste, which showed great vigour at first in the exercise of discipline. For the latter, ZWINGLI, BULLINGER, HALLER, the abuse of the severer discipline and the extreme falling away under the *Papacy*—were the cause of them not abolishing discipline, excommunication and ecclesiastical judgments, but restraining them in the light of the times as well as by the compulsion of the state of the realm, as the *Conf. Helv.* C. 17 says."

53.—All these powers are the attributes of Church discipline proper, which the Church herself exercises. But parallel to them is to be considered the power which belongs to the State in Church matters, the State or worldly government; the *gubernatio ecclesiae civilis.*—HEIDEGGER (*Med.* XXVII, 43): "The government of the Church has been ecclesiastical in the past. It is civil, so far as the believing magistrate, armed with the sword, also cares for the Church along with the State and furthers and protects the pure worship of God, as the custodian of the two tables."

54.—The State has the right to make laws and to watch over their observance; and all that the State ordains without conflicting with the Law of God, obligates the individual to obey and binds him in his conscience, because government is of God.—PICTET (XIII, 13, 2): "What are the functions of the magistrate ? Ans. (1) To institute equitable and just laws and to sanction them with penalties that fit the crime; (2) to administer justice according to the law."—HEIDEGGER (*Med.* XXVII, 46): "The power of the magistrate consists in legislation and in the dispensing of judgments.—But the human laws of the civil power have no validity at all in regard to anything enjoined or forbidden by divine law. They are only valid for things which, where divine laws are not explicit, make for the preservation of order in human society. And so long as they do not sanction anything base or dishonourable, any laws of this kind bind conscience, because obedience depends not only on wrath but also on conscience, Rom. 13. 5 (not only because of the wrath, but also for conscience' sake). Not because conscience of itself is subject to human laws, but because the magistracy is a divine ordinance and so receives from God who ordains it the power to pass laws. And since the power to legislate is invalid without judgments, judicial power also belongs to the magistrate."

55.—But the government's power extends still further. It comprises not only the sphere of civic life but also extends into the Church sphere— but here within quite definite limits, which the government must not pass without hurting the Church.—PICTET (XIII, xiii, 3): "The magistrate deals not only with things civil but also with things sacred, whence to him is entrusted the custody of God's law."—TURRETIN (XVIII, xxxiv, 3): "The orthodox—lay it down, that the godly and believing magistrate cannot and ought not to be excluded from all care of religion and things sacred; such care is demanded of him by God; but that this right must be circumscribed within certain limits, to avoid confusion between the functions of ecclesiastical and political order."— The *Christian* government, as all dogmaticians agree, is the "custodian of the two tables."

56.—Church government proper does not belong to the State.— TURRETIN (XVIII, xxix, 20): "The power of the magistrate in sacred things ought not to abrogate the power which belongs to the rulers of the Church, because although they deal with the same object materially, it is not the same formally. The power of the magistrate is outward, that of the pastor inward. The former is compulsory and corporal, armed as it is with the right and power of the sword; the latter is spiritual, coercing and convincing with spiritual weapons, i.e., with the word of God, and with censures applied to conscience. The former includes *dominium*, the latter only *ministerium*. The former is concerned with the Church and holy things κατὰ τὸ ἔξω, the latter resides in the actual Church and is concerned κατὰ τὸ ἔσω. The former is called ecclesiastical objectively only and improperly; the latter formally and strictly."

57.—The civil government's power extends only *circa sacra* (not *in sacra*); as God's servant it is entitled, or more correctly, bound to further the well-being of the Church in every connection; especially to give her the outward means for achieving her purposes, to support the Church's servants in the exercise of their office, to take measures for upholding Church order, to remove unworthy servants of the Church, to lead the more comprehensive Synods, to found schools, to take up oppressed communions of related faith: on the other hand to prevent the outcropping of false doctrines, and also to give protection against the misuse of Church authority.—HEIDEGGER (*Med.* XXVII, 52): "Anything but simple is the care and power which belongs to the magistrate in religion and the Church. And indeed generally, so far as he is ὁμόπιστος and an excellent member of the Church, he has a share of the same power that belongs to the whole Church. In that case the magistrate's power as such regarding the Church consists in his being able and not able only but also bound to do that, by which he can serve Christ and His kingdom by the power granted him by God and to expand that kingdom. He is God's minister alike to the individuals under him and also to the Church subjected to his *imperium*.—Therefore as regards Christ it is not power but διακονία and κηδεμονία (*ministerium et procuratio*, ministry and delegated rule).—BURMANN (VIII, x, 15): "(The magistrate's duties in things sacred) consist pretty much in the following: (1) It is his to constitute and duly order public rites and ceremonies, so that they may accord with the word of God, by fixing for their exercise suitable places and times and other details requiring to be arranged but not defined in the word of God; to remove hindrances to divine worship and in particular to see to it that God's name is not blasphemed in his territories and that things heretical and unseemly do not obtain publicly. (2) To care for the public ministry and ministers, that the former is pure and complete, and that the latter do their duty. Although in their offices ministers are not the magistrate's representatives, any more than is the paterfamilias in ruling a household, the office having been instituted by Christ and deriving its authority from him; nevertheless his public care was given to the magistrate [by God], nor are ministers to be withdrawn from his inspection in the execution of their office. (3) In fact he should even preside at the callings of them and take precautions in entrusting these offices, that none but worthy men are put in charge of assemblages (*coetus*), and not tolerate others in their territory, also honour faithful teachers and support them with revenues publicly appointed. (4) In this direction also tends the power to depose a minister both on other charges and for defilement of doctrine or character after King Solomon's example, 1 K. 2. 26-28. 35-36 (the extrusion of Abiathar and the appointment of Zadok). Deposition and abdication from public office are part of his jurisdiction. (5) It is also his to call Synods to discuss ecclesiastical cases, and to take part in the pastors' deliberations and moderate in them; in short to lend his authority to their decrees, and, that they may pass into public laws, to confirm them by his edicts. (6) Further he may admit the complaints of those who complain of injury from ecclesiastical measures and order a fresh cognisance of the case and grant other judges. And finally where he sees a man oppressed by a faction, he may judge of the whole matter. (7) Schools also and public establishments of good repute and seminaries of Christian doctrine he is bound to erect and equip and protect according to his powers.—(8) Where religion is corrupt and where the state of the Church has collapsed, the task of cleansing it again and restoring it to its former glory belongs quite pre-eminently to the magistrate.—(9) And since Christ's spouse and Church is one, the guardianship of which as a whole and its oversight so to speak is entrusted not to one singly but to one and all in common, princes must not only provide for the Churches in their jurisdiction, but where the brethren elsewhere are harassed and oppressed, succour them with help, advice, intercession and in other ways.—16: (10) Finally also he ought to do his duty by the heterodox and heretics, both in curing them and in composing and restraining them and in warding off creeping decay from the churches."

CHAPTER XXVIII.

GLORIFICATION.

1.—Since the glorification of God is the purpose of all things, and since as the original source of all blessedness God wills to be glorified in the faithful, the latter are called by the Father not only to the enjoyment of Christ's grace but also to Christ's glory, which however, is not imparted to the elect in its entire perfection until after death.— a DIEST (p. 486): "The state of grace having been explained, follows lastly the state of glory".—ALTING p. 119: "There remains the means of applying (salvation), which looks to life and the age to come and is but one. It is called glorification, which begins in this life, 2 Cor. 3. 18 (we all, with unveiled face reflecting as a mirror the glory of the Lord, are transformed into the same image from glory to glory, even as from the Lord the Spirit) but is consummated in the second, Rom. 8. 17 (if children, then heirs; heirs of God and joint-heirs with Christ; if so be that we suffer with him, that we may be also glorified with him)."—AMESIUS (I, xli, 2): "Then the end of their calling will be present to all the called; for we are called to the eternal glory of God".—WITSIUS (III, xiv, 1): "As all God's actions tend to His glory, so they also tend to the glorification of His elect. It is of course God's glory to show Himself in the elect as He is to Himself, the source of bliss achieved. When He does this, He is glorified in His saints, and becomes admirable among believers, 2 Th. 2. 10 (with all deceit of unrighteousness for them that are perishing; because they received not the love of truth, that they might be saved)."

2.—Since therefore death for the believer is essentially nothing else than the sure road to glorification, the terrors have thereby ceased for him.— HEIDEGGER (Med. XXVIII, 2): "Glorification is either of the soul separately or of the whole man.—3: The separation of soul from body takes place in death, by which the tabernacle of its earthly house is dissolved.—The death of believers is quite different from this, toto caelo.—4: None the less death is still to be feared to a certain extent by believers; —but the Spirit soothes that fear by faith and hope, contains it within the barriers of godliness, refers it to God's glory and the mortification of the flesh."—COCCEIUS (Summ. theol. XCIV, 7): "Wherefore also the death of the godly or any affliction, though they seem to be sad things, ought not to be received as a punishment. For thereby we are freed from sin."

3.—The glorification of the elect person originates in the first instance in his soul, since separated from the body by death it is at once carried to heaven,—whereas the soul of one who dies in unbelief reaches hell

695

at once.—*Conf. Helv.* (II, 26): "We believe that the faithful pass straight from bodily death to Christ and that therefore they have no need of the suffrages or prayers of the living on behalf of the deceased, or indeed of any of their offices. We also believe that unbelievers are hurled straight to hell (*tartara*), from which no issue is opened up for any godless persons through any offices of the living."—Cf. HEIDEGGER (*Med.* XXVIII, (12).—BEZA (Epist. 82).—GÜRTLER p. 940.—BERNSAU p. 384.

4.—This glorification of the believing soul, which of course maintains the full identity of its being after death, consists in its being freed from the body of sin and death and its achievement of complete sanctification and arrival in heaven, where in the enjoyment of heavenly bliss and in eternal praising of the Lord it persists till the perfection of its own glorification by reunion with its body and till the final completion of the kingdom of God.—ALTING p. 119: "The glorification of the separated soul consists in several steps; as (1) full and accomplished sanctification, the body of sin and death having been laid aside; (2) transportation by the angels to heaven; (3) immunity from the miseries of this life; (4) the fruition of heavenly joy and glory; (5) the praising and lauding of God and Christ; (6) the longing for and expectation of full glorification, both by the restoration of its own body, and by God's final deliverance of the Church."—CALVIN (III, xxv, 6): "To inquire curiously into their (the souls') intermediate state is neither right nor expedient [see CALVIN in the *Psychopannychia*]. Many torture themselves outrageously by discussing what place they occupy and whether or not they enjoy heavenly glory. And yet it is foolish and rash to inquire into matters unknown more deeply than God allows us to know.—No less foolish and futile is it to ask about the place, when we know that this dimension is not of soul but of body."

5.—By its separation from the body the soul does not reach its perfect glorification yet. That rather directly presupposes the reunion of the soul with the body, since God has adopted us into the covenant of grace not in soul only but also in body (OLEVIAN p. 93). In order therefore to raise believers to perfect glory and bliss and to give thereby the final conclusion to his work of redemption, Christ will one day return to the earth in a real, visible and local manner.—ALTING p. 119 : "In man's glorification there are three steps: the resurrection of the dead, the last judgment and eternal life."—AMESIUS (I, xli, 9): "This final perfection of administration demands the personal arrival and presence of Christ himself."—POLAN (VI, 65): "This arrival of Christ will be true, visible and local, not phantastic or imaginary or invisible or placeless."—Similarly ZANCHIUS p. 286.

6.—The day of this reappearance of Christ on earth (*dies novissimus, dies Domini*), which will be manifested when all the elect are introduced to the enjoyments of the covenant of grace, is known only to God; but its near approach will certainly be announced by signs. To this sign especially belongs the spreading of the Gospel over all the earth, the rise in the Church of antichrist, who arrayed in great power will try quite directly to destroy the work of the Lord, before its final completion and the conversion of Israel.—POLAN (VI, 66): "The universal (general) resurrection of the dead is the work of God, by which, after the fulfilment of the number of the elect, all men dead from the beginning of the world shall rise again from the dust of the earth, their souls having been reunited to their bodies."—RIISSEN (XVIII, 5): The "diagnostic signs" of Christ's approaching parousia are "either common or proper and special. Common are those reviewed by Christ, Mt. 24, Mk. 13, Lk. 21, where the references to the destruction of Jerusalem also belong to the end of the world", above all "the universal preaching of the Gospel over the whole earth."—"The proper and special signs are: (1) the revelation of antichrist and the extreme corruption of the truth in the Christian Church, of which Paul speaks, 2 Th. 2. 3 (let no man beguile you in any wise: for it will not be, except the falling away come first, and the man of sin be revealed, the son of perdition).—(2) The conversion of the Jews, Rom. 11. 12, 15, 16 (if their fall is the riches of the world, and their loss the riches of the Gentiles; how much more their fulness?)—(3) Changes in heaven, in the sun, the moon and the stars (Mt. 24; Mk. 13; Lk. 21). —(4) Finally there is the concomitant sign, with which Christ deals, Mt. 24. 40 (then shall two men be in the field; one is taken and one is left), namely the mysterious "sign of the Son of man in heaven—over which the commentators harass themselves in vain."

For the covenant of grace the hope of Christ's return is of essential moment. Thereby believers have the certainty that sometime there will come a day of consummation, in which the slave form of God's kingdom ceases, when sin in them is completely slain and God will be glorified in them. Then the Son of God, who suffered on earth as an evildoer, will be manifested before all the world as God's righteous one, who gives life to all who believe in his name (OLEVIAN p. 155).

7.—With Christ's return to earth there will follow first of all the resurrection of the dead, in fact of all the dead. "The resurrection of the dead is the action of God, Father, Son and H. Spirit, whereby by His almighty power, at the archangel's trumpet, at the end of the ages, the bodies of all men, godly and ungodly alike, even though reduced to dust, shall be restored by Him to the same souls from which they were separated by death, to be united and informed by them for an endless duration, in order that the godless may pay the penalties of their crimes, the godly, being presented with eternal bliss, may enjoy the same eternally" (LEIDEN SYNOPSIS LI, 16). This hope, which must remain eternally incomprehensible, to which yet is joined for the believer the sure comfort of the dissolution some day of the covenant of works (COCCEIUS, *Summ. de foed.* XVI, 669), belongs to the most essential and individual signs of the Christian consciousness, since precisely in faith in Christ's resurrection and in the rearousing of their own bodies is preserved faith in the new order of life and in its eventual victory, which God has set up in opposition to the natural order of things, according to which death is the end of all earthly life.—LEIDEN SYNOPSIS (LI, 3): "This article (on the resurrection) makes a distinction between *ethnici* and Christians, as *Tertullian* has rightly observed that the *fiducia* of Christians is the resurrection of the dead. And what *Augustine* said of the Head is applicable to all the members: that Christ died, pagans and enemies believe; but that Christ rose, is the peculiar faith of Christians: that all men are thus liable to death, all ethnics see and agree; but when it comes to resurrection, it seems ληρώδης λόγος (Ac. 17. 32)."

8.—The resurrection of the dead is the work of the creative omnipotence of the triune God, in that Christ is thereby effective in relation to believers as the Prince of life, and in relation to the ungodly as their future Judge. —HEIDEGGER (*Med.* XXVIII, 33): "God alone by His almighty word will recall His dead.—Yet in a unique way is assigned to Christ, as the second Adam made εἰς πνεῦμα ζωοποιοῦν, 1 Cor. 15. 45, the work of resuscitation, because he will raise both the godly as the Avenger (*vindex*) of their blood, Jn. 5. 29 (they that have done good, unto the resurrection of life; they that have done ill, unto the resurrection of judgment) and the ungodly as their future Judge."—LEIDEN SYNOPSIS (LI, 22): "This effect, which is common to the three persons (of the Deity), cannot be accomplished by the virtue of any natural cause, but solely by the divine power. No natural cause can reproduce the same thing numerically. And there is no such thing in nature as a regress from privation to habit, such as is required from death to resurrection."

9.—The faith that some day God will really execute this work rests generally, on the one hand upon the evidences of Scripture which guarantee that at the end of days God wills to raise the dead; and on the other hand upon faith in God's omnipotence, according to which God can also execute what He wills and according to which He will therefore really execute the promise given in the covenant of grace, that His benefits shall be for the benefit of the whole man in body and in soul.—LEIDEN SYNOPSIS (LI, 5): "We shall sustain our faith on the two levers indicated to us by Christ, Mt. 22. 29 (. . . ye do err, not knowing the Scriptures, nor the power of God), when in their denial of the resurrection he recalled the Sadducees to Scripture and the power of God, ignorance of which he disclosed as the source of their error; on the other hand for faith he laid two foundations concerning this article, knowledge of the divine will out of Scripture and of the divine power from the nature of it. Since the resuscitation of the dead is a divine action and since there are two necessary and sufficient principles, will and faculty, we must also have regard to them in this work of resurrection. These two things, being conjoined in God, in whom there is no ἀδυναμία, put the thing in action, because our Lord in heaven hath done whatsoever things he would."— The Scripture passages by which the resurrection of the dead is proved are (RIISSEN XVIII, 2): Ps. 16. 9-10 (therefore my heart is glad, and my glory rejoiceth: my flesh also shall dwell in safety. For thou wilt not leave my soul in Sheol: neither wilt thou suffer thy holy one to see corruption) 17. 15 (as for me, I shall behold thy face in righteousness: I shall be satisfied, when I awake, with thy likeness) Is. 25. 7 (and he will destroy in this mountain the face of the covering that is cast over all peoples, and the veil that is spread over all nations. He hath swallowed up death for ever . . .) 26. 19 (thy dead shall live; my dead bodies shall arise. Awake and sing, ye that dwell in the dust: for thy dew is as the dew of herbs, and the earth shall cast forth the dead), Ezek. 37. 1-3 (the valley of dry bones) Dan. 12. 1-2 (And at that time shall Michael stand up, the great prince which standeth for the children of thy people: and there shall be a time of trouble, such as never was since there was a nation even to that same time; and at that time thy people shall be delivered, every one that shall be found written in the book. And many of them that sleep in the dust of the earth shall awake, some to everlasting life, and some to shame and everlasting contempt, Hos. 13. 14 (I will ransom them from the power of the grave; I will redeem them from death: O death, where are thy plagues? O grave where is thy destruction? Repentance shall be hid from mine eyes), Jn. 5. 28-29 (Marvel not at this: for the hour cometh, in which all that are in the tombs shall hear his voice, and shall come forth; they that have done good unto the resurrection of judgment) 6. 39 (and this is the will of him that sent me, that of all that which he hath given me I should lose nothing, but should raise it up at the last day) 11. 24 (Martha saith unto him, I know that he shall rise again in the resurrection at the last day), Ac. 4. 2 (being sore troubled because they taught the people and proclaimed in Jesus the resurrection from the dead) 17. 18 (and certain also of the Epicurean and Stoic philosophers encountered him. And some said, What would this babbler say? other some, He seemeth to be a setter forth of strange gods: because he preached Jesus and the resurrection) 23. 6 (But when Paul perceived that the one part were Sadducees, and the other Pharisees, he cried out in the council, Brethren, I am a Pharisee, a son of Pharisees; touching the hope and resurrection of the dead I am called in question) etc.—RIISSEN sets out in addition the following arguments for the resurrection (XVIII, 2, 1) : " (1) from God's covenant, because, since it necessarily involves perfect felicity and eternal life, it cannot be fulfilled in us unless along with the immortality of spirits resurrection of the bodies is also given, so that the whole man may participate in the benefits of the covenant for ever.—(2) from God's righteousness, which orders rewards to be paid to the good and punishments to the bad also, in the body which sinned. Since this is not always done in this life, it must be done after this life, when bodies have been raised, 2 Cor. 5. 10 (we must all be made manifest before the judgment seat of Christ; that each one may receive the things done in the body, according to what he hath done, whether it be good or bad) 2 Th. 1. 6-7 (if so be that it is a righteous thing with God to recompense affliction to them that afflict you, and to you that are afflicted rest with us, at the revelation of the Lord Jesus from heaven with the angels of his power).—(3) from the examples of those who have already been raised in OT and NT, 1 K. 17. 21 (And he stretched himself upon the child three times, and cried unto the LORD, and said, O Lord, my God, I pray thee, let this child's soul come into him again. And the LORD hearkened unto the voice of Elijah; and the soul of the child came into him again, and he revived. . .etc.) 2 K. 4 (Elishah and the Shunnamite's son), 2 K. 13 (Joash and the LORD's arrow for victory), Mk. 5. 41 (Talitha, coumi), Lk. 7. 15 (widow of Nain), Jn. 11 (raising of Lazarus).

10.—And God will so effect the raising, that every soul will be re-united with its own body, with which it was clothed on earth. The risen bodies will therefore be identical in number and substance with those who have lived on earth; for "this" flesh will be resuscitated.—CALVIN (III, xxv, 7): "Equally phenomenal is the error of those who imagine that souls will not receive the bodies with which they are clothed at present, but will be endued with other fresh ones. And the *Manichees*' reasoning was pretty bad, that it is anything but agreeable that flesh which is unclean should rise again. As if there is no uncleanness in souls, whom yet they did not cut off from the hope of heavenly life. Thus it was just as if they said that it cannot be divinely cleansed because it has been infected with the defilement of sin.—If God were forming new bodies, wherein would this change in quality consist? 1 Cor. 15. 53 (this corruptible must put on incorruption etc. . . . .)."—LEIDEN SYNOPSIS (LI, 24): "Now we must deal with the substance (of resurrection), which is called by some *subjectum quo*. Well, it is strictly the flesh (*caro*) or body of a man, because resurrection takes place according to the body, not strictly according to the soul. Neither does a man's soul perish, being immortal; and when a body is restored to earth, the spirit returns to God who made it, Eccl. 12. 7.—25: Now we say that the body will rise the same in number and substance."—HEIDEGGER (*Med.* XXVIII, 37): "The body which has died will rise again the same numerically, for we believe in the resurrection of this flesh."

11.—Of course the bodies of the godless as of the pious are raised in a higher state, namely in that of imperishability, so that never again shall they become death's prey. Yet they will retain in essence the fleshly nature of their substance and even their sexuality, though without making use of it.—WOLLEB p. 158: "The form (of the resurrection) is contemplated in —deliverance from corruption;—the godly will also be beautified with glory."—BUCAN (XXXVII, 2): "Resurrection is the restoration of the same human body to life in the same substance, less mortality.—14: The bodies of the unrighteous will rise again immortal and incorruptible, it is true, yet passible."—LEIDEN SYNOPSIS (LI, 37): "With *Augustine* we do not hesitate to assert that in the resurrection there will be distinction of séxes, which is a right inference from the fact that, when asked whose of the seven brothers she would be the wife, whom each of them had married, Christ did not deny that there would be women in the resurrection; which would have been a complete answer, had it been true; he only denied that there would be marriages. That there would still be a female sex he established, by declaring that they shall not marry, referring to women, nor take in marriage, referring to men. Therefore there will be women who normally get married here, there will also be those who normally take in marriage; but they will not do so there (*De civit. Dei, lib.* 22, *cap.* 17)."

12.—This resurrection of the dead will be a general one. Therefore a particular resurrection of the righteous and the institution of a 1,000 year kingdom of them before the end of the times and before the last judgment is not to be assumed.—HEIDEGGER (*Med.* XXVIII, 37): "The resurrection will be universal, not only of the just, but also of the unjust." Similarly RIJSSEN (XVIII, 2, 2).

13.—At the same time the resuscitation of the righteous will result differently from that of the godless. The former, in virtue of their living unity with Christ the Prince of life, and in virtue of the Spirit of God dwelling in them, will be reunited by Christ to their bodies and will at once be taken to their Lord to meet him; whereas in the resuscitation of the godless it is purely the omnipotence of God that is displayed."—AMESIUS (XLI,

18): "All will be raised by Christ, not however in one and the same way: the resurrection of believers is to life and is accomplished in virtue of that union which they have with Christ as their life, and by the operation of his quickening Spirit who dwells in them. But the resurrection of others is by that power of Christ's by which he executes punishing righteousness."—BUCAN (XXXVII, 9): "(The godless) shall indeed rise, but not by the benefit, power and efficacy of Christ's resurrection—by the necessity and efficacy of the divine decree."—ZANCHIUS p. 209: "We believe that when Christ appears in his majesty and glory all the godly will go to meet him, translated to the clouds from earth to heaven 1 Th. 5. 1 (concerning the times and the seasons . . . the day of the Lord so cometh as a thief in the night) Mt. 24. 3 (when shall these things be ? . . . the sign of thy coming and of the end of the world ? . . . Take heed!) 25. 31 (when the Son of man shall come in his glory, and all the angels with him, then shall he sit on the throne of his glory)—GUERTLER p. 928: "We shall be rapt into the clouds to meet the Lord in the air, as the fable is foolish, that the last judgment will be accomplished in the valley of Jehoshaphat, having arisen from an ill understood prophecy of Joel."

14.—For believers therefore Christ's resurrection is the God-given guarantee of their own resuscitation, since the Head cannot possibly be without the members; and at the same time Christ's merit is for them the guarantee of the glory and bliss in which their bodies will rise.—LEIDEN SYNOPSIS (LI, 20): "It follows that not even for the elect did Christ merit resurrection *simpliciter*, but resurrection of a kind, i.e. *blessed* and *glorious*."—ARETIUS, p. 57: "In this (resurrection of Christ) the hope has been confirmed for us of the resurrection of our bodies. For since the Head shall have risen, it is altogether necessary that the several members must be raised."

15.—This general resurrection of the dead must at the same time result in the accompanying change of those still alive into the new and higher status of those who rise.—RIISSEN (XVIII, 3): "Thus we assert the general resurrection of all men, except that we should wish those to be excepted, who at the time of Christ's advent are destined to survive, and who, we learn from Paul, 1 Cor. 15. 51-52 (Behold, I tell you a mystery: We shall not all sleep, but we shall all be changed, in a moment, in the twinkling of an eye, at the last trump: for the trumpet shall sound, and the dead shall be raised incorruptible, and we shall be changed) 1 Thess. 4. 15-16-17 (this we say unto you by the word of the Lord, that we that are alive, that are left unto the presence of the Lord, shall in no wise precede them that are fallen asleep. The Lord himself shall descend from heaven with a shout, with the voice of the archangel, and with the trump of God: and the dead in Christ shall rise first: then we that are alive, that are left, shall together with them be caught up in the clouds, to meet the Lord in the air: and so shall we ever be with the Lord), are not there-fore to be aroused from a death which they are not destined to feel, but only to be changed."—Similarly ALTING p. 119 and others.—The view that the unintelligent creation also would be resurrected is rejected by POLAN (VI, 66): "Further, there will be no resurrection of brute beasts. —What is said in Rom. 8. 21 (the creation itself also shall be delivered from the bondage of corruption into the liberty of the glory of the children of God) is not understood of brute beasts, but of the heavenly mechanism of the world (mundus) and of the ethereal region, which will be put into that happy state of incorruption, instead of the corruption to which they are now bound because of man's sins." [The Russians pray for the 'innocent animals' who give their innocent lives for man].

16.—Herewith is prepared the judgment, which Christ will hold after his return. "The last judgment is the judicial act by which on the last day, immediately upon the resurrection of the dead, Christ in great majesty and glory will pronounce sentence on all men, will separate the elect from the reprobate, and adjudge the former to life eternal, the latter to unquenchable fire" (BUCAN XXVIII, 4). This court is held by the triune God, but consummated personally by the God-man—yet so that he will not act as the mere commissioner of the Father, but as Lord over all (which he is by the Father's will) and as the king of his kingdom (which he is in virtue of his merit). As a man, therefore Christ will appear visibly and act visibly, and as the Father's Son he will deliver judgment with divine infallibility and power.

LEIDEN SYNOPSIS (LI, 47): "The chief efficient cause of this judgment is God the Father, Son and H. Spirit, if we view the authority in the utterance of the sentence and the power behind the execution of it. But this judgment will be administered in visible form through the Son in the assumed human nature. He will judge not only according to the divine, but also according to the human nature, to which by grace was given autocratic power, from which there will be no appeal, because by his death he acquired for himself the right of Lordship over all men Rom. 14. 9 (to this end Christ died, and lived again, that he might be Lord of both the dead and the living). Now part of his dominium is judgment."—RIISSEN (XVIII, 9): "As judge Christ will be in that actual nature, in which he was condemned for us. Although judicial power is common to the whole Trinity, it will be exercised specially through the incarnate Son. Judgment is said to have been delivered to him by the Father Jn. 5. 22 (neither doth the Father judge any man, but hath given all judgment to the Son) Ac. 10. 42 (he charged us . . . to testify that this is he which is ordained of God to be the judge of quick and dead) 17. 31 (inasmuch as he hath appointed a day, in the which he will judge the world in righteousness by the man whom he hath ordained; whereof he hath given assurance unto all men, in that he hath raised him from the dead), as the king of his Church, the champion of his elect, avenger against the godless, the Lord of all, etc. Moreover both Christ's natures should concur here in the exercise of that office. From the divine nature emanate heavenly authority, rule and wisdom, to scrutinise the secrets and the dark places of hearts,—by which indeed a human being will appear conspicuously in visible majesty on the clouds as on a judgment-seat, will present himself as judge and will pronounce the sentence delivered in sight of all."—AMESIUS (I, xli): "The final judgment is exercised by Christ as by a king; the power of delivering judgment is part of a king's office.—21: As regards the believing it proceeds from grace and is the function of the kingdom of grace essential to Christ the Mediator; but as regards unbelievers it is only of the power and dominion granted by the Father, looking indeed to a perfection of mediation, but not an essential perfection."

17.—Before Christ's presence, then, all men, good and bad, who have ever lived, as well as the bad angels, shall appear, while the good angels meet him only to glorify his manifestation.—LEIDEN SYNOPSIS (LI, 59): " The *materia circa quam* or the object of the last judgment, if we look at persons, are all bad angels and all men, good and bad alike."

18.—The norm according to which Christ will pronounce judgment upon individuals is the gospel revealed by him, whereby Christ will consider man's works as the fruits and proofs of his faith or unbelief in himself.— WENDELIN (*Coll.* p. 498): "The norm of this judgment will be: Whosoever believeth shall be saved, Jn. 3. 18 (he that believeth on him is not judged; he that believeth not hath been judged already, because he hath not believed on the only begotten Son of God) and 12. 49 (I spake not from myself: but the Father which sent me, he hath given me commandment, what I should say, and what I should speak. He that rejecteth me and receiveth not my sayings, hath one that judgeth him: the word that I spake, the same shall judge him in the last day (v. 48): and, Rom. 2. 16 [through conscience, etc.] in the day when God shall judge the secrets of men, according to my gospel, by Jesus Christ)."— BUCAN (XXXVIII, 12): "Although the godly will also be acquitted by the voice of the law, so far as Christ fulfilled it on their behalf, and by the same law—the ungodly will be condemned, yet the voice, not so much of the law as of the gospel, which the apostles preached, will be the norm (of the last judgment)."

19.—But Christ will deal with the elect godly otherwise than with the ungodly. The former, whose good works Christ will manifest as effects of his gracious fellowship already bestowed upon them, he will acknowledge before all the world as his own who belong to him, so that there will be no mention of their sins, forgiveness of which has long ago been assured to them. Hence the godly will not really be judged, but Christ will separate them from the others, that they may be witnesses of the righteousness of his real judgments, by which he turns over ungodly angels and men from their own works to their godlessness and worthy condemnation.—WOLLEB (p. 160): "The godless will be judged according to and on account of their works, the godly according to their works of faith, but not on account of their works.—Both their infidelity and their godlessness will so be put before the eyes of the ungodly, that they will be unable to deny or contradict anything."—The reason is the following (AMESIUS, I, xli): 29: "Believers will also judge along with Christ, by their presence, not taking counsel but approving, as much by judgment and will, as by compassion for their own life and works.—22: Hence the sins of believers will not come up for judgment. Since in this life they have been covered and removed by the sentence of justification, and since the last judgment will be the confirmation and manifestation of the same sentence, it would not be congruous that they should be brought to light afresh at this juncture."

TURRETIN (XX, vi, 17): "If here asked whether the sins of the godly as well as of the ungodly are to be revealed, we reply that the negative seems more probable: (1) because of the judge who, since he has made the fullest satisfaction for us and now intercedes in heaven on our behalf will then come as redeemer and saviour, not to reproach his own with their sins, but to fulfil his promises in them and to manifest the wonders of his grace; (2) the process of judgment with the godly is such that mention is made of good works but not of bad, Mt. 25 (the virgins, the talents [the "well done!"] and then Gethsamane), the godly do not hear the publication of their sins, but an account of their love and well-doing; (3) by God's free mercy He no longer wishes to remember our sins, but casts them behind his back; what God has once willed to be covered in this life, He is not likely to reveal in the next; (4) if sins were revealed, this would amount to disgrace and confusion for the godly, in whom He should exult, since Christ is to return on purpose to be glorious in his saints and admirable in His believers."—Hence AMESIUS teaches precisely, that only the ungodly should be described as the object of judgment (I, xli, 30) : "Judgment will be pronounced not only on ungodly men, but also on bad angels."

20.—The purpose of God's judgment is first of all for God's glory to be manifested in His saints, and for God's eternal consent to be completely realised in the bliss of the righteous and the eternal punishment of the ungodly.—LEIDEN SYNOPSIS (LI, 55): "The ultimate end of the judgment is, that God be glorified in His saints and be admirable in all who have believed in that day, 2 Thess. 1. 10 ; also that by the manifestation of His truth in righteousness towards the ungodly all the nations should come and worship before Him, because His judgments have been made manifest Rev. 15. 4. The subordinate end will be the salvation and blessed state of the godly, the rejection of the godless, the deliverance of Christ's Church, the execution of the eternal decree, and the declaration of God's righteousness in the reprobate and His mercy in the elect."

21.—After the judgment will come the end of this world (*finis mundi consummatic huius saeculi*, συντέλεια τοῦ αἰῶνος τούτου), since God will destroy its present state by fire, i.e. not destroy the world but out of the old make a new world, a new heaven and a new earth which shall not pass away.—GUERTLER p. 946: "When we are changed into this glory, the present *saeculum* will be accomplished and created things redeemed from the vanity to which they are subjected because of sin, to be restored to their pristine state of integrity."—ARETIUS p. 504: "Theologians and philosophers seem to agree that this φθορὰ of the world is not to be referred to its οὐσία, but is only of its form : this view needs proof."—HEIDEGGER (*Med.* XXVIII, 46): "The end of the world and the consummation of the *saeculum* will herald the last judgment."—LEIDEN SYNOPSIS (LII, 56): "Just as the destruction of the world by a flood of waters came first, so too H. Scripture bears witness that the final perishing of the world will be by fire Is. 66. 15 (Behold, the Lord will come with fire and his chariots will be like the whirlwind; to render his anger with fury, and his rebuke with flames of fire) 2 Pet. 3. 7 (the heavens that now are, and the earth, have been stored up for fire, having been reserved against the day of judgment and destruction of ungodly men)." Similarly RIISSEN (XVIII, 6): WENDELIN (*Collat.* p. 484): AMESIUS (I, xli): 31: "The fire appointed for cleansing and renewing the world will not precede but will follow the judgment.—33: The elements will not be removed but changed. For we expect not other heavens and another earth, but new heavens and a new earth."

22.— The bliss which the righteous shall then enjoy is eternal life, which is given them in Christ. "Life eternal is the glorious state in which, after the coming resurrection of the dead, the elect, united most fully to Christ their Head, are to know God in heaven along with the angels, to enjoy

His presence and to celebrate it eternally, to obtain the highest good acquired for us by Christ, to be conformed in body and soul to His image, so far as he is man" (BUCAN XXXIX, 6). Hence the bliss of the righteous rests upon their direct communion with God, since with the bodily eye in sight of Christ they see the full glory of the Father and behold Himself directly with the eye of the Spirit and by the light which the H. Spirit turns upon it [the glory]; since further they rejoice in the most perfect loving fellowship with God and since at the same time they are raised to the perfection of a nature the image of God and thereby to the real possession of the glory of God.—WALAEUS p. 1025: "By eternal life we mean not natural life born of the union of soul and body (because after the resurrection it will also be common to the reprobate and damned, and yet in Scripture their life is rather called eternal death), but that happy and blessed life, which God promises to the faithful as the end, reward and gain for all their miseries and toils.—1028: So we say that this extreme and perfect bliss of man consists in the vision of God, together with plenary sanctification and glorification, from which things follows ineffable joy, which far exceeds man's grasp here."—ALTING p. 120: "The form of eternal life consists in (1) the clearest vision of God, which is the *intuitive* awareness of God; and the *mental* [vision] if God's spiritual essence is in view, the *ocular* [vision] in God incarnate such as the angels have."—[Similarly WALAEUS p. 1030: "We agree that God's glory will be most fully seen in Christ's human nature — yet we grant that this actual vision, which is as it were the supreme basis of eternal life, will be not of the bodily, but of the soul's eye][1]; (2) the full and most pleasant sense of God's favour; (3) the glorious and perfect fellowship of God's image, by which we are made participators in the divine virtues of wisdom, righteousness, holiness, glory."—BUCAN (XXXIX, 1): "There are three kinds of life, (1) the life of nature, or natural life; (2) the life of grace, by which the sons of God alone enjoy Christ in the spiritual kingdom in this world; (3) the life of glory, by which the soul shall live again in union with its body."

23.—In the bodily state of the blessed will also be shewn forth the glorification imparted to them by the real imparting of eternal life, since they will be not merely non-transient, but also beyond passion, independent of matter, in no wise hindered or oppressed in their living expression, and like Christ's glorified body a blessed instrument of the revelation of God's glory, so that the righteous shall shine as the sun in their Father's kingdom.—BUCAN (XXXIX, 13 6): "There will be added the

---

[1] "Hence W. assumes a kind of middle light, whereby spiritual viewing of the divine nature is mediated to the blessed."

clarification of their bodies, supreme beauty and majesty, by which they will be made like to Christ's glorious body."—RIISSEN (XVIII, 24): "The bodies of the glorified are to be changed not in substance but only in qualities, which the word μετασχηματίζεσθαι suggests, which Paul uses, Phil. 3. 21 (who shall fashion anew the body of our humiliation, that it may be conformed to the body of his glory, according to the working whereby he is able even to subject all things unto himself) in the sense in which Christ is said to have been μεταμορφωθείς, Mt. 17. 2 (he was transfigured before them; and his face did shine as the sun, and his garments became white as the light) before his disciples, not in bodily substance but because the fashion of his countenance was altered and his raiment became white and dazzling, Lk. 9. 29. Now these qualities of glorified bodies are (1) incorruption and immortality." — In this connection we are to notice (a) that risen bodies are immortal, not by their own essentiality but *per gratiam* and (b) that this immortality (otherwise than in Adam's original state) is an "absolute impossibility of dying;" for because the blessed will no more be able to sin any more, so too neither will they be able to die—(2) impassibility, by which they are not liable to passions at all, inward or outward;—(3) clarity and glory, by which the elect are said to be about to "shine forth as the sun in the kingdom of the Father," Mt. 13. 43;——(4) power and virtue, situated both in the strength of their bodies and in their agility and swiftness. At the same time this is not so to be taken, "that bodies are to be destitute of flesh and blood, skin and bones and organic parts, as the *Socinians* would have it, nor that they are to be unplaceable, invisible, untouchable, penetrable, as the *Ubiquitistae* would have it in their readiness to patronise their own hypothesis; but both so far as bodies will be perfectly purged of all earthly lees and dregs, all senses rendered purer, all movements and actions more perfect, and because they will be removed from the necessities of this animal life [!?], sleep, rest, food, drink, medicines, clothes, etc., and because they will be perfectly subject to the H. Spirit, and their souls regenerated by It and so they will have leisure for spiritual actions only." —On the other hand for glorified bodies the need for matter ceases and dependence on it, above all animal life, since its sheer principle of life is the Spirit; LEIDEN SYNOPSIS (LII, 29): "Removed from glorified man are not only all those things which result from sin and are of the nature of a penalty, but also those regarding man's animal estate, in virtue of the first creation in this world."

24.—Thus what believers already possess in germ here on earth, is imparted to them there in its perfection.—ALSTED p. 846: "Eternal life is felt by us in this world, but it is after this life that it touches us fully;

and in this sense it is divided into imperfect and perfect, inchoate and consummated.—HEIDEGGER (*Med.* XXVIII, 64): "God, man's highest good, imparts Himself to him to be enjoyed in His entirety.—65: The good therefore of this and of the next life is the same, but it admits of difference in the degrees of perfection. Whatever there is of imperfection belongs to this life, whatever of perfection to the next."

25.—It is not thereby excluded, that there are degrees of glorification, *gradus gloriae* in eternity, which correspond to the fruits of righteousness which each has produced in the temporal life, but in which there is manifested to knowledge no graduation of acquired merit, but the wealth and variety of grace in the unity of Christ's mystical body, to the glorifying of which they all contribute.—COCCEIUS (*Summ. theol.* XCVII, 4-5): "In glory there will be disparity (*differitas*) in individuals; but without jealousy and with an overflow upon all of the greatest glory, also that of the Head, 1 Cor. 15. 41-42 (there is one glory of the sun, and another glory of the moon, and another glory of the stars; for one star differeth from another star in glory. So also is the resurrection of the dead. It is sown in corruption it is raised in incorruption, etc.) 2 Cor. 5. 10 (we must all be made manifest before the judgment-seat of Christ; that each one may receive the things done through the body, according to that which he hath done, whether it be good or bad) Dan. 12. 3 (they that be wise shall shine as the brightness of the firmament; and they that turn many to righteousness as the stars for ever and ever), cf, 1 Cor. 12. 24-25-26-27 (. . . God tempered the body together, giving more abundant honour to that part which lacked; that there should be no schism in the body; but that the members should have the same care one for another. And whether one member suffereth, all the members suffer with it; or one member is honoured, all the members rejoice with it. Now ye are the body of Christ, and severally members thereof). The difference is not the different proportion of merit, nor does it argue a discrepancy in justification; it will be in accord with the grace of God, by which Christ was given a body in which God's manifold wisdom might be displayed.—5: There will also be degrees in punishment"—(*Summ. de foed.* XVI, 647): "There are also degrees in glory, not according to the merit of works, but in a way corresponding to the fruits of righteousness which each has borne in life."—BUCAN (XXXIX, 14): "Is the glory of eternal life to be common to all the elect in equal measure? No; but as God imparts His gifts unequally to the elect in this life, so He will crown these gifts of His in heaven among the elect in an unequal manner of· glory."—To avoid misunderstandings WENDELIN remarks (*Coll.* p. 534): "Inequality of fruits does not necessarily argue inequality of blessedness, but of glory conjoined with blessedness."—In the same way

PISCATOR (p. 108) also distinguishes between "life eternal" (which he conceives as " a full sense of God's favour and communion with His nature") and the "heavenly glory" with which the blessed are glorified in different degrees according to the measure of the gifts bestowed upon them.

26.—As then the bliss of the righteous rests upon their communion with God, the non-blessedness of the damned, eternal death, rests upon separation from God. Hence the punishment which they suffer in the fire of hell is not a mere dispensing with bliss (*poena damni*). The soul must necessarily feel the unbliss of abandonment by God, along with a positive suffering of punishment (*poena sensus*); this consists above all in the anguish which its own conscience brings, in the feeling of divine wrath and in the despair proceeding therefrom—WALAEUS p. 1051: " As we show that eternal life strictly consists in man's union with God, so too eternal death is rightly said to consist in man's separation from God."— RIISSEN (XVIII, 20): "The punishment of hell is not mere annihilation, as the *Socinians* would like; or punishment of loss, as though it consisted in simple deprivation of good without any sense of evils. Both these in this case undoubtedly contribute to increasing the torments of the ungodly.—*Mala στερητικά* (*privative* evils) are separation from God and Christ, and deprivation of the divine vision in which rests the felicity of the blest, separation from the angels and the blessed, deprivation of light, joy, glory, felicity and life. The positive evils are manifold, being adumbrated by pains and tortures, by racks etc. and other things of the kind, which usually import evils of every sort, as much to soul as to body." In addition to this RIISSEN (XVIII, 22) adduces the "adjuncts of infernal punishments"; these are (1) inequality according to the varying nature of the crimes, Mt. 11, 22 (it shall be more tolerable for Tyre and Sidon in the day of judgment, than for you), Lk. 12, 47-48 (that servant, which knew his lord's will, and made not ready, nor did according to his will, shall be beaten with many stripes; but he that knew not, and did things worthy of stripes, shall be beaten with few stripes. And to whomsoever much is given, of him shall much be required: and to whom they commit much, of him will they ask the more), Mk. 12. 40 (they which devour widows' houses, and for a pretence make long prayers; these shall receive greater condemnation [Lk. 20. 47] Mt. 23. 14 [in AV only]." The punishments are "unequal" not "by reason of extension" (for they are all eternal), but "by reason of intension or gravity";—(2) the "greatness and intensity of the penalty, which should be so great, as cannot be conceived by the mind or expressed in words;—(3) by the duration and extensity of the punishment, not only in their unbroken continuity so far as the damned are not to have any rest or relaxation, but also in their perpetuity and eternity.—From this, finally, will arise despair and groaning as the inevitable consequence."—That the bodies of the damned are tortured by "some physical fire", RIISSEN considers probable. —COCCEIUS (*Summ. de foed.* XVI, 644): "These punishments are both of loss and of feeling (*tum damni tum sensus*); whence they are compared with fire and the worm. To be given punishment by loss without punishment by feeling is a fairy tale (*fabula*). What more absurd than to say that a soul can be without feeling ? Where there is feeling, if the feeling is pleasant, there is no punishment by loss; if it is unpleasant it is punishment by loss.—645: There are also degrees of punishment, Lk. 12. 47-48 (p. 710), Mt. 11. 22 (*ibid.*) 24 (=22), 5. 22 (. . . everyone who is angry with his brother shall be in danger of the judgment; and whosoever shall say unto his brother, *Raca,* shall be in danger of the council; and whosoever shall say *Moreh,* shall be in danger unto the hell of fire) Rom. 2. 5-6 (but after thy hardness and impenitent heart treasurest up for thyself wrath in the day of wrath and revelation of the righteous judgment of God; who will render unto every man according to his works). Similarly RAVENSPERGER p. 273; COCCEIUS (*De foed.* 646): "Despair will accompany punishment, because there is no redemption from hell Lk. 16. 26 (beside all this, between us and you a great gulf is fixed, that they which would pass from hence to you may not be able, and that none may cross over from thence to us) nor do those who are there cross over to us. There is no repentance in hell, or sanctification."—These punishments the damned suffer in the "inferno", in hell; HEIDEGGER (*Med.* XXVII, 52): "Hell is the place of the damned, in which the devil, his angels and all damned humans shall eternally suffer the punishment of loss and sense or torture by fire." How the fire of hell is to be conceived is questionable; WENDELIN (*Coll.* p. 510): "But whether the infernal fire appointed for the tortures of the godless is to be natural or physical, there is no agreement; Scripture is silent here. But even if it were to be the most natural or elemental, it still would not necessarily corrupt bodies, as it in fact corrupts them in this life, because God could very readily prevent such corruption and preserve those bodies numerically and rack them with eternal tortures."

27.—The incorruptibility of their bodies bestowed on the ungodly is not crowned with the glory of eternal life, but only serves to make their agony a never-ending one.—WENDELIN (*Coll.* p. 494): "Incorruptibility alone the godless shall have, but they shall be utterly destitute of any glory, power of spiritual dignity."

28.—For the damnation of the ungodly has or course, like the bliss of the righteous, its gradations in individual cases, but will keep them in each instance for eternity; therefore the opinion is to be rejected of those who assume a finite cessation of damnation and a finite conversion of it.— GUERTLER p. 940: "After this life no place is given for repentance or for satisfaction of crimes."—LEIDEN SYNOPSIS (LII, 47) declares that "erroneous is the opinion of the *Origenists* and certain *Anabaptists*, who have imagined that there will at last be an end of these tortures."

29.—Now if the judgment has been held and if God's merciful love to the righteous and His punitive righteousness towards the ungodly has been manifested to the whole world, then the Father's good pleasure in Christ has been accomplished. Then the Son restores the kingdom to the Father's hands—not as though he ceased to be the Head of the elect and the King of his kingdom, since he remains this eternally; nor as though the Father did not reign now: but because then the Father will be all in all in God's eternal kingdom through the Son.—BERNSAU p. 393: "Then the Lord Jesus shall obtain for ever the glory of the absolute mediatorial office"; for "he has actually provided all that God Himself could exact from the Mediator between Himself and man.".—COCCEIUS (*Summ. de foed.* XVI, 639): "The last foe defeated, the Son shall deliver the kingdom to the Father, not because the Father does not reign now, but because (1) it might be more evidently recognised that the Father is in the Son and reigns in him; and next (2) the Father will plainly fill the Church with His own and the Son's grace, that He may be all things in them, i.e. so that in perfect holiness, all viciousness uprooted, they may be united to God and with Him, according to the capacity (*captus*) of human nature, share in the joy of glory without any lack. This fulfilling (*impletio*) of the Church is Christ's as true God and Head, Eph. 1, 23 (the church, which is his body, the fulness of him that filleth all in all) 4, 13 (till we all attain unto the unity of the faith, and of the knowledge of the Son of God, unto a full-grown man, unto the measure of the stature of the fulness of Christ); and the Father's, so far as the divine work of grace has been administratively secured by the Son, 1 Cor. 15, 24-28 (then the end, when he shall deliver up the kingdom to the God and Father; when he shall have abolished all rule and all authority and power . . . and when all things have been subjected unto him, then shall the Son also himself be subjected to him that did subject all things to him, that God may be all in all)."—AMESIUS (I, xli): 34: "After the day of judgment Christ will also remain King and Mediator for eternity. He will not deliver the kingdom to the Father in such wise as to cease reigning himself, but as restoring the kingdom to the Father complete, as it is to remain to eternity."

THE END

LIST OF THE MOST IMPORTANT
SOURCES QUOTED

(The editions used by Heppe were not completely ascertained; the year dates given by him are in brackets; mistakes are amended).

1. JOHN CALVIN, *Institutio Christianae Religionis*. Edn. A. Tholuck, Berlin, 1834.
2. HEINRICH BULLINGER, *Compendium Christianae Religionis decem libris comprehensum*. Tiguri, 1559 (1556).
3. PETRI MARTYRI VERMILII, Florentini praestantissimi nostra aetate theologi, *Loci Communes*. Ed. *R. Massonius*. London, 1576.
4. MATTHAEUS VIRELLIUS, *Religionis Christianae Compendium*. Geneva 1582.
5. LAMBERTUS DANAEUS, *Christianae Isagoges ad Christianorum theologorum Locos Communes libri II; cum praefatione Theodori Bezae*. Geneva, 1588.
6. WOLFGANG MUSCULUS DUSANUS, *Loci Communes Theologiae Sacrae*. Basel (no date; 1599).
7. BENEDICTUS ARETIUS, a Berne theologian, *SS. Theologiae Problemata seu Loci Communes et Miscellaneae Quaestiones*. Geneva, 1589.
8. THEODORI BEZAE, *Opera, Tom. I—III*. Geneva, 1582 (1583).
9. GULIELMUS BUCANUS, *Institutiones Theologicae seu Locorum Communium Christianae Religionis ex Dei Verbo et praestantissimorum theologorum orthodoxo consensu expositorum Analysis*, Geneva, 1609.
10. STEPHANUS SZEGEDINUS PANNONIUS, *Theologiae Sincerae Loci Communes de Deo et Homine perpetuis Tabulis explicati et Scholasticorum dogmatis illustrati*. Basel, 1593.
11. AMANDUS POLANUS a POLANSDORF, *Syntagma Theologiae Christianae*. Hanover, 1624 (1625).
12. JOHANNES WOLLEBUIS, *Christianae Theologiae Compendium*. Basel, 1626.
13. ANDREAE HYPERII, *Methodi theologiae sive praecipuorum Christianae religionis Locorum Communium Libri Tres iam denuo in lucem editi*. Basel, 1568 (1566).
14. PETRUS BOQUINUS, *Exegesis Divinae atque humanae κοινωνίας*. Heidelberg (no date, 1561).
15. GASPAR OLEVIANUS, *De Substantia Foederis Gratuiti inter Deum et electos itemque de mediis, quibus ea ipsa substantia nobis communicatur, libri duo*. Geneva, 1585.
16. D. ZACHARIAE URSINI, *Opera Theologica*. Heidelberg, 1612. Vol. I (*Didaskalia Scripta*). Includes:
    1. *Loci Theologici* (1562).
    2. *Explicationes Catacheseos Palatinae sive Corpus Theologiae* (cited *Expl. Catech.*). In addition :
    3. *Explicationum Catecheticarum D. Zachariae Ursini Silesii absolutum opus totiusque theologiae purioris quasi novum corpus; Davidis Parei opera extrema recognitum*. Neustadt in the Palatine, 1598 (cited, *Expl. catech, 1598*).

713

17. CHRISTOPHERUS PEZELIUS, *Argumentorum et Objectionum de praecipuis Articulis Doctrinae Christianae cum Responsionibus, quae passim extant in Scriptis reverendi Viri Domini Philippi Melanchthonis. Pars I—VII.* Neapoli Nemetum (Neustadt) 1582—1588. *Loci theologici Strigellii, quibus loci communes Melanchthonis illustrantur.* Neustadt 1582-3.

18. GEORGIUS SOHNIUS, *Opera; Tom. I—IV.* Herborn, Nassau, 1591 (1609).

19. HIERONYMI ZANCHII, *De Religione Christiana Fides.* Neustadt in the Palatine (no date, 1585).

20. JOHANNES PISCATOR, *Aphorismi Doctrinae Christianae, maximam Partem ex Institutione Calvini* (sic) *exerpti, seu Loci communes theologici, brevibus sententiis expositi.* Second Edition; Herborn, 1592.

21. BARTHOLOMAEUS KECKERMANN DANTISCANUS, *Systema Sacrosanctae Theologiae, tribus libris adornatum.* Geneva, 1611.

22. DANIEL BERNHARD EILSHEMIUS, *Oestfriesslaendisch Kleinod des wahren Glaubens.* Emden, 1612.

23. JOHANNES HENRICUS ALSTEDIUS, *Theologia Scholastica Didactica exhibens Locos communes theologicos Methodo scholastica.* Hanover, 1618.

24. MARCUS FRIDERICUS WENDELINUS, *Christianae Theologiae Systema maius duobus libris comprehensum. Opus posthumum.* Cassel, 1656. *Collatio Doctrinae Christianae Reformatorum et Lutheranorum.* Cassel, 1660.

25. LUDOVICUS CROCIUS, *Syntagma Sacrae Theologiae.* Bremen, 1636.

26. RAPHAELIS EGLINI ICONII TIGURINI (Zuerich ?) D. *Tractatus theologicus De Coena Domini et Foedere Gratiae quinis Disputationibus interstinctus (Disputatio IV; Diexodus theologica de magno illo insitionis nostrae in Christum Mysterio; Disputatio V; De Foedere Gratiae).* Marburg, 1614.

27. HERMANN RAVENSPERGER, *Wegweiser, i.e. The wrong and right Explanation of all necessary points of doctrine in the Christian Religion.* Groeningen, 1615.

28. MATTHAEUS MARTINIUS, *Christianae Doctrinae Summa Capita, quae continentur in Symbolo Apostolico, Decalogo, Oratione Dominica, Institutione Disciplinae ecclesiasticae, s. baptismi et s. Coenae.* Herborn in Nassau, 1603.

29. LUCAS TRELCATIUS, *Scholastica et methodica Locorum communium s. Theologiae Institutio.* Hanover, 1610.

30. ANTONIUS WALAEUS, *Loci communes s. Theologiae.* Leiden, 1640.

31. GULIELMUS AMESIUS, *Medulla Theologica.* Amsterdam, 1634 (1628).

32. HENRICI a DIEST, *Theologia Biblica.* Deventer, 1643.

33. DOCTORUM ET PROFESSORUM IN ACADEMIA LEIDENSI JOH. POLYANDRI, ANDR. RIVETI, ANT. WALAEI et ANT. THYSSII *Synopsis purioris Theologiae.* Leiden 1581; editio sexta: (1652).

34. SAMUELIS MARESIUS, *Collegium theologicum sive Systema breve universae Theologiae comprehensum octodecim disputationibus. Editio sexta iuxta exemplar quartae et quintae ab authore ultimo recognitae excusa. Huic tres accesserunt Disputationes celebres, I, De syncretismo et reconciliatione partium in religione dissidentium; II, De legitimis causis nostrae ab Ecclesia Romana secessionis; III, De peccato in Spiritum Sanctum.* Geneva, 1662.

35. MELCHIORIS LEYDECKERI, *De Veritate Religionis reformatae seu evangelicae Libri VII.* Utrecht, 1688.
36. GISBERTUS VOETIUS, *Selectarum Disputationum theologicarum Pars. I—V.* Utrecht, 1648-1669.
37. JOHANNES COCCEIUS, *Summa Theologiae ex Scriptura repetita.* Amsterdam, 1665. *Summa Doctrinae de Foedere et Testamento Dei. 1648. (Opera, Tom. VI.* Amsterdam 1673).
38. FRANCISCUS BURMANNUS, *Synopsis Theologiae et speciatim oeconomiae foederum Dei ab Initio Saeculorum usque ad Consummationem eorum.* Amsterdam 1699.
39. HERMANNUS WITSIUS, *De Oeconomia Foederum Dei cum hominibus libri quattuor.* Editio tertia. Utrecht 1694. (Leovard, 1685).
40. JOHANNES BRAUNIUS, *Doctrina Foederum sive Systema Theologiae didacticae et elencticae.* Amsterdam, 1688.
41. JACOBUS ALTINGIUS, *Methodus Theologiae didacticae (Opera,* Amsterdam, 1687).
42. JOH. HENRICUS HOTTINGERUS, *Cursus theologicus Methodo Altingiana.* Heidelberg, 1660.
43. PETRUS VAN MASTRICHT, *Theoretico-practica Theologia.* Editio nova. Utrecht and Amsterdam, 1725 (1714).
44. ABRAHAMUS HEIDANUS, *Corpus Theologiae Christianae in quindecim locos digestum.* Leiden, 1686 (1687).
45. SALOMON VAN TIL, *Theologiae utriusque Compendium cum naturalis tum revelatae.* Leiden, 1704. *s. Compendium Theologiae.* Bern, 1705. The Ὑποτύπωσις τῶν ὑγιαινόντων λόγων seu Compendium Theologiae, Bern, 1705, could not be proved from the Information Bureau of the German Libraries. We have therefore attributed to it the quotations from v. TIL not found in the first-named work. (note by BIZER, the Bonn Editor of the German Edition).
46. JOHANNES HENRICUS HEIDEGGERUS, *Corpus Theologiae.* Zuerich, 1700. *Medulla Theologiae Christianae,* Zuerich, 1696.
47. BENEDICTUS PICTETUS, *Theologia Christiana ex puris SS. Literarum fontibus hausta.* Geneva, 1696. (*Dissertationis de Consensu et Dissensu inter Reformatos et Augustanae Confessionis Fratres Vindiciae adversus Animadversiones, quas edidit Lutheranus.* Geneva, 1700.
48. FRANCISCUS TURRETTINUS, *Institutio Theologiae elencticae.* Editio nova. Utrecht and Amsterdam, 1701 (Geneva 1688).
49. LEONARDUS RIISSENIUS, *Francisci Turretini Compendium Theologiae didactico-elencticae ex theologorum nostrorum Institutionibus auctum et illustratum.* Amsterdam, 1695.
50. JOHANNES MARCKIUS, *Compendium Theologiae Christianae didactico-elencticum.* Amsterdam, 1690. (Groningen, 1686).
51. HENRICUS GULIELMUS BERNSAU, *Compendium Theologiae dogmaticae.* Franekker, 1755.
52. NICOLAUS GUERTLERUS, *Institutiones theologicae Ordine maxime naturali dispositae ac variis accessionibus auctae.* Marburg, 1732.
53. DAN. WYTTENBACHIUS, *Tentamen Theologiae dogmaticae Methodo scientifica pertractatae.* Tom. I—III; Frankfort-on-Main, 1747-1749 (Bern, 1741-1747).

54. Fried. Adolph Lampe, *Einleitung zu dem Geheimnis des Gnadenbundes;* Marburg and Frankfurt, 1782.

55. Sam. Endemann, *Institutiones theologicae dogmaticae.* Tom. I—II. Hanover, 1777 and 1778. *Compendium Theologiae dogmaticae in Usum Auditorum.* Frankfort-on-Main, 1782.

56. H. A. Niemeyer, *Collectio Confessionum in Ecclesiis Reformatis publicatorum.* Leipzig, 1840.

57. Heinrich Heppe, *Die Bekenntnisschriften der reformierten Kirchen Deutschlands.* Elberfeld, 1860.
Dogmatik des deutschen Protestantismus im sechszehnten Jahrhundert. Gotha, 1857.

INDEX

A

Adamites 315
Adam cc. XI, XIII, XIV, XV, 342
Adiphora 688
Adminicula (supports) 23
Administration of :
    (i) Baptism 611f., 613
    (ii) Covenant of Grace 394f.
    (iii) Lord's Supper 627
    (iv) Sacraments 604ff.
Admission to the Supper 653ff.
Adoption 552
Adoration of Christ 438
Advent 696, 702
Affects of God's Will 92f.
Affectations of the Soul 225
Agyrtae 37
Ambrose 613
Amyraldus 295, 398
Anabaptists 13, 67, 315, 540, 553, 661, 682, 712
Analogy of Faith 36
Angels Ch. x.
    Guardian 212
Antidico-Marianites 423
Antitrinitarianism 109
Antitrinitarians 108
Apocryphi 14
Apotelesma 258, 445
Application of H. Scripture 38
Arians 122, 614
Aristotle 55, 191, 198
Arminius, Arminians 7, 44, 77, 87, 105, 139, 377
Arnold 37
Articles (fundamental) 43
    pure and mixed 11
Ascension of Christ 500f.
Assent of Faith 508, 527ff.
Assumption of Humanity 316ff.
Athanasius 102, 414, 430
Attributes of God Ch. 5, 57ff.
    H. Scripture 21f.
Augsburg Confession 494
Augustani 170, 175, 617
Augustine 23, 38, 54, 78, 101, 102, 106, 130, 158, 169, 173, 185, 187, 192, 194, 233, 236, 297, 312, 324, 343, 350, 356, 422, 424, 507, 538, 650, 653, 698, 701
Aureolus 202
Authenticity of Scripture 26f.
Authority of Church 23, 40
    Scripture 9, 15, 16, 21f., 23, 25, 26f.
Averroes 256
Aymon 669

B

Balduin 64
Baptism 542, 611ff.
    of Christ 448
    by Heretics 613f.
    by John Baptist 625f.
Basil 102, 440
Beatitude of God 68
Becanus 78
Bellarmine 338, 659
Bernard 52, 53, 507
Biel, Gabriel 103, 340
Blasphemy against H. Spirit 352ff.
Body of Angels 202, 213
    Man 221
Boethius 69
Bonaventure 202
Bougot, Stephen 351
Bright, Timothy 230
Bread in Supper 634-641
Brownists 682
Bucer 691
Buddeus 375
Bullinger 691
Burgess, Cornelius 542

C

Canonical Books 13
Capito 691
Cardin 37
Cargius 319
Caritas 535, 561
Cartesians 62, 99, 108
Castellio 78, 289
Cases requiring Baptism (None!) 613f.
Catiline 350
Cause of Creation 195-6
    Election 163, 176ff.
    Fall of Adam 303ff.
    Sin 326
Causes, second 258ff.
Certainty of Election 175ff.
    Faith 536ff.
    Salvation 389ff., 584ff.
    Scripture (Cocceian) 18ff.
Chalcedon (against Eutyches) 433
Chamier 36, 213
Chaos 197
Charenton, Synod of 333
Chemnitz 543
Chrysostom 91
Circulati (Agyrtae) 37
Clauberg 108
Clemency of God 96
Cloppenburg 377
Coleman 690
Combach 230

717

twin brooks series BOOKS IN THE SERIES